DISTRICT OF COLUMBIA
MARRIAGE RECORDS INDEX
June 28, 1877 to October 19, 1885
(Marriage Record Books 11 to 20)

Wesley E. Pippenger
Dorothy S. Provine

WILLOW BEND BOOKS
2008

WILLOW BEND BOOKS
AN IMPRINT OF HERITAGE BOOKS, INC.

Books, CDs, and more—Worldwide

For our listing of thousands of titles see our website
at
www.HeritageBooks.com

Published 2008 by
HERITAGE BOOKS, INC.
Publishing Division
100 Railroad Ave. #104
Westminster, Maryland 21157

Copyright © 1997 Wesley E. Pippenger

All rights reserved. No part of this book may be reproduced or transmitted in any form or by any means, electronic or mechanical, including photocopying, recording or by any information storage and retrieval system without written permission from the author, except for the inclusion of brief quotations in a review.

International Standard Book Numbers
Paperbound: 978-1-58549-563-4
Clothbound: 978-0-7884-7203-9

DISTRICT OF COLUMBIA
MARRIAGE RECORDS INDEX

June 28, 1877 to October 19, 1885

INTRODUCTION

This work represents marriage records for not only residents of the District of Columbia, but also neighboring Virginia, Maryland, and elsewhere. To be married in the District of Columbia was by some thought an adventure, an excursion, or an escape from tradition—particularly for those who resided afar.

Marriage Record Books

The primary source of information in this work is taken from ten bound marriage record books found in the District of Columbia Archives, part of the District of Columbia Office of Public Records. Pages in these books are titled "Record of Marriages." Marriage record books number 11 through 20 cover approximately 14,682 marriage licenses issued between June 28, 1877 and October 19, 1885. The record series is scattered with instances where a marriage occurred quite some time past date of license, and also later than 1885. In most instances this record series provides both the date a marriage license was issued and information about the marriage performed. In the latter case, the record book is often signed by the officiating minister who was to enter the church of his affiliation and the place of the marriage.

One might presume that if the marriage record book (of licenses) is absent information about an actual marriage, that a license was not returned to the D.C. clerk. This is not necessarily true, as many cases are found where the return is on file while the space for the appropriate marriage information is absent from the marriage record book. In all cases, it is suggested researchers check the bound marriage returns.

Breakout of the bound marriage record books:

Book 11	June 28, 1877	to	April 10, 1878
Book 12	April 10, 1878	to	December 31, 1878
Book 13	January 1, 1879	to	November 21, 1879
Book 14	November 21, 1879	to	October 18, 1880
Book 15	October 18, 1880	to	September 30, 1881
Book 16	October 1, 1881	to	August 31, 1882
Book 17	August 31, 1882	to	June 18, 1883
Book 18	June 19, 1883	to	May 3, 1884
Book 19	May 3, 1884	to	December 31, 1984
Book 20	January 1, 1885	to	October 19, 1885

Marriage Return Books

In addition to the above, there is for just under half the cases, a corresponding marriage application and minister return. These are bound in separate volumes that are also found at the D.C. Archives. In some instances, one may discover that although the marriage record book is absent information to confirm a marriage took place, the information exists in other public records and was not copied and reconciled to all records. Further, one finds in studying the returns that it is common for the records to differ in spelling, and sometimes provide conflicting information. Numerous instances were noted where the date of marriage given precedes date of license.

The compilers compared the marriage record books described above with bound marriage returns in books labeled 9 to 36. Returns reviewed are numbered 2,000 through 8,999. Therefore, approximately 7,000 returns are found for 14,682 marriage licenses issued during the period. What this shows is that we do not have a separate return for over half of the licenses issued.

A word of caution regarding the marriage returns. Researchers should know that these small books do not have their own index, but rather the D.C. Archives has separate index volumes for the returns. The individual certificates in these are only in **very** rough chronological order. Arrangement is numerical and chronological by when the return arrived in the recording office. The bound books have dates inscribed on the spine, but these dates often cause more confusion than help in locating a record. One may find sequences grouped by minister, as that minister only periodically brought returns into the recording office. In some cases this may be over a year after the date inscribed on the volume spine. For instance, dozens of returns by minister Thomas G. Addison are bound in volume 10, inscribed for the period December 21, 1877 to April 22, 1878. Among this group are 27 returns for 1875 and 1876, and a number for the first few months of 1877. Researchers may find any number of other oddities.

One version (1883) of the "return" form bears the following legal citation:

> Section 2. That it shall be the duty of every clergyman, magistrate, or other person who shall perform any marriage ceremony within the District of Columbia, to report each marriage ceremony solemnized by him to the Registrar, aforesaid, within forty-eight hours thereafter, giving the full name, age, color, occupation, birthplace (State or Country), and legal residence of each person married, and the date of such marriage.

> Section 9. That any person who shall violate, or aid and abet in violating any of the provisions of the foregoing regulations, shall, upon conviction thereof by competent judicial authority, be punished by a fine of not less than twenty-five nor more than two hundred dollars for each and every such offense.

A marriage return, officially inscribed "Certificate of Marriage," contain blanks to enter the following information: (1) Date of Marriage; (2) Full Name of Husband; (3) Age; (4) Color; (5) Place of Residence; (6) Occupation; (7) Husband's Birthplace; (8) Number of Husband's Marriage; (9) Maiden Name of Wife; (10) Age; (11) Color; (12) Place of Residence; (13) Wife's Birthplace; (14) Number of Wife's Marriage; (15) Signatures; (16) Certification by Minister. See later in this work for examples of forms used. Marriage return forms called for signatures of the bride and groom along with the officiating minister. With these present, another opportunity exists to verify correct spelling.

Every effort has been made to correctly interpret handwriting of each of the many brides, grooms, ministers and record keepers. We request that any errors be reported to the compilers.

Wesley E. Pippenger
Arlington, Virginia

ABBREVIATIONS AND EXPLANATION

Marriage record entries followed with "L" indicate the date given is the date a marriage license was issued. Entries followed by "R" are dates of marriage taken from the marriage return. Otherwise, the date provided is the date of marriage provided in the record of marriage book. Samples of the various forms used for marriage record keeping are provided on the following pages.

Abbreviations

Typical abbreviations found use in this work are as follows:

A.M.E.	African Methodist Episcopal
C	License Returned Unused
C.M.E.	Colored Methodist Episcopal
Capt.	Captain
Corp.	Corporal
Dr.	Doctor
L	Date License Issued, No Date of Marriage Found
Lt.	Lieutenant
M.E.	Methodist Episcopal
M.G.	Minister of the Gospel
Mr./Mrs.	
P.E.	Protestant Episcopal
R	Marriage Return, Bound Volume
Rev.	Reverend

Explanation

If the compilers located a marriage return, the date of marriage is followed by an "R". If no marriage return was found and the date of marriage is not given in the record book, the date given here is followed by an "L" to indicate date of license. Dates without an "R" or "L" represent date of marriage as found in the marriage record book. Book and page numbers typically refer to the marriage record volume. In cases where no record was found in the marriage record volume but a marriage return is found, the book and page given refer to the marriage return book location.

Record No. 8844

To the Registrar of Vital Statistics,
Board of Health, District of Columbia.

CERTIFICATE OF MARRIAGE.

1. Date of Marriage **21st Dec.** 1886
2. Full Name of Husband, **Charles H. Zier**
3. Age, **26** years,
4. Color, **White**
5. Place of Residence, **Washington D.C.**
6. Occupation, **Metropolitan R.R. Co**
7. Husband's Birthplace, **Montgomery Co. Md**
8. No. of Husband's Marriage, **First**
9. Maiden Name of Wife, **Jennie B. Cork**
10. Age, **23** years,
11. Color, **White**
12. Place of Residence, **Washington D.C.**
13. Wife's Birthplace, **Westmoreland Co. Virginia**
14. No. of Wife's Marriage, **First**

We, the contracting parties, do certify that the foregoing information is correct.

Signatures: { **Charles H. Zier** / **Jennie B. Cork** }

THIS CERTIFIES that on the **21st** day of **Dec.** 1886, I joined in Holy Matrimony the parties above described.

Name, **J. S. Wynkoop**
Official Station, **Minister Western Presb. Church**
Residence, **1906 H St., Washington** D. C.

Sample Marriage Record Form, Style 1

16   RECORD OF MARRIAGES.

To any Minister of the Gospel authorized to Celebrate Marriages in the District of Columbia, Greeting:

You are hereby LICENSED to solemnize the RITES OF MARRIAGE between _Alexander Barnes_, of _Hillsdale D.C._ AND _Fannie Addison_, of _Stanton town D_ if you find no lawful impediment thereto; and having so done, you are commanded to appear in the Clerk's Office of the Supreme Court of said District and certify the same.

Witness my hand and the seal of said Court this _13_ day of _Jany_, 18_85_.

R. J. Meigs, Clerk.

By _R. J. Meigs Jr._, Asst. Clerk.

I, _____, Minister of _____ Church in _____, hereby certify that, by authority of a License of the same tenor as the foregoing, I solemnized the marriage of the parties aforesaid on the _____ day of _____, 18__, at _____, in the District of Columbia.

To any Minister of the Gospel authorized to Celebrate Marriages in the District of Columbia, Greeting:

You are hereby LICENSED to solemnize the RITES OF MARRIAGE between _Jeremiah Crowley_, of _Washington DC_ AND _Nellie Briscoe_, of _Alexandria, Va_ if you find no lawful impediment thereto; and having so done, you are commanded to appear in the Clerk's Office of the Supreme Court of said District and certify the same.

Witness my hand and the seal of said Court this _13_ day of _Jany_, 18_85_.

R. J. Meigs, Clerk.

By _L. P. Williams_, Asst. Clerk.

I, _E. D. Huntley_, Minister of _Metropolitan M.E._ Church in _Washington D.C._, hereby certify that, by authority of a License of the same tenor as the foregoing, I solemnized the marriage of the parties aforesaid on the _14_ day of _Jan_, 18_85_, at _333 C St. NW Washington_, in the District of Columbia.

E. D. Huntley

MARRIAGE LICENSE.

No. ....

To any Minister, or other person, authorized to celebrate marriages in the District of Columbia, Greeting:

You are hereby authorized to solemnize the rites of marriage between Joseph Paxton of Montgomery Co., Md. and Ann Maria Wolford of London Co., Va. and having done so, you are commanded to make return of the same to the Clerk's Office of the Supreme Court of the said District within TEN days, as the law directs.

Witness my hand and seal of said Court this 10 day of Sept, Anno Domini 1884.

R. J. Meigs, Clerk.
By J. R. Young, Assistant Clerk.

No. ....

RETURN.

I, J. S. Teasdale, who have been duly authorized to celebrate the rites of marriage in the District of Columbia, do hereby certify that, by authority of license of corresponding number herewith, I solemnized the marriage of .... and .... named therein, on the 10 day of September, 1884, at Tenallytown, in said District.

J. S. Teasdale

Address: ....

Clerk's Office, Supreme Court of the District of Columbia.

I, J. R. Young, Clerk of the Supreme Court of the District of Columbia, hereby certify that the foregoing License and Certificate of Marriage are truly copied from Originals of Record on file in said Office.

Witness my hand and the seal of said Court, the 15th day of Feby, 1898.

J. R. Young, Clerk.
By R. Mings J., Assistant Clerk.

District of Columbia, to wit:

I, E. F. Bingham, Chief Justice of the Supreme Court of the District of Columbia, do certify that the foregoing attestation by J. R. Young, Clerk of the said Court, is in due form. Witness my hand and seal, this 15th day of Feby, 1898.

E. F. Bingham, Chief Justice, etc. [SEAL]

Sample Marriage Record Form, Style 3

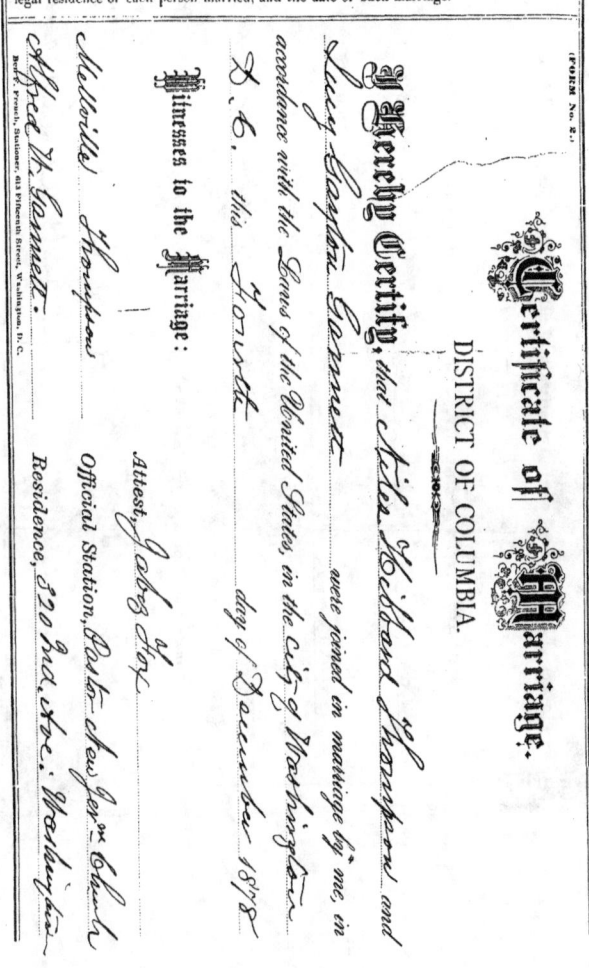

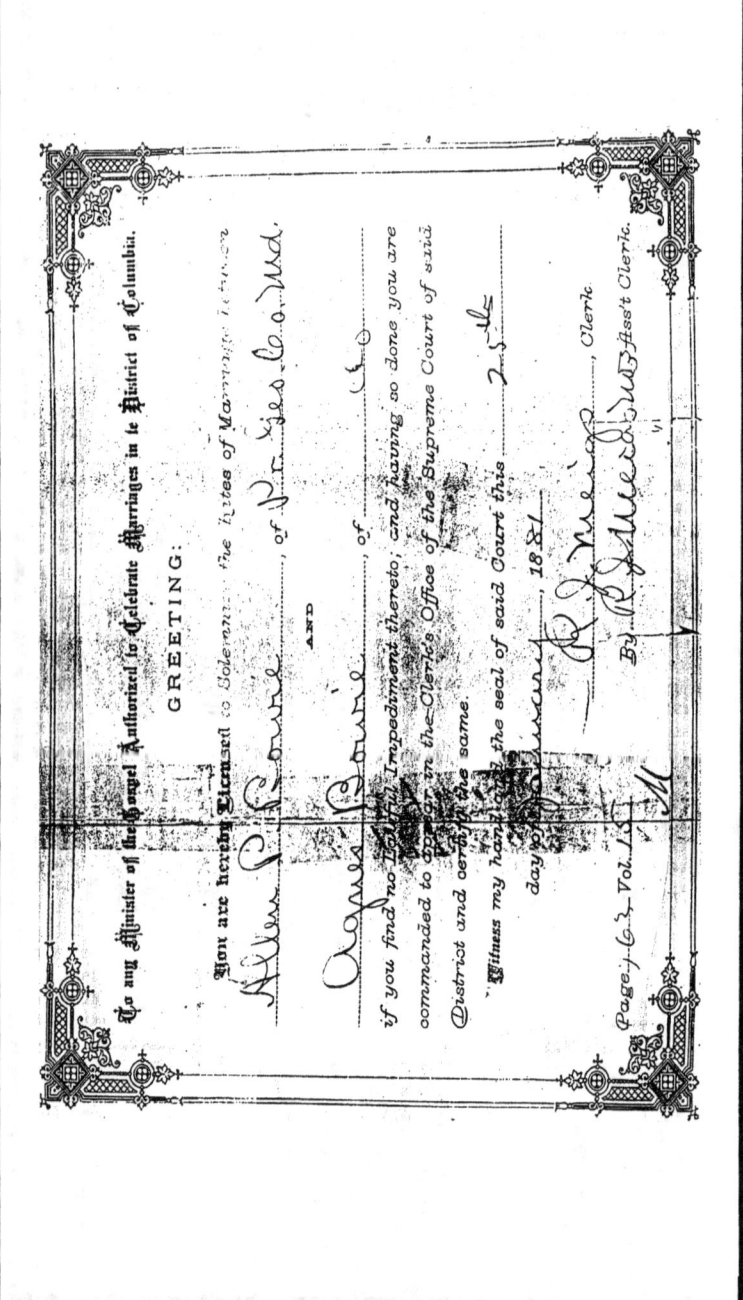

Sample Marriage Record Form, Style 5

Extract from Regulations Governing Vital Statistics in the District of Columbia.

"SECTION 2. That it shall be the duty of every clergyman, magistrate, or other person who shall perform any marriage ceremony within the District of Columbia, to report each marriage ceremony solemnized by him to the Registrar aforesaid, within forty-eight hours thereafter, giving the full name, age, color, occupation, birthplace, (State or Country,) and legal residence of each person married, and the date of such marriage."

"SECTION 9. That any person who shall violate, or aid and abet in violating, any of the provisions of the foregoing regulations, shall, upon conviction thereof by competent judicial authority, be punished by a fine of not less than twenty-five nor more than two hundred dollars for each and every such offense."

No. 6238

CERTIFICATE OF MARRIAGE.

TO THE HEALTH OFFICER, DISTRICT OF COLUMBIA.

1. Date of Marriage, November 29th, 1882
2. Full Name of HUSBAND, William Lothorop Smoot
3. Age, Thirty three years.
4. Color, White
5. Place of Residence, Langley Fairfax County Virginia
6. Occupation, Farmer
7. Husband's Birthplace, Poolesville Montgomery County Maryland
8. Number of Husband's Marriage, First Marriage
9. Maiden Name of WIFE, Jane Mosher Kurtz
10. Age, Twenty seven years.
11. Color, White
12. Place of Residence, Minneapolis Minnesota
13. Wife's Birthplace, Georgetown D.C.
14. Number of Wife's Marriage, No previous marriage

We, the contracting parties, do certify that the foregoing information is correct.

Signatures: { William Lothorop Smoot
{ Jane Kurtz Smoot

THIS CERTIFIES, That on the 29th day of Nov. 1882, I joined in Holy Matrimony the parties above described.

Name, Albert R. Stuart
Official Station, Rector of Christ Church Parish, Georgetown
Residence, 3330 P St. W Washington D.C.

Sample Marriage Record Form, Style 6

DISTRICT OF COLUMBIA MINISTERS

Following is a list of ministers and their churches as found for specific years on a sample of marriage records for the period, June 28, 1877 to October 19, 1885. Ministers usually served a span of years.

A

ADAMS, T.H.	Mt. Zion M.E. Church (1881); residence at 2523 P St., N.W.
ADDISON, Thomas G.	Trinity P.E. Church, 3rd & C Sts., N.W. (1880)
AHERN, J.A.	St. Matthew's Church (1885)
ALEXANDER, Sandy	First [Colored] Baptist Church, 27th St. & Dumbarton Ave., N.W., Georgetown, D.C. (1881); residence at 2026 M St., N.W. (1883)
ALEXANDER, W.G.	A.M.E. Church (1882)
ALIG, Matthew	St. Mary's Catholic Church (1881)
AMES, Alfred H.	McKendree M.E. Church (1877); residence at 921 Massachusetts Ave. (1880)
AMES, John G.	Protestant Episcopal Church, D.C. (1883); residence at 1300 13th St., N.W.
ANDREWS, Charles D.	Christ Episcopal Church, G & 7th Sts., S.E. (1880); residence at 620 G St., S.E. (1881)
ANDREWS, Edward G.	Bishop of the Methodist Episcopal Churches (1881); residence at 1545 Rhode Island Ave., N.W. (1883)
ARMSTRONG, Amzi L.	Presbyterian Church, Dutch Neck, Mercer Co., N.J. (1882)
ARMSTRONG, Joseph	Galbreath Chapel (1877); residence at 467 New York Ave., N.W. (1877)
ARNOLD, William R.	St. Paul's A.M.E. Chapel, 8th & D Sts., S.W. (1882)
AVERY, William B.	Methodist Episcopal Church, Washington, D.C. (1882)
AVIRETT, James B.	Protestant Episcopal Church, Silver Spring Parish, Montgomery Co., Md. (1881)

B

BAER, Robert N.	Metropolitan Memorial M.E. Church, 333 C St., N.W. (1880); Waugh M.E. Church (1885)
BAILEY, Henry	Abyssinian [Colored] Baptist Church (1881)
BAILEY, Henry	Fourth Baptist Church (1881); residence 1814 Vermont Ave. (1881)
BAILEY, Henry	Beulah Church, Alexandria, Va. (1883)
BAILOR, Henry	Rehobeth [Colored] Baptist Church, 1322 1st St., N.W. (1883); residence at 1243 3rd Street, S.W. (1881)
BAKER, Robert M.	Grace P.E. Church, 32nd St. below the canal, Georgetown, D.C. (1883); residence at 3417 Prospect Ave., Georgetown, D.C. (1881)
BALDWIN, Charles W.	Union Methodist Episcopal Church (1885)
BALL, Benjamin F.	M.G., M.E. Church South (1885)
BALL, R.H.	Foundry M.E. Church (1881)
BANKS, Edgar	Macedonian Baptist Church, Hillsdale, D.C. (1877)
BARBER, Theodore P.	Great Choptank Parish, Dorchester Co., Md. (1879)
BARKER, William M.	St. Paul's Parish Church, 919 23rd St., N.W. (1882)
BARNARD, J.H.	St. Mark's P.E. Church, Tonawanda, N.Y. (1885)
BARNES, Joshua	Prince George's Circuit (1877)
BAROTTI, Felix	St. Augustine's Church (1877)
BARTLETT, William A.	New York Avenue Presbyterian Church, 13th St. & New York Ave., N.W., 1882-1894
BATCHELOR, Ward	Bethany Presbyterian Chapel, 13th & C Sts., N.W. (1883)
BATES, L.W.	Methodist Protestant Church, Georgetown, D.C. (1885)
BEALL, G.W.	Gay St. Baptist Church, Georgetown, D.C. (1877)
BECKETT, D.J.	African Methodist Church, Hillsdale, D.C. (1885)
BELL, John	Beulah [Colored] Baptist Church, 3rd & P Sts., N.W. (1881)
BELL, J.W.	Israel Methodist Church (1877)
BENDER, A.J.	M.G.; residence at 456 L St., S.W. (1877)
BENNETT, Edward	Baptist Church (1885)

District of Columbia Ministers

BERRY, George M.	Mount Zion M.E. Church, Tennallytown, D.C. (1881); Little Falls M.E. Church, Canal Rd. (1883)
BITTINGER, Benjamin F.	Westminster Church, 7th & D Sts., S.W. (1880); residence at 638 F St., S.W. (1883)
BLACK, R.W.	Hamlin M.E. Church (1877); Methodist Church, Baltimore, Md. (1885); residence at 1506 9th Street, N.W. (1877)
BLACK, W.H.	Methodist Episcopal Church (1885)
BLOUNT, C.M.	M.G., Hillsdale, D.C. (1879)
BOLAND, John D.	St. Matthew's Church (1880)
BOOTHE, Thomas W.	Mt. Zion [Colored] M.E. Church, 29th St. near Dumbarton Ave., N.W. (1882)
BOSLEY, George	Zion A.M.E. Church (1885)
BOTELER, J. Wesley	Methodist Episcopal Church South (1881)
BOULDEN, Jesse F.	19th Street Baptist Church (1877); residence at 1123 19th St. (1881)
BOULDEN, Z.F.	12th Street Baptist Church (1880)
BOULDIN, Albert	Third [Colored] Baptist Church, N & 4th Sts., N.W. (1880)
BOWSER, Jacob W.	Ebenezer A.M.E. Church (1885)
BOYLE, Francis E.	St. Matthew's Church (1880)
BRISCOE, George	M.E. Church (1883)
BRODHEAD, Augustus	New York Avenue Presbyterian Church (1877)
BROOKE, Pendleton	Protestant Episcopal Church, Westmoreland Co., Va. (1882)
BROOKS, Henry	Residence at 1121 8th St., N.W. (1881)
BROOKS, John H.	Fifth [Colored] Baptist Church, Q St. & Vermont Ave. (1880)
BROOKS, Walter H.	19th Street [Colored] Baptist Church, 19th & I Sts., N.W. (1882); residence at 1232 20th St., N.W. (1883)
BROUILLET, J.B.A.	No church identified (1881)
BROWN, Benjamin, Jr.	No church identified (1879); residence at Waterford, Loudoun Co., Va.
BROWN, Benjamin Peyton	Foundry Church, 1876-1878; M.E. Church (1881)
BROWN, John M.	Bishop A.M.E. Church (1882)
BROWN, Stephen	M.E. Church (1883); residence at 930 B Street, S.W.
BUCK, James A.	St. Paul's Rock Creek, Rock Creek Rd. near the Soldier's Home (1883)
BULLOCK, Joseph J.	Presbyterian Church (1882)
BURDICK, Frank H.	Sixth Presbyterian Church, 6th St. near Maryland Ave., S.W. (1885)
BUSAM, Joseph	Assistant Pastor, St. Joseph's Catholic Church (1880)
BUSH, Stephen, D.D.	Presbyterian Church, Waterford, N.Y. (1885)
BUSHNELL, Ebenezer	Presbyterian Church, Cleveland, Ohio (1883)
BUTLER, J. George	Memorial Lutheran Church, 14th & N Sts., N.W. (1881); residence at 1107 10th St.

C

CALL, P.C.	St. Dominick's Catholic Church, 6th and E Sts., S.W. (1883)
CAMP, Norman W.	Protestant Episcopal Church (1883); residence at 1004 New Hampshire Ave.
CAMPBELL, T.G.	Zion A.M.E. Church (1881)
CARGILL, John Marcus	Ebenezer [Colored] M.E. Church, O & 28th Sts., N.W., Georgetown, D.C. (1881); St. Paul's Church, Washington, D.C. (1885)
CARROLL, D.A.	A.M.E. Church (1877)
CARROLL, Nathaniel M.	Asbury [Colored] M.E. Church, K & 11th Sts., N.W. (1881); Jackson Street M.E. Church, Lynchburg, Va. (1883)
CARROLL, T.O.	Mt. Zion M.E. Church, 1030 R St., N.W. (1885)
CHAPMAN, William H.	Ryland M.E. Church (1885)
CHAPPELLE, Placide Louis	St. Matthew's Catholic Church, 15th & H Sts., N.W.,1882-1891
CHEEK, Robert M.	Washington Mission (1879); residence at 1518 M St,
CHENOWITH, George D.	Methodist Episcopal Church (1877)
CHESTER, John	Metropolitan Presbyterian Church, 4th & B Sts., S.E. (1881); residence at 639 Pennsylvania Ave., S.E.
CHEW, John H.	St. Albans Church (1877); residence near Georgetown, D.C. (1879)

District of Columbia Ministers

CHICK, Farris H. — Shiloh [Old School] Baptist Church (1877)
CHICKERING, John W., Jr. — Congregational Church (1877)
CHILDS, Thomas S. — Western Presbyterian Church (1880); residence at 1449 Massachusetts Ave. (1883)
CIAMPI, A.F. — Trinity Church, Georgetown, D.C. (1880)
CLARK, James W. — St. James' [Episcopal] Chapel, 9th & H Sts., N.E. (1881)
CLARKSON, S.A. — St. Dominic's Catholic Church (1879)
COBB, Nehemiah — M.G. (1883)
COLE, Isaac — Second Baptist Church (1880)
COOK, Fields — Ebenezer Baptist Church, Alexandria, Va. (1885)
COOKE, Wm. D. — A.M.E. Church (1881)
COWLES, Jesse S. — John Wesley A.M.E. Zion Church, Connecticut Ave. (1883); residences at 1417 Hopkins St., and 2117 Boundary St., N.W. (1883)
COX, Samuel K. — Mount Vernon Place M.E. Church South, 9th & K Sts., N.W. (1882)
CRIST, Philip A. — Methodist Episcopal Church (1883)
CROISSANT, J.D. — Methodist Church (1877)
CROSS, Isaac — M.E. Church, Newark, N.J. (1877)
CROSS, Thomas H. — A.M.E. Zion (1880)
CRUMMELL, Alexander — St. Luke's [Colored] P.E. Church, 15th & Sampson Sts., N.W. (1880)
CRUMPTON, Jacob — Mount Zion Church (1885)
CUMPSTON, Edw. — Presbyterian Church, Alexandria, Va. (1883)
CUTHBERT, James H. — First Baptist Church, 13th and G streets, N.W. (1881)

D

DANIEL, Robert J. — Zion Wesley [Colored] M.E. Church, D & 2nd Sts., S.W. (1880); residence at 217 D Street, S.W. (1881)
DAVIS, Giles L. — Miles' Chapel (1885)
DAVIS, Richard T. — St. John's Church, Loudoun Co., Va. (1881)
DEALE, John S. — Wesley Chapel M.E. Church (1880)
DENNIS, A. — Mt. Zion M.E. Church, Georgetown, D.C. (1883)
DeWOLF, D. — St Matthews Catholic Church (1877)
DeWOLF, John B. — Holy Trinity Parish, 1875-1879
DILLARD, Noah — Pilgrim Baptist Church (1881); Rock Creek [Colored] Baptist Church, Tennallytown, D.C. (1885)
DILLINGHAM, Pitt — Harvard Church, Charleston, Mass. (1883)
DOMER, Samuel — St. Paul's English Lutheran Church, Washington, D.C. (1883); residence at 738 11th St., N.W. (1881)
DOWNS, Wilford — Waugh M.E. Church, 3rd & A Sts., N.W.; residence at 111 3rd St., N.E. (1881)
DRAPER, Daniel — St. Paul Chapel (1879); residence at 9th St.
DRAPER, Wm. H. — Central M.E. Church (1883); residence 1031 17th St. (1883)
DULIN, B.P. — Tennallytown Church, Tennallytown, D.C. (1880)
DUNSBURY, Jas. W. — Mt. Zion M.E. Church (1879); residence at West St., Georgetown, D.C.
DYSON, Robert H.G. — John Wesley Church (1885)

E

EBBINGHAUS, J.W. — First Reformed Church (1877)
EDWARDS, W.S. — McKendree M.E. Church (1883)
EELLS, Edward, Sr. — Presbyterian Church (1885)
ELBERT, Henry R. — Asbury [Colored] Mission Church, 967 Boundary St., N.W. (1882)
ELLIOTT, John H. — Ascension Episcopal Church, Massachusetts Ave. & 12th St., N.W. (1880); residence at 908 H St., N.W. (1881)
ELLYSON, O. — Queenstown Baptist Church (1883); Kendall Chapel [Baptist] Mission (1883); residence at 1535 8th St., N.W.
EMMONS, Richard — No church identified, Washington, D.C. (1883)

District of Columbia Ministers

EUTSLER, D.F. — Methodist Episcopal Church South (1883)
EVANS, French S. — Methodist Episcopal Church (1883)
EVANS, Wm. B. — Methodist Episcopal Church (1883)
EWAN, John W. — Methodist Episcopal Church South (1885); residence at 1253 9th St., N.W.

F

FALLS, Neilson — St. Alban's Parish, between Georgetown and Tennallytown (1883)
FAUNCE, Daniel W. — E Street Baptist Church (1881); residence at 931 G St.
FINLEY, J. Randolph — Mt. Vernon Place M.E. Church (1877)
FLIPPO, O.F. — First Baptist Church, Alexandria, Va. (1885)
FLOYD, W.J. — First M.P. Church (1877)
FORHAN, Patrick, S.J. — Roman Catholic Church (1877)
FORREST, Douglas F. — Trinity Church (1880); residence at 339 C St. (1881)
FORT, William S. — Methodist Episcopal Church (1885)
FORTUNE, C.B. — Catholic Priest (1877); residence at 6th and F Sts., S.W.
FOX, Jabez — New Jerusalem [Swedenborgian] Church, North Capitol near B St., N.W. (1881); residence at 320 Indiana Ave. (1881)
FRANCE, Henry S. — Grace M.E. Church (1883); residence at 1713 6th St., N.W. (1879)
FRANCE, Joseph (1819-1889) — 4th Street M.E. Church, 4th & E Sts., S.E. (1882)
FRENCH, John L. — Presbyterian Church, Boyds, Md. (1885)
FRISBY, Wm. B. — Protestant Episcopal Church, West New Brighton, N.Y. (1885)
FULLERTON, Thomas — West Street Presbyterian Church, Georgetown, D.C., 1884-c.1893

G

GAINES, J.W., Dr. — Salem Baptist Church (1885)
GANT, Benjamin J. — Ebenezer M.E. Church (1883); residence at 210 F St., S.W.
GARDNER, Leonard M. — Mount Zion Methodist Episcopal Church, R & 15th Sts., N.W. (1880)
GASKINS, Madison H. — Second [Colored] Baptist Church, 3rd & H Sts., N.W. (1880)
GIBBONS, William — Zion [Colored] Baptist Church, 335 F St., S.W. (1883)
GIBSON, Edward H. — Bethlehem Baptist Church (1885)
GIERY, Samuel H. — Epiphany Episcopal Church (1885)
GILES, Chauncey — New Church, Philadelphia, Pa. (1877)
GILLIAT, Francis — Grace Protestant Episcopal Church, D & 8th Sts., S.W. (1882); residence at 1102 Maryland Ave. (1881)
GRAVES, John A. — Protestant Episcopal Church (1883)
GRAY, E.H. — North Baptist Church (1877)
GRAY, James W. — First Methodist Protestant Church, Virginia Ave. near 5th St., S.E. (1880), residence at 500 Virginia Ave., S.E. (1881)
GRAY, John H.T. — Mount Zion A.M.E. Church, Hillsdale, D.C. (1881)
GREEN, Adam — Mount Zion [Colored] Baptist Church, 12th & E Sts., N.E. (1883); Mount Calvary Church (1885)
GREEN, J.W. — African M. Protestant Church (1877)
GREEN, Nathaniel J. — Galbraith A.M.E.Z. Church, 6th near L St., N.W. (1885)
GREEN, Thomas L. — Hillsdale C.M.E. Church, Hillsdale, D.C. (1883)
GREENE, Columbus — Residence at 1114 10th St., N.W. (1881)
GREENE, Samuel Harrison — Calvary Baptist Church (1880); residence at 1114 10th St., N.W. (1881)
GREENIGE, E.P. — Mt. Pisgah Chapel (1877)
GRIFFITH, Samuel H. — Grace Episcopal Church, Georgetown, D.C. (1885)
GRIMKE, Francis J. — Providence [15th Street] [Colored] Presbyterian Church, 15th & I Sts., N.W. (1881); residence at 1608 R St., N.W.
GUENTHER, August — First (Trinity) Evangelical Reformed Church, 6th & N Sts., N.W. (1882)

H

HAGEY, J. Clarke — Union M.E. Church (1880); Grace M.E. Church, 9th and S Sts., N.W. (1883); North Capitol M.E. Church (1885); residence at 812 20th St., N.W. (1881)

District of Columbia Ministers

HAINES, John	E. Washington Station, Washington, D.C. (1877)
HALL, Aquilla	Israel C.M. Church (1881)
HALL, Philip T.	Methodist Protestant Church (1881)
HAMER, Jacob P.	Galbraith [Colored] Chapel, L St. W. between 4th and 5th Sts. (1880)
HAMILTON, F.M.	East Washington Station C.M.E. Church, 14th & C Sts., N.E. (1882)
HAMMACK, W. McK.	Methodist Episcopal Church, Bladensburg, Md. (1881); Memorial M.E. Church, 818 8th Street, N.E., Washington, D.C. (1881)
HANDY, James A.	Union Bethel African M.E. Church, 15th & M Sts., N.W. (1883)
HARGRAVES, B.J.	C.M.E. Church (1883)
HARRIS, William A.	St. Andrews Church (1881)
HARROLD, James A.	Holy Cross P.E. Church, Massachusetts Ave. near 18th St., N.W. (1882); residence at 1424 N St. (1883)
HARTSOCK, Samuel M.	Hamlin M.E. Church, 9th & P Sts., N.W.; residence at 1506 9th Street, N.W., (1881)
HATCHER, W.E.	Grace Street Baptist Church, Richmond, Va. (1885)
HAVENNER, Franch H.	North Capitol M.E. Church (1881); residence at 33 K Street, N.E.
HAWLEY, M.L.	M.G., Methodist Episcopal Church (1883)
HAY, Lewis	Church of the Reformation (1877)
HAYES, Peter	Mt. Bethel Baptist Church (1882)
HAYGHE, John L.	Waugh Chapel (1881)
HAYNES, John H.	C.M.E. Church, Petersburg, Va. (1883)
HAYWARD, Richard	Epiphany Church (1883)
HEALY, P.F., S.J.	Roman Catholic Church, Georgetown, D.C. (1880)
HEISSE, J. Fred	Wesley Chapel M.E. Church (1877)
HENRY, J.R.	Allen Chapel (1880)
HEWETH, Wm. H.	M.G., 18 I St., N.W. (1883)
HEYDE, Geo. W.	12th St. Methodist Episcopal Church (1880); residence at 1012 Pennsylvania Ave., S.E. (1879)
HICKS, William	Mt. Zion Church, Georgetown, D.C. (1881)
HICKS, Wm. W.	The Tabernacle M.E. Congregational Church, 9th & B Sts., S.W. (1882)
HOBBS, G.W.	Methodist Episcopal, Elkridge Landing, Md. (1877)
HOLLAND, Wm. II.	St. John's M.P. Church (1882)
HOLMEAD, Alfred	Grace Church (1879); residence at 12th St., South
HOLMES, Addison	Zion Baptist Church, Annapolis, Md. (1877)
HOLMES, James R.	Mount Vernon Baptist Church (1882); residence at 1205 R St. (1883)
HOLMES, Robert	Mont. Baptist Church (1877)
HOLMES, Washington	No church associated (1885)
HOMRIGHAUS, Albert	Church of the Fatherland [Lutheran], 6th & P Sts., N.W. (1883); residence at 929 O St., N.W.
HOOD, Samuel	Methodist Episcopal Church (1883)
HOOVER, S.H.	Methodist Episcopal Church, Philadelphia, Pa. (1881)
HOUSE, Chas. T.	Douglas Memorial M.E. Church (1883)
HOWARD, James	Macedonian [Colored] Baptist Church, Hillsdale, D.C. (1883)
HOWARD, William James	Zion Baptist Church (1883)
HOWE, Samuel H.	West Street Presbyterian Church, P & 31st Sts., N.W., Georgetown, D.C., 1873-1883; residence at 3121 R St., N.W. (1881)
HUBLER, John Brewster	St. Paul's Church (1883)
HUNTINGTON, A.J.	Baptist Church (1877)
HUNTLEY, E.D.	Metropolitan M.E. Church (1883)

I

INGERSOLL, W.M.	Metropolitan Baptist Church, 6th & A St., N.E. (1883)
INGLE, Edward H.	Ascension Church (1882)

District of Columbia Ministers

J

JACKSON, Nathaniel	Jones Chapel (1877)
JACKSON, Noah	Mount Hall [Colored] Baptist Church, 16th & B, N.E. (1883); residence at 2249 8th St. near Grant Ave., N.W.
JANNEY, George E.	Eastern Station Church (1877)
JEFFERIS, Mortimer T.	Protestant Episcopal Church, Diocese of Long Island (1883); residence 150 Lexington Ave., New York City
JEFFERSON, William B.	Third [Colored] Baptist Church, Franklin & 4th Sts., N.W. (1882); residence at Trumbull St. (1881)
JENKINS, Charles K., S.J.	Roman Catholic Church (1880)
JOHNSON, Robert	Metropolitan Baptist Church (1883); Fourth [Colored] Baptist Church, 12th & R St., N.W. (1883)
JOHNSON, Morris	Mt. Zion Church, Georgetown, D.C. (1880)
JOHNSON, Samuel M.	Mt. Pleasant A.M.E. Church (1883)
JOHNSON, William B.	Second Baptist Church (1885)
JOHNSTON, John B.	Whitney Avenue Union Mission, Whitney Ave. near 7th St. Rd. (1883)
JONES, Arthur	African M.E. Church (1877)
JONES, I.S.	Methodist Church (1883)
JOYCE, J. Jay	St. John's Protestant Episcopal Church (1877)

K

KELLY, Joseph T.	Fourth Presbyterian Church, 9th & G Sts., N.W. (1880); residence at 519 4th St., N.W. (1881)
KELLY, Stephen A.	Holy Trinity Catholic Parish, 36th & O St., N.W., 1881-1890
KENT, Alexander	First Universalist Church, 13th & L Sts., N.W. (1880)
KERNS, W.S.	Baptist Church, Va. (1882)
KERVICK, Thomas J.	Catholic Church (1885)
KING, Charles	M.E. Church, Virginia Conference (1877)
KRAMER, Samuel R.	Seaman's Bethel and Reading Room M.E. Church, 714 L St., S.E. (1883); acting chaplain at U.S. Navy Yard (1881); residence at 102 C Street, S.E. (1881)
KRATT, Martin	German Evangelical Concordia Church (1880); residence at 611 20th St., N.W. (1881)
KURTZ, Frederick	German Evangelical Church (1877)
KURZ, R.	St. John's Lutheran Church (1877)

L

LANAHAN, John	Foundry Church, 1878-1881; residence at 1335 G St., N.W. (1879)
LANCASTER, Clement S.	St. John's Church, Frederick, Md. (1882)
LANDAN, G.W.J.	Evangelical Lutheran Church (1877); German Presbyterian Zion Church, Washington, D.C. (1880)
LANE, John F.	A.M.E. Church, Good Hope Hill, D.C. (1883)
LANEY, William H.	Gorsuch Methodist Episcopal Church, 4½ & L Sts., N.W. (1885)
LASSELL, James T.	9th Street Methodist Protestant Church, 515 9th St., N.W. (1882)
LATANE, William C.	Protestant Episcopal Church, Westmoreland Co., Va. (1881)
LAWS, Robert S.	Virginia Avenue [Colored] Baptist Church, Virginia Ave. & 6th St., S.W. (1883)
LEAR, John I.	Colored M.E. Church in America, Hillsdale, D.C. (1881); Bethlehem Baptist Church, Washington, D.C. (1885)
LEE, A.H.	First Methodist Church (1885)
LEE, R.R.	M.E. Asbury Church, Tennallytown, D.C. (1885)
LEE, William H.	South Washington First [Colored] Baptist Church, 705 6th St., S.W. (1881)
LEECH, George V.	4th Street Methodist Episcopal Church (1880)
LEHNERT, Ernest	St. John's German Evangelical Lutheran Church, 4½ & D Sts., S.W. (1882)
LEONARD, William Andrew	St. John's Parish Church, 16th & H Sts., N.W., 1881-c.1889

District of Columbia Ministers

LEWIS, John Vaughan	St. John's Church (1877)
LEWIS, Madison	Mt. Horeb Baptist Church (1877); Israel [Colored] Baptist Church, A & 7th Sts., N.E. (1880)
LEWIS, Peter	Salem Baptist Church (1880); residence at 470 S Street, S.W. (1883)
LEWIS, W.H.	Southwest (Virginia Avenue) Baptist Church (1881)
LIGHTHIPE, L.H.	Trinity Church, Vincentown, N.J. (1881)
LINDSAY, James H.	Mt. Zion Baptist Church (1883)
LINDSAY, John J.	St. John's Church, O St. & Potomac Ave., N.W., Georgetown, D.C. (1880); Union M.E. Church (1883); residence at 3236 O St. (1883)
LITTLE, George O.	Assembly Presbyterian Church, 5th & I Sts., N.W. (1881); residence at 216 I Street, N.W. (1883)
LIVINGSTON, W.F.	Methodist Protestant Church, Alexandria Co., Va. (1885)
LODGE, J.L.	Gay Street Baptist Church, West Washington, D.C. (1885)
LOGAN, B.F.	Roman Catholic Church, Washington, D.C. (1885)
LOUIS, Peter C.	C.M.E. Church, Hillsdale, D.C. (1885)
LOVING, Junius I.	M.G., Baptist Church (1885)
LOWRIE, Randolph W.	Protestant Episcopal Church, Diocese of Md. (1883)
LOWRY, John	Presbyterian Church, Whitehall, N.Y. (1880)
LUEBKERT, Wm. C.H.	German Evangelical Trinity Congregation of the Unaltered Augsburg Confession, 4th & E Sts., N.W. (1881)
LYONS, J.F.	Wesley Zion Church (1877)

M

MacCAULEY, Clay	All Souls Church, 1877-1880
MACLEAN, John, M.G.	No church identified (1881)
MADDEN, S.W.	First Baptist Church, Alexandria, Va. (1880)
MAITRIGUES, Julius, Fr.	Trinity Church, Georgetown, D.C. (1877)
MARRIOTT, O.C.	M.E. Church, Uniontown, D.C. (1877)
MASON, A.F.	Calvary Baptist Church (1877)
MATTHEWS, Joseph	Mt. Zion Baptist Church, Arlington, Va. (1881)
MAYNADIER, Ebenezer E.	St. Ann's Catholic Church, Tennallytown, D.C. (1881)
McCOOK, Henry C.	Tabernacle Presbyterian Church, Philadelphia, Pa. (1880)
McELROY, Irving	Epiphany Church (1885)
McKEE, John M. Ezekiel	Emanuel P.E. Church, Anacostia, D.C. (1881)
McKENNEY, Wm. I.	Hamlin M.E. Church (1880); Wesley Chapel M.E. Church, 5th & F Sts., N.W. (1883)
McLAREN, James	Methodist Episcopal Church (1880)
McNALLY, John	St. Stephen's Catholic Church, Pennsylvania Ave. & 25th St., N.W., 1867-1889; residence 2426 Pennsylvania Ave. (1883)
MEAD, Charles H.	Church of the Epiphany Mission, 1216 Maryland Ave., S.W. (1881); residence at 1332 G St., N.W.
MEADOR, Chastain C.	Fifth Baptist Church (1881); residence at 903 13th St., N.W.
MEIER, Henry A.	M.G., Reformed Trinity Church (1885)
MEIGS, Harry Ingersoll	Montgomery Co., Pa. (1881)
MICHAEL, J.T.	Free Methodist Church (1881)
MIDDLETON, Charles H.	Baptist Church (1882)
MILLER, Jos.	A.M.E. Church (1880)
MILLER, Shelton	St. Luke's Baptist Church, Magnolia Lane, Brightwood, D.C. (1880); residence at 2009 11th St., N.W. (1883)
MILLS, Joseph L.	9th Street Methodist Protestant Church (1883); residence at 1536 Columbia St., N.W.
MIRICK, Stephen H.	E Street Baptist Church (1881)
MITCHELL, Jacob M.	Israel Mission [Colored] M.E. Church, Stanton Ave. and Pomeroy Ave., Hillsdale, D.C. (1882)
MITCHELL, Walter A.	Protestant Episcopal Church, c.1861-post 1896
MITCHELL, Samuel S.	New York Avenue Presbyterian Church (1877)

District of Columbia Ministers

MOORE, J.W.	Lincoln Memorial Congregation (1885)
MORGAN, Tillotson A.	12th Street M.E. Church, 12th & E Sts., S.E. (1881)
MORRIS, James T.	Bethel A.M.E. Church, 26th & P Sts., N.W., Georgetown, D.C. (1880)
MORRISON, Wm. Foster	Ascension Church (1880)
MULLIGAN, John A.	Galbraith Chapel (1883)
MURPHY, Edgar	Mt. Zion M.E. Church (1883)
MURPHY, John J.	Holy Trinity Parish, 1877-1878; St. Aloysius Catholic, North Capitol and I Sts., N.W. (1883)
MURRAY, J.T.	Methodist Protestant Church, Georgetown, D.C. (1880)
MYTINGER, Charles H.	Methodist Episcopal Church (1882); residence at 71 DeFrees St. (1877)

N

NAYLOR, Henry R.	Foundry Methodist Episcopal Church, 1884-1887
NEEPIER, W.J.	North Carolina Avenue M.P. Church (1883)
NEUMAN, J.P.	Methodist Episcopal Church (1877)
NEWMAN, Stephen M.	First Congregational Church (1885)
NICE, Henry	Methodist Episcopal Church, 12th Street, S.E. (1877)
NICHOLS, John H.	Sampson Street Baptist Church (1885)
NIXDORFF, George A.	English Evangelical Lutheran Church, Q & 32nd Sts., N.W., Georgetown, D.C., 1871-1894
NOBLE, Mason	Sixth Presbyterian Church (1881)
NORRIS, Richard	Ryland M.E. Church, 10th & D Sts., S.W. (1882); residence at 414 10th St., S.W. (1883)
NORTON, F.L.	St. John's Episcopal Church (1880)
NOURSE, James M.	M.G., Presbyterian Church, Alexandria, Va. (1885)
NOURSE, Robert	Tabernacle Congregational Church (1885)

O

O'SULLIVAN, Jeremiah	St. Peter's Catholic Church, 2nd & C Sts., S.E. (1882); residence at 2nd and C Streets, S.E. (1879)
OCKERMAN, J.F.	Mt. Zion M.E. Church (1885)
OWEN, E.D.	Ryland M.E. Church (1877); Mt. Zion Church (1877, 1880); Gorsuch M.E. Church (1885); residence at 1432 T St., N.W. and 414 10th St., S.W.
OWENS, George W.	North Capitol M.E. Church, K & North Capitol Sts., N.W. (1883)

P

PARET, William	Epiphany P.E. Church, G & 13th Sts., N.W. (1880); residence at 1334 New York Ave. (1881)
PARKER, Jacob E.	Methodist Episcopal Church (1883)
PARKER, J.W.	E. Baptist Church (1877)
PARSON, William E.	Church of the Reformation [Lutheran], B St. & Pennsylvania Ave., S.E. (1880)
PATCH, George B.	Unity Presbyterian Church, 1630 14th St., N.W. (1880)
PAXTON, John R.	New York Avenue Presbyterian Church (1880)
PAYNE, Robert A.	Trinity Ind. Methodist Church (1885)
PEARSALL, Z.T.	Wesley Zion Church (1885)
PECK, Edward W.S.	Methodist Episcopal Church (1880); residence at 1003 M St., N.W. (1879)
PECK, Eugene	First Presbyterian Church (1883)
PEEL, William T.	Plymouth Congregational [Colored] Church, 18th & L Sts., N.W. (1882)
PERRY, Josiah B.	St. Andrews' Protestant Episcopal Church, 14th & Corcoran Sts., N.W. (1883); St. Andrew's Church (1885); residence at 1630 15th Street, N.W. (1883)
PETTIS, W.M.	Protestant Episcopal Church, Newport, Ky. (1882)
PEYTON, Randolph V.	Mt. Herman Church (1883)
PHELPS, E.P.	Methodist Episcopal Church (1877)

District of Columbia Ministers

PHILIPBAR, Charles	Emanuel Church (1883)
PHILLIPS, Bartlet L.	First Baptist Church (1883)
PHILLIPS, John W.	St. Paul's P.E. Church (1881); Grace Episcopal Church, Washington, D.C. (1885); residence at 419 New Jersey Ave., S.E. (1881)
PINKNEY, Henry	Asbury M.E. Church (1883); residence at 1220 N St., N.W.
PINKNEY, William	Bishop of Maryland (1881); residence Bladensburg, Md.
PITZER, Alexander W.	Central Presbyterian Church, 3rd & I Sts., N.W. (1880); residence at 42 I St. (1881)
PLUMMER, Henry V.	Mt. Carmel [Colored] Baptist Church, 4th & K Sts., N.W. (1881)
POTTER, John F.	St. Mary's [Colored] Chapel, mission of John's Episcopal Church, 23rd & G Sts., N.W. (1881)
POULSON, A.	No church identified (1881)
POWER, Frederick D.	Vermont Avenue Christian Church, Vermont Ave. near N St., N.W. (1881); residence at 1321 Corcoran St.
PRICE, J.A.	Hamlin M.E. Church (1885)
PRIMROSE, Hanson	C.M.E. Church (1885)
PROCTOR, John	Asbury Church (1877)
PRYOR, John H.	Baptist Church (1885); residence at Pomeroy St., N.W.

R

RABBIA, Sebastian	St. Peter's Church (1877); residence at 313 2nd Street, S.W.
RAMSDELL, Charles B.	North Presbyterian Church, N & 9th Sts., N.W. (1881); residence at 11 16 10th St., N.W.
RANKIN, James E.	First Congregational Church, 10th & G Sts., N.W. (1880); residence at 9 Grant Pl. (1883)
READ, R.A.	Gospel Mt. Zion Church, Georgetown, D.C. (1877); Asbury M.E. Church, Washington, D.C. (1885)
REAZOR, F.B.	St. John's Chapel and Parish Church (1885)
REED, James	Israel Church (1877)
REED, W. Hurst	Memorial M.E. Chapel, 11th & H Sts., N.E. (1882)
REID, B.G.W.	Methodist Episcopal Church (1877)
REID, Newton P.	Zion Primitive Baptist Church (1880)
REID, W.J.O.	M.E. Church, Uniontown, D.C. (1883)
REILEY, J. McKendree	Dumbarton Street Methodist Episcopal, Georgetown, D.C. (1880); residence at 3130 Beall "O" Street, West Washington, D.C. (1881)
RENNALDS, Lewis Paul	Catholic Church
REVILLE, D., O.P.	St. Dominic's Church (1877)
RICE, Maartin F.B.	Fourth Street M.E. Church (1885)
RICH, Alex. M.	Trinity P.E. Parish Hall (1883)
RICHARDSON, Chas. Herbert	McKendree M.E. Church, Massachusetts Ave. near 10th St., N.W. (1880)
ROANE, J. Wm.	Central [Colored] Baptist Church, L & 3rd Sts., N.W. (1882); residence at 59 P Street, N.W. (1883)
ROBBINS, Nathaniel	Gurley Presbyterian Chapel, Boundary between 6th & 7th Sts., N.W. (1883)
ROBERTS, Albert A.	No church associated. Residence at 1707 17th Street, N.W. (1877)
ROBINSON, Clement	Beulah Baptist Church, Alexandria, Va. (1877); Bethesda [Colored] Baptist Church, 2728 M St., N.W. (1883)
ROBINSON, Fielding	White Oak [Colored] Baptist Church, Madison Ave. near 15th St., N.W. (1883); residence 20 Pierce St. (1881)
ROBINSON, Jacob	No church associated. (1877)
ROBINSON, James	Salem Baptist Church (1880); residence at 120 Laurence St. (1883)
ROBINSON, Temple S.	Mount Jezreel [Colored] Baptist Church, 5th & E Sts., S.E. (1883); 7th and I Streets, S.E. (1881); residence at 324 E St., S.W. (1881)
ROBINSON, William Temple	Mount Olivet [Colored] Baptist Church, 1128 6th St., N.E. (1883)
ROSS, M.H.	John Wesley M.E. Zion Church (1880)
ROSS, Jacob	Methodist Protestant Church, Georgetown, D.C. (1880)
ROWE, Robert S.	Methodist Protestant Church, Baltimore, Md. (1882)

District of Columbia Ministers

RYAN, P.J.	Assistant Pastor, Immaculate Conception Catholic, 8th & N Sts., N.W. (1883)
RYAN, Stanislaus F.	St. Theresa Catholic Church, Washington & Fillmore, Anacostia, D.C. (1883)
RYLAND, J.H.	Uniontown M.E. Church, Uniontown [Anacostia], D.C. (1880); residence at 1012 Pennsylvania Ave., S.E. (1883)

S

SAMUELS, I.W.	Adas Israel Congregation, 6th & G Sts., N.W. (1885); residence at 723 6th St., N.W. (1879)
SAUNDERS, Samuel	Second Baptist Church, Virginia Ave. and 4th, S.E. (1882)
SCHARF, J.G.	Emanuel's Church (1880)
SCHELL, William H.	Christian Church, Rockville, Md. (1883)
SCHLEUTER, John T.M.	St. Joseph's Roman Catholic Church, 2nd & C Sts., N.E. (1880)
SCHNEIDER, Louis H.	Evangelical Lutheran Concordia Church, 20th & G Sts., N.W. (1883)
SCHUBERT, Wm. Augustus	Episcopal Church (1881)
SCOTT, Edward D.	Gethsemane Baptist Church (1885)
SCOTT, Henry	Bethlehem [Colored] Baptist Church, Nichols Ave., Hillsdale, D.C. (1881); residence at Navy Yard, S.E.
SCOTT, Samuel	Enon [Colored] Baptist Church, 6th & C Sts., S.E. (1883)
SHARP, Henry T.	Grace P.E. Church, Alexandria, Va. (1883)
SHIPPEN, Rush A.	All Souls [Unitarian] Church, 14th & L Sts., N.W., 1881-1895
SHIRAS, Alexander	Protestant Episcopal Church (1877)
SHORT, John T.	Congregational Church in Central Ohio (1881)
SHORTS, Thomas H.	Garfield Baptist Church, Clarke Co., Va. (1882)
SHUTE, Samuel M., M.G.	Baptist Church (1881, 1885)
SHREEVE, Jesse	North Carolina Avenue Church (1877)
SHREEVES, J.P.	St. Paul's A.M.E. Chapel, S.W. Washington, D.C. (1881)
SIMEON, James	St. Joseph Church (1877)
SIMPSON, T.W.	Presbyterian Church, Montgomery Co., Md. (1883)
SMITH, John C.	Fourth Presbyterian Church (1877)
SMITH, John W.	Grace M.E. Church (1881)
SMITH, Joseph T.	Central Presbyterian Church, Baltimore, Md. (1882)
SMITH, Presley B.	M.E. Church South, Falls Church, Va. (1881)
SMITH, Simon P.	Lincoln Memorial [Colored] Mission Church, 11th & R Sts., N.W. (1880)
SMITH, Warner	Ebenezer Church, Georgetown, D.C. (1883)
SMOOT, Wm. M.	Primitive Baptist Church, Prince William Co., Va. (1880)
SNELL, M. Porter	Congregational Church (1882)
SONTAG, Charles F.	Grace Mission Reformed Church, 15th St. between Vermont Ave. and P St., N.W. (1881)
SOUTHERLAND, Silas B.	Methodist Protestant Church, 1238 31st St., N.W., Georgetown, D.C. (1881)
SOUTHGATE, William S.	Episcopal Church, Annapolis, Md. (1877)
ST. JAMES, Osmund	Heavenly Rest [Colored] Episcopal Church, 105 2nd St., S.E. (1883)
STANSBERRY, J.B.	St. Paul's Methodist Church (1877)
STANTON, Elias M.	Galbraith [Colored] M.E. Church, 428 L St., N.W. (1883)
STARR, Jesse C.	M.E. Church, Tennallytown, D.C. (1877); Gorsuch M.E. Church, Washington, D.C. (1880); residence at 456 L St., S.W. (1879)
STEELE, A. Floridus	St. Mark's Protestant Episcopal Church, 3rd & A Sts., S.E. (1885); residence at 600 A St., N.E. (1881)
STEELE, Robert	Ebenezer [Colored] M.E. Church, D & 4th Sts., S.E. (1881); residence at 124 3rd St., S.E.
STELTZER, Joseph	Emanuel Church of the Evangelical Association, 1114 6th St., N.W. (1880); residence at 1114 6th St., N.W. (1883)
STEMPLE, Isaac	Adas Israel Jewish Congregation (1885)
STERN, Herman I.	German Reformed Trinity Church (1881)
STERN, Louis	Rabbi, Washington Hebrew Reform Congregation, 8th & H Sts., N.W. (1877); residence at 1448 9th St. (1883)

District of Columbia Ministers

STEVENS, H.S.	Baptist Church, Cromwell, Conn. (1883)
STONE, W.H.	North Carolina Avenue Church (1880)
STUART, Albert R.	Christ P.E. Church Parish, 31st & O Sts., N.W. (1881); residence at 3030 P St., N.W. (1883)
STUBBS, Alfred H.	St. Barnabas Episcopal Church, Greensboro, N.C. (1885)
STUBBS, Nathaniel	Union Wesley [Colored] M.E. Church, 23rd near L St., N.W. (1883); residence at 1118 26th St., N.W.
SUNDERLAND, Byron	First Presbyterian Church, 4-1/2 St. near Louisiana Ave., N.W. (1877, 1880); residence at 328 6th St., N.W.
SWALLOW, Benjamin	Baptist Church (1885)
SWEM, Edmond Hez.	Second Baptist Church (1885)

T

TACKETT, John O.	Methodist Episcopal Church South, Fauquier Co., Va. (1880)
TAGG, Frank T.	Methodist Protestant, Georgetown, D.C. (1883); residence at 1236 Congress Street, Georgetown, D.C.
TARRO, P.	No church associated. Residence at 1118 15th Street, N.W. (1877)
TASCO, Stephen	Bennings [Colored] M.E. Church, Bennings, D.C. (1883)
TEASDALE, John H.	Mount Tabor [Colored] Baptist Church, Tennallytown, D.C. (1881)
TEWES, Francis J.	St. Mary's German Catholic Church, 5th & H Sts., N.W. (1883)
THOMAS, Cornelius F.	St. Patrick's Roman Catholic Church (1883); residence at corner of 10th and G Sts., N.W.
THOMAS, Walter T.	Israel C.M.E. Church, 1st and B Sts., S.W. (1881)
THOMAS, W.S.O.	Baptist Church, Rockville, Montgomery Co., Md. (1885)
TILGHMAN, William H.	Arlington A.M.E. Church, Arlington, Va. (1883); M.E. Zion Church, Laurel, Md. (1885)
TIMOTHY, B.W.	A.M.E. Church, Hillsdale, D.C. (1881)
TOWNSEND, Israel L.	Incarnation Church, 12th & N Sts., N.W. (1881)
TREADWAY, S.B.	Methodist Protestant Church (1885)
TRESSEL, Emanuel G.	Grace Evangelical Lutheran Church, 13th & Q Sts., N.W. (1881)
TROUT, J.W.	N.C. Avenue Methodist Protestant Church (1881); Eutaw M.P. Church, Baltimore, Md. (1882)
TROWBRIDGE, Wm. H.	Free Will Baptist Church, Mountain Grove, Mo. (1885)
TUCKER, G.W.	John Wesley Church (1881)
TUDOR, W.V.	Methodist Episcopal Church South, St. Louis, Mo. (1881)
TURNER, Matthew A.	Methodist Episcopal Church (1885)
TYLER, Geo. T.	Methodist Episcopal Church South, Rockville, Md. (1881)

U

UPSHAW, A.W.	Mt. Pisgah Church (1885)
UREEL, Charles R.	First Independent Christ Church, Baltimore, Md. (1881)
USHER, George W.	Israel C.M.E. and A.M.E. Church (1883)

V

VALENTINE, John W.	Trinity Church (1883); Mount Pisgah [Colored] M.E. Church, 10th & R Sts., N.W. (1883)
VAN DOREN, Wm. Theo.	Presbyterian Church (1885); residence at 647 East Capitol (1883)

W

WALES, S.S.	John Wesley A.M.E. Church, residence at 1733 H Street, N.W. (1881)
WALKER, Joseph	Georgetown [Gay Street] Baptist Church, Georgetown, D.C. (1882)
WALKER, Wm. J.	Shiloh [Colored] Baptist Church, 16th & L Sts., N.W. (1880), residence at 1707 19th St., N.W. (1881)
WALKER, P.G.	Ebenezer M.E. Church (1877)

District of Columbia Ministers

WALLEN, Samuel S.	Eastern Presbyterian Church, 8th & F Sts., N.E. (1882)
WALLER, Washington	Mt. Olivet Church, Arlington, Va. (1881); residence 1608 11th St. (1877)
WALSH, Michael J.	St. Augustine [Colored] Catholic Church, 15th & L Sts., N.W. (1883)
WALTER, Jacob Ambrose	St. Patrick's Catholic Church, G & 9th Sts., N.W.,1860-1894; residence at 619 10th St., N.W. (1881)
WARD, Cato	St. Paul's M.E. Church (1881)
WARD, William F.	Foundry M.E. Church, G & 14th Sts., N.W., 1881-1884; residence at 1335 3rd St., N.W. (1883)
WARING, William	Berean [Colored] Baptist Church, 18th and L Sts., N.W. (1880)
WASHINGTON, Samuel	Jerusalem Baptist Church, Montgomery Co., Md. (1877)
WATERS, William H.	A.M.E. Church (1877, 1880); residence at 432 Delaware Avenue, S.W. (1877)
WATKINS, George T.	Union Bethel Church (1885)
WATTS, Augustus A.	First Union [Colored] Baptist Church, Sherman Ave., N.W. (1883)
WATSON, Edward L.	Methodist Episcopal Church, Montgomery Co., Md. (1883)
WEBSTER, Joseph J.G.	Dumbarton Street M.E. Church, Dumbarton Ave. near 32nd St., N.W., Georgetown, D.C. (1882); residence at 3130 O St. (1883)
WEDERMAN, L.G.	U.S. M.E. Church (1880)
WEECH, William T.L.	Union Chapel M.E. Church, 20th & H Sts., N.W. (1882); residence at 812 20th St., N.W. (1883)
WEEDE, Charles T.	North Capitol M.E. Church (1877); Tennallytown M.E. Church, Tennallytown, D.C. (1880); residence at 622 New Jersey Ave., N.W. (1877)
WELCH, John H.	Mount Sinai [Colored] M.E. Church, 14th and B Sts., N.E. (1883); Mt. Zion A.M.E. Church, Hillsdale, D.C. (1885)
WELLS, David	Western Presbyterian Church (1877)
WHEELER, J.R.	Waugh Church (1877); residence at 111 3rd Street, N.E.
WHITEFORD, John	Providence Mission, 2nd & I Sts., N.E. (1883)
WHITTLESEY, E.	Congregational Church (1885)
WILLIAMS, James T.	Emory Chapel (1879); residence Brightwood, D.C.
WILLIAMS, John B.	St. Matthews Episcopal Church, Bladensburg, Md. (1877); Protestant Episcopal Church, St. Matthew's Parish, Md. (1881); All Saints Chapel, Bennings Station on B & P.R.R. (1883)
WILLIAMS, John C.	A.M.E. Church, Bladensburgh, Md. (1882)
WILLIAMS, R.S.	Israel C.M.E. Church (1885)
WILLIS, Edward J.	Liberty [Colored] Baptist Church, E & 17th St., N.W. (1880)
WILLS, David	Chaplain, U.S.A. (1881)
WILSON, A.B.	Ebenezer Methodist Episcopal Church (1880)
WILSON, David	9th Street M.P. Church (1877); residence at 517 9th St., N.W.
WILSON, William H.	Emery Chapel, Brightwood, D.C. (1883)
WINSTON, John H.	Seventh [Colored] Baptist Church, 19th & R Sts., N.W. (1880)
WOLFE, J.W.	Enon M.E. Church South, Brightwood, D.C. (1885)
WOLFF, William	German Concordia Church (1883)
WORTHINGTON, William	Episcopal Church (1883)
WRIGHT, William H.	Union Wesley Church, Montgomery Co., Md. (1880)
WYNKOOP, Theodoe S.	Western Presbyterian Church, 1313 H St., N.W. (1882)
WYNNE, Lewis B.	Baptist Church (1880); residence at 1110 14th St. (1877)

Y

YANCY, Jeremiah	Baptist Church, Fluvanna Co., Va. (1882); St. James Church in Va. (1883)
YATES, Charles L.	Baptist Church, Rappahannock Co., Va. (1885)
YORK, Levi H.	Methodist Episcopal Church (1885)
YOUNG, W.H.	East Washington Station C.M.E. Church (1881)
YOUNG, William Henry	Metropolitan Baptist Church (1885)

DISTRICT OF COLUMBIA
MARRIAGE RECORDS INDEX
June 28, 1877 to 1885
Marriage Record 11 through 20

A

Abbot, Edna	Petitt, James W.	03 OCT 1878	12	253
Abbott, Ellen	Hobbs, Frank D.	01 OCT 1879 R	13	395
Abbott, Ernest E.	Stratton, Jennie	22 AUG 1885 R	20	361
Abbott, George Albert	Otis, Harriet Elizabeth	20 MAR 1883	17	352
Abbott, Harriet	Brenner, William	04 MAR 1881 R	15	214
Abbott, Julius	Forster, Johanmah	23 MAY 1880 R	14	279
Abbott, Sarah E., Mrs.	Frühnch, John	29 OCT 1881 L	16	052
Abbott, W.E.	Gove, Hattie E.	24 JAN 1878	11	317
Abel, Fritz	Bohraus, Kathrina	26 OCT 1878 L	12	292
Abel, Thomas	Watson, Mary	10 AUG 1885	20	363
Abell, Flora	Henley, George F.	25 OCT 1884	19	335
Abell, Laney	Field, Lewis O.	08 FEB 1883	17	300
Abell, Leila Kate	Stephenson, Joseph G.	27 JAN 1881 R	15	165
Abell, Lydia S., Mrs.	Button, George P.	21 AUG 1877	11	059
Able, Dulcie	Kendall, John	30 APR 1879	13	168
Able, Roxie Ann	Sutherland, Mobeary	25 SEP 1879	13	387
Able, Selone	Syncox, James T.	13 SEP 1883	18	129
Abner, Edward	Engels, Helene	09 NOV 1878 L	12	319
Abraham, Clara	Barnes, James Wallace	28 DEC 1881 R	16	162
Abraham, Jacob	Harding, O.P., Mrs.	29 MAR 1883 L	17	370
Accardi, Adrian J.P.	Rock, Laura Cecilia	02 OCT 1877 R	11	119
Ace, Annie	Langton, Henry	14 MAY 1885	20	223
Acher, Ella, Mrs.	Fairfax, John A.	20 OCT 1880	15	006
Acker, William Jacob	Burgess, Jessie	11 DEC 1884 R	19	450
Acton, Annie May	Colné, Thaddeus A.	04 OCT 1881 L	16	006
Acton, Josephine	Smith, Joseph T.	05 JUN 1884 L	19	064
Acton, Mary E.	Woods, Samuel M.	02 FEB 1885 L	20	047
Adam, Charles Fox Frederick	Palmer, Juliet	29 NOV 1877 R	11	209
Adam, Lucretia	Martin, Lewis	10 SEP 1878 L	12	208
Adams, Aaron	Mason, Katie	21 APR 1881 L	15	269
Adams, Amos S.	Waugh, Sallie R.	09 OCT 1879	13	411
Adams, Annie	Mercy, Charles E.	14 JUL 1877 L	11	019
Adams, Annie	Hall, James	02 JAN 1878	11	287
Adams, Annie R.	Sims, Frederick G.	16 JAN 1878	11	306
Adams, Arthur C.	Schneider, Mary F.	15 APR 1879 R	13	146
Adams, Asbury	Digges, Adeline	04 AUG 1881 R	15	432
Adams, Benjamin Bela, Dr.	DeMotte, Ella	20 OCT 1881 R	15	004
Adams, Byron S.	Holtzman, Estelle P.	21 NOV 1882 L	17	140
Adams, Charles Emery	Collins, Amanda V.	05 JUN 1882 R	16	385
Adams, Charles Frederic	Rozer, Henrietta Frances	05 AUG 1885 R	20	351
Adams, David	Reeves, Sarah	23 DEC 1884 R	19	481
Adams, Eliza	Arnold, Willie Lawrence	26 MAY 1881 R	15	329
Adams, Elizabeth	Jenkins, Charles	06 MAY 1881	15	295
Adams, Ellen	Johnson, Washington	17 DEC 1877 L	11	239
Adams, Emma	Hunter, William	07 OCT 1878	12	258
Adams, Emma	Waters, William Henry	17 JUN 1880 L	14	325
Adams, Fannie W.	Moore, Jacob G.	18 SEP 1883 R	18	135
Adams, Frank C.	Windsor, Eva R.	20 NOV 1884 R	19	398
Adams, George S.	Johnson, Catherine	19 MAR 1879 L	13	107
Adams, George S.	Proctor, Rose	01 NOV 1881 R	16	054

D.C. Marriage Records Index, June 28, 1877 to October 19, 1885

Name	Spouse	Date	Vol	Page
Adams, George W.	Bowler, Almira	15 NOV 1877 R	11	189
Adams, George W.	Robey, Mary Virginia	29 JUN 1881 R	15	331
Adams, George W.	Robey, Mary E.	16 OCT 1882 L	17	073
Adams, Hamilton	Rodier, Frances Louise	28 FEB 1881 L	15	205
Adams, Hattie	Scott, George W.	09 MAR 1882 R	16	272
Adams, Henrietta	Gassaway, Richard	27 APR 1883 L	17	418
Adams, Isaiah	Brooker, Milley	20 JUN 1881 L	15	368
Adams, James W.	Lackey, Elizabeth M.	03 MAY 1878 L	12	036
Adams, John	Banks, Mary E.	17 APR 1882 L	16	319
Adams, John	Batson, Mary	01 JUN 1882	16	377
Adams, John Henry	Contee, Alice	04 SEP 1880	14	432
Adams, John T.	Walker, Mary Jane	13 DEC 1879 L	14	045
Adams, Jonah	Davis, Alice	06 DEC 1883 L	18	301
Adams, Josephine	Warwick, Alfred	09 JAN 1878	11	249
Adams, Judy	Janey, Samuel	29 OCT 1880 L	15	022
Adams, Julius	Claggett, Louisa	21 NOV 1883 L	18	270
Adams, Katie	Johnson, Benjamin	21 AUG 1884 R	18	314
Adams, Katie E. Brown	Hamilton, F.M.	25 OCT 1883	18	214
Adams, Lizzie A.	Hurley, James E.	13 FEB 1878 R	11	323
Adams, Louisa	Washington, Charles	10 JUN 1884 R	19	051
Adams, Lucy Ann	Key, William	20 OCT 1884 L	19	319
Adams, Lula	Ewers, Thomas Armistead	18 DEC 1883	18	322
Adams, Mamie E.	Collins, Albert G.	26 APR 1882 R	16	336
Adams, Manning J.	McKelden, Mary W.	18 DEC 1884	19	467
Adams, Mary	Dickson, Thomas	19 FEB 1881 L	15	195
Adams, Mary	Wright, William	09 MAR 1882 R	16	271
Adams, Mason P., Dr.	Petteys, Nellie	16 JUN 1880	14	324
Adams, Nancy	Hall, Edward	26 OCT 1882	17	097
Adams, Nicholas J.	Redman, Martha J.	07 NOV 1878 R	12	310
Adams, Noble	Clagett, Mary	25 DEC 1878 L	12	401
Adams, Perry M.	Kiskadden, Annie F.	20 APR 1881 R	15	271
Adams, Phillip	Coleman, Olivia	14 MAR 1878 L	11	382
Adams, Rebecca	Lee, Richard	03 SEP 1879 L	13	348
Adams, Richard A.	Wade, Alice L.	08 APR 1885	20	153
Adams, Richard R.	Lynn, Mary E., Mrs.	04 DEC 1878	12	366
Adams, Robert	Alexander, Evalena	20 MAY 1884 R	19	029
Adams, Robert C.	Donnelly, Kate M.	20 FEB 1882 L	16	251
Adams, Samuel	Dorsey, Florence	14 OCT 1881 R	16	017
Adams, Samuel W.	Smith, Georgianna	16 NOV 1882	17	133
Adams, Sarah	Johnson, Hamilton	30 AUG 1877 L	11	071
Adams, Sarah M.	Lewis, Clarence H.	10 FEB 1880 R	14	147
Adams, Sevi	Brown, Carrie	29 DEC 1881	16	164
Adams, Susie Rachel	Holmes, Jacob W.	17 MAY 1883	17	450
Adams, Thomas	Red, Maria	28 JUL 1877 L	11	033
Adams, Thomas F.	Crabster, Ella	03 JUN 1881 L	15	342
Adams, Thomas H.	Hamer, Mamie J.	20 DEC 1882 R	17	196
Adams, Thomas N.	Bouis, Annie E.	09 NOV 1880 R	15	037
Adams, Wesley	Ryder, Josephine	20 NOV 1879 R	13	498
Adams, West B.	Bland, Anna M.	10 MAR 1880 R	14	181
Adams, William	Mills, Evalina	10 AUG 1881 R	15	433
Adams, William	Taylor, Sallie	14 MAY 1883	17	442
Adams, William	Lyon, Anna L., Mrs.	09 NOV 1884	19	369
Adamson, Richard Alvin	Lacey, Mary Jane	13 FEB 1879 R	13	059
Adamson, William	Lynn, Ida	25 MAY 1885 R	20	238
Addis, Alice M.	Floyd, Albert C.	02 APR 1878	11	402
Addis, Charles M.	Scroggins, Indiana M.	18 JUN 1879 R	13	234
Addis, Georgia Eugenia	Stenger, Charles Robert	15 OCT 1879 L	13	424
Addision, Lizzie	Williams, Henry	03 NOV 1881	16	055

Addison, Annie	Gibbs, Lemuel	30 NOV 1879	14	011
Addison, Anthony	Driver, Mary	21 AUG 1882	16	488
Addison, Arthur D.	Steele, Caroline H.	21 FEB 1882 L	16	253
Addison, Emily	Contee, Edward	10 APR 1882 R	16	304
Addison, Fannie	Barnes, Alexander	13 JAN 1885 L	20	016
Addison, Hattie	Colbert, Henry	22 SEP 1884 R	19	262
Addison, Jere M.	Ashton, Lucy Frances	12 MAR 1885 L	20	110
Addison, Jerre M.	Harris, Liberta	07 JUL 1881 L	15	393
Addison, John	Hawkins, Johanna	27 FEB 1879 L	13	082
Addison, Josephine	Johnson, James	09 SEP 1880 L	14	438
Addison, Julia	Ashton, MacDaniel	24 OCT 1877 L	11	154
Addison, Maggie M.M.	Woodward, Arthur	05 MAY 1879 L	13	173
Addison, Margaret B.	Jackson, William	04 OCT 1879 L	13	403
Addison, Mary	Diggs, Oscar	02 JUN 1881	15	339
Addison, Mary Lizzie	Scott, Henry	28 MAY 1885	20	246
Addison, Nathan	Terry, Sarah Ellen	27 JAN 1881 R	15	168
Addison, Thomas	Brown, Lucindia	18 DEC 1879 R	14	058
Addison, Virgin P.	Jackson, Maria E.	19 NOV 1878	12	335
Addler, Cora H.	Berlimer, Emile	26 OCT 1881 R	16	043
Adkins, Thomas	Dotson, Louisa	06 OCT 1881	16	009
Adler, Cora	Behrend, Albert	22 JAN 1885 R	20	030
Adler, Edmund	Liesch, Mary	16 SEP 1880 R	14	448
Adlung, John	Gunser, Christine Wilhemine	19 DEC 1880 R	15	109
Adt, Alex	Bergmann, Sophia	02 AUG 1877 L	11	058
Ager, Emma J.	Tippett, Samuel F.	08 AUG 1884	19	176
Ager, Josey L.	McCuller, Peter C.	22 NOV 1881 L	16	088
Ages, Anna	Johnson, Hillary	05 MAR 1885	20	059
Ages, Martha	Craige, Spencer E.	13 JUL 1882 L	16	446
Aglien, John Benjamin	Brown, Ida M.	30 MAR 1882 L	16	294
Agnor, Theodore T.	Shields, Rachel T.	27 OCT 1881 L	16	048
Ahern, James	Malone, Isabella A.	30 APR 1883 L	17	423
Ahern, John	Keenan, Theresa	15 AUG 1881 L	15	445
Ahern, Joseph E.	Duggan, Mary	29 APR 1880 L	14	245
Ahern, Josepheria T.	Kelly, James	24 JUN 1884 L	19	099
Ahern, Laurence J.	Kelly, Catherine C.	03 SEP 1884 L	19	222
Ahern, William J.	McCartney, Alice	29 JUN 1880 R	14	337
Aherne, Anna M.	Aherne, John W.	08 JUN 1880	14	307
Aherne, John W.	Aherne, Anna M.	08 JUN 1880	14	307
Aigland, Mary	Dorsey, Chapman	23 DEC 1879 R	14	065
Aiken, Catharine Raingeard	Carpenter, Thomas Hicks	23 JAN 1884 R	18	389
Aiken, Clara R.	Campagna, Cyprian C.	21 OCT 1884	19	322
Aiken, George R.	Kearney, Sarah C.	14 MAY 1878	12	050
Aiken, Matthew	Mitchell, Susan Brown	06 NOV 1879 R	13	463
Ailes, Louisa Bass	Wright, Henry	05 MAR 1881 R	15	215
Aimes, James Franklin	Brown, Elizabeth	21 NOV 1884	19	394
Aitcheson, Annie	Connell, Thomas B.	26 NOV 1884 R	19	413
Aitcheson, Kate	Lindsey, Noble	21 AUG 1878	12	175
Aitchoson, Robert	Whipps, Sarah Elizabeth	09 JUN 1884	19	069
Aitken, George	Middleton, S. Agnes	14 OCT 1880 R	14	493
Aitkenhead, Wilfred C.	O'Donnoghue, Mary E.	14 JAN 1879 R	13	017
Akers, James O.	Ford, E.L.	23 JAN 1878 L	11	314
Akers, Maggie	Thomas, Daniel	15 APR 1878 R	12	004
Albaugh, Mollie A.M.	Norris, Henry J.	28 APR 1884 R	18	536
Albee, Henry Worsle	Williams, Hester Eliza	04 FEB 1880 R	14	135
Albee, Seth V.	Doren, Mollie J.	21 JAN 1885	20	031
Alber, August	Tilling, Ella	10 JUL 1878	12	132
Alber, William	Wilson, Annie F.	01 AUG 1878 L	12	155
Albers, Annie D.	Taylor, George M.	31 OCT 1883	18	224

Name	Spouse	Date	Vol	Page
Albinson, Annie M.	Thomas, William A.	04 JUN 1878	12	083
Albinson, James Edwin	Trusheim, Caroline	22 JUN 1882 R	16	423
Albot, Calbot	Albot, Sarah	27 SEP 1883 L	18	156
Albot, Sarah	Albot, Calbot	27 SEP 1883 L	18	156
Albrecht, Katie	Berghauser, Hermann	02 OCT 1883	18	163
Albriton, Ida Virginia	Steel, John T.	04 APR 1878	11	405
Alcorn, Lizzie	Alcorn, Robert	06 SEP 1881 R	15	472
Alcorn, Robert	Alcorn, Lizzie	06 SEP 1881 R	15	472
Alden, Mattie	Carroll, Walter	02 JUL 1882	16	433
Aldrich, Francis	Smith, Sarah	17 AUG 1881 R	15	450
Aldrich, Ossian F.	Smith, Sarah Elizabeth	31 MAY 1880 R	14	194
Aleider, John E.	Hefner, Josephine	19 OCT 1880	15	002
Alexander, A.A.	Chappelle, Nona	16 AUG 1880	14	400
Alexander, Abraham Lin.	Pinkett, Mary Eliz.	05 AUG 1885 R	20	354
Alexander, Albert	Price, Bettie	05 JUN 1884 R	19	064
Alexander, Amanda	Dorsey, Luther	05 JUL 1881 R	15	389
Alexander, Annie	Corbine, James W.	28 MAY 1885 R	20	244
Alexander, Apolline M.	Blair, James L.	21 FEB 1883	17	312
Alexander, Blandina Kate	Bloomer, Arthur Finley	04 DEC 1878 R	12	366
Alexander, Charlotte	Chapman, Silas	15 FEB 1882 R	16	241
Alexander, Chas. Wm.	Smith, Daisy Ethelberta	05 OCT 1885 R	20	456
Alexander, Douglass B.	Swain, Augusta	17 SEP 1878	12	224
Alexander, Edgar May	Thayer, Ella V.	26 JAN 1881 R	15	164
Alexander, Eliz. S., Mrs.	Turner, Edwin	07 OCT 1885 R	20	467
Alexander, Eliza	Parker, James	05 OCT 1882	17	056
Alexander, Evalena	Adams, Robert	20 MAY 1884 R	19	029
Alexander, Fannie	Redmond, Richard	05 FEB 1879 L	13	046
Alexander, George W.	Cook, Rachel J.	10 OCT 1877	11	127
Alexander, Grant	Robertson, Addie	03 MAY 1879 R	13	173
Alexander, Hiram	Jackson, Susan	04 DEC 1878 L	12	365
Alexander, Isaac	Crockett, Sallie	24 JUN 1878 L	12	123
Alexander, James	Washington, Eliza	08 NOV 1877 R	11	176
Alexander, James Henry	Burnham, Kate	24 JUN 1881 R	15	378
Alexander, John Henry	Wormley, Fannie	28 JUL 1882	16	460
Alexander, John St. Clair	Hilleary, Mary Matilda	23 OCT 1883 R	18	207
Alexander, Joseph N.	Walker, Ella E.	20 JAN 1880 R	14	113
Alexander, Lewis	Poindexter, Katie	03 JAN 1881 R	14	300
Alexander, Lewis W.	Todd, Sarah P.	06 NOV 1878 R	12	311
Alexander, Lizzie	Lewis, Richard	10 DEC 1884	19	447
Alexander, Malinda	Johnson, John	10 JUL 1878 R	13	272
Alexander, Martha	Jackson, Samuel	30 OCT 1877	11	160
Alexander, Martha	Berry, Horace	04 APR 1882	16	297
Alexander, Mary	Dudley, Paul	08 JUN 1878	12	093
Alexander, Mary Shahan	Johnson, John	02 APR 1878 R	11	400
Alexander, Milly	Bell, Louis Alexander	26 NOV 1882	17	149
Alexander, Nathan H.	Shaw, Victoria D.	21 DEC 1882	17	200
Alexander, Sarah	Smith, William	26 NOV 1879 R	14	002
Alexander, Sarah	Miner, David	22 DEC 1881 L	16	151
Alexander, Seymore	Blackburn, Susan	31 JUL 1883	18	068
Alexander, Thomas	Bean, Martha	02 JUN 1880 L	14	300
Alexander, Thomas A.	Brent, Martha E.	17 JAN 1880 L	14	110
Alexander, Thomas E.	Johnson, Elizabeth Jane	14 MAY 1878	12	051
Alexandria, Lettie	Bingham, Moses	22 NOV 1883 L	18	273
Alfred, Walter J.	Carmack, Kate Moore	12 JAN 1880 R	14	101
Allabach, Gertrude B.	Moss, George W.	12 FEB 1878 R	11	338
Allaire, Alice	Campbell, Wm. Walter	16 SEP 1884 R	19	251
Allan, Charles, Dr.	Sanford, Mary F.	08 NOV 1883 L	18	243
Allan, John	Hill, Delia	09 DEC 1879 L	14	039

D.C. Marriage Records Index, June 28, 1877 to October 19, 1885

Name	Spouse	Date	Vol	Page
Alleman, John S.	Domer, Delia Irene	11 OCT 1882 R	17	063
Allen, Alexander	Beckwith, Isabella	15 JUN 1882 L	16	412
Allen, Alfred	Moore, Ann	28 DEC 1880	15	125
Allen, Alice Frances	Barrett, George	08 OCT 1884	19	294
Allen, Amelia	Hamilton, William	21 JUL 1881 L	15	412
Allen, Ann	Quander, William	30 AUG 1883 R	18	106
Allen, Anna	Francis, Charles	10 NOV 1880 L	15	042
Allen, Annie May	Saffel, Albin F.	28 SEP 1882	17	043
Allen, Annie S.	Fagan, James	07 AUG 1879 L	13	310
Allen, Barney	Vessels, Nancy	21 JUN 1884 L	19	096
Allen, Benjamin	Henson, Louisa	10 JUN 1879	13	227
Allen, Benjamin	Greenhow, Florida	08 DEC 1881 R	16	121
Allen, Berta	Hall, George	02 AUG 1877 L	11	037
Allen, Catherine	Payne, Albert	20 FEB 1879 L	13	071
Allen, Catherine R.	Allen, Thomas E.	13 NOV 1877	11	180
Allen, Charlotte	Mahoney, William	10 APR 1879 R	13	136
Allen, Charlotte Virginia	Oliver, Alexander Weems	26 DEC 1882 R	17	212
Allen, Cinderella L.	Baker, James W.	19 SEP 1878	12	225
Allen, Clarence G.	McKee, Martha J.	20 OCT 1884	19	317
Allen, Cyrus M.	Moulden, Lillia E.	08 FEB 1882 R	16	232
Allen, David	McNamara, Mary	30 APR 1885 L	20	200
Allen, Edith	Webb, Harry Edwin	23 MAY 1881 R	15	321
Allen, Edward	Mahoney, Emma	20 JUN 1878 L	12	108
Allen, Eliza Norcesley Va.	Hardy, Frank Benj.	28 DEC 1882 R	17	210
Allen, Elizabeth J.	Simpson, James T.	03 SEP 1878	12	191
Allen, Emily E.	Baker, William W.	14 NOV 1878	12	328
Allen, Emma	Carmine, George W.	11 JUN 1878 R	12	096
Allen, F. Welton	Van Pelt, Lydia Ann	03 MAY 1881	15	289
Allen, Ferdinand	Bodine, Maggie	08 DEC 1881 R	16	120
Allen, Frank	Lewis, Carrie Virginia	25 OCT 1884	19	336
Allen, George	Murray, Margaret J.	07 MAR 1881	15	217
Allen, George W.	Poore, Mary	21 JAN 1878 L	11	311
Allen, Harriet	Parker, William	28 SEP 1882 R	17	039
Allen, Henry	Watson, Margaret	17 APR 1885 L	20	174
Allen, Henry Charles	Hein, Mary	23 JUL 1881 R	15	414
Allen, Hester	Gaskins, James	02 AUG 1877	11	030
Allen, James	Coleman, Mary	12 DEC 1881	16	125
Allen, James T.	Pinkney, Susan	11 JUL 1881 L	15	398
Allen, James T.	Allen, Lena Blan, Mrs.	22 NOV 1882 R	17	144
Allen, James T.	Burkhart, Lizzie C.	14 FEB 1885 R	20	066
Allen, James W.	Fowler, Alice V.	29 SEP 1881 L	15	503
Allen, Jennie	Baker, John W.	19 AUG 1885	20	380
Allen, Jeremiah	Cook, Martha	15 AUG 1878	12	168
Allen, John E.	Haven, Maggie R.	10 OCT 1877	11	126
Allen, John Ethan	Searle, Lodoiska Elizabeth	04 OCT 1881 R	16	006
Allen, John F.	Dunnington, Mary E.	10 AUG 1881 L	15	438
Allen, John P.	Hardwick, Sallie F.	30 APR 1879	13	166
Allen, Joseph	Johnson, Anna	01 JUL 1878 L	12	119
Allen, Joseph	Clavin, Annie	28 SEP 1881 R	15	502
Allen, Joseph B.	Day, Josephine	13 DEC 1883	18	313
Allen, Josephene	Stewart, James	03 JUL 1883	18	031
Allen, Josephine	Hamilton, Charles	25 JUN 1885 L	20	294
Allen, Julia	Buckner, Robert H.	20 NOV 1879 R	13	487
Allen, Langston W.	Holmes, Virginia E.	19 OCT 1880 L	15	002
Allen, Lemuel	Brown, Emma	15 APR 1885	20	168
Allen, Lena Blan, Mrs.	Allen, James T.	22 NOV 1882 R	17	144
Allen, Letitia	Mackey, Jefferson	02 AUG 1883	18	071
Allen, Lillian E.	Markell, Charles F.	08 AUG 1878 L	12	159

Name	Spouse	Date		
Allen, Lillian J.	Lynn, James W.	21 FEB 1882	16	249
Allen, Lizzie	Warfield, Harry L.	13 JUL 1885 R	20	321
Allen, Mamie Salter	Berry, Allen Preston	28 JUN 1883 R	18	021
Allen, Marcellus	Smith, Lillie E.	26 MAR 1885 R	20	133
Allen, Margaret A.	O'Leary, David	18 AUG 1881	15	452
Allen, Maria	Frazier, Ben	21 AUG 1877	11	060
Allen, Maria	Jones, John William	10 MAR 1885 R	20	104
Allen, Marina	Wilson, Elias	08 OCT 1880 L	14	483
Allen, Martha	Rex, Samuel	04 OCT 1883 R	18	153
Allen, Mary	Washington, Lewis	05 APR 1879 L	13	129
Allen, Mary	Ewell, Henry	12 AUG 1882	16	477
Allen, Mary A.	Sullivan, Henry E.	11 APR 1885 L	20	160
Allen, Mary Ann	Latimer, William James	14 FEB 1878 R	11	340
Allen, Mary E.	Smith, George E.	12 JUL 1881	15	398
Allen, Mary E.	Smith, John	29 JUN 1882 R	16	431
Allen, Mary E.	Kidwell, Beauregard	14 NOV 1883 R	18	246
Allen, Mary Elizabeth	Salisbury, William H.	08 JAN 1883	17	243
Allen, Mary Ellen	Carter, Truman	13 DEC 1884 R	19	456
Allen, Matilda E.	Perrie, James C.	22 OCT 1884	19	329
Allen, Mattie	Jackson, Andrew	17 SEP 1878 L	12	223
Allen, Minnie V.	Cameron, Charles B.	03 AUG 1885 L	20	349
Allen, Nancy L.	Clift, James E.	13 FEB 1882 R	16	237
Allen, Nathaniel	Stansbury, Susanna R.	18 SEP 1879 R	13	375
Allen, Nellie	Croft, Jacob M.	19 FEB 1883 R	17	311
Allen, Notley	Robinson, Amelia	17 FEB 1880 L	14	155
Allen, Oley	Soper, Elizabeth	01 AUG 1878	12	154
Allen, Rena	Hayes, Harry	18 SEP 1882 L	17	027
Allen, Richard	DeLong, Vena	27 MAY 1880 R	14	294
Allen, Richard	Lewis, Mary	19 SEP 1883 L	18	141
Allen, Robert	Harris, Mary Louisia	31 DEC 1879 R	14	084
Allen, Robert	Carroll, Laura V.	18 APR 1882 R	16	323
Allen, Robert F.	Ferguson, Amelia Virginia	16 APR 1884 R	18	514
Allen, Sarah	Haines, Joseph	29 OCT 1877 R	11	157
Allen, Sarah A.	Taylor, R.W.	02 JUL 1883 L	18	029
Allen, Sophie I.	Marshall, Joseph M.	30 JUN 1880 L	14	340
Allen, Thomas E.	Allen, Catherine R.	13 NOV 1877	11	180
Allen, Thomas E.	Givens, Matilda	14 NOV 1878 R	12	329
Allen, Tillie	Baldwin, William E.	08 AUG 1883	18	080
Allen, Virginia	Bowie, Thomas	17 DEC 1884 L	19	466
Allen, William	Taliaferro, Anna S.	26 FEB 1878	11	357
Allen, William H.	Bowens, Celia Ann	26 DEC 1878 R	12	396
Allen, William T.	Crown, Ida E.	27 AUG 1878	12	182
Allen, Wm. H.	Hamilton, Minnie	29 JUN 1880 L	14	338
Allens, Henry	Harris, Sophia	16 OCT 1884	19	299
Aller, Ophelia	Marshall, William H.	06 MAR 1879 R	13	054
Allison, Charles H.	Poland, Fanny D.	19 JUN 1884 R	19	093
Allison, John H.	Scheel, Margaret W.	16 DEC 1879	14	051
Allison, Mary	Washington, George	17 AUG 1881 L	15	449
Allman, James J.	O'Brien, Missouri	06 JUN 1885 L	20	259
Allman, John E.	Collins, Joanna T.	27 MAY 1884 L	19	040
Allman, Julia A.	Collins, John W.	22 OCT 1879 L	13	434
Allman, Mary A.	Hurd, Alexander	03 JUL 1884 L	19	118
Allmann, John Henry	Goss, Louisa J.	22 JUL 1880	14	373
Alimendinger, Christine	Scherble, Gottlob	25 SEP 1884 L	19	267
Allmiendinger, Andrew	Corotifski, Mary	14 APR 1885 R	20	157
Allnutt, Joseph T.	Miller, Ella M.W.	02 SEP 1885 R	20	397
Allsworth, Ella Lillian	Washburn, Dwight Hamilton	16 DEC 1882 R	17	187
Allvine, John F.	Sommer, Kate L.	10 JUN 1884	19	071

D.C. Marriage Records Index, June 28, 1877 to October 19, 1885

Ally, C.H.	Cantell, Nellie	19 OCT 1881 L	16 034
Alman, Katie	Schnepler, Joseph	30 SEP 1882 L	17 045
Almond, Maggie	Putner, William S.	08 JUL 1882 R	16 443
Almond, Margaret	Connor, James	21 NOV 1883 L	18 274
Aloas, Amelia	Fales, Lawrence	10 JAN 1885 L	20 011
Alsop, Jackson L.	Hiller, Louisa Augusta	24 JUN 1885 R	20 288
Alsop, Melvin B.	Cavell, Helen M.	13 DEC 1881 R	16 126
Alsop, Thaddeus	Frank, Katie	03 AUG 1879	13 304
Alsop, Thomas	Hiller, Mary	05 AUG 1879	13 306
Alsop, William L.	Heider, Minnie	14 DEC 1882 L	17 186
Alston, Philip C.	Freeman, Rachel T.	08 NOV 1877	11 172
Alt, Kate	Schaffert, John Leonhard	09 FEB 1879 R	13 051
Althoff, J. Elmer	Bibb, Lulu J.	18 MAR 1885 R	20 122
Altman, Samuel	Cook, Ida E.	31 OCT 1879 L	13 457
Alton, Ann	Williams, Fanzy	17 MAR 1880	14 181
Alton, John Wesley	Pennill, Nancy Ann	13 NOV 1877 L	11 181
Altschuh, Perdita	Schmid, Ernst	16 JAN 1883 L	17 260
Alvord, Emily Louise	Craig, Thomas	04 MAY 1880 R	14 248
Amberger, Frederick	Fallen, Martha Ellen	01 AUG 1879 L	13 302
Ambler, Charles F.	Wilson, Almira G.	16 JUN 1881 R	15 363
Ambler, Julia B.	Young, Robert D.	05 NOV 1884	19 364
Ambrose, Mamie Virginia	Snowden, Gurden	08 MAR 1883 L	17 338
Ambrose, Mary Frances	Torrey, Charles Henry	02 JUL 1879 R	13 261
Ambroselli, Joseph B.	Mayo, Minnie A.	08 OCT 1878	12 260
Ambush, Samuel	Willis, Johanna	24 FEB 1880 R	14 164
America, George Edward	Scott, Frances Virginia	15 JUN 1881 R	15 362
America, Joseph P.	Rokenheiser, Elizabeth L.	20 JUL 1884	19 146
America, Sallie Y.	Nash, James R.	18 JUN 1879 R	13 237
America, Thomas F.	Fiersinger, Carrie M.	08 APR 1885 R	20 154
Ames, John Thomas	Garrison, Mary M.	21 MAR 1878 R	11 389
Ames, Rosa	Smith, James Nelson	05 AUG 1879 L	13 306
Amidon, James M.	Williams, Annie V.	15 SEP 1880	14 447
Amiss, Laura L.	Crittenden, William L.	03 JAN 1883 R	17 233
Amiss, Melvilla J.	Stranahan, G.N.	01 OCT 1878	12 246
Ammann, Henry E.	Schultz, Barbara E.	03 JAN 1883 L	17 235
Ammann, Robert	Boyle, Mary	20 SEP 1880	14 452
Ammon, George Q.	Dant, Annie E.	22 AUG 1882	16 480
Ammons, Edward V.	Edwards, Nannie Lee	01 JUN 1882 R	16 386
Ammons, Israel H.	Winston, Louisa	10 OCT 1882 L	17 064
Amoroso, Alfonso	Pascuccio, Grazia	01 JUN 1880 L	14 298
Amos, James T.	Frankland, Emma M.	31 JAN 1879 R	13 040
Amos, Louise	Bowen, Raymond	05 SEP 1882 R	17 004
Amos, Mollie S.	Shrader, Houston D., Dr.	29 MAR 1881	15 241
Anadale, Andrew M.	Walsh, Josephine	25 FEB 1884 L	18 441
Anadale, Sarah F.	Means, John W.	07 NOV 1877	11 171
Ancona, John F.	Flinn, Sarah E.	29 OCT 1878 R	12 293
Anders, George W.	Holbrunner, Maria L.	22 JAN 1881 L	15 161
Anders, John A.	Ruppert, Mary E.	31 MAY 1885	20 154
Anderson, Addie	Young, Harry A.	06 SEP 1883	18 115
Anderson, Adeline	Henderson, Gustus	28 DEC 1880 R	15 129
Anderson, Agnes M.	Clarke, J. Thomas	18 AUG 1885 R	20 374
Anderson, Alexander	Washington, Emily	03 SEP 1881 L	15 470
Anderson, Alexander	Green, Matilda	19 JUL 1883	18 053
Anderson, Alice	Wilson, Julius J.	31 OCT 1878 L	12 301
Anderson, Amy	Russell, Charles	20 JUN 1882 L	16 420
Anderson, Amy	Toliver, Frank	15 AUG 1883 L	18 088
Anderson, Andrew	Lodge, Katrine	23 APR 1881 L	15 270
Anderson, Annie	Jones, Thomas	03 NOV 1882	17 108

Name	Spouse	Date	Vol	Page
Anderson, Annie	Thelon, Etienne Joseph	07 JUN 1882 R	16	397
Anderson, Archie	Carter, Annie	09 SEP 1885	20	401
Anderson, Catherine D.	Keithley, John T.	26 APR 1882	16	338
Anderson, Charles Joseph	Waters, Mary Josephine	08 JUL 1880 R	14	350
Anderson, Charles P.	Barnes, Mary A.	22 DEC 1881 L	16	150
Anderson, Charlie B.	Anderson, Nannie D.	06 NOV 1882	17	112
Anderson, Christian	Dugan, Harriet Shore	19 NOV 1879 R	13	493
Anderson, Christian	Exkstein, Lizzie	02 AUG 1883	18	073
Anderson, Daniel	Axen, Maria	15 OCT 1877	11	137
Anderson, David	Boswell, Sarah	01 NOV 1881 R	16	056
Anderson, David	Johnson, Rosa	11 NOV 1884 R	19	373
Anderson, Dennis	Snow, Harriet	03 JUL 1884 L	19	121
Anderson, Dora E.	Furr, Charles E.	21 FEB 1881 L	15	197
Anderson, Edgar S.	Streeks, Emma L.	18 MAR 1884	18	476
Anderson, Edward	Thompson, Alice	03 DEC 1883 L	18	293
Anderson, Edward	Joyce, Margaret	22 NOV 1884 L	19	402
Anderson, Eliza	Dennison, Samuel	08 NOV 1882 L	17	118
Anderson, Elizabeth A. Garner	Lawson, Benjamin F.	06 JUL 1880 R	14	348
Anderson, Ellen	Williams, John	28 OCT 1879 L	13	447
Anderson, Ellen N.	Butler, Augustus F.	12 APR 1882	16	311
Anderson, Fanny	Sumby, Samson	28 MAY 1885 L	20	244
Anderson, Florida Virginia	Hale, Charles Frederick	01 NOV 1880 R	15	024
Anderson, Gabrielle	Fletcher, William	08 OCT 1885	20	470
Anderson, George W.	Stewart, Jennie	06 APR 1882 L	16	302
Anderson, Georgie	Fraser, Charles E.	25 OCT 1883 R	18	212
Anderson, Gillespie B.	Thorton, Virginia	20 OCT 1881	16	037
Anderson, H.P.	Thompson, Susie E.	06 AUG 1877	11	042
Anderson, Harriet	Carick, Albert	08 DEC 1881 L	16	121
Anderson, Ira Imri	Matthews, Georgetta	25 JAN 1882	16	207
Anderson, Ira Lewis	Bovie, Lizzie	05 JUL 1882 R	16	438
Anderson, James Archibald	Daingerfield, Bettie Rozier	11 DEC 1879 R	14	033
Anderson, James F.	Peake, Mary L.	21 OCT 1879 R	13	435
Anderson, James W.	Riley, Delia	13 SEP 1883	18	130
Anderson, James Wm.	Terrill, Mary L.	17 MAY 1881 R	15	312
Anderson, Jane	Clark, Samuel	04 SEP 1884	19	225
Anderson, Jeannetta	Batkins, William T.	30 JUL 1884	19	161
Anderson, Jefferson D.	Carrick, Annie R.	14 DEC 1884	19	455
Anderson, John	Johnson, Laura	24 APR 1879 L	13	159
Anderson, John E.	Robinson, Martha J.	08 MAY 1883	17	432
Anderson, John Henry	Treynor, Katie May	14 OCT 1885 R	20	481
Anderson, John V.	Tolson, Hattie	29 DEC 1884	19	497
Anderson, Josephus	Gardiner, Louisa M.	18 JAN 1883 R	17	265
Anderson, Joshua	Kilburn, Catherine A.	25 JUN 1884	19	103
Anderson, Julia	Vigle, Frank	12 NOV 1878 R	12	299
Anderson, Laura A.	Nelson, Parker A.	23 DEC 1878	12	394
Anderson, Lavinia C.	Bryan, John S.	09 FEB 1878 L	11	335
Anderson, Maggie L.	Palmer, Philip C.	17 NOV 1884	19	386
Anderson, Mary	Henderson, Lee E.	23 FEB 1882 R	16	257
Anderson, Mary C.	Coleman, Reuben T.	30 MAY 1878	12	077
Anderson, Mary E.	Green, Thomas E., Sr.	20 OCT 1880	15	006
Anderson, Mary Eugenia	Green, John	27 JUN 1883 R	18	020
Anderson, Mary S.	Jones, Charles W.	27 DEC 1881 L	16	158
Anderson, Matthew	Bell, Ella	22 MAR 1884 L	18	479
Anderson, Nannie D.	Anderson, Charlie B.	06 NOV 1882	17	112
Anderson, Nathan	Simms, Annie	03 MAY 1878	12	035
Anderson, Nellie E.	Snelling, George E.	25 DEC 1880 R	15	124
Anderson, Oppy	Brown, Katie	20 AUG 1884 L	19	197
Anderson, Pauline	Wilson, Burnet	08 JUL 1884	19	128

D.C. Marriage Records Index, June 28, 1877 to October 19, 1885

Anderson, R.T.	Baker, R.V.	05 AUG 1885 L	20	354
Anderson, Richard D.	White, M. Carrie	30 NOV 1881 L	16	104
Anderson, Richard H.T.	Francis, Mary L.	07 MAY 1885 R	20	210
Anderson, Richard H.T.	Hungerford, Mary Ann	25 JUN 1885	20	292
Anderson, Robert L.	Richards, Rosa E.	20 NOV 1879 R	13	495
Anderson, Robert W.	Lucas, Catherine Jane	12 MAR 1885 R	20	106
Anderson, Sallie Josephine	Crupper, Robert Douglass	28 FEB 1883 R	17	322
Anderson, Sarah	Brooks, Henry T.	18 JUN 1879 L	13	236
Anderson, Sarah	Hill, Charles	29 OCT 1879 R	13	450
Anderson, Sarah	Western, Clemnes	11 SEP 1882 R	17	016
Anderson, Seymour	Washington, Cydonia	03 MAY 1883 L	17	429
Anderson, Stephen	Brown, Laura B.	27 FEB 1879 R	13	083
Anderson, Stephen	Moxley, Alice	07 JUN 1882	16	369
Anderson, Susie C.	Ott, George G.	18 DEC 1877 L	11	243
Anderson, Thomas H.	Jones, Mary Elizabeth	03 OCT 1883	18	164
Anderson, Wallace	Ewell, Clara	17 AUG 1885 L	20	373
Anderson, Wella Percy	Bartlett, Mary Beall	07 JUL 1880 R	14	349
Anderson, William	Cross, Mary I.	15 OCT 1878	12	273
Anderson, William A.	Beavers, Annie, Mrs.	08 OCT 1878	12	261
Anderson, William D.	Thornton, Nellie	12 APR 1881 R	15	254
Anderson, William H.	Hughes, Mattie B.	09 FEB 1885 R	20	058
Anderson, William Henry	Thornton, Lee	03 MAY 1885	20	210
Anderson, William M.	Lumpkin, Alice	11 DEC 1884 R	19	451
Anderson, William R.	Jasper, Mary Jane	07 OCT 1878	12	226
Anderson, William W.	Bradley, Martha H.	15 DEC 1881 R	16	133
Anderson, William Weldon	Cartwell, Nellie Natalie	16 JAN 1878 R	11	307
André, Lillie E.	Beaton, Malcolm S.	23 SEP 1880 R	14	459
Andresen, Josephine G.	Gordon, Francis H.	14 FEB 1880 L	14	153
Andrews, Albert Slacum	Barnard, Constance Kate	21 SEP 1882 R	17	033
Andrews, Amelia C.	Boynton, Henry S.	29 JUL 1884	19	161
Andrews, Catherine R.	Wilson, Samuel S.	26 AUG 1882 L	16	494
Andrews, Frank	Owens, Lydia O.	21 FEB 1881	15	197
Andrews, Helen	Nixon, William G.	02 JUN 1881	15	335
Andrews, Joseph	Gray, Alice	24 DEC 1883 L	18	338
Andrews, Louisa	Bouldin, Julius	15 MAY 1879	13	192
Andrews, Loulie E.	Graves, Henry	09 APR 1885	20	158
Andrews, Reuben H.	Stanley, Amelia K.	30 JAN 1879 R	13	040
Andrews, William T.	Miller, Fannie K.	21 JUL 1883	18	055
Angel, Edward C.	Butler, Annie E.	21 JAN 1884 L	18	386
Angel, Lottie	Joseph, Frederick	13 JUN 1882 R	16	408
Angel, Maria I.	Sanders, Zachanah T.	13 MAY 1880	14	270
Angell, Alice E.	Compton, Ludwell	08 JAN 1878	11	296
Angell, Annie	Lusby, William T.	29 OCT 1878	12	295
Angell, Eva C.	Carey, Martin V.	29 OCT 1884	19	347
Angell, Thomas	Weal, Mary Ann	10 DEC 1884 R	19	445
Angle, Ella	Rauber, Jacob	05 JAN 1882 L	16	183
Angraman, Amelia F.	Hueke, Hugh L.	15 DEC 1880 L	15	099
Anholt, Fredevich W.	Taylor, Maggie	08 SEP 1878	12	203
Annadale, Josephine	Daly, Joseph	22 JUN 1885 L	20	283
Anthony, Mary E.	Mann, Wm. E.	16 DEC 1884 R	19	458
Anthony, Sallie L.	Ogle, Albert C.	26 DEC 1877 L	11	268
Apel, Wilhelm	Dorzman, Julia	19 JAN 1879 R	13	020
Appich, John	Koetzner, Mary A.	18 JUN 1879	13	212
Apple, David K.	Collins, Mollie	03 DEC 1879 R	14	025
Appleby, Ellen King	DeValin, Charles Edward	26 OCT 1882 R	17	093
Appleby, Geo. Franklin	Steele, Katharine Barney	28 JUL 1885 R	20	344
Appler, Charles W.	Snyder, Fannie C.	04 DEC 1878 R	12	365
Appler, Clara B.	Hollinger, Arthur C.	02 OCT 1884	19	272

Name	Spouse	Date	Vol	Page
Applewhite, Henry B.	Carter, Kate C.	29 MAY 1884	19	044
Appold, Ellen R.	Grant, James M.	17 SEP 1884 R	19	250
Aquilla, Celia Virginia	Washington, Daniel L., Rev.	23 MAY 1883 L	17	460
Arata, Madalena	Laurenzi, Cesare	12 APR 1880 R	14	221
Arberly, Abraham J.	La Fetra, Anna M.	13 AUG 1885	20	368
Archer, Agnes L.	Smith, Marshall L.	07 OCT 1884 L	19	291
Archer, Henry S.	Williams, Julia	19 AUG 1885 R	20	378
Archer, James A.	Lunsford, Elizabeth R.	28 DEC 1882 L	17	217
Archibald, William	Miller, Anna May	30 SEP 1885	20	448
Arendes, Mary	Schaefer, George M.	26 NOV 1884 L	19	412
Argyle, Fanny Farrar	Glazebrook, Marshall Ambler	23 MAY 1883 R	17	459
Arlow, Mary A., Mrs.	Hall, John R.	31 JAN 1884 R	18	403
Armbrecht, Augustus	Lingebach, Louise	06 NOV 1878	12	304
Armentrout, Annie L.	Van Pelt, Robert A.	07 FEB 1884	18	416
Armes, Aaron	Williams, Alice	17 APR 1878 L	12	010
Armistead, Fannie H.	Coleman, Josiah L.	30 APR 1878 R	12	032
Armistead, Leland	Thomas, Lucinda	26 MAY 1879 L	13	205
Armistead, Mary	Simms, Simon	27 OCT 1883 R	18	190
Armistead, Mary Loudon	Leache, Robert Willett	23 AUG 1877	11	063
Armistead, Rose A.	Powers, John S.	11 JUN 1884	19	077
Armistead, Thomas H.	Lockhard, Emma E.	28 NOV 1877	11	206
Armistead, Wm. Christ.	Salf, Julia Ann	26 JUL 1877 R	11	032
Armor, Ella Maria	Donn, Albert Alonzo	08 APR 1885 R	20	152
Armor, John E.	Goodwin, Annie E.	30 OCT 1878 L	12	300
Armour, Elenor J.	Eckerson, Theodore H.	12 AUG 1884	19	181
Armour, Isabel Louise	Scala, William Franklin	20 DEC 1877 L	11	255
Armour, Maggie	Fanning, Joseph	01 FEB 1882 R	16	216
Arms, Ben	Green, Margt.	04 OCT 1881	16	008
Armstead, Bartlett	Lee, Sarah	02 OCT 1884 L	19	284
Armstead, Carrie	Carter, Louis	25 MAR 1880 L	14	197
Armstead, Edward	Henderson, Letha	10 OCT 1878 L	12	265
Armstead, James Ryan	Bird, Sue	28 JUN 1882	16	424
Armstrong, Alexander	Washington, Josephine	19 NOV 1884	19	391
Armstrong, Charlotte	Falls, Robert Wilson	15 MAY 1883 R	17	441
Armstrong, Ella V.	Nash, Nicholas M.	30 JAN 1882 R	16	215
Armstrong, Elvie J.	Hughes, Edward A.	06 SEP 1882 L	17	008
Armstrong, Gemima	Lee, Elie	06 AUG 1878 L	12	157
Armstrong, George	Heagem, Margaret	22 DEC 1881 L	16	152
Armstrong, George H.	Wilson, Mary E.	30 APR 1885 R	20	199
Armstrong, James	Matthews, Maria	28 JUN 1880 L	14	336
Armstrong, James	Caffey, Josephine Ann	15 APR 1882	16	316
Armstrong, Jennie B.	Williams, John M.	04 SEP 1877	11	075
Armstrong, John B.	Halton, Mary R.	29 DEC 1880	15	131
Armstrong, John F.	Chappelle, Katie	22 DEC 1884	19	476
Armstrong, Jordan	Hall, Elizabeth	27 NOV 1882 L	17	149
Armstrong, Joseph S.	Bolding, Carrie	07 AUG 1878 L	12	158
Armstrong, Luther Kelley	Brown, Marion Rebecca	30 DEC 1884 R	19	500
Armstrong, Mary C.	Johnson, William H.	14 OCT 1885 L	20	480
Armstrong, Minnie	Duvall, William T.	06 JUN 1881	15	347
Armstrong, Susie	Robinson, Joshua	21 FEB 1882 R	16	254
Arndt, Ruth	Weedon, John Henry	09 SEP 1884	19	149
Arnett, Adella J.	Cord, William P.	04 SEP 1884 L	19	225
Arnold, Anne Mary	Oswald, Louis Oscar	19 OCT 1885 R	20	496
Arnold, David C.	Miller, Maggie	31 AUG 1882 R	16	500
Arnold, David C.	Miller, Maggie	31 AUG 1882 L	17	001
Arnold, Edgar	Sydnor, Anna	22 JUL 1880 L	14	372
Arnold, Edmund C.	Wasselle, Lizzie G.	15 APR 1882 R	16	315
Arnold, Elbert	Bias, Eliza	26 DEC 1884 L	19	493

D.C. Marriage Records Index, June 28, 1877 to October 19, 1885   11

Name	Spouse	Date	Vol	Page
Arnold, Eliza	Mills, George	08 OCT 1880 L	14	483
Arnold, Ella	Watson, Harold	27 NOV 1882 R	17	150
Arnold, Ezzie	Landvoigt, William H.	14 MAR 1878 L	11	381
Arnold, George W.	Jones, Jane	21 JUN 1879 L	13	242
Arnold, Henry	Brawner, Harriet	17 APR 1882 L	16	321
Arnold, Henry F.	Riggles, Molly	21 MAY 1884	19	031
Arnold, John F.	Flurrey, Sarah F.	01 JUN 1882 L	16	389
Arnold, Kate A.	Colt, Charles L.	13 JUN 1881	15	356
Arnold, Katie A.	Smith, Wendell A.	20 JUN 1883	18	003
Arnold, Lillie	Rowley, Charles P.	07 SEP 1878 R	12	204
Arnold, Mary Jane Brooke	Hantzman, Robert	06 JUL 1881 R	15	392
Arnold, Mary S.	Spencer, Frank A.	29 NOV 1884 L	19	425
Arnold, Paul	Fracker, Sarah K.	29 APR 1884 R	18	540
Arnold, Priscilla	Johnson, George	15 MAR 1883 L	17	347
Arnold, Robert	Wood, Lizzie	07 MAY 1885	20	207
Arnold, Sarah J.	Englehart, Charles	14 MAY 1884 R	19	006
Arnold, William H.	Nelson, Missouri C.	01 AUG 1881 L	15	429
Arnold, Willie Lawrence	Adams, Eliza	26 MAY 1881 R	15	329
Arpenstaen, Annie Oertele	Knoor, William H.A.	15 DEC 1884 L	19	459
Arrata, Vittoria	Schneider, Carmillo	29 JUN 1880 L	14	338
Arrington, Andrew J.	Kerr, Mary A.	23 OCT 1884 L	19	333
Arrington, Benjamin F.	Cornell, Louisa	07 NOV 1883	18	239
Arrington, Julia A.	Higgins, James B.	03 MAY 1882 R	16	347
Artes, Mary	Kreuter, William George	08 DEC 1879	14	035
Artes, Sophia	Kennelly, Edward M.	18 SEP 1882 L	17	025
Arteuzer, Mathias	Leim, Mary A.	19 JAN 1884	18	384
Arth, John William	Mansell, Amy Priscilla	20 FEB 1882 R	16	244
Arthur, Ann C.	Brooks, Solomon	04 NOV 1884 L	19	357
Artis, Isabelle	Kern, George	19 MAR 1885	20	124
Artz, Martin L.	Crabill, Lucy C.	29 JUL 1882 R	16	460
Artz, Samuel	Stearn, Emma J.	18 MAY 1880 R	14	275
Arundell, Charles A.	Rogers, Louisianna	26 AUG 1884	19	208
Arundell, James T.	Tennyson, Ada T.	22 APR 1884	18	521
Asfield, Jno. McFarland	Dailey, Gertrude Frances	02 JUL 1877 R	11	005
Ash, Emma E.	Hulse, Austin B.	03 APR 1879 R	13	127
Ash, Frank	Oswell, Katie	03 DEC 1878 R	12	363
Ash, Frank Thomas	Robey, Mary E.	25 DEC 1878 R	12	395
Ash, James	Countee, Elizabeth B.	12 DEC 1884 L	19	455
Ash, Maria A.	Reilly, Dennis	03 NOV 1880 R	15	027
Ash, Orvillie J.	Goldsmith, Edwin F.	11 APR 1878	11	415
Ash, Thomas F.	Joy, Mollie E.	04 APR 1881 L	15	245
Ashburn, George W.	Browne, Juda	12 NOV 1878 R	12	323
Ashburn, Roland	Pankens, Ellen	17 NOV 1880 R	15	052
Ashby, Ellen	Butler, Jacob	16 NOV 1882 R	17	132
Ashby, Irving G.	Upperman, Kate	11 DEC 1879 R	14	041
Ashby, Lucy B.	Cook, Llewellyn M.	26 MAR 1879 R	13	115
Ashby, Mary A.	Ryer, Henry C.	15 AUG 1881 R	15	446
Ashby, Mollie C.	Howell, Samuel B.	24 APR 1879 R	13	159
Ashby, Molly	Banks, Henry	25 MAY 1885 R	20	235
Ashby, Rebecca J. (Harris)	McAllister, John Ferguson	24 JUL 1882 R	16	455
Ashby, Richard	Moncure, Lilla J.	31 JUL 1878	12	304
Ashby, Roburta	Clark, Jack	21 MAY 1885 L	20	233
Ashby, William Todd	McKnew, Nina	18 APR 1883 R	17	397
Asher, Samuel	Crandell, Maggie F.	30 JUN 1880 L	14	339
Ashford, Annie E.	Proctor, Abr. M.	09 JUN 1880 R	14	313
Ashford, Florence V.	Simons, Samuel H.	06 MAY 1879 R	13	176
Ashford, Henry C.	Simmons, Emma	16 FEB 1880 L	14	156
Ashford, Henry C.	Eally, Roberta M.	22 MAR 1885 R	20	127

Ashford, Mary S.	Bivens, Charles H.	07 APR 1885	20	150
Ashley, Wm. M.	Brock, M.E.	12 NOV 1879 R	13	480
Ashman, William	Thiede, Louise E.	01 AUG 1884	19	164
Ashton, Alice	Rady, Henry	18 SEP 1883 L	18	140
Ashton, Basil	Estrich, Isabel	23 DEC 1884	19	470
Ashton, Charles	Denton, Louisa	21 JAN 1878 L	11	312
Ashton, Cornelius	Watson, Bettie	31 DEC 1881 R	16	171
Ashton, Emma	Porter, Thomas	30 JUL 1885	20	345
Ashton, Fred	Turner, Henrietta	20 JUN 1882 R	16	419
Ashton, George W.	Young, Nettie, Mrs.	23 DEC 1883 R	18	333
Ashton, Gurden C.	Garner, Emily F.	28 JUL 1878 R	12	149
Ashton, Harriet A.E.	Waynes, Henson	25 JUN 1885	20	292
Ashton, Ida	Brooker, William H.	11 DEC 1883	18	309
Ashton, John P.	Hines, Sarah Jane	15 JUN 1881 L	15	363
Ashton, Joseph	Thomas, Julia	12 JAN 1882	16	170
Ashton, Laura Ann	Galey, Benjamin	20 MAR 1879 R	13	104
Ashton, Lewis	Lewis, Birdie	02 DEC 1880 L	15	083
Ashton, Lucy Frances	Addison, Jere M.	12 MAR 1885 L	20	110
Ashton, MacDaniel	Addison, Julia	24 OCT 1877 L	11	154
Ashton, Maggie L.	Robinson, Andrew J.	11 FEB 1880 R	14	148
Ashton, Martha	Taylor, Henry	10 AUG 1882 L	16	475
Ashton, Mary	Rice, Cephas	14 AUG 1884	19	184
Ashton, Massouria	Young, James	14 JUN 1883 R	17	493
Ashton, Nathan	Walker, Anney	23 MAR 1882 R	16	253
Ashton, Nellie	Kelly, William	30 DEC 1884 R	19	500
Askins, Isaac	Lewis, Catherine	13 DEC 1881 L	16	129
Asmussen, Louise	Veerhoff, W.H.	06 MAY 1878	12	033
Assu, Karalina	Guyon, Daniel W.	05 JAN 1881 R	15	139
Asterline, George	Shields, Sarah E.	15 NOV 1882 L	17	129
Aston, George W.	Dabney, Sarah	27 JUN 1878 R	12	115
Atchinson, Alzine	Bidwell, Lewis T.	01 OCT 1877 L	11	116
Atchison, Claude B.	Gormley, Mary Elizabeth	31 MAY 1880 L	14	296
Atchison, Eliza	Sayers, Franklin P.	16 DEC 1884	19	463
Atchison, Eugene A.	Gilchrist, Mary Harriett	29 APR 1880 R	14	242
Atchison, Welford C.	Minnick, Lydia C.	22 DEC 1881 R	16	153
Atchison, William	Rainey, Catherine	30 DEC 1879 L	14	078
Atherton, Emma Frances	St. Clair, Gilbert	20 OCT 1877 L	11	146
Athey, George Anna	Burrows, George W.	07 MAR 1883 L	17	336
Athey, Ida I.	Croxton, Richard A.	16 MAY 1885	20	225
Athey, Katie	Bridgett, Jerome	23 OCT 1879 R	13	436
Atkins, Alice	Miller, Timothy	06 NOV 1880	15	034
Atkins, Elizabeth	Hoye, Robert	19 OCT 1877	11	144
Atkins, Henry	Carter, Elizabeth	05 OCT 1880 R	14	469
Atkinson, Ada	Riggins, Samuel	01 SEP 1883 L	18	107
Atkinson, Annie E.	Sisson, Armstead C.	15 MAY 1879 L	13	191
Atkinson, Charles	Cudlipp, Ida	10 DEC 1884 R	19	447
Atkinson, Cora A.	Overton, Charles H.	04 FEB 1878 R	11	325
Atkinson, Edna	Burton, Walter T.	22 APR 1884 R	30	7325
Atkinson, Elmer E.	Smith, Maggie L.	06 MAR 1880 L	14	179
Atkinson, Fannie E.	Pate, William A.	06 FEB 1883 L	17	296
Atkinson, Julia Ann	White, Henry	05 JAN 1882 L	16	183
Atkinson, Minnie R.	Bradley, J. Wharton, Rev.	11 MAR 1879	13	096
Atkinson, R.W.	Martin, Laura L.	05 JUL 1881 R	15	389
Atkinson, Rebecca	Tolliver, William P.R.	03 JUN 1885	20	255
Atkinson, Richard W.	Enroughty, Mary F.	22 OCT 1884	19	328
Atkinson, Robert Harbottle	Bogert, Alice	20 FEB 1883 R	17	311
Atkinson, Rosetta	Hill, Henry	11 DEC 1879 R	13	199
Atkinson, Virginia Lee	Enroughty, Francis	08 JUN 1881 R	15	353

Atkinson, W.B.	Day, Millie A.	07 JAN 1878 R	11	294
Atwell, Benjamin F.	Curtis, Rosa V.	25 MAY 1878	12	066
Atwell, Ida	Byroad, Frank M.	16 JUL 1885	20	329
Atwell, John	Barnes, Ellen	08 OCT 1878 L	12	260
Atwell, John W.	Keller, Margaret F., Mrs.	23 OCT 1879	13	441
Atwell, John W.	Powers, Cora	15 MAY 1883 R	17	443
Atwood, Belle	Clum, John P.	06 FEB 1883 R	17	292
Atz, Charles	Collins, Barbara E.	26 AUG 1880	14	416
Atz, Mary	Hodges, G.H.	30 MAY 1878 R	12	029
Atzell, John Fred	Verneu, Elizabeth	03 FEB 1881 R	15	177
Atzerodt, Ida N.	Hazard, Henry C.	17 MAY 1881 L	15	312
Auerbach, Carl	Rosenberg, Hanna	02 JUN 1878 R	12	067
Aufrecht, Carl Gottlob	Bartel, Augusta Agnes	23 MAR 1881 R	15	231
Aufrecht, Caroline	Miller, Adam	18 NOV 1880 R	15	052
Augell, George B.	Wilkinson, Ella M.	02 FEB 1882	16	222
August, Benjamin E.	Owens, Sarah J.	14 OCT 1884 L	19	306
Auguste, George G.	Scott, Annie C.	19 NOV 1879 R	13	496
Auguste, Gertrude	Meyers, William R.	16 OCT 1884	19	316
Auguste, Mary A.	Herfurth, Charles A.	18 MAY 1885 R	20	226
Augustine, Bell	Quisenbery, Joseph L.	24 DEC 1878 R	12	400
Austin, Edward	McGolerich, Mary	23 SEP 1879 R	13	383
Austin, Fannie	Dixon, Sheldon	02 JAN 1884 R	18	361
Austin, Fredrick R.	Dougherty, A.C.	28 MAR 1881 L	15	240
Austin, George L.	Burford, Eleanor L.	02 FEB 1881	15	173
Austin, Mary V.	Shelton, James B.	12 APR 1882 R	16	309
Austin, Samuel M.	Smith, Georgiana	17 DEC 1879 L	14	052
Austin, Sarah Forward	Bradshaw, Moses	04 AUG 1881 R	15	432
Auters, Kate V.	Shoemaker, David W.	29 MAR 1883 L	17	371
Auth, Columba	Spatz, Ludavig	28 NOV 1879	14	018
Auth, John	Pozner, Mary	09 OCT 1877	11	124
Auth, Mary	Dorr, George	06 SEP 1877	11	059
Auth, Paulina	Hoch, Wilhelm	19 JUN 1882 L	16	415
Auth, Paulina	Poch, Wilhelm	17 JUN 1882	16	417
Averill, John W.	Downing, Emily A.	06 JAN 1879 R	13	006
Avery, Frank T.	Moran, May	24 JUL 1879 R	13	291
Avery, Georgianna	Schlosser, William H.	14 DEC 1882 R	17	185
Avery, John B.	Vaughan, Susan E.	02 APR 1884 L	18	492
Awkard, James C.	Duffey, Martha V.	15 SEP 1880 L	14	447
Awkward, Emma D.	Brent, Amos D.	07 MAY 1885 R	20	211
Axen, Maria	Anderson, Daniel	15 OCT 1877	11	137
Ayer, Alice	Curtis, William	07 MAY 1884 R	19	009
Ayes, Julia	Stewart, Edward	11 JAN 1885 R	20	004
Aylor, Blanche	Aylor, H.H.	26 JAN 1882 R	16	210
Aylor, Charles Milton	Hawkins, Nannie B.	17 APR 1882 R	16	318
Aylor, H.H.	Aylor, Blanche	26 JAN 1882 R	16	210
Aymé, Louis Henry	Harrison, Florence	01 MAR 1880 R	14	166
Aynes, Mary B.	Gayle, Edward E.	09 MAR 1881	15	221
Ayres, Charles G.	Fairfax, Mary Elizabeth	16 APR 1884 R	18	508
Ayres, Chauncey Lewis	Stancliff, Annie Clark	04 JUL 1883 R	18	034
Ayres, Emily D.	Howell, Rezin G.	05 FEB 1884 L	18	410
Ayres, Frederick	Davis, Eva	03 NOV 1881	16	060
Ayres, Joseph	Henderson, Mary	05 SEP 1879	13	354

B

Babbitt, Charles E.	Seymour, Ida McLean	17 AUG 1882 R	16	484
Babcock, Daniel A.	Thompson, Minette	27 NOV 1878 L	12	353
Babcock, Stephen	Taylor, Henrietta Van Patten	10 JUL 1878	12	130
Babendreier, Fred L.	Mylins, Mary L.	17 SEP 1885 R	20	425
Baber, Daniel	Lathan, Lydia	21 JAN 1879	13	026
Babikow, Augusta	Obinger, John	07 JUN 1880 L	14	307
Babson, Mary Winnifred	French, William B.	05 NOV 1877	11	168
Bacchus, Anna	Wilbrand, Ernst	14 APR 1881 R	15	253
Bacey, Emanuel	Young, Chlory Ann	02 AUG 1877 L	11	038
Bacey, Richard	Simms, Mary	02 APR 1885	20	141
Bache, Frederick C.	Eckloff, Emma C.	13 MAY 1885 L	20	219
Bachrach, Moses	Mailhouse, Cecilia	16 NOV 1879 R	13	488
Bachschmid, Paul	Poggensee, Johannah Martha	04 SEP 1883 R	18	109
Bacigaluppo, Joseph	Cavagarro, Cornelia	11 JAN 1884 L	18	373
Backus, Amelia, Mrs.	Brown, Jordan	29 NOV 1878 R	12	372
Backus, Robertha V.	Bouis, Stephen G.	13 OCT 1879 R	13	417
Backus, William M.	Beall, Constance H.	29 DEC 1881 R	16	170
Bacon, Arthur A.	Springmann, Rose V.	23 OCT 1879 R	13	441
Bacon, Gus	Wood, Katie	10 JUL 1884	19	126
Bacon, Harry R.	Hopkins, Florence J.	19 JAN 1882 R	16	200
Bacon, Isabella	Bond, Charles H.	01 MAY 1883 R	17	393
Bacon, Sarah	Sims, Henry	31 MAR 1879 L	13	119
Baden, Alfred	Dorsey, Harriet	11 JUL 1877	11	014
Baden, Annie W.	Low, A. Maurice	23 OCT 1884	19	329
Baden, Susie V.	Yates, James W.	05 MAR 1884 L	18	459
Badger, Annie Mansfield	Elliott, George Frank	06 JAN 1880 R	14	088
Bäeker, Bertha	Hausmann, William	10 MAY 1885 R	20	214
Baer, Mary E.	Dean, Albert L.	29 JAN 1880	14	125
Baer, Sophie	Heilprin, Giles F.	09 NOV 1879	13	469
Baerman, Charlotte	Cozzen, James	24 NOV 1881 R	16	094
Baeschlin, Carile	Phelps, Joseph A.	17 FEB 1885 L	20	072
Baeschlin, Lavinia M.	Harper, James E.	15 JAN 1880 L	14	106
Bagaley, Sarah Elizabeth	McAllister, Richard	21 APR 1879 R	13	152
Bagaley, Wateman	Livingston, Annie M.	05 NOV 1881	16	063
Bagaley, Waterman Palmer	Livingston, Anna M.	22 JAN 1878	11	313
Bagby, George W.	Palmer, Laura R.	25 FEB 1885 L	20	085
Bagby, Montgomery	Jackson, Louisa	09 SEP 1879 L	13	360
Bagby, Nettie	Pinkett, Benjamin	13 JUN 1878 L	12	097
Bagby, Thomas	Herbert, Charlotte	17 OCT 1883 L	18	200
Bagby, Walker	Howe, Ellen	08 FEB 1878	11	332
Bagby, William W.	Suttle, C. Broaddus	24 FEB 1880 R	14	165
Bageon, Mary C.	Day, John W.	04 JAN 1883 R	17	238
Baggott, Levi	Rodgers, Rebecca Ann	26 DEC 1882 R	17	210
Baggott, Robert	Grimsley, Anna Jane	28 MAR 1882 R	16	291
Bagley, Mary E.	Crowder, Walter F.	27 MAY 1884	19	040
Bagley, Sarah	Haskins, D.H.	10 SEP 1880 R	14	431
Bagley, Thomas	Phillipson, Anne Walker	31 OCT 1878 R	12	303
Bahrs, Joanna Heneretta	Padgett, Charles Edward	15 OCT 1878 L	12	273
Baier, William	Boyle, Mary	15 FEB 1882 R	16	225
Bailey, Addison	Pinn, Hannah	01 MAY 1878	12	031
Bailey, Aimee E.	Jones, John J.	01 JUN 1878	12	079
Bailey, Alice	Reed, John F.	18 OCT 1883	18	193
Bailey, Alice	Green, Thornton	12 JAN 1885 L	20	013
Bailey, Bernard	Pettit, Emily B.	02 MAR 1881 R	15	207
Bailey, Calista	Pierce, Charles B.	25 OCT 1877 L	11	155
Bailey, Caroline	Cox, John	24 OCT 1882	17	085
Bailey, Catherine	Middleton, Edward	22 JUN 1880	14	330

D.C. Marriage Records Index, June 28, 1877 to October 19, 1885

Name	Spouse	Date		
Bailey, Charles	King, Annie	25 FEB 1885	20	085
Bailey, Charles E.	Jewell, Ida M.	17 OCT 1882 R	17	076
Bailey, Charlotte E.	Brennan, David	01 MAR 1883 R	17	331
Bailey, Clayton L.	Drake, Carrie E.	20 FEB 1884	18	432
Bailey, Elmira	Campbell, Cornelius	03 JAN 1884 R	18	352
Bailey, Emma J.	Barron, John Oliver	28 MAY 1879 R	13	208
Bailey, Etway	Howard, Robert F.	01 AUG 1880	14	382
Bailey, Fannie	Epps, Matthew	27 DEC 1882 R	17	213
Bailey, Fannie	Steinert, William	11 SEP 1884 L	19	241
Bailey, Florence D.	Conaway, James R.	22 DEC 1884 L	19	475
Bailey, George	Buckner, Maggie	30 AUG 1882	16	496
Bailey, George Henry	Boone, Carrie	06 JUL 1885	20	310
Bailey, Guinette	Morris, George A.	29 JUL 1879 R	13	298
Bailey, Hattie K.	Bradshaw, J.T.	03 AUG 1885	20	348
Bailey, Henrietta, Mrs.	Day, Joseph S.	04 JAN 1881 R	15	138
Bailey, Henry	Owens, Alice M.	28 JAN 1879	13	036
Bailey, Horace	Waters, Ada	24 FEB 1883 L	17	320
Bailey, Howard T.	Minor, Millie	03 JUN 1884 L	19	052
Bailey, Ida	Nightingale, John A.	02 JUN 1882 R	16	390
Bailey, James E.	Smith, Marandar C.	27 OCT 1880	14	123
Bailey, James F.	Hennis, Margaret	04 AUG 1885 L	20	351
Bailey, James Lewis	Hamilton, Julia Eliza	19 NOV 1884 L	19	397
Bailey, James R.	Harrison, Harriet Rebecca	28 MAR 1882	16	292
Bailey, James S.	Shaw, Sarah	20 OCT 1884 L	19	323
Bailey, Jane Titus	Breen, Thomas Henry	13 FEB 1878 R	11	336
Bailey, Janie	Monroe, Charles	25 MAY 1882	16	376
Bailey, John J.C.	Hayden, Laura B.	19 SEP 1877	11	100
Bailey, John Wm.	Murphy, Mary Henrietta Luvina	20 FEB 1883	17	312
Bailey, Levi	Perry, Jane	07 JAN 1880 R	14	086
Bailey, Levi J.	Martin, Anna D.	04 JUL 1878	12	121
Bailey, Levi J.	Robrecht, Mary E.	17 MAY 1882	16	363
Bailey, Lidia E.	Lamb, Francis R.	23 FEB 1882	16	258
Bailey, Lizzie	Carter, George	10 JUN 1884 L	19	071
Bailey, Lorenzo Alton	Brooke, Louisa Hamilton	04 NOV 1882 R	17	110
Bailey, Luretta	Brooks, James Edward	11 JAN 1883	17	251
Bailey, Mamie F.	Young, William A.	11 DEC 1884 R	19	453
Bailey, Margaret	Donohue, Edward	10 JUN 1880 R	14	316
Bailey, Marietta	Strothers, James	02 JUL 1885	20	305
Bailey, Martha A.	Curtis, Peter C.	13 JAN 1880 R	14	095
Bailey, Mary	Holly, George	09 NOV 1882 L	17	120
Bailey, Mary	Horner, Firmin	13 MAY 1884	19	016
Bailey, Mary E.	Mansfield, Charles H.	07 MAR 1879 L	13	093
Bailey, Richard H.	Weber, Kate	09 SEP 1885	20	410
Bailey, Stephen A.	Bean, Benetta	08 SEP 1881 R	15	472
Bailey, Susan L.	Dandelet, Jerome F.	09 FEB 1880 R	14	075
Bailey, Susie C.	Harrison, James T.	20 AUG 1878	12	174
Bailey, Theodore	Mortimer, Missouri O.	26 MAR 1879 R	13	113
Bailey, Theodore F.	Jackson, Francis F.	29 NOV 1883 L	18	285
Bailey, William	Payne, Elizabeth	30 AUG 1880	14	423
Bailey, William	Moran, Mary Elizabeth	05 NOV 1883	18	233
Bailey, William	Steward, Louisa	21 JAN 1885	20	033
Bailey, William H.	Love, Mary Jane	24 DEC 1884 R	19	487
Bailey, William Jenks	Talbott, Virginia	08 FEB 1883 R	17	298
Baillieux, Clementine M.	Maddox, William F.	14 JUL 1884 L	19	137
Baily, Anna R.	King, William H.	19 DEC 1878	12	393
Bain, Edward A.	Dalton, Josie	22 JUL 1881 R	15	413
Bain, James E.	Harris, Mary E.	20 AUG 1885 L	20	381
Bain, James Robert	Elmore, Inez [Carlisle]	20 DEC 1882 R	17	194

Name	Spouse	Date	Vol	Page
Bain, William V.	Landrick, Virginia	03 FEB 1879 L	13	043
Bain, William V.	Reynolds, Agness	25 SEP 1883 R	18	154
Baird, Ella C.	Baird, J.M.	16 FEB 1882 R	14	398
Baird, George D.	Dade, Eliza Minor	25 APR 1879 L	13	160
Baird, J.M.	Baird, Ella C.	16 FEB 1882 R	14	398
Baird, Sarah	McNew, Frank O.	22 OCT 1884	19	321
Baker, A. Florence	Frey, Victor K.	12 MAR 1884	18	466
Baker, Alice	Callahan, Timothy	16 MAY 1881 L	15	308
Baker, Charles	Nalley, Mary Ellen	21 OCT 1877	11	147
Baker, Charles Thos. Morrison	Johns, Mary Elizabeth	01 JUN 1882 R	16	389
Baker, Collie M.	Gunnell, Joshua C.	08 JUL 1885 L	20	317
Baker, Eliza Ellen	Street, Peter W.	05 NOV 1884 L	19	365
Baker, Ellen	Tolson, Isaac	03 FEB 1885	20	050
Baker, Emma J.	Wex, Henry	24 OCT 1882 R	17	089
Baker, Fannie	Martin, George	20 MAY 1880 R	14	279
Baker, Frank B.	Woodard, Janette	28 MAY 1881 R	15	330
Baker, Harry C.	Linville, Annie H.	22 OCT 1878	12	284
Baker, Jacob	Briscoe, Alice B.	03 OCT 1878 R	12	248
Baker, James	Bundy, Lucy, Mrs.	12 JAN 1881	15	149
Baker, James S.	Magruder, Lavinia	29 JUL 1883	18	064
Baker, James W.	Allen, Cinderella L.	19 SEP 1878	12	225
Baker, Jennie	Baker, William	18 MAY 1885 R	20	226
Baker, Jesse Elliott	Gow, Lizzie Baker, Mrs.	08 DEC 1878 R	12	372
Baker, Jesse M.	Wallace, Courtenay Hamilton	26 JAN 1882 R	16	210
Baker, John	Pollock, Anne Louise	21 JUN 1881 R	15	369
Baker, John L.	Jones, Maggie E.	10 DEC 1884 L	19	449
Baker, John P.	Douglass, Katie Francis	09 MAY 1880 R	14	254
Baker, John W.	Allen, Jennie	19 AUG 1885	20	380
Baker, Joseph S.A.	Howlett, Mary E.	31 OCT 1882	17	103
Baker, Josephine	Dawson, Henry Americus	03 DEC 1879 R	14	024
Baker, Julian George	Lynch, Olivia Jessie	31 JUL 1881 R	15	425
Baker, Katie L.B.	Dean, James W.	10 JUL 1879 R	13	277
Baker, Louisa	Smith, Alexander	18 AUG 1881 L	15	451
Baker, Mary A.	Bellermann, William E.	06 NOV 1883	18	236
Baker, Mary Eliza	Lacy, Oliver	13 AUG 1883 L	18	084
Baker, Mary Elizabeth	Farr, Charles N.	13 FEB 1882	16	236
Baker, Mary H.	Bing, Nathaniel J.	19 OCT 1880 L	15	004
Baker, Matilda	Bause, George E.	07 DEC 1882 R	17	175
Baker, Mattie A.	Tinsley, John	24 JAN 1884 R	18	395
Baker, Millie W.	Woody, George D.	30 DEC 1884	19	499
Baker, Oscar	Clear, Maggie B.	17 JAN 1878	11	310
Baker, Philip	Cole, Sybella R.	19 SEP 1882 R	17	029
Baker, R.V.	Anderson, R.T.	05 AUG 1885 L	20	354
Baker, Sadie	Constantini, Benedetto	28 AUG 1881 R	15	435
Baker, William	Ellis, Jennie	21 OCT 1880 L	15	007
Baker, William	Baker, Jennie	18 MAY 1885 R	20	226
Baker, William C.	Irby, Sallie E.	29 DEC 1877	11	281
Baker, William H.	Jenkins, Hosanna	03 OCT 1878 R	12	245
Baker, William W.	Allen, Emily E.	14 NOV 1878	12	328
Bakersmith, John	Bradley, Julia	16 SEP 1884 L	19	252
Balch, Matilda	Jackson, Armistead	27 FEB 1878 L	11	362
Balcher, Elizabeth	Purdy, John W. Larman	18 SEP 1879 R	13	376
Balderston, Joseph W.	Meads, Lizzie G.	30 MAY 1883 R	17	467
Balderstone, Charles	Dillays, Effie	07 FEB 1882 R	16	222
Baldwin, Agnes B.	Perry, James A.	27 FEB 1878	11	362
Baldwin, Brenton L.	Foley, Caroline	03 DEC 1879	14	028
Baldwin, Chricelia	Miller, Perry R.	21 MAY 1884 L	19	033
Baldwin, John W.	O'Connell, Maggie J.	31 JUL 1880 L	14	381

D.C. Marriage Records Index, June 28, 1877 to October 19, 1885

Name	Spouse	Date		
Baldwin, Leander	Johnson, Laura Ester Joyce	18 JAN 1881 R	15	153
Baldwin, Mary	Schwab, Hermann Caspar	04 JUN 1885 R	20	256
Baldwin, Mary Ann, Mrs.	Ogden, John	15 AUG 1882 R	16	464
Baldwin, Sallie	Bogue, George W.	01 JUN 1882 R	16	387
Baldwin, Samuel	Fuller, Harriet	29 JUL 1878 L	12	150
Baldwin, William	Bell, Ellen	17 OCT 1884 L	19	317
Baldwin, William B.	Bassett, Fannie C.	23 SEP 1885	20	436
Baldwin, William E.	Allen, Tillie	08 AUG 1883	18	080
Balenger, Lucy Ann	Howard, James Henry	22 DEC 1880 R	15	116
Bales, Alice	Lee, George F.	05 JUN 1879 R	13	220
Bales, Sarah	Brawner, Calvin	15 FEB 1882	16	241
Baley, George	Brown, Ida	23 JUN 1884	19	098
Balinger, Richard Clinton	Passeno, Isabelle May	30 SEP 1885 R	20	450
Ball, Andrew F.	Reed, Mamie E.	31 JAN 1882 L	16	217
Ball, Barbara	Ricketts, John A.	23 JUN 1881	15	375
Ball, Benjamin	Sanders, Jane	15 AUG 1882 L	16	480
Ball, Carrie E.V.	Medley, George D.	14 OCT 1885 R	20	485
Ball, Cecilia A., Mrs.	Blake, Isaac	13 OCT 1879 R	13	415
Ball, Charles	Banyan, Catharine	17 JAN 1883 R	18	345
Ball, Charles A.	Hutchinson, Linda	07 APR 1880	14	213
Ball, Charles C.	Henson, Jennie E.	26 JUN 1879 L	13	254
Ball, David	Rummels, Sarah	17 JAN 1880	14	110
Ball, George A.	Hanson, Mary E.	19 AUG 1879 L	13	326
Ball, George W.	Stewart, Josephine Adger	28 APR 1881 R	15	274
Ball, Henrietta	Smith, Jordan	19 MAR 1879 R	13	103
Ball, I.L.	Hedgman, F.C.	20 JAN 1881 L	15	159
Ball, John Robert	Jones, Henrietta	19 SEP 1883 R	18	141
Ball, Laura V.	Harrison, Wesley	07 JAN 1880 R	14	094
Ball, Laurie J.	Wilkins, Franklin P.	13 JAN 1881 R	15	150
Ball, Lucy	Cook, Israel	09 AUG 1877 L	11	047
Ball, Marshel T.	Shipman, Nellie	08 AUG 1881 L	15	435
Ball, Mary	Mattill, Henry	10 JUL 1880 L	14	355
Ball, Mary E.	Reed, George W.	17 JAN 1882	16	196
Ball, Mary Elizabeth	Sebastian, Nicholas	15 FEB 1880	14	147
Ball, Mary F.	Parker, Charles F.	29 MAY 1878	12	072
Ball, Robert	Stuart, Sidonia	03 APR 1884 L	18	495
Ball, Sallie	Hunton, H.C.	01 OCT 1880 L	14	468
Ball, Sarah C.	Saunders, James	04 MAR 1880 R	14	178
Ball, Susie	Burgess, John E.	12 DEC 1878	12	379
Ball, Thomas A.T.	Cage, Sarah Ellen	05 FEB 1880	14	139
Ball, Thomas Latham	Hunter, Zaidee Price	15 NOV 1881 R	16	078
Ball, William M.	Eimer, Mary F.	10 OCT 1884 L	19	299
Ball, William T.	Kidwell, Julia Ann	12 FEB 1880 R	14	149
Ballard, Augustus W.	Briggs, Mary[1]	14 DEC 1878 L	12	380
Ballard, Augustus Warwick	Lathrop, Flora Elizth.	30 MAR 1880 R	14	202½
Ballard, Fannie	Boston, Odsey	13 DEC 1881	16	128
Ballard, James H.	Thomas, Victoria	14 APR 1880 L	14	222
Ballard, Lillian	Coughlan, J. Aloysius	14 AUG 1879 L	13	320
Ballauf, Minnie	German, Samuel	12 JAN 1881	15	148
Ballauff, Robert Benedict	Williams, Mary Ildergerte	05 NOV 1884 L	19	363
Ballenger, Joseph	Grady, Nellie	13 OCT 1878 R	12	268
Ballenger, Maggie	Wister, Philip	15 MAY 1879 R	13	190
Ballenger, Richard F.	Davis, Elizabeth E.	25 AUG 1879 R	13	333
Ballenger, Richard F.	Davis, Elizabeth E.	25 AUG 1879	13	500
Ballinger, William H.	McCabe, Maria	13 OCT 1884 L	19	303
Ballman, Mary	Burnham, Elgie L.	29 JUN 1884 R	19	109

[1] Cancelled license because of Lady's death, 30 MAR 1880.

Ballock, Kate	Lake, James Randall	14 JUN 1882 R	16	408
Ballot, Hattie	Holmes, Thomas	05 APR 1882 L	16	302
Balluff, Annie	Kelley, David	15 SEP 1885 L	20	417
Bally, Frederick	Corboner, Maria Jane	05 MAY 1882 R	16	350
Balsam, Fannie	Holmes, Thomas	17 JUN 1880 R	14	321
Balthis, French A.	Wise, Lillie Lee	19 SEP 1878 L	12	227
Baltz, Henry Edward	Widmayer, Rosa Mary	27 APR 1885 R	20	189
Baltz, Mary	Michel, George	29 JAN 1884 R	18	398
Baltzley, Edwin	Kaemmerer, Edith M.	27 DEC 1883	18	341
Banes, Albert	Dickson, Louise	06 NOV 1879 R	13	470
Banes, Eliza	Bradley, Edward	31 DEC 1878 R	12	405
Banes, Warner P.	Berry, Elizabeth L.	30 JUL 1878 L	12	152
Bangs, Annie Eliza	Parks, Frederick James	20 OCT 1877	11	147
Bangs, J. Howard	Hines, Fannie J.	20 SEP 1882 L	17	031
Bangs, Susanna E.A.	Burrows, Frederick W.	26 NOV 1877	11	203
Banket, Phillis	Harris, Minor	16 JAN 1879 R	13	024
Bankhead, Carry	Kelley, John Edward	26 JAN 1881 R	15	164
Banks, Adeline	Coleman, George	18 MAY 1880 L	14	274
Banks, Amanda	Harvey, Frank	16 OCT 1884	19	305
Banks, Anida Elizabeth	Ward, William E.	16 MAY 1878 L	12	056
Banks, Bradley	Churchhill, Harriet	24 JUL 1879	13	290
Banks, Broadus	Ferguson, Rachel	06 SEP 1883 L	18	116
Banks, Christopher J.C.	Green, Susan, Mrs.	27 FEB 1879 R	13	082
Banks, Clara E.	Grimes, William H.	08 JAN 1878 L	11	295
Banks, Cora	Collins, John F.	16 APR 1883 L	17	395
Banks, Ellen	Clayton, John	09 AUG 1878 R	12	162
Banks, Fanny	Burnett, Edward W.	18 JUN 1879 L	13	237
Banks, Gracie	Brown, Charles C.	14 DEC 1881 L	16	130
Banks, Henry	Ashby, Molly	25 MAY 1885 R	20	235
Banks, James	Lear, Frances	06 NOV 1870	12	312
Banks, James	Douglas, Susanna	28 SEP 1881 R	15	501
Banks, Jesse	Brown, Elizabeth	18 AUG 1884	19	192
Banks, John	Nash, Melvina	16 SEP 1880 R	14	448
Banks, John F.	Robinson, Catherine	15 NOV 1881 R	16	077
Banks, John Mitchell	Waters, Minnie	17 NOV 1881 L	16	082
Banks, Martha	Lee, Jerry	26 OCT 1882 L	17	097
Banks, Martha Ellen	Washington, Lee	13 NOV 1878 R	12	317
Banks, Martha Ellen	Lee, Richard Henry	08 NOV 1881 R	16	055
Banks, Mary	Henry, James W.	12 SEP 1880	14	434
Banks, Mary	Lawson, Fleetwood	18 SEP 1884 L	19	260
Banks, Mary E.	Adams, John	17 APR 1882 L	16	319
Banks, Matilda B.	Jenkins, Talbot M.	06 NOV 1883 L	18	238
Banks, Mattie	Dickinson, Daniel	27 DEC 1883 R	18	339
Banks, Nannie E.	Southworth, Harrison	14 MAY 1879	13	189
Banks, Nathaniel P.	Brooks, Belle	24 FEB 1885 L	20	084
Banks, Nellie I.	Smith, Jeremiah	25 MAR 1880	14	197
Banks, Robert	Coates, Annie J.	24 JAN 1881 L	15	161
Banks, Robert	Hayes, Nancy	13 MAY 1882 L	16	359
Banks, Sarah M.	Johnson, William H.	10 JUL 1884 L	19	133
Banks, William	Brown, Alice	18 JUL 1878 L	12	141
Banks, William H.	Jones, Lizzie E.	02 JAN 1879	13	005
Banks, William Henry	Newman, Annie Elizabeth	01 MAY 1883 R	17	425
Bannan, Eliza	Watson, James	09 DEC 1882 L	17	175
Banneker, Ettie	Stewart, Daniel H.	12 MAY 1885	20	015
Banner, Edward	Johnson, Keseiah	20 FEB 1879 R	13	067
Bannion, Pleasy	Butler, Delozier I.	24 NOV 1880 L	15	063
Bannister, George	Wood, Maggie	25 JUL 1882 R	16	455
Bannister, Susie	Hill, Reuben B.	20 APR 1880 L	14	228

Name	Spouse	Date	Vol	Page
Banville, George W.W.	Graney, Catherine	25 AUG 1879 L	13	334
Banyan, Catharine	Ball, Charles	17 JAN 1883 R	18	345
Banyan, Robert	Carpenter, Eliza	21 SEP 1877	11	104
Baptis, Mary E.	Gibson, Thomas A.	01 NOV 1882	17	105
Baptist, Jennie	Meredith, Charles	08 NOV 1883 L	18	243
Barber, Allan	Williams, Winnie	03 FEB 1882 L	16	224
Barber, Carrie	Page, Henry C.	20 SEP 1883 L	18	144
Barber, Charley	Beckett, Blanche	07 JUL 1885 R	20	311
Barber, David	Walters, Louisa Davis	23 OCT 1879 R	13	439
Barber, Elenora	Kissner, Lawrence	17 JUN 1879	13	233
Barber, Ella	Ross, Thomas	03 JUN 1880 R	14	303
Barber, George E.	Cox, Fannie M.	21 SEP 1880	14	454
Barber, Henry	Mickins, Josephine	06 MAR 1878	11	371
Barber, Ida Belle	Stone, Jay	05 OCT 1881 R	16	005
Barber, Maggie	Brown, Thomas	18 NOV 1880 R	15	054
Barber, Oregon L.	Green, Andrew M.	17 JUN 1884	19	089
Barber, Patsey	Jackson, Henry	18 JUL 1881 L	15	408
Barber, Robert T.J.	Hayden, Lucy B.	18 MAY 1885	20	226
Barber, William D.	Burr, Jennie	09 MAY 1882 R	16	355
Barber, William W.	Dixon, Mary H.	22 FEB 1883 R	17	308
Barbour, Anderson H.	McKenzie, Kate	22 MAR 1882	16	287
Barbour, J.E.	Brown, J.S.	15 JAN 1885	20	015
Barbour, Jane C.	Gulick, Robert M.	26 MAR 1883 L	17	360
Barbour, Mary Imogene	Phillips, Robert A.	27 DEC 1880 L	15	127
Barbour, Samuel	Clay, Anna	18 NOV 1879 L	13	493
Barbour, Susanna D.	Lombard, Andrew J.	31 OCT 1878 R	12	301
Barclay, Edgar L.	Hough, Sarah J.	12 SEP 1878 R	12	216
Barclay, Joseph J.	Willard, Alice R.	24 SEP 1884	19	266
Bare, George E.	Holmes, Bettie H.	17 MAY 1883 R	17	449
Bare, Louisa E.	Dentinger, Louis C.	08 AUG 1878 R	14	3401
Barfoot, Cassa	Garrett, Charles	02 JAN 1882 R	16	175
Barfoot, John A.	Beadle, Annie M.	23 JUL 1879	13	291
Barghausen, Marley	Diller, Charles	12 OCT 1884	19	300
Barister, W.L.	Frances, Annie E.	18 AUG 1881 R	22	5304
Barker, Bertie E.	Isel, John C.	13 AUG 1885 R	20	367
Barker, Bettie	Cline, Henry	29 MAY 1882 L	16	380
Barker, Charles A.	Moore, Anna	03 NOV 1881 R	16	060
Barker, Elsie	Oliver, Francis R.	02 OCT 1885	20	452
Barker, Georgie A. (Blundon)	Smith, Richard T., Capt.	19 JAN 1882 R	16	203
Barker, Harrison S.	Hudson, Lizzie E.	12 DEC 1883	18	312
Barker, James C.	Belt, Martina	06 DEC 1883	18	303
Barker, John B.	West, Julia G.	16 FEB 1878 L	11	345
Barker, Mary	Thomson, Charles P.	06 DEC 1883	18	304
Barker, Mary E.	Wanstall, Frank B.	13 DEC 1880 R	15	093
Barker, Nammie E.	Carpenter, Thomas W.	20 OCT 1881 L	16	038
Barker, Nelson	McGill, Harriet A.	06 DEC 1877 L	11	224
Barker, Soffie	Tolbert, James	07 JUN 1883 R	17	483
Barkley, John A.	Oker, Sophie	05 JUN 1881	15	343
Barlow, Alfred	Queen, Fannie M.	24 FEB 1883 R	17	320
Barnaclo, Alice	Poore, Bushard W.	10 JUN 1882	16	403
Barnaclo, Eliza L.	Danenhauer, John	23 FEB 1879 R	13	075
Barnaclo, James K.	Crowley, Johanna A.	28 APR 1884 L	18	535
Barnaclo, William Alphonso	Neidfeldt, Carrie M.	18 JUN 1881 R	15	367
Barnard, Constance Kate	Andrews, Albert Slacum	21 SEP 1882 R	17	033
Barnard, Egbert G.	Bradley, Sarah A.	26 SEP 1883 R	18	154
Barnard, Francis F.	Bartley, Alice	03 OCT 1877 R	11	119
Barnard, George B.	Chew, Margaret E.	30 APR 1884 L	18	543
Barnard, Helena Emma	Hall, Evelyn Smith	20 MAY 1880 R	14	280

Name	Spouse	Date	Vol	Page
Barnard, Josephine F.	McDonald, Joseph E.	12 JAN 1881	15	146
Barnard, Lucy A.	Thomas, J.M.F.A.	24 JUL 1879	13	292
Barnard, Luther W.	Duty, Elizabeth	26 JUL 1882 R	16	458
Barnard, Minnie Lenore	Harvey, William, Jr.	28 JUN 1884	19	110
Barnard, William H.	Dickson, Clara	03 MAY 1880 R	14	250
Barnes, Ada Virginia	Hurdle, George W.	27 FEB 1879	13	084
Barnes, Adelaide	Loughlin, Frank	06 OCT 1885 L	20	460
Barnes, Agnes R.	Postell, Porcher	02 NOV 1884	19	353
Barnes, Alexander	Addison, Fannie	13 JAN 1885 L	20	016
Barnes, Alfred	Ganes, Annie	24 MAR 1884 L	18	479
Barnes, Aloysius	Soper, Fannie	16 OCT 1879	13	431
Barnes, Andrew	Nelson, Estella	19 JUN 1884 R	19	091
Barnes, Anne	Cook, Wesley	06 MAR 1879 R	13	051
Barnes, Annie	Johnson, Thomas	06 FEB 1882 L	16	227
Barnes, Annie	Scott, Frank T.	22 JAN 1882	16	198
Barnes, Charles H.	Myers, Sadie G.	10 FEB 1884 R	18	411
Barnes, Columbus	Soper, Emma	24 JUN 1880	14	334
Barnes, Edgar	Shelton, Annie	24 JUN 1879 L	13	246
Barnes, Edward	Campbell, Alice	15 JUL 1878 L	12	135
Barnes, Eliza	Jackson, George T.	12 NOV 1878 L	12	323
Barnes, Elizabeth A.	Stevens, Henry M.	18 JAN 1883 R	17	268
Barnes, Ellen	Atwell, John	08 OCT 1878 L	12	260
Barnes, Elzy	Poindexter, Julia A.	04 NOV 1880 R	15	030
Barnes, Everard F.	Johnson, Bernice	25 SEP 1879 L	13	386
Barnes, Frank	Bradley, Elizabeth	10 MAY 1883 R	17	435
Barnes, Helen	Shedrick, James Andrew	21 JAN 1885 L	20	032
Barnes, Henry C.	Marlow, Cornelia	08 FEB 1881 L	15	182
Barnes, Henry Francis	Moten, Edith	01 AUG 1882	16	461
Barnes, James Wallace	Abraham, Clara	28 DEC 1881 R	16	162
Barnes, John F.	Mattingly, Josephine	16 OCT 1884 L	19	311
Barnes, Joseph E.	Fraser, Lillie P	10 MAY 1881 R	15	299
Barnes, Joseph H.	Johnson, Kate	13 MAY 1884 L	19	017
Barnes, Kate	Butler, Nathaniel	30 DEC 1880	15	133
Barnes, Lena	Gwynn, Benjamin	05 JAN 1881 L	15	141
Barnes, Lewis	Magee, Catherine	02 DEC 1880 R	15	077
Barnes, Louie M.	McKenney, Clara E.	17 SEP 1878 R	12	221
Barnes, Margaret	Toy, William	05 MAR 1878	11	371
Barnes, Mary	Cook, Charles C.H.	28 MAY 1883 L	17	466
Barnes, Mary A.	Anderson, Charles P.	22 DEC 1881 L	16	150
Barnes, Mary E.	Hausmann, August F.	27 APR 1880 R	14	238
Barnes, Mary E.	Sanders, Charles	15 JAN 1880 R	14	107
Barnes, Mary F.	Tinsley, John C.	29 AUG 1877 R	11	067
Barnes, Mary Frances	Harris, Joseph R.	26 JAN 1880 L	14	120
Barnes, Mary Frances	Clarke, Harrison	01 JAN 1885	19	515
Barnes, Maude M.	Clarvoe, John T.	09 OCT 1879 R	13	411
Barnes, Minnie	Scriber, George W.	23 JAN 1882	16	205
Barnes, Mollie C.	DeAtley, James F.	20 SEP 1877	11	103
Barnes, Raymond F.	Van Slyck, Mattie M.	07 DEC 1881 R	16	116
Barnes, Sadie A.	Wright, Robert F.	21 SEP 1878	12	205
Barnes, Sarah	Scott, James	25 JUN 1885	20	294
Barnes, Sarah O.	Tracy, W.H.	27 JUN 1883	18	019
Barnes, Susie	Free, Robert	14 MAY 1881 L	15	306
Barnes, Thomas Henry	Dyson, Matilda	20 JUL 1882 R	16	453
Barnes, William	Willis, Bettie	11 JUN 1884 L	19	078
Barnes, William	Williams, Alice	17 FEB 1885 L	20	075
Barnes, William H.	Soper, Maggie	18 DEC 1877 L	11	244
Barnes, Winnie A.	Frazier, Alexander	03 JUN 1880	14	302
Barnesley, Sallie	Harris, Orlando	23 APR 1883 L	17	405

D.C. Marriage Records Index, June 28, 1877 to October 19, 1885

Barnett, Alice M.	Wilson, William J.	04 MAY 1882 L	16	349
Barnett, Gussie V.	Cole, Peter L.	17 OCT 1883 R	18	197
Barnett, K.J.	Landon, G.W.	24 JUL 1879	13	292
Barnett, Lou M.	Slee, Robert H.S.	25 NOV 1881 R	16	099
Barnett, Sarah	Cady, Patrick	25 FEB 1878 L	11	355
Barnett, William	Langley, Margaret S.	15 JUN 1883 R	17	496
Barnett, William A.	Dean, Delia	26 JUN 1884 R	19	106
Barnhouse, Isaac P.	Smith, Lizzie M.	30 JAN 1878	11	322
Barns, Dulcenia	Collins, Andrew J.	01 OCT 1878 L	12	246
Barns, Lucretia	Lee, Emery	09 OCT 1877 R	11	126
Barns, Sarah	Mandul, Berry	01 OCT 1878	12	245
Baron, Bernard	Schwartz, Rachel	10 AUG 1880 R	14	390
Barr, Annie Isadora	Raum, Henry	27 MAY 1880 R	14	294
Barr, Annie Webb	Israel, Robert Otho	18 MAR 1880 L	14	188
Barr, Frances A.	Robertson, William F.	19 APR 1884	18	520
Barr, James H.	Webb, Margaret	02 AUG 1881 R	15	428
Barr, Jennie	Walker, George	07 APR 1881	15	250
Barr, John	Bickford, Jennie L.	30 OCT 1882 L	17	101
Barr, Mary	Collins, Millard F.	11 MAY 1880 L	14	265
Barr, Robert McClelland	Davis, Fannie Queen	28 SEP 1885 R	20	447
Barrand, Mary C.	Davis, Harry A.	29 NOV 1883	18	278
Barrett, Anna Theresa	Harkness, Robert Henry	20 MAR 1884 R	18	478
Barrett, Bessie Christopher	Dentinger, Charles Joseph	15 JAN 1879	13	021
Barrett, Carrie L.	Purman, Louis C.	26 AUG 1880 L	14	418
Barrett, Elbert G.	Kramer, Mary D.	19 DEC 1883 L	18	328
Barrett, Elizabeth	Reagan, Patrick F.	20 SEP 1879 R	15	3508
Barrett, Franklin	Kidwell, Mary	15 JAN 1884 R	18	374
Barrett, George	Allen, Alice Frances	08 OCT 1884	19	294
Barrett, Hannah M.	Prather, Charles S.	09 SEP 1884 L	19	235
Barrett, James D.	Webster, Emily Frances	30 MAR 1882 R	16	290
Barrett, James P.	Reagan, Margaret A.	11 NOV 1884 L	19	373
Barrett, John W.	McKenney, Lizzie	30 JUN 1880	14	337
Barrett, John W.	Gore, Sarah A. Carr	22 SEP 1885 R	20	433
Barrett, Maggie F.	Loveless, John T.	14 JUL 1882 L	16	448
Barrett, Michael	Shields, Catherine	22 JUL 1879 R	13	288
Barrett, Michael	Myers, Mary	16 JUN 1883 L	17	497
Barrett, Michael F.	Buckley, Ella D.	16 JUN 1885 L	20	277
Barrett, Michael J.	Walsh, Mary	13 NOV 1884 L	19	380
Barrett, Norah	Mooney, Thomas H.	26 NOV 1880 L	15	068
Barrett, Sophie Cecelia	Collins, Thomas Jasper	05 JAN 1881 R	15	139
Barrett, Susie A.	Fowler, Joseph O.	11 JUN 1879 R	13	227
Barrett, Theodore H.	McKee, Georgie Brubaker	05 JUN 1879 R	13	219
Barrett, William Henry	Bellducket, Clara	28 DEC 1880 R	15	127
Barrett, Wm. Claude	Parkhurst, Mabel A.	15 APR 1884 R	18	509
Barrick, Annie M.	Sharpless, Frank	22 FEB 1882 R	16	255
Barriere, Fannie	Mosely, George C.	23 FEB 1883 R	17	319
Barriere, Mary F.	House, Henry J.	21 JAN 1885	20	030
Barrister, Susie C.	Copeland, Wm. Warren	24 JAN 1885 R	20	035
Barron, Ada R.	Koontz, Thomas L.	07 FEB 1882 R	16	229
Barron, Carrie	Boyd, Chas. A.B.	20 NOV 1883 L	18	266
Barron, Elizabeth	Proctor, James	29 OCT 1883 R	18	200
Barron, Florence L., Mrs.	Sullivan, William J.	10 JUN 1884	19	072
Barron, Gertrude	Kerkham, Robert E.	29 SEP 1881 R	15	507
Barron, Harry W.	Coleman, Mary Ella	23 APR 1883 L	17	404
Barron, John	Elton, Fannie H.	04 JUL 1878 R	12	124
Barron, John Oliver	Bailey, Emma J.	28 MAY 1879 R	13	208
Barron, Maggie	Burns, James	22 OCT 1882	17	085
Barron, Mattie	Rose, William L.	18 JUL 1883	18	052

Barron, Owen F.	Hartnett, Mary E.	27 SEP 1883 L	18	157
Barrow, Margaret E.	Travers, John C., Jr.	28 APR 1884 L	18	537
Barrus, Johnson C.	Berkley, Catherine	11 SEP 1877	11	085
Barry, Alice	Bell, William B.	05 JUL 1883	18	036
Barry, Clifton	Kelly, Mary M.	13 APR 1882	16	298
Barry, David Sheldon	Bonney, Cora	19 APR 1883 R	17	401
Barry, Ella E.	Gray, John	17 MAY 1883 R	17	448
Barry, Emily	Creagan, Francis	20 SEP 1879 L	13	379
Barry, James	Swope, Kate	10 DEC 1877 L	11	228
Barry, Jeremiah	Thompson, Florida	02 MAY 1880 R	14	247
Barry, Jerry	Green, Evelina	14 JAN 1880 L	14	104
Barry, Julia	McHale, Anthony	04 NOV 1883	18	291
Barry, Mary	O'Donnell, Henry	03 DEC 1877 R	11	210
Barry, Mary M.	O'Connor, Jeremiah J.	16 OCT 1882 R	17	074
Barry, Mary S.	Norfolk, Charles K.	05 AUG 1885	20	355
Barry, Michael	Walsh, Catharine Phelan	14 SEP 1880 R	14	444
Barry, Patrick	Welsh, Johanna	08 OCT 1877	11	125
Barry, Patrick	Sullivan, Mary	10 SEP 1881 R	15	480
Barry, Thomas Henry	Bestor, Ellen	23 JAN 1884 R	18	388
Barry, Virginia	Brooks, Charles W.	01 AUG 1885	20	346
Barry, William	King, Margaret	16 AUG 1883	18	091
Barry, William H.	Worthington, Juana	26 NOV 1883 L	18	277
Barshall, Fannie	Kissner, Robert	01 FEB 1882	16	220
Bartel, Augusta Agnes	Aufrecht, Carl Gottlob	23 MAR 1881 R	15	231
Bartel, Priscilla	Robinson, Joseph T.	16 JAN 1878 L	11	306
Barthlomeai, Albert S.	Rawlings, Annie E.	26 NOV 1883 L	18	276
Bartholomae, Emma	Miller, Edwin	13 FEB 1878 L	11	339
Bartholow, John B.	Gambrill, Mary M.	06 JUN 1882	16	395
Bartles, Joseph	True, Mabel	22 DEC 1883 D	18	333
Bartlett, Emma	Fletcher, Edward	16 APR 1878	12	008
Bartlett, Fitz J.	Wiber, Annah N., Mrs.	15 FEB 1883	17	309
Bartlett, Frederick H.	Gunter, Mary	21 AUG 1885	20	382
Bartlett, James W.	Reamy, Annie L.	06 OCT 1883 R	18	175
Bartlett, Mary Beall	Anderson, Wella Percy	07 JUL 1880 R	14	349
Bartlett, Phoenix	Mathews, Jennie S.	14 NOV 1883 R	18	254
Bartlett, William U.	Whelan, Anna E.	02 JUL 1885 L	20	306
Bartley, Alice	Barnard, Francis F.	03 OCT 1877 R	11	119
Bartley, James W.	Guigon, Mary Josephine	31 JUL 1878 L	12	152
Bartley, Lillie A.	Linkins, John R.	04 AUG 1879 R	13	305
Bartley, Minnie H.	Reese, William K.	11 OCT 1877 R	11	130
Bartley, Roger S.	Hall, Carrie B.	26 DEC 1877 L	11	271
Bartley, Thomas W.	McCoy, Ellen Espy	17 SEP 1878 L	12	223
Barton, Albert	Thomas, Elvira	14 APR 1885 L	20	166
Barton, Alice S.	Cowell, George H.	11 NOV 1878 R	12	320
Barton, Elmer E.	Hill, Esther I.	15 JAN 1884	18	377
Barton, George	Hill, Louisa	11 MAR 1882 L	16	273
Barton, Henry	Young, Catherine	25 APR 1882 L	16	334
Barton, Martha	Ferguson, James E.	13 APR 1881	15	256
Barton, Mary	Norris, Reuben	09 NOV 1879	13	468
Barton, William W.	Murray, Mary	03 JUL 1883 L	18	034
Baruch, Allen	Callisher, Leah	11 DEC 1881 R	16	124
Basey, Gabriel	Gibson, Matilda	04 DEC 1882 R	17	166
Basey, Richard	Waters, Alice	03 JUN 1879 L	13	218
Bashears, Frank	Timmons, Emma L.	24 AUG 1881 L	15	456
Baskall, Catharine	Conovy, Warren	24 AUG 1885 L	20	384
Baskerville, Ada V.	Smith, Hillary	12 JAN 1885 R	20	013
Bass, Hamilton	Jones, Louisa	13 SEP 1877 L	11	091
Bass, Louis	Pifferling, Zelinda	25 OCT 1884 L	19	337

D.C. Marriage Records Index, June 28, 1877 to October 19, 1885

Bass, Marian C.	Pitts, Laban W.	12 MAR 1884	18	466
Bass, William M.	Hart, Rosalie	18 SEP 1878 R	12	223
Bassell, Henry	Jackson, Emma	31 DEC 1878	12	408
Bassett, Fannie C.	Baldwin, William B.	23 SEP 1885	20	436
Bassett, George W.	Cline, Maggie	10 OCT 1878 R	12	264
Bassfield, Emma	Matthews, Robert	14 DEC 1882 R	17	186
Bassford, John N.	Mitchell, Ellen C.	05 DEC 1883	18	295
Bassford, Sarah E.	Bowen, Winter E.	08 SEP 1880 R	14	436
Bastianelli, Adrian	Johnston, Kate Arlena	22 NOV 1882 R	17	138
Batchelor, Julia J.	Gibbs, John B.	28 JAN 1882 R	16	213
Bateman, Frances S.	Foley, Beverly R.	09 JUL 1881 L	15	396
Bateman, John Thomas	Meredith, Charlotte	21 FEB 1883 R	17	314
Bateman, Laura L.	McKinney, William W.	29 MAR 1884 R	18	486
Bateman, W. Grafton	Collton, Angie E.	20 NOV 1884	19	394
Baten, Alice	Dutch, Edward	03 MAY 1882 L	16	347
Bates, Annie E.	Brown, William S.	23 MAY 1881 L	15	322
Bates, Bertie	Robinson, Lee	20 DEC 1877 R	11	252
Bates, Clarence D.	Collins, David M.	07 JUN 1880	14	308
Bates, Edward T.	Scarff, M. Alice	12 JUL 1882 R	16	446
Bates, Emma F.	Wileman, Miles H.	13 MAY 1885	20	217
Bates, Emory H.	Read, Mary Anna	14 NOV 1878 R	12	330
Bates, Fannie Warren	Burke, Lawrence Wm.	11 DEC 1882 R	17	177
Bates, Jeanie M., Mrs.	Routh, John	20 JAN 1881 R	15	160
Bates, Lillie M.	Shieber, William F.	03 SEP 1883 L	18	108
Bates, Mary	Johnson, William Thomas	28 JUL 1881 R	15	422
Bates, Mason	Morton, Alice	18 SEP 1879 R	13	377
Bates, Maud D.	Biondi, Charles P.	15 SEP 1884 R	19	243
Bates, Mollie	Robinson, Henry	09 OCT 1880 L	14	485
Bates, Nelly M.	Stone, William Jay	14 MAY 1881 R	15	307
Bates, Robert	Douglass, Laura	04 FEB 1884 L	18	407
Bates, Samuel Brown	Gill, Mary Eliz.	20 DEC 1882 R	17	194
Bates, William J.	Morrison, Mary Ellen	03 AUG 1885	20	348
Batkins, William T.	Anderson, Jeannetta	30 JUL 1884	19	161
Batley, Georgie A.	Ricks, William C.	05 JUL 1884	19	124
Batson, Henson	Shorter, Margaret	24 DEC 1877	11	264
Batson, John	Smothers, Charity E.	12 FEB 1880 R	14	151
Batson, Mary	Adams, John	01 JUN 1882	16	377
Battenfield, John E.	Sutton, Kate R.	16 OCT 1884	19	313
Battie, Allece	Brown, Henry	25 AUG 1881 L	15	458
Battle, Annie	Williams, Ed	20 DEC 1879 L	14	060
Battle, John	Parker, Harriet	21 JUN 1883 L	18	009
Batts, George M.	Redding, Margaret Ann Evans	30 JUL 1879 R	13	298
Bauer, Andrew	Schickler, Katie	24 MAR 1879	13	112
Bauer, Christina	Iager, Henry A.	16 OCT 1877 L	11	139
Bauer, Dora	Kramer, Alois	02 FEB 1882	16	219
Bauer, John C.	Hyland, Mary E.	21 AUG 1879 L	13	330
Bauer, Louis	Pfitzmaier, Mary	15 JAN 1880 R	14	105
Bauer, Sophia	Beckstedt, Henry	10 OCT 1881 L	16	016
Baughn, James N.	Lucas, Alice A.	29 MAY 1882 R	16	379
Baum, Emmie C.	Lewis, Dio W.	17 SEP 1885 R	20	421
Baum, Fannie	Luchs, Joseph	11 MAY 1879 R	13	183
Baum, Frances	Brock, Jacob	21 OCT 1880 R	15	009
Baum, Mary S.	Foster, Thomas	28 DEC 1878 R	12	400
Baumann, Barbara A.	Hammer, John H.	03 JAN 1880 R	13	390
Baumann, William C.	Wolz, Annie B.	27 JUL 1879 R	13	294
Baumbach, Mollie (Webber)	Waldron, Edward	31 DEC 1881 R	16	173
Baumgras, Erwin Cyrus	Greenland, Emma Belle	28 APR 1885 R	20	194
Baur, Joseph Anton	Pfeiffer, Elizabeth Madaline	26 OCT 1879 R	13	442

Baurman, Augustus B.	Koepf, Louise	24 MAR 1885	20	129
Bause, George E.	Baker, Matilda	07 DEC 1882 R	17	175
Bawsel, Edward	Borland, Eliza J.	11 FEB 1880 L	14	149
Baxter, Annie	Thompson, George S.	23 JUL 1884 R	19	152
Baxter, G.H.	Koon, Clara H.	24 APR 1878	12	022
Baxter, George O.	May, Allie	11 FEB 1884	18	418
Baxter, Hattie H.	Graeme, John K.	21 FEB 1884	18	436
Baxter, Walter W.	Hogue, Marie Alma	06 SEP 1881 R	15	473
Bayard, James T.E.	Foreman, Victoria	14 JUL 1884 L	19	138
Bayard, Mabel	Warren, Samuel Dennis, Jr.	25 JAN 1883 R	17	270
Bayard, T. Jefferson	Craig, Ella	28 FEB 1884 R	18	451
Bayless, Ezra	Tillett, Eliza J.	23 APR 1885 R	20	185
Bayley, Cornelius P.	Burroughs, Mary Emma	03 DEC 1878 R	12	360
Bayley, Henry B.	Hammett, Blanche	15 APR 1884 R	18	509
Bayley, S.P., Jr.	Clagett, Elise M.	14 OCT 1878	12	270
Bayliss, C.B.	Smith, E.G.	20 JUN 1882	16	419
Bayliss, Clara V.	Reese, John	13 OCT 1879 R	13	418
Bayliss, Georgiana	Hall, Elihu	30 DEC 1880 R	15	132
Bayliss, Hillman	Fahnline, Catherine A.	13 SEP 1882	17	020
Bayliss, Margaret A.	Reid, Eugenius N.	15 SEP 1884 L	19	247
Bayliss, Mary E.	Monroe, Richmond	15 JAN 1878 R	10	2460
Bayliss, McElmer	Wilson, Mary E.	31 JUL 1880 R	14	379
Bayliss, Robert Vinton	Jenkins, Mary, Mrs.	08 MAY 1884 R	19	004
Bayliss, William F.	Quigley, Mollie E.	22 APR 1885	20	183
Bayliss, William T.	Tillett, Sallie L.	02 JUL 1885 R	20	307
Baylor, Allen	Whittey, Julia	15 AUG 1885 L	20	371
Baylor, Gussie	Miller, Webster	12 JAN 1882 R	16	187
Baylor, James	Ruffins, Louisa Miles	29 SEP 1882 R	17	044
Baylor, Mary E.	White, Dennis E.	08 JUN 1881	15	351
Baylor, Milly	Dennis, John H.	27 NOV 1878 R	12	052
Baylor, Sarah	Jones, William M.	19 JUN 1884 L	19	093
Baylor, William	Winfield, Martha	18 FEB 1878	11	346
Bayne, Sarah A.	Crane, Willie F.	25 SEP 1882	17	036
Baynes, Margaret	Forrest, John W.	08 JUL 1883	18	039
Baynum, William	Tasco, Margaret	11 AUG 1880 R	14	397
Beach, Anna	Thomas, James M.	11 DEC 1884	19	451
Beach, Annie A.	Newman, Henry	10 NOV 1879 R	13	474
Beach, Annie Laura	Rollins, William Henry	11 JUL 1882 R	16	444
Beach, Benjamin F.	Stone, Sallie E.	17 FEB 1884	18	427
Beach, Cecilia M.	Gonzales, M.	31 AUG 1879	13	345
Beach, Daniel Webster	Ridgely, Mary Stella	19 JUN 1879 R	13	238
Beach, Frank	Massey, Helen	07 FEB 1881 R	15	180
Beach, Frank L.	Meyers, Henrietta	01 SEP 1880 L	14	425
Beach, Frank L.	Meyers, Henrietta	08 SEP 1881 L	15	477
Beach, Frederick	Sutherland, Alcinda	21 AUG 1884	19	201
Beach, George W.	Worster, Martha	02 JUL 1877	11	004
Beach, James H.	Sanford, Mary E.	10 OCT 1883 R	18	184
Beach, James H.	Welch, Josephine	10 APR 1884 R	18	504
Beach, James L.	Dobson, Malvena	22 AUG 1883 L	18	095
Beach, Jennie C.	Curren, William E.	06 DEC 1882 R	17	170
Beach, Laura C.	Williamson, Alexander	26 DEC 1884 L	19	493
Beach, Lillie Lee	Cook, John Thomas	08 OCT 1882 R	17	047
Beach, Lilly Mary	Dean, Harry Clinton	13 OCT 1885 L	20	479
Beach, Louisa	Bryant, Stewart L.	11 JAN 1885	20	012
Beach, Martha F.	Morsell, Robert L.	12 NOV 1877	11	178
Beach, Mary C.	Maley, John E.	12 JUN 1884 R	19	079
Beach, Mary E.	Trumble, Samuel H.	19 JAN 1882 L	16	201
Beach, Mary F.	Burns, Wm. F.	02 MAY 1881 R	15	288

D.C. Marriage Records Index, June 28, 1877 to October 19, 1885

Beach, Sanford A.	Payne, Sarah V., Mrs.	13 DEC 1880	15	093
Beach, Walter L.	Marcy, Matilda	04 JUN 1878	12	085
Beach, William T.	Devers, Maggie J.	08 SEP 1879	13	356
Beach, Wm. Calvin McDaniel	Garrison, Sarah Elizabeth	30 JAN 1884 R	18	401
Beach, Zera Rose	Sutherland, James Buchanan	29 MAR 1883 R	17	370
Beadle, Annie M.	Barfoot, John A.	23 JUL 1879	13	291
Beadle, Henry M.	Remingham, Mary	06 NOV 1880 L	15	035
Beagle, Ida M.	Galloway, John R.	16 JAN 1879 R	13	020
Beagle, James	Roberts, Mittie	04 APR 1885 R	20	144
Beal, Burton A.	Coleman, Fannie P.	11 DEC 1879 R	14	044
Beal, Horace	Carter, Julia, Mrs.	01 JAN 1882 R	16	173
Beal, James A.	Morton, Rena	24 OCT 1883 L	18	212
Beal, Josephine	Taylor, Charles H.	23 DEC 1878 R	12	393
Beal, Ruberta Thrift	Self, Robert W.	05 DEC 1877 R	11	223
Beale, Alice	Warfield, Columbus	17 OCT 1878	12	280
Beale, Allison F.	Givens, Susie A.	02 OCT 1879 R	13	401
Beale, C.E.	Clements, M.E.	21 JUN 1883 L	18	009
Beale, Edward	Joyce, Mary	13 MAY 1883 R	17	436
Beale, Edward M.	Lilly, Clara Alphonsa	04 JUN 1884 R	19	055
Beale, Emily T.	McLean, John R.	06 OCT 1884 L	19	289
Beale, John Wheeler	Carroll, Katharine D.B.	13 DEC 1877 R	11	234
Beale, Laura Jane	Clift, James Edward	04 NOV 1878 R	12	306
Beale, Violet Blair	Bloomer, George Craft	02 FEB 1881 R	15	172
Beales, Amanda	Minor, John Thomas	08 SEP 1879 R	13	348
Beales, Mary	Watkins, John	29 APR 1880 R	14	243
Beall, A.V.	Weeden, A.M.	26 FEB 1878	11	359
Beall, Ann Eliza Wallingsforth	Johnson, George	04 NOV 1882 R	17	111
Beall, Annie C.	Osborn, Alfred G.	06 OCT 1885	20	459
Beall, Annie J.	Miller, Richard A.	17 NOV 1884	19	388
Beall, Annie J.L.	Johnson, Thomas C.	14 JUN 1884 L	19	084
Beall, Catherine	Wood, Charles	12 NOV 1877	11	179
Beall, Constance H.	Backus, William M.	29 DEC 1881 R	16	170
Beall, Geo. Washington	Ogle, Mary Elizabeth	17 JAN 1878 L	11	310
Beall, George	Hayes, Lemuel	20 OCT 1881 L	16	036
Beall, George I.	King, Elizabeth	06 OCT 1883 R	18	174
Beall, George M.	Offield, Mary E.	05 APR 1881	15	247
Beall, Ida M.	Money, Nathaniel B.	14 FEB 1882 L	16	239
Beall, James A.	Beers, M. Virginia	24 OCT 1878 R	12	288
Beall, James Lemuel	Trissler, Hattie A.	20 JAN 1885 R	20	029
Beall, John W.	Wagner, Elizabeth C.	16 MAR 1882	16	280
Beall, John W.	Clements, Mary E.	20 NOV 1883 L	18	266
Beall, Louis Erwin	Clark, Harriet Morgan	04 DEC 1884 R	19	434
Beall, Mary Eleanor	Bowie, Richmond Irving	05 FEB 1880 R	14	136
Beall, Mattie A.	Jackson, William J.	12 APR 1882 L	16	312
Beall, Richard H.	Brown, Mary Ann, Mrs.	24 JUL 1879	13	289
Beall, Richard S.	Crandall, Jennie B.	09 APR 1885	20	155
Beall, Sarah L.	Crupper, F.R.	29 MAY 1884 L	19	046
Beall, Warren H.	Weaver, Lucy H.	18 JUL 1881 R	15	407
Beall, William J.	Walling, Annie L.	04 FEB 1884 L	18	408
Beall, William W.	Rose, Edith	15 NOV 1877 L	11	186
Bealle, Chas. Albert	Hicks, Mary T.	07 NOV 1877 R	11	173
Beam, Cora E.	Wilkins, Charles	05 JUL 1878	12	125
Beam, Ophelia	Silver, John	05 FEB 1884	18	406
Beaman, Addie M.	Neale, Charles A.	09 JAN 1883 L	17	246
Beaman, Mills	Lyons, Lucy Ellen	09 SEP 1879 L	13	361
Bean, Benetta	Bailey, Stephen A.	08 SEP 1881 R	15	472
Bean, Benjamin A.	Blundon, Mary F.	27 DEC 1881 R	16	157
Bean, Carrie V.	Milstead, W. Edward	23 JAN 1878 R	11	315

Bean, Ella E.	Herfurth, Herman	14 JAN 1885	20	018
Bean, John A.	Burr, Lille	26 FEB 1884 L	18	445
Bean, Lillie	Staub, Amandos	15 AUG 1884 L	19	188
Bean, Margaret Catharine	Hebb, Walter Hanson Jenifer	26 NOV 1877 R	11	202
Bean, Martha	Alexander, Thomas	02 JUN 1880 L	14	300
Bean, Mary Ida	Graham, William E.	15 JAN 1878	11	304
Bean, Sophronia J.	Magruder, Jonathan	08 SEP 1880 R	14	438
Bean, Thaddeus	Melson, Annie E.	19 NOV 1879 R	13	494
Bean, Thomas	Brady, Lavena	02 JAN 1884 L	18	361
Bean, Wm. Thos.	Harris, Annie	11 JAN 1883 L	17	253
Beander, Geo. Thomas	Lewis, Cora	17 DEC 1878 R	12	384
Beander, James	Dixon, Ellen	16 OCT 1884 R	19	312
Beane, Lizzie M.	McCartney, Bernard T.	06 JUL 1879 R	13	269
Bear, Louisa E.	Dentinger, Lewis C.	08 AUG 1878	12	158
Bear, Mariella Twaddell	Hanford, Charles Barnum	30 JUN 1885 R	20	297
Beard, James	Bouze, Mary A.	11 AUG 1884	19	179
Beard, Jeannette	Lewis, James Henry	16 FEB 1881 R	13	370
Beard, Julian Mortimer	Phelps, Ellen Virginia Sibley	30 DEC 1884	19	500
Beard, Lloyd W.	Hillary, Christiana	15 SEP 1880 L	14	446
Beasler, Mary J.	Dailey, John Samuel	15 MAR 1883 R	17	347
Beasley, Annie E.	Hopkins, Eugene A.	09 JAN 1878	11	298
Beasley, Josephene	Gaddis, George H.	26 NOV 1878 R	12	346
Beaton, John F.	Cooley, Fannie H.	05 JAN 1884	18	366
Beaton, Malcolm S.	André, Lillie E.	23 SEP 1880 R	14	459
Beaton, Susie L.	Fowler, Edwin C.	31 DEC 1883 R	18	357
Beattie, James A.	Maubry, Ella	25 AUG 1885	20	387
Beatty, Charles A.	Lafontine, Alice	19 OCT 1877 L	11	146
Beatty, Joseph	White, Matilda	28 OCT 1879 R	13	449
Beatty, Kate F.	Cook, George T.	07 MAY 1884	19	012
Beatty, Mary Frances	Gould, John Henry	23 SEP 1877 R	11	095
Beatty, Sadie	Wood, William A.	23 DEC 1878 R	12	396
Beau, Diana M.	Thomason, Frank D.	24 NOV 1881	16	095
Beaude, Julia	Williams, George A.	20 JUN 1878 L	12	107
Beaver, Charles H.	Gallivian, Maggie	14 JUN 1881	15	360
Beaver, Charlotte	Lewis, Robert	27 JUN 1882 L	16	428
Beaver, Randolph W.	Webster, Ella M.	24 FEB 1885 R	20	081
Beavers, Annie, Mrs.	Anderson, William A.	08 OCT 1878	12	261
Beavers, Leona W.	Redder, W. Pierce	15 AUG 1878 L	12	170
Beavers, Sadie W.	Walsh, Harry H.	22 NOV 1881	16	085
Beavin, Fidelia A.	Grimes, Henry W.	22 AUG 1878 L	12	176
Beavin, Luvina	Mallonee, Oliver Winfield	08 JUL 1880	14	352
Beazley, Alva N.	Bray, C.A.	07 MAY 1884	19	010
Beazley, M.J.	Durette, T.D.	05 JAN 1884	18	366
Bechler, Maria	Kübler, Carl August	04 JUN 1884 R	19	061
Bechold, Christiana	Freeman, John	26 DEC 1879 L	14	076
Beck, August H.	Umhau, Margaret	12 DEC 1882	17	179
Beck, Clarence E.	Cook, Ella R.	15 JUN 1880 L	14	323
Beck, Dora	DeVilliers, Francis	22 JUN 1882 L	16	422
Beck, Frank	Davis, Josephine	31 DEC 1878	12	409
Beck, Jacob J.	Summers, Catherine L.	22 NOV 1880 L	15	059
Beck, James Hopkins	Morgan, Lizzie Lawton	21 FEB 1884 R	18	437
Beck, John, Jr.	King, Alice A.	22 MAY 1884	19	035
Beck, Lyman Seely	Jones, Roberta J.	02 NOV 1883 R	18	229
Beck, Maggie	Biggane, William J.	26 NOV 1884 L	19	419
Becker, Anna M.	Owings, James H.	10 NOV 1878 R	12	317
Becker, Diederich	Neumann, Margaretta	27 OCT 1877 L	11	158
Becker, Edward	Ragan, Mary Jane	09 FEB 1880	14	145
Becker, Helen C.	Johnson, At Lee	26 DEC 1882	17	208

Becker, John	Bretsch, Magdalena	02 JUN 1881	15	338
Becker, Lewis	Hoy, Catherine	15 AUG 1881 R	15	444
Becker, Mary J.	Combs, William H.	16 APR 1884 R	18	515
Becker, Michael H.	Mackin, Annie	29 SEP 1880 L	14	465
Beckert, Nellie C.	White, Frank H.	02 AUG 1880 R	14	382
Becket, Louisa, Mrs.	Groves, Arkarey	24 MAR 1881 R	15	239
Beckett, Albert C.	Gales, Roberta	13 SEP 1881	15	475
Beckett, Blanche	Barber, Charley	07 JUL 1885 R	20	311
Beckett, Catherine	Matthews, Carter	26 JUL 1884 L	19	158
Beckett, Daniel C.	Keese, Mary Jane	07 MAY 1884 L	19	010
Beckett, David	Buckner, Lucy Ann	14 AUG 1879 R	13	322
Beckett, Florence E.	Washington, Willis	07 JAN 1880 R	14	094
Beckett, Frank	Williams, Catherine	03 AUG 1880	14	385
Beckett, George	Downey, Mary	19 SEP 1881 R	15	491
Beckett, Hattie	Redman, Arthur F.	27 OCT 1882 L	17	098
Beckett, James	Quince, Josephine	02 DEC 1880 L	15	079
Beckett, James W.	Curtis, Margaret J.	08 OCT 1880 R	14	477
Beckett, John H.	Budd, Mary	13 MAY 1880 R	14	267
Beckett, Julia	Chaney, Joseph	05 APR 1883	17	379
Beckett, Julia	Henson, George W.	10 NOV 1884	19	371
Beckett, Laura	Scott, Albert	13 DEC 1877	11	234
Beckett, Lemuel M.	Giles, Mary C.	05 NOV 1884 L	19	363
Beckett, Maggie	Clarke, James	12 FEB 1881 L	15	188
Beckett, Marcellina S.	Williams, Richard F.	29 JAN 1880 R	14	125
Beckley, Charles	Peyton, Sarah	22 APR 1885 L	20	184
Beckley, Ella B.	Welborne, Walter S.	15 OCT 1884	19	310
Beckman, Elizabeth	William, Henry A.	09 JUL 1883	18	040
Beckman, Josephine	Stein, Otto J.H.	02 OCT 1880	14	469
Beckman, Mary E.	O'Dwyer, William G.	03 JUL 1883 R	18	031
Beckmann, August	Kracka, Bertha	20 JUN 1883	17	466
Beckstedt, Henry	Bauer, Sophia	10 OCT 1881 L	16	016
Beckwith, Francis E.	Taylor, Eleanora	18 OCT 1880 R	15	001
Beckwith, Isabella	Allen, Alexander	15 JUN 1882 L	16	412
Beckwith, John	Moseley, Nancy	13 DEC 1877 L	11	234
Beckwith, John Henry	Dudley, Emma	18 AUG 1882 L	16	487
Beckwith, Nelly	Fox, Charles Eben	10 JUN 1884 R	19	067
Becraft, Clara E.	Retaliata, Joseph A.	21 AUG 1885 L	20	382
Beebe, Mary E.	Galt, Frank	19 SEP 1882 R	17	028
Beecher, Lucinda	Duckett, Randolph	20 JUL 1882 R	16	452
Been, Henry	Van Horn, Mary E.	10 JAN 1878 R	11	301
Beers, Harry C.	Thompson, Mary E.	06 JUN 1881 L	15	347
Beers, M. Virginia	Beall, James A.	24 OCT 1878 R	12	288
Beetle, Carrie E., MRs.	Greene, James A.	01 DEC 1884 R	19	428
Beetly, Mary M.	Smith, Charles W.	08 JUL 1880 R	14	353
Behler, Paulus	Schulz, Elizabeth	13 JAN 1885 R	20	011
Behr, Eva Maria	Merten, Henry	27 JAN 1878	11	315
Behrend, Albert	Adler, Cora	22 JAN 1885 R	20	030
Behrend, Elon	Hanlein, Carrie	04 NOV 1883 R	18	230
Behrend, Rebecca	Nathanson, Edward	12 JUN 1883 R	17	482
Behrens, Ernst	Ruhl, Anna	29 SEP 1885 R	20	446
Belcher, Lucius C.	Martin, Maggie E.	14 MAR 1881 R	15	224
Belfield, William E.	Taliaferro, Retta	20 DEC 1882	17	198
Belfils, Alice	Jewell, Malvern H.	05 MAR 1882	16	267
Belford, Jonas	Griffin, Susan Jane	25 JUL 1882 R	16	456
Bell, Amanda A.R.	Quander, Charles Henry	18 DEC 1878	12	385
Bell, Bertha E.	Jackson, Henry	05 JAN 1885	20	003
Bell, Bruce	Blagden, Lizzie	28 JUN 1877 L	11	002
Bell, Charles A.	Holmes, Marianna	07 MAR 1883 R	17	335

Bell, Charles H.	Warren, Clora	30 JAN 1879 L	13	039
Bell, Charles Milton	Colley, Annie	16 NOV 1880 L	15	050
Bell, Chlora	Tyer, George	25 DEC 1877 R	11	263
Bell, Christine	Lee, Thomas	06 AUG 1885 L	20	359
Bell, David H.	Walker, Annie	26 OCT 1882	17	098
Bell, Dionysius	King, Alice	16 SEP 1885 R	20	421
Bell, Edmonia	Hall, Opieisia	27 SEP 1883	18	130
Bell, Edward Eugene	Conover, Katie E.	09 OCT 1881 R	16	012
Bell, Eleazer	Fletcher, Laura	30 OCT 1877	11	158
Bell, Elizabeth	Johnson, Olmstead	25 OCT 1877 R	11	154
Bell, Ella	Anderson, Matthew	22 MAR 1884 L	18	479
Bell, Ellen	Burch, Stephen	09 OCT 1880 L	14	485
Bell, Ellen	Baldwin, William	17 OCT 1884 L	19	317
Bell, Emily	Queen, William	29 AUG 1878 L	12	188
Bell, Enoch	Johnson, Ida	13 MAY 1880	14	264
Bell, Fannie	Queen, Chailley	01 JUL 1880 R	14	343
Bell, Fannie	Johnson, Barney	25 JAN 1883 R	17	272
Bell, Florence	Hayes, William	03 APR 1879 R	13	125
Bell, Florence Serena	Smith, William Edward	31 JAN 1881 R	15	170
Bell, Frances	Coleman, Clayton	15 AUG 1883	18	089
Bell, Henry	Toodle, Susannah	17 NOV 1880 L	15	053
Bell, Ida	Seymour, Arthur	12 SEP 1878	12	213
Bell, Ida B.	Grinder, Joseph B.	18 MAR 1882	16	282
Bell, James Alfred	Steward, Jennie	05 FEB 1879 L	13	047
Bell, James, Corp.	Wilson, Ellen, Mrs.	16 MAY 1881 L	15	310
Bell, James R.	Magruder, Annie	22 FEB 1883 R	17	311
Bell, Jane Ann	Rollins, William	20 DEC 1882 L	17	199
Bell, Jane E.	Washington, Peyton	18 DEC 1884 L	19	470
Bell, Joanna	Miller, Richard	22 APR 1878 L	12	019
Bell, John	Grant, Francis Amanda	01 NOV 1822 R	17	105
Bell, John	Snow, Catharine	17 OCT 1878 R	12	281
Bell, John	Tolson, Carrie	24 AUG 1880	14	411
Bell, John Henry	Ennis, Mary	21 FEB 1003 L	17	316
Bell, John M.	Oden, Marian C.	21 FEB 1878 R	11	352
Bell, John T.	Blackburne, Ella	30 APR 1878	12	025
Bell, Joseph S.	Wilcox, Mary E.	16 MAY 1883	17	445
Bell, Joshua	Lawrence, Sylvia	22 NOV 1880 L	15	060
Bell, Katie G.	Price, Edwin F.	06 DEC 1882	17	169
Bell, Katie V.	Valiant, Theodore G.	30 APR 1878	12	030
Bell, Laura	Stevenson, William	26 JUN 1884 L	19	106
Bell, Lethe	Blaine, I.B.	15 JAN 1883 L	17	258
Bell, Lettie	Buckner, Joshua	20 DEC 1877 R	11	254
Bell, Lottie	Cooper, James	22 APR 1880	14	235
Bell, Louis Alexander	Alexander, Milly	26 NOV 1882	17	149
Bell, Martha	Jackson, Charles	26 JUN 1879 L	13	254
Bell, Martha	Fisher, Nelson	16 SEP 1882 L	17	024
Bell, Mary	Martin, John	16 SEP 1878 L	12	219
Bell, Mary	Thomas, Henry	18 OCT 1880 L	14	500
Bell, Mary	McDaniel, John	26 NOV 1884 L	19	412
Bell, Mary F.S.	Wilson, Frank	10 JUL 1879	13	278
Bell, Mary Jane	Linn, Thomas	30 DEC 1880 R	15	131
Bell, Mary Q. Ella	Parker, William H.F.	03 NOV 1881	16	059
Bell, Matthew N.	Tolliver, Sallie	05 APR 1883 R	17	382
Bell, Nathan	Clagett, Maggie	15 MAR 1883 L	17	346
Bell, Pinkney	Snowdon, Mary	24 OCT 1883 L	18	209
Bell, Priscilla	Snell, James	27 OCT 1881 L	16	049
Bell, R.A., Mrs.	Brandenburg, Joseph	26 AUG 1877	11	064
Bell, R.R.	Poole, E.C.	08 NOV 1883	18	244

Name	Spouse	Date	Vol	Page
Bell, Rachel A.	Narl, Henry	02 DEC 1884	19	429
Bell, Robert	Smith, Sarah	18 OCT 1877 R	11	143
Bell, Robert Alexander	Hume, Mamie	06 MAR 1884 R	18	461
Bell, Robert, Jr.	Sanno, Emma J.	22 OCT 1877	11	148
Bell, Rouzo Berry	Carey, Lucy	11 JUN 1885 L	20	268
Bell, Solomon	King, Margaret	01 MAR 1883	17	329
Bell, Solon L.	Jones, Mattie E.	02 DEC 1880 R	15	077
Bell, Sophia	Thomas, Lemuel	08 OCT 1878 L	12	260
Bell, Sophy	Brown, John William	13 FEB 1883	17	297
Bell, Susan A.	Franklin, George W.	15 MAY 1884 L	19	023
Bell, Susie B.	Hutton, George	01 JUL 1880 L	14	344
Bell, Thomas	Campbell, Charlotte	08 DEC 1881 L	16	120
Bell, Thomas P.	Robinson, Isabella	03 NOV 1881	16	059
Bell, Thomas Reuben	Cook, Mary Ellen	10 OCT 1881 R	16	015
Bell, Thomas S.	Wise, Rosa J.	04 OCT 1882 R	17	053
Bell, Venson	Dorsey, Levina	22 NOV 1883 L	18	271
Bell, Wallace	Holland, Margaret	03 MAY 1879 L	13	172
Bell, Walter E.	Merritt, Bettie E.	23 DEC 1884 R	19	481
Bell, William B.	Barry, Alice	05 JUL 1883	18	036
Bell, William H.	Diffenbaugh, Mollie C.	11 AUG 1879 R	13	315
Bell, William H.	Norris, Jane	08 JUL 1880	14	352
Bell, William R.	Wilson, Annie G.	13 MAY 1880	14	271
Bell, William S.	Robey, Virginia E.	27 DEC 1881 R	16	160
Bell, William W.	Nelson, Sarah A.	06 SEP 1883	18	115
Bell, Zidonia	Brown, William J.	02 FEB 1882 R	16	221
Bellducket, Clara	Barrett, William Henry	28 DEC 1880 R	15	127
Bellefille, Charlotte	Ransom, John Wm.	17 OCT 1882	17	075
Bellen, Maggie J.	Topley, Henry T.	29 JUN 1885 L	20	300
Beller, James H.	Munroe, Ella	29 NOV 1882 R	17	157
Bellermann, William E.	Baker, Mary A.	06 NOV 1883	18	236
Bellew, Mary E.	Harleston, George B.	15 APR 1884 L	18	512
Bellew, William R.	Jennings, Laura	26 MAY 1884	19	037
Bellfield, Benjamin B.	Jennings, Emma	24 MAY 1883 L	17	460
Bellford, James	Robinson, Sarah	12 SEP 1882 L	17	017
Bellman, Fannie	Birch, George A.	23 JUN 1879 R	13	243
Belmont, Susie	Byng, Robert H.	11 MAY 1882 R	16	356
Belt, Andrew	Hall, Louisa	30 JAN 1879 L	13	038
Belt, Annie R.	Jenkins, Roy C.	15 MAR 1882 R	16	278
Belt, Benjamin	Gill, Minnie	15 APR 1882	16	317
Belt, George W.	Gant, Louisa	24 JAN 1884 L	18	393
Belt, Martina	Barker, James C.	06 DEC 1883	18	303
Belt, Susan E.	Jacob, Christopher C.	22 APR 1880 L	14	232
Belt, Thomas Daniel	Collins, Susie	23 APR 1878 R	12	016
Belt, William	Eastern, Ella	16 DEC 1880 L	15	105
Beltz, Paulina	Stumpf, Edward	19 SEP 1880 R	14	448
Bembry, John H.	Brown, Caroline	21 APR 1881 R	15	267
Bender, Carrie Monroe	Ray, George Elmore	16 DEC 1882 R	17	187
Bender, Catharine A.	Posey, Francis A.	02 JUL 1883 L	18	030
Bender, Charles	Wege, Margaret, Mrs.	05 SEP 1879 L	13	354
Bender, Harry F.	Simpson, Fannie M.	01 AUG 1883	18	069
Bender, Lillie C.	Winters, Bernard M.	05 JUN 1882 R	16	226
Bender, Matilda A.	Railey, Robert M.	06 OCT 1880 L	14	478
Benedict, James E.	Junken, Elizabeth M.	22 NOV 1883 R	18	271
Benedict, James Sackett	Chase, Cora Blanche	09 JAN 1879 R	13	012
Benhan, Isaac	Brennan, Catharine M.C.	28 JAN 1880 R	14	124
Benhardt, Catharine	Neitzey, Augustus	05 AUG 1885	20	354
Benke, Annie A.	Schroeder, George G.	18 JAN 1885	20	014
Benner, Fannie	Gray, David E.	17 SEP 1884	19	254

Name	Spouse	Date	Vol	Page
Benner, George L.	Muddiman, Anne E.	21 MAY 1884 R	19	030
Bennett, Andrew J.	Grandin, Mary S.S.	28 OCT 1879	13	447
Bennett, Annie	Marshall, Frank	21 JUL 1877 L	11	028
Bennett, Annie E.	Sullivan, John J.	17 OCT 1877 L	11	143
Bennett, C.F.	Lucas, Sadie V.	14 FEB 1883 R	17	306
Bennett, Catharine	Gregory, Manfred	26 APR 1883 R	17	409
Bennett, Catherine E.	Gallivan, John	08 SEP 1879 L	13	358
Bennett, Charles S.	Laws, Medora P.	15 NOV 1877 R	11	190
Bennett, Clara	Harrison, William H.	21 AUG 1882	16	487
Bennett, Francis A.	Kern, Ada R.	20 OCT 1881	16	033
Bennett, George A.	McClosky, Rose A.	22 SEP 1881 L	15	495
Bennett, George T.	Tatum, Kate V. [Miller]	03 MAY 1883 R	17	427
Bennett, Helen May	Robinson, Alfred S.	03 JUL 1882 R	16	216
Bennett, John	Keys, Emma	30 MAR 1878 L	11	399
Bennett, Louisa	Collins, Carter	30 APR 1885	20	181
Bennett, Martha	Thornley, Jesse	03 NOV 1881 R	16	057
Bennett, Mary	Dotson, Alphonso	06 FEB 1883 L	17	295
Bennett, Mary C.	Pernell, William L.	30 DEC 1881 R	16	164
Bennett, Mary E.	King, Edward E.	02 APR 1878 L	11	402
Bennett, Mary E.	Hibbs, Ernest L.	01 DEC 1884	19	428
Bennett, Mary Josephine	Dee, William Joseph	10 SEP 1885 L	20	411
Bennett, Philo Henry	Davis, Hattie Virginia	15 JUN 1881 R	15	362
Bennett, Richard	Kane, Mary	23 JUN 1881 L	15	376
Bennett, Rosa A.	Biggs, John W.E.	22 DEC 1883 L	18	335
Bennett, William A.	Lynn, Phebe	22 JUL 1884	19	150
Bensinger, Emma	Strasburger, Myer	03 JAN 1883 R	17	231
Bensinger, May	Newmyer, Louis	22 NOV 1882 R	17	139
Bensley, William James	Gunther, Mary Ellen	30 NOV 1882 R	17	156
Benson, Clara V.	Jackson, Charles I.	19 NOV 1880 R	15	072
Benson, Clarence	Williams, Laura	30 MAR 1879 R	13	114
Benson, Elbert G.	Lord, Ella D.	20 AUG 1880 R	14	409
Benson, Isaac	Tolliver, Eliza	15 AUG 1882	16	479
Benson, J. Hepburn P.	Evans, Susan M.	01 SEP 1884 L	19	218
Benson, Lillian M.	Herr, M.M.	26 FEB 1884	18	443
Benson, Mary	Mudd, Daniel H.	07 APR 1883 L	17	385
Benson, Richard J.	Murphy, Isbell Neal	22 APR 1880 R	14	233
Benson, Rosetta L.	Price, Thomas W.	21 DEC 1882 L	17	200
Benson, Sarah E.L., Mrs.	Saffold, Milton Whiting	15 DEC 1882 R	17	187
Benson, Thomas E.	Murphy, Julia E.	18 JAN 1883	17	263
Benter, Maximillian A.	Smith, Jennie H.	10 APR 1883 R	17	388
Bentley, Nellie B.	McAbee, M. Broderick	12 SEP 1877	11	089
Bentley, Rosa	Daley, William H.	18 OCT 1881 R	16	030
Bentley, William	Holmes, Charlotte	14 AUG 1877 R	11	053
Bentley, William Henry	Logan, Alice Ann	11 JUL 1879 L	13	279
Benton, Edward V.	Davis, Lillie Ida	28 JUN 1881 R	15	381
Benton, Emma H.	Hollida, David	25 DEC 1878 L	12	415
Benton, J.H.	MacIntosh, Annie	31 JAN 1885 L	20	046
Benton, John	Logan, Alice	10 FEB 1883 L	17	301
Benton, Mary P.	Payne, Samuel H.	30 OCT 1878 R	12	299
Benzler, Hermann	Helmuth, Louise Mary	11 JUN 1884 R	19	077
Berg, Joseph S.	Turner, Annie	23 MAR 1883 L	17	357
Berg, Julius O.	Young, Minnie E.	06 MAY 1880 R	14	255
Berger, Auguste	Kuhlmann, Henry	22 JUN 1881	15	369
Berger, Henry	Stello, Louisa	11 SEP 1878 R	12	206
Berger, Johan Anton	Dilger, Helene	09 MAY 1882	16	351
Berger, Oscar L.	Guttenson, Lizzie	29 MAY 1878 L	12	075
Berger, Oscar S.	Herbert, Amelia C.	08 NOV 1882	17	119
Berghauser, Hermann	Albrecht, Katie	02 OCT 1883	18	163

Bergling, Bernard	Krepps, Helen V.	14 NOV 1884 L	19	381
Bergling, Henry G.	Johnson, Ida L.	26 JUN 1883 R	18	015
Bergling, John	Thompson, Lillie S.	07 DEC 1881 L	16	117
Bergmann, Etta M.	Westnedge, James	05 FEB 1885 R	20	054
Bergmann, Fred W.	Ewald, Catherine	14 FEB 1878 L	11	342
Bergmann, Hedwig	Lauer, Heinrich F.W.	24 APR 1881 R	15	257
Bergmann, Henry Hermann	Meyer, Ida Louisa Carolina	27 DEC 1879 R	14	069
Bergmann, Sophia	Adt, Alex	02 AUG 1877 L	11	058
Berk, Katherina	Schneider, Gottlieb	20 JUL 1884	19	146
Berk, Nelson	Washington, Louise	16 FEB 1884 L	18	427
Berkeley, Guy	McPherson, Kate	15 MAY 1879 R	13	185
Berkeley, Kate	Rennert, Edward	13 JUN 1885 R	20	272
Berkeley, Mary Blanch	Gill, William	01 MAR 1885 R	20	090
Berkely, Adeline	Delaney, Cassius	10 APR 1885	20	159
Berkley, Annie F.	Herbert, George R.	08 FEB 1881 R	15	182
Berkley, Catherine	Barrus, Johnson C.	11 SEP 1877	11	085
Berkley, Christopher	Zells, Emma J.	13 JAN 1880 R	14	102
Berkley, Cornelius A.	Carter, Isabel	18 JUL 1878	12	139
Berkley, Enos R.	Jenkins, Emma E.	23 APR 1882	16	330
Berkley, Maria	Whitney, Charles	14 OCT 1880 R	14	492
Berkley, Rosetta	Russ, Charles	16 AUG 1879 L	13	324
Berlimer, Emile	Addler, Cora H.	26 OCT 1881 R	16	043
Berlin, Grace M.	Stoddart, Armat	24 MAR 1881 R	15	238
Berlin, Mary	Davidson, Robert	17 JUL 1882 L	16	451
Bernalio, Frank J.	Wagner, Maggie M.	30 JUN 1884	19	111
Bernard, Annette C.	Stinzing, John P.	15 SEP 1880	14	445
Bernard, Cornelia C.	Mullen, John T.	16 MAY 1878	12	054
Bernard, Elizabeth B.	Cole, David A.	21 APR 1885 L	20	180
Bernard, Mary J.	McCarthy, Jerome J.	22 SEP 1879 R	13	380
Bernau, Louis	Schwemke, Mary	30 NOV 1882 R	17	146
Berner, Charles J.V.	Hornbach, Mary A.	20 JUN 1880	14	324
Bernhard, E.J.	Tippett, Grace	23 MAY 1883 L	17	460
Bernhard, Katie Genevieve	Speake, John William, Jr.	21 MAR 1883 R	17	353
Bernhardt, William	Kessler, Mary	11 APR 1880	14	206
Bernharth, Jessy	Mason, Maria Margareth	16 JUL 1878 L	12	136
Beron, John	Schifaly, Amelia	30 APR 1879	13	168
Berrell, George	Brown, Rosa	08 MAY 1879 R	13	180
Berril, Sallie	Christian, Anthony	03 MAY 1881 R	15	287
Berry, Agnes	Shannon, William A.	11 OCT 1882	17	065
Berry, Albert Gleaves	Merriman, Lillian Reed	28 SEP 1881 R	15	498
Berry, Allen Preston	Allen, Mamie Salter	28 JUN 1883 R	18	021
Berry, Anna E.	Kindrick, William H.	31 MAY 1881 L	15	331
Berry, Annie	Smith, John	30 JUN 1881 R	15	316
Berry, Annie	Wilkerson, Henry	09 OCT 1883 R	18	179
Berry, Annie	Sheridan, Charles F.	22 NOV 1884 L	19	401
Berry, Annie M.	Ennis, George T.	24 DEC 1882 R	17	204
Berry, Annie Powell Field	Craighill, James Morsell	17 FEB 1885 R	20	070
Berry, Caroline M.	Berry, Norman	08 JAN 1880 L	14	097
Berry, Carrie	Sanders, Clements	21 DEC 1880 R	15	112
Berry, Charles	Green, Jennie	03 JAN 1883 L	17	235
Berry, Charles H.	Jones, Frances E.	03 NOV 1884 R	19	430
Berry, Charlotte	Frank, William B.	13 DEC 1883	18	313
Berry, Christiana	Curtis, William	03 JUN 1878 L	12	080
Berry, Eliza	Lewis, George	17 OCT 1877	11	142
Berry, Eliza	Paul, Nicholas	01 SEP 1884	19	215
Berry, Elizabeth	Palmer, Charles Ernest	10 AUG 1881 R	15	438
Berry, Elizabeth L.	Banes, Warner P.	30 JUL 1878 L	12	152
Berry, Emma	Cole, John C.	29 NOV 1882 L	17	161

Name	Spouse	Date	Vol	Page
Berry, Emma L.	Yoder, Charles T.	20 AUG 1877	11	058
Berry, Emory E.	Johnson, Carrie Eliza	20 SEP 1877 L	11	102
Berry, Enoch	Jefferson, Josephine C.	10 DEC 1879 R	14	040
Berry, Estella	Boone, Victor Emanuel	15 JUN 1885 L	20	274
Berry, Fannie	Dixon, William H.	17 SEP 1878 L	12	221
Berry, Ferdinand V.	Evans, Emma V.	05 NOV 1877	11	168
Berry, Fred	Starters, Sarah	23 JUN 1881	15	377
Berry, George R.	Wilkerson, Susie	12 OCT 1879 R	13	416
Berry, H.A.	Monteiro, Margaret	10 FEB 1884 L	18	418
Berry, Horace	Alexander, Martha	04 APR 1882	16	297
Berry, Ida M.	Padgett, James E.	24 MAY 1880	14	284
Berry, James P.	Lucas, Louisa	29 DEC 1884 L	19	499
Berry, James W.	Diggs, Bessie E.	20 DEC 1881	16	159
Berry, John	Cox, Marian	13 JAN 1879 L	13	015
Berry, John	O'Day, Delia	03 MAY 1881	15	290
Berry, John	Stewart, Anna	28 NOV 1882 R	17	154
Berry, John Crusen	Gaskins, Jane	27 MAR 1885 R	20	135
Berry, Julia A.	Shreve, J.W.	08 JUN 1881	15	351
Berry, Julia H.	Taylor, George E.	05 MAY 1884 R	19	005
Berry, Lucy C.	Moore, Fred	09 FEB 1883	17	291
Berry, Marcellena O.	Roberts, Joseph M.	29 SEP 1879 R	13	391
Berry, Martha E.	Kemp, Richard R.	28 DEC 1881 R	16	108
Berry, Mary	Brown, Charles	05 JUN 1879	13	221
Berry, Mary	Smith, Albert	19 SEP 1883 R	18	142
Berry, Mary H.	Langley, John H.	19 DEC 1878 R	12	386
Berry, Norman	Berry, Caroline M.	08 JAN 1880 L	14	097
Berry, Richard	Maguire, Mary E.	21 FEB 1881 R	15	196
Berry, Rosena	Johnson, Harrison	20 AUG 1884 L	19	197
Berry, Smith	Young, Maggie	19 AUG 1885	20	379
Berry, William H.	Roland, Rachel E.	06 SEP 1878 R	12	202
Berry, Winnie	Thompson, Smith	19 NOV 1884 R	19	396
Berry, Wm. R.	Brown, Helen	15 OCT 1885	20	484
Berryman, Louisa	Blackston, John	01 JUN 1885	20	249
Berryman, Robert	Jones, Lucy	31 JUL 1879 R	13	296
Berryman, Wilson W.	Moseley, Ardella	04 DEC 1879 L	14	030
Besley, Bertha E.	Green, Frederick F.	28 MAR 1884 R	18	485
Bessels, Emil, Dr.	Ravené, Bertha	20 JUN 1885 L	20	282
Bessler, Bertha	Newland, Andrew	17 MAR 1885 L	20	118
Bessler, Frank Bonifox	Miller, Mary Theresa	17 FEB 1882 L	16	247
Best, Henry	Gorum, Mary E.	08 MAY 1879 R	13	179
Best, Jane	Harmon, William H.	24 OCT 1878 L	12	291
Bestor, Ellen	Barry, Thomas Henry	23 JAN 1884 R	18	388
Betker, John K.	Browning, N.E.	07 MAY 1885	20	212
Betters, John	Crimmins, Catherine	21 OCT 1880 L	15	010
Betts, E.A.	Sherzer, Charles P.	26 DEC 1883 R	18	343
Betts, Mary	Kelly, James	06 NOV 1884 L	19	366
Betts, Susan	Moens, Frank	31 JUL 1879 R	13	302
Bettus, John	Stewart, Rebecca	10 SEP 1883 L	18	120
Betz, Ernest	Gerard, Sadie	19 DEC 1882 L	17	195
Beukert, Maria	Loeckel, Ludwig	10 AUG 1879 R	13	312
Bevan, Joseph H.	Herbert, Georgie Frances	29 DEC 1884 L	19	496
Bevans, Elmira	Dean, Albert	15 JUL 1880 L	14	364
Bevans, Fannie E.	Towles, Henry O.	01 JUN 1882 R	16	386
Bevans, Mary B.	Edwards, John	28 APR 1880 R	14	244
Beverly, Delphia	Johnson, Fleming	25 JUL 1882 R	16	413
Beverly, Julia	Burkley, Richard	19 DEC 1878 R	12	387
Beverly, Julia	Reynolds, Archie	29 JAN 1885 L	20	043
Beverly, Matilda	Brown, Theophilus	04 JUN 1881 L	15	344

Name	Spouse	Date	Vol	Page
Beverly, Richard	Hawkins, Agnes	27 MAY 1884 R	19	016
Beverly, Richard H.	Ward, Mary A.	18 SEP 1883 L	18	138
Beverly, Robert	Jarvis, Mary	09 MAR 1885 L	20	102
Beyea, Georgianna C.	Tiernan, John	08 OCT 1879 R	13	410
Beyer, Annie E.	Butt, George H.	19 DEC 1878 R	12	392
Beyer, James V.	Maloney, Maggie	01 NOV 1883 L	18	226
Beyer, Mary Magdalen	Lusby, Lemuel Franklin	30 NOV 1881 R	16	106
Bias, Eliza	Arnold, Elbert	26 DEC 1884 L	19	493
Bias, Fannie	Brent, John	25 JAN 1882 L	16	210
Bias, Henry	Brent, Jane	21 MAR 1878 R	11	389
Bias, Lucinda	Terrell, David	27 JUL 1877 L	11	033
Bibb, Albert Burnley	Hanson, Julia	30 SEP 1880 R	14	467
Bibb, Lulu J.	Althoff, J. Elmer	18 MAR 1885 R	20	122
Bibb, William D.	Shannon, Mary C.	01 APR 1885	20	140
Bickford, Jennie L.	Barr, John	30 OCT 1882 L	17	101
Bicking, Augusta	Rupprecht, Richard	07 APR 1885 R	20	143
Bicksler, Alice Eugenie	Carraher, John Victor	09 JAN 1879 R	13	013
Bicksler, Veturia C.	Eberly, Daniel C.	06 JAN 1881 R	15	143
Biddle, Eliza	Seltman, William B.	17 JUN 1880 L	14	326
Biddle, Hiram R.	Sanford, Mamie E.	24 OCT 1878 R	12	288
Biddle, Maggie	Leavy, Nels	10 MAY 1878 L	12	047
Biddle, Marcia H.	Garner, William F.	16 MAR 1879 R	13	100
Bidwell, Lewis T.	Atchinson, Alzine	01 OCT 1877 L	11	116
Bigelow, Edward R.	Clear, Helen B.	07 OCT 1884 L	19	292
Bigelow, George S.	House, Ida G.	10 MAY 1881	15	297
Biggan, M.F.	Evans, M.E.	16 APR 1884 L	18	516
Biggan, Mary	Cantwell, John	15 NOV 1881 L	16	079
Biggane, William J.	Beck, Maggie	26 NOV 1884 L	19	419
Biggin, Mary Jane	O'Day, John J.	22 APR 1884 L	18	526
Biggins, Catharine	O'Brien, William T.	10 OCT 1883 R	18	181
Biggs, John W.E.	Bennett, Rosa A.	22 DEC 1883 L	18	335
Biggs, Wilhelmina	Turner, James F.	17 DEC 1884	19	464
Biggs, William E.	Queen, Catharine	01 JUL 1884 L	19	114
Billings, Rolland B.	Kersey, Matilda J.	30 OCT 1884 L	19	348
Billingsley, Lura K.	Henderson, George W.	15 JAN 1884	18	378
Billingsley, Mary Mildred	Trew, James Thomas	10 NOV 1877 R	11	170
Billingsly, Ellen	Jones, James	05 JUL 1885 L	20	054
Billingsly, Lou	Boarman, James	11 JUN 1879 L	13	228
Binder, John F.	Haker, Katie	06 SEP 1885 R	20	400
Binds, Lewis	Boyd, Rebecca	24 DEC 1884 R	19	486
Bing, Nathaniel J.	Baker, Mary H.	19 OCT 1880 L	15	004
Bingham, Emma V.	Tchlosser, William T.	27 AUG 1884	19	212
Bingham, Lafayette	Latham, Anna	06 APR 1880 L	14	212
Bingham, Moses	Alexandria, Lettie	22 NOV 1883 L	18	273
Bingham, Sarah	Brooks, Philip	23 SEP 1882 L	17	034
Binnix, Roberta	Thiel, Niclaus	29 OCT 1878 L	12	296
Binns, John Alexander	Ormsbee, Mary Ellen	20 FEB 1881 R	15	195
Biondi, Charles P.	Bates, Maud D.	15 SEP 1884 R	19	243
Birch, Annie	Blunt, John S.	19 MAY 1880	14	277
Birch, Bessie	Morrow, Thomas G.	06 JUN 1883 L	17	479
Birch, Carrie F.	Bonneville, Columbus J.	02 OCT 1878 R	12	325
Birch, Carrie F.	Bornievill, Columbus J.	02 OCT 1878 L	12	256
Birch, Corbin	Carroll, Almira Rawlings	18 NOV 1884 L	19	390
Birch, George A.	Bellman, Fannie	23 JUN 1879 R	13	243
Birch, Isaac	Graves, Minnie M.	01 OCT 1879 R	13	395
Birch, Isabella	Miller, Emanuel	11 NOV 1882	17	115
Birch, Jacob	O'Brien, Julia Anne	16 OCT 1878	12	276
Birch, Mary	Simms, Samuel	10 JAN 1882	16	187

Name	Spouse	Date	Vol	Page
Birch, Mary Estelle	Jones, Owen W.	14 OCT 1885 R	20	483
Birch, Philip Wilbur	Moore, Jessie L.	15 JUN 1883 R	17	496
Birch, Richard	O'Brien, Cordelia E.	09 OCT 1884	19	296
Birch, William Taylor	Simms, Ida R.	27 NOV 1878 R	12	349
Birchett, Mary P.	Boisseau, William E.	14 SEP 1881 R	15	483
Birckhead, I.G.	Clowes, A.L.	30 MAY 1883	17	469
Birckhead, Middleton	Joyce, Charlotte M.	16 DEC 1880	15	107
Bird, Alexander	Jones, Harriet	14 OCT 1880	14	493
Bird, Alice	Young, Thomas C.	29 OCT 1884	19	347
Bird, Cornelia	Ross, William F.	04 NOV 1884	19	351
Bird, Ella	Jordan, William	27 NOV 1877 R	11	203
Bird, Ella	Dixson, Philip	12 AUG 1885 L	20	365
Bird, Florence	Lancaster, John	09 MAY 1881 L	15	297
Bird, Frances [Fanny]	Day, Tyler	16 OCT 1884 R	19	312
Bird, Harvey	Johnson, Julia	00 OCT 1879 R	13	399
Bird, Lucy	Green, Spencer	10 SEP 1879 L	13	362
Bird, Mary E.	Mealey, Thomas S.	01 DEC 1881	16	117
Bird, Minnie C.	Wood, Samuel A.	04 APR 1883 L	17	378
Bird, Sue	Armstead, James Ryan	28 JUN 1882	16	424
Bird, William	Glascoe, Harriet Ann	30 AUG 1877 L	11	071
Birmingham, William Otis	Wilson, Jennie Boyd	31 MAR 1885 R	20	138
Birney, Geogeanna	Johnson, John Wesley	01 MAY 1882 R	16	343
Birrell, John	Bradfield, Lewellen Virginia	03 SEP 1878	12	196
Birth, Emma J. Wagner	Towers, Lewis E.	18 JUL 1880 R	14	367
Birtwell, Daniel, Jr.	Erickson, Alice	21 MAY 1879 R	13	197
Bisbee, Horace F.	Norfleet, Mildred	13 MAY 1884	19	018
Bischoff, Charles H.	Stiebeling, Elisabetha	16 JUL 1882 R	16	449
Biscoe, Ida M.	Davis, R.S.	04 DEC 1882 R	17	165
Bishop, Cassie A.	Braxton, Charles Ely	12 SEP 1877	11	087
Bishop, Henrietta	Henderson, J.H.	22 MAR 1879 L	13	111
Bishop, Joseph E.	Cooke, Mary C.	12 SEP 1882 L	17	017
Bishop, Mollie	Knight, Jackson	31 OCT 1883	18	222
Bispham, Lou H.	May, James B.	22 NOV 1877	11	198
Bissham, Samuel T.	Connor, Mary	27 JAN 1879	13	034
Bitting, Charles Carroll	Rayfield, Eva H.	18 FEB 1880 R	14	157
Bivens, Charles H.	Ashford, Mary S.	07 APR 1885	20	150
Black, Asbury	Brown, Annie	06 SEP 1879 L	13	355
Black, Frankie	Talbot, Horace	04 SEP 1879 R	13	349
Black, James A.	Garber, Josephine J.	15 SEP 1885	20	415
Black, James H.	Hankey, Mary	27 NOV 1879 R	14	014
Black, Joseph S.	Fairall, Henrietta P.	15 NOV 1881 R	16	075
Black, Joshua	Boston, Annie E.	12 AUG 1880	14	393
Black, Miranda	Kenney, Tucker	08 SEP 1883 L	18	118
Blackburn, Annie	Bushwood, Geo. Wash.	14 DEC 1877 L	11	238
Blackburn, Arthur	Gordon, Mary	13 FEB 1880	14	151
Blackburn, Fannie	Coleman, John	06 MAR 1884 R	18	454
Blackburn, Henry H.	McHenry, Mamie E.	10 OCT 1878	12	267
Blackburn, Susan	Alexander, Seymore	31 JUL 1883	18	068
Blackburne, Ella	Bell, John T.	30 APR 1878	12	025
Blackiston, Minnie D.	McBee, Randolph	19 JUL 1877 R	11	026
Blackley, Ida J.	Blaydes, Samuel C.	16 NOV 1880 R	15	049
Blacklock, Elizabeth Va.	Maury, Fontaine	06 JUN 1885 R	20	257
Blackman, Laura E.	Burdette, Elmer W.	25 SEP 1883 R	18	153
Blackman, Samuel Stockton	Stuart, Ida M.	18 SEP 1883 R	18	140
Blackman, William F.	Worthington, Lucy	01 JUL 1884	19	112
Blackmen, Elizabeth	Richardson, William L.	11 APR 1878 R	11	411
Blackson, Lucy	Tolbort, John F.	10 JAN 1878	11	294
Blackstine, Margaret A.	Newman, Dennis E.	29 APR 1880	14	246

Blackston, John	Berryman, Louisa	01 JUN 1885	20	249
Blackstone, Harriete	Jackson, Oscar	26 DEC 1882 R	17	212
Blackstone, Henry	Shorter, Mary	21 DEC 1877 L	11	257
Blackstone, Walter	Simpson, Charity	21 JAN 1878 L	11	312
Blackus, August	Granby, Anna	09 NOV 1880 L	15	039
Blackwell, Anne E.	Middleton, William P.	11 OCT 1881 R	16	018
Blackwell, Charles	Herbert, Mary Theresa	14 OCT 1879 L	13	422
Blackwell, Emma	Nicholas, Otway	14 MAY 1878 R	12	055
Blackwell, George	Davis, Mary Elleanor	12 AUG 1882 R	16	471
Blackwell, Jane	Brown, John Samuel	26 MAR 1879 L	13	115
Blackwell, John	Wiggins, Alice	06 APR 1882	16	303
Blackwell, Lavinia	Ward, George	22 JAN 1878 L	11	312
Blackwill, Americus	Magruder, Helen Ann	30 OCT 1877 R	11	157
Bladen, Alice E.	Reiser, William F.	13 APR 1882 L	16	314
Bladen, Andrew	Norton, Adele	10 JUN 1879 L	13	226
Bladen, George William	Padgett, Margaret Louisa	26 MAR 1879 R	13	116
Bladen, John H.	Broderick, Bridget E.	19 FEB 1881 L	15	194
Bladen, Martin Luther	Dutton, Mary C.	22 APR 1880 L	14	234
Bladen, Rosier T.	Gray, Laura V.	27 FEB 1884 L	18	446
Bladnon, Saly	Forbes, Thomas	23 JAN 1879 R	12	407
Bladon, Sallie A.	Watson, W.C.	15 OCT 1884	19	309
Blagden, Lizzie	Bell, Bruce	28 JUN 1877 L	11	002
Blaine, Alice Stanwood	Coppinger, John Joseph, Col.	06 FEB 1883	17	292
Blaine, I.B.	Bell, Lethe	15 JAN 1883 L	17	258
Blair, Ada	Bland, Joseph	17 JUN 1885 L	20	278
Blair, Bettie	Shields, Eleas	17 FEB 1885 R	20	069
Blair, Emeline	Butler, Emmanuel	27 JAN 1879	13	035
Blair, Emma	Nelson, Phillip	15 APR 1879	13	142
Blair, George P.	West, Annie	07 APR 1879 R	13	130
Blair, James L.	Alexander, Apolline M.	21 FEB 1883	17	312
Blair, John [the Baptist]	Morsell, Annie	01 NOV 1884 L	19	386
Blair, Minna	Richey, Stephen O.	15 NOV 1884 R	19	384
Blair, Pat	Tentman, Mary	02 MAY 1884 L	19	002
Blair, Pat	Tentman, Mary	02 MAY 1884 L	18	547
Blair, Regina Agnes	McKeon, Robert W.	22 SEP 1884 L	19	265
Blake, Daniel F.	Rhodes, Lillian F.	25 OCT 1882	17	092
Blake, E.J.	Cathell, J.H.	20 DEC 1877 L	11	249
Blake, Edwin Myers	Donn, Maggie Kate	23 NOV 1881	16	095
Blake, Ella J.	Cathell, James H.	03 JAN 1878	11	293
Blake, Frances	Stubbs, Edward C.	16 OCT 1879 R	13	429
Blake, Isaac	Ball, Cecilia A., Mrs.	13 OCT 1879 R	13	415
Blake, William F.	Lewis, Cora B.	27 NOV 1884 R	19	420
Blake, William Reed	Williams, Sarah	30 MAR 1880 R	14	195
Blakely, Mary Ann	Chism, George A.	12 DEC 1877	11	229
Blakey, Gertrude B.	Taylor, John Wm.	30 APR 1884 R	18	545
Blakey, Tabitha Ann	Jackson, Giles	20 FEB 1879	13	069
Blakey, William E.	Wilson, Rosa L.	12 JUN 1882 R	16	406
Blakey, William O.	Landrum, Blanche L.	21 OCT 1884 R	19	327
Blaky, Frances E.	Harrod, Lucius	25 OCT 1877 R	11	154
Blanchard, Mary Lenthall	Towers, Winfield Scott	17 NOV 1880 R	15	051
Blanchard, Mattie	Bosher, Robert	06 JUN 1881 R	15	346
Blanchard, Meda A.	Coyle, John F.	25 MAR 1878 L	11	392
Blanchard, Nellie McCay	Warren, Benjamin B.	17 JUN 1885 R	20	277
Blanchard, William F.	Wade, Emma C.	11 AUG 1880 R	14	395
Bland, Allie F.	Nott, William T.	03 OCT 1878	12	242
Bland, Anna M.	Adams, West B.	10 MAR 1880 R	14	181
Bland, Dolly	Lyle, Charles	16 JUL 1878 L	12	136
Bland, Irene	Jones, Frank W.	05 SEP 1885	20	400

Bland, James Arthur	Cornwall, Alice Virginia	01 OCT 1885 R	20	451
Bland, John Bolling	Boyd, Mary Eliza	02 FEB 1878	11	325
Bland, John H.	Pierce, Annie J.	28 APR 1881 L	15	276
Bland, Joseph	Robertson, Rosetta	23 JUL 1884 L	19	151
Bland, Joseph	Blair, Ada	17 JUN 1885 L	20	278
Blank, Robert B.	Faulkner, Eugenia C.	08 AUG 1880 R	14	391
Blankline, Anne Eliza	Carroll, Walter W.	22 MAR 1879 L	13	112
Blantaker, Lewis	Smith, Hodena	24 DEC 1879 L	14	068
Blanton, George W.	Mountjoy, Catherine H.	16 SEP 1880 R	14	449
Blau, Antoinette H.	Lambie, Edward L.	02 FEB 1881 R	15	171
Blaxton, Maria	Bogus, Charley	29 MAY 1884 L	19	047
Blaydes, Samuel C.	Blackley, Ida J.	16 NOV 1880 R	15	049
Bleecker, Cornelia	Wheeler, Langden P.	26 OCT 1881 R	16	046
Bleifus, Amalia	Hatzfeld, Adam	28 APR 1878	12	026
Blenck, William	Shanahan, Mary	17 MAY 1878 L	12	067
Blenheim, Sarah	Chin, James	07 OCT 1880 L	14	479
Blenner, Rose	Wallner, W.M.	14 MAY 1883	17	438
Bligh, John	Kennedy, Catharine	31 JUL 1877 L	11	035
Bligh, John A.	Glynn, Mary A.	29 MAR 1883 R	17	368
Blincoe, Albert F.	Webster, Emma Grace	15 JUL 1884	19	140
Blincoe, Joseph	Jenkins, Laura A.	27 JUN 1878	12	117
Blinkard, William W.	Neujahr, Maggie A.	24 APR 1879 R	13	158
Bliss, Amelia Ann	Speake, Rufus Henry	16 APR 1878 L	12	008
Bliss, Clara Bell	Hinds, Jerome Jasper	17 JUN 1878 R	12	102
Bliss, Ellis B.	Jackson, Ellenore Frances	20 APR 1880 R	14	230
Blodget, Carrie A.	Upton, Cassius M.	14 MAY 1884 R	19	018
Blondel, Emma V.	Klopfer, Harry C.	26 MAR 1884 L	18	482
Blondel, Maggie W.	Klopfer, Walter H.	28 DEC 1881 L	16	166
Blondelle, Eugenia	Waggener, Norris M.	20 FEB 1878 L	11	350
Blondheim, Henry	Breslauer, Adeline	17 JAN 1883 R	17	261
Bloomer, Arthur Finley	Alexander, Blandina Kate	04 DEC 1878 R	12	366
Bloomer, Eliza S.	Priddy, E.O. Clifford	18 JUL 1878	12	139
Bloomer, George Craft	Beale, Violet Blair	02 FEB 1881 R	15	172
Bloudon, Martha Jane	Mullican, John E.	10 FEB 1880 R	14	144
Bloxton, James S.	Fritter, Lulu	15 APR 1880	14	225
Blue, Samuel	Johnson, Sarah A.	14 FEB 1881 L	15	189
Blue, Sophy	Nicholson, George	28 APR 1884 R	18	535
Blue, Willy Ann	Ford, Samuel	09 FEB 1881	15	184
Blueit, Ella	Jones, Matthew	29 MAY 1882 L	16	381
Bluet, Mildred S.	Kahlert, William	16 NOV 1882 R	17	133
Blum, Rosa	Eiseman, Lewis	24 JUN 1883 R	18	007
Blumenthal, Hannah	Newmeyer, Solomon	15 JAN 1882 R	16	188
Blumenthal, Henrietta	Sommers, Joseph	01 MAR 1885 R	20	089
Blundon, Kate M.	Mayfield, Mercer B.	23 SEP 1885	20	437
Blundon, Laura V.	Dann, Wm. F.	20 JAN 1880 R	14	113
Blundon, Lewis A.	Ray, Gertrude T.	05 OCT 1885 L	20	458
Blundon, Mary F.	Bean, Benjamin A.	27 DEC 1881 R	16	157
Blunt, Fannie	Hanes, Walter	23 MAY 1885 R	20	236
Blunt, John S.	Birch, Annie	19 MAY 1880	14	277
Blunt, Mary Virginia	Gates, Richard	18 DEC 1878 R	12	381
Blunt, Susan	Dorsey, Lewis	09 AUG 1877 R	11	049
Boadley, Daniel	Gillis, Nancy	12 JUN 1879	13	229
Boaman, Lillie	Wheatley, John W.	17 FEB 1879 L	13	063
Boardman, Myron	Stutzman, Annie G.	02 OCT 1878	12	249
Boarman, Elizabeth	Williams, Augustus	20 DEC 1883 L	18	330
Boarman, James	Billingsly, Lou	11 JUN 1879 L	13	228
Boas, Rachel	Queene, Charles	21 JUL 1884 L	19	149
Boatman, Mary J.	Sanders, Robert W.	20 DEC 1883	18	331

Bobb, Rosa	Walsh, Martin J.	05 MAR 1885 R	20	096
Bobee, Ida	Heydon, Charles S.	01 AUG 1883 L	18	070
Bock, Ella	Nichols, Theodore	05 MAR 1884 L	18	459
Bock, Henry Michael	Smith, Margaret Ann	28 MAR 1880 R	14	199
Bock, Louise	Noah, Morris Sampson	05 JUL 1880 R	14	347
Bocock, James D.	Walter, Regina M.	30 NOV 1881 R	16	104
Bode, Richard	Miller, Augusta D.	11 JAN 1881	15	147
Bodenseck, Katy S.	Simms, James B.	14 APR 1878	12	411
Bodenseck, Katy S.	Timms, James B.	10 APR 1878 L	11	416
Bodensick, Sarah V.	Fowler, Alfred H.	30 OCT 1879 L	13	454
Bodieu, Fannie M.	Byers, Jaames W.	22 OCT 1884	19	327
Bodin, Henry Armand	Torrens, Mary C. Roy	23 JUL 1877 R	11	030
Bodin, Lucy J.	Sanders, Harrison	11 AUG 1883 L	18	083
Bodine, Hiram D.	Johnson, Clara E.	27 MAR 1883 R	17	360
Bodine, Maggie	Allen, Ferdinand	08 DEC 1881 R	16	120
Bodine, Rose E.	Megby, Frank	17 DEC 1884 R	19	463
Body, John H.	Jefferson, Elizabeth	01 JUN 1882 L	16	388
Boegeholz, Emma G.	Troulard, Robert A.	23 MAY 1883	17	458
Boehmer, George H.	Schultze, Lucie C.	03 NOV 1878	12	305
Boehnaann, William C.	Chrisman, Maggie	10 JUN 1884	19	074
Boem, Josephine	Hobbs, William	10 JUN 1880 R	14	315
Boernstein, Henry N.	Schlegel, Lottie M.	21 DEC 1881 R	16	146
Bogan, J.F.	Hobbs, M.E.	17 AUG 1880	14	402
Bogel, Essick	Johnson, Mary	20 OCT 1879 R	13	430
Bogert, Alice	Atkinson, Robert Harbottle	20 FEB 1883 R	17	311
Bogger, William	Lawrence, Cordelia F.	30 OCT 1877 L	11	160
Boggs, Cyrus E.	McElfresh, Vannetta C.	29 JUN 1878	12	118
Boggs, William Benjamin	Work, Ida Georgianna	07 JUN 1882 R	16	398
Bogles, Lucy	Craig, John	04 OCT 1883 R	18	171
Bogue, George W.	Baldwin, Sallie	01 JUN 1882 R	16	387
Bogus, Charley	Blaxton, Maria	29 MAY 1884 L	19	047
Bohannon, Joseph	Chambers, Carrie M.	10 JUN 1880 R	14	315
Bohlyer, George	Padgett, Fannie McClelland	07 DEC 1880 R	15	028
Bohn, August	Rabbe, Margaretha	11 SEP 1881	15	479
Bohn, Theresa Marie	Johnson, Edwin J.	26 MAY 1880	14	285
Bohnhardt, Augusta A.	Waite, John P.	03 SEP 1878	12	195
Bohnke, Hubert	Hellmuth, Anna	27 AUG 1884	19	210
Bohraus, Kathrina	Abel, Fritz	26 OCT 1878 L	12	292
Bohrer, Corine C.	Doom, Alexander R.	27 AUG 1877 L	11	064
Bohrer, Marion Willett	McKenny, Sarah A.	16 SEP 1879 R	13	371
Bohrer, Mary E.	Guy, Benjamin Walter	21 SEP 1881 R	15	493
Bohrer, Minnie R.	Maxson, Louis Wm.	25 DEC 1884 R	19	483
Bohrer, Wm. P.	Savage, Susie	03 NOV 1884 L	19	354
Boisseau, William E.	Birchett, Mary P.	14 SEP 1881 R	15	483
Boisseaux, C. Gray	Tyler, Clara W.	16 NOV 1880 R	15	051
Bolac, Henry	Sullivan, Margaret	13 MAY 1885 L	20	217
Bolan, Mary Margaret	Reynolds, William	20 AUG 1882	16	488
Boland, Patrick	Sullivan, Annie	14 OCT 1885 L	20	484
Boldan, Ida E.	Brown, Willis R.M.	20 DEC 1880 R	15	111
Bolden, Charles	Sanders, Amelia	26 JUN 1878 R	12	109
Bolden, Charles Francis	King, Mary	19 APR 1882 R	16	325
Bolden, Frances E.	Brooks, John C.F.	12 MAY 1879 L	13	185
Bolden, Joseph	Holly, Agnes	13 SEP 1880 R	14	443
Bolden, Samuel Henry	Marshall, Laura	01 JUL 1884 L	19	115
Bolden, Wilson	Page, Ellen O.	15 JAN 1880 R	14	109
Bolding, Carrie	Armstrong, Joseph S.	07 AUG 1878 L	12	158
Boler, Abraham	Carter, Letitia V.	08 AUG 1883 L	18	081
Bolling, Alice	Smith, Edward	16 JAN 1884 L	18	382

Bolling, James M.	Eimer, Emma	22 APR 1880 R	14	228
Bolling, Mary A.	Grill, George	16 JUL 1883	18	048
Bollison, Roderick	Rowe, Emily	04 DEC 1878	12	363
Bolls, Margaret	Penn, Jesse	31 OCT 1878 R	12	299
Boltenfield, Rosa C.	Gold, Joseph H.	19 OCT 1881 L	16	035
Bolton, Mary	Fitzpatrick, James	17 JUN 1879 L	13	234
Boman, Annie Virginia	Hutchinson, Alexander	09 DEC 1878 R	12	373
Boman, John R.	Harrison, Martha Virginia	23 DEC 1882 R	26	6283
Bombray, Elsie	Phillips, Edward	25 SEP 1879 L	13	385
Bombray, Joseph	Dandridge, Mary C.	05 SEP 1884	19	224
Bombray, Lucy	Stewart, George	29 NOV 1878 R	12	351
Bomievill, Columbus J.	Birch, Carrie F.	02 OCT 1878 L	12	256
Bond, Carrie E.	Willis, William J.	14 MAY 1885	20	222
Bond, Charles H.	Bacon, Isabella	01 MAY 1883 R	17	393
Bond, Charles T.	Morgan, Margaret M.	12 SEP 1878	12	215
Bond, Edwin Hilton	Robertson, Rachel	20 DEC 1883	18	325
Bond, Ella D.	Hendle, John E.	27 JAN 1880 R	14	122
Bond, Elmer H.	Simpson, Annie L.	28 OCT 1884 L	19	341
Bond, Emma L.	Smith, Benjamin F.	20 JUN 1883	18	001
Bond, Gertrude B.	Gibb, Frederick Sommerfield	29 JUN 1881 R	15	382
Bond, James Henry G.	White, Julia Ann Elizabeth	10 NOV 1880 R	15	033
Bond, James T.	Mahoney, Flora Elizabeth	17 DEC 1884	19	366
Bond, Kate	Dunlop, Matthew	24 JUN 1880 R	14	333
Bond, Leonia J.	Trumbo, Louis	01 JUL 1884	19	108
Bond, Lillie K.	Thomas, Edward H.	27 JUL 1884	19	159
Bond, Maggie	Lockett, Scott	16 FEB 1885 R	20	071
Bond, Maria, Mrs.	Watkins, James	01 AUG 1878 R	12	153
Bond, Mary C.	Hall, James D.J.	25 JUN 1878	12	112
Bond, R. Matilda	Todd, William B.	22 JAN 1885 R	20	033
Bond, Rebecca	Tills, Ambrose	28 APR 1880 R	14	208
Bond, Samuel	Swann, Celia	19 NOV 1877	11	189
Bone, Wallace G.	Leavy, Cary A.	21 DEC 1882	17	199
Bones, Thomas Arthur	Parker, Marietta Matilda Wilkins	20 MAR 1881 R	15	231
Bonini, Jennie	Kelley, John H.	04 OCT 1883	18	170
Bonnell, Lizzie Claiborne	Compton, Joseph William	01 JUN 1881 R	15	337
Bonnelle, Frank Jackson	Whiton, Emma Sumner	23 DEC 1880 R	15	114
Bonner, James R.	Bonner, Margaret A.	21 JAN 1879	13	029
Bonner, Margaret A.	Bonner, James R.	21 JAN 1879	13	029
Bonneville, Columbus J.	Birch, Carrie F.	02 OCT 1878 R	12	325
Bonney, Cora	Barry, David Sheldon	19 APR 1883 R	17	401
Bonney, Florence Estelle	Keech, William Cyril	16 JAN 1878	11	308
Bontz, Fairfax	Viehmann, Catharine R.	28 JUN 1883 L	18	025
Booker, Annie	Holmes, William	30 OCT 1879 R	13	453
Booker, Benjamin	Davis, Mary C.	08 MAY 1878	12	043
Booker, Coleman	Watson, Rebecca F.	15 AUG 1878 L	12	170
Booker, Moses	Paine, Martha	25 DEC 1881 R	16	156
Booker, William L.	Lias, Nannie	02 APR 1883 R	17	372
Bookman, Ella A.	Scouter, Gavin	16 SEP 1878	12	220
Bool, George	Engleke, Mary	10 SEP 1877	11	084
Boom, William	Downmus, Lizzie	07 MAY 1881	15	296
Boon, Emma	Smith, George	04 SEP 1878 L	12	199
Boone, Annie A.	Elias, James	26 DEC 1879 L	14	076
Boone, Arianna I.	Crumpton, Eugene	05 FEB 1882	16	181
Boone, Carrie	Bailey, George Henry	06 JUL 1885	20	310
Boone, Eliza Ann	Medford, Daniel	03 APR 1883	17	376
Boone, Elizabeth E.	Tolliver, James H.	30 APR 1885	20	198
Boone, Florence	Brown, Charles H.	30 OCT 1884 L	19	352
Boone, Jacob	Garnett, Leanna	26 JUL 1877 L	11	032

D.C. Marriage Records Index, June 28, 1877 to October 19, 1885   39

Name	Spouse	Date	Vol	Page
Boone, Victor Emanuel	Berry, Estella	15 JUN 1885 L	20	274
Boone, William	Dent, Mary	29 APR 1882 R	16	340
Boorhardt, Wilhelmine	Decker, John	08 OCT 1884 L	19	295
Boose, Florence R.	Brown, Charles H.	30 OCT 1884 L	19	351
Boose, Frank	Carroll, Lizzie	05 AUG 1884 L	19	169
Boose, Mary	Kelly, Richard S.	12 APR 1882 R	16	313
Booth, Addison	Herns, James	18 SEP 1883 R	18	137
Booth, Charles Alfred	Lockwood, Florence	27 FEB 1878 R	11	359
Booth, Elizabeth	Smith, Joseph	28 NOV 1883 L	18	283
Booth, John	Edwards, Nancy	09 NOV 1883 L	18	244
Booth, Joseph	Sullivan, Katie	13 JUL 1878 L	12	134
Booth, Margaret A.	Martin, John	08 SEP 1880 R	14	437
Booth, Mary L.	Laughlin, John T.	24 MAY 1880 R	14	284
Booth, Mattie W. (Parraday)	Brown, David H.P.	29 SEP 1884 R	19	272
Booth, Moses Z.	Oliver, Elizabeth	24 NOV 1880 L	15	064
Booth, Rose Ella	Crawford, John	26 OCT 1880 L	15	015
Boothe, George C.	Stant, Rosella	16 JUL 1877	11	021
Bootwright, Orlando A.	Francis, Nannie M.	31 DEC 1884	19	508
Booze, Alice	Scott, Charley	05 JUN 1878 L	12	087
Booze, Mary Agnes	Pendleton, Almiles	14 MAY 1880	14	271
Bopp, Mary R.	Ray, Frank P.	18 MAY 1883	17	451
Borden, Alanson	Kent, Mary F.	25 DEC 1877	11	259
Borden, William N.	Wilson, Eleanor Caldwell	05 MAR 1885 R	20	097
Bordon, Daniel L.	Ward, Harriet E.	28 AUG 1883	18	102
Borger, Mary Theresa	Bosse, John H.	05 JUL 1882 L	16	437
Borland, Eliza J.	Bawsel, Edward	11 FEB 1880 L	14	149
Borland, Lillian B.	Willson, John E.	03 JUN 1885 R	20	251
Borland, Mary Estelle	Duryee, Albertus Redfield	27 DEC 1882 R	17	214
Born, John Columbus	Butler, Delia Ann	03 DEC 1878 R	12	360
Bornett, Georgianna	Harris, James	18 OCT 1877 R	11	140
Bornheim, Moses	Laveen, Laura	13 OCT 1880 R	14	490
Boroughs, Rosa	Garrett, Frank	16 JAN 1879	13	024
Borsekowski, Ferdinand	Elkins, Mary Eliza	12 DEC 1877	11	232
Bosher, Robert	Blanchard, Mattie	06 JUN 1881 R	15	346
Bosher, Wm. Pemberton	Clayton, Susanna B.	24 JUN 1884 R	19	098
Bosley, Ada A.	Owings, Thomas H.	01 APR 1882 L	16	295
Bosley, Cornelius	Johnson, Lina	23 MAR 1881 L	15	236
Bosley, Cornelius Henry	Weems, Mary	17 DEC 1878 L	12	385
Bosley, Laura J.	Brown, Alexander D.	21 AUG 1880 R	14	386
Boss, Anna Estelle	Phair, Thomas Elwood	25 JUN 1879 R	13	245
Boss, Robert Lake	Curtin, Mary J.	04 JUN 1878	12	084
Boss, Samuel D.	Weaver, Jessie S.	18 SEP 1883	18	136
Boss, Sarah Virginia	Van Horn, William G.	05 MAR 1880 L	14	178
Boss, Stewart H.	King, Laura V.	18 NOV 1884 L	19	392
Bosse, John H.	Borger, Mary Theresa	05 JUL 1882 L	16	437
Bossett, Amelia F.	Clark, William Frank	25 APR 1881	15	271
Bossfield, Frances	Jackson, Andrew	18 OCT 1877 R	11	141
Bost, Jennie L.	Hilton, William H.	18 OCT 1882	17	077
Bostic, John A.	Thomas, Mamie E.	24 OCT 1883	18	211
Bostick, Peter	Reed, Amanda	17 JAN 1884 R	18	383
Boston, Adaline	Johnson, William H.	27 SEP 1877 L	11	112
Boston, Adline	Diggs, Robert	27 SEP 1882	17	003
Boston, Annie E.	Black, Joshua	12 AUG 1880	14	393
Boston, Eugene	Williams, Dora	01 OCT 1885 L	20	453
Boston, George W.	Shade, Mary A.	26 JUN 1884 L	19	105
Boston, Joseph	Bowie, Ella	01 JAN 1885	19	493
Boston, Josephine	Simmons, John Thomas	18 JUL 1882	16	451
Boston, Julia	Martin, Hillray	15 JAN 1885	20	020

Boston, Nathaniel	Taylor, Alice	22 APR 1880	14	234
Boston, Odsey	Ballard, Fannie	13 DEC 1881	16	128
Boston, Thomas	Clark, Harriet	09 OCT 1879 L	13	413
Boston, William S.	Syphax, Julia W.	26 OCT 1882	17	096
Bostrom, Augustus O.	Hallstrom, Christina	10 SEP 1878	12	210
Bostwick, Philip Denny	Dixon, Fannie	08 SEP 1878 R	12	205
Boswell, Adelia A.	Collins, James E.	16 SEP 1878 R	12	220
Boswell, Alice	Davis, John H.	10 JUN 1879 R	13	223
Boswell, Charles	Carroll, Emma	16 SEP 1880 R	14	453
Boswell, Elmira	Jones, George W.	09 APR 1880 R	14	218
Boswell, Ignatius	Salor, Nettie Aanna	04 DEC 1879 R	14	028
Boswell, James E.	Fraas, Katie M.	29 JAN 1880 R	14	126
Boswell, John B.	Mills, Ellen Florence	18 OCT 1883 R	18	201
Boswell, Josephine	Pinkard, Robert O.	26 FEB 1880 L	14	167
Boswell, Mary V.	Turner, Joseph W.	05 JUL 1883	18	038
Boswell, Samuel	Jones, Laura	04 MAR 1880 L	14	175
Boswell, Sarah	Anderson, David	01 NOV 1881 R	16	056
Boswell, William H.	Shipman, Mary E.	30 JUL 1883 L	18	066
Bosworth, Charles M.	Grant, Jennie	16 SEP 1881 R	15	487
Bosworth, Joseph H.	Davis, Mary A.	16 JUL 1881 R	15	403
Bosworth, Maria Ryan (Jones)	Sipe, Andrew Gibbon Corouther	28 MAY 1883 R	17	464
Boteler, Edward M.	Taltavull, Edith E.	24 NOV 1880	15	063
Boteler, Mary B.	Pentz, John J.	24 NOV 1880	15	066
Bottomley, Louis	Ruppert, Katie	23 AUG 1882 R	16	446
Bottriell, John W.	Jones, Alice C.	03 JUN 1879	13	216
Botts, Isabella	Dozier, Ike	15 DEC 1881 R	16	131
Botts, Sanford H.	Budd, Ludy W.	04 FEB 1884 L	18	408
Botts, Thomas	Young, Annie	31 MAR 1885 L	20	139
Boudinot, Elias Cornelius	Minear, Clara C.	16 APR 1885 R	20	173
Boudren, James E.	Macnamara, Kate	25 NOV 1879	14	003
Bouduiot, Ella Cornelia	Flenner, Jesse Weirick	02 OCT 1882 R	17	047
Bouduiot, George Stockton	Boyd, Jessie I.M.	14 SEP 1882 R	17	020
Boudurant, Henry	Sapp, Sallie	08 JUN 1885	20	260
Boughton, Wilfred E.	Rodier, Effie	12 NOV 1884	19	376
Boughton, William DeL.	Butterfield, Marian A.	02 JUN 1885 L	20	251
Bouis, Annie E.	Adams, Thomas N.	09 NOV 1880 R	15	037
Bouis, Stephen G.	Backus, Robertha V.	13 OCT 1879 R	13	417
Boulden, Charles F.	Green, Lena L.	14 JUL 1880 L	14	361
Boulden, Charlotte	Johnson, Charles H.	05 FEB 1879	13	044
Boulden, James A.	Brooks, Cecilia	11 APR 1881 L	15	253
Boulden, Martha	Colbert, William T.	16 SEP 1880 R	14	447
Boulden, Samuel	Tasca, Cressy	10 APR 1879	13	132
Bouldin, Agnes	Place, Charles H.	10 APR 1885 R	20	151
Bouldin, Frances	Herbert, Rinaldo	31 OCT 1878 L	12	302
Bouldin, Indiana F.	Nicholas, James L.	15 AUG 1877 L	11	055
Bouldin, Joseph	Mason, Lucy	14 DEC 1882 L	17	184
Bouldin, Josephine	Johnson, Alexander	06 OCT 1880	14	476
Bouldin, Julia M.	Harrison, John H.	31 DEC 1881 L	16	174
Bouldin, Julius	Andrews, Louisa	15 MAY 1879	13	192
Bouldin, Robert	McPherson, Julia	05 JUL 1881 L	15	388
Bouldin, Rosa	Henry, Thomas	21 NOV 1878 R	12	342
Bouler, Charlie E.	Jordan, Ida Frances	19 MAY 1882	16	365
Bounds, Evan	Meeks, Martha	14 OCT 1877 R	11	136
Bourn, James	Livingston, Athenia	26 MAR 1879 R	13	113
Bourne, Thomas C.	Young, Linnie M.	10 FEB 1881 R	15	183
Bouze, Mary A.	Beard, James	11 AUG 1884	19	179
Bovie, Lizzie	Anderson, Ira Lewis	05 JUL 1882 R	16	438
Bowen, Burton Lee	Menhorn, Caroline Matilda	13 JUN 1882 R	16	408

D.C. Marriage Records Index, June 28, 1877 to October 19, 1885

Bowen, Charles	Childress, Dora A.	14 JUN 1881	15	360
Bowen, James	Cissell, Cassie	03 NOV 1880	15	028
Bowen, James E.M.	Cooke, Sophie	15 OCT 1879 R	13	426
Bowen, Jane	Davis, William Thomas	09 OCT 1884	19	297
Bowen, John Wayne	Briscoe, Emma	27 NOV 1877 R	11	205
Bowen, Maggie E.	Clarke, Samuel A.	01 JUN 1882 R	16	389
Bowen, Maria	Moore, Alexander	11 AUG 1880 L	14	397
Bowen, Marion A.	Holman, Edward H.	04 SEP 1878 R	12	197
Bowen, Mary	Smith, Lewis	31 MAR 1884 R	30	7296
Bowen, Raymond	Amos, Louise	05 SEP 1882 R	17	004
Bowen, Rebecca	Butler, Sammuel	27 NOV 1880 L	15	069
Bowen, Richard T.	Butler, Elizabeth	11 OCT 1884	19	300
Bowen, Sallie E.	Mathaney, Thomas H.	19 AUG 1880 R	14	409
Bowen, Winter E.	Bassford, Sarah E.	08 SEP 1880 R	14	436
Bowens, Anna	West, Lloyd	10 MAY 1879	13	183
Bowens, Celia Ann	Allen, William H.	26 DEC 1878 R	12	396
Bowens, Randall	Walker, Annie	05 DEC 1878 L	12	370
Bowers, Eliza Frances	Stringfellow, James W.	15 NOV 1883	18	255
Bowers, Jordan	Nugent, Maria Louisa	30 DEC 1878 R	12	407
Bowers, Louisa	Johnson, Samuel	15 AUG 1877 R	11	056
Bowers, Rudolph P.	Heinz, Amelia A.	15 SEP 1885 R	20	415
Bowie, Agnes	Bowie, Allen P.	27 JAN 1881 R	15	162
Bowie, Agnes W.	Perry, James M.	26 APR 1883 R	17	415
Bowie, Alice R.	Haight, Horace	20 DEC 1877 R	11	243
Bowie, Allen P.	Bowie, Agnes	27 JAN 1881 R	15	162
Bowie, Anna A.	Whiting, Philip	22 MAR 1883 L	17	356
Bowie, Annie S.	Langley, Richard Warren	12 SEP 1878	12	209
Bowie, Armenia	McGrath, Wallock	15 FEB 1884 R	18	426
Bowie, Carrie	Watkins, Williams	10 AUG 1877 L	11	050
Bowie, Celia	Marks, Joseph	06 MAY 1884 R	19	009
Bowie, Charles	Gaines, Annie	10 FEB 1881 L	15	186
Bowie, Ella	Green, George	07 MAY 1883 R	17	430
Bowie, Ella	Boston, Joseph	01 JAN 1885	19	493
Bowie, Ethelbert	Sanders, Mollie	23 OCT 1878	12	287
Bowie, George Thomas	Hutt, Mary Jane Virginia	16 JUL 1880 L	14	365
Bowie, Hamilton	Wilbur, Bertha E.	06 OCT 1885 R	20	464
Bowie, Isaac	Garnett, Eliza	18 SEP 1883 R	18	135
Bowie, Jesse S.	Herbert, Mary C.	06 DEC 1883 L	18	303
Bowie, John	Duffin, Celia	27 DEC 1880	15	126
Bowie, John F.	Bowie, T.H., Mrs.	26 DEC 1883 L	18	342
Bowie, Louisa	Yarborough, Thomas S.	09 APR 1885	20	157
Bowie, Maggie	Strauthers, Warren	17 FEB 1885 R	20	075
Bowie, Margaret	Byass, Jacob	03 NOV 1879 L	13	461
Bowie, Maria	Johnson, William	10 JAN 1878 R	11	297
Bowie, Mary	Rawlings, James	11 MAR 1878	11	376
Bowie, Matilda	Turner, William Thomas	15 SEP 1883 L	18	134
Bowie, Millie	Holt, Moses	08 OCT 1879 R	13	402
Bowie, Rachel	Johnson, John Wesley	10 NOV 1879	13	474
Bowie, Richmond Irving	Beall, Mary Eleanor	05 FEB 1880 R	14	136
Bowie, Samuel	Reeves, Ella	10 OCT 1882 L	17	063
Bowie, Sarah	Jackson, Adam	18 NOV 1880 L	15	057
Bowie, T.H., Mrs.	Bowie, John F.	26 DEC 1883 L	18	342
Bowie, Thomas	Allen, Virginia	17 DEC 1884 L	19	466
Bowker, Frances Drummond	Stanwood, Robert Given	08 APR 1879 R	13	130
Bowler, Almira	Adams, George W.	15 NOV 1877 R	11	189
Bowles, Belle A.	Napier, Edward A.	23 JUL 1883	18	056
Bowles, Carrie Grace	Whitmore, Alfred H.	23 DEC 1882 L	17	206
Bowles, Lee P.	Shaw, Sarah E.	13 NOV 1884	19	380

Bowles, Martha	Tibbs, Henry	04 JAN 1882 R	16	182
Bowles, Otelia A.	Slick, John E.	31 JAN 1878 R	11	323
Bowles, Ruth	Messler, Cornelius N.	23 JUL 1883	18	056
Bowles, Sarah	Matthews, Joshua	20 NOV 1882 L	17	137
Bowles, Virginia	Johnson, James	12 MAY 1881 L	15	303
Bowling, Thomas W.	Hurley, Ida A.	08 MAY 1879	13	179
Bowman, Amelia	Bradley, Francis	15 OCT 1879 L	13	426
Bowman, Ann	Thompkins, Robert	24 MAY 1879 R	13	204
Bowman, Annie	Phipps, Robert	10 MAY 1883	17	434
Bowman, Columbus S.	Crown, Ida S.	13 NOV 1878 R	12	323
Bowman, Dora	Lee, George Henry	31 DEC 1883 R	18	353
Bowman, Ella F.	Jenkins, Joseph E.	25 DEC 1883	18	335
Bowman, Emma	Slater, James W. [John]	02 APR 1878 R	11	401
Bowman, Frank Hubbard	Shue, Minnie J.	05 JUL 1884 R	19	122
Bowman, George Wm.	Craig, Ella Irena	28 OCT 1884	19	342
Bowman, Ida L.	Hawkins, George W.	01 NOV 1881	16	055
Bowman, Ida Sophronia	Wilburn, John William	24 SEP 1878 R	12	233
Bowman, Imogene	Morrow, James	27 OCT 1881	16	048
Bowman, James	Lewis, Victoria	05 JUN 1884 L	19	063
Bowman, John	Perry, Lizzie	29 DEC 1880 R	15	130
Bowman, Josephine	Gibson, George W.	27 SEP 1882 R	17	039
Bowman, Letha Virginia	Jefferson, Simon Peter	03 OCT 1882 R	17	049
Bowman, Lizzie	Cole, William Alexander	13 MAY 1884 R	19	004
Bowman, Maggie E.	Wood, William N.	04 JUN 1885 L	20	256
Bowman, Mary	Jenkins, Thomas J.	26 DEC 1883	18	343
Bowman, Mary A.	James, Charles	19 DEC 1881 L	16	138
Bowman, Samuel Stillman	Peterson, Janet West	13 OCT 1884 R	19	302
Bowman, Serena	Wilson, William	06 NOV 1879	13	470
Bowman, Susan	Smith, Timothy	26 FEB 1884	18	439
Bowman, Thomas	Grant, Louisa	25 NOV 1884 L	19	410
Bowman, William A.	Gilbert, Sadie H.	20 SEP 1878 L	12	229
Bowman, William J.	Quintor, Mary Ann	25 SEP 1884 L	19	269
Bowser, James	Brown, Martha	06 APR 1885 L	20	146
Bowser, Joseph	Grimm, Eliza M.	03 JUL 1878 L	12	123
Box, Martha (Carter)	Johnson, J.W.	21 JUN 1883 R	18	005
Boyce, Silas	Emerson, Sarah M. [Bartlett]	25 SEP 1883 R	18	150
Boyce, Stansbury	Taylor, Fannie	11 DEC 1882	17	177
Boyce, Walter J.	Mockabee, Susie A.	08 OCT 1877	11	125
Boyd, Augustus	Sonomon, Emma	12 JAN 1882 L	16	192
Boyd, Catharine	Wise, Charles	19 JUN 1884 L	19	094
Boyd, Charles W.F.	Howard, Katie D.	28 OCT 1879 R	13	448
Boyd, Chas. A.B.	Barron, Carrie	20 NOV 1883 L	18	266
Boyd, Edwin W.	Thurman, Selia	01 OCT 1884	19	279
Boyd, Geo. Washington	Esch, Clara R.	23 APR 1884 R	18	529
Boyd, Harry F.	Peters, Eliza	23 JUL 1881 L	15	415
Boyd, Jeemes	Brown, Fannie	20 AUG 1879	13	323
Boyd, Jessie I.M.	Bouduiot, George Stockton	14 SEP 1882 R	17	020
Boyd, Louisa	Jones, Thomas	12 NOV 1879	13	480
Boyd, Lulie A.	Wood, Charles L.	05 MAR 1879	13	089
Boyd, Maggie J.	Cash, Walter S.	07 DEC 1881 L	16	116
Boyd, Mary	Brewer, James	02 MAR 1882 L	16	264
Boyd, Mary	Thorne, S. Morris	09 FEB 1882 R	16	234
Boyd, Mary Agnes	Lynch, Charles A.	25 NOV 1879 R	14	004
Boyd, Mary Eliza	Bland, John Bolling	02 FEB 1878	11	325
Boyd, Mary Jane	Saunders, Walter Turner	03 FEB 1880 R	14	131
Boyd, Mattie V.	Saltzer, James E.	22 NOV 1881 L	16	088
Boyd, Milton P.	Moynihan, Catherine	08 OCT 1881 R	16	014
Boyd, Minnie A.	Upperman, William B.	28 JUL 1879	13	295

Boyd, Nellie R.	Mangum, William H.	17 OCT 1877 R	11	142
Boyd, Rebecca	Binds, Lewis	24 DEC 1884 R	19	486
Boyd, Russell N.	Cook, Tulip V.	03 OCT 1883 R	18	168
Boyd, Virginia E.	Green, Randolph T.	08 OCT 1885 R	20	469
Boyd, William	Rhodes, Ella	06 JUL 1885 L	20	312
Boyd, William F.	Kelley, Sarah Ann	23 JAN 1884 R	18	391
Boyd, William G.	Reed, Anna Bell	21 FEB 1883	17	315
Boyden, Annie T.	Garrison, John S.	13 OCT 1877 R	11	133
Boyden, Helen Jane	Davidson, John E.	08 SEP 1882 R	17	012
Boyer, Andrew J.	Moore, Anna M.	14 OCT 1885	20	483
Boyer, Katie B.	Trundle, C. Newton	13 OCT 1880 L	14	491
Boyer, Margaret	Miller, William H.	20 OCT 1884 L	19	322
Boyer, Richard	Reeves, Barbara	22 MAR 1882 R	16	286
Boyer, Romulus W.	Goodwin, Victoria R.	22 APR 1880 R	14	234
Boyer, sarah	Ellis, Jacob	20 OCT 1883 L	18	204
Boyer, Thomas Webster	Day, Della	09 FEB 1880 R	14	143
Boyland, John H.	Downey, Nellie E.	17 NOV 1880 L	15	055
Boyland, Michael	Doyle, Catherine, Mrs.	05 JAN 1881 L	15	140
Boyle, Bridget	Chipman, Charles M.	24 NOV 1880 R	15	047
Boyle, Ellen	Quackenbush, Geo. D.	30 SEP 1880	14	464
Boyle, Mary	Ammann, Robert	20 SEP 1880	14	452
Boyle, Mary	Baier, William	15 FEB 1882 R	16	225
Boyle, Mary Jane	Welsh, Michael Raymond	21 NOV 1878 L	12	343
Boyle, Patrick A.	O'Connor, Katie E.	04 FEB 1883 R	17	283
Boyle, Richard	Ford, Delia	20 OCT 1878 R	12	283
Boyle, Thomas	Casey, Lizzie	25 JAN 1883 L	17	274
Boylen, Amelia T.	Graf, Fredrich	03 FEB 1882 L	16	224
Boynton, Charles A.	Lowell, Emma N.	12 MAY 1880 R	14	264
Boynton, Henry S.	Andrews, Amelia C.	29 JUL 1884	19	161
Bozeman, Ada A.	Jones, Andrew J.	10 OCT 1883	18	185
Bozeman, Euretta B.	Matthews, William E.	03 JAN 1883	17	236
Bozzell, Charles S.	Means, Marian M.	28 APR 1881	15	279
Bozzell, Marion E.	Finch, Eugene C.	16 OCT 1879 R	13	424
Brachhoogel, Udo	Müller, Kathinka	12 JAN 1878 L	11	302
Brackett, John E.	Foster, Jeanie D.	21 NOV 1878 R	12	340
Bradburn, C.E.	Thomas, J.E.	10 MAR 1880 L	14	181
Bradburn, Enola V.	Hull, James M.	19 MAY 1885	20	228
Bradburn, Washington	Crown, Lizzie E.	10 JUL 1877 R	11	014
Bradbury, Maggie Bross	Platt, William	02 NOV 1877 R	11	164
Braddock, Denton Scott	Rodier, Iola E.	28 JUL 1885 R	20	343
Bradfield, Lewellen Virginia	Birrell, John	03 SEP 1878	12	196
Bradford, Emily M.	Simms, James H.	21 NOV 1884 L	19	400
Bradford, Grace	Johnson, Dennis	19 MAY 1880 L	14	277
Bradford, Ida F.	McIntyre, Bernard	09 AUG 1881	15	436
Bradford, Julia	Nelson, Julius	06 JUL 1882 L	16	440
Bradford, Samuel	Greenfield, Mollie	12 SEP 1878	12	214
Bradford, William Russell	Donoho, Ida Indiana	05 JUN 1882 R	16	392
Bradley, Alice	Vinton, William	25 OCT 1884 L	19	338
Bradley, Alice F.	Coleman, John B.	23 JAN 1879 L	13	031
Bradley, Edward	Banes, Eliza	31 DEC 1878 R	12	405
Bradley, Edward J.	Landram, Sarah L.	10 AUG 1882 L	16	476
Bradley, Eliza	Garnett, John Henry	03 MAR 1880 L	14	173
Bradley, Elizabeth	Barnes, Frank	10 MAY 1883 R	17	435
Bradley, Francis	Bowman, Amelia	15 OCT 1879 L	13	426
Bradley, George W.	Smith, Mary J.	25 OCT 1882	17	094
Bradley, Georgia L.	Upton, William H.	23 JUN 1881	15	376
Bradley, Henry H.	Reed, Laura A.	15 FEB 1881 R	15	190
Bradley, Henry J.	Sherman, Gussie E.	06 NOV 1883	18	234

Bradley, J. Wharton, Rev.	Atkinson, Minnie R.	11 MAR 1879	13	096
Bradley, James H.	Perry, Annie Lee	06 AUG 1885 R	20	357
Bradley, John E.	Hardy, George Anna	05 OCT 1882 R	17	055
Bradley, John L.	Graham, Elizabeth	14 SEP 1882 L	17	022
Bradley, Julia	Bakersmith, John	16 SEP 1884 L	19	252
Bradley, Lulu	Pumphrey, Frank	26 FEB 1884 L	18	445
Bradley, Lulu M.	Garland, Rush M.	09 JUL 1884	19	130
Bradley, Maria L.	Shackleford, Lloyd M.	02 JAN 1883 R	17	230
Bradley, Martha H.	Anderson, William W.	15 DEC 1881 R	16	133
Bradley, Mary Emma	Ross, Lemuel	04 DEC 1877 L	11	218
Bradley, Patrick H.	Hagan, Mary A.	22 NOV 1881 L	16	088
Bradley, Polly, Mrs.	Broadus, John S.	06 JAN 1880 R	14	092
Bradley, Robert Edmond	Hercus, May Sherman	29 NOV 1884 R	19	424
Bradley, Sarah A.	Barnard, Egbert G.	26 SEP 1883 R	18	154
Bradshaw, Aaron	Leech, Mary E.	25 JUN 1879 R	13	247
Bradshaw, Ida C.	Presgrave, Eugene W.	27 FEB 1883 L	17	322
Bradshaw, J.T.	Bailey, Hattie K.	03 AUG 1885	20	348
Bradshaw, John T.	Cooksie, Georgie V.	09 SEP 1879	13	359
Bradshaw, Moses	Austin, Sarah Forward	04 AUG 1881 R	15	432
Bradt, Albert H.	Grove, Annie M.	29 APR 1883	17	420
Brady, Bernard L.	Case, Elizabeth Caroline	14 MAR 1878	11	369
Brady, C. Owen	Day, Mary	14 JUL 1885	20	326
Brady, Catherine	Wilson, Solmon	24 NOV 1881 L	16	097
Brady, Charlotte Ann	Brady, Joseph F.	27 JAN 1880 R	14	121
Brady, Cyrus Townsend	Guthrie, Clarissa Sidney	10 SEP 1884	19	237
Brady, Elizabeth Ann	Silence, George P.	08 MAY 1880 R	14	259
Brady, George W.	Dorsey, Mary C.	01 SEP 1879 R	13	346
Brady, Henry	Ennis, Lucy	24 MAR 1884 L	18	480
Brady, Joseph F.	Brady, Charlotte Ann	27 JAN 1880 R	14	121
Brady, Lavena	Bean, Thomas	02 JAN 1884 L	18	361
Brady, Lydia S.C.M.	Dease, George W.	19 JUN 1878 L	12	105
Brady, Margaret	Gill, Phillip	13 FEB 1870 L	13	060
Brady, Peyton	Brown, Lillie A.	23 JUL 1884	19	145
Brady, Robert	Bruce, Rosa	22 MAR 1882 R	16	287
Brady, Sarah, Mrs.	Grigsby, William Henry	07 JUL 1879 R	13	266
Brady, Sarita Morrison	Hutchins, Stilson	06 MAR 1883 L	17	335
Braendel, Fredolino	O'Byrne, Rosa A.	05 JUN 1878 L	12	086
Brahler, George W.	Klug, Lizzie Mary	17 SEP 1885 L	20	425
Brahler, John H.	Klug, Elizabeth	23 NOV 1880	15	059
Branagan, Mary	Smith, Silas	10 NOV 1880 R	15	040
Branch, Edward C.	Hunter, Jane	27 SEP 1877 R	11	111
Brand, Edward James	Stofer, Mary	09 MAR 1882 R	16	271
Brandebury, Henry F.	Taylor, Ella P.	11 JUN 1885	20	265
Brandenburg, Frederick H.	Zeh, Virginia P.	29 NOV 1881 R	16	102
Brandenburg, Joseph	Bell, R.A., Mrs.	26 AUG 1877	11	064
Brandenburg, Pauline	Imhof, Friedrich	01 OCT 1882 R	17	045
Brandlinger, Lizzie	Newcomer, Frank	26 MAY 1879 R	13	205
Brandon, Virginia	Williams, Solomon	26 JAN 1882 L	16	212
Brandon, William	Williams, Mary	13 MAY 1880 R	14	218
Brandt, Adam	McDonald, Lizzie S.	04 FEB 1884	18	408
Brandt, Emma	Grosskurth, William	21 SEP 1884	19	261
Brandt, George	Heinemann, Marian S.	24 JUN 1884 L	19	099
Brandt, Rosa G.	Walsh, William	20 JUN 1883 L	18	006
Brandum, Maggie	Johnson, Henry	20 FEB 1882 R	16	250
Braner, Charles Fent	Corcoran, Millie	25 AUG 1885 L	20	386
Branham, Ella	Sewell, James B.	28 APR 1881	15	277
Branham, Samuel	Powell, Mary	29 DEC 1877 L	11	280
Branham, Wilson A.	Henry, Fannie B.	12 JUL 1877 R	11	018

Brannagin, William	Butler, Elizabeth	25 OCT 1880 R	15	012
Brannan, Susan	Nelson, Henry	23 AUG 1877 L	11	063
Brannum, Sally	Moore, Madison	20 OCT 1883 L	18	203
Bransom, John James	Myers, Margaret	24 OCT 1883	18	208
Branson, Clara B.	Taylor, Robert	02 APR 1883	17	374
Branson, Fred Douglass	Parker, Maria	28 JUN 1883 L	18	024
Branson, Hannah	Smith, Richard	04 APR 1881 L	15	246
Branson, Louis Whitman	Only, Bertha W.	02 FEB 1885 R	19	451
Branson, Thomas	Scott, Addie	22 MAR 1878	11	389
Branson, William A.	Moulton, Laurelia L.	03 DEC 1884 L	19	435
Brant, Alice	Shepherd, Samuel	18 JUL 1883	18	052
Braselman, Carrie N.	Butt, S. Holland	25 SEP 1884	19	268
Braselman, Helen Marr	Simmons, Leo	10 NOV 1884 R	19	370
Braselman, Joseph R.	Southall, Ella C.	24 SEP 1878 R	12	232
Brashear, M. Larn	Kinsey, Kate B.	25 OCT 1883	18	213
Brashears, Ellen	Kent, Douglas	18 DEC 1879 L	14	057
Brashears, James T.	Wood, Hattie E.	20 FEB 1884	18	433
Braun, John	Filz, Susanne Marie	09 MAY 1880 R	14	261
Braund, Alice B.	King, R.F.	02 FEB 1880 L	14	132
Braund, Annie Phillips	Brice, Edward Clifton	04 DEC 1884	19	431
Brauninger, William	Denmead, Margaret	27 FEB 1883 L	17	321
Braunstein, Emma	Jordan, Richard E.	02 MAR 1880 R	14	170
Braunstein, Louis	Jones, Emily A.G.	18 SEP 1884	19	258
Brawner, Andrew	Howard, Sarah	25 DEC 1877 L	11	268
Brawner, Bettie E.	Lynn, Thomas H.	19 FEB 1880 R	14	160
Brawner, Calvin	Bales, Sarah	15 FEB 1882	16	241
Brawner, George W.	Studds, Laura A.	10 NOV 1881 R	16	071
Brawner, Harriet	Arnold, Henry	17 APR 1882 L	16	321
Brawner, Louisa P.	King, James W.	07 NOV 1878	12	312
Brawner, Mollie T.	Carr, John C.	04 OCT 1882 R	17	052
Brawner, William	Dutton, Ida	11 AUG 1879 L	13	315
Braxon, Virginia	Ford, Harrison	06 OCT 1885	20	421
Braxton, Annie	Smith, Elias	04 OCT 1884 L	19	285
Braxton, Charles Ely	Bishop, Cassie A.	12 SEP 1877	11	087
Braxton, Durry	Crosby, Amanda	23 JAN 1884 L	18	392
Braxton, Eliza	Carter, Patrick	23 NOV 1880 R	15	062
Braxton, Eliza	Squals, James	20 NOV 1883 R	18	252
Braxton, Ella M.	Tines, Simon	24 OCT 1878 L	12	292
Braxton, Fanny	Phillips, Samuel	11 APR 1878 R	12	001
Braxton, Ida J.	Warren, George K.	11 JUN 1884	19	076
Braxton, John	Poindexter, Sarah	13 FEB 1885 R	20	041
Braxton, John W.	Taylor, Carrie C.	14 NOV 1878 R	12	313
Braxton, Louisa N.	Pryor, Ellsworth	23 AUG 1884	19	204
Braxton, Martha	Scipieo, Charles William	15 MAR 1883 L	17	347
Braxton, Nora	James, William	16 SEP 1884 L	19	251
Braxton, Sallie Ann	Carter, Mansfield	02 DEC 1883	18	289
Braxton, Thomas	Kenney, Sarah Jane	07 FEB 1883 R	17	299
Braxton, Washington	Simmons, Melinda	21 AUG 1878 R	12	183
Braxton, Washington	Brown, Ruth Anna	22 JAN 1884	18	390
Bray, C.A.	Beazley, Alva N.	07 MAY 1884	19	010
Bray, George	Tyre, Rosa, Mrs.	28 APR 1881 R	15	278
Bray, Henry	Curtis, Hannah	17 AUG 1885	20	373
Brayton, S.W.	Wheeler, F.M.	14 APR 1879 L	13	141
Braywood, Julia	Gregan, John	28 DEC 1881 R	16	167
Brebaker, George Henry	Yockel, Mary Josephine	12 JUN 1883 R	17	489
Brecht, Mamie J.	Griffith, Joseph I.	26 FEB 1885 R	20	087
Breck, Annie C.	Tilp, Frederick	13 FEB 1879 R	13	055
Breckenridge, Hattie	Johnson, Gilbert	12 SEP 1885 R	20	412

Name	Spouse	Date	Vol	Page
Bredekamp, Ellanora	Lipphard, William A.	16 JUL 1878 R	12	133
Bredekamp, Henry	Nessenson, Sophia	28 FEB 1884	18	449
Breen, Thomas Henry	Bailey, Jane Titus	13 FEB 1878 R	11	336
Breeze, Caroline	Schultz, Ludwig E.	25 MAY 1884 R	19	036
Bregstone, Miles	Levi, Fannie	08 FEB 1885 R	20	057
Breithaupt, Riggie	Glück, John Peter	16 NOV 1884	19	384
Brelsford, Frances Cornelia	Kiesecker, William	20 MAR 1880 R	14	191
Bremann, J.I.	Chrisall, Josephine	15 NOV 1884 L	19	383
Bremer, John T.	Brien, Dora	18 AUG 1880 R	14	404
Bremerman, Clara	Lenz, George A.	21 OCT 1878 L	12	284
Bremerman, Phoebe S.	Kirby, Frank E.	15 MAY 1883 L	17	440
Bremmehl, Lillie	Richards, Benjamin R.	14 OCT 1877	11	131
Bremmer, William	Nasser, Emily Virginia	19 OCT 1880 R	14	491
Brennan, Bridget Agnes	Malley, John O.	05 APR 1885	20	143
Brennan, Catharine M.C.	Benhan, Isaac	28 JAN 1880 R	14	124
Brennan, David	Bailey, Charlotte E.	01 MAR 1883 R	17	331
Brennan, John	Hunter, Maria	07 APR 1885 R	20	147
Brenner, William	Abbott, Harriet	04 MAR 1881 R	15	214
Brennon, Kate, Mrs.	Hughes, Thomas	03 FEB 1878 R	11	325
Brenoten, Rosie E.	Donalson, Emmet	30 SEP 1884 L	19	274
Brent, Amos D.	Awkward, Emma D.	07 MAY 1885 R	20	211
Brent, Elizabeth A.	Dewalt, William C.	28 MAR 1883 L	17	365
Brent, Hattie	Cook, Thomas	26 JUN 1884	19	107
Brent, Jane	Bias, Henry	21 MAR 1878 R	11	389
Brent, Jennie D.	Johnson, William H.	27 NOV 1877	11	197
Brent, John	Bias, Fannie	25 JAN 1882 L	16	210
Brent, Louis	Kattenberg, Minna	15 JUL 1882 R	16	449
Brent, Martha E.	Alexander, Thomas A.	17 JAN 1880 L	14	110
Brent, Mary	Parker, Charles	07 NOV 1877 R	11	170
Brent, Robert	Coleman, Clara	15 MAY 1879 R	13	172
Brent, William	Jackson, Mary	02 JUN 1884 L	19	049
Brent, William H.	Smith, Carrie L.	04 AUG 1881	15	420
Brent, William Henry	Taylor, Charlotte	29 NOV 1880	15	071
Brent, William R.	Steele, Minnie Ann	14 APR 1881 L	15	258
Bresenhan, Hanorah	Trainor, Eugene	26 MAY 1885	20	240
Breslauer, Adeline	Blondheim, Henry	17 JAN 1883 R	17	261
Breslauer, Ferdinand	Gross, Clara	05 AUG 1877 R	11	040
Bresnahan, Catharine Cecilia	Evans, Richard May	17 FEB 1879 R	13	062
Bresnahan, Johanna A.	Robey, Lucien E.	23 JUN 1884 L	19	096
Bresnahan, Katie E.	Newham, Thomas J.	13 MAY 1878 L	12	049
Bresnahan, Margaret	O'Connell, Michael	22 JAN 1885 L	20	033
Bresnahan, P.J.	Byrnes, Cecilia	16 SEP 1882 L	17	024
Bresnan, Mary	Keliher, Jams	28 MAR 1883 R	27	6598
Brethauer, August	Herfurth, Augusta	11 JUL 1883 L	18	043
Bretsch, Charles M.	Deboy, Mary E.	06 MAY 1883	17	425
Bretsch, Magdalena	Becker, John	02 JUN 1881	15	338
Brett, John A.	Godmell, Annie E.	29 NOV 1877	11	211
Brewer, Archibald	Dade, Lizzie	25 APR 1878 R	12	024
Brewer, Elizabeth Patten	Fisher, Flavius Josephus	27 JUN 1883 R	18	021
Brewer, Fanny	Tenley, Andrew F.	13 NOV 1881 R	16	064
Brewer, George J.	Finley, Laura	19 DEC 1883	18	325
Brewer, Harrison Gaston	Elliott, Marcie	19 OCT 1881 R	16	031
Brewer, James	Boyd, Mary	02 MAR 1882 L	16	264
Brewer, Mary	Burgee, Samuel M.	30 NOV 1883 L	18	288
Brewer, Mary	Jackson, Ernest	07 AUG 1883 L	18	076
Brewer, Nannie B.	Graves, John W.	28 NOV 1883	18	284
Brewer, Nathan	Dotson, Lizzie	21 NOV 1881	16	086
Brewer, Philip	Duvall, Anna	07 SEP 1882 L	17	012

D.C. Marriage Records Index, June 28, 1877 to October 19, 1885

Brewster, Mary Walker	Koons, Robert John W.	06 FEB 1883 R	17	291
Brewster, Robert J.W.	Shoemaker, Leila	19 OCT 1885 R	20	493
Brewton, William W.	Duvall, Emma A.	29 MAY 1884 L	19	045
Brian, Sophia	Johnson, Chester	13 NOV 1878 R	12	324
Briant, Margaret Eliza	Muse, William Henry	20 SEP 1880	14	452
Brice, Amanda	Honesty, Asbury	27 DEC 1877 L	11	275
Brice, Edward Clifton	Braund, Annie Phillips	04 DEC 1884	19	431
Brice, Maude	Thompson, Augustus	04 MAR 1884 R	18	456
Brice, Robert	Phillips, Alice	14 OCT 1885 R	20	482
Bricker, Joseph W.	Schlorb, Katie	18 JUN 1883 R	17	498
Brickhead, Charles E.	Fowler, Ella A.	18 MAY 1881	15	313
Bridge, Anna H.	Webb, Asbury M.	10 JUL 1883 L	18	041
Bridges, Benjamin, Jr.	Palmer, Alice V.	29 APR 1880 R	14	244
Bridges, Hattie Maria	Hyer, Charles Statler	22 APR 1885 R	20	183
Bridget, Emma	Sanner, Harry	05 OCT 1880 R	14	474
Bridget, Katie V.	Everett, Joseph Samuel	23 SEP 1879 R	13	382
Bridget, Sarah A.	Burns, John	02 AUG 1879 L	13	304
Bridgett, Jerome	Athey, Katie	23 OCT 1879 R	13	436
Bridgman, Harriett M.	Sterling, Daniel G.	13 AUG 1884	19	183
Bridwell, Adelaide	Fowler, Marion M.	23 APR 1884	18	527
Brien, Dora	Bremer, John T.	18 AUG 1880 R	14	404
Briggs, Alfred Benthall	Shryock, Carrie Biddle	08 AUG 1882 R	16	471
Briggs, Edmund B.	Combs, Leonora J.	01 JAN 1881	15	135
Briggs, Mary[2]	Ballard, Augustus W.	14 DEC 1878 L	12	380
Briggs, Orlando	Washington, Rebecca	27 DEC 1882 R	17	211
Briggs, Rachel	Lewis, David E.	29 MAR 1881 R	15	240
Briggs, Solomon R.	Kleinhause, Susie E.	03 APR 1879 R	13	122
Brightwell, Elizabeth	Kibble, Alexander	19 AUG 1879 R	13	325
Brightwell, John W.	McCormick, Matilda	07 NOV 1882	17	113
Brightwell, Sarah Virginia	Keonig, Peter E.	17 JUL 1884	19	144
Briles, Maggie	Carroll, Edward	20 JUL 1881	15	410
Briles, William A.	Clark, Elizabeth	22 FEB 1881 L	15	198
Brill, Louis	Schulz, Annie	05 JUN 1882	16	391
Briner, William B.	Conley, Mary L.	02 JUL 1884 L	19	116
Briney, Elizabeth C.	Taylor, Robert V.	20 MAY 1878 L	12	059
Bringas, Luis	West, Susan Elizabeth	22 DEC 1884 L	19	477
Brinkerhoff, Henry S.	Warren, Margaret	18 SEP 1878 R	12	224
Brinkley, Alice R.	Lewis, Albert E.	26 NOV 1884 R	19	421
Brinkley, Cora M.	Hayden, Richard B.	28 APR 1881 R	15	280
Brinkley, Minnie J.	Taltavull, Peter A.	15 JUL 1885 L	20	328
Brinkmann, W. Henry	Weber, Emilie K.	09 SEP 1885	20	406
Brintnall, Catherine J.	Curry, Levi	08 JAN 1885 R	20	009
Brisco, Frank	Washington, Ella	07 NOV 1878	12	314
Briscoe, Abraham L.	Washington, Ella E.	01 MAR 1883 R	17	328
Briscoe, Alexander	Moseley, Sophia	09 JUL 1878 L	12	130
Briscoe, Alice B.	Baker, Jacob	03 OCT 1878 R	12	248
Briscoe, Benjamin Franklin	Prather, Annie Darius	25 SEP 1879 R	13	384
Briscoe, Charles M.	Simms, nannie	20 JUN 1883	18	007
Briscoe, Eliza	Chiffins, Richard	29 DEC 1882	16	069
Briscoe, Emma	Bowen, John Wayne	27 NOV 1877 R	11	205
Briscoe, Emma	Burley, Benjamin J.	15 NOV 1882 L	17	130
Briscoe, Geo. Wash.	Duckett, Martha	03 JAN 1882 L	16	177
Briscoe, Henrietta	Smith, Fred	20 JUN 1881 L	15	368
Briscoe, James	Clark, Annie	15 FEB 1883 R	17	306
Briscoe, James	Turner, Louisa	13 JUN 1884 R	19	064
Briscoe, James W.	Butler, Annie E.	22 FEB 1883 L	17	318

[2] Cancelled license because of Lady's death, 30 MAR 1880.

Briscoe, John	Brooks, Emma	09 JUN 1880 R	14	293
Briscoe, John W.	Carroll, Mary E.	07 SEP 1885 L	20	402
Briscoe, Maud M.	Henson, David J.	07 MAY 1885 L	20	214
Briscoe, Moses	Lomax, Julia	21 AUG 1884 L	19	198
Briscoe, Nellie	Crowley, Jeremiah	14 JAN 1885	20	016
Briscoe, Sargent	Cryler, Margaret	09 SEP 1885 R	20	409
Briscoe, Spencer	Douglas, Julia	01 MAY 1884 L	19	001
Briscoe, Spencer	Douglass, Julia	01 MAY 1884 L	18	546
Briscoe, William	Morgan, Frances	01 FEB 1881 L	15	172
Briscoll, Mary Ann	Malloy, Edwin	18 MAR 1879 R	13	105
Brissey, Agnes	Cornell, John B.	23 JUN 1879	13	244
Brissey, Louisa	Jeffries, John T.	23 JUN 1879 R	13	244
Britt, G.S.	Frazier, Fannie M.	21 FEB 1880	14	162
Britt, Mary A.	Robinson, Charles G.	19 MAY 1880 R	14	274
Britt, Pierce	Tounay, Johanna	04 OCT 1883 L	18	174
Britt, Sallie H.	Cross, Francis E.	26 DEC 1883 R	18	340
Brittain, Clara Belle	King, John J.	09 JAN 1885 R	19	516
Brittain, Milton J.	Knight, Lizzie G.	31 JUL 1877 L	11	034
Britten, Belle	Galt, Walter Allen	09 FEB 1884 R	18	417
Broach, Alice	Mayo, George W.	14 AUG 1882	16	478
Broadbent, William	David, Lizzie	18 AUG 1883 R	18	076
Broadis, Millie M.	Wallace, William S.	24 DEC 1877 L	11	261
Broadus, Elizabeth	Stanton, Frank	31 MAR 1885 L	20	139
Broadus, John S.	Bradley, Polly, Mrs.	06 JAN 1880 R	14	092
Broadus, Mary Jane	Daison, Alexander	09 FEB 1882 R	16	235
Broadus, Rosa Ann	Mantrow, Thos. Alexander	04 DEC 1879 L	14	031
Broadway, Richard R.	Freeman, Malinda Jane	15 AUG 1877 L	11	054
Broche, Gustavus	Solomon, Milanie	02 MAY 1883	17	426
Brock, Charles A.	Hevener, Lizzie C.	31 DEC 1877 L	11	281
Brock, Eveline	Green, James W.	15 OCT 1879 R	13	420
Brock, Jacob	Baum, Frances	21 OCT 1880 R	15	009
Brock, M.E.	Ashley, Wm. M.	12 NOV 1879 R	13	180
Brock, William S.	Kelly, Julia S.	15 DEC 1881 R	16	134
Brockenborough, Edmund T.	Kay, Elizabeth	20 JUL 1878 L	12	143
Brockenborough, Lettie	Lively, Thomas	08 MAR 1881 L	15	219
Brockenbrough, Alice Bland	Plater, Mayhew	29 NOV 1883	18	280
Brocker, Jennie	Schneider, George W.	17 MAR 1884 R	18	473
Brockhaus, Anna	Nephutt, Andrew	08 JAN 1882	16	186
Brockwell, Roselle	Williams, Edith C.	29 SEP 1885 R	20	445
Brod, Charles Emile	Phillippi, Mane Josephine	16 AUG 1880 R	14	400
Brodekamp, Mary C.	Helvin, George W.	08 SEP 1879	13	356
Broden, Mary	Palmer, John M.	19 JUL 1880 R	14	342
Broderick, Bridget E.	Bladen, John H.	19 FEB 1881 L	15	194
Broderick, Dennis	Odenhall, Ellen	04 DEC 1879 R	14	027
Broderick, Mary Ella	Gray, Charles Clinton	12 APR 1882 R	16	310
Broderick, Michael	Daley, Ellen	07 FEB 1882 L	16	228
Brodie, Albert K.	Syphax, Mary Ellinor	05 APR 1881 R	15	248
Brodie, Charles Cameron	Watson, Lucy Marion	19 FEB 1883 R	17	312
Brodie, Jenettie A.	Shirley, James Woodford	18 DEC 1877 R	11	245
Brodiecamp, Matilda	Owens, John H.	10 JUN 1882 L	16	404
Brodnax, Robert W.	Foster, Mary Elizabeth	23 MAR 1883	17	356
Brodracht, Marie E.	Sheehy, Henry	18 JUL 1883	18	051
Broeker, Mary	Kober, Charles	10 JUL 1884	19	134
Brogden, Josiah	Taylor, Sallie Ann	05 SEP 1878 L	12	202
Brokenborough, Rachel	Gilton, Doctor	19 DEC 1878 R	12	392
Broman, Andrew	McKenna, Laura	27 NOV 1877 R	11	205
Bromley, Frank C.	Peckham, Willimine W.	30 OCT 1884	19	344
Brond, Emilie	Wilson, Perry	02 JUN 1885 R	20	283

Bronson, George W.	Craig, Emeline A.	08 FEB 1880	14	140
Bronson, Ida	Henry, James	31 OCT 1881 L	16	053
Bronson, Maggie	Salusbury, John M.	27 DEC 1877	11	276
Brook, Caroline	Payne, James	19 JUL 1877 L	11	027
Brook, Felix Q.	Cory, Lillian A.	27 NOV 1884	19	419
Brook, Nancy	Norman, William	24 OCT 1878	12	288
Brooke, Albert	Taylor, Bettie Ambler	01 DEC 1881 R	16	105
Brooke, Alexander M.	Fenwick, Catherine E.	20 NOV 1877 L	11	194
Brooke, Alice	Malone, William J.	09 FEB 1881 R	15	185
Brooke, Annie F.	Magruder, Samuel F.	20 NOV 1884 L	19	398
Brooke, John W.	Sheckells, Annie J.	30 OCT 1877 R	11	160
Brooke, Kate	Johnson, John	06 OCT 1885 R	20	460
Brooke, Louisa Hamilton	Bailey, Lorenzo Alton	04 NOV 1882 R	17	110
Brooke, Mary E.	Cox, Stephen A.	07 OCT 1880 R	14	481
Brooke, Sarah Acklin	Cartwright, Levin T.	30 SEP 1885 R	20	450
Brooke, Susan	Wills, Samuel	10 SEP 1884 L	19	239
Brooke, Thomas H., Jr.	Kirby, Susan V.	05 JUL 1884	19	126
Brooke, William E.	Clarvoe, A.M.C.	23 DEC 1879 R	14	065
Brooker, Aaron M.	Hatcher, Margaret	25 JUL 1883 R	18	060
Brooker, Laura	Mason, F.M.	29 MAR 1883 L	17	369
Brooker, Milley	Adams, Isaiah	20 JUN 1881 L	15	368
Brooker, Sarah	Eastland, Richard	27 NOV 1879	14	012
Brooker, William	Guy, Martha Etta	26 AUG 1880 R	14	412
Brooker, William H.	Ashton, Ida	11 DEC 1883	18	309
Brookes, Stephen	Towles, Martha	16 DEC 1884	19	460
Brooking, Peter G.	Richardson, Margaret	08 SEP 1881 L	15	479
Brooks, Albert	Ware, Lucinda	23 SEP 1880	14	456
Brooks, Alcena	Queen, Frank	25 FEB 1881 R	15	204
Brooks, Alex. H.	Smith, Mary E.	06 MAY 1880 R	14	255
Brooks, Alexander	Edderson, Laura	21 APR 1881 R	15	267
Brooks, Alice	Carroll, William	09 JUN 1880 L	14	313
Brooks, Anastatia E.	Thomas, Walter S.	12 FEB 1880 R	14	150
Brooks, Anna R.	Green, William W.F.	24 JAN 1884	18	394
Brooks, Annie	Smith, Henry	20 DEC 1877 R	11	252
Brooks, Annie	Butler, Nathaniel	13 APR 1885 L	20	161
Brooks, Annie E.	Meredith, Peter B.	17 DEC 1884 L	19	466
Brooks, Annie P.	Swann, Richard J.	26 DEC 1877 R	11	270
Brooks, Arthur J.	Jefferson, Carrie	07 OCT 1880 L	14	479
Brooks, Aurelia	Digges, Alfred P.	03 MAR 1885	20	090
Brooks, Belle	Banks, Nathaniel P.	24 FEB 1885 L	20	084
Brooks, Bellzora	Penn, Isaiah G.	12 APR 1882	16	311
Brooks, Bettie	Makle, Brook	09 FEB 1884 L	18	417
Brooks, Carrie	Wells, Daniel	07 MAR 1883 L	17	337
Brooks, Cecilia	Boulden, James A.	11 APR 1881 L	15	253
Brooks, Charles	Chase, Jennie	15 NOV 1883	18	256
Brooks, Charles	McKenzie, Cannetta	22 NOV 1883 L	18	272
Brooks, Charles	Hawkins, Mary	05 MAR 1885	20	098
Brooks, Charles E.	Brown, Susie C.	11 JAN 1883 R	17	248
Brooks, Charles W.	Barry, Virginia	01 AUG 1885	20	346
Brooks, Clarke J.	Washburn, Susie F.	19 SEP 1882 L	17	027
Brooks, Daniel	Matney, Jennie	12 APR 1884	18	464
Brooks, David	Craig, Emma J.	31 AUG 1882 R	16	497
Brooks, Eli	Martin, Sarah	09 MAR 1882 L	16	272
Brooks, Eliza	Thomas, Dennis	01 SEP 1881 R	15	467
Brooks, Eliza	Harridy, Richard	01 FEB 1883	17	284
Brooks, Eliza Jane	Grady, Lewis	25 DEC 1880 R	15	120
Brooks, Ella Geneva	Lane, Andrew Jackson	13 OCT 1881 R	16	022
Brooks, Ellen N.C.	Freeburger, Peter V.	23 JUL 1882 R	16	450

Brooks, Elmira Cora	Eskridge, Albert	07 OCT 1880 R	14	479
Brooks, Emma	Taylor, Arthur	13 AUG 1877 R	11	036
Brooks, Emma	Rainey, Ferdinand	25 JUN 1879 R	13	247
Brooks, Emma	Briscoe, John	09 JUN 1880 R	14	293
Brooks, Emma Adelle	Schneider, Louis H.	17 JAN 1883	17	263
Brooks, Eva S.	Johnston, Henry A.	10 NOV 1880 R	15	041
Brooks, Frank	Jenkins, Maria	29 MAR 1880	14	201
Brooks, George	Henson, Annie	16 DEC 1880 R	15	093
Brooks, George H.	Richards, Annie Bradocks	07 JUL 1878 R	12	125
Brooks, Harriet	Buchanan, Dennis	15 JUL 1877 R	11	007
Brooks, Harriet	Holland, Edward	22 JUL 1879 R	13	286
Brooks, Hattie	Calvert, William	25 APR 1882 L	16	333
Brooks, Hattie F.	Coombs, Charles C.	16 APR 1882	16	322
Brooks, Henry	Parker, Columbia	16 JUN 1879 R	13	198
Brooks, Henry	Wilson, Adaline Hester	17 SEP 1884 L	19	254
Brooks, Henry J.	Walker, Elizabeth M.	12 JUL 1877 R	11	015
Brooks, Henry T.	Anderson, Sarah	18 JUN 1879 L	13	236
Brooks, Henson	Murray, Virginia	05 DEC 1884 L	19	437
Brooks, Isabella	Lancaster, Benjamin	13 OCT 1880 R	14	492
Brooks, Jackson D.	Larkin, Attie A.	21 APR 1880 L	14	231
Brooks, James	Evans, Nancy	26 MAR 1879 L	13	116
Brooks, James	Smith, Catherine	02 AUG 1883	18	067
Brooks, James	Stepney, Mary	10 MAR 1885 R	20	058
Brooks, James Edward	Bailey, Luretta	11 JAN 1883	17	251
Brooks, James N.	Taylor, Clara S.	16 MAY 1885 L	20	225
Brooks, Jane	Hill, Henry	13 DEC 1883 L	18	315
Brooks, Janie W.	Stewart, John T.	20 AUG 1884	19	194
Brooks, Jennie E.	White, Simon	14 JUN 1883 R	17	495
Brooks, John	Parker, Frances, Mrs.	20 MAR 1882 L	16	283
Brooks, John C.F.	Bolden, Frances E.	12 MAY 1879 L	13	185
Brooks, John E.	Jones, Georgie	26 AUG 1879 R	13	336
Brooks, John H.	Travis, Maria	23 DEC 1879 R	14	007
Brooks, John Thomas	Reed, Eliza	19 JUL 1877	11	027
Brooks, Joseph	Sidney, Lizzie	09 DEC 1879 L	14	036
Brooks, Julia A.	Curtis, Wallace L.	14 AUG 1878 L	12	168
Brooks, Kate	Jackson, John Henry	31 NOV 1877 L	11	196
Brooks, Kate	Dixon, Carter	03 JUL 1883 L	18	033
Brooks, Landonia	Turner, Isaac	26 JUN 1879 L	13	252
Brooks, Levi	Jones, Elizabeth	16 NOV 1881	16	074
Brooks, Lewis	Thomas, Clara	16 NOV 1880	15	049
Brooks, Lizzie	Johnson, Lee	03 JAN 1884 L	18	364
Brooks, Lloyd B.	Easby, Esther R.	25 DEC 1879	14	007
Brooks, Lovely	Skinner, Charles	27 DEC 1877 L	11	275
Brooks, Lucy Ellen	Young, Anderson	05 SEP 1882	17	004
Brooks, Maria W.	Hayson, Abraham	11 SEP 1877	11	086
Brooks, Mary	Martin, Edward	21 JUL 1880 R	14	370
Brooks, Mary	Smith, Henry	19 MAY 1884 R	19	028
Brooks, Mary	Taylor, Thornton	23 OCT 1884 L	19	335
Brooks, Mary Ann	Holland, Alexander	08 SEP 1879 R	13	357
Brooks, Mary Bettie	Chase, Silas	17 OCT 1883	18	179
Brooks, Mary E.	Dyson, William	22 JUL 1880 L	14	373
Brooks, Mary V.	Dickson, Charles	02 AUG 1883 R	18	073
Brooks, Milton T.	Gray, Mary E.	11 AUG 1884	19	168
Brooks, Nanie	Hill, Robert W.	26 JUN 1883	18	016
Brooks, Nellie	Harris, David	22 JAN 1880 R	14	110
Brooks, Orlando	Dyer, Alice	16 OCT 1882	17	074
Brooks, Oscar	Jackson, Anna	27 AUG 1884 L	19	212
Brooks, Patsey A.	Peters, Harry	24 NOV 1884 L	19	405

Brooks, Peter	Key, Lucinda	11 NOV 1878	12	321
Brooks, Peter	Bruce, Elivina	07 AUG 1884	19	173
Brooks, Philip	Bingham, Sarah	23 SEP 1882 L	17	034
Brooks, Philip	Taylor, Ann	18 MAR 1884 L	18	474
Brooks, Phobe	Smith, Samuel	03 MAR 1881 R	15	212
Brooks, Preston	Dodson, Victoria	06 MAY 1884 R	19	003
Brooks, Preston	Dodson, Victoria	03 MAY 1884	18	549
Brooks, Rosetta	Minnis, Thomas M.	29 APR 1879 R	13	162
Brooks, Rufus C.	Goetz, Julia	13 SEP 1877 R	11	091
Brooks, Sarah	West, Joseph	27 MAR 1879 R	13	104
Brooks, Sarah	Turner, Franklin P.	14 MAR 1883 L	17	343
Brooks, Sarah	Logan, Toliver	14 AUG 1884	19	186
Brooks, Solomon	Arthur, Ann C.	04 NOV 1884 L	19	357
Brooks, Sophia	Vier, James	04 DEC 1879 R	14	028
Brooks, Susanna	Logans, Robert	19 JUN 1879	13	240
Brooks, Susannah V.	Gaither, James B.	19 JUN 1879	13	238
Brooks, Theodore	Jackson, Mattie	10 OCT 1878 L	12	265
Brooks, Theresa V.	Fairfax, Robert T.	27 JAN 1885 L	20	039
Brooks, Thomas	Hill, Rachel	24 APR 1884 L	18	531
Brooks, Thomas B.	Nourse, Mamie W.	23 DEC 1879 R	14	068
Brooks, Thomas H.	Lucas, Maria A.	11 DEC 1884 L	19	453
Brooks, Tracey	Brown, Jeremiah	13 OCT 1877 L	11	133
Brooks, William	Rivers, Jane	26 SEP 1878	12	238
Brooks, William B.	Washington, Caroline	13 AUG 1884	19	183
Brooks, William F.	Scarff, Margaret J.	14 JUN 1882 R	16	411
Brooks, William H.	Richardson, Julia C.	09 MAY 1882 R	16	354
Brooks, William H.	Carroll, Sarah C.	05 NOV 1882 R	17	106
Broom, Andrew J.	Morgan, Lizzie	17 AUG 1882 L	16	483
Broomall, Clara	Grove, George	05 DEC 1879 L	14	031
Bros, Mary	Keli, James	06 JUL 1881 L	15	392
Brosius, George	Walters, Lizzie	01 JAN 1885 R	19	514
Brosnan, John	Roche, Katie A.	30 MAY 1878 L	12	076
Brosnan, Patrick A.	Harmon, Ella	03 OCT 1881 L	16	002
Brosshan, Mary D.	Suttle, James D.	13 JAN 1883 L	17	256
Brothers, Alcenia E.	White, Volney	12 JUN 1884	19	082
Brothers, Annie (Blondin)	Deans, Charles	26 MAY 1884 R	19	038
Brotherton, Isaac B.	French, Georgia J.	09 MAY 1878 R	12	046
Brotzell, Sarah Jane	Cumberland, George W.	02 JUN 1879 R	13	215
Brough, John H.	Woods, Elizabeth M.	11 DEC 1884	19	450
Broun, Charles Albert	Wrisley, Mary Louise	25 MAY 1881 R	15	324
Broune, William E.	Pridgeon, Mary Virginia	04 AUG 1885 L	20	350
Brower, Jane A.N.	Fales, Willard Noice	06 APR 1878 L	11	408
Brown, A.H.	Meserole, M.L., Mrs.	02 MAY 1878	12	036
Brown, Abraham	Green, Harriet Lucinda	05 APR 1882 R	16	300
Brown, Adaline C.	Gleason, John J.	30 SEP 1880	14	468
Brown, Addell	Freeman, Columbus	09 DEC 1880 R	15	088
Brown, Addie	Thomas, James	13 JUL 1878 L	12	134
Brown, Adeline	Carter, James	09 AUG 1880 R	14	321
Brown, Adeline	Hill, James T.	23 APR 1883 L	17	406
Brown, Agnes	Brown, Samuel L.	27 NOV 1879 R	14	006
Brown, Albert	Pinn, Mary	02 DEC 1880 R	15	077
Brown, Albert	Wilkerson, Martha	29 DEC 1881 L	16	169
Brown, Alex	Oda, Minnie	27 DEC 1883	18	346
Brown, Alexander D.	Bosley, Laura J.	21 AUG 1880 R	14	386
Brown, Alice	Banks, William	18 JUL 1878 L	12	141
Brown, Alice	Somerville, G. Alex	23 DEC 1879 R	14	066
Brown, Alice	Lewis, Henry F.	30 OCT 1883 L	18	222
Brown, Alice	Smothers, Joseph E.	10 JUL 1883 L	18	042

Brown, Alice	Hennigan, John	11 JUN 1885 R	20	052
Brown, Alice E.	Jordon, Harry B.	24 MAR 1880 L	14	195
Brown, Alice R.	Lambert, Henry	02 JUL 1879 R	13	260
Brown, Alice V.	Yates, Henry P.	17 DEC 1879 L	14	052
Brown, Allen G.P.	Commons, Mary C.	31 MAR 1879 R	13	120
Brown, Ambrose M.	Selby, Bettie E.	25 JUN 1885 R	20	292
Brown, Amelia A.	Robertson, John	14 FEB 1884 L	18	427
Brown, Andrew	Hill, Frazier	03 MAY 1881 L	15	290
Brown, Andrew A.	Digges, Maria L.	26 SEP 1882 R	17	036
Brown, Andrew R.	Thompson, Sallie E.	08 OCT 1878 R	12	262
Brown, Anna A.	Hutchinson, Alexander	16 AUG 1877 R	11	055
Brown, Anne	Dorsey, Lewis	09 FEB 1881 R	15	185
Brown, Annie	Brown, Henry F.	11 SEP 1877 L	11	088
Brown, Annie	Black, Asbury	06 SEP 1879 L	13	355
Brown, Annie	Moore, Squire	30 JUL 1879 R	13	299
Brown, Annie	Tilley, Joseph R.	08 OCT 1879 L	13	411
Brown, Annie	Bush, Chapman	07 DEC 1882	17	171
Brown, Annie	Dyson, John	26 DEC 1882 L	17	210
Brown, Annie	Harris, Joseph	16 AUG 1882 R	16	481
Brown, Annie	Hannan, Michael	12 SEP 1882 L	17	018
Brown, Annie	Thompson, James	08 DEC 1884 L	19	441
Brown, Annie Cooney	O'Brien, William	07 MAR 1880 R	14	176
Brown, Annie E.	Weller, M. Scott	13 MAY 1885 R	20	220
Brown, Annie Steele	Semple, Frank Buchanan	07 FEB 1882 R	16	226
Brown, Anthony	Jackson, Henrietta	03 FEB 1879 L	13	044
Brown, Arthur	Holmes, Mary J.	15 MAR 1883	17	342
Brown, Arthur	Fredrick, Mary Agnes	01 JAN 1884	18	338
Brown, Arthur	Payne, Martha	18 DEC 1884 L	19	472
Brown, Belle M.	Ward, Randolph G.	13 NOV 1882 L	17	124
Brown, Benjamin	Garnett, Gracie	25 SEP 1879 L	13	386
Brown, Benjamin F.	Lockwood, Lillie M.	20 SEP 1883 R	18	146
Brown, Benjamin H.	Wright, Rosa V.	18 APR 1878	12	011
Brown, Caroline	Nicholson, George	13 SEP 1879	13	367
Brown, Caroline	Bembry, John H.	21 APR 1881 R	15	267
Brown, Carrie	Jackson, Jesse	03 DEC 1877 L	11	215
Brown, Carrie	Elliot, Andrew	03 FEB 1879 R	13	042
Brown, Carrie	Adams, Sevi	29 DEC 1881	16	164
Brown, Carrie	Warfield, Richard	28 FEB 1881 R	15	207
Brown, Carrie	Wade, Frank	03 DEC 1883 L	18	292
Brown, Carrie A.	Waring, James H.N.	04 APR 1883 R	17	379
Brown, Catharine	Chesley, Washington	27 DEC 1877	11	257
Brown, Cecilia	Brown, John Francis	28 DEC 1877	11	272
Brown, Charles	Berry, Mary	05 JUN 1879	13	221
Brown, Charles	Whitney, Carrie	01 NOV 1879 L	13	458
Brown, Charles	Grandison, Ella	01 APR 1880 R	14	205
Brown, Charles	Freeman, Nancy	03 APR 1880 L	14	206
Brown, Charles	Mount, Ellen	02 MAY 1883 R	17	423
Brown, Charles C.	Banks, Gracie	14 DEC 1881 L	16	130
Brown, Charles E.	Tinney, A.B., Mrs.	20 MAR 1880 L	14	190
Brown, Charles E.	Reight, Emma	16 FEB 1884 L	18	428
Brown, Charles H.	Magruder, Henrietta	16 JAN 1879	13	023
Brown, Charles H.	Lacy, Jennie	27 MAY 1880 L	14	290
Brown, Charles H.	Moore, Lannia	27 SEP 1883 R	18	156
Brown, Charles H.	Boose, Florence R.	30 OCT 1884 L	19	351
Brown, Charles H.	Boone, Florence	30 OCT 1884 L	19	352
Brown, Charles H.	Holly, Carrie	17 JUN 1885 L	20	278
Brown, Charles L.	Van Dyck, Rose	05 MAR 1884 R	18	459
Brown, Charlotte	Johnson, Edward	26 APR 1883 R	17	413

D.C. Marriage Records Index, June 28, 1877 to October 19, 1885

Brown, Charlotte M.	Conger, Franklin Barker	14 JAN 1879 R	13	016
Brown, Clara	Tucker, Alexander	28 NOV 1878	12	354
Brown, Clara V.	Hogeland, D.M.	13 APR 1885	20	162
Brown, Cornelia	Brown, Joseph	04 AUG 1880	14	384
Brown, Corrie	Johnson, Charles H.	19 NOV 1878 L	12	337
Brown, Daniel	Brown, Rose	11 MAR 1882	16	271
Brown, David	Salzmann, Mary S.	22 JAN 1878 L	11	313
Brown, David	Shelton, Kaokie	17 NOV 1884 L	19	388
Brown, David H.P.	Booth, Mattie W. (Parraday)	29 SEP 1884 R	19	272
Brown, Doreter L.	Farris, Allan H.	24 OCT 1883 L	18	212
Brown, Douglas	Winston, Matilda	28 AUG 1879 R	13	343
Brown, Douglas A.	Donaldson, Ella E.	14 FEB 1883 R	17	305
Brown, Edgar J.	Butterhof, Mary M.	04 OCT 1883	18	169
Brown, Edward	Johnson, Lydia	12 SEP 1877 R	11	089
Brown, Edward	Kenney, Martha	31 OCT 1878	12	301
Brown, Edward	Jones, Marian	09 MAR 1880 R	14	180
Brown, Edward	Srays, Kate	03 NOV 1881 L	16	058
Brown, Edward F.	O'Brien, Jennie	20 DEC 1881 R	16	141
Brown, Edward H.	Hawkins, Amanda Ella	22 FEB 1883 L	17	319
Brown, Edward P.	Vaughan, Chaney	10 JAN 1878	11	299
Brown, Eliza	Reed, James Henry	11 OCT 1883	18	186
Brown, Eliza	Reese, John Wm. Henry	06 APR 1883 L	17	384
Brown, Eliza E.	Johnson, John	26 FEB 1880 R	14	164
Brown, Eliza E.	Johnson, William Henry	27 AUG 1885	20	386
Brown, Elizabeth	Washington, John E.	22 AUG 1878	12	177
Brown, Elizabeth	Aimes, James Franklin	21 NOV 1884	19	394
Brown, Elizabeth	Banks, Jesse	18 AUG 1884	19	192
Brown, Ella	King, Joseph E.	14 NOV 1878	12	331
Brown, Ella	Watts, John	25 DEC 1884	19	484
Brown, Ella	Wheeler, Thomas	25 MAR 1885	20	130
Brown, Emma	Hall, George Washington	11 AUG 1881 R	15	440
Brown, Emma	Fisher, Samuel D.	26 JUN 1883 R	18	015
Brown, Emma	Gannett, James	15 JAN 1883 L	17	258
Brown, Emma	Allen, Lemuel	15 APR 1885	20	168
Brown, Emma J.	Evans, Charles	27 AUG 1877	11	067
Brown, Emma J.	Magruder, William H.	02 DEC 1879 L	14	022
Brown, Emma J.	Gill, Stephen Fr., Jr.	24 SEP 1885 R	20	441
Brown, Emma V.	Montgomery, Henry P.	06 MAR 1879	13	093
Brown, Emma V.	Pierce, William W.	26 OCT 1880 R	15	011
Brown, Esther Ann	Fletcher, George Henry	08 JUL 1880 R	14	353
Brown, F. Oskie	Slater, John W.	20 OCT 1882 L	17	083
Brown, Fannie	Boyd, Jeemes	20 AUG 1879	13	323
Brown, Fannie	Smith, Lewis	07 AUG 1880	14	392
Brown, Fannie	Newman, Richard P.	15 OCT 1885 L	20	490
Brown, Fillmore	Scaggs, Alice	17 NOV 1884 R	19	389
Brown, Fisher	Fields, Fannie	19 AUG 1880 L	14	407
Brown, Florence E.	Dorsey, Noble	22 APR 1878 L	12	014
Brown, Francene L.	Sidman, George D.	24 JUN 1885 R	20	286
Brown, Frances	Robinson, Lewis	07 APR 1881 L	15	251
Brown, Francis Milton	Webster, Adele	17 FEB 1881 R	15	194
Brown, Frank	Cook, Catherine	11 NOV 1879 R	13	477
Brown, Frank	Wall, Rachel	19 DEC 1882 L	17	191
Brown, Frank A.	Duvall, Louisa M.	05 JUL 1883	18	038
Brown, Frederick	Williamson, Julia	24 JUL 1883 R	18	059
Brown, George	Feen, Chloe	24 OCT 1881 L	16	042
Brown, George	Jackson, Anna	14 DEC 1882	17	185
Brown, George Henry Johnson	Watts, Georgie Cornelia	26 FEB 1880 R	14	158
Brown, George Robert	Wright, Ella Elizabeth	15 MAR 1881 R	15	226

Brown, George W.	Page, Lucy	26 DEC 1881 L	16	159
Brown, George W.	Wiley, Frances M.	05 AUG 1885	20	355
Brown, Georgianna	Vogel, George	31 MAY 1880 R	14	297
Brown, Gracie	Hall, Henson	26 AUG 1879	13	334
Brown, Hannah Maria	Hicks, Silas	07 MAY 1884 R	19	010
Brown, Harriet	Johnson, James	23 OCT 1877 R	11	150
Brown, Harriet Jane	Gorain, Henry	15 FEB 1883 R	17	308
Brown, Harrison Bradley	Wilmouth, Delphine	19 OCT 1883 L	18	203
Brown, Harry A.	Tully, Cora B.	31 MAR 1880 R	14	179
Brown, Harry B.	McChesney, Mary Alice	12 JUN 1884	19	079
Brown, Harvey	Jackson, Eliza	28 MAR 1882 L	16	291
Brown, Helen	Woods, William Henry	27 MAR 1884 R	18	482
Brown, Helen	Berry, Wm. R.	15 OCT 1885	20	484
Brown, Henrietta	Parker, William	03 JUN 1884 L	19	053
Brown, Henrietta	Rich, Claybourn	25 DEC 1884	19	491
Brown, Henry	Taylor, Lucy	05 JAN 1878 L	11	293
Brown, Henry	Johnson, Ellenora	18 SEP 1879 L	13	377
Brown, Henry	Jenkins, Mary	01 SEP 1880 L	14	426
Brown, Henry	Battie, Allece	25 AUG 1881 L	15	458
Brown, Henry	Lambert, Connorn	05 DEC 1882 L	17	167
Brown, Henry	King, Emma	27 SEP 1883 R	18	158
Brown, Henry F.	Brown, Annie	11 SEP 1877 L	11	088
Brown, Henry T.	McElfresh, Rose E.	15 APR 1885 R	20	167
Brown, Hettie E.	Miller, Nelson	07 JAN 1883 R	17	240
Brown, Hodge	Smith, Mattie	20 SEP 1882 L	17	030
Brown, Horace	Rochbuck, Clarrisa B.	10 JUN 1880 R	14	312
Brown, Hugh F.	Gordan, Nancy J.	15 SEP 1884 L	19	247
Brown, Ida	Holmes, Thomas	27 AUG 1878	12	182
Brown, Ida	Baley, George	23 JUN 1884	19	098
Brown, Ida	Ford, Henry	22 SEP 1885	20	435
Brown, Ida E.	Stant, George W.	06 SEP 1880 R	14	429
Brown, Ida M.	Aglien, John Benjamin	30 MAR 1882 L	16	294
Brown, Isaac	Plummer, Mary	20 JUL 1880	14	369
Brown, Isaac	Pinckney, Gabriella	16 AUG 1881 L	15	447
Brown, Isaac	Watts, Mary E.	10 JAN 1882 L	16	188
Brown, Isaac	Thomas, Fannie	18 MAY 1882	16	366
Brown, Isaac B.	Coakley, Gertrude	28 NOV 1883 L	18	283
Brown, J. Ingalls	West, Nettie A.	15 FEB 1883 R	17	307
Brown, J.S.	Barbour, J.E.	15 JAN 1885	20	015
Brown, J.W.	Henson, Katie	06 JAN 1885	20	006
Brown, James	Jackson, Melinda	28 NOV 1877 L	11	211
Brown, James	Griffin, Fannie	24 OCT 1878	12	289
Brown, James	Kane, Sarah	29 JUL 1880 R	14	378
Brown, James	Dent, Isabella	18 OCT 1883 L	18	202
Brown, James S.	Hansbrough, Fannie C.	15 JUL 1880 R	14	359
Brown, James W.	Dutton, Elizabeth M.	23 JUN 1881 L	15	375
Brown, Jane	Reynolds, Samuel C.A.	15 MAY 1878	12	051
Brown, Jane	Gantt, John Wesley	27 MAR 1883 L	17	362
Brown, Jane R.	Williams, Beverly D.	12 DEC 1882	17	180
Brown, Jennie Catherine	Roberson, Thomas Gordon	25 APR 1883 R	18	409
Brown, Jeremiah	Brooks, Tracey	13 OCT 1877 L	11	133
Brown, Joanna F.	Rose, Willis	27 OCT 1881 L	16	051
Brown, John	Smith, Elizabeth	21 DEC 1877 R	11	256
Brown, John	Taylor, Fanny	08 MAY 1878	12	040
Brown, John	Paine, Lillie	01 APR 1880 L	14	204
Brown, John	Magruder, Elizabeth Ellen	08 MAR 1883 R	17	339
Brown, John	Smith, Elizabeth	18 MAR 1884 R	18	468
Brown, John B.	Lanham, Rachel	02 JUL 1881 L	15	384

D.C. Marriage Records Index, June 28, 1877 to October 19, 1885

Brown, John Francis	Brown, Cecilia	28 DEC 1877	11	272
Brown, John H.	Williams, Harriet	26 MAY 1881	15	323
Brown, John H.	Craig, Rhoda	02 MAY 1883 L	17	426
Brown, John H.	Green, Ella M.	03 JUL 1883	18	032
Brown, John Henry	Dean, Carrie	11 MAY 1882 L	16	357
Brown, John M.	Folkes, Susan A.	16 OCT 1877 L	11	138
Brown, John M.	Johnson, Maria B.	06 JAN 1879 R	13	007
Brown, John R.	McGuire, Blanche S.	08 SEP 1880 L	14	436
Brown, John R.	Francis, Sarah Elizabeth	20 SEP 1883 R	18	143
Brown, John Samuel	Blackwell, Jane	26 MAR 1879 L	13	115
Brown, John William	Bell, Sophy	13 FEB 1883	17	297
Brown, Jordan	Backus, Amelia, Mrs.	29 NOV 1878 R	12	372
Brown, Joseph	Brown, Cornelia	04 AUG 1880	14	384
Brown, Joseph	Paine, Martha	06 DEC 1883 L	18	300
Brown, Joseph	Jones, Margaret	04 MAY 1885 R	20	203
Brown, Josephine	Nalls, Bryant B.	21 JAN 1879 R	13	025
Brown, Josephine	Newton, Francis	06 MAY 1880 R	14	256
Brown, Josephine	Gray, Andrew Ellsworth	16 SEP 1885 R	20	420
Brown, Josephine N.	McCallister, Charles D.	12 AUG 1882 R	16	478
Brown, Joshua A.	Robson, mary Ann	23 JUN 1883 L	18	012
Brown, Julius	Stern, Selina	03 JUN 1883 R	17	471
Brown, Kate	Griffin, George M.	31 MAR 1884 L	18	488
Brown, Kate E.	Harvey, Robert W.	11 JAN 1882 R	16	190
Brown, Katie	Anderson, Oppy	20 AUG 1884 L	19	197
Brown, Katie	Price, Albert Sidney Johnson	28 MAY 1884 R	19	041
Brown, Katie A.	Hands, John	14 JAN 1884 L	18	376
Brown, Katie F.	Ingle, Samuel S.	18 SEP 1882 L	17	025
Brown, Laura	Gorham, Charles E.	26 NOV 1879 R	14	010
Brown, Laura B.	Anderson, Stephen	27 FEB 1879 R	13	083
Brown, Laura R.A.	Janifer, George C.	03 JUL 1879	13	267
Brown, Lewis	Smith, Dolly	14 AUG 1882	14	019
Brown, Libbie G.	Simpson, Elmer E.	21 MAY 1884	19	031
Brown, Lillie A.	Brady, Peyton	23 JUL 1884	19	145
Brown, Lizzie	Hawkins, James	01 MAY 1882	16	342
Brown, Lizzie	Butler, Joseph A.	09 APR 1883 L	17	388
Brown, Lizzie A.	Welsh, John E.	12 MAR 1883 L	17	341
Brown, Lottie	Washington, John	15 APR 1881 R	15	256
Brown, Lou	Mahoney, Bub	29 MAY 1882 L	16	381
Brown, Louisa	Dunmore, Benjamin	19 DEC 1878	12	382
Brown, Louisa	Holmes, Edward	04 SEP 1879	13	353
Brown, Louisa	Thomas, William H.W.	02 APR 1879 L	13	124
Brown, Louisa Alberta	Robinson, Robert E.	22 AUG 1878 R	12	147
Brown, Louise Palmer	Crossfield, Amasa Scott	04 APR 1883 R	17	373
Brown, Lucie B.	Carter, Robert R.	06 JUL 1881 L	15	393
Brown, Lucinda	Harrity, John	28 SEP 1881 L	15	502
Brown, Lucindia	Addison, Thomas	18 DEC 1879 R	14	058
Brown, Lucy	Nelson, Augustus	10 JAN 1878 R	11	300
Brown, Lucy Dora	Jones, Moses	25 AUG 1879	13	333
Brown, Lucy R.	Flint, Weston	14 JUN 1883 R	17	492
Brown, Lulie J.	Clark, Edward B.	03 DEC 1878 L	12	362
Brown, Lydia	Terry, Lawrence	20 DEC 1877 R	11	244
Brown, Maggie	Burrs, Henry	20 DEC 1877	11	253
Brown, Maggie	Simms, John T.	17 JAN 1884 L	18	382
Brown, Maggie	Williams, John F.	07 JUL 1885 L	20	313
Brown, Malinda	Grimes, David	04 OCT 1883 R	18	169
Brown, Mallie M.	Smith, Moses H.	30 JAN 1883 R	17	279
Brown, Margaret	Edmonson, John	26 AIG 1884 L	19	207
Brown, Maria L.	Middleton, Samuel	27 AUG 1884 L	19	211

D.C. Marriage Records Index, June 28, 1877 to October 19, 1885

Brown, Marion	Norris, Amos	11 JAN 1883 R	17	254
Brown, Marion Rebecca	Armstrong, Luther Kelley	30 DEC 1884 R	19	500
Brown, Martha	Reed, Alexander	22 SEP 1877	11	095
Brown, Martha	Taylor, John W.	21 OCT 1880 L	15	009
Brown, Martha	Bowser, James	06 APR 1885 L	20	146
Brown, Martha Louisa	Small, Joseph Edward	08 NOV 1882 R	17	118
Brown, Martha Virginia	Mangum, John Thomas	04 MAY 1878 L	12	037
Brown, Mary	Delaney, George	18 SEP 1879 L	13	377
Brown, Mary	Mason, Amos	26 JUN 1879 R	13	252
Brown, Mary	Tunia, William H.	13 MAY 1879	13	186
Brown, Mary	Smallwood, Wm. Henry	05 AUG 1880 L	14	388
Brown, Mary	Carter, James	09 OCT 1882	17	061
Brown, Mary	Magruder, William	02 FEB 1882 L	16	223
Brown, Mary	Mead, James	08 AUG 1882 L	16	474
Brown, Mary	Wilson, John S.	09 NOV 1882 R	17	114
Brown, Mary	Lee, Alexander	24 SEP 1883 L	18	150
Brown, Mary	Weims, Robert	12 APR 1883	17	393
Brown, Mary	Carter, Robert L.	28 FEB 1884	18	442
Brown, Mary	Johnson, William	01 OCT 1885 L	20	451
Brown, Mary	Scott, Joseph	21 JUL 1885	20	334
Brown, Mary Ann, Mrs.	Beall, Richard H.	24 JUL 1879	13	289
Brown, Mary Elizabeth	Dorsey, James Thomas	06 SEP 1884	19	229
Brown, Mary Ellen	Harris, Henry	04 MAR 1878 L	11	368
Brown, Mary Jane	Hearns, James	27 SEP 1877 R	11	112
Brown, Mary Josephine	Langston, Lemuel	22 DEC 1877 L	11	260
Brown, Mary K.	Clarkson, Joseph	12 JUL 1883	18	045
Brown, Mary O.	Green, William F.	21 SEP 1880	14	454
Brown, Mary V.	Monroe, Richard H.	03 OCT 1883 R	18	168
Brown, Mary Virginia	Cissel, William Fisk	23 DEC 1879 R	14	064
Brown, Matilda	Lee, George Thomas	13 DEC 1879 L	14	045
Brown, Matilda	Gross, Basil	05 OCT 1885	20	458
Brown, Mattie L.	Williams, John H.	03 JAN 1881 R	15	135
Brown, McKenzie	Carlton, Homazelle	15 MAR 1882 L	16	279
Brown, Melvina	West, Frank	02 FEB 1882 R	16	222
Brown, Michael J.	McVarrey, Mary Ann	04 NOV 1877 R	11	165
Brown, Mildred R.	Jackson, Charles L.	30 JAN 1878 L	11	321
Brown, Millie	Diggs, Faut Leroy	04 JUL 1884	19	124
Brown, Mitchell	French, Lizzie	29 DEC 1884 R	19	498
Brown, Nammie	Cox, George	18 OCT 1881	16	032
Brown, Nancy Ann	Stubbs, Edward	27 DEC 1877	11	274
Brown, Nannie C.	Sabine, Andrew, Dr.	28 OCT 1879 R	13	444
Brown, Nathan	Rollins, Fanny J.	05 DEC 1877	11	220
Brown, Nellie	Redd, William H.	06 NOV 1879 L	13	472
Brown, Nellie E.	Morgan, James E.	16 DEC 1880 L	15	105
Brown, Nellie T.	Kelser, William W.	25 SEP 1878 R	12	234
Brown, Oliver P.	Donn, Ella G.	03 FEB 1882	16	225
Brown, Oscar	Matthews, Josephine E.	13 NOV 1884	19	381
Brown, Oscar J.	Kennedy, Theresa	16 JUN 1879 L	13	234
Brown, Parthenia	Coleman, William	10 NOV 1880 L	15	042
Brown, Rachel	Harrison, Charles	08 NOV 1883 L	18	242
Brown, Rachel	Johnson, William	14 AUG 1883 L	18	086
Brown, Rachel	Cole, George W.	29 APR 1884	18	540
Brown, Reason	Payne, Ida	15 OCT 1885 R	20	489
Brown, Rebecca	Carter, George	04 JAN 1882 L	16	179
Brown, Reuben	Jackson, Jane	18 SEP 1878 R	12	171
Brown, Richard	Ross, Elizabeth	04 APR 1881	15	245
Brown, Richard	Smith, Lucinda	05 OCT 1882 R	17	056
Brown, Richard B.	Webster, Belle F.	14 NOV 1883	18	255

D.C. Marriage Records Index, June 28, 1877 to October 19, 1885

Brown, Robert	Williams, Martha	07 APR 1881	15	251
Brown, Robert	Stanton, Rose	10 JAN 1883	17	249
Brown, Robert	Johnson, Hannah	05 MAY 1883 R	17	430
Brown, Robert	Kohl, Mamie L.	13 OCT 1884 L	19	301
Brown, Robert	Smith, Lucy W.	22 JAN 1885 R	20	028
Brown, Rosa	Berrell, George	08 MAY 1879 R	13	180
Brown, Rosa L.	Rogers, Thomas L.	02 JUN 1884	19	051
Brown, Rose	Miles, John D.	31 JAN 1880 R	14	128
Brown, Rose	Brown, Daniel	11 MAR 1882	16	271
Brown, Rosie E.	Bush, Charles H.	11 JAN 1883 L	17	253
Brown, Ruth Anna	Braxton, Washington	22 JAN 1884	18	390
Brown, Sallie W.	Pleasants, Charles L.	29 MAY 1882 R	16	380
Brown, Samuel	Young, Sarah	10 OCT 1877 R	11	130
Brown, Samuel	Simpson, Celia	09 JAN 1879 R	13	013
Brown, Samuel	Gant, Annie V.	23 OCT 1879 R	13	440
Brown, Samuel	Thomas, Mary Ann	10 SEP 1883 R	18	122
Brown, Samuel	Chapman, Alice	30 SEP 1884 R	19	274
Brown, Samuel L.	Brown, Agnes	27 NOV 1879 R	14	006
Brown, Sarah	Wade, Harrison	26 MAY 1881 L	15	328
Brown, Sarah	Bryan, James	08 JAN 1884 L	18	370
Brown, Sarah	Sumby, John	14 APR 1884 R	18	504
Brown, Sarah A.	Cash, Thomas M.	04 SEP 1884	19	227
Brown, Sarah E.	Wood, Edward J.	19 MAY 1881 R	15	317
Brown, Sarah Elizabeth	Mason, Charles W.	14 AUG 1879	13	322
Brown, Sarah Jane	Sweeney, A.A.	02 JAN 1878	11	290
Brown, Sewellon Alden	Phelps, Sally Maynadier	05 FEB 1880 R	14	138
Brown, Silas M.	Kaiser, Adelaide G.	02 FEB 1881 R	15	171
Brown, Susan	Lyles, Thomas	07 AUG 1879	13	309
Brown, Susie	Travis, Phil	01 NOV 1883 R	18	226
Brown, Susie A.	Shutt, J.C.	02 JUL 1878	12	126
Brown, Susie Ann	Cole, James E.	16 MAY 1881 R	15	309
Brown, Susie C.	Brooks, Charles E.	11 JAN 1883 R	17	248
Brown, T.R.	Thompson, Louisa	01 APR 1880 L	14	205
Brown, Theophilus	Beverly, Matilda	04 JUN 1881 L	15	344
Brown, Thomas	Jackson, Fannie	13 APR 1879 R	13	121
Brown, Thomas	Barber, Maggie	18 NOV 1880 R	15	054
Brown, Thomas	Butler, Eliza	13 APR 1882 R	16	315
Brown, Thomas	Johnson, Annie E.	26 APR 1883 R	17	415
Brown, Thomas D.	Tyler, Annie	04 DEC 1878 R	12	364
Brown, Thomas Isaac	Johnson, Rachel Ann	11 NOV 1880 R	15	031
Brown, Thomas Jefferson	Hull, Florence May	31 OCT 1877 R	11	159
Brown, Townley	Douglas, Lucy	05 SEP 1878	12	200
Brown, Vada	Lindsey, Charles	03 JAN 1884	18	360
Brown, Victorine	Gross, John W., Jr.	10 OCT 1880 R	14	486
Brown, Virgie	Jackson, James	12 MAR 1885 L	20	111
Brown, Waite E.	Freeman, Jannie	03 DEC 1884 L	19	433
Brown, Walker	Chisley, Nannie	13 DEC 1880 L	15	094
Brown, Walter S.	Hunter, Minnie	05 OCT 1880	14	473
Brown, Wendell A.	Denton, Anna	08 NOV 1884 R	19	369
Brown, William	Stewart, Annie	30 JAN 1879 L	13	039
Brown, William	Dorsey, Philomena	09 JUN 1880 L	14	314
Brown, William	Jackson, Maria	31 AUG 1882 L	17	001
Brown, William	Jackson, Maria	31 AUG 1882 L	16	499
Brown, William	Jackson, Catherine	07 DEC 1882 L	17	174
Brown, William	Morrison, Lizzie	19 JUN 1883 L	18	002
Brown, William	Burke, Alice	14 SEP 1885 L	20	413
Brown, William Edward	Giddings, Elizabeth A.	16 JAN 1879 R	13	022
Brown, William F.	Holroyd, Sarah E.	11 FEB 1885 R	20	064

Brown, William F.	Crawford, Caroline	03 JUL 1885 R	20	264
Brown, William H.	Clark, Nancy A.	19 JUL 1879 R	13	285
Brown, William H.	White, Patsy	20 MAY 1880 L	14	279
Brown, William H.	Smith, Mary L.	15 FEB 1883 R	17	307
Brown, William Henry	Gross, Mary E.	23 OCT 1879 L	13	440
Brown, William J.	Bell, Zidonia	02 FEB 1882 R	16	221
Brown, William Lee	Jeffries, Henrietta Linn	12 DEC 1878 R	12	373
Brown, William M., Jr.	Jullien, Frances E.	02 DEC 1880 R	15	082
Brown, William P.	Christopher, Julia	16 OCT 1879 R	13	428
Brown, William S.	Bates, Annie E.	23 MAY 1881 L	15	322
Brown, Willis R.M.	Boldan, Ida E.	20 DEC 1880 R	15	111
Brown, Wilson E.	Simpson, Mattie M.	17 NOV 1879 R	13	490
Brown, Winfield S.	Johnson, Marian A.	10 SEP 1879 L	13	362
Brown, Wm. W.	Wall, Minnie	03 NOV 1879 L	13	460
Browne, A.K.	Dunn, Cyrene E.	31 JAN 1880	14	129
Browne, Aldis Birdsey	Delahay, Mary Barry	01 DEC 1880	15	075
Browne, Carrie J.	Taylor, William G.	26 AUG 1879 R	13	299
Browne, James	Irving, Mary	09 AUG 1879 L	13	314
Browne, James H.	Henderson, Lucy	06 APR 1881 L	15	249
Browne, Juda	Ashburn, George W.	12 NOV 1878 R	12	323
Browne, Julia Janet	Stepney, Franklin	24 APR 1883 L	17	406
Browne, Sarah Lizzie	Wagner, John West	29 MAY 1878 R	12	074
Browner, John W.	Lynch, Catherine	01 NOV 1880 R	15	023
Browning, Arthur	Ringgold, Nellie D.	06 NOV 1879 R	13	441
Browning, Florence J.	Crawford, John N.	12 FEB 1879	13	053
Browning, Frank Temple	Kennedy, Susie E.	11 JAN 1882 L	16	191
Browning, Joseph S.	Fisher, Ella V.	14 JUL 1879 R	13	279
Browning, Livingston	Evans, Mollie M.	20 OCT 1878	12	283
Browning, Maggie E.	Shepard, James H.	07 JUN 1883 R	17	481
Browning, Mary E.	Smith, Edmond F.	11 FEB 1884 R	18	413
Browning, N.E.	Betker, John K.	07 MAY 1885	20	212
Browning, Ringgold W.	McCauslen, Nellie H	03 JUL 1885	20	308
Browning, Sarah S.	Hurley, John F.	17 OCT 1885	20	493
Browning, Titia	Wilson, John H.	01 MAR 1882 L	16	262
Brubaker, Jonas M.	Mutersbaugh, Georgie Etta	25 NOV 1879 R	14	004
Bruce, Alice F.	Dobbins, William J.	24 NOV 1880 L	15	066
Bruce, Edwin	Quesenberry, Alice	21 SEP 1882 L	17	032
Bruce, Elivina	Brooks, Peter	07 AUG 1884	19	173
Bruce, Elizabeth	Simms, Charles Henry	09 NOV 1878 L	12	319
Bruce, Emma J.	Suttle, William H.	24 MAY 1885 R	20	237
Bruce, Fannie E. Swift	Ware, Charles Howard	07 AUG 1883	18	077
Bruce, George	Davis, Lucinda	25 DEC 1878 R	12	340
Bruce, Henry T.	Pierson, Ida M.	31 MAY 1882 R	16	382
Bruce, Jennie	Davis, Thomas	11 SEP 1879 L	13	365
Bruce, John Thomas	Nelson, Mary Ann	22 DEC 1879 R	14	066
Bruce, Joseph	Davis, Margaret	08 NOV 1877	11	173
Bruce, Katie	Smith, John W.H.	08 APR 1880 R	14	217
Bruce, Lewis	Lyles, Anna	08 AUG 1884	19	174
Bruce, Lucy J.	Smoot, George L.	15 MAR 1885	20	112
Bruce, Minnie Maud	Von Nevta, George Oehlmann	22 JAN 1880 R	14	117
Bruce, Nathan	Enders, Mary E.	28 MAY 1878 L	12	072
Bruce, Nathan	Enders, Mary	12 AUG 1884	19	181
Bruce, Robert E.	Taylor, Mary J.	18 AUG 1885 L	20	375
Bruce, Rosa	Brady, Robert	22 MAR 1882 R	16	287
Bruce, Samuel	West, Rebecca	01 JAN 1883	17	226
Bruce, Sophie	Cook, Alfred	24 JUL 1884	19	157
Bruehl, Clara A.	Mansfield, John R.	08 APR 1880 R	14	214
Bruehl, Clara L.	Wasser, Henry R.	13 AUG 1885 R	20	367

D.C. Marriage Records Index, June 28, 1877 to October 19, 1885

Name	Spouse	Date	Vol	Page
Bruehl, Emilie Charlotte	Motz, Werner Carl	19 APR 1880 R	14	227
Brumagin, Ella M.	Vanderbergh, Benjamin	25 FEB 1884 R	18	216
Brundage, Joseph Smith	Fishback, Fannie M.	28 MAR 1878	11	397
Brunner, Samuel W.	Wirtz, Matilda	20 JAN 1883 L	17	269
Bruno, Harry	Johnson, Lola	23 JUN 1883 L	18	011
Brusecke, Annie	Sweitzer, John	09 OCT 1884	19	296
Bryan, Annie A.	Moore, Isaac J.	18 SEP 1879 R	13	378
Bryan, Annie E.	Stanford, Edward H.	11 JUN 1885	20	270
Bryan, Bernard, Jr.	Malatesta, Virginia	10 MAR 1884 L	18	464
Bryan, Carrie P.	Moses, S. Preston, Jr.	01 JUN 1880 L	14	299
Bryan, Carrie P.	Morgan, Wm. P.	29 JAN 1880 R	14	128
Bryan, Charles	Bryan, Emma	08 SEP 1884	19	233
Bryan, Edward	Mills, Matilda	27 FEB 1879 R	13	083
Bryan, Ella	Williams, Thomas W.	16 AUG 1884 L	19	190
Bryan, Emma	Bryan, Charles	08 SEP 1884	19	233
Bryan, Frances Heiskell	Gatewood, Richard	13 SEP 1881 R	15	480
Bryan, Henry Lewis	McClery, Marion	15 OCT 1878 R	12	271
Bryan, James	Brown, Sarah	08 JAN 1884 L	18	370
Bryan, Jeannie E.	True, Edward R.	10 SEP 1878 R	12	211
Bryan, John A.	Lewis, Ida V.	28 APR 1882 R	16	334
Bryan, John S.	Anderson, Lavinia C.	09 FEB 1878 L	11	335
Bryan, John Thomas	Cook, Frances	17 MAR 1882	16	277
Bryan, Kate L.	Gross, Joseph H.	14 SEP 1884 R	19	245
Bryan, Maggie	Pollard, Thomas	15 JUL 1880	14	363
Bryan, Mary	Janes, George	15 JUL 1885 L	20	327
Bryan, Mary I. Augustin	Owens, Edmund W.	04 DEC 1878 R	12	364
Bryan, Nathaniel	Norman, Frances	30 JAN 1884 L	18	402
Bryan, Octavia E.	Green, John Rush	16 MAR 1880 R	14	186
Bryan, R. Hughlett	Mayhew, Georgie	04 DEC 1882	17	165
Bryan, Sarah Savilla	Thompson, William E.	28 MAY 1878	12	070
Bryan, W.S.	Veige, Rosa	30 APR 1884	18	546
Bryan, William	Colloway, Mary	16 MAY 1878 R	12	042
Bryant, Alexander P.	Jackson, Eliza Thomas	26 APR 1881	15	272
Bryant, Catherine	Patram, Thomas W.	05 DEC 1883 L	18	295
Bryant, Cornelia	Colbert, John	06 NOV 1878	12	309
Bryant, Frank	Ogle, Annie Cora	17 APR 1879	13	149
Bryant, George H.	Newton, Bessie	19 JUN 1883	18	002
Bryant, George W.	Williams, Ann E.	30 OCT 1882 L	17	101
Bryant, James Derby	Parker, Rosa	30 AUG 1878 L	12	187
Bryant, Jane	Grayson, Lee	26 DEC 1879 R	14	074
Bryant, Louis	Coke, Addie	11 APR 1883 R	17	390
Bryant, Napoleon B.	Walbridge, Louisa J.	05 JUL 1877	11	009
Bryant, Sarah	Draper, Philip	17 MAY 1883	17	450
Bryant, Stewart L.	Beach, Louisa	11 JAN 1885	20	012
Bryant, Thomas H.	Sutherland, Virginia A.	30 MAR 1880 R	14	203
Bryant, William	Johnson, Mattie	19 APR 1882 L	16	326
Bryant, William H.	Wilburn, Elisabeth	06 MAR 1881 R	15	215
Bryne, Emma D.	Duvall, James E.	16 JAN 1880 R	14	106
Bubb, Frederick L.	Simpson, Mary A.	10 JUL 1883	18	040
Buchanan, Albert	Frazier, Katie	22 JUN 1880 R	14	331
Buchanan, Charles H.	Webb, Catharine A.	05 JUN 1884 L	19	065
Buchanan, Charles T.	Lightfoot, Annie	23 JUN 1881 R	15	378
Buchanan, Daniel	Carter, Eliza Ann	24 OCT 1883 R	18	206
Buchanan, Dennis	Brooks, Harriet	15 JUL 1877 R	11	007
Buchanan, E. Key	Lee, Minnie A.	30 APR 1880	14	207
Buchanan, Israel	Pleasant, Sallie	15 NOV 1877	11	187
Buchanan, John	Haslup, Antonia	18 OCT 1877 R	11	144
Buchanan, margaret	Harris, Frederick	28 AUG 1884 L	19	213

Buchanan, Mary J.	Weaver, Thomas A.	15 FEB 1881 R	15	191
Buchanan, William H.	Chase, Mary E.	18 AUG 1881 L	15	453
Buchanan, William Henry	Richardson, Lizzie	10 FEB 1885 L	20	060
Bucheler, Herman C.	Gregory, Mintty	04 JUN 1881 R	15	343
Buchert, William	Lederer, Linie	01 MAR 1884 L	18	452
Buchly, Alice T.	Casey, John A.	24 DEC 1884 L	19	490
Bucigaluppi, John	Künzig, Fraziska	06 JUN 1884	19	066
Buck, Thomas O.	Pear, Ella	30 MAR 1880 R	14	203
Buckey, Alice	Hoover, William Bartlett	21 FEB 1884	18	435
Buckingham, Virginia	Steele, Rush C.	16 NOV 1881 R	16	081
Buckingham, William E.	Porter, Venora E.	14 JUL 1885 R	20	323
Buckland, Daniel	Simms, Susan I.	29 JUL 1878 L	12	151
Buckley, Alice S.	Mansfield, Philip	27 JUN 1883 R	17	488
Buckley, Ella D.	Barrett, Michael F.	16 JUN 1885 L	20	277
Buckley, Johanna	Richter, Joseph	15 SEP 1879 L	13	370
Buckley, Johanna	Campbell, John	03 FEB 1880 L	14	134
Buckley, John M.	Cronan, Catherine	08 AUG 1878 R	12	162
Buckley, Joseph F.	Zeigler, Louisa E.	20 NOV 1878 R	12	337
Buckley, Margaret V.	Lawler, D.J.	15 AUG 1877 L	11	054
Buckley, Mary M.	Mulholland, John	28 JAN 1880 R	14	124
Buckley, Phillip Maury	Russell, Cora J.	16 JAN 1879 R	13	019
Buckley, Robert	Fletcher, Mamie	28 DEC 1881 R	16	168
Buckley, Rosa L.	Hayre, Frank G.	06 OCT 1881 L	16	012
Buckley, Rosa L.	Lowe, Earnest C.	26 JUN 1883	18	014
Bucklin, John E.	Frere, Frances	26 DEC 1878 R	12	404
Buckman, Ida	Jackson, Wesley	17 OCT 1878	12	278
Buckman, John Harrison	McCabe, Mary E.	02 SEP 1881 R	15	469
Buckman, Kittie	Young, John	23 DEC 1879	14	062
Buckman, Sarah	Diggs, Alexander	10 FEB 1885 L	20	062
Buckner, Eliza	Rich, Joseph	31 AUG 1881 L	15	466
Buckner, Frederick	Lovett, Eliza	10 DEC 1883 L	18	306
Buckner, Georgianna	Upsher, Albert	13 MAY 1880 R	14	243
Buckner, Hellen	Morris, James H.	10 APR 1879 R	13	135
Buckner, Jacob	Woodfolk, Martha	15 NOV 1877 L	11	189
Buckner, Joshua	Bell, Lettie	20 DEC 1877 R	11	254
Buckner, Laura	Winslow, Wm. Frederick	06 AUG 1883	18	074
Buckner, Lucinda A.	Waters, Charles	15 JAN 1880	14	100
Buckner, Lucy Ann	Beckett, David	14 AUG 1879 R	13	322
Buckner, Maggie	Bailey, George	30 AUG 1882	16	496
Buckner, Priscilla	Turner, George	29 JUL 1880 R	14	378
Buckner, Randolph	Johnson, Agnes	26 DEC 1884 L	19	492
Buckner, Robert H.	Allen, Julia	20 NOV 1879 R	13	487
Buckner, Robert H.	Lucas, Hannah A.	10 SEP 1880	14	441
Buckner, William	Edwards, Eliza [Wood]	18 DEC 1884 R	19	468
Budd, Alexander	Washington, Dora	14 OCT 1884 R	19	304
Budd, Christiana	Selvy, Joshua	11 DEC 1884 R	19	450
Budd, Ludy W.	Botts, Sanford H.	04 FEB 1884 L	18	408
Budd, Mary	Beckett, John H.	13 MAY 1880 R	14	267
Budd, Mary Jane	Taliaferro, Thomas T.	14 NOV 1877 L	11	184
Budd, Rosie	Johnson, James	05 JUL 1883 L	18	035
Buecheler, Emilie	Koppen, William	02 SEP 1885 R	20	393
Buechler, Mary	Glick, John H.	02 SEP 1879 R	13	347
Buechling, John B.	Lewis, Katharine Anna	19 MAR 1878 L	11	386
Buell, Alice V.	Tracey, James	25 DEC 1878 L	12	391
Buell, Augustus C.	Polk, Madeleine Tascar	11 MAR 1878 R	11	376
Buell, Clayton Henry	Finley, Leila Lawrence	30 APR 1885 R	20	197
Buesher, Mary	Stecher, Joseph	26 JAN 1882 L	16	211
Buhler, Anne	Greff, Charles	19 FEB 1879	13	066

D.C. Marriage Records Index, June 28, 1877 to October 19, 1885 61

Name	Spouse	Date	Vol	Page
Buhler, Katherine	Mohler, Herrman	06 MAR 1885	20	126
Buil, Ella L.	Cole, Joseph	22 JUN 1881 R	15	371
Buil, Mary Elizabeth	Noland, Samuel D.	13 SEP 1877 L	11	092
Bulifant, Elvira Harrison	Evans, Jno. Blackwell	15 DEC 1883 R	18	321
Bull, Clara Matilda	Shubkagel, William Henry	23 MAR 1882 R	16	288
Bull, Emma V.	Clarkson, William H.	01 MAY 1884 L	19	001
Bull, Emma V.	Clarkson, William H.	01 MAY 1884	18	547
Bull, Laban L.	Hoshall, Lizzie B.	16 FEB 1881 R	15	191
Bullard, Maggie M.	Willis, Blucher	25 OCT 1882	17	095
Bullard, Mary E.	Matthews, Joseph O.	22 MAY 1879 R	15	3724
Bullock, Emma Spottswood	Stevens, William Presley	16 AUG 1879 R	13	324
Bullock, Sousan	Manning, Payton	03 JUN 1880 R	14	304
Bullock, William Broadus	Hammett, Ella	11 JAN 1882 R	16	189
Bumbach, Amandus	Jones, Catharine	24 JUL 1879 L	13	290
Bumbray, Ruberta F.	Curtiss, Ottawa H.	09 AUG 1880	14	393
Bumbrey, Eliza	Thomas, Justus	05 JUL 1879	13	270
Bumpas, Thomas B.	Heurich, Sallie B.	07 OCT 1882 R	17	058
Bumrie, Mary	Dyson, William	19 FEB 1878	11	348
Bumry, Martha	Johnson, John	15 DEC 1881 R	16	132
Bunce, Mary	Ward, Thomas G.	05 JUN 1878	12	087
Bundick, Thomas E.	Halley, Ellen	19 JUN 1879 R	13	240
Bundy, Austin	Eppes, Gracie	10 NOV 1877 L	11	178
Bundy, Emma	Neal, Benjamin F.	03 JUL 1879 R	13	258
Bundy, James F.	Freeman, Delila	05 JUN 1884	19	062
Bundy, John H.	Jackson, Phillis	16 DEC 1880 R	15	098
Bundy, Julius L.	Jacobs, Sophia	07 NOV 1822	17	113
Bundy, Lucy, Mrs.	Baker, James	12 JAN 1881	15	149
Bundy, Martha Stella	Coleman, James	09 DEC 1877	11	218
Bundy, Mary	Offutt, James	04 JUL 1882	16	436
Bundy, Millie Jane	Lewis, George	05 JAN 1882 L	16	184
Bundy, William Henry	Nelson, Annie	07 JUN 1881 L	15	349
Bunnell, Annie Elizabeth	Taylor, John W.	13 NOV 1884 R	19	379
Bunting, Harry C.	Harris, Addie L.	01 JUL 1885	20	304
Burbridge, Georgia	Hughes, Wormley H.	20 FEB 1885 L	20	079
Burch, Alice G.	Foster, David L.	15 DEC 1881 R	16	132
Burch, Andrew	Hasselbach, Lizzie	22 DEC 1883 L	18	358
Burch, Catharine M.	Warner, Leslie	30 NOV 1880	15	071
Burch, David O.	Wallen, Emma J.	31 DEC 1877	11	283
Burch, Ellen	Robinson, Charles J.	13 NOV 1879 L	13	484
Burch, George Robert	Sluper, Bertha J.	26 NOV 1884 R	19	404
Burch, Henry W.	Christmann, Auguste H.	08 OCT 1885 R	20	472
Burch, Jessie E.	Zimmerman, William M.	01 DEC 1883	18	290
Burch, Joseph O.	Geary, Elizabeth C.	27 NOV 1878 R	12	352
Burch, Lizzie	Morris, James P.	10 OCT 1881	14	501
Burch, Mamie R.	Gordon, Graham L.	18 AUG 1881 R	15	453
Burch, Mary D.	Herbert, W.K.	07 MAY 1883 L	17	431
Burch, Robert R.	Jones, Lucy A.	07 NOV 1882 L	17	115
Burch, Rosie	Penn, Charles T.	04 SEP 1877 L	11	074
Burch, Sidonia	Jenkins, Edward	18 MAY 1884	19	025
Burch, Stephen	Bell, Ellen	09 OCT 1880 L	14	485
Burchard, George C.	Kilby, Addie C.	01 SEP 1885 R	20	394
Burchell, Sarah Frances	Burt, Arthur	24 JUN 1885 R	20	289
Burden, Louise E.	Gales, Joseph	22 NOV 1877 L	11	199
Burden, Mary	Johnson, James	04 NOV 1881 R	15	431
Burdett, Annie B.	Gooch, Charles J.	26 NOV 1879 L	14	009
Burdett, George	Fields, Mary E.	31 JUL 1879 R	13	300
Burdett, John H.	Throop, Laura W.	07 OCT 1879 R	13	405
Burdette, Elmer W.	Blackman, Laura E.	25 SEP 1883 R	18	153

Burdine, James W.	Connor, Josephine M.	15 SEP 1884 L	19	247
Burdine, Mary I.	Langley, Preston F.B.	10 JUN 1884 L	19	073
Burdine, William A.	Spaight, Mary	12 FEB 1883	17	302
Burfoot, Ellen Catharine	Sheild, Alfred Prentis	26 SEP 1879 R	13	389
Burford, Eleanor L.	Austin, George L.	02 FEB 1881	15	173
Burford, William E.	Drury, Josephine	19 NOV 1877 L	11	195
Burgdorf, Albert O.	Casler, Sarah E.	31 DEC 1883 L	18	356
Burgdorf, Charles	Thomas, Ella	03 DEC 1883 L	18	292
Burgee, Samuel M.	Brewer, Mary	30 NOV 1883 L	18	288
Burger, Mary S.	Hoover, Charles H.	04 NOV 1882 R	17	111
Burger, Peter	Gensslen, Virginia E.	03 APR 1884	19	275
Burgess, Abner	Fink, Carrie E.	16 OCT 1877	11	139
Burgess, Alexander	Hayward, Sarah	24 MAY 1879	13	203
Burgess, Charles A.	Oakland, Catherine	21 JUL 1881 L	15	412
Burgess, Eliza	Davis, Charles	22 AUG 1878 L	12	177
Burgess, Elizabeth	Talbot, Edmund R.	17 AUG 1882 R	16	481
Burgess, Ella Carrie	Cann, David C.	12 JUN 1883	17	488
Burgess, Henry Edwin	Shepherd, Lucy Ellen	13 DEC 1884 R	19	457
Burgess, Jacob	Ricks, Julia	27 JUL 1877 L	11	033
Burgess, James H.	Johnson, Fannie R.	29 AUG 1883	18	103
Burgess, Jessie	Acker, William Jacob	11 DEC 1884 R	19	450
Burgess, John B.	Ryan, Ella C.	01 JUN 1881 L	15	337
Burgess, John E.	Ball, Susie	12 DEC 1878	12	379
Burgess, John J.A.	Miller, Eleanora	07 DEC 1882 L	17	174
Burgess, Louisa	Clifton, William	05 JUN 1884 L	19	062
Burgess, Martha	Dent, John	29 MAR 1883 R	17	369
Burgess, Mary Hannah	Summers, Edward W.	07 AUG 1877 R	11	044
Burgess, Rosa E.	Dunan, Lewis A.	12 MAY 1879	13	186
Burgess, Susan	Landon, Isaac	07 JAN 1879 L	13	009
Burgess, Thomas	Davis, Katie V.	13 MAR 1883 L	17	341
Burgess, William	Lee, Eliza	27 JUL 1878 L	12	149
Burgess, William	White, Annie E.	04 DEC 1879 R	14	001
Burgess, William	Parker, Mary E.	18 FEB 1883 R	17	301
Burgess, William Henry	Byrant, Willie A.	26 APR 1882 R	16	338
Burgess, William R.	Rawlings, Nellie A.	05 NOV 1883 L	18	231
Burgoyne, Harriet	Christine, Fleming	21 DEC 1883	18	322
Burgy, Emile	Waters, Eliza	27 JUN 1882 R	16	426
Burhell, Lizzie	Crampton, Daniel	17 OCT 1878	12	280
Burk, Ann	Davison, Charles D.	10 DEC 1881	16	047
Burk, Bessie E.	Custerd, William A.	19 JAN 1881	15	158
Burk, Bridget	Burk, Michael	20 FEB 1879 L	13	069
Burk, Ellen J.	Simmons, Miles	18 JAN 1884 R	18	384
Burk, James E.	Hopson, Carrie	21 SEP 1885 R	20	431
Burk, James O.	Greaves, Julia	25 FEB 1879 L	13	078
Burk, John H.	Cross, Malvina	24 JUL 1884 L	19	157
Burk, Julian F.	Douglass, Melvina	09 OCT 1878	12	263
Burk, Michael	Burk, Bridget	20 FEB 1879 L	13	069
Burk, Michael	Hurley, Mary	15 JUL 1884 L	19	140
Burkart, Tillie	Zentgraf, Frank	07 JUN 1881	15	349
Burke, Ada Marie	Noel, John Snider	18 OCT 1882	17	077
Burke, Addie M.	Edwards, William M.	18 DEC 1882 R	17	188
Burke, Alice	Jackson, Washington	15 MAR 1882 L	16	277
Burke, Alice	Brown, William	14 SEP 1885 L	20	413
Burke, Annie	Clarke, John	21 NOV 1877 L	11	196
Burke, Annie	Nelygan, Henry	20 APR 1878 L	12	013
Burke, Annie	Drescher, Frederick W.	25 SEP 1879 R	13	386
Burke, Annie	Davis, Charles	01 DEC 1881 R	16	100
Burke, Catherine	Gaines, William	30 JUL 1882 R	16	498

Burke, Charles Sumner	Oatman, Nellie Louise	31 DEC 1879 R	14	082
Burke, Clara J.	Keating, Chester B.	28 JUL 1878 R	12	146
Burke, Daniel J.	Moore, Adlade	18 MAR 1884 R	18	476
Burke, Delia	Zerega, Luigi	13 MAY 1879	13	187
Burke, Dora	Sands, Ellsworth	01 AUG 1882	16	464
Burke, Edmund	Haskins, Laura C.	15 JUN 1880	14	321
Burke, Eliza	Richson, Thomas	05 MAR 1885 R	20	097
Burke, Fannie E.	Butchel, John H.	18 FEB 1885 L	20	076
Burke, Fanny E.	Matthews, John T.	27 SEP 1877 L	11	113
Burke, Frank P.	O'Hare, Mary E.N.	06 MAR 1883 L	17	335
Burke, George H.	Smetnam, Mary E.	12 DEC 1883	18	311
Burke, Harriet J.	Holmes, Charles A.	27 AUG 1880	14	417
Burke, James Henry	Maynard, Elizabeth E.	17 MAY 1882 L	16	364
Burke, James W.	Payne, Mary L.	11 DEC 1879 R	14	045
Burke, Jennie E.	Jenkins, Thomas T.	06 DEC 1882 R	17	171
Burke, Katie E.	Vosser, John	13 NOV 1882 L	17	123
Burke, Lawrence W.	Smith, Barbara	22 MAY 1879 L	13	201
Burke, Lawrence Wm.	Bates, Fannie Warren	11 DEC 1882 R	17	177
Burke, Louisa	Sorrel, Sandy	07 OCT 1880 R	14	481
Burke, Maggie A.	Mulhare, Joseph F.	23 AUG 1884 L	19	205
Burke, Margaret	Connolly, James B.	25 NOV 1884 L	19	409
Burke, Mariah A.	Salb, Charles F.	02 JUN 1884 R	19	050
Burke, Michael	Ratry, Mary	23 FEB 1878 L	11	355
Burke, Michael J.	Wasney, Mary A.	02 JAN 1879 R	13	002
Burke, Michael J.	Harrington, Maria T.	07 NOV 1882	17	113
Burke, Mollie E.	Sanford, Charles E.	24 APR 1884 L	18	532
Burke, Ophelia	Hennerson, Anthony	05 FEB 1878	11	327
Burke, Patrick	O'Hare, May E.	01 MAR 1883 L	17	330
Burke, Richard O'H.	Sheehy, Norah	20 JAN 1881 R	15	156
Burke, Sadie E.	Linthicum, Edwin S.	11 MAR 1881	15	221
Burke, Sallie Burdon	Cunigan, Benjamin Lewis	13 MAR 1879 R	12	407
Burke, Solomon	Coleman, Clara	22 DEC 1881 R	16	151
Burke, Thomas J.	Edmonds, Mary	28 NOV 1883	18	281
Burke, William	O'Farrell, Ida M.	21 FEB 1882 R	16	248
Burket, Alice Mary	Garvin, Joseph M.	18 DEC 1878 R	12	387
Burket, Joseph U.	Rhees, Fannie A.	04 JUN 1884	19	056
Burket, Lincoln	Rodier, Emma Elizabeth	05 AUG 1881 L	15	434
Burket, Sallie M.	Clarke, Mortimer	20 DEC 1883 L	18	331
Burkhardt, John George	Spalding, Sarah Annie Davidson	03 MAY 1880 R	14	249
Burkhardt, Tina C.	White, William O.	14 JUL 1881 L	15	403
Burkhart, Lizzie C.	Allen, James T.	14 FEB 1885 R	20	066
Burkins, Catherine	Sloane, John	20 OCT 1881 L	16	038
Burkley, Joseph	Letter, Emma	09 OCT 1879 R	13	412
Burkley, Richard	Beverly, Julia	19 DEC 1878 R	12	387
Burklin, George	Hoover, Hattie E.	03 MAR 1881	15	213
Burks, Charles	Winfrey, Rebecca	31 JUL 1877	11	035
Burks, Nelson	Porter, Alice	19 FEB 1884 L	18	430
Burley, Benjamin J.	Briscoe, Emma	15 NOV 1882 L	17	130
Burley, C. St. Clair	Marshall, Harriet A.	24 NOV 1882 L	17	148
Burley, Hattie	Jones, Lewis	10 MAR 1885 R	20	098
Burley, John	Ross, Fanny	04 OCT 1881	16	005
Burley, Mary Lizzie	Morrow, William Nelson	05 OCT 1879 R	13	403
Burley, Richard T.	Scott, Ary	19 JUN 1879 R	13	239
Burlingame, Fannie M.	Reed, Bushrad W.	21 OCT 1884	19	326
Burlingame, Frederick H.	Mills, Katie F.	04 AUG 1884	19	166
Burn, James D.	Dant, Lottie L.	15 DEC 1884 R	19	459
Burn, Mary V.	Lavezzi, Joseph Sylvester	21 OCT 1880	15	008
Burnaught, George	Homes, Catherine	17 SEP 1885 L	20	427

Burnaw, Martha	Shelton, Robert	22 APR 1880	14	224
Burnes, Ella	Harrence, William	27 MAY 1880 R	14	284
Burnes, Susie M.R.	Paul, James	18 FEB 1879 R	13	064
Burnett, Edward W.	Banks, Fanny	18 JUN 1879 L	13	237
Burnett, Etta	O'Rork, Charles E.	04 JUL 1881	15	387
Burnett, James	Wiggins, Mary	27 JAN 1885 L	20	040
Burnett, John T.	Roots, Fannie	09 SEP 1885 R	20	408
Burnett, Mary Cummings	Harrison, Luther Jackson	25 OCT 1881 R	16	044
Burnett, Mary F.	Godfrey, Francis	01 AUG 1881 R	15	428
Burnett, Mary P.	Haynes, James	08 OCT 1884	19	286
Burnett, Simon C.	West, Nellie G.	30 JUL 1881 L	15	427
Burnett, William H.	King, Eliza J.	07 NOV 1878	12	311
Burnette, Thomas	Davis, Mary	24 NOV 1877 L	11	201
Burnham, Elgie L.	Cox, Mamie E.	07 FEB 1880	14	141
Burnham, Elgie L.	Ballman, Mary	29 JUN 1884 R	19	109
Burnham, Emma	Freeman, Benj.	20 JUN 1881 R	15	366
Burnham, Henry W.	Johnson, Sallie	27 SEP 1881 R	15	495
Burnham, Kate	Alexander, James Henry	24 JUN 1881 R	15	378
Burnison, Jennie F.	DeVaughn, Walter E.	19 OCT 1885 R	20	497
Burns, Annie B.	Hawkins, James B.	06 AUG 1885	20	357
Burns, Belle	Magruder, George L., Dr.	21 NOV 1882 L	17	141
Burns, J. Eldridge	Markley, Emma A.	30 APR 1884 R	18	544
Burns, James	Barron, Maggie	22 OCT 1882	17	085
Burns, John	Bridget, Sarah A.	02 AUG 1879 L	13	304
Burns, Joseph D.	Thornton, Mary A.	28 OCT 1880	15	018
Burns, Joseph R.	Downey, Ella J.	30 OCT 1879	13	452
Burns, Lillie	Turner, Charles L.	22 JUL 1885 R	20	335
Burns, Lizzie	Pfiel, John K., Jr.	01 MAY 1882	16	344
Burns, Mary Ann	Slattery, Daniel	02 OCT 1877 L	11	118
Burns, Sallie	Porter, William R.	27 JAN 1885 R	20	038
Burns, William G.	Overall, Fannie L.	17 OCT 1883	18	195
Burns, William H.	Washington, Almira	04 AUG 1885	20	362
Burns, Wm. F.	Beach, Mary F.	02 MAY 1881 R	15	288
Burnside, Alice Edgehill	Paret, John Francis	29 APR 1884 R	18	536
Burnside, James Bradford	Whiting, Mary Gray	05 OCT 1882 R	17	052
Burnside, Lizzie M.	Rice, Henry D.	13 OCT 1881 R	16	021
Burnside, Robert W.	Fisher, Louise A.	29 APR 1882 R	16	341
Burr, Charles E.	Proctor, Emma J.	26 MAR 1885 R	20	133
Burr, Charles R.	Frost, Mary	23 OCT 1879 R	13	440
Burr, Fredrick H.	Keech, Anna Eliza	15 MAR 1880 R	14	184
Burr, Harrison	Holland, Ada	01 NOV 1877 R	11	162
Burr, Jennie	Barber, William D.	09 MAY 1882 R	16	355
Burr, Lille	Bean, John A.	26 FEB 1884 L	18	445
Burr, Mary	Johnston, William E.	15 OCT 1884	19	310
Burr, Melbourne C.	Cain, Alice	20 JUN 1883	18	006
Burr, Nellie M.	Smithson, Daniel C.	13 FEB 1884	18	423
Burr, Thomas Washington	Peacock, Sallie B.	27 SEP 1881 R	15	499
Burrage, Margaret M.	Clarkson, Edward H.	20 DEC 1877	11	255
Burrage, Mary E.	Morris, Thomas L.	28 AUG 1878 R	12	184
Burrel, Elizabeth	Stewart, William Henry	17 APR 1878	12	007
Burrell, Jane	Taylor, Matthews	29 JUL 1880 L	14	377
Burrell, Mary	Lewis, Isaiah	28 FEB 1883 R	17	327
Burrell, William H.	Young, Maria L.	29 MAY 1884	19	046
Burrhus Fredrick C., Jr.	Lynch, Flora B.	03 JAN 1881 L	15	136
Burrill, Edward	Guirge, Carrie	07 SEP 1885 R	20	401
Burrill, Susan	White, George H.	13 JUN 1881 L	15	358
Burris, Benjamin	Jones, Ellen	18 APR 1881	15	260
Burriss, Reuben A.	Gallahorn, Mary Jane	08 MAR 1883 R	17	337

Burrough, Hanson G.	Coghill, Robertie	17 JAN 1884 R	18	381
Burrough, Howard	Ferguson, Alice	27 JUN 1881 R	15	371
Burroughs, Evannah	Sherwood, James Edward	10 OCT 1878 R	12	266
Burroughs, Jennie	Hurley, William	24 AUG 1880 R	14	413
Burroughs, Mary	O'Brien, Richard A.	02 JUL 1883 L	18	028
Burroughs, Mary A.	Jones, Francis A.	15 JAN 1880 R	14	103
Burroughs, Mary Emma	Bayley, Cornelius P.	03 DEC 1878 R	12	360
Burrows, Annie	Heiss, Michael	29 JAN 1878 L	11	320
Burrows, Campson	Tyler, Emma	14 JUL 1880 R	14	359
Burrows, Ella F.	Hudson, James N.	03 JUL 1877 R	11	004
Burrows, Ella M.	Sherwood, James C.	22 JUN 1880 R	14	330
Burrows, Fannie C.	Morrow, James P.	26 DEC 1883	18	277
Burrows, Frederick W.	Bangs, Susanna E.A.	26 NOV 1877	11	203
Burrows, George E.	Teachum, Annie E.	23 MAR 1880 R	14	194
Burrows, George F.	Cleaves, Cassie L.	10 AUG 1885 L	20	362
Burrows, George Francis	Pyles, Mary Elizabeth	08 DEC 1880 R	15	087
Burrows, George W.	Athey, George Anna	07 MAR 1883 L	17	336
Burrows, J. Lemuel	Mansfield, Alice R.	15 MAR 1885 R	20	112
Burrows, James	Connell, Mary	02 NOV 1879	13	458
Burrows, John R.	Riley, Laura C.	10 JAN 1878 R	11	299
Burrows, Lola B.K.	Ingersoll, John Carter	16 NOV 1884 R	19	385
Burrows, Nettie	Stone, Alfred	30 MAY 1885 L	20	248
Burrows, Otto M.	Reynolds, Sarah E.	28 FEB 1884	18	450
Burrows, Sallie L.	Ward, Ignatus H.	03 MAR 1881	15	214
Burrows, Wm. T.	Harry, Helen M.	07 JAN 1884 R	18	367
Burrs, Celia	Diggs, Jacob	02 OCT 1883 R	18	162
Burrs, Henry	Brown, Maggie	20 DEC 1877	11	253
Burrs, Mary E.	Elmore, William	21 NOV 1877	11	197
Burrus, Mary	Hawkins, Robert	28 DEC 1882 R	17	218
Burrus, Nelson	Emerson, Emma	03 OCT 1884 L	19	284
Burrus, Robert	Steele, Annie M.	01 MAR 1881 L	15	209
Burruss, Maggie S.	Harrison, W.H.	17 DEC 1880 R	15	107
Burruss, Molly B.	Hoffman, George W.	31 AUG 1878 L	12	189
Burson, Rosalie	Dishman, Charles E.	19 NOV 1884	19	392
Burt, Arthur	Burchell, Sarah Frances	24 JUN 1885 R	20	289
Burt, S. Bertha	Clark, William	01 SEP 1884 L	19	218
Burton, Cora Ann	Wertheim, Isaac C.	05 JUL 1879 R	13	269
Burton, Edward	Snell, Maggie	21 OCT 1884 L	19	325
Burton, Eliza	Green, Daniel	06 MAR 1883 L	17	333
Burton, Frank	Croasdale, Mary A.	16 AUG 1877 R	11	055
Burton, Henrietta	Galt, Ralph Lee	21 APR 1885 R	20	177
Burton, John	Stewart, Mary	13 AUG 1878 R	12	157
Burton, John	Lowrey, Maggie	10 SEP 1885 R	20	411
Burton, Marian	Washington, Lewis	08 SEP 1884 R	19	231
Burton, Robert A.	Way, Fannie S.	11 FEB 1879 R	13	054
Burton, Walter	Johnson, May	03 MAR 1879	13	086
Burton, Walter T.	Atkinson, Edna	22 APR 1884 R	30	7325
Bury, Annie Eliz.	Keithley, Arthur	10 JUL 1885 R	20	319
Bury, E. Matilda	Cook, Jesse	12 NOV 1878 R	12	324
Bury, George B.	Johnston, Annie E.	18 JUN 1885 L	20	280
Bury, Mary I.	Wilkison, Charles C.	16 APR 1878 R	12	007
Bury, William T.	Lusby, Annie G.	23 JUL 1878	12	145
Busbee, Perrin	Worden, Olivia Steele	19 NOV 1879 R	13	490
Busey, Alfred	Gaites, Mary	03 MAY 1880 L	14	249
Busey, Edward E.	Bush, Talulah M.	23 FEB 1884 L	18	438
Busey, Louisa	Soloman, Robert	20 JAN 1879 R	13	025
Busey, Mary Ann	Washington, James	05 OCT 1882 R	17	055
Busey, Paris Worthington	Wells, Cornelia Ann	18 AUG 1880 L	14	406

Bush, Amy Ann	Young, Soloman	19 MAR 1879 L	13	108
Bush, Arthur Augustus	Simms, Rose	08 SEP 1885 L	20	405
Bush, Basell	Butler, Sophia	31 JUL 1878 L	12	152
Bush, Chapman	Brown, Annie	07 DEC 1882	17	171
Bush, Charles H.	Brown, Rosie E.	11 JAN 1883 L	17	253
Bush, Charles W.	Collins, Olivia Ann	15 NOV 1881	16	073
Bush, Edward D.C.	Charleston, Emma D.	26 JUN 1878 L	12	116
Bush, Fannie	Hollan, Joseph	25 JUN 1885	20	281
Bush, James Clark	Stanton, Eleanor Adams	08 JAN 1880 R	14	095
Bush, Josephine	Jackson, John H.	29 SEP 1881 R	15	505
Bush, Kate G.	Moore, Morgan M.	02 JAN 1880 R	14	087
Bush, Mary	Taylor, Jesse	09 SEP 1880 R	14	440
Bush, Mattie E.	Miller, Henry T.	16 NOV 1883 L	18	260
Bush, Talulah M.	Busey, Edward E.	23 FEB 1884 L	18	438
Bush, Thomas Oliver	Dover, Mary Elizabeth Magdalena	23 AUG 1878 L	12	178
Bush, Thomas Oliver	Shorter, Annie	20 SEP 1885	20	426
Bushby, Charles D.	Dunham, Aimée E.	20 MAY 1878 R	12	060
Bushby, James H.	Constable, Kate	18 OCT 1877 R	11	141
Bushby, William R.	Crews, Mary A.	01 OCT 1879 R	13	396
Busher, Henry A.	Walz, Matilda B.	28 OCT 1880	15	020
Busher, John H.	May, Annie	06 MAR 1878	11	371
Busher, Lizzie	Sheckels, William Henry	08 NOV 1882 L	17	119
Bushie, Laura	Lemmon, Wm. Lee	25 MAY 1880 R	14	285
Bushing, Augusta	Sheid, John T., Jr.	02 MAY 1878 R	12	035
Bushman, Joseph T.	Lutz, Cora Barbara	01 JAN 1878	11	284
Bushnell, Albert B.	King, Charlotte P.	13 SEP 1883	18	129
Bushnell, Katharine	Hay, George W.	03 SEP 1884	19	222
Bushnell, T. Howard	Pleasants, Katie	18 MAY 1878 L	12	058
Bushroyd, Wesley	Watkins, Lucy	25 AUG 1880	14	414
Bushwood, Geo. Wash.	Blackburn, Annie	14 DEC 1877 L	11	238
Bussman, Sophie E.D.	Zulauf, Henry	25 JUN 1883 R	18	010
Busy, George	Johnson, Olivia	06 APR 1879	13	127
Butchel, John H.	Burke, Fannie E.	18 FEB 1885 L	20	076
Butcher, Henry	Stewart, Martha	02 JAN 1879 L	13	004
Butcher, Joseph	Shiles, Isabella	16 DEC 1880 R	15	102
Butcher, Robert	Champ, Eliza	19 FEB 1880	14	150
Butler, Albert	Gray, Virginia	10 NOV 1880 L	15	043
Butler, Alice	Winder, Charles Henry	26 MAR 1880 L	14	199
Butler, Andrew	[Blank], Margaret	06 MAY 1880 L	14	256
Butler, Anne	Teel, James H.	20 NOV 1882 R	17	135
Butler, Annie E.	Briscoe, James W.	22 FEB 1883 L	17	318
Butler, Annie E.	Angel, Edward C.	21 JAN 1884 L	18	386
Butler, Annie R.	Edwards, James E.	19 JUN 1879 L	13	241
Butler, Anthony F.	Green, Susan A.	27 SEP 1877 L	11	109
Butler, Augustus F.	Anderson, Ellen N.	12 APR 1882	16	311
Butler, Benjamin	Jackson, Martha	04 APR 1885 R	33	8248
Butler, Benjamin	Jackson, Martha	04 MAY 1885 L	20	204
Butler, Bertie J.	Greaver, William A.	24 APR 1884 L	18	532
Butler, Buck	Price, Jane	24 JUN 1885 L	20	290
Butler, Caroline	Frazier, Beverly	30 AUG 1884 R	18	130
Butler, Carrie	Snowden, Danie Webster, Dr.	13 MAY 1880 L	14	270
Butler, Catherine	Simms, Jimmy	25 MAY 1880 L	14	287
Butler, Charles	Miller, Edith	04 MAR 1882 L	16	267
Butler, Charles E.	Kemp, Julia A.	21 FEB 1878 R	11	350
Butler, Charles H.	Gordon, Mary Louise	10 JAN 1884 L	18	373
Butler, Cora V.	Shepherd, John H.	08 FEB 1883 L	17	300
Butler, David	Matthews, Ella	14 JUN 1882 L	16	410
Butler, Delia Ann	Born, John Columbus	03 DEC 1878 L	12	360

D.C. Marriage Records Index, June 28, 1877 to October 19, 1885   67

Butler, Delozier I.	Bannion, Pleasy	24 NOV 1880 L	15	063
Butler, Delozier Jerry	Proctor, Cordelia	28 JUL 1880 L	14	377
Butler, Eliza	Brown, Thomas	13 APR 1882 R	16	315
Butler, Elizabeth	Brannagin, William	25 OCT 1880 R	15	012
Butler, Elizabeth	Bowen, Richard T.	11 OCT 1884	19	300
Butler, Ella	Deneal, Church	19 MAR 1885 R	20	122
Butler, Ella A.	Seville, Dorsey F.	28 JAN 1881 L	15	169
Butler, Emma E.	Swann, William F.	15 MAY 1884	19	023
Butler, Emma L.	Ferris, John R.	17 MAR 1878	11	385
Butler, Emmanuel	Blair, Emeline	27 JAN 1879	13	035
Butler, Fannie	Magor, Lewis	18 FEB 1885 R	20	031
Butler, Florence D.	Turner, Stephen K.	16 FEB 1879 R	13	061
Butler, Frances	Thomas, James	23 OCT 1884 L	19	334
Butler, Frank	Jones, Lucy	19 JUN 1878	12	104
Butler, Frank	Jackson, Annie	27 DEC 1881 L	16	163
Butler, Frank G.	Thomas, Mary Virginia	13 FEB 1882 R	16	239
Butler, Geneva	Davis, William H.	01 MAR 1884 L	18	453
Butler, George	White, Mariah	05 AUG 1884	19	167
Butler, George M.	Colman, D.S.	26 AUG 1880 R	14	417
Butler, George N.	Hawkins, Marian S.	24 JUN 1884 R	19	099
Butler, George W.	Smith, Amelia	15 JAN 1879 L	13	021
Butler, Harriet, Mrs.	Williams, John	10 MAR 1881 R	15	187
Butler, Hattie	Eaglend, Charles H.	03 NOV 1883 L	18	230
Butler, Henry	Lee, Loretta	04 DEC 1878	12	368
Butler, Isaac	Munroe, Jennie	21 AUG 1882 R	17	033
Butler, Jacob	Ashby, Ellen	16 NOV 1882 R	17	132
Butler, James	Marshall, Maria	15 JAN 1883 L	17	257
Butler, James	Goens, Sarah	22 NOV 1883 R	18	272
Butler, James	Lewis, Evelina	20 JUN 1885 L	20	282
Butler, Jane	Pinckney, Hanson	29 OCT 1879 R	13	449
Butler, Jane M.	Dodson, Lewis A.	17 MAY 1883 R	17	445
Butler, Jennie	Scott, George A.	27 DEC 1881 L	16	160
Butler, Jennie	Garner, Ignatius	14 SEP 1882 L	17	021
Butler, Jennie	Steward, John	23 SEP 1884 L	19	263
Butler, John	Stephinson, Catherine	06 SEP 1880 L	14	433
Butler, John	Wilson, Mary Frances	15 APR 1885 L	20	169
Butler, Joseph	Davis, Sarah A.	02 OCT 1879 R	13	399
Butler, Joseph	Thomas, Matilda	15 JUL 1880	14	362
Butler, Joseph A.	Brown, Lizzie	09 APR 1883 L	17	388
Butler, Levi	Butler, Lizzie	13 NOV 1884	19	379
Butler, Lewis	Henson, Rachel	23 OCT 1879 L	13	439
Butler, Lizzie	Snowden, Henry	16 JUL 1879 R	13	282
Butler, Lizzie	Butler, Levi	13 NOV 1884	19	379
Butler, Loie M.	Sullivan, W.F.	01 APR 1884	18	490
Butler, Louisa	Mudd, John F.	02 SEP 1882	17	002
Butler, Mack	Harry, Mary E.	17 SEP 1877 L	11	097
Butler, Madison	Morris, Martha	15 APR 1884	18	511
Butler, Margaret	Coats, Moses	03 MAY 1884 L	18	548
Butler, Margaret	Coats, Moses	03 MAY 1884 L	19	002
Butler, Martha	Dunmore, Benjamin	04 NOV 1880	14	407
Butler, Mary	Hewit, Charles B.	27 JUL 1878 R	12	137
Butler, Mary	Lawlor, James	10 JAN 1880 L	14	098
Butler, Mary A.	Norton, Robert H.	01 OCT 1879 R	13	395
Butler, Mary A.	Skidmore, Patrick H.	06 APR 1880 L	14	212
Butler, Mary F.	Wilson, Robert A.	16 MAR 1883	17	348
Butler, Mary Jefferson	Cockrill, James W.	31 OCT 1877 L	11	163
Butler, Mary R.	Clay, Henry	31 OCT 1883	18	223
Butler, Mary T.	Cornick, William	26 DEC 1877	11	261

Name	Spouse	Date	Vol	Page
Butler, Nathaniel	Barnes, Kate	30 DEC 1880	15	133
Butler, Nathaniel	Brooks, Annie	13 APR 1885 L	20	161
Butler, Orlando Robinson	Oswold, Helen	19 MAR 1880 R	14	189
Butler, Richard T.	Hall, Lizzie E.	17 NOV 1884	19	389
Butler, Robert	Johnson, Sophia	28 FEB 1883 L	17	327
Butler, Robert	Tubman, Frances	09 AUG 1885 R	20	360
Butler, Sammuel	Bowen, Rebecca	27 NOV 1880 L	15	069
Butler, Sarah	Thomas, Robert	08 JAN 1879 R	13	004
Butler, Sarah A.	Young, Joshua T.	11 MAR 1879 L	13	096
Butler, Simon	Williams, Eliza Coleman	29 AUG 1880 R	14	420
Butler, Sophia	Bush, Basell	31 JUL 1878 L	12	152
Butler, Teresa	Whipps, Adam, Jr.	13 OCT 1884 L	19	302
Butler, Theresa	Sweetnin, Augustus	11 JAN 1881 L	15	146
Butler, Theresa	Young, Frederick	19 MAR 1885 L	20	125
Butler, Virginia V.	Waters, John F.	20 NOV 1883 R	18	266
Butler, William	Payne, Jane	28 AUG 1879 R	13	341
Butler, William	Jackson, Julia	30 JAN 1883 L	17	278
Butler, William	Giles, Julia	24 NOV 1883 L	18	275
Butler, William D.	Gascon, Mary	10 SEP 1878 L	12	210
Butler, William H.	Middleton, Mary Isabel	05 SEP 1883	18	110
Butler, William Henry	Tasco, Rebecca Ann	05 JUN 1883 R	17	477
Butler, William J.	Warfield, Martha J.	29 AUG 1885	20	391
Butler, Winfield	Grant, Susan	20 SEP 1878	12	206
Butt, Eva E.	Keller, Samuel P.	16 SEP 1884 L	19	252
Butt, George H.	Beyer, Annie E.	19 DEC 1878 R	12	392
Butt, S. Holland	Braselman, Carrie N.	25 SEP 1884	19	268
Butterfield, George	Weston, Jeannette E.	23 DEC 1880 R	15	120
Butterfield, Marian A.	Boughton, William DeL.	02 JUN 1885 L	20	251
Butterhof, Mary M.	Brown, Edgar J.	04 OCT 1883	18	169
Butterhoff, Barbara	Clever, William E.	30 DEC 1882	17	197
Buttet, George	Launay, Jane	22 AUG 1884 L	19	203
Button, George P.	Ahell, Lydia S., Mrs.	21 AUG 1877	11	059
Button, Mary F. [Harris]	Wade, George A.	16 MAY 1883 R	17	446
Butts, Charles	Padgett, Katie	29 SEP 1878 R	12	240
Butts, Fannie M.	Laughlin, William H.	12 JUN 1882 R	16	406
Butts, Hattie	Yarnell, Robert S.	24 DEC 1877 R	11	262
Butts, Jennie L.	Moore, Marl	25 JAN 1880 R	14	119
Butty, Joseph	Trotman, Hattie V.	02 JUN 1881 R	15	341
Butz, Mary	Collins, Francis	28 JUN 1878 R	12	117
Buxbaum, Ferdinand	Hanlein, Lizzie	25 MAR 1883 R	17	357
Buxton, James Leonard	Duley, Frances Ardella	22 OCT 1879 R	13	437
Buxton, Lillian B.	Wilson, Charles C.	25 DEC 1880	15	124
Byass, Jacob	Bowie, Margaret	03 NOV 1879 L	13	461
Byerly, Edward V.	Byerly, Samuella M.	16 APR 1884	18	516
Byerly, Samuella M.	Byerly, Edward V.	16 APR 1884	18	516
Byers, Jaames W.	Bodieu, Fannie M.	22 OCT 1884	19	327
Byes, Jacob	Geesy, Jainey	05 SEP 1881 L	15	471
Byington, Arthur Wm.	Hurst, Ellen Amelia	18 MAR 1880 L	14	187
Byington, George Richmond	Morrison, Emma M.	03 APR 1878 R	11	404
Byles, Emma	Dame, Jonathan C.	29 APR 1884 L	18	542
Byng, Robert H.	Belmont, Susie	11 MAY 1882 R	16	356
Byram, Carrie E.	Griffith, Aloysius B.	26 NOV 1884 R	19	408
Byram, John L.	Fulton, Clora Anne	24 JAN 1879 L	13	033
Byrant, Willie A.	Burgess, William Henry	26 APR 1882 R	16	338
Byrd, John Henry	Carter, Georgiana	19 NOV 1884 L	19	393
Byrd, Logan A.	Grayson, Maggie	01 AUG 1883 L	18	069
Byrne, Dennis	Taaff, Bridget	04 JUN 1884 L	19	059
Byrne, Maria Teresa	Schweinshant, Francis	15 JAN 1882 R	16	194

Byrne, Mary	O'Neil, James J.	07 NOV 1878 R	12	315
Byrne, Mary Catharine	Clements, William Walter	28 DEC 1881 R	16	165
Byrnes, Cecilia	Bresnahan, P.J.	16 SEP 1882 L	17	024
Byrnes, Edward M.	Wise, Emma F.	21 AUG 1882 L	16	490
Byrnes, Edward Malcolm	Wise, Sallie Ellen	10 OCT 1878 R	12	264
Byrnes, Elizabeth	Connell, David	20 APR 1879 R	13	145
Byrnes, John Joseph	VandeWater, Nellie G. Sherman	10 FEB 1880 R	14	144
Byrnes, Lewis M.	Corcoran, Annie	09 SEP 1880 L	14	439
Byrns, Maria	McDermott, Peter D.	23 FEB 1884 L	18	440
Byrns, Teresa	Neenan, Stephen J.	15 MAY 1883 L	17	443
Byrns, William F.	Wall, Mary E. Berry	24 JUL 1882 R	16	454
Byroad, Frank M.	Atwell, Ida	16 JUL 1885	20	329
Byron, Annie	Warder, John W.	18 JUL 1883	18	050
Byron, Richard	Chauncey, Eliza	06 MAY 1880 R	14	258
Byron, W.J. Osborne	Hall, A.C.	08 FEB 1882 L	16	233

C

Name	Spouse	Date	Vol	Page
Cabe, Julia C.	Heath, Edward E.	30 APR 1883 L	17	421
Cade, Alice	Schaefer, Gustav	10 MAR 1879	13	094
Cadey, Julia	McIntryre, Thomas F.	08 APR 1885	20	153
Cadey, Maggie	Cadey, Patrick	07 AUG 1882 L	16	470
Cadey, Patrick	Cadey, Maggie	07 AUG 1882 L	16	470
Cadman, Mary J.	Duffy, Edward P.	07 MAY 1885	20	209
Cadwell, Maggie	Gross, William	02 JAN 1879 R	13	004
Cady, Benjamin J.	Zimmerman, Minnie B.	08 AUG 1878	12	160
Cady, Bridget	Faherty, James	06 MAY 1880 R	14	247
Cady, Bridget Ellen	Foley, Thomas	25 APR 1878	12	014
Cady, Bridget Ellen	McClelland, James Robert	08 JUL 1884 L	19	129
Cady, Ellen A.	Carley, Bernard J.	10 APR 1883 L	17	389
Cady, Emma Cleveland	Sutton, John Suter	13 OCT 1877 R	11	132
Cady, Mary J.	Murray, Owen	30 JUL 1881 L	15	427
Cady, Matthew	McGraw, Honora	04 JUN 1884	19	052
Cady, Michael	Griffin, Annie	25 JUN 1883	18	012
Cady, Patrick	Barnett, Sarah	25 FEB 1878 L	11	355
Cady, Patrick	Noonan, Bridget	11 MAY 1882 L	16	358
Cady, William R.	Smith, Fannie E.	13 JAN 1881	15	149
Caffey, Josephine Ann	Armstrong, James	15 APR 1882	16	316
Cage, Catherine E.	Kirbey, Joseph C.	08 APR 1884 R	18	499
Cage, Jeannette M.	Murray, James A.	15 MAY 1881	15	307
Cage, Lemuel P.	McInturff, Emily W.	01 DEC 1879 L	14	021
Cage, Leonard P.	McInturff, Emily W.	02 DEC 1879 R	14	017
Cage, Sarah Ellen	Ball, Thomas A.T.	05 FEB 1880	14	139
Cager, Isaac	Cooper, Louisa	13 AUG 1882	16	491
Cages, Sarah Maria	Mitchell, Peter	04 DEC 1881 R	16	111
Cahill, Fielding	Scott, Lizzie	24 NOV 1881 R	16	093
Cahill, Patrick	Small, Emma Frances	26 JUN 1879 R	13	248
Cahill, William	Dentz, Catherine	16 NOV 1878 L	12	332
Cahill, William	Robey, Ella Virginia	29 OCT 1878 L	12	297
Cahn, Felix	Raff, Isabell	14 OCT 1877 R	11	134
Cain, Alice	Burr, Melbourne C.	20 JUN 1883	18	006
Cain, Charles C.	Holmes, Susie	15 DEC 1881 L	16	134
Cain, Cornelius	Shane, Maggie	09 MAY 1880 R	14	260
Cain, Ida E.	Crossman, William D.	16 DEC 1880	15	105
Cain, John T.	Morwood, Agnes V.	09 SEP 1885 L	20	407
Cain, Joseph Guien	John, Lena Augusta	04 JUL 1883	18	019
Cain, Lindsey	Hauff, Virginia	23 MAR 1882 R	16	283
Cain, William	Lyons, Catherine	31 OCT 1877 L	11	162
Calbert, Delia	Jackson, Thomas	11 DEC 1878	12	375
Calbert, Harry	Cammell, Eliza	16 MAY 1878 R	12	041
Caldbert, Robert R.	Tasker, Alice	16 OCT 1884 L	19	314
Caldwell, Charles W.	Mahoney, Julia A.	05 SEP 1882 L	17	004
Caldwell, John T.	Martin, Katie E.	07 APR 1883 L	17	386
Caldwell, Joseph B.S.	Dallas, Eda A.	21 NOV 1883 R	18	268
Caldwell, Joseph W.L.	Perry, Mary Elizabeth	31 AUG 1883 R	18	106
Caldwell, Katie	Hunter, William H.	23 APR 1881	16	023
Caldwell, Mary	Simms, John	22 APR 1885	20	179
Caldwell, Mary Elizabeth	Clagett, Charles Thomas	06 FEB 1884 L	18	414
Calhoun, Etta E.	Simmons, Walter L.	22 JUL 1884 L	19	150
Calhoun, Robert W.	Schweitzer, Rosa E.	15 APR 1879 R	13	145
Calinan, Hester E.	Cornell, George W.	04 MAY 1882	16	346
Callaghan, Dennis	Lalley, Katie	08 JUL 1879 L	13	274
Callaghan, Eliza Virginia	Clarke, Frank	30 MAR 1882 R	16	292
Callaghan, Mary	Grimes, Francis J.	17 JUN 1880 L	14	325
Callaghan, Richard	McCarthy, Margaret	12 JUL 1885 L	20	321

D.C. Marriage Records Index, June 28, 1877 to October 19, 1885

Name	Spouse	Date	Vol	Page
Callahan, Adolphus W.	Penn, Grace	02 NOV 1877	11	164
Callahan, Ella	Kilroy, Patrick	28 NOV 1882 L	17	154
Callahan, Francis R.	Kennedy, Julia	13 FEB 1879	13	060
Callahan, Margaret	Folan, John	05 NOV 1878	12	308
Callahan, Mary J.	King, Alexander S.	13 FEB 1884 L	18	423
Callahan, Michael	Fahey, Mary	17 APR 1879 R	13	150
Callahan, Sarah	Carter, Anthony	11 APR 1880 R	14	220
Callahan, Timothy	Baker, Alice	16 MAY 1881 L	15	308
Callaman, Frances M.	Smackum, John T.	13 DEC 1883 L	18	317
Callan, Catherine C.	Smith, Thomas J.	25 AUG 1880 R	14	412
Callan, James C.	Hubner, Maggie C.	20 SEP 1882 R	17	031
Callbut, Rebecca	Robinson, William	08 JUL 1880 R	14	348
Callis, Walter S.	Jordan, Lucie D.	10 APR 1885 R	20	159
Callisher, Leah	Baruch, Allen	11 DEC 1881 R	16	124
Callohan, Ellen	Sullivan, John W.	18 APR 1878	12	010
Callon, William C.M.	Watson, Rosa L.	28 JUN 1880 L	14	336
Callow, Robert	O'Hare, Maggie	30 MAY 1880 R	14	295
Calloway, Catherine	Gray, William	29 DEC 1881 R	16	167
Calver, Henry	Waters, Fannie A.	17 DEC 1877	11	239
Calvert, Amelia	Johnson, Thomas	18 JAN 1881 L	15	152
Calvert, Annie L.	Shackleford, Bage	15 JAN 1880 R	14	104
Calvert, Cecil	Wagener, Kate	01 JUN 1881 R	15	334
Calvert, Charles Washington	Williams, Maggie Brown	10 FEB 1880 R	14	146
Calvert, Dennis J.	Windsor, Annie C.	20 JAN 1885 R	20	027
Calvert, Jennie	Tyler, George S.	17 FEB 1880 L	14	156
Calvert, Mary Jane	West, Francis	02 FEB 1882	16	223
Calvert, Richard	Howard, Annie Louise	07 JUN 1883 R	17	482
Calvert, Robert M.	Cowles, Helen	29 JAN 1883 R	17	277
Calvert, Rose Antoinette	Schuermann, Carl Wm.	09 DEC 1879 R	14	036
Calvert, William	Brooks, Hattie	25 APR 1882 L	16	333
Calvert, William F.	McPherson, Agnes	18 JUL 1878 L	12	140
Camden, Horsely B.	Campbell, Willie T.	27 JUL 1885	20	341
Cameron, Charles B.	Allen, Minnie V.	03 AUG 1885 L	20	349
Cameron, Shelton T.	Freeland, Roberta A.	16 AUG 1883 L	18	091
Cameron, Theodore R.	McCully, Emma E.	18 SEP 1884	19	258
Cameron, Virginia Rolette	Rodgers, Alexander	11 JAN 1883	17	238
Cammack, Virginia H.	Whitcomb, James A.	23 APR 1882 R	16	330
Cammell, Eliza	Calbert, Harry	16 MAY 1878 R	12	041
Camolier, George A.	Fearing, Irene	26 MAY 1880 L	14	292
Camp, Elisha	Disney, Annie L.	23 JUL 1880 L	14	374
Camp, Marie Caroline Vivans	Carr, Camello Casalti C.	27 NOV 1878 R	12	347
Campagna, Cyprian C.	Aiken, Clara R.	21 OCT 1884	19	322
Campbell, Alice	Barnes, Edward	15 JUL 1878 L	12	135
Campbell, Amelia	Smith, William	26 APR 1884 L	18	534
Campbell, Anna	Carter, Robert	17 JAN 1878 R	11	309
Campbell, Annie	Mack, Robert	01 JAN 1878 R	11	283
Campbell, Archibald	Winters, Elisabeth	06 OCT 1879 R	13	405
Campbell, Benjamin S.	Mitchell, Maggie	06 DEC 1882 L	17	171
Campbell, Bettie	Jackson, Arthur	15 OCT 1885 R	20	487
Campbell, Blanche Kennedy	Towson, Dorsey E.W.	18 OCT 1883 R	18	201
Campbell, Charles	Grey, Eliza	31 OCT 1882	17	103
Campbell, Charles Oscar	Cummings, Mary Louise	16 JUL 1879 R	13	283
Campbell, Charlotte	Bell, Thomas	08 DEC 1881 L	16	120
Campbell, Cornelius	Moore, Sallie	15 DEC 1880 R	15	098
Campbell, Cornelius	Bailey, Elmira	03 JAN 1884 R	18	352
Campbell, D. Kate	McLean, Richard	21 APR 1884 L	18	523
Campbell, Dora	Cook, John T.	29 AUG 1885 R	20	391
Campbell, Elizabeth	McKenney, John	17 SEP 1878 L	12	222

Campbell, Elizabeth	Washington, George	15 OCT 1884	19	308
Campbell, Ella B.	Nalley, Charles K.	29 SEP 1881 L	15	510
Campbell, Emily	Johnson, Aleck	15 SEP 1881 L	15	485
Campbell, Enoch	Hill, Anna	08 FEB 1878 L	11	333
Campbell, Enoch J.	Ebert, Christine	05 FEB 1884	18	216
Campbell, Florence	Shamwell, Lewis	25 OCT 1884 L	19	337
Campbell, George	Scott, Emma	25 FEB 1880 R	14	120
Campbell, George W.	Massey, Lola	05 OCT 1885 R	20	456
Campbell, Gertrude May	Fry, Henry Davidson	20 FEB 1884 R	18	434
Campbell, Gussie	Digney, Daniel	30 APR 1884	18	543
Campbell, Harriet Rebecca	Roth, Julius	08 MAY 1881 R	15	296
Campbell, Henrietta	Patterson, William E.	23 JUL 1884 R	19	473
Campbell, Hester B.	Colter, Willis H.	03 NOV 1881 R	16	060
Campbell, Horace	Lewis, Jennie	27 JAN 1885	20	038
Campbell, James	Weaver, Mary S.	25 SEP 1884	19	269
Campbell, Jennie	Huff, William	12 MAY 1881	15	302
Campbell, Jennie	Walker, Henry	16 MAY 1882 L	16	361
Campbell, John	Buckley, Johanna	03 FEB 1880 L	14	134
Campbell, John	Clancy, Kate	16 DEC 1881 R	16	124
Campbell, John G., Hon.	Malezieux, Marguerite	20 MAY 1880	14	278
Campbell, John H.	Kendrick, Mary E.	06 FEB 1880 L	14	141
Campbell, John H.	Taylor, Catherine	07 AUG 1883 L	18	078
Campbell, Joseph	Johnson, Caroline	03 JAN 1883 L	17	234
Campbell, Joshua	Eskridge, Caria	10 FEB 1881 R	15	222
Campbell, Julia	McDowell, Dan	01 NOV 1881 L	16	056
Campbell, Kate	Robinson, George S.	04 AUG 1882	16	464
Campbell, Kate A.	Hunnell, William S.	28 MAY 1884 L	19	043
Campbell, Katie A.	Spaulding, James J.	01 SEP 1885 L	20	395
Campbell, Marg. Cornelia	Reid, Robert A.C.	02 JAN 1878 L	11	286
Campbell, Margaret	O'Brien, John	25 NOV 1877	11	201
Campbell, Margaret	Duncan, William	02 NOV 1883	18	229
Campbell, Martha	Claiborne, Robert Lee	09 MAR 1881	15	216
Campbell, Martha	Webster, Addison	17 MAR 1881	15	230
Campbell, Mary	Robison, Richard	27 JUN 1878 R	12	116
Campbell, Mary	Warner, William	11 APR 1878 L	12	002
Campbell, Mary	Sauntry, Jeremiah	26 NOV 1879 L	14	012
Campbell, Mary A.	Gett, Clarence R.	19 JUL 1884 L	19	146
Campbell, Mary Jane	Mooney, Bernard	30 JUN 1884 L	19	110
Campbell, Mary T.	Reddick, J.F.	20 SEP 1877 R	11	101
Campbell, Moses Alexa.	Smith, Mary E.	04 MAY 1885 L	20	204
Campbell, Norah	McProuty, William L.	28 NOV 1883 L	18	282
Campbell, Peter	Thomas, Lizzie	27 AUG 1883 L	18	100
Campbell, Ritchard T.	Hagan, Anna	21 JUL 1884	19	148
Campbell, Rosa E.	Lawton, A. Bradley	22 APR 1884	18	522
Campbell, Thedore	Fox, Sallie	15 MAY 1882 R	16	360
Campbell, Thomas H.	Lawrence, Emma J.	06 JAN 1884	18	366
Campbell, William	Carpenter, Ellen	28 MAY 1883	18	275
Campbell, William	Dorcas, Laura	18 DEC 1884 L	19	471
Campbell, William Alex. Lamb	Gant, Frances Victoria	21 AUG 1879 R	13	330
Campbell, Willie T.	Camden, Horsely B.	27 JUL 1885	20	341
Campbell, Winnie	Shanklin, Richard	25 APR 1883 L	17	412
Campbell, Wm. Walter	Allaire, Alice	16 SEP 1884 R	19	251
Camper, N. Gibson	Greene, Georgia J.	17 DEC 1884	19	465
Camper, Sarena A.	Lomack, Lewis T., Jr.	18 DEC 1883 L	18	323
Canabury, Mary	Girard, Pasqual H.	15 APR 1884 R	18	508
Canavin, James	Roase, Jane	01 NOV 1883 L	18	291
Canby, Emma	Henry, John S.	09 JUL 1878	12	131
Cane, John	Valentine, Ida V.	03 JUL 1879 R	13	257

Canfield, Charles H.	Vosburgh, Annie E.	14 OCT 1879	13	422
Cann, David C.	Burgess, Ella Carrie	12 JUN 1883	17	488
Cannoday, Ann Eliza	Smith, Moses	27 DEC 1881	16	158
Cannon, George E.	Scroggins, Nannie R.	07 OCT 1885 R	20	465
Cannon, George M.	Gunnell, Frances	24 JUL 1884	19	154
Cannon, Henry W.	Curtis, Jennie O.	21 NOV 1879 R	13	496
Cannon, Mary	McLane, John	31 AUG 1880 L	14	424
Cannon, Mary	Zeis, Adams	21 APR 1885	20	176
Cannon, Mary A.	Kendrick, Thomas J.	18 OCT 1882 R	17	080
Cannon, Sallie F.	Goode, John C.	25 JUN 1885 R	20	293
Cannon, William H.	Lightfoot, Laura L.	23 JAN 1883 R	17	271
Cantell, Nellie	Ally, C.H.	19 OCT 1881 L	16	034
Canter, Florence V.	Gates, Andrew M.	15 OCT 1885 R	20	486
Cantwell, John	Biggan, Mary	15 NOV 1881 L	16	079
Canty, Lizzie	Stewart, Columbus	08 FEB 1882 L	16	231
Canty, Patrick	Horrigan, Mary	30 DEC 1882 L	17	226
Caplan, Fannie	Sachs, Jacob	27 MAY 1883 R	17	462
Cappen, Annie	Dries, John F.	30 JUL 1883	18	066
Capps, James S.	Richards, Louisa	08 SEP 1879 R	13	357
Capps, Joseph E.	Derby, Martha A.	16 APR 1882	16	318
Capps, Wilton R.	Chandler, Florence V.	10 MAY 1883 R	17	434
Car, George	Newman, Mary	28 JUL 1881 R	15	423
Carberry, M.A.	Lasser, Oscar	31 JUL 1882 L	16	463
Cardew, William H.	Murphy, Josephine	24 MAY 1881 L	15	323
Cardozo, Annie L.	Dunning, Samuel L.	12 OCT 1882 R	17	070
Cardwell, Martha L.	Richardson, Charley E.	10 JUL 1884	19	132
Carey, Annie	Wells, Beverly	04 JUL 1880 R	14	346
Carey, Jane	Watts, Richard	04 JUN 1879 L	13	219
Carey, Julia	Marston, George	16 JUL 1879 R	13	283
Carey, Katie	Curtin, John	07 OCT 1879 L	13	408
Carey, Lucy	Bell, Rouzo Berry	11 JUN 1885 L	20	268
Carey, Martha C.	Herbert, Charles H.	23 OCT 1883 R	18	206
Carey, Martin V.	Angell, Eva C.	29 OCT 1884	19	347
Carick, Albert	Anderson, Harriet	08 DEC 1881 L	16	121
Carick, Fannie	Tayler, Lewis	09 JUN 1884 R	19	070
Carleton, Maude Clinton	Courtis, Frank	17 APR 1883 R	17	395
Carley, Bernard J.	Cady, Ellen A.	10 APR 1883 L	17	389
Carley, Kate E.	Schmalhoff, William L.	02 OCT 1882 R	17	046
Carlin, Belle	Grimes, Thomas W.	13 MAR 1879 L	13	099
Carlin, James S.	Thompson, Mary Antonia	02 SEP 1880 R	14	427
Carlin, Jno. Frank	Rudd, Sarah V.	16 AUG 1881 R	15	447
Carlin, Mary Ann	Parker, John T.	05 JUL 1877	11	009
Carlin, Thomas L.	Thornton, Ella A.	29 DEC 1879	14	078
Carlisle, George J.	Crump, Carrie	04 JUN 1884	19	051
Carlisle, Inez	Elmore, Yates H.	19 MAR 1878 R	11	385
Carlisle, Stephen H.	Dufief, Nettie	27 JAN 1885	20	038
Carlton, Ella	Hyatt, Frank, M.D.	09 OCT 1878 R	12	263
Carlton, Homazelle	Brown, McKenzie	15 MAR 1882 L	16	279
Carlyle, Frederic W.	Ferrall, Fannie Watson	16 OCT 1884	19	315
Carmack, Kate Moore	Alfred, Walter J.	12 JAN 1880 R	14	101
Carmack, Sarah A.	Dyer, John C.	30 NOV 1881	16	102
Carman, Jesse Seaman	Pleasants, Margaret Cassandra	27 OCT 1881 R	16	046
Carmine, George W.	Allen, Emma	11 JUN 1878 R	12	096
Carmody, Hanorah	McVarry, Michael L.	30 APR 1879 R	13	167
Carmody, Mary	Costello, John C.	29 SEP 1878 R	12	239
Carneal, Dora	Dickinson, Edward B.	17 SEP 1883	18	134
Carney, John	Dougherty, Katie	19 APR 1881 L	15	262
Carney, Mary	Schofield, William S.	04 JUN 1878 R	12	085

Carney, William	Skidmore, Mary	18 JAN 1883 L	17	267
Carpenter, Albert L.	Hawkins, Annie	10 SEP 1881 L	15	481
Carpenter, Annie	Pendleton, Muscow	22 JUL 1882 L	16	454
Carpenter, Annie E.	Randall, Francis G.	03 JUL 1883	18	032
Carpenter, Daniel W.	Lyles, Mary E.	07 APR 1880	14	213
Carpenter, Eli	Parker, Mary	16 AUG 1880 L	14	401
Carpenter, Eliza	Banyan, Robert	21 SEP 1877	11	104
Carpenter, Ellen	Campbell, William	28 MAY 1883	18	275
Carpenter, Emma	Sparks, Lorenzo	26 SEP 1882 R	17	037
Carpenter, George A.	Tucker, Mary A.	07 SEP 1877 R	11	082
Carpenter, Henry	Edmonds, Lulie	19 AUG 1884 R	19	193
Carpenter, John	Tucker, Ella	28 AUG 1877 R	11	063
Carpenter, Katie	Lloyd, Morris D.	03 FEB 1883 L	17	288
Carpenter, Lillie Thomas	Yowell, Jefferson Davis	29 MAR 1882 R	16	292
Carpenter, Louisa Victoria	Morris, Henry	10 APR 1879 R	13	128
Carpenter, Mary	Lingenbaugh, Charles	27 SEP 1877 L	11	111
Carpenter, Mattie	Turner, Edward	03 JUL 1884 L	19	120
Carpenter, Mattie E.	Coffin, John R.	11 DEC 1877	11	229
Carpenter, Sarah	Thomas, Robert	08 JUL 1885 L	20	317
Carpenter, Sophia L.	Gordon, John A.	18 DEC 1883	18	321
Carpenter, Thomas Hicks	Aiken, Catharine Raingeard	23 JAN 1884 R	18	389
Carpenter, Thomas W.	Barker, Nammie E.	20 OCT 1881 L	16	038
Carr, Allen	Price, Nannie	14 FEB 1884 R	18	424
Carr, Ashel	Shoemaker, Elizabeth Jane	08 APR 1884 L	18	500
Carr, Camello Casalti C.	Camp, Marie Caroline Vivans	27 NOV 1878 R	12	347
Carr, Emma	Hurst, William Daniel	26 NOV 1884 R	19	422
Carr, Henry	Garner, Betsy	04 NOV 1880	15	030
Carr, J. Gertrude	Robinson, R. Brannon	02 SEP 1880 R	14	428
Carr, John	Lee, Harriet	11 JUL 1883 R	18	041
Carr, John C.	Brawner, Mollie T.	04 OCT 1882 R	17	052
Carr, John Richard	Cook, Nancy	08 OCT 1878	12	257
Carr, John W.	Young, Emma J.	15 SEP 1880	14	446
Carr, Julia	Trunnell, Thyson T.	07 AUG 1879 R	13	308
Carr, Lucy	Roots, Howard	24 JUL 1877 R	11	029
Carr, Lula M.	Mason, George H.	02 MAR 1878 L	11	370
Carr, Mollie Virginia	Griggs, Wm. Lewis	08 MAR 1881 R	15	220
Carr, Sebina C.	Parker, Francis D.	18 NOV 1880 R	15	055
Carr, William E.	Quigley, Maggie	16 FEB 1882 L	16	246
Carr, William K.	Van Riswick, Martina	04 JUN 1885	20	256
Carraher, John Victor	Bicksler, Alice Eugenie	09 JAN 1879 R	13	013
Carraher, Mary E.	Marsden, Frank L.	27 SEP 1883 L	18	157
Carrick, Annie R.	Anderson, Jefferson D.	14 DEC 1884	19	455
Carrick, Ella F.	Stewart, John T.	21 JAN 1882 L	16	204
Carrick, Joseph C.	Nolan, Elizabeth	20 APR 1882 L	16	328
Carrick, Martha Is. Va.	Miller, Nelson	07 OCT 1885 R	20	466
Carrick, William Everest	Ward, Mary Frances	30 SEP 1879 R	13	382
Carrico, Annie F.	Foos, William D.	21 FEB 1882 R	16	253
Carrico, William C.	Kyle, Emma G.	14 SEP 1885 R	20	415
Carrie, Banks	Woodyard, William H.L.	22 MAR 1883 L	17	355
Carrier, Leona Abigail	Hall, J.N.	26 NOV 1879 L	14	014
Carrington, Campbell	Ricketts, Laura V.	12 SEP 1877	11	085
Carrington, Charles	Meredith, Josephine	03 JUL 1885 L	20	309
Carrington, David C.	Ross, Laura D.	16 APR 1879	13	140
Carrington, Jacob	Robinson, Sarah, Mrs.	12 APR 1881	15	251
Carrington, Mollie	Richardson, J.F.	18 SEP 1877	11	098
Carrington, Solomon M.	Gibbs, Fannie L.	05 OCT 1882 R	17	052
Carrington, Thomas A.	Seaton, Constance Gertrude	06 MAR 1878 L	11	374
Carrison, Eva	Scott, William	22 JAN 1884 L	18	389

D.C. Marriage Records Index, June 28, 1877 to October 19, 1885

Carrol, Mary	Robinson, Charles	14 NOV 1878	12	330
Carrol, Richard	Redman, Alice	04 FEB 1879	13	045
Carrol, Robert C.	Ogdon, Emma	13 MAR 1884 R	18	471
Carroll, Almira Rawlings	Birch, Corbin	18 NOV 1884 L	19	390
Carroll, Annie J.	O'Neal, William	27 SEP 1883 R	18	147
Carroll, Carrie	Nicholson, Philip Walter	20 MAY 1884 R	19	029
Carroll, Catharine	Murphy, William	20 MAY 1879 R	13	197
Carroll, Charles H.	Herbert, Letha M.	03 APR 1883 L	17	377
Carroll, Clara E.	Mockabee, William	07 JUN 1884	19	068
Carroll, David	Williams, Annie	16 AUG 1877 R	11	054
Carroll, David Winfield	Watson, Mary Jane	07 SEP 1881 L	15	474
Carroll, Dennis	Morgan, Alice	30 OCT 1877	11	161
Carroll, Edward	Lancaster, Henrietta	30 JUN 1880 L	14	339
Carroll, Edward	Briles, Maggie	20 JUL 1881	15	410
Carroll, Eliza	Jackson, James	28 FEB 1884	18	450
Carroll, Elizabeth Lucille	Tucker, Tarlton Webb	20 SEP 1883	18	141
Carroll, Emma	Swan, Moses M.	18 FEB 1879 L	13	064
Carroll, Emma	Boswell, Charles	16 SEP 1880 R	14	453
Carroll, Eugene	Clark, Emma	16 AUG 1880 L	14	400
Carroll, Eugene	Jackson, Rachel A.	01 DEC 1883 L	18	289
Carroll, George H.	Chapman, Alice V.	05 APR 1882	16	300
Carroll, Georgiana	Harper, George A.	08 OCT 1883 L	18	176
Carroll, Hannora	McCathran, Benjamin F.	29 APR 1883 R	17	421
Carroll, Harriet L.	Smallwood, John T.	30 OCT 1884	19	349
Carroll, Henry	James, Mary E.	29 JAN 1880	14	041
Carroll, James	Coats, Emma	26 AUG 1884 L	19	208
Carroll, James P.	Farron, Amanda M.	06 MAY 1879 R	13	177
Carroll, James W.	Colclaser, Ellen E.	08 SEP 1880 R	14	437
Carroll, John	Gray, Eliza	29 OCT 1878 R	12	298
Carroll, John	Fitzgerald, Ellen	08 JUN 1880	14	307
Carroll, John Henry	Fry, Mary Frances	30 JAN 1878	11	292
Carroll, John William	Sullivan, Hannah	18 JUL 1879 R	13	281
Carroll, Julia	Shorter, Charles	14 MAY 1885	20	222
Carroll, Julia A.	Folks, David T.	23 FEB 1881 L	15	201
Carroll, Kate	Padgett, William L.	23 FEB 1881 R	15	199
Carroll, Kate B.	Trego, Albert	07 NOV 1883 D	18	239
Carroll, Katharine D.B.	Beale, John Wheeler	13 DEC 1877 R	11	234
Carroll, Laura V.	Allen, Robert	18 APR 1882 R	16	323
Carroll, Lizzie	Boose, Frank	05 AUG 1884 L	19	169
Carroll, Louisa	Wright, John H.	09 OCT 1877	11	125
Carroll, Lucy	Simms, Wallace	03 JUN 1879	13	216
Carroll, M. Alice	Faunce, Phillip P.	19 NOV 1883	18	263
Carroll, Martha	Saunders, Thornton	04 SEP 1879 R	13	350
Carroll, Mary	Harris, George W.	24 JUL 1884	19	154
Carroll, Mary A.	Shoemaker, Isaac W.	03 APR 1879 L	13	125
Carroll, Mary A.	Killafoyle, John J.	02 JUN 1880 L	16	390
Carroll, Mary E.	Webster, James H.	07 OCT 1877	11	123
Carroll, Mary E.	Richardson, John Francis	23 FEB 1878 L	11	354
Carroll, Mary E.	Wilson, Frank	07 FEB 1883	17	295
Carroll, Mary E.	Briscoe, John W.	07 SEP 1885 L	20	402
Carroll, Mary Ellen	Clagett, Edward	27 JUN 1878 L	12	115
Carroll, Mary Ellen	Moore, Charles T.	29 JUN 1882 R	16	432
Carroll, Minnie	Herbert, Thomas	04 OCT 1877	11	122
Carroll, O.D.	Green, M.A.	09 DEC 1884 L	19	444
Carroll, Oden	Parker, Isabella	08 APR 1883 R	17	384
Carroll, Patrick	Kerrick, Sue Franklin	12 MAY 1879 R	13	185
Carroll, Patrick H.	Sanders, Emma A.	26 AUG 1879 L	13	338
Carroll, Richard H.	Minor, Isabella	01 OCT 1878	12	244

Carroll, Robert	Thomas, Augusta	07 FEB 1883 L	17	298
Carroll, Sarah	King, George	02 DEC 1878 L	12	357
Carroll, Sarah C.	Brooks, William H.	05 NOV 1882 R	17	106
Carroll, Thomas	Hodge, Hannah	20 NOV 1882 L	17	137
Carroll, Walter	Alden, Mattie	02 JUL 1882	16	433
Carroll, Walter W.	Blankline, Anne Eliza	22 MAR 1879 L	13	112
Carroll, Wesley	Smith, Emma	05 FEB 1885	20	053
Carroll, William	Milburn, Mary	08 NOV 1877 L	11	176
Carroll, William	Whitney, Marcella	05 AUG 1879	13	307
Carroll, William	Brooks, Alice	09 JUN 1880 L	14	313
Carroll, William	Simms, Jane	09 OCT 1884 L	19	298
Carroll, William A.	Thompson, Annie	09 APR 1881 R	15	235
Carroll, William C.	Washington, Mary E.	16 SEP 1883	18	133
Carroll, William C.	Walton, Julia C.	22 SEP 1885 L	20	435
Carson, Adolph B.	Kernon, Helen S.	08 APR 1884 R	18	500
Carson, William Henry	Darr, Nellie Agnes	09 FEB 1881 R	15	184
Carstens, Anna P.	Riston, Charles Thos.	03 JUN 1885 R	20	252
Carston, Maggie	Norriss, Jacob	20 NOV 1879 R	13	496
Carter, Addison	Turner, Sally	29 MAY 1878 L	12	073
Carter, Adelaide	Kelpy, Anthony	10 JAN 1881 R	15	145
Carter, Andromeda C.	Meagher, Francis	17 JUL 1882	16	447
Carter, Ann	Hutchinson, George	29 NOV 1877 R	11	197
Carter, Annie	Davenport, Isaac	31 JUL 1879	13	300
Carter, Annie	Anderson, Archie	09 SEP 1885	20	401
Carter, Annisetta	Saunders, Christopher W.	13 AUG 1883	18	084
Carter, Anthony	Callahan, Sarah	11 APR 1880 R	14	220
Carter, Armstead	Gaston, Matilda	02 OCT 1883 L	18	165
Carter, Benjamin G.	Reeves, Rosa B.	07 MAY 1884	19	011
Carter, Berta Verginia	Noyes, Galveston	26 SEP 1883 R	18	155
Carter, Bettie	Walker, William	15 SEP 1884 L	19	248
Carter, Burrell	Halkins, Emelin	21 DEC 1882 R	17	202
Carter, C.H.	Grayson, Mary E.	26 APR 1881 L	15	273
Carter, Champ	Johnson, Fanny	02 APR 1878 R	11	401
Carter, Charles	Pinckney, Georgiana	30 OCT 1879 R	13	453
Carter, Charles	Dixon, Martha	27 NOV 1879	14	013
Carter, Charles	Jackson, Mary	16 OCT 1883 R	18	194
Carter, Charles	Davis, Mary	04 SEP 1884 L	19	228
Carter, Charles C.	Douglas, Martha R.	10 DEC 1880 L	15	104
Carter, Charles Edward	Tolley, Emily Jane	10 NOV 1879 R	13	475
Carter, Charles F.	Mudd, Anna C.	25 SEP 1879 R	13	387
Carter, Charles H.	Clark, Jane Estella	07 DEC 1882 R	17	173
Carter, Churchill	Miller, Susanna	07 MAY 1884 L	19	011
Carter, Daniel	Thomas, Maria	21 FEB 1878 L	11	351
Carter, E.F.	Lucas, Mary E.	05 JUN 1879 L	13	221
Carter, Edward	Thompson, Eliza	23 NOV 1882 R	17	130
Carter, Elias	Davis, Fannie	20 JUN 1885 L	20	282
Carter, Eliza	Miles, George	02 JUL 1883 L	18	029
Carter, Eliza Ann	Buchanan, Daniel	24 OCT 1883 R	18	206
Carter, Eliza R.	Rossi, Eugene	17 FEB 1885	20	065
Carter, Elizabeth	Atkins, Henry	05 OCT 1880 R	14	469
Carter, Elizabeth	Hart, George H.	27 FEB 1883 R	17	322
Carter, Elizabeth	Williams, John H.	02 MAY 1883 L	17	426
Carter, Ella A.	Godwin, Lucien J. Bonaparte	22 APR 1879 R	13	153
Carter, Emma	Odelions, Frank	18 JUL 1881 L	15	408
Carter, Enoch	Neal, Fannie	20 OCT 1881 L	16	037
Carter, Eugean	Curtley, Alice	10 SEP 1883 R	18	121
Carter, Fannie	Gaskins, Randolph	03 NOV 1881 R	16	054
Carter, Frank	Pendleton, Amanda	24 MAY 1882 R	16	374

D.C. Marriage Records Index, June 28, 1877 to October 19, 1885

Carter, Frank	Pinion, Rachel	18 FEB 1884 R	18	430
Carter, Franklin	Jackson, Mary L.	04 FEB 1884 R	18	407
Carter, Frederick	Wallace, Emma	17 MAR 1885 R	20	120
Carter, George	Grandison, Mary Florence	26 MAY 1879	13	199
Carter, George	Brown, Rebecca	04 JAN 1882 L	16	179
Carter, George	Johnson, Annie	09 DEC 1882 L	17	175
Carter, George	Bailey, Lizzie	10 JUN 1884 L	19	071
Carter, George W.	Shaw, Susannah	12 JUN 1879	13	231
Carter, Georgiana	Byrd, John Henry	19 NOV 1884 L	19	393
Carter, Harrison	Smith, Lillie	02 JUN 1884	19	048
Carter, Henrietta	White, Thomas	28 AUG 1881	15	438
Carter, Henrietta E.	Crawford, William T.	25 JAN 1882 L	16	208
Carter, Henry	Webb, Ella M.D.	22 SEP 1880 R	14	456
Carter, Henry	Dixon, Alice	16 JUL 1885 L	20	330
Carter, Horace	Thomas, Susan	09 JAN 1883 L	17	245
Carter, Horace	Snowdon, Anna	27 SEP 1883 L	18	158
Carter, Horace	Thomas, Isabella	10 FEB 1885 L	20	061
Carter, Isabel	Berkley, Cornelius A.	18 JUL 1878	12	139
Carter, J.W.	Peed, L.A.	21 JUN 1883	18	009
Carter, James	Kent, Maria	12 JUL 1877 R	11	016
Carter, James	Maith, Mildreth	31 DEC 1879 L	14	085
Carter, James	Brown, Adeline	09 AUG 1880 R	14	321
Carter, James	Brown, Mary	09 OCT 1882	17	061
Carter, James	Smith, Martha	17 MAY 1883 R	17	448
Carter, James A.	Parker, Julia A.	09 DEC 1880 R	15	081
Carter, James William	Falconer, Ella	19 APR 1882 R	16	326
Carter, Jane	Holmes, Charles H.	17 OCT 1881	16	025
Carter, Jennie	Coleman, William	24 SEP 1885 R	20	423
Carter, John	Fitzhugh, Maria	22 APR 1878 L	12	015
Carter, John	Washington, Mary E.	02 SEP 1878 L	12	192
Carter, John	Shields, Marian D.	21 AUG 1879	13	328
Carter, John F.	Daymude, Anna E. "Lizzie"	15 OCT 1880 R	14	496
Carter, John Lewis	Lewis, Milwood Eddy	01 OCT 1884	19	278
Carter, John M.	Wiley, Lena	01 FEB 1883	17	282
Carter, John T.	Veney, Emiline	10 MAY 1884 L	19	013
Carter, John Wesley	Smith, Mary Frances	04 OCT 1880 L	14	473
Carter, Joseph	Covington, Ella E.	18 MAR 1884	18	477
Carter, Julia J.	Harrison, Robert H.	20 OCT 1879 R	13	439
Carter, Julia, Mrs.	Beal, Horace	01 JAN 1882 R	16	173
Carter, Kate C.	Applewhite, Henry B.	29 MAY 1884	19	044
Carter, Katie M.	Washington, George W.	16 SEP 1882 L	17	023
Carter, L.T.	Turner, Viola	05 FEB 1878	11	328
Carter, Lena N.	Loury, George C.R.	23 JAN 1879	13	032
Carter, Letitia V.	Boler, Abraham	08 AUG 1883 L	18	081
Carter, Lewis	Walker, Emily	20 SEP 1883 L	18	142
Carter, Lizzie	Harris, Andrew	17 AUG 1882 L	16	484
Carter, Louis	Armstead, Carrie	25 MAR 1880 L	14	197
Carter, Louisa	Lawler, Samuel	21 DEC 1881 R	16	146
Carter, Lucinda	Webster, William Henry	18 DEC 1877 L	11	243
Carter, Lucy A.	McPherson, Richard	02 OCT 1884	19	283
Carter, Lucy Ann	Jones, William Francis	03 FEB 1881 R	15	176
Carter, Mansfield	Braxton, Sallie Ann	02 DEC 1883	18	289
Carter, Marshall[3]	Hudnall, Roberta	24 AUG 1881	15	457

---

[3] Western Union Telegraph attached to record, spelling preserved: "Warrenton, Va., Aug. 23, 1881. Roberta Chalahan and Marshall Carter leave for Washington tomorrow for marriage certificate. She has a husband, don't issue without Evidence to contrary from this county." [signed] A. Carter. "Cyrus H. Newhouse of Fauquier, Va., came with Marshall Carter to ask for the license, & explained that the marriage with Calahan was void because Callahan is a white man & Hudnall is Colored."

Carter, Martha	Whidnon, Jesse	27 NOV 1879 R	14	018
Carter, Martha	Dyson, Charles	03 JAN 1884	18	354
Carter, Martha C.	Peterson, David	22 FEB 1882 R	16	257
Carter, Mary	Sudduth, Joseph A.	19 MAR 1879	13	108
Carter, Mary	Jones, Charles Wash.	16 MAR 1885 L	20	115
Carter, Mary E.	Thomas, Wilemon	27 JUL 1882 L	16	459
Carter, Mary E.	Waters, Henry	05 JUN 1882	16	393
Carter, Mary E.	Schweizer, William T.	15 OCT 1883	18	192
Carter, Mary Ellen	McGee, George Francis	15 SEP 1879 R	13	369
Carter, Matilda	Jackson, John B.	15 SEP 1883 L	18	132
Carter, May	Dove, William	06 NOV 1884	19	367
Carter, Millie	Johnson, Moses	05 NOV 1884 L	19	361
Carter, Miney	Henderson, Charles Henry	20 SEP 1877 R	11	089
Carter, Morton	Randall, Julia	30 MAY 1882	16	378
Carter, Noah Albert	Crowley, Katie C.	27 AUG 1877	11	066
Carter, Patrick	Braxton, Eliza	23 NOV 1880 R	15	062
Carter, Pinkey	Fortune, Eugene	18 OCT 1881 L	16	033
Carter, Polly	Mason, Samuel	24 AUG 1881 L	15	456
Carter, Polly [Dickson]	Williams, John	05 FEB 1883 R	17	290
Carter, Richard W., Jr.	Tenly, Georgie I.	04 OCT 1883 L	18	169
Carter, Robert	Campbell, Anna	17 JAN 1878 R	11	309
Carter, Robert	Roberts, Bettie L.	30 DEC 1879 R	16	3865
Carter, Robert	Wilson, Evelina	25 MAR 1880 R	14	196
Carter, Robert B.	Schneider, Lavinia M.	28 MAR 1884 L	18	486
Carter, Robert Daniel	Robinson, Edie	24 JAN 1878 L	11	316
Carter, Robert L.	Brown, Mary	28 FEB 1884	18	442
Carter, Robert R.	Brown, Lucie B.	06 JUL 1881 L	15	393
Carter, Rosa L.	Tolson, Francis E.	05 MAY 1881 R	15	293
Carter, Samuel Powh., Capt.	Williams, Martha Custis	03 OCT 1877	11	118
Carter, Sarah	Green, William	14 DEC 1877	11	235
Carter, Sarah	Johnson, Daniel	25 JUN 1883 R	18	013
Carter, Sarah	Dickson, James	03 JUL 1884 L	19	119
Carter, Sarah A.	Slade, Jesse B.	17 MAR 1881 L	15	230
Carter, Silas	Holmes, Annie Elizabeth	19 JUL 1879 L	13	286
Carter, Stephen	Shepherd, Elizabeth	26 SEP 1885 L	20	088
Carter, Strawther	Robinson, Annie	09 DEC 1880 R	15	085
Carter, Susan	King, Benjamin	01 APR 1880 R	14	196
Carter, Susan	Montgomery, Isaac	14 AUG 1884 L	19	185
Carter, Thomas	Glover, E. Victoria	20 AUG 1879 R	13	321
Carter, Thomas	James, Sarah	21 MAY 1885 R	20	234
Carter, Truman	Allen, Mary Ellen	13 DEC 1884 R	19	456
Carter, Walter	Stewart, Lucy	13 MAY 1884	19	007
Carter, Wilbur E.	Soper, Elizabeth	09 OCT 1877	11	128
Carter, William	Hall, Lucy	15 JAN 1878 R	11	304
Carter, William	Morton, Viney	28 FEB 1878 L	11	366
Carter, William	Young, Mary	25 MAR 1884 L	18	481
Carter, William B., Rev.	Patten, Ellen D.	01 JUL 1884	19	111
Carter, William Frank	Feaster, Alice	21 JAN 1885	20	032
Carter, William H.	Lewis, Virginia	01 OCT 1884	19	297
Carter, Willie Catherine	Hildebrand, Abraham	28 DEC 1880 R	15	128
Carter, Winnie Ann	Mason, Samuel	20 NOV 1877 L	11	193
Cartes, Nannie	Chew, Thomas	20 JUL 1883 L	18	056
Carttter, George A.	Dade, Lucy M.	24 MAY 1881 L	15	322
Cartwell, Nellie Natalie	Anderson, William Weldon	16 JAN 1878 R	11	307
Cartwright, Alice	Harris, Fenton	06 NOV 1879 R	13	471
Cartwright, Celestine	Garner, Thomas	15 JAN 1884 L	18	379
Cartwright, Harriet A.	Paul, Joseph R.	30 DEC 1884 L	19	503
Cartwright, Levin T.	Brooke, Sarah Acklin	30 SEP 1885 R	20	450

Cartwright, Richard T.	Tredway, Catherine A.	05 APR 1880 R	14	209
Carty, Susan A.	Harper, Stephen V.	16 NOV 1883 R	18	260
Carver, Alpha E.H.	Hinson, Clara Beall	23 MAR 1881 R	15	236
Carver, Luellen	Raynor, Martin	10 OCT 1879 R	13	407
Carver, Margaret	Shackelford, William M.	13 NOV 1878 R	12	325
Cary, Louisa M.	Noble, Horace E.	06 SEP 1883 R	18	117
Casassa, Agnes R.	Parham, Ellsworth C.	23 MAY 1878	12	064
Case, Elizabeth Caroline	Brady, Bernard E.	14 MAR 1878	11	369
Case, Francis H.	Traylor, Sarah E.	23 OCT 1884	19	332
Case, Marion Hill	Lang, Oscar	18 JUL 1883	18	052
Case, Wm. W.	Hutton, Maggie S.	02 JAN 1881 R	20	4769
Casey, Catherine	Daly, Joseph E.	06 JUN 1885 L	20	258
Casey, Ellen E.	Mannix, John B.	26 JUN 1880 L	14	335
Casey, Fannie	Magruder, William P.	18 NOV 1878 R	12	333
Casey, John	Havenner, Laura V.	01 APR 1882 L	16	295
Casey, John A.	Buchly, Alice T.	24 DEC 1884 L	19	490
Casey, Lizzie	Boyle, Thomas	25 JAN 1883 L	17	274
Casey, Maggie	Connor, Patrick	12 JAN 1885 L	20	012
Casey, Mary	Lynch, Martin	27 AUG 1883 L	18	127
Casey, Mary	Riley, James	11 AUG 1883 L	18	083
Casey, Mary	Sullivan, Michael	08 FEB 1885	20	055
Casey, Patrick Jas.	Tobin, Mary E.	26 OCT 1881 R	16	041
Cash, Katie	Massie, Byron	22 OCT 1883	18	205
Cash, Thomas M.	Brown, Sarah A.	04 SEP 1884	19	227
Cash, Walter S.	Boyd, Maggie J.	07 DEC 1881 L	16	116
Cashell, George T.	Wilkerson, Mollie C.	23 MAY 1884	18	527
Casler, Sarah E.	Burgdorf, Albert O.	31 DEC 1883 L	18	356
Caspar, Frank	Depierri, Rosa	28 JUN 1877 L	11	001
Caspari, John	Lutz, Annie	23 APR 1883 L	17	405
Cass, Kate	Kappler, Gregory, Jr.	07 FEB 1878 L	11	331
Cassady, Samuel T.	Eubank, Camille A.	04 FEB 1884 R	18	216
Cassasa, Joseph	Ratte, Annie	26 JUL 1879	13	293
Casseen, Annie	Soper, Edward	26 AUG 1879 R	13	333
Cassell, Lou A.	Pope, N.Q.	03 APR 1878 R	11	405
Cassell, Washington F.	Laignel, Marie	25 JUN 1884 R	19	103
Cassidy, Edward F.	Murray, Mary A.	17 APR 1884 R	18	517
Cassidy, Fannie	Free, William F.	08 JUN 1884	19	128
Cassidy, Henry Harrison	Davis, Susan Ellen	20 JUN 1881 R	14	431
Cassidy, Nellie L.	Keyser, Earl A.	18 OCT 1882 R	17	079
Cassin, Bridget	Culhane, Thomas	16 JAN 1883 L	17	259
Cassin, Margaret Batty	Gladmon, Edwin	27 MAR 1884 R	18	484
Cassin, Virgina Lee	Kinkaid, Thomas Wright	03 APR 1883 R	17	373
Cassosa, Louisa	Rocca, John B.	14 JAN 1883	17	256
Castafneto, Maria	Riani, Gandenzio	27 OCT 1881 L	16	050
Castell, Annie M.	Colleflower, Charles E.	20 FEB 1882 R	16	248
Castello, Dan, Jr.	Smith, Gertrude Frazier	10 OCT 1883 L	18	183
Casten, Henry	Klein, Amelia	25 SEP 1881 R	15	491
Castle, Walter L.	Crim, Mary	29 JAN 1884	18	399
Castor, Mary E.	Watson, Joseph	25 APR 1878	12	023
Cate, Fernando C.	Whittier, Clara O.	18 MAY 1882	16	363
Cate, Holmes	McCleary, Maggie W.	26 AUG 1879 R	13	337
Cate, Nellie F.	Patterson, Walter B.	21 FEB 1884	18	436
Cater, Benjamin	Lovelace, Laura	28 AUG 1877	11	066
Cathcart, Frank H.	Dienelt, Bertha	24 DEC 1884 R	19	485
Cathell, J.H.	Blake, E.J.	20 DEC 1877 L	11	249
Cathell, James H.	Blake, Ella J.	03 JAN 1878	11	293
Cathell, Margaret Jane	Fuller, Wilson Neville	25 NOV 1880 R	15	063
Catis, Kate	Scrivener, Theodore A.	19 JUL 1877	11	019

Catlet, Cassie	Thomas, Walker	08 DEC 1884 L	19	439
Catlet, Lucy Ann	Jones, George J.	18 MAR 1879 L	13	103
Catlett, Albert H.	Fleshman, Minnie	15 OCT 1885	20	487
Catlett, Eliza	Dyer, Alexander F.	19 DEC 1881 L	16	139
Catlett, James M., Jr.	Tredick, Fannie L.	13 DEC 1881 R	16	127
Caton, George D.	Mulquin, Mary A.	30 OCT 1879 L	13	454
Caton, Jennie A.	Nitzel, Charles A.	13 AUG 1879 L	13	319
Caton, Margaret	Doherty, William	09 JUL 1877 L	11	013
Caton, Mary A.	Reynolds, Henry W.	23 AUG 1884 L	19	204
Caton, Mary E.	Donahue, John M.	18 FEB 1882 L	16	248
Caton, William H.	Elliot, Mary C.S.	22 JAN 1878 R	11	313
Cator, Albert R.	Watson, E. Lavinia	23 NOV 1880	15	059
Cator, Annie M.	Wise, William	01 JUL 1880 L	14	343
Cator, Martha Ann	Walker, Henry	11 MAR 1878 L	11	377
Cattell, Lizzie M.	Woods, William	12 DEC 1877	11	230
Caulder, Laura	Yeakle, John A.	21 MAY 1881 L	15	321
Caulfield, Charles J.	Prentiss, Eunice A.	17 JUL 1880 R	14	366
Caulfield, Genevieve	Fox, Charles B.	05 NOV 1878	12	305
Causten, Fanny C.	Crusor, William	05 AUG 1879 L	13	307
Causten, George P.	Smith, Ida May	24 OCT 1878	12	289
Cautions, Mary Eliza Sewall	Lane, William Andrew	21 APR 1881 R	15	258
Cavagarro, Cornelia	Bacigaluppo, Joseph	11 JAN 1884 L	18	373
Cavanaugh, Joseph	Woods, Ella	30 NOV 1883 L	18	288
Cavanaugh, Margaret	Downs, Henry	21 AUG 1882 L	16	489
Cavanaugh, Rosa	Gibbs, William Henry	27 SEP 1877 R	11	106
Cavell, Helen M.	Alsop, Melvin B.	13 DEC 1881 R	16	126
Cavender, Joseph	Tibbs, Annie L., Mrs.	14 JAN 1884 L	18	376
Cavill, Robert	Chew, Mary E.	05 APR 1883	17	380
Cavis, Ada P.	Williss, Rodolph	27 SEP 1882	17	039
Cavis, Annie Hamilton	Holden, Augustus Randall	07 DEC 1882 R	17	172
Cavis, Belle	Potee, Robert L.	06 APR 1885 R	20	145
Cavis, Belle	Thomson, William	07 FEB 1885 L	20	056
Cawldwell, Mary	Culver, Charles Z.	03 JAN 1882	16	177
Cawood, Thos. Marion	Marsh, Blanche W.	03 NOV 1884 R	19	355
Caynor, Alice B.	Degges, Elmer E.	21 MAY 1883 L	17	454
Caywood, John B.	Ricketts, Emeline	07 OCT 1880 R	14	480
Ceals, Frank	Patton, Sarah	14 MAR 1882	16	275
Ceas, Ella M.	Sisson, Armstead C.	07 JUN 1883 R	17	484
Ceas, Fannie M.	Souder, John W.	12 OCT 1881 L	16	019
Cecil, William H.	Earp, Mary E.	03 OCT 1883	18	167
Ceiss, John L.	Smith, Annie V.	03 NOV 1882	17	110
Center, Henry R.	McCulloch, Kitty	17 APR 1879 R	13	150
Chadwick, Robert P.	Mahoney, Mary Magdaline	21 AUG 1882	16	490
Chaffee, Kate	Greenwood, James	28 OCT 1882 L	17	099
Chalk, Charles S.	Hill, Mary J.	12 SEP 1883	18	127
Chalk, George F.	Mills, Virginia	20 JAN 1880	14	112
Chalker, Chas. Webster	Otler, Hellen Elizabeth	25 JUL 1878	12	148
Chamberlain, Alice	Cumberland, John	09 DEC 1884	19	443
Chamberlain, Clara C.	Daw, Robert A.	08 OCT 1878 R	12	262
Chamberlain, Henry	Evans, Isabel L., Mrs.	10 SEP 1884	19	240
Chamberlain, Mary E.	Rollings, John Henry	26 JUL 1881 L	15	419
Chamberlain, William	Graham, Lizzie C.	14 FEB 1882 L	16	240
Chamberlin, Kate	Gore, John Edward	27 DEC 1884 R	19	494
Chamberlin, Susie A.	Colburn, James R.	18 OCT 1877	11	145
Chamberlin, William Nelson	Marks, Edwina Pierrepont	25 OCT 1880 R	15	010
Chambers, Carrie M.	Bohannon, Joseph	10 JUN 1880 R	14	315
Chambers, Dabney M.	Hughes, Laura	07 OCT 1884 L	19	289
Chambers, Emma	Green, William	18 JAN 1883 R	17	266

D.C. Marriage Records Index, June 28, 1877 to October 19, 1885 — 81

Chambers, Georgie Delrean	Moore, Leopold Fred.	05 SEP 1883	18	109
Chambers, Maggie E.	Owens, Samuel H.	19 FEB 1885 R	20	077
Chamblin, Manie	Munroe, Thomas Eugene	24 SEP 1885 R	20	439
Champ, Charles P.	Powell, Malinda	24 APR 1884 R	18	515
Champ, Eliza	Butcher, Robert	19 FEB 1880	14	150
Champ, Isabella	Smith, Benjamin	25 JUL 1877 L	11	031
Champlin, William	Kydd, Eleanor M.	09 APR 1878	12	046
Chandler, Florence V.	Capps, Wilton R.	10 MAY 1883 R	17	434
Chandler, Morton	Grimes, Cornelia	20 OCT 1885 R	20	495
Chandler, Oliver M.	Smith, Annie F.	09 APR 1878	11	416
Chandler, Richard	Williams, Martha Eliz. Bell	19 FEB 1880 R	14	160
Chaney, Alice G.	Hall, Peter F.	24 JAN 1884 R	18	390
Chaney, Andrew W.	Marsh, Rosa E.	24 DEC 1877	11	262
Chaney, Belle	Willie, William W.	25 JUL 1885 L	20	341
Chaney, Emma E.	McCollam, Edward F.W.	22 MAY 1883	17	456
Chaney, Joseph	Beckett, Julia	05 APR 1883	17	379
Chaney, Martina	Thompson, George H.	14 JUL 1879 L	13	280
Chaney, Mary	King, John W.	24 FEB 1881 L	15	203
Chapin, Charles T.	Stanhope, Ida J.	11 JUN 1882 R	16	404
Chapin, Mattie D.	Ellery, Albert S.	19 NOV 1884 R	19	395
Chapman, Alice	Brown, Samuel	30 SEP 1884 R	19	274
Chapman, Alice J.	St. John, J.F.	23 OCT 1884 L	19	333
Chapman, Alice V.	Carroll, George H.	05 APR 1882	16	300
Chapman, Celia	Ray, William	21 NOV 1883 L	18	270
Chapman, Charles W.	Ross, Fannie M.	24 OCT 1880	15	011
Chapman, E. Rose	McAvoy, George F.	26 NOV 1884 L	19	416
Chapman, E.K.	Knight, E.E.	12 MAY 1879 R	13	186
Chapman, Edward	Reinburg, Honora	09 APR 1885 L	20	156
Chapman, Elijah	Washington, Mary	26 APR 1882 L	16	335
Chapman, Ella	Moor, Jacob	29 NOV 1878	12	355
Chapman, Frank R.	Crabbin, Emma L.	24 SEP 1878	12	232
Chapman, George P.	Haines, Mary E.	28 FEB 1880	14	168
Chapman, Ignatius	Dison, Martha E.	18 FEB 1879	13	065
Chapman, Katherine P.	Gregory, George Wm.	16 MAY 1883	17	444
Chapman, Martha	Gross, William	06 AUG 1884 L	19	171
Chapman, Olivia	Richard, Carter	22 APR 1882 L	16	329
Chapman, Richard	Matthews, Mary Francis	28 JUN 1877	11	003
Chapman, Silas	Alexander, Charlotte	15 FEB 1882 R	16	241
Chappel, Charles H.	Koon, Jennie L.	24 APR 1878	12	021
Chappelear, Harry L.	Chappelear, Mary Ellen	30 JUL 1885 R	20	345
Chappelear, Mary Ellen	Chappelear, Harry L.	30 JUL 1885 R	20	345
Chappell, Ida H.	Paxton, James A.	10 JAN 1880 R	14	096
Chappell, Minnie Jennetta	McElfresh, Frank Spindler	12 FEB 1884 R	18	420
Chappell, Oliver F.	Van Slyke, Rachel	04 SEP 1884	19	227
Chappelle, Katie	Armstrong, John F.	22 DEC 1884	19	476
Chappelle, Nona	Alexander, A.A.	16 AUG 1880	14	400
Charles, W.B.	Neale, Ida F.	27 FEB 1878 L	11	361
Charleston, Emma D.	Bush, Edward D.C.	26 JUN 1878 L	12	116
Charlton, Sarah	Hudnall, James	30 APR 1878	12	029
Charlton, William	Robinson, Martha	31 AUG 1885 L	20	392
Chartters, William S.	Simpson, Laurette	31 MAY 1882	16	382
Chase, Amelia	Millice, Tony	02 MAR 1880	14	170
Chase, Ann	Hegeman, Eli	08 OCT 1883 L	18	177
Chase, Augustus	McGrath, Catherine	14 MAR 1881 L	15	225
Chase, Constantine	Mosher, Mary M.	06 APR 1878 R	11	409
Chase, Cora Blanche	Benedict, James Sackett	09 JAN 1879 R	13	012
Chase, David	Morris, Maria	14 DEC 1882 L	17	184
Chase, Eliza	Thomas, Benjamin	16 MAR 1880 R	14	186

Chase, Ella V.	Williams, Emery W., Rev.	05 DEC 1882 R	17	167
Chase, Elmar	Chun, Florence	05 NOV 1878 L	12	307
Chase, Emma	Kane, John	26 APR 1878 R	12	018
Chase, Emma	Magruder, Allan	23 DEC 1880 L	15	119
Chase, Evlyn M.	Harvey, Edward W.	07 OCT 1885 R	20	466
Chase, Fannie R.	Pool, Benjamin G.	20 DEC 1882 R	17	194
Chase, Greenbury	Powell, Ella	07 SEP 1877 R	11	070
Chase, Greenbury	Powell, Ella	29 OCT 1877 R	09	2164
Chase, Henrietta P.	Plant, George H.	02 JUN 1879	13	215
Chase, Isaac Henry	Kenealy, Mary J.	25 NOV 1884 R	19	405
Chase, Isaac McKim	Hall, Emeline, Mrs.	01 APR 1878 R	11	399
Chase, James	Matthews, Mary	05 JUN 1883 L	17	475
Chase, Jane	Johnson, Philip	05 JUN 1882 L	16	394
Chase, Jennie	Brooks, Charles	15 NOV 1883	18	256
Chase, Joseph	Singleton, Mariah	15 MAY 1884 R	19	022
Chase, Josephine A.	Palmer, Clinton C.	29 APR 1881 L	15	285
Chase, Laura	Dietz, John	15 OCT 1881	16	024
Chase, Lincoln Melville	Richard, Marion Genevieve	25 SEP 1882 R	17	036
Chase, Lizzie Ambush	McWill, William H.	28 APR 1880 R	14	239
Chase, Louisa	Wallace, Thomas	24 OCT 1878	12	291
Chase, Martha	Stewart, Henry	20 OCT 1879 L	13	434
Chase, Martha	Frazer, Hamilton	02 AUG 1884	19	165
Chase, Mary	Jenkins, Daniel	23 DEC 1884 L	19	479
Chase, Mary Ann	Johnson, John Randall	22 AUG 1877 R	11	060
Chase, Mary E.	Buchanan, William H.	18 AUG 1881 L	15	453
Chase, Mary L.	Payne, George W.	16 JUL 1884	19	142
Chase, Minnie	Peters, Abraham	01 APR 1882	16	463
Chase, Paul	Danden, Ester	05 APR 1884 L	18	496
Chase, Robert A.	Jones, Ann R.	26 APR 1879 R	13	158
Chase, Samuel C.	Ford, Lucy	04 JUL 1878 R	12	122
Chase, Sarah Frances	Jones, William Henry	18 JUN 1880	14	325
Chase, Silas	Brooks, Mary Bettie	17 OCT 1883	18	179
Chase, Sophronia	West, Charles	02 AUG 1879 L	13	305
Chase, Susan	Reed, William	09 JUL 1880 R	14	354
Chase, Susie	Green, John W.	07 MAR 1884 L	18	462
Chase, Walter Edward	McIntosh, Mary Claiborne Stevens	06 MAY 1884 R	19	007
Chase, William	Readings, Rose	26 DEC 1883 L	18	350
Chase, William	Johnson, Mary Ellen	05 SEP 1885 R	20	400
Chase, William A.	Ridgley, Mary E.	15 SEP 1881 L	15	486
Chase, William H.	Johnson, Eliza	21 MAY 1879	13	199
Chase, William O.	Fahrmeier, Annie	21 DEC 1883 L	18	334
Chase, William Woodbury	Goodno, Mary Norris	18 MAY 1881 R	15	314
Chasley, George	Coakley, Mary C.	02 JUN 1880 L	14	301
Chatman, Annie	Mercer, Fenton	08 MAR 1883 R	17	334
Chauncey, Eliza	Byron, Richard	06 MAY 1880 R	14	258
Cheatam, Ida G.	Cogswell, Nathan H.	23 JUL 1885 L	20	337
Cheatham, Mary E.	Hallback, W.M.	16 DEC 1884 L	19	463
Check, Susie B.	Tucker, Creed R.	27 DEC 1883 R	18	348
Cheeks, Robert M., Rev.	Foreman, Martha E.	21 AUG 1884 L	19	201
Cheese, Thomas	Lewis, Nancy A.	06 SEP 1884	19	231
Chenault, Ann Elizabeth	Moore, Abner L.	14 JUL 1879	13	281
Chenery, James Harris	Taylor, Ida Burnley	25 JAN 1882 R	16	208
Cheney, Thomas	Miller, Ellen	03 NOV 1881	16	061
Chenoweth, Elizabeth Crawford	Sloan, John	14 NOV 1881 R	16	073
Chenoweth, Jennie	Sullivan, Marcus Wm.	03 JUN 1878 R	12	081
Chephas, Bailey W.	Walker, Elmonia	13 NOV 1879 L	13	483
Cherry, Annie	Cronein, George	14 JAN 1884 L	18	375
Cherry, M.E.	Linkhow, J.C.	17 AUG 1880 R	14	403

Name	Spouse	Date	Vol	Page
Cherry, Susan M.	Skinner, William L.	23 MAY 1878 L	12	064
Cherry, Willie A.	Goodman, Mollie E.	14 NOV 1883	18	249
Chery, Ella Carnana	Orme, James W.	31 JUL 1882 R	16	461
Cherz, William T.	Eaton, Clara S.	17 FEB 1885 R	33	8023
Cheseldine, Annie Sophia	Knott, James William	22 DEC 1881 R	16	149
Cheseldine, Aug. Dunn.	Myers, Janie Frances	05 JUN 1884 R	19	061
Cheseltine, Sarah M.	Gibson, John J.	28 SEP 1882 R	17	043
Cheshire, Ellen R.	Iden, Joseph J.	04 DEC 1879 R	14	029
Chesley, James Belt, Dr.	Gibson, Mamie Faulkner	29 AUG 1883 R	18	099
Chesley, John	Craig, Matilda	10 NOV 1884 R	19	370
Chesley, Louisa	Harrison, Elias	21 SEP 1880 L	14	454
Chesley, Washington	Brown, Catharine	27 DEC 1877	11	257
Chesser, John E.	Waters, Maggie A.	14 NOV 1883 R	18	254
Chester, John C.	McDermott, Dorothea	10 OCT 1879 R	13	415
Chester, Mary	Thompson, James	16 JUL 1885 R	20	328
Chevalier, Alphonse M.	Doyle, Katie	30 DEC 1879 L	14	081
Chevallié, Belle Eugenie	Greene, Francis Vinton	25 FEB 1879 R	13	068
Chevremont, Eugene	Grandjean, Marie	30 MAR 1878	11	388
Chew, Abraham	Mars, Alice	13 SEP 1877 L	11	090
Chew, Charles H.	Hamilton, Mary C.	28 JAN 1885 L	20	041
Chew, Emmeline	Chew, Philip R.	06 DEC 1877	11	225
Chew, Lemuel	Medlock, Annie	27 JAN 1881 L	15	168
Chew, Leonard Covington	Wallace, Helen Leigh	17 APR 1879 R	13	146
Chew, Margaret E.	Barnard, George B.	30 APR 1884 L	18	543
Chew, Mary E.	Cavill, Robert	05 APR 1883	17	380
Chew, Monroe Grayson	Hester, Marguerite Winsborough	09 OCT 1883 R	18	179
Chew, Philip R.	Chew, Emmeline	06 DEC 1877	11	225
Chew, Robert	Willis, Lizzie	07 FEB 1884 L	18	415
Chew, Robert	Jackson, Malinda D.	16 OCT 1884 L	19	313
Chew, Samuel	Green, Elizabeth	09 NOV 1882	17	121
Chew, Sarah	Robinson, William	03 FEB 1885 L	20	049
Chew, Thomas	Cartes, Nannie	20 JUL 1883 L	18	056
Chewning, Annie Payne	Finks, James Oliver	18 FEB 1885 R	20	076
Chezum, James H.	Furse, Elizabeth J.C.	18 SEP 1877 R	11	099
Chick, Charles T.	Dyer, Annie L.	28 NOV 1880 R	15	069
Chick, Henry C.	Spates, Henrietta C.	30 NOV 1878 L	12	356
Chick, Mamie	Chism, Edward	02 AUG 1877	11	039
Chicker, Nettie S.	Hoffman, Albert D.	27 MAY 1885 R	20	243
Chidister, Thomas E.	Marshall, Lizzie E.	25 SEP 1878 R	12	235
Chiffins, Richard	Briscoe, Eliza	29 DEC 1882	16	069
Child, Frank Linus	Harlan, Edith Shanklin	25 OCT 1881	16	040
Childress, Dora A.	Bowen, Charles	14 JUN 1881	15	360
Childress, Garnett L.	Childress, William P.	15 AUG 1881 R	15	443
Childress, John A.	Lee, Sarah E.	04 OCT 1879 R	13	404
Childress, William P.	Childress, Garnett L.	15 AUG 1881 R	15	443
Childrey, Henrietta	Jackson, Eli	24 DEC 1877	11	247
Childs, Carrie B.	Denham, William R.	26 APR 1883 R	17	416
Childs, Charles	Webster, Maggie E.	28 APR 1884 R	18	537
Childs, Ella	Scott, Charles D.	13 SEP 1879 R	13	368
Childs, Frank H.	Shepherd, Jane F.	29 SEP 1879 R	13	390
Childs, George B.	Taylor, Jenettie	08 AUG 1883	18	078
Childs, George H.	Taylor, Violet	06 AUG 1884 L	19	172
Childs, Ida	Denham, George E.	25 JAN 1882	16	209
Childs, Louisa	Hicks, William A.	06 DEC 1882	17	167
Childs, Mamie	Gaines, Edward	14 JAN 1885 L	20	019
Childs, Mary Emma	Dean, Samuel	28 JUN 1881 L	15	381
Childs, Washington	Johnson, Louisa	21 APR 1881 R	15	268
Childs, Wm. Emmes, Dr.	Henry, Mabel Irene	28 MAY 1885 R	20	245

Chilton, Joseph C.	Peach, Helen M.	14 JUL 1884	19	137
Chin, James	Blenheim, Sarah	07 OCT 1880 L	14	479
Chinn, B.W.	Smith, Rosa	02 MAY 1878 L	12	034
Chinn, Catherine	Wright, John Henry	17 DEC 1878 L	12	383
Chinn, Charles E.	Hunt, Fannie	18 SEP 1877 L	11	099
Chinn, Henry W.	Nash, Candus Ann	29 NOV 1877	11	213
Chinn, James	Monteith, Emma	12 JUN 1882 R	16	405
Chinn, Leslie T.	Green, William T.	04 APR 1882 R	16	298
Chinn, Mary A.	Collins, Peyton	24 SEP 1885	20	440
Chipley, William R.	Thorn, Annie Laura	15 JUN 1880 R	14	319
Chipman, Charles M.	Boyle, Bridget	24 NOV 1880 R	15	047
Chisley, David	Tyler, Estella	09 APR 1883	17	387
Chisley, Elizabeth	McCoy, William	06 MAY 1882	16	351
Chisley, John Henry	Johnson, Christie	20 APR 1882	16	323
Chisley, Nannie	Brown, Walker	13 DEC 1880 L	15	094
Chisley, Richard T.	Sewell, Sallie	06 JUL 1879 R	13	271
Chisley, Samuel L.	Holmes, Fannie	10 DEC 1877 L	11	228
Chism, Edward	Chick, Mamie	02 AUG 1877	11	039
Chism, Frederick	Collins, Laura	17 SEP 1884 L	19	255
Chism, George A.	Blakely, Mary Ann	12 DEC 1877	11	229
Chism, Mary J.	Dunn, William F.	29 DEC 1878 R	12	404
Chism, Tilly A.	Murphy, Mary J.	18 MAR 1879 L	13	106
Chitams, Joseph	Hamesley, Mary A.	04 FEB 1884 L	18	406
Chivell, Joseph H.	Husemann, Julia H.	27 JUL 1885	20	342
Cholet, Jules	Cordovado, Emma	19 MAR 1885 R	20	123
Chorpenning, Harry W.	Levy, Katie	30 SEP 1878 R	12	240
Chris, Julia	Miles, Robert	15 FEB 1881 L	15	191
Chrisall, Josephine	Bremann, J.I.	15 NOV 1884 L	19	383
Chrisman, Benjamin F.	Mansfield, Ella E.	21 MAY 1882 R	16	370
Chrisman, George William	White, Eliza Fletcher	14 MAY 1882 R	16	358
Chrisman, Maggie	Boehnaann, William C.	10 JUN 1884	19	074
Chrisman, Robert E.	Harrison, Clara	00 AUG 1883 R	18	082
Chrissinger, William, Dr.	Morrison, Mary E.	06 DEC 1883	18	304
Christian, Albert P.	Jones, Sarah E.	22 MAR 1883 R	17	354
Christian, Anthony	Berril, Sallie	03 MAY 1881 R	15	287
Christian, Belle T.	Davis, Peyton H.	17 AUG 1885 R	20	372
Christian, Jefferson	Henderson, Josephine	31 JAN 1884 L	18	403
Christian, Leander	Snowden, Eliza Ann	25 DEC 1879	14	062
Christian, Lucy Ellen	Proctor, William	17 NOV 1881	16	083
Christian, Martha	Hawkins, George	23 MAY 1882 L	16	372
Christiani, Charles	DeSilver, Antoinette	09 MAR 1882 R	16	272
Christine, Fleming	Burgoyne, Harriet	21 DEC 1883	18	322
Christine, Katie Josephine	Pole, Samuel Boyce	02 SEP 1880 R	14	427
Christmann, Auguste H.	Burch, Henry W.	08 OCT 1885 R	20	472
Christmon, Arthur	Dilli, Elizabeth	21 FEB 1882 R	16	251
Christon, Annie	Jackson, William	26 JUL 1883	18	063
Christon, Kate	Wells, Lewis	05 JUN 1884 R	19	061
Christopher, James	Harrover, Jane Elizabeth	21 MAY 1879 R	13	200
Christopher, Joseph B.	Seibert, Delia	21 MAY 1884	19	032
Christopher, Julia	Brown, William P.	16 OCT 1879 R	13	428
Christopher, Louise	Peters, John B.	28 JUL 1883 R	18	064
Chum, Florence	Smith, Albert	24 DEC 1884 L	19	489
Chum, John H.	Norris, Eliza Jane	19 JUL 1881 R	15	407
Chun, Florence	Chase, Elmar	05 NOV 1878 L	12	307
Church, Charles D.	Skinner, Julia	20 APR 1880	14	229
Church, Fannie	Selby, William H.	28 FEB 1878 R	11	366
Church, Joseph B.	Murdock, Laura V.	06 JUN 1882	16	395
Church, Maria	Triplett, Cephas	15 JUN 1880 L	14	320

Church, Melville	Durant, Sarah Heyliger	05 MAY 1881 R	15	293
Church, William A. H.	Clark, Margaret E.	07 JAN 1880 R	14	094
Churchhill, Harriet	Banks, Bradley	24 JUL 1879	13	290
Churchwell, Elias	Smith, Eliza	12 DEC 1882	17	176
Churchwell, Mary Ann	Gaskins, Tom	03 NOV 1879 L	13	459
Churn, Charles H.	Jenkins, Mary Josephine	25 SEP 1879 R	13	385
Chyle, Maria	Lucas, James Henry	12 NOV 1884 L	19	375
Ciscle, George E.	Preller, Mary Irene	28 OCT 1884 L	19	341
Cison, Katie	Lewis, William	17 MAR 1884	18	473
Cissel, Charles H.	Williams, Lettie	29 SEP 1881 R	15	504
Cissel, Emily Virginia	Rabbit, James E.	29 NOV 1882 R	17	155
Cissel, Eugene E.	Derrick, Agnes	18 SEP 1878 R	12	225
Cissel, Mary A.	Walker, James H.	03 OCT 1878	12	249
Cissel, William Fisk	Brown, Mary Virginia	23 DEC 1879 R	14	064
Cissell, Cassie	Bowen, James	03 NOV 1880	15	028
Cissell, Elizabeth	Coates, Lewis	14 OCT 1885 L	20	485
Cissell, Mary Julia	Glascow, Alexius C.	09 AUG 1883	18	079
Cladwell, Benjamin M.	Ransel, Georgetta W.	17 SEP 1878	12	222
Clagett, Alice	Tolson, Isaac	06 JAN 1883 R	17	241
Clagett, Bettie	Robinson, Henry	18 SEP 1882	17	026
Clagett, Charles Thomas	Caldwell, Mary Elizabeth	06 FEB 1884 L	18	414
Clagett, Edward	Carroll, Mary Ellen	27 JUN 1878 L	12	115
Clagett, Elise M.	Bayley, S.P., Jr.	14 OCT 1878	12	270
Clagett, Henry B.	Laws, Corrie L.	16 JAN 1884 R	18	379
Clagett, Howard Clare	DuHamel, Mary M.	04 JAN 1882 R	16	178
Clagett, John B.	Gunnell, Alice I.	31 AUG 1882 R	16	499
Clagett, Maggie	Bell, Nathan	15 MAR 1883 L	17	346
Clagett, Maria	Hayes, George H.D.	15 JAN 1885	20	021
Clagett, Martha	Tolliver, William	22 SEP 1877	11	104
Clagett, Mary	Adams, Noble	25 DEC 1878 L	12	401
Clagett, Maurice J.	Noble, Emma L.	28 OCT 1884	19	340
Clagett, Sarah Matilda	Toney, James Wm.	27 JUL 1882 R	16	459
Clagett, William	Pinkney, Rachel	10 JUN 1878 L	12	094
Claggett, Louisa	Adams, Julius	21 NOV 1883 L	18	270
Claiborne, Robert Lee	Campbell, Martha	09 MAR 1881	15	216
Clair, Edward G.	Potter, Susan Virginia	11 DEC 1877 L	11	230
Clampitt, Katie M.	Minick, John B.	15 SEP 1880 R	14	446
Clancey, Daniel	Maloney, Margaret	03 MAY 1884 L	19	002
Clancey, Daniel	Maloney, Margaret	04 MAY 1884	18	548
Clancy, Ella	Dobson, Edward	27 APR 1881 R	15	282
Clancy, Frank Willey	Swallow, Charlotte Jane Cawthorn	30 OCT 1879	13	452
Clancy, Kate	Campbell, John	16 DEC 1881 R	16	124
Clancy, Thomas	Mahloy, Julia	09 DEC 1880 L	15	089
Clapp, William W.	Withington, Caroline F.	01 FEB 1883	17	281
Clare, Ella A.	Elliott, John L.	12 NOV 1879 R	13	481
Clarence, Henry	Holly, Florence	26 JUL 1883	18	060
Clark, Agnes	Jackson, Cornelius	02 AUG 1877 R	11	039
Clark, Alexander	Holland, Rachael A.	01 NOV 1883 L	18	224
Clark, Alice	Wadsworth, Edward	29 OCT 1878	12	294
Clark, Alice	Edwards, John	05 AUG 1880 R	14	389
Clark, Alice Ella	Gonter, Thomas S.	28 APR 1881 R	15	284
Clark, Allen C.	Pearce, Sarah	21 NOV 1882 R	17	142
Clark, Ann Jordan	Pullen, John Fountani	10 JUL 1880 L	14	355
Clark, Annie	Briscoe, James	15 FEB 1883 R	17	306
Clark, Annie F.	Darby, Rufus H.	11 DEC 1879 L	14	042
Clark, Annie M.	Heflebower, George W.	20 APR 1880 R	14	229
Clark, B. Thomas	Henry, Elizabeth	07 MAR 1882	16	269
Clark, C.J., Mrs.	Skinner, Horan L.	10 NOV 1880	15	040

Clark, Charles	Thompson, Emma	28 MAR 1878 R	11	397
Clark, Charles C.	Schooler, Maggie L.	06 SEP 1883 L	18	116
Clark, Charles H.	Terry, Willie	01 JAN 1884 R	18	359
Clark, Charles H.	Hines, Mary C.	11 NOV 1884 L	19	374
Clark, Cornelia	Fisher, William	28 DEC 1882 L	17	217
Clark, David A.	Coulter, Virginia E.	24 NOV 1880	15	066
Clark, Edward	Watson, Laura	06 DEC 1877 L	11	223
Clark, Edward	Pipsico, Letitia	05 MAR 1878 L	11	372
Clark, Edward B.	Brown, Lulie J.	03 DEC 1878 L	12	362
Clark, Elizabeth	Briles, William A.	22 FEB 1881 L	15	198
Clark, Emma	Carroll, Eugene	16 AUG 1880 L	14	400
Clark, Emma J.	Sewell, Thomas J.	19 JUL 1880 L	14	368
Clark, Emma J.	Trott, Charles Vernon	08 NOV 1880 R	15	035
Clark, Ennis S.	Coates, Mary A.	01 SEP 1881	15	469
Clark, Eugene Bradley	Harriet, Harriet Miller	13 NOV 1878 R	12	326
Clark, Ferdinard	Lukes, Mary M.	03 MAR 1880 R	14	171
Clark, Florence Lathin	Scofield, John Cowles	18 MAR 1885 R	20	121
Clark, Florence R.	Gray, George W.	21 DEC 1882 R	17	189
Clark, Gabriel	Pony, Martha	08 NOV 1877	11	175
Clark, George	Matthews, Lucy A.	27 FEB 1879 L	13	083
Clark, George Washington	Robinson, Sara Eaton Gregg	15 DEC 1880 R	15	098
Clark, Hannah	Jhonson, Archey	06 APR 1885 R	20	146
Clark, Harriet	Boston, Thomas	09 OCT 1879 L	13	413
Clark, Harriet Morgan	Beall, Louis Erwin	04 DEC 1884 R	19	434
Clark, Henry	Myers, Mary	04 APR 1878	11	403
Clark, Henry L.	Davis, Manassa V.	04 OCT 1883	18	173
Clark, Horace	Whitley, Mary	11 FEB 1885 L	20	064
Clark, Isabel Collington	Clark, John Forney	02 FEB 1881 R	15	174
Clark, J. Jerome	Wright, Nellie	27 MAR 1883 L	17	363
Clark, Jack	Ashby, Roburta	21 MAY 1885 L	20	233
Clark, James	Goddard, Flora	05 AUG 1880 L	14	300
Clark, James	Garnett, Celia	14 DEC 1882 R	17	183
Clark, James	Williamson, Ella	07 FEB 1883 R	17	299
Clark, James A.	Thompson, Marian V.	02 APR 1881 R	15	244
Clark, James R.	Payne, Emma C.	06 SEP 1877 R	11	081
Clark, Jane C.	Scott, Clifton B.	09 FEB 1882 R	16	234
Clark, Jane Estella	Carter, Charles H.	07 DEC 1882 R	17	173
Clark, John	Somerville, Rosa	31 JUL 1879 R	13	294
Clark, John Black	Curtin, Mary Cecilia	20 MAY 1878 L	12	061
Clark, John Bullock, Jr.	Weil, Cornelia Jacoby	10 NOV 1880 R	15	037
Clark, John Forney	Clark, Isabel Collington	02 FEB 1881 R	15	174
Clark, Joseph	Smith, Helen	06 APR 1885	20	147
Clark, Joseph Edward	Peck, Ophelia Gertrude	21 AUG 1884	19	202
Clark, Julia	Morgan, Richard	21 DEC 1881	16	142
Clark, Laura S.	Whitaker, Grenville A.	05 FEB 1880	14	137
Clark, Lemuel F.	Lester, Elizabeth	18 SEP 1877 R	11	100
Clark, Lillie	Koats, Charles A.	25 FEB 1884 L	18	442
Clark, Linda E.	Wherrett, William H.	10 FEB 1885	20	062
Clark, Lizzie Margret	Davis, James Sanford	05 JUL 1883	18	037
Clark, Lizzie Pauline	Sawyers, Kincaid	21 DEC 1881 R	16	147
Clark, Margaret E.	Church, William A. H.	07 JAN 1880	14	094
Clark, Marshall	Jackson, Maria	04 APR 1878 L	11	407
Clark, Martha	Winters, Humphreys	03 AUG 1880 L	14	385
Clark, Mary	Redcroft, Scott	12 SEP 1878 L	12	216
Clark, Mary	Miles, Richard E.	30 OCT 1883	18	221
Clark, Mary	Tilghman, Charles	07 AUG 1884	19	173
Clark, Mary A.	Demonet, Charles J.	27 AUG 1879	13	339
Clark, Mary Ann	Kaldenbach, James Henry	12 AUG 1879 R	13	316

Name	Spouse	Date	Vol	Page
Clark, Mary E.	Vigle, Henry	18 SEP 1878	12	197
Clark, Mary Ida	Sedgwick, Baker	06 JUN 1878 R	12	089
Clark, Mary M.	Jones, Richard R.	22 DEC 1877 L	11	259
Clark, Morris	Nachman, Hannah	18 JAN 1882 R	16	197
Clark, Nancy A.	Brown, William H.	19 JUL 1879 R	13	285
Clark, Nelson	Lee, Emma Jane	14 SEP 1878 R	12	217
Clark, Norris A.	Palmer, Jennie F.	30 SEP 1884 L	19	276
Clark, Prentiss M.	Sabine, Adeleide W.	11 MAR 1884 L	18	465
Clark, R. Bentley	Waters, Eva S.	15 SEP 1885 R	20	419
Clark, Richard T.	Jacobs, Katie Elizabeth	09 FEB 1880 R	14	142
Clark, Robert	Walker, Angelina	06 JAN 1879 L	13	006
Clark, Rosa	Slick, John E.	30 NOV 1881	16	104
Clark, Rose	Farquher, Patrick	13 OCT 1877 L	11	135
Clark, Samuel	Mitchell, Alice	31 MAR 1880	14	202
Clark, Samuel	Anderson, Jane	04 SEP 1884	19	225
Clark, Sarah	Williams, John	28 DEC 1882 L	17	222
Clark, Susie	Phillips, John	23 JUN 1881 R	15	378
Clark, Susie	Munford, Elijah	04 FEB 1885 R	20	047
Clark, Susie V.	Massey, James L.	26 MAY 1880 R	14	291
Clark, T.D. Douglas	Holtzman, Sallie M.	27 MAY 1884 L	19	040
Clark, Thomas	Richardson, Mary	12 MAY 1880 R	14	258
Clark, Thomas J.	Curtin, Maggie H.	28 NOV 1881 R	16	100
Clark, Victoria	Taulman, Dan'l Jay	11 MAR 1885 R	20	107
Clark, William	Contee, Julia	31 MAY 1879 L	13	212
Clark, William	Ford, Ida	26 AUG 1880 R	14	413
Clark, William	Burt, S. Bertha	01 SEP 1884 L	19	218
Clark, William Frank	Bossett, Amelia F.	25 APR 1881	15	271
Clark, William H.	Towles, Celia	25 MAR 1879 L	13	115
Clark, William Henry	Washington, Jane Rebecca	03 JUN 1885 L	20	254
Clark, Williams Smith	Thorpe, Frances Isabelle	09 MAY 1878 R	12	044
Clarke, Addie	Smith, James T.	08 JUN 1884	19	065
Clarke, Albert S.	Murphy, Mary Morrissey	27 NOV 1879 R	14	017
Clarke, Benjamin F.	Lynn, Ocea A.	12 JAN 1882	16	191
Clarke, Blanche	Kerrick, Edward	02 AUG 1883	18	071
Clarke, Charles I.	Hobson, Annie C.	19 AUG 1885	20	379
Clarke, Charles, M.D.	Neale, Julia V.	17 MAY 1883 R	17	446
Clarke, Clara Ellen	Turner, Charles Smoot	25 APR 1878 R	12	020
Clarke, Daisy Octavia	Smith, Frank St. C.	08 NOV 1882 R	17	116
Clarke, Eliza	Lloyd, Frederick Morgan	29 APR 1878 R	12	028
Clarke, Ella	Parker, Walter	12 DEC 1883	18	308
Clarke, Ella P.G.	Harding, Richard N.	24 NOV 1880 R	15	065
Clarke, Ellen	Jackson, John H.	22 DEC 1881 R	16	148
Clarke, Ellen M.	Morse, Alexander Porter	17 APR 1883	17	397
Clarke, Fannie	Young, Clement Chapman	14 JUN 1883 R	17	490
Clarke, Fannie Adaline	Fairbrother, Frank Lazolin	20 DEC 1877 R	11	246
Clarke, Frank	Callaghan, Eliza Virginia	30 MAR 1882 R	16	292
Clarke, George R.	Latimer, Clementine R.	20 JUL 1885 R	20	315
Clarke, Harrison	Barnes, Mary Frances	01 JAN 1885	19	515
Clarke, J. Thomas	Anderson, Agnes M.	18 AUG 1885 R	20	374
Clarke, James	Beckett, Maggie	12 FEB 1881 L	15	188
Clarke, James W.W.	Haislip, Kezia E.	26 JAN 1882 L	16	212
Clarke, John	Burke, Annie	21 NOV 1877 L	11	196
Clarke, John T.	McDonnell, Ella	15 SEP 1881 L	15	486
Clarke, Julia F.	Selecman, James A.	04 JUN 1884	19	058
Clarke, Katherine Phillips	Nicholson, Augustus Archibald	25 JUN 1879 R	13	249
Clarke, Lucien A.	Lynn, Lucy M.	09 JUN 1880 R	14	314
Clarke, Luretta	Mackenzie, P.R.	16 JUL 1883	18	046
Clarke, Mary E.	Mack, Samuel H.	03 JAN 1884 L	18	364

Groom	Bride	Date	Vol	Page
Clarke, Mortimer	Burket, Sallie M.	20 DEC 1883 L	18	331
Clarke, Robert	Keyes, Margaret	24 JUL 1882 L	16	455
Clarke, Samuel A.	Bowen, Maggie E.	01 JUN 1882 R	16	389
Clarke, Stephen C.	Cook, Frances A.	23 MAR 1881 L	15	236
Clarke, William D.	Lynn, Estella J.	16 AUG 1882 L	16	482
Clarke, William H.	Johnson, Julia A.	11 DEC 1878 R	12	377
Clarke, William H.	Hawes, Margaret	22 JUL 1882 L	16	453
Clarke, William S.	Herbst, Amelia	14 JUL 1882 R	16	447
Clarkson, Cecilia M.	Johnston, Matthew B.	28 APR 1883 L	17	419
Clarkson, Edward H.	Burrage, Margaret M.	20 DEC 1877	11	255
Clarkson, Joseph	Brown, Mary K.	12 JUL 1883	18	045
Clarkson, M.A.	Haight, E.R.	30 JUN 1880	14	341
Clarkson, William G.H.	Webster, Katie E.	17 DEC 1879 R	14	053
Clarkson, William H.	Bull, Emma V.	01 MAY 1884 L	19	001
Clarkson, William II.	Bull, Emma V.	01 MAY 1884	18	547
Clarvoe, A.M.C.	Brooke, William E.	23 DEC 1879 R	14	065
Clarvoe, John T.	Barnes, Maude M.	09 OCT 1879 R	13	411
Clarvoe, Mary Rose	Tucker, George H.	16 OCT 1879 R	13	430
Clarvoe, Mattie R.	Thompson, William N.	04 AUG 1881 L	15	432
Clarvoe, R.G.	Lamb, Jennie M.	28 DEC 1882	17	220
Claterbrooks, Sarah	Guthries, Henry	15 AUG 1881	15	445
Claughton, Blanche	West, George W.	11 SEP 1877 L	11	087
Clavin, Annie	Allen, Joseph	28 SEP 1881 R	15	502
Claxton, Mary F.	Williams, Charles H.	12 AUG 1880	14	383
Clay, Andrus	Wood, Mary Ellen	26 JUL 1883 L	18	063
Clay, Anna	Barbour, Samuel	18 NOV 1879 L	13	493
Clay, Cassius H.	Seal, Alice M.	17 FEB 1885	20	077
Clay, Henry	James, Lizzie	09 AUG 1878 L	12	162
Clay, Henry	Butler, Mary R.	31 OCT 1883	18	223
Clay, Hyrel A.	Jones, Judith A.	05 MAY 1879	13	174
Clay, James Henry, Jr.	Turner, Lucilia Helen	16 AUG 1882 L	16	482
Clayter, Isaac	Dodson, Mary M.	12 MAR 1878	11	378
Clayton, Airy E.	Lane, Daniel	13 MAY 1880 L	14	269
Clayton, Bettie	Greenwood, Middleton H.	17 AUG 1883	18	092
Clayton, Henry	Warfield, Ida	26 JUN 1879 R	13	257
Clayton, John	Banks, Ellen	09 AUG 1878 R	12	162
Clayton, Susanna B.	Bosher, Wm. Pemberton	24 JUN 1884 R	19	098
Clear, Helen B.	Bigelow, Edward R.	07 OCT 1884 L	19	292
Clear, Lillie Helen	Dyer, Harry Linden	21 JAN 1880 R	14	116
Clear, Maggie B.	Baker, Oscar	17 JAN 1878	11	310
Clear, Mary Alline	Lamont, John Charles	16 SEP 1885 R	20	423
Cleary, Annie	Keogh, John M.	29 JAN 1880 R	14	127
Cleary, Florence Josephine	Wimsatt, William A.	30 SEP 1879 R	13	393
Cleary, Kate	Sullivan, George N.	05 JUN 1879	13	221
Cleary, Katie	Welch, John	06 OCT 1885 L	20	460
Cleaves, Cassie L.	Burrows, George F.	10 AUG 1885 L	20	362
Cleavland, Luther	Ryan, Mary A.	08 JAN 1884 L	18	369
Cleggett, Mary	Weathers, Churchwell	17 NOV 1877 L	11	190
Cleggett, William	Lee, Jessie	01 FEB 1883 L	17	282
Clem, Lizzie	Tamkin, Edwin	11 AUG 1880 R	14	398
Clemens, Mary Elizabeth	Loveless, Charles	13 OCT 1885 R	20	475
Clements, Amanda	Simmons, George Clarkson	24 NOV 1884 R	19	403
Clements, Cecilia V.	Walker, Joseph E.	14 MAY 1879 R	13	188
Clements, Charles A.	McGraw, Mary Louise	26 JAN 1881 R	15	166
Clements, Charles A.	Pfluger, Katie R.	14 JAN 1885 R	20	017
Clements, Clara V.	Markward, Geo. Clinton	10 OCT 1877	11	130
Clements, Eleanor	Nelson, James B.	16 MAY 1878 L	12	052
Clements, Francis M.	Gaston, Isabella	22 DEC 1884	19	476

Clements, James H.	Padgett, Rebecca	24 NOV 1880	15	067
Clements, John R.	Collins, Jennie	18 NOV 1878 R	12	321
Clements, John S.	Thompson, Mary	09 APR 1884	18	502
Clements, John T.	Spencer, Alice	29 APR 1880 R	14	245
Clements, Joseph C.	Smith, Amelia Jones, Mrs.	12 APR 1881 R	15	255
Clements, Lucinda	Dow, Henson	14 MAY 1885	20	221
Clements, M. Rosalie	Moran, J. Milton	13 OCT 1885 L	20	478
Clements, M.E.	Beale, C.E.	21 JUN 1883 L	18	009
Clements, Margaret	Rollins, Oliver	22 APR 1879 R	13	152
Clements, Mary E.	Beall, John W.	20 NOV 1883 L	18	266
Clements, Mary Ida	Pomeroy, James S.	26 DEC 1883 R	18	344
Clements, Mary S.	Leavers, Lafayette	18 JUN 1884	19	090
Clements, Noah A.	Harrover, Ella B.	02 OCT 1877 R	11	117
Clements, Stephen A.	McCauley, Bettie C.	04 OCT 1882 L	17	051
Clements, William C.	Hurley, Emma J.	01 FEB 1881	15	172
Clements, William Walter	Byrne, Mary Catharine	28 DEC 1881 R	16	165
Clementson, Olivia J.	Davis, William Colbert	13 NOV 1877 L	11	180
Clemerson, Ella	Frizell, Andrew	12 APR 1879 R	13	138
Clemmer, Mary	Hudson, Edmund	18 JUN 1883 L	17	499
Clemmonds, Katy	Parker, Andrew	02 AUG 1881 R	15	430
Cleveland, Annie M.	Roberts, Richard H.	03 APR 1879 R	13	127
Cleveland, Burton	Luckett, Jane	30 SEP 1877	11	115
Cleveland, Caleb	Sauls, Emma	06 MAR 1879 R	13	087
Cleveland, Cora F.	Harrison, William H.	24 DEC 1879	14	072
Cleveland, David G.	Ferguson, Mary	03 JUN 1885 L	20	254
Cleveland, Elijah	Sweeney, Hattie C.	01 FEB 1882	16	217
Cleveland, J.D. Green	Tyler, Catherine	29 JAN 1878	11	318
Cleveland, Philip B.	Sweeney, Mollie J.	20 APR 1885 R	20	173
Cleveland, William	Day, Mary	23 JUL 1885 L	20	339
Cleveland, Wm. H.	McCellicett, Laura	23 DEC 1879	14	061
Clevenger, Elizabeth Kate	Sewell, John Fletcher	04 JUL 1880 R	14	260
Clever, William E.	Butterhoff, Barbara	30 DEC 1882	17	197
Clifford, Thomas	Miller, Helen	14 AUG 1878 L	12	166
Clift, James B.	McKenney, Mollie	07 MAR 1882 R	16	269
Clift, James E.	Allen, Nancy L.	13 FEB 1882 R	16	237
Clift, James Edward	Beale, Laura Jane	04 NOV 1878 R	12	306
Clifton, John	Pryor, Julia E. Anderson	28 AUG 1879 R	13	342
Clifton, Minnie C.	Crown, James F.	26 SEP 1878	12	237
Clifton, William	Burgess, Louisa	05 JUN 1884 L	19	062
Cliggett, Julia	Hayes, Robert	11 AUG 1885 R	20	365
Cline, George Thomas	Linkins, Alice Louisa	08 JUL 1878 R	12	129
Cline, Henry	Barker, Bettie	29 MAY 1882 L	16	380
Cline, John William	Myers, Katie	04 MAY 1878	12	036
Cline, Maggie	Bassett, George W.	10 OCT 1878 R	12	264
Clingan, Amanda S.A.	Firmin, Orange Scott	24 OCT 1882 R	17	087
Clinkett, Isaac E.	Sanders, Mary A.	10 MAY 1881 L	15	301
Clinton, Charles C.	Taylor, Rosa	08 AUG 1883 L	18	081
Clinton, Edward	Kirby, Annie, Mrs.	19 SEP 1881 R	15	483
Cloey, James F.	Murray, Mary C.	18 DEC 1883	18	324
Clomas, Griffin	Johnson, Emily	04 AUG 1885 R	20	335
Clopper, Ella C.	Wade, William H.	25 JUL 1879 R	13	293
Clore, Elizabeth J.	Nelson, Charles E.	21 AUG 1879 L	13	330
Clore, Joseph Angus	Diggs, Fannie	04 JAN 1881 R	15	138
Cloud, Martha P.	Reinhart, William L.	18 APR 1883	17	399
Clowes, A.L.	Birckhead, I.G.	30 MAY 1883	17	469
Cloyd, Albert	Frazier, Mary	11 SEP 1882	17	016
Cloyd, Alfred	Jones, Emma	31 MAY 1882 L	16	383
Club, Edward	Moore, Josephine Elizabeth	26 AUG 1884 R	19	207

Club, Henry H.	Hodson, Elizabeth	26 DEC 1878 L	12	402
Clubb, Frances A.	Hill, Edward L.	02 NOV 1822 L	17	108
Clubb, Sophia	Rockett, George T.	22 APR 1884	18	524
Clum, Andrew Herbert Wade	Sefton, Ida Constance	02 DEC 1878 R	12	357
Clum, John P.	Atwood, Belle	06 FEB 1883 R	17	292
Cluney, Lizzie	Conley, Edwin F.	26 AUG 1881 L	15	461
Cluss, Mary	Kimball, Edwin S.	10 DEC 1881 R	15	285
Clute, Charles P.	Mumford, Emma	17 MAR 1885	20	118
Clutter, Noah D.	Kelley, Kate McPherson	19 MAR 1879 R	13	108
Coagy, Katie M.	Hall, Alfred J.	14 MAY 1883 L	17	438
Coakley, Ellen N.	Dawson, George W.	06 SEP 1881	15	473
Coakley, Gertrude	Brown, Isaac B.	28 NOV 1883 L	18	283
Coakley, Mary C.	Chasley, George	02 JUN 1880 L	14	301
Coakley, Rosetta E.	Lawson, Jesse	17 DEC 1884 R	19	465
Coakley, Seraphine F.	Pulley, Perry W.	18 OCT 1881 R	16	032
Coale, Annie May	Weisbacker, William	28 JUN 1879 L	13	256
Coalman, Annie E.	Vigle, William H.	17 OCT 1878	12	266
Coalman, Lucy	Crupper, William	30 AUG 1877 R	11	071
Coates, Annie J.	Banks, Robert	24 JAN 1881 L	15	161
Coates, Anthony	Turner, Elizabeth	12 DEC 1878 R	12	379
Coates, Christopher Columbus	Webster, Mary Ellen	02 JUL 1882 R	16	434
Coates, David S.	Derrick, Melissa L.	12 OCT 1882 R	17	069
Coates, Ellen	Lias, Robert	03 AUG 1881 R	15	428
Coates, Emma B.	Morgan, Richard W.	23 JUN 1880 R	14	332
Coates, James	Robey, Amanda E.	21 AUG 1882	16	489
Coates, Lewis	Cissell, Elizabeth	14 OCT 1885 L	20	485
Coates, Lewis, Maj.	Quenan, Mary Nettie	04 MAY 1881 R	15	292
Coates, Louisa	Jennings, Henry	25 DEC 1877	11	262
Coates, Mary A.	Clark, Ennis S.	01 SEP 1881	15	469
Coates, Mollie A.	Ratcliffe, Conway B.	25 JUL 1885 R	20	341
Coates, Singleton	Montgomery, Anna	10 JAN 1880 L	14	100
Coates, Willie P	Gilman, Lucy C.	16 FEB 1885	20	070
Coats, Ananias	Monroe, Mary	06 OCT 1878	12	253
Coats, Charles H.	Johnson, Martha A.	19 NOV 1884 R	19	393
Coats, Edward	Fortune, Sarah	25 NOV 1879 L	14	005
Coats, Emma	Carroll, James	26 AUG 1884 L	19	208
Coats, Jane	Lane, Robert Alexander	09 OCT 1877 R	10	2328
Coats, John	Coats, Mary	02 JAN 1879 R	12	316
Coats, Laura	Phoenix, Sylvester	24 OCT 1882 L	17	089
Coats, Lewis	Lawson, Melvina	27 NOV 1877	11	200
Coats, Louisa	Scott, Joseph	14 OCT 1880 L	14	496
Coats, Mary	Coats, John	02 JAN 1879 R	12	316
Coats, Mary C.	Winfield, Benjamin F.	06 FEB 1878 R	11	330
Coats, Moses	Butler, Margaret	03 MAY 1884 L	19	002
Coats, Moses	Butler, Margaret	03 MAY 1884 L	18	548
Coats, Patrick	Green, Annie	18 OCT 1883 R	18	200
Coats, Robert	Mitchell, Annie	25 SEP 1884 L	19	268
Coats, Sarah	Humphreys, Albert	28 AUG 1880 R	14	420
Cobb, Mary C.	Shoemaker, Wm. Alfred	13 MAR 1879	13	098
Cobb, Norvell H.	Jones, Mary C.	27 JAN 1880 R	14	121
Cobb, Robert	Dawson, Letitia	17 JAN 1882	16	198
Cobb, Sybel	Hockam, Lucian	01 OCT 1883 L	18	162
Cober, Louisa Jane	West, Albert	15 JUL 1880	14	364
Cobin, John	Thompson, Kate	25 DEC 1877 R	11	264
Coburn, Benjamin H.	Urie, Mary C.	24 OCT 1882 R	17	092
Coburn, Charles Eli	Shaley, Mary Elen	26 FEB 1881 L	15	205
Coburn, Turley	Shalloo, Marie A.	25 JUN 1879 L	13	249
Coburn, Walter G.	Denham, Lulu C.	15 MAR 1883 R	17	345

Groom	Bride	Date	Vol	Page
Cochran, Joseph	Parker, Kate E.	04 AUG 1883	18	073
Cochran, Sallie	Harban, James Hamilton	24 DEC 1884 R	19	480
Cocke, Cora M.	Hillyard, John	09 MAY 1882 R	16	352
Cocke, Grace Russell	Smith, Harry Burton	10 APR 1882 R	16	307
Cocke, Thomas W.	Isbell, Mary Jane	27 AUG 1877 R	11	066
Cockerill, Mollie	Garrett, James	09 JUN 1881 R	15	355
Cockerill, Sarah	Mead, John H.	10 JAN 1880 L	14	099
Cocking, Joseph	Millar, Fannie P.	27 DEC 1883 R	18	332
Cockrell, Elnora	Sisk, James H.	27 JAN 1885	20	040
Cockrell, J.J.	Dearing, Ann L.	13 JUL 1880	14	358
Cockrell, Lizzie	Martin, Samuel E.	02 JUL 1878	12	121
Cockrill, Eliza Victoria	Thompson, James Albert	20 SEP 1877 R	11	103
Cockrill, Fannie	Talbert, Perry	10 AUG 1880	14	396
Cockrill, James W.	Butler, Mary Jefferson	31 OCT 1877 L	11	163
Coda, Andrea	Schneider, Giosephina	28 AUG 1880 L	14	419
Codley, Archie	Jones, Jane	05 OCT 1885 L	20	456
Codrick, Cora A.	Mattingly, Joseph S.	17 MAY 1881 L	15	313
Codrick, Frederick Milton	McDaniel, Marian Jackson	15 MAR 1882 R	16	278
Coe, S.A.	White, Katherine	17 JUL 1885	20	278
Coe, Walker Peyton Conway	Prigg, Ada Ball	25 MAR 1885 R	20	131
Coethen, Alfred	Yost, Josephine	06 JAN 1879 R	13	006
Coeyman, William H.	Hatton, Mary C.	01 JAN 1878 R	11	279
Coffee, Cornelia Ann	Warren, John H.	04 APR 1882	16	299
Coffey, Margaret A.	Mullen, Daniel P.	14 OCT 1879 R	13	420
Coffey, Margaret A.	Hutchinson, Charles W.	05 FEB 1883 L	17	293
Coffey, Patrick Joseph	Hickey, Catherine	05 NOV 1877 R	11	167
Coffey, Thomas J.	Howison, Ada F.	30 JAN 1880 L	14	128
Coffin, Edwin Chapin	Lang, Fannie Wing	30 APR 1878 R	12	027
Coffin, Helen Olcott	Paine, Sumner Cummings	27 FEB 1878 R	11	358
Coffin, John R.	Carpenter, Mattie E.	11 DEC 1877	11	229
Coffin, Mary	Penhallow, Charles Sherburne	28 APR 1881 R	15	277
Coffman, Delman J.	Marks, Annie	04 JUN 1879 R	13	218
Cogey, Eliza	Wright, Lewis	01 DEC 1881 L	16	106
Coggie, Frank	West, Caroline	27 NOV 1882 R	17	149
Coggins, Ella E.	Nash, George J.	28 NOV 1882 R	17	154
Coggins, I. Louise	Gheen, Frederick	17 APR 1884	18	518
Coggins, Louisa	Heinz, Peter J.	27 MAR 1885 L	20	134
Coghill, John H.	Giles, Louisa	23 JUN 1881	15	372
Coghill, Malvina	Manning, Alex. E.	18 MAR 1880 R	14	188
Coghill, Robertie	Burrough, Hanson G.	17 JAN 1884 R	18	381
Cogswell, Nathan H.	Cheatam, Ida G.	23 JUL 1885 L	20	337
Cogy, Mary	Corly, William	11 SEP 1877 R	11	127
Cohan, Margaret	Donovan, John	23 FEB 1884 L	18	439
Cohen, Augusta	Selinger, Julius	11 JUN 1884 R	19	074
Cohen, C. Henry	Sneed, Nora V.	28 DEC 1882 R	17	219
Cohen, Emma	Presbrey, Frank Spencer	12 JUN 1878 R	12	095
Cohen, John C.	Gregsbey, Jane	18 AUG 1884	19	192
Cohen, Rachel	Curtain, James	07 FEB 1878	11	329
Cohen, Rachel	Salinger, Fred	11 JAN 1880 R	14	099
Cohen, William K.	Simpson, R. Louise	17 JUN 1884	19	087
Cohill, Ada Lindsey	Hartmann, Charles A.	23 OCT 1884	19	331
Cohill, William A.	Ferrill, May G.	07 MAY 1885 R	20	212
Coignet, Charles Eugene	Kempf, Julie	28 SEP 1879	13	389
Coke, Addie	Bryant, Louis	11 APR 1883 R	17	390
Coker, Rosanna L.	Fester, William	15 FEB 1878 R	11	342
Cokey, Mary	Young, James	20 MAY 1880 L	14	278
Colbert, Daniel	Hicks, Lizzie	26 DEC 1878 L	12	401
Colbert, Edward N.	Pye, Mary C.	29 JAN 1883 L	17	277

Colbert, Frank	Martin, Mary	23 JAN 1879 R	13	028
Colbert, Henry	Addison, Hattie	22 SEP 1884 R	19	262
Colbert, James	Proctor, Mary Ellen	07 NOV 1879 L	13	472
Colbert, James F.	Ross, Anna Rebecca	25 DEC 1884	19	440
Colbert, John	Bryant, Cornelia	06 NOV 1878	12	309
Colbert, Lizzie	Slater, Stephen	12 JUN 1884 R	19	025
Colbert, Luther	Hackley, Cora	16 DEC 1880 R	15	106
Colbert, Nicholas A.	Osborne, Mary A.	27 APR 1882 R	16	336
Colbert, William M.	Hughes, Rebecca W.	26 SEP 1878 L	12	238
Colbert, William T.	Boulden, Martha	16 SEP 1880 R	14	447
Colbert, Wm. H.	Gibson, Martha Jane	11 JUL 1881 L	15	398
Colburn, James R.	Chamberlin, Susie A.	18 OCT 1877	11	145
Colby, Eugene A.	Hess, Josephene Helene	13 NOV 1878 R	12	324
Colby, Franklin Green	Horner, Jessy	19 JUL 1882 R	16	445
Colby, Walter	Drupe, Lena	06 SEP 1879 L	13	356
Colcasier, Hattie	Kraft, John	17 OCT 1880 L	14	499
Colclaser, Ellen E.	Carroll, James W.	08 SEP 1880 R	14	437
Coldensroth, Dora W.	Wiseman, Joseph B.	21 FEB 1884 L	18	437
Cole, Alexander M.	Denty, Annie M.	12 AUG 1884 L	19	182
Cole, Alice	Taylor, McKensie	27 MAY 1884 L	19	042
Cole, Alice M.	Montgomery, C.F.	04 NOV 1879 L	13	463
Cole, Allen H.	Hoffmaan, Harriet B.	15 NOV 1884 L	19	384
Cole, Annie M.	Payne, Gibson	14 JUL 1881	15	402
Cole, Barney	Simmons, Annie	03 FEB 1882 L	16	225
Cole, Benjamin F.	Jackson, Barbara E.	16 JAN 1884 L	18	380
Cole, Canterbury	Simms, William	09 JUL 1879 R	13	277
Cole, Charles	Hoskinson, Martha E.	30 DEC 1882 L	17	227
Cole, Charles D.	Giessler, Augusta M.	02 OCT 1884 R	19	281
Cole, Charles F.	Cole, Martha Eugenia	20 JUN 1883 R	27	6711
Cole, Charles N.	Moore, Virginia M.	14 APR 1879 L	13	143
Cole, Daniel Webster	Darnes, Sarah Elizabeth	26 JUL 1884	19	159
Cole, David	Litner, Mary	13 NOV 1879 L	13	485
Cole, David A.	Bernard, Elizabeth B.	21 APR 1885 L	20	180
Cole, Ella	Johnson, Hiram	24 FEB 1883 L	17	320
Cole, Frank	Davis, Ruth A.	11 OCT 1882 L	17	066
Cole, Fred W.	Nally, Maggie	30 APR 1884 R	18	545
Cole, George	Simmons, Amanda	05 SEP 1878 L	12	201
Cole, George Heath	Palmer, Mary Letitia	16 JUL 1881	15	405
Cole, George W.	Brown, Rachel	29 APR 1884	18	540
Cole, Georgiana	Henderson, Erastus	03 JUL 1878 L	12	122
Cole, Harry	McKenney, Bettie	08 SEP 1880 L	14	435
Cole, Henry	Davis, Anlucretia	22 FEB 1883 L	17	318
Cole, Ignacious	Jackson, Frances	23 SEP 1884 R	19	264
Cole, Imogen A.	Hanna, Benjamin W.	30 MAY 1882 R	16	378
Cole, James	Wallace, Belle	26 FEB 1880 L	14	167
Cole, James E.	Brown, Susie Ann	16 MAY 1881 R	15	309
Cole, Jeremiah	Smallwood, Lovina	13 NOV 1879 R	13	482
Cole, Jerry	Perry, Catherine	27 DEC 1883	18	350
Cole, Jessie R.	McLaughlin, John	07 DEC 1881 R	16	115
Cole, John C.	Berry, Emma	29 NOV 1882 L	17	161
Cole, John T.	Shepherd, Emma K.	27 FEB 1882	16	260
Cole, Joseph	Day, Ida	11 DEC 1879 R	14	043
Cole, Joseph	Buil, Ella L.	22 JUN 1881 R	15	371
Cole, Julia I.	Zepp, James H.	11 NOV 1880 R	15	045
Cole, Laura A.V.	Cooke, William E.	25 DEC 1883	18	333
Cole, Lawrence	Dewdney, Jennie	15 APR 1885 R	20	166
Cole, Martha	Frazier, Charles	18 JUL 1880 L	14	367
Cole, Martha Eugenia	Cole, Charles F.	20 JUN 1883 R	27	6711

D.C. Marriage Records Index, June 28, 1877 to October 19, 1885

Name	Spouse	Date	Vol	Page
Cole, Mary A.	Smith, Wm. C.	14 JUL 1885 R	20	326
Cole, Mary Aggness	Keifer, Elwood	05 OCT 1879 R	13	404
Cole, Mary L.E.	Snow, Arnold	11 OCT 1881 R	16	016
Cole, Nannie V.	Hobbs, Millard F.	31 DEC 1877	11	259
Cole, Nettie C., Mrs.	McGee, Edward	17 APR 1879 R	13	149
Cole, Patrick Henry	Penn, Victorine	30 DEC 1879 R	14	079
Cole, Peter L.	Barnett, Gussie V.	17 OCT 1883 R	18	197
Cole, Sarah	Richardson, Burley	09 OCT 1881 R	16	014
Cole, Susan E.	Page, William H.	05 SEP 1878 L	12	201
Cole, Sybella R.	Baker, Philip	19 SEP 1882 R	17	029
Cole, Thaddeus P.	Davis, Susie B.	26 AUG 1879	13	335
Cole, William	Fraim, Sarah	20 APR 1881	15	263
Cole, William	Frain, Sarah	12 MAY 1881 R	21	5027
Cole, William Alexander	Bowman, Lizzie	13 MAY 1884 R	19	004
Cole, William Thomas	Vaughan, Maria	22 AUG 1885 R	20	383
Colegate, Augusta McBlair	Mosher, Theodore, Lt.	28 NOV 1877 L	11	206
Colegate, Cornelia Thos.	Getty, Robert Nelson	14 OCT 1885 R	20	475
Colelazier, Frances J.	Hall, William M.	15 OCT 1879 R	13	425
Coleman, Addison	Holmes, Martha	28 MAR 1878 R	11	396
Coleman, Adele A.	Slye, John A.	15 MAY 1884 L	19	024
Coleman, Alexander B.	Jones, Mary Catherine	30 NOV 1880 R	15	073
Coleman, Anderson	Peck, Anna	03 JUL 1879	13	262
Coleman, Annie	Makell, Lemuel	30 AUG 1881 L	15	465
Coleman, Annie	Evans, John	02 JAN 1883 R	17	232
Coleman, Annie	Sands, Johnny	17 JUN 1884 L	19	088
Coleman, Betsy	Crawford, Samuel	22 JUN 1881 R	15	374
Coleman, Caroline	Price, John	04 MAR 1878 L	11	369
Coleman, Charles	Williams, Eliza	05 SEP 1882 L	17	006
Coleman, Charles A.	Jenkins, Georgianna	20 SEP 1885 R	20	429
Coleman, Charles H.	Woods, Sarah	09 OCT 1882 R	17	081
Coleman, Clara	Brent, Robert	15 MAY 1879 R	13	172
Coleman, Clara	Burke, Solomon	22 DEC 1881 R	16	151
Coleman, Clayton	Bell, Frances	15 AUG 1883	18	089
Coleman, Edgar A.	Daughton, Kate H.	07 JAN 1884 R	18	412
Coleman, Fannie P.	Beal, Burton A.	11 DEC 1879 R	14	044
Coleman, George	Banks, Adeline	18 MAY 1880 L	14	274
Coleman, Hanna	Walace, Henry	24 OCT 1878	12	289
Coleman, Henry	Howard, Sarah	12 OCT 1885	20	474
Coleman, Howard	Hall, Josephine	18 MAR 1880 R	14	187
Coleman, James	Bundy, Martha Stella	09 DEC 1877	11	218
Coleman, James	Honesty, Sarah	02 OCT 1883 L	18	163
Coleman, Jere	Gibson, Frances	19 APR 1879 R	13	149
Coleman, John	Blackburn, Fannie	06 MAR 1884 R	18	454
Coleman, John	Giles, Frances	10 JUN 1885 L	20	267
Coleman, John B.	Bradley, Alice F.	23 JAN 1879 L	13	031
Coleman, Josiah L.	Armistead, Fannie H.	30 APR 1878 R	12	032
Coleman, Julia	Randall, William	15 DEC 1877 R	11	238
Coleman, Julia	Simms, Geo. Jos. Martin	26 SEP 1878 L	12	237
Coleman, Julia	Smith, Henson	25 DEC 1884 R	19	479
Coleman, Lawerence	Robinson, Julia	06 JUN 1882 L	16	397
Coleman, Lewis	Finks, Elizabeth	19 JUN 1884	19	093
Coleman, Lucy Ann	Polston, James Edward	06 DEC 1877	11	222
Coleman, Lydia Anne	Johnson, Benjamin	05 DEC 1878 R	12	361
Coleman, Malvina	Sanders, Charles	08 DEC 1877 L	11	227
Coleman, Margaret	Gant, Rezin	05 SEP 1882 R	16	484
Coleman, Mary	Talioferro, William	13 NOV 1878	12	327
Coleman, Mary	Allen, James	12 DEC 1881	16	125
Coleman, Mary	Swales, Wesley	11 MAY 1882	16	356

Coleman, Mary	Ware, Stephen	25 APR 1882 L	16	334
Coleman, Mary Ella	Barron, Harry W.	23 APR 1883 L	17	404
Coleman, Mary Louisa	Johnson, John Thomas	19 FEB 1883 R	17	310
Coleman, Mary Malvina	Streets, John H.	19 DEC 1878 R	12	390
Coleman, Mildred	Smith, Wilson	08 JAN 1883 L	17	243
Coleman, Nannie A.	Lewis, Everett	02 DEC 1884 R	19	429
Coleman, Nelson	Smith, Serena	30 DEC 1880 L	15	133
Coleman, Olivia	Adams, Philip	14 MAR 1878 L	11	382
Coleman, Peter	Looney, Julia	05 NOV 1877	11	169
Coleman, Rachel Ann	Henderson, Charles	29 JAN 1880 R	14	125
Coleman, Reuben T.	Anderson, Mary C.	30 MAY 1878	12	077
Coleman, Richard	Parker, Ella	30 MAY 1879 R	13	203
Coleman, Robert	Mathes, Mary Louisa	15 OCT 1885	20	442
Coleman, Sadie A.	Wood, John E.	21 APR 1885	20	181
Coleman, Sallie	Cook, Lewis	04 JUN 1884	19	013
Coleman, Thomas	Lee, Sallie	29 MAR 1883 R	17	366
Coleman, Thomas	Lee, Alice Mary	03 JUL 1883 L	18	033
Coleman, Thomas Emery	Roberts, Annie	03 MAR 1882 R	16	266
Coleman, Thomas Lewis	Frye, Minnie	09 APR 1884 R	18	501
Coleman, William	Swales, Janet	14 FEB 1878 R	11	336
Coleman, William	Brown, Parthenia	10 NOV 1880 L	15	042
Coleman, William	Carter, Jennie	24 SEP 1885 R	20	423
Coleman, William D.	Hazel, Nannie E.	26 MAY 1881 L	15	327
Coleman, William H.	Germon, Belle	11 JAN 1882 L	16	190
Coles, Mary V.	Middleton, Henry M.	30 APR 1885 R	20	201
Colignon, Louise	Kuhblank, Emil	21 JAN 1884 R	18	235
Collamer, Warren I.	France, Florence Ida	21 JAN 1880	14	116
Colleflower, Charles E.	Castell, Annie M.	20 FEB 1882 R	16	248
College, Lydia Elizabeth Cogswell	Hadley, Samuel H.	09 MAR 1879 R	13	094
Colleton, Thomas	Keenan, Mary	22 APR 1885	20	177
Collett, John H.	Murray, Ruth	22 JUN 1882 L	16	422
Colley, Annie	Bell, Charles Milton	16 NOV 1880 L	15	050
Collier, Lewis C.	Jordan, Julia C.	23 DEC 1879 R	14	061
Collier, Mollie E.	Henderson, John B.	12 SEP 1882 R	17	019
Collier, Nancy Street	Jackson, Reuben R.	20 NOV 1877 R	11	149
Colliflower, Clemie	Heitinger, Charles	26 DEC 1881	13	481
Colliflower, Ollie	Hilton, William	04 DEC 1879 R	13	499
Collins, Ada Genevieve	Gaskins, Samuel A.	13 JUN 1883 L	17	490
Collins, Albert G.	Adams, Mamie E.	26 APR 1882 R	16	336
Collins, Alice A.	Snowden, Walter	04 NOV 1879 L	13	462
Collins, Amanda V.	Adams, Charles Emery	05 JUN 1882 R	16	385
Collins, Amelia H.	Nichols, Thomas	12 OCT 1885 L	20	476
Collins, Andrew J.	Barns, Dulcenia	01 OCT 1878 L	12	246
Collins, Annie M.	Lake, Wilmot	08 JAN 1885 L	20	008
Collins, Barbara A.	King, James E.	03 JUL 1884 L	19	118
Collins, Barbara E.	Atz, Charles	26 AUG 1880	14	416
Collins, Carter	Bennett, Louisa	30 APR 1885	20	181
Collins, Charles C.	Taylor, Adalaide C.	06 FEB 1879	13	049
Collins, Charles H.	Taylor, Cora Lee	07 MAY 1885 R	20	099
Collins, Charles Henry	Tallent, Sarah Virginia	26 JUN 1879 R	13	250
Collins, Clara E.	Watts, Samuel R.	19 NOV 1878	12	336
Collins, Cornelius	Ellis, Jane E.	26 OCT 1881 R	16	044
Collins, David M.	Bates, Clarence D.	07 JUN 1880	14	308
Collins, Douglas	Streets, Martha	02 SEP 1879 R	13	338
Collins, Edgar A.	Talbot, Lizzie E.	12 APR 1880	14	219
Collins, Ellen C.	Goodrick, William	02 SEP 1879	13	347
Collins, Emma	Donaldson, James	15 SEP 1880	14	444
Collins, Florence M.	Dowden, John L.	30 APR 1884	18	544

D.C. Marriage Records Index, June 28, 1877 to October 19, 1885

Name	Spouse	Date	Vol	Page
Collins, Francis	Butz, Mary	28 JUN 1878 R	12	117
Collins, Geneta L.	Collins, Stephen R.	16 MAY 1885 R	20	227
Collins, George W.	Murphy, Mary E.	30 JUN 1882 R	16	432
Collins, Homer Krum	Scarff, Martha Emma	01 OCT 1878 R	12	246
Collins, Honora	Kennedy, Patrick	06 FEB 1880 L	14	140
Collins, Jacob W.	Darley, Susan B.	26 JAN 1881 R	15	162
Collins, James E.	Boswell, Adelia A.	16 SEP 1878 R	12	220
Collins, James M.	Giddings, Martha A.	16 DEC 1879 L	14	051
Collins, Jennie	Clements, John R.	18 NOV 1878 R	12	321
Collins, Jennie	Hill, Joseph	24 NOV 1883 L	18	275
Collins, Jennie	Proctor, Lewis	02 JUL 1884 L	19	116
Collins, Joanna T.	Allman, John E.	27 MAY 1884 L	19	040
Collins, Johannah	McDonough, Patrick	13 FEB 1879 R	13	057
Collins, John	Redding, Anna	01 MAR 1878 R	11	361
Collins, John	Reed, Lizzie A.	10 MAY 1881	15	300
Collins, John	Long, Julia	06 FEB 1883 L	17	297
Collins, John	McDonogh, Mary	08 SEP 1883 L	18	120
Collins, John B.J.	Pelouze, Kate	25 OCT 1880 L	15	012
Collins, John C.	Werner, Emily	16 MAY 1881 L	15	311
Collins, John F.	Banks, Cora	16 APR 1883 L	17	395
Collins, John W.	Allman, Julia A.	22 OCT 1879 R	13	434
Collins, Joseph	Hickey, Mary Ann	02 JUL 1879 L	13	262
Collins, Julia	Dorsey, John H.	16 AUG 1883 L	18	090
Collins, Julia E.	Neal, Horatio	22 MAY 1883	17	455
Collins, Laura	Chism, Frederick	17 SEP 1884 L	19	255
Collins, Laura J.	Gladmon, William O.	02 JUN 1881 R	15	340
Collins, Lewis	Jones, Georgie	11 MAR 1885 R	20	108
Collins, Lucy Ann	Harvey, Augustus	31 MAY 1880 L	14	297
Collins, Maggie	Cook, John	03 JUL 1883	18	032
Collins, Maria	Diggs, Moses	25 MAY 1882	16	373
Collins, Maria Virginia	Redmon, James Lewis	29 OCT 1879 R	13	451
Collins, Martha	Downey, Patrick	29 SEP 1883 L	18	160
Collins, Mary	Noyes, Albert	27 SEP 1880 L	14	461
Collins, Mary J.	Harris, John R.	22 FEB 1883	17	316
Collins, Mary Josephine	Doyle, John Hadley Ing	19 JAN 1881	15	155
Collins, Michael	McVarry, Katie	16 MAY 1881 L	15	311
Collins, Michael	McNery, Kate	11 FEB 1881 L	15	186
Collins, Millard F.	Barr, Mary	11 MAY 1880 L	14	265
Collins, Minnie Gertrude	Reynolds, Wm. Edward	09 MAR 1885 R	20	100
Collins, Mittie	Keltin, James R.	10 AUG 1881	15	439
Collins, Mollie	Apple, David K.	03 DEC 1879 R	14	025
Collins, Olivia Ann	Bush, Charles W.	15 NOV 1881	16	073
Collins, Peyton	Chinn, Mary A.	24 SEP 1885	20	440
Collins, R. Walter	Yeatman, Edith Morgan	30 NOV 1879 R	14	020
Collins, Robert	Marshall, Fanny	08 JUL 1879 L	13	275
Collins, Rosa V.	Holmes, Thomas J.	10 APR 1883 R	17	389
Collins, Samuel	Golden, Georgeanna	23 AUG 1879 R	13	332
Collins, Sophia M.	Gilfeather, Michael	16 JUN 1884	19	087
Collins, Stephen R.	Collins, Geneta L.	16 MAY 1885 R	20	227
Collins, Susie	Belt, Thomas Daniel	23 APR 1878 R	12	016
Collins, Thomas J.	Stephens, Dora	04 SEP 1884	19	230
Collins, Thomas Jasper	Barrett, Sophie Cecelia	05 JAN 1881 R	15	139
Collins, Thomas M.	Winkler, Mary E.	09 AUG 1880 R	14	391
Collins, Victoria	Hall, John	02 DEC 1880 R	15	076
Collins, William F.	Queen, Eliza V.	03 JUL 1883 R	18	033
Collins, William M.	Hope, Agnes	04 NOV 1884	19	359
Collins, Wm. H.	Cross, Mary V.	08 NOV 1877 R	11	176
Collison, Annie V.	Livingston, Robert L.R.	29 NOV 1882	17	156

Collison, Catherine Alice	Russell, Benj. Theodore	09 NOV 1882	17	120
Collison, George W.	Cox, Lizzie M.	30 APR 1878	12	028
Colloway, Mary	Bryan, William	16 MAY 1878 R	12	042
Collton, Angie E.	Bateman, W. Grafton	20 NOV 1884	19	394
Colman, Charles D.	Stilwell, Anna M.	29 MAY 1879 R	13	209
Colman, D.S.	Butler, George M.	26 AUG 1880 R	14	417
Colné, Charles C.	Ribnitzkey, Annie	30 MAR 1880 R	14	201
Colné, Thaddeus A.	Acton, Annie May	04 OCT 1881 L	16	006
Cologne, Michael	Hughes, Eliza	06 SEP 1882 L	17	008
Colston, Annie V.	Washington, William H.	01 MAR 1881	15	209
Colston, Hattie	Duncan, Edward	20 SEP 1883 L	18	144
Colston, Ralph Edward	Mitchell, Laura Eunice (Collier)	27 JUN 1883 R	18	020
Colston, William	Williams, Charlotte	11 JUL 1880	14	355
Colt, Charles L.	Arnold, Kate A.	13 JUN 1881	15	356
Colt, Elizabeth	Zevely, Henry B.	04 JAN 1883	17	236
Colten, William Henry	Fox, Susie	14 MAY 1879	13	189
Colter, Willis H.	Campbell, Hester B.	03 NOV 1881 R	16	060
Colton, Maria	Lennox, Frank	03 OCT 1878	12	248
Columbus, A.A.	Hayden, H.L.	02 NOV 1880	15	026
Columbus, Archibald C.	Williams, Laura	31 MAY 1882 R	16	385
Columbus, Christopher M.	Feeley, Mary T.	22 JAN 1879 L	13	030
Columbus, Ella E.	Fitzhugh, William R.	25 JAN 1882 L	16	209
Columbus, John B.	Perrott, Minnie J.	19 OCT 1885 L	20	498
Columbus, Lewis E.	Cowling, Annie H.	19 SEP 1881 L	15	490
Columbus, William F.	Gormley, Martha	16 OCT 1878 R	12	275
Colvert, Enoch	Lowmax, Mary F.	22 SEP 1885	20	432
Colville, Melvina	Thomas, Joe	31 DEC 1879 L	14	084
Colvin, John R.	Knox, Fannie	24 DEC 1878 R	12	388
Colvin, Katherine	Tapscott, Murray	09 SEP 1885 L	20	410
Colvin, Thomas B.	Weaver, Lillie	10 JAN 1883	17	249
Combes, Alice	Williams, Jesse	04 MAY 1879 R	13	172
Combes, Edward R.	Gunnell, Mamie V.	30 JUL 1884	19	162
Combes, Mary H.	Hanvey, Edgar W.	11 FEB 1885 R	20	063
Combs, Agatha B.	Wilkins, Alonzo A.	31 JAN 1883	17	280
Combs, Emma J.	Springsteen, Ahram F.	22 JUL 1885 L	20	336
Combs, Ignatius George	Hunt, Ardella Vannette	10 AUG 1880 R	14	390
Combs, Kate J.	Dooley, Michael T.	05 FEB 1883 L	17	290
Combs, Leonora J.	Briggs, Edmund B.	01 JAN 1881	15	135
Combs, Sallie C.	Reamy, William D.	23 APR 1878	12	015
Combs, William H.	Becker, Mary J.	16 APR 1884 R	18	515
Comer, Peter	Roche, Maggie	05 NOV 1881 L	16	063
Commodore, Holdsworth	Slater, Catherine	28 JUL 1881 R	15	418
Commons, Mary C.	Brown, Allen G.P.	31 MAR 1879 R	13	120
Compton, Henry	Diggs, Priscilla	03 JUL 1880 L	14	346
Compton, James	Doll, Ellen Letcher	27 APR 1881 R	15	276
Compton, Joseph William	Bonnell, Lizzie Claiborne	01 JUN 1881 R	15	337
Compton, Ludwell	Angell, Alice E.	08 JAN 1878	11	296
Comstock, Walter Jay	Forney, Clara Sherk	04 FEB 1880 R	14	134
Conaway, Alexander	Waddy, Julia	17 NOV 1884	19	385
Conaway, Eliza	Credic, Ruffy	22 MAY 1884 L	19	033
Conaway, James R.	Bailey, Florence D.	22 DEC 1884 L	19	475
Conaway, John C.	Long, Rebecca	18 MAY 1883 R	17	437
Conaway, M.	Tucker, B.L.	18 MAY 1881 L	15	315
Conaway, Will	Green, Sylvester	10 JAN 1882 R	16	189
Conaway, William H.	Malvan, Ella F.	12 FEB 1884	18	419
Condie, Charlotte	Pumphrey, Columbus	18 FEB 1880 R	14	158
Condon, Edward M.	Smith, Annie T.K.	10 SEP 1880 R	14	440
Condon, Mary	Condon, Patrick	10 OCT 1880 R	14	485

D.C. Marriage Records Index, June 28, 1877 to October 19, 1885 97

Name	Spouse	Date	Vol	Page
Condon, Mary E.	Wylie, Geo. Washington	19 MAR 1885 R	20	124
Condon, Patrick	Condon, Mary	10 OCT 1880 R	14	485
Condron, John Lawrence	Eastwood, Lottie Jeanette	02 APR 1884 R	18	491
Conger, Franklin Barker	Brown, Charlotte M.	14 JAN 1879 R	13	016
Conkling, Annie Mary Wise	Tanner, Millard Fillmore	17 FEB 1885 R	20	071
Conkling, Frances Helen	Robinson, Henry S.	13 NOV 1883 R	18	250
Conley, Annie	Krause, William	07 SEP 1885 L	20	402
Conley, Edwin F.	Cluney, Lizzie	26 AUG 1881 L	15	461
Conley, Frederick G.	Toliver, Rosa	10 APR 1884 R	18	498
Conley, Julia	Richards, Alfred A.	10 DEC 1880 L	15	090
Conley, Lottie A.	Mansfield, Edward	15 MAR 1885 R	20	112
Conley, Mary L.	Briner, William B.	02 JUL 1884 L	19	116
Connel, John	Hopkins, Bridget	21 NOV 1877 L	11	195
Connell, Alice Virginia	Green, John H.	21 JUL 1884	19	149
Connell, David	Byrnes, Elizabeth	20 APR 1879 R	13	145
Connell, Dennis	McPherson, Ella	22 NOV 1881 R	16	089
Connell, George E.	Roose, Mary C.	21 APR 1880 R	14	231
Connell, Ida R.	Sturgis, Joseph	12 OCT 1879	13	416
Connell, Jeremiah T.	Reilly, Maggie	24 FEB 1879	13	075
Connell, John	Dillon, Ellen	10 AUG 1880	14	396
Connell, Josephine	Fowler, William C.	22 APR 1885	20	184
Connell, Laura	Talent, Arthur	15 JUL 1878 R	12	135
Connell, Lizzie	McRae, Edward W.	23 DEC 1884 L	19	478
Connell, Maggie	Meinekhein, George	07 JUL 1881 R	15	392
Connell, Mary	Burrows, James	02 NOV 1879	13	458
Connell, Mary Agnes	McCabe, James A.	08 AUG 1881 R	15	435
Connell, Robert	Stouffer, Mary	03 APR 1883 R	17	375
Connell, Samuel S.	Taylor, Elizabeth	18 APR 1883 R	17	399
Connell, Sue A.	McNally, Richard	30 AUG 1880 L	14	422
Connell, Thomas B.	Aitcheson, Annie	26 NOV 1884 R	19	413
Connelly, John T.	Jackson, Ella	25 DEC 1884	19	488
Conner, Ella Vashti	Edwards, Wm. E.	07 DEC 1882 R	17	173
Conner, George	Higgs, Ann Priscilla	27 NOV 1877 R	11	204
Conner, James T.	Lewis, Laura R.	07 JUL 1880 R	14	351
Conner, John W.	Nichols, Katie R.	06 MAY 1884	19	006
Conner, Marshal R.	Nick, Mary E.	19 OCT 1880 R	15	003
Conner, Mary C.	Crawford, John H.	05 OCT 1881 R	16	010
Conner, Richard	Detter, Alberta	21 OCT 1884 L	19	326
Conner, Samuel	Hutcherson, Walter Ann	04 SEP 1882 R	17	002
Conners, Daniel	Shanahan, Winnie	30 NOV 1881 L	16	103
Conners, Michael	McMahon, Catherine	16 OCT 1878 L	12	275
Connix, Elizabeth M.	Jackson, William J.	25 APR 1883 R	17	410
Connolly, James B.	Burke, Margaret	25 NOV 1884 L	19	409
Connolly, Theresa M.	Peake, Charles P.	01 NOV 1880 R	15	023
Connor, Ella	Connor, James C.	14 NOV 1877 R	11	183
Connor, James	McCallan, Honora	03 AUG 1880	14	382
Connor, James	Duffy, Annie J.	31 JUL 1882 R	16	462
Connor, James	Almond, Margaret	21 NOV 1883 L	18	274
Connor, James C.	Connor, Ella	14 NOV 1877 R	11	183
Connor, John F.	Kyne, Mamie A.	02 SEP 1884 L	19	221
Connor, John Fred.	Waugh, Ada V.	14 MAY 1883 R	17	439
Connor, Josephine M.	Burdine, James W.	15 SEP 1884 L	19	247
Connor, Julia	O'Dea, Michael	21 OCT 1884	19	324
Connor, Lawrence	Cook, Sallie J.	16 SEP 1884 L	19	251
Connor, Maggie C.	Kidwell, Charles G.	28 APR 1884 L	18	539
Connor, Margaret	Hayes, John	17 JUL 1879 L	13	284
Connor, Martin	Nevin, Mary	28 JAN 1878 L	11	319
Connor, Mary	Hays, Robert W.	19 MAR 1878	11	386

Connor, Mary	Bissham, Samuel T.	27 JAN 1879	13	034
Connor, Mary	Sullivan, Jeremiah	15 APR 1885 L	20	171
Connor, Mary A.	Regan, John E.F.	04 JUN 1878 L	12	084
Connor, Mary Catherine	McClellan, George Robert	21 JUN 1879 R	13	285
Connor, Michael J.	Walsh, Mary E.	04 APR 1885 L	20	145
Connor, Patrick	Meeny, Ann	02 NOV 1878	12	411
Connor, Patrick	Keane, Julia	16 JAN 1879 R	13	022
Connor, Patrick	Casey, Maggie	12 JAN 1885 L	20	012
Connor, Susan	Smith, George	31 MAY 1879	13	206
Connor, Thomas	Donohue, Bridget	21 JUL 1884 L	19	148
Connor, Valentine	Crampzey, Cora Virginia	15 APR 1878	12	005
Connors, Ellen O.	Donahue, Daniel D.	17 JUL 1877 L	11	050
Connors, Mary Jane	Packenham, Philip	05 MAY 1881 L	15	294
Connors, Nora	Cunningham, William	23 MAY 1884	18	518
Conover, Katie E.	Bell, Edward Eugene	09 OCT 1881 R	16	012
Conovy, Warren	Baskall, Catharine	24 AUG 1885 L	20	384
Conoway, Lizzie	Stephens, Horace	01 FEB 1879 L	13	041
Conrad, Annie	McClintock, John M.	07 JAN 1884 R	18	367
Conrad, Charles T.	Lyon, Mary M.	30 OCT 1878 R	12	300
Conrad, George	Gertman, Caroline	30 AUG 1878	12	187
Conrad, Robert W.	Poole, Katie A.	30 SEP 1878 R	12	243
Conrad, Sallie M.	Quinn, Daniel P.	11 SEP 1885 R	20	412
Conradis, Emma	Hartig, Louis	12 MAY 1881 R	15	304
Conroy, Katie A.	Welsh, Charles E.	16 APR 1883 L	17	396
Considine, James William	Duggan, Margaret M.	04 SEP 1877 R	11	074
Considine, John	Shanahan, Mary	01 SEP 1877 L	11	073
Constable, Kate	Bushby, James H.	18 OCT 1877 R	11	141
Constantine, Adolphus C., Jr.	Smith, Rebecca E.	07 FEB 1882	16	228
Constantine, Al W.	Lukowitz, Antoinette von	16 MAY 1878 R	12	053
Constantine, G.W.	Miller, Lillie L.	11 APR 1878 R	12	001
Constantini, Benedetto	Baker, Sadie	28 AUG 1881 R	15	435
Contoo, Alice	Adams, John Henry	04 SEP 1880	14	432
Contee, Ann	Thomas, Henry	05 JAN 1878	11	270
Contee, Edward	Addison, Emily	10 APR 1882 R	16	304
Contee, George	Maynard, Lucy	17 MAY 1883	17	447
Contee, James B.	Jannifer, Rosa	07 NOV 1883 L	18	239
Contee, Julia	Clark, William	31 MAY 1879 L	13	212
Contee, Lucinda S.	Mitchell, Isaiah	20 JAN 1881	15	159
Contee, Marcellus	Thomas, Eliza	29 SEP 1877 L	11	114
Contee, Mary	Stewart, Henry	03 SEP 1885	20	399
Contee, Robert	Naylor, Amanda	14 JUN 1881 L	15	359
Contee, Solomon	Peck, Nancy	01 DEC 1883 L	18	291
Contee, William	Foreman, Emma	13 APR 1882 R	15	125
Conti, Antonina	Giardino, Joseph	20 JAN 1884	18	385
Conti, John T.	Lipscomb, Lizzie W.	26 MAY 1885 R	20	240
Contine, Charles R.	Sweatmn, Isabella, Mrs.	11 NOV 1879 R	16	3776
Contnor, Emma Jean	Ide, Edward Milo	19 OCT 1885 R	20	494
Converse, George Leroy, Jr.	Jenkins, Antonia Thornton	12 OCT 1882 R	17	067
Conway, George	King, Elizabeth	27 NOV 1877 L	11	206
Conway, George	Hicks, Matilda	23 DEC 1884	19	482
Conway, Jeremiah	Mitchell, Bettie	18 SEP 1884 L	19	260
Conway, Lettie	Davis, Edward	02 AUG 1882 R	16	465
Conway, Louisa	Warner, Watty	10 JUL 1885 L	20	319
Conway, Mary Frances	Wright, Samuel B.	14 MAY 1884 R	19	019
Conway, Sarah Elizabeth	Lynch, James S.	29 MAR 1884 L	18	486
Conway, Shadrach	Robinson, Caroline	16 NOV 1878 R	12	237
Conway, William	Nary, Sarah	10 AUG 1882 R	16	475
Conwell, Florence	Hughes, David J.	27 APR 1884 R	18	535

D.C. Marriage Records Index, June 28, 1877 to October 19, 1885

Coogan, Thomas E.	Relye, Ella	05 JUL 1884 L	19	122
Cook, Alexander J.	McKenny, Martha	01 NOV 1877	11	165
Cook, Alfred	Bruce, Sophie	24 JUL 1884	19	157
Cook, Alice E.	Jones, Worthington L.	05 APR 1878 R	11	407
Cook, Alice J.	Weaver, Charles H.	29 AUG 1883 R	18	104
Cook, Andrew	Tipplet, Susie G.	30 JAN 1881 R	15	170
Cook, Annie	Krey, Charles H.	27 NOV 1884 R	19	411
Cook, Catherine	Brown, Frank	11 NOV 1879 R	13	477
Cook, Charles	Young, Lizzie	06 MAR 1884 L	18	461
Cook, Charles C.H.	Barnes, Mary	28 MAY 1883 L	17	466
Cook, Eliza	Gilbert, Lewis	01 NOV 1883 R	18	228
Cook, Ella R.	Beck, Clarence E.	15 JUN 1880 R	14	323
Cook, Frances	Bryan, John Thomas	17 MAR 1882	16	277
Cook, Frances A.	Clarke, Stephen C.	23 MAR 1881 L	15	236
Cook, Frank H.	Hull, Ella C.	24 JUL 1884	19	157
Cook, Frank W.	Ware, Josephine A.	28 NOV 1881 R	16	066
Cook, Franklin	Parker, Sarah J.	15 APR 1884 R	18	511
Cook, Geo. T.	Lawson, Ada	17 AUG 1882 R	16	485
Cook, George H.	Wallace, Mary	15 JUL 1885 R	20	323
Cook, George T.	Beatty, Kate F.	07 MAY 1884	19	012
Cook, Ida E.	Altman, Samuel	31 OCT 1879 L	13	457
Cook, Israel	Ball, Lucy	09 AUG 1877 L	11	047
Cook, James	Page, Rosa	12 AUG 1885 R	20	363
Cook, James E.	Payne, Medora Lee	27 SEP 1884	19	271
Cook, James Henry	Parker, Frances	11 DEC 1879 R	14	043
Cook, Jane	Davis, Wallace	22 APR 1884	18	524
Cook, Jane E.	Wells, Charles C.	17 APR 1884	18	517
Cook, Jesse	Bury, E. Matilda	12 NOV 1878 R	12	324
Cook, John	Collins, Maggie	03 JUL 1883	18	032
Cook, John George	Flynn, Isabella Jane	28 SEP 1881 R	15	335
Cook, John T.	Campbell, Dora	29 AUG 1885 R	20	391
Cook, John Thomas	Beach, Lillie Lee	08 OCT 1882 R	17	047
Cook, John Waters	Klopfer, Laura Viriginia	25 FEB 1880	14	166
Cook, Joseph	Scott, Eva	07 NOV 1877 L	11	173
Cook, Josephine Ida	Cook, Richard	31 JAN 1885 L	20	045
Cook, Lewis	Hungerford, Rosa	31 DEC 1879 L	14	084
Cook, Lewis	Whiting, Mahalah, Mrs.	19 JAN 1881 R	15	155
Cook, Lewis	Coleman, Sallie	04 JUN 1884	19	013
Cook, Llewellyn M.	Ashby, Lucy B.	26 MAR 1879 R	13	115
Cook, Louisa	Purcell, Benjamin F.	08 APR 1884	18	501
Cook, Mahala Virginia	Yarmann, Gustav Oscar	01 APR 1880 L	14	205
Cook, Mark	Nilant, Mary	10 AUG 1878 L	12	163
Cook, Martha	Allen, Jeremiah	15 AUG 1878	12	168
Cook, Mary	Thomas, Michael B.	12 APR 1881 L	15	255
Cook, Mary E.	Jones, P.B.	25 SEP 1879	13	500
Cook, Mary Ellen	Bell, Thomas Reuben	10 OCT 1881 R	16	015
Cook, Mary F.	Townley, Charles T.	26 JUL 1883	18	061
Cook, Mary Virginia Scrivner	Sonnenschmidt, Charles W.	20 MAY 1882 R	16	369
Cook, Matthew	Schmuck, Sophia	08 APR 1882 L	16	304
Cook, Mollie E.	Johnson, Joseph L.	09 FEB 1882 R	16	233
Cook, Nancy	Carr, John Richard	08 OCT 1878	12	257
Cook, Nellie M.	Johnson, Henry	14 JUL 1881 R	15	400
Cook, Philip H.	Van Horn, Mary E.	23 JUL 1877 L	11	030
Cook, Rachel J.	Alexander, George W.	10 OCT 1877	11	127
Cook, Rebecca	Hackett, Gustavus	12 JUN 1879	13	231
Cook, Richard	Thomas, Annie	04 SEP 1878 L	12	198
Cook, Richard	Fletcher, Mary E.	02 FEB 1880 L	14	131
Cook, Richard	Cook, Josephine Ida	31 JAN 1885 L	20	045

Cook, Sallie J.	Connor, Lawrence	16 SEP 1884 L	19	251
Cook, Samuel F.	Ward, Bertha E.	26 DEC 1878	12	403
Cook, Sarah	Logan, John	26 AUG 1884 L	19	209
Cook, Sarah J.	McCann, Michael H.	03 DEC 1881 L	16	112
Cook, Sellman	Weeden, Ida V.	12 OCT 1880	14	487
Cook, Theodore Freling	Wingfield, Louise Violet	24 NOV 1881 R	16	096
Cook, Thomas	Young, Sarah	14 JUN 1883 R	17	494
Cook, Thomas	Brent, Hattie	26 JUN 1884	19	107
Cook, Thomas F.	Curran, Agnes A.	09 APR 1885 L	20	157
Cook, Tulip V.	Boyd, Russell N.	03 OCT 1883 R	18	168
Cook, Violet E.	Myers, Edward E.	03 SEP 1884	19	220
Cook, Wesley	Barnes, Anne	06 MAR 1879 R	13	051
Cook, William F.	Henderson, Sarah	09 SEP 1882 L	17	014
Cook, William F.	Leary, Louisa	21 APR 1885 L	20	177
Cooke, Ella S.	George, Wilbur F.	07 JUN 1882 R	16	395
Cooke, Kate Moorhead	Magruder, John Rose	19 FEB 1879 L	13	066
Cooke, Margaret E.	Warfield, Joshua D.	18 JAN 1883	17	255
Cooke, Mary C.	Bishop, Joseph E.	12 SEP 1882 L	17	017
Cooke, Pitt	Nicholson, Helen M.	28 APR 1881 R	15	276
Cooke, Robert R.	Morrow, Alice V.	03 OCT 1883 R	18	161
Cooke, Sarah J.	Riley, Richard R.	07 OCT 1884	19	288
Cooke, Sarah V.	Curry, William L.	24 FEB 1885 R	20	082
Cooke, Sophie	Bowen, James E.M.	15 OCT 1879 R	13	426
Cooke, William E.	Cole, Laura A.V.	25 DEC 1883	18	333
Cooksey, Charles E.	Smith, Sarah V.	21 OCT 1879 R	13	436
Cooksey, Charles W.	Smithson, Ida V.	14 NOV 1882	17	125
Cooksey, Charlotte G.	Thomas, Joseph B.	06 AUG 1884	19	171
Cooksey, Ellen A.	Whitemore, Henry H.	05 APR 1881 R	15	248
Cooksey, Francis B.	Price, Rena	18 OCT 1880	14	498
Cooksey, J. Walter	Yates, Ada B.	26 FEB 1884 L	18	445
Cooksey, Katie	Thom, George	21 AUG 1879 R	13	331
Cooksey, Maggie J.P.	Emmons, Oliver A.	01 AUG 1881 R	15	429
Cooksie, Georgie V.	Bradshaw, John T.	09 SEP 1879	13	359
Cool, Annie	Peters, Conrad F.	14 FEB 1884 R	18	425
Cool, Betty	Gibson, Wesley	29 NOV 1877 R	09	2218
Cooley, Benjamin	White, Letitia Lettie	14 NOV 1883 R	18	236
Cooley, Fannie H.	Beaton, John F.	05 JAN 1884	18	366
Cooley, Lillie F.	Stallings, John S.	31 MAY 1881 R	15	333
Cooley, Sarah A.	Dailey, Charles F.	13 OCT 1881 R	16	022
Coolidge, James Abernethy	Moodey, Helen Quamer	04 MAY 1880 R	14	253
Coombs, Alice Leiby	Getchell, Addison Cole	03 NOV 1881 R	16	057
Coombs, Charles C.	Brooks, Hattie F.	16 APR 1882	16	322
Coombs, Mary	Powell, Tobias	30 SEP 1880 L	14	466
Coombs, Sarah	Wilson, William	21 JUN 1878 L	12	109
Coomes, Charles	Imhof, Hulda	01 MAY 1881 R	15	273
Coomes, Charles	Imhof, Hulda	01 MAY 1881	15	269
Coomes, Lewis Walter	Harper, Anna Malisa Kelly	10 AUG 1881 R	15	437
Coomes, Mary	Handy, George K.	28 APR 1880 L	14	242
Coomes, Sarah M.	Farr, Walter P.	05 FEB 1884 R	18	409
Coon, Byron C.	McPherson, Janet D.	29 APR 1879 L	13	165
Coon, Frank W.	Sullivan, Maggie	05 SEP 1882 L	17	006
Coon, Rosa	McLean, John W.	16 OCT 1883 R	18	195
Coon, William Henry	Shoemaker, Lizzie E.	24 MAR 1885 R	20	129
Cooney, Mollie	Schooley, Elmer E.	08 OCT 1885 R	20	471
Coons, Mary V.	Harris, Ritchie B.	04 SEP 1884	19	227
Cooper, Alice	Sawnders, Edward	22 DEC 1881 R	16	152
Cooper, Callie Thatcher, Mrs.	Genet, Louis Franklin F.	14 SEP 1881 R	15	482
Cooper, Carrie	Thomas, Robert	18 MAY 1885 R	20	219

D.C. Marriage Records Index, June 28, 1877 to October 19, 1885 101

Name	Spouse	Date	Vol	Page
Cooper, Geo. Wash.	Walker, Martha	04 MAR 1880 R	14	177
Cooper, George S.	Stier, Margaret H.	26 SEP 1884	19	267
Cooper, George W.	Johnson, Mary E.	13 MAY 1879	13	187
Cooper, J.E.	Hodges, L.E.	26 APR 1885	20	169
Cooper, James	Bell, Lottie	22 APR 1880	14	235
Cooper, James	Parley, Julia Ann	05 JUL 1884	19	124
Cooper, James H.	Head, Lillian Lee	25 MAR 1879 L	13	114
Cooper, James W.	Graves, Mary	30 SEP 1884 L	19	276
Cooper, John	Stewart, Lizzie	31 JUL 1880	14	380
Cooper, John A.	Nyce, Ella C.	19 AUG 1878 R	12	171
Cooper, Jonas	Green, Esther	05 AUG 1880	14	384
Cooper, Joseph H.	Robinson, Lizzie	05 MAY 1878 R	12	037
Cooper, Leah Virginia	Wilson, William L.	28 APR 1884	18	539
Cooper, Lewis F.	DeFrouville, Marie Louise	04 OCT 1883 R	18	173
Cooper, Lottie	Fox, Harrison	30 JUN 1885	20	296
Cooper, Lottie E.	Linthicum, Benjamin F.	12 SEP 1884	19	243
Cooper, Louisa	Cager, Isaac	13 AUG 1882	16	491
Cooper, M. Charlotte	Thomas, Joseph B.	13 AUG 1884	19	181
Cooper, Mary	Winslow, Frederick	16 JUN 1879 L	13	233
Cooper, Mary	Meeks, Sandy	21 JUN 1883 R	18	010
Cooper, Mary Ann	Smith, George N.R.	09 AUG 1880 L	14	394
Cooper, Mary Eleanor	Hall, Thomas Thornton	29 OCT 1881 R	16	051
Cooper, Mary J.	Speaks, Edward	15 NOV 1881	16	076
Cooper, Mary Jane	Franklin, Benjamin	03 JUL 1882 L	16	437
Cooper, Mary Julia	Geare, Randolph	28 FEB 1881	15	208
Cooper, Morris	Thomas, Susan	23 JAN 1879 R	13	031
Cooper, Nelson	Magruder, Louisa	06 SEP 1879 L	13	355
Cooper, Robert Simpson	Roberts, Madeleine Rosalie	10 JAN 1883 R	17	245
Cooper, Thomas H.	Green, Martha	01 DEC 1881 R	16	110
Cooper, Virginia C.	Kelly, Theophilus J.	13 AUG 1885 L	20	370
Copeland, Frances	Holt, Jesse	23 NOV 1882 R	17	147
Copeland, Guild Anderson	Pettit, Amelia L.	30 APR 1885 R	20	195
Copeland, Howard S.	Gray, Fannie	24 DEC 1884 R	19	487
Copeland, Soloman	Jewricks, Georgia	21 MAR 1878 L	11	390
Copeland, Thomas	Riggs, Isabella	30 DEC 1879 R	14	081
Copeland, Wm. Warren	Barrister, Susie C.	24 JAN 1885 R	20	035
Copely, Henry	Lincoln, Sally	17 JUL 1878	12	137
Copp, Walter S.	Parrott, Abner A.	19 SEP 1881	15	490
Coppar, Richard R.	Thomas, Jane T.	19 DEC 1878	12	383
Copper, Lydia	Phenix, Samuel	06 JUN 1878	12	091
Coppin, Levi J.	Jackson, Fannie M.	21 DEC 1881 L	16	145
Coppinger, John Joseph, Col.	Blaine, Alice Stanwood	06 FEB 1883	17	292
Coquire, John Francis	Ford, Rosa	07 JAN 1878 L	11	294
Coquire, Mary Henrietta	Hutchinson, Tobias	12 OCT 1881 L	16	018
Corbelt, George W.	Hanrahan, Helen	03 OCT 1878 R	12	2904
Corbett, Charles F.	Strong, Lidia Eudore	11 JAN 1879 R	13	014
Corbett, Charles F.	Wibert, Minnie B.	30 MAY 1883	17	468
Corbett, George W.	Henrahan, Ellen	04 OCT 1877 L	11	121
Corbin, Alexander	Green, Alice, Mrs.	04 SEP 1879 R	13	353
Corbin, Ann	Sherman, John	25 MAR 1879	13	099
Corbin, Augustine	Louis, Ferderiand	02 JUL 1881 R	15	384
Corbin, Elizabeth	Spotts, Charles	29 OCT 1877 L	11	159
Corbin, J.	[Blank], [Blank]	04 DEC 1878 L	12	368
Corbin, James Wm. Bird	Dorsey, Fanny F.	01 AUG 1878	12	154
Corbin, Jimison R.	Helm, Emma E.	18 JAN 1883 R	17	266
Corbin, John	Streets, Cora	05 AUG 1880 L	14	389
Corbin, Joseph Anna	Webster, Addison	12 JUN 1879	13	206
Corbin, Susan	Taylor, Joseph	03 APR 1884 R	18	494

Corbine, James W.	Alexander, Annie	28 MAY 1885 R	20	244
Corbitt, Amanda M.	Hughes, John F.	06 MAY 1878 L	12	039
Corbley, Mary	Smith, John	14 JUN 1881 L	15	358
Corboner, Maria Jane	Bally, Frederick	05 MAY 1882 R	16	350
Corcoran, Annie	Byrnes, Lewis M.	09 SEP 1880 L	14	439
Corcoran, Annie E.	White, John J.	22 FEB 1881 R	15	196
Corcoran, Edward Boyd	Harmon, Annie Virginia	22 OCT 1879 R	13	437
Corcoran, Jesse A.	Thoma, Charlotte	24 DEC 1883 R	18	337
Corcoran, Lizzie A.	McGee, James F.	08 NOV 1882 L	17	116
Corcoran, Michael	Derban, May A.	23 JUN 1884 L	19	098
Corcoran, Millie	Braner, Charles Fent	25 AUG 1885 L	20	386
Corcoran, Richard J.	Prout, Ellen Teresa	23 JAN 1884 L	18	392
Corcoran, Sarah	Mead, John H.	15 MAY 1879 L	13	191
Corcoran, W.L.	Meyers, Katie M.	28 NOV 1883 L	18	283
Cord, Ida M.	Warren, Edward F.	07 JUL 1880 L	14	351
Cord, Louise	Ruppert, Henry J.	20 NOV 1883 L	18	265
Cord, William P.	Arnett, Adella J.	04 SEP 1884 L	19	225
Cordes, Friederika Karoline D.	Joachim, John	29 APR 1883 R	17	419
Cordovado, Emma	Cholet, Jules	19 MAR 1885 R	20	123
Coriell, Octavia, Mrs.	Shauer, J.S.	07 APR 1883 R	17	385
Corley, Nellie A.	Norris, William P.	11 JUN 1885 L	20	270
Corly, William	Cogy, Mary	11 SEP 1877 R	11	127
Cornell, Betty Ann	Dean, John A.	14 OCT 1877 R	11	135
Cornell, Charles	England, Mary Davis, Mrs.	03 SEP 1880 R	14	430
Cornell, George W.	Calinan, Hester E.	04 MAY 1882	16	346
Cornell, John B.	Brissey, Agnes	23 JUN 1879	13	244
Cornell, Louisa	Arrington, Benjamin F.	07 NOV 1883	18	239
Cornell, Maggie M.	Trammell, Charles A.	27 JUN 1885	20	295
Cornett, Thomas H.	Culver, Mary Louise	01 JAN 1885	19	510
Cornick, William	Butler, Mary T.	26 DEC 1877	11	261
Corning, Albert Edward	Reid, Anna Laura	18 MAR 1885 R	20	123
Corning, Cora Hamilton	DeSaules, Julius Edward	19 AUG 1878 R	12	170
Cornish, Washington	Hays, Frances	07 OCT 1885 L	20	469
Cornwall, Alice Virginia	Bland, James Arthur	01 OCT 1885 R	20	451
Cornwall, Luther M.	Hepburn, Maud E.	26 JAN 1881 L	15	165
Cornwell, Clara V.	Gessford, George W.	23 NOV 1882	17	145
Cornwell, John L.	Page, Mary Virginia	15 MAY 1883 R	17	440
Cornwell, Newton	Story, Jane	06 JUL 1879 R	13	270
Cornwell, Thompson	Lambert, Josephine	15 OCT 1879 R	13	427
Corotifski, Mary	Allmiendinger, Andrew	14 APR 1885 R	20	157
Corrick, Charles J.	Griffith, Jennie S.	25 JUN 1879 R	13	248
Corrick, Edwin M.	Hurdle, Nettie L.	24 JAN 1883 R	17	271
Corrick, Jenny Amelia	Young, John Taylor	02 JAN 1879 R	13	003
Corrigan, Ann	Frawly, James	01 SEP 1878 R	12	181
Corrigan, Maria Aanne	Driscoll, Timothy	26 SEP 1878 R	12	238
Corrigan, Mary Ann	Driscoll, Timothy	26 SEP 1878 L	12	236
Corry, Robert	Simpson, Alice	29 MAR 1883 L	17	368
Corse, Julie Grenville	Marshall, William J.	02 JUN 1879 L	13	212
Corse, Mary Eltinge	McBee, Elias Alexander	18 FEB 1882 R	16	320
Corson, Annie	Spinning, Dewitt C.	20 MAR 1883 R	17	353
Corson, Millie	Hall, Nathaniel	18 AUG 1877 L	11	057
Cory, Lillian A.	Brook, Felix Q.	27 NOV 1884	19	419
Cosby, George W.	Holmes, Mildred	17 MAY 1880 L	14	273
Cosby, Leppie	Jones, G.E.	20 NOV 1883 L	18	276
Cosby, Martin	Grinnip, Maggie	29 JAN 1883 L	17	276
Cosby, Teppie	Jones, G.E.	26 NOV 1883 R	29	7111
Cosey, Jane J.	Thomas, Isaac	18 JUN 1878 L	12	103
Cosman, Charles T.	Roberson, Ida	29 AUG 1878 L	12	185

Cost, Charles	Guess, Carrie	09 AUG 1882 R	16	473
Costello, John C.	Carmody, Mary	29 SEP 1878 R	12	239
Costello, Maggie	Dowling, James	17 JUN 1884 L	19	088
Costello, Margaret	More, Martin	26 APR 1882 L	16	335
Coster, Stephen K.	Martin, Ida	30 MAY 1879 R	12	412
Coster, Susie E.	Rupp, Albert E.	04 OCT 1880 L	14	471
Costin, James	Syphax, Annie	28 JUN 1883 R	18	023
Cotter, Annie C.	Sherry, James P.	01 OCT 1879 R	13	394
Cotter, Joseph W.	Poor, Ada T.	26 JAN 1882 L	16	211
Cotter, Mary	Sullivan, Thomas F.	10 JAN 1884	18	372
Cotter, Mary C.	Frank, Jacob B.	24 JAN 1882 R	16	207
Cottingham, Maggie	Noonan, James H.	23 JUN 1885 L	20	287
Cotton, James S.W.	Whitley, Julia F.	08 AUG 1883 L	18	079
Cottrell, Willard M.	Williams, Matilda A.	29 OCT 1884	19	345
Coughlan, J. Aloysius	Ballard, Lillian	14 AUG 1879 L	13	320
Coughlein, James	Jones, Lelia	03 NOV 1884	19	356
Coughlin, Daniel	Walch, Katie	16 FEB 1885 L	20	068
Coughlin, David	Dogget, Elvira V.	15 AUG 1881 R	15	444
Coughlin, Mary E.	O'Connell, Patrick B.	03 OCT 1882	17	050
Coulter, Virginia E.	Clark, David A.	24 NOV 1880	15	066
Coumbe, Oscar H.	Larman, Emma G.	14 SEP 1881 R	15	485
Councill, William Boardman	Hare, Florence Bell	18 DEC 1879 R	14	054
Countee, Amy	Lewis, John	25 JUL 1878 R	12	148
Countee, Charles Robert	Jamison, Matilda	02 OCT 1879 L	13	398
Countee, Elizabeth B.	Ash, James	12 DEC 1884 L	19	455
Countee, Laura	Johnson, Washington	01 FEB 1883 R	17	285
Countee, Mary Jane	Price, Basil	05 AUG 1880	14	388
Countee, Philip	Lee, Virginia	28 DEC 1882	17	221
Countee, Rachel Jane	Crown, John Francis	02 DEC 1880 R	15	080
Countee, Richard	Johnson, Mary Jane	30 JUN 1881 R	15	383
Countee, William	Jones, Harriet	09 JUN 1881 L	15	354
Course, Julia	Sommers, Uriah	07 AUG 1877 L	11	044
Courtis, Florence	Wheeler, James	04 NOV 1884 L	19	360
Courtis, Frank	Carleton, Maude Clinton	17 APR 1883 R	17	395
Courtney, Frederick W.	Taylor, Sarah Elizabeth	01 JAN 1879 R	12	408
Courtney, John R.	Krochel, Lena	27 JAN 1879	13	035
Coves, John Willis	Toliver, Maggie	26 DEC 1883 R	18	345
Covey, Mariah	Green, Wm. O.	03 JUL 1885 R	20	285
Covey, Tollever Preston	Dean, Emma Elizabeth	03 SEP 1885 R	20	399
Covill, Emma H., Mrs.	Harris, Bruce	22 FEB 1883 R	17	316
Covington, Ella E.	Carter, Joseph	18 MAR 1884	18	477
Covington, Ellen T.	Knapp, Gustav	05 APR 1882 L	16	298
Covington, William E.R.	Crown, Ellen	14 JUN 1882 R	16	407
Cowaen, Alexander	Gunnell, Nancy L. Cummings	20 MAR 1879 R	13	109
Cowan, Edward J.	Long, Ada B.	28 AUG 1883 R	18	102
Cowarding, Eugenia	Sonnemann, William	02 APR 1884	18	491
Cowell, George H.	Barton, Alice S.	11 NOV 1878 R	12	320
Cowen, Henry	Voltz, Eliza	07 MAR 1881 R	15	216
Cowie, Fred G.	Williams, Lylie H.	16 NOV 1880 L	15	050
Cowie, Thomas J., U.S.N.	Gedney, Susie Ada	15 FEB 1881 R	15	189
Cowles, Helen	Calvert, Robert M.	29 JAN 1883 R	17	277
Cowling, Annie H.	Columbus, Lewis E.	19 SEP 1881 L	15	490
Cowling, Emma J.	Smoot, Hobart A.	30 APR 1878	12	026
Cowling, Florence D.	Ellis, John P.	14 NOV 1883 R	18	250
Cowling, Frances Ann	Reynolds, Charles Leslie	08 JUN 1880 R	14	311
Cowling, Mary	Goodman, Thos. Augustus	22 JAN 1879 R	13	030
Cowne, Charles H.	Gouldman, Annie P.	12 JUN 1882 R	16	406
Cox, Anne R.	Jackson, Horace B.	28 FEB 1878	11	364

Cox, Annie B.	Larner, Charles N.	09 DEC 1884	19	443
Cox, Bettie Govanni	Francis, John Richard, Dr.	28 DEC 1881 R	16	164
Cox, Charles W.	Dean, Ellen A.	17 JAN 1878 R	11	301
Cox, Edward D.	Jones, Isabella	25 MAY 1880 R	14	287
Cox, Elizabeth	Tyree, Henry	21 JUN 1884 R	19	095
Cox, Ella	Mackel, Charles	02 JAN 1878 L	11	286
Cox, Fannie M.	Barber, George E.	21 SEP 1880	14	454
Cox, George	Hill, Louisa	23 DEC 1880 L	15	118
Cox, George	Brown, Nammie	18 OCT 1881	16	032
Cox, Gussie	Langworthy, S. Ransom	16 JUN 1884 L	19	086
Cox, Harriet	Richardson, Harry	07 NOV 1884 R	19	358
Cox, Harriet A.	Minor, George	26 FEB 1880 L	14	168
Cox, J.P.	Meiggs, Georgie C.	17 AUG 1880	14	403
Cox, James L.	Scaggs, M. Georgette	21 AUG 1878	12	174
Cox, James L.	Skinner, Laura V.	28 JUL 1881 R	15	421
Cox, James W.	Devlin, Elizabeth	28 FEB 1878 R	11	363
Cox, Jennie E.	Wolfe, James M.	25 MAY 1885 R	20	239
Cox, John	Bailey, Caroline	24 OCT 1882	17	085
Cox, John F.	Owen, Helen G.	23 OCT 1883 R	18	208
Cox, Lizzie M.	Collison, George W.	30 APR 1878	12	028
Cox, Maggie L.	Monroe, Morgan L.	18 AUG 1885	20	498
Cox, Marnie E.	Burnham, Elgie L.	07 FEB 1880	14	141
Cox, Marian	Berry, John	13 JAN 1879 L	13	015
Cox, Mary	Parker, William T.	03 MAR 1879 L	13	085
Cox, Mary	Rich, Washington	27 MAY 1885 R	20	243
Cox, Mary Ann	Germeroth, Christian	08 JUN 1878 L	12	092
Cox, Mary Ann Elizabeth	Sullivan, Charles	05 DEC 1883 L	18	297
Cox, Mary C.	Streeks, Andrew	14 NOV 1880 R	15	047
Cox, Minnie	Stith, J.P.	02 JUN 1880 L	14	301
Cox, Mollie E.	Masten, Ed S.	04 MAR 1885	20	094
Cox, Owen A.	Nokes, Mary H.	17 SEP 1885 R	20	427
Cox, Owen Augustus	Oliver, Maggie	05 FEB 1879	13	046
Cox, Patrick	Cross, Mary	09 AUG 1879 L	13	313
Cox, Peter	Fines, Mary M.	26 MAR 1883	17	361
Cox, Richard J.	Green, Rebecca M.	05 NOV 1883 L	18	232
Cox, Robert Lee	Shoemaker, Edith L.	25 OCT 1877	11	153
Cox, Robert W.	Moreland, Mary L.	19 NOV 1881 L	16	085
Cox, Samuel Baker	Haddon, Julia M.	31 MAR 1879 R	13	119
Cox, Samuel Henry	Lambert, Alice M. Williams	20 DEC 1880 R	15	112
Cox, Stephen A.	Brooke, Mary E.	07 OCT 1880 R	14	481
Cox, Susan	Williams, Wilson	14 NOV 1878 R	12	180
Cox, Susanna	Hayes, William	19 AUG 1879 R	13	326
Cox, William	Hill, Mary J.V.	16 OCT 1884 L	19	309
Cox, William B.	Vertongen, Maria J.	31 OCT 1881 R	16	052
Cox, William T.	Price, Sandonia	18 FEB 1885	20	074
Cox, Wm. Washington	McGill, Emma L.	21 JUN 1881 R	15	373
Coxen, George W.	Herbert, Lizzie	06 AUG 1881 L	15	434
Coxen, Mary Elizabeth	Finney, John Thomas	01 APR 1880 R	14	204
Coxen, Thomas E.	Martin, Lizzie	06 SEP 1880 L	14	433
Coxson, James H.W.	Fodor, Eunice C.	24 FEB 1880 L	14	163
Coyle, John F.	Blanchard, Meda A.	25 MAR 1878 L	11	392
Cozzen, James	Baerman, Charlotte	24 NOV 1881 R	16	094
Crabbe, Cornelius C.	Neal, P.D.	26 JUN 1878	12	114
Crabbin, Emma L.	Chapman, Frank R.	24 SEP 1878	12	232
Crabbin, Mollie M.	Walsh, George M.	24 JUL 1884	19	155
Crabill, Lucy C.	Artz, Martin L.	29 JUL 1882 R	16	460
Crabster, Ella	Adams, Thomas F.	03 JUN 1881 L	15	342
Crabtree, Charlotte	Huss, O. Edwin	02 JUL 1883 L	18	031

D.C. Marriage Records Index, June 28, 1877 to October 19, 1885

Name	Spouse	Date	Vol	Page
Crabtree, Thomas	Harrison, Priscilla	23 MAR 1880	14	194
Craddle, William	Marshall, Lucinda	20 OCT 1885	20	492
Crager, Sarah S.	Thorn, Albert W.	05 NOV 1879 R	13	464
Cragg, Mary E.	Jaeger, Thomas S.	10 AUG 1880 R	14	394
Cragin, Annette F.	McCarteney, Charles M.	30 APR 1878	12	031
Cragin, Harry W.	Stamper, Mary E.	20 JAN 1880	14	111
Craig, A. Franklin	Sale, Ida Lee	07 OCT 1878 R	12	259
Craig, Addie	Warner, Alford	03 OCT 1878 L	12	251
Craig, Alice	Fuller, Wm. Henry	20 NOV 1879 R	13	491
Craig, Alice Elizabeth	Jony, Pierre Louis	26 JUN 1879 R	13	253
Craig, Andrew Cyrus	Johnson, Elizabeth L. Dora	30 JAN 1884 R	18	401
Craig, Charlotte C.	Simms, John T.	29 SEP 1879 R	13	331
Craig, David	Gardner, Jemima	24 JUL 1884 R	19	153
Craig, Ella	Bayard, T. Jefferson	28 FEB 1884 R	18	451
Craig, Ella Irena	Bowman, George Wm.	28 OCT 1884	19	342
Craig, Emeline A.	Bronson, George W.	08 FEB 1880	14	140
Craig, Emma	Yates, William	27 NOV 1878 R	12	349
Craig, Emma J.	Brooks, David	31 AUG 1882 R	16	497
Craig, Georgianna	Duff, George	19 MAY 1885	20	229
Craig, John	Bogles, Lucy	04 OCT 1883 R	18	171
Craig, John J.	Crow, Virginia E.	18 JUN 1879	13	236
Craig, Josephine	Smith, James H.	23 DEC 1884 R	19	444
Craig, Mary	Gardiner, David	10 JUN 1882 L	16	403
Craig, Matilda	Chesley, John	10 NOV 1884 R	19	370
Craig, Rhoda	Brown, John H.	02 MAY 1883 L	17	426
Craig, Thomas	Alvord, Emily Louise	04 MAY 1880 R	14	248
Craig, Thomas	Johnson, Annie	03 JUL 1884 R	19	118
Craig, William	Shillen, Mollie A.	03 NOV 1881 R	16	059
Craige, Spencer E.	Ages, Martha	13 JUL 1882 L	16	446
Craighill, James Morsell	Berry, Annie Powell Field	17 FEB 1885 R	20	070
Cram, N.D.	Queen, Mary	13 MAR 1884	18	469
Cramer, Benjamin D.	Speer, Kittie L.	10 OCT 1883 R	18	185
Cramer, James	Hinson, Lillure	07 MAY 1878	12	041
Crammell, George W.	Wells, Elvira	26 MAR 1885 L	20	133
Crampsey, Welford E.	Gonter, Lillie	16 OCT 1881 R	16	026
Crampton, Daniel	Burhell, Lizzie	17 OCT 1878	12	280
Crampton, James C.	Talbot, Mary Jane	14 AUG 1883	18	087
Crampton, James William	West, Mollie E.	02 NOV 1882 R	17	107
Crampton, John	Wells, Emma	12 OCT 1884	19	298
Crampton, Julia	Gross, Charles	15 OCT 1885 R	20	488
Crampton, Mary E.	Taylor, James E.	24 DEC 1883	18	337
Crampton, Sophie C.	Roberts, John S.	06 DEC 1883	18	301
Crampton, Thomas H.	Young, Mary Ellen	17 DEC 1879 R	14	050
Crampton, William H.	Lee, Mary	25 JUL 1882 R	16	430
Crampzey, Cora Virginia	Connor, Valentine	15 APR 1878	12	005
Cranage, Mary Elizabeth	McQuin, George H.	20 APR 1881 R	15	261
Crandall, Charles P.	Gibbs, Isabel B.	25 OCT 1883	18	215
Crandall, Clarke P.	Lahey, Mollie	26 JAN 1885	20	036
Crandall, Jennie B.	Beall, Richard S.	09 APR 1885	20	155
Crandall, Milton R.	Johnson, Belle	24 OCT 1879 R	13	427
Crandall, Milton R.	Smith, Lena	14 APR 1885 L	20	164
Crandell, Maggie F.	Asher, Samuel	30 JUN 1880 L	14	339
Crandell, Richard A.	Dutton, Ella H.	05 OCT 1880 L	14	474
Crandell, W.V.	Eaton, Emma	11 AUG 1877	11	051
Crane, George Francis	Moore, Mollie Whaley	26 MAY 1881 R	15	326
Crane, Mary	King, Edward J.	08 FEB 1885	20	056
Crane, Willie F.	Bayne, Sarah A.	25 SEP 1882	17	036
Crangle, Nannie	Lucas, George H.	01 OCT 1884	19	280

Cranston, Sallie M.	McCarthy, John J.	17 MAY 1881 R	15	310
Craun, Emma B.	Henkle, Charles L.	09 JUN 1885 R	20	262
Craves, Rose	Ellis, George	16 JUL 1881 R	25	6046
Crawford, Albert	Stuart, Isabella	30 DEC 1880 L	15	134
Crawford, Caroline	Brown, William F.	03 JUL 1885 R	20	264
Crawford, Carrie R.	Smith, Henry F.	13 MAR 1879 R	13	101
Crawford, Charles M.	Isaac, Henrietta	15 JUN 1878	12	100
Crawford, Eliza S.	Gousha, Valentine B.	17 JAN 1883 L	17	264
Crawford, George A.	Marceron, Bernice B.	13 JUL 1877 L	11	049
Crawford, George A.	Marceron, Bernice B.	21 AUG 1877	11	164
Crawford, Griffin	Thomas, Mary Ellen	20 JUN 1884 R	19	095
Crawford, Joel B.	Sullivan, Maggie F.	17 AUG 1880 L	14	402
Crawford, John	Evans, Sophia	26 AUG 1879	13	335
Crawford, John	Booth, Rose Ella	26 OCT 1880 L	15	015
Crawford, John H.	Conner, Mary C.	05 OCT 1881 R	16	010
Crawford, John J.	Lyles, Fanny	09 MAR 1882	16	270
Crawford, John James	Miller, Minerva Rose	21 NOV 1882 R	17	138
Crawford, John N.	Browning, Florence J.	12 FEB 1879	13	053
Crawford, Joseph O.	Gantt, Celestin	17 APR 1884 L	18	518
Crawford, Josephine	Lewis, Lewis	02 DEC 1884 L	19	432
Crawford, Kate	Richards, William M.	28 APR 1885 R	20	194
Crawford, Lillie	Harrod, Robert	06 JAN 1879 L	13	008
Crawford, M. Alice	Henry, William F.	03 JUL 1884	19	120
Crawford, Mary	Smith, William	29 DEC 1877 L	11	280
Crawford, Mary R.	Swift, Joseph	04 AUG 1880	14	386
Crawford, Medorem	Goodall, Lola	14 JAN 1885 R	20	016
Crawford, Nathan	Matthews, Amanda	12 APR 1883 R	17	392
Crawford, Samuel	Coleman, Betsy	22 JUN 1881 R	15	374
Crawford, William	Smith, Malvina	05 MAR 1883 L	17	332
Crawford, William F.	Goode, Ellsler T.	19 JUN 1883	18	001
Crawford, William P.	White, Mary E.	20 JUL 1882 L	16	452
Crawford, William T.	Carter, Henrietta E.	25 JAN 1882 L	16	208
Crawford, Wm. Stewart	Snelling, Ellie Eugenia	17 MAR 1885 R	20	118
Crawley, Bridget	Kennedy, James	26 SEP 1878 R	12	235
Crawley, Nathaniel	Nutt, Laura	23 JUL 1885 R	20	338
Creagan, Francis	Barry, Emily	20 SEP 1879 L	13	379
Creagh, James F.	Naddy, Maggie J.	08 MAY 1882 L	16	352
Creamer, James	Hulahan, Emma	31 OCT 1879 R	13	456
Creamer, Samuel L.	Swain, Elizabeth Ann	24 OCT 1877 L	11	153
Creaven, John	Foy, Mary	05 FEB 1884 R	18	411
Credic, Ruffy	Conaway, Eliza	22 MAY 1884 L	19	033
Creecy, William B.	King, Lillie M.	25 DEC 1883 R	18	335
Creegan, Ellen	Malley, Thomas	01 OCT 1878 R	12	241
Creegan, Michael	Kinslow, Ida	15 APR 1885 L	20	170
Creek, Eliza Sophia	Hurley, Henry	24 MAR 1885 L	20	128
Creek, Rachel	Hill, John Wesley	09 NOV 1878 L	12	318
Crehan, Margaret	Loveless, James W.	07 SEP 1878 L	12	204
Cremling, Peter	Glench, Dora	26 JUL 1883 L	18	060
Cremmer, Nelson	Williams, Laura	04 JAN 1885 R	20	002
Creswell, Francis McC.	Stacy, Adaline A.	26 MAR 1884 L	18	482
Crewe, John	Smith, Lena	07 DEC 1881 L	16	119
Crews, Enos	Sincell, Emma Margaret	16 APR 1884 R	18	516
Crews, Mary A.	Bushby, William R.	01 OCT 1879 R	13	396
Crews, Rosa	Whitehurst, Manning E.	15 JUL 1884	19	138
Crider, Genevieve A.	Lewis, William H.	04 OCT 1883 R	18	172
Cridler, Thomas Wilbur	Prosperi, Adelaide Aug.	26 FEB 1885 R	20	087
Crier, Emma Elizabeth	Ford, Thomas	18 APR 1881 R	15	261
Crier, Henry A.	Lee, Mary E.	19 APR 1883 R	17	399

Crier, Sarah	Smallwood, Joseph H.	25 DEC 1882 L	17	209
Crim, Mary	Castle, Walter L.	29 JAN 1884	18	399
Crimmins, Catherine	Betters, John	21 OCT 1880 L	15	010
Crimmins, Mary E.	Wall, George W.	23 MAY 1883 L	17	459
Crippen, Americus N.	Denig, Florence (Smith)	06 MAY 1884 R	18	487
Crippen, Elizabeth	Glorius, Andrew G.	27 NOV 1877	11	204
Crismond, James	Staples, Annie M.	26 MAR 1883 R	17	359
Crismond, Sudie Stewart	Grogan, Robert Riddell	19 OCT 1885 R	20	465
Crissey, Sallie E.	Talks, Arthur T.	22 JAN 1884 R	18	388
Crist, Amelia C.	New, John P.	24 JAN 1882 R	16	207
Cristofani, Felice	Malatesta, Colomba L.	27 NOV 1880 L	15	070
Criswell, Hattie M.	Graham, George F.	17 APR 1878 L	12	010
Crittenden, Mary E.	Davis, Thornton	04 SEP 1884 L	19	228
Crittenden, William L.	Amiss, Laura L.	03 JAN 1883 R	17	233
Crittenton, Mary	Proctor, James	26 MAR 1885 L	20	134
Croasdale, Marion S.	Phair, John H.	13 FEB 1879 R	13	058
Croasdale, Mary A.	Burton, Frank	16 AUG 1877 R	11	055
Crocker, Edward A.	Townley, Kate	03 JUL 1882	16	435
Crocker, Willis Francis	Metcalfe, Annie Hodge	05 NOV 1879 R	13	465
Crocket, Laura Virginia	King, Simon Peter	13 OCT 1884 L	19	303
Crockett, Alfred	Willis, Mary	16 JUN 1880 L	14	324
Crockett, Alfred	Johnson, Anna	15 SEP 1883 L	18	131
Crockett, Lillian Patton	Jones, H. Clay	21 NOV 1882 R	17	140
Crockett, Sallie	Alexander, Isaac	24 JUN 1878 L	12	123
Croenin, George	Cherry, Annie	14 JAN 1884 L	18	375
Crofoot, Carrie V.	McMorran, Samuel	03 JAN 1884 R	18	364
Croft, Jacob M.	Allen, Nellie	19 FEB 1883 R	17	311
Croggan, William N.	Stone, Elizabeth J.	14 OCT 1879 L	13	421
Croghan, Cornelia	Widdecombe, Thomas W.	21 FEB 1878 L	11	352
Crombaugh, Daniel	Woody, Ellen Annie	23 AUG 1881 L	15	456
Crompton, Alice	Wilson, Thomas	26 APR 1883 R	17	410
Cromwell, Mary Isabel	Lewis, Robert Eldon	18 DEC 1883	18	320
Cronan, Catherine	Buckley, John M.	08 AUG 1878 R	12	162
Cronan, Janey	Keese, Samuel	20 AUG 1878	12	173
Cronin, Katie A.	Smith, Clarence B.	15 OCT 1881 L	16	027
Crooker, William L.	Utt, Mary A.	02 MAY 1878 R	12	033
Cropper, Allie B.	Wright, Stephen H.	28 DEC 1881	16	165
Cropper, John	McLane, Anne	22 NOV 1881 R	16	086
Cropper, Mary E.B.	Mettert, Joseph G., Jr.	27 MAY 1882 R	16	380
Cropsey, James Clement	Talbot, Mary A.	22 JUN 1880 R	14	328
Crosby, Amanda	Braxton, Durry	23 JAN 1884 L	18	392
Crosby, Annie M.	Jackson, Thomas H.	03 JAN 1885 L	20	002
Crosby, Nellie C.	McCarthy, John B.	29 JUN 1883	18	026
Crosor, Julies C.	McNunty, F.	09 DEC 1878	12	371
Cross, Alice R.	Marche, Thomas Everett	12 OCT 1882 R	17	069
Cross, Charles	Taylor, Mary	20 AUG 1880 L	14	410
Cross, Charles T.	Money, Valvia D.	26 APR 1881 R	15	273
Cross, Emma G.	Ross, Henry L.	01 NOV 1883 L	18	227
Cross, Francis E.	Britt, Sallie H.	26 DEC 1883 R	18	340
Cross, George W.	Smoot, Cordelia V.	09 JAN 1884 R	18	372
Cross, H. Emma	Frasier, Edgar D.	19 APR 1882 R	16	325
Cross, Harriet T.	King, Thomas	05 JUL 1877 R	11	009
Cross, Hattie	Gray, Jesse	02 MAR 1882 L	16	265
Cross, Henry C.	O'Holioran, Helena M.	20 NOV 1877 R	11	194
Cross, Ida F.	Fant, Andrew Lovingston	13 DEC 1882 R	17	180
Cross, Jane	Lewis, Peter	29 SEP 1880 L	14	464
Cross, John J.	Joy, Bridget C.	14 JUN 1881 L	15	361
Cross, Kate	Whails, George	21 MAR 1882 R	16	268

Name	Spouse	Date	Vol	Page
Cross, Lillie M.	Lapham, William R.	24 APR 1879	13	159
Cross, Lucy	Triplett, Washington	07 APR 1880 L	14	213
Cross, Malvina	Burk, John H.	24 JUL 1884 L	19	157
Cross, Marian G.	West, Amos	17 APR 1882 L	16	318
Cross, Mary	Cox, Patrick	09 AUG 1879 L	13	313
Cross, Mary E.	Marshall, Joseph A.	07 APR 1884 R	18	493
Cross, Mary I.	Anderson, William	15 OCT 1878	12	273
Cross, Mary V.	Collins, Wm. H.	08 NOV 1877 R	11	176
Cross, Richard W.	Rabbitt, Emma	29 AUG 1883 R	18	103
Cross, Sarah Ann	Foster, Charles E.	18 JUN 1885 R	20	281
Cross, Washington	Webster, Rachel	06 JAN 1881 R	15	143
Cross, Washington	Green, Mattie	03 JUN 1882 L	16	391
Cross, William R.E.	Riley, Araminta	14 FEB 1883 R	17	304
Crossfield, Amasa Scott	Brown, Louise Palmer	04 APR 1883 R	17	373
Crossman, William D.	Cain, Ida E.	16 DEC 1880	15	105
Crouch, Edwin D.	Oches, Mollie M.	05 NOV 1879 R	13	467
Crouch, Margaret	Smith, George W.	20 JUN 1878	12	106
Crouch, Walter Francis	Stadler, Maggie	27 MAY 1879 L	13	207
Croueberg, Anna	Rice, John	21 MAR 1882 L	16	285
Crounse, Ida	Herbert, Ernest	27 OCT 1884	19	339
Crow, Susie W.	Whelan, William T.	01 FEB 1882 L	16	219
Crow, Virginia E.	Craig, John J.	18 JUN 1879	13	236
Crowder, Walter F.	Bagley, Mary E.	27 MAY 1884	19	040
Crowe, Peter	Noonan, Honora	26 NOV 1884 L	19	418
Crowe, Sallie B.	Skidmore, John T.	10 NOV 1880 R	15	043
Crowley, D.J.F.	Feeley, Mary A.	12 OCT 1880	14	488
Crowley, Estella	Wright, Frank B.	27 OCT 1881	16	050
Crowley, Horace	Gant, Mary Ann	02 AUG 1883 L	18	070
Crowley, Jeremiah	Briscoe, Nellie	14 JAN 1885	20	016
Crowley, Johanna A.	Barnaclo, James K.	28 APR 1884 L	18	535
Crowley, Katie C.	Carter, Noah Albert	27 AUG 1877	11	066
Crowley, Patrick F.	Herbert, Helen	28 APR 1881 R	15	280
Crowley, William B.	Seidenspinner, Josephine	28 JUN 1877 L	11	002
Crown, Ellen	Covington, William E.R.	14 JUN 1882 R	16	407
Crown, French C.	Landon, Cordelia A.	28 JAN 1885	20	042
Crown, Henrietta	Jackson, Albert	18 SEP 1884	19	259
Crown, Ida E.	Allen, William T.	27 AUG 1878	12	182
Crown, Ida S.	Bowman, Columbus S.	13 NOV 1878 R	12	323
Crown, James F.	Clifton, Minnie C.	26 SEP 1878	12	237
Crown, John A.	McDonough, Annie L.	27 MAR 1878 R	11	395
Crown, John Francis	Countee, Rachel Jane	02 DEC 1880 R	15	080
Crown, Lizzie E.	Bradburn, Washington	10 JUL 1877 R	11	014
Crown, Mary Eugene	Vermillion, James Fish	04 OCT 1883 R	18	171
Crown, Mary M.	Schnopp, John Adam	28 DEC 1880 R	15	126
Crown, William S.	Keeser, Margaret A.	20 OCT 1880	15	005
Crowther, Addison B.	Hennaman, Sarah M.	17 DEC 1877	11	240
Crowther, Fannie C.	Edwards, Isaac Newton	21 DEC 1884 R	19	473
Crowther, M.J.	Jackson, W.W.	06 OCT 1879 R	13	406
Crowther, William	Shelton, Julia	09 OCT 1879 R	13	415
Croxton, Richard A.	Athey, Ida I.	16 MAY 1885	20	225
Crubaugh, Wesley W.	Mifflin, Alice F.	01 JAN 1884	18	355
Cruit, John W.	Myers, Lucy L.	08 JAN 1884	18	369
Crumbaugh, Edward	Walker, Ella M.	06 SEP 1877	11	079
Crummey, Emma	Miller, Henry	28 FEB 1883 R	17	326
Crummins, Annie	Lilly, Frank	04 JUN 1878	12	084
Crump, Armistead	Rhodes, Cora	23 NOV 1882 R	17	114
Crump, Carlisle F.	Matthews, Sarah	15 JUL 1879 R	13	282
Crump, Carrie	Carlisle, George J.	04 JUN 1884	19	051

D.C. Marriage Records Index, June 28, 1877 to October 19, 1885   109

Name	Spouse	Date	Vol	Page
Crump, Cora V.	King, William F.	10 FEB 1879 R	13	052
Crump, Edward	Woodland, Katie	23 APR 1885	20	187
Crump, Fannie	Davis, Alfred	14 APR 1881 R	15	234
Crump, Frances Ann	Dilks, Charles L.	03 NOV 1877 L	11	167
Crump, George A.	Towers, Marion D.	24 DEC 1882 R	17	203
Crump, George D.	Wisely, Marsella	04 JUN 1880 L	14	306
Crump, Henry	Honesty, Annie	24 MAR 1881 R	15	237
Crump, Ida M.	Duty, Charles E.	05 MAR 1885	20	095
Crump, James Edward	Dells, Annie E.	30 OCT 1877	11	161
Crump, John	Howard, Susan	13 NOV 1878	12	329
Crump, Sarah	Taylor, Nero	29 MAR 1883 R	17	365
Crumpsey, Laura J.	Pierce, Clark Sweet	07 MAR 1883 R	17	331
Crumpton, Eugene	Boone, Arianna I.	05 FEB 1882	16	181
Crumpton, Jacob	Peck, Laura	05 MAY 1885	20	206
Crumpton, John T.	Wilson, Lavinia, Mrs.	03 FEB 1880 R	14	133
Crupper, Cora A.	Felton, Charles W.	30 MAR 1881 L	15	242
Crupper, F.R.	Beall, Sarah L.	29 MAY 1884 L	19	046
Crupper, Robert Douglass	Anderson, Sallie Josephine	28 FEB 1883 R	17	322
Crupper, William	Coalman, Lucy	30 AUG 1877 R	11	071
Cruser, Collin Barton, Dr.	Davenport, Bettie	26 FEB 1885 R	20	088
Crusoe, Frank R.	Gasway, Annie	20 DEC 1882 R	17	197
Crusor, William	Causten, Fanny C.	05 AUG 1879 L	13	307
Crutchet, Emma	Gibson, William Henry	17 JAN 1883 R	17	262
Crutchett, Sarah E.	Wenzel, George W.	11 NOV 1879 R	13	476
Crutchfield, Robert	Dabney, Martha Ellen	01 NOV 1883 L	18	225
Cryer, Eliza A.	Harden, T.L.	08 JUN 1881	15	352
Cryler, Margaret	Briscoe, Sargent	09 SEP 1885 R	20	409
Cuddihy, Maggie	Donohue, Thomas	22 MAY 1883 R	17	456
Cuddihy, Mary	Shanahan, Thomas	18 APR 1881 R	15	252
Cudlipp, Ida	Atkinson, Charles	10 DEC 1884 R	19	447
Culbertson, Josephine	Syford, George H.	11 FEB 1885	20	063
Culby, Samuel	Dennison, Annie	27 OCT 1881	16	037
Culhane, Catherine A.	Holohan, Charles E.	07 SEP 1885 L	20	401
Culhane, Thomas	Cassin, Bridget	16 JAN 1883 L	17	259
Culligan, Mary	Fitzgerald, Patrick	08 APR 1880 R	14	215
Cullinan, Martin F.	O'Leary, Mary E.	11 FEB 1885	20	064
Cullison, Ida	Holland, Edward E.	06 APR 1878 R	11	408
Culotta, Concetta	Falisi, Vincenzo	25 APR 1883 L	17	410
Culton, John R.	Patterson, Margaret	27 AUG 1877	11	067
Culver, Charles Z.	Cawldwell, Mary	03 JAN 1882	16	177
Culver, Mary Louise	Cornett, Thomas H.	01 JAN 1885	19	510
Culver, Reuben Dillon	Todd, Mazie Brooke	30 DEC 1883 R	18	352
Cumbach, Mary	Offutt, Frank	26 NOV 1884 L	19	412
Cumber, James H.	Johnson, Julia A.	22 AUG 1882 L	16	491
Cumberland, Ann Rebecca	Joy, Edward F.	10 MAR 1885 L	20	104
Cumberland, George W.	Brotzell, Sarah Jane	02 JUN 1879 R	13	215
Cumberland, John	Chamberlain, Alice	09 DEC 1884	19	443
Cumberland, John Hews	Hurbert, Mary Annie	24 MAY 1880 R	14	283
Cumberland, Mary Frances	Smith, Charles W.	26 MAY 1879 R	13	204
Cumberland, Mary Roberta	Zachary, George Wash.	14 NOV 1883 R	18	253
Cumberland, Susie	McDermott, George	19 APR 1882 L	16	324
Cuming, Valentine H.	Dawson, Virginia A.	19 JUN 1878 L	12	104
Cumins, Addie	Hawkins, John	09 MAR 1885 R	20	102
Cummings, Doctor	Fritter, Dora	04 DEC 1883 L	18	295
Cummings, Mary Louise	Campbell, Charles Oscar	16 JUL 1879 R	13	283
Cunigan, Benjamin Lewis	Burke, Sallie Burdon	13 MAR 1879 R	12	407
Cunningham, Annie E.	Hershaw, Charles W.	08 OCT 1879 R	13	409
Cunningham, Carrie R.	Phillips, John J.	28 JAN 1885 R	20	024

Cunningham, Emma	Fletcher, Augusta C.	26 NOV 1883 L	18	276
Cunningham, Fannie	Lewis, John H.	04 OCT 1883 R	18	172
Cunningham, George A.	Meade, Julia A.	21 JAN 1884 L	18	387
Cunningham, George D.	Leeman, Elizabeth M.	15 AUG 1883 L	18	088
Cunningham, Harry T.	Mangan, Agnes	05 FEB 1883 L	17	292
Cunningham, Ida C.	Sebree, Wm. E.	20 NOV 1883 R	18	265
Cunningham, Leanora	Snyder, John F.	09 JAN 1879 R	13	014
Cunningham, Mark	Sheahan, Mary	28 APR 1883 L	17	420
Cunningham, Mary	Karr, Patrick	26 FEB 1878 L	11	357
Cunningham, Mary	O'Neill, Martin	25 APR 1881 L	15	271
Cunningham, Mary E.	Horgan, Edmond	27 OCT 1879 R	13	443
Cunningham, William	Connors, Nora	23 MAY 1884	18	518
Curl, Edward C.	Fowler, Ella	30 APR 1885	20	199
Curley, Albert	Davis, Annie V.	08 MAY 1883 R	17	433
Curley, Maria	Duffy, James	17 SEP 1079 L	13	375
Curran, Agnes A.	Cook, Thomas F.	09 APR 1885 L	20	157
Curran, Clarence E.	Eccleston, Henrietta M.	17 JAN 1884 R	18	380
Curran, Helen Givin	Sanderson, John Thomas	15 OCT 1878 R	12	274
Curran, Nellie G.	Lynch, James F.	20 JUN 1883 R	18	005
Curran, Rosanna	Leland, Theo F.	03 JUL 1878 L	12	123
Currell, Virginia F.	Mitchell, Geo. Wash.	16 SEP 1880	14	450
Curren, Annie E.	Kerr, William J.	11 JUN 1884	19	085
Curren, William E.	Beach, Jennie C.	06 DEC 1882 R	17	170
Curriden, Samuel W.	Kelly, Mary E.	19 OCT 1880 R	15	003
Currier, Sallie Ella	Rinehart, Charles	09 MAY 1882 R	16	355
Curry, Annie C.	Daniels, Joseph W.	09 MAR 1885 L	20	103
Curry, Christiana	Hawkins, John E.	03 DEC 1884 L	19	434
Curry, Edward	Dandridge, Mary Jane	05 APR 1883 R	17	191
Curry, George	Harris, Ann Maria	05 JUN 1884	19	066
Curry, James Benjamin	Hazel, Louisa	10 DEC 1882 R	17	178
Curry, Levi	Brintnall, Catherine J.	08 JAN 1885 R	20	009
Curry, Mary E.	Taylor, James W P	02 OCT 1881 R	16	001
Curry, William L.	Cooke, Sarah V.	24 FEB 1885 R	20	082
Curtain, Bettie Ann	Curtain, George T.	15 APR 1884 R	18	513
Curtain, George T.	Curtain, Bettie Ann	15 APR 1884 R	18	513
Curtain, Ida	Kyle, James	07 FEB 1878	11	333
Curtain, James	Cohen, Rachel	07 FEB 1878	11	329
Curlin, Elizabeth A.	O'Hagan, James T.	12 DEC 1882 L	17	178
Curtin, Jennette S.	Hudson, George J.	09 APR 1882 R	16	305
Curtin, John	Carey, Katie	07 OCT 1879 L	13	408
Curtin, Katie F.	Scanlon, Patrick	10 SEP 1879	13	363
Curtin, Maggie H.	Clark, Thomas J.	28 NOV 1881 R	16	100
Curtin, Mary Cecilia	Clark, John Black	20 MAY 1878 L	12	061
Curtin, Mary J.	Boss, Robert Lake	04 JUN 1878	12	084
Curtin, Nettie M.	Riley, Thomas	04 FEB 1884 R	18	405
Curtin, Oliver	Thomas, Josephine F.	10 JUL 1884	19	132
Curtin, Teresa B.	Lusby, James E.	20 AUG 1884 L	19	195
Curtis, Christiana	Mountjoy, Anthony	11 SEP 1884 L	19	242
Curtis, Clifton Henry	Simms, Rachel, Mrs.	29 SEP 1880 R	14	462
Curtis, Ednah A.	Dorman, George R.	17 APR 1878	12	009
Curtis, Edwin L.	Downs, Maggie D.	09 SEP 1882	17	010
Curtis, F.	Lewis, Elizabeth	10 APR 1878 L	11	415
Curtis, Frank	Dyson, Mary	19 APR 1884 L	18	521
Curtis, Hannah	Bray, Henry	17 AUG 1885	20	373
Curtis, Ida M.	Waddey, Benjamin F.	25 MAY 1878	12	066
Curtis, James	Hill, Annie	28 JUN 1877	11	001
Curtis, James	Gibson, Esther	12 OCT 1882 R	17	068
Curtis, James	Nichols, Sarah	29 NOV 1883	18	285

Curtis, James M.	Turton, Florence A.	09 NOV 1882 L	17	121
Curtis, Jennie O.	Cannon, Henry W.	21 NOV 1879 R	13	496
Curtis, John Henry	Marshall, Susanna	13 NOV 1884	19	373
Curtis, Leonora Clara	Rogers, William Isaac	15 MAY 1878 R	12	048
Curtis, Margaret J.	Beckett, James W.	08 OCT 1880 R	14	477
Curtis, Mary	Henderson, Gilson	20 JAN 1883 R	17	269
Curtis, Mary Bell	Menagh, Preston S.	02 SEP 1885	20	394
Curtis, Mary Ellen	Savoy, Frank	11 OCT 1883 R	18	189
Curtis, Mary V.	Jackson, Arthur E.	06 FEB 1883 L	17	297
Curtis, Peter C.	Bailey, Martha A.	13 JAN 1880 R	14	095
Curtis, Rosa V.	Atwell, Benjamin F.	25 MAY 1878	12	066
Curtis, Sarah Jane	Hutchins, Julius	07 AUG 1884 L	19	174
Curtis, Wallace L.	Brooks, Julia A.	14 AUG 1878 L	12	168
Curtis, William	Berry, Christiana	03 JUN 1878 L	12	080
Curtis, William	Ayer, Alice	07 MAY 1884 R	19	009
Curtiss, John Klink	May, Elizabeth Boss	28 OCT 1878 R	12	291
Curtiss, Ottawa H.	Bumbray, Ruberta F.	09 AUG 1880	14	393
Curtley, Alice	Carter, Eugean	10 SEP 1883 R	18	121
Cushing, Frank H.	McGill, Emma T.	10 JUL 1882	16	442
Cushman, Frederick A.	Saffell, Annie T.	17 JAN 1885 L	20	025
Cusick, Maggie	Hilbus, George J.	22 JAN 1878	11	314
Cusick, Patrick F.	Danaher, Mary C.	23 NOV 1881 L	16	091
Cusick, William	Ryan, Annie	02 JAN 1883 L	17	232
Custard, Mary Jane	Hearns, Jeemes	22 JUN 1882	16	424
Custerd, William A.	Burk, Bessie E.	19 JAN 1881	15	158
Custis, Ellen	Hatton, Charles	01 MAR 1880 R	14	169
Custis, Henry	Pryor, Emily	07 DEC 1881 L	16	119
Cutler, Jennie Whitmore	Woodman, Francis Jos.	30 JUN 1884	19	112
Cutler, Louise F.	McClure, Alfred J.	01 JAN 1880	14	083
Cutler, William Gifford	Pelouze, Minnie E.	20 SEP 1882 R	17	027
Cuvillier, Maggie	Mister, Frederick M.	01 DEC 1879 R	14	020

D

Name	Spouse	Date	Vol	Page
Dabner, Alick	Hillery, Sophia	05 JAN 1883 L	17	240
Dabney, Charles	Haskins, Martha Ellen Dabney	14 JUN 1881 L	15	358
Dabney, Charles	Simmons, Mary A.	18 SEP 1883 L	18	137
Dabney, Frank W.	Saunders, Roberta J.	04 JUL 1883 L	18	035
Dabney, James H.	Ross, Lottie	09 MAY 1878 L	12	045
Dabney, Louise	Jackson, John Lewis	21 DEC 1882 R	17	201
Dabney, Mamie	Rollins, Daniel	27 NOV 1883 L	18	278
Dabney, Martha Ellen	Crutchfield, Robert	01 NOV 1883 L	18	225
Dabney, Sarah	Aston, George W.	27 JUN 1878 R	12	115
Dacey, Mary	Harper, Charles	09 AUG 1880 R	14	395
Dade, Bettie Jane	Gilbert, James W.H.	07 FEB 1881 L	15	179
Dade, Charles T.	Savoy, Mary C.	22 SEP 1884	19	262
Dade, Daniel B.	Nelson, Mary Susan	15 FEB 1879 R	13	061
Dade, Effie	Fields, Isaac	08 JAN 1885 L	20	010
Dade, Eliza Minor	Baird, George D.	25 APR 1879 L	13	160
Dade, John F.	Fields, Carrie E.	04 SEP 1879	13	349
Dade, Julia A.	Fields, John A.	18 DEC 1878	12	387
Dade, Lewis A.	Green, Margaret	17 APR 1883 L	17	397
Dade, Lizzie	Brewer, Archibald	25 APR 1878 R	12	024
Dade, Lucy M.	Cartter, George A.	24 MAY 1881 L	15	322
Dade, Peter	Ewell, Mary	20 DEC 1880 R	15	111
Dadmun, Elizabeth	Wilson, Orrin S.	19 DEC 1877 R	11	240
Dafney, John H.	Henry, Mary F.	21 AUG 1884 L	19	203
Daggs, Delia	Dixon, Frank	27 NOV 1884 L	19	416
Daggs, Ella	Fantroy, Robert	11 AUG 1881	15	441
Dahler, Sophie	Hauser, Ernest	03 MAY 1885 R	20	200
Dailey, Annie M.	Richardson, Willard S.	29 JUL 1884 L	19	161
Dailey, Charles F.	Cooley, Sarah A.	13 OCT 1881 R	16	022
Dailey, Charles H.	Doremus, Mary	01 JAN 1883	17	230
Dailey, Gertrude Frances	Asfield, Jno. McFarland	02 JUL 1877 R	11	005
Dailey, John M.	Roach, Mary E.	30 OCT 1004	19	274
Dailey, John Samuel	Beasler, Mary J.	15 MAR 1883 R	17	347
Daily, Edward	Perry, Mary	11 APR 1885 L	20	160
Daily, Hattie B.	Strine, William R.	12 SEP 1879	13	367
Daily, Mary E.	Roche, William J.	16 FEB 1885 R	20	068
Daily, Patrick R.	Stone, Lottie M.	13 DEC 1882 R	17	180
Daines, Matilda	Morgan, George G.W.	22 DEC 1877 R	11	227
Daingerfield, Bettie Rozier	Anderson, James Archibald	11 DEC 1879 R	14	033
Dairy, Delia	Ender, James	08 NOV 1877 R	11	175
Daison, Alexander	Broadus, Mary Jane	09 FEB 1882 R	16	235
Dale, Charley	Nelson, Hattie	28 JUN 1883 R	18	023
Daley, Annie	Osterman, John F.	07 JUN 1882 L	16	399
Daley, Annie M.	Harris, John W.	03 DEC 1884 R	19	432
Daley, Ellen	Broderick, Michael	07 FEB 1882 L	16	228
Daley, Jacob Edwar	Greever, Ida	12 SEP 1880 R	14	441
Daley, James A.	Martin, Kate C.	04 AUG 1883	18	074
Daley, John C.	McCarty, Mary L.	29 MAY 1883 L	17	467
Daley, Uriah	Vanderpool, Annie	20 SEP 1883 L	18	145
Daley, William H.	Bentley, Rosa	18 OCT 1881 R	16	030
Dallas, Eda A.	Caldwell, Joseph B.S.	21 NOV 1883 R	18	268
Dallas, Mary	Read, Daniel	26 OCT 1882 R	17	097
Dalrymple, James A.D.	Torbert, Lilla W.	20 DEC 1882 R	17	193
Dalton, Josie	Bain, Edward A.	22 JUL 1881 R	15	413
Dalton, Kate J.	Finch, John Summerfield	16 OCT 1881	16	026
Daly, Annie J.	Gant, Ambrose C.	14 JAN 1881 R	15	151
Daly, Eugene	O'Connell, Nora	14 MAY 1882 R	16	360
Daly, Frederick F.	Norman, Lucy E.	03 JUN 1882 L	16	392

Daly, James A.	Martin, Kate C.	20 JUL 1883 L	18	054
Daly, Jefferson D.	Herbert, Mary A.	12 JUL 1882 L	16	445
Daly, John A.	Esputa, Josephine	07 NOV 1882	17	112
Daly, Joseph	Annadale, Josephine	22 JUN 1885 L	20	283
Daly, Joseph E.	Casey, Catherine	06 JUN 1885 L	20	258
Daly, Katie Mary Camelia	Glassgow, George Wm.	24 SEP 1881 L	15	497
Daly, Margaret	Lane, William	15 OCT 1877 R	11	134
Daly, Martin	Russel, Florence	29 APR 1881	15	286
Daly, Mary Ellen	Handy, William	15 NOV 1881 L	16	078
Daly, Ross	Fletcher, Addie	22 DEC 1881 R	16	118
Daly, Walter H.	Nightingale, Emily	29 APR 1880 R	14	245
Daly, William B.	Parsons, Julia	13 JAN 1881 L	15	151
Daly, William W.	Thour, Margaret M.	21 NOV 1882 R	17	141
Dame, Jonathan C.	Byles, Emma	29 APR 1884 L	18	542
Damens, John Andrew	Morris, Martha, Mrs.	02 NOV 1882 R	16	384
Dammann, Emma O.	May, John G.	28 OCT 1881 L	16	051
Danaher, Mary C.	Cusick, Patrick F.	23 NOV 1881 L	16	091
Dandelet, Jerome F.	Bailey, Susan L.	09 FEB 1880 R	14	075
Dandelet, Lucile J.	Fessenden, Stephen D.	14 JUN 1883 R	17	493
Danden, Ester	Chase, Paul	05 APR 1884 L	18	496
Dandridge, George	Green, Sarah	26 APR 1883 R	17	392
Dandridge, Mary C.	Bombray, Joseph	05 SEP 1884	19	224
Dandridge, Mary Jane	Curry, Edward	05 APR 1883 R	17	191
Danenhauer, John	Barnaclo, Eliza L.	23 FEB 1879 R	13	075
Danforth, Charles A.	Holt, Laura V.	10 JUN 1880 R	14	317
Danforth, Fanny Harriet (Northup)	Eldert, Nessel	30 MAY 1883 R	17	468
Danforth, Helene	Gray, Samuel	14 JUL 1881 R	15	402
Danforth, James A.	Martin, Fannie Louise	06 MAY 1879 R	13	177
Dangerfield, carrie	Wiggins, Benjamin	20 AUG 1884 L	19	198
Dangerfield, Eliza A.	Willard, Lewis	14 AUG 1884	19	188
Dangler, Mattie P.	Mahagan, J. Robert	22 NOV 1882 L	17	144
Dangler, Susie Lovina	Smith, Charles Coltman	19 MAY 1885 R	20	229
Daniel, Adelaide E.	Luke, Vyvyan	07 DEC 1883	18	305
Daniel, Alonzo	Symcox, Frances	18 DEC 1883	18	317
Daniel, Celia	Wye, James	20 JUN 1879	13	244
Daniel, Edward B.	Stevens, Julia M.	17 OCT 1877 R	11	138
Daniel, Fernando	Riley, Mollie	23 SEP 1885 R	20	432
Daniel, Lafayette W.	Tillett, Hattie B.	29 SEP 1880	14	466
Daniel, Sallie W.	Turpin, Perry B.	30 AUG 1882 L	16	497
Daniel, Samuel Greenhow	Fitzhugh, Virginia Meade	03 AUG 1882 R	16	467
Daniel, William	Whitback, Emma	25 SEP 1878	12	233
Daniels, Ara M.	Whitmore, Emma V.	07 DEC 1882	17	174
Daniels, Benjamin	Johnson, Elizabeth	13 NOV 1878 R	12	283
Daniels, Emma	Johnson, Moses	09 JAN 1879 R	13	005
Daniels, Fannie	Finecy, James	03 JUL 1878 R	12	124
Daniels, Harriet	Wilson, William	12 JUN 1883 R	17	484
Daniels, John W.	Fisher, Maritia	19 MAY 1884 L	19	027
Daniels, Joseph W.	Curry, Annie C.	09 MAR 1885 L	20	103
Daniels, Mary	Davis, Wesley	10 APR 1879 R	13	135
Daniels, Mary	Thompson, Wales	25 JAN 1882	16	208
Daniels, Robert	Day, Sarah	15 JUN 1879 R	13	200
Daniels, Rosa A.	McDonald, John D.	24 OCT 1883 L	18	210
Daniels, Walter W.	Wells, Emma M.	31 DEC 1877	11	283
Danison, Francis W.	Hayes, Rosa	18 SEP 1881 R	15	488
Danison, Joseph E.	Fudge, Ida	22 JAN 1880 R	14	118
Dann, Wm. F.	Blundon, Laura V.	20 JAN 1880 R	14	113
Dannison, Annie	Hayes, William	19 JUL 1881 L	15	408
Dant, Annie E.	Ammon, George Q.	22 AUG 1882	16	480

Dant, Edward E.	Murray, Alice E.	09 SEP 1885	20	435
Dant, Lottie L.	Burn, James D.	15 DEC 1884 R	19	459
Dant, Thomas E.	McGarraghy, Mary Reddy	21 FEB 1882 R	16	252
Dante, Drancis	Tricker, Annie Serena	29 NOV 1883 L	18	287
Dante, Verdie S.	Woodward, Herbert E.	03 JUN 1885	20	253
Danz, Louis	Digel, Louise	11 NOV 1884 L	19	374
Darby, Ella R.	Iglehart, Basil R.	28 MAY 1884 R	19	041
Darby, Hattie	Pugh, Thomas O.	03 OCT 1882 R	17	050
Darby, Rezin W.	Esther, Clara M.	15 JAN 1880 R	14	109
Darby, Rufus H.	Clark, Annie F.	11 DEC 1879 L	14	042
Darden, Andrew J.	Reiley, Gertrude	06 DEC 1884	19	439
Darden, Martha Eleanor	Hyatt, Robert James	28 APR 1881 R	15	281
Dare, Joseph W.	Wallace, Fannie	20 DEC 1882	17	196
Darley, Elizabeth Fenton	Horsey, Martin	15 SEP 1884	19	246
Darley, Susan B.	Collins, Jacob W.	26 JAN 1881 R	15	162
Darling, Charles A.	Hudders, Isabella L.	08 OCT 1884	19	293
Darlington, Gerturde	Zamzaw, Albert	06 NOV 1883 L	18	236
Darlington, Joseph J.	Meador, Elizabeth R.	21 JUL 1885	20	333
Darmstead, Teny	Padgett, William R.	05 OCT 1880 R	14	475
Darnall, J.E.	Griffin, L.V.	28 JUL 1884 L	19	160
Darnall, Katie A.	Parker, Robert H.	25 NOV 1884	19	407
Darnall, Marion D.	Dunn, Annie E.	04 JAN 1881	15	138
Darnall, Percival Y.	Simonds, Mary A.H.	18 JUL 1880 R	14	365
Darnall, Sarah E.	Lewis, Julius	20 DEC 1877 R	11	255
Darnall, Thomas A.	Hemmersey, Louisa	30 SEP 1884 L	19	277
Darne, R.H.	Oliver, Octavia	05 MAY 1881	15	291
Darnell, Reuben	Tavener, Mary V.	28 APR 1885	20	193
Darnes, Sarah Elizabeth	Cole, Daniel Webster	26 JUL 1884	19	159
Darr, John Francis	Pillage, Annie Elizabeth	19 JUN 1881 R	15	368
Darr, Nellie Agnes	Carson, William Henry	09 FEB 1881 R	15	184
Darr, Philip	Lawless, Annie	20 OCT 1883 L	18	204
Darr, Robert W.	Mahler, Kate M.	14 OCT 1884	10	305
Dartt, James F.	Ray, Florence	19 MAY 1881	15	316
Dashields, Robert Benjamin	Payne, Anna Rose	20 JUN 1880 R	14	322
Dashiell, George B.	Wheeler, M. Clara	22 JUL 1884 L	19	150
Datcher, Emily	Mills, George	12 APR 1879 L	13	139
Datcher, Thomas Henry	Smith, Anna	31 DEC 1881 R	16	171
Dature, Lizzie	Davis, William Thomas	05 OCT 1881 L	16	008
Dauch, Laura	Haueke, John	13 APR 1879	13	130
Daughton, Dixon M.	Koch, Katie	24 OCT 1883	18	210
Daughton, Emma	Krahling, Herman	16 OCT 1884 R	19	314
Daughton, Kate H.	Coleman, Edgar A.	07 JAN 1884 R	18	412
Dauterich, Henry L.	Helmuth, Amelia C.	14 MAR 1883	17	344
Davenport, Belle	Robinson, Warner	24 JUL 1884	19	156
Davenport, Benjamin	Goodhue, Minnie K.	17 AUG 1880 R	14	404
Davenport, Bettie	Cruser, Collin Barton, Dr.	26 FEB 1885 R	20	088
Davenport, Christopher	James, Mary	01 MAY 1879 L	13	170
Davenport, Christopher	Lindsay, Maria Annie	2y DEC 1883 R	18	340
Davenport, Edward	Hughes, Louisa	04 OCT 1882	17	051
Davenport, Emma	Ford, William	27 OCT 1879 R	13	446
Davenport, Isaac	Carter, Annie	31 JUL 1879	13	300
David, Lizzie	Broadbent, William	18 AUG 1883 R	18	076
Davidge, James	Parker, Annie	26 APR 1881 L	15	275
Davidson, Alexander S.	Moore, Sarah M.	23 MAY 1883 L	17	457
Davidson, John E.	Boyden, Helen Jane	08 SEP 1882 R	17	012
Davidson, John Frank	Shoemaker, Eliza	06 DEC 1877 R	11	217
Davidson, Margaret A.	Parker, John E.	29 FEB 1884 R	18	452
Davidson, Martha	Detwiler, William S.	06 AUG 1884	19	170

Davidson, Robert	Berlin, Mary	17 JUL 1882 L	16	451
Davidson, Sophie P.	Miller, Douglass G.	28 MAR 1881	15	240
Davidson, Thomas	Mahoney, Ida	06 SEP 1882 L	17	010
Davidson, William J.	Morrison, Rosina R.	12 APR 1883 R	17	381
Davidsson, Maggie	Nicholson, Augustus L.	27 OCT 1883 L	18	217
Davies, Charles	Warren, Louisa Malvina	30 AUG 1883 R	18	105
Davies, Frank	Thorn, Effie	18 OCT 1877	11	145
Davis, Ada	Davis, French J.	11 JUN 1885	20	268
Davis, Agnes	Solus, Charlie	05 JAN 1882 L	16	184
Davis, Albert	Reddick, Rose, Mrs.	03 JUL 1879 R	13	266
Davis, Alfred	Crump, Fannie	14 APR 1881 R	15	234
Davis, Alice	Fowler, Samuel	01 AUG 1877	11	037
Davis, Alice	Queen, Charles	01 JUN 1878	12	079
Davis, Alice	Adams, Jonah	06 DEC 1883 L	18	301
Davis, Alice C.	Purcell, James H.	28 OCT 1884	19	343
Davis, Alice E.	Dredge, William C.	29 NOV 1882 R	17	155
Davis, Alice Virginia	Lyons, Philip W.	03 JAN 1884	18	365
Davis, Anlucretia	Cole, Henry	22 FEB 1883 L	17	318
Davis, Anna L.	Reynolds, Richard H.	07 NOV 1883	18	240
Davis, Anne	Reamer, Frank	15 OCT 1878	12	274
Davis, Annie	Jenkins, Edward	09 AUG 1877 R	11	046
Davis, Annie	Monroe, Lewis	19 SEP 1880	14	440
Davis, Annie A.	Della, Edward L.	11 FEB 1884 R	18	419
Davis, Annie E.	Geese, Edward	26 OCT 1882 R	17	095
Davis, Annie Laurie	Dennis, Frank	31 DEC 1884 R	19	494
Davis, Annie V.	Curley, Albert	08 MAY 1883 R	17	433
Davis, Bayliss	Ellis, Ellen	27 APR 1883 L	17	418
Davis, Benjamin F.	Downey, Mary R.	16 AUG 1884 L	19	190
Davis, Bettie L.	Spalding, John H.	26 APR 1881 L	15	274
Davis, Carrie A. Harnes, Mrs.	McMurray, Robert A.	21 OCT 1880 R	14	495
Davis, Celia	Gant, Thomas	17 OCT 1878 L	12	281
Davis, Charles	Burgess, Eliza	22 AUG 1878 L	12	177
Davis, Charles	Gordin, Julia	20 JUL 1881 L	15	411
Davis, Charles	Burke, Annie	01 DEC 1881 R	16	100
Davis, Charles E.	Scott, Epsey	30 SEP 1880 R	14	467
Davis, Charles L.	Jackson, Mary Ellen	04 SEP 1877 L	11	075
Davis, Edmund Walter	Steuart, Maria Hunter	30 NOV 1880 R	15	072
Davis, Edward	Foley, Katie	19 AUG 1880	14	408
Davis, Edward	Conway, Lettie	02 AUG 1882 R	16	465
Davis, Edward F.	Pope, Minnie B.	03 FEB 1881	15	177
Davis, Effie	Tichenor, Clarendon L.	05 AUG 1885 R	34	8427
Davis, Effie V.	Mathiot, Harry B.	04 JUN 1884	19	053
Davis, Elias	Rawlings, Eliza	30 JUN 1881 R	15	350
Davis, Elizabeth	Johnson, Joseph	15 MAY 1879 L	13	191
Davis, Elizabeth E.	Ballenger, Richard F.	25 AUG 1879 R	13	333
Davis, Elizabeth E.	Ballenger, Richard F.	25 AUG 1879	13	500
Davis, Ella	Hill, William	10 SEP 1884	19	238
Davis, Ella	O'Connor, Michael	26 AUG 1884 L	19	209
Davis, Ella V.	Tallant, John M.	08 FEB 1883 R	17	300
Davis, Ellen	Robinson, Columbus	04 MAR 1880 L	14	176
Davis, Emma E.	Hardy, Thomas G.	18 MAY 1882 R	16	366
Davis, Emma Jane	Peoples, Cary Henry	02 OCT 1884	19	257
Davis, Eva	Ayres, Frederick	03 NOV 1881	16	060
Davis, Fannie	Rennoe, Chapman	13 SEP 1877 R	11	093
Davis, Fannie	Carter, Elias	20 JUN 1885 L	20	282
Davis, Fannie L.	Weed, A.L.	26 JUL 1881	15	418
Davis, Fannie L.	Taylor, Will B.	02 JAN 1884 R	18	361
Davis, Fannie Queen	Barr, Robert McClelland	28 SEP 1885 R	20	447

Davis, Franklin R.	May, Elizabeth	10 NOV 1880	15	034
Davis, French J.	Davis, Ada	11 JUN 1885	20	268
Davis, Frisby Francis	Shipley, Mary Jane	06 JUL 1879 R	13	260
Davis, George	Queen, Annie	09 AUG 1877 R	11	045
Davis, George	Smith, Emma	02 JUL 1883 L	18	029
Davis, George A.	Thompson, Mary Olivia	03 JUL 1881 R	15	385
Davis, George H.	Roberts, Emily	27 JUL 1880 R	14	376
Davis, George W.	Parker, Sarah E.	02 DEC 1879 R	14	021
Davis, George W.	Sutton, Susan Isabella	04 FEB 1884 R	18	406
Davis, Harriet	Maddox, W.M.	27 FEB 1884	18	448
Davis, Harrison	Peake, Bertha	08 JUL 1885 R	20	316
Davis, Harry A.	Barrand, Mary C.	29 NOV 1883	18	278
Davis, Harry C.	Schneider, Ida J.	09 OCT 1882 R	17	061
Davis, Hattie	Elms, James W.	09 JUN 1882	16	402
Davis, Hattie Virginia	Bennett, Philo Henry	15 JUN 1881 R	15	362
Davis, Henry	Simonds, Louisa	16 AUG 1880 L	14	401
Davis, Henry	Harris, Allice	09 OCT 1884 R	19	297
Davis, Henry Edgar	Riddle, Harriet	17 JAN 1882 R	16	196
Davis, Henry P.	Washington, Elenora	07 MAR 1881 R	15	217
Davis, Ida Eliz.	Rathvon, Robert Hind.	19 NOV 1884 R	19	395
Davis, India	Wells, William L.	28 AUG 1877 L	11	068
Davis, Isaac	Farr, Ella	07 FEB 1878	11	331
Davis, Jacob	Hamilton, Sophia	25 NOV 1884 L	19	409
Davis, James	Ogden, Martha	28 OCT 1880 L	15	021
Davis, James	Francis, Jennie	14 JUL 1884	19	136
Davis, James H.	Green, Ellen	02 MAY 1878	12	034
Davis, James S.	Irland, Kate Latimer	21 MAR 1883	17	354
Davis, James Sanford	Clark, Lizzie Margret	05 JUL 1883	18	037
Davis, James T.J.	Fayman, Roberta	02 JUN 1880 R	14	299
Davis, James W.	Foote, Hattie	08 MAR 1880 R	14	179
Davis, Jane	Miles, William	06 MAR 1878 L	11	373
Davis, Jerome F.	Thompson, Frances D.	05 JAN 1885 R	20	003
Davis, John	Saunders, Mary	28 AUG 1879	13	343
Davis, John	Williams, Alice	26 APR 1880 L	14	237
Davis, John Fisher	Ellis, Hattie R.	22 SEP 1885 R	20	434
Davis, John H.	Boswell, Alice	10 JUN 1879 R	13	223
Davis, John, Rev.	Jones, Elizabeth A.	03 OCT 1882	17	049
Davis, John Wm. Henry	Terry, Eliza	13 AUG 1885 R	20	368
Davis, Joseph Gilbert	Lehman, Mary Helena	19 DEC 1878 R	12	373
Davis, Joseph M.T.	Morse, Mary A.	30 JAN 1883 R	17	279
Davis, Josephine	Gauges, Robert	05 SEP 1877 L	11	077
Davis, Josephine	Beck, Frank	31 DEC 1878	12	409
Davis, Josie E.	Funk, John J.	29 JAN 1885 R	20	042
Davis, Kate	Pulitzer, Joseph	19 JUN 1878	12	106
Davis, Katie S.	Tribby, Charles E.	17 JUL 1885	20	328
Davis, Katie V.	Burgess, Thomas	13 MAR 1883 L	17	341
Davis, Laura	Gebhard, George	18 JUN 1878 R	12	101
Davis, Laura	Dredge, William C.	26 JAN 1881 L	15	166
Davis, Lewis	Whitney, Mary	27 DEC 1883 L	18	348
Davis, Lewis Henry	Meeks, Arrene	19 NOV 1878 L	12	336
Davis, Lillie Ida	Benton, Edward V.	28 JUN 1881 R	15	381
Davis, Lily V.	Schafer, Henry William	21 SEP 1881 R	15	489
Davis, Lizzie	Reed, Henry	22 SEP 1879 R	13	380
Davis, Lizzie	Robey, John Thomas	30 JUN 1885	20	302
Davis, Lloyd T.	Thomas, Winnie	13 AUG 1884 L	19	184
Davis, Lon S.	Nash, Susie	26 OCT 1881	16	046
Davis, Lucinda	Bruce, George	25 DEC 1878 R	12	340
Davis, Lucinda	Freeman, John	30 JUN 1879 R	13	241

D.C. Marriage Records Index, June 28, 1877 to October 19, 1885

Davis, Lucy Hansford	Gordon, William Henry	04 JAN 1883 R	17	237
Davis, Lycurgus F.	Pettit, Viemma	23 MAR 1880	14	192
Davis, Maggie	Pelouze, Frank H.	23 APR 1879 R	13	156
Davis, Malinda	Gordon, Frederick	14 JUL 1881 L	15	402
Davis, Manassa V.	Clark, Henry L.	04 OCT 1883	18	173
Davis, Margaret	Bruce, Joseph	08 NOV 1877	11	173
Davis, Maria	Page, Isaac	24 OCT 1878 R	12	290
Davis, Marian R.	Sangston, William R.	22 APR 1879 R	12	412
Davis, Martha J.	Vaughan, Samuel J.	25 OCT 1882	17	094
Davis, Mary	Burnette, Thomas	24 NOV 1877 L	11	201
Davis, Mary	Carter, Charles	04 SEP 1884 L	19	228
Davis, Mary	Thomas, Fred	26 AUG 1885 L	20	388
Davis, Mary A.	Bosworth, Joseph H.	16 JUL 1881 R	15	403
Davis, Mary Ann	McQueen, David William	26 FEB 1880 R	14	166
Davis, Mary Ann	Moore, Primus	26 NOV 1880 RL	15	068
Davis, Mary C.	Booker, Benjamin	08 MAY 1878	12	043
Davis, Mary Elleanor	Blackwell, George	12 AUG 1882 R	16	471
Davis, Mary L.	Sterne, Charles M.	22 FEB 1883 R	17	317
Davis, Mary M.	Finckel, William H.	02 JUN 1880 L	14	302
Davis, Mary M.	Lowry, William H.	16 MAR 1881 L	15	228
Davis, Mary V.	Payne, Charles A.	03 DEC 1878 R	12	362
Davis, Matthew A.	Helem, E., Mrs.	06 JAN 1882 L	16	185
Davis, Milton	Hopson, Violetta S.	03 SEP 1884	19	224
Davis, Minnie	Poole, George	18 MAY 1882 L	16	367
Davis, Minnie Ellsworth	Jones, Thomas Rozzel	02 FEB 1882 R	16	218
Davis, Mollie	Yeatman, Bernard	21 JAN 1884 R	18	386
Davis, Mollie E.	Miller, John	27 FEB 1879	13	073
Davis, Nona	Plowman, Jesse W.	09 APR 1881 R	15	252
Davis, Olive	Robinson, Samuel	04 JUN 1878 R	12	081
Davis, Patrick	Rhone, Mary	14 MAR 1885 L	20	113
Davis, Peyton H.	Christian, Belle T.	17 AUG 1885 R	20	372
Davis, Philip	Willis, Jane	12 JUL 1877 L	11	017
Davis, Pinkey A.	Scott, James E.	27 APR 1882	16	339
Davis, Pracilla	Quarles, Henry	31 DEC 1883 L	18	356
Davis, R.S.	Biscoe, Ida M.	04 DEC 1882 R	17	165
Davis, Rachel	Green, George	11 MAR 1879 L	13	097
Davis, Rebecca	Thomas, Robert	14 JUN 1883	17	495
Davis, Roberta E.	Jacobs, William A.	06 FEB 1884 R	18	413
Davis, Roger	O'Leary, Mary	23 AUG 1882 L	16	492
Davis, Ruth A.	Cole, Frank	11 OCT 1882 L	17	066
Davis, Sallie	Toliver, Shedrick	06 JUN 1882 L	16	396
Davis, Sallie C. Blades	Houck, Albert P.	03 SEP 1879 R	14	3460
Davis, Sallie F.	Garland, Peter W.	31 DEC 1877	11	281
Davis, Samuel	Rankins, Elizabeth Jane	24 AUG 1880	14	413
Davis, Samuel	Marshall, Ella	07 JUN 1882	16	399
Davis, Samuel	Smith, Annie	16 NOV 1882	17	132
Davis, Samuel	Turnburke, Mary E.	11 JUL 1885 L	20	320
Davis, Sandy A.	Smith, Evelyn B.	11 DEC 1884 R	19	449
Davis, Sarah	McQuay, William	17 MAR 1881 R	15	228
Davis, Sarah	Gilliard, Howard	26 MAY 1884 R	19	338
Davis, Sarah A.	Butler, Joseph	02 OCT 1879 R	13	399
Davis, Sarah A.	Gladman, Jacob F.	10 SEP 1879 L	13	364
Davis, Sarah A.	Gladmon, Jecomias F.	22 OCT 1881 L	16	039
Davis, Sarah A.E.	McNamara, William	19 OCT 1885 L	20	497
Davis, Sarah Jane	Gaham, William T.	21 DEC 1881 R	16	146
Davis, Sibbie	Mason, Amos	26 NOV 1884 L	19	414
Davis, Susan A.	St. Lawrence, Philip A.	26 AUG 1879 L	13	336
Davis, Susan Ellen	Cassidy, Henry Harrison	20 JUN 1881 R	14	431

Davis, Susie	Taylor, Lewis	08 MAY 1884 L	19	012
Davis, Susie B.	Cole, Thaddeus P.	26 AUG 1879	13	335
Davis, Susie V.	Humphries, William D.	07 MAR 1883 R	17	336
Davis, Thomas	Johnson, Willie	27 SEP 1877	11	114
Davis, Thomas	Bruce, Jennie	11 SEP 1879 L	13	365
Davis, Thomas	Lee, Hattie	29 MAY 1885	20	237
Davis, Thornton	Crittenden, Mary E.	04 SEP 1884 L	19	228
Davis, W. Dana	Harding, Louisa	03 APR 1880	14	207
Davis, Wallace	Cook, Jane	22 APR 1884	18	524
Davis, Wesley	Daniels, Mary	10 APR 1879 R	13	135
Davis, William	Prater, Rachael A.	05 DEC 1881	16	109
Davis, William B.T.	Simms, Rosa R.	19 OCT 1881	16	035
Davis, William Colbert	Clementson, Olivia J.	13 NOV 1877 L	11	180
Davis, William H.	Newman, Elizabeth	30 DEC 1880 L	15	134
Davis, William H.	Raynor, Eddie	26 APR 1883	17	413
Davis, William H.	Butler, Geneva	01 MAR 1884 L	18	453
Davis, William Thomas	Dature, Lizzie	05 OCT 1881 L	16	008
Davis, William Thomas	Bowen, Jane	09 OCT 1884	19	297
Davison, Charles D.	Burk, Ann	10 DEC 1881	16	047
Davison, Edward W.	Williams, Mary L., Mrs.	23 NOV 1881	16	097
Davison, Garland Hamner, Dr.	Early, Mary Margaret	28 APR 1881 R	15	280
Davison, George Alfred	Summers, Alice Sophronia	27 NOV 1877 R	11	202
Davison, Joseph C.	Johnson, Ida L.	20 AUG 1882 R	16	486
Daw, Mary Emma	Hough, Perry V.	22 SEP 1880 L	14	457
Daw, Robert A.	Chamberlain, Clara C.	08 OCT 1878 R	12	262
Dawes, Frederick	Paine, Lucy	07 FEB 1881	15	179
Dawes, Hattie E.	Lockley, Wm. H.	15 JAN 1880 R	14	107
Dawson, Americus	Trundell, Rachel W.	17 FEB 1885	20	072
Dawson, Charles E.	Hawkins, Anna E.	17 SEP 1881 L	15	488
Dawson, Clara	Taylor, S.B., Jr.	10 OCT 1882 R	17	065
Dawson, Florence Elizabeth	Hansen, Sophus Christian	06 FEB 1070 R	11	330
Dawson, Frances E.	Thompson, John H.	23 JUN 1879 L	13	243
Dawson, George C.	Weaver, Sarah Louise	04 JAN 1883 R	17	238
Dawson, George W.	Coakley, Ellen N.	06 SEP 1881	15	473
Dawson, Georgeana	Gardner, Julius	03 APR 1884 L	18	494
Dawson, Henry Americus	Baker, Josephine	03 DEC 1879 R	14	024
Dawson, John Francis	Washington, Mary E.	23 MAR 1882	16	287
Dawson, Letitia	Cobb, Robert	17 JAN 1882	16	198
Dawson, Lynch	Shields, Mary Jane	29 AUG 1878 R	12	179
Dawson, Mary M.	Gibbs, James H.	27 DEC 1883	18	346
Dawson, Virginia A.	Cuming, Valentine H.	19 JUN 1878 L	12	104
Dawson, Zernah	Richardson, Thomas E.	01 NOV 1884	19	353
Day, Andrew	Robinson, Hannah	15 OCT 1885 R	20	488
Day, Andrew Edward	Nichols, Lizzie	24 DEC 1882 R	17	206
Day, Catherine E.	Ogden, John W.	06 SEP 1877	11	078
Day, Daniel	Ray, Hester	15 JUL 1882 R	16	448
Day, David P.	Meeker, Alice	17 JUL 1879	13	282
Day, Della	Boyer, Thomas Webster	09 FEB 1880 R	14	143
Day, Edward	Landren, Lizzie	12 JUN 1879 L	13	232
Day, Elizabeth	Day, Samuel	26 JUN 1877	11	031
Day, Emma J.	Wood, Charles M.	15 JUN 1885 R	20	276
Day, Fanny	Johnson, Thomas	27 MAY 1881 R	15	212
Day, George	Robison, Hagar	20 FEB 1883 L	17	314
Day, George W.	Moore, Laura	29 APR 1879 R	13	162
Day, Hannah	Sanders, George	30 JUN 1883 L	18	027
Day, Harriet	Lewis, James	16 APR 1878 L	12	006
Day, Hattie	Golden, George W.	15 JAN 1884 L	18	378
Day, Ida	Cole, Joseph	11 DEC 1879 R	14	043

Day, James	Ware, Emma	03 DEC 1879 R	14	025
Day, James Henry	Washington, Henrietta	14 NOV 1882 L	17	126
Day, Jennie	Lee, Roland	08 AUG 1883 L	18	081
Day, John W.	Bageon, Mary C.	04 JAN 1883 R	17	238
Day, John W.	Sanders, Belle A.	22 MAR 1884 L	18	478
Day, Joseph	King, Sarah	13 APR 1880 L	14	222
Day, Joseph S.	Bailey, Henrietta, Mrs.	04 JAN 1881 R	15	138
Day, Josephine	Allen, Joseph B.	13 DEC 1883	18	313
Day, Julia	Wilson, John	20 FEB 1878	11	349
Day, Lewis W.	McCormick, Julia R.	22 MAR 1882 R	16	286
Day, Mary	Brady, C. Owen	14 JUL 1885	20	326
Day, Mary	Cleveland, William	23 JUL 1885 L	20	339
Day, Mary E.O.	Hurvey, Thomas	31 AUG 1878 L	12	190
Day, Mary Elizabeth, Mrs.	Payne, William H.	24 NOV 1878 R	12	343
Day, Mary O.	Reilly, James	23 NOV 1881 L	16	096
Day, Millie A.	Atkinson, W.B.	07 JAN 1878 R	11	294
Day, Orrin	Sunderland, Rosalie	30 OCT 1878 R	12	300
Day, Patsy	Johnson, Charles	22 MAR 1883 L	17	355
Day, Samuel	Day, Elizabeth	26 JUN 1877	11	031
Day, Sarah	Daniels, Robert	15 JUN 1879 R	13	200
Day, Sarah Frances	Thomas, Geo. Williams	03 JUL 1882	16	436
Day, Tyler	Bird, Frances [Fanny]	16 OCT 1884 R	19	312
Day, William	Mason, Ellen	28 AUG 1884 L	19	212
Dayhoff, Florence Katherine	Forrest, Clarence Rosewell	05 AUG 1885 R	20	356
Daymude, Anna E. "Lizzie"	Carter, John F.	15 OCT 1880 R	14	496
De Leon, George Henry	Townley, Sallie Edna	19 FEB 1880 R	14	160
Deacon, Virginia Lee	Meeks, George W.	18 FEB 1882	16	247
Deagle, Mary	Weaver, John Henry	10 JUN 1885	20	264
Deakins, Alice	Walter, Charles H.	30 DEC 1882 R	17	224
Deale, William G.	Hickok, Clara Bell	03 FEB 1878 R	11	324
Dealy, Honora	Macnamara, Thomas	09 FEB 1885 L	20	059
Dean, Albert	Bevans, Elmira	15 JUL 1880 L	14	364
Dean, Albert L.	Baer, Mary E.	29 JAN 1880	14	125
Dean, Anna	Schlichting, Henry A.	01 NOV 1883 L	18	227
Dean, Annie	Elbert, Mathew B.	17 APR 1883 L	17	396
Dean, Annie L.	Story, Joseph W.	13 MAY 1884 R	19	015
Dean, Carrie	Brown, John Henry	11 MAY 1882 L	16	357
Dean, Charles	Fairfax, Julia	14 OCT 1879 R	13	410
Dean, Charles Thomas	Wrightson, Annie Stewart	24 MAR 1885 L	20	128
Dean, Della	Barnett, William A.	26 JUN 1884 R	19	106
Dean, Ellen A.	Cox, Charles W.	17 JAN 1878 R	11	301
Dean, Emma Elizabeth	Covey, Tollever Preston	03 SEP 1885 R	20	399
Dean, Frances	Murray, Clarence	01 JUN 1882 L	16	388
Dean, Harry Clinton	Beach, Lilly Mary	13 OCT 1885 L	20	479
Dean, Henry	Settles, Mary Ellen	21 MAY 1885	20	232
Dean, James Edward	Goodrick, Emma	26 JUN 1879	13	251
Dean, James W.	Baker, Katie L.B.	10 JUL 1879 R	13	277
Dean, John A.	Cornell, Betty Ann	14 OCT 1877 R	11	135
Dean, John T.	Sayres, Susie	04 MAR 1884	18	457
Dean, Katie	Payne, James H.	31 MAY 1878	12	078
Dean, Katie E.	Schultz, Henry W.	25 NOV 1879 L	14	006
Dean, Malisha V.	Myers, Joseph H.	27 JUL 1881 R	15	420
Dean, Martha J.	Walling, Charles E.	03 JUN 1881 R	15	342
Dean, Richard L.	Kendrick, Mary L.	06 NOV 1883 L	18	234
Dean, Rosa	Walker, Dabney	27 JAN 1881 L	15	167
Dean, Samuel	Childs, Mary Emma	28 JUN 1881 L	15	381
Dean, Walker	Long, Sallie	29 DEC 1883 R	18	348
Dean, Ward H.	Simmons, Katie Lee	01 JUN 1884	19	048

Dean, William E.	Fugett, Ellen R.	29 MAY 1883	17	465
Dean, William Francis	Faulkner, Sarah Eliza	16 APR 1884 R	18	514
Dean, Willie K.	Williamson, Charles H.	15 NOV 1880	15	048
Deane, Morris W.	Downey, Charlotte	24 JUN 1880 R	14	334
Deans, Charles	Brothers, Annie (Blondin)	26 MAY 1884 R	19	038
Dearing, Ann L.	Cockrell, J.J.	13 JUL 1880	14	358
Dearing, Sarah M., Mrs.	Walter, Joseph C.	19 OCT 1884	19	318
Dease, George W.	Brady, Lydia S.C.M.	19 JUN 1878 L	12	105
DeAtley, Benjamin F.	Mehring, Emma	18 DEC 1884 R	19	472
DeAtley, James F.	Barnes, Mollie C.	20 SEP 1877	11	103
Deavers, Belle	Diggins, Thomas P.	27 APR 1882 L	16	338
Deavers, Mary Frances	Hall, Peter	01 MAY 1883 R	17	424
DeBarry, Julia C.F.	Harriot, Charles J.E.	15 NOV 1879 R	13	487
Deboy, Mary E.	Bretsch, Charles M.	06 MAY 1883	17	425
DeChard, Emanuel A.	Herlihy, Kate E.	21 NOV 1882 L	17	139
Decker, John	Boorhardt, Wilhelmine	08 OCT 1884 L	19	295
Decker, John Lewis	Dushel, Therese Elisabeth	10 MAR 1885 R	20	101
Decker, Wm. Odey Hudson	Simmons, Annie Laurie	20 APR 1884 R	18	503
Deckman, Elizabeth	Steiver, Henry	03 OCT 1878 L	12	250
Dee, William Joseph	Bennett, Mary Josephine	10 SEP 1885 L	20	411
Deeble, Silas W.	McNally, Annie E.	24 JUL 1879 L	13	292
Deery, Thomas	Smith, Rose	28 APR 1878 R	12	014
Deeton, Andrew D.	Moore, Alice R.	08 SEP 1879	13	357
Deeton, George B.	Suthard, Sallie A.	02 JAN 1878 R	11	288
Deffinbaugh, B.W.	Mitchell, Sarah Wilmot	27 NOV 1878 R	12	347
Defreese, Samuel Edward, Jr.	DeGroat, Catherine Lavinia	08 NOV 1879 R	13	473
DeFrouville, Marie Louise	Cooper, Lewis F.	04 OCT 1883 R	18	173
Degges, Charles A.	Kline, Jane	14 AUG 1877 L	11	053
Degges, Elmer E.	Caynor, Alice B.	21 MAY 1883 L	17	454
Degges, Henry H.	Hill, Bettie M.	06 SEP 1882 L	17	007
Degges, Nellie B.	Hopkins, Frank H.	06 JUN 1883 L	17	480
Degges, Sophie Alice	Galloway, Thos. Franklin	29 JUN 1882 L	16	430
DeGrain, Reinhold F.	Hemm, Maria	25 FEB 1878	11	354
DeGrange, J. William	Shupe, Laura	23 FEB 1880 R	14	159
DeGraw, Elizabeth Pauline	Souder, William Charles	15 DEC 1880	15	101
DeGroat, Catherine Lavinia	Defreese, Samuel Edward, Jr.	08 NOV 1879 R	13	473
DeHaan, Jennie	Rosenthall, Charles	19 MAY 1879 R	13	195
Deitemann, Emma	Loeliker, John	03 NOV 1877	11	166
Deitrick, John W.	Leake, Mary G.	16 FEB 1881 R	15	192
DeKrafft, Harriet Scott	Woods, Arthur Tannatt	02 SEP 1884	19	217
DeKrafft, John W.	Smith, Sarah E., Mrs.	13 MAR 1879	13	099
del Bondio, Texanita	Keller, John L.	05 DEC 1882 R	17	166
DeLacy, William H.	Myers, Mary Eveline	20 FEB 1884 R	18	434
Delahay, Mary Barry	Browne, Aldis Birdsey	01 DEC 1880	15	075
Delahunty, John	Leahy, Nellie	01 FEB 1884 L	18	404
DeLand, Ida May	McPherson, Dorsey Mahon	29 DEC 1880 R	15	130
DeLand, Nellie Sarah	Drexel, Charles Francis	23 NOV 1881 R	16	095
Delaney, Alexander	Taylor, Sarah E.	02 MAR 1878 L	11	367
Delaney, Anne M.	Gant, James H.	08 AUG 1878 L	12	161
Delaney, Caroline	Hatton, Thomas	20 JAN 1885 L	20	029
Delaney, Cassius	Berkely, Adeline	10 APR 1885	20	159
Delaney, Edward	Meeds, Mary	21 OCT 1884	19	321
Delaney, George	Brown, Mary	18 SEP 1879 L	13	377
DeLaney, Richard	Wells, Maria	31 JUL 1883 L	18	067
Delany, Ellen	Minnis, Richard	02 APR 1878	11	402
Delany, Shadrach	Ford, Susan	03 JUN 1880 L	14	303
Delany, Thomas	Rucker, Martha	21 SEP 1881 R	15	492
Delarue, Beulah	Stackpole, Edward C.	30 DEC 1884 R	19	501

Delavergne, Nathan E.	Thomson, Annie C.	17 JUN 1880	14	326
Delcandio, Francesco	Papa, Maria	21 JAN 1882 L	16	204
Dell, Maggie H.	Peck, Melvin D.	29 MAY 1878 R	12	073
Della, Edward L.	Davis, Annie A.	11 FEB 1884 R	18	419
Della, Henry T.	Pillsbeaury, Mary E.	12 JUN 1878 R	12	097
Della, Lillie	Roberts, John T.	08 SEP 1881 L	15	476
Dells, Annie E.	Crump, James Edward	30 OCT 1877	11	161
Dellwig, Louis A.	Engel, Emma	07 MAY 1882 L	16	353
Delly, W.C.	Hudnall, Cora	27 DEC 1877	11	277
DeLoffre, Augustus A., Dr.	Eliot, Fannie	17 DEC 1878 R	12	381
Delong, Vina	Sparshott, Alfred	04 JUN 1883 R	17	472
DeLong, Vena	Allen, Richard	27 MAY 1880 R	14	294
Delphy, Annie G.	Eliason, William A.	30 JUN 1880 R	14	341
DeLyons, Rosa	Turner, John R.	20 AUG 1884 L	19	196
Demaine, Henry	Wilson, Mary	21 JAN 1880 R	14	114
DeMeissner, Wladimir	Radford, Sophia Adelaide	20 NOV 1878 R	12	333
Dement, Annie Elizabeth	Goddin, William Frankin	16 MAY 1878 R	12	052
Dement, Annie V., Mrs.	Sherman, George S.	07 FEB 1884 R	18	414
Dement, Edward N.	Jones, Ella T.	27 JUN 1882 R	16	425
Dement, Mary E.	Steele, Charles N.	08 JUN 1885	20	262
DeMiends, Tressey	Johnson, George	21 SEP 1880 L	14	453
Demines, Alice	Smallwood, Howard	30 JAN 1884 R	18	397
DeMoll, Theodore G.	Stinzing, Mary L.	15 OCT 1879 R	13	426
Demonet, Aug. C.	Gleasons, Mary E.	26 APR 1882	16	337
Demonet, Charles J.	Clark, Mary A.	27 AUG 1879	13	339
Demonet, George H.	O'Dowd, Maggie	06 MAY 1885	20	207
DeMotte, Ella	Adams, Benjamin Bela, Dr.	20 OCT 1880 R	15	004
Dempsey, Ann C.	Padgett, Robert L.	19 MAR 1885 R	20	123
Dempsey, Joseph A.	Smith, Emma Lee	08 SEP 1885 R	20	261
Denamore, Mary G.	Steadman, William H.	31 AUG 1884	19	216
Deneal, Church	Butler, Ella	19 MAR 1885 R	20	122
DeNeal, Irene	Jackson, Bynedon	06 MAR 1883 L	17	334
DeNeale, Annie E.	Reardon, Thomas	29 MAR 1880 L	14	200
DeNeale, Franklin T.	Johnson, Sadie F.	28 SEP 1880 R	14	461
DeNeale, Jeannett Y.	Lashhorn, Charles S.H.	10 JUL 1884	19	131
Denham, Cora Virginia	Lange, George William	18 JAN 1881 R	15	154
Denham, George E.	Childs, Ida	25 JAN 1882	16	209
Denham, Lewis C.	Kelly, Irene A.	12 OCT 1881 R	16	020
Denham, Lizzie E.	Taylor, George W.	12 APR 1882 R	16	313
Denham, Louise	Harkness, J. Williams	18 DEC 1878 R	12	388
Denham, Lulu C.	Coburn, Walter G.	15 MAR 1883 R	17	345
Denham, Mary Josephine	Miller, Albert G.	26 DEC 1882 R	17	216
Denham, William	Meeds, Carrie V.	20 MAR 1882 L	16	284
Denham, William R.	Childs, Carrie B.	26 APR 1883 R	17	416
Denig, Florence (Smith)	Crippen, Americus N.	06 MAY 1884 R	18	487
Denigri, Mollie F.	Ellis, Ben D.	12 JUN 1884 L	19	085
Denmead, Margaret	Brauninger, William	27 FEB 1883 L	17	321
Denning, James L.	Smith, Emma E.	03 APR 1884 L	18	495
Dennis, Alexander	Martin, Sarah	29 SEP 1885 L	20	447
Dennis, Emma Frances	Frizzell, George Henry	02 SEP 1885 R	20	395
Dennis, Frank	Davis, Annie Laurie	31 DEC 1884 R	19	494
Dennis, Ida V.	May, George C.	13 JAN 1883 L	17	255
Dennis, John H.	Baylor, Milly	27 NOV 1878 R	12	352
Dennis, William G.	Garnett, Catherine	29 NOV 1882 R	17	155
Dennison, Annie	Culby, Samuel	27 OCT 1881	16	037
Dennison, Annie L.	Zimmerman, William	01 JUL 1880 R	14	342
Dennison, Catherine C.	Ewin, William	17 APR 1880	14	226
Dennison, John E.	Hellmuth, Mollie R.	27 FEB 1884	18	446

D.C. Marriage Records Index, June 28, 1877 to October 19, 1885

Name	Spouse	Date	Vol	Page
Dennison, Minnesota	Semmes, James Hall	17 OCT 1881 R	16	026
Dennison, Samuel	Anderson, Eliza	08 NOV 1882 L	17	118
Denny, Mary	Mockabee, Frank	22 DEC 1877 L	11	260
Denny, William H.	Talbert, Sarah E.	08 JAN 1879 R	13	011
Dent, Alice	Graham, Charles	03 MAR 1881	15	210
Dent, Annie	Dunmar, William	20 FEB 1883 L	17	313
Dent, Annie Ellen	Owens, Marshall	28 JUN 1883	18	018
Dent, Catherine F.	Mankin, Henry D.	29 DEC 1881 L	15	509
Dent, Cornelia	Thomas, William	23 SEP 1879	13	358
Dent, Edward	Winkler, Clara	09 APR 1883 R	17	386
Dent, Frances Lillia	Dent, Joseph Hugh	23 APR 1885 R	20	182
Dent, George	Maddox, Laura W.	30 JUL 1885 R	20	346
Dent, Georgie	Smackum, John P.	28 NOV 1878 R	12	350
Dent, Henry	Taylor, Selina	27 NOV 1879 R	14	003
Dent, Isabella	Brown, James	18 OCT 1883 L	18	202
Dent, James H.	Wills, Sarah	07 JUN 1883 L	17	484
Dent, James W.	Thomas, Harriet Ann	28 JUN 1879	13	257
Dent, John	Burgess, Martha	29 MAR 1883 R	17	369
Dent, Joseph Hugh	Dent, Frances Lillia	23 APR 1885 R	20	182
Dent, Louis A.	Yost, Estelle K.	03 JUN 1884	19	038
Dent, Mary	Boone, William	29 APR 1882 R	16	340
Dent, Mary Alice	Holly, William Henry	07 MAY 1878 L	12	040
Dent, Milton C.	Marr, R. Josephine	12 FEB 1879 R	13	058
Dent, Nellie	Henderson, Nathan	25 AUG 1881 L	15	460
Dent, Samuel	Newton, Sarah J.	07 FEB 1882 R	16	229
Dent, Samuel F.	Norris, Sarah Jane	11 SEP 1880 R	14	441
Dent, Thomas I.	France, Eveline	05 MAR 1881 L	15	215
Dentinger, Charles Joseph	Barrett, Bessie Christopher	15 JAN 1879	13	021
Dentinger, Lewis C.	Bear, Louisa E.	08 AUG 1878	12	158
Dentinger, Louis C.	Bare, Louisa E.	08 AUG 1878 R	14	3401
Dentinger, Mary M.	Kendrick, Abraham L.	04 SEP 1884	19	225
Denton, Anna	Drown, Wendell A.	08 NOV 1884 R	19	369
Denton, Louisa	Ashton, Charles	21 JAN 1878 L	11	312
Denton, Noyes	Snowden, Georgianna	16 MAY 1878 L	12	055
Denty, Annie C.	Lyles, George L.	09 AUG 1877 L	11	048
Denty, Annie M.	Cole, Alexander M.	12 AUG 1884 L	19	182
Dentz, Catherine	Cahill, William	16 NOV 1878 L	12	332
Denzler, John	Harris, Rosa B.	13 FEB 1883 R	17	303
Depierri, Rosa	Caspar, Frank	28 JUN 1877 L	11	001
Derban, May A.	Corcoran, Michael	23 JUN 1884 L	19	098
Derby, Martha A.	Capps, Joseph E.	16 APR 1882	16	318
DeRemer, James R.	Roche, Anna M.	14 JUL 1885	20	324
Dermody, Mary E.	Dieste, Frank	27 FEB 1881	15	205
Derrick, Agnes	Cissel, Eugene E.	18 SEP 1878 R	12	225
Derrick, Anna L.	Joyner, Littleton J.	12 AUG 1884	19	178
Derrick, Melissa L.	Coates, David S.	12 OCT 1882 R	17	069
Derricks, Waymon	Wilson, Mary A.	19 APR 1881 L	15	262
Derry, Absalom R.	Yantis, Amelia R.	19 FEB 1885 R	20	077
DeSaules, Emily E.	Humrickhouse, Charles Breslin	22 NOV 1881 R	16	089
DeSaules, Julius Edward	Corning, Cora Hamilton	19 AUG 1878 R	12	170
DeSaules, Susie H.	Magruder, Willis B.	20 DEC 1883	18	331
Deshon, Richard P.	Herndon, Mary E.	18 FEB 1880 R	14	157
DeSilver, Antoinette	Christiani, Charles	09 MAR 1882 R	16	272
Desio, Girolamo	Sosick, Maggie	01 OCT 1877 L	11	117
Desio, Mary	Geracci, Ignatius	19 OCT 1885 R	20	492
Desio, Salvatore	Lochboehler, Mary Mag.	22 SEP 1885 R	20	434
Deske, Karl	Klabunde, Louisa	01 JAN 1881	15	125
Desmond, Jerry	Leary, Mary	26 APR 1883 L	17	414

Desmond, Katie	Ragan, Daniel	10 SEP 1884 L	19	240
Despeaux, Carrie Virginia	Nice, William A.	12 DEC 1881 R	16	125
Desper, Sandy B.	Young, Eleanor B.	17 JUL 1877	11	024
Desport, Daniel	Harlan, Isabella	15 JAN 1880 R	14	074
Dessez, Charles E.	Serrin, Cora C.	06 NOV 1884	19	365
Dester, Amanda	Hardin, Albert	29 JUL 1881 R	15	425
DesVerney, Clara E.	Valentine, John W.	10 JUL 1884	19	133
deThierry, Alphonse, Vis.	Frere, Mary Theresa	10 NOV 1884 L	19	369
Detrick, Irene	Lauder, Charles	13 MAY 1884 L	19	015
Detter, Alberta	Conner, Richard	21 OCT 1884 L	19	326
Detter, Isabella	Gilbert, Frank	25 JUN 1878	12	112
Detterer, Auguste	Konig, Bertha	03 DEC 1877 L	11	215
Detweiler, Ada	Simpson, Charles Washington	28 FEB 1883 R	17	324
Detwiler, William S.	Davidson, Martha	06 AUG 1884	19	170
DeValin, Charles Edward	Appleby, Ellen King	26 OCT 1882 R	17	093
DeVan, Susan J.	Fawcett, Charles F.	14 NOV 1883 R	18	253
DeVaughn, James M.	Edelen, Georgiana C.	26 NOV 1879 R	14	002
DeVaughn, Lizzie, Mrs.	Havenner, Joseph C.	15 FEB 1883 R	17	309
DeVaughn, Luther	Lovejoy, Emma Rebecca	08 OCT 1884 L	19	293
DeVaughn, Walter E.	Burnison, Jennie F.	19 OCT 1885 R	20	497
DeVeale, William	Gibson, Emma	06 JAN 1880 R	14	091
Devers, Albina	Devers, Horace E.	07 OCT 1880	14	477
Devers, Benjamin F.C.	Tyler, Rebecca	28 MAR 1883 L	17	364
Devers, George	Fuller, Mary F.	20 DEC 1877	11	253
Devers, Horace E.	Devers, Albina	07 OCT 1880	14	477
Devers, John W.	Petitt, Elizabeth	10 AUG 1880 R	14	395
Devers, Maggie J.	Beach, William T.	08 SEP 1879	13	356
Devers, Susannah	Dove, William R.	10 APR 1883	17	389
Devileant, Annie E.	King, Isaac Millard Filmore	27 FEB 1883	17	324
DeVilliers, Francis	Beck, Dora	22 JUN 1882 L	16	422
DeVilliers, Francis	Lovelace, Annie	28 JUN 1883 R	18	024
Devine, Julia C.	Kremer, C.H.	21 FEB 1884 L	18	435
Devine, Kate A.	McCulloch, George M. Dallas	16 OCT 1879 R	13	428
Devine, Mary	Ryan, Patrick	08 JUL 1877	11	003
Deviny, Edward	Sullivan, Joe	16 JUL 1881 L	15	404
Devis, Sarah Jane	Javins, Harrison, Jr.	06 JAN 1880 R	14	080
Devlin, Elizabeth	Cox, James W.	28 FEB 1878 R	11	363
Devlin, Mary C.	Sallaba, Henry R.	29 APR 1880 R	14	246
Dew, Etta	Merillat, Charles E.	21 DEC 1881 L	16	143
Dewalt, William C.	Brent, Elizabeth A.	28 MAR 1883 L	17	365
Dewar, Charles Alex.	Walbridge, Martha Maria	15 MAR 1881 R	15	227
Dewdney, Jennie	Cole, Lawrence	15 APR 1885 R	20	166
DeWees, Irene	Sadler, Harry Warren	14 SEP 1881 R	15	484
Dewey, Albert N.	Dove, Fida S.	13 NOV 1878 L	12	326
Dewey, Silas J.	Dickson, Bell R.	25 APR 1882 R	16	335
Dewey, Thomas	Woodjet, Doxy	09 NOV 1881 L	16	068
Diamonds, Mary E.	Engel, Theodore P.	18 SEP 1884 L	19	258
Dibble, Emma	Gass, Henry	04 NOV 1880	15	032
Dice, Robert McLelland	Wiebking, Carlina W.M.	13 AUG 1885	20	368
Dick, Isabella C.	King, John Thomas	28 FEB 1878 L	11	363
Dick, William	West, Frances	26 JUN 1878	12	113
Dickas, George H.	Frailer, Mary R.	20 FEB 1884 L	18	434
Dickens, Katie Arnott	Dunbar, Homer White	31 JAN 1883 R	17	281
Dickerson, Betty Brown	Edwards, Lea A.	11 DEC 1883 L	18	308
Dickerson, Charles E.	Dickerson, Julia E.	01 AUG 1877	11	035
Dickerson, Fannie	Loyd, Lawrence	06 SEP 1881 R	15	473
Dickerson, Ida M.	Fallon, Daniel F.	29 DEC 1881 R	16	160
Dickerson, Jennie	Reeves, James E.	06 SEP 1880	14	433

Dickerson, Julia	Nelson, Lewis	12 JUN 1879 L	13	232
Dickerson, Julia E.	Dickerson, Charles E.	01 AUG 1877	11	035
Dickerson, Louise	Sherwin, Frank Remington	03 JUL 1883 R	18	025
Dickerson, Peter	Watson, Annie	13 FEB 1880 R	14	152
Dickinson, Charles H.	Wharton, Mamie S.	12 NOV 1884 L	19	376
Dickinson, Daniel	Banks, Mattie	27 DEC 1883 R	18	339
Dickinson, Edward B.	Carneal, Dora	17 SEP 1883	18	134
Dickman, Ernest	Grattan, Bessie A.	28 DEC 1882 L	17	223
Dickson, Amanda	Scott, James H.	27 NOV 1884	19	410
Dickson, Bell R.	Dewey, Silas J.	25 APR 1882 R	16	335
Dickson, Charles	Brooks, Mary V.	02 AUG 1883 R	18	073
Dickson, Clara	Barnard, William H.	03 MAY 1880 R	14	250
Dickson, James	Carter, Sarah	03 JUL 1884 L	19	119
Dickson, Lettie	Smith, George B.	02 JUN 1880	14	302
Dickson, Louise	Banes, Albert	06 NOV 1879 R	13	470
Dickson, Mary	Hackett, Junior	15 APR 1879 R	13	144
Dickson, Mary	Ware, Joseph	26 MAY 1884 R	19	037
Dickson, Mime	Johnson, Benjamin	18 DEC 1883	18	323
Dickson, Patsy	Matthews, Reuben	05 APR 1883 R	17	381
Dickson, Rosa	Henson, George	04 MAY 1885	20	204
Dickson, Thomas	Adams, Mary	19 FEB 1881 L	15	195
Dienelt, Bertha	Cathcart, Frank H.	24 DEC 1884 R	19	485
Diener, A. Laberta	Richardson, James L.	18 NOV 1884	19	393
Dierkopf, Louisa (Reiter)	Schroder, Gerrit Henry	08 APR 1884 R	18	464
Dieste, Frank	Dermody, Mary E.	27 FEB 1881	15	205
Dieste, Kate M.	Wilkins, John L.	09 NOV 1880 R	15	040
Dietel, Margarethe	Grünelieng, Friedr. Wm.	21 JUN 1884	19	094
Dieterich, Annie K.	Lerch, George A.	07 APR 1885 R	20	149
Dieterich, Fred G.	Krause, Bertha L.	07 OCT 1879 R	13	406
Dietz, Augusta	Herfurth, William	05 SEP 1878	12	200
Dietz, Charles	Goebel, Lizzie	26 NOV 1879 R	14	008
Dietz, Frank H	Evans, Isabella	18 DEC 1882 L	17	189
Dietz, John	Chase, Laura	15 OCT 1881	16	024
Dietz, Philip	Gartrell, Blanche	30 SEP 1884 R	19	273
Diffenbaugh, Mollie C.	Bell, William H.	11 AUG 1879 R	13	315
Digel, Louise	Danz, Louis	11 NOV 1884 L	19	374
Digelé, Marie Luise	Olsen, Johan Frederik	08 MAY 1884 L	19	012
Diges, Millie	Harris, Henry	17 JUL 1879 R	13	283
Digges, Adeline	Adams, Asbury	04 AUG 1881 R	15	432
Digges, Alfred P.	Brooks, Aurelia	03 MAR 1885	20	090
Digges, Maria L.	Brown, Andrew A.	26 SEP 1882 R	17	036
Digges, Samuel S.	Washington, Lucinda	24 DEC 1883 L	18	336
Diggins, Thomas P.	Deavers, Belle	27 APR 1882 L	16	338
Diggs, Aaron	Snowden, Frances	17 JUL 1879	13	274
Diggs, Alexander	Buckman, Sarah	10 FEB 1885 L	20	062
Diggs, Alice	Fitzhugh, Lewis	11 DEC 1877	11	231
Diggs, Alice	Jackson, Lloyd	25 JUN 1883	18	013
Diggs, Ann Eliza	Reed, Thomas Randolph	16 MAY 1881 R	15	310
Diggs, Annie	Williams, Anderson	18 DEC 1884	19	470
Diggs, Bessie E.	Berry, James W.	20 DEC 1881	16	159
Diggs, Charles	Watts, Anna	14 MAR 1883 L	17	344
Diggs, Charlie	Turner, Matilda	22 NOV 1883 R	18	273
Diggs, Cora	Warren, Julius	05 APR 1883	17	380
Diggs, Cornelia Almira	Noland, John Edward	11 NOV 1878 R	12	319
Diggs, Elizabeth	Owden, William C.	12 AUG 1879 R	13	316
Diggs, Fannie	Clore, Joseph Angus	04 JAN 1881 R	15	138
Diggs, Faut Leroy	Brown, Millie	04 JUL 1884	19	124
Diggs, Hannibal	Franklin, Elizabeth	01 AUG 1885 L	20	347

Diggs, Henson	Selvey, Mary Jane	13 NOV 1883 R	18	247
Diggs, Jacob	Burrs, Celia	02 OCT 1883 R	18	162
Diggs, Katie	Gross, Benjamin	06 APR 1882	16	297
Diggs, Louis	Simms, Jane R.	02 OCT 1884 L	19	282
Diggs, Lucy	Sim, L.E.	04 AUG 1885 R	20	350
Diggs, Mary	Green, Robert	29 DEC 1881 R	16	161
Diggs, Mathias	Holmes, Clara	07 APR 1885 L	20	148
Diggs, Matilda	Straightner, Perry Wm.	05 AUG 1882 L	16	469
Diggs, Matilda	Straitner, William	31 DEC 1883 R	18	355
Diggs, Meredith Smith	Perry, Mary Catharine	15 NOV 1882 R	17	127
Diggs, Moses	Collins, Maria	25 MAY 1882	16	373
Diggs, Nancy	Lee, John	29 MAY 1885 L	20	247
Diggs, Oscar	Addison, Mary	02 JUN 1881	15	339
Diggs, Priscilla	Compton, Henry	03 JUL 1880 L	14	346
Diggs, Richard	Jackson, Louisa	25 MAY 1882 L	16	376
Diggs, Richard E.N.	Summerville, Georgeana	27 DEC 1883	18	342
Diggs, Robert	Boston, Adline	27 SEP 1882	17	003
Diggs, Robert W.	Dodson, Nannie	14 NOV 1883 R	18	253
Diggs, Robert William	Robinson, Hattie Bladen	17 FEB 1881 R	15	194
Diggs, Samuel	Walker, Polly	03 JAN 1881 L	15	137
Diggs, Thomas A.	Williams, Lena	01 APR 1884 L	18	488
Diggs, Thomas J.	Whiting, Flora	03 JUN 1880 L	14	304
Diggs, William	Plater, Martha	23 JUL 1880 R	14	362
Diggs, William F.	Dixon, Susie	07 NOV 1878	12	315
Diggs, William J.	Soper, Mary E.	20 JUL 1881 L	15	411
Digney, Daniel	Campbell, Gussie	30 APR 1884	18	543
Dilber, Lavinia	Williams, John S.	02 AUG 1883	18	005
Dilger, Hanna	Lerch, John Henry P.	02 MAY 1882 R	16	340
Dilger, Helene	Berger, Johan Anton	09 MAY 1882	16	351
Dilks, Charles L.	Crump, Frances Ann	03 NOV 1877 L	11	167
Dill, Henry Houck	English, Marie DuBant	17 DEC 1878 R	12	384
Dillard, Annie W.	Wright, Paul B.	22 DEC 1878 R	12	397
Dillard, Clarence, Rev.	Hamer, Annie L.	30 OCT 1884	19	346
Dillays, Effie	Balderstone, Charles	07 FEB 1882 R	16	222
Diller, Charles	Barghausen, Marley	12 OCT 1884	19	300
Dilli, Elizabeth	Christmon, Arthur	21 FEB 1882 R	16	251
Dilli, Mary	Haefliger, R.	06 DEC 1877 L	11	226
Dillon, Elizabeth	Ebert, John	23 JAN 1881	15	133
Dillon, Ellen	Connell, John	10 AUG 1880	14	396
Dillon, John W.	Henderson, Cora L.	14 MAY 1883	17	437
Dillon, Mary E.	Horigan, Michael	28 OCT 1880 R	15	019
Dillon, Michael	Holmes, Selestia Frances	09 NOV 1882 R	17	115
Dilworth, Mary Lillie	Jackson, Wm. Strother	28 NOV 1881 R	16	101
Dimmick, Edgar C.	McGinily, Elizabeth J.	17 SEP 1884	19	254
Dimpfel, Fredrick Pierre, Jr.	Gill, Theresa M.	25 OCT 1880 R	15	013
Dimsey, John Edward	Green, Sallie V.	11 OCT 1883	18	187
Dine, Daniel	Phillips, Malvina	23 MAY 1885 R	20	232
Dines, Joseph	Mockabee, Elizabeth	07 NOV 1882 R	17	114
Dines, Philip	Portlock, Fannie	15 JUN 1885	20	271
Dinges, Sarah C.	Long, Philip P.	04 FEB 1884 R	18	409
Dinguid, John T.	Peters, Winnie G.	20 APR 1885 R	20	175
Dinneen, Nellie	Monahan, John	09 JUL 1884 L	19	131
Dinquid, William Alphonse	Prince, Martha	12 FEB 1880 R	14	151
Dinwiddie, Robert, Jr.	Donn, Cora Louise	22 JUN 1881 R	15	371
Dinwiddie, William A.	Killpatrick, Ella J.	27 FEB 1878	11	356
Dipert, Annie Leonora	Meredith, Gustave A.	04 JUL 1881 R	15	385
Dirks, Isabel	Ware, Richard	02 JAN 1880 L	14	086
Dishman, Annie B.	Harrison, Oliver L.W.	24 AUG 1880 L	14	414

Dishman, Charles E.	Burson, Rosalie	19 NOV 1884	19	392
Dishman, Mary Ann	Trice, William	02 JUN 1879 L	13	214
Dishman, Mary L.	Gregory, Manfred	08 JAN 1879 R	13	011
Disney, Annie L.	Camp, Elisha	23 JUL 1880 L	14	374
Disney, Emma J.	Olden, John W.	09 SEP 1884	19	236
Disney, Frank	Marschauer, Annie	10 MAY 1885	20	215
Disney, John Thomas	Verr, Kate	31 AUG 1879 R	13	344
Disney, Thomas H.	Harrison, M. Blanche	15 JUL 1880 R	14	362
Dison, Martha E.	Chapman, Ignatius	18 FEB 1879	13	065
Diven, Thomas M.	Taylor, Sarah Ann	12 APR 1883	17	385
Divens, Elizabeth	Gray, Eugene S.	04 JUL 1882 R	16	437
Divine, Fannie	Mann, Franklin P.	09 AUG 1877	11	048
Divine, Mary E.	Phillips, James E.	16 NOV 1880 R	15	049
Divine, Virginia Wise	Trew, Bushrod Washington	05 APR 1882 R	16	301
Dixon, Aaron	Matthews, Helen	08 JAN 1884	18	455
Dixon, Alice	Carter, Henry	16 JUL 1885 L	20	330
Dixon, Bettie	Hill, Archie	02 MAY 1878 L	12	035
Dixon, Carter	Johnson, Lizzie	02 JAN 1883 L	17	231
Dixon, Carter	Brooks, Kate	03 JUL 1883 L	18	033
Dixon, Charles	Hawkins, Hattie	11 SEP 1879 R	13	335
Dixon, Effie V.	Wood, Charles E.	16 JAN 1884	18	381
Dixon, Elizabeth	Jackson, Charles A.W.	03 DEC 1881 L	16	112
Dixon, Ellen	Beander, James	16 OCT 1884 R	19	312
Dixon, Ellen F.	Dyer, Alonzo D.	03 APR 1883 R	17	376
Dixon, Fannie	Bostwick, Philip Denny	08 SEP 1878 R	12	205
Dixon, Frank	Pettey, Fannie	10 JUN 1884	19	075
Dixon, Frank	Daggs, Delia	27 NOV 1884 R	19	416
Dixon, George	Rogers, Mary Ann, Mrs.	06 JUL 1880 L	14	349
Dixon, Jennie A.	Reiss, J.H.H.	07 JUL 1885	20	315
Dixon, Jerusha Frances	Greene, Adam Francis	01 OCT 1885	20	453
Dixon, John	Lee, Sarah	30 MAY 1878	12	076
Dixon, Josephine	Pflasterer, Francis	04 DEC 1883	18	294
Dixon, Lucy	Hall, John T.	27 MAY 1881	15	328
Dixon, Martha	Carter, Charles	27 NOV 1879	14	013
Dixon, Mary H.	Barber, William W.	22 FEB 1883 R	17	308
Dixon, Nancy	Williams, Paxton	04 JUL 1883 R	18	034
Dixon, Rosetta	Harris, Sam	10 MAY 1881 L	15	300
Dixon, Sadie L., Mrs.	Fletcher, W.H.	24 MAY 1882 R	16	374
Dixon, Samuel	Randall, Laura	05 MAR 1879 L	13	091
Dixon, Sheldon	Austin, Fannie	02 JAN 1884 R	18	361
Dixon, Susie	Diggs, William F.	07 NOV 1878	12	315
Dixon, Thomas	James, Sonnie	16 MAR 1882 L	16	279
Dixon, William H.	Berry, Fannie	17 SEP 1878 L	12	221
Dixon, William S.	Myers, Henrietta B.	11 JUN 1884 R	19	076
Dixson, Fannie	Standard, Charles H.	23 JUN 1881 R	15	375
Dixson, John T.	Dunnington, Deliah	26 JAN 1881 R	15	166
Dixson, Philip	Bird, Ella	12 AUG 1885 L	20	365
Dobbins, Ella	Lawson, William	29 OCT 1879 L	13	452
Dobbins, Emma	Miller, Jerry	31 AUG 1880 R	14	423
Dobbins, Marietta	Worsham, Richard S.	03 OCT 1881 R	16	001
Dobbins, William J.	Bruce, Alice F.	24 NOV 1880 L	15	066
Dobson, Edward	Clancy, Ella	27 APR 1881 R	15	282
Dobson, Hattie	Walker, Robert	24 JUN 1882 L	16	424
Dobson, John W.	Richardson, Maggie L.	07 OCT 1878	12	259
Dobson, Malvena	Beach, James L.	22 AUG 1883 L	18	095
Docherty, Lizzie	Kidwell, James W.	24 APR 1884	18	533
Dockett, Nora E.	Laws, John E.	20 SEP 1883 L	18	146
Dodd, Ernest L.	Grubb, Minnie C.	19 JUN 1884	19	092

Dodd, Richard Joseph	Wilson, Alice Jane	28 JUL 1885 R	20	344
Doddrell, M. Ellen	Leonard, William	27 AUG 1879 R	13	337
Dodds, James	Merryman, Kate L.	11 DEC 1884	19	454
Dodge, A.G.P.	Dodge, E.A.P.	02 SEP 1878 L	12	191
Dodge, Alice M.	White, William B.	07 FEB 1883	17	298
Dodge, Carrie Roberta	Hagner, Randall	03 NOV 1881 R	16	062
Dodge, E.A.P.	Dodge, A.G.P.	02 SEP 1878 L	12	191
Dodge, Eliza	Hopkins, Frank Ellsworth	07 APR 1885 R	20	213
Dodge, Mary A.	Wells, Charles W.	25 AUG 1881	15	459
Dodge, Neenah	Townsend, George Y.	16 OCT 1884	19	307
Dodge, William Waldo	Parker, Mary Amelia	26 APR 1883	17	414
Dodson, Addie	Spriggs, William	18 APR 1882 L	16	322
Dodson, Ann Maria	Howard, Henry	21 JUL 1885 L	20	333
Dodson, Edie	Harrison, Sidney	31 MAY 1880	14	298
Dodson, Edwatd	Williams, Emma	27 JUN 1885 L	20	298
Dodson, Frank D.	Jett, Maria R.	02 DEC 1884 L	19	431
Dodson, George Waugh	Flanagan, Maggie Lucretia	06 FEB 1883	17	293
Dodson, Henry	Young, Caroline Virginia	06 JAN 1880 L	14	093
Dodson, Hernetta	Middleton, George	21 JAN 1880 R	14	117
Dodson, James	Lawson, Julia	09 SEP 1879 L	13	360
Dodson, Joseph	Hawkins, Mary	18 SEP 1884 L	19	261
Dodson, Julia A.	Robinson, William H.	23 OCT 1884 L	19	332
Dodson, Lewis A.	Butler, Jane M.	17 MAY 1883 R	17	445
Dodson, Mary	Gaither, George	25 OCT 1883 L	18	218
Dodson, Mary M.	Clayter, Isaac	12 MAR 1878	11	378
Dodson, Nannie	Diggs, Robert W.	14 NOV 1883 R	18	253
Dodson, Peter A.	Sparrow, Rosa	22 AUG 1878	12	178
Dodson, Rufus H.	Winstrum, Christina	01 NOV 1882 R	17	104
Dodson, Sarah	Williams, John Edward	25 OCT 1881	16	042
Dodson, Victoria	Brooks, Preston	06 MAY 1884 R	19	003
Dodson, Victoria	Brooks, Preston	03 MAY 1884	18	549
Dogans, Henry	Kent, Matilda	22 MAY 1880 L	14	282
Dogans, John	Williams, Malvina	15 JAN 1880 L	14	106
Dogget, Elvira V.	Coughlin, David	15 AUG 1881 R	15	444
Doggett, Fannie A.	Peters, William	20 NOV 1879 L	13	497
Doggett, Melvinia	McBride, Patrick	11 JUN 1884	19	077
Doggett, Susie	Rodgers, George H.	03 NOV 1880	15	027
Doherty, John H.	Ready, Catherine	21 FEB 1879 L	13	072
Doherty, William	Caton, Margaret	09 JUL 1877 L	11	013
Doigens, Daniel	Jackson, Jennie	20 MAY 1880 L	14	277
Dolan, Grace R.	Jasper, William C.	30 JUN 1885 R	20	301
Dolan, Thomas J.	Harrison, Ellen J.	24 NOV 1880 R	15	061
Doleman, Charles M.	Nash, Annie	20 MAR 1880 R	14	190
Doleman, Eliza	Thomas, Alfred H.	29 SEP 1884 L	19	272
Doll, Ellen Letcher	Compton, James	27 APR 1881 R	15	276
Dolle, Mary E.	Johnson, Charles M.	03 JAN 1881	15	047
Dolle, Mary E.	Johnson, Charles M.	03 JAN 1881 R	20	4767
Dombhart, George E.	Hillman, Mary A.	14 APR 1885 R	20	163
Domer, Delia Irene	Alleman, John S.	11 OCT 1882 R	17	063
Domhart, Annie	Hayes, Columbus	09 JUL 1879 R	13	275
Donaghe, F.L.	Hutchinson, C.D.	18 DEC 1883 L	18	322
Donahue, Daniel D.	Connors, Ellen O.	17 JUL 1877 L	11	050
Donahue, Ellen	Hurdell, Samuel	07 SEP 1878 L	12	204
Donahue, Ellen	O'Neal, John	31 MAR 1883 L	17	372
Donahue, John M.	Caton, Mary E.	18 FEB 1882 L	16	248
Donahue, Mary	Meloy, James	08 DEC 1878	12	372
Donahue, Mary	McGee, Patrick	19 FEB 1884	18	431
Donald, John Wm.	Parsley, Margaret Victor	09 SEP 1880	14	439

Donald, R.B.	Wright, Mary A.	27 SEP 1883	18	160
Donaldson, Anna Bruce	Lewis, James Hall	24 OCT 1882 R	17	087
Donaldson, Blanche E.	Shepperson, James F.	02 JUL 1884	19	116
Donaldson, Ella E.	Brown, Douglas A.	14 FEB 1883 R	17	305
Donaldson, Emma E.	Stewart, William A.	14 APR 1881 R	15	257
Donaldson, Fillmore	Williams, Annie	23 DEC 1879 R	14	067
Donaldson, George	Hickey, Maggie A.	13 NOV 1878 L	12	328
Donaldson, George Wm.	Fowler, Martha Ellen	21 APR 1883 L	17	403
Donaldson, Ida B.	Rye, John	14 SEP 1880 R	14	443
Donaldson, Ida N.	Williams, John T.	10 FEB 1880 R	14	140
Donaldson, James	Collins, Emma	15 SEP 1880	14	444
Donaldson, John Thomas	Hamptman, Maria Louise	14 APR 1884 R	18	507
Donaldson, Jonah R.	Fisher, Alice Sarah	17 OCT 1883 R	18	198
Donaldson, Laura	Shreve, John W.	05 JAN 1882	16	179
Donaldson, Laura F.	Stephens, William H.	04 JUN 1878	12	082
Donaldson, Lucy Dawes	Lauck, Horatio Jones	13 MAR 1884 R	18	468
Donaldson, M.V.	Sewell, J.P.	03 OCT 1879 L	13	402
Donaldson, Naaman	Murchant, Fannie M.	24 FEB 1881	15	203
Donaldson, Sandy	Green, Mary E.	30 AUG 1877 L	11	072
Donaldson, Silas	Mahony, Jennie	24 APR 1884	18	530
Donaldson, Thomas A.	Knott, Jennie V.	25 APR 1885 L	20	189
Donaldson, Tillie E.K.	Wardon, David W.	02 DEC 1884	19	431
Donaldson, Walter Alexander	Slosson, Irene	08 FEB 1882 R	16	231
Donaldson, Webster Clay	Strother, Sarah Virginia	26 JAN 1880 R	14	112
Donalson, Anna	Shreve, Robert	28 FEB 1884 R	18	448
Donalson, Emmet	Brenoten, Rosie E.	30 SEP 1884 L	19	274
Donalson, Mary Ella	Schlorb, George L.	02 JUN 1885	20	249
Donegan, Mary	Stevens, John T.	15 JUN 1882 L	16	413
Donelly, Catharine A.	Walter, William J.	06 OCT 1884 L	19	288
Donifer, John Davis	Maddox, Mary	06 NOV 1883 L	18	238
Doniphan, Florence	Searle, Allan R.	02 FEB 1882	16	221
Donn, Albert Alonzo	Armor, Ella Maria	08 APR 1885 R	20	152
Donn, Cora Louise	Dinwiddie, Robert, Jr.	22 JUN 1881 R	15	371
Donn, Ella G.	Brown, Oliver P.	03 FEB 1882	16	225
Donn, Frank C.	Schneiderwin, Elizabeth	13 NOV 1879 L	13	485
Donn, Katie C.	Webel, Charles	07 JUL 1885 L	20	314
Donn, Lillian V.	Kane, James	29 JAN 1879 R	13	038
Donn, Maggie Kate	Blake, Edwin Myers	23 NOV 1881	16	095
Donn, Millard Fillmore	Walker, Mary Emma	05 OCT 1880 R	14	457
Donnell, Emma	Willard, George F.	08 AUG 1882	16	473
Donnelly, Annie	Meredith, Rodger	27 DEC 1883 L	18	349
Donnelly, Bridget	Lynch, John	25 JUL 1885 L	20	340
Donnelly, Daniel G.	Hammett, Frances E.	19 AUG 1883	18	094
Donnelly, Francis P.	Quinn, Annie	17 JAN 1878	11	301
Donnelly, Helen L.	Myers, J.P.	24 JAN 1880 L	14	119
Donnelly, James	Nash, Frances	25 JAN 1879 R	13	034
Donnelly, Jennie Agnes	Hughes, Francis P.	04 OCT 1877	11	122
Donnelly, Kate M.	Adams, Robert C.	20 FEB 1882 L	16	251
Donnelly, Mary T.	Sword, Robert B.	14 APR 1879 L	13	139
Donner, Susan	Ricks, John	31 MAY 1883 R	17	470
Donoghu, Nora A.	Hildreth, Leaming	12 DEC 1878	13	378
Donoho, Ida Indiana	Bradford, William Russell	05 JUN 1882 R	16	392
Donohoe, James W.	Thorn, Olivia Jenkins	15 JAN 1879 R	13	018
Donohoo, Commodore	Griffin, Mary	26 JUN 1879	13	251
Donohue, Bridget	McNaney, Edward	12 MAY 1880	14	264
Donohue, Bridget	Connor, Thomas	21 JUL 1884 L	19	148
Donohue, Columbus C.	McDermott, Julia	19 OCT 1879 R	13	432
Donohue, Edward	Bailey, Margaret	10 JUN 1880 R	14	316

Donohue, George A.	Yadley, Mary Ellen	23 NOV 1884 R	19	403
Donohue, James F.	Dudley, Lottie	29 NOV 1884 L	19	426
Donohue, Janey T.	Garrett, David T.	02 AUG 1884 L	19	166
Donohue, Kate	O'Dea, Martin	04 FEB 1883 R	17	283
Donohue, Thomas	Cuddihy, Maggie	22 MAY 1883 R	17	456
Donovan, Annie C.	Kraft, Philip	17 AUG 1880 R	14	403
Donovan, Jeremiah E.	Murphy, Annie	26 SEP 1885 L	20	443
Donovan, John	Cohan, Margaret	23 FEB 1884 L	18	439
Donovan, John J.	Pepper, Mary J.	03 MAY 1883 R	17	429
Donovan, John P.	Weilacher, Louisa F.	12 APR 1880 R	14	220
Donsion, William B.	Mehrling, Mary E.	20 JUN 1878	12	107
Dooley, Michael T.	Combs, Kate J.	05 FEB 1883 L	17	290
Doom, Alexander R.	Bohrer, Corine C.	27 AUG 1877 L	11	064
Doppe, Pauline	Dresher, Jacob, Jr.	21 APR 1884	18	522
Doram, Ella	Howard, James H.	29 MAR 1883 R	17	367
Doran, Sarah Ellen	Fisher, Charles Freemont	02 JUL 1884 R	19	117
Dorcas, Jackson	Priest, Lucy	13 AUG 1885 L	20	369
Dorcas, Laura	Campbell, William	18 DEC 1884 L	19	471
Dorcas, Lucinda	Upshur, Peter	05 JUL 1877 R	11	010
Doremus, Charles Avery, Dr.	Ward, Bessie Johnson	04 AUG 1880 R	14	387
Doremus, Mary	Dailey, Charles H.	01 JAN 1883	17	230
Doren, Margaret	Wilson, Charles Harrison	30 MAR 1880 R	14	203
Doren, Mollie J.	Albee, Seth V.	21 JAN 1885	20	031
Dorian, Annie R.	Fulton, William J.	26 APR 1883	17	414
Dorian, Marion	Silvers, Lulu A.	02 OCT 1882 R	17	046
Dorman, George R.	Curtis, Ednah A.	17 APR 1878	12	009
Dorn, Barbara	Franks, W.E.D.	05 APR 1883	17	383
Dorney, Johanna	Mahoney, John	15 MAY 1884 L	19	021
Dornin, Louisa	Green, Boston	05 JUN 1883 L	17	477
Dorr, Emma Minnie	Johnson, Charles Edwin	18 APR 1883 R	17	398
Dorr, George	Auth, Mary	06 SEP 1877	11	059
Dorr, Lewis	Flowers, Annie C.	06 SEP 1877 L	11	082
Dorrell, George A.	Farr, Georgie L.	16 JAN 1883	17	258
Dorsett, Laura Louisa	Thomas, William E.	24 DEC 1879 R	14	073
Dorsey, A.N.J. Henry	Gray, Alice Rosina	09 MAY 1881 L	15	298
Dorsey, Albert	Smith, Sarah C.	10 JUL 1884 L	19	133
Dorsey, Alfred	Rich, Susan Ann	24 JAN 1883 L	17	273
Dorsey, Annie	Taylor, John	29 DEC 1883 L	18	352
Dorsey, Barbara Ellen	Thompson, John W.	12 MAR 1878 R	11	379
Dorsey, Carrie A.	Johnston, Thomas H.	22 JUL 1884 R	19	151
Dorsey, Catherine	Snowden, Henry	05 MAY 1879	11	233
Dorsey, Chapman	Aigland, Mary	23 DEC 1879 R	14	065
Dorsey, Charles	Jackson, Henrietta, Mrs.	16 APR 1878 R	12	005
Dorsey, Charles W.H.	Richardson, Eliza	13 MAR 1879 R	13	086
Dorsey, Clara V.	Williamson, William A.	15 NOV 1881 R	16	075
Dorsey, Clifton S.	Morgan, Annie Tobitha	04 JUN 1881 R	15	339
Dorsey, Daniel	Jenkins, Maggie	23 JUL 1885 L	20	338
Dorsey, Elijah	Grimes, Sarah Virginia	30 DEC 1880 R	15	131
Dorsey, Elijah	Young, Rosa A.	05 JUN 1884 L	19	065
Dorsey, Eliza	Lewis, Richard	14 SEP 1882 L	17	021
Dorsey, Elizabeth	Rosier, John T.	04 MAR 1878 L	11	368
Dorsey, Fanny F.	Corbin, James Wm. Bird	01 AUG 1878	12	154
Dorsey, Florence	Adams, Samuel	14 OCT 1881 R	16	017
Dorsey, Frances	Moore, James H.	28 JUL 1881 R	15	423
Dorsey, Georgeanna	Holland, Richard	20 NOV 1880 L	15	058
Dorsey, Grace M.	Pitchlynn, Thomas	12 JAN 1881	15	149
Dorsey, Hannah E.	Seaton, Frederick A.	07 JUN 1883	17	482
Dorsey, Harriet	Baden, Alfred	11 JUL 1877	11	014

Dorsey, Henry	Thomas, Lucy	26 SEP 1879 R	15	3523
Dorsey, Ida M.	Minor, Thomas N.	31 DEC 1877	11	282
Dorsey, Isabella	Smith, James	06 OCT 1885 L	20	462
Dorsey, James H.	Gray, Alice R.	21 JUN 1883 R	17	468
Dorsey, James Henry	Gray, Alice	13 MAR 1882 L	16	274
Dorsey, James Thomas	Brown, Mary Elizabeth	06 SEP 1884	19	229
Dorsey, Jennie	Moore, Thomas	20 NOV 1882 L	17	152
Dorsey, John H.	Collins, Julia	16 AUG 1883 L	18	090
Dorsey, John Henry	Hawkins, Rachel	16 DEC 1878 L	12	381
Dorsey, John Thomas	LeBarre, Mary Frances	19 JUN 1882 R	16	418
Dorsey, Joseph	Thomas, Louisa	27 NOV 1879 R	14	016
Dorsey, Joseph C.	Fitzhugh, Mary	24 APR 1884 L	18	531
Dorsey, Joseph H.	Smoot, Mary P.	26 DEC 1884 R	19	492
Dorsey, Levina	Bell, Venson	22 NOV 1883 L	18	271
Dorsey, Lewis	Blunt, Susan	09 AUG 1877 R	11	049
Dorsey, Lewis	Brown, Anne	09 FEB 1881 R	15	185
Dorsey, Luther	Alexander, Amanda	05 JUL 1881 R	15	389
Dorsey, Margaret	Mason, John H.	30 OCT 1881	16	052
Dorsey, Maria Izenna	Johnson, Henry	14 NOV 1883	18	252
Dorsey, Martha	Howard, Frank	06 JUL 1885 L	20	311
Dorsey, Mary	Warris, Beverly	03 MAR 1884 R	18	454
Dorsey, Mary	King, James	09 JUL 1885 L	20	318
Dorsey, Mary Ann	Minor, Henry	10 JUL 1880 R	14	354
Dorsey, Mary C.	Brady, George W.	01 SEP 1879 R	13	346
Dorsey, Matilda	Johnson, Charley	03 JAN 1885 L	20	003
Dorsey, Morgan J.	Maloney, Annie M.	14 JUL 1881 R	15	401
Dorsey, Moses A.	Logan, Aldah Amelia	10 SEP 1883 L	18	122
Dorsey, Moses H.	Rhodes, Martha E.	26 NOV 1878	12	348
Dorsey, Nathaniel	Robinson, Eliza	08 OCT 1884 L	19	294
Dorsey, Nicholas	Scales, Adeline	30 OCT 1882	17	100
Dorsey, Noble	Brown, Florence E.	22 APR 1878 L	12	014
Dorsey, Noble	Hawkins, Matilda	31 JUL 1884	19	104
Dorsey, Philomena	Brown, William	09 JUN 1880 L	14	314
Dorsey, Priscilla	Washington, George	21 JUN 1884 L	19	095
Dorsey, Richard	Levy, Louisa	27 NOV 1879 R	14	016
Dorsey, Richard P.	Rankins, Emeline	30 SEP 1878 R	12	243
Dorsey, Solomon	Waddey, Sarah	05 APR 1883 R	17	382
Dorsey, Sophia	Locks, Albert A.	15 JUN 1882 R	16	411
Dorsey, Susan Annie	Willis, George W.	17 AUG 1885 L	20	374
Dorsey, Thomas	Murphy, Amanda	21 JAN 1880 L	14	114
Dorsey, Thomas	Hill, Joanna	11 MAY 1882	16	357
Dorsey, Thomas Edward	Pyles, Barbara Ellen	24 JUL 1879 R	13	290
Dorsey, Walter	Young, Fannie K.	07 FEB 1883	17	296
Dorsey, William	Jackson, Lucy	25 SEP 1879 L	13	385
Dorsey, William	Washington, Emma	27 DEC 1884 R	19	494
Dorsey, Wm. Edward	Simmons, Maria	31 OCT 1877 L	11	163
Dorsey, Wm. W.	Winters, Izetta	12 NOV 1879 L	13	479
Dorsy, Sarah A.	Young, Thadeus S.	14 MAR 1878 R	11	381
Dorum, James S.	Queen, Annie M.	16 JUL 1884	19	141
Dory, Eliza	Hall, Fenton	15 MAY 1883	17	441
Dorzman, Julia	Apel, Wilhelm	19 JAN 1879 R	13	020
Dosey, Catherine	Snowden, Henry	05 MAY 1879 R	13	3189
Dosier, Albert	Parker, Jane	30 JUL 1879 L	13	299
Dotry, Annie	Smith, Edward	13 NOV 1883 L	18	250
Dotson, Alphonso	Bennett, Mary	06 FEB 1883 L	17	295
Dotson, John Henry	Jackson, Maria	25 SEP 1879 L	13	387
Dotson, John Wesley	Wood, Ella	17 NOV 1881 R	16	009
Dotson, Laura E.	Washington, Kemp Wm.	20 NOV 1877 R	11	192

Dotson, Lizzie	Brewer, Nathan	21 NOV 1881	16	086
Dotson, Louisa	Adkins, Thomas	06 OCT 1881	16	009
Dotson, Mary	Marshal, Isaac	11 JAN 1883 L	17	252
Douden, Bertolomeo	Rettagliutil, Maria	03 APR 1878 L	11	403
Doudge, Charles B.	Jackson, Elizabeth O.	04 DEC 1884 R	19	429
Dougal, Helen	Herr, Charles	14 JUN 1881 R	15	359
Dougherty, A.C.	Austin, Fredrick R.	28 MAR 1881 L	15	240
Dougherty, Daniel	Welch, Annie	30 NOV 1877 L	11	213
Dougherty, Katie	Carney, John	19 APR 1881 L	15	262
Doughty, Cecelia	Searle, Charles Robinson	02 JAN 1884 R	18	360
Douglas, Carrie	Watson, Wharton B.	16 NOV 1881 R	16	080
Douglas, E.E.	Masterson, D.W.	07 JUL 1885	20	313
Douglas, Emaline	Jones, John	08 AUG 1878	12	161
Douglas, Frazier T.	Jones, William H.	27 NOV 1883 L	18	279
Douglas, Harry James	Warren, Georgie	12 APR 1882 R	16	309
Douglas, Harry R.	Lomax, Marian	30 AUG 1884	19	216
Douglas, Henry H.	Keith, Mattie	13 MAR 1879 R	13	101
Douglas, John	Parker, Anna	28 FEB 1881 L	15	208
Douglas, Julia	Briscoe, Spencer	01 MAY 1884 L	19	001
Douglas, Louisa T.	Jackson, William	19 JUN 1879	13	238
Douglas, Lucy	Brown, Townley	05 SEP 1878	12	200
Douglas, Margaret	Lee, Spencer G.	09 AUG 1877 L	11	048
Douglas, Maria	Fletcher, Andrew	03 FEB 1883 L	17	286
Douglas, Martha R.	Carter, Charles C.	16 DEC 1880 L	15	104
Douglas, Mary Eliza Wise	Hackett, Nelson	12 JUN 1879 R	13	228
Douglas, Ranald	Stevens, Lizzie Adelaide	20 MAY 1882 R	16	339
Douglas, Susanna	Banks, James	28 SEP 1881 R	15	501
Douglass, Ambrose M.	Murphy, Mary E.	22 DEC 1877	11	258
Douglass, Annie Rebecca	Simons, Francis	27 NOV 1879 R	14	009
Douglass, Floyd	Schwartz, Justina J.	31 DEC 1877 L	11	284
Douglass, Frances	Martin, William	02 MAR 1882 R	16	266
Douglass, Frederick	Pitts, Helen	24 JAN 1884 R	18	395
Douglass, Frederick	Johnson, Sophia C.	20 JAN 1885	20	029
Douglass, George Lyon	Stone, Elizabeth Newton	04 JUN 1878 R	12	080
Douglass, George T.	Evans, Martha Virginia	07 MAY 1884 L	19	009
Douglass, Isabella V.	Small, Reuben A.	03 JAN 1883	17	235
Douglass, Jane	Slaughter, William	23 JUN 1881 L	15	377
Douglass, Jennie	Johnson, John H.	22 AUG 1884	19	203
Douglass, John A.	Henning, Catharine	03 MAR 1884 L	18	455
Douglass, Julia	Briscoe, Spencer	01 MAY 1884 L	18	546
Douglass, Katie Francis	Baker, John P.	09 MAY 1880 R	14	254
Douglass, Laura	Bates, Robert	04 FEB 1884 L	18	407
Douglass, Lewis	Marshall, Mary	09 JUN 1879 L	13	224
Douglass, Macdonald	Paulding, Helen Offley	05 OCT 1881 R	16	005
Douglass, Mary E.	Minnis, George W.	13 JUL 1882 L	16	447
Douglass, Mary Huntington	Rives, Lockwood Chafin	28 MAY 1885 R	20	245
Douglass, Melvina	Burk, Julian F.	09 OCT 1878	12	263
Douglass, William	Johnson, Sarah	19 MAY 1884 R	19	028
Douglass, William Edw.	Smith, Josephine	05 JUL 1881	15	389
Douglass, William O.	Porter, Mary A.	04 AUG 1885	20	352
Dove, Annie V.	Gunnell, Robert	23 DEC 1878 L	12	396
Dove, Bernadine J.	Dussne, Mary A.	24 JUN 1885 L	20	289
Dove, Eugenia C.	Nuthall, John T.	17 SEP 1877 R	11	097
Dove, Fida S.	Dewey, Albert N.	13 NOV 1878 L	12	326
Dove, Franklin P.	Hillary, Clara L.	11 FEB 1879 L	13	054
Dove, Henry	Price, Aurelia	10 MAR 1880 L	14	182
Dove, James	McCauliffe, Kate D.W.	14 OCT 1880	14	494
Dove, John W.	Grimsley, Rebecca	13 NOV 1879 R	13	484

Dove, Lida Lawrence	Smith, Fred Percy	25 NOV 1884 R	19	406
Dove, Lydia Ann	Jacobs, James Thomas	14 JUN 1881 R	15	356
Dove, Mamie C.	Robinson, John W.	12 JUL 1880 L	14	357
Dove, Margaret R.	Talbot, James Robert	17 JAN 1878 R	11	302
Dove, Mary	O'Hare, John	23 OCT 1878 L	12	287
Dove, Mary E.	Worthan, John L.	16 SEP 1880 R	14	450
Dove, Mary J.	Ridgeway, Hayden	21 NOV 1882 R	17	142
Dove, Robert A.	Tobin, Mary M.	11 OCT 1882 L	17	066
Dove, William	Carter, May	06 NOV 1884	19	367
Dove, William M.	Whiteley, Mary B.	12 MAY 1880 R	14	263
Dove, William R.	Devers, Susannah	10 APR 1883	17	389
Dover, Mary Elizabeth Magdalena	Bush, Thomas Oliver	23 AUG 1878 L	12	178
Dow, Henson	Clements, Lucinda	14 MAY 1885	20	221
Dow, Sarah	Mallory, John	14 MAY 1879	13	190
Dowbiggin, Agnes	Padgett, Jonathan Francis	06 OCT 1885 R	20	464
Dowd, Eva E.	Switzer, Charles J.	14 MAY 1884 R	19	019
Dowd, Johanna Sullivan	Stewart, John Thomas	01 JAN 1879 R	12	393
Dowd, Julia M.	Lynch, James P.	10 APR 1882 L	16	306
Dowden, Charles B.	Hall, Cora A.	14 FEB 1884 R	18	425
Dowden, John L.	Collins, Florence M.	30 APR 1884	18	544
Dowden, William	Hall, Jennie	02 JUN 1885 R	20	253
Dowdy, Robert	Wise, Hester	14 MAR 1883 R	17	343
Dowe, William H.	Downing, Emily	25 OCT 1883 L	18	214
Dowell, Emma	Lambourne, George F.	08 NOV 1882 R	17	119
Dowell, Lulah O.	Gingrich, Cyrus M., Dr.	04 JAN 1881 R	15	136
Dowell, William L.	Holden, Matilda	10 DEC 1884 R	19	446
Dowling, Fillmore	Everett, Annie V.	07 SEP 1885 L	20	402
Dowling, James	Costello, Maggie	17 JUN 1884 L	19	088
Dowling, Jennie	Tobin, James E.	13 MAY 1885 R	20	218
Dowling, Mary A.	Maisak, George H.	01 JUL 1884 L	19	114
Downey, Alice E.	Schreyer, George	27 OCT 1881 L	16	049
Downey, Annie M.	Wannell, Henry Clay	17 MAR 1884 L	18	472
Downey, Bridget L.	Leahy, William	22 MAY 1884 L	19	034
Downey, Charlotte	Deane, Morris W.	24 JUN 1880 R	14	334
Downey, Dennis J.	Flynn, Katie	01 JUN 1885 L	20	250
Downey, Ella J.	Burns, Joseph R.	30 OCT 1879	13	452
Downey, Hanna	Knighton, Michael	24 DEC 1883 L	18	339
Downey, Jeremiah Francis	Frawley, Mary Ann	11 JUN 1881 L	15	355
Downey, Jesse A.	Snapp, Mollie E.	19 DEC 1880 R	15	108
Downey, Mary	Beckett, George	19 SEP 1881 R	15	491
Downey, Mary A.	Sheahan, Daniel S.	03 FEB 1883 R	17	287
Downey, Mary Elizabeth	Wannall, William Tell,	23 AUG 1883	18	096
Downey, Mary J.	Grindall, William E.	06 JAN 1883 R	17	241
Downey, Mary M.	Fitzgerald, John J.	14 OCT 1884 L	19	306
Downey, Mary R.	Davis, Benjamin F.	16 AUG 1884 L	19	190
Downey, Nellie E.	Boyland, John H.	17 NOV 1880 L	15	055
Downey, Patrick	Collins, Martha	29 SEP 1883 L	18	160
Downey, Susie L.	Pulman, Henry B.	20 NOV 1884	19	399
Downing, Belle	Moran, William H.	09 APR 1879	13	131
Downing, Elizabeth E.	Wheeler, Charles S.	28 JAN 1879 L	13	035
Downing, Emily	Dowe, William H.	25 OCT 1883 L	18	214
Downing, Emily A.	Averill, John W.	06 JAN 1879 R	13	006
Downing, Emma [Reinle]	Hahn, Gottlob	06 AUG 1885 R	20	358
Downing, Joseph G.	Edmonston, Ada V.	12 JUL 1880 L	14	357
Downing, Thomas Myers	Stephenson, Ella Rebecca	01 JAN 1878	11	285
Downmus, Lizzie	Boom, William	07 MAY 1881	15	296
Downs, Ella V.	Halley, John M.	27 DEC 1877 R	11	273
Downs, Henry	Cavanaugh, Margaret	21 AUG 1882 L	16	489

D.C. Marriage Records Index, June 28, 1877 to October 19, 1885   133

Downs, Ida V.	Minter, Theophilus F.	02 OCT 1884	19	283
Downs, Josephine	Flamer, Bascom	20 DEC 1881	16	138
Downs, Joshua	Wright, Sarah	18 SEP 1884	19	256
Downs, Lizzie	Joseph, William B.	16 OCT 1882 R	17	073
Downs, Maggie D.	Curtis, Edwin L.	09 SEP 1882	17	010
Downs, Mary E.	Miller, John Thomas	20 MAY 1879 R	13	198
Downs, Peter	Laner, Mary R.	05 FEB 1882	16	218
Downs, Rachel	Hall, Joseph	03 SEP 1884 L	19	275
Downs, Samuel I.	Lasano, Anna M.	29 DEC 1880 R	15	126
Downs, Thomas B.	Murray, Maud M.	23 FEB 1881 R	15	199
Doyle, Annie	Ennis, George Jacob	29 OCT 1877	11	159
Doyle, Annie	Tuohy, Aloysius G.	13 JUN 1882 R	16	407
Doyle, Burton Thomas	Jarvis, Virginia Austin	22 NOV 1881 R	16	084
Doyle, Catherine, Mrs.	Boyland, Michael	05 JAN 1881 L	15	140
Doyle, George E.	Reed, Jane C.	25 AUG 1881 L	15	459
Doyle, John Hadley Ing	Collins, Mary Josephine	19 JAN 1881	15	155
Doyle, John P.	Sullivan, Mary Ann	19 AUG 1878	12	173
Doyle, John T.	Hughes, Mary E.	21 FEB 1882 L	16	252
Doyle, Katie	Chevalier, Alphonse M.	30 DEC 1879 L	14	081
Doyle, Katie E.	Sell, Frank A.	30 JUL 1881 L	15	426
Doyle, Laura F.	Simmons, Lloyd A.	09 OCT 1883 R	18	178
Doyle, Mary E.	Green, Nelson W.	20 MAR 1878 L	11	388
Doyle, Thomas F.	Shehan, Mary A.	28 OCT 1879 L	13	448
Dozer, Walter	Givins, Sarah Margaret	13 MAR 1884 R	18	470
Dozier, Edward	Taylor, Frances	02 SEP 1880 R	14	428
Dozier, Ike	Botts, Isabella	15 DEC 1881 R	16	131
Dozier, Jennie	White, William L.	21 JAN 1885 L	20	030
Dozier, Jeremiah	Tibbs, Betsy	02 SEP 1880 R	14	428
Dozier, Moses	Ware, Alice	10 SEP 1880 R	14	436
Drach, John Henry, Dr.	Mallonee, Mary Ida	13 JUN 1883 R	17	471
Draeger, George	Nalley, Kathrin	11 MAR 1878 L	11	377
Drake, Carrie E.	Bailey, Clayton L.	20 FEB 1884	18	432
Drake, Mary Inman	Sherman, Roger M.	28 FEB 1885 R	20	089
Drane, Thomas W.	Langley, Lizzie T.	03 APR 1878 L	11	416
Draper, Amos G.	Merrill, Luella B.	16 JUN 1879	13	233
Draper, Annie E., Mrs.	Moran, Frank M.	17 AUG 1884 R	19	191
Draper, Annie G.	McClelland, John, Capt.	06 JAN 1881	15	144
Draper, Mary J.	Jackson, Geo. L.	10 APR 1880 R	14	217
Draper, Philip	Bryant, Sarah	17 MAY 1883	17	450
Draper, Rose DeL.	Gill, DeLancey W.	25 MAY 1881	15	325
Dredge, Laura Virginia	Koenig, John M.	20 JAN 1881 R	15	160
Dredge, William C.	Davis, Laura	26 JAN 1881 L	15	166
Dredge, William C.	Davis, Alice E.	29 NOV 1882 R	17	155
Dreer, Thomas	Scott, Emma	26 NOV 1884 R	19	420
Dreifus, Sarah	Loewenthal, William	20 MAR 1881 R	15	230
Drennan, Daniel Ogilvie	Merrill, Lucy Frances	22 MAY 1884 R	19	031
Drescher, Eliza	Kernill, John A.	24 JUN 1884 L	19	100
Drescher, Frederick W.	Burke, Annie	25 SEP 1879 R	13	386
Dresdner, Simon	Eisenmann, Lena	23 AUG 1885 R	20	383
Dresher, Jacob, Jr.	Doppe, Pauline	21 APR 1884	18	522
Drew, George J.	Fraser, Ella May	28 OCT 1884	19	342
Drew, Katie	Lee, Samuel	01 AUG 1883 L	18	069
Drew, Robert	Morton, Martha	24 AUG 1880 L	14	412
Drexel, Charles Francis	DeLand, Nellie Sarah	23 NOV 1881 R	16	095
Dreyer, Mary	Martens, William	27 MAY 1883	17	463
Dreyfuss, Jacob	Robinson, Fannie H.	03 NOV 1880 R	15	029
Dries, John F.	Cappen, Annie	30 JUL 1883	18	066
Driscole, Maggie Ellen	Warwick, George L.	07 MAY 1883 L	17	431

Driscoll, Caroline K., Mrs.	Fulton, Charles C.	30 JUN 1879 R	13 394
Driscoll, Cornelius	Kane, Ellen	19 JUL 1877 L	11 026
Driscoll, Cornelius	Scully, Annie	16 JAN 1879 R	13 023
Driscoll, Dennis	Driscoll, Maggie	17 JUN 1884 L	19 088
Driscoll, Ellen	Naughton, Patrick	11 JUN 1885 L	20 270
Driscoll, Ellen V.	Sullivan, Eugene F.	15 MAY 1883	17 443
Driscoll, Humphrey	Sheehy, Nora	27 JUN 1885 L	20 296
Driscoll, Louisa	Warren, William	26 OCT 1882	17 095
Driscoll, Maggie	Driscoll, Dennis	17 JUN 1884 L	19 088
Driscoll, Mary	Kenney, Thomas M.	16 MAY 1879	13 194
Driscoll, Timothy	Corrigan, Maria Aanne	26 SEP 1878 R	12 238
Driscoll, Timothy	Corrigan, Mary Ann	26 SEP 1878 L	12 236
Driver, Golden	Miller, Harriet N.	24 SEP 1881 L	15 496
Driver, Jeannette	Jackson, L.W.	10 APR 1879 L	13 134
Driver, Mary	Addison, Anthony	21 AUG 1882	16 488
Droege, Wilhelmina C.	Wetzel, Charles J.	31 MAR 1884 R	18 487
Drum, Henrietta Margaret	Hunt, Henry Jackson	25 JUN 1883 L	18 012
Drummer, Leonad	Johnson, John	11 MAR 1885	20 106
Drummer, Martha	Moxley, Charles	05 FEB 1885	20 060
Drummond, Ada	Holland, Richard Bowie	02 FEB 1881 R	15 171
Drummond, Samuel D.	Gillet, Talupher	08 MAY 1878 L	12 044
Drummond, Sidney	Tinder, Fannie	19 NOV 1884	19 385
Drummond, William N.	Johns, Jenny	14 NOV 1880 R	15 046
Drupe, Lena	Colby, Walter	06 SEP 1879 L	13 356
Drury, Charles Scott	Wells, Ida Lavinia	05 NOV 1884	19 362
Drury, Charles Scott	Wells, Ida Lavinia	05 NOV 1884 L	19 361
Drury, George A.	Wright, Mary A.	27 MAR 1883 L	17 363
Drury, George W.	Moxley, Ida B.	06 MAR 1883 R	17 332
Drury, Hattie E.	Riley, Edgar B.	27 SEP 1883 R	18 154
Drury, John S.	Mason, Alice M.	15 APR 1884 L	18 512
Drury, Josephine	Burford, William E.	19 NOV 1877 L	11 195
Drury, Lillie	Gulluk, George	12 DEC 1883 L	18 313
Drury, Louise Marie	Nicodemus, Charles V.	27 MAY 1879 R	13 205
Drury, Rose M.	Schaeffer, E.M.	18 OCT 1882	17 076
Dubant, Hattie	Sammons, Joseph H.	11 FEB 1885 R	20 061
Dubaut, William M.	Weyrich, Annie D.	14 FEB 1884 R	18 424
Dubois, Juliette	Thoma, Frank	26 MAR 1883	17 353
Ducat, Arthur Charles, Jr.	Stellwagen, Elise	15 AUG 1885 R	20 370
Ducket, Henry	Walker, Mary	18 DEC 1877 R	11 241
Ducket, Lucy	Morris, Nehemiah	26 AUG 1884 L	19 207
Ducket, Odelia	Rollins, Charles	23 FEB 1882 R	16 256
Duckett, Alice H.	Whalen, James W.	19 APR 1881 L	15 262
Duckett, Daniel	Hickman, Harriet	28 JAN 1878 L	11 319
Duckett, Dennis	Skinner, James	11 DEC 1879 R	14 032
Duckett, Flora	Waugh, Harry	04 JAN 1883 R	17 225
Duckett, Grace B.	Leapley, P.F.	10 JUL 1879	13 278
Duckett, Harriet R.	Gittings, Richard P.	30 OCT 1884 L	19 349
Duckett, Ida C.	Robinson, Scipio	14 APR 1885 L	20 165
Duckett, James	Lair, Martha A.	19 DEC 1878	12 391
Duckett, James	Garner, Mary Alice	14 MAY 1879 L	13 189
Duckett, James	Fairfax, Virginia	14 AUG 1884	19 186
Duckett, Martha	Briscoe, Geo. Wash.	03 JAN 1882 L	16 177
Duckett, Randolph	Beecher, Lucinda	20 JUL 1882 R	16 452
Duckett, Rhoda	Galloway, Thomas	05 MAR 1883 L	17 332
Duckett, Samuel	Johnson, Emma	27 FEB 1879 R	13 055
Duckett, William	Hall, Huster	02 AUG 1883	18 072
Duddenhausen, August	House, Mollie L.	04 NOV 1880 R	15 030
Dudley, Alice A.	Parker, William T.	25 JAN 1883 R	17 244

Dudley, Emma	Beckwith, John Henry	18 AUG 1882 L	16	487
Dudley, Lottie	Donohue, James F.	29 NOV 1884 L	19	426
Dudley, Mary	Russell, Patrick	17 AUG 1883 L	18	092
Dudley, Paul	Alexander, Mary	08 JUN 1878	12	093
Dudman, Lizzie E.	Ellis, William	17 JUL 1881	15	405
Duehring, August F.C.	Thiel, Anna Martha	02 JUL 1878 L	12	120
Duehring, Carl	Fischer, Anna E.	14 JAN 1883	17	250
Duehring, Edward, Jr.	Lahey, Katie	16 OCT 1881 R	16	024
Duehring, Rosa	Schultz, Charles A.	05 APR 1885 R	20	145
Duer, Virgio A.	Peregoy, Henry H.	06 DEC 1883 L	18	301
Duesberry, Americus B.	Odel, Mary E.	28 APR 1883 L	17	418
Dufee, Charlotte	Savoy, Samuel W.	09 FEB 1881 L	15	184
Duff, George	Craig, Georgianna	19 MAY 1885	20	229
Duffey, Catherine	Mathers, James W.	18 AUG 1884	19	190
Duffey, Martha V.	Awkard, James C.	15 SEP 1880 L	14	447
Duffey, Mary A.	Ramsey, William H.	25 SEP 1879 R	13	383
Duffey, Sarah Jane	Padgett, Millard Filmore	16 JUL 1877 R	11	022
Duffie, John Smiley	Sullivan, Florence Patten	12 JUL 1883	18	042
Duffield, Harriet A.	Lee, Israel S.	27 AUG 1881	15	462
Duffin, Celia	Bowie, John	27 DEC 1880	15	126
Duffins, Robert D.	Fox, Fannie	17 NOV 1880 R	15	053
Duffy, Annie J.	Connor, James	31 JUL 1882 R	16	462
Duffy, Edward P.	Cadman, Mary J.	07 MAY 1885	20	209
Duffy, James	Curley, Maria	17 SEP 1879 L	13	375
Duffy, Margaret C.	Little, Charles F.	05 NOV 1879 R	13	466
Duffy, Maria	Gray, Jesse	24 JUN 1885 R	20	291
Duffy, Peter	Holmes, Mary Ellen	11 FEB 1882 R	16	237
Duffy, Rebecca	Snowden, Ignatius	21 OCT 1884 L	19	324
Duffy, Thomas	Yancey, Elizabeth	09 OCT 1882	17	061
Dufief, Maggie W.	Magruder, Walter F.	15 JAN 1885 L	20	020
Dufief, Nettie	Carlisle, Stephen H.	27 JAN 1885	20	038
DuFour, Clarence R.	Hughes, Cora	19 FEB 1884 R	18	429
Dugan, Harriet Shore	Anderson, Christian	19 NOV 1879 R	13	493
Dugan, John F.	Twomey, Mary Ellen	24 JUL 1885 L	20	339
Dugan, Michael	Harrington, Mary	24 OCT 1882 L	17	090
Dugan, Patrick	Feeny, Norah	29 APR 1885 L	20	196
Dugan, Rachel A.	McCauley, Daniel L.	21 OCT 1884 L	19	327
Dugan, Stephen	Rooney, Maggie	10 FEB 1878 R	11	335
Dugan, William J.	Gibson, Virginia C.	01 MAY 1882	16	342
Duggan, John	Shaffer, Mary J.	31 AUG 1882 L	16	500
Duggan, Margaret M.	Considine, James William	04 SEP 1877 R	11	074
Duggan, Mary	Ahern, Joseph E.	29 APR 1880 L	14	245
Duguid, Isabella	Noyes, Clarence	28 SEP 1881	15	499
DuHamel, Mary M.	Clagett, Howard Clare	04 JAN 1882 R	16	178
Duhneen, John F.	McDonald, Bridget D.	09 AUG 1881 L	15	437
Dukhant, Fredrick	Herbel, Lizzie Frawzes	31 DEC 1881 L	16	172
Duley, Frances Ardella	Buxton, James Leonard	22 OCT 1879 R	13	437
Duley, Ida W.	Kramer, J.C.	19 AUG 1880 L	14	408
Duley, Louisa R.	Garner, John L.	21 DEC 1881 R	16	125
Dulin, John F.	Russell, Laura R.S.C.	20 AUG 1879 R	13	325
Dulin, Thaddeus C.	Stinemetz, Irene D.	17 MAY 1882 R	16	362
Dulin, William S.	Gordon, Mary S.	09 JAN 1885 R	20	012
Dull, Samuel R.	McAllister, Willie T.	26 JUN 1882 L	16	425
Dumbhart, Charles H.	Gray, Sarah A.	28 JAN 1884 R	18	396
Dummer, Anna	Randall, Charles	10 SEP 1878 L	12	210
Dunan, Emma	Inch, Richard	09 NOV 1881	16	067
Dunan, Lewis A.	Burgess, Rosa E.	12 MAY 1879	13	186
Dunan, Molly O.	Meader, Henry I.	17 APR 1882 R	16	319

Dunawin, William H.	Major, Annie S.	19 DEC 1878 R	12	389
Dunbar, Homer White	Dickens, Katie Arnott	31 JAN 1883 R	17	281
Duncan, Amanda A.G.	Scott, David W.	30 AUG 1884	19	216
Duncan, Annie E.	Parker, John H.	05 JUN 1883 R	17	476
Duncan, Charity A.	Steward, William W.	15 NOV 1882	17	128
Duncan, Edward	Colston, Hattie	20 SEP 1883 L	18	144
Duncan, Lillie	Twyman, Albert	07 FEB 1882 L	16	229
Duncan, Lizzie	Peverill, Thomas	13 FEB 1878 R	11	337
Duncan, Thomas	Robinson, Georgie	30 DEC 1882	17	225
Duncan, William	Campbell, Margaret	02 NOV 1883	18	229
Dungan, Ezekial S.	Polglase, Emma G.	13 APR 1878	12	003
Dunham, Aimée E.	Bushby, Charles D.	20 MAY 1878 R	12	060
Dunham, Edward Jay	Owens, Olivia Jane	03 MAR 1880 R	14	172
Dunham, Samuel C.	Seyholt, Laura L.	29 APR 1885 L	20	198
Dunlap, Leander	Smith, Dorothea	23 DEC 1880 R	15	118
Dunlap, Martha E.	Penn, Delaware	13 JUN 1881 L	15	357
Dunlop, Elizabeth Rachel	Harrold, Joseph Franklin	10 SEP 1885 R	20	409
Dunlop, Florence	Sirine, Fred'k E.	15 DEC 1883 L	18	321
Dunlop, Florence	Sirine, Frederick E.	16 DEC 1884	18	550
Dunlop, Matthew	Bond, Kate	24 JUN 1880 R	14	333
Dunmar, William	Dent, Annie	20 FEB 1883 L	17	313
Dunmore, Benjamin	Brown, Louisa	19 DEC 1878	12	382
Dunmore, Benjamin	Butler, Martha	04 NOV 1880	14	407
Dunmore, Elizabeth	Mason, Isaiah	22 DEC 1878	12	394
Dunmore, Ellen	Richards, James	24 OCT 1883 R	18	211
Dunn, Annie	McKnight, John	27 DEC 1884 R	19	495
Dunn, Annie E.	Darnall, Marion D.	04 JAN 1881	15	138
Dunn, Cyrene E.	Browne, A.K.	31 JAN 1880	14	129
Dunn, Dennis	Murphy, Annie	19 FEB 1878 L	11	349
Dunn, Emma Mary Louisa	Morrison, Charles Clifford	30 APR 1879	13	164
Dunn, Mary	Pike, William H.	01 JUL 1884 I	19	113
Dunn, Mary Ellen	Schlosser, James F.E.	05 DEC 1884 L	19	438
Dunn, Peter	Keely, Mary	06 MAY 1882 L	16	352
Dunn, William F.	Chism, Mary J.	29 DEC 1878 R	12	404
Dunn, Winfield S.	Wall, Susannah V.	05 JUN 1882 R	16	393
Dunning, John W.	Swan, Lula A.	06 NOV 1879	13	470
Dunning, Mary Ann	Kaiser, John W.	25 JAN 1881 L	15	162
Dunning, Mary Ann	Kaiser, John William	05 JUN 1882 R	16	393
Dunning, Samuel L.	Cardozo, Annie L.	12 OCT 1882 R	17	070
Dunnington, Deliah	Dixson, John T.	26 JAN 1881 R	15	166
Dunnington, George G.	Jordan, Ida Blanche	29 OCT 1884	19	346
Dunnington, Mary E.	Allen, John F.	10 AUG 1881 L	15	438
Dunnington, Mary H.	McDonald, Judson R.	02 NOV 1880	15	024
Dunnovan, Daniel	O'Brien, Kate	11 JUN 1877	11	005
Dunson, Alice	Hayes, Jacob	28 OCT 1880 L	15	020
Durant, Mary Harper	Todd, Edward Jesse	27 DEC 1881 R	16	161
Durant, Sarah Heyliger	Church, Melville	05 MAY 1881 R	15	293
Durette, T.D.	Beazley, M.J.	05 JAN 1884	18	366
Durfee, George W.	Yeatman, Mattie H.	13 AUG 1883	18	085
Durham, Bridget A.	White, Frank W.	20 NOV 1884 R	19	378
Durham, Sarah D.	Hobbs, Henry Waldo	12 NOV 1884 R	19	375
Durity, Ida V.	St. Clair, William W.	06 JUN 1878 R	12	088
Durkin, John	Ogle, Elizabeth	22 APR 1882 L	16	330
Durse, Elizabeth	Rogers, Joseph I.	26 DEC 1878 R	12	358
Duryee, Albertus Redfield	Borland, Mary Estelle	27 DEC 1882 R	17	214
Duryee, Sacket	Long, Lizzie Constance	09 OCT 1879	13	414
Duryee, Sacket	Long, Lizzie Constance	09 OCT 1879 R	13	413
Dushel, Therese Elisabeth	Decker, John Lewis	10 MAR 1885 R	20	101

Dusing, Sophronia	Stockett, William A.	04 SEP 1884	19	229
Dussne, Mary A.	Dove, Bernadine J.	24 JUN 1885 L	20	289
Dutch, Decy	Williams, Anthony	06 FEB 1879	13	049
Dutch, Edward	Baten, Alice	03 MAY 1882 L	16	347
Dutch, Louise	Gilmore, James	10 OCT 1884 L	19	299
Dutch, Martha	Smith, Lewis H.	05 MAR 1884 R	18	458
Dutch, Moses	Fractim, Eddie Benton	20 MAY 1880 R	14	275
Dutton, Donnie A., Rev.	Graves, A.W., Rev.	22 MAR 1881 L	15	234
Dutton, Elizabeth M.	Brown, James W.	23 JUN 1881 L	15	375
Dutton, Ella H.	Crandell, Richard A.	05 OCT 1880 L	14	474
Dutton, Ida	Brawner, William	11 AUG 1879 L	13	315
Dutton, Leila V.	Pritchard, George J.	08 OCT 1884	19	294
Dutton, Lydia B.	Joy, John C.	04 OCT 1883 L	18	173
Dutton, Maria S.	Franklin, Samuel R.	10 JAN 1883	17	244
Dutton, Mary C.	Bladen, Martin Luther	22 APR 1880 L	14	234
Duty, Charles E.	Crump, Ida M.	05 MAR 1885	20	095
Duty, Elizabeth	Barnard, Luther W.	26 JUL 1882 R	16	458
Duval, Everett Bennett	Waters, Lenore Tom	25 OCT 1881 R	15	504
Duvall, Albert	Johnson, Emma	22 DEC 1884 R	19	475
Duvall, Alfred	Terry, Bessie	23 FEB 1878 L	11	354
Duvall, Anna	Brewer, Philip	07 SEP 1882 L	17	012
Duvall, Annie E.	Heffner, John T.	25 OCT 1883 R	18	213
Duvall, Benjamin F., Jr.	Van Ness, Lizzie E.	27 AUG 1884	19	210
Duvall, Clara M.	Goldsmith, Albert	08 FEB 1880 R	14	142
Duvall, Emelius Lafere	Slyer, Ella Virginia	27 FEB 1879 R	13	081
Duvall, Emma A.	Brewton, William W.	29 MAY 1884 L	19	045
Duvall, Fannie	Lee, Munroe	03 FEB 1885 L	20	051
Duvall, Florence A.	Riley, Henry C.	11 JAN 1882 R	16	190
Duvall, George W.	Sewell, Jeanie A.	08 JUL 1878	12	127
Duvall, George W.	Price, Rosa A.	19 AUG 1882 R	16	487
Duvall, Ina N.	Singleton, William H.	23 JUL 1885 R	20	338
Duvall, J. Walter	Moore, Rebecca O.	09 JUL 1878	12	129
Duvall, James E.	Bryne, Emma D.	16 JAN 1880 R	14	106
Duvall, John William	Wilson, Lillie Cora	16 FEB 1879	13	062
Duvall, Katherine Hyde	Walters, George F.M.	04 SEP 1884	19	223
Duvall, Lizzie	Grace, James	30 DEC 1878 L	12	406
Duvall, Lizzie	Simpson, W I.	31 MAY 1881 R	15	333
Duvall, Louisa M.	Brown, Frank A.	05 JUL 1883	18	038
Duvall, Manadier Mason	Mayhugh, Frances	10 NOV 1884 R	19	368
Duvall, Pattie	Fisher, James Summers	16 MAY 1878 R	12	053
Duvall, Robert Edward	Kent, Georgiana	23 DEC 1884 L	19	477
Duvall, Samuel	Keefe, Elizabeth	29 APR 1885	20	196
Duvall, Sarah A. Grandell	Purcell, John Fleet	26 JUN 1879 R	13	253
Duvall, Susan D.	Reese, Theoliver	07 AUG 1879 R	13	310
Duvall, W. Clarence	Gilfillan, May E.	18 OCT 1882 R	17	078
Duvall, William A.	Robey, Laura V.	28 NOV 1877 R	11	208
Duvall, William T.	Armstrong, Minnie	06 JUN 1881	15	347
Duvall, William T., Jr.	Tenley, Hattie V.	25 JUN 1884	19	102
Duvant, Lucretia, Mrs.	Gregory, Welfried	25 FEB 1879 R	13	079
Düvel, Friedrick Aug. Chris.	Sohn, Anna N.	21 SEP 1883	18	147
Dwilley, Mary S.	Mercer, George P.	05 OCT 1882	17	055
Dwire, Edward F.	Neenan, Katie A.	29 APR 1885 R	20	195
Dwyer, Bettie	Ogle, Harry	02 JUN 1881 L	15	341
Dwyer, Edwin	Van Horn, Mattie R.	20 MAR 1882 R	16	282
Dwyer, Henry	Sage, Harriet R.	18 MAY 1880	14	272
Dwyer, Laura F.	Waddey, Hodgson B.	29 JUN 1881 R	15	382
Dwyer, Thomas D.	Salsbury, Mary	16 MAY 1883 L	17	445
Dye, Andrew	Jordan, Margaret	04 MAR 1879 R	13	087

Dye, Henry	Shackelford, Mary Ellen	06 NOV 1883 D	18	235
Dye, Lucius Cary	Shreeve, Mary Virginia	15 NOV 1883 R	18	257
Dyer, Abby	Kinzy, Isaac	14 APR 1878 R	12	003
Dyer, Alexander F.	Catlett, Eliza	19 DEC 1881 L	16	139
Dyer, Alice	Brooks, Orlando	16 OCT 1882	17	074
Dyer, Alonzo D.	Dixon, Ellen F.	03 APR 1883 R	17	376
Dyer, Andrew Stanislaus	Murphy, Mamie	16 MAY 1882 L	16	362
Dyer, Anne Mason	Taylor, James Lockerman	24 OCT 1877 R	11	152
Dyer, Annie L.	Chick, Charles T.	28 NOV 1880 R	15	069
Dyer, Edward F.	Kirby, Flora C.	12 JUL 1877 R	11	013
Dyer, Elizabeth	Whitehead, Joel H.	24 AUG 1879	13	332
Dyer, George O.	Hamilton, Anna	17 NOV 1881 L	16	083
Dyer, Grace King	Smith, Frank B.	25 NOV 1880 R	15	067
Dyer, Harry Linden	Clear, Lillie Helen	21 JAN 1880 R	14	116
Dyer, James	Jackson, Eliza	16 APR 1878	12	006
Dyer, James W.	Mead, Ann Maria	02 JUL 1878	12	118
Dyer, John C.	Carmack, Sarah A.	30 NOV 1881	16	102
Dyer, John F.	Elgin, Sallie A.	15 MAR 1881 L	15	227
Dyer, John W.	Koontz, Medora	01 MAR 1879	13	085
Dyer, Martha A.	Wilt, Jeremiah	19 MAR 1883	17	350
Dyer, Mary E.R.	Sebastian, Edward B.	03 JAN 1878 R	11	291
Dyer, Mary R.	Jones, John	11 NOV 1879 R	13	476
Dyer, Nathaniel	Porter, Margaret Ann	27 OCT 1880 R	15	016
Dyer, Robert C.	Gordon, Norah E.	01 JUN 1882 R	16	388
Dyer, Rosina	Hawkins, Henry	12 NOV 1880 L	15	046
Dyer, Sidney S.	Wurdeman, J. Henry	26 SEP 1882	17	038
Dyer, William Robert	Winckelman, Annie M.D.	30 NOV 1880 R	15	074
Dyrerg, Mollie	Pindle, Jerome	25 FEB 1884 R	18	438
Dyson, Adella	Woodard, Isaiah	02 MAY 1882	16	345
Dyson, Charles	Carter, Martha	03 JAN 1884	18	354
Dyson, Eliza	Robinson, Richard	03 SEP 1884	19	223
Dyson, Henry	Rhodes, Margaret	16 SEP 1884	19	259
Dyson, Henson	Rhodes, Julia	21 NOV 1877	11	198
Dyson, John	Brown, Annie	26 DEC 1882 L	17	210
Dyson, John	Possey, J'An	01 NOV 1883 R	18	229
Dyson, John E.	Phillips, Jane, Mrs.	03 DEC 1879 R	14	020
Dyson, John F.	Frazer, Lucinda	29 DEC 1881 R	16	168
Dyson, Lucy	King, Abraham	29 NOV 1882	17	161
Dyson, Mary	Curtis, Frank	19 APR 1884 L	18	521
Dyson, Mary A.	Smallwood, William	05 SEP 1877 R	11	077
Dyson, Mary Cordelia	Mitchell, Abraham	03 APR 1885 R	20	136
Dyson, Matilda	Barnes, Thomas Henry	20 JUL 1882 R	16	453
Dyson, Nelly	Lee, Charles H.	11 MAR 1880 L	14	182
Dyson, Sallie	Jones, Blake	28 DEC 1881 R	25	6108
Dyson, Sarah	Simms, Janett	13 DEC 1883 L	18	316
Dyson, William	Bumrie, Mary	19 FEB 1878	11	348
Dyson, William	Brooks, Mary E.	22 JUL 1880 L	14	373
Dyson, William	Simmons, Lucinda	13 JAN 1881 R	15	150
Dyson, William R.	Warren, Kate	01 AUG 1878	12	153

E

Eagan, Annie E.	Steele, Willmer	24 SEP 1883 L	18	151
Eager, Francis H.	Robinson, Annie J.	26 NOV 1884	19	422
Eaglend, Charles H.	Butler, Hattie	03 NOV 1883 L	18	230
Eagleston, Edward C.	Glick, Kate M.	16 MAR 1882 L	16	279
Eaglin, William Francis	Payne, Mary Lucretia	22 MAY 1882 L	16	372
Eally, Roberta M.	Ashford, Henry C.	22 MAR 1885 R	20	127
Earl, Edward Frank	Leypoldt, Annie	13 SEP 1885 R	20	412
Earley, Frederick D.	Middleton, Mary E.	12 JUN 1879 R	13	229
Earley, John H.	Gruber, Hallie	02 SEP 1885 R	20	396
Early, Martha Jane	Mudd, William H.	16 JUN 1881 R	15	317
Early, Mary L.	Phelan, James	15 OCT 1881 R	16	024
Early, Mary Margaret	Davison, Garland Hamner, Dr.	28 APR 1881 R	15	280
Early, William	Jones, Martha	20 AUG 1884	19	196
Earnest, Henry Taylor	Kirby, Laura Virginia	23 OCT 1883 R	18	207
Earp, Mary E.	Cecil, William H.	03 OCT 1883	18	167
Easby, Esther R.	Brooks, Lloyd B.	25 DEC 1879	14	007
Ease, William H.S.	Somby, Belle M.	06 DEC 1877	11	226
Eastburn, Gibbons S.	Smithson, Lydia A.	16 JUL 1885 R	20	312
Easter, Louisa Frances	Snowden, Henry	18 DEC 1884 L	19	469
Eastern, Ella	Belt, William	16 DEC 1880 L	15	105
Eastland, Richard	Brooker, Sarah	27 NOV 1879	14	012
Eastman, Annie	Keys, W.H.	22 DEC 1884	19	476
Easton, Edward Denison	Jefferis, Helen Mortimer	24 MAY 1883 R	17	461
Easton, Lydia	Jones, George	13 FEB 1883 L	17	303
Eastwood, Lottie Jeanette	Condron, John Lawrence	02 APR 1884 R	18	491
Eastwood, Sallie	Gephart, Jackson	19 FEB 1885 R	20	078
Eaton, Clara S.	Cherz, William T.	17 FEB 1885 R	33	8023
Eaton, Emma	Crandell, W.V.	11 AUG 1877	11	051
Eaton, Frank S.	Waters, Emmie W.	28 SEP 1878 L	12	240
Eaton, Josephine A.	Harrison, Thomas B.	24 JUN 1879 R	13	245
Eaton, Reuben	Malad, Ella	09 JUN 1884 L	19	070
Eaton, Samuel Oscar	Lynn, Pammie	08 APR 1884 R	18	499
Eaton, W. Frank I.	Rawlings, Mary E.	09 SEP 1884	19	237
Eberle, Frank	Franklin, Rebecca S.	05 APR 1883 L	17	381
Eberly, August F.	Johnson, Mamie T.	23 JAN 1879 R	13	025
Eberly, Daniel C.	Bicksler, Veturia C.	06 JAN 1881 R	15	143
Eberly, George Lewis	Schenck, Eliz. Catherine	12 NOV 1878	12	322
Eberly, John A.	Senkind, Friederike Juliane Maria	30 DEC 1877 R	11	279
Eberlyer, Wilhelmina	Hunecke, Henry	18 JAN 1884 R	18	385
Ebert, Christine	Campbell, Enoch J.	05 FEB 1884	18	216
Ebert, John	Dillon, Elizabeth	23 JAN 1881	15	133
Ebert, Joseph C.	Mook, Margaret	16 SEP 1885 L	20	422
Ebert, Julius	Peehsa, Wilhelmine	14 MAY 1885 L	20	222½
Ebert, Julius	Peeksa, Wilhelmina	16 MAY 1885	20	231
Eccleston, Henrietta M.	Curran, Clarence E.	17 JAN 1884 R	18	380
Eckels, William A.	Wright, Lucy (Lawrence)	21 AUG 1882 R	16	490
Eckenrode, Mary Jane	Zulauf, Edward	10 DEC 1883	18	307
Eckerson, Theodore H.	Armour, Elenor J.	12 AUG 1884	19	181
Eckert, Hedwig	Hirte, Adelbert	30 MAR 1883 L	17	371
Eckert, Lizzie E.	Smith, John G.	08 JUL 1885 L	20	317
Eckhardt, Henrietta	Winck, Louis	21 APR 1881 R	15	260
Eckloff, Emma C.	Bache, Frederick C.	13 MAY 1885 L	20	219
Eckloff, Harry A.	Lippold, Annie B.	14 DEC 1882 R	17	186
Eckloff, Kate C.	Weyrich, William H.	20 APR 1881 L	15	266
Eckloff, Randolph J.	Judd, Laura L.	07 MAY 1884 L	19	011
Eckloff, William R.	Ellis, Indiana	13 APR 1879	13	138
Eckoff, Frederick T.	Shepperson, Jennie	18 DEC 1883	18	324

Eckridge, Matilda	Heitzler, Hermann	01 AUG 1877	11	036
Eckstein, Charles A.	Heath, Margaret	16 FEB 1885 L	20	070
Eckwood, Chaney Ann	Gray, Thornton	27 AUG 1885 R	20	375
Edderson, Laura	Brooks, Alexander	21 APR 1881 R	15	267
Eddingberg, Rebecca	Steele, James	04 NOV 1884 L	19	359
Edel, Hermann	Fryling, Isabella	26 FEB 1879 R	13	076
Edel, Johanna	Erskine, George	16 JAN 1883	17	260
Edelen, Georgiana C.	DeVaughn, James M.	26 NOV 1879 R	14	002
Edelen, Joshua T.	Norfolk, Martha Ann Swayne	22 APR 1880 R	14	232
Edelin, Clayton A.	Kersey, Sallie E.	17 APR 1882 R	16	319
Edelin, Emma Florence	Wilson, James P.	15 FEB 1879 R	13	062
Edelin, Esther Jane	Sherlock, Robert	04 MAY 1880 R	14	250
Edelin, Jane	Kent, Joseph	30 JUN 1879 R	13	259
Edelin, Josephine	Milburn, Charles H.	08 JAN 1885 L	20	010
Edelin, Mary A.	Shipley, Enos A.	24 MAY 1881 R	15	324
Edelin, Robley Dunglison	Merillat, Charlotte Amy	22 APR 1885 R	20	180
Edelin, Virginia	Taylor, Charles Henry	14 SEP 1885	20	414
Eden, Carrie V.	Myers, Thomas	14 JUL 1881	15	396
Edgar, James Alexander	Hitchcock, Emma Alice	03 MAY 1880 R	14	250
Edinburg, Martha	King, John	09 SEP 1879 R	13	352
Edinburgh, Martha	Harvey, Edward G.	19 DEC 1882 R	17	195
Edlin, John	Harris, Maggie	20 DEC 1882	17	193
Edmonds, James	Powell, Mary	20 MAY 1884 L	19	028
Edmonds, Kate	Sullivan, William	12 SEP 1885 R	20	408
Edmonds, Lulie	Carpenter, Henry	19 AUG 1884 R	19	193
Edmonds, Mary	Burke, Thomas J.	28 NOV 1883	18	281
Edmonson, John	Brown, Margaret	26 AIG 1884 L	19	207
Edmonston, Ada	King, George A.	14 JUN 1881 R	15	356
Edmonston, Ada V.	Downing, Joseph G.	12 JUL 1880 L	14	357
Edmonston, Elizabeth Linger	Parris, Joseph	20 NOV 1879 R	13	490
Edmonston, Kate E.	Pearson, George W.	13 DEC 1877	11	207
Edmonston, Robert O.	Naylor, Maggie A.	06 APR 1880 L	14	212
Edmonston, Samuel Sherwood	Miller, Mary Eleanor	03 NOV 1880	15	026
Edmunds, Hattie	Webb, James W.	12 OCT 1881 L	16	019
Edmunds, Richard	Rowe, Mary	24 OCT 1877 L	11	152
Edmunds, Richard	Lewis, Harriet	18 MAR 1880 R	14	188
Edmunds, Webster	Thompson, Vertie	25 MAR 1880 L	14	155
Edson, Emma E.	Knode, Thomas	02 AUG 1882 L	16	466
Edward, James	Fennell, Coorie C.	30 APR 1885 R	20	199
Edwards, Alpheus L.	Lloyd, Nancy	01 SEP 1881 L	15	468
Edwards, Eliza [Wood]	Buckner, William	18 DEC 1884 R	19	468
Edwards, Ella	Watkins, George D.	26 MAY 1881 L	15	327
Edwards, Ellen	Wise, William	23 NOV 1880	15	061
Edwards, George	Fowler, Rachel A.	14 DEC 1881 R	16	129
Edwards, George	Smith, Lizzie	27 SEP 1883	18	159
Edwards, George A.	Webb, Alice B.	09 SEP 1879 R	13	360
Edwards, George B.	Valentine, Annie A.	21 NOV 1883	18	267
Edwards, George T.	Keiley, Winifred	18 JUL 1878 L	12	139
Edwards, George W.	Green, Frances	12 MAY 1878	12	042
Edwards, Helen	Thomas, Hugh	27 MAR 1879	13	117
Edwards, Isaac Newton	Crowther, Fannie C.	21 DEC 1884 R	19	473
Edwards, Isabella S.	Keeney, Joseph	03 MAY 1884 L	18	549
Edwards, Isabella S.	Keeney, Joseph	04 MAY 1884 L	19	003
Edwards, James E.	Butier, Annie R.	19 JUN 1879 L	13	241
Edwards, John	Bevans, Mary B.	28 APR 1880 R	14	244
Edwards, John	Clark, Alice	05 AUG 1880 R	14	389
Edwards, John	Golden, Kate	09 DEC 1880 R	15	086
Edwards, John	Jackson, Caroline	23 NOV 1880 L	15	062

Edwards, Josephine S.	Sherwood, Columbus F.	21 SEP 1882 R	17	032
Edwards, Lea A.	Dickerson, Betty Brown	11 DEC 1883 L	18	308
Edwards, Louisa	Jones, William H.	22 AUG 1878 R	12	169
Edwards, Mary Anne	Foster, Silus	21 SEP 1878 L	12	229
Edwards, Nancy	Booth, John	09 NOV 1883 L	18	244
Edwards, Nannie Lee	Ammons, Edward V.	01 JUN 1882 R	16	386
Edwards, Ned	Lewis, Fanny	04 DEC 1878 L	12	367
Edwards, Samuel E.	Herbert, Rosa A.	22 APR 1879 R	13	156
Edwards, Sarah E.	Shepherd, Henderson	06 DEC 1882 R	17	169
Edwards, William I.	Liston, Ellen	29 JUN 1885 L	20	299
Edwards, William M.	Burke, Addie M.	18 DEC 1882 R	17	188
Edwards, Wm. E.	Conner, Ella Vashti	07 DEC 1882 R	17	173
Edwood, Isaac	Watson, Emma Virginia	06 JUL 1882 R	16	439
Ege, John F.	Friess, Katie C.	01 JAN 1882 R	16	171
Ege, Porter F.	Hauptman, Hattie E.	04 SEP 1884	19	226
Eggensberger, Veronica	Rabbitt, Samuel P.	28 APR 1884 R	18	538
Eggleston, Jos. Mortimer	Hill, Mary Alice	22 MAY 1884 R	19	034
Eggleston, William H.	Lord, Katie M.	09 SEP 1884	19	234
Eglin, James	Peterson, Lucy	19 NOV 1877 R	11	191
Eglin, Mary E.	Knott, John	15 NOV 1880 R	14	500
Eglin, Robert B.	Osborn, Mildred E.	08 OCT 1885 L	20	472
Egloff, Melchion	Groh, Antonia	07 OCT 1883	18	175
Egood, Lemuel	Seybolt, Lucy J. (Davis)	09 JUN 1885 R	20	263
Ehrhardt, Kate	Rainey, Charles	18 NOV 1880 L	15	055
Ehrmantraut, Leonard A.	Linkins, Blanche	01 SEP 1885 L	20	396
Ehrmantraut, Mary	Shipley, Charles E.	22 JUN 1880 L	14	330
Ehrmantrout, Sophie	Ellis, Everett	12 AUG 1879 L	13	317
Ehrnantraut, Edward	St. John, Ada	02 MAY 1881	15	286
Eichberg, Kate (Morse)	Morse, Marx	27 AUG 1885 R	20	390
Eichholtz, Helena Augusta	Hall, George W.	30 DEC 1878 R	12	406
Eichhorn, Barbara F.	Handy, Charles W.	28 APR 1881 L	15	283
Eichhorn, Eleanor M.	Waldecker, William	07 AUG 1883 L	18	077
Eickel, Henry	Neger, Caroline E. Geiger	01 DEC 1880 R	15	074
Eiker, James M.	Strobel, Agnes A.	29 OCT 1878 R	12	296
Eilenberger, Fannie R.	Williamson, J.C.	10 NOV 1880	15	041
Eils, Bette Edward Julius	Quinn, Florence	01 NOV 1877 R	11	163
Eimer, Charles G.	Marsden, Lillie J.	15 AUG 1881 R	15	442
Eimer, Emma	Bolling, James M.	22 APR 1880 R	14	228
Eimer, John Philip	Jones, Ella	09 JUL 1878	12	125
Eimer, Lizzie	Rackey, William Henry	17 NOV 1884 R	19	389
Eimer, Mary F.	Ball, William M.	10 OCT 1884 L	19	299
Eisebraum, Gottieb	Hoffman, Rutha	07 FEB 1882 R	16	230
Eisele, Johanna Francisca Julia	Fischer, William	08 AUG 1882 R	16	472
Eiseman, Lewis	Blum, Rosa	24 JUN 1883 R	18	007
Eisenbeiss, Bertha J.R.	Sullivan, Daniel J.	19 JUN 1880 L	14	327
Eisenmann, Lena	Dresdner, Simon	23 AUG 1885 R	20	383
Elam, Daniel N.	Winne, Annie	17 JUL 1885	20	331
Elbert, Jeremiah	Wood, Maggie	08 FEB 1881 L	15	182
Elbert, Mathew B.	Dean, Annie	17 APR 1883 L	17	396
Elder, Maggie F.	Skinner, Eustace J.	26 JAN 1885 R	20	037
Eldert, Nessel	Danforth, Fanny Harriet (Northup)	30 MAY 1883 R	17	468
Eldridge, Lillian I.	Linkins, William W.	08 JAN 1880 R	14	096
Eldridge, May Amelia	Eldridge, Wm. Watson	28 MAY 1885 R	20	243
Eldridge, Nellie	Smith, Henry	26 DEC 1878 R	12	395
Eldridge, Wm. Watson	Eldridge, May Amelia	28 MAY 1885 R	20	243
Elgin, Rebecca J.	Fairfax, Thaddeus	05 JUN 1879 R	13	220
Elgin, Sallie A.	Dyer, John F.	15 MAR 1881 L	15	227
Elias, James	Boone, Annie A.	26 DEC 1879 L	14	076

Eliason, Annie O.	Linkins, Joseph	02 MAY 1883	17	427
Eliason, James U.	Magill, Jennie V.	02 DEC 1883	18	290
Eliason, William A.	Delphy, Annie G.	30 JUN 1880 R	14	341
Eliot, Catharine Llewellin	McNally, Valentine	17 OCT 1883 L	18	199
Eliot, Fannie	DeLoffre, Augustus A., Dr.	17 DEC 1878 R	12	381
Eliot, Leila Rebecca	Moran, Elasah French	12 OCT 1884	19	301
Eliot, Llewellyn	Lancaster, Mary S.	15 APR 1885	20	169
Eliot, Mary J.	Stroud, William D.	15 NOV 1877	11	188
Elkins, Mary Eliza	Borsekowski, Ferdinand	12 DEC 1877	11	232
Ellart, Margaret	Masson, James E.W.	08 MAY 1878 R	12	042
Ellen, Mary	Lomis, Isaac	26 JUL 1881 L	15	416
Eller, Mary	Jones, Isaac	26 OCT 1881 R	22	5312
Ellerbruck, Dora	Puvogel, Diedrich	08 SEP 1882	17	014
Ellery, Albert S.	Chapin, Mattie D.	19 NOV 1884 R	19	395
Ellery, George H.	Moore, Amelia H.	06 SEP 1881	15	471
Ellery, Stephen B.	McLaughlin, Eleanor E.	28 FEB 1881 R	15	206
Ellett, Martha J.	Lanckton, Thomas W.	06 SEP 1877	11	078
Ellicott, Charles P.	Munson, Ollie	19 DEC 1881 R	16	137
Ellinger, George	Wilson, Katy	29 AUG 1878 L	12	184
Elliot, Albert D.	Pugh, Sallie S.	09 SEP 1884	19	231
Elliot, Andrew	Brown, Carrie	03 FEB 1879 R	13	042
Elliot, Cecilia M.	Ross, John R.	20 FEB 1879 L	13	069
Elliot, Charles A.	Posthwait, Clara D.	07 OCT 1878 L	12	257
Elliot, Clara M.	Ents, John H.	29 MAY 1884 L	19	043
Elliot, Fanny	Lindsey, James E.	09 JUN 1878	12	093
Elliot, Mary C.S.	Caton, William H.	22 JAN 1878 R	11	313
Elliott, Annie S.	Lancaster, Henry Clay	30 OCT 1882 R	17	100
Elliott, Franklin	Payne, Sarah	29 MAY 1884 L	19	046
Elliott, George Frank	Badger, Annie Mansfield	06 JAN 1880 R	14	088
Elliott, John G.	Young, Alice	16 OCT 1879	13	429
Elliott, John L.	Clare, Ella A.	12 NOV 1879 R	13	481
Elliott, John W.	Walker, Alice	17 MAY 1883 L	17	417
Elliott, Josiah	Sisco, Henrietta	09 OCT 1883 L	18	180
Elliott, Marcie	Brewer, Harrison Gaston	19 OCT 1881 R	16	031
Elliott, Perry	Gurtchell, Annie	28 OCT 1879 R	13	444
Elliott, Thomas H. McN.	Trapp, Rosa	27 JAN 1881 R	15	164
Elliott, Thomas Munroe	Galt, Marian Virginia	16 OCT 1877 R	11	138
Ellis, Annie	Mellin, William A.	11 AUG 1881 L	15	441
Ellis, Ben D.	Denigri, Mollie F.	12 JUN 1884 L	19	085
Ellis, Betsey	Willis, John	26 AUG 1878	12	180
Ellis, Carrie Maria	Lyon, Horace Freeman	26 JUL 1882 R	16	458
Ellis, Charles A.	Long, Mary F.	24 NOV 1879 R	14	001
Ellis, Daniel	Tibble, Viney	14 JUL 1885 L	20	325
Ellis, Edward	Laton, Annie	07 AUG 1879 R	13	309
Ellis, Eliza	Jones, Henry	13 JUL 1885	20	322
Ellis, Ella E.	Lynch, Patrick	06 NOV 1877 R	11	167
Ellis, Ella E.	Richardson, William H.	10 MAR 1885 R	20	105
Ellis, Ellen	Davis, Bayliss	27 APR 1883 L	17	418
Ellis, Emma Eubank	Saunders, Abram Warrick	09 MAY 1885 R	20	216
Ellis, Everett	Ehrmantrout, Sophie	12 AUG 1879 L	13	317
Ellis, Frederick	Younger, Lucinda	31 OCT 1877 L	11	162
Ellis, Genevieve	White, John M.	29 NOV 1879 L	14	019
Ellis, George	Craves, Rose	16 JUL 1881 R	25	6046
Ellis, George	Graves, Rosa	17 AUG 1882 L	16	483
Ellis, George F.	Triplett, Emma	20 JUL 1882	16	453
Ellis, George W.	Williams, Clara E.	13 AUG 1884	19	183
Ellis, Georgiana	Erskine, Samuel	27 APR 1882 R	16	336
Ellis, Hattie R.	Davis, John Fisher	22 SEP 1885 R	20	434

Ellis, Henry P.	Van Horn, Retta D.	20 APR 1881 L	15	263
Ellis, Herman L.	Lee, Henrietta	22 MAR 1883 R	17	340
Ellis, Indiana	Eckloff, William R.	13 APR 1879	13	138
Ellis, Jacob	Boyer, sarah	20 OCT 1883 L	18	204
Ellis, James R.	Shoemaker, Ida	06 JUL 1885 L	20	313
Ellis, Jane	Johnson, William	25 SEP 1880 L	14	459
Ellis, Jane E.	Collins, Cornelius	26 OCT 1881 R	16	044
Ellis, Jennie	Baker, William	21 OCT 1880 L	15	007
Ellis, John D.	Payne, Sarah E.	09 OCT 1879	13	414
Ellis, John P.	Cowling, Florence D.	14 NOV 1883 R	18	250
Ellis, Lewis Y.	Rosenbaum, Rosa H.	18 NOV 1879	13	494
Ellis, Lucy A.C.	Ryal, Ferdinand	02 SEP 1880 R	14	421
Ellis, Mary	Suit, James E.	10 FEB 1878	11	333
Ellis, Mary	Tucker, Floyd W.	29 JAN 1880 R	14	127
Ellis, Mary A.	Lewis, Henry	24 NOV 1881 L	16	098
Ellis, Mary C.	Jones, Levi	19 FEB 1878 L	11	347
Ellis, Matilda C.	King, J.E.	12 APR 1881 L	15	254
Ellis, May	Magans, Robert	13 SEP 1883 R	18	129
Ellis, Moses	Spurlock, Eliza	19 OCT 1880 R	15	004
Ellis, Nelson	Husemann, Alice	28 MAY 1883 L	17	465
Ellis, Robert H.	Greenwells, Alice M.	12 APR 1881 L	15	253
Ellis, Sarah	Gray, Harvey	08 AUG 1885 L	20	361
Ellis, William	Dudman, Lizzie E.	17 JUL 1881	15	405
Ellis, William B.	Ware, Martha A.	14 AUG 1883	18	087
Ellis, William Francis	McAuliffe, Mary	14 SEP 1879 R	13	298
Ellison, Eliza Ann	Shamwell, Charles H.	10 NOV 1877 L	11	178
Ellison, Margaret	Robison, Henry	02 OCT 1884	19	283
Ellsworth, Henry L.	Wadkins, Bell M.	20 FEB 1883 R	17	313
Ellwood, Thomas	Moore, Mary	04 AUG 1882 L	16	469
Elmenreich, Hermann	Niebuhr, Dora	30 JAN 1884 R	18	395
Elmore, Alice E.	Isham, Francis H.	24 DEC 1879 R	14	069
Elmore, Inez [Carlisle]	Bain, James Robert	20 DEC 1882 R	17	194
Elmore, William	Burrs, Mary E.	21 NOV 1877	11	197
Elmore, Yates H.	Carlisle, Inez	19 MAR 1878 R	11	385
Elms, James W.	Davis, Hattie	09 JUN 1882	16	402
Elms, Lida A.	McLaughlin, James A.	26 JUL 1881 R	15	419
Elsey, Louisa	Lanam, George	13 MAR 1883	17	340
Elsie, Martha Ann	Huff, Moses	18 NOV 1882 R	17	135
Elton, Fannie H.	Barron, John	04 JUL 1878 R	12	124
Ely, Judson	Magee, Bertie	14 AUG 1880 L	14	399
Ely, Louis H.	Ubhoff, Clara C.	15 JUN 1882 L	16	414
Ely, Maria E.	Hess, George W.	19 FEB 1884	18	428
Ely, Sophie	Hood, Edwin M.	04 OCT 1883	18	172
Emberson, Noah R.	Mahaney, Barbara Ellen	29 AUG 1878 R	12	186
Embrey, Margaret Virginia	Hines, Lawrence Augustus	29 SEP 1883 R	18	160
Emerson, Emma	Burrus, Nelson	03 OCT 1884 L	19	284
Emerson, Emma Virginia	Harris, William Washington	19 JUN 1882 R	16	417
Emerson, Eudosia Sutor	Sanner, Jerome F.	20 SEP 1879 R	13	382
Emerson, Lillie E.	Parsons, Joseph Hepburn	12 JAN 1883 R	17	255
Emerson, Sarah M. [Bartlett]	Boyce, Silas	25 SEP 1883 R	18	150
Emery, Clara K.	Henkle, Saul S.	21 JUL 1880	14	371
Emery, Ellen	Lasier, Thomas Jefferson	23 OCT 1878 R	12	285
Emicks, Mary	Robinson, William F.	22 MAR 1883 R	17	354
Emmerich, L. Blanche	Simons, Henry A.	20 FEB 1879	13	070
Emmerman, Mary	Slater, Wm. P.	17 NOV 1877 R	11	191
Emmert, Anna M.W.	Germann, Wm. Henry	29 JAN 1885 R	20	043
Emmert, Christine	Rükert, Joseph	25 JUN 1884 R	19	104
Emmert, John H.	Myers, Katie H.	06 APR 1881 L	15	249

Emmett, John	Moonshine, Lena	30 OCT 1882 L	17	101
Emmons, Howard O.	Scott, Kate A.	06 APR 1880	14	211
Emmons, Oliver A.	Cooksey, Maggie J.P.	01 AUG 1881 R	15	429
Emory, Albert	Proctor, Mary	02 APR 1885	20	142
Emrich, Appolonia	Garrity, William J.	17 FEB 1885 L	20	074
Emrick, F.X.A.O.	Heide, Carolena Vonder	25 MAY 1884	19	023
Ender, James	Dairy, Delia	08 NOV 1877 R	11	175
Enders, Mary	Bruce, Nathan	12 AUG 1884	19	181
Enders, Mary E.	Bruce, Nathan	28 MAY 1878 L	12	072
Engel, Christian	Strobel, Margaretta	30 JAN 1879	13	039
Engel, David L.	Newmyer, Mamie	17 SEP 1878 R	12	219
Engel, Emma	Dellwig, Louis A.	07 MAY 1882 L	16	353
Engel, George W.	Schneider, Rosa E.	14 OCT 1885 R	20	484
Engel, Mary	Lee, Edward	13 JUL 1885 R	20	323
Engel, Theodore P.	Diamonds, Mary E.	18 SEP 1884 L	19	258
Engelhardt, Frank	Schultz, Clara Angusta	12 MAR 1884 R	18	462
Engelke, Augusta	Giesler, Daniel	21 MAY 1882	16	370
Engels, Helene	Abner, Edward	09 NOV 1878 L	12	319
England, Mary Davis, Mrs.	Cornell, Charles	03 SEP 1880 R	14	430
England, Robert Ezra	Murdock, Mary Eliz.	17 FEB 1885 R	20	072
Englebright, Katie	Walsh, John E.	03 OCT 1879 L	13	401
Englehardt, Catherine	Molfenter, William	31 MAY 1884 L	19	048
Englehart, Annie	Schloz, Christian	20 OCT 1884 R	19	320
Englehart, Charles	Arnold, Sarah J.	14 MAY 1884 R	19	006
Engleke, Mary	Bool, George	10 SEP 1877	11	084
Englert, Josephine	Rick, Alois	05 OCT 1878	12	254
English, Benjamin S.	Sutton, Eveline	06 JAN 1885 R	20	006
English, Marie DuBant	Dill, Henry Houck	17 DEC 1878 R	12	384
English, Thomas	Flanagan, Mary J.	13 APR 1883 L	17	393
English, William Henry	Zell, Ella Susannah	21 JUN 1881 R	15	370
Ennels, William Matthew	Johnson, Mary V.	05 MAY 1881 R	15	291
Ennis, Albert	Pindle, Diana	21 DEC 1883 L	18	334
Ennis, Edward	Popkins, Ella F.	10 JUN 1884	19	074
Ennis, George Jacob	Doyle, Annie	29 OCT 1877	11	159
Ennis, George T.	Berry, Annie M.	24 DEC 1882 R	17	204
Ennis, James Edward	Mills, Flora Ellen	21 JUL 1881 R	15	412
Ennis, Lucy	Brady, Henry	24 MAR 1884 L	18	480
Ennis, Mary	Bell, John Henry	21 FEB 1883 L	17	315
Ennis, Mary Elizabeth	Fick, John Rolph	16 DEC 1879 R	14	049
Ennis, Peter T.	William, Lucy	21 FEB 1878 R	11	356
Ennis, Thomas	Tasker, Barbara	12 OCT 1877 L	11	133
Enns, Richard	Jackson, Susie	10 NOV 1881 R	16	062
Enroughty, Francis	Atkinson, Virginia Lee	08 JUN 1881 R	15	353
Enroughty, Mary F.	Atkinson, Richard W.	22 OCT 1884	19	328
Enselman, Christopher	Speckman, Fredericka	23 DEC 1877	11	257
Ensor, Harry G.	Ryan, Lydia	20 JAN 1885	20	027
Ensor, Rachel A.	Price, John S.	13 NOV 1878 R	12	326
Ents, John H.	Elliot, Clara M.	29 MAY 1884 L	19	043
Epperson, William	Thomas, Hellen	25 DEC 1884	19	484
Eppes, Gracie	Bundy, Austin	10 NOV 1877 L	11	178
Epping, Carl A.	McDevitt, Annie W.	07 AUG 1883 L	18	077
Epps, Harry	Wilson, Ellen	19 JUN 1878 R	12	105
Epps, Matthew	Bailey, Fannie	27 DEC 1882 R	17	213
Erberbach, Matilda W.	Schambra, Edward L.	08 SEP 1880	14	438
Ergood, Lemuel	Fitzgerald, Mamie J.	25 NOV 1879	14	005
Erickson, Alice	Birtwell, Daniel, Jr.	21 MAY 1879 R	13	197
Erickson, Lucy	Wilson, John Edwin	07 APR 1885 R	20	152
Ernest, Mary Emma	Viehmeyer, John F.	15 MAY 1883 R	17	439

Erney, Charles A.	Riggles, Hannah E.	18 OCT 1877	11	142
Ernst, Frederick K.	Herbert, Lulu P.	02 APR 1884	18	492
Erpenbeck, Katharine	Smith, George P., Jr.	28 JUL 1880 R	14	376
Erskine, George	Edel, Johanna	16 JAN 1883	17	260
Erskine, Samuel	Ellis, Georgiana	27 APR 1882 R	16	336
Ertter, Sarah Jane	Keene, Charles Henry	17 MAY 1880 R	14	272
Ervenbeck, Margaret	Mennier, Louis	29 APR 1879 R	13	163
Esch, Clara R.	Boyd, Geo. Washington	23 APR 1884 R	18	529
Escott, Annie	Summerville, William H.	14 NOV 1883 R	18	251
Esko, Kause	Mackabee, Martha	30 DEC 1884 L	19	501
Eskridge, Albert	Brooks, Elmira Cora	07 OCT 1880 R	14	479
Eskridge, Caria	Campbell, Joshua	10 FEB 1881 R	15	222
Eskridge, Daniel	Towles, Jennie	17 JAN 1878 R	11	307
Eskridge, Edgar Peyton	Terrell, Rosamund G.	26 APR 1884 R	18	533
Eskridge, Eliza	Johnson, Gabriel	31 AUG 1882 R	16	494
Eskridge, Osborne	Pryor, Alice	16 DEC 1882	17	188
Eslin, George McClellan	Stutz, Anna Maria Babette	12 AUG 1885 R	20	364
Eslin, James William	Gier, Lilly Elizabeth	16 SEP 1878 L	12	220
Espey, Maria V.	Ryon, John T.	24 OCT 1882 L	17	090
Esputa, John	Esputa, Mary	15 FEB 1882 L	16	243
Esputa, Josephine	Daly, John A.	07 NOV 1882	17	112
Esputa, Mary	Esputa, John	15 FEB 1882 L	16	243
Essex, Jannie	Sonnemann, Theodore	20 DEC 1881 L	16	140
Estes, Dana	Page, Grace D.	10 NOV 1884	19	354
Estes, Elisha B.	Harding, Alice G.	01 OCT 1878 R	12	245
Estes, Martha	Reed, William	09 SEP 1884	19	232
Estes, Robert W.	Harvey, Mary W.	21 APR 1881 R	15	267
Esther, Clara M.	Darby, Rezin W.	15 JAN 1880 R	14	109
Estler, Theodore W.	Moore, Ida C.	26 JUN 1884 R	19	106
Estrich, Isabel	Ashton, Basil	23 DEC 1884	19	470
Etchison, Thomas H.	Thompson, Alice V.	15 DEC 1881 R	16	136
Ether, Robert Morton	Peterson, Emma	26 DEC 1877 L	11	268
Etherington, Mary Ellen	Glasgow, Clurmont	18 OCT 1883 R	18	202
Etter, Walter	Sherwood, Ella G.	29 AUG 1881 L	15	463
Eubank, Camille A.	Cassady, Samuel T.	04 FEB 1884 R	18	216
Eury, Emma O.	Hudson, Alpheus W.	06 JUN 1878	12	090
Evans, Alice G.	Gross, Milton	10 JUL 1884	19	111
Evans, Anna J.	Murray, Daniel	02 APR 1879	13	121
Evans, Annie A.	Evans, Cornelius P.	23 DEC 1884 R	19	478
Evans, Carrie D.	Vanhook, J. Clifford	03 AUG 1882 L	16	468
Evans, Carrie Durer	Van Hook, J. Clifford	10 JUL 1883	18	040
Evans, Catherine Wade	Warder, Charles Edward	21 JAN 1880 R	14	115
Evans, Celia	Sharp, Paul	15 OCT 1879 L	13	427
Evans, Champ	Washington, Cecelia	04 MAY 1882 R	16	349
Evans, Charles	Brown, Emma J.	27 AUG 1877	11	067
Evans, Charles Alfred	Myers, Genevive E.	26 NOV 1879 R	14	011
Evans, Charles P.	McGill, Harriet V.	15 JUN 1878 L	12	100
Evans, Cornelius P.	Evans, Annie A.	23 DEC 1884 R	19	478
Evans, Emma	Pool, Wm. Alex	14 SEP 1881 R	14	233
Evans, Emma V.	Berry, Ferdinand V.	05 NOV 1877	11	168
Evans, Frederick Walter	Monahan, Eleanor Augusta	26 JUL 1882 R	16	459
Evans, French S.	Mowbray, Frank de	31 MAR 1885 R	20	138
Evans, George H.	Latimer, Mary P.	12 DEC 1877 L	11	231
Evans, Georgie	Patterson, William Hart	13 JAN 1881 R	15	150
Evans, Helen M.	Magruder, Walter F.	03 OCT 1877 R	11	120
Evans, Ida E., Mrs.	Hudson, Richard	17 NOV 1883 L	18	262
Evans, Isabel L., Mrs.	Chamberlain, Henry	10 SEP 1884	19	240
Evans, Isabella	Dietz, Frank H.	18 DEC 1882 L	17	189

Name	Spouse	Date		
Evans, James	Higgins, Ida	22 APR 1885 R	20	120
Evans, Jennie G.	Graham, Andrew B.	09 JAN 1884	18	370
Evans, Jennie L.	Stuart, George W.	20 JUL 1882 R	16	448
Evans, Jno. Blackwell	Bulifant, Elvira Harrison	15 DEC 1883 R	18	321
Evans, John	Coleman, Annie	02 JAN 1883 R	17	232
Evans, John D.	Streamer, Marie B.	26 JUL 1881 R	15	415
Evans, John R.	Matthias, Sallie J.	22 DEC 1884 R	19	475
Evans, Laura J.	Saunders, Page	27 FEB 1884 L	18	446
Evans, Lewis S.	Savoy, Sarah C.	03 AUG 1881	16	117
Evans, M.E.	Biggan, M.F.	16 APR 1884 L	18	516
Evans, Madge Randolph	Rogers, Robert Cummins	24 MAR 1885 R	20	127
Evans, Martha Virginia	Douglass, George T.	07 MAY 1884 L	19	009
Evans, Mary Louisa	Taylor, John	21 FEB 1881 L	15	196
Evans, Mary R.	McLeod, Angus A.	05 OCT 1882 R	17	057
Evans, Mollie M.	Browning, Livingston	20 OCT 1878	12	283
Evans, Nancy	Brooks, James	26 MAR 1879 L	13	116
Evans, Nina	Zevely, Bartram	30 JAN 1879 R	13	037
Evans, Nina Florence	Mackall, James Mc., Dr.	30 APR 1880 R	14	282
Evans, Richard Kennon	Shunk, Jane Findley	11 NOV 1880 R	15	045
Evans, Richard May	Bresnahan, Catharine Cecilia	17 FEB 1879 R	13	062
Evans, Richard Penhallow	Smith, Emeline Franter	15 JUN 1880 R	14	322
Evans, Robert	Richardson, Annie	08 OCT 1885	20	470
Evans, Robert Kennon, Lt.	Shunt, Jane Lindley	11 NOV 1880	15	039
Evans, Sallie	Lang, William H.	08 JAN 1880 R	14	096
Evans, Samuel B.	Woodworth, Mary L.	26 OCT 1879	13	443
Evans, Sarah I.	Johnson, Louis C.	27 JUN 1883	18	018
Evans, Sophia	Crawford, John	26 AUG 1879	13	335
Evans, Susan M.	Benson, J. Hepburn P.	01 SEP 1884 L	19	218
Evans, Waring E.	Judd, Kate I.	04 OCT 1882 L	17	053
Evans, William M.	Wade, Nannie L.	08 JAN 1883 R	17	242
Evarts, Raymond M.	Tully, Annie E.	06 FEB 1884 R	18	413
Evatt, Maggie L.	Wharton, William M.	07 SEP 1882 R	17	011
Evely, Mary A.	Morgan, Morris A.	08 JAN 1880	14	097
Everard, Mary A.	Shekel, A.B., Dr.	09 OCT 1877 L	11	128
Everest, J.M.	Fox, Lillie	12 OCT 1880 R	14	489
Everet, Georgie	Young, Henry	28 NOV 1883 L	18	284
Everett, Annie V.	Dowling, Fillmore	07 SEP 1885 L	20	402
Everett, John Coleman, Dr.	Martin, Nellie Geraldine	26 AUG 1885 R	20	388
Everett, Joseph Samuel	Bridget, Katie V.	23 SEP 1879 R	13	382
Everett, Julia R.	Liggan, Robert L.	08 AUG 1883	18	080
Everett, Mary	Uhfelder, Benjamin	20 JUL 1881 R	15	411
Everett, Mary L.	Wilson, E.J.	07 AUG 1883 L	18	078
Everett, Robert	Scaggs, Emma L.	08 MAY 1879	13	181
Everett, Rosanna	Thom, William G.B.	26 JAN 1885 R	20	037
Everett, William K.	French, Fannie V.	26 AUG 1880 R	14	418
Everhart, Katie	Violett, Alfred Lee	19 AUG 1885	20	379
Everly, Rebecca	Perry, Erasmus	13 MAR 1884 R	18	469
Everton, Florence	James, Morris M.	30 APR 1880	14	247
Everts, Virginia	Kleindienst, Joseph B.	11 JUN 1885 L	20	269
Ewald, Catherine	Bergmann, Fred W.	14 FEB 1878 L	11	342
Ewald, Hermann C.	Henry, Rosa	11 SEP 1877 L	11	086
Ewald, Louise	Schmidtman, Hermann	26 NOV 1882 R	17	148
Ewald, Rose	Kraemer, William	18 NOV 1877	11	188
Ewell, Clara	Anderson, Wallace	17 AUG 1885 L	20	373
Ewell, Eliza	Walker, William Henry	22 NOV 1880 R	15	053
Ewell, Henry	Allen, Mary	12 AUG 1882	16	477
Ewell, Mary	Stanley, Marshal	08 AUG 1877 L	11	046
Ewell, Mary	Dade, Peter	20 DEC 1880 R	15	111

D.C. Marriage Records Index, June 28, 1877 to October 19, 1885   147

Ewell, William Henry	Mercer, Sadie	05 JAN 1881 R	15	140
Ewer, Mary Ella	Ridgeway, William Henry	09 AUG 1877	11	050
Ewers, Thomas Armistead	Adams, Lula	18 DEC 1883	18	322
Ewin, Deborah D.	Lamb, Francis H.	20 MAY 1880	14	276
Ewin, James L.	King, Janie Y.	14 DEC 1880 R	15	096
Ewin, William	Dennison, Catherine C.	17 APR 1880	14	226
Ewing, John Wm.	Norman, Hattie	16 JUL 1885 R	20	330
Exel, Christian	Schafer, Emma Elise	25 APR 1883 R	17	411
Exel, Leonhard	Sohn, Elise	04 MAY 1882 L	16	350
Exkstein, Lizzie	Anderson, Christian	02 AUG 1883	18	073
Ezell, John	Hickey, Margaret	13 NOV 1879 R	13	486

F

Faber, Louis	Urich, Mary J.	09 JUL 1879 R	13	275
Faerber, Julius I.	Rowe, Lavinia B.	17 MAR 1885 R	20	119
Fagan, James	Allen, Annie S.	07 AUG 1879 L	13	310
Fagan, Margaret	Fitzgerald, Edmund	17 APR 1882	16	321
Fague, Thomas W.	Ferguson, Mary E.	11 NOV 1884	19	372
Faherty, James	Cady, Bridget	06 MAY 1880 R	14	247
Fahey, Daniel C.	Whyte, Katie R.	18 NOV 1884	19	392
Fahey, Delia L.	Sullivan, John J.	06 NOV 1878 R	12	163
Fahey, Mary	Callahan, Michael	17 APR 1879 R	13	150
Fahnline, Catherine A.	Bayliss, Hillman	13 SEP 1882	17	020
Fahrenbruch, A.D.	Hagemeyer, H.W.	06 MAY 1879 R	13	174
Fahrmeier, Annie	Chase, William O.	21 DEC 1883 L	18	334
Fairall, Henrietta P.	Black, Joseph S.	15 NOV 1881 R	16	075
Fairall, Mary E.	Shelton, John R.	29 MAY 1878	12	074
Fairall, Mary M.	Young, Richard	25 OCT 1882 R	17	086
Fairbanks, William	Watts, Eliza	21 AUG 1884 R	19	200
Fairbrother, Frank Lazolin	Clarke, Fannie Adaline	20 DEC 1877 R	11	246
Fairfax, Alice	Gray, Thomas	18 NOV 1879	13	491
Fairfax, Arthur Percy	Hoge, Nannie Hunter	02 FEB 1882 R	16	221
Fairfax, Catherine	Fossett, David	18 JUN 1883	17	499
Fairfax, Emma L.	Johnston, J.R.	14 JUN 1881 L	15	362
Fairfax, John A.	Acher, Ella, Mrs.	20 OCT 1880	15	006
Fairfax, Julia	Dean, Charles	14 OCT 1879 R	13	410
Fairfax, Lucy D.	Honesty, Henry W.	05 SEP 1880	14	422
Fairfax, Lucy M.	Saunders, James M.	27 JUL 1882 R	16	440
Fairfax, Mary	Mahoney, George	13 NOV 1884 R	19	380
Fairfax, Mary Elizabeth	Ayres, Charles G.	16 APR 1884 R	18	508
Fairfax, Robert T.	Brooks, Theresa V.	27 JAN 1885 L	20	039
Fairfax, Rosie L.	Shepard, Mark	30 SEP 1884	19	273
Fairfax, Susie C.	Simpson, Silas E.	19 MAR 1883 R	17	351
Fairfax, Thaddeus	Elgin, Rebecca J.	05 JUN 1879 R	13	220
Fairfax, Victorine	Makely, Cassius E.	20 DEC 1882	17	197
Fairfax, Virginia	Duckett, James	14 AUG 1884	19	186
Fairfax, William T.	Lewis, Ida	27 MAR 1878 L	11	394
Fairlamb, Fannie	Stevens, Alphonso	12 JUN 1882 R	16	407
Falconer, Ella	Carter, James William	19 APR 1882 R	16	326
Fales, Lawrence	Aloas, Amelia	10 JAN 1885 L	20	011
Fales, Minnie E.	Martin, Millard F.	20 MAY 1878	12	060
Fales, Willard Noice	Brower, Jane A.N.	06 APR 1878 L	11	408
Faley, Katie A.	Lyons, Daniel J.	06 JAN 1880 L	14	092
Falisi, Vincenzo	Culotta, Concetta	25 APR 1883 L	17	410
Falkner, Margaret A.	Keefe, John J.	28 SEP 1878	12	239
Fall, Jane	Gould, James	08 OCT 1882 R	17	059
Fall, Martin	Martin, Lizzie	10 JUN 1883 R	17	485
Fallen, Martha Ellen	Amberger, Frederick	01 AUG 1879 L	13	302
Fallon, Daniel F.	Dickerson, Ida M.	29 DEC 1881 R	16	160
Fallon, John T.	Summerscales, Elizabeth	22 APR 1879 L	13	154
Falls, Robert Wilson	Armstrong, Charlotte	15 MAY 1883 R	17	441
Falvey, John H.	Frizzell, Laura Virginia	28 APR 1885 L	20	192
Falvey, Nannie	Henderson, John D.	28 MAY 1878	12	068
Falvey, William	Linsley, Elizabeth	16 JUL 1877	11	023
Fanning, John W.	Summons, Jennie	15 NOV 1881 L	16	079
Fanning, Joseph	Armour, Maggie	01 FEB 1882 R	16	216
Fanning, William H.	Parker, Florence L.	17 MAR 1885	20	120
Fant, Alice Norton	Keller, Thomas White	28 DEC 1882 R	17	221
Fant, Andrew Lovingston	Cross, Ida F.	13 DEC 1882 R	17	180
Fant, Joseph N.	Mears, Mariana B.	02 FEB 1880 L	14	130

Fant, Mary Emilie	Reardon, George Evett	13 NOV 1878 R	12	338
Fant, Nellie L.	Payne, George R.	25 DEC 1879	14	075
Fantleroy, Richard H.	Parker, Martha A.	06 JAN 1881 R	15	143
Fantroy, Cornealous	Quill, Anna	05 SEP 1881 R	22	5286
Fantroy, John	James, Mary E.	12 NOV 1878 R	12	296
Fantroy, Mary	Jenkins, John	31 MAY 1883 L	17	470
Fantroy, Mary J.	Foster, James H.	13 OCT 1881 R	16	020
Fantroy, Robert	Daggs, Ella	11 AUG 1881	15	441
Farden, James D.	Rutherford, Annie	10 SEP 1884	19	236
Farell, Patrick	Halpin, Mary	30 MAY 1884	19	025
Fargo, Mary A.	Greenleef, George	10 APR 1880	14	219
Farless, Benjamin A.	Mirick, Emily	22 JUN 1881	15	373
Farley, James	Stone, Mary	08 APR 1880 L	14	215
Farlor, William	Gerhardt, Elizabeth	27 AUG 1884	19	211
Farmer, Ida	Stith, Paul J.	18 MAY 1881 R	15	315
Farmer, James	Thomas, Sarah	22 DEC 1881	16	143
Farmer, Mary	Golly, Benjamin	14 JUL 1877 L	11	021
Farmer, Mary	Stanton, Thomas	15 MAR 1881 L	15	225
Farmer, Sarah Aloysie	Flynn, Samuel W.	11 JAN 1884 L	18	374
Farnes, Mary	Gallivan, John J.	08 APR 1880 R	14	210
Farnsworth, Wealthey A.	Smith, Jay B.	14 DEC 1880	15	096
Farquhar, Patrick	Sands, Mary, Mrs.	27 DEC 1882	17	213
Farquher, Patrick	Clark, Rose	13 OCT 1877 L	11	135
Farr, Charles N.	Baker, Mary Elizabeth	13 FEB 1882	16	236
Farr, Clarke L.	Lewis, Ella V.	19 DEC 1883	18	328
Farr, Clementia, Mrs.	Jones, George	06 DEC 1882 R	17	164
Farr, Ella	Davis, Isaac	07 FEB 1878	11	331
Farr, Georgie L.	Dorrell, George A.	16 JAN 1883	17	258
Farr, Middleton	Watson, Fannie	11 SEP 1879 R	13	366
Farr, Richard R.	Malone, Margaret E.	12 FEB 1879	13	058
Farr, Walter P.	Coomes, Sarah M.	05 FEB 1884 R	18	409
Farr, Wm. Thomas	Hurley, Kate	20 MAY 1880 R	14	281
Farr, Zadie L.	Miskell, William A.	03 AUG 1880 R	14	384
Farrar, R. Blanche	Sutherland, Moses H.	25 APR 1882 R	16	332
Farrar, Watson W.	Harvey, Clara C.	10 APR 1883 L	17	388
Farrell, Helen C.	Lusby, Charles C.	29 SEP 1883 L	18	161
Farrell, J.	Nalley, Nona C.	30 DEC 1884 L	19	506
Farrell, John	Hurley, Ellen	29 NOV 1883 L	18	286
Farrell, Katie	Norris, Millard A.	11 OCT 1885	20	474
Farrell, Margaret E.	Maguire, John	13 FEB 1879 R	13	060
Farrelly, Mary J.	Stanton, Edward G.	14 APR 1879 R	13	141
Farrington, Frederick	Rainsford, Charlotte Mary	24 JAN 1882 R	16	204
Farrington, Mary A.	Murphy, James J.	11 DEC 1879 L	14	044
Farris, Allan H.	Brown, Doreter L.	24 OCT 1883 L	18	212
Farron, Amanda M.	Carroll, James P.	06 MAY 1879 R	13	177
Farrow, Anna E.	Treadwell, John	19 OCT 1880	15	001
Fassett, Flora	Hodge, Clark R.	16 JUN 1880 R	14	322
Faubel, Alice H.	Koester, Lewis	02 JUN 1879	13	213
Faulhaher, Alexander	Heurich, Elisabetta	19 AUG 1878 L	12	172
Faulk, James E.	Tait, Sarah Ann	29 DEC 1881 R	16	168
Faulkener, Mary A.	Walker, Joseph S.	28 FEB 1885	20	090
Faulkner, Albert	Matthews, Marie	03 SEP 1884 L	19	222
Faulkner, Eugenia C.	Blank, Robert B.	08 AUG 1880 R	14	391
Faulkner, Ida M.	Gatten, Henry	20 NOV 1883 R	18	264
Faulkner, Sarah Eliza	Dean, William Francis	16 APR 1884 R	18	514
Faunce, Annie	Runby, L.	07 NOV 1881	16	064
Faunce, Jennie	Galliher, Charles E.	15 NOV 1883 R	18	256
Faunce, John	Haneke, Agatha	25 MAY 1883 L	17	462

Name	Spouse	Date	Vol	Page
Faunce, Margaret E.	Paige, Charles H.	09 NOV 1882 R	17	122
Faunce, Mary A.	Smith, John T.	19 MAR 1883 L	17	349
Faunce, Mary L.	Sebree, William E.	23 JAN 1879 R	13	032
Faunce, Phillip P.	Carroll, M. Alice	19 NOV 1883	18	263
Fauntleroy, Annie	White, Charles	18 MAY 1881 L	15	316
Fauntleroy, Benjamin	Griffin, Jennie	19 JUN 1879	13	239
Fauntleroy, Emma	Wars, Lewis W.	30 JUL 1883 L	18	068
Fauntleroy, Henry	Jackson, Lizzie	09 OCT 1883	18	178
Fauntleroy, Rachel	Miller, George	06 FEB 1883 R	17	294
Fauntleroy, William M.	Hamilton, Annie R.	12 SEP 1882 L	17	018
Fauth, Charles	Keller, Elizabeth	27 JUN 1882 L	16	427
Fauth, Frank	Hopkins, Mary Van Ness	24 APR 1884 R	18	525
Fautroy, Eliza	Hunt, Moses	13 JUN 1878 L	12	099
Favill, Annie R.	Woltz, Charles H.	02 JAN 1878	11	289
Fawcett, Charles F.	DeVan, Susan J.	14 NOV 1883 R	18	253
Fawcett, Mary Elizabeth	Gray, George Ryland	18 DEC 1878 R	12	388
Fayman, Roberta	Davis, James T.J.	02 JUN 1880 R	14	299
Fealy, Patrick A.	O'Connell, Annie L.	07 OCT 1882 L	17	059
Fearing, Irene	Camolier, George A.	26 MAY 1880 L	14	292
Fearson, Charles Dallas	Plummer, Julia Ella	03 JUN 1879 F	13	214
Fearson, Ella S.	Mudd, Rufus H.	19 JUN 1882 L	16	418
Fearson, James S.	Hutcheson, Jennie F.	03 FEB 1880 R	14	132
Fearson, Lizzie	Sutton, Robert G.	19 OCT 1882 L	17	080
Fearson, William Jesse	Gooding, Frances E.	21 FEB 1882 R	16	254
Feast, John, Jr.	Serrin, Ella Catharine	06 NOV 1883 R	18	234
Feaster, Alice	Carter, William Frank	21 JAN 1885	20	032
Febiger, John C., U.S.N.	Johnson, Ellen T.	01 JUN 1882	16	387
Febrey, Sadie E., Mrs.	Granger, John L.	23 APR 1885 L	20	186
Febrey, Wallace A.	Short, Sadie	21 JUN 1883 L	18	008
Febrey, William N.	Hughes, Eliza Frances	21 MAR 1882	16	285
Fechet, Eugene Oscar	Montgomery, Mary Emily	03 DEC 1879 R	14	026
Federwisch, H. Louis	Frank, Kunigunda	03 NOV 1877 L	11	166
Feeley, Mary A.	Crowley, D.J.F.	12 OCT 1880	14	488
Feeley, Mary T.	Columbus, Christopher M.	22 JAN 1879 L	13	030
Feen, Chloe	Brown, George	24 OCT 1881 L	16	042
Feeney, William J.	McDermott, Eliza	04 AUG 1885 L	20	351
Feeny, Norah	Dugan, Patrick	29 APR 1885 L	20	196
Feester, Maggie	Jenkins, James	08 JUN 1878 R	12	092
Fegan, Hugh J.	Wise, Catharine V.	18 FEB 1878 L	11	347
Fegan, James M.	Steuart, Katie	22 APR 1884 L	18	524
Feggans, Peter H.	Gordon, Frances	21 AUG 1879 R	13	328
Feile, Magdalena	Michel, Adam	31 JUL 1883 L	18	067
Feldman, Christoph Frederick	Krone, Maria Lisette	17 OCT 1880 R	14	497
Feldman, Shiman	Rubinstein, Minnie	27 SEP 1885 R	20	443
Feldross, Annie M.	Vierbuchen, John P.	26 NOV 1884 R	19	416
Fell, Edward Nelson	Palmer, Anne Mumford	25 MAY 1885 R	20	239
Fellows, Barnard T.	Luckett, Ellen A.	19 FEB 1879 R	13	068
Felton, Charles W.	Crupper, Cora A.	30 MAR 1881 L	15	242
Fender, Maria	Washington, Henry	30 AUG 1882 L	16	497
Fendrick, Sarah	Ross, James	09 FEB 1882 L	16	234
Fennell, Coorie C.	Edward, James	30 APR 1885 R	20	199
Fennell, Robert A.	Lunsford, Kate	14 JAN 1882 L	16	195
Fenton, Charles B.	Scheckell, Ida J.	11 JUL 1883 R	18	044
Fenton, Charles W.	Walch, Clara H.	21 DEC 1881 R	16	141
Fenton, Edwin L.	Zelner, Ellen S.	21 OCT 1884 L	19	325
Fenton, Joseph B.	Smith, Helen	01 MAR 1881 R	15	206
Fenton, Julia G.	Nunes, William Joseph	31 DEC 1882 R	17	224
Fenton, Maggie A.	Fitzgerald, Edward A.	13 NOV 1877 R	11	182

Fenwick, Addie Lavinia	Hayes, James E.	06 NOV 1878 R	12	309
Fenwick, Alice G. (Evans)	Wallach, Richard L.	28 MAY 1883 R	17	464
Fenwick, Catherine E.	Brooke, Alexander M.	20 NOV 1877 L	11	194
Fenwick, Sarah	Parker, William Henry	16 DEC 1878 R	12	358
Ferguson, Alice	Burrough, Howard	27 JUN 1881 R	15	371
Ferguson, Amelia Virginia	Allen, Robert F.	16 APR 1884 R	18	514
Ferguson, Anna Elizabeth	Gray, Joseph William	27 JUL 1877 L	11	032
Ferguson, Anna Laura	Rumpf, Lewis	24 JUL 1883	18	058
Ferguson, Charles E.	Hebbron, Amelia A.	27 FEB 1879 R	13	084
Ferguson, Clarence R.	Hoffman, Anna R.	23 OCT 1877 L	11	151
Ferguson, Ella M.	Jones, Frank Y.	15 SEP 1885 R	20	418
Ferguson, Esther Jane	Henderson, Richard Wilson	15 MAY 1883 R	17	442
Ferguson, Fannie	Windsor, Eugene	10 NOV 1884 R	19	371
Ferguson, J. Edwin	Maginnis, Florence	20 JUL 1884 L	19	148
Ferguson, J.C., M.D.	Parker, Octavia	30 JUN 1880	14	341
Ferguson, James E.	Barton, Martha	13 APR 1881	15	256
Ferguson, Mary	Cleveland, David G.	03 JUN 1885 L	20	254
Ferguson, Mary E.	Fague, Thomas W.	11 NOV 1884	19	372
Ferguson, Nancy	Giles, Edward	24 DEC 1884 L	19	490
Ferguson, Rachel	Banks, Broadus	06 SEP 1883 L	18	116
Ferguson, William	Worcester, Rosella	23 OCT 1877 R	11	150
Ferguson, William	Fox, Annie	24 DEC 1879 L	14	072
Ferguson, William	Jackson, Maria	28 MAR 1883 R	17	363
Ferguson, William	Standard, Alice	18 SEP 1883 R	18	139
Ferguson, William A.	Garner, Jeanette E.	17 JUL 1881 R	15	405
Fergusson, Amanda	Olden, Fred	23 AUG 1883 L	18	097
Ferrall, Fannie Watson	Carlyle, Frederic W.	16 OCT 1884	19	315
Ferrill, May G.	Cohill, William A.	07 MAY 1885 R	20	212
Ferris, John R.	Butler, Emma L.	17 MAR 1878	11	385
Ferriter, Maggie R.	Ingersoll, Charles E.	11 AUG 1884 R	19	180
Ferry, James Thomas	Runnells, Sarah McClellan	17 JUL 1883 R	18	050
Ferry, Julia N.	Rowzee, Charles R.	20 JAN 1881 R	15	157
Ferry, Laura Isabella	Sullivan, Millard Fillmore	01 JAN 1882 R	16	175
Fessenden, Stephen D.	Dandelet, Lucile J.	14 JUN 1883 R	17	493
Fester, William	Coker, Rosanna L.	15 FEB 1878 R	11	342
Fichter, George	Rye, Mary McElfresh	03 MAR 1880	14	175
Fick, John Rolph	Ennis, Mary Elizabeth	16 DEC 1879 R	14	049
Fickling, Austin	Stuart, Cora	01 OCT 1877	11	116
Fiedler, Madison	Jouvenal, Emma	29 JAN 1882 R	16	214
Field, Bessie	Reinhart, Daniel	12 NOV 1884 R	19	378
Field, Emeline Van S.	Kinsella, Thomas	19 MAY 1880 R	14	276
Field, George W.	Norris, Martha F.	16 SEP 1879 L	13	373
Field, John M.	Wills, Caroline W.	29 JAN 1880	14	126
Field, Lewis O.	Abell, Laney	08 FEB 1883	17	300
Field, Lucy	Rigney, William	01 JUL 1885 R	20	305
Fielding, William S.	Root, Harriet C.	03 AUG 1882 R	16	468
Fields, Bailey	Tolliver, Rachel	06 MAY 1880 L	14	257
Fields, Carrie E.	Dade, John F.	04 SEP 1879	13	349
Fields, Fannie	Brown, Fisher	19 AUG 1880 L	14	407
Fields, Isaac	Dade, Effie	08 JAN 1885 L	20	010
Fields, J.W.	Fisher, Isadore V.	30 APR 1878	12	027
Fields, James	Scott, Eliza	16 OCT 1884 L	19	311
Fields, Jennie Hellen	Hansen, Thomas	08 SEP 1883 L	18	119
Fields, John A.	Dade, Julia A.	18 DEC 1878	12	387
Fields, Laura A.	Scott, W.H.	16 MAR 1880	14	185
Fields, Louisa	Pollard, Griffin	26 MAY 1880 L	14	288
Fields, Louvinia	Pollard, Griffith	02 JAN 1878 L	11	287
Fields, M. Phemie	Hager, Myron D.	15 APR 1882 R	16	316

Fields, Mary E.	Burdett, George	31 JUL 1879 R	13	300
Fields, Mary R.	Spilman, George N.	24 SEP 1883 R	18	149
Fields, Mary Virginia	Hamlit, William	13 OCT 1880 L	14	491
Fields, Rebecca	Wilson, John	28 FEB 1883	17	326
Fields, Samuel	James, Maggie	01 SEP 1881 L	15	468
Fields, Susan	Morton, Robert	18 FEB 1878	12	227
Fields, Thomas	Henderson, Annie	17 NOV 1881 R	16	084
Fields, William	Levyman, Susie	03 SEP 1884	19	223
Fiersinger, Carrie M.	America, Thomas F.	08 APR 1885 R	20	154
Fife, Mary A.	Tracey, John T.	17 NOV 1882 L	17	134
Figgins, Enoch	Garrett, Corra	31 OCT 1884	19	353
Filler, Maud	Purcell, Mahlon	23 FEB 1881 R	15	200
Fillins, Capitolia V.	Hollinberger, Joseph T.	18 MAY 1880	14	275
Fillins, Katie Eliz.	Kenney, John Manns	01 SEP 1885 R	20	392
Filz, Susanne Marie	Braun, John	09 MAY 1880 R	14	261
Finagin, Margaret Cath.	Simmons, John Benjamin	03 OCT 1880 R	14	468
Finch, Edwin Jr.	Robinson, Nannie A.	03 OCT 1882 R	17	049
Finch, Erastus M.	Lesh, Annette	06 NOV 1879 R	13	469
Finch, Eugene C.	Bozzell, Marion E.	16 OCT 1879 R	13	424
Finch, Jerusa K.	Simm, James T.	30 JUL 1881 L	15	427
Finch, John Summerfield	Dalton, Kate J.	16 OCT 1881	16	026
Finch, Lauron	Holmes, John	06 NOV 1884 R	19	366
Finch, Paul	Thecker, Mary J.	04 AUG 1877 L	11	040
Finckel, William H.	Davis, Mary M.	02 JUN 1880 L	14	302
Findley, Elizabeth	Howe, Edward	24 OCT 1881 L	16	040
Finecy, James	Daniels, Fannie	03 JUL 1878 R	12	124
Finegan, John	Murray, Margaret A.	28 SEP 1885 L	20	444
Fines, Mary M.	Cox, Peter	26 MAR 1883	17	361
Fink, Carrie E.	Burgess, Abner	16 OCT 1877	11	139
Finkmann, Elizabeth C.	Schmid, Edward S.	15 MAY 1883 R	17	440
Finks, Elizabeth	Coleman, Lewis	19 JUN 1884	19	093
Finks, James Oliver	Chewning, Annie Payne	18 FEB 1885 R	20	076
Finley, John Park	Larkin, Julia Villet	18 NOV 1879 R	13	492
Finley, Joseph James	Kyne, Bridget	10 JUL 1880 L	14	356
Finley, Kate Palmer	McElfresh, John J.S.	10 OCT 1882 L	17	062
Finley, Katie	Harper, Joseph Franklin	01 JUL 1884 R	19	109
Finley, Laura	Brewer, George J.	19 DEC 1883	18	325
Finley, Leila Lawrence	Buell, Clayton Henry	30 APR 1885 R	20	197
Finley, William L.	Morris, Elienor B.	15 OCT 1884	19	306
Finly, Sarah H.	Kneas, Adolph	08 NOV 1881	16	067
Finn, John F.	Pyles, Annie	17 MAR 1884	18	473
Finn, William J.	Redthka, Mina	12 SEP 1884 L	19	243
Finnell, Lucy	Jones, Edward	16 MAY 1885 R	20	225
Finney, John Thomas	Coxen, Mary Elizabeth	01 APR 1880 R	14	204
Finney, Mary E.	Fowler, Samuel R.	08 JUL 1884	19	127
Finney, Mary M.J.	Phelps, George B.	08 JUN 1880 R	14	309
Finney, Sally	Tyler, John	20 APR 1882 R	16	327
Firmin, Orange Scott	Clingan, Amanda S.A.	24 OCT 1882 R	17	087
Firth, Fannie P.	Perry, Lewis P.	24 DEC 1880 R	15	122
Fisburne, B.P., Dr.	Redon, E. Alice	01 JUN 1881	15	336
Fischer, Anna E.	Duehring, Carl	14 JAN 1883	17	250
Fischer, Emma K.	Regnier, Charles N.	07 APR 1880 R	14	209
Fischer, Florence	Sweetman, George Jay	01 FEB 1884	18	405
Fischer, Pauline A.	Lamb, John Melvin, Dr.	08 SEP 1885 R	20	405
Fischer, William	Eisele, Johanna Francisca Julia	08 AUG 1882 R	16	472
Fishback, Fannie M.	Brundage, Joseph Smith	28 MAR 1878	11	397
Fishback, Sallie	Putnam, Benjamin	19 JUN 1878 R	12	110
Fishback, William Owen	Kauffman, Mary Emma	06 DEC 1877 R	11	221

Fishel, Adolf Morris	Goodman, Rebecca	20 APR 1884 R	18	520
Fisher, Ada	Guggenheimer, Samuel	17 AUG 1879 R	13	321
Fisher, Alice	Snowden, James R.	07 JUN 1883 L	17	481
Fisher, Alice Sarah	Donaldson, Jonah R.	17 OCT 1883 R	18	198
Fisher, Alice V.	Phenix, James	25 DEC 1877 R	11	263
Fisher, Alvina	Steward, Charles	30 AUG 1884 L	19	215
Fisher, Amanda	Williams, Lewis	13 AUG 1885 L	20	369
Fisher, Annie	Taylor, Bartlett	03 DEC 1877 L	11	215
Fisher, Annie	Moser, Christian	09 DEC 1879 L	14	037
Fisher, Barbara	Neven, William Henry	12 FEB 1878 L	11	337
Fisher, Bertha Virginia	McKnew, Thomas Willson	16 JUN 1885 R	20	275
Fisher, Charles B.	King, Cora D.	16 NOV 1885	20	473
Fisher, Charles Freemont	Doran, Sarah Ellen	02 JUL 1884 R	19	117
Fisher, Charlotte Margaret	Stellwagen, Edward James	29 SEP 1880 R	14	462
Fisher, Charlotte Muir	Scheffer, Julius Caesar	10 APR 1878 R	11	414
Fisher, Ella V.	Browning, Joseph S.	14 JUL 1879 R	13	279
Fisher, Flavius Josephus	Brewer, Elizabeth Patten	27 JUN 1883 R	18	021
Fisher, George	Howell, Carrie	03 APR 1882 R	16	296
Fisher, George Everett	Loveless, Mary Ann	31 JUL 1881 R	15	425
Fisher, Hannah	Sickle, Eli	18 OCT 1885 R	20	491
Fisher, Hattie	Jones, Joseph	14 DEC 1882	17	183
Fisher, Helen	Stokes, Sewell Lewis	15 OCT 1885 R	20	488
Fisher, Ida May	Gale, Thomas Monroe	24 JUN 1880 R	14	332
Fisher, Isabella	Spencer, John E.	15 SEP 1885	20	418
Fisher, Isadore V.	Fields, J.W.	30 APR 1878	12	027
Fisher, James Summers	Duvall, Pattie	16 MAY 1878 R	12	053
Fisher, John Henry	Smith, Mary Ellen	08 DEC 1881 R	16	120
Fisher, Louise A.	Burnside, Robert W.	29 APR 1882 R	16	341
Fisher, Margaret	Miner, Thomas	02 JUL 1879	13	264
Fisher, Maritia	Daniels, John W.	19 MAY 1884 L	19	027
Fisher, Mary	Jones, Louis	10 MAY 1883 R	17	435
Fisher, Mary B.	Wingate, Oliver A.	24 OCT 1882 L	17	089
Fisher, Nelson	Bell, Martha	16 SEP 1882 L	17	024
Fisher, Robert B.	Garner, Minnie Ann	04 AUG 1880 R	14	387
Fisher, Rosalie	Winston, Miles	29 OCT 1880 R	15	021
Fisher, Samuel D.	Brown, Emma	26 JUN 1883 R	18	015
Fisher, Sarah	Wheeler, Nicholas	18 APR 1878 R	11	2504
Fisher, Sarah E.	Jackson, William P.H.	18 JUN 1885	20	277
Fisher, Sophia S.	Parsons, Francis H.	03 JUN 1880 R	14	300
Fisher, William	Clark, Cornelia	28 DEC 1882 L	17	217
Fisher, William	Watkins, Lucy	08 OCT 1885 L	20	470
Fisher, William A.	Hobson, Carrie	26 JAN 1881 R	15	163
Fisher, William Thomas	McCormick, Ellen Morgan	12 SEP 1877 L	11	090
Fisher, William Thos.	Watson, Mattie Leonore	26 OCT 1881 R	16	045
Fiske, Henry B.	Hollinger, Lizzie	16 JUN 1884	19	086
Fister, William H.	McDonald, Mary A.	04 NOV 1881	16	062
Fitan, James	Murphey, Bridget	08 JAN 1884 L	18	368
Fitch, Charles H.	Stevens, Mary C.H.	26 APR 1882 R	16	332
Fitch, May Perkins	Oberteuffer, Herman F.	30 JAN 1883 L	17	278
Fitchett, Cordie Jane	Jarvis, Christopher	07 SEP 1881 R	15	474
Fitnan, Laura V.	Wells, Albert H.	10 NOV 1884 L	19	371
Fitton, Mary S.	Norton, Willie E.	26 NOV 1884	19	413
Fitz, Ella	Hart, William	29 FEB 1878	11	365
Fitz, Mary C.	Kancher, Theodore	29 AUG 1878 L	12	185
Fitzgerald, Annie Y.	Mitchell, Patrick H.	18 NOV 1884 L	19	391
Fitzgerald, Belle	Kerr, Robert H.	07 AUG 1884	19	175
Fitzgerald, Catherine	Wells, William H.	02 JAN 1885 L	20	001
Fitzgerald, David	Sinton, Esther	09 APR 1878	11	409

Fitzgerald, Edmund	Fagan, Margaret	17 APR 1882	16	321
Fitzgerald, Edward	Shea, Mary	02 DEC 1877 R	11	193
Fitzgerald, Edward A.	Fenton, Maggie A.	13 NOV 1877 R	11	182
Fitzgerald, Edward D.	Robinson, Lillie J.	18 JAN 1883	17	265
Fitzgerald, Ella	Mangan, Timothy	23 MAR 1884	18	479
Fitzgerald, Ella	Price, George W.	09 FEB 1885 L	20	058
Fitzgerald, Ellen	Carroll, John	08 JUN 1880	14	307
Fitzgerald, Ellen L.	Seitz, Charles N.	16 OCT 1879	13	419
Fitzgerald, George	Ricketts, Margaret M.	03 MAY 1881 L	15	289
Fitzgerald, Jenkins A.	Jefferis, Ida F.	03 NOV 1882 R	17	109
Fitzgerald, John J.	Downey, Mary M.	14 OCT 1884 L	19	306
Fitzgerald, John P.	Roth, Annie M.	28 APR 1884 L	18	537
Fitzgerald, Joseph R.	Tupper, Aggie	28 APR 1880	14	240
Fitzgerald, Mamie J.	Ergood, Lemuel	25 NOV 1879	14	005
Fitzgerald, Martha	Wells, Eldridge Wash.	19 SEP 1881 L	15	490
Fitzgerald, Mary	Gessner, John	23 NOV 1884	19	401
Fitzgerald, Mary Ann	Hess, Augustus	20 OCT 1877 L	11	146
Fitzgerald, Michael E.	Wilson, Ellen T.	13 APR 1884	18	505
Fitzgerald, Michael J.	McMahon, Annie A.	20 AUG 1884 L	19	194
Fitzgerald, Patrick	Culligan, Mary	08 APR 1880 R	14	215
Fitzgibbon, Edward J.	Liston, Maggie E.	10 MAY 1881 L	15	300
Fitzhugh, Annie Eliz.	Triplet, James Edward	13 AUG 1885 R	20	369
Fitzhugh, James S.	Page, Louisa	17 FEB 1881 L	15	193
Fitzhugh, Joseph D.	Miller, Lena C.	16 JAN 1885	20	025
Fitzhugh, Lewis	Diggs, Alice	11 DEC 1877	11	231
Fitzhugh, Lulu Bright	Simmes, Bennett Barton	21 SEP 1880	14	455
Fitzhugh, Maria	Carter, John	22 APR 1878 L	12	015
Fitzhugh, Mary	Toy, Mary	06 MAR 1879 L	13	092
Fitzhugh, Mary	Dorsey, Joseph C.	24 APR 1884 L	18	531
Fitzhugh, Norman R., Jr.	Linton, Bertha A.	01 OCT 1885 R	20	445
Fitzhugh, Roberta	Strange, George	05 FEB 1879	13	043
Fitzhugh, Samuel	Jordan, Mary E.	02 AUG 1883 I	18	071
Fitzhugh, Taylor	Hill, Maria	29 NOV 1883	18	279
Fitzhugh, Virginia Meade	Daniel, Samuel Greenhow	03 AUG 1882 R	16	467
Fitzhugh, William R.	Columbus, Ella E.	25 JAN 1882 L	16	209
Fitzmorris, John	Trader, Martha Elizabeth	18 APR 1881 L	15	259
Fitzpatrick, James	Bolton, Mary	17 JUN 1879 L	13	234
Fitzpatrick, Katie	Vucinovich, Joseph	08 DEC 1883	18	306
Fitzpatrick, Mary A.	Grace, Richard R.	22 JUN 1878	12	109
Fitzpatrick, Mary E.	Sullivan, Michael P.	26 SEP 1883	18	155
Fitzpatrick, Susie	Payne, George W.	21 JUL 1885 R	34	8410
Flack, Florence A.	Mankin, George B.	12 JUN 1884 R	19	078
Flagg, Henry T.	Whelpley, Adeline	15 NOV 1877	11	188
Flagg, William	Padgett, Ida Adelaide	16 APR 1878 R	12	007
Flagler, Sarah P.	Lugenbeel, John W.	02 MAY 1885 L	20	201
Flaherty, Ananias	Tillett, Lucy E.	19 DEC 1882	17	192
Flaherty, Catherine E.	Hagan, Michael E.	17 NOV 1883 L	18	261
Flaherty, Edward	Gleason, Minnie	27 JAN 1885 L	20	040
Flaherty, Johanna	Matthews, Edward	12 MAR 1884	18	466
Flaherty, Margaret C.	McAllister, Thomas A.	08 FEB 1882 R	16	232
Flaherty, Mary A.	Spaulding, Patrick H.	07 APR 1884 L	18	498
Flaherty, Mary J.	White, Richard E.	08 NOV 1880	15	034
Flaherty, Mollie	Sammons, James E.	15 OCT 1877	11	136
Flaith, Louisa (Knell), Mrs.	Seward, Simon	10 JUN 1885 R	20	251
Flamer, Bascom	Downs, Josephine	20 DEC 1881	16	138
Flammer, William	Hirsch, Katie F.	21 DEC 1880 R	15	114
Flanagan, Maggie Lucretia	Dodson, George Waugh	06 FEB 1883	17	293
Flanagan, Mary A.	Lynch, Thomas	16 SEP 1882 L	17	024

Flanagan, Mary J.	English, Thomas	13 APR 1883 L	17	393
Flanigan, Kate	Flynn, Daniel	30 OCT 1884 L	19	352
Flavin, Katie	Ritz, John	21 NOV 1883 L	18	270
Fleet, Mary M.	Lemos, Beverly R.	21 APR 1881	15	265
Fleet, Mozart B.	Shewalter, Addie V.	08 OCT 1878	12	261
Fleetwood, Moses	Neal, Sophia E.	08 MAY 1879	13	180
Fleischmann, H.H.	Waddell, A.P.	26 NOV 1881 R	16	101
Fleishman, Israel S.	Goodman, Fannie	18 JAN 1885 R	20	024
Fleishman, Lehman	Rice, Regina	03 OCT 1880 R	14	466
Fleming, Abraham	Newman, Minnie	29 NOV 1877 R	11	209
Fleming, Amanda	Swann, Thomas	08 DEC 1880 L	15	087
Fleming, Harry	Martyne, Susie S.J.L.	18 NOV 1883	18	260
Fleming, Joseph S.	Gise, Ora	09 MAR 1885 L	20	100
Fleming, Roberta	McCoy, Augustus	23 APR 1880	14	236
Flemmons, Harriet	Steward, Edward	08 MAY 1879 R	13	175
Flemons, Ross	Nelson, Ella	04 MAR 1885 R	20	094
Flenner, Jesse Weirick	Bouduiot, Ella Cornelia	02 OCT 1882 R	17	047
Fleshman, Minnie	Catlett, Albert H.	15 OCT 1885	20	487
Fletcher, Addie	Daly, Ross	22 DEC 1881 R	16	118
Fletcher, Andrew	Douglas, Maria	03 FEB 1883 L	17	286
Fletcher, Annie C.	McCartney, Peter	05 JAN 1882 R	16	184
Fletcher, Archibald	Green, Agnes	12 OCT 1885	20	475
Fletcher, Augusta C.	Cunningham, Emma	26 NOV 1883 L	18	276
Fletcher, Catharine	Foster, Daniel	14 APR 1885 L	20	162
Fletcher, Edward	Bartlett, Emma	16 APR 1878	12	008
Fletcher, Eleanor	Honester, Geo. Francis	04 APR 1878	11	400
Fletcher, Emma	Johnson, Edward	20 AUG 1884	19	196
Fletcher, Franzeona M.	Myers, Ellis Gregg	31 DEC 1883 R	18	356
Fletcher, George Henry	Brown, Esther Ann	08 JUL 1880 R	14	353
Fletcher, Hamilton W.	Jackson, Mary Ella	19 AUG 1881 L	15	454
Fletcher, Henrietta	Young, Spencer	04 NOV 1879 L	13	461
Fletcher, Henry	Murry, Ellen	29 JAN 1880 R	14	122
Fletcher, Ida L.	Wetzel, John A.	14 APR 1884 L	18	508
Fletcher, Inazella F.	Jones, G. Tucker	01 JAN 1879	13	001
Fletcher, J. Harrison	Wallace, Sarah G.	16 OCT 1880 L	14	497
Fletcher, John	Hall, Mollie	26 MAR 1878	11	393
Fletcher, Joseph	Frizzell, Annie	20 MAY 1879 R	13	198
Fletcher, Joseph	Moffett, Henrietta	25 APR 1882 R	16	329
Fletcher, Laura	Bell, Eleazer	30 OCT 1877	11	158
Fletcher, Louisa	Warren, Albert	07 MAR 1885 L	20	099
Fletcher, Mamie	Buckley, Robert	28 DEC 1881 R	16	168
Fletcher, Mariah	Matthews, William	26 JUN 1884 R	19	101
Fletcher, Mary	Taylor, Stephen	15 AUG 1878	12	164
Fletcher, Mary E.	Cook, Richard	02 FEB 1880 L	14	131
Fletcher, Nellie M.	Perkins, Daniel W.	12 FEB 1884 R	18	421
Fletcher, Nellie R.	Zevely, Douglass	17 OCT 1885 L	20	493
Fletcher, Rebecca	Moseby, John	05 SEP 1878	12	199
Fletcher, Roseanna	Rigner, Firmer	18 MAY 1884 R	19	026
Fletcher, W.H.	Dixon, Sadie L., Mrs.	24 MAY 1882 R	16	374
Fletcher, Washington	Hawkins, Henrietta	04 APR 1885 R	20	142
Fletcher, William	Semmes, Mary	29 AUG 1882 L	16	495
Fletcher, William	Tucker, Carrie	20 JUL 1885 L	20	332
Fletcher, William	Anderson, Gabrielle	08 OCT 1885	20	470
Flick, Nettie B.	Lokey, David	23 JAN 1884	18	391
Fling, James A.	Stadman, Alice Mary	03 SEP 1885 R	20	397
Flinn, Michael W.	Wiley, Ida R.	28 AUG 1880 R	14	421
Flinn, Sarah E.	Ancona, John F.	29 OCT 1878 R	12	293
Flint, Albert Stowell	Thomas, Helen Alfreda	22 OCT 1884 R	19	330

Flint, Charles	Ruoff, Julia Spencer	02 OCT 1878 R	12	248
Flint, Weston	Brown, Lucy R.	14 JUN 1883 R	17	492
Flipper, William M.	Jackson, Annie	17 JUN 1878 R	12	101
Floegel, Ernest	Gruenke, Lessie	28 MAR 1880 R	14	198
Flood, Anna V.	Hill, Robert W.	22 OCT 1884	19	328
Flood, James	Spottswood, Maria	21 FEB 1882 L	16	255
Flood, Martha S.	Garvitt, J.W.	09 MAR 1885	20	100
Flood, William F.	Kerper, Lizzie	16 JUN 1884	19	085
Flournoy, Lettie Carrington	Jones, William Wright	14 MAY 1883 R	17	437
Flowers, Annie C.	Dorr, Lewis	06 SEP 1877 L	11	082
Floyd, Albert C.	Addis, Alice M.	02 APR 1878	11	402
Floyd, Charles J.	Lazenby, Sarah E.	03 DEC 1878 L	12	362
Floyd, Frank Brooks	Steele, Rachel Jane	23 DEC 1879 R	14	066
Floyd, John B.	Mills, Ella L.	07 JUN 1880 R	14	308
Floyd, Robert	Rollins, Maria	29 NOV 1878 R	12	346
Fluehart, John C.	Pool, Mary W.	22 JAN 1879 R	13	031
Flurrey, Sarah F.	Arnold, John F.	01 JUN 1882 L	16	389
Flurry, Sarah Frances	McHugh, Charles M.	22 JAN 1878 R	11	311
Flynn, Annie M. Randolph	Hackney, Fielder Poston	07 OCT 1880 R	14	482
Flynn, Annie T.	Johnston, W.J.	09 DEC 1879 L	14	038
Flynn, Daniel	Flanigan, Kate	30 OCT 1884 L	19	352
Flynn, Isabella Jane	Cook, John George	28 SEP 1881 R	15	335
Flynn, Katie	Downey, Dennis J.	01 JUN 1885 L	20	250
Flynn, Mary Ann	Webster, Benjamin F.	16 JUN 1877	11	309
Flynn, Morris B.	Hartnett, Annie	20 APR 1885 L	20	175
Flynn, Nellie	Main, Robert	24 DEC 1880 L	15	123
Flynn, Samuel W.	Farmer, Sarah Aloysie	11 JAN 1884 L	18	374
Flynn, Thomas	McGraw, Mary	28 JUL 1884 L	19	160
Fockler, S. Eugenia	Quenzel, Charles A.H.	27 NOV 1882 R	17	150
Foder, Blanche F.	Mallonee, John P.	26 SEP 1882	17	037
Fodor, Eunice C.	Coxson, James H.W.	24 FEB 1880 L	14	163
Fogg, Virginia D.	Furtner, James W.	18 OCT 1882 R	17	078
Fogle, George F.	Wasmann, Dora	23 OCT 1877	11	148
Folan, John	Callahan, Margaret	05 NOV 1878	12	308
Foley, Angela	Harvey, Arsenuis Thomas	02 OCT 1879 R	13	397
Foley, Beverly R.	Bateman, Frances S.	09 JUL 1881 L	15	396
Foley, Caroline	Baldwin, Brenton L.	03 DEC 1879	14	028
Foley, Catharine C.	McGrath, Richard	14 APR 1884 L	18	507
Foley, Catherine	Quinlan, Timothy	29 MAY 1882 L	16	381
Foley, Catherine C.	McGrath, Richard	27 JUN 1883 L	18	018
Foley, Daniel P.	McCaffrey, Katie	24 SEP 1882 R	17	035
Foley, Edward	Hanlan, Sarah	08 AUG 1883 L	18	079
Foley, Eva R.	Rector, Edward B.	25 JUL 1882	16	457
Foley, John	Green, Jane	10 JAN 1878 L	11	300
Foley, Katie	Davis, Edward	19 AUG 1880	14	408
Foley, Maggie	Wilson, Marcellus	16 FEB 1878 L	11	343
Foley, Michael	Welsh, Annie	27 DEC 1878 R	12	404
Foley, Michael P.	Westberg, Bertha M.	01 NOV 1883 R	18	227
Foley, Theophilus	Pelton, Jane, Mrs.	23 JUL 1881 R	15	414
Foley, Thomas	Cady, Bridget Ellen	25 APR 1878	12	014
Foley, William J.	Lyons, Johanna A.	24 DEC 1884 L	19	486
Folie, Agnes	Matthews, John N.	27 MAR 1885 L	20	135
Folkes, Susan A.	Brown, John M.	16 OCT 1877 L	11	138
Folkmann, Caroline	Loes, Adam	15 JUL 1882 R	16	442
Folks, David T.	Carroll, Julia A.	23 FEB 1881 L	15	201
Follansbee, Lambert T.	Tucker, Bessie	16 AUG 1881 L	15	448
Follin, Annie M.	Walker, Benjamin F.	26 APR 1883 R	17	415
Follin, Thomas	Mattingly, Mary	10 DEC 1880	15	083

Follin, William Thos.	Goldin, Alice Willard	26 NOV 1877 R	11	200
Foltz, John Calhoun	Hall, Susan Laura	01 JAN 1879 R	13	001
Fonda, Charles Bradford	Mundell, Mary Martha	25 OCT 1882 R	17	093
Fontroy, Cornelius	Washington, Charlotte	02 MAY 1881 L	15	287
Fontz, Charles Stewart	Glenn, Nora	15 APR 1885 L	20	170
Foos, Kate V.	Mullin, Edward J.	29 NOV 1882 R	17	156
Foos, William D.	Carrico, Annie F.	21 FEB 1882 R	16	253
Foote, Eliza B.	Hunter, Joseph H.	30 DEC 1884 R	19	496
Foote, Hattie	Davis, James W.	08 MAR 1880 R	14	179
Foote, Martha A.	James, George W.	05 JUN 1883 R	17	475
Forbes, Dennis	Williams, Bettie	28 OCT 1880	15	002
Forbes, Nestor H., Jr.	McGilvray, Ida	25 AUG 1877	11	065
Forbes, Thomas	Bladnon, Saly	23 JAN 1879 R	12	407
Force, Mary	Stead, Robert	10 APR 1882 R	16	306
Ford, William	Johnson, Sarah F.	26 NOV 1879	14	015
Ford, Agnes Lutetia	Robinon, Charles Henry	20 DEC 1882 R	17	202
Ford, Alberta	Lewis, Edward	08 JUN 1880 R	14	306
Ford, Alice	Williams, William H.	14 NOV 1883 R	18	246
Ford, Alice V.	Harrington, Claude M.	29 NOV 1882 R	17	158
Ford, Andrew	Johnson, Rosa	12 MAY 1881 L	15	304
Ford, Anna M.	Johnson, A.J.	11 APR 1882	16	310
Ford, Annie	Lacy, George	21 FEB 1883	17	316
Ford, Belle	Marshall, Henry	25 OCT 1877 L	11	155
Ford, Bettie	Hawkins, Robert	08 APR 1880 R	14	216
Ford, Charles E.	Grantham, Laura	30 SEP 1885	20	449
Ford, Delia	Boyle, Richard	20 OCT 1878 R	12	283
Ford, Delia	Scott, Robert D.	06 MAR 1884 L	18	460
Ford, E.L.	Akers, James O.	23 JAN 1878 L	11	314
Ford, Fannie	Plater, Benjamin	04 MAY 1882 L	16	348
Ford, Frank B.	McKnee, Victoria V.	19 MAR 1884 R	18	475
Ford, Frederick	Posey, Annie Eliza	04 OCT 1885 R	20	454
Ford, George	Smith, Sarah	28 JUN 1883	18	019
Ford, Gerty	Jones, George Alfred	08 SEP 1881 L	15	477
Ford, Harriet	Mills, Benjamin	10 FEB 1881 R	15	185
Ford, Harrison	Braxon, Virginia	06 OCT 1885	20	421
Ford, Henry	Mason, Mary	15 DEC 1881 R	16	112
Ford, Henry	Brown, Ida	22 SEP 1885	20	435
Ford, Hester Ann	West, Julius	26 FEB 1880	14	167
Ford, Ida	Clark, William	26 AUG 1880 R	14	413
Ford, Isabella	Johnson, Charles H.	07 NOV 1878	12	311
Ford, James	Johns, Alice J.	09 FEB 1882 R	16	230
Ford, James A.	Thornton, Mary J.	28 MAY 1878 L	12	071
Ford, John	Gates, Mary	04 JUL 1883	17	435
Ford, John T.	Lewis, Bettie R.	31 JUL 1879 R	13	297
Ford, Joseph	Philips, Anna	10 SEP 1884 L	19	239
Ford, Julia E.	Hunter, William F.	20 APR 1883	17	402
Ford, Lavinia	Parker, Thomas	30 APR 1878 R	12	027
Ford, Lucy	Chase, Samuel C.	04 JUL 1878 R	12	122
Ford, Maggie	Plater, Henry	27 FEB 1882 R	16	260
Ford, Mary	Lewis, Edward	20 FEB 1879 L	13	070
Ford, Mary	Keane, Patrick	05 FEB 1884 R	18	410
Ford, Mary A.	Kerin, James A.	06 JAN 1885 L	20	007
Ford, Mary D.	Hailstork, Nathan	18 MAR 1880 R	14	187
Ford, Mary M.	Henderson, Thomas	24 SEP 1883 L	18	152
Ford, Mittie E.	Gibbons, W.P.	04 OCT 1882 L	17	054
Ford, Mollie T.	Swetmamn, Ecca R.	03 FEB 1881 L	15	175
Ford, Nathan	Hawkins, Sarah	20 DEC 1882 L	17	195
Ford, Oscar Irven	McDonald, Mary Ann	19 MAY 1881 L	15	319

Ford, Patty C.	Swetnam, Thomas R.	03 FEB 1881 L	15	176
Ford, Richard	Queen, Lydia Ann	11 SEP 1879	13	365
Ford, Robert H.	Macon, Mary E.	13 DEC 1877	11	237
Ford, Robert H.	Salinas, Anna E.	21 APR 1878 R	12	013
Ford, Rosa	Coquire, John Francis	07 JAN 1878 L	11	294
Ford, Samuel	Blue, Willy Ann	09 FEB 1881	15	184
Ford, Saulsbury	Stewart, Dora	14 FEB 1882 L	16	240
Ford, Susan	Delany, Shadrach	03 JUN 1880 L	14	303
Ford, Thomas	Crier, Emma Elizabeth	18 APR 1881 R	15	261
Ford, William	Davenport, Emma	27 OCT 1879 R	13	446
Fordham, Mary A.	Wayson, Edward	15 MAR 1883	17	348
Foreman, Alexander	Parker, Sally	30 OCT 1877 R	11	155
Foreman, Emma	Contee, William	13 APR 1882 R	15	125
Foreman, Hattie M.	Kraft, Philip H.	30 OCT 1884 L	19	350
Foreman, Martha E.	Cheeks, Robert M., Rev.	21 AUG 1884 L	19	201
Foreman, Thomas	Green, Nettie	21 JUN 1883 R	17	494
Foreman, Victoria	Bayard, James T.E.	14 JUL 1884 L	19	138
Forman, John	Matthews, Alice	05 JUL 1881 R	15	390
Forney, Andrew H.	Schwiering, Elizabeth	04 JUN 1884 R	19	058
Forney, Annie K.	Kemp, William A.	03 MAR 1881 L	15	213
Forney, Clara Sherk	Comstock, Walter Jay	04 FEB 1880 R	14	134
Forney, Edward Otis	Hanna, Anna R.	22 NOV 1881 L	16	090
Forney, Pierce W.	Greer, Julia A.	01 MAY 1879 L	13	170
Fornshill, Julia	Stone, Oliver	05 AUG 1877	11	041
Forrest, Arthur	Harris, Fanny	15 JAN 1884 R	18	378
Forrest, Clarence Rosewell	Dayhoff, Florence Katherine	05 AUG 1885 R	20	356
Forrest, James F.	Ward, Laura L.	14 JUL 1879	13	276
Forrest, John W.	Baynes, Margaret	08 JUL 1883	18	039
Forrest, Julia V.	Matthews, Stephen T.M.	14 OCT 1878 R	12	270
Forrest, Laura	Smith, Robert H.	25 JUL 1883 L	18	098
Forrest, Samuel	Green, Jennie	24 FEB 1881	15	201
Forrest, William H.	Sauer, Carry M.	20 SEP 1878 L	12	229
Forrester, George H.	McKenney, Annie	05 AUG 1884 L	19	167
Forrester, Peter	McCauley, Kate	01 JAN 1878	11	285
Forrester, Rachel Adella	Hildebrand, Herman G.	07 SEP 1881 R	15	475
Forsberg, Helen	Murray, William J.	14 MAY 1878 R	12	050
Forsberg, Helge	Parham, Lydia S.	07 JUL 1879 R	13	271
Forster, Johanmah	Abbott, Julius	23 MAY 1880 R	14	279
Forten, Charlotte L.	Grimke, Francis J.	09 DEC 1878	12	391
Fortin, Leon Sosthenes	Larmier, Leonide Elise	22 DEC 1880 R	15	113
Fortune, Delia T.	Taylor, Erasmus Spencer	16 JAN 1879 R	13	014
Fortune, Eugene	Carter, Pinkey	18 OCT 1881 L	16	033
Fortune, Isaiah	Sanders, Annie M.	05 SEP 1884	19	169
Fortune, John	Green, Henrietta	27 APR 1884 R	18	525
Fortune, Sarah	Coats, Edward	25 NOV 1879 L	14	005
Fortune, T.T.	Smille, C.C.	21 FEB 1878 L	11	353
Fosdick, Dering	Whiting, Eliza Macomb	16 MAY 1882 R	16	360
Fosque, Solomon Porterfield	Watts, Annie Elizabeth	15 DEC 1880 R	15	102
Fossett, David	Fairfax, Catherine	18 JUN 1883	17	499
Foster, Albert	Jackson, Laura	11 APR 1878 R	11	379
Foster, Annie	Price, Jacob	16 DEC 1881 R	16	134
Foster, Charles E.	Cross, Sarah Ann	18 JUN 1885 R	20	281
Foster, Daniel	Fletcher, Catharine	14 APR 1885 L	20	162
Foster, David L.	Burch, Alice G.	15 DEC 1881 R	16	132
Foster, Edward	White, Isabella	28 DEC 1882 R	17	157
Foster, Edward	Jones, Mary	28 MAR 1883	17	367
Foster, Emma	Jackson, Harry	10 JUN 1885	20	265
Foster, Flora	Smith, Henry Randolph	16 OCT 1883 R	18	196

Name	Spouse	Date	Vol	Page
Foster, Frank	Shelton, Mary J.	23 FEB 1881 L	15	200
Foster, Irene	Franklin, Benjamin	08 OCT 1881 R	16	015
Foster, Irene	Hawkins, John Henry	29 AUG 1883 L	18	104
Foster, J. William	Mitchell, Mary	15 APR 1880 R	14	224
Foster, James H.	Fantroy, Mary J.	13 OCT 1881 R	16	020
Foster, Jeanie D.	Brackett, John E.	21 NOV 1878 R	12	340
Foster, Jennie Elizabeth	Richard, Archibald	21 APR 1882 R	16	328
Foster, John	Tait, Ella	22 AUG 1877 L	11	061
Foster, John	Harris, Margaret	23 JUN 1881 R	15	374
Foster, Magnolia E.	Harris, Rosser V.	15 SEP 1878 R	12	219
Foster, Mary E.	Payne, John T.	24 APR 1883 R	17	407
Foster, Mary Elizabeth	Brodnax, Robert W.	23 MAR 1883	17	356
Foster, Mary Frances	Neal, Lewis Wm. Henry	31 AUG 1885 L	20	393
Foster, Ross H.	Murray, Augusta L.	12 MAY 1884	19	014
Foster, Silus	Edwards, Mary Anne	21 SEP 1878 L	12	229
Foster, Thomas	Baum, Mary S.	28 DEC 1878 R	12	400
Foster, William N.	Vance, Amanda	07 SEP 1881 R	15	472
Foulkes, George L.	Mitchell, Ida R.	06 AUG 1883	18	076
Fountain, Mary E.	Lawson, Adam	29 JUN 1880 L	14	338
Fountain, Susan	Mahoney, Isaac	14 NOV 1877 R	11	182
Foust, James F.	Mattingly, Rosa Lee	27 MAY 1885	20	242
Fowcus, Martha A.	Miller, Leonard D.	08 JUL 1885 R	20	316
Fowler, Alfred H.	Bodensick, Sarah V.	30 OCT 1879 L	13	454
Fowler, Alice V.	Allen, James W.	29 SEP 1881 R	15	503
Fowler, Ambrose	Mudd, Hattie	17 FEB 1878	11	344
Fowler, Annie S.	Ogden, Leonard R.W.	18 MAR 1880 L	14	187
Fowler, Carrie R.	Watt, George	26 APR 1883	17	416
Fowler, Charles E.	King, Josephine	19 NOV 1877 L	11	191
Fowler, Edwin C.	Beaton, Susie L.	31 DEC 1883 R	18	357
Fowler, Elizabeth E.	Herbert, Edgar C.	05 AUG 1877	11	042
Fowler, Ella	Curl, Edward C.	30 APR 1885	20	199
Fowler, Ella A.	Brickhead, Charles E.	18 MAY 1881	15	313
Fowler, Fannie J.	Willis, Henry M.	07 OCT 1885 R	20	461
Fowler, Florence A.	Hill, William E.	02 APR 1884	18	490
Fowler, Florence T.	Hardy, John Thomas	17 OCT 1877	11	141
Fowler, Florence Virginia	Middleton, Robert Parker	08 NOV 1877 R	11	174
Fowler, Frank Stephen	Prosise, Ida Virginia	28 SEP 1881 R	15	499
Fowler, Gilbert J.	Owens, Annie S.	08 JAN 1883 L	17	242
Fowler, James G.	Goerner, Clara E.	09 FEB 1878	11	334
Fowler, John H.A.	Stephen, Annie Louise	07 JUN 1881 L	15	350
Fowler, Joseph O.	Barrett, Susie A.	11 JUN 1879 R	13	227
Fowler, Julius Edwin	Hays, Mary Estelle	04 AUG 1881 R	15	433
Fowler, Margaret V.	Mason, Richard	02 SEP 1879 R	13	346
Fowler, Marion M.	Bridwell, Adelaide	23 APR 1884	18	527
Fowler, Martha Ellen	Donaldson, George Wm.	21 APR 1883 L	17	403
Fowler, Martha V.	Fowler, Thomas J.J.	05 APR 1882 R	16	297
Fowler, Norman	Gordon, Mary A.	24 NOV 1878	12	344
Fowler, Rachel A.	Edwards, George	14 DEC 1881 R	16	129
Fowler, Samuel	Davis, Alice	01 AUG 1877	11	037
Fowler, Samuel R.	Finney, Mary E.	08 JUL 1884	19	127
Fowler, Thomas J.J.	Fowler, Martha V.	05 APR 1882 R	16	297
Fowler, Walter	Jones, Celia Ann	04 OCT 1881 R	15	505
Fowler, William C.	Connell, Josephine	22 APR 1885	20	184
Fowler, William E.	White, Mary G.	15 AUG 1878	12	167
Fowles, Thomas	Nickens, Julia	07 MAR 1878 L	11	375
Fox, Annie	Ferguson, William	24 DEC 1879 L	14	072
Fox, Charles B.	Caulfield, Genevieve	05 NOV 1878	12	305
Fox, Charles Eben	Beckwith, Nelly	10 JUN 1884 R	19	067

Fox, Charlotte A.	Hanson, Hoban	18 MAR 1883	17	349
Fox, Ella Leonora	Smith, James Henry	15 DEC 1884 R	19	459
Fox, Fannie	Duffins, Robert D.	17 NOV 1880 R	15	053
Fox, Frederick A.	Hazel, Rose	22 AUG 1885 L	20	383
Fox, Gilbert D.	Wright, Marion Jeanitte	30 MAY 1878	12	075
Fox, Harrison	Cooper, Lottie	30 JUN 1885	20	296
Fox, James Dallas	Waters, Malinda	19 JUN 1879	13	239
Fox, Joseph W.	Galey, Matilda	17 AUG 1881 R	15	449
Fox, Lillie	Everest, J.M.	12 OCT 1880 R	14	489
Fox, Lucinda	Thomas, John I.B.	11 SEP 1878	12	212
Fox, Martha L.	Hicks, Jeremiah	29 SEP 1885 R	20	430
Fox, Nella	Perry, Daniel E.	21 AUG 1884	19	200
Fox, Roberta K.	Oberteuffer, William G.	05 MAR 1884 L	18	458
Fox, Sallie	Campbell, Thedore	15 MAY 1882 R	16	360
Fox, Sallie	Johnson, John Henry	24 APR 1882 L	16	332
Fox, Silas	Keleher, Katie	23 DEC 1881 R	16	154
Fox, Sofia C.	Snyder, Thomas L.	24 JAN 1884 R	18	393
Fox, Susie	Colten, William Henry	14 MAY 1879	13	189
Foy, Mary	Creaven, John	05 FEB 1884 R	18	411
Fraas, John M.	Nicholson, Sarah A.	21 FEB 1878 L	11	351
Fraas, Katie M.	Boswell, James E.	29 JAN 1880 R	14	126
Fracker, Sarah K.	Arnold, Paul	29 APR 1884 R	18	540
Fractim, Eddie Benton	Dutch, Moses	20 MAY 1880 R	14	275
Fractions, Nancy E.	Harken, Joseph Alex.	19 APR 1883 L	17	401
Fraeler, Ella Marc.	Krause, Charles Adolph	11 JUN 1884 R	19	075
Fraile, Manuel	Gahagan, Mary A.	12 APR 1885	20	158
Frailer, Mary R.	Dickas, George H.	20 FEB 1884 L	18	434
Frailey, Robert T.	Prather, Beatrice	01 JUL 1885 R	20	302
Fraim, Sarah	Cole, William	20 APR 1881	15	263
Frain, John N.	McLaughlin, Mary J.	24 JUN 1881 R	15	377
Frain, Michael	Mullin, Mary	05 MAY 1879 R	13	173
Frain, Sallie	Shay, William	04 MAR 1882 L	16	267
Frain, Sarah	Cole, William	12 MAY 1881 R	21	5027
Fran, William	Young, M.	24 MAY 1883	17	462
Franc, Louis	Hollander, Lena	24 SEP 1879 R	13	383
France, Augusta Bertha	Koehler, William F.	25 JUN 1885 R	20	293
France, Eveline	Dent, Thomas I.	05 MAR 1881 L	15	215
France, Florence Ida	Collamer, Warren I.	21 JAN 1880	14	116
France, Rebecca	Howard, James Albert	10 APR 1881 R	15	252
Frances, Annie E.	Barister, W.L.	18 AUG 1881 R	22	5304
Francis, Charles	Allen, Anna	10 NOV 1880 L	15	042
Francis, George W.C.	Shaw, Louisa	14 AUG 1883	18	087
Francis, Henry E.	Marshall, Katie E.	01 MAR 1880	14	169
Francis, Jennie	Davis, James	14 JUL 1884	19	136
Francis, John Richard, Dr.	Cox, Bettie Govanni	28 DEC 1881 R	16	164
Francis, Martha E.	Suit, Charles J.	21 JUN 1883	18	008
Francis, Mary Ann	Williams, Frank	07 JUL 1882 R	16	362
Francis, Mary L.	Anderson, Richard H.T.	07 MAY 1885 R	20	210
Francis, Matilda	Snowden, Richard	02 JAN 1883 R	17	223
Francis, Nannie M.	Bootwright, Orlando A.	31 DEC 1884	19	508
Francis, Sarah Elizabeth	Brown, John R.	20 SEP 1883 R	18	143
Frank, Abraham D.	Hart, Pauline	01 DEC 1880 R	15	072
Frank, Benjamin	Kaufman, Bertha C.	14 OCT 1885 R	20	477
Frank, Cornelius A.	Owens, Mary	05 AUG 1885	20	356
Frank, Ferdinand	Rosenberg, Emma	28 FEB 1883 R	17	321
Frank, Jacob B.	Cotter, Mary C.	24 JAN 1882 R	16	207
Frank, Katie	Alsop, Thaddeus	03 AUG 1879	13	304
Frank, Kunigimda	Federwisch, H. Louis	03 NOV 1877 L	11	166

Name	Spouse	Date	Vol	Page
Frank, Lena M.	Hiller, John	17 JUN 1881 R	15	324
Frank, Mary A.	Miller, James M.	30 NOV 1878 R	12	356
Frank, Mary Selina	Towner, Oscar T.	15 NOV 1881 R	16	075
Frank, William B.	Berry, Charlotte	13 DEC 1883	18	313
Frankel, Andreas	Leonberger, Hannah M.	23 JUN 1880 R	14	329
Frankel, Friederika	Kurtz, Lewis	25 MAY 1878 L	12	066
Frankland, Emma M.	Amos, James T.	31 JAN 1879 R	13	040
Franklin, Benjamin	Warren, Ada	24 AUG 1878	12	178
Franklin, Benjamin	Foster, Irene	08 OCT 1881 R	16	015
Franklin, Benjamin	Cooper, Mary Jane	03 JUL 1882 L	16	437
Franklin, Clara B.	Franklin, Harry C.	15 AUG 1881 R	15	443
Franklin, Elizabeth	Diggs, Hannibal	01 AUG 1885 L	20	347
Franklin, George W.	Bell, Susan A.	15 MAY 1884 L	19	023
Franklin, Harry C.	Franklin, Clara B.	15 AUG 1881 R	15	443
Franklin, J. Chauncey	Reardon, Agnes B.	15 JUN 1885 L	20	275
Franklin, James	Ross, Fanny	15 DEC 1877 R	11	238
Franklin, Jeannie Wood	Wilson, Whitwell H.	17 AUG 1882 R	16	486
Franklin, John	Humphreys, Martha	16 JUL 1885 L	20	329
Franklin, Rachel	Taplett, John	02 FEB 1881 L	15	174
Franklin, Rebecca S.	Eberle, Frank	05 APR 1883 L	17	381
Franklin, Rosabella M.J.	Payne, William L.	10 JAN 1880 L	14	099
Franklin, Samuel R.	Dutton, Maria S.	10 JAN 1883	17	244
Franklin, William	Rhodes, Lena	30 JUL 1884	19	162
Franks, Julia Ann	Walker, Stephen Miller	16 DEC 1880 R	15	103
Franks, W.E.D.	Dorn, Barbara	05 APR 1883	17	383
Franz, Ernestine	Schmidt, August	02 APR 1882 R	16	290
Fraser, Annie P.	Hull, John D., Rev.	27 NOV 1879 R	14	016
Fraser, Charles E.	Anderson, Georgie	25 OCT 1883 R	18	212
Fraser, Ella May	Drew, George J.	28 OCT 1884	19	342
Fraser, Lillie P.	Barnes, Joseph E.	10 MAY 1881 R	15	299
Fraser, M. Agnes	Reeves, James C.	16 SEP 1885	20	422
Fraser, Sarah E.	Henry, Wm. Daingerfield	25 JUN 1884 R	19	101
Frasier, Edgar D.	Cross, H. Emma	19 APR 1882 R	16	325
Frawley, Mary Ann	Downey, Jeremiah Francis	11 JUN 1881 L	15	355
Frawly, James	Corrigan, Ann	01 SEP 1878 R	12	181
Frayser, John	O'Laughlin, Bridget	13 JUL 1883 L	18	046
Frazer, Hamilton	Chase, Martha	02 AUG 1884	19	165
Frazer, Lucinda	Dyson, John F.	29 DEC 1881 R	16	168
Frazier, Adah S.	Torrey, William A.	25 NOV 1879 R	14	002
Frazier, Alexander	Barnes, Winnie A.	03 JUN 1880	14	302
Frazier, Arthur F.	Robinson, Ida V.	20 MAR 1883 R	17	352
Frazier, Ben	Allen, Maria	21 AUG 1877	11	060
Frazier, Beverly	Butler, Caroline	30 AUG 1884 R	18	130
Frazier, Charles	Cole, Martha	18 JUL 1880 L	14	367
Frazier, Fannie M.	Britt, G.S.	21 FEB 1880	14	162
Frazier, Fanny	Smith, Robert	29 JUL 1884	19	162
Frazier, Georgianna	Hawkins, Peter	31 MAR 1881 L	15	243
Frazier, Harriet	Street, Walter	19 MAY 1881 L	15	318
Frazier, J. Arthur	Thomas, Christine Elise	27 OCT 1881 R	16	045
Frazier, Katie	Buchanan, Albert	22 JUN 1880 R	14	331
Frazier, Lewis	Moore, Rosa	16 DEC 1878 L	12	382
Frazier, Mary	Cloyd, Albert	11 SEP 1882	17	016
Frazier, McHenry Grafton	Moon, Florence	13 JUN 1885 R	20	272
Frazier, Samuel L.	Whiting, Amelia Ann	13 JUN 1882 R	16	343
Frazier, William Henry	Thompson, Bertha	28 JUL 1881 L	15	422
Fred, Mathilda	Lecomte, Alfred	10 MAY 1882 R	16	353
Frederich, Leon L., M.D.	Joost, Fanny Genevieve	05 APR 1881 R	15	246
Frederick, Julia Ann	Robertson, John Walter	10 OCT 1880 R	14	484

Fredick, Amasa C.	Stewart, Sarah E.	19 OCT 1881 R	16	033
Fredrick, Mary Agnes	Brown, Arthur	01 JAN 1884	18	338
Free, Robert	Barnes, Susie	14 MAY 1881 L	15	306
Free, William F.	Cassidy, Fannie	08 JUN 1884	19	128
Freeburger, Peter V.	Brooks, Ellen N.C.	23 JUL 1882 R	16	450
Freedman, Charles	Rietmüller, Lizzie	31 DEC 1878 R	12	409
Freeland, Roberta A.	Cameron, Shelton T.	16 AUG 1883 L	18	091
Freeman, Anne	Lyles, Milton	15 JAN 1878	11	303
Freeman, Benj.	Burnham, Emma	20 JUN 1881 R	15	366
Freeman, Charles	Wheeler, Ella	02 MAR 1881 L	15	211
Freeman, Columbus	Brown, Addell	09 DEC 1880 R	15	088
Freeman, Delila	Bundy, James F.	05 JUN 1884	19	062
Freeman, Emma	Johnson, Benjamin F.	09 SEP 1885 R	20	407
Freeman, Frank	Straub, Maggie	30 SEP 1879 L	13	393
Freeman, J.R.	Weaver, Marie Ellen	26 NOV 1879	14	015
Freeman, Jannie	Brown, Waite E.	03 DEC 1884 L	19	433
Freeman, John	Davis, Lucinda	30 JUN 1879 R	13	241
Freeman, John	Bechold, Christiana	26 DEC 1879 L	14	076
Freeman, Julia Ann	Miller, Thomas	17 DEC 1879	14	054
Freeman, Malinda Jane	Broadway, Richard R.	15 AUG 1877 L	11	054
Freeman, Martha	Johnson, George Allen	06 SEP 1883 R	18	114
Freeman, Mary Teresa	Norton, A. Howard	08 DEC 1879 L	14	033
Freeman, Nancy	Brown, Charles	03 APR 1880 L	14	206
Freeman, Rachel T.	Alston, Philip C.	08 NOV 1877	11	172
Freeman, Reah	Lancaster, Isaih	16 DEC 1880 L	15	104
Freeman, Thomas	Wallace, Sarah	17 OCT 1883 L	18	198
Freeman, Wm. Spencer	Washington, Mary F.	22 APR 1885 R	20	093
Freer, Emma Jane, Mrs.	Holder, Joseph	23 OCT 1884 R	19	331
Freirick, Clara	Marx, Marx	07 MAY 1882 R	16	349
Freitag, Gertrude M.	Herbert, Charles C.	15 NOV 1882 R	17	127
Fremont, George W.	Penn, Jennie	17 OCT 1885	20	483
Fremont, James	Jackson, Lucy	08 OCT 1877 R	11	124
French, Adah B.	Sauer, Charles L.	05 MAY 1880 R	14	254
French, Amanda	Parham, John	15 JUL 1885 R	20	325
French, Clarence E.	McLaughlin, Lida A.	04 JUN 1884 R	19	057
French, Dorathea B.	Power, Robert H., Dr.	17 AUG 1881 R	15	449
French, Edith	LePreux, Manning	14 AUG 1884	19	186
French, Edward E.	Washington, Elmira	24 AUG 1881 R	15	457
French, Fannie M.	Kirby, Samuel G., Jr.	10 OCT 1882 R	17	060
French, Fannie V.	Everett, William K.	26 AUG 1880 R	14	418
French, Fitzhugh	Webster, Mannie	11 AUG 1882 L	16	476
French, Frances M.	Young, Arthur	02 JUL 1879 R	13	262
French, George	Horner, Maggie A.	07 FEB 1879	13	050
French, George Norris	Hamblin, Isabella Gray	19 SEP 1877 R	11	099
French, Georgia J.	Brotherton, Isaac B.	09 MAY 1878 L	12	046
French, Henrietta	Tibbs, William A.	19 JUN 1885	20	280
French, James W.	Price, Mollie B.	31 OCT 1883 R	18	224
French, John M.	Holland, Florence D.	15 OCT 1884 R	19	293
French, Lizzie	Brown, Mitchell	29 DEC 1884 R	19	498
French, Mary	Patten, John W.	26 MAY 1880 R	14	286
French, Mary E.	Ryan, Thomas F.	13 OCT 1881 L	16	023
French, William B.	Babson, Mary Winnifred	05 NOV 1877	11	168
French, William E.P.	Ogilvie, Marion J.	03 MAR 1880	14	176
Frere, Frances	Bucklin, John E.	26 DEC 1878 R	12	404
Frere, Mary Theresa	deThierry, Alphonse, Vis.	10 NOV 1884 L	19	369
Freudenberger, Catherine	Treiber, Ernst F.	29 AUG 1878 L	12	184
Freudenthal, Leonora Louise	Varnell, Thomas O.	09 NOV 1880	15	038
Freund, John	Freund, Maria Elizabeth	15 NOV 1877 L	11	187

Freund, Maria Elizabeth	Freund, John	15 NOV 1877 L	11	187
Frey, Isacac	Sleigh, Hannah Putnam	05 JUN 1883 R	17	474
Frey, Jacob	Moran, Elizabeth	31 DEC 1878 L	12	410
Frey, Levin Sothoron	Hall, Alberta Blanche	25 SEP 1878 R	12	235
Frey, Victor K.	Baker, A. Florence	12 MAR 1884	18	466
Fridley, B.F.	Hammond, Sarah M.	18 FEB 1878	11	344
Fridley, P.B.	White, Margaret Crawford	31 AUG 1878 L	12	190
Fridley, Sarah E.	Leesnitzer, Henry J.	26 NOV 1884	19	419
Fridley, William H.	Matlock, Josie F.	17 SEP 1878 R	12	221
Friederick, Friedrick Franz	Wahansen, Anna Maria	15 JUL 1883	18	046
Friedlander, Harry	Spanier, Sarah	22 JUL 1885 R	20	334
Friedmann, Fredrick	Hornischer, Sophia	30 OCT 1880	15	013
Friedrich, Ludolph H.	Van Sciver, Mary A. Courell	09 DEC 1880 R	15	090
Friedrich, Mary Elizabeth	Mills, Theodore A.	29 NOV 1877 R	11	210
Friel, Emily	Philp, Mansel B.	06 JUN 1880	14	306
Frieland, Mahala	Pendleton, John	09 MAY 1885 L	20	215
Frieman, John W.	Thurm, Auguste Louise Agnes	02 MAR 1880 R	14	159
Friendrick, Lottie	Minor, James	05 AUG 1885 L	20	356
Friess, Frederick W.	Riordan, Mary E.	23 DEC 1881 L	16	155
Friess, John Henry	Spence, Grace	13 SEP 1879 R	13	368
Friess, Katie C.	Ege, John F.	01 JAN 1882 R	16	171
Frigon, Louis T.	Saul, Frances E.	11 FEB 1879	13	052
Frilling, Johanna	Sieber, Frederick	09 AUG 1885 R	20	361
Frinks, Laura	Harrison, John	27 DEC 1882 R	17	211
Frisbie, Josephine	Holmes, Peter L.	06 MAR 1884 L	18	462
Frisby, Richard A.	Waites, Bessie	31 MAY 1885 R	20	248
Fritter, Dora	Cummings, Doctor	04 DEC 1883 L	18	295
Fritter, Lulu	Bloxton, James S.	15 APR 1880	14	225
Fritz, Katie	Weber, John	08 MAR 1883 R	17	338
Frizell, Andrew	Clemerson, Ella	12 APR 1879 R	13	138
Frizzell, Annie	Fletcher, Joseph	20 MAY 1879 R	13	198
Frizzell, Charles R.	Holt, Lottie M.	02 JAN 1883 R	17	232
Frizzell, George Henry	Dennis, Emma Frances	02 SEP 1885 R	20	395
Frizzell, Laura Virginia	Falvey, John H.	28 APR 1885 L	20	192
Frost, Charles A.	Winn, Elizabeth A.	13 AUG 1884	19	180
Frost, John W.	Keys, Julia A.	14 AUG 1879 R	13	320
Frost, Mary	Burr, Charles R.	23 OCT 1879 R	13	440
Frost, William H.	Stanard, Sallie	12 SEP 1878	12	218
Fry, Angelina	Wise, Hiram	13 AUG 1884	18	509
Fry, Annie E.D.	Jarboe, James A.	06 NOV 1879 R	13	464
Fry, Charles B.	Grayson, Nellie T.	15 JUL 1880	14	364
Fry, Dennis W.	White, Matilda	06 SEP 1883 R	18	115
Fry, Henry Davidson	Campbell, Gertrude May	20 FEB 1884 R	18	434
Fry, Ida L.	Richardson, William H.	25 JUN 1885	20	290
Fry, Mary Frances	Carroll, John Henry	30 JAN 1878	11	292
Fry, Robert	Johnson, Mary	15 MAR 1878	11	383
Fry, Samuel B.	Pfeil, Sophie M.	08 APR 1879 R	13	131
Fry, Sarah F.	Owen, George	27 SEP 1877 R	11	107
Fryatt, Henry Clay	Smith, Maggie Lee	22 MAY 1882 R	16	368
Frye, Elizabeth G.	Poffenberger, Martin L.	06 JUN 1883 R	17	480
Frye, Minnie	Coleman, Thomas Lewis	09 APR 1884 R	18	501
Fryling, Isabella	Edel, Hermann	26 FEB 1879 R	13	076
Fr[ ]hch, John	Abbott, Sarah E., Mrs.	29 OCT 1881 L	16	052
Fudge, Ida	Danison, Joseph E.	22 JAN 1880 R	14	118
Fuelling, William L.	Steiner, Lena	14 JUL 1880 R	14	360
Fuer, George	Garner, Sarah	09 DEC 1880	15	088
Fuersinger, Mary Louise	Scharr, George Gottlob	31 JUL 1879 R	13	301
Fugett, Ellen R.	Dean, William E.	29 MAY 1883	17	465

Fugitt, Eugene	Skinner, Miriam	18 JAN 1885	20	025
Fugitt, Lemuel	Woodfield, Sarah O.	30 NOV 1884	19	427
Fuller, A.M.	Weiner, William G.	20 JUL 1881 L	15	410
Fuller, Catherine	Jones, James	29 AUG 1881 L	15	464
Fuller, Charles F.	Gray, Ruth A.	11 APR 1883 R	17	387
Fuller, Harriet	Baldwin, Samuel	29 JUL 1878 L	12	150
Fuller, Helen	Johnson, Frank	06 SEP 1877 L	11	080
Fuller, Johanna	Sullivan, John	07 JUL 1883 L	18	039
Fuller, John J.	Sullivan, Nannie	31 DEC 1881 L	16	174
Fuller, Lizzie B.	Herrmann, Franz	02 DEC 1882 L	17	164
Fuller, Mary F.	Devers, George	20 DEC 1877	11	253
Fuller, Miles	Swing, Nora Maud	27 MAY 1884 R	19	039
Fuller, Minnie	Johnston, Robert	15 NOV 1881	16	076
Fuller, Minnie Harriet	Parker, Alfred Curtis	26 FEB 1885 R	20	087
Fuller, Ruth H.	Medford, William C.	28 SEP 1881	15	500
Fuller, Wilson Neville	Cathell, Margaret Jane	25 NOV 1880 R	15	063
Fuller, Wm. Henry	Craig, Alice	20 NOV 1879 R	13	491
Fullings, Frank Harrison	Love, Virginia Lillian	29 NOV 1882 R	17	158
Fulmer, John A.	Richardson, Nellie P.	30 APR 1884 R	18	540
Fulton, Charles C.	Driscoll, Caroline K., Mrs.	30 JUN 1879 R	13	394
Fulton, Clora Anne	Byram, John L.	24 JAN 1879 L	13	033
Fulton, Elizabeth	Saunders, John	08 JAN 1885 L	20	010
Fulton, Mary	Vanalstine, W.W.	09 OCT 1881	16	013
Fulton, William J.	Dorian, Annie R.	26 APR 1883	17	414
Funk, John J.	Davis, Josie E.	29 JAN 1885 R	20	042
Funtner, Samuel E.	Minniter, Lizzie C.	15 MAR 1880	14	185
Furlong, Emma	Pilkerton, Alexander	07 OCT 1879 L	13	407
Furlong, Irwin	Wren, Julia T.	04 AUG 1879	13	305
Furnald, Francis P.	Weed, Charlotte A.	07 MAY 1885 R	20	211
Furr, Charles E.	Anderson, Dora E.	21 FEB 1881 L	15	197
Furr, Eli C.	Tolliver, Alice V.	20 JUN 1878 L	12	106
Furrer, Jacob A.	Pfaumann, Laura E.	16 NOV 1879 R	13	486
Furse, Elizabeth J.C.	Chezum, James H.	18 SEP 1877 R	11	099
Furtner, James W.	Fogg, Virginia D.	18 OCT 1882 R	17	078
Fuse, Charles B.	Roche, Nellie B.	14 JUL 1877 L	11	020
Fuss, John A.	Grey, Annie P.	29 APR 1884 R	18	534

G

Gabriel, Elizabeth Ann	McCalman, Peter	14 AUG 1883 L	18	086
Gaddis, Adam	Trimble, Mary	12 JUN 1883 R	17	487
Gaddis, George H.	Beasley, Josephene	26 NOV 1878 R	12	346
Gade, Gustav Chr. Theod.	Heitmuller, Maria Ch. Ant.	19 JUN 1884 R	19	092
Gadsby, Mary Augusta	Lee, William	09 APR 1885 R	20	155
Gaegler, Barbara E.	Meintel, Joseph W.	22 DEC 1882 L	17	204
Gaegler, Rosa J.	Scott, R. Thomas	10 AUG 1882 L	16	476
Gaghan, John	McFaul, Anna	12 SEP 1883	18	128
Gahagan, Mary A.	Fraile, Manuel	12 APR 1885	20	158
Gaham, William T.	Davis, Sarah Jane	21 DEC 1881 R	16	146
Gahell, Henry	Scanlan, Kate	29 OCT 1883 L	18	221
Gahn, Henrick	Wilhelmina, Henriette	16 AUG 1884 L	19	189
Gailey, Annie	Kite, Thomas O.	31 MAY 1881	15	334
Gainer, Marsella	Regan, Edward	24 MAR 1883 L	17	358
Gaines, Annie	Wilkerson, Peter	29 APR 1880 R	14	244
Gaines, Annie	Bowie, Charles	10 FEB 1881 L	15	186
Gaines, Annie Elizabeth	Wells, Jacob R.	09 NOV 1882	17	120
Gaines, Edward	Childs, Mamie	14 JAN 1885 L	20	019
Gaines, Emma	Johnson, Edward	04 DEC 1884 R	19	436
Gaines, George	Shankland, Anna	06 MAR 1878	11	373
Gaines, Jennie A.	Simmons, Edward E.	14 JUL 1885 L	20	326
Gaines, John	Whiting, Susan	25 JUL 1880 R	14	295
Gaines, John S.	Green, Charity	28 APR 1879 L	13	161
Gaines, Margaret Catherine	Lawrence, Wayman C.	23 JUL 1884	19	152
Gaines, Sarah	Gross, Thomas	13 DEC 1883 L	18	315
Gaines, William	Burke, Catherine	30 JUL 1882 R	16	498
Gains, Frank	Quonn, Addie	27 JUN 1885 R	20	297
Gains, Richard	Morton, Jennie	28 APR 1880 R	14	240
Gaites, Mary	Busey, Alfred	03 MAY 1880 L	14	249
Gaither, George	Dodson, Mary	25 OCT 1883 L	18	218
Gaither, Harry	Smallwood, Sarah S.	24 DEC 1884 L	19	484
Gaither, Henry	Redd, Floretta	29 NOV 1882 L	17	159
Gaither, James B.	Brooks, Susannah V.	19 JUN 1879	13	238
Galaway, Annie	Gordon, Henry	04 OCT 1883 R	18	143
Galbraith, William John	Liddle, Mary Helen	05 NOV 1882 R	17	112
Gale, Thomas Monroe	Fisher, Ida May	24 JUN 1880 R	14	332
Gales, Amie Neoma	Hutchinson, Christopher T.	03 NOV 1882 R	17	109
Gales, Everett	Smith, Hattie	17 JAN 1885 L	20	024
Gales, Joseph	Burden, Louise E.	22 NOV 1877 L	11	199
Gales, Roberta	Beckett, Albert C.	13 SEP 1881	15	475
Galey, Benjamin	Ashton, Laura Ann	20 MAR 1879 R	13	104
Galey, Matilda	Fox, Joseph W.	17 AUG 1881 R	15	449
Gallagher, James	McGarvey, Ellen	25 FEB 1879 L	13	078
Gallagher, James	Reardon, Julia	11 JUN 1883 L	17	486
Gallagher, James	Stanton, Sophia	25 FEB 1884 L	18	441
Gallagher, John H.	Selby, Ida M.	29 NOV 1884	19	425
Gallagher, Kate	O'Donoghue, Martin J.	11 NOV 1879 R	13	475
Gallagher, Rosa	Lennon, John J.	13 MAY 1884 R	19	017
Gallagher, Timothy A.	McGarver, Margaret	03 DEC 1879 L	14	027
Gallagher, William T.	McIntire, Annie Laura	02 OCT 1877 R	11	116
Gallahan, Annie	Tayman, Zedock	21 OCT 1884	19	326
Gallaher, Edmond M.	Keeseman, Lillie B.	12 OCT 1885 L	20	476
Gallahorn, Mary Jane	Burriss, Reuben A.	08 MAR 1883 R	17	337
Galleher, William R.	Webb, Martha	19 NOV 1883	18	262
Galliher, Charles E.	Faunce, Jennie	15 NOV 1883 R	18	256
Gallivair, Bridget	O'Neill, Edward	18 AUG 1880 L	14	405
Gallivan, John	Bennett, Catherine E.	08 SEP 1879 L	13	358

Name	Spouse	Date		
Gallivan, John J.	Farnes, Mary	08 APR 1880 R	14	210
Gallivian, Maggie	Beaver, Charles H.	14 JUN 1881	15	360
Galloway, Basil P.	Red, Alice C.	28 DEC 1882	17	218
Galloway, John R.	Beagle, Ida M.	16 JAN 1879 R	13	020
Galloway, Thomas	Duckett, Rhoda	05 MAR 1883 L	17	332
Galloway, Thos. Franklin	Degges, Sophie Alice	29 JUN 1882 L	16	430
Galloway, Washington	Harper, Nancy	19 OCT 1885 L	20	496
Gally, Joseph E.	Williams, Caroline C.	04 DEC 1877	11	216
Galt, Frank	Beebe, Mary E.	19 SEP 1882 R	17	028
Galt, Marian Virginia	Elliott, Thomas Munroe	16 OCT 1877 R	11	138
Galt, Ralph Lee	Burton, Henrietta	21 APR 1885 R	20	177
Galt, Walter Allen	Britten, Belle	09 FEB 1884 R	18	417
Galvin, Barbara	Gill, Charles Frank	05 JUL 1883 R	18	037
Galway, Kate	Pinkwood, Emanuel	19 JUL 1877 R	11	027
Gambrell, Madora	Thompson, Frederick	08 JAN 1884	18	370
Gambrill, Mary M.	Bartholow, John B.	06 JUN 1882	16	395
Gamer, James E.	Tyler, Mary	14 MAY 1878 L	12	051
Gandy, Mary Bell	Wilson, Joshua J.	21 AUG 1884 L	19	201
Ganes, Annie	Barnes, Alfred	24 MAR 1884 L	18	479
Ganley, Kate A.	McGuire, John	07 JUL 1881	15	394
Gannaway, Thomas H.	Johnson, Alice	06 DEC 1883 L	18	304
Gannett, James	Brown, Emma	15 JAN 1883 L	17	258
Gannett, Lucy Gayton	Thompson, Niles Hibbard	05 DEC 1878 R	12	367
Gannon, Annie	Shillinglaw, James G.	05 AUG 1884 L	19	170
Gannon, Catherine	Horigan, Dennis	02 DEC 1882	17	163
Gant, Ambrose C.	Daly, Annie J.	14 JAN 1881 R	15	151
Gant, Ann	Sim, John Wesley	23 MAY 1885 L	20	236
Gant, Annie V.	Brown, Samuel	23 OCT 1879 R	13	440
Gant, Benjamin	Paine, Nannie	12 JUL 1880 L	14	358
Gant, Charles	Mackall, Phillis	11 NOV 1880	15	043
Gant, Charles B.	Ward, Mattie J.	28 DEC 1882 L	17	219
Gant, Daniel E.	Price, Alice	06 JUN 1878 R	12	089
Gant, Edward	Taylor, Rebecca	23 DEC 1884 L	19	481
Gant, Edward A., Jr.	Scott, Josephine	25 OCT 1882	17	091
Gant, Ellen	Slingerland, E.J.	15 AUG 1878	12	168
Gant, Frances Victoria	Campbell, William Alex. Lamb	21 AUG 1879 R	13	330
Gant, Frank	Lawson, Frances	04 SEP 1882 R	17	002
Gant, George	Johnson, Anna	15 MAY 1879 L	13	193
Gant, George	Stephenson, Annie	26 AUG 1879 L	13	337
Gant, George	Toy, Margaret	08 AUG 1883 L	18	080
Gant, George M.	Jac, Bertha	16 JAN 1882 L	16	195
Gant, George S.	Johnson, Eva	07 AUG 1879	13	312
Gant, James	Talliaferno, Delia	04 MAY 1880 L	14	252
Gant, James H.	Delaney, Anne M.	08 AUG 1878 L	12	161
Gant, James W.	Tolliver, Josie	30 DEC 1880 R	15	092
Gant, Joseph	Spriggs, Mary	20 OCT 1879 R	13	425
Gant, Louisa	Belt, George W.	24 JAN 1884 L	18	393
Gant, Mary	Holmes, James H.	25 DEC 1883	18	296
Gant, Mary Ann	Crowley, Horace	02 AUG 1883 L	18	070
Gant, Mary Anne	Smith, Edward	07 OCT 1878	12	255
Gant, Mary C.	White, Abner	25 FEB 1879 L	13	080
Gant, Mary E.	Humphreys, George	31 JUL 1884 L	19	164
Gant, Mary Jane	Guilom, Samuel	07 OCT 1878 L	12	258
Gant, Paul	Smothers, Kitty	09 AUG 1877 R	11	047
Gant, Rezin	Coleman, Margaret	05 SEP 1882 R	16	484
Gant, Sarah	Spriggs, Peter	01 JAN 1884 R	18	223
Gant, Thomas	Davis, Celia	17 OCT 1878 L	12	281
Gant, Willis	Scott, Harriet	03 MAR 1880 L	14	173

Gantt, Agnes	Nevet, William	07 JUL 1884	19	125
Gantt, Celestin	Crawford, Joseph O.	17 APR 1884 L	18	518
Gantt, Edward	Harden, Mary Frances	06 FEB 1879 R	13	048
Gantt, Edward L.	Tadoldi, Mary A.	29 JAN 1880 R	14	126
Gantt, Frederick R.	Vowles, Annie A.	21 FEB 1881 L	15	197
Gantt, Helen Mary	Harbaugh, George Hastings	11 FEB 1880 R	14	148
Gantt, John Wesley	Brown, Jane	27 MAR 1883 L	17	362
Gantt, Susan	Jordan, Cherry	04 DEC 1877 L	11	219
Ganzhoon, Lizzie	Smith, George	11 DEC 1883	18	309
Ganzhorn, George P.	Zeller, Margaret D.	03 FEB 1884 R	18	405
Garber, Josephine J.	Black, James A.	15 SEP 1885	20	415
Garden, Peter G.	Soper, Mary I.	03 OCT 1877	11	120
Gardener, Margaret	Robinson, John	01 JUL 1879 L	13	260
Gardener, Martha	Taylor, William	24 MAR 1884 L	18	480
Gardiner, Columbia R.	McMahon, John W.	24 JUL 1883	18	059
Gardiner, David	Craig, Mary	10 JUN 1882 L	16	403
Gardiner, Louisa M.	Anderson, Josephus	18 JAN 1883 R	17	265
Gardiner, Mary Alice	Jones, J. Moulton	07 JUL 1885	20	314
Gardner, Alexander	Johnson, Jennie	22 DEC 1881 L	16	149
Gardner, Alexander	Thomas, Nancy	14 NOV 1883	18	136
Gardner, C. Clinton	Kealey, Annie R.	08 AUG 1885 L	20	360
Gardner, Gussie B.	Montague, Benjamin F., Dr.	07 JUL 1879 L	13	273
Gardner, J. Anthony	Schoenecker, Josephine	31 DEC 1884	19	519
Gardner, Jacob	York, Jane	25 OCT 1882 L	17	094
Gardner, James R.	Mason, Carrie C.	28 APR 1885 L	20	194
Gardner, Jemima	Craig, David	24 JUL 1884 R	19	153
Gardner, Julius	Dawson, Georgeana	03 APR 1884 L	18	494
Gardner, Richard L.	Hichen, Mary E.	06 APR 1880 R	14	211
Gardner, Virginia C.	Harris, Alexander F.	06 DEC 1882	17	172
Gardner, William H.	Jones, Annie N.	13 OCT 1880 R	14	482
Gardner, William Henry	Lewis, Carrie Elizabeth	26 FEB 1880 R	14	163
Garey, Mary Jane	Hundley, James J.	04 NOV 1879 R	13	462
Garges, Abraham	Walde, Leona	31 OCT 1881	16	053
Garland, Hattie E.	Simpson, James C.	29 JAN 1883 L	17	276
Garland, James	Webb, Larica	24 MAY 1878	12	068
Garland, Peter W.	Davis, Sallie F.	31 DEC 1877	11	281
Garland, Rush M.	Bradley, Lulu M.	09 JUL 1884	19	130
Garland, Sanders	Henning, Anna M.	17 FEB 1885 R	20	073
Garmaroth, Kitty Louise	Hoaglan, J. Henry	24 NOV 1877 L	11	202
Garmeroth, Caroline	Pachmayer, John M.	17 DEC 1878 R	12	379
Garner, Agnes V.	Lawson, John E.	24 FEB 1881 R	15	202
Garner, Betsy	Carr, Henry	04 NOV 1880	15	030
Garner, Effie G.	Lawson, J. William	19 DEC 1883 L	18	326
Garner, Emily F.	Ashton, Gurden C.	28 JUL 1878 R	12	149
Garner, Hannah M.	Hutchins, Rosser D.	23 OCT 1884 R	19	331
Garner, Harry	Messiah, Martha	20 DEC 1880	15	111
Garner, Henry	Williams, Henrietta	05 OCT 1877 R	11	123
Garner, Ignatius	Butler, Jennie	14 SEP 1882 L	17	021
Garner, Jeanette E.	Ferguson, William A.	17 JUL 1881 R	15	405
Garner, John L.	Duley, Louisa R.	21 DEC 1881 R	16	125
Garner, John W.	Jones, Marian	20 APR 1880	14	227
Garner, Julia	Lyles, Ledger Benjamin	29 MAY 1879	13	195
Garner, Lafayette J.	Thomas, Annie C.	07 JUL 1880	14	351
Garner, Lillie V.	Henderson, William G.	03 AUG 1880 L	14	385
Garner, Mary Alice	Duckett, James	14 MAY 1879 R	13	189
Garner, Minnie Ann	Adair, Joseph	04 AUG 1880 R	14	387
Garner, Mollie F.	Fisher, Robert B.	13 MAY 1880 R	14	269
Garner, Moten	Mueller, Heinrich, Jr.	02 MAR 1884 R	18	453
	Williams, Mary			

Garner, Nellie	Lawson, Albert	10 JAN 1881 L	15	145
Garner, Noah	Weaver, Sarah Ann	30 JUL 1884	19	163
Garner, Sarah	Fuer, George	09 DEC 1880	15	088
Garner, Stephen G.	Ollifer, Sarah Louisa	18 DEC 1877 R	11	240
Garner, Thomas	Cartwright, Celestine	15 JAN 1884 L	18	379
Garner, Thomas A.	Green, Clara H.	05 FEB 1885 R	20	054
Garner, William	Peyser, Sarah	01 FEB 1885 R	20	044
Garner, William E.	Weaver, Jennie A.	10 APR 1878	11	414
Garner, William F.	Biddle, Marcia H.	16 MAR 1879 R	13	100
Garnet, Emma Lee	Weems, Thomas	19 MAR 1883	17	351
Garnett, Catherine	Dennis, William G.	29 NOV 1882 R	17	155
Garnett, Celia	Clark, James	14 DEC 1882 R	17	183
Garnett, Charles	Johnson, Malinda	01 MAR 1882 L	16	262
Garnett, Eliza	Bowie, Isaac	18 SEP 1883 R	18	135
Garnett, George L.	Lyon, Celestia G.	08 AUG 1882 R	16	472
Garnett, Gracie	Brown, Benjamin	25 SEP 1879 L	13	386
Garnett, James	Young, Martha Jane	26 OCT 1882	17	096
Garnett, John Henry	Bradley, Eliza	03 MAR 1880 L	14	173
Garnett, Leanna	Boone, Jacob	26 JUL 1877 L	11	032
Garnett, May L.	Hamilton, J.W.	06 NOV 1884	19	367
Garnett, Riter Case	Spindle, Susan Marcella	12 DEC 1881 R	16	126
Garnett, Sophia L. [Turner]	Kilroy, John	11 DEC 1884 R	19	439
Garrett, Carrie E.	Johnston, George M.	19 SEP 1883 R	18	142
Garrett, Charles	Barfoot, Cassa	02 JAN 1882 R	16	175
Garrett, Cornelia A.	Sparshott, Frank C.	17 JAN 1883	17	264
Garrett, Corra	Figgins, Enoch	31 OCT 1884	19	353
Garrett, David T.	Donohue, Janey T.	02 AUG 1884 L	19	166
Garrett, Frank	Boroughs, Rosa	16 JAN 1879	13	024
Garrett, James	Cockerill, Mollie	09 JUN 1881 R	15	355
Garrett, Jesse L.	McCullough, Ruth Buckley	09 JAN 1881 R	15	145
Garrett, Katie	Rupp, John N.	07 JUN 1881 L	15	348
Garrett, Laura V.	Mothersead, Charles C.	31 JUL 1879 R	13	302
Garrison, George Edward	Lacey, Carrie Virginia	14 APR 1884 R	18	506
Garrison, John S.	Boyden, Annie T.	13 OCT 1877 R	11	133
Garrison, Laura Virginia	Seaton, Hiram	12 JUN 1878 L	12	097
Garrison, Martha C.	Rains, William R.	06 MAY 1883	17	430
Garrison, Mary Emma	Randolph, Henry	15 JAN 1879	13	019
Garrison, Mary M.	Ames, John Thomas	21 MAR 1878 R	11	309
Garrison, Nettie	Sion, John H.	23 SEP 1885	20	436
Garrison, Sarah Elizabeth	Beach, Wm. Calvin McDaniel	30 JAN 1884 R	18	401
Garrison, Virginia	Moran, John W.	20 JUL 1881 R	15	409
Garrity, William J.	Emrich, Appolonia	17 FEB 1885 L	20	074
Garrrison, John	Simons, Bettie Lewis	12 JUL 1881 R	15	399
Gartnell, Fannie Israel	Israel, George Robert	19 JUN 1883	18	002
Gartrell, Annie J.	Howard, Joseph W.	04 NOV 1879 R	13	461
Gartrell, Blanche	Dietz, Philip	30 SEP 1884 R	19	273
Gartrell, Ella Harkness	Stokes, George W.R.	20 DEC 1883	18	328
Garvey, Mary	Jelka, Anthony F.	12 AUG 1880 L	14	398
Garvin, Joseph M.	Burket, Alice Mary	18 DEC 1878 R	12	387
Garvin, Madison A.	Smoot, Emma L.	27 JAN 1880 L	14	123
Garvitt, J.W.	Flood, Martha S.	09 MAR 1885	20	100
Gary, James	Williams, Annie	21 JUN 1879 R	13	242
Gary, Robert Lee	Larrabee, Bertha E.L.	26 JUN 1884 R	19	104
Gasaway, Henrietta	Lomax, Henry	12 JUL 1883 L	18	045
Gasch, Lissetta M.	Kolb, Charles A.	18 JUN 1884 R	19	089
Gascon, Mary	Butler, William D.	10 SEP 1878 L	12	210
Gaskin, Caroline	Terrill, David B.	07 MAR 1879 L	13	094
Gaskin, Frances	Newton, Marshall	25 JUL 1885 L	20	340

D.C. Marriage Records Index, June 28, 1877 to October 19, 1885

Name	Spouse	Date	Vol	Page
Gaskins, Arthur	Hamilton, Mary Ellen	19 JUN 1879	13	237
Gaskins, Charles H.	Mullin, Mollie M.	12 OCT 1880 R	14	487
Gaskins, Elizabeth	Twine, John	10 NOV 1879	13	473
Gaskins, James	Allen, Hester	02 AUG 1877	11	030
Gaskins, Jane	Berry, John Crusen	27 MAR 1885 R	20	135
Gaskins, Mary A.	Turner, Charles H.	30 OCT 1884 R	19	350
Gaskins, Mollie	Taylor, Edward	11 JAN 1878 R	11	287
Gaskins, Moses	Johnson, Leanna	15 MAR 1880 L	14	185
Gaskins, Nancy	Harris, Robert	22 MAY 1878	12	063
Gaskins, Randolph	Carter, Fannie	03 NOV 1881 R	16	054
Gaskins, Samuel A.	Collins, Ada Genevieve	13 JUN 1883 L	17	490
Gaskins, Sarah Virginia	Lee, Herbert	10 JUL 1884	19	130
Gaskins, Susannah	Green, Samuel	05 FEB 1885 L	20	055
Gaskins, Susie E.	Jefferson, John L.[4]	08 MAR 1884 R	18	463
Gaskins, Tom	Churchwell, Mary Ann	03 NOV 1879 L	13	459
Gaskins, William	Jones, Isabella	24 JUN 1885 R	20	284
Gass, Frederick William	Norriss, Mary Jane	19 JUN 1879	13	240
Gass, Georgeanna D.	Skinner, Thomas E.	08 APR 1884	18	501
Gass, Henry	Dibble, Emma	04 NOV 1880	15	032
Gassaway, Julia Ann	Williams, William	31 MAR 1881	15	243
Gassaway, Richard	Payne, Emma	06 OCT 1880	14	470
Gassaway, Richard	Adams, Henrietta	27 APR 1883 L	17	418
Gassaway, Sarah	Lawson, Mark F.E.	19 JUN 1884 R	19	091
Gassenheimer, Bertha	Hechinger, Jonas	18 OCT 1884 L	19	318
Gassmann, Elizabeth Diana, Mrs.	Rickes, Lorenz	07 JAN 1883 R	17	239
Gastoll, Mary C.	Spencer, Charles	05 JUN 1880 L	14	305
Gaston, Isabella	Clements, Francis M.	22 DEC 1884	19	476
Gaston, Matilda	Carter, Armstead	02 OCT 1883 L	18	165
Gasway, Annie	Crusoe, Frank R.	20 DEC 1882 R	17	197
Gatehell, Addie	Street, Daniel B.	22 JUL 1885	20	335
Gately, Mary Jane	Kellerman, John	13 APR 1885 L	20	161
Gately, Patrick	Kiernan, Elizabeth	27 JUL 1884	19	158
Gater, William	Miner, Patsy	17 MAR 1879 L	13	105
Gates, Andrew M.	Canter, Florence V.	15 OCT 1885 R	20	486
Gates, Anne V.	Harry, William C.	16 OCT 1884 L	19	310
Gates, Fanny	Leypoldt, Christopher	29 DEC 1877 L	11	279
Gates, Florence Virginia	Hardester, John Thomas	16 FEB 1880 R	14	154
Gates, George W.	Musgrove, Ella M.	12 DEC 1880 R	15	092
Gates, Mary	Ford, John	04 JUL 1883	17	435
Gates, Mary C.	Lee, Thacker E.	23 JUL 1883	18	057
Gates, Richard	Blunt, Mary Virginia	18 DEC 1878 R	12	381
Gates, Walter N.	Pritchard, Jessie R.	15 SEP 1885 R	20	419
Gatewood, James W.	Patterson, Ida Minetta	05 APR 1883 R	17	378
Gatewood, Richard	Bryan, Frances Heiskell	13 SEP 1881 R	15	480
Gatten, Henry	Faulkner, Ida M.	20 NOV 1883 R	18	264
Gatto, Joseph	Ronz, Johanna	16 MAR 1879 R	13	095
Gatton, Ada	Warner, James J.	02 MAY 1881 L	15	288
Gauges, Robert	Davis, Josephine	05 SEP 1877 L	11	077
Gauss, Samuel	Gusdorf, Ida	15 MAR 1885 R	20	113
Gaver, Henry	Love, Hannah A.	13 NOV 1879 R	13	483
Gavit, Allen	Miner, Jennie	19 APR 1884 R	18	519
Gavoin, Margaret	Noonan, Matthias	26 NOV 1881 L	16	099
Gawler, Albert H.	Gihon, Maggie	25 MAR 1878 L	11	392
Gay, Hattie	Matthews, Charles	30 APR 1884 L	18	545
Gay, James W.	Hauthman, Lucy	19 NOV 1884 L	19	396
Gayle, Edward E.	Aynes, Mary B.	09 MAR 1881	15	221

[4]This return #8,989, for a marriage performed 8 MAR 1884, is found bound amidst returns of early 1886.

Name	Spouse	Date	Vol	Page
Geare, Randolph	Cooper, Mary Julia	28 FEB 1881	15	208
Geary, Elizabeth C.	Burch, Joseph O.	27 NOV 1878 R	12	352
Geary, Margaret J.	May, Edward L.	18 MAY 1879	13	194
Gebhard, George	Davis, Laura	18 JUN 1878 R	12	101
Geckel, Peter	Smith, Addie C.	07 APR 1879	13	129
Geddes, Jane	Scott, John	29 NOV 1877 R	11	209
Geddes, Maggie	Leitch, Alexander Archibald	20 OCT 1879 R	13	433
Gedney, Charles Deforest	Wasney, J. Catherine	05 FEB 1881 R	15	178
Gedney, Susie Ada	Cowie, Thomas J., U.S.N.	15 FEB 1881 R	15	189
Gee, David	Johnson, Mary	09 OCT 1884 L	19	298
Gee, Samuel P.	Morehouse, Mary J. White	28 SEP 1882 R	16	495
Gees, Richard H.	Mansfield, Emma C.	10 MAY 1879 R	13	184
Geese, Edward	Davis, Annie E.	26 OCT 1882 R	17	095
Geesy, Jainey	Byes, Jacob	05 SEP 1881 L	15	471
Gehr, Lou A.	Mittag, Thomas E.	03 JUN 1881 R	15	342
Geier, Annie	Kuhlman, Fredrick	18 SEP 1881	15	489
Geier, Bernard J.	Murphy, Annie	19 SEP 1882 L	17	028
Geier, Mary	Hohmann, Henry	27 NOV 1880 L	15	070
Geiger, Babette	Schmidt, Robert	19 JUN 1879 L	13	241
Geigger, Mory	Gundling, Frederick	05 SEP 1878 L	12	200
Geisendaffer, Lucy M.	Martin, George E.	22 DEC 1884 R	19	482
Genella, William B.	McNerhany, Emily L.	03 DEC 1879 R	14	023
Genesse, Peter	Hallinen, Sarah	24 NOV 1884	19	365
Genet, Louis Franklin F.	Cooper, Callie Thatcher, Mrs.	14 SEP 1881 R	15	482
Gennori, Joseph	Schleucher, Mary	08 AUG 1885 R	20	359
Gensslen, Virginia E.	Burger, Peter	03 APR 1884	19	275
Gentner, Mary B.	Newman, George J.	15 JAN 1884 R	18	377
Gentner, Mary Virginia	Schmid, Alexander	05 AUG 1885 R	20	357
George, Bessie C.	Hill, William Wallace	08 JUN 1880 R	14	309
George, Charles Andrew	Simmes, Mary Elizabeth	24 MAY 1882 L	16	374
George, Charles Peaslee, Lt.	Graham, Jennie Piercy	08 NOV 1883 R	18	241
George, John E.	Virts, Orra B.	13 DEC 1877	11	233
George, Nettie E.	Lyons, John	31 DEC 1884 L	19	512
George, Wilbur F.	Cooke, Ella S.	07 JUN 1882 R	16	395
Georges, Louise	O'Hare, Edward	03 JUN 1885	20	247
Georgii, Eugenia Anna Frederika	Petersen, Christian Fred. Peter	01 MAR 1883 L	17	328
Gephart, Jackson	Eastwood, Sallie	19 FEB 1885 R	20	078
Geracci, Ignatius	Desio, Mary	19 OCT 1885 R	20	492
Gerah, George	Sprigs, Clara	27 NOV 1878 L	12	350
Gerard, Sadie	Betz, Ernest	19 DEC 1882 L	17	195
Gerardi, Vincenigo	Lauria, Maria L.	22 NOV 1880 L	15	060
Gerhardt, Elizabeth	Farlor, William	27 AUG 1884	19	211
Gerhardt, Julius I.	Salzig, Katie P.	04 SEP 1881	15	470
Gerhardt, Pauline	Haltnorth, Otto	29 MAR 1880 R	14	202
Gerhold, Henry	Perks, Rosa	13 OCT 1881	16	013
Gerhold, John F.	Nolte, Mary L.	26 AUG 1879 R	13	336
Gering, John J.	Zanner, Margaret	28 NOV 1883	18	280
German, Emma J.	Romain, Arthur	21 SEP 1877 L	11	104
German, Samuel	Ballauf, Minnie	12 JAN 1881	15	148
German, William G.	Thompson, Clara B.	27 JUN 1883	18	017
Germann, Daniel M.	Hunt, Mattie V.	28 MAY 1878	12	072
Germann, Wm. Henry	Emmert, Anna M.W.	29 JAN 1885 R	20	043
Germeroth, Annie	Thuringer, Joseph F.	20 DEC 1883	18	329
Germeroth, Christian	Cox, Mary Ann	08 JUN 1878 L	12	092
Germeroth, Mary	Johnson, Edward	19 MAR 1883 R	17	339
Germon, Belle	Coleman, William H.	11 JAN 1882 L	16	190
Germond, Laura V.	McLean, George H.	01 SEP 1877 R	11	073
Germuiller, Julius	Lohman, Christina	27 JAN 1885 L	20	039

Name	Spouse	Date	Vol	Page
Gerry, Fanny	Waters, John T.	12 JUL 1881 R	15	388
Gersdorff, Charles A.	Spiess, Marie L.	05 AUG 1884	19	165
Gertman, Caroline	Conrad, George	30 AUG 1878	12	187
Gessford, George W.	Cornwell, Clara V.	23 NOV 1882	17	145
Gessford, Ida V.	McClure, William J.	30 OCT 1879 R	13	456
Gessford, Susie E.	Handy, Levin C.	17 NOV 1879 R	13	491
Gessford, William T.	Shepperson, Ida	21 AUG 1883	18	095
Gessner, John	Fitzgerald, Mary	23 NOV 1884	19	401
Getchell, Addison Cole	Coombs, Alice Leiby	03 NOV 1881 R	16	057
Gett, Clarence R.	Campbell, Mary A.	19 JUL 1884 L	19	146
Gettinger, James G.	McKenney, Mary J.	28 DEC 1882 R	17	220
Gettings, Mary E.	Meyer, Edward F.	20 MAY 1885	20	231
Getty, Caroline	Page, Washington Edw.	07 APR 1885 R	20	144
Getty, Robert Nelson	Colegate, Cornelia Thos.	14 OCT 1885 R	20	475
Gheen, Frederick	Coggins, I. Louise	17 APR 1884	18	518
Gheen, John S.	Roberts, Mary E.	06 MAY 1880 R	14	003
Ghiselli, Angeline	Giovannitti, Vincenzo	12 SEP 1883	18	126
Giacchetti, Joseph	Lohr, Julia M.	20 JUN 1887 R	15	366
Giardina, Francesca Pavola	Manchino, Rosario	10 NOV 1883 L	18	245
Giardino, Joseph	Conti, Antonina	20 JAN 1884	18	385
Gibb, Frederick Sommerfield	Bond, Gertrude B.	29 JUN 1881 R	15	382
Gibbins, Chas. Matthew	Jones, Alice Cornelia	09 OCT 1878	12	263
Gibbons, Ella P.	Hoskinson, George P.	17 JAN 1883 R	17	262
Gibbons, George Walter	Kookogey, Adah Naomi	01 JAN 1884 R	18	349
Gibbons, Maggie Virginia	Young, James Henry	08 APR 1878 R	11	410
Gibbons, Mary	Stanton, Thomas J.	26 NOV 1879 L	14	014
Gibbons, Mary E.	Proctor, Arthur B.	10 JUN 1885 R	20	266
Gibbons, Robert A.	Tinsley, Sarah E.	27 NOV 1878 L	12	349
Gibbons, Sarah Alice	Saunders, James Thornton	15 MAY 1881 R	15	308
Gibbons, W.P.	Ford, Mittie E.	04 OCT 1882 L	17	054
Gibbs, Aaron	Rosher, Emma	03 JUL 1879 R	13	268
Gibbs, Ada Nettie	Osborn, Eugene Ernest	27 AUG 1879	13	338
Gibbs, Arthur	Harris, Sarah	22 NOV 1877 R	11	199
Gibbs, Catherine E., Mrs.	Stanton, Elias M., Rev.	07 SEP 1882 R	17	011
Gibbs, Charles E.	Thomas, Maggie E.	02 JAN 1879 R	13	002
Gibbs, Fannie L.	Carrington, Solomon M.	05 OCT 1882 R	17	052
Gibbs, Fanny	Parker, Jackson	24 DEC 1877	11	263
Gibbs, Isabel B.	Crandall, Charles P.	25 OCT 1883	18	215
Gibbs, James H.	Dawson, Mary M.	27 DEC 1883	18	346
Gibbs, John B.	Batchelor, Julia J.	28 JAN 1882 R	16	213
Gibbs, Lemuel	Addison, Annie	30 NOV 1879	14	011
Gibbs, Mary W.	Reynolds, James W.	17 SEP 1885	20	427
Gibbs, William Henry	Cavanaugh, Rosa	27 SEP 1877 R	11	106
Gibney, Elizabeth (Gardner)	Young, Charles E.	14 SEP 1885 R	20	414
Gibson, Alfred	Webb, Harriet	15 OCT 1883 R	18	194
Gibson, Alice	Plummer, Milton	03 OCT 1878 L	12	251
Gibson, Annie E.	Penn, James H.	05 SEP 1878 L	12	202
Gibson, Annie E.	Gibson, William B.	17 DEC 1883	18	318
Gibson, Caleb	Watson, Annie Eliza	20 MAY 1879 R	13	196
Gibson, David	Lawson, Ella	30 JAN 1878	11	322
Gibson, Elizabeth	Johnson, Thomas	27 MAY 1880	14	292
Gibson, Elizabeth	Scott, John Fortune	28 JUL 1881	15	424
Gibson, Emma	DeVeale, William	06 JAN 1880 R	14	091
Gibson, Esther	Curtis, James	12 OCT 1882 R	17	068
Gibson, Frances	Coleman, Jere	19 APR 1879 R	13	149
Gibson, George W.	Bowman, Josephine	27 SEP 1882 R	17	039
Gibson, Hattie E.	Smiles, James	14 NOV 1881 R	16	067
Gibson, Ida K.	Merrill, John B.	16 DEC 1880 R	15	101

Name	Spouse	Date	Vol	Page
Gibson, Ida May	Harvey, James F.	26 SEP 1878 R	12	239
Gibson, Jane	Mooney, William	11 JUN 1884 L	19	078
Gibson, John	Hart, Mary L.	03 JUL 1879 R	13	268
Gibson, John E.	White, Annie G.	06 MAR 1883 R	17	333
Gibson, John Henry	Handler, Annie Amelia	03 AUG 1885	20	349
Gibson, John J.	Cheseltine, Sarah M.	28 SEP 1882 R	17	043
Gibson, Joshua E.	Mead, Annie	20 MAY 1882 R	16	370
Gibson, Julia Ann	Smith, John Phillip	03 JUL 1878 R	12	122
Gibson, Laura V.	Keene, Herbert N.	25 OCT 1882	17	092
Gibson, Lizzie	Williams, Caleb	29 JAN 1878	11	318
Gibson, Louisa P.	Sands, Joseph R.	04 APR 1878 R	11	405
Gibson, Mamie Faulkner	Chesley, James Belt, Dr.	29 AUG 1883 R	18	099
Gibson, Martha Jane	Colbert, Wm. H.	11 JUL 1881 L	15	398
Gibson, Mary E.	Mahoney, Jackson S.	28 OCT 1880 R	15	018
Gibson, Matilda	Parker, Page	27 DEC 1877	11	278
Gibson, Matilda	Basey, Gabriel	04 DEC 1882 R	17	166
Gibson, Nancy Ann	Jardiner, Amos J.	18 AUG 1885 L	20	376
Gibson, Nannie	Shaw, William H.	07 NOV 1884	19	368
Gibson, Nicholas	Hall, Lydia	08 NOV 1880 L	15	035
Gibson, Pamelia M.J.	Johnson, Martin G.W.	08 JUN 1878 L	12	092
Gibson, Peter	Willett, Ellen	12 JUL 1879 R	13	279
Gibson, Sandy	Rex, Virginia	27 AUG 1885 L	20	390
Gibson, Thomas A.	Baptis, Mary E.	01 NOV 1882	17	105
Gibson, Thomas H.	Taylor, Winifred A.	23 MAY 1885 L	20	237
Gibson, Virginia C.	Dugan, William J.	01 MAY 1882	16	342
Gibson, Wesley	Cool, Betty	29 NOV 1877 R	09	2218
Gibson, William	Walker, Rosa	05 AUG 1880 R	14	388
Gibson, William B.	Gibson, Annie E.	17 DEC 1883	18	318
Gibson, William Henry	Crutchet, Emma	17 JAN 1883 R	17	262
Giddings, Elizabeth A.	Brown, William Edward	16 JAN 1879 R	13	022
Giddings, Mamie Anna	Thomas, Wm. Arthur	16 OCT 1885 R	20	489
Giddings, Martha A.	Collins, James M.	16 DEC 1879 L	14	051
Giddings, Rosa E.	McFarland, W.C.	12 NOV 1879 R	13	400
Giddings, William	Law, Laura Harding	13 JAN 1882	16	193
Giddings, William Virginius	Millar, Sallie Dunbar	06 JUN 1883 R	17	478
Gier, Lilly Elizabeth	Eslin, James William	16 SEP 1878 L	12	220
Giese, Francis J.	Oliver, Jennette B.	07 JUL 1881 L	15	393
Gieseke, August	Leebode, Lena	31 AUG 1878	12	189
Gieseke, Emilie	Smith, John F.	14 SEP 1880 R	14	443
Gieseking, Amelia H.	Naylor, Charles E.	14 APR 1885 R	20	163
Gieseking, Fredrick C.	Steinle, Rosa Bertha	12 FEB 1884 R	18	420
Giesler, Daniel	Hornisher, Theresia	19 OCT 1878	12	282
Giesler, Daniel	Engelke, Augusta	21 MAY 1882	16	370
Giesler, Julia	Kraemer, John	10 JAN 1883	17	248
Giesmar, Albert	Walton, Louisa	07 DEC 1884 L	12	371
Giessler, Augusta M.	Cole, Charles D.	02 OCT 1884 R	19	281
Gihon, Maggie	Gawler, Albert H.	25 MAR 1878 L	11	392
Gilam, Carrie	Hill, Lewis H.	23 AUG 1883	18	097
Gilbert, Caroline Saltillo	Offutt, Charles Alphonse	26 NOV 1884 R	19	417
Gilbert, Edith Estelle	King, William Bruce	29 JUN 1885 R	20	298
Gilbert, Frank	Detter, Isabella	25 JUN 1878	12	112
Gilbert, George	West, Laura	20 DEC 1877	11	253
Gilbert, Isaac	Porter, Jane	15 JAN 1879 L	13	018
Gilbert, James W.H.	Dade, Bettie Jane	07 FEB 1881 L	15	179
Gilbert, John W.	Lewis, Mary F.	10 MAR 1885 R	20	093
Gilbert, Lewis	Cook, Eliza	01 NOV 1883 R	18	228
Gilbert, Sadie H.	Bowman, William A.	20 SEP 1878 L	12	229
Gilbert, Sallie S.	Ketcham, Ellis M.	25 DEC 1884	19	487

D.C. Marriage Records Index, June 28, 1877 to October 19, 1885

Name	Spouse	Date	Vol	Page
Gilchrist, Annie E.	Terrill, Silas	07 JAN 1879 R	13	009
Gilchrist, Mary Harriett	Atchison, Eugene A.	29 APR 1880 R	14	242
Giles, Charles	Hamilton, Lizzie	06 SEP 1882 L	17	009
Giles, Edward	Ferguson, Nancy	24 DEC 1884 L	19	490
Giles, Elizabeth	Pocher, Simon	05 SEP 1878	12	199
Giles, Frances	Coleman, John	10 JUN 1885 L	20	267
Giles, George H.	Michler, Rebecca	14 FEB 1878	11	340
Giles, James H.	Johnson, Lucy Jane	19 MAR 1879 L	13	109
Giles, John M.	Lancaster, Sarah E.	05 NOV 1879 L	13	465
Giles, Julia	Butler, William	24 NOV 1883 L	18	275
Giles, Louisa	Coghill, John H.	23 JUN 1881	15	372
Giles, Mary C.	Beckett, Lemuel M.	05 NOV 1884 L	19	363
Giles, William	Rasor, Sarah	21 OCT 1882	17	084
Gilfeather, Michael	Collins, Sophia M.	16 JUN 1884	19	087
Gilfillan, May E.	Duvall, W. Clarence	18 OCT 1882 R	17	078
Gilkeson, Henry B.	Paxton, Mary C.	18 NOV 1884	19	390
Gill, Albert E.	Nash, Emma J.	30 JUL 1877 L	11	034
Gill, Bettie L.	Woodward, Charles W.	04 JUL 1881 R	15	387
Gill, Charles Frank	Galvin, Barbara	05 JUL 1883 R	18	037
Gill, DeLancey W.	Draper, Rose DeL.	25 MAY 1881	15	325
Gill, Elizabeth M.	Turpin, William B.	15 NOV 1883 L	18	259
Gill, Frances	Whiting, Allen	30 MAY 1881 R	15	331
Gill, Herbert A.	Smith, Monita Wederstradt	27 JUN 1882	16	429
Gill, John	Huth, Clara	23 MAY 1882	16	363
Gill, Joseph A.	Parker, Annie	19 JUL 1881 L	15	409
Gill, Laura V.	Richardson, William H.	08 APR 1878	11	411
Gill, Levi C.	Wilson, Augusta	05 FEB 1879 R	13	045
Gill, Mary Eliz.	Bates, Samuel Brown	20 DEC 1882 R	17	194
Gill, Mary Emma	Lung, Fred J.	08 JUN 1881 R	15	352
Gill, Mary Virginia	Metzgar, Charles Watson	11 APR 1883 R	17	390
Gill, Minnie	Belt, Benjamin	15 APR 1882	16	317
Gill, Nancy J.	Gordon, John H.	16 JUL 1883	18	047
Gill, Phillip	Brady, Margaret	13 FEB 1879 L	13	059
Gill, Stephen Fr., Jr.	Brown, Emma J.	24 SEP 1885 R	20	441
Gill, Theresa M.	Dimpfel, Fredrick Pierre, Jr.	25 OCT 1880 R	15	013
Gill, William	Berkeley, Mary Blanch	01 MAR 1885 R	20	090
Gillam, Richard	Teagle, Abelinda	21 MAY 1877	11	248
Gillbritzer, Mary E.	Wright, Charles E.	15 APR 1879 R	13	145
Gillem, Caroline St. Clair	McMillan, Alexander	16 JAN 1883	17	259
Gillem, Eliza	Wallace, Warren	08 OCT 1881	16	014
Gillem, Josephine	Washington, Alexander	07 FEB 1878 L	11	331
Gillen, John R.	Wood, Edna	30 NOV 1883 L	18	288
Gillespie, Andrew J.	May, Arcie A.	10 SEP 1884	19	238
Gillet, Talupher	Drummond, Samuel D.	08 MAY 1878 L	12	044
Gilliam, Lulu May	Hance, James H.	08 JUN 1885 L	20	261
Gilliard, Howard	Davis, Sarah	26 MAY 1884 R	19	338
Gilliland, James C.	McChesney, Alice V.	08 NOV 1883 L	18	242
Gillingham, Cora	Shenton, Raymond	05 DEC 1878 R	12	370
Gillingham, Henry R.	Morrice, Lizzie, Mrs.	30 SEP 1879 R	13	393
Gillis, Nancy	Boadley, Daniel	12 JUN 1879	13	229
Gillis, Narcissa J.	Shipley, John R.	27 FEB 1879 R	13	084
Gillison, Lanzy	Scroggins, Agnes	18 FEB 1880 R	14	148
Gillott, Joseph L.	Moore, Josaphene	18 DEC 1879	14	057
Gilis, Charles	Jones, Sally	22 JAN 1880 R	14	104
Gilluly, Annie Catherine	Kibble, Columbus	27 JAN 1881 L	15	168
Gillum, Mary A.	Greenlease, Joseph E.	11 DEC 1879 R	14	042
Gilman, Ida Mary	Hall, Orville D.	22 OCT 1879 R	13	437
Gilman, Julia	Tiffany, Walton Cuyler	09 APR 1879 R	13	132

Gilman, Laura V.	Norton, John T.	04 APR 1878	11	399
Gilman, Lucy C.	Coates, Willie P.	16 FEB 1885	20	070
Gilmore, George	Rosier, Mary	11 SEP 1879 R	13	364
Gilmore, Ida	Offutt, Henry	17 FEB 1885 R	20	073
Gilmore, James	Dutch, Louise	10 OCT 1884 L	19	299
Gilmore, Mary Leonard	McLeod, Edwin Markham	02 NOV 1882 R	17	107
Gilton, Doctor	Brokenborough, Rachel	19 DEC 1878 R	12	392
Gingell, Alice	Kirby, Thomas	07 JUL 1885 L	20	057
Gingell, Laura V.	Veirs, John H.	16 OCT 1883 L	18	196
Gingrich, Cyrus M., Dr.	Dowell, Lulah O.	04 JAN 1881 R	15	136
Ginnaty, James A.	Walsh, Mary L.	07 JUL 1877 L	11	012
Giovannitti, Vincenzo	Ghiselli, Angeline	12 SEP 1883	18	126
Gipson, Alfred	Johnson, Sarah	31 MAY 1881 R	15	333
Girard, Pasqual H.	Canabury, Mary	15 APR 1884 R	18	508
Gise, Ora	Fleming, Joseph S.	09 MAR 1885 L	20	100
Gist, Elmer E.	Matheney, Sarah E.	06 AUG 1885	20	359
Gist, George W.	Sloane, Mary S.	29 MAY 1878	12	076
Gittings, Jedidiah, Jr.	McClees, Sallie Endicott	27 OCT 1880 R	15	017
Gittings, Lottie	Hefft, John	18 JUL 1878 L	12	141
Gittings, Richard P.	Duckett, Harriet R.	30 OCT 1884 L	19	349
Gittings, William Edward	Naylor, Jane Elizabeth	09 JAN 1882 R	16	186
Gittings, Wm. Thos.	Lesher, Mollie J.	30 NOV 1884 R	19	425
Given, Emma	Griffith, William D.	01 JAN 1884	18	355
Givens, Annie	Young, Beverly	27 AUG 1879 L	13	339
Givens, Mary, Miss	King, William H.	25 APR 1885 L	20	188
Givens, Matilda	Allen, Thomas E.	14 NOV 1878 R	12	329
Givens, Susie A.	Beale, Allison F.	02 OCT 1879 R	13	401
Givins, Sarah Margaret	Dozer, Walter	13 MAR 1884 R	18	470
Gladden, Joseph	Livingston, Victoria V.	09 APR 1878	11	412
Gladding, Charles Davenport	Townshend, Willie Lumsdon	25 SEP 1882 R	17	035
Gladman, Jacob F.	Davis, Sarah A.	10 SEP 1879 L	13	364
Gladman, Mary Jane	Tyler, Noble S.	25 FEB 1879 L	13	077
Gladmon, Edwin	Cassin, Margaret Batty	27 MAR 1884 R	18	484
Gladmon, Jecomias F.	Davis, Sarah A.	22 OCT 1881 L	16	039
Gladmon, William O.	Collins, Laura J.	02 JUN 1881 R	15	340
Glancy, John P.	McCarthy, Sophia A.	08 OCT 1883 L	18	177
Glasco, David Benjamin	Jankey, Amelia	29 JAN 1884 R	18	400
Glascock, Abner L.	Lindsey, Maggie B.	27 AUG 1878	12	181
Glascoe, Emma J.	Walker, Samuel H.	07 OCT 1885 R	20	468
Glascoe, Harriet Ann	Bird, William	30 AUG 1877 L	11	071
Glascow, Alexius C.	Cissell, Mary Julia	09 AUG 1883	18	079
Glasgow, Ann Elizabeth	Proctor, Daniel Brads.	16 OCT 1877	11	137
Glasgow, Clurmont	Etherington, Mary Ellen	18 OCT 1883 R	18	202
Glass, Robert R.	Jeter, Bettie	19 JUN 1883 R	18	001
Glassgow, George Wm.	Daly, Katie Mary Camelia	24 SEP 1881 L	15	497
Glassgow, William M.	Penn, Janie E.	07 NOV 1883	18	240
Glazebrook, Marshall Ambler	Argyle, Fanny Farrar	23 MAY 1883 R	17	459
Gleason, Henry M.	Phillips, Emily R.	27 DEC 1882 L	17	215
Gleason, James A.	Thompson, Agnes E.	05 MAR 1878 R	11	370
Gleason, John J.	Brown, Adaline C.	30 SEP 1880	14	468
Gleason, Minnie	Flaherty, Edward	27 JAN 1885 L	20	040
Gleason, Nellie C.	Walsh, William J.	15 APR 1884 L	18	512
Gleason, Sarah	King, Jno. Samuel	24 JAN 1884 L	18	394
Gleason, Sarah	Simms, Frank M.	06 MAY 1885 R	20	209
Gleasons, Mary E.	Demonet, Aug. C.	26 APR 1882	16	337
Glench, Dora	Cremling, Peter	26 JUL 1883 L	18	060
Glenn, Annie Grace	Young, Tapley Webb	20 SEP 1882 R	17	029
Glenn, Minnie Sherburne	Porter, Harvey J.	29 FEB 1884	18	449

Glenn, Nora	Fontz, Charles Stewart	15 APR 1885 L	20	170
Glenn, William G.	Weigand, Katherine	19 FEB 1883 R	17	309
Glennan, Arthur H., Dr.	Rayner, Susie Polk	28 APR 1881 R	15	279
Glick, John H.	Buechler, Mary	02 SEP 1879 R	13	347
Glick, John H.F.	Streb, Magadalena	16 APR 1879 R	13	144
Glick, Kate M.	Eagleston, Edward C.	16 MAR 1882 L	16	279
Glidden, Charles	Manning, Anna Belle	13 SEP 1877 R	11	092
Gloom, John W.	Kuhn, Lena	14 OCT 1883	18	191
Glorius, Andrew G.	Crippen, Elizabeth	27 NOV 1877	11	204
Glorius, Ignatius G.	Hines, Eleanora	03 JUN 1884 L	19	052
Glotzbach, Lizza	Winfield, John Joseph	18 SEP 1883 L	18	138
Glover, Blanche Meade	Semkens, Henry Milton	14 JUN 1883 R	17	491
Glover, Charles Carroll	Poor, Annie Cunningham	10 JAN 1878 R	11	300
Glover, Cora J.	Savage, James W.	18 OCT 1881 R	16	028
Glover, E. Victoria	Carter, Thomas	20 AUG 1879 R	13	321
Glover, George W.	Harris, Ahna A.	06 JUL 1880	14	348
Gloyd, Lizzie S. Clagett	Lawson, James H.	16 OCT 1883 R	18	195
Glück, John Peter	Breithaupt, Riggie	16 NOV 1884	19	384
Glutting, Andrew F.	Krauskopf, Katie M.	27 JAN 1885 R	20	036
Glynn, Mary A.	Bligh, John A.	29 MAR 1883 R	17	368
Gockeler, Emma	Wilson, Jacob F.	04 JUN 1884 R	19	059
Goddard, Flora	Clark, James	05 AUG 1880 L	14	390
Goddard, Ida	Thorpe, Benjamin R.	24 MAY 1883	17	461
Goddard, Maggie E.	Sioussa, John E.	22 DEC 1879 L	14	061
Goddard, Mary A.	Robinson, James F.	18 SEP 1878	12	225
Goddard, William R.	Shay, Annie A.	05 JUL 1877 L	11	010
Goddin, Rosalie W.	O'Neill, John J.	01 DEC 1881 L	16	108
Goddin, William Frankin	Dement, Annie Elizabeth	16 MAY 1878 R	12	052
Godey, Edward	Smith, Katie W.	03 DEC 1878 R	12	361
Godey, Katie M.	Perry, John W.	19 DEC 1878	12	390
Godey, Rachel E.	Ourand, Thomas D.D.	15 NOV 1883	18	257
Godfrey, Francis	Burnett, Mary F.	01 AUG 1881 R	15	428
Godman, S.C.	Martin, Lillie B.	27 MAR 1884	18	485
Godmell, Annie E.	Brett, John A.	29 NOV 1877	11	211
Godron, Barbara	Kottmann, Henry	21 MAR 1882	16	280
Godrow, Lena	Teagle, Edward	21 FEB 1882	16	250
Godson, George	Prout, Alice	17 DEC 1879	14	050
Godwin, Jean	Underwood, John C.	22 OCT 1883 L	18	206
Godwin, Lucien J. Bonaparte	Carter, Ella A.	22 APR 1879 R	13	153
Goebel, George	Nass, Carlena	12 SEP 1878	12	211
Goebel, Lizzie	Dietz, Charles	26 NOV 1879 R	14	008
Goebel, Othilia	Kolb, Edward L.	10 JUN 1884 R	19	073
Goebel, Rosina	Helene, Paul	25 SEP 1884	19	268
Goens, Sarah	Butler, James	22 NOV 1883 R	18	272
Goerner, Clara E.	Fowler, James G.	09 FEB 1878	11	334
Goetz, George W.	Pfeil, Louisa K.	17 MAR 1878	11	384
Goetz, Julia	Brooks, Rufus C.	13 SEP 1877 R	11	091
Goetzinger, Walter	Lochbehler, Laura	15 FEB 1881	15	169
Goff, Caroline E.	Nealy, Sid H.	25 MAY 1881 R	15	326
Goff, Doretta F.	Talcott, A.B.	13 FEB 1878	11	338
Goff, Letty Payne	Lee, Samuel	17 SEP 1879 R	13	374
Goff, Mollie E.	Whiting, Benjamin C.	05 APR 1882	16	301
Goheens, Frank	Petignat, Augusta	16 JAN 1883 R	17	225
Goines, George W.	Holmes, Lavinia	04 JAN 1883	17	239
Going, Mildred	Nash, Willie	25 JUL 1882	16	457
Goings, Annie	Hill, Spencer	14 JUL 1877 L	11	020
Goings, George W.	Washington, Carrie	14 MAY 1885 L	20	223
Goings, Lewis	Smith, Hannah	26 NOV 1884 L	19	417

Gold, Joseph H.	Boltenfield, Rosa C.	19 OCT 1881 L	16	035
Golden, Caldwell D.	Greenfield, Alice Florence	03 MAY 1882 R	16	347
Golden, Cornelia G.	Jones, Samuel M.	21 JAN 1885 R	20	027
Golden, George W.	Day, Hattie	15 JAN 1884 L	18	378
Golden, Georgeanna	Collins, Samuel	23 AUG 1879 R	13	332
Golden, Harry H.	Hoover, Sallie E.	16 SEP 1885 R	20	422
Golden, Ida V.	King, Richard C.	16 OCT 1881 R	16	025
Golden, John Arthur	Murphy, Ida M.	13 JAN 1882 R	16	193
Golden, Joseph W.	Gooding, Jane R.	21 OCT 1880 R	15	007
Golden, Kate	Edwards, John	09 DEC 1880 R	15	086
Golden, William Thomas	Vessey, Sallie Elizabeth	09 NOV 1882 R	17	117
Goldin, Alice Willard	Follin, William Thos.	26 NOV 1877 R	11	200
Goldin, Rosa	Taylor, Charles	26 SEP 1877 R	11	109
Goldin, Willie Jane	Hawkins, Henry	09 JUL 1885	20	318
Golding, Harriet L.	Mount, William J.	22 JUN 1880 R	14	329
Goldsmith, Albert	Duvall, Clara M.	08 FEB 1880 R	14	142
Goldsmith, Clara	Lauphelmer, Michael	16 OCT 1878 L	12	275
Goldsmith, Edwin F.	Ash, Orvillie J.	11 APR 1878	11	415
Goldstein, Bertha	Stierman, Joseph	25 MAR 1883 R	17	357
Goldstein, Rachel Annah	Stargardter, Leopold	04 OCT 1885 R	20	454
Golly, Benjamin	Farmer, Mary	14 JUL 1877 L	11	021
Golly, Benjamin	McAuliffe, Katie	05 OCT 1878	12	255
Gonter, Lillie	Crampsey, Welford E.	16 OCT 1881 R	16	026
Gonter, Thomas S.	Clark, Alice Ella	28 APR 1881 R	15	284
Gonter, William M.	Osborne, Lizzie E.	06 FEB 1883 L	17	296
Gonzales, M.	Beach, Cecilia M.	31 AUG 1879	13	345
Gonzenbach, Charles H.	Suman, Teresa A.R.	18 OCT 1877	11	137
Gonzenbach, Susie D.	McNally, Thomas	06 DEC 1877	11	224
Gooch, Charles J.	Burdett, Annie B.	26 NOV 1879 L	14	009
Goodall, Kate Hayes	Townsend, Henry Clark	23 APR 1879 R	13	155
Goodall, Lola	Crawford, Medorem	14 JAN 1885 R	20	016
Goodall, William	Johnson, Abbie	14 MAR 1878 R	11	382
Goode, Ellsler T.	Crawford, William F.	19 JUN 1883	18	001
Goode, Helen Shaaff	Rittenhouse, Charles E., Jr.	16 FEB 1880 R	14	153
Goode, John C.	Cannon, Sallie F.	25 JUN 1885 R	20	293
Goodell, Charles F.	Graham, Ada V.	15 MAY 1883 L	17	442
Goodhart, Adelaide	Pendleton, John Richardson	20 AUG 1879 R	13	324
Goodhue, Isaac W.	Lillebridge, Annie W.	16 APR 1884 R	18	513
Goodhue, Minnie K.	Davenport, Benjamin	17 AUG 1880 R	14	404
Gooding, Frances E.	Fearson, William Jesse	21 FEB 1882 R	16	254
Gooding, Jane R.	Golden, Joseph W.	21 OCT 1880 R	15	007
Goodman, Cordelia E.	Moseby, Thomas L.	29 OCT 1878 L	12	298
Goodman, Fannie	Fleishman, Israel S.	18 JAN 1885 R	20	024
Goodman, Isham C.	Thomas, Rosa	06 JUL 1883 R	17	486
Goodman, Mary	Latimer, Frederick	02 OCT 1879 R	13	400
Goodman, Mollie E.	Cherry, Willie A.	14 NOV 1883	18	249
Goodman, Rebecca	Fishel, Adolf Morris	20 APR 1884 R	18	520
Goodman, Richard D.	Kerr, Caroline	04 JUL 1885	20	309
Goodman, Samuel	King, Fannie E.	26 MAY 1881 R	15	327
Goodman, Thos. Augustus	Cowling, Mary	22 JAN 1879 R	13	030
Goodno, Charles E.	Lake, Annie	26 MAR 1878 R	11	393
Goodno, Mary Norris	Chase, William Woodbury	18 MAY 1881 R	15	314
Goodrich, Edward P.	Wannall, Lizzie M.	07 OCT 1879 R	13	408
Goodrich, Elizabeth Elliot	Porter, Thomas K.	22 JAN 1879	13	030
Goodrich, Elizabeth R.	Paxton, George M.	18 MAY 1882	16	365
Goodrich, Ida	McKenna, Joseph M.	30 OCT 1879 R	13	451
Goodrick, Aaron M.	Ingraham, Mary	26 NOV 1877 R	11	196
Goodrick, Emma	Dean, James Edward	26 JUN 1879	13	251

Goodrick, Martha	Knott, Isaiah	21 SEP 1878 L	12	230
Goodrick, Samuel	Powers, Sophie Jane	03 DEC 1879 R	14	023
Goodrick, William	Collins, Ellen C.	02 SEP 1879	13	347
Goodrick, William	Lucas, Kate S.	26 NOV 1884 L	19	415
Goodridge, Kate F. Andrews	Hall, Henry W.	01 SEP 1879 R	13	345
Goods, James W.	Shacklett, Carrie V.	14 JAN 1885	20	017
Goodwin, Annie E.	Armor, John E.	30 OCT 1878 L	12	300
Goodwin, Eliza	Martin, Sidney	10 DEC 1881 R	16	124
Goodwin, John J.	Sullivan, Nellie T.	16 MAY 1883 R	17	444
Goodwin, Kitty W.	Pendleton, Charles E.	26 AUG 1882 R	16	493
Goodwin, Mattie J.	Martin, Luther J.	18 OCT 1882 R	17	078
Goodwin, Roberta	Ham, Peter	17 MAY 1881 R	15	312
Goodwin, Victoria R.	Boyer, Romulus W.	22 APR 1880 R	14	234
Gorahm, Ann Virginia	Pettit, Elias	02 JUL 1885 R	20	306
Gorain, Henry	Brown, Harriet Jane	15 FEB 1883 R	17	308
Gordan, Charles H.	Pritchett, M. Blanche	26 FEB 1878	11	358
Gordan, Nancy J.	Brown, Hugh F.	15 SEP 1884 L	19	247
Gorden, Ida C.	Lewis, Edward H.	15 JAN 1885 L	20	022
Gordin, Julia	Davis, Charles	20 JUL 1881 L	15	411
Gordon, Anderson	Swann, Maria	15 APR 1882 R	16	317
Gordon, Anna T.	Hall, Francis	18 APR 1878	12	012
Gordon, Anthony	Woodfork, Laura	23 DEC 1879 L	14	064
Gordon, Carrie E.	Jacobs, A. Issac	01 MAR 1880 R	14	170
Gordon, Charles H.	Mays, Georgeanna, Mrs.	22 NOV 1884 L	19	402
Gordon, Ella V.	Herenberg, Fred C.G.	08 OCT 1884	19	295
Gordon, Ellen	Smith, Jacob	30 OCT 1879 L	13	456
Gordon, Fannie C.	Jenkins, Arthur	20 OCT 1881	16	036
Gordon, Florence R.	Hood, William H.	18 AUG 1883	18	093
Gordon, Frances	Feggans, Peter H.	21 AUG 1879 R	13	328
Gordon, Francis H.	Andresen, Josephine G.	14 FEB 1880 L	14	153
Gordon, Frederick	Davis, Malinda	14 JUL 1881 L	15	402
Gordon, G.W.	Nelson, Mary Jane	08 DEC 1881 L	16	121
Gordon, Graham L.	Burch, Mamie R.	18 AUG 1881 R	15	453
Gordon, Harriet S.	McMahon, William J.	19 DEC 1877 L	11	250
Gordon, Henry	Galaway, Annie	04 OCT 1883 R	18	143
Gordon, Herbert C.	Wright, Effie W.	16 DEC 1884 R	19	462
Gordon, James	Harrity, Emma	16 JAN 1882 L	16	195
Gordon, James A.	Weser, Annie M.	26 DEC 1883 L	18	342
Gordon, James G.	Jones, Beckie	24 JAN 1883 L	17	274
Gordon, Jerry	Wood, Elizabeth	14 OCT 1878 R	12	284
Gordon, John A.	Carpenter, Sophia L.	18 DEC 1883	18	321
Gordon, John H.	Gill, Nancy J.	16 JUL 1883	18	047
Gordon, Laura	Hall, James A.	28 AUG 1879 L	13	342
Gordon, Margaret	Tyler, John	21 JUN 1883	17	483
Gordon, Mary	White, Richard	31 DEC 1879 L	14	083
Gordon, Mary	Blackburn, Arthur	13 FEB 1880	14	151
Gordon, Mary A.	Fowler, Norman	24 NOV 1878	12	344
Gordon, Mary Elizabeth	Matthews, Moses A.	03 JUL 1884	19	121
Gordon, Mary Jane Arnold	Noakes, George Washington	04 FEB 1878 R	11	328
Gordon, Mary Louise	Butler, Charles H.	10 JAN 1884 L	18	373
Gordon, Mary S.	Dulin, William S.	09 JAN 1885 R	20	012
Gordon, Norah E.	Dyer, Robert C.	01 JUN 1882 R	16	388
Gordon, Sallie E.	Scaggs, Willie E.	10 APR 1884	18	503
Gordon, Thomas M.	Washington, Mary E.	05 APR 1884	18	494
Gordon, William	Walker, Susan	12 FEB 1880 R	14	137
Gordon, William F.	Kelly, Fanny Wiggins	05 MAY 1880 R	14	254
Gordon, William H.	Lemon, Lizzie W.	12 OCT 1883	18	186
Gordon, William Henry	Davis, Lucy Hansford	04 JAN 1883 R	17	237

Gordon, William T.	Hurd, Molly A.	19 AUG 1885 L	20	376
Gore, John Edward	Chamberlin, Kate	27 DEC 1884 R	19	494
Gore, Sarah A. Carr	Barrett, John W.	22 SEP 1885 R	20	433
Goree, Patsy	Lee, Thomas S.	06 NOV 1878	12	310
Gorham, Aaron S.	Morrison, Harriet R.	17 MAR 1881 L	15	229
Gorham, Charles E.	Brown, Laura	26 NOV 1879 R	14	010
Gorham, Mary Victoria	Warren, Robert	05 AUG 1885 R	20	353
Gorman, Susan	Gray, George	21 MAY 1885 L	20	234
Gormley, Martha	Columbus, William F.	16 OCT 1878 R	12	275
Gormley, Mary	Noordzy, Harry C.	20 AUG 1884 L	19	194
Gormley, Mary Elizabeth	Atchison, Claude B.	31 MAY 1880 L	14	296
Gorringe, Jern Blanche	Hiland, Thomas	07 AUG 1878	12	159
Gorum, Mary E.	Best, Henry	08 MAY 1879 R	13	179
Gosham, Virginia	Williams, Joseph	24 SEP 1883 L	18	148
Goss, Frances Eva	Howard, Fred. Fritz-Henry	15 JUL 1880	14	363
Goss, Louisa J.	Allmann, John Henry	22 JUL 1880	14	373
Goss, Mary G.	Saur, William F.	09 MAY 1885	20	214
Goss, Maud E.	Kell, James H.	19 SEP 1884	19	259
Goss, Thomas J.	Mathews, Lydia	28 MAY 1878	12	071
Got, Ching	Kellum, Katie E.	06 NOV 1882 R	17	073
Gott, Frank Pierce	Leland, Hester Annie	20 APR 1881 R	15	264
Gotthold, Frederick	Wolf, Florence A.	12 JUN 1878	12	095
Gottridge, Estella	Thorton, Moses	16 MAY 1881 R	15	309
Gottsmann, Sophia M.	Trede, Fretz	20 OCT 1878	12	282
Gough, Marietta	Simons, Wellington F.	29 JAN 1884 L	18	399
Gould, Ellen L.	Russell, Edward M.	06 DEC 1877 R	11	220
Gould, James	Fall, Jane	08 OCT 1882 R	17	059
Gould, John Henry	Beatty, Mary Frances	23 SEP 1877 R	11	095
Gould, Samuel	Thomas, Susan	23 MAR 1882	16	278
Goulder, Harvey D.	Rankin, Mary F.	11 NOV 1878 R	12	320
Gouldman, Annie P.	Cowne, Charles H.	12 JUN 1882 R	16	406
Gourley, James	Tarr, Louisa J.	03 OCT 1881 R	16	002
Gousha, Valentine B.	Crawford, Eliza S.	17 JAN 1883 L	17	264
Gouverneur, Ruth Monroe	Johnson, Wm. Crawford, Dr.	06 DEC 1882 R	17	168
Gove, Caddie E.	Kent, Alexander	24 JAN 1878	11	316
Gove, Hattie E.	Abbott, W.E.	24 JAN 1878	11	317
Gover, Robert Carey	Weaver, Louisa Hunter	19 APR 1880 R	14	227
Gow, Lizzie Baker, Mrs.	Baker, Jesse Elliott	08 DEC 1878 R	12	372
Gown, Adaline	Zeirmann, George W.	11 JUN 1878 L	12	096
Grace, James	Duvall, Lizzie	30 DEC 1878 L	12	406
Grace, Richard R.	Fitzpatrick, Mary A.	22 JUN 1878	12	109
Grady, Anne	Jackson, Andrew	18 SEP 1878 R	12	226
Grady, Annie M.	Stegmaier, George W.	13 OCT 1878 R	12	268
Grady, James	Jenness, Maggie	14 SEP 1884	19	244
Grady, Lewis	Brooks, Eliza Jane	25 DEC 1880 R	15	120
Grady, Nellie	Ballenger, Joseph	13 OCT 1878 R	12	268
Grady, William E.	Murray, Mary	29 MAR 1881 R	15	241
Graefe, Lena	Kraemmer, Lorenz Theodor	19 AUG 1880 L	14	406
Graeme, John K.	Baxter, Hattie H.	21 FEB 1884	18	436
Graf, Fredrich	Boylen, Amelia T.	03 FEB 1882 L	16	224
Graff, Caroline M.	Howard, William H.	16 JUL 1884	19	140
Graham, Ada V.	Goodell, Charles F.	15 MAY 1883 L	17	442
Graham, Andrew B.	Evans, Jennie G.	09 JAN 1884	18	370
Graham, Ann	Weems, Jerry	07 APR 1884 L	18	497
Graham, Charles	Dent, Alice	03 MAR 1881	15	210
Graham, Eliza, Mrs.	North, George	01 NOV 1882 L	17	104
Graham, Elizabeth	Marll, John S.	27 JUL 1881 R	15	421
Graham, Elizabeth	Bradley, John L.	14 SEP 1882	17	022

Graham, Emma G.	Thompson, Richard L.	28 AUG 1883 L	18	102
Graham, Florence J.	Noland, Walter F.	06 NOV 1884	19	364
Graham, Florence Louise	Manning, James Forrest	15 SEP 1884 L	19	248
Graham, George F.	Criswell, Hattie M.	17 APR 1878 L	12	010
Graham, George W.	Green, Amanda Ann	16 MAY 1885	20	224
Graham, Horace A.	Wright, Laura E.	09 AUG 1882 R	16	475
Graham, Jennie Piercy	George, Charles Peaslee, Lt.	08 NOV 1883 R	18	241
Graham, John H.	Hartman, Lena	21 MAY 1878	12	061
Graham, John Robert	Sweeny, Bertie	01 JAN 1884 R	18	360
Graham, John T.	Wallis, Hattie C.	27 SEP 1877 L	11	112
Graham, John W.	Russ, Geneva M.	11 NOV 1878 L	12	322
Graham, Lizzie	Tyler, George	10 APR 1879	13	134
Graham, Lizzie C.	Chamberlain, William	14 FEB 1882 L	16	240
Graham, Lucinda	Hill, James A.	12 DEC 1877 R	11	233
Graham, Matilda	Sims, Thomas Judson	25 MAR 1885 L	20	131
Graham, Oscar	Rollins, Mary	19 DEC 1883	18	325
Graham, Rebecca	Shipley, John	20 DEC 1877 R	11	250
Graham, Rosa	Green, John	21 MAY 1885 L	20	235
Graham, Sarah A.	Wellman, Edwin H.	17 JUN 1880 R	14	323
Graham, Tillie	Yates, John William	12 FEB 1879 R	13	057
Graham, Wesley F.	Shields, Josie A.	12 MAR 1884	18	467
Graham, William E.	Bean, Mary Ida	15 JAN 1878	11	304
Grain, Thomas	Thomas, Minnie	06 MAY 1879 L	13	175
Grainer, Elizabeth	Watson, John W.	25 FEB 1885	20	086
Gramlich, John P.	Klug, Mary	25 SEP 1883	18	151
Granby, Anna	Blackus, August	09 NOV 1880 L	15	039
Grandin, M. Gussie	Quinn, William	14 JUN 1883 R	17	490
Grandin, Mary S.S.	Bennett, Andrew J.	28 OCT 1879	13	447
Grandison, Eliza	Mason, Charles	21 APR 1884 L	18	523
Grandison, Ella	Brown, Charles	01 APR 1880 R	14	205
Grandison, Henry	Overton, Emma J.	03 OCT 1884 L	19	285
Grandison, Mary Florence	Carter, George	26 MAY 1879	13	199
Grandjean, Marie	Chevremont, Eugene	30 MAR 1878	11	388
Grandy, Annie	Jones, George William	04 SEP 1879 R	13	350
Granery, Michael	Nalley, Matilda	13 DEC 1882 R	17	182
Granet, Adelaide	Machette, Henry C.	13 APR 1885	20	160
Graney, Catherine	Banville, George W.W.	25 AUG 1879 L	13	334
Granger, John L.	Febrey, Sadie E., Mrs.	23 APR 1885 L	20	186
Granger, Robert	Williams, Mima	25 SEP 1884	19	270
Graninger, Balthaser	Kraus, Catherine L.	09 SEP 1883	18	117
Grant, Donald S.	Miller, Mary D.	10 FEB 1878	11	335
Grant, Edward M.	Lutton, Jennie	17 MAR 1885 L	20	119
Grant, Electa S.	Lawton, William T.	03 SEP 1878 L	12	196
Grant, Francis Amanda	Bell, John	01 NOV 1822 R	17	105
Grant, James L.	Short, Rebecca C.	15 SEP 1879 R	13	369
Grant, James M.	Appold, Ellen R.	17 SEP 1884 R	19	250
Grant, Jennie	Bosworth, Charles M.	16 SEP 1881 R	15	487
Grant, John	Herbert, Mollie Virginia	15 DEC 1881 R	16	131
Grant, Julia D.	Stocks, Anthony A.	14 JUL 1879 R	13	280
Grant, Louisa	Bowman, Thomas	25 NOV 1884 R	19	410
Grant, Mamie	Robertson, William H.	20 MAY 1885 L	20	230
Grant, Maria	Williams, Andrew	26 APR 1883 R	17	416
Grant, Mary	Sweetnin, Lewis	06 APR 1882	16	301
Grant, Susan	Butler, Winfield	20 SEP 1878	12	206
Grantham, Joanna M.	Sparks, Richard M.	25 SEP 1883	18	152
Grantham, Laura	Ford, Charles E.	30 SEP 1885	20	449
Grantlin, Richard A.	Tuckson, Emma	01 FEB 1883 R	17	285
Grantlin, Samuel	Jackson, Josephine	25 DEC 1879 R	14	063

Name	Spouse	Date	Vol	Page
Grape, Anna Wilhelmi	Schwarz, Louis A.	27 APR 1885 R	20	189
Grattan, Bessie A.	Dickman, Ernest	28 DEC 1882 L	17	223
Graves, A.W., Rev.	Dutton, Donnie A.	22 MAR 1881 L	15	234
Graves, Amelia	Hunt, George Washington	18 SEP 1881 R	15	489
Graves, Gertrude L.	Newton, Frank E.	02 JUL 1883 L	18	030
Graves, Henry	Andrews, Loulie E.	09 APR 1885	20	158
Graves, James P.	Kite, Cora L.	15 OCT 1883 R	18	193
Graves, John W.	Brewer, Nannie B.	28 NOV 1883	18	284
Graves, Lewis H.	McCormick, Mary E.	15 NOV 1883	18	258
Graves, Lizzie S.	Ramsey, John H.	10 SEP 1879 R	13	362
Graves, Mary	Cooper, James W.	30 SEP 1884 L	19	276
Graves, Mary E.	Smith, Geo. W.	02 NOV 1879 R	13	459
Graves, Mary E.	Woodward, William	17 JAN 1883 R	17	262
Graves, Minnie M.	Birch, Isaac	01 OCT 1879 R	13	395
Graves, Rosa	Ellis, George	17 AUG 1882 L	16	483
Graves, Sallie A.	McDonald, James F.	14 FEB 1878 L	11	340
Gray, Adele Bertha	Thompson, Oliver Thos.	25 MAR 1885 R	20	132
Gray, Alice	Dorsey, James Henry	13 MAR 1882 L	16	274
Gray, Alice	Andrews, Joseph	24 DEC 1883 L	18	338
Gray, Alice R.	Dorsey, James H.	21 JUN 1883 R	17	468
Gray, Alice Rosina	Dorsey, A.N.J. Henry	09 MAY 1881 L	15	298
Gray, Andrew Ellsworth	Brown, Josephine	16 SEP 1885 R	20	420
Gray, Anna	Stoks, Emmet	09 OCT 1879 R	13	391
Gray, Annie Laura	Hutton, Mesach	04 JUN 1885	20	255
Gray, Augusta A.	Paul, Henry M.	27 AUG 1878 R	12	179
Gray, Caroline	Jenkins, Tilman	27 MAR 1884 R	18	484
Gray, Celia	Mack, Lane	06 JUN 1878 R	12	086
Gray, Charles	Hurdle, Emily Jane	22 NOV 1881 L	16	090
Gray, Charles B.	Robinson, Marion E.	26 MAY 1880 R	14	289
Gray, Charles Clinton	Broderick, Mary Ella	12 APR 1882 R	16	310
Gray, Charlotte	Howard, Reuben	16 JUN 1885 L	20	276
Gray, Cornelius	Nourse, Mary Jane	09 JAN 1878 L	11	297
Gray, David E.	Benner, Fannie	17 SEP 1884	19	254
Gray, Eliza	Carroll, John	29 OCT 1878 R	12	298
Gray, Elizabeth	Matthews, George	06 JAN 1879 L	13	007
Gray, Eugene S.	Divens, Elizabeth	04 JUL 1882 R	16	437
Gray, Fannie	Young, John	14 APR 1880 L	14	223
Gray, Fannie	Copeland, Howard S.	24 DEC 1884 R	19	487
Gray, George	Kyler, Mary Allen	14 MAR 1878	11	343
Gray, George	Jenning, Mary Jane	27 MAY 1878 L	12	068
Gray, George	Gorman, Susan	21 MAY 1885 L	20	234
Gray, George Ryland	Fawcett, Mary Elizabeth	18 DEC 1878 R	12	388
Gray, George W.	Clark, Florence R.	21 DEC 1882 R	17	189
Gray, Georgianna	Mumford, Moses	08 MAR 1881 L	15	220
Gray, Harry W.	Hoard, Martha	27 FEB 1879 R	13	079
Gray, Harvey	Ellis, Sarah	08 AUG 1885 R	20	361
Gray, Hattie	Powell, Robert C.	22 JUL 1879	13	288
Gray, Ida	Harrison, William H.	22 DEC 1880 L	15	115
Gray, Isabella Frances	Sweeney, George	03 JUL 1877 L	11	007
Gray, James	Smith, Bertha	05 MAR 1883	17	321
Gray, Jesse	Cross, Hattie	02 MAR 1882 L	16	265
Gray, Jesse	Duffy, Maria	24 JUN 1885 R	20	291
Gray, John	Stewart, Marrie	06 FEB 1878 R	11	321
Gray, John	Barry, Ella E.	17 MAY 1883 R	17	448
Gray, John Edmond	Green, Amelia E.	29 MAR 1883 R	17	368
Gray, John H.	Venable, Kate	25 APR 1878	12	023
Gray, John W.	Jasper, Jennette E.	02 OCT 1884	19	281
Gray, Joseph William	Ferguson, Anna Elizabeth	27 JUL 1877 L	11	032

Gray, Julia Ann	Williams, Charles Henry	22 DEC 1881 R	16	147
Gray, Julia Eliza	Palmer, Charles	07 APR 1881 L	15	250
Gray, Katharine	Shuster, Ernest Alvin	15 DEC 1879 R	14	046
Gray, Katie	Henson, John	02 JUL 1885 L	20	308
Gray, Laura Louisa	Martin, William Franklin	27 JUN 1881 R	15	380
Gray, Laura V.	Bladen, Rosier T.	27 FEB 1884 L	18	446
Gray, Leander	Gross, Henrietta	01 MAR 1883 L	17	328
Gray, Lena	Norfolk, Buddy	30 SEP 1879 R	13	391
Gray, Madison	Moten, Annie	14 DEC 1881 L	16	130
Gray, Margaret Ann	Harris, Henry	20 JUL 1880 L	14	369
Gray, Mary	Minor, William	28 MAY 1885 R	20	246
Gray, Mary Cacharine	Hays, Columbus Horatio	25 SEP 1879 R	13	384
Gray, Mary E. Alice	Winans, William	02 OCT 1879 R	13	401
Gray, Mary E.	Brooks, Milton T.	11 AUG 1884	19	168
Gray, Mary Ella	Simpson, Henry Kedglie	23 APR 1884 R	18	530
Gray, Mary Matilde	Younger, George L.	06 FEB 1879 R	13	050
Gray, Milton R.	Hays, Rosannah	21 NOV 1881 L	16	086
Gray, Richard L.	Lusby, Annie Victoria	10 DEC 1879 R	14	038
Gray, Robert	Smith, Lucy	05 FEB 1885 L	20	053
Gray, Robert H.	Robinson, Molly	15 JAN 1880 R	14	105
Gray, Ruth A.	Fuller, Charles F.	11 APR 1883 R	17	387
Gray, Samuel	Danforth, Helene	14 JUL 1881 R	15	402
Gray, Samuel	Lucas, Maria	16 MAR 1885 R	20	116
Gray, Sarah	Wilson, Morgan C.	27 SEP 1877	11	110
Gray, Sarah	Lemore, John	05 JUL 1883	18	037
Gray, Sarah A.	Dumbhart, Charles H.	28 JAN 1884 R	18	396
Gray, Thomas	Fairfax, Alice	18 NOV 1879	13	491
Gray, Thornton	Eckwood, Chaney Ann	27 AUG 1885 R	20	375
Gray, Town	Miner, Belle	16 JUN 1885	20	274
Gray, Virginia	Butler, Albert	10 NOV 1880 L	15	043
Gray, Virginia	Susco, Charles	22 JUN 1884	19	096
Gray, William	Calloway, Catherine	29 DEC 1881 R	16	167
Gray, William F.	Leasenby, Catharine	07 JUL 1879 R	13	263
Gray, William H.	Thomas, Jennie	23 MAY 1878 L	12	065
Gray, William L.	Smith, Sallie V.	05 JUN 1884	19	066
Grayson, Alcinda	Watson, James	04 JAN 1883 R	17	237
Grayson, Charles B.	Stewart, Elizabeth	03 MAR 1879 L	13	086
Grayson, Eliza	Horner, Coleman	13 MAY 1880 R	14	262
Grayson, Eliza	Williams, Joseph	23 NOV 1881 R	16	092
Grayson, George W.	Lee, Anna	06 DEC 1883 L	18	300
Grayson, Lavinia	Thomas, David	15 OCT 1883 R	18	194
Grayson, Lee	Bryant, Jane	26 DEC 1879 R	14	074
Grayson, Maggie	Byrd, Logan A.	01 AUG 1883 L	18	069
Grayson, Mary E.	Carter, C.H.	26 APR 1881 L	15	273
Grayson, Nellie T.	Fry, Charles B.	15 JUL 1880	14	364
Greaver, Jacob A.	Yeager, Katie	17 OCT 1883	18	197
Greaver, William A.	Butler, Bertie J.	24 APR 1884 L	18	532
Greaves, James T.	Ossire, Julia A.	07 AUG 1879	13	311
Greaves, Julia	Burk, James O.	25 FEB 1879 L	13	078
Green, Agnes	Fletcher, Archibald	12 OCT 1885	20	475
Green, Agnes Louisa	White, Oscar William	04 JUN 1883 R	17	473
Green, Alice, Mrs.	Corbin, Alexander	04 SEP 1879 R	13	353
Green, Amanda Ann	Graham, George W.	16 MAY 1885	20	224
Green, Amelia E.	Gray, John Edmond	29 MAR 1883 R	17	368
Green, Andrew	Robinson, Susie	18 MAY 1880 R	14	273
Green, Andrew M.	Barber, Oregon L.	17 JUN 1884	19	089
Green, Anna P.	Van Arsdale, Joseph S.	15 JAN 1879 R	13	017
Green, Annie	Roberts, George	29 MAY 1879 R	13	210

Green, Annie	Coats, Patrick	18 OCT 1883 R	18	200
Green, Annie B.	Wells, Millard F.	07 AUG 1883	18	074
Green, Annie G.	Wilkinson, William H.	23 MAY 1878 R	12	058
Green, Betty A.L.	Williams, Winston W.	09 NOV 1882 R	17	122
Green, Boston	Dornin, Louisa	05 JUN 1883 L	17	477
Green, Brittan B.	Hall, Ida T.	28 MAY 1883	17	464
Green, Caroline	Williams, Augustus	17 DEC 1880 L	15	108
Green, Catharine	Jackson, Charles Olmstead	11 NOV 1878 L	12	320
Green, Catharine E.	Simms, Charles E.	29 NOV 1883 L	18	286
Green, Cathey, Mrs.	Queen, Samuel Fitch	09 NOV 1882 R	25	6176
Green, Charity	Gaines, John S.	28 APR 1879 L	13	161
Green, Charles	Pfluger, Lizzie	09 JUN 1879	13	225
Green, Charlotte	Quesenbery, Taylor	28 FEB 1878	11	364
Green, Clara H.	Garner, Thomas A.	05 FEB 1885 R	20	054
Green, Daniel	Burton, Eliza	06 MAR 1883 L	17	333
Green, Edward	Hungerford, Winnie	20 MAR 1879 L	13	110
Green, Edward	Johnson, Nettie	24 DEC 1883 L	18	336
Green, Edward C.	Reed, Julia S.	05 JUL 1883 L	18	035
Green, Edward E.	Howarth, Mary Ellen	03 JUL 1879 R	13	266
Green, Edward Harris, Dr.	Pickrell, Carrie Salome	17 DEC 1884 R	19	457
Green, Elizabeth	Chew, Samuel	09 NOV 1882	17	121
Green, Ella M.	Brown, John H.	03 JUL 1883	18	032
Green, Ella Virginia	Watson, John Thomas	26 MAY 1880 R	14	290
Green, Ellen	Davis, James H.	02 MAY 1878	12	034
Green, Ellen L.	Odrick, John W.	17 JAN 1884 R	18	383
Green, Esther	Cooper, Jonas	05 AUG 1880	14	384
Green, Evelina	Barry, Jerry	14 JAN 1880 L	14	104
Green, Frances	Edwards, George W.	12 MAY 1878	12	042
Green, Francis	Stuart, Addie	27 AUG 1878	12	181
Green, Frederick F.	Besley, Bertha E.	28 MAR 1884 R	18	485
Green, George	Davis, Rachel	11 MAR 1879 L	13	097
Green, George	Wright, Celia	08 MAY 1880 R	14	261
Green, George	Bowie, Ella	07 MAY 1883 R	17	430
Green, George H.	Mahoney, Katie H.	16 MAY 1882 L	16	361
Green, George Wm.	Wayne, Rachel Ann	08 JUL 1877 R	11	011
Green, Gracie A.	Moffitt, Stephen	12 AUG 1879 R	13	317
Green, Harriet	Powell, Wm. H.	11 MAY 1882 L	16	357
Green, Harriet Lucinda	Brown, Abraham	05 APR 1882 R	16	300
Green, Helen	Wilson, William Henry	26 JUL 1881 R	15	419
Green, Henrietta	Fortune, John	27 APR 1884 R	18	525
Green, Ida M.	Londerman, George F.	16 JUN 1882	16	415
Green, Israel	Minor, Maria	03 SEP 1883 L	18	107
Green, James W.	Brock, Eveline	15 OCT 1879 R	13	420
Green, Jane	Foley, John	10 JAN 1878 L	11	300
Green, Jennie	Robeson, Charles	18 DEC 1879 R	14	056
Green, Jennie	Forrest, Samuel	24 FEB 1881	15	201
Green, Jennie	Berry, Charles	03 JAN 1883 L	17	235
Green, John	Simms, Alice R.	29 AUG 1879 L	13	344
Green, John	Nelson, Eva	21 OCT 1879 L	13	434
Green, John	Howard, Mary S.	10 MAR 1881 L	15	223
Green, John	Anderson, Mary Eugenia	27 JUN 1883 R	18	020
Green, John	Graham, Rosa	21 MAY 1885 L	20	235
Green, John H.	Connell, Alice Virginia	21 JUL 1884	19	149
Green, John Marshall	McGregor, Inez	10 MAY 1885 R	20	215
Green, John R.	Nichols, Kate	10 JUL 1879 L	13	278
Green, John Rush	Bryan, Octavia E.	16 MAR 1880 R	14	186
Green, John W.	Johnson, Susie	27 SEP 1882 L	17	040
Green, John W.	Chase, Susie	07 MAR 1884 L	18	462

Green, Joseph	Wells, Annie	31 OCT 1883 L	18	222
Green, Julia	Peyton, William Henry	10 JUL 1883	18	042
Green, Julia Ada	Petitt, David L.	25 JAN 1881 R	15	163
Green, Lena L.	Boulden, Charles F.	14 JUL 1880 L	14	361
Green, Lewis	Price, Bettie	03 APR 1882	16	296
Green, Lottie	Snowden, John	12 MAY 1881 R	15	303
Green, Lottie	Holmes, James	01 APR 1885	20	141
Green, Louisa	Simmons, William	05 OCT 1878 R	12	252
Green, Lucinda	Thockmorton, Charles	06 APR 1881	15	249
Green, Lucy	Wilmer, Harry	14 AUG 1884 L	19	187
Green, Lucy	Smith, Samuel	03 MAR 1885 L	20	092
Green, M.A.	Carroll, O.D.	09 DEC 1884 L	19	444
Green, Mabel	Jay, Leonard Brewer	28 JAN 1884 R	18	398
Green, Maggie	Lee, William H.	17 AUG 1880 L	14	404
Green, Margaret	Dade, Lewis A.	17 APR 1883 L	17	397
Green, Margt.	Arms, Ben	04 OCT 1881	16	008
Green, Marion C.	Smith, James A.	22 MAY 1879 L	13	202
Green, Martha	Cooper, Thomas H.	01 DEC 1881 R	16	110
Green, Mary	West, Matthew	19 JUL 1883 L	18	054
Green, Mary	Tyler, John	04 FEB 1885 L	20	052
Green, Mary A.	Phelps, J.W.	16 JUL 1881 L	15	406
Green, Mary Alice	Roub, Philip	29 MAR 1883 R	17	369
Green, Mary Ann	Young, Mulberry	19 APR 1883 L	17	400
Green, Mary C.	Saunders, Lorin M.	16 NOV 1881	16	081
Green, Mary E.	Donaldson, Sandy	30 AUG 1877 L	11	072
Green, Mary F.	Hamilton, Charles E.	31 MAR 1885 R	20	126
Green, Matilda	Anderson, Alexander	19 JUL 1883	18	053
Green, Mattie	Cross, Washington	03 JUN 1882 L	16	391
Green, Mattie	Young, James E.	16 JAN 1883 R	17	256
Green, Michael	Jackson, Victoria	23 DEC 1878	12	394
Green, Minnie V.	Hofer, Charles A.	27 DEC 1882	17	215
Green, Mollie	Robinson, Wash. W.	12 MAY 1880 R	14	266
Green, Nancy	Lewis, Edward	20 MAY 1878 R	12	016
Green, Nelson W.	Doyle, Mary E.	20 MAR 1878 L	11	388
Green, Nettie	Foreman, Thomas	21 JUN 1883 R	17	494
Green, Randolph T.	Boyd, Virginia E.	08 OCT 1885 R	20	469
Green, Rebecca	Mason, Sol Labran	25 FEB 1885 L	20	085
Green, Rebecca M.	Cox, Richard J.	05 NOV 1883 L	18	232
Green, Riburn	Marbury, Malvina	01 DEC 1880 L	15	076
Green, Richard	Ross, Lucy E.	17 OCT 1877 R	11	140
Green, Richard	Reeves, Mary C.	27 JAN 1884 R	18	387
Green, Robert	Diggs, Mary	29 DEC 1881 R	16	161
Green, Robert H.	Jackson, Matilda	27 JUL 1881 L	15	421
Green, Robert H.	Jenkins, Millie	14 MAY 1883	17	436
Green, Sallie	James, Lafayette	18 OCT 1878 R	12	292
Green, Sallie V.	Dimsey, John Edward	11 OCT 1883	18	187
Green, Samuel	Gaskins, Susannah	05 FEB 1885 L	20	055
Green, Sarah	Dandridge, George	26 APR 1883 R	17	392
Green, Sarah A.	Levy, Henry	05 NOV 1878 L	12	308
Green, Sarah Ann	Tolson, John F.	14 DEC 1884 R	19	457
Green, Solomon	Howell, Matilda	23 MAY 1878	12	065
Green, Spencer	Robinson, Anna B.	21 JAN 1879 R	13	027
Green, Spencer	Bird, Lucy	10 SEP 1879 L	13	362
Green, Susan	Ruffins, Benjamin	23 FEB 1878 R	11	342
Green, Susan	White, Thomas	01 JUL 1878 R	12	119
Green, Susan A.	Butler, Anthony F.	27 SEP 1877 L	11	109
Green, Susan, Mrs.	Banks, Christopher J.C.	27 FEB 1879 R	13	082
Green, Susie	Harris, Joseph	20 MAY 1879 R	13	196

Name	Spouse	Date	Vol	Page
Green, Sylvester	Conaway, Will	10 JAN 1882 R	16	189
Green, Theodore L.	Jackson, Margaret	24 DEC 1878 L	12	399
Green, Thomas	Scriver, Mary	21 NOV 1878 L	12	342
Green, Thomas E., Sr.	Anderson, Mary E.	20 OCT 1880	15	006
Green, Thornton	Bailey, Alice	12 JAN 1885 L	20	013
Green, Virginia	Keve, John	15 JAN 1885 L	20	021
Green, William	Carter, Sarah	14 DEC 1877	11	235
Green, William	Chambers, Emma	18 JAN 1883 R	17	266
Green, William	Johnson, Kittie	27 JUN 1884 L	19	107
Green, William	King, Elizabeth	08 SEP 1885 R	20	404
Green, William Burton	Ricketts, Ella	11 JAN 1883	17	253
Green, William E.	Ruckcer, Ella G.	15 NOV 1882 L	17	128
Green, William F.	Brown, Mary O.	21 SEP 1880	14	454
Green, William H.	Johnson, Harriet C.	27 NOV 1881 R	16	099
Green, William T.	Chinn, Leslie T.	04 APR 1882 R	16	298
Green, William W.F.	Brooks, Anna R.	24 JAN 1884	18	394
Green, Willis H.	Taylor, Maria C.	16 SEP 1879 R	13	372
Green, Wm. O.	Covey, Mariah	03 JUL 1885 R	20	285
Greenappel, Tely H.	Hepner, Fannie	15 MAR 1885 R	20	114
Greene, Adam Francis	Dixon, Jerusha Frances	01 OCT 1885	20	453
Greene, Clinton	Porter, Magga	07 OCT 1883 R	18	220
Greene, Emma J.	Watson, William H.	05 AUG 1880 R	14	383
Greene, Francis Vinton	Chevallié, Belle Eugenie	25 FEB 1879 R	13	068
Greene, Georgia J.	Camper, N. Gibson	17 DEC 1884	19	465
Greene, James A.	Beetle, Carrie E., MRs.	01 DEC 1884 R	19	428
Greene, John W.	Marshall, Anna C.	03 FEB 1885 R	20	049
Greenfield, Alice Florence	Golden, Caldwell D.	03 MAY 1882 R	16	347
Greenfield, Christie	Wells, William H.	05 JUN 1885 L	20	257
Greenfield, James	Williams, Agnes	07 MAR 1882 R	16	268
Greenfield, Mollie	Bradford, Samuel	12 SEP 1878	12	214
Greenfield, William W.	Ramsburg, Eliza Emma	06 FEB 1879 R	13	048
Greenhow, Catharine	Merdoc, Frederick	14 JAN 1884	18	371
Greenhow, Florida	Allen, Benjamin	08 DEC 1881 R	16	121
Greenland, Emma Belle	Baumgras, Erwin Cyrus	28 APR 1885 R	20	194
Greenlaw, Marian B.	Settle, Edwin B.	15 OCT 1884 R	19	307
Greenleaf, Betsy	Smith, Enoch	15 FEB 1882 L	16	243
Greenleaf, John Thomas	Johnson, Annie	09 NOV 1877	11	177
Greenleaf, Letitia	Parker, Richard H.	15 NOV 1883 R	18	259
Greenleaf, Tillman	Jones, Sarah	23 MAR 1880 R	14	157
Greenlease, Joseph E.	Gillum, Mary A.	11 DEC 1879 R	14	042
Greenleaf, George	Fargo, Mary A.	10 APR 1880	14	219
Greenwell, Alice	Orbella, Cesare P.	31 MAY 1882 L	16	383
Greenwell, Annie Adelaide	Kelly, William Benson	29 NOV 1882 R	17	153
Greenwells, Alice M.	Ellis, Robert H.	12 APR 1881 L	15	253
Greenwood, Alice McGuire	Perry, Benjamin Oliver	10 MAY 1883 R	17	434
Greenwood, James	Chaffee, Kate	28 OCT 1882 L	17	099
Greenwood, Middleton H.	Clayton, Bettie	17 AUG 1883	18	092
Greer, Effie	Payne, Robert L.	12 MAR 1883	17	340
Greer, Everlyn	Wilkerson, Edward O.	19 DEC 1878	12	392
Greer, Fannie	Martin, J.M.	11 MAY 1881 L	15	301
Greer, John J.	Ingle, Rosina C.	12 NOV 1879 R	13	478
Greer, Julia A.	Forney, Pierce W.	01 MAY 1879 L	13	170
Greer, Marcus	Murphy, Annie	04 JUN 1884 R	19	056
Greer, Robert Franklin	Jenkins, Virginia U.	11 SEP 1883 R	18	124
Greever, Ida	Daley, Jacob Edwar	12 SEP 1880 R	14	441
Greff, Charles	Buhler, Anne	19 FEB 1879	13	066
Gregan, John	Braywood, Julia	28 DEC 1881 R	16	167
Gregory, Charles Richmond	Waters, Annah	30 NOV 1881 R	16	103

Gregory, Frederick	Huntington, Lillie R.	06 MAR 1878 R	11	374
Gregory, George Wm.	Chapman, Katherine P.	16 MAY 1883	17	444
Gregory, Hannah Lewis	Ladson, Henry James	22 OCT 1879 R	13	438
Gregory, John R.	Wilcox, Floie D.	03 JUN 1883 R	17	474
Gregory, Manfred	Dishman, Mary L.	08 JAN 1879 R	13	011
Gregory, Manfred	Bennett, Catharine	26 APR 1883 R	17	409
Gregory, Mintty	Bucheler, Herman C.	04 JUN 1881 R	15	343
Gregory, Welfried	Duvant, Lucretia, Mrs.	25 FEB 1879 R	13	079
Gregory, William B.	Lundy, Alice R.	20 DEC 1877	11	256
Gregsbey, Jane	Cohen, John C.	18 AUG 1884	19	192
Greif, Helenei	Grüser, Karl	06 MAY 1878 L	12	038
Gresham, Sarah	McReynolds, Curren T.	29 DEC 1881 R	16	131
Gressom, Mary Frances	Jackson, John	06 MAY 1882 R	16	344
Grey, Annie P.	Fuss, John A.	29 APR 1884 R	18	534
Grey, Eliza	Campbell, Charles	31 OCT 1882	17	103
Grice, Arie	Smith, Frank	20 MAR 1882 L	16	283
Grice, Edward	Washington, Lena	15 MAR 1883 R	17	342
Grice, Josephine	Williams, James	22 NOV 1877 R	11	199
Gridley, Lucius Egbert	Walker, Edith Augusta	05 FEB 1880 R	14	138
Griemsbey, Emma J.	Nelson, George H.	01 JUN 1882	16	386
Grier, Ralph H.	Seymour, Ella T.	07 JUN 1881 R	15	345
Grier, Sarah (Robinson)	Smallwood, Joseph A.	27 DEC 1881 R	16	145
Grieve, Mary E.	Southard, John F.	01 MAY 1882 R	16	343
Griffin, Annie	Cady, Michael	25 JUN 1883	18	012
Griffin, Annie	Williams, Edward	22 MAY 1884	19	035
Griffin, Catherine	O'Connor, James L.	07 DEC 1880	15	085
Griffin, Catherine	Walsh, Daniel	26 MAY 1883 L	17	463
Griffin, Fannie	Brown, James	24 OCT 1878	12	289
Griffin, George M.	Brown, Kate	31 MAR 1884 L	18	488
Griffin, Hannah	Palmer, John M.	12 SEP 1884 L	19	242
Griffin, Hattie	Harris, John	15 JUN 1885 R	20	273
Griffin, James A.	Woodward, Mary E.	20 NOV 1877	11	194
Griffin, Jennie	Fauntleroy, Benjamin	19 JUN 1879	13	239
Griffin, John A.	Jacobs, Henrietta	19 JUL 1883	18	054
Griffin, L.V.	Darnall, J.E.	28 JUL 1884 L	19	160
Griffin, Levi	Toliver, Mary	05 JUL 1877 R	11	006
Griffin, Lucy	Neal, Asbury	04 MAY 1880	14	252
Griffin, Mary	Donohoo, Commodore	26 JUN 1879	13	251
Griffin, Mary T.	McNamara, Patrick E.	01 OCT 1884 L	19	279
Griffin, Nellie	Robinson, Thomas M.	20 AUG 1884 L	19	197
Griffin, Oliver	Madison, Rose	01 DEC 1877	11	214
Griffin, Oliver	Johnson, Mary	18 DEC 1884 L	19	471
Griffin, Richard B.	Hinkelbein, Theresa F.M.	04 MAY 1885 L	20	203
Griffin, Robert W.	Simonds, Anna M.	24 NOV 1880 R	15	065
Griffin, Sarah E.	Lee, Willie	08 AUG 1885 R	20	360
Griffin, Susan Jane	Belford, Jonas	25 JUL 1882 R	16	456
Griffin, Thomas H.	West, Mary E.	26 DEC 1883 L	18	344
Griffin, Tyson	Jenifer, Mary	27 AUG 1884 L	19	210
Griffin, Wm. H.	Thomas, Janie E.	09 MAR 1883	17	339
Griffing, Edward B.	Van Winkle, Annie E.	23 SEP 1884 L	19	264
Griffith, Aloysius B.	Byram, Carrie E.	26 NOV 1884 R	19	408
Griffith, George H.	Gross, Mary I.	09 AUG 1880 R	14	394
Griffith, Jennie S.	Corrick, Charles J.	25 JUN 1879 R	13	248
Griffith, Joseph I.	Brecht, Mamie J.	26 FEB 1885 R	20	087
Griffith, Mary C.	Shipley, Fourose	29 JUL 1883	18	065
Griffith, Missouri V.	Hawling, Eugene	04 DEC 1884 R	19	437
Griffith, Nancy	Lewis, Joseph	17 APR 1879	13	150
Griffith, Samuel H.	Watmough, Ellen Coxe	04 OCT 1883	18	167

Griffith, William D.	Given, Emma	01 JAN 1884	18	355
Griffo, Mary	Kellum, Zed B.	10 OCT 1882 L	17	062
Griggs, Able E.	Hooper, Emily	17 MAY 1879 L	13	195
Griggs, Charles A.	Wood, Fannie G.	16 OCT 1881	16	027
Griggs, Newton	West, Emily	11 SEP 1877 R	11	129
Griggs, Wm. Lewis	Carr, Mollie Virginia	08 MAR 1881 R	15	220
Grigsby, James	Hughes, Georgia Johanna	27 AUG 1883 L	18	099
Grigsby, Milton T.	Sorrell, Annie E.	08 APR 1885 R	20	154
Grigsby, William Henry	Brady, Sarah, Mrs.	07 JUL 1879 R	13	266
Grill, George	Bolling, Mary A.	16 JUL 1883	18	048
Grills, William A.	White, Eleanor	16 SEP 1884 L	19	249
Grimes, Amanda	Tramell, Lewis Thomas	28 FEB 1878 L	11	365
Grimes, Andrew	Johnson, Agnes	17 DEC 1883	18	318
Grimes, Cornelia	Chandler, Morton	20 OCT 1885 R	20	495
Grimes, David	Brown, Malinda	04 OCT 1883 R	18	169
Grimes, Emma E.	Grimes, Willie	28 FEB 1884 R	18	449
Grimes, Francis J.	Callaghan, Mary	17 JUN 1880 L	14	325
Grimes, Henry W.	Beavin, Fidelia A.	22 AUG 1878 L	12	176
Grimes, Jennie V.	Plowman, Jesse W.	09 SEP 1883 R	18	119
Grimes, Josephine A.	Sydenstricker, Oliver P.	26 NOV 1878	12	345
Grimes, Katie	Smith, Samuel A.	06 NOV 1879 R	13	468
Grimes, Laura J.	Jenkins, William	12 JAN 1881 R	15	148
Grimes, Maria	Johnson, Harry	07 APR 1881	15	247
Grimes, Sarah C.	Stewart, Caleb	11 DEC 1877 R	11	230
Grimes, Sarah Virginia	Dorsey, Elijah	30 DEC 1880 R	15	131
Grimes, Thomas W.	Carlin, Belle	13 MAR 1879 L	13	099
Grimes, William H.	Banks, Clara E.	08 JAN 1878 L	11	295
Grimes, Willie	Grimes, Emma E.	28 FEB 1884 R	18	449
Grimke, Francis J.	Forten, Charlotte L.	09 DEC 1878	12	391
Grimm, Eliza M.	Bowser, Joseph	03 JUL 1878 L	12	123
Grimsley, Anna Jane	Baggott, Robert	28 MAR 1882 R	16	291
Grimsley, Rebecca	Dove, John W.	13 NOV 1879 R	13	484
Grindall, William E.	Downey, Mary J.	06 JAN 1883 R	17	241
Grinder, Bettie	McCondach, James	15 NOV 1882	17	129
Grinder, Ida	Story, James	01 JAN 1878	11	284
Grinder, Joseph B.	Bell, Ida B.	18 MAR 1882	16	282
Griner, Josephine	Keenan, John Francis	23 DEC 1881 R	16	154
Grinnell, Bettie E.	Lewis, Walter L.	20 SEP 1882 L	17	030
Grinnell, Harriet	Rhoden, Robert	12 FEB 1885 L	20	065
Grinnip, Maggie	Cosby, Martin	29 JAN 1883 L	17	276
Grissett, James A.	Kilbman, Margaret A.	07 DEC 1881	16	115
Grissett, Mary E.	Mangum, John	20 JAN 1879	13	024
Griswold, Dwight T.	Spaulding, Fannie	24 AUG 1882 L	16	493
Groener, Charles	Schoepflen, Katharina	27 DEC 1877	11	275
Groff, Bessie	Rothrock, Hamilton Irving	04 DEC 1884	19	433
Grogan, Mary	McCarthy, John	03 MAY 1884 L	18	550
Grogan, Robert Riddell	Crismond, Sudie Stewart	19 OCT 1885 R	20	465
Groh, Antonia	Egloff, Melchior	07 OCT 1883	18	175
Grooves, Lemuel	Williamson, Alice	18 JUN 1880	14	327
Grose, Annie	Howell, Hercules J.	30 AUG 1883	18	105
Grose, Daniel Charles	Smith, Hattie Estelle	25 MAY 1881 R	15	326
Grosendorf, John	Reinhardt, Rebecca	29 DEC 1877 L	11	280
Groshon, Nettie A.	Morris, John	09 JUN 1885 R	20	263
Gross, Alice	Mason, William	21 SEP 1885 R	20	431
Gross, Basil	Brown, Matilda	05 OCT 1885	20	458
Gross, Benjamin	Diggs, Katie	06 APR 1882	16	297
Gross, Charles	Crampton, Julia	15 OCT 1885 R	20	488
Gross, Clara	Breslauer, Ferdinand	05 AUG 1877 R	11	040

Gross, Henrietta	Gray, Leander	01 MAR 1883 L	17	328
Gross, James H.	Warner, Mary	11 NOV 1877 R	11	179
Gross, James H.	Hodge, Sina	07 OCT 1880 L	14	482
Gross, John W., Jr.	Brown, Victorine	10 OCT 1880 R	14	486
Gross, Joseph H.	Bryan, Kate L.	14 SEP 1884 R	19	245
Gross, Julia C.	Hughs, William R.	31 MAY 1884 L	19	047
Gross, Maggie E.	McNamara, M.T.	29 DEC 1882 L	17	223
Gross, Mamie V.	Morris, William	15 APR 1885 R	20	170
Gross, Mary E.	Brown, William Henry	23 OCT 1879 L	13	440
Gross, Mary Frances Parrish	Holmead, Alfred	20 JUN 1883 R	18	006
Gross, Mary I.	Griffith, George H.	09 AUG 1880 R	14	394
Gross, Mary M.	Pinkney, Eugene K.	10 JUL 1878	12	132
Gross, Matilda	Warren, F.W.	12 JUL 1877	11	020
Gross, Milton	Evans, Alice G.	10 JUL 1884	19	111
Gross, Sarah	Tibb, Emanuel	08 NOV 1881 R	16	066
Gross, Sarah	Simmons, George H.	25 MAR 1884 L	18	481
Gross, Soloman	Smith, Laura	10 SEP 1877 R	11	083
Gross, Thomas	Gaines, Sarah	13 DEC 1883 L	18	315
Gross, William	Cadwell, Maggie	02 JAN 1879 R	13	004
Gross, William	Chapman, Martha	06 AUG 1884 L	19	171
Grosskurth, William	Brandt, Emma	21 SEP 1884	19	261
Grossman, Maurice Neville	Hubbard, Gertrude McCurdy	17 JAN 1880	14	102
Grove, Annie M.	Bradt, Albert H.	29 APR 1883	17	420
Grove, Berkley	Marshal, Rebecca	26 MAY 1880 R	14	291
Grove, Elijah F.	McConike, Isabella G.	05 MAR 1879 R	13	092
Grove, George	Broomall, Clara	05 DEC 1879 L	14	031
Grove, Virginia May	McChesney, Junius Baylor	30 APR 1884 R	18	547
Grover, John F.	Harding, Ann E.	25 JUN 1883	18	013
Grover, Martha	Stover, John	31 OCT 1877 L	11	161
Grover, Martha Jerusha	Henley, William George	16 MAY 1878	12	054
Groves, Arkarey	Becket, Louisa, Mrs.	24 MAR 1881 R	15	239
Groves, George	Nelson, Ellen	21 JUN 1883 L	18	007
Groves, Margaret A.	Humphreys, William W.	05 JUL 1877 L	11	011
Groves, Matilda	Kendrick, John J.	14 DEC 1881 R	16	130
Groves, William Henry	Lovejoy, Annie Ellen	18 SEP 1879 R	13	376
Grubb, Mary A.	Saltmer, George H.	19 DEC 1877	11	245
Grubb, Minnie C.	Dodd, Ernest L.	19 JUN 1884	19	092
Grubbs, Augustine S.	Keller, Kate	17 OCT 1878	12	276
Grubbs, Emma W.	Nelson, Ira C.	06 MAY 1885 R	20	208
Grube, Minna	Schwerdtmann, Ludolph	04 SEP 1885	20	399
Gruber, Hallie	Earley, John H.	02 SEP 1885 R	20	396
Gruenke, Frances A.	Hailer, William H.	25 OCT 1881	16	044
Gruenke, Lessie	Floegel, Ernest	28 MAR 1880 R	14	198
Grumley, Edward Clark	Williams, Flora Nettie	01 JUL 1883	18	027
Grünelieng, Friedr. Wm.	Dietel, Margarethe	21 JUN 1884	19	094
Grüser, Karl	Greif, Helenei	06 MAY 1878 L	12	038
Gude, Edward B.	Hulcher, Mary	15 AUG 1881 R	15	444
Gude, George	Joyce, Annie W.	24 APR 1878 L	12	021
Gude, Henry	Kissner, Clara	21 JUL 1880 L	14	370
Guess, Carrie	Cost, Charles	09 AUG 1882 R	16	473
Guess, Magretta	Zelbernagle, Wladyas	28 OCT 1878	12	293
Guest, George W.	McCathran, Maggie	11 MAR 1880 R	14	182
Guggenheimer, Samuel	Fisher, Ada	17 AUG 1879 R	13	321
Guggenhein, Simon	Hexter, Carrie	29 JAN 1882 R	16	213
Guigon, Mary Josephine	Bartley, James W.	31 JUL 1878 L	12	152
Guild, Alexander	Kennedy, Mary E.	23 APR 1879	13	157
Guilford, Harry A.	Wood, Alice G. (Caton)	30 DEC 1882 L	17	227
Guilford, Lottie	McCormick, Millard P.	11 APR 1882	16	303

Guilom, Samuel	Gant, Mary Jane	07 OCT 1878 L	12	258
Guinand, Alice E.	McKenzie, Alexander	12 APR 1882 R	16	312
Guinn, Annie Marie	Machenheimer, Charles Page, Dr.	25 OCT 1877 R	11	156
Guinniss, Guinn	Warder, Mary Eleanor	10 FEB 1885 R	20	061
Guire, Annie	Johnson, Stephen R.	03 APR 1883 L	17	375
Guirge, Carrie	Burrill, Edward	07 SEP 1885 R	20	401
Guiss, Amelia	Pfeil, John K., Jr.	11 MAY 1879 R	13	183
Gulick, George	Drury, Lillie	12 DEC 1883 L	18	313
Gulick, James H.	Miller, Mary K. McPherson	28 APR 1878 R	12	026
Gulick, Robert M.	Barbour, Jane C.	26 MAR 1883 L	17	360
Gundaker, Samuel W.	Williams, Mary	27 JAN 1885 R	20	015
Gundling, Frederick	Geigger, Mory	05 SEP 1878 L	12	200
Gunnell, Alice I.	Clagett, John B.	31 AUG 1882 R	16	499
Gunnell, Carrie	Rollins, Lewis F.	31 AUG 1885	20	393
Gunnell, Catherine	Malone, Edward E.	18 AUG 1877 L	11	056
Gunnell, Frances	Cannon, George M.	24 JUL 1884	19	154
Gunnell, George W.	Hicks, Emma G.	11 APR 1878 R	12	002
Gunnell, Joshua	Nelson, Edmonia	27 MAR 1878 L	11	393
Gunnell, Joshua C.	Baker, Collie M.	08 JUL 1885 L	20	317
Gunnell, Laura	Jones, Jeff	24 MAY 1883 R	17	461
Gunnell, Mamie V.	Combes, Edward R.	30 JUL 1884	19	162
Gunnell, Nancy L. Cummings	Cowaen, Alexander	20 MAR 1879 R	13	109
Gunnell, Robert	Dove, Annie V.	23 DEC 1878 L	12	396
Gunser, Christine Wilhemine	Adlung, John	19 DEC 1880 R	15	109
Gunter, Mary	Bartlett, Frederick H.	21 AUG 1885	20	382
Gunther, Mary Ellen	Bensley, William James	30 NOV 1882 R	17	156
Günther, Caroline	Loth, Wilhelm	20 JUL 1884	19	147
Gunzer, Rosa	Hudson, Edward J.	13 SEP 1882 R	17	019
Gurley, Laura	Tyler, James Madison	02 DEC 1884 L	19	430
Gurley, Martha	Seuter, Albert	15 DEC 1877 R	11	237
Gurley, William Brooks	Shields, Elizabeth Howard	09 OCT 1879	13	412
Gurrath, Rosina, Mrs.	Langer, Joseph R.	15 MAY 1881 R	15	305
Gurtchell, Annie	Elliott, Perry	28 OCT 1879 R	13	444
Gusdorf, Fannie	Stern, Louis	12 OCT 1879	13	414
Gusdorf, Ida	Gauss, Samuel	15 MAR 1885 R	20	113
Güthler, Max	Rothsehn, Margaret	21 AUG 1881 R	15	453
Guthridge, Jules	Sterling, Anna	20 OCT 1884 L	19	320
Guthrie, Clarissa Sidney	Brady, Cyrus Townsend	10 SEP 1884	19	237
Guthries, Henry	Claterbrooks, Sarah	15 AUG 1881	15	445
Gutridge, Mary Jane	McNiel, John	10 OCT 1882	17	063
Guttenson, Lizzie	Berger, Oscar L.	29 MAY 1878 L	12	075
Guy, Benjamin Walter	Bohrer, Mary E.	21 SEP 1881 R	15	493
Guy, Eliza	Henderson, George T.	24 DEC 1877 L	11	261
Guy, Frank Morsell	West, Gertrude Morse	18 FEB 1879 R	13	065
Guy, James T.	Schrepler, Catherine	15 APR 1885 L	20	171
Guy, Josephine	Jackson, James A.	15 OCT 1885 R	20	486
Guy, Martha Etta	Brooker, William	26 AUG 1880 R	14	412
Guy, Minnie	Mugler, Hamlet M.	08 JAN 1883 R	17	243
Guy, Peter	Harrison, Mary	02 JAN 1878 R	11	286
Guy, Rosa B.	Talbot, John M.	30 SEP 1880	14	467
Guyon, Daniel W.	Assu, Karalina	05 JAN 1881 R	15	139
Guyvers, Louisa	Smith, Thomas	21 NOV 1882 R	17	140
Gwin, William	Lamar, Martha Ann	10 OCT 1877 R	11	129
Gwynn, Benjamin	Barnes, Lena	05 JAN 1881 L	15	141

H

Haag, Gustave E.	Sauer, Emma	31 JAN 1880 R	14	129
Haas, Lotta	Voigt, Edward, Jr.	26 MAR 1883 L	17	361
Haase, Wilhelm August	Rheb, Sophia	12 MAR 1878	11	378
Habermamn, Clara	Walker, Carlile S.	10 AUG 1881 R	15	439
Hablemann, Annie M.	Nadin, Arthur	19 JUL 1880 R	14	367
Habram, John	Sullivan, Ellen	02 OCT 1882 R	17	048
Haburk, Conrad	Kinzel, Christina	16 APR 1879 R	13	142
Hack, Oliver Clarence	Storer, Laura Lorraine	26 SEP 1880 R	14	460
Hackenyos, Charles W.	Lewis, Mary L.	19 APR 1883 R	17	391
Hackett, Gustavus	Cook, Rebecca	12 JUN 1879	13	231
Hackett, Junior	Dickson, Mary	15 APR 1879 R	13	144
Hackett, Mary Ann	McDonald, Pierce	06 JUN 1879 L	13	222
Hackett, Nelson	Douglas, Mary Eliza Wise	12 JUN 1879 R	13	228
Hackley, Cora	Colbert, Luther	16 DEC 1880 R	15	106
Hackley, Lucy A.	Stone, Oscar F.	08 MAY 1878 R	12	043
Hackley, Martha	Harris, J.	11 APR 1882 L	16	309
Hackley, William H.	Williams, Isabella	22 JUL 1880 L	14	373
Hackney, Fielder Poston	Flynn, Annie M. Randolph	07 OCT 1880 R	14	482
Haddaway, Charles A.	McKim, Harriet Hutchins	15 OCT 1884	19	309
Haddon, Julia M.	Cox, Samuel Baker	31 MAR 1879 R	13	119
Hadfeld, Harry	Noon, Katie	29 MAR 1880 R	14	198
Hadfield, Alexander	Whibking, Dora	03 JUN 1881 L	15	343
Hadley, Samuel H.	College, Lydia Elizabeth Cogswell	09 MAR 1879 R	13	094
Hadley, Sarah E.	Keese, John Henry	30 MAR 1882 R	16	294
Haefliger, R.	Dilli, Mary	06 DEC 1877 L	11	226
Hafner, Augustus P.	Rogers, Ella	06 DEC 1883	18	303
Hagan, Anna	Campbell, Ritchard T.	21 JUL 1884	19	148
Hagan, James	Sheehan, Mary Ann	10 NOV 1883 L	18	245
Hagan, Marion W.	Hays, Lewis N.	27 SEP 1881	15	498
Hagan, Mary A.	Bradley, Patrick H.	22 NOV 1881 L	16	088
Hagan, Michael E.	Flaherty, Catherine E.	17 NOV 1883 L	18	261
Hagar, Caroline	Whitemore, David B.	13 DEC 1881 R	16	127
Hagemeyer, Clara E.	Smith, Samuel W.	02 JAN 1883	17	230
Hagemeyer, H.W.	Fahrenbruch, A.D.	06 MAY 1879 R	13	174
Hager, Myron D.	Fields, M. Phemie	15 APR 1882 R	16	316
Hagerty, Lizzie C.	O'Shurland, George C.	13 MAY 1878 L	12	049
Haggenmaker, James M.	Ries, Julia	16 FEB 1880 R	14	153
Haggin, Cassie M.	Jones, Thomas	17 SEP 1884	19	255
Hagner, Randall	Dodge, Carrie Roberta	03 NOV 1881 R	16	062
Hahn, Charles	Smith, Mollie	03 AUG 1881 R	15	431
Hahn, Gottlob	Downing, Emma [Reinle]	06 AUG 1885 R	20	358
Hahn, Johanna	Hoffmann, Max	14 NOV 1884 L	19	382
Haight, E.R.	Clarkson, M.A.	30 JUN 1880	14	341
Haight, Horace	Bowie, Alice R.	20 DEC 1877 R	11	243
Haight, Mary L.	Tucker, Milton T.	15 OCT 1878	12	272
Hailer, William H.	Gruenke, Frances A.	25 OCT 1881	16	044
Hailey, Thomas	Rolfe, Kate	27 MAY 1880 R	14	290
Hailstock, Charles J.	Saunders, Margaret J.	18 NOV 1884 L	19	391
Hailstock, Joshua	Herndon, Mary	20 DEC 1879 R	14	060
Hailstork, Nathan	Ford, Mary D.	18 MAR 1880 R	14	187
Hain, Ida	Kelley, Joseph Van Dorn	22 MAR 1883 R	17	351
Haines, Bessie	Magee, John	13 DEC 1879 L	14	046
Haines, Clara V.	Harris, John R.	14 APR 1880 R	14	223
Haines, Emma N.	Pullman, Edgar J.	30 DEC 1883	18	354
Haines, Joseph	Allen, Sarah	29 OCT 1877 R	11	157
Haines, Laura	Morris, James	15 OCT 1877	11	132
Haines, Mary E.	Chapman, George P.	28 FEB 1880	14	168

Haines, Mary R.	Harrison, Alexander L.	23 OCT 1884 L	19	333
Hainey, Susie A.	Scott, Aquilla D.	05 JAN 1881 R	15	137
Haislip, Kezia E.	Clarke, James W.W.	26 JAN 1882 L	16	212
Haislip, Mary	West, Hezekiah	27 DEC 1877 L	11	271
Haislip, William Walter	Simmons, Allie E.	12 FEB 1884	18	420
Haithman, William I.	Lee, Lucretia	20 DEC 1881 L	16	142
Haker, Katie	Binder, John F.	06 SEP 1885 R	20	400
Hale, Charles Frederick	Anderson, Florida Virginia	01 NOV 1880 R	15	024
Hale, Conrad L.	Hess, Tillie E.	01 JAN 1885 R	20	001
Hale, Martha Rogers	Hampson, Thomas	29 MAY 1878 R	12	069
Hales, Martha P.	Martin, Bernard	01 NOV 1879 R	13	459
Haley, Edward	O'Neill, Kate	20 JAN 1878	11	311
Haley, John	Rector, Martha	15 APR 1885 R	20	167
Haley, Lucy	Heflin, Gilson	14 SEP 1877 R	11	094
Halfert, Katie	Ritter, John B.	19 OCT 1885 L	20	495
Halkins, Emelin	Carter, Burrell	21 DEC 1882 R	17	202
Hall, A.C.	Byron, W.J. Osborne	08 FEB 1882 L	16	233
Hall, A.L.	McCathran, F.C.	01 AUG 1881 L	15	429
Hall, Ada E.	Owings, G.A.	04 DEC 1882	17	165
Hall, Albert Green	Stouffer, Anna May	03 APR 1883	17	372
Hall, Alberta Blanche	Frey, Levin Sothoron	25 SEP 1878 R	12	235
Hall, Alfred J.	Coagy, Katie M.	14 MAY 1883 L	17	438
Hall, Alice	Wilson, John Francis	03 JUL 1879 R	13	250
Hall, Annie	Jones, Charles	18 OCT 1881	16	030
Hall, Annie	Hogan, Peter	05 NOV 1885	17	035
Hall, Annie	Jones, Sylvester	24 SEP 1885 L	20	441
Hall, Annie Mary	Toyer, George Benjamin	05 MAR 1885 R	20	089
Hall, Annie S., Mrs.	Hamilton, Andrew P.	01 AUG 1881 R	15	430
Hall, Asbury R.	Hotman, Mary	04 DEC 1879 R	14	030
Hall, Caroline Choate	Howes, Edward Everett	04 DEC 1879 R	14	029
Hall, Carrie B.	Bartley, Roger S.	26 DEC 1877 L	11	271
Hall, Charles	Shorter, Rebecca Ann	10 JUL 1879 R	13	273
Hall, Charles	Walls, Patsey	06 MAR 1885 R	20	099
Hall, Charles W.	Pace, Emma D.	22 OCT 1884	19	328
Hall, Charles William	Olverson, Alice Robinson	07 JUN 1883	17	483
Hall, Cora A.	Dowden, Charles B.	14 FEB 1884 R	18	425
Hall, Dora Lee	Nelson, John Benjamin	28 AUG 1884	19	214
Hall, Edward	Adams, Nancy	26 OCT 1882	17	097
Hall, Elihu	Bayliss, Georgiana	30 DEC 1880 R	15	132
Hall, Elizabeth	Armstrong, Jordan	27 NOV 1882 L	17	149
Hall, Ellen	Hall, James F.	26 DEC 1877 L	11	271
Hall, Emeline, Mrs.	Chase, Isaac McKim	01 APR 1878 R	11	399
Hall, Evelyn Smith	Barnard, Helena Emma	20 MAY 1880 R	14	280
Hall, F.P.	Lacy, Jennie R.	08 JUL 1880	14	353
Hall, Fenton	Dory, Eliza	15 MAY 1883	17	441
Hall, Francis	Gordon, Anna T.	18 APR 1878	12	012
Hall, George	Allen, Berta	02 AUG 1877 L	11	037
Hall, George	Ware, Sarah Ann	11 AUG 1881	15	440
Hall, George B.	Hart, Jane E.	13 OCT 1879 R	13	418
Hall, George W.	Eichholtz, Helena Augusta	30 DEC 1878 R	12	406
Hall, George Washington	Brown, Emma	11 AUG 1881 R	15	440
Hall, Gertrude U. Hall	Hawes, John B.	21 APR 1879 R	13	153
Hall, Hannibal	Holmes, Rhoda	28 APR 1881 R	15	282
Hall, Harriet	Russell, Daniel	16 JAN 1885 L	20	023
Hall, Henry	Jordan, Margaret E.	12 MAY 1879 L	13	184
Hall, Henry	Tyler, Mary E.	27 JUN 1885 L	20	297
Hall, Henry W.	Goodridge, Kate F. Andrews	01 SEP 1879 R	13	345
Hall, Henson	Brown, Gracie	26 AUG 1879	13	334

Hall, Huster	Duckett, William	02 AUG 1883	18	072
Hall, Ida T.	Green, Brittan B.	28 MAY 1883	17	464
Hall, J.N.	Carrier, Leona Abigail	26 NOV 1879 L	14	014
Hall, James	Adams, Annie	02 JAN 1878	11	287
Hall, James	Rawls, Mary F.	11 DEC 1879 R	14	042
Hall, James A.	Gordon, Laura	28 AUG 1879 L	13	342
Hall, James D.	Rudd, Laura M.	20 JUL 1884	19	143
Hall, James D.J.	Bond, Mary C.	25 JUN 1878	12	112
Hall, James F.	Hall, Ellen	26 DEC 1877 L	11	271
Hall, James Henry	Hatch, Lizzie E.	20 MAR 1883 R	17	350
Hall, James Hiram Barney	Niermann, Margaret Ellen	13 OCT 1880 R	14	489
Hall, Jane	Jackson, Chapman H.	11 FEB 1879 L	13	053
Hall, Jennie	Dowden, William	02 JUN 1885 R	20	253
Hall, John	Collins, Victoria	02 DEC 1880 R	15	076
Hall, John	Hardy, May	26 JUN 1884 L	19	105
Hall, John F.	Phair, Jane L.	06 DEC 1883 L	18	300
Hall, John R.	Arlow, Mary A., Mrs.	31 JAN 1884 R	18	403
Hall, John T.	Dixon, Lucy	27 MAY 1881	15	328
Hall, John T.	Stweart, Cordelia	13 MAR 1884 L	18	470
Hall, Joseph	Warren, Alice	24 OCT 1883 R	18	209
Hall, Joseph	Downs, Rachel	03 SEP 1884 L	19	275
Hall, Josephine	Coleman, Howard	18 MAR 1880 R	14	187
Hall, Josephine	Jones, David	06 DEC 1883 L	18	302
Hall, Josephine	Pryor, Robert James	09 FEB 1884 L	18	416
Hall, Julian M.	Maguire, Alice E.	06 FEB 1883 L	17	294
Hall, Lewis K.	Maxwell, Emma R.	12 MAY 1880	14	266
Hall, Lillian Hammond	McGinn, Robert Wright	19 MAR 1881 R	15	233
Hall, Lizzie E.	Butler, Richard T.	17 NOV 1884	19	389
Hall, Lizzie F.	Wood, Stan King	20 FEB 1884 R	18	432
Hall, Louisa	Belt, Andrew	30 JAN 1879 L	13	038
Hall, Lucy	Carter, William	15 JAN 1878 R	11	304
Hall, Lutha	Pritchet, Mattie	20 SEP 1878	12	228
Hall, Lydia	Gibson, Nicholas	08 NOV 1880 L	15	035
Hall, Mack	Johnson, Annie	11 AUG 1885	20	358
Hall, Margaret	Swinborne, John	11 DEC 1884 R	19	454
Hall, Martha	Handy, George	05 AUG 1879	13	306
Hall, Martha L.	Mansfield, Walter N.	15 FEB 1882 R	16	243
Hall, Martimore S.	Saffee, Emma L.	16 JUL 1884	19	136
Hall, Mary	Milburn, Thomas	30 OCT 1882	17	056
Hall, Mary	Washington, William	10 DEC 1883 L	18	307
Hall, Mary Alice	Wright, George	06 APR 1878 L	11	408
Hall, Mary Ellen	Harris, George W.	01 JUL 1880 L	14	344
Hall, Mary Lizzie	Mines, James M.	02 JUN 1881 L	15	341
Hall, Mary Susan	Kenny, Edmund	08 OCT 1878 L	12	259
Hall, Mollie	Fletcher, John	26 MAR 1878	11	393
Hall, Nathaniel	Corson, Millie	18 AUG 1877 L	11	057
Hall, Nora P.	Wall, Henry Wooford	06 JUN 1883	17	473
Hall, Oden	Stewart, Minty	15 OCT 1885 R	20	489
Hall, Opieisia	Bell, Edmonia	27 SEP 1883	18	130
Hall, Orville D.	Gilman, Ida Mary	22 OCT 1879 R	13	437
Hall, Peter	Deavers, Mary Frances	01 MAY 1883 R	17	424
Hall, Peter	Jones, Alice Leeatha	11 SEP 1884 R	19	241
Hall, Peter F.	Chaney, Alice G.	24 JAN 1884 R	18	390
Hall, Philip	Johnson, Mary Ann	09 DEC 1879 R	14	034
Hall, Philip Thomas	Weaver, Mary E.	30 APR 1878 R	12	031
Hall, Rachel	McKnight, Cassius	14 JUL 1883 L	18	047
Hall, Rosa A.	Shultz, John A.	29 NOV 1884	19	337
Hall, Sallie Evelyn	Pinkerton, David C.	23 DEC 1880	15	117

Hall, Sarah A.	Purdum, J. Rufus	01 MAY 1883 R	17	420
Hall, Sarah Jane	Spaulding, Daniel J.	17 OCT 1881	16	028
Hall, Susan Laura	Foltz, John Calhoun	01 JAN 1879 R	13	001
Hall, Thomas	Welch, Louisa	03 JAN 1878 R	11	290
Hall, Thomas L.	Ludwig, Phebe Henrietta	09 SEP 1885 R	20	407
Hall, Thomas Thornton	Cooper, Mary Eleanor	29 OCT 1881 R	16	051
Hall, William M.	Colelazier, Frances J.	15 OCT 1879 R	13	425
Hall, William W.	Peach, Rebecca A.	25 AUG 1881 L	15	458
Hall, Woolsey P.	Matthews, Matilda	16 APR 1879 R	13	147
Hallback, W.M.	Cheatham, Mary E.	16 DEC 1884 L	19	463
Halleck, William Edward	Stone, Lucinda Ridgely	26 NOV 1878 R	12	348
Halleck, William Filmore	McVay, Charlotte	14 NOV 1882 R	17	124
Haller, Eveline	Tolbert, William	15 JUN 1880 L	14	320
Haller, Nicholas	McClelland, Lola	06 MAR 1878 R	11	374
Haller, Nicholas T.	Squires, Fannie E.	21 APR 1885	20	178
Haller, Vialetta	Horman, Augustus	02 AUG 1883 R	18	065
Halley, Ellen	Bundick, Thomas E.	19 JUN 1879 R	13	240
Halley, John E.	McKerichar, Mary S.	23 FEB 1882 R	16	258
Halley, John M.	Downs, Ella V.	27 DEC 1877 R	11	273
Halliday, Francis A., Dr.	Shaw, Laura Belle	21 DEC 1881	16	144
Hallinen, Sarah	Genesse, Peter	24 NOV 1884	19	365
Hollock, Edward D.	Pennington, Mary C.	01 DEC 1880 L	15	078
Halloran, Jennie B.	Springer, Horace P.	02 FEB 1879 R	13	042
Hallstrom, Christina	Bostrom, Augustus O.	10 SEP 1878	12	210
Halpin, Bridget Adele	Keefe, Jeremiah	26 SEP 1883 L	18	156
Halpin, James	Walsh, Mary E.	08 JUL 1884 L	19	127
Halpin, Mary	Farell, Patrick	30 MAY 1884	19	025
Halter, Christine Nellie	Vliet, Edgar	15 JUL 1880 R	14	360
Haltnorth, Otto	Gerhardt, Pauline	29 MAR 1880 R	14	202
Halton, Mary R.	Armstrong, John B.	29 DEC 1880	15	131
Ham, Jeemes	Roane, Carrie	25 SEP 1883 L	18	152
Ham, Peter	Goodwin, Roberta	17 MAY 1881 R	15	312
Hambleton, Henry	Washington, Rosa Lee	03 NOV 1884	19	356
Hamblin, Isabella Gray	French, George Norris	19 SEP 1877 R	11	099
Hamer, Annie L.	Dillard, Clarence, Rev.	30 OCT 1884	19	346
Hamer, Mamie J.	Adams, Thomas H.	20 DEC 1882 R	17	196
Hamersly, John Robert	Webb, Emma Jane	25 AUG 1879	13	334
Hamesley, Mary A.	Chitams, Joseph	04 FEB 1884 L	18	406
Hamill, Ida Malvina	Robertson, Henry	29 MAY 1881 R	15	330
Hamilton, Agnes	Henson, Richard	19 AUG 1880	14	406
Hamilton, Andrew P.	Hall, Annie S., Mrs.	01 AUG 1881 R	15	430
Hamilton, Anna	Dyer, George O.	17 NOV 1881 L	16	083
Hamilton, Annie R.	Fauntleroy, William M.	12 SEP 1882 L	17	018
Hamilton, Asa H.	Mangum, Rachel Sophia	22 NOV 1883 L	18	271
Hamilton, Charles	Miles, Julia	28 JAN 1884 L	18	398
Hamilton, Charles	Allen, Josephine	25 JUN 1885 L	20	294
Hamilton, Charles	Powell, Evelina	17 SEP 1885 L	20	424
Hamilton, Charles E.	Green, Mary F.	31 MAR 1885 R	20	126
Hamilton, Charlotte	Meridith, Henry	18 JAN 1881 L	15	154
Hamilton, Charlotte, Mrs.	Nordenstrahl, Thor	04 NOV 1882 R	17	106
Hamilton, Clara	Waters, John W.	27 AUG 1885 L	20	389
Hamilton, Cora L.	Knox, William Salsbury	14 OCT 1885 R	20	479
Hamilton, Cornelia	Lloyd, Thomas	13 AUG 1879 R	13	312
Hamilton, Eliza	Scott, Thomas	05 JUL 1881	15	391
Hamilton, Elizabeth Blanch	Wilker, James A.	05 OCT 1885 R	20	455
Hamilton, Ellen	Ouden, Lewis	30 JAN 1883 L	17	279
Hamilton, F.M.	Adams, Katie E. Brown	25 OCT 1883	18	214
Hamilton, Fannie E.	Miller, Daniel	28 JUL 1884	19	160

Hamilton, Frances	Parker, Miles	21 AUG 1884 L	19	202
Hamilton, Henry	Jones, Lottie	08 AUG 1882 R	16	470
Hamilton, J.W.	Garnett, May L.	06 NOV 1884	19	367
Hamilton, John	Lewis, Lizzie D.	29 OCT 1882	17	099
Hamilton, Joseph	Lawkins, Rosa	06 AUG 1883 L	18	075
Hamilton, Julia Eliza	Bailey, James Lewis	19 NOV 1884 L	19	397
Hamilton, Lelia	Parker, Edward F.	29 NOV 1882	17	151
Hamilton, Lizzie	Giles, Charles	06 SEP 1882 L	17	009
Hamilton, Lydia J.	Sargeant, John L.	17 FEB 1884 R	18	428
Hamilton, Mamie	Hellen, Joseph	25 APR 1883 R	17	408
Hamilton, Mary A.	Kearney, Charles E.	23 DEC 1880 R	15	118
Hamilton, Mary C.	Chew, Charles H.	28 JAN 1885 L	20	041
Hamilton, Mary Ellen	Gaskins, Arthur	19 JUN 1879	13	237
Hamilton, Minnie	Allen, Wm. H.	29 JUN 1880 L	14	338
Hamilton, Ross	Knox, M.B.	18 MAY 1885 L	20	228
Hamilton, Sophia	Davis, Jacob	25 NOV 1884 L	19	409
Hamilton, Stanislaus M.	Olds, Catherine M.	28 SEP 1880 L	14	463
Hamilton, Susie N.	King, Charles R.	17 APR 1884 L	18	517
Hamilton, Washington	Thornton, Laura	16 JAN 1879	13	016
Hamilton, William	Long, Esther	07 APR 1878	11	404
Hamilton, William	Allen, Amelia	21 JUL 1881 L	15	412
Hamlet, Harriet Miller	Clark, Eugene Bradley	13 NOV 1878 R	12	326
Hamlin, Theodore R.	Wilson, Eva E.	21 JUN 1881	15	367
Hamlit, William	Fields, Mary Virginia	13 OCT 1880 L	14	491
Hamm, Allen	Warrington, Ella	22 JUN 1882 R	16	423
Hammacher, Catherine E.	Meredith, John P.	25 JUL 1883	18	059
Hammack, William L.	Sexton, Ella C.	23 OCT 1882 L	17	086
Hammack, William M.	Markward, Celia	04 APR 1882 L	16	299
Hammer, Andersen	York, Emma E.	10 OCT 1883	18	184
Hammer, George H.	Saur, Emma	28 NOV 1877	11	212
Hammer, John H.	Baumann, Barbara A.	03 JAN 1880 R	13	390
Hammer, Rosa	Lombardy, Charles	09 DEC 1879 R	14	038
Hammer, William	Richter, Mary A.	12 OCT 1878 L	12	267
Hammerly, Edward L.	Hayden, Emma E.	13 MAR 1884 R	18	468
Hammersly, Laura	McCormick, Michael George	26 JAN 1885 L	20	036
Hammett, Blanche	Bayley, Henry B.	15 APR 1884 R	18	509
Hammett, Charles N.	Maryman, Harriet E.	23 NOV 1881 L	16	092
Hammett, Ella	Bullock, William Broadus	11 JAN 1882 R	16	189
Hammett, Frances E.	Donnelly, Daniel G.	19 AUG 1883	18	094
Hammett, John A.	Stollager, Carrie	27 AUG 1883	18	100
Hammett, Susan Lydia	Stewart, John	17 MAY 1883 R	17	448
Hammond, Addie Ursula	May, George C.	06 SEP 1883 R	18	110
Hammond, Ella J.	Murray, Charles D.	05 AUG 1884 R	19	168
Hammond, George W.	Steinmeyer, Josephine	06 FEB 1880 R	14	133
Hammond, Henry	Parker, Annie	12 OCT 1881 L	16	018
Hammond, Katie	Speer, William F.	10 JUL 1882 R	16	444
Hammond, Marie Louise	Snyder, William Tayloe	26 MAR 1883 R	17	360
Hammond, Robert	Roberts, Annie	27 JUL 1882 R	16	317
Hammond, Sarah M.	Fridley, B.F.	18 FEB 1878	11	344
Hammond, Thomas Victor	Hopkins, Bertha	03 JUN 1884 R	19	050
Hammond, Virginia	Johnson, Edward	21 NOV 1883 L	18	269
Hammond, Willie D.	Lamb, Laura E.W.	08 JUN 1885	20	261
Hamod, Elias	Hayes, Christiana	18 OCT 1877 R	11	143
Hamond, William T.	Manfield, Eliza	23 JUN 1880 R	14	333
Hampson, Charles	Vaughan, Mary E.	01 JUN 1885 R	20	250
Hampson, Thomas	Hale, Martha Rogers	29 MAY 1878 R	12	069
Hamptman, Maria Louise	Donaldson, John Thomas	14 APR 1884 R	18	507
Hampton, Alice	Scott, Rochester	08 AUG 1885 R	20	347

Hampton, John	Walker, Emma J.	25 JAN 1883	17	275
Hampton, John W.	Young, Lottie	15 MAY 1884 R	19	020
Hance, James H.	Gilliam, Lulu May	08 JUN 1885 L	20	261
Hancock, James M.	Jackson, Lillie M.	22 SEP 1885 R	20	433
Hand, Mary J.	Perkins, Thomas	30 JUN 1878	12	117
Handler, Annie Amelia	Gibson, John Henry	03 AUG 1885	20	349
Handley, Josephine A.	Hunter, James T.	03 JUN 1878	12	080
Handley, Margaret L.	Ryan, William S.	25 DEC 1883 R	18	336
Handrup, Ferdinand A.	Raab, Antoinette	23 JUN 1883 L	18	011
Hands, Adam C.	Thompson, Mary V. Ratcliff	30 SEP 1878 R	12	243
Hands, John	Brown, Katie A.	14 JAN 1884 L	18	376
Handy, Charles W.	Eichhorn, Barbara F.	28 APR 1881 L	15	283
Handy, George	Hall, Martha	05 AUG 1879	13	306
Handy, George K.	Coomes, Mary	28 APR 1880 L	14	242
Handy, Levin C.	Gossford, Susie E.	17 NOV 1879 R	13	491
Handy, Thomas	Rhodes, Hannah	23 OCT 1882 L	17	085
Handy, William	Daly, Mary Ellen	15 NOV 1881 L	16	078
Handy, William B.	Hughes, Mary A.	24 MAR 1880 R	14	196
Handy, William Edward	Hickenlooper, Ettie	04 MAY 1882 R	16	348
Haneke, Agatha	Faunce, John	25 MAY 1883 L	17	462
Haneke, Christine	Ockershausen, Henry	12 JUN 1879	13	230
Haner, Etta G.	Jonas, LeRoy D.	26 MAY 1885	20	241
Hanes, Walter	Blunt, Fannie	23 MAY 1885 R	20	236
Haney, Amanda	Jackson, Samuel	03 OCT 1878	12	252
Haney, Annie V.	Newman, John H.	07 JUN 1883	17	479
Hanford, Charles Barnum	Bear, Mariella Twaddell	30 JUN 1885 R	20	297
Hanford, Fannie Lawson	Young, Constantine W.	28 FEB 1882 R	16	260
Hankey, Mary	Black, James H.	27 NOV 1879 R	14	014
Hankins, Jacob	Jones, Sina	16 JUN 1882 R	16	414
Hanlan, Sarah	Foley, Edward	08 AUG 1883 L	18	079
Hanlein, Augusta	Immrich, Daniel B.	30 SEP 1878 R	12	242
Hanlein, Carrie	Behrend, Elon	04 NOV 1883 R	18	230
Hanlein, Lizzie	Buxbaum, Ferdinand	25 MAR 1883 R	17	357
Hanna, Anna R.	Forney, Edward Otis	22 NOV 1881 L	16	090
Hanna, Benjamin W.	Cole, Imogen A.	30 MAY 1882 R	16	378
Hanna, Robert	Thomas, Sarah	03 SEP 1879 L	13	348
Hannah, Susie	Thomas, Henry	29 OCT 1883 R	18	220
Hannal, Georgiana	Stuart, William	19 JUN 1884 R	19	092
Hannan, Frank	Monahan, Ella J.	27 NOV 1884 L	19	423
Hannan, Michael	Brown, Annie	12 SEP 1882 L	17	018
Hannen, Maggie	Watson, William W.	09 SEP 1884 L	19	236
Hannum, Jennie	Knight, Charles D.	20 FEB 1884	18	432
Hanover, Minnie	Schmidt, Charles G.L.	11 SEP 1881	15	470
Hanover, Sarah E.	Ramey, John W.	08 JUN 1882	16	400
Hanrahan, Helen	Corbelt, George W.	03 OCT 1878 R	12	2904
Hansbrough, Fannie C.	Brown, James S.	15 JUL 1880 R	14	359
Hansbrough, Maria	Peck, William H.	28 APR 1880 L	14	240
Hansen, John	Meyenberg, Pauline	02 SEP 1878 L	12	192
Hansen, John H.	Lamkin, Alice V.	12 OCT 1878	12	271
Hansen, Sophus Christian	Dawson, Florence Elizabeth	06 FEB 1878 R	11	330
Hansen, Thomas	Fields, Jennie Hellen	08 SEP 1883 L	18	119
Hanson, Charles L.	Warmbold, Helen	28 MAR 1883	17	364
Hanson, Hoban	Fox, Charlotte A.	18 MAR 1883	17	349
Hanson, James	Slaughter, Louisa	04 OCT 1883	18	168
Hanson, John	McCoy, Rachel	28 NOV 1877	11	211
Hanson, Julia	Bibb, Albert Burnley	30 SEP 1880 R	14	467
Hanson, Mary E.	Ball, George A.	19 AUG 1879 L	13	326
Hanson, Susan	Hanson, William	06 NOV 1877	11	171

Hanson, William	Hanson, Susan	06 NOV 1877	11	171
Hantzman, Robert	Arnold, Mary Jane Brooke	06 JUL 1881 R	15	392
Hanvey, Edgar W.	Combes, Mary H.	11 FEB 1885 R	20	063
Harban, James Hamilton	Cochran, Sallie	24 DEC 1884 R	19	480
Harban, Walter Simpson	Higgins, Isabelle	26 OCT 1881 R	16	043
Harbaugh, Christina	Ratcliff, Richard A.	13 OCT 1883 L	18	190
Harbaugh, Edgar G.	Washington, Julia Cady	10 DEC 1877	11	227
Harbaugh, George Hastings	Gantt, Helen Mary	11 FEB 1880 R	14	148
Harbeck, Theodore	Quistorff, Hellen Louise	11 AUG 1885 R	20	364
Harbin, James S.	Worthan, Miriam S.	04 MAY 1878	12	037
Harbin, James T.	Mitchell, Jennie A.	23 SEP 1882 L	17	034
Harbin, John H.	Skinner, Mary A.	29 DEC 1884 R	19	499
Hard, Margaret	Mack, George	16 JUN 1881 L	15	364
Hard, Mary	Young, Isaac	23 DEC 1879	14	062
Hardaway, Mary	Johnson, Robert	29 MAY 1884	19	044
Hardell, Robert C.	Soper, Julia E.	16 NOV 1880 L	15	050
Harden, Mary Frances	Gantt, Edward	06 FEB 1879 R	13	048
Harden, Mary Jane	Knott, John	07 MAR 1878 L	11	376
Harden, T.L.	Cryer, Eliza A.	08 JUN 1881	15	352
Hardester, John Thomas	Gates, Florence Virginia	16 FEB 1880 R	14	154
Hardester, Mollie E.	Mitchell, John A.	26 MAR 1885 R	20	134
Hardesty, Anna J.	Mudd, Ernest F.	06 JUN 1878 L	12	090
Hardick, Henry	Thomas, Bertie	16 DEC 1884 L	19	460
Hardie, William H.	Towles, Sarah	10 FEB 1885	33	8009
Hardin, Albert	Dester, Amanda	29 JUL 1881 R	15	425
Hardin, Margaret	Morgan, Thomas	21 SEP 1881	15	492
Harding, Alice G.	Estes, Elisha B.	01 OCT 1878 R	12	245
Harding, Ann E.	Grover, John F.	25 JUN 1883	18	013
Harding, C.T.	Langworthy, Villie M.	02 JUN 1880 R	14	301
Harding, George W.	Nash, Mollie	17 OCT 1882	17	077
Harding, Hezekiah	Jennings, Sarah A.	08 SEP 1882 R	17	013
Harding, Jennie	Parker, Charles W.	05 OCT 1880 R	14	475
Harding, John	Stone, Emma	16 JUL 1885	20	331
Harding, John E.	Kidwell, Sarah V.	03 MAY 1883 R	17	428
Harding, Katie	Thomas, George	08 JUL 1878 L	12	128
Harding, Louisa	Davis, W. Dana	03 APR 1880	14	207
Harding, O.P., Mrs.	Abraham, Jacob	29 MAR 1883 L	17	370
Harding, Richard N.	Clarke, Ella P.G.	24 NOV 1880 R	15	065
Harding, Thomas H.	Murphy, Nellie B.	17 OCT 1882 L	17	075
Hardister, James A.	Smith, Mary J.E.	22 SEP 1880 L	14	455
Hardwick, Sallie F.	Allen, John P.	30 APR 1879	13	166
Hardy, Annie	Teuly, Albert C.	27 APR 1881 L	15	277
Hardy, Elmira	Hickerson, Charles E.	17 AUG 1885 L	20	372
Hardy, Francis B.	Richardson, Cora J.	16 DEC 1884 R	19	461
Hardy, Frank Benj.	Allen, Eliza Norcesley Va.	28 DEC 1882 R	17	210
Hardy, George Anna	Bradley, John E.	05 OCT 1882 R	17	055
Hardy, Henry	Hatton, Helen Ruth	10 SEP 1882	17	028
Hardy, John Thomas	Fowler, Florence T.	17 OCT 1877	11	141
Hardy, Kate M.	Wiley, John T.	27 SEP 1880	14	461
Hardy, Louisa	Rockafellow, Andrew D.	30 MAY 1878	12	073
Hardy, Mary E.	Warrick, John B.	21 OCT 1880 R	15	009
Hardy, Mary S.	Robinson, James	01 DEC 1880 R	15	074
Hardy, May	Hall, John	26 JUN 1884 L	19	105
Hardy, Richard	Moore, Alice	09 JUL 1885 L	20	319
Hardy, Samuel F.	Smoot, Rosa E.	29 OCT 1884 L	19	344
Hardy, Thomas G.	Davis, Emma E.	18 MAY 1882 R	16	366
Hardy, William H.	Toles, Sarah E.	05 DEC 1884 L	19	438
Hare, Florence Bell	Council, William Boardman	18 DEC 1879 R	14	054

Hare, Francis G.	Ward, Sarah Ann	10 JAN 1883 R	17	246
Hargrove, Silas	Jennings, Pug	13 AUG 1877 L	11	051
Harken, Joseph Alex.	Fractions, Nancy E.	19 APR 1883 L	17	401
Harkness, Cora P.	Rupp, William H.	20 NOV 1878 R	12	338
Harkness, J. Williams	Denham, Louise	18 DEC 1878 R	12	388
Harkness, John A.	Wright, Mary	25 FEB 1879 R	13	079
Harkness, Kate Elizabeth	Manson, Joseph Oscaar	12 APR 1882 R	16	313
Harkness, Robert Henry	Barrett, Anna Theresa	20 MAR 1884 R	18	478
Harlan, Edith Shanklin	Child, Frank Linus	25 OCT 1881	16	040
Harlan, Isabella	Desport, Daniel	15 JAN 1880 R	14	074
Harlan, Thomas	Runnells, Maria	08 MAR 1883 R	17	338
Harleston, Charles W.	Keys, Ellen	30 MAY 1883 L	17	469
Harleston, George B.	Bellew, Mary E.	15 APR 1884 L	18	512
Harley, Irene	Newman, Robert	06 FEB 1883 L	17	293
Harley, Jane A.	McKenney, Charles E.	21 APR 1882	16	327
Harley, John A.	Mann, Hesta L.	23 APR 1884	18	528
Harley, John J.	Porter, Susie E.	06 SEP 1882 L	17	009
Harley, Laura	Otis, William	05 JUL 1883	18	038
Harley, Lizzie	Smith, James	21 JUL 1885 R	20	327
Harlins, Winston	Webb, Julia	26 AUG 1884 L	19	208
Harman, David	Todd, Harriet	02 JAN 1882 R	16	176
Harman, Rosalie	Smith, Robert M.	22 FEB 1880 R	14	161
Harman, William H.	Mulcahy, Mary E.	15 NOV 1879 L	13	489
Harmon, Amelia	Sparrow, William	06 JUL 1880	14	350
Harmon, Annie Virginia	Corcoran, Edward Boyd	22 OCT 1879 R	13	437
Harmon, Ella	Brosnan, Patrick A.	03 OCT 1881 L	16	002
Harmon, Grace G.	Lipscomb, Andrew A.	21 SEP 1881	15	492
Harmon, John D., Jr.	King, Florence	02 APR 1883 L	17	375
Harmon, William H.	Best, Jane	24 OCT 1878 L	12	291
Harold, Charles	Maddox, Virginia	26 JUN 1883 R	18	016
Harold, John	Milstead, Emma	02 APR 1878 L	11	401
Harover, Emma J.	Love, William	04 JUN 1884 R	19	055
Harper, Anna Malisa Kelly	Coomes, Lewis Walter	10 AUG 1881 R	15	437
Harper, Charles	Dacey, Mary	09 AUG 1880 R	14	395
Harper, Clara M.	Scott, John A.	15 JUN 1882	16	413
Harper, Edward	Keys, Delia Ann	22 SEP 1885 L	20	434
Harper, Eliza	Harris, Thomas P.	11 SEP 1884 L	19	241
Harper, George A.	Carroll, Georgiana	08 OCT 1883 L	18	176
Harper, Georgianna C.	Wilson, Taylor	25 AUG 1883	18	092
Harper, James	Thomas, Matilda	12 FEB 1881 L	15	187
Harper, James	West, Fannie	07 JUN 1883 L	17	481
Harper, James E.	Baeschlin, Lavinia M.	15 JAN 1880 L	14	106
Harper, John H.	Sterne, Susie	20 NOV 1882	17	136
Harper, Joseph Franklin	Finley, Katie	01 JUL 1884 R	19	109
Harper, Laura Virginia	Hodgkin, Charles Edwin	14 MAY 1885 R	20	222
Harper, Lurena E.	Jones, George W.	04 JUL 1882	16	432
Harper, Mamie F.	Yates, Richard H.	18 APR 1882 L	16	323
Harper, Mary	Hawkins, Frank	02 MAR 1880 L	14	171
Harper, Mary E.	Nalley, James E.	21 APR 1885 L	20	178
Harper, Nancy	Galloway, Washington	19 OCT 1885 L	20	496
Harper, Samuel A.	Young, Mary F.	24 DEC 1877 L	11	265
Harper, Stephen V.	Carty, Susan A.	16 NOV 1883 R	18	260
Harper, T. Dennis	Odell, Matie M.	07 AUG 1877 L	11	044
Harper, Thomas	Parker, Melinda	12 OCT 1881 R	16	019
Harper, William Mercer	Smith, Eulalie	25 JAN 1881 R	15	163
Harrence, William	Burnes, Ella	27 MAY 1880 R	14	284
Harri, Millie	Lewis, Leonidas A.	05 SEP 1883	18	113
Harridy, Richard	Brooks, Eliza	01 FEB 1883	17	284

D.C. Marriage Records Index, June 28, 1877 to October 19, 1885

Harries, George H.	Langley, Lizzie S.	23 APR 1884	18	530
Harries, Laura	Harris, James	30 OCT 1877 R	09	2161
Harrigan, Kate E.	Long, Edward F.	20 AUG 1883 L	18	095
Harrin, Mary A.	Purcell, Thomas P.	29 JUN 1882	16	430
Harrington, Charles Albert	Streaker, Mary Genila	06 JUN 1882 R	16	396
Harrington, Claude M.	Ford, Alice V.	29 NOV 1882 R	17	158
Harrington, Daniel	Sullivan, Mary E.	16 APR 1879 L	13	148
Harrington, David J.	Murphy, Nellie A.	16 APR 1884 R	18	514
Harrington, Julia	Sullivan, Michael	03 APR 1883 L	17	377
Harrington, Maria T.	Burke, Michael J.	07 NOV 1882	17	113
Harrington, Mary	Dugan, Michael	24 OCT 1882 L	17	090
Harrington, Mary I.	Shreve, Walter E.	02 OCT 1878 R	12	247
Harrington, Nannie V.	Shreves, Ben	19 JUN 1880 L	14	327
Harriot, Charles J.E.	DeBarry, Julia C.F.	15 NOV 1879 R	13	487
Harris, Abraham	Marcus, Rebecca	05 NOV 1877	11	168
Harris, Addie L.	Bunting, Harry C.	01 JUL 1885	20	304
Harris, Ahna A.	Glover, George W.	06 JUL 1880	14	348
Harris, Albert	Mack, Rose	18 APR 1878 R	12	002
Harris, Alberta	Williams, James H.	10 JUN 1885 L	20	266
Harris, Alexander F.	Gardner, Virginia C.	06 DEC 1882	17	172
Harris, Alfred	Seems, Caroline	18 OCT 1883 R	18	199
Harris, Alice	Harris, Edmund	13 MAR 1879 R	13	100
Harris, Alice A.	Proctor, Samuel	13 OCT 1877 L	11	134
Harris, Allice	Davis, Henry	09 OCT 1884 R	19	297
Harris, Amelia	Snowden, Edward	17 MAY 1878	12	057
Harris, Andrew	Carter, Lizzie	17 AUG 1882 L	16	484
Harris, Ann Maria	Curry, George	05 JUN 1884	19	066
Harris, Annie	Mason, Edward	26 MAY 1881 L	15	329
Harris, Annie	Bean, Wm. Thos.	11 JAN 1883 L	17	253
Harris, Annie	Olin, James H.	16 SEP 1884	19	253
Harris, Annie	Thomas, William	24 SEP 1885 R	20	428
Harris, Annie C.	Pearman, John N.	16 JUL 1883	18	048
Harris, Annie Lee	Jones, Andrew Coles	04 JUL 1881 R	15	386
Harris, Archibald	Tolliver, Sarah	04 JAN 1880 R	14	088
Harris, Augusta	White, David	09 NOV 1877 R	11	177
Harris, Benjamin F.	Tait, Mary Ann	30 DEC 1880 L	15	132
Harris, Bruce	Covill, Emma H., Mrs.	22 FEB 1883 R	17	316
Harris, Charity Tinney	Robinson, William	23 MAY 1881 R	15	321
Harris, Charles	Perry, Carrie	10 NOV 1881	16	028
Harris, Clara	West, John	07 SEP 1880 R	14	435
Harris, David	Brooks, Nellie	22 JAN 1880 R	14	110
Harris, E. Samuel	Richardson, Mary Ellen	05 DEC 1878 R	12	369
Harris, Edmund	Harris, Alice	13 MAR 1879 R	13	100
Harris, Elijah	Terry, Mary	10 MAY 1881 R	15	298
Harris, Eliza	Reynolds, Jarett	21 JUL 1885 L	20	336
Harris, Elizabeth	Pierce, James F.	07 JUL 1879 L	13	272
Harris, Ellen	Young, William	07 OCT 1884 L	19	289
Harris, Emma	Williams, Philip	20 MAY 1878 R	12	045
Harris, Emma	Haskins, Simon	09 JAN 1883	17	247
Harris, Emma C.	Smith, David R.	31 DEC 1882 R	17	227
Harris, Fannie	Johnson, William	17 DEC 1880 L	15	107
Harris, Fanny	Forrest, Arthur	15 JAN 1884 R	18	378
Harris, Fenton	Cartwright, Alice	06 NOV 1879 R	13	471
Harris, Florence	Henson, John	15 MAY 1879 L	13	192
Harris, Florence O.	Taylor, Henry	18 JAN 1881	15	153
Harris, Frank	Mason, Laura	02 NOV 1881 R	15	467
Harris, Frederick	Jones, Bettie	23 APR 1884 R	18	528
Harris, Frederick	Buchanan, margaret	28 AUG 1884 L	19	213

Harris, George W.	Hall, Mary Ellen	01 JUL 1880 L	14	344
Harris, George W.	Carroll, Mary	24 JUL 1884	19	154
Harris, George W.	Vallen, Sarah	21 AUG 1884	19	199
Harris, Gracie	Thomas, James L.	13 MAR 1884	18	470
Harris, Harriet	Humphrey, Henry	27 NOV 1879	14	018
Harris, Henrietta	Winbush, S.H.	19 AUG 1878 L	12	172
Harris, Henry	Brown, Mary Ellen	04 MAR 1878 L	11	368
Harris, Henry	Diges, Millie	17 JUL 1879 R	13	283
Harris, Henry	Gray, Margaret Ann	20 JUL 1880 L	14	369
Harris, J.	Hackley, Martha	11 APR 1882 L	16	309
Harris, J.T.	Jordan, R.S.	10 SEP 1879 L	13	364
Harris, James	Bornett, Georgianna	18 OCT 1877 R	11	140
Harris, James	Harries, Laura	30 OCT 1877 R	09	2161
Harris, James	Tebbs, Carrie V.	01 AUG 1878	12	150
Harris, James H.	Nichols, Mary E.	12 JAN 1879	13	015
Harris, James P.	Makle, Maria	14 NOV 1882 L	17	126
Harris, James W.	Heming, Katie F.	18 NOV 1879 L	13	493
Harris, Jane	Hill, Julius	12 JUL 1877 R	11	018
Harris, Jane	Luce, Robert	18 JUL 1885 L	20	331
Harris, Jinnie	Jenkins, William Francis	01 FEB 1883	17	283
Harris, John	Wilson, Amelia	26 JUL 1880 L	14	375
Harris, John	Griffin, Hattie	15 JUN 1885 R	20	273
Harris, John H.	Herbert, Mary K.	05 NOV 1879 R	13	468
Harris, John R.	Haines, Clara V.	14 APR 1880 R	14	223
Harris, John R.	Collins, Mary J.	22 FEB 1883	17	316
Harris, John W.	Williams, Louisa	06 AUG 1883 L	18	075
Harris, John W.	Daley, Annie M.	03 DEC 1884 R	19	432
Harris, Joseph	Green, Susie	20 MAY 1879 L	13	196
Harris, Joseph	Brown, Annie	16 AUG 1882 R	16	481
Harris, Joseph C.	Miles, Alice	17 MAR 1881 L	15	229
Harris, Joseph H.	Winters, Mary A.	25 FEB 1885	20	084
Harris, Joseph R.	Barnes, Mary Frances	26 JAN 1880 L	14	120
Harris, Katie	Mackenzie, James B.	12 JAN 1880 R	14	102
Harris, Katie	Lancaster, Augustus, Jr.	01 SEP 1885	20	394
Harris, Laura S.	Lyvers, Paris	05 APR 1882	16	300
Harris, Liberta	Addison, Jerre M.	07 JUL 1881 L	15	393
Harris, Lizzie	Jackson, Charles H.	19 APR 1882 R	16	303
Harris, Lorenzo	Marshall, Cecelia	11 APR 1883 L	17	391
Harris, Lucinda	Wallace, Charles	28 NOV 1877 L	11	208
Harris, Lucinda	Washington, George	12 JUL 1883	18	044
Harris, Lucy	Newell, Charles	14 SEP 1877	11	094
Harris, Maggie	Edlin, John	20 DEC 1882	17	193
Harris, Maggie	Matthews, John	02 AUG 1883	18	072
Harris, Mamie M.	Smith, Charles B.	06 SEP 1882 R	17	009
Harris, Margaret	Foster, John	23 JUN 1881 R	15	374
Harris, Maria	Joiner, Samuel	10 MAY 1882 L	16	355
Harris, Mary	Tenny, John	27 OCT 1883 R	18	218
Harris, Mary A.	Moton, Armstead	06 DEC 1877 R	11	225
Harris, Mary E.	Bain, James E.	20 AUG 1885 L	20	381
Harris, Mary Louisa	Allen, Robert	31 DEC 1879 R	14	084
Harris, Mason	Robertson, Martha	03 JUL 1879	13	265
Harris, Matilda	Newman, Charles	17 OCT 1883 R	18	197
Harris, Michael	Lachmann, Mary	19 JUN 1883 L	18	004
Harris, Millie W.	Martin, R.H.	29 NOV 1881	16	101
Harris, Minor	Banket, Phillis	16 JAN 1879 R	13	024
Harris, Morgan B.	Linney, Mary Agnes	29 MAR 1880 R	14	200
Harris, Morris	Richelson, Fannie	06 JAN 1883 L	17	240
Harris, Moses	Pettiford, Edmonia	11 NOV 1880 R	15	044

D.C. Marriage Records Index, June 28, 1877 to October 19, 1885

Name	Spouse	Date		
Harris, Nancy	Johnson, Willis	15 DEC 1883 L	18	317
Harris, Orlando	Barnesley, Sallie	23 APR 1883 L	17	405
Harris, Patrick	Lewis, Louisa	18 DEC 1884 R	32	7901
Harris, Patrick	Lewis, Sophia	05 DEC 1884	19	440
Harris, Philip B.	Thomas, Annie	04 JUN 1878	12	083
Harris, Philip B.	Thomas, Annie, Mrs.	04 JUN 1879 R	14	3256
Harris, Phoebe	Morewood, George Palmer	25 MAY 1882 R	16	376
Harris, Preston P.	Johnson, Mary E.	03 OCT 1883 R	18	166
Harris, Rachel	Montague, William	23 MAY 1883 R	17	458
Harris, Reuben	Newmyer, Hattie	01 SEP 1880 R	14	425
Harris, Richard	Sayles, Mary	27 JUN 1879 R	13	242
Harris, Rickson T.	Waller, Eddie F.	28 OCT 1880 R	15	021
Harris, Ritchie B.	Coons, Mary V.	04 SEP 1884	19	227
Harris, Robert	Gaskins, Nancy	22 MAY 1878	12	063
Harris, Robert	Shields, Anna	24 MAR 1879	13	110
Harris, Rosa B.	Denzler, John	13 FEB 1883 R	17	303
Harris, Rosetta	Stroder, John	20 DEC 1884	19	474
Harris, Rosser V.	Foster, Magnolia E.	15 SEP 1878 R	12	219
Harris, Russell	Taylor, Frances	28 DEC 1882 L	17	222
Harris, S.	Wiley, E.F.	31 MAR 1878	11	398
Harris, Sadie F.	Prufer, William J.	10 SEP 1878	12	208
Harris, Sam	Dixon, Rosetta	10 MAY 1881 L	15	300
Harris, Samuel C.	Madison, James A.	19 JUL 1880 R	14	369
Harris, Samuel H.	Morris, Rebecca	25 MAR 1880 R	14	197
Harris, Sarah	Gibbs, Arthur	22 NOV 1877 R	11	199
Harris, Sarah V.	Ochard, James F.	15 SEP 1880 L	14	445
Harris, Shepherd Augustus	Richardson, Alice R.	28 APR 1881 R	15	284
Harris, Sophia	Allens, Henry	16 OCT 1884	19	299
Harris, Sophronia	Snowden, Samuel	05 JUN 1883	17	476
Harris, Thomas P.	Harper, Eliza	11 SEP 1884 L	19	241
Harris, Vinsent	Wilkerson, Vincent	02 APR 1884 L	18	491
Harris, Viola	Smith, Hartway	12 JUN 1884	19	080
Harris, Walter S.	Tinsley, Rosa B.	10 SEP 1878 L	12	209
Harris, Walter S.	Stockton, Lucy B.	23 APR 1885 R	20	187
Harris, Washington R.	Johnson, Annie E.	14 APR 1881 R	15	233
Harris, Wesley	Williams, Martha	20 JUN 1878 L	12	108
Harris, William	Jackson, Mary	09 JUN 1881 R	15	354
Harris, William E.	Wallingford, Mollie E.	04 OCT 1881 L	16	007
Harris, William H.	Hawkins, Martha E.	12 JUN 1884 L	19	080
Harris, William James	Wilson, Belle	15 APR 1885 R	20	168
Harris, William T.	Williams, Mary E.	23 NOV 1882 L	17	147
Harris, William Washington	Emerson, Emma Virginia	19 JUN 1882 R	16	417
Harris, Willis	Scott, Fannie	09 OCT 1879 L	13	412
Harrison, Alexander L.	Haines, Mary R.	23 OCT 1884 L	19	333
Harrison, Carrie	Harrison, Joseph	18 MAR 1880	14	189
Harrison, Charles	Brown, Rachel	08 NOV 1883 L	18	242
Harrison, Charles M.	Upton, Annie Amelia	21 DEC 1880	15	110
Harrison, Clara	Chrisman, Robert E.	09 AUG 1883 R	18	082
Harrison, Daniel C.	Hurdle, Harriet A., Mrs.	28 APR 1880 R	14	243
Harrison, Edward M.	Slack, Lizzie H.	28 FEB 1883 R	17	326
Harrison, Elias	Chesley, Louisa	21 SEP 1880 L	14	454
Harrison, Ellen J.	Dolan, Thomas J.	24 NOV 1880 R	15	061
Harrison, Fillmore	Shillenn, Harriet Wynn	30 AUG 1881 R	15	463
Harrison, Florence	Swart, J.H.	06 NOV 1879 R	13	471
Harrison, Florence	Aymé, Louis Henry	01 MAR 1880 R	14	166
Harrison, Francis M.	Hicks, Mary F.	05 APR 1883 R	17	380
Harrison, George F.E.	Ray, Mamie R.	13 FEB 1882	16	236
Harrison, George W.	Mavrans, Annie Josephine	25 DEC 1878 R	12	395

Harrison, George W.	Watson, Ida E.	03 JUN 1879 R	13	218
Harrison, George W.	Hopkins, Emma E.	11 MAR 1884 L	18	465
Harrison, Harriet Rebecca	Bailey, James R.	28 MAR 1882	16	292
Harrison, Hattie	Marshall, Vincent	24 MAR 1883 L	17	358
Harrison, J.H.	Keller, Mattie A.	27 FEB 1878	11	362
Harrison, James	Whitley, Catherine	12 FEB 1881 L	15	187
Harrison, James, Jr.	Ingram, Mollie B.	03 SEP 1878 R	12	192
Harrison, James T.	Bailey, Susie C.	20 AUG 1878	12	174
Harrison, James W.	Neal, Emma	12 JUN 1879	13	229
Harrison, John	Travis, Dora	30 JAN 1879	13	034
Harrison, John	Frinks, Laura	27 DEC 1882 R	17	211
Harrison, John	Jackson, Frances	31 JAN 1884	18	399
Harrison, John H.	Bouldin, Julia M.	31 DEC 1881 L	16	174
Harrison, John Thomas	Latchford, Mary Etta	05 MAY 1880 R	14	251
Harrison, Joseph	Harrison, Carrie	18 MAR 1880	14	189
Harrison, Luther Jackson	Burnett, Mary Cummings	25 OCT 1881 R	16	044
Harrison, M. Blanche	Disney, Thomas H.	15 JUL 1880 R	14	362
Harrison, Maggie E.	Lang, William	16 NOV 1879 R	13	488
Harrison, Martha Virginia	Boman, John R.	23 DEC 1882 R	26	6283
Harrison, Mary	Guy, Peter	02 JAN 1878 R	11	286
Harrison, Mary	Watson, George	20 NOV 1882 L	17	138
Harrison, Mary J.	West, Joseph	15 JAN 1878	11	305
Harrison, Nicholas	Hebron, Louisa	02 JUN 1881 L	15	337
Harrison, Oliver L.W.	Dishman, Annie B.	24 AUG 1880 L	14	414
Harrison, Priscilla	Crabtree, Thomas	23 MAR 1880	14	194
Harrison, Robert H.	Carter, Julia J.	20 OCT 1879 R	13	439
Harrison, Sarah R.	Minnis, J.W.	11 MAY 1880	14	262
Harrison, Sidney	Dodson, Edie	31 MAY 1880	14	298
Harrison, Thomas B.	Eaton, Josephine A.	24 JUN 1879 R	13	245
Harrison, W.H.	Burruss, Maggie S.	17 DEC 1880 R	15	107
Harrison, Wesley	Ball, Laura V.	07 JAN 1880 R	14	094
Harrison, William	Ward, Sophia	08 MAY 1879	13	180
Harrison, William	Taylor, Emma	24 JUL 1880 L	14	374
Harrison, William	Mitchell, Sarah	18 JAN 1882 R	16	200
Harrison, William	Pierson, Mary	13 OCT 1883	18	189
Harrison, William H.	Cleveland, Cora F.	24 DEC 1879	14	072
Harrison, William H.	Gray, Ida	22 DEC 1880 L	15	115
Harrison, William H.	Bennett, Clara	21 AUG 1882	16	487
Harrison, William H.	Tubman, Elizabeth	08 SEP 1885 R	20	404
Harrison, William Henry	Pettit, Mary Jefferson	20 SEP 1879 R	13	380
Harrison, William S.	Rector, Catherine J.	25 JUL 1882	16	456
Harrity, Emma	Gordon, James	16 JAN 1882 L	16	195
Harrity, John	Brown, Lucinda	28 SEP 1881 L	15	502
Harrod, Lucius	Blaky, Frances E.	25 OCT 1877 R	11	154
Harrod, Robert	Crawford, Lillie	06 JAN 1879 L	13	008
Harrod, Sarah	Reynolds, Jerry	03 APR 1884	18	493
Harrold, J.	Schaeffer, George C.	08 JUN 1881 R	15	352
Harrold, Joseph Franklin	Dunlop, Elizabeth Rachel	10 SEP 1885 R	20	409
Harron, Elizabeth M.	Raum, George	26 MAY 1881 R	15	328
Harron, Ella	Renoe, Arthur	20 JUN 1883	18	004
Harron, Leighton Greg.	Spencer, Catherine	04 DEC 1877 R	11	217
Harrover, Alma	Isparhecher [Indian]	04 JUN 1884	19	060
Harrover, Ella B.	Clements, Noah A.	02 OCT 1877 R	11	117
Harrover, James R.	Hughes, Margaret M.	09 JAN 1883 L	17	245
Harrover, Jane Elizabeth	Christopher, James	21 MAY 1879 R	13	200
Harry, Helen M.	Burrows, Wm. T.	07 JAN 1884 R	18	367
Harry, Mary E.	Butler, Mack	17 SEP 1877 L	11	097
Harry, William C.	Gates, Anne V.	16 OCT 1884 L	19	310

Harryday, Stephen Daniel	Ruffin, Matilda Catharine	01 JUN 1880 R	14	289
Harryman, William D.	Palmer, Victoria B.	02 FEB 1885 R	20	048
Hart, Archie M.	Kane, Mary Jane	11 DEC 1878 L	12	377
Hart, Dora	Wheeler, Robert	01 JUN 1885 L	20	250
Hart, Ettie	Lupton, Jesse Monroe	19 JAN 1881 R	15	157
Hart, George H.	Carter, Elizabeth	27 FEB 1883 R	17	322
Hart, Jane E.	Hall, George B.	13 OCT 1879 R	13	418
Hart, John Cornelius	Thompson, Aurelia	09 MAY 1878 R	12	046
Hart, Joseph B.	Keefe, Deborah	07 APR 1885 L	20	150
Hart, Lillian P.	Marias, William	26 DEC 1883	18	341
Hart, Mamie E.	Jones, John H.	29 NOV 1882 R	17	157
Hart, Martha E.	Holmes, William	05 MAY 1884 L	19	006
Hart, Mary L.	Gibson, John	03 JUL 1879 R	13	268
Hart, Pauline	Frank, Abraham D.	01 DEC 1880 R	15	072
Hart, Rosalie	Bass, William M.	18 SEP 1878 R	12	223
Hart, William	Fitz, Ella	29 FEB 1878	11	365
Hart, William	Kelly, Lizzie	11 SEP 1881	15	482
Hartbower, William	Helmuth, Virginia	23 FEB 1881 R	15	200
Hartbrecht, Josephine E.	Ott, Joseph W.	12 MAY 1885 L	20	217
Hartig, Louis	Conradis, Emma	12 MAY 1881 R	15	304
Harting, Bertha	Helzle, John	05 JAN 1882 R	16	181
Hartley, Jennie	Stotts, Jesse	07 APR 1881 L	15	250
Hartley, Leanna	Wilson, James W.	27 SEP 1881 R	15	497
Hartman, Lena	Graham, John H.	21 MAY 1878	12	061
Hartmann, Charles A.	Cohill, Ada Lindsey	23 OCT 1884	19	331
Hartnett, Annie	Flynn, Morris B.	20 APR 1885 L	20	175
Hartnett, Bridget	King, Michael	13 NOV 1877 R	11	177
Hartnett, John	Moriarty, Josephine E.	21 NOV 1878 R	12	338
Hartnett, Mary E.	Barron, Owen F.	27 SEP 1883 L	18	157
Hartnett, William	Manion, Mary	20 JUN 1881 L	15	367
Hartt, Lizzie J.	Lotz, Jeremiah Carpenter	05 DEC 1877 R	11	219
Hartung, Teresa L.A.	Lauman, John H.	13 SEP 1884	19	245
Hartwick, Emma	Kline, James H.G.	07 APR 1880 R	14	214
Harvard, M.E.S.	Johnstone, W.B.	01 DEC 1881	16	110
Harvey, Arsenuis Thomas	Foley, Angela	02 OCT 1879 R	13	397
Harvey, Augustus	Collins, Lucy Ann	31 MAY 1880 L	14	297
Harvey, B. Fenwick	Robinson, C. Blanche	03 OCT 1881 L	16	004
Harvey, Charles A., Jr.	Prather, Ida Kate	25 DEC 1879 R	14	073
Harvey, Clara C.	Farrar, Watson W.	10 APR 1883 L	17	388
Harvey, Edward G.	Edinburgh, Martha	19 DEC 1882 R	17	195
Harvey, Edward W.	Chase, Evlyn M.	07 OCT 1885 R	20	466
Harvey, Ella M.	Sherwood, Henry	27 MAY 1879	13	207
Harvey, Frank	Banks, Amanda	16 OCT 1884	19	305
Harvey, Isabella	Miller, John W.	20 MAY 1884	19	038
Harvey, Jacob Henry	Tanner, Harriet Louisa	20 AUG 1883 R	18	094
Harvey, James F.	Gibson, Ida May	26 SEP 1878 R	12	239
Harvey, James M.	Huntt, Lizzie	28 JAN 1881 L	15	169
Harvey, John B.	Wilkinson, Martha L.	24 OCT 1882 R	17	086
Harvey, Mary W.	Estes, Robert W.	21 APR 1881 R	15	267
Harvey, Peyton	MacWill, Louisa E.	13 JAN 1880 R	14	090
Harvey, Robert W.	Brown, Kate E.	11 JAN 1882 R	16	190
Harvey, Susan	Toler, Philip	02 NOV 1881 R	16	056
Harvey, William, Jr.	Barnard, Minnie Lenore	28 JUN 1884	19	110
Harvey, William K.	Yoos, Mary C.	19 DEC 1883	18	326
Hascus, Hennie	Offutt, Wesley	12 JUL 1877	11	018
Hasker, Charles Edmund	Weisiger, Adelaide Amelia	21 NOV 1877	11	193
Haskins, D.H.	Bagley, Sarah	10 SEP 1880 R	14	431
Haskins, Laura C.	Burke, Edmund	15 JUN 1880	14	321

Haskins, Martha Ellen Dabney	Dabney, Charles	14 JUN 1881 L	15	358
Haskins, Simon	Harris, Emma	09 JAN 1883	17	247
Haskins, Susie A.	Smith, Abram M.	21 DEC 1881 L	16	149
Hasler, Antonian B.	Tippett, William B.	29 SEP 1884	19	271
Haslup, Antonia	Buchanan, John	18 OCT 1877 R	11	144
Hasselbach, Lizzie	Burch, Andrew	22 DEC 1883 L	18	358
Hasselbusch, Lottie W.D.	Schwiering, Augustus E.L.	17 APR 1883 R	17	396
Hastings, Russell	Platt, Emily	19 JUN 1878	12	103
Hatch, Lizzie E.	Hall, James Henry	20 MAR 1883 R	17	350
Hatcher, Edward W.	McDermot, Mary Ann	06 OCT 1881 R	16	007
Hatcher, Jeannette W.	Murray, George E.	25 APR 1884 R	18	533
Hatcher, Margaret	Brooker, Aaron M.	25 JUL 1883 R	18	060
Hathman, Edward	Winters, Charlotte	13 SEP 1880 L	14	442
Hatto, Annie	Kennedy, James	02 OCT 1880	14	470
Hatton, Alice M.M.	Vincel, William D.	24 SEP 1877 R	11	105
Hatton, Charles	Custis, Ellen	01 MAR 1880 R	14	169
Hatton, Charles E.S.	Sewell, Annie E.	21 DEC 1881 L	16	144
Hatton, Eliza J.	Smith, Thomas D.	25 MAR 1879	13	113
Hatton, Helen Ruth	Hardy, Henry	10 SEP 1882	17	028
Hatton, Maggie	Sheriff, Ebbie	29 NOV 1881 R	16	100
Hatton, Mary C.	Coeyman, William H.	01 JAN 1878 R	11	279
Hatton, Sophia	Nickens, L.T.	29 MAY 1879	13	211
Hatton, Thomas	Delaney, Caroline	20 JAN 1885 L	20	029
Hattoo, Annie	Morgan, Richard	01 JUN 1881 L	15	336
Hatzfeld, Adam	Bleifus, Amalia	28 APR 1878	12	026
Haueke, John	Dauch, Laura	13 APR 1879	13	130
Hauf, John L.	Mulvahill, Mary E.	21 MAY 1883 R	17	454
Hauff, Virginia	Cain, Lindsey	23 MAR 1882 R	16	283
Hauptman, Hattie E.	Ege, Porter F.	04 SEP 1884	19	226
Hauptman, Mary M.	King, Borrows W.	15 DEC 1881 R	16	136
Hauser, Ernest	Dahler, Sophie	03 MAY 1885 R	20	200
Hauser, J.W.	Raurer, Catherine	16 DEC 1879 L	14	050
Hausmann, August F.	Barnes, Mary E.	27 APR 1880 R	14	238
Hausmann, William	Bäeker, Bertha	10 MAY 1885 R	20	214
Hauthman, Lucy	Gay, James W.	19 NOV 1884 L	19	396
Haven, Maggie R.	Allen, John E.	10 OCT 1877	11	126
Haven, Priscilla	McCubbin, Edward	27 MAR 1879	13	116
Havener, Marion I.	Slack, Olivia M.	03 JAN 1883	17	234
Havener, Mason A.	Walker, Sarah E.	12 DEC 1878 R	12	378
Havenner, Joseph C.	DeVaughn, Lizzie, Mrs.	15 FEB 1883 R	17	309
Havenner, Laura V.	Casey, John	01 APR 1882 L	16	295
Hawes, John B.	Hall, Gertrude U. Hall	21 APR 1879 R	13	153
Hawes, Margaret	Clarke, William H.	22 JUL 1882 L	16	453
Hawkens, Robert	Johnson, Lidy	13 DEC 1884 R	32	7900
Hawking, William J.	Scott, Carrie	04 DEC 1882 R	17	121
Hawkins, Abraham	McEntee, Elizabeth	11 AUG 1881 L	15	441
Hawkins, Agnes	Beverly, Richard	27 MAY 1884 R	19	016
Hawkins, Alfred	Huton, Julia	03 DEC 1877 L	11	216
Hawkins, Alice	Scott, Alexander	26 AUG 1882	16	494
Hawkins, Amanda Ella	Brown, Edward H.	22 FEB 1883 L	17	319
Hawkins, Anna E.	Dawson, Charles E.	17 SEP 1881 L	15	488
Hawkins, Annie	Jannifer, John	19 FEB 1879 L	13	067
Hawkins, Annie	Carpenter, Albert L.	10 SEP 1881 L	15	481
Hawkins, Barbara	Williams, Edward	17 MAR 1881 R	15	228
Hawkins, Barclay	McDonald, Mattie	23 APR 1885 L	20	186
Hawkins, Benjamin	Tyler, Cora	08 SEP 1884 L	19	232
Hawkins, Bettie	Jones, Peter	26 JUL 1883	18	062
Hawkins, Charles	Stanton, Annie	20 FEB 1882 L	16	251

Hawkins, Charles Allen	Swan, Laura Ellen	15 DEC 1879 L	14	048
Hawkins, Cornelius	Snyder, Maria	05 JUN 1883 R	17	457
Hawkins, Eldridge	Holmes, Nannie Maria	27 DEC 1881 R	16	150
Hawkins, Ella	Wills, Henry	27 DEC 1883	18	351
Hawkins, Frank	Harper, Mary	02 MAR 1880 L	14	171
Hawkins, Geo. Samuel	Marlow, Sarah Elizabeth	14 OCT 1879 R	13	420
Hawkins, George	Christian, Martha	23 MAY 1882 L	16	372
Hawkins, George	Wilson, Christiana	16 JUN 1883 L	17	497
Hawkins, George H.	Mahoney, Mary L.	07 NOV 1882 L	17	116
Hawkins, George W.	Bowman, Ida L.	01 NOV 1881	16	055
Hawkins, Georgiana	Young, James Edward	15 SEP 1883	18	131
Hawkins, Georgie	Milburn, Charles	23 FEB 1881 L	15	201
Hawkins, H. Cray	Smith, Sarah E.	29 MAY 1884	19	044
Hawkins, H. Lewis	Henderson, Jennie	04 DEC 1884 L	19	436
Hawkins, Hattie	Dixon, Charles	11 SEP 1879 R	13	335
Hawkins, Henrietta	Fletcher, Washington	04 APR 1885 R	20	142
Hawkins, Henry	Dyer, Rosina	12 NOV 1880 L	15	046
Hawkins, Henry	Goldin, Willie Jane	09 JUL 1885	20	318
Hawkins, Horace	Tucker, Matilda	18 MAY 1881	15	314
Hawkins, Isaac S.	Nolen, Ella M.	07 DEC 1880 L	15	086
Hawkins, James	Brown, Lizzie	01 MAY 1882	16	342
Hawkins, James B.	Burns, Annie B.	06 AUG 1885	20	357
Hawkins, Joanna	Humphreys, Robert B.	23 JUN 1881	15	364
Hawkins, Johanna	Addison, John	27 FEB 1879 L	13	082
Hawkins, John	Iglon, Virginia	05 JAN 1880 L	14	088
Hawkins, John	Cumins, Addie	09 MAR 1885 R	20	102
Hawkins, John D.	Smith, May M.	18 DEC 1879 L	14	055
Hawkins, John E.	Curry, Christiana	03 DEC 1884 L	19	434
Hawkins, John H.	O'Connor, Bridget	30 MAR 1880	14	202½
Hawkins, John Henry	Foster, Irene	29 AUG 1883 L	18	104
Hawkins, John L.	McMeanes, Mary A.	13 MAR 1880	14	184
Hawkins, Josephine	Hill, Walter	09 APR 1879 L	13	133
Hawkins, Laura	Patterson, Abraham	17 JUL 1884	19	144
Hawkins, Lewis	Plant, Louisa	19 NOV 1878 L	12	337
Hawkins, Lewis C.	Vanlentine, Maggie S.	02 MAR 1881 L	15	210
Hawkins, Lizzie	Lyles, Richard	05 DEC 1881 L	16	113
Hawkins, Maggie	Strodus, Charles	10 APR 1882 L	16	307
Hawkins, Marian S.	Butler, George N.	24 JUN 1884 R	19	099
Hawkins, Martha E.	Harris, William H.	12 JUN 1884 L	19	080
Hawkins, Mary	Dodson, Joseph	18 SEP 1884 L	19	261
Hawkins, Mary	Brooks, Charles	05 MAR 1885	20	098
Hawkins, Mary C.	Lee, Thomas	06 NOV 1883 R	18	237
Hawkins, Mary E.	Johnson, James D.	28 JUN 1877	11	002
Hawkins, Mary Olivia	Marshall, Ignatius A.	28 OCT 1879 R	13	444
Hawkins, Matilda	Dorsey, Noble	31 JUL 1884	19	164
Hawkins, Matilda	Whiting, Frank	13 JUL 1884	19	135
Hawkins, May	Simms, John	08 MAY 1880 L	14	260
Hawkins, Nannie B.	Aylor, Charles Milton	17 APR 1882 R	16	318
Hawkins, Peter	Frazier, Georgianna	31 MAR 1881 L	15	243
Hawkins, Rachel	Dorsey, John Henry	16 DEC 1878 L	12	381
Hawkins, Randolph	Jackson, Hannah	03 JUN 1884	19	054
Hawkins, Richard	Johnson, Mary E.	06 JAN 1880 L	14	090
Hawkins, Robert	Ford, Bettie	08 APR 1880 R	14	216
Hawkins, Robert	Burrus, Mary	28 DEC 1882 R	17	218
Hawkins, Robert	Robertson, Lina	04 DEC 1884	19	438
Hawkins, Robert H.	Nelson, Sarah Jane	26 JUL 1884	19	159
Hawkins, Sarah	Ford, Nathan	20 DEC 1882 L	17	195
Hawkins, Sarah J.	Middleton, Walter	02 MAR 1880 L	14	171

Hawkins, Sarah Jane	Peed, James	31 DEC 1881	16	165
Hawkins, Thomas D.	Johnson, Eliza	24 MAR 1881 L	15	238
Hawkins, Thomas F.	Thorn, Mary A.	22 APR 1885 L	20	182
Hawkins, William Henry	Sampson, Mary	07 OCT 1884	19	291
Hawkins, Wilson	Starvit, Maggie	26 DEC 1883	18	341
Hawkshaw, Mary Josephine	Sheid, Harry	15 AUG 1883	18	089
Hawley, John H.	Hinley, Lucretie	21 NOV 1883	18	268
Hawley, Lucian	Jennings, Lida W.	18 DEC 1877	11	242
Hawling, Eugene	Griffith, Missouri V.	04 DEC 1884 R	19	437
Hawthorne, Emma	Randall, Charles S.	02 AUG 1880 R	14	381
Hawthorne, Hartwell K.	Tupper, Charlotte R.	11 MAY 1884	19	014
Hay, George W.	Bushnell, Katharine	03 SEP 1884	19	222
Hayden, Andrew	Smith, Charlotte	04 OCT 1880 R	14	469
Hayden, Emma E.	Hammerly, Edward L.	13 MAR 1884 R	18	468
Hayden, H.L.	Columbus, A.A.	02 NOV 1880	15	026
Hayden, John T.W.	Lyons, Mary E.	27 DEC 1882 R	17	216
Hayden, Laura B.	Bailey, John J.C.	19 SEP 1877	11	100
Hayden, Lucy B.	Barber, Robert T.J.	18 MAY 1885	20	226
Hayden, Richard B.	Brinkley, Cora M.	28 APR 1881 R	15	280
Hayden, Robert	Jackson, Mary	21 MAR 1878 R	11	390
Hayden, Samuel Alexander	Wood, Mollie	04 APR 1882 R	16	299
Hayes, John	Connor, Margaret	17 JUL 1879 L	13	284
Hayes, Alexander O.	Hill, Mary Virginia	21 FEB 1885 L	20	080
Hayes, Benjamin T.	Hurdle, Barbara A.	27 DEC 1881	16	157
Hayes, Christiana	Hamod, Elias	18 OCT 1877 R	11	143
Hayes, Columbus	Domhart, Annie	09 JUL 1879 R	13	275
Hayes, Florence B.	Raines, Edward M.	19 OCT 1883 R	18	203
Hayes, Florence L.	O'Connor, Eugene A.	17 OCT 1878 R	12	281
Hayes, Frank	Moulding, Anna	24 SEP 1881 R	22	5285
Hayes, Frank L.	Walker, Cora M.	26 JUN 1884	19	101
Hayes, George H.D.	Clagett, Maria	15 JAN 1885	20	021
Hayes, Harry	Allen, Rena	18 SEP 1882 L	17	027
Hayes, Helena Cole	Salmon, Joseph H.	25 NOV 1878 R	12	342
Hayes, Hester Edith	Pumphrey, Edward	16 AUG 1883	18	090
Hayes, Jacob	Dunson, Alice	28 OCT 1880 L	15	020
Hayes, James E.	Fenwick, Addie Lavinia	06 NOV 1878 R	12	309
Hayes, John	Lee, Sarah	29 JAN 1885 R	20	042
Hayes, John	Watkins, Kate	21 APR 1885 L	20	179
Hayes, Joseph Capin	Turner, Louisa Virginia	02 MAR 1882	16	261
Hayes, Lemuel	Beall, George	20 OCT 1881 L	16	036
Hayes, Marian T.	Maddox, Highland	29 APR 1879	13	164
Hayes, Mary F.	Roach, Joseph E.	23 MAY 1882	16	371
Hayes, Nancy	Banks, Robert	13 MAY 1882 L	16	359
Hayes, Robert	Cliggett, Julia	11 AUG 1885 R	20	365
Hayes, Rosa	Danison, Francis W.	18 SEP 1881 R	15	488
Hayes, William	Bell, Florence	03 APR 1879 R	13	125
Hayes, William	Cox, Susanna	19 AUG 1879 R	13	326
Hayes, William	Dannison, Annie	19 JUL 1881 L	15	408
Hayne, Daniel H.	Sheriff, Nannie E.	23 AUG 1884	19	205
Hayne, James Henry	Mills, Lavinia	04 OCT 1882 R	17	051
Haynes, George A.	Small, Georgie A.	16 JUN 1883 R	17	497
Haynes, Henry	Smith, Mary	16 FEB 1880	14	155
Haynes, James	Burnett, Mary P.	08 OCT 1884	19	286
Haynie, Marian F.	Newton, Celestine D.	02 MAR 1882 R	16	265
Haynie, Mary K.	Hickey, W.	07 JUN 1878 L	12	091
Hayre, Frank G.	Buckley, Rosa L.	06 OCT 1881 R	16	012
Hayre, Mary E.	Mitchell, Filmore	22 OCT 1883 R	18	204
Hays, Charles Bogue	Snowden, Ada S.	16 APR 1878 R	12	004

Hays, Columbus Horatio	Gray, Mary Cacharine	25 SEP 1879 R	13	384
Hays, Edward L.	Waring, Anna T.	18 NOV 1880 R	15	057
Hays, Frances	Cornish, Washington	07 OCT 1885 L	20	469
Hays, Lewis N.	Hagan, Marion W.	27 SEP 1881	15	498
Hays, Mary Estelle	Fowler, Julius Edwin	04 AUG 1881 R	15	433
Hays, Robert W.	Connor, Mary	19 MAR 1878	11	386
Hays, Rosannah	Gray, Milton R.	21 NOV 1881 R	16	086
Hayslock, Maria	Miles, John Vincent	01 SEP 1880	14	421
Hayson, Abraham	Brooks, Maria W.	11 SEP 1877	11	086
Hayward, Delia	Thomas, William R.	28 AUG 1883 R	18	101
Hayward, Sarah	Burgess, Alexander	24 MAY 1879	13	203
Hazard, Henry C.	Atzerodt, Ida N.	17 MAY 1881 L	15	312
Hazard, Marion V.	Helton, Addison S.	27 OCT 1883 R	18	218
Hazard, Robert Houston	Penfield, Jessie Mary	19 OCT 1882 R	17	082
Hazel, Addie Marie	Kengla, George M.	05 MAY 1880 L	14	253
Hazel, Frank	Peck, Georgia M.	15 AUG 1880 R	14	399
Hazel, John T.	Soper, Emma	04 OCT 1877	11	121
Hazel, Louisa	Curry, James Benjamin	10 DEC 1882 R	17	178
Hazel, M. Susie	Hizer, Thomas O.	19 DEC 1882	17	192
Hazel, Nannie E.	Coleman, William D.	26 MAY 1881 L	15	327
Hazel, Rose	Fox, Frederick A.	22 AUG 1885 L	20	383
Hazen, Eugenia	Hepburn, Jerry M.	17 NOV 1880	15	054
Hazen, William P.C.	Wood, Catharine E.	08 JAN 1878 R	11	295
Hazle, John T.	Wood, Mary J.	16 OCT 1878 L	12	278
Head, Benjamin Franklin	McIntosh, Arabella F.	25 AUG 1880 R	14	416
Head, Ethelberta	Ready, Maurice J.	27 OCT 1883 L	18	217
Head, James M.	Rotchford, Annie	17 DEC 1879 R	14	053
Head, Lillian Lee	Cooper, James H.	25 MAR 1879 L	13	114
Head, Thaddeus	Jackson, Sarah	03 JAN 1878 L	11	293
Heagem, Margaret	Armstrong, George	22 DEC 1881 L	16	152
Healy, Ellen	McGarr, John R.	05 FEB 1881 R	15	178
Healy, John P.	Worthington, Kate V.	14 NOV 1884	19	382
Heaney, Julia	Whitney, Patrick	20 MAY 1881 L	15	319
Heap, Annie Ellen	Nicholson, Reginald F.	05 JUL 1877 R	11	006
Hearns, James	Brown, Mary Jane	27 SEP 1877 R	11	112
Hearns, Jeemes	Custard, Mary Jane	22 JUN 1882	16	424
Hearns, Mary	Lewis, Andrew	19 MAY 1881 R	15	317
Hearty, Sarah	McLaughlin, Charles	27 APR 1882	16	339
Heath, Annie E.	Johnson, George A.	06 DEC 1883	18	302
Heath, Augusta Louise	Jarvis, John Fillis	25 DEC 1878 R	12	399
Heath, Edward E.	Cabe, Julia C.	30 APR 1883 L	17	421
Heath, Margaret	Eckstein, Charles A.	16 FEB 1885 L	20	070
Heathman, Maria L.	Leftridge, Robert P.	05 DEC 1878 R	12	359
Hebb, Walter Hanson Jenifer	Bean, Margaret Catharine	26 NOV 1877 R	11	202
Hebbron, Amelia A.	Ferguson, Charles E.	27 FEB 1879 R	13	084
Hebren, Peter	Vigle, Henrietta	15 SEP 1884	19	249
Hebrew, John A.	King, Ida L.	19 JUL 1877	11	025
Hebron, Louisa	Harrison, Nicholas	02 JUN 1881 L	15	337
Hebsacker, Robert	Rudhart, Anna	29 OCT 1882	17	099
Hechinger, Jonas	Gassenheimer, Bertha	18 OCT 1884 L	19	318
Hechinger, Julia	Stein, Jacob	11 SEP 1881 R	15	481
Heck, Nettie	Reed, Wm. H.	06 OCT 1885 R	20	457
Heckheimer, Abraham	Saks, Rebecca	17 MAR 1878 R	11	380
Hedgman, F.C.	Ball, I.L.	20 JAN 1881 L	15	159
Hedgman, Sarah	Mason, Richard	24 MAY 1879	13	206
Hedrick, Alice	Olcott, Wareham Harry	10 MAR 1884 R	18	463
Heeter, Uriah	Nessline, Lizzie	02 DEC 1877 R	11	213
Heffer, Daniel	Reithmüller, Louisa	15 AUG 1878	12	167

Hefflin, Lucy	Plaskett, Joseph	31 OCT 1879 R	13	457
Heffner, Francis Eugene	Worthmiller, Jane Rebecca	16 JAN 1879 R	13	016
Heffner, John T.	Duvall, Annie E.	25 OCT 1883 R	18	213
Heffner, William C.	Wurtmiller, Rosa A.	27 JAN 1881 L	15	167
Hefft, John	Gittings, Lottie	18 JUL 1878 L	12	141
Heflebower, George W.	Clark, Annie M.	20 APR 1880 R	14	229
Heflin, Gilson	Haley, Lucy	14 SEP 1877 R	11	094
Heflin, Henry W.	Robinson, Caroline B.	01 APR 1885	20	140
Hefner, Josephine	Aleider, John E.	19 OCT 1880	15	002
Hegeman, Eli	Chase, Ann	08 OCT 1883 L	18	177
Heiberger, Franz J.	Nairn, Mary J.	03 SEP 1878 R	12	194
Heide, Carolena Vonder	Emrick, F.X.A.O.	25 MAY 1884	19	023
Heider, Louisa	Heitmüller, Henry Wm.	29 OCT 1879 L	13	450
Heider, Louisa Eleonore	Heitmüller, Charles G.	08 SEP 1885 R	20	403
Heider, Minnie	Alsop, William L.	14 DEC 1882 L	17	186
Heider, William	King, Sarah	01 DEC 1881 L	16	107
Heiliger, Minnie M.M.	Seebo, Charles W.	22 AUG 1880 R	14	410
Heilprin, Giles F.	Baer, Sophie	09 NOV 1879	13	469
Heilprin, Henrietta	Kleinberger, William	09 DEC 1879 L	14	036
Hein, Agnes W.	McChesney, Algernon R.	06 MAY 1885 R	20	210
Hein, Mary	Allen, Henry Charles	23 JUL 1881 R	15	414
Heine, Edward	Oppenheimer, Rose	18 NOV 1883 R	18	249
Heine, Maria	Miller, William	24 APR 1879 R	13	157
Heine, Wilhelm	Heitmüller, Mary	09 MAY 1878 R	12	045
Heinemann, Marian S.	Brandt, George	24 JUN 1884 L	19	099
Heinline, Amanda	Keller, William H.	23 FEB 1885 R	20	082
Heinline, Katie E.	Holland, Richard H.	07 DEC 1881 R	16	114
Heinline, Rosie C.	Starr, Alfred A.	07 FEB 1881 R	15	181
Heinrich, Christina	Huss, Carl	12 JUN 1880 L	14	318
Heinz, Amelia A.	Bowers, Rudolph P.	15 SEP 1885 R	20	415
Heinz, Peter J.	Coggins, Louisa	27 MAR 1885 L	20	134
Heise, Carrie L.	Hunter, George R.E.	20 JUN 1878	12	108
Heise, Eli	Makeley, Ada	20 APR 1884	18	502
Heisey, Mary L.	Pike, Charles A.	27 SEP 1882 L	17	040
Heiss, Michael	Burrows, Annie	29 JAN 1878 L	11	320
Heiter, James	Payne, Rebecca	14 FEB 1878 L	12	099
Heitinger, Charles	Colliflower, Clemie	26 DEC 1881	13	481
Heitinger, Lena C.	Smith, Nathan A.C.	08 AUG 1882	16	473
Heitmuller, Charles G.	Heider, Louisa Eleonore	08 SEP 1885 R	20	403
Heitmuller, Ferdinand A.	Toepper, Louisa M.	23 JUN 1885 R	20	287
Heitmuller, Maria Ch. Ant.	Gade, Gustav Chr. Theod.	19 JUN 1884 R	19	092
Heitmuller, Mary L.H.	Miller, Thomas	20 SEP 1883 L	18	145
Heitmüller, Augusta D.A.	Meyer, Johann Heinrich	10 FEB 1885 R	20	063
Heitmüller, Charles	Korster, Johana Buchsteiner	10 MAR 1881 R	15	222
Heitmüller, Henry Wm.	Heider, Louisa	29 OCT 1879 L	13	450
Heitmüller, Mary	Heine, Wilhelm	09 MAY 1878 R	12	045
Heitzler, Hermann	Eckridge, Matilda	01 AUG 1877	11	036
Heitzmann, Rosalie	Taylor, William Wirt	15 JUL 1878	12	134
Held, Mary	Spindler, William F.	26 MAY 1884 R	19	039
Helem, E., Mrs.	Davis, Matthew A.	06 JAN 1882 L	16	185
Helene, Paul	Goebel, Rosina	25 SEP 1884	19	268
Hellen, Joseph	Hamilton, Mamie	25 APR 1883 R	17	408
Hellen, Walter	Jackson, Carrie M.	15 SEP 1881 R	15	486
Heller, Annie	Kraft, Henson C.	16 SEP 1883	18	133
Hellmuth, Anna	Bohnke, Hubert	27 AUG 1884	19	210
Hellmuth, Martin	Smith, Annie	09 JUL 1878	12	112
Hellmuth, Mollie R.	Dennison, John E.	27 FEB 1884	18	446
Hellriegel, Michael	Mundlein, Charlotte	22 MAY 1879	13	201

D.C. Marriage Records Index, June 28, 1877 to October 19, 1885   207

Name	Spouse	Date	Vol	Page
Helm, Corrina L.	Mareau, Fred. G.	03 JUN 1884	19	053
Helm, Edwin L.	Sydnor, Emma J.	10 JUN 1884	19	071
Helm, Emma E.	Corbin, Jimison R.	18 JAN 1883 R	17	266
Helmick, Howard Franklin	Meacham, Mary Emma	03 DEC 1883	18	292
Helmsen, Charles J.	McLeod, Minnie C.	12 DEC 1882	17	179
Helmuth, Amelia C.	Dauterich, Henry L.	14 MAR 1883	17	344
Helmuth, Emma Christine	Seufferle, Wm. Lowndes	10 FEB 1885 R	20	059
Helmuth, Louise Mary	Benzler, Hermann	11 JUN 1884 R	19	077
Helmuth, Virginia	Hartbower, William	23 FEB 1881 R	15	200
Helton, Addison S.	Hazard, Marion V.	27 OCT 1883 R	18	218
Helvin, George W.	Brodekamp, Mary C.	08 SEP 1879	13	356
Helvin, Jennie	West, Benjamin O.	04 DEC 1878 R	12	360
Helzle, John	Harting, Bertha	05 JAN 1882 R	16	181
Heming, Katie F.	Harris, James W.	18 NOV 1879 L	13	493
Hemingway, Charles B.	Stewart, Mary K.	03 NOV 1883 L	18	231
Hemm, Maria	DeGrain, Reinhold F.	25 FEB 1878	11	354
Hemmersey, Louisa	Darnall, Thomas A.	30 SEP 1884 L	19	277
Hemming, Annie F.	Mills, William H.	27 MAY 1885 L	20	242
Hempstone, Snowden Lee	Smith, Ellen M.	28 DEC 1880	15	124
Hemsley, Luther	Ward, Jane Elizabeth	20 SEP 1881 L	15	491
Hemsley, William H.	Rainey, Isabel	10 DEC 1878 L	12	375
Henault, Robert Emile	White, Martha A.	29 NOV 1881 R	16	094
Henderson, Adam W.	Ware, Mary Jane	19 MAY 1884	19	027
Henderson, Anne	Snowden, Wm. Albert	08 MAR 1881	15	220
Henderson, Annie	Fields, Thomas	17 NOV 1881 R	16	084
Henderson, Annie	Hill, Edward	15 NOV 1881 L	16	077
Henderson, Asbury	King, Nellie S.	23 AUG 1882 R	16	492
Henderson, C.W.	Potts, Bertha L.	21 JUL 1885	20	337
Henderson, Catherine	Shields, William	18 AUG 1881 R	15	451
Henderson, Charles	Coleman, Rachel Ann	29 JAN 1880 R	14	125
Henderson, Charles Henry	Carter, Miney	20 SEP 1877 R	11	089
Henderson, Clara C.	Merritt, Washington C.	26 JUN 1883 R	18	015
Henderson, Cora L.	Dillon, John W.	14 MAY 1883	17	437
Henderson, Ella	Miller, Alexander	06 NOV 1877	11	171
Henderson, Erastus	Cole, Georgiana	03 JUL 1878 L	12	122
Henderson, George T.	Guy, Eliza	24 DEC 1877 L	11	261
Henderson, George W.	Billingsley, Lura K.	15 JAN 1884	18	378
Henderson, Gilson	Curtis, Mary	20 JAN 1883 R	17	269
Henderson, Gustus	Anderson, Adeline	28 DEC 1880 R	15	129
Henderson, Henry	Taylor, Sarah	28 DEC 1881 L	16	166
Henderson, J.H.	Bishop, Henrietta	22 MAR 1879 L	13	111
Henderson, James Alfred	Hollins, Mary	04 DEC 1879	14	024
Henderson, James E.	Tolson, Sarah	26 FEB 1880 L	14	168
Henderson, James H.	Thomas, Agnes	26 FEB 1878	11	360
Henderson, James H.	Morgan, Mary Margaret	06 NOV 1881 R	16	064
Henderson, Janie M.	Murdock, Robert A.	12 DEC 1878	12	377
Henderson, Jennie	Hawkins, H. Lewis	04 DEC 1884 L	19	436
Henderson, John	Hill, Mary L.	25 MAR 1879 L	13	114
Henderson, John B.	Collier, Mollie E.	12 SEP 1882 R	17	019
Henderson, John D.	Falvey, Nannie	28 MAY 1878	12	068
Henderson, John William	Kirk, Marian Frances	01 NOV 1882 R	17	104
Henderson, Joseph	Temple, Emma	23 JAN 1879 L	13	032
Henderson, Joseph	Proctor, Eliza	27 OCT 1884	19	339
Henderson, Josephine	Christian, Jefferson	31 JAN 1884 L	18	403
Henderson, Lee E.	Anderson, Mary	23 FEB 1882 R	16	257
Henderson, Lena	Hill, Henry	29 SEP 1880 L	14	463
Henderson, Letha	Armstead, Edward	10 OCT 1878 L	12	265
Henderson, Lina M.	Norton, Charles Edward	25 FEB 1884 L	18	441

Henderson, Lottie	Scott, Henry E.	03 OCT 1879 R	13	403
Henderson, Lucy	Browne, James H.	06 APR 1881 L	15	249
Henderson, Lucy	Hume, Henry	07 JAN 1885 L	20	007
Henderson, Luvenia	Smith, Manuel	22 SEP 1878 R	12	172
Henderson, Luvinia	Johnson, J.W.	15 JUN 1885	20	273
Henderson, Margaret Ellen	King, Alex	05 SEP 1885	20	406
Henderson, Mary	Ayres, Joseph	05 SEP 1879	13	354
Henderson, Mary	Robison, Asbury	01 JAN 1880 R	14	087
Henderson, Mary	Hyde, Edward	19 APR 1882 L	16	326
Henderson, Mary V.	Simms, Maurice A.	03 FEB 1883 L	17	290
Henderson, Nathan	Dent, Nellie	25 AUG 1881 L	15	460
Henderson, Rachel A.	Jackson, James A.	04 DEC 1879 R	14	025
Henderson, Richard Wilson	Ferguson, Esther Jane	15 MAY 1883 R	17	442
Henderson, Robert Alexander	Hutchinson, Rosie Moss	28 DEC 1882 R	17	221
Henderson, Sarah	Cook, William F.	09 SEP 1882 L	17	014
Henderson, Sarah A.	Shipman, Washington E.	04 SEP 1883 R	18	108
Henderson, Thomas	Ford, Mary M.	24 SEP 1883 L	18	152
Henderson, Thomas	Johnson, Mary E.	28 OCT 1884 L	19	342
Henderson, William	Mars, Lulu	21 FEB 1883 L	17	315
Henderson, William G.	Garner, Lillie V.	03 AUG 1880 L	14	385
Henderson, William T.	Riley, Mary	07 JUL 1885 L	20	314
Henderson, Winslow	Washington, Carrie	17 DEC 1884 L	19	466
Hendle, John E.	Bond, Ella D.	27 JAN 1880 R	14	122
Hendley, James T.	Trotter, Harriet E.	27 DEC 1880 R	15	127
Hendley, James William	Marnaker, Josephine	20 DEC 1877	11	251
Hendley, Julian P.	Mills, Annie E.	05 OCT 1882 R	17	057
Hendley, Peter	Lowndes, Loveanna	11 AUG 1884	19	178
Hendley, William	Lee, Mary A.	07 APR 1878	11	410
Hendrix, Thomas J.	Sprigg, Annie Florence	10 JUL 1878 R	12	132
Henison, Lucy	Lyles, Lewis	24 MAY 1879 L	13	203
Henkel, Catherine	Hunt, John C.	13 MAY 1879 R	13	162
Henkle, Charles L.	Craun, Emma B.	09 JUN 1885 R	20	262
Henkle, Saul S	Emory, Clara K.	21 JUL 1880	14	371
Henley, George F.	Abell, Flora	25 OCT 1884	19	335
Henley, H. Thomas	Huhn, H. Elizabeth	03 DEC 1878 L	12	359
Henley, Hamilton H.	Knowles, Sarah E., Mrs.	07 JAN 1879 L	13	010
Henley, William George	Grover, Martha Jerusha	16 MAY 1878	12	054
Hennaman, Sarah M.	Crowther, Addison B.	17 DEC 1877	11	240
Hennerson, Anthony	Burke, Ophelia	05 FEB 1878	11	327
Hennessy, Martha	Nelson, Peter	29 APR 1882 L	16	340
Hennicke, Helen J.	Mungen, Theodore	28 JUN 1878	12	116
Hennigan, Eliza	Johnson, Clarence	31 JAN 1884	18	396
Hennigan, John	Brown, Alice	11 JUN 1885 R	20	052
Hennige, Christina F.	Zitting, William F.	04 OCT 1883	18	170
Henning, Aloysius	Sanford, Alice Ada	26 APR 1882 R	16	337
Henning, Anna M.	Garland, Sanders	17 FEB 1885 R	20	073
Henning, Betty	Hueter, Charles	12 OCT 1878 L	12	269
Henning, Catharine	Douglass, John A.	03 MAR 1884 L	18	455
Henning, James G.	Howes, Mary C.	08 OCT 1878 R	12	261
Henning, Sidney	Lynch, Catherine	06 FEB 1879 R	13	050
Hennis, Margaret	Bailey, James F.	04 AUG 1885 L	20	351
Henrahan, Ellen	Corbett, George W.	04 OCT 1877 L	11	121
Henry, C.O.	Mills, Annie	08 SEP 1877	11	083
Henry, Elizabeth	Clark, B. Thomas	07 MAR 1882	16	269
Henry, Fannie B.	Branham, Wilson A.	12 JUL 1877 R	11	018
Henry, George B.	Johnson, Ida D.	20 JAN 1882 L	16	203
Henry, James	Bronson, Ida	31 OCT 1881 L	16	053
Henry, James W.	Banks, Mary	12 SEP 1880	14	434

D.C. Marriage Records Index, June 28, 1877 to October 19, 1885

Henry, John G.	Wise, Caroline L.	18 DEC 1883	18	319
Henry, John S.	Canby, Emma	09 JUL 1878	12	131
Henry, Mabel Irene	Childs, Wm. Emmes, Dr.	28 MAY 1885 R	20	245
Henry, Maggie	Scott, Robert D.	16 NOV 1882 R	17	132
Henry, Mary F.	Dafney, John H.	21 AUG 1884 L	19	203
Henry, Mary Jane	Thomas, George	27 SEP 1881 L	15	498
Henry, Norma W., Mrs.	Wills, Walter H.	07 JAN 1882 R	16	185
Henry, Rachel	Young, Abraham	28 SEP 1885 L	20	446
Henry, Rosa	Ewald, Hermann C.	11 SEP 1877 L	11	086
Henry, Thomas	Bouldin, Rosa	21 NOV 1878 R	12	342
Henry, Washington	Jones, Agnes	19 OCT 1880 R	14	493
Henry, William	Sales, Julia	01 DEC 1877 L	11	214
Henry, William	Moore, Jennie	02 NOV 1880	15	025
Henry, William F.	Crawford, M. Alice	03 JUL 1884	19	120
Henry, Wilmore John	Oar, Anna Martha	04 OCT 1881 R	16	007
Henry, Wm. Daingerfield	Fraser, Sarah E.	25 JUN 1884 R	19	101
Hensey, Alex. Thomas	Rheem, Louise Rosine	19 FEB 1885 R	20	078
Hensin, John H.	Johnson, Josephine	14 JUN 1883 R	17	023
Hensley, Martha A., Mrs.	Robrecht, Frank	22 FEB 1884 R	18	437
Henson, Albert Tiberias	Rollins, Caroline Alice	25 SEP 1879 R	13	388
Henson, Annie	Brooks, George	16 DEC 1880 R	15	093
Henson, David J.	Briscoe, Maud M.	07 MAY 1885 L	20	214
Henson, Frank E.	Parker, Mary L.	24 NOV 1884 L	19	406
Henson, George	Dickson, Rosa	04 MAY 1885	20	204
Henson, George W.	Beckett, Julia	10 NOV 1884	19	371
Henson, James	Johnson, Celia	06 OCT 1879 L	13	406
Henson, James E.	Parker, Sarah J.	02 SEP 1884 L	19	220
Henson, Jennie E.	Ball, Charles C.	26 JUN 1879 L	13	254
Henson, John	Harris, Florence	15 MAY 1879 L	13	192
Henson, John	Middleton, Mary	29 MAR 1883 R	17	371
Henson, John	Gray, Katie	02 JUL 1885 L	20	308
Henson, Katie	Brown, J.W.	06 JAN 1885	20	006
Henson, Llewellyn	Lyon, Bettie	11 JAN 1883 R	17	252
Henson, Louisa	Allen, Benjamin	10 JUN 1879	13	227
Henson, Mary E.	Simms, John Wesley	14 DEC 1882	17	185
Henson, Rachel	Butler, Lewis	23 OCT 1879 R	13	439
Henson, Richard	Hamilton, Agnes	19 AUG 1880	14	406
Henson, Robert	Matthews, Sophia	10 DEC 1881 L	16	123
Henson, Thomas Bruce	Porter, Adalaide	26 FEB 1885 R	20	083
Henson, William H.	Speakes, Charlotte	15 JAN 1880 R	14	108
Henson, William Henry	Williams, Eliza	29 MAY 1878	12	074
Henson, Yarmouth	Nutt, Ella	18 DEC 1884	19	473
Hepburn, Charles W.	Madigan, Bridget H.	04 FEB 1879 R	13	043
Hepburn, Jerry M.	Hazen, Eugenia	17 NOV 1880	15	054
Hepburn, John H.	Reidrick, Harriet	05 DEC 1877 R	11	222
Hepburn, Maud E.	Cornwall, Luther M.	26 JAN 1881 L	15	165
Hepner, Fannie	Greenappel, Tely H.	15 MAR 1885 R	20	114
Herbel, Lizzie Frawzes	Dukhant, Fredrick	31 DEC 1881 L	16	172
Herberger, Lawrence	Huth, Theresa	19 MAY 1882 L	16	368
Herbert, Albert A.	Sullivan, Mary E.	15 FEB 1882 L	16	242
Herbert, Amelia C.	Berger, Oscar S.	08 NOV 1882	17	119
Herbert, Ananias	Scott, Fannie	27 SEP 1883 L	18	159
Herbert, Anna	Kemp, James H.	04 JAN 1883 L	17	239
Herbert, C. Victoria	Taylor, E. Winston	09 JAN 1879	13	011
Herbert, Charles C.	Montague, Julia C.	19 FEB 1879 L	13	068
Herbert, Charles C.	Freitag, Gertrude M.	15 NOV 1882 R	17	127
Herbert, Charles H.	Carey, Martha C.	23 OCT 1883 R	18	206
Herbert, Charles R.	Reese, Harriet E.	15 AUG 1880 R	14	392

Herbert, Charlotte	Bagby, Thomas	17 OCT 1883 L	18	200
Herbert, Clement	Lee, Caroline	01 NOV 1877 R	11	165
Herbert, Edgar C.	Fowler, Elizabeth E.	05 AUG 1877	11	042
Herbert, Edward H.	Phillips, Mary E.	21 AUG 1884	19	199
Herbert, Eliza J.	Shelton, James S.	05 FEB 1878	11	326
Herbert, Ella L.	Sanzio, D.E.	10 OCT 1882 R	17	064
Herbert, Emma M.	Mason, Charles A.	19 JAN 1880	14	111
Herbert, Ernest	Javins, Lillie	14 JUN 1883 L	17	491
Herbert, Ernest	Crounse, Ida	27 OCT 1884	19	339
Herbert, George R.	Berkley, Annie F.	08 FEB 1881 R	15	182
Herbert, Georgie	Jarvis, William	23 NOV 1882 R	17	148
Herbert, Georgie Frances	Bevan, Joseph H.	29 DEC 1884 L	19	496
Herbert, Hattie C.	Minor, Eugene P.	16 OCT 1885 L	20	491
Herbert, Helen	Crowley, Patrick F.	28 APR 1881 R	15	280
Herbert, Henrietta, Mrs.	Wood, John	26 DEC 1883 L	18	344
Herbert, James J.	Walsh, Elizabeth E.	12 NOV 1879	13	479
Herbert, Jennie A.	Saddler, William D.	08 JUN 1882 R	16	401
Herbert, John R.	Loudon, Onimeral	29 NOV 1882 L	17	159
Herbert, Lawerence M.	Tolson, Annie E.	27 DEC 1881 R	16	161
Herbert, Letha M.	Carroll, Charles H.	03 APR 1883 L	17	377
Herbert, Levi	Simms, Winnie	20 DEC 1877 L	11	252
Herbert, Lizzie	Coxen, George W.	06 AUG 1881 L	15	434
Herbert, Lucy	Nichols, Julius	01 OCT 1885 L	20	453
Herbert, Lulu P.	Ernst, Frederick K.	02 APR 1884	18	492
Herbert, Martha	Robertson, George	12 JUL 1877 R	11	017
Herbert, Mary A.	Daly, Jefferson D.	12 JUL 1882 L	16	445
Herbert, Mary C.	Bowie, Jesse S.	06 DEC 1883 L	18	303
Herbert, Mary E.	Howe, James E.	15 SEP 1885 L	20	419
Herbert, Mary K.	Harris, John H.	05 NOV 1879 R	13	468
Herbert, Mary Theresa	Blackwell, Charles	14 OCT 1879 L	13	422
Herbert, Mollie Virginia	Grant, John	15 DEC 1881 R	16	131
Herbert, Nathan Francis	Williams, Mary A.	21 DEC 1882 R	17	200
Herbert, Nathaniel O T	Hogan, Millio	20 SEP 1877	11	102
Herbert, Pierson	Keys, Carrie	15 MAY 1883 L	17	441
Herbert, Rinaldo	Bouldin, Frances	31 OCT 1878 L	12	302
Herbert, Rosa A.	Edwards, Samuel E.	22 APR 1879 R	13	156
Herbert, Thomas	Carroll, Minnie	04 OCT 1877	11	122
Herbert, W.A.	McLeod, Ambrosia M.	14 AUG 1877 L	11	053
Herbert, W.K.	Burch, Mary D.	07 MAY 1883 L	17	431
Herbert, William E.	Williams, Monterey T.	04 DEC 1883	18	294
Herbertons, Emmy	Ryan, Joseph	19 AUG 1885 L	20	377
Herbst, Amelia	Clarke, William S.	14 JUL 1882 R	16	447
Hercus, May Sherman	Bradley, Robert Edmond	29 NOV 1884 R	19	424
Herd, Elizabeth	Howard, Isaac	14 MAY 1885 L	20	220
Herd, Frankie	Johnson, Jordan	01 SEP 1881	15	467
Herdnell, Charlotte	Holmes, Robert A.	26 SEP 1878	12	231
Herdon, Learen	Holmes, Elizabeth	09 MAY 1885	20	206
Herenberg, Fred C.G.	Gordon, Ella V.	08 OCT 1884	19	295
Herfurth, Augusta	Brethauer, August	11 JUL 1883 L	18	043
Herfurth, Charles A.	Auguste, Mary A.	18 MAY 1885 R	20	226
Herfurth, Herman	Bean, Ella E.	14 JAN 1885	20	018
Herfurth, John	York, Mary Christine	03 MAR 1885	20	091
Herfurth, Theresa	Miller, Edward H.	12 MAR 1882	16	270
Herfurth, William	Dietz, Augusta	05 SEP 1878	12	200
Hering, August	Schickler, Sophia	30 MAY 1883	17	466
Herlihy, Kate E.	DeChard, Emanuel A.	21 NOV 1882 L	17	139
Herman, Bertha	Strauss, David	11 APR 1880 R	14	215
Herman, Bridget	Hunt, William	15 SEP 1880 R	14	434

Herman, Linda	Klotz, Henry E.	03 OCT 1881	16	002
Herman, Louise	Pearce, Stanley	24 DEC 1884 R	19	485
Herndon, Alice	Lee, Alexander	21 MAY 1881 L	15	320
Herndon, Mary	Hailstock, Joshua	20 DEC 1879 R	14	060
Herndon, Mary E.	Deshon, Richard P.	18 FEB 1880 R	14	157
Herndon, Moses	Lewis, Agnes	10 JUL 1884 L	19	134
Herns, James	Booth, Addison	18 SEP 1883 R	18	137
Herold, Charles	Pfeiffer, Annetta A.	13 NOV 1877 L	11	181
Herold, Elizabeth Capitola	Magruder, Edward	22 NOV 1883 R	18	272
Herold, Mary A., Mrs.	Williams, John M.	02 APR 1878	11	403
Herr, Charles	Dougal, Helen	14 JUN 1881 R	15	359
Herr, Fannie	Niblack, William Caldwell	10 FEB 1880 R	14	145
Herr, M.M.	Benson, Lillian M.	26 FEB 1884	18	443
Herreford, R.W.	Mitchellmore, Katie	26 FEB 1885	20	088
Herrit, Ella	Washington, John	12 FEB 1880 R	14	152
Herrmann, Franz	Fuller, Lizzie B.	02 DEC 1882 L	17	164
Herron, J. Whit	Partridge, Charlotte P.	25 DEC 1877	11	265
Herron, James L.	Linthicum, Amanda L.	09 MAR 1885 R	20	101
Hershaw, Charles W.	Cunningham, Annie E.	08 OCT 1879 R	13	409
Herzberger, Mary	Metcalf, Francis S.	18 SEP 1880 L	14	451
Herzog, Friedrick	Oppermann, Maria Katharina	23 FEB 1880 R	14	161
Herzog, Joseph	Pinkus, Rosa	18 MAR 1885 R	20	121
Hesen, Harmon O.	Rall, Susie	21 APR 1885	20	178
Hess, Augustus	Fitzgerald, Mary Ann	20 OCT 1877 L	11	146
Hess, George W.	Ely, Maria E.	19 FEB 1884	18	428
Hess, Josephene Helene	Colby, Eugene A.	13 NOV 1878 R	12	324
Hess, Julie Caroline	Southard, Harry Codding	08 APR 1885 R	20	149
Hess, Mary Katie	Vermillion, Charles F.	03 APR 1884 R	18	489
Hess, Tillie E.	Hale, Conrad L.	01 JAN 1885 R	20	001
Hesselbach, Fanny	Schmitt, Ewold	13 OCT 1881 L	16	022
Hesselbach, Olga M.	Spier, George W.	20 JAN 1883 L	17	269
Hessian, Julia A.	Wise, Albert M.	19 OCT 1885 L	20	498
Hesson, William	McNamara, Annie, Mrs.	26 AUG 1879 R	13	307
Hester, Gertrude	Mohler, Jacob Rupert	18 JAN 1881 R	15	152
Hester, J. Lester A.	Lacey, Eliza I.	28 AUG 1884	19	215
Hester, Marguerite Winsborough	Chew, Monroe Grayson	09 OCT 1883 R	18	179
Hettinger, Wm. L.	Lederer, Magdalene B.	04 FEB 1883	17	287
Heunigs, Henry	Kemmauf, Maggie	30 NOV 1884	19	424
Heurich, Elisabetta	Faulhaber, Alexander	19 AUG 1878 L	12	172
Heurich, Sallie B.	Bumpas, Thomas B.	07 OCT 1882 R	17	058
Hevener, Lizzie C.	Brock, Charles A.	31 DEC 1877 L	11	281
Hewit, Charles B.	Butler, Mary	27 JUL 1878 R	12	137
Hewitt, Etta M.	Perkins, Edwy	30 MAY 1884	19	047
Hewitt, Ida W.	Maring, Delos T.	14 JAN 1885	20	018
Hewitt, Samuel S.	Jones, Virginia E.	05 AUG 1879 L	13	308
Hewlett, Aronella Molyneaux	Scott, Edward D.	16 FEB 1882 R	16	246
Hexter, Carrie	Guggenhein, Simon	29 JAN 1882 R	16	213
Heyde, Helen W.	Padgett, James E.	15 DEC 1880 R	15	099
Heydon, Charles S.	Bobee, Ida	01 AUG 1883 L	18	070
Heyl, Elizabeth Rebecca	Lancaster, Andrew Jackson	30 JUL 1882 R	16	458
Hibbs, Bettie	Kerrick, Charles C.	08 JAN 1879 R	13	010
Hibbs, Ernest L.	Bennett, Mary E.	01 DEC 1884	19	428
Hichen, Mary E.	Gardner, Richard L.	06 APR 1880 R	14	211
Hichew, John D.	Lyons, Mary E., Mrs.	21 DEC 1880 L	15	113
Hickcox, John Howard, Jr.	Hughlett, Lula Lee	11 APR 1882 R	16	304
Hickenlooper, Carrie	Seebring, Francis A.	21 OCT 1884	19	324
Hickenlooper, Ettie	Handy, William Edward	04 MAY 1882 R	16	348
Hickerson, Charles E.	Hardy, Elmira	17 AUG 1885 L	20	372

Hickey, Catherine	Coffey, Patrick Joseph	05 NOV 1877 R	11	167
Hickey, Ellen	Walker, William	28 MAY 1878 L	12	070
Hickey, Maggie A.	Donaldson, George	13 NOV 1878 L	12	328
Hickey, Margaret	Ezell, John	13 NOV 1879 R	13	486
Hickey, Mary Ann	Collins, Joseph	02 JUL 1879 L	13	262
Hickey, Mary J.	Holland, James M.	01 JUL 1879 L	13	261
Hickey, Patrick	Sanford, Amanda	13 FEB 1884	18	422
Hickey, W.	Haynie, Mary K.	07 JUN 1878 L	12	091
Hickman, Ellen F.	Loudon, John A.	07 AUG 1884	19	174
Hickman, Etchison H.	Slater, Effie L.	06 OCT 1885 R	20	458
Hickman, Harriet	Duckett, Daniel	28 JAN 1878 L	11	319
Hickman, Henry	Warren, Mary	29 NOV 1883	18	287
Hickman, Lewis W.	Smallwood, Cornelia F.	27 FEB 1884	18	447
Hickman, Samuel T.	Wenner, Sallie J.	21 JUL 1885 R	20	334
Hickman, Sarah	Perry, William	16 APR 1881 L	15	259
Hickman, William Purnell	Hilton, Anne Virginia	02 JUN 1881 R	15	338
Hickok, Clara Bell	Deale, William G.	03 FEB 1878 R	11	324
Hicks, Emma G.	Gunnell, George W.	11 APR 1878 R	12	002
Hicks, Georgiana	Howard, Charles H.	21 APR 1881 L	15	269
Hicks, Henry	Ross, Mary C.	29 SEP 1885	20	429
Hicks, Ida Matilda	Smart, John Pearson	19 JAN 1882 R	16	201
Hicks, Jeremiah	Fox, Martha L.	29 SEP 1885 R	20	430
Hicks, Joseph	Tibbs, Mary Jane	14 NOV 1883	18	254
Hicks, Julia	Warren, Columbus	19 JAN 1882	16	201
Hicks, Lizzie	Colbert, Daniel	26 DEC 1878 L	12	401
Hicks, Mary F.	Harrison, Francis M.	05 APR 1883 R	17	380
Hicks, Mary T.	Bealle, Chas. Albert	07 NOV 1877 R	11	173
Hicks, Matilda	Conway, George	23 DEC 1884	19	482
Hicks, Phillips E.	Wright, Josephine A.	19 NOV 1884 L	19	397
Hicks, Reuben	Wiley, Martha	10 MAY 1884 L	19	370
Hicks, Robert L.	Welch, Lena	24 AUG 1885	20	384
Hicks, Rosa	Jones, John Wm.	08 OCT 1884	19	292
Hicks, Samuel H.	Kepler, Lizzie F.	27 FEB 1878	11	360
Hicks, Silas	Brown, Hannah Maria	07 MAY 1884 R	19	010
Hicks, Susie	Pierce, M.C.	09 JUN 1879 L	13	225
Hicks, William A.	Childs, Louisa	06 DEC 1882	17	167
Hicks, William W.	Higgins, Sarah Ann	17 NOV 1879 R	13	489
Hierling, Mary Adelaide	Krause, Franz	19 JUL 1884	19	147
Hieth, James	Stanmore, Harriet	03 JUL 1882 L	16	435
Higby, Celinda	Preall, Andrew J.	12 JUN 1883	17	488
Higdon, Florence R.	Julihn, M.L.	06 OCT 1885 L	20	462
Higginbottom, Lucy Jane	Tucker, Beverly, Capt.	06 OCT 1881 R	16	011
Higgins, Carrie Andrews	Hutchins, Hamilton	04 APR 1881	15	248
Higgins, Ida	McKnew, Wm. Harrison	22 NOV 1882 R	17	143
Higgins, Ida	Evans, James	22 APR 1885 R	20	120
Higgins, Isabelle	Harban, Walter Simpson	26 OCT 1881 R	16	043
Higgins, James B.	Arrington, Julia A.	03 MAY 1882 R	16	347
Higgins, John deBree	Williams, Anna Brown	07 FEB 1884 R	18	412
Higgins, Lloyd	Magruder, Emma	23 JUN 1878	12	110
Higgins, Lucius Cornelius	Myers, Susie P.	06 NOV 1879 R	13	464
Higgins, Maimie H.	Shipe, Frank H.	30 APR 1879 R	13	169
Higgins, Reason	Proctor, Martha	21 NOV 1878 L	12	341
Higgins, Sarah Ann	Hicks, William W.	17 NOV 1879 R	13	489
Higginson, William L.	Jones, Julia N.	13 MAR 1885 L	20	140
Higgs, Ann Priscilla	Conner, George	27 NOV 1877 R	11	204
Higgs, Wm. Thompson	Laughlin, Mary A.	13 DEC 1877 R	11	236
High, Henry	Lynch, Emma J.	04 OCT 1877	11	122
Highfield, Mary E.	Newton, John W.	09 JUN 1884 L	19	068

D.C. Marriage Records Index, June 28, 1877 to October 19, 1885

Name	Spouse	Date	Vol	Page
Hiland, Thomas	Gorringe, Jern Blanche	07 AUG 1878	12	159
Hilbrandt, Alonzo E.	Williams, Edmonia	13 NOV 1877	11	180
Hilbus, George J.	Cusick, Maggie	22 JAN 1878	11	314
Hildebrand, Abraham	Carter, Willie Catherine	28 DEC 1880 R	15	128
Hildebrand, Eliza J.	Hunt, James A.	25 OCT 1880 R	15	012
Hildebrand, Herman G.	Forrester, Rachel Adella	07 SEP 1881 R	15	475
Hildebrand, Mary	Ramsberg, Sammuel	06 OCT 1880 L	14	476
Hildreth, Leaming	Donoghu, Nora A.	12 DEC 1878	13	378
Hildrup, Jessie Sophia	Tullock, Seymour Wilcox	22 NOV 1882 R	17	142
Hile, Margaret	Moore, Joseph B.	09 NOV 1879 R	13	486
Hill, Alexander P., Jr.	Munro, Mary Catherine	25 APR 1883	17	406
Hill, Anna	Campbell, Enoch	08 FEB 1878 L	11	333
Hill, Annie	Curtis, James	28 JUN 1877	11	001
Hill, Annie	Lewis, John	19 MAR 1879 L	13	109
Hill, Archie	Dixon, Bettie	02 MAY 1878 L	12	035
Hill, Benjamin F.	White, Sallie	26 MAR 1885 R	20	132
Hill, Bettie	Simpson, Lloyd	04 MAR 1880 R	14	174
Hill, Bettie M.	Degges, Henry H.	06 SEP 1882 L	17	007
Hill, Charles	Anderson, Sarah	29 OCT 1879 R	13	450
Hill, Charles	Wright, Sarah	15 MAY 1882 R	16	359
Hill, Charlotte	Wilson, William	28 JUL 1879 L	13	296
Hill, Daniel	Simms, Mary	08 SEP 1880 L	14	435
Hill, Delia	Allan, John	09 DEC 1879 L	14	039
Hill, Edward	Henderson, Annie	15 NOV 1881 L	16	077
Hill, Edward	Moore, Margaret A.	23 MAY 1883	17	457
Hill, Edward L.	Clubb, Frances A.	02 NOV 1822 L	17	108
Hill, Eliza	Terrell, Scott	26 NOV 1879 L	14	009
Hill, Eliza B.	Sipes, John H.	15 JUN 1883 R	17	485
Hill, Elizabeth A.	Mason, Alexander	11 MAR 1885 L	20	107
Hill, Emma	Linsey, Philip	24 SEP 1885 L	20	439
Hill, Emma P.	Young, Alfred	18 OCT 1877 R	11	144
Hill, Esther I.	Barton, Elmer E.	15 JAN 1884	18	377
Hill, Frazier	Brown, Andrew	03 MAY 1881 L	15	290
Hill, Georgianna	Merrick, Edwin	04 AUG 1883	18	070
Hill, Helena Marie	Sommners, Frank Pierce	28 FEB 1881 R	15	207
Hill, Henrietta	Skidmore, Samuel Charles	25 AUG 1880	14	415
Hill, Henry	Atkinson, Rosetta	11 DEC 1879 R	13	199
Hill, Henry	Henderson, Lena	29 SEP 1880 L	14	463
Hill, Henry	Brooks, Jane	13 DEC 1883 L	18	315
Hill, Horace L.	Sterling, Julia H.	03 MAR 1883 L	17	331
Hill, Ida	Ridgway, George T.	05 SEP 1883	18	112
Hill, Ida V.	MacNalty, William P.	01 MAY 1884 R	19	001
Hill, Ida V.	McNalty, William P.	01 MAY 1884 L	18	546
Hill, James	Richardson, Annie	08 SEP 1881 R	15	471
Hill, James A.	Graham, Lucinda	12 DEC 1877 R	11	233
Hill, James Henry	Marten, Cora Z.	16 NOV 1882 R	17	124
Hill, James T.	Brown, Adeline	23 APR 1883 L	17	406
Hill, James W.	Lewis, Anna M. Haslup	21 JUL 1880 R	14	371
Hill, Joanna	Dorsey, Thomas	11 MAY 1882	16	357
Hill, John	Thomas, Margaret J.	31 JUL 1883 L	18	068
Hill, John Wesley	Creek, Rachel	09 NOV 1878 L	12	318
Hill, Joseph	Ware, Rachel	08 MAY 1882 R	16	346
Hill, Joseph	Collins, Jennie	24 NOV 1883 L	18	275
Hill, Josephine	Waugh, Clinton	23 DEC 1880 R	15	119
Hill, Julius	Harris, Jane	12 JUL 1877 R	11	018
Hill, Lena	Severs, John	04 AUG 1882	16	465
Hill, Levi	Marsden, Julia	20 FEB 1879 R	13	071
Hill, Lewis H.	Gilam, Carrie	23 AUG 1883	18	097

Hill, Lloyd	Littleford, Catherine L.	03 FEB 1881	15	177
Hill, Louisa	Cox, George	23 DEC 1880 L	15	118
Hill, Louisa	Barton, George	11 MAR 1882 L	16	273
Hill, Louise L.	Ramsay, Dennis McCarty	13 FEB 1880 R	14	152
Hill, Lucretia	Lee, Samuel	18 JUL 1878 L	12	141
Hill, Lucy Ann	Oman, Barney	31 MAR 1879 L	13	118
Hill, Mamie F.	Tyler, William Edward	25 AUG 1883	18	098
Hill, Maria	Johnson, Henson	18 JAN 1881 L	15	153
Hill, Maria	Fitzhugh, Taylor	29 NOV 1883	18	279
Hill, Mary	McCollum, H.A.	21 AUG 1877	11	061
Hill, Mary	Randall, William	19 NOV 1882	17	135
Hill, Mary Alice	Eggleston, Jos. Mortimer	22 MAY 1884 R	19	034
Hill, Mary Isabel	Sargent, Nathan	26 APR 1879 R	13	161
Hill, Mary J.	Chalk, Charles S.	12 SEP 1883	18	127
Hill, Mary J.V.	Cox, William	16 OCT 1884 L	19	309
Hill, Mary Jane	Meredith, John Henry	21 NOV 1878 L	12	341
Hill, Mary L.	Henderson, John	25 MAR 1879 L	13	114
Hill, Mary Virginia	Hayes, Alexander O.	21 FEB 1885 L	20	080
Hill, Mary W.	Paine, Robert E.	23 SEP 1878 L	12	230
Hill, Melinda E.	Moran, Horatio H.	15 MAR 1883 L	17	348
Hill, Mildred C.	Langston, Richard	23 APR 1885 L	20	186
Hill, Nicholas	Hughes, Alice	11 MAY 1885 L	20	216
Hill, Rachel	Brooks, Thomas	24 APR 1884 L	18	531
Hill, Reuben B.	Johnson, Musette	20 APR 1880	14	228½
Hill, Reuben B.	Bannister, Susie	20 APR 1880 L	14	228
Hill, Robert W.	Brooks, Nanie	26 JUN 1883	18	016
Hill, Robert W.	Flood, Anna V.	22 OCT 1884	19	328
Hill, Rosa	Jones, Thomas A.	13 OCT 1883 L	18	190
Hill, Sam	Young, Maria	20 MAR 1883 L	17	352
Hill, Spencer	Goings, Annie	14 JUL 1877 L	11	020
Hill, Thomas	Tolson, Malvina	04 SEP 1883 L	18	111
Hill, Thomas O.L.	Nowland, Mary Lee	02 APR 1883 R	17	374
Hill, Walter	Hawkins, Josephine	09 APR 1879 L	13	133
Hill, William	Krisman, Emma	18 JUL 1878 L	12	140
Hill, William	Davis, Ella	10 SEP 1884	19	238
Hill, William	Johnson, Sarah C.	01 JUN 1885	20	246
Hill, William Cocoran	Phenix, Sallie	23 OCT 1877 R	11	149
Hill, William E.	Fowler, Florence A.	02 APR 1884	18	490
Hill, William M.	Leftwich, Martha J.	04 JUN 1884 R	19	060
Hill, William Wallace	George, Bessie C.	08 JUN 1880 R	14	309
Hill, Willie F.	Neal, Georgie	01 JAN 1880 R	14	076
Hillary, Christiana	Beard, Lloyd W.	15 SEP 1880 L	14	446
Hillary, Clara L.	Dove, Franklin P.	11 FEB 1879 L	13	054
Hillary, William	Spriggs, Grace Anna	15 APR 1880 L	14	224
Hilleary, Clarence Worthing	Wheeler, Charlotte Oram	25 JAN 1882 R	16	206
Hilleary, George C.	Reed, Catharine	27 JUN 1883 L	18	021
Hilleary, Mary Matilda	Alexander, John St. Clair	23 OCT 1883 R	18	207
Hiller, John	Frank, Lena M.	17 JUN 1881 R	15	324
Hiller, Louisa Augusta	Alsop, Jackson L.	24 JUN 1885 R	20	288
Hiller, Mary	Alsop, Thomas	05 AUG 1879	13	306
Hillery, Lewis W.	Willis, Alice J.	12 JUL 1880 L	14	356
Hillery, Sophia	Dabner, Alick	05 JAN 1883 L	17	240
Hillman, Charles	Lacy, Virginia	15 SEP 1884	19	249
Hillman, Clara	Marsh, Frank A.	18 JUN 1884	19	090
Hillman, Mary A.	Dombhart, George E.	14 APR 1885 R	20	163
Hillstock, John Tyler	Hillstock, Mary	01 MAR 1883 L	17	327
Hillstock, Mary	Hillstock, John Tyler	01 MAR 1883 L	17	327
Hillyard, John	Cocke, Cora M.	09 MAY 1882 R	16	352

Hilton, Abraham L.	Rockey, Emma	07 JUN 1885	20	258
Hilton, Anne Virginia	Hickman, William Purnell	02 JUN 1881 R	15	338
Hilton, Annie E.	Long, Israel	05 JUN 1882 R	16	394
Hilton, Hattie M.	Scheitlin, Rudolph	15 OCT 1881 R	16	027
Hilton, James H.	Murray, Mary	16 JAN 1878 L	11	305
Hilton, Mary Frances	Toulson, Arthur Richard	15 DEC 1880 R	15	095
Hilton, William	Colliflower, Ollie	04 DEC 1879 R	13	499
Hilton, William H.	Bost, Jennie L.	18 OCT 1882	17	077
Hiltz, Maggie	Williams, John	24 APR 1878 L	12	022
Hindmarsh, Henry Edward	Randall, Clara G. Gassaway	16 NOV 1881 R	16	079
Hinds, Jerome Jasper	Bliss, Clara Bell	17 JUN 1878 R	12	102
Hines, Albert B.	Serrin, Marion V.	28 APR 1881 R	15	283
Hines, Albert E.	Nichols, Alice E.	06 MAY 1885	20	208
Hines, Eleanora	Glorius, Ignatius G.	03 JUN 1884 L	19	052
Hines, Ellen	Slater, William C.	24 SEP 1878	12	232
Hines, Fannie J.	Bangs, J. Howard	20 SEP 1882 L	17	031
Hines, Lawrence Augustus	Embrey, Margaret Virginia	29 SEP 1883 R	18	160
Hines, Mary C.	Clark, Charles H.	11 NOV 1884 L	19	374
Hines, Mary E.	Young, George W.	23 JAN 1881 R	15	161
Hines, Sarah Jane	Ashton, John P.	15 JUN 1881 L	15	363
Hines, William	Mattingly, Eliza	24 FEB 1885 R	20	081
Hinke, Carl M.W.	Schifner, Catherine L.	23 APR 1883	17	404
Hinkelbein, Theresa F.M.	Griffin, Richard B.	04 MAY 1885 L	20	203
Hinley, Lucretie	Hawley, John H.	21 NOV 1883	18	268
Hinson, Clara Beall	Carver, Alpha E.H.	23 MAR 1881 R	15	236
Hinson, Lillure	Cramer, James	07 MAY 1878	12	041
Hinton, Florence	Lower, Cyras Benson	08 NOV 1881 R	16	065
Hipkins, Bertie	Wyatt, Cullin	20 DEC 1877 L	11	254
Hipkins, Mariah	Young, Noah	25 SEP 1884	19	263
Hipkins, Moses	Kinslow, Charlotte	14 FEB 1884 R	18	422
Hipkins, Penny	Muse, William	27 AUG 1880	14	419
Hirsch, Katie F.	Flammer, William	21 DEC 1880 R	15	114
Hirschfield, Rose	Robinson, Bernard	18 JAN 1885 R	20	023
Hirsh, Morris	Strasburger, Bertha	16 SEP 1884 L	19	253
Hirte, Adelbert	Eckert, Hedwig	30 MAR 1883 L	17	371
Hiser, Daniel	Wunderlich, Barbara	28 AUG 1881	15	461
Hiser, Paul, Jr.	Wunderlich, Kate	15 MAY 1881	15	307
Hitchcock, Emma Alice	Edgar, James Alexander	03 MAY 1880 R	14	250
Hitchins, Owen	Powell, Nancy	14 MAR 1885 R	20	113
Hitner, Mary	Cole, David	13 NOV 1879 L	13	485
Hitnor, William	Newman, Annie A.	10 FEB 1885 L	20	060
Hizer, Thomas O.	Hazel, M. Susie	19 DEC 1882	17	192
Hoaglan, J. Henry	Garmaroth, Kitty Louise	24 NOV 1877 L	11	202
Hoagland, John H.	Steel, Annie	27 NOV 1879 L	14	017
Hoagland, John Henry	Steel, Annie Eliza	07 JAN 1880 R	14	141
Hoard, Martha	Gray, Harry W.	27 FEB 1879 R	13	079
Hoban, Henry	McCarter, Sarah	22 JUN 1881 L	15	373
Hoban, James	Mitchel, Elise A.	28 JUL 1880 R	14	376
Hobbs, Frank B.	Walker, Florence O.	16 APR 1885 R	20	172
Hobbs, Frank D.	Abbott, Ellen	01 OCT 1879 R	13	395
Hobbs, Henry Waldo	Durham, Sarah D.	12 NOV 1884 R	19	375
Hobbs, Laura V.	Thompson, John B.	24 FEB 1880 R	14	162
Hobbs, M.E.	Bogan, J.F.	17 AUG 1880	14	402
Hobbs, Mary Linda	Johnson, John Altheus	12 SEP 1883 R	18	126
Hobbs, Millard F.	Cole, Nannie V.	31 DEC 1877	11	259
Hobbs, Susan J.	Simons, Gaylord C.	20 JAN 1879 R	13	026
Hobbs, William	Boem, Josephine	10 JUN 1880 R	14	315
Hobelmann, Herman	Peters, Bettie	22 JAN 1880 R	14	115

Hobson, Annie C.	Clarke, Charles I.	19 AUG 1885	20	379
Hobson, Carrie	Fisher, William A.	26 JAN 1881 R	15	163
Hoch, Wilhelm	Auth, Paulina	19 JUN 1882 L	16	415
Hockam, Lucian	Cobb, Sybel	01 OCT 1883 L	18	162
Hodgdon, Micah W.	Sterling, Mary E.	15 SEP 1881 L	15	487
Hodge, Annie	Lomax, Moses	01 AUG 1884	19	141
Hodge, Clark R.	Fassett, Flora	16 JUN 1880 R	14	322
Hodge, Hannah	Carroll, Thomas	20 NOV 1882 L	17	137
Hodge, Sina	Gross, James H.	07 OCT 1880 L	14	482
Hodgen, Annie M.	Prather, Jesse J.	06 JUL 1885 R	20	056
Hodges, Clara W.	Morsell, William A.	10 SEP 1883	18	123
Hodges, G.H.	Atz, Mary	30 MAY 1878 R	12	029
Hodges, Ida D.	McCargo, Peyton R.	22 SEP 1881 R	15	494
Hodges, L.E.	Cooper, J.E.	26 APR 1885	20	169
Hodges, Margaret E.	Petty, Henry S.	12 JUL 1877 R	11	016
Hodges, William H.	Williams, Emma M.	01 DEC 1880 L	15	078
Hodgkin, Charles Edwin	Harper, Laura Virginia	14 MAY 1885 R	20	222
Hodgkin, M.A.	Price, C.C.	02 JAN 1878	11	289
Hodgkins, Cora	King, Theo. Ingalls	04 FEB 1885 R	20	050
Hodgkins, J.S.	Meyers, Annie H.	21 FEB 1880	14	162
Hodgkins, S. Elizabeth	Swingle, Morgan	16 OCT 1884	19	313
Hodgson, Charles S.	Irving, Katie S.	10 JAN 1882 R	16	188
Hodgson, Laura C.	Purington, Joseph W.	11 MAY 1881	15	302
Hodgson, Thomas A.	Johnston, Mary E.	13 DEC 1882 L	17	181
Hodson, Elizabeth	Club, Henry H.	26 DEC 1878 L	12	402
Hodson, Lizzie A.	Smith, James S.F.	03 MAR 1881	15	211
Hodson, William M.	Levy, Rachel	17 JUL 1878 L	12	137
Hoeke, John	Kahlert, Louisa	30 DEC 1879	14	081
Hoesch, Anna	Lohr, Charles W.	17 NOV 1884 R	19	386
Hofer, Charles A.	Green, Minnie V.	27 DEC 1882	17	215
Hoff, Alice A.	Kinstendorff, Charles A., Jr.	23 FEB 1880	14	163
Hoffa, Lena	Schembeck, Emanuel	17 OCT 1883 R	18	199
Hoffmaan, Harriet B.	Cole, Allen H.	15 NOV 1884 L	19	384
Hoffman, Albert D.	Chicker, Nettie S.	27 MAY 1885 R	20	243
Hoffman, Anna R.	Ferguson, Clarence R.	23 OCT 1877 L	11	151
Hoffman, Augusta	Ziegler, Gottlieb	30 SEP 1877	11	108
Hoffman, Charles	Kohlert, Katie	25 JUN 1881 L	15	379
Hoffman, Emma F.	Robertson, Daniel	04 JUL 1879 R	13	268
Hoffman, Ernest Emil	Kuhlman, Mary Louise	24 JAN 1878 R	11	316
Hoffman, Fred	Neuchter, Katherine	15 OCT 1883	18	193
Hoffman, George W.	Thompson, Elizabeth	11 MAY 1878 L	12	048
Hoffman, George W.	Burruss, Molly B.	31 AUG 1878 L	12	189
Hoffman, Henry	Thoma, Lena	02 SEP 1880 L	14	429
Hoffman, Marie A.	Kines, Frances W.	18 MAY 1882 R	16	364
Hoffman, Rutha	Eisebraum, Gottieb	07 FEB 1882 R	16	230
Hoffmann, George N.	Reder, Caroline	27 DEC 1881	16	162
Hoffmann, Maria	Walter, Frederick	11 NOV 1883	18	244
Hoffmann, Max	Hahn, Johanna	14 NOV 1884 L	19	382
Hofheimer, Alexander T.	Rosenberg, Fannie	18 AUG 1880 R	14	402
Hogan, Fannie Austin	Smellie, Robert	23 DEC 1877 R	11	258
Hogan, John F.	Pumphrey, Emma A.	26 DEC 1877 R	11	265
Hogan, Leonard T.	Prescott, Clara C.	22 OCT 1884	19	320
Hogan, Mary	Knowles, David O.	28 NOV 1880	15	064
Hogan, Mary	McFarland, Sidney M.	03 JUN 1885 L	20	255
Hogan, Millie	Herbert, Nathaniel O.T.	20 SEP 1877	11	102
Hogan, Peter	Hall, Annie	05 NOV 1885	17	035
Hogans, John J.	Sulavan, Ella	16 OCT 1880 L	14	499
Hogans, Mary H.	Thomas, David W.	26 NOV 1878 R	12	346

Hoge, Nannie Hunter	Fairfax, Arthur Percy	02 FEB 1882 R	16	221
Hogeland, D.M.	Brown, Clara V.	13 APR 1885	20	162
Hogg, William S.	Owens, Gertrude	11 MAR 1885	20	104
Hogue, George W.	Hutchinson, Annie O.	23 JUN 1880	14	332
Hogue, Marie Alma	Baxter, Walter W.	06 SEP 1881 R	15	473
Hohbein, Annie	Jost, John B.	20 NOV 1883	18	264
Hohbein, Kate	Lerch, Thomas J.	30 MAY 1880 R	14	294
Höhlein, Margaretha	Juster, Gerritt	30 JAN 1879 R	13	038
Hohlpien, Mortin	Waltz, Lena	08 JUL 1884	19	127
Hohmann, Henry	Geier, Mary	27 NOV 1880 L	15	070
Hohn, Christine	Wanner, Franz	10 SEP 1877 L	11	084
Holbrook, Mary A.	Jackson, Frank H.	07 DEC 1881 R	16	118
Holbrunner, Maria L.	Anders, George W.	22 JAN 1881 L	15	161
Holcombe, John Hite Lee	Taylor, Ida Hilton	27 APR 1881 R	15	274
Holden, Augustus Randall	Cavis, Annie Hamilton	07 DEC 1882 R	17	172
Holden, Henry	Warren, Mary	23 OCT 1877 L	11	151
Holden, Matilda	Dowell, William L.	10 DEC 1884 R	19	446
Holder, Joseph	Freer, Emma Jane, Mrs.	23 OCT 1884 R	19	331
Holer, Emil	Pfahrer, Elise	13 FEB 1879 R	13	060
Holl, Eugene A.	Pendleton, Louisa M.	19 DEC 1883	18	324
Hollan, Alexander	Lisber, Mary	02 JAN 1883	17	233
Hollan, Joseph	Bush, Fannie	25 JUN 1885	20	281
Holland, Ada	Burr, Harrison	01 NOV 1877 R	11	162
Holland, Alexander	Brooks, Mary Ann	08 SEP 1879 R	13	357
Holland, Charles R.	Jones, Annie M.	06 MAR 1879 R	13	087
Holland, Daniel	Smith, Josephine	29 NOV 1882 L	17	161
Holland, Edward	Brooks, Harriet	22 JUL 1879 R	13	286
Holland, Edward E.	Cullison, Ida	06 APR 1878 R	11	408
Holland, Estelle M.	Koehler, George	30 SEP 1885 L	20	448
Holland, Florence D.	French, John M.	15 OCT 1884 R	19	293
Holland, James	Warren, Lizzie	21 DEC 1880 R	15	113
Holland, James M.	Hickey, Mary J.	01 JUL 1879 L	13	261
Holland, Margaret	Bell, Wallace	03 MAY 1879 L	13	172
Holland, Mary	Wells, William J.	02 OCT 1883 L	18	165
Holland, Mary C.	McCleary, Andrew H.	02 MAR 1883 R	17	330
Holland, Mary D.	Wren, Edward L.	22 FEB 1878	11	353
Holland, Mollie E.	Kraus, Charles A.	11 AUG 1884 L	19	179
Holland, Rachael A.	Clark, Alexander	01 NOV 1883 L	18	224
Holland, Richard	Dorsey, Georgeanna	20 NOV 1880 L	15	058
Holland, Richard Bowie	Drummond, Ada	02 FEB 1881 R	15	171
Holland, Richard H.	Heinline, Katie E.	07 DEC 1881 R	16	114
Holland, Robert	Wormley, Frances	05 MAR 1885 L	20	096
Hollander, Edward	Kaufman, Bertha	15 OCT 1885 R	20	482
Hollander, Justus	Kaufman, Treasa	01 FEB 1882 R	16	217
Hollander, Lena	Franc, Louis	24 SEP 1879 R	13	383
Holle, Anna Viola	Maguire, Francis A.	15 FEB 1882 R	16	244
Holler, Amelia	Melton, A.L.	28 DEC 1880 R	15	128
Hollida, David	Benton, Emma H.	25 DEC 1878 L	12	415
Holliday, Henniretta	Luckett, Frank	07 JUN 1882 L	16	399
Hollin, Delia	Manning, Bernard	09 DEC 1884 L	19	442
Hollinberger, Joseph T.	Fillins, Capitolia V.	18 MAY 1880	14	275
Holling, Charles	Jones, Mary	14 APR 1879	13	142
Hollinger, Arthur C.	Appler, Clara B.	02 OCT 1884	19	272
Hollinger, Daniel	Loskam, Barbara	16 AUG 1880 R	14	401
Hollinger, Lizzie	Fiske, Henry B.	16 JUN 1884	19	086
Hollingshead, John S.	Willson, Mary W.	07 JAN 1879 R	13	008
Hollins, Mary	Henderson, James Alfred	04 DEC 1879	14	024
Hollister, George H.	Sharpe, Caroline	20 OCT 1877 L	11	148

Hollman, Alfred	Taylor, Annie	08 AUG 1879 R	13	310
Hollohan, Mary	Siebert, J.M.	21 MAY 1878 L	12	062
Holloran, Mary	O'Brien, William	26 FEB 1878	11	357
Holly, Agnes	Bolden, Joseph	13 SEP 1880 R	14	443
Holly, Carrie	Brown, Charles H.	17 JUN 1885 L	20	278
Holly, Florence	Clarence, Henry	26 JUL 1883	18	060
Holly, George	Bailey, Mary	09 NOV 1882 L	17	120
Holly, Harriet	Hutchinson, William H.	27 OCT 1880 L	15	016
Holly, Mary	Williams, Richard	05 DEC 1882 R	17	168
Holly, Peter	Washington, Caroline	29 MAR 1883 R	17	350
Holly, William Henry	Dent, Mary Alice	07 MAY 1878 L	12	040
Holman, Edward H.	Bowen, Marion A.	04 SEP 1878 R	12	197
Holmead, Alfred	Gross, Mary Frances Parrish	20 JUN 1883 R	18	006
Holmes, Albert	Lewis, Mary	12 SEP 1878 L	12	214
Holmes, Alexander	Washington, Elizabeth	19 MAY 1883 L	17	451
Holmes, Alfred	Scott, Georgianna	14 JUN 1882 L	16	411
Holmes, Annie	Talburt, Isaac	14 MAR 1884 R	18	469
Holmes, Annie Elizabeth	Carter, Silas	19 JUL 1879 L	13	286
Holmes, Annie Laura	Nolan, John W.	09 DEC 1880 R	14	331
Holmes, Armstead	McCullum, Lizzie	08 APR 1884 L	18	500
Holmes, Benjamin T.	Southall, Louisa T.	20 DEC 1877 R	11	242
Holmes, Bettie H.	Bare, George E.	17 MAY 1883 R	17	449
Holmes, Carrie	Lee, William	16 APR 1885 L	20	173
Holmes, Carrie	Mable, Henry	22 OCT 1885	20	496
Holmes, Charles	Smart, Alice	08 JUL 1878 R	12	126
Holmes, Charles A.	Burke, Harriet J.	27 AUG 1880	14	417
Holmes, Charles E.	Jones, Sallie	14 JUN 1883 R	17	487
Holmes, Charles H.	Carter, Jane	17 OCT 1881	16	025
Holmes, Charlotte	Bentley, William	14 AUG 1877 R	11	053
Holmes, Clara	Diggs, Mathias	07 APR 1885 L	20	148
Holmes, Edward	Brown, Louisa	04 SEP 1879	13	353
Holmes, Edwin P.	Holmes, S. Lina	24 DEC 1880 R	18	332
Holmes, Elizabeth	Herdon, Learen	09 MAY 1885	20	206
Holmes, Fannie	Chisley, Samuel L.	10 DEC 1877 L	11	228
Holmes, George W.	Jones, Catherine C.	04 MAR 1879 L	13	089
Holmes, Henry A.	Washington, Elizabeth	18 MAR 1880 L	14	189
Holmes, Jacob W.	Adams, Susie Rachel	17 MAY 1883	17	450
Holmes, James	Green, Lottie	01 APR 1885	20	141
Holmes, James F.	Hough, Eliza	23 JUN 1883 R	18	011
Holmes, James H.	Gant, Mary	25 DEC 1883	18	296
Holmes, James O.	Wright, Sarah E.	09 MAY 1878 L	12	047
Holmes, Jane	Wracks, Allen	28 NOV 1878	12	336
Holmes, John	Johnson, Patsey	24 DEC 1877 L	11	266
Holmes, John	Finch, Lauron	06 NOV 1884 R	19	366
Holmes, Lavinia	Goines, George W.	04 JAN 1883	17	239
Holmes, Madalaine M.	Howard, Melville H.	21 DEC 1881	16	144
Holmes, Maggie	Smith, James	20 NOV 1877 L	11	195
Holmes, Maria	McKenney, Stephen	14 DEC 1882 R	17	182
Holmes, Maria	Perry, William	06 NOV 1884	19	368
Holmes, Marianna	Bell, Charles A.	07 MAR 1883 R	17	335
Holmes, Martha	Coleman, Addison	28 MAR 1878 R	11	396
Holmes, Mary	James, Robert	13 AUG 1878	12	165
Holmes, Mary	Lancster, John	17 NOV 1881 R	16	084
Holmes, Mary	Robinson, William	17 DEC 1884 L	19	464
Holmes, Mary A.	Wilson, Hamilton M.	08 DEC 1881 L	16	122
Holmes, Mary Elizabeth	Shorter, Charles Marshall	14 OCT 1880 R	14	487
Holmes, Mary Ellen	Duffy, Peter	11 FEB 1882 R	16	237
Holmes, Mary J.	Brown, Arthur	15 MAR 1883	17	342

Holmes, Mildred	Cosby, George W.	17 MAY 1880 L	14	273
Holmes, Milo	Ridgley, Florence	23 SEP 1884	19	264
Holmes, Nannie Maria	Hawkins, Eldridge	27 DEC 1881 R	16	150
Holmes, Nannie T.	Lafayette, Pierce	27 DEC 1877	11	273
Holmes, Peter	Tasker, Lucy, Mrs.	18 OCT 1877 R	11	139
Holmes, Peter L.	Frisbie, Josephine	06 MAR 1884 L	18	462
Holmes, Rhoda	Hall, Hannibal	28 APR 1881 R	15	282
Holmes, Robert A.	Herdnell, Charlotte	26 SEP 1878	12	231
Holmes, Rosa Lee	Kelsey, Philip P.	27 NOV 1884 R	19	413
Holmes, S. Lina	Holmes, Edwin P.	24 DEC 1883 R	18	332
Holmes, Selestia Frances	Dillon, Michael	09 NOV 1882 R	17	115
Holmes, Susan P.	Wiggins, George H.	03 MAR 1884 L	18	455
Holmes, Susie	Cain, Charles C.	15 DEC 1881 L	16	134
Holmes, Thomas	Oden, Maggie	04 FEB 1878 L	11	326
Holmes, Thomas	Brown, Ida	27 AUG 1878	12	182
Holmes, Thomas	Balsam, Fannie	17 JUN 1880 R	14	321
Holmes, Thomas	Ballot, Hattie	05 APR 1882 L	16	302
Holmes, Thomas J.	Collins, Rosa V.	10 APR 1883 R	17	389
Holmes, Virginia E.	Allen, Langston W.	19 OCT 1880 L	15	002
Holmes, Warren	Robinson, Eliza Fox	02 DEC 1880 R	15	075
Holmes, Washington	Williams, Mary	20 DEC 1882 L	17	198
Holmes, William	Booker, Annie	30 OCT 1879 R	13	453
Holmes, William	Nicholas, Mary	19 OCT 1880 R	14	486
Holmes, William	Hart, Martha E.	05 MAY 1884 L	19	006
Holmes, William Henry	Osgood, Kate Clifton	17 OCT 1883 R	18	196
Holmes, William J.	Marks, Eva H.	04 JUN 1884 L	19	059
Holohan, Charles E.	Culhane, Catherine A.	07 SEP 1885 L	20	401
Holroyd, Arthur E.	Shoemaker, Jennie	03 DEC 1881 L	16	111
Holroyd, Julia	Talbert, Harry	25 NOV 1884	19	409
Holroyd, Sarah E.	Brown, William F.	11 FEB 1885 R	20	064
Holschuh, Josephine C.	Webster, John Eddy	22 JUN 1881 R	15	372
Holson, Eliza A.	Welsh, William P.	22 MAY 1882	16	372
Holston, Dora	Provis, William	23 JUL 1878 L	12	145
Holt, George W., Jr.	Osborne, Bertha A.	10 NOV 1884 L	19	372
Holt, Ida Virginia	Williams, Richard Thos.	02 JUL 1879 R	13	264
Holt, Jesse	Copeland, Frances	23 NOV 1882 R	17	147
Holt, Laura V.	Danforth, Charles A.	10 JUN 1880 R	14	317
Holt, Lottie M.	Frizzell, Charles R.	02 JAN 1883 R	17	232
Holt, Martha A.	Williams, Andrew J.	29 NOV 1882 R	17	160
Holt, Moses	Bowie, Millie	08 OCT 1879 R	13	402
Holt, Thomas W.	Warren, Margaret Gray	22 APR 1885 R	20	185
Holton, Hoyt A.	Larman, Melvie M.	16 JAN 1883 R	17	257
Holtzclaw, C. Taylor	Taite, Mary E.	11 JUL 1877	11	016
Holtzclaw, Chas. Taylor	Taite, Emma J.	10 AUG 1881 L	15	439
Holtzclaw, Lucien Dade	Shumate, Bettie	14 AUG 1883	18	086
Holtzclaw, William B.	Hurdle, Gracie	29 NOV 1882	17	159
Holtzman, Annie M.	Quinn, John	16 MAY 1881 L	15	309
Holtzman, Catharine Celestine	Jones, Joseph J.	02 OCT 1879 R	13	398
Holtzman, Estelle P.	Adams, Byron S.	21 NOV 1882 L	17	140
Holtzman, Flora	Matney, Thomas H.	27 MAY 1880	14	293
Holtzman, Robert C.	Scior, Ella G.	20 NOV 1877 R	11	192
Holtzman, Sallie M.	Clark, T.D. Douglas	27 MAY 1884 L	19	040
Homer, Lizzie L.	Smith, John H.P.	07 JUN 1884	19	067
Homes, Catherine	Burnaught, George	17 SEP 1885 L	20	427
Homes, Frances	Smith, Charles	25 FEB 1879 L	13	078
Homes, Thomas	Wiles, Ida	16 JAN 1884 L	18	380
Homstead, Henry	Streets, Amelia	07 OCT 1884 L	19	290
Honest, Margaret	Lee, John T.	06 JAN 1881 R	15	141

Honester, Geo. Francis	Fletcher, Eleanor	04 APR 1878	11	400
Honesty, Annie	Crump, Henry	24 MAR 1881 R	15	237
Honesty, Asbury	Brice, Amanda	27 DEC 1877 L	11	275
Honesty, Carrie	Hughes, Charles	29 OCT 1884 L	19	345
Honesty, Henry W.	Fairfax, Lucy D.	05 SEP 1880	14	422
Honesty, Ida	Warren, John	02 OCT 1879 R	13	399
Honesty, James	McEntee, Laura E.	03 JUN 1878	12	082
Honesty, Martha	Simms, Alexander	27 JUL 1883	18	064
Honesty, Martha Celina	Smallwood, William H.	13 NOV 1884 L	19	379
Honesty, Mary Ann, Mrs.	Robinson, Isaac	16 DEC 1880 R	15	100
Honesty, Sarah	Coleman, James	02 OCT 1883 L	18	163
Honesty, William	Richardson, Julia	04 AUG 1881	15	433
Hood, Charles Dennis	Lunsford, Addie Edmonds	21 NOV 1883 R	18	268
Hood, Edwin M.	Ely, Sophie	04 OCT 1883	18	172
Hood, Florence	Tines, Simon S.	25 SEP 1883 L	18	153
Hood, William H.	Gordon, Florence R.	18 AUG 1883	18	093
Hooker, Mary D.	Kendall, John B.	31 JAN 1883	17	276
Hooper, Emily	Griggs, Able E.	17 MAY 1879 L	13	195
Hooper, George	Langhorn, Annie	20 OCT 1882 L	17	083
Hooper, Mary J.	Robertson, William E.	20 APR 1883	17	402
Hoover, Andrew B.F.	Williams, Ella F.	11 DEC 1882 L	17	178
Hoover, Annie C.	Shands, Elverton A.	19 FEB 1884 R	18	431
Hoover, Arthur H.	Walker, Fannie	28 SEP 1882	17	042
Hoover, Charles H.	Burger, Mary S.	04 NOV 1882 R	17	111
Hoover, Clara E.	Nace, Charles L.	16 AUG 1882 R	16	482
Hoover, Dickerson Naylor	Scheitlin, Annie M.	17 SEP 1879 R	13	374
Hoover, Edward C.	McCubbin, Mary Geneva	16 AUG 1881 R	15	448
Hoover, Hattie E.	Burklin, George	03 MAR 1881	15	213
Hoover, Sallie E.	Golden, Harry H.	16 SEP 1885 R	20	422
Hoover, William Bartlett	Buckey, Alice	21 FEB 1884	18	435
Hope, Agnes	Collins, William M.	04 NOV 1884	19	359
Hope, Lady Blanche	Nuckols, Clarence Pend.	06 JAN 1885 R	20	005
Hope, William F	Scoggin, Blanche V.	14 SEP 1885	20	413
Hopkins, Archibald	Wise, Charlotte Everett	14 NOV 1878 R	12	322
Hopkins, Bertha	Hammond, Thomas Victor	03 JUN 1884 R	19	050
Hopkins, Bridget	Connel, John	21 NOV 1877 L	11	195
Hopkins, Charles	Johnson, Lulie	15 APR 1881 L	15	258
Hopkins, Edward E.	Pullen, Janie T.	31 JAN 1883	17	281
Hopkins, Emma E.	Harrison, George W.	11 MAR 1884 L	18	465
Hopkins, Eugene A.	Beasley, Annie E.	09 JAN 1878	11	298
Hopkins, Florence J.	Bacon, Harry R.	19 JAN 1882 R	16	200
Hopkins, Frank Ellsworth	Dodge, Eliza	07 APR 1885 R	20	213
Hopkins, Frank H.	Degges, Nellie B.	06 JUN 1883 L	17	480
Hopkins, Frederick W.	Lenoir, Ida V.	07 FEB 1881 R	15	179
Hopkins, Henry	Lindsey, Maggie E.	05 JUL 1881 L	15	390
Hopkins, Ira W.	Riggles, Anna M.	07 JUL 1885 R	20	315
Hopkins, James	Lee, Amelia	25 AUG 1885 L	20	387
Hopkins, Mary Van Ness	Fauth, Frank	24 APR 1884 R	18	525
Hopkins, Ressia	Jackson, Peter N.	13 AUG 1878 R	12	165
Hopkins, Sallie P.	Woodward, Matthew	17 OCT 1883 R	18	180
Hopkins, Sarah E.	Maltby, Sidney	30 AUG 1877 R	11	072
Hopkins, Utah E.	Smith, Jesse T.	02 APR 1885 R	20	141
Hopkins, Wesley	Pinggold, Hester	29 NOV 1883	18	286
Hoppkins, Moses	Smith, Annie	12 NOV 1883 R	18	248
Hopson, Carrie	Burk, James E.	21 SEP 1885 R	20	431
Hopson, Lucien	Keep, Mary E.	27 AUG 1885 R	20	390
Hopson, Violetta S.	Davis, Milton	03 SEP 1884	19	224
Horan, Joseph H.	Phillips, Lucy E.	27 MAY 1884 L	19	041

Horgan, Edmond	Cunningham, Mary E.	27 OCT 1879 R	13	443
Horgan, Kate C.	Weber, John F.	16 JUL 1885 L	20	330
Horidan, Patrick	Mahoney, Mary V.	30 JUN 1884 L	19	110
Horigan, Dennis	Gannon, Catherine	02 DEC 1882	17	163
Horigan, Michael	Dillon, Mary E.	28 OCT 1880 R	15	019
Horman, Augustus	Haller, Vialetta	02 AUG 1883 R	18	065
Hornbach, Mary A.	Berner, Charles J.V.	20 JUN 1880	14	324
Hornbach, William T.	Viedt, Amelia D.	28 OCT 1883	18	213
Hornblower, Helen	Stevenson, Eugene	11 JUN 1884 R	19	070
Horner, Coleman	Grayson, Eliza	13 MAY 1880 R	14	262
Horner, Emma C.	Leprew, Louis	16 DEC 1879 R	16	3836
Horner, Firmin	Bailey, Mary	13 MAY 1884	19	016
Horner, Jessy	Colby, Franklin Green	19 JUL 1882 R	16	445
Horner, Maggie A.	French, George	07 FEB 1879	13	050
Hornig, Rosa	West, Christopher	11 MAY 1880 L	14	263
Hornischer, Sophia	Friedmann, Fredrick	30 OCT 1880	15	013
Hornisher, Theresia	Giesler, Daniel	19 OCT 1878	12	282
Hornity, Ellen	O'Brien, Joseph	08 SEP 1885 L	20	404
Hornor, Alice Lee	Snelling, Walter Comonfort	20 OCT 1879 R	13	432
Horrigan, Dennis	Maloney, Hanora Ellen	23 FEB 1879 R	13	072
Horrigan, Mary	Canty, Patrick	30 DEC 1882 L	17	226
Horseman, Nettie	Simpson, William G.	30 SEP 1882 R	17	044
Horsey, Martin	Darley, Elizabeth Fenton	15 SEP 1884	19	246
Horsman, Martha A.	Kendrick, William L.H.	07 AUG 1884 L	19	173
Horton, Lewis	Semple, Lucinda	08 JUL 1884	19	129
Horton, Margaret Elizabeth	Powell, Samuel	15 JUN 1885	20	273
Hoshall, Lizzie B.	Bull, Laban L.	16 FEB 1881 R	15	191
Hoskinson, George P.	Gibbons, Ella P.	17 JAN 1883 R	17	262
Hoskinson, Martha E.	Cole, Charles	30 DEC 1882 L	17	227
Hosman, Ida May	Stokes, William Brown	03 JAN 1883 R	17	233
Hosman, Victoria	Lawrence, Thomas Henry	05 MAR 1882 R	16	268
Hosmer, Jessie	Ridenour, Charles Howard	16 AUG 1882 R	16	481
Hotman, Mary	Hall, Asbury R.	04 DEC 1879 R	14	030
Houck, Albert P.	Davis, Sallie C. Blades	03 SEP 1879 R	14	3460
Hough, Caldwell C.	Stiner, Ella A.	15 APR 1884	18	519
Hough, Eliza	Holmes, James F.	23 JUN 1883 R	18	011
Hough, Hector T.C.	Shumaker, Jane E.	24 MAR 1880 R	14	198
Hough, Perry V.	Daw, Mary Emma	22 SEP 1880 L	14	457
Hough, Samuel J.	Slacum, Novella	01 MAY 1883 R	17	424
Hough, Sarah J.	Barclay, Edgar L.	12 SEP 1878 R	12	216
Houghton, Arthur J.	Shattuck, Minnie A.	06 OCT 1880 R	14	471
Houghton, Hattie M.	Roach, William H.	01 SEP 1880 R	14	426
Houghton, Wilson H.	Keys, Clara M.	05 SEP 1877	11	074
Houk, Julia	Kasten, William	02 FEB 1879 R	13	041
House, Henry J.	Barriere, Mary F.	21 JAN 1885	20	030
House, Ida G.	Bigelow, George S.	10 MAY 1881	15	297
House, Jennie	Prosperi, Fredrick	11 JUN 1878 R	12	102
House, Joseph S.	Mayne, Laura C.	01 NOV 1880 L	15	024
House, Mollie L.	Duddenhausen, August	04 NOV 1880 R	15	030
House, Thomas L.	Rawlings, Jennie E.	15 NOV 1881 R	16	077
Houseman, Maggie L.	Magruder, Zebedee B.	30 NOV 1882 R	17	162
Houst, William	Parker, Eliza Ann	10 JAN 1878 R	11	298
Houst, William R.	Mack, Mary E.	03 NOV 1880	15	026
Houston, Ella G.	Williams, William E.	05 SEP 1882 R	17	003
Houston, Fanny S.	Williams, J. Hale	28 SEP 1878 R	12	247
Howaldt, George J.	Zeigler, Carrie	14 JUN 1884	19	083
Howard, Alexander E.	McKenney, Martha E.	16 OCT 1878	12	276
Howard, Alice R.	Schaper, John	19 JUN 1883	18	003

Howard, Annie Louise	Calvert, Richard	07 JUN 1883 R	17	482
Howard, Beverly W.	Moran, Josephine	18 DEC 1884 L	19	468
Howard, Charles H.	Olden, Elizabeth	10 SEP 1878	12	207
Howard, Charles H.	Hicks, Georgiana	21 APR 1881 L	15	269
Howard, Eli C.	Whiting, Amanda	25 APR 1878	12	023
Howard, Emily	Standard, William	05 MAR 1878 L	11	372
Howard, Emily J.	Tillet, William	21 JAN 1880 R	14	115
Howard, Emma	Lee, William	18 DEC 1879 L	14	058
Howard, Emma	Jones, Philip	18 SEP 1883 L	18	139
Howard, Francis	Kaelin, Mary A.L.	05 DEC 1880	15	081
Howard, Frank	White, Sarah	17 JAN 1878	11	309
Howard, Frank	Dorsey, Martha	06 JUL 1885 L	20	311
Howard, Fred. Fritz-Henry	Goss, Frances Eva	15 JUL 1880	14	363
Howard, George	Lindsey, Mary Eliza	08 JAN 1880 R	14	093
Howard, George B.	Pletsch, Rosa	17 DEC 1883 L	18	319
Howard, George Francis	Woody, Ellen Addie	20 APR 1885 R	20	175
Howard, George L.	Nappel, Annie	13 MAR 1882 L	16	275
Howard, George W.	Warden, Rachel V.	03 JUN 1879 R	13	216
Howard, Harriet (Gandy)	Merrick, Caleb Cornwell	29 JUN 1883 R	18	014
Howard, Henrietta	Wells, Thomas	28 AUG 1879 L	13	341
Howard, Henry	Dodson, Ann Maria	21 JUL 1885 L	20	333
Howard, Isaac	Herd, Elizabeth	14 MAY 1885 L	20	220
Howard, James	McBride, Maggie	13 MAR 1883 L	17	341
Howard, James Albert	France, Rebecca	10 APR 1881 R	15	252
Howard, James H.	Doram, Ella	29 MAR 1883 R	17	367
Howard, James Henry	Balenger, Lucy Ann	22 DEC 1880 R	15	116
Howard, James M.	Yaste, H. Jane A.	12 AUG 1884	19	180
Howard, John	Thomas, Charlotte S.	02 DEC 1881 L	16	111
Howard, John H.	Littles, Jennie	24 NOV 1884 L	19	404
Howard, Joseph W.	Gartrell, Annie J.	04 NOV 1879 R	13	461
Howard, Katie D.	Boyd, Charles W.F.	28 OCT 1879 R	13	448
Howard, Katie H.	Shipe, William R.	09 APR 1885 L	20	156
Howard, Mack	Whiby, Mary	02 OCT 1885 R	20	450
Howard, Martha C.	Plowden, James H.	13 MAR 1882 L	16	275
Howard, Mary A.	Smith, Charles Carrington	21 AUG 1878 R	12	175
Howard, Mary S.	Green, John	10 MAR 1881 L	15	223
Howard, Melville H.	Holmes, Madalaine M.	21 DEC 1881	16	144
Howard, Oscar D.	Taylor, Lucy J.	20 NOV 1879	13	498
Howard, Reuben	Gray, Charlotte	16 JUN 1885 L	20	276
Howard, Robert F.	Bailey, Etway	01 AUG 1880	14	382
Howard, Robert S.	Selby, Ida Amelia	15 NOV 1880 R	15	048
Howard, Rosa E.	Mead, Elgar J.	01 JUN 1878	12	078
Howard, Sarah	Brawner, Andrew	25 DEC 1877 L	11	268
Howard, Sarah	Coleman, Henry	12 OCT 1885	20	474
Howard, Sidney	Seevers, Ella	23 DEC 1879 R	14	065
Howard, Susan	Crump, John	13 NOV 1878	12	329
Howard, Thomas Allen	Hunt, Fannie Calderson	01 NOV 1882 R	17	103
Howard, William	Williams, Sarah E.	18 APR 1881 L	15	260
Howard, William	Monroe, Mary E.	17 NOV 1881	16	080
Howard, William	Morris, Jennie	30 AUG 1883 R	18	104
Howard, William C.	Young, Lottie	20 FEB 1878 L	11	350
Howard, William H.	Graff, Caroline M.	16 JUL 1884	19	140
Howard, William J.	Schlerogt, Lizzie	18 JAN 1883 R	17	266
Howard, William Robert	Knight, Anna Ruth	26 MAR 1883 R	17	361
Howarth, John Thomas	Payne, Nannie E.	20 JUN 1883 R	17	498
Howarth, Lillie P.	Owens, James F.	16 JAN 1879 R	13	021
Howarth, Mary Ellen	Green, Edward E.	03 JUL 1879 R	13	266
Howe, Catherine C.	Stockett, Charles A.	06 FEB 1879 R	13	048

D.C. Marriage Records Index, June 28, 1877 to October 19, 1885

Name	Spouse	Date	Vol	Page
Howe, Edward	Findley, Elizabeth	24 OCT 1881 L	16	040
Howe, Ellen	Bagby, Walker	08 FEB 1878	11	332
Howe, Frank H.	Ray, Ella	18 JUN 1879 R	13	235
Howe, James E.	Herbert, Mary E.	15 SEP 1885 L	20	419
Howe, John D.	Scott, Josephine	29 SEP 1884	19	271
Howe, Josephine L.	Waltemeyer, John S.	25 NOV 1878 R	12	345
Howell, Carrie	Fisher, George	03 APR 1882 R	16	296
Howell, Grace	Nolen, William Geo.	12 SEP 1883 R	18	128
Howell, Harriett, Mrs.	Hummel, Charles	23 SEP 1880 R	14	457
Howell, Hercules J.	Grose, Annie	30 AUG 1883	18	105
Howell, James Notley	Muir, Mabel Olive	01 SEP 1880 R	14	424
Howell, L.R.	Trailer, Mary E.	01 MAR 1884 L	18	452
Howell, Matilda	Green, Solomon	23 MAY 1878	12	065
Howell, Rezin G.	Ayres, Emily D.	05 FEB 1884 L	18	410
Howell, Samuel B.	Ashby, Mollie C.	24 APR 1879 R	13	159
Howell, Sanders	James, Harriet	19 JUL 1877	11	023
Howes, Edward Everett	Hall, Caroline Choate	04 DEC 1879 R	14	029
Howes, Mary C.	Henning, James G.	08 OCT 1878 R	12	261
Howes, Nicholas M.	Walker, Bettie M.	24 NOV 1881 R	16	098
Howison, Ada F.	Coffey, Thomas J.	30 JAN 1880 L	14	128
Howison, Ella I.	Steinmeyer, William E.	27 DEC 1881	16	158
Howland, Edwin P.	Mason, Virginia Fairfax	15 OCT 1877 R	11	135
Howlett, Ella	Jones, William J.	31 JAN 1883	17	280
Howlett, Mary E.	Baker, Joseph S.A.	31 OCT 1882	17	103
Howlin, Patrick Henry	Nelson, Margaret A.	02 FEB 1880 R	14	130
Howser, Ida	Shipman, Frank	26 JUN 1883 R	18	017
Hoxie, Richard Leveridge, Lt.	Ream, Vinnie	28 MAY 1878	12	067
Hoy, Catherine	Becker, Lewis	15 AUG 1881 R	15	444
Hoye, Robert	Atkins, Elizabeth	19 OCT 1877	11	144
Hoyle, Henry J.	Jenkins, Annie	22 OCT 1878 R	12	286
Hoyt, Frederick A.	Murphey, Florence S.	03 APR 1883 L	17	377
Hubbard, Gertrude McCurdy	Grossman, Maurice Neville	17 JAN 1880	14	102
Hubbard, Valeria E.	Swearingen, Henry Hartmell	15 DEC 1880 R	19	4700
Hubner, Maggie C.	Callan, James C.	20 SEP 1882 R	17	031
Huckstep, W.W.	Stephens, Linda W.	13 DEC 1884	19	458
Hudders, Isabella L.	Darling, Charles A.	08 OCT 1884	19	293
Huddleson, Willie Everett	Walther, Rosalia	01 DEC 1881 R	16	108
Huddleston, Cordelia U.	Leyhan, John	12 DEC 1882 L	17	179
Hudlow, James	Mills, Mary	02 FEB 1878	11	324
Hudlow, Samuel	Sullivan, Abby	23 JUL 1878	12	146
Hudnall, Cora	Delly, W.C.	27 DEC 1877	11	277
Hudnall, James	Charlton, Sarah	30 APR 1878	12	029
Hudnall, Roberta	Carter, Marshall[5]	24 AUG 1881 R	15	457
Hudson, Alpheus W.	Eury, Emma O.	06 JUN 1878	12	090
Hudson, Edmund	Clemmer, Mary	18 JUN 1883 L	17	499
Hudson, Edward J.	Gunzer, Rosa	13 SEP 1882 R	17	019
Hudson, Esther	Thomas, William	21 JUL 1879 L	13	287
Hudson, George	Pistorio, Eliza C.	28 OCT 1879 R	13	445
Hudson, George J.	Curtin, Jennette S.	09 APR 1882 R	16	305
Hudson, James N.	Burrows, Ella F.	03 JUL 1877 R	11	004
Hudson, Jamie E.	Stoddard, John G.	04 APR 1881 L	15	246
Hudson, Lizzie E.	Barker, Harrison S.	12 DEC 1883	18	312
Hudson, M.E.	Morton, A.H.	16 OCT 1879	13	429

[5] Western Union Telegraph attached to record, spelling preserved: "Warrenton, Va., Aug. 23, 1881. Roberta Chalahan and Marshall Carter leave for Washington tomorrow for marriage certificate. She has a husband, don't issue without Evidence to contrary from this county." [signed] A. Carter. "Cyrus H. Newhouse of Fauquier, Va., came with Marshall Carter to ask for the license, & explained that the marriage with Calahan was void because Callahan is a white man & Hudnall is Colored."

Name	Spouse	Date			
Hudson, Nettie Bell	Ross, James	28 MAR 1883	L	17	366
Hudson, Richard	Evans, Ida E., Mrs.	17 NOV 1883	L	18	262
Hudson, William H.	Raybold, Lizzie T.	18 JUN 1884		19	090
Huebner, Richard	Terry, Ames	06 NOV 1883	L	18	235
Hueke, Hugh L.	Angraman, Amelia F.	15 DEC 1880	L	15	099
Hueter, Charles	Henning, Betty	12 OCT 1878	L	12	269
Hueter, Susie C.	Reinhardt, Henry C.	20 SEP 1883	L	18	145
Huff, John	Monahan, Julia	04 DEC 1882		17	153
Huff, Moses	Elsie, Martha Ann	18 NOV 1882	R	17	135
Huff, Randolph	Parker, Kate	04 NOV 1880	L	15	031
Huff, William	Campbell, Jennie	12 MAY 1881		15	302
Hughes, Alice	Hill, Nicholas	11 MAY 1885	L	20	216
Hughes, Benjamin F.	Thompson, Rebecca	25 JUL 1885	L	20	340
Hughes, Bernard Richard	Sanders, Eunice Wentworth	31 DEC 1884	R	19	509
Hughes, Carrie Melissa	Stephens, Lewis Charles	16 JAN 1879	R	13	020
Hughes, Charles	Honesty, Carrie	29 OCT 1884	L	19	345
Hughes, Clara W.	Rowzee, William S.	04 MAY 1878		11	406
Hughes, Cora	DuFour, Clarence R.	19 FEB 1884	R	18	429
Hughes, David J.	Conwell, Florence	27 APR 1884	R	18	535
Hughes, Edward A.	Armstrong, Elvie J.	06 SEP 1882	L	17	008
Hughes, Eli H.	Johnson, Florence A.	11 OCT 1882	L	17	065
Hughes, Eliza	Cologno, Michael	06 SEP 1882	L	17	008
Hughes, Eliza Frances	Febrey, William N.	21 MAR 1882		16	285
Hughes, Ella	Johnson, Bailey	06 DEC 1882	L	17	170
Hughes, Francis P.	Donnelly, Jennie Agnes	04 OCT 1877		11	122
Hughes, George	Hughes, Sarah	04 FEB 1884		18	438
Hughes, Georgia Johanna	Grigsby, James	27 AUG 1883	L	18	099
Hughes, Jennie E.	Torreyson, William	21 JUN 1882	L	16	421
Hughes, John	Nelligan, Mary	19 SEP 1878	L	12	228
Hughes, John F.	Corbitt, Amanda M.	06 MAY 1878	L	12	039
Hughes, Joseph	Marneaux, Marguerite	28 APR 1880	R	14	239
Hughes, Laura	Chambers, Dabney M.	07 OCT 1884	L	19	289
Hughes, Lilly	Jones, James	08 JAN 1885	R	20	009
Hughes, Lottie	Johnson, Thomas	28 MAR 1883	L	17	366
Hughes, Louisa	Davenport, Edward	04 OCT 1882		17	051
Hughes, Louisa T.	Peach, Thomas F.	11 JUL 1877		11	015
Hughes, Maggie	O'Brien, James	06 APR 1883	L	17	383
Hughes, Margaret M.	Harrover, James R.	09 JAN 1883	L	17	245
Hughes, Marian	Scaggs, Edward O.	05 NOV 1877	L	11	169
Hughes, Martha	Waters, William	06 JUL 1881		15	391
Hughes, Mary A.	Handy, William B.	24 MAR 1880	R	14	196
Hughes, Mary A.	Owens, James C.	08 DEC 1883	L	18	306
Hughes, Mary E.	Doyle, John T.	21 FEB 1882	L	16	252
Hughes, Mattie B.	Anderson, William H.	09 FEB 1885	R	20	058
Hughes, Rebecca W.	Colbert, William M.	26 SEP 1878	L	12	238
Hughes, Sarah	Hughes, George	04 FEB 1884		18	438
Hughes, Sarah Ann	Palmer, James Hervey	27 DEC 1877	R	11	276
Hughes, Thomas	Brennon, Kate, Mrs.	03 FEB 1878	R	11	325
Hughes, Wormley H.	Burbridge, Georgia	20 FEB 1885	L	20	079
Hughey, Mary	Miller, John	07 MAR 1878		11	366
Hughlett, Julius	Stevens, Agnes V.	29 MAR 1885		20	136
Hughlett, Julius	Stevens, Agnes Vadieux	01 JUL 1885	R	20	303
Hughlett, Lula Lee	Hickcox, John Howard, Jr.	11 APR 1882	R	16	304
Hughs, Lewis	Wallace, Becky	23 JUN 1881		15	372
Hughs, William R.	Gross, Julia C.	31 MAY 1884	L	19	047
Hugo, Louis C.F.	Young, Lizzie	09 MAR 1880	R	14	180
Huguley, James F.	King, Katie A.	29 OCT 1878		12	297
Huhn, H. Elizabeth	Henley, H. Thomas	03 DEC 1878	L	12	359

D.C. Marriage Records Index, June 28, 1877 to October 19, 1885   225

Name	Spouse	Date	Vol	Page
Huhn, Henry	Ruppel, Josephine	14 NOV 1878 L	12	329
Huhn, William	McAuliff, Nellie	17 NOV 1884 L	19	387
Huitt, Churchwell H.	Johnson, Hattie	30 APR 1884	18	544
Hulahan, Emma	Creamer, James	31 OCT 1879 R	13	456
Hulcher, Mary	Gude, Edward B.	15 AUG 1881 R	15	444
Hulien, Charles H.	Lerch, Minnie E.	20 NOV 1881 R	16	085
Hulien, Ella	Neidomanski, Fred J.	29 JUL 1878	12	149
Hull, Bessie M.	Linden, James F.	31 DEC 1884 R	19	517
Hull, Ella C.	Cook, Frank H.	24 JUL 1884	19	157
Hull, Evaline W.	Pierce, Joseph H.	09 SEP 1884 L	19	235
Hull, Florence May	Brown, Thomas Jefferson	31 OCT 1877 R	11	159
Hull, James M.	Bradburn, Enola V.	19 MAY 1885	20	228
Hull, John D., Rev.	Fraser, Annie P.	27 NOV 1879 R	14	016
Hullfish, Henry Augustus	Skerrett, Annie Louise	18 APR 1883 R	17	398
Hullings, Mary E.	Hunter, John C.	20 AUG 1884	19	195
Hulse, Austin B.	Ash, Emma E.	03 APR 1879 R	13	127
Hulse, Florence C.	Moore, Douglass	18 JAN 1881 R	15	155
Hume, Henry	Henderson, Lucy	07 JAN 1885 L	20	007
Hume, Jennie	Knott, John Francis	01 SEP 1881 R	15	469
Hume, Mamie	Bell, Robert Alexander	06 MAR 1884 R	18	461
Hume, Sue Ellen	Johnson, John Clinton	14 OCT 1885 R	20	477
Humes, Ida	Smith, Arthur G.	01 MAY 1878 L	12	033
Hummel, Charles	Howell, Harriett, Mrs.	23 SEP 1880 R	14	457
Hummer, John W.	Keene, Mary Elizabeth	10 JAN 1878 R	11	293
Humphrey, Fred H.	Parker, Louise Alfretta	15 JAN 1880 R	14	105
Humphrey, Henry	Harris, Harriet	27 NOV 1879	14	018
Humphrey, John	Owens, Rebecca	27 AUG 1885	20	388
Humphrey, Lillian E.	Wright, Abner O.	05 DEC 1883	18	296
Humphreys, Albert	Coats, Sarah	28 AUG 1880 R	14	420
Humphreys, Annie E.	Nichols, Edmond S.	20 AUG 1885 L	20	380
Humphreys, Arcelia	Ward, Samuel	16 JAN 1878	11	308
Humphreys, George	Scott, Charity	26 OCT 1880 L	15	014
Humphreys, George	Gant, Mary E.	31 JUL 1884 L	19	164
Humphreys, George W.	Long, Bettie A.	06 AUG 1885 L	20	358
Humphreys, Kate	May, David	06 DEC 1884 R	19	437
Humphreys, Lee	Smith, Harriet A.	28 JUN 1883 R	18	023
Humphreys, Martha	Johnson, Henry	01 NOV 1880 R	15	023
Humphreys, Martha	Franklin, John	16 JUL 1885 L	20	329
Humphreys, Mary	Murray, John	20 MAR 1882	16	281
Humphreys, Robert B.	Hawkins, Joanna	23 JUN 1881	15	364
Humphreys, William W.	Groves, Margaret A.	05 JUL 1877 L	11	011
Humphries, Kate F.	Simpson, Philip H., Jr.	03 MAY 1882 L	16	346
Humphries, Lucy A.	Thompson, James H.	06 JAN 1885 R	20	005
Humphries, William D.	Davis, Susie V.	07 MAR 1883 R	17	336
Humrickhouse, Charles Breslin	DeSaules, Emily E.	22 NOV 1881 R	16	089
Hunaker, Harry	James, Lula	28 SEP 1882 L	17	041
Hunaker, Mary E.	Parker, Charles W.	30 SEP 1882 L	17	044
Hundley, James J.	Garey, Mary Jane	04 NOV 1879 R	13	462
Hunecke, Henry	Eberlyer, Wilhelmina	18 JAN 1884 R	18	385
Huneke, Minnie R.C.	Weide, George E.	28 MAY 1881 L	15	330
Hungerford, Mary Ann	Anderson, Richard H.T.	25 JUN 1885	20	292
Hungerford, Rosa	Cook, Lewis	31 DEC 1879 L	14	084
Hungerford, Winnie	Green, Edward	20 MAR 1879 L	13	110
Hunnaker, Katie	Tenley, William A.	07 MAY 1881 R	15	218
Hunnell, William S.	Campbell, Kate A.	28 MAY 1884 L	19	043
Hunneman, Ellen	Jackson, James	21 JUL 1877 L	11	029
Hunster, Thomas Watkins	Lewis, Susan Alice	06 OCT 1880 R	14	475
Hunt, Ardella Vannette	Combs, Ignatius George	10 AUG 1880 R	14	390

Name	Spouse	Date		
Hunt, E. Blanche	Wise, James D.	14 FEB 1883	17	305
Hunt, Electa	Keech, John Reeder	31 MAY 1883	17	470
Hunt, Ellen Ann	Scott, John Wesley	08 OCT 1885 R	20	469
Hunt, Fannie	Chinn, Charles E.	18 SEP 1877 L	11	099
Hunt, Fannie Calderson	Howard, Thomas Allen	01 NOV 1882 R	17	103
Hunt, George Washington	Graves, Amelia	18 SEP 1881 R	15	489
Hunt, Georgia Anna	Murphy, Wm. Augustus	08 APR 1885 R	20	149
Hunt, Henry Jackson	Drum, Henrietta Margaret	25 JUN 1883 L	18	012
Hunt, J.R.	Wanser, E.	19 DEC 1881 L	16	139
Hunt, James	McMann, Ellen	02 MAR 1882 L	16	264
Hunt, James A.	Hildebrand, Eliza J.	25 OCT 1880 R	15	012
Hunt, James Elias	Ward, Rosa	14 AUG 1879 R	13	319
Hunt, John	McDowell, Hattie M.	06 JUN 1882 R	16	396
Hunt, John C.	Henkel, Catherine	13 MAY 1879 R	13	162
Hunt, John S.	Lynn, Florian M.	06 AUG 1881 L	15	434
Hunt, Mattie V.	Germann, Daniel M.	28 MAY 1878	12	072
Hunt, Moses	Fautroy, Eliza	13 JUN 1878 L	12	099
Hunt, Taresa	Roony, Morris	05 FEB 1884 L	18	411
Hunt, William	Herman, Bridget	15 SEP 1880 R	14	434
Hunt, William	Tate, Ella	04 AUG 1885 L	20	352
Hunt, William Franklin	Knight, Marie Lillian	07 NOV 1878 R	12	314
Hunter, Annie	Thornton, Reuben	03 APR 1880 L	14	207
Hunter, Edward B.	Williams, Alice A.	31 MAY 1883 L	17	471
Hunter, George R.E.	Heise, Carrie L.	20 JUN 1878	12	108
Hunter, George W.	Sinclair, Lucy	21 MAY 1884 L	19	030
Hunter, Harriet	Wilson, Elias	26 NOV 1884 R	19	421
Hunter, Hattie J.	Smith, James H.	24 SEP 1883 R	18	150
Hunter, Hester	Page, John	02 OCT 1879 R	13	396
Hunter, Horace	Scott, Mary T.	19 FEB 1885 R	20	078
Hunter, Irene	Stansbury, Charles F.	30 APR 1879 L	13	166
Hunter, James T.	Handley, Josephine A.	03 JUN 1878	12	080
Hunter, Jane	Branch, Edward C.	27 SEP 1877 R	11	111
Hunter, John	Wiley, Lucy	23 MAR 1880 L	14	193
Hunter, John C.	Hullings, Mary E.	20 AUG 1884	19	195
Hunter, Joseph H.	Foote, Eliza B.	30 DEC 1884 R	19	496
Hunter, Louisa	Jones, Everet	02 APR 1879 L	13	124
Hunter, Lydia McElfresh	Stansell, Dwight Daniel	25 JUN 1878 R	12	111
Hunter, Mabel M.	Peake, James A.	12 APR 1883 L	17	392
Hunter, Maria	Brennan, John	07 APR 1885 R	20	147
Hunter, Marion V.	Thomas, John W.	02 JAN 1883 R	17	231
Hunter, Mary C.	Stuart, Benjamin S.	22 OCT 1877 R	11	149
Hunter, Minnie	Brown, Walter S.	05 OCT 1880	14	473
Hunter, Mollie R.	Seitz, Clinton A.	05 NOV 1884 L	19	362
Hunter, Rebecca K.	Offutt, Dorsey W.	23 FEB 1881 L	15	199
Hunter, Robert	Vine, Alice	06 JUN 1885	20	257
Hunter, Rose A.	Miller, Thomas H.	13 AUG 1879 L	13	320
Hunter, Selina	Sappington, Turner	03 NOV 1881 R	16	048
Hunter, Viola B.	Seay, Richard B.	18 SEP 1882 R	17	008
Hunter, William	Adams, Emma	07 OCT 1878	12	258
Hunter, William F.	Ford, Julia E.	20 APR 1883	17	402
Hunter, William H.	Caldwell, Katie	23 APR 1881	16	023
Hunter, William Henry	Sanford, Mary Elizabeth	17 DEC 1877 R	11	241
Hunter, Winnie Yardley	Roan, Patrick	18 JUN 1884 R	19	089
Hunter, Zaidee Price	Ball, Thomas Latham	15 NOV 1881 R	16	078
Huntington, Craven	Tyler, Patsie	22 FEB 1882 R	16	256
Huntington, Lillie R.	Gregory, Frederick	06 MAR 1878 R	11	374
Huntington, Peter	Lyles, Ellenora	01 SEP 1881	15	468
Hunton, H.C.	Ball, Sallie	01 OCT 1880 L	14	468

D.C. Marriage Records Index, June 28, 1877 to October 19, 1885

Huntress, William F.	Whitehouse, Lottie M.	07 MAY 1885	20	179
Huntt, Lizzie	Harvey, James M.	28 JAN 1881 L	15	169
Hunziker, Adolph	King, Sarah	31 JUL 1884	19	163
Hurbert, Mary Annie	Cumberland, John Hews	24 MAY 1880 R	14	283
Hurbert, Thomas William	Snowdon, Mary Ellen	26 JUL 1883 L	18	063
Hurd, Alexander	Allman, Mary A.	03 JUL 1884 L	19	118
Hurd, Lizzie	Jordan, James	29 JAN 1884 L	18	401
Hurd, Margaret	Palmer, Henry	10 SEP 1885 L	20	411
Hurd, Molly A.	Gordon, William T.	19 AUG 1885 L	20	376
Hurdel, Ella C.	Plunkett, Frank	16 NOV 1878 L	12	332
Hurdell, Samuel	Donahue, Ellen	07 SEP 1878 L	12	204
Hurdle, Barbara A.	Hayes, Benjamin T.	27 DEC 1881	16	157
Hurdle, Bettie C.	Omohundro, William R.	13 DEC 1881 R	16	128
Hurdle, Charles H.[6]	Miller, Annie M.	11 MAY 1880 L	14	263
Hurdle, Emily Jane	Gray, Charles	22 NOV 1881 L	16	090
Hurdle, George W.	Barnes, Ada Virginia	27 FEB 1879	13	084
Hurdle, Gracie	Holtzclaw, William B.	29 NOV 1882	17	159
Hurdle, Harriet A., Mrs.	Harrison, Daniel C.	28 APR 1880 R	14	243
Hurdle, Hester	Miller, Francis, Jr.	18 MAR 1882 L	16	282
Hurdle, Irene C.	King, William F.	17 APR 1879	13	148
Hurdle, James Richard	Simpson, Mary Elizabeth	25 AUG 1884 L	19	206
Hurdle, Joseph	Taylor, Mary E.	11 NOV 1879 R	13	475
Hurdle, Lavinia	Hurley, Charles W.	22 OCT 1878 R	12	286
Hurdle, Lulu May	Wilson, George W.	21 AUG 1884	19	202
Hurdle, Nettie L.	Corrick, Edwin M.	24 JAN 1883 R	17	271
Hurdle, Pinky	Sherwood, Morgan A.	13 DEC 1877 R	11	236
Hurdle, Thomas T.	Payne, Mary C.	22 JAN 1885 L	20	034
Hurley, Addie	Krause, John	12 FEB 1884 R	18	422
Hurley, Catherine	Mahorney, Michael	26 JUN 1880 L	14	335
Hurley, Charles W.	Hurdle, Lavinia	22 OCT 1878 R	12	286
Hurley, Ellen	Farrell, John	29 NOV 1883 L	18	286
Hurley, Emma J.	Clements, William C.	01 FEB 1881	15	172
Hurley, Henry	Creek, Eliza Sophia	24 MAR 1885 L	20	128
Hurley, Ida A.	Bowling, Thomas W.	08 MAY 1879	13	179
Hurley, Isabella	Shorter, Charles Henry	11 MAR 1879 L	13	096
Hurley, James Dennis	Toner, Rosannah	07 JUL 1880 L	14	350
Hurley, James E.	Adams, Lizzie A.	13 FEB 1878 R	11	323
Hurley, John F.	Browning, Sarah S.	17 OCT 1885	20	493
Hurley, John W.	Major, Levia W.	27 DEC 1877 L	11	277
Hurley, Josephine	Keithly, William A.	05 SEP 1883 R	18	112
Hurley, Kate	Farr, Wm. Thomas	20 MAY 1880 R	14	281
Hurley, Mamie F.	Lacey, William L.	02 MAY 1883 R	17	427
Hurley, Mary	Burk, Michael	15 JUL 1884 L	19	140
Hurley, Salem Henry	Tucker, Margaret Rebecca	02 APR 1878	11	400
Hurley, William	Burroughs, Jennie	24 AUG 1880 R	14	413
Hurst, Ellen Amelia	Byington, Arthur Wm.	18 MAR 1880 L	14	187
Hurst, Lucy Ann	Wells, Samuel	13 NOV 1880 R	15	020
Hurst, Robert J.	Perry, Maria D.	21 JUL 1881 R	15	413
Hurst, William Daniel	Carr, Emma	26 NOV 1884 R	19	422
Hurvey, Thomas	Day, Mary E.O.	31 AUG 1878 L	12	190
Husemann, Alice	Ellis, Nelson	28 MAY 1883 L	17	465
Husemann, Julia H.	Chivell, Joseph H.	27 JUL 1885	20	342
Hush, Eliza Theresa	Larrabee, Clinton	04 SEP 1880 L	14	432
Huss, Carl	Heinrich, Christina	12 JUN 1880 L	14	318
Huss, O. Edwin	Crabtree, Charlotte	02 JUL 1883 L	18	031
Huston, Hannah D.	Ware, William O.	12 JUL 1877	11	017

---

[6] May 11th 1880. This license is issued without my consent or knowledge-- I protest against it. /signed/ Charles H. Hurdle.

Hutcherson, John F.	Manion, Maggie	03 JUN 1880 R	14	304
Hutcherson, Walter Ann	Conner, Samuel	04 SEP 1882 R	17	002
Hutcherson, Wm. Andrew	Steiner, Annie M.	07 OCT 1884	19	291
Hutcheson, David	Thayer, Helen	11 SEP 1883	18	121
Hutcheson, Jennie F.	Fearson, James S.	03 FEB 1880 R	14	132
Hutcheson, John W.	Maddox, Willie A.	14 JAN 1878 L	11	303
Hutchings, John Booker	Williams, Hattie Belle	01 JUL 1880 R	14	345
Hutchins, Hamilton	Higgins, Carrie Andrews	04 APR 1881	15	248
Hutchins, Julius	Curtis, Sarah Jane	07 AUG 1884 L	19	174
Hutchins, Rosser D.	Garner, Hannah M.	23 OCT 1884 R	19	331
Hutchins, Stilson	Brady, Sarita Morrison	06 MAR 1883 L	17	335
Hutchinson, Alexander	Brown, Anna A.	16 AUG 1877 R	11	055
Hutchinson, Alexander	Boman, Annie Virginia	09 DEC 1878 R	12	373
Hutchinson, Annie O.	Hogue, George W.	23 JUN 1880	14	332
Hutchinson, Belle	Markward, George A.	12 JUN 1879 R	13	230
Hutchinson, C.D.	Donaghe, F.L.	18 DEC 1883 L	18	322
Hutchinson, Catherine Abbott	Olmstead, John F.	08 NOV 1882	17	117
Hutchinson, Charles W.	Coffey, Margaret A.	05 FEB 1883 L	17	293
Hutchinson, Christopher T.	Gales, Amie Neoma	03 NOV 1882 R	17	109
Hutchinson, David	Williams, Mary E.	16 MAY 1885 L	20	224
Hutchinson, Emma Jane	Keithley, Josiah	15 JAN 1884 R	18	377
Hutchinson, Geo. Wm.	Van Gueder, Clara	10 SEP 1877 R	11	083
Hutchinson, George	Carter, Ann	29 NOV 1877 R	11	197
Hutchinson, George Washington	Trunnell, Amelia	13 MAR 1882 R	16	274
Hutchinson, Josephine Ann	Tibbs, Vivian	15 MAR 1883 R	17	346
Hutchinson, Linda	Ball, Charles A.	07 APR 1880	14	213
Hutchinson, Lucy A.	Shaw, Richard A.	07 MAR 1878	11	375
Hutchinson, Maggie E.	Johnson, Charles H.	24 MAY 1882	16	375
Hutchinson, Rachel	Jackson, John William	29 NOV 1877 R	11	183
Hutchinson, Rosie Moss	Henderson, Robert Alexander	28 DEC 1882 R	17	221
Hutchinson, Tobias	Coquire, Mary Henrietta	12 OCT 1881 L	16	018
Hutchinson, William H.	Holly, Harriot	27 OCT 1880 L	15	016
Hutchison, Charles L.	Mankin, Mollie L.	25 JAN 1882 R	16	209
Hutchison, Columbus P.	Whaley, Lelia Virginia	14 FEB 1882 R	16	242
Hutchison, Elijah	Travers, Margaret	27 APR 1885 R	20	191
Huth, Charles H.	Osbern, Ada	18 DEC 1884	19	464
Huth, Clara	Gill, John	23 MAY 1882	16	363
Huth, Louis C.	Vogel, Maggie M.	18 MAR 1884 R	18	474
Huth, Minnie	Lerch, H.F.	18 JUN 1879	13	222
Huth, Theresa	Herberger, Lawrence	19 MAY 1882 L	16	368
Huton, Julia	Hawkins, Alfred	03 DEC 1877 L	11	216
Hutson, Katie J.	Sease, William H.	13 FEB 1881	15	178
Hutt, Mary Jane Virginia	Bowie, George Thomas	16 JUL 1880 L	14	365
Hutton, Della T.	Pennell, Andrew	24 DEC 1879 R	14	070
Hutton, George	Bell, Susie B.	01 JUL 1880 L	14	344
Hutton, Katie B.	Linney, John J.	12 FEB 1879 L	13	057
Hutton, Lola C.	Shomo, Oscar V.	06 AUG 1884 R	19	172
Hutton, Maggie S.	Case, Wm. W.	02 JAN 1881 R	20	4769
Hutton, Margaret	Scott, Frank	28 JUN 1883	18	024
Hutton, Mesach	Gray, Annie Laura	04 JUN 1885	20	255
Hutton, Sophia	Johnson, John	20 MAY 1878 L	12	061
Huysman, Anna Maaria	Kraft, Philip C.	05 NOV 1878 R	12	307
Huysman, Elizabeth V.C.	Schwigert, Edward C.	19 MAY 1885 L	20	229
Huysman, John Sidney	Weaver, Sallie Elisabeth	30 APR 1878 L	12	025
Hyatt, Frank, M.D.	Carlton, Ella	09 OCT 1878 R	12	263
Hyatt, Helen M.	McCeney, John S.	12 MAR 1884 R	18	467
Hyatt, L. Dorcas	Wolfe, Jesse Hyatt	31 MAY 1878	12	078
Hyatt, Margaret A., Mrs. [Eliz.]	Ricketts, Richard	18 FEB 1879 R	13	065

Hyatt, Robert James	Darden, Martha Eleanor	28 APR 1881 R	15	281
Hyde, Edward	Henderson, Mary	19 APR 1882 L	16	326
Hyde, George Augustus	Kidwell, Ida West	08 FEB 1881	15	181
Hyde, May	Moriarty, Richard	28 MAY 1884 L	19	043
Hyde, Nettie	Steel, T.M.	27 SEP 1883	18	158
Hyde, William Edgar	Kelly, Mary Agnes	27 JUN 1881 R	15	379
Hyer, Charles Statler	Bridges, Hattie Maria	22 APR 1885 R	20	183
Hyland, Mary E.	Bauer, John C.	21 AUG 1879 L	13	330
Hynes, Ellen	Maddan, John	09 OCT 1880 L	14	484
Hynes, Thomas	Morris, Jessie P.	04 AUG 1882	16	465
Hynson, William Thomas	Undith, Joanna Elizabeth	03 JAN 1884	18	363
Hyson, Frank	Smallwood, Theresa	01 JAN 1880 R	14	085

I

Name	Spouse	Date	Vol	Page
Iager, Henry A.	Bauer, Christina	16 OCT 1877 L	11	139
Ide, Edward Milo	Contnor, Emma Jean	19 OCT 1885 R	20	494
Iden, Joseph J.	Cheshire, Ellen R.	04 DEC 1879 R	14	029
Iglehart, Basil R.	Darby, Ella R.	28 MAY 1884 R	19	041
Iglon, Virginia	Hawkins, John	05 JAN 1880 L	14	088
Ignon, Lizzie	Stuart, John	19 NOV 1878	12	334
Imbrie, J. Rankin	Whitney, Lelia E.	09 OCT 1877	11	124
Imes, Cecelia	Monroe, James	26 NOV 1884 L	19	420
Imes, Simon	Kelly, Carrie	04 SEP 1883 L	18	110
Imhof, Friedrich	Brandenburg, Pauline	01 OCT 1882 R	17	045
Imhof, Hulda	Coomes, Charles	01 MAY 1881	15	269
Imhof, Hulda	Coomes, Charles	01 MAY 1881 R	15	273
Imhof, Karoline	Schneider, John F.	13 JUN 1882 R	16	409
Immore, Dorothea	Neuhaus, Ido	27 DEC 1879 R	16	3886
Immrich, Daniel B.	Hanlein, Augusta	30 SEP 1878 R	12	242
Imwald, Mary A.	Marshall, John	07 OCT 1879 R	13	408
Inch, Richard	Dunan, Emma	09 NOV 1881	16	067
Ingersoll, Charles E.	Ferriter, Maggie R.	11 AUG 1884 R	19	180
Ingersoll, John Carter	Burrows, Lola B.K.	16 NOV 1884 R	19	385
Ingle, John	Shad, Elizabeth C.	18 JUN 1878 L	12	104
Ingle, Millard F.	Walker, Anna C.	15 NOV 1879 R	13	487
Ingle, Rosina C.	Greer, John J.	12 NOV 1879 R	13	478
Ingle, Samuel S.	Brown, Katie F.	18 SEP 1882 L	17	025
Ingraham, John	Nichols, Eva	10 AUG 1884 R	19	175
Ingraham, Mary	Goodrick, Aaron M.	26 NOV 1877 R	11	196
Ingraham, Thomas	Middleton, Florence	25 APR 1878 L	12	024
Ingram, Mollie B.	Harrison, James, Jr.	03 SEP 1878 R	12	192
Ingram, Thomas G.	Young, Cora L.	20 FEB 1884 L	18	433
Inloins, Margaret Etta	Summerville, John F.	24 SEP 1885 L	20	440
Inslee, Hannah Armstrong	Randall, George	20 SEP 1882	17	029
Ions, Robert A.	Nevine, Cecile	05 SEP 1879 R	13	354
Irby, Sallie E.	Baker, William C.	29 DEC 1877	11	281
Ireland, Robert	Rutherford, Mary A.	02 AUG 1877 L	11	038
Irland, Kate Latimer	Davis, James S.	21 MAR 1883	17	354
Ironing, Thomas W.	Jackson, Martina	07 NOV 1881 L	16	065
Irving, Carrie	Scott, William	02 NOV 1880 L	15	025
Irving, Kate G.	Tyree, William W.	28 OCT 1880 R	15	019
Irving, Katie S.	Hodgson, Charles S.	10 JAN 1882 R	16	188
Irving, Mary	Browne, James	09 AUG 1879 L	13	314
Irving, Nelson	Wilson, Eliza	13 OCT 1885 R	20	478
Irwin, H. May	Leech, Mary Louise	11 SEP 1879 R	13	366
Irwin, James	Ridenour, Florence	08 JUN 1882	16	398
Irwin, John	Noerr, Susie C.	09 FEB 1881	15	174
Isaac, Henrietta	Crawford, Charles M.	15 JUN 1878	12	100
Isaacs, S.J.	Moten, S.B.	26 JUL 1880 L	14	375
Isaacs, Sarah Jane	Moten, Sylvester B.	01 AUG 1880 R	14	303
Isbell, Mary Jane	Cocke, Thomas W.	27 AUG 1877 R	11	066
Isel, John C.	Barker, Bertie E.	13 AUG 1885 R	20	367
Isemann, Sophie	Naecker, Ludwig	03 JUN 1879	13	217
Isham, Francis H.	Elmore, Alice E.	24 DEC 1879 R	14	069
Isparhecher [Indian]	Harrover, Alma	04 JUN 1884	19	060
Israel, George Robert	Gartnell, Fannie Israel	19 JUN 1883	18	002
Israel, Ida Ella	Mertz, William Corrigan	21 JAN 1879 R	13	029
Israel, Robert Otho	Barr, Annie Webb	18 MAR 1880 L	14	188
Iverson, Millie	Lee, William Henry	03 NOV 1881 R	16	038
Iverson, Soloman	Peale, Nancy	31 JAN 1878 R	11	322
Ives, Ella K.	Pierce, James H.	04 OCT 1881	16	003

J

Jac, Bertha	Gant, George M.	16 JAN 1882 L	16	195
Jack, Sophia C.	Pope, Frederick C.	18 DEC 1884 L	19	472
Jackson, A.D.	Smith, Ellen	03 MAY 1881 L	15	290
Jackson, Ada	Morgan, George	12 MAY 1881	15	296
Jackson, Adam	Bowie, Sarah	18 NOV 1880 L	15	057
Jackson, Addealia	Peyton, Alexander	29 SEP 1880 R	14	451
Jackson, Albert	Crown, Henrietta	18 SEP 1884	19	259
Jackson, Andrew	Bossfield, Frances	18 OCT 1877 R	11	141
Jackson, Andrew	Grady, Anne	18 SEP 1878 R	12	226
Jackson, Andrew	Allen, Mattie	17 SEP 1878 L	12	223
Jackson, Andrew	Murray, Addie	11 FEB 1880	14	147
Jackson, Andrew	Robinson, Bettie B.	24 FEB 1880	14	165
Jackson, Andrew	Massey, Emma	16 SEP 1880	14	449
Jackson, Andrew	Moore, Elvie	05 APR 1881	15	247
Jackson, Andrew	Wells, Lizzie	16 JUN 1881 R	15	365
Jackson, Andrew	Thomas, Mollie	16 JUN 1881 L	15	364
Jackson, Ann Eliza	Silvey, Robert W.	05 APR 1882 R	16	293
Jackson, Ann Mary	Langston, Ralph E.	14 MAR 1881 L	15	224
Jackson, Anna	Shipley, Fernando	10 SEP 1877 L	11	084
Jackson, Anna	Sanders, Stephen	16 JAN 1878 L	11	308
Jackson, Anna	Brown, George	14 DEC 1882	17	185
Jackson, Anna	Brooks, Oscar	27 AUG 1884 L	19	212
Jackson, Anna M.	Johnson, Jerome A.	30 NOV 1878 L	12	357
Jackson, Annie	Flipper, William M.	17 JUN 1878 R	12	101
Jackson, Annie	Johnson, Lawson	29 AUG 1880	14	418
Jackson, Annie	Butler, Frank	27 DEC 1881 L	16	163
Jackson, Annie E.	Sale, Leonard D.	06 OCT 1885	20	454
Jackson, Annie M.	Taggart, Hugh T.	15 OCT 1877 L	11	181
Jackson, Annie P.	Kattell, John C.	28 AUG 1879 R	13	340
Jackson, Armistead	Balch, Matilda	27 FEB 1878 L	11	362
Jackson, Arthur	Taylor, Louisa	16 DEC 1880 L	15	103
Jackson, Arthur	Campbell, Bettie	15 OCT 1885 R	20	487
Jackson, Arthur E.	Curtis, Mary V.	06 FEB 1883 L	17	297
Jackson, Barbara E.	Cole, Benjamin F.	16 JAN 1884 L	18	380
Jackson, Benjaamin	Watson, Julia	08 SEP 1884 L	19	233
Jackson, Betsey	Wheeler, Albert	29 NOV 1877 R	11	204
Jackson, Bynedon	DeNeal, Irene	06 MAR 1883 L	17	334
Jackson, Caroline	Edwards, John	23 NOV 1880 L	15	062
Jackson, Carrie M.	Hellen, Walter	15 SEP 1881 R	15	486
Jackson, Catharine	Price, Lemuel	19 JUN 1879 R	13	196
Jackson, Catherine	Brown, William	07 DEC 1882 L	17	174
Jackson, Chapman H.	Hall, Jane	11 FEB 1879 L	13	053
Jackson, Charles	Jordan, Mary Fannie	02 JAN 1879 L	13	005
Jackson, Charles	Bell, Martha	26 JUN 1879 L	13	254
Jackson, Charles A.W.	Dixon, Elizabeth	03 DEC 1881 L	16	112
Jackson, Charles H.	Harris, Lizzie	19 APR 1882 R	16	303
Jackson, Charles Henry	Jackson, Rose Ann	06 SEP 1883 L	18	113
Jackson, Charles I.	Benson, Clara V.	19 NOV 1880 R	15	072
Jackson, Charles L.	Brown, Mildred R.	30 JAN 1878 L	11	321
Jackson, Charles Olmstead	Green, Catharine	11 NOV 1878 L	12	320
Jackson, Clara P.	Lacy, Sylvester S.	30 MAR 1882 L	16	293
Jackson, Cornelia	Walker, Robert	13 JUN 1878	12	099
Jackson, Cornelia	Threat, John H.	06 DEC 1883 L	18	302
Jackson, Cornelius	Clark, Agnes	02 AUG 1877 R	11	039
Jackson, D.B.	Smith, Aggie E.	18 JUN 1883 L	17	499
Jackson, Dennis	Walker, Milly	23 NOV 1880 R	15	060
Jackson, Edmund	Sayles, Hattie	06 JUN 1883	17	478

Jackson, Edward	Ricks, Lena	02 DEC 1880 R	15	083
Jackson, Edward	Rich, Georgie	21 FEB 1884 L	18	436
Jackson, Eli	Childrey, Henrietta	24 DEC 1877	11	247
Jackson, Eliza	Dyer, James	16 APR 1878	12	006
Jackson, Eliza	Parker, William M.	20 NOV 1879 R	13	473
Jackson, Eliza	Thornhill, John	26 FEB 1881 R	15	204
Jackson, Eliza	Brown, Harvey	28 MAR 1882 L	16	291
Jackson, Eliza	Williams, Charles H.	20 FEB 1884 L	18	433
Jackson, Eliza Thomas	Bryant, Alexander P.	26 APR 1881	15	272
Jackson, Elizabeth	Sauer, Peter G.	29 APR 1880	14	246
Jackson, Elizabeth	Robinson, Hiram	04 JAN 1882 R	16	182
Jackson, Elizabeth O.	Doudge, Charles B.	04 DEC 1884 R	19	429
Jackson, Ella	Rosell, Henry	26 SEP 1883	18	148
Jackson, Ella	Connelly, John T.	25 DEC 1884	19	488
Jackson, Ellen	Sparks, Philip	24 SEP 1877 L	11	105
Jackson, Ellen	Winfield, John	16 OCT 1884 L	19	315
Jackson, Ellenore Frances	Bliss, Ellis B.	20 APR 1880 R	14	230
Jackson, Emma	Bassell, Henry	31 DEC 1878	12	408
Jackson, Enoch	Wilson, Mary	26 APR 1883 R	17	404
Jackson, Ernest	Brewer, Mary	07 AUG 1883 L	18	076
Jackson, Estelle E.	Rowzel, Edward G.	11 NOV 1879	13	477
Jackson, Fannie	Brown, Thomas	13 APR 1879 R	13	121
Jackson, Fannie M.	Coppin, Levi J.	21 DEC 1881 L	16	145
Jackson, Fannie W.	King, James	16 MAR 1885 L	20	116
Jackson, Fenton	Matthews, Ida	18 JUN 1885 R	20	281
Jackson, Florence	Newton, John Alexander	30 MAR 1882 R	16	288
Jackson, Frances	Cole, Ignacious	23 SEP 1884 R	19	264
Jackson, Frances	Harrison, John	31 JAN 1884	18	399
Jackson, Frances	Johnson, William	01 JUL 1885 R	20	304
Jackson, Francis F.	Bailey, Theodore F.	29 NOV 1883 L	18	285
Jackson, Frank	Smith, Victoria	08 APR 1880 L	14	210
Jackson, Frank	Noland, Elizabeth	16 DEC 1880 R	15	102
Jackson, Frank A.	Woodard, Mary J.	21 MAY 1883 R	17	453
Jackson, Frank H.	Holbrook, Mary A.	07 DEC 1881 R	16	118
Jackson, Geo. L.	Draper, Mary J.	10 APR 1880 R	14	217
Jackson, George T.	Barnes, Eliza	12 NOV 1878 L	12	323
Jackson, Giles	Blakey, Tabitha Ann	20 FEB 1879	13	069
Jackson, Hannah	Hawkins, Randolph	03 JUN 1884	19	054
Jackson, Harriet	Jones, Aaron	30 SEP 1885	20	449
Jackson, Harriet	Tylor, John H.	11 MAY 1885 R	20	213
Jackson, Harry	Foster, Emma	10 JUN 1885	20	265
Jackson, Hattie	Steward, John	11 AUG 1882	16	477
Jackson, Hattie	Payne, Lineas	04 OCT 1884 L	19	285
Jackson, Henrietta	Brown, Anthony	03 FEB 1879 L	13	044
Jackson, Henrietta, Mrs.	Dorsey, Charles	16 APR 1878 R	12	005
Jackson, Henry	Ranson, Lou	27 NOV 1879 R	14	012
Jackson, Henry	Barber, Patsey	18 JUL 1881 L	15	408
Jackson, Henry	Madison, Amanda	09 OCT 1883 R	18	174
Jackson, Henry	Mercer, Della	19 NOV 1884 L	19	395
Jackson, Henry	Bell, Bertha E.	05 JAN 1885	20	003
Jackson, Henry Alfonso	Jordan, Mary E.	03 JUN 1884 L	19	054
Jackson, Horace B.	Cox, Anne R.	28 FEB 1878	11	364
Jackson, Humphrey P.	Washington, Julia A.	02 DEC 1880 L	15	081
Jackson, Irene	Kirk, George W.	22 OCT 1878 R	12	286
Jackson, J. Thornton	Logan, Georgianna	30 NOV 1882	17	150
Jackson, James	Joshua, Ida	11 OCT 1877 R	11	131
Jackson, James	Hunneman, Ellen	21 JUL 1877 L	11	029
Jackson, James	Somersville, Olivia	16 MAY 1878	12	055

Jackson, James	McCoy, Mollie	09 JAN 1879	13	013
Jackson, James	Walker, Bettie	04 JAN 1883 R	17	237
Jackson, James	Thornton, Sallie	31 OCT 1883 L	18	223
Jackson, James	Carroll, Eliza	28 FEB 1884	18	450
Jackson, James	Brown, Virgie	12 MAR 1885 L	20	111
Jackson, James A.	Henderson, Rachel A.	04 DEC 1879 R	14	025
Jackson, James A.	Guy, Josephine	15 OCT 1885 R	20	486
Jackson, James William	Ross, Elizabeth	27 SEP 1877	11	111
Jackson, Jane	Brown, Reuben	18 SEP 1878 R	12	171
Jackson, Jane	Mosby, Joseph	09 DEC 1880 R	15	089
Jackson, Jane	Wilson, R.H.	02 JUL 1884	19	113
Jackson, Jennie	Doigens, Daniel	20 MAY 1880 L	14	277
Jackson, Jennie	Pendleton, Muscoe R.	13 SEP 1884 L	19	244
Jackson, Jesse	Brown, Carrie	03 DEC 1877 L	11	215
Jackson, Jesse Lewis	Reely, Mary, Mrs.	28 MAY 1881 R	15	325
Jackson, John	Toy, Sophie Anne	20 FEB 1879 L	13	070
Jackson, John	Wells, Elizabeth	26 MAY 1880 L	14	292
Jackson, John	Gressom, Mary Frances	06 MAY 1882 R	16	344
Jackson, John	Jackson, Mary	12 MAR 1885 L	20	109
Jackson, John B.	Carter, Matilda	15 SEP 1883 L	18	132
Jackson, John H.	Nixon, Penny E.	08 JAN 1880 R	14	097
Jackson, John H.	Bush, Josephine	29 SEP 1881 R	15	505
Jackson, John H.	Clarke, Ellen	22 DEC 1881 R	16	148
Jackson, John H.	Murray, Rosa	23 NOV 1882 L	17	145
Jackson, John Henry	Brooks, Kate	31 NOV 1877 L	11	196
Jackson, John Lewis	Dabney, Louise	21 DEC 1882 R	17	201
Jackson, John Richard	Washington, Almira	09 AUG 1877	11	047
Jackson, John William	Hutchinson, Rachel	29 NOV 1877 R	11	183
Jackson, Joseph	Matthews, Lulu	08 DEC 1884 R	19	441
Jackson, Joseph S.	Smith, Millie E.	30 OCT 1879 R	13	455
Jackson, Josephine	Spiggs, Richard	20 DEC 1877	11	251
Jackson, Josephine	Grantlin, Samuel	25 DEC 1879 R	14	063
Jackson, Julia	Phoenix, Richard	03 AUG 1878 L	12	156
Jackson, Julia	Butler, William	30 JAN 1883 L	17	278
Jackson, Julius	Jackson, Martha	05 MAY 1879 L	13	174
Jackson, Kate	Seals, Franklin	24 JUN 1885	20	290
Jackson, L.J.	Prior, William	18 JUL 1878	12	142
Jackson, L.W.	Driver, Jeannette	10 APR 1879 L	13	134
Jackson, Laura	Foster, Albert	11 APR 1878 R	13	379
Jackson, Lemuel	Lane, Hannah	20 MAR 1879	13	110
Jackson, Lewis	James, Harriet	19 JUN 1882 L	16	417
Jackson, Lillie M.	Hancock, James M.	22 SEP 1885 R	20	433
Jackson, Lizzie	Johnson, James	20 AUG 1877 R	11	057
Jackson, Lizzie	Fauntleroy, Henry	09 OCT 1883	18	178
Jackson, Lizzie	Johnson, George	15 NOV 1884	19	372
Jackson, Lloyd	Diggs, Alice	25 JUN 1883	18	013
Jackson, Louisa	Jones, Robert H.	08 JAN 1878	11	296
Jackson, Louisa	Bagby, Montgomery	09 SEP 1879 L	13	360
Jackson, Louisa	Diggs, Richard	25 MAY 1882 L	16	376
Jackson, Lucilia	Thompson, Jerry	04 JUN 1884 L	19	058
Jackson, Lucy	Fremont, James	08 OCT 1877 R	11	124
Jackson, Lucy	Dorsey, William	25 SEP 1879 L	13	385
Jackson, Lucy	Williams, Joseph C.	22 AUG 1882	16	491
Jackson, Lucy	Oden, Anthony	06 NOV 1884	19	363
Jackson, Lucy J.	Smith, Henry	30 AUG 1885 L	20	391
Jackson, Luena	Johnston, Middleton	07 AUG 1884	19	175
Jackson, Maggie	Richardson, Charles	28 AUG 1879 R	13	343
Jackson, Malinda D.	Chew, Robert	16 OCT 1884 L	19	313

Jackson, Margaret	Green, Theodore L.	24 DEC 1878 L	12	399
Jackson, Margaret	Shaw, Francis	24 FEB 1881 R	16	170
Jackson, Margaret	Keys, Nelson	12 JUN 1884	19	082
Jackson, Margarett	Page, Thos.	10 JUN 1880 L	14	314
Jackson, Maria	Clark, Marshall	04 APR 1878 L	11	407
Jackson, Maria	Dotson, John Henry	25 SEP 1879 L	13	387
Jackson, Maria	Williams, Elzie	02 JUN 1881 R	15	338
Jackson, Maria	Brown, William	31 AUG 1882 L	17	001
Jackson, Maria	Brown, William	31 AUG 1882 L	16	499
Jackson, Maria	Robinson, Spencer	20 SEP 1882 L	17	031
Jackson, Maria	Ferguson, William	28 MAR 1883 R	17	363
Jackson, Maria E.	Addison, Virgin P.	19 NOV 1878	12	335
Jackson, Maria M.	West, Russell	10 MAR 1882 R	16	273
Jackson, Martha	Jackson, Julius	05 MAY 1879 L	13	174
Jackson, Martha	Butler, Benjamin	04 MAY 1885 L	20	204
Jackson, Martha	Butler, Benjamin	04 APR 1885 R	33	8248
Jackson, Martha Ann, Mrs.	Swarn, James Nelson	26 SEP 1882 R	17	038
Jackson, Martina	Ironing, Thomas W.	07 NOV 1881 L	16	065
Jackson, Mary	Hayden, Robert	21 MAR 1878 L	11	390
Jackson, Mary	Redman, Basil	20 DEC 1878 R	12	385
Jackson, Mary	Southerland, Richard	06 NOV 1878 L	12	312
Jackson, Mary	Paine, John	13 MAR 1879	13	097
Jackson, Mary	Yates, Thomas	16 SEP 1880	14	450
Jackson, Mary	Harris, William	09 JUN 1881 R	15	354
Jackson, Mary	Carter, Charles	16 OCT 1883 R	18	194
Jackson, Mary	Brent, William	02 JUN 1884 L	19	049
Jackson, Mary	Jackson, John	12 MAR 1885 L	20	109
Jackson, Mary A.	Williams, William H.	12 MAR 1884 R	18	467
Jackson, Mary Elizabeth	Smith, John H.	20 DEC 1882 L	17	198
Jackson, Mary Ella	Fletcher, Hamilton W.	19 AUG 1881 L	15	454
Jackson, Mary Ellen	Davis, Charles L.	04 SEP 1877 L	11	075
Jackson, Mary L.	Carter, Franklin	04 FEB 1884 R	18	407
Jackson, Mary O.	Rollins, Isaac	21 DEC 1882	17	203
Jackson, Mary V.	Kraft, Clarence O.	23 JAN 1882 L	16	205
Jackson, Matilda	Mars, William	03 DEC 1879 R	13	001
Jackson, Matilda	Green, Robert H.	27 JUL 1881 L	15	421
Jackson, Mattie	Brooks, Theodore	10 OCT 1878 L	12	265
Jackson, Melinda	Brown, James	28 NOV 1877 L	11	211
Jackson, Melvin M.	Young, Martha E.	13 OCT 1881 R	16	023
Jackson, Oscar	Blackstone, Harriete	26 DEC 1882 R	17	212
Jackson, Paul Ardean	Wilson, Maggie	30 DEC 1879 L	14	079
Jackson, Peter N.	Hopkins, Ressia	13 AUG 1878 R	12	165
Jackson, Philip	Peterson, Ellen	22 MAY 1884 R	19	032
Jackson, Philip M.	Scott, Fannie	04 DEC 1880 L	15	084
Jackson, Phillis	Bundy, John H.	16 DEC 1880 R	15	098
Jackson, Rachel	Stewart, George, Jr.	09 SEP 1880 R	14	439
Jackson, Rachel A.	Carroll, Eugene	01 DEC 1883 L	18	289
Jackson, Randolph	Smith, Alice	22 MAY 1884	19	034
Jackson, Rebecca	Moulton, Charles	25 DEC 1879	14	064
Jackson, Reuben R.	Collier, Nancy Street	20 NOV 1877 R	11	149
Jackson, Richard J.	Todd, Margaret J.	15 JAN 1878 R	11	302
Jackson, Richard J.	Smith, Anna E.	03 OCT 1878	12	254
Jackson, Robie St. Clair	McMichael, Alexander Ausle	19 JUL 1882 R	16	451
Jackson, Rose Ann	Jackson, Charles Henry	06 SEP 1883 L	18	113
Jackson, Rozetta	Robinson, Henry	06 DEC 1883 L	18	297
Jackson, Sadie	Snowden, John	13 AUG 1877 L	11	051
Jackson, Samuel	Alexander, Martha	30 OCT 1877	11	160
Jackson, Samuel	Haney, Amanda	03 OCT 1878	12	252

Jackson, Samuel	York, Jane	02 JUL 1879 L	13	263
Jackson, Samuel	Nelson, Mary	22 JUN 1880 R	14	328
Jackson, Sarah	Head, Thaddeus	03 JAN 1878 L	11	293
Jackson, Sarah	Watts, Henry	05 FEB 1878	11	327
Jackson, Sarah	Johnson, French	04 SEP 1883 R	18	109
Jackson, Sarah E.	Jackson, Wm. H.	29 APR 1880	14	241
Jackson, Sarah E.	King, Charles	04 JUN 1884 L	19	060
Jackson, Sarah Jane	Scott, James	23 JUL 1883 L	18	057
Jackson, Sarah M.	Simmons, Zachariah E.	21 JAN 1879 R	13	027
Jackson, Susan	Alexander, Hiram	04 DEC 1878 L	12	365
Jackson, Susan	Monroe, Frank	06 FEB 1883 R	17	294
Jackson, Susie	Enns, Richard	10 NOV 1881 R	16	062
Jackson, Susie	Morton, Peter	30 APR 1885 R	20	200
Jackson, Thomas	Smith, Maria	22 AUG 1878 R	12	176
Jackson, Thomas	Calbert, Delia	11 DEC 1878	12	375
Jackson, Thomas H.	Crosby, Annie M.	03 JAN 1885 L	20	002
Jackson, Thomas R.	Park, Henrietta	10 FEB 1880 R	14	144
Jackson, Valdamar	Webb, Amanda	22 OCT 1879 R	13	438
Jackson, Victoria	Green, Michael	23 DEC 1878	12	394
Jackson, W.H.	Wilson, Amelia	30 OCT 1879	13	454
Jackson, W.H.	Lee, Mary L.	02 APR 1884 L	18	492
Jackson, W.W.	Crowther, M.J.	06 OCT 1879 R	13	406
Jackson, Washington	Burke, Alice	15 MAR 1882 L	16	277
Jackson, Washington	Johnson, Annie	11 AUG 1884 L	19	179
Jackson, Wayneboro	Tasco, Martha	17 APR 1884 R	18	510
Jackson, Wesley	Buckman, Ida	17 OCT 1878	12	278
Jackson, William	Lewis, Emma	04 JUN 1878 R	12	083
Jackson, William	Douglas, Louisa T.	19 JUN 1879	13	238
Jackson, William	Thomas, Eliza Ann	10 APR 1879	13	136
Jackson, William	Addison, Margaret B.	04 OCT 1879 L	13	403
Jackson, William	Tolson, Amelia	25 AUG 1879 R	13	326
Jackson, William	Rideout, Eliza	25 MAR 1880 R	14	183
Jackson, William	Christon, Annie	26 JUL 1883	18	063
Jackson, William	Jones, Gertrude	24 JAN 1884	18	393
Jackson, William	Marshall, Emma	29 DEC 1884 L	19	498
Jackson, William	Thornhill, Eliza	17 MAR 1885 R	20	119
Jackson, William H.	White, Alice	18 SEP 1883 R	18	139
Jackson, William J.	Beall, Mattie A.	12 APR 1882 L	16	312
Jackson, William J.	Connix, Elizabeth M.	25 APR 1883 R	17	410
Jackson, William P.H.	Fisher, Sarah E.	18 JUN 1885	20	277
Jackson, Wm. H.	Jackson, Sarah E.	29 APR 1880	14	241
Jackson, Wm. Strother	Dilworth, Mary Lillie	28 NOV 1881 R	16	101
Jacob, Christopher C.	Belt, Susan E.	22 APR 1880 L	14	232
Jacob, John W.	Robey, Rosa D.	19 JAN 1885 L	20	026
Jacobs, A. Issac	Gordon, Carrie E.	01 MAR 1880 L	14	170
Jacobs, Charles P.	Riddle, Mary P.	02 OCT 1883	18	162
Jacobs, George M.	Prather, Jessie M.	15 AUG 1885	20	371
Jacobs, Harry H.	Lansburgh, Carrie	25 MAR 1885 R	20	129
Jacobs, Henrietta	Griffin, John A.	19 JUL 1883	18	054
Jacobs, Henry	Preston, Anne	21 JUN 1881 R	15	370
Jacobs, Ida M.	Jerman, M.G.	28 JUN 1883	18	025
Jacobs, Ida May	Miller, James Edgar	02 MAR 1881 R	15	211
Jacobs, James Thomas	Dove, Lydia Ann	14 JUN 1881 R	15	356
Jacobs, Katie Elizabeth	Clark, Richard T.	09 FEB 1880 R	14	142
Jacobs, Mary E.	Ray, Charles G.	05 FEB 1879 L	13	047
Jacobs, Norman	Smith, Martha	07 OCT 1882 R	17	059
Jacobs, Sophia	Bundy, Julius L.	07 NOV 1822	17	113
Jacobs, William A.	Davis, Roberta E.	06 FEB 1884 R	18	413

Jacobson, Jacob	Werr, Mary	31 DEC 1877 L	11	282
Jaeger, Henry	Theilkuhl, Rosa L.	25 JUN 1884	19	103
Jaeger, Thomas S.	Cragg, Mary E.	10 AUG 1880 R	14	394
Jaegle, Joseph A.	Schoenborn, Mary A.	26 SEP 1885 L	20	444
Jaeschke, Charles	Schiskler, Mary	01 JUL 1883	18	028
James, Ada	McVeigh, George H.	04 SEP 1884	19	226
James, Alice Louisa	Wakeman, Stephen Herrick	07 APR 1885 R	20	148
James, Amanda	Smallwood, James	02 AUG 1879 L	13	304
James, Anne Price	Raymond, Stephen	20 NOV 1877 R	11	174
James, Charles	Bowman, Mary A.	19 DEC 1881 L	16	138
James, Charlie	Knight, Annie E.	29 APR 1879	13	156
James, George H.	Sales, Bettie	31 JAN 1885 L	20	046
James, George W.	Foote, Martha A.	05 JUN 1883 R	17	475
James, George Watson	Southall, Mary Whitfield	07 JAN 1879 R	13	010
James, Harriet	Howell, Sanders	19 JUL 1877	11	023
James, Harriet	Jackson, Lewis	19 JUN 1882 L	16	417
James, Henry C.	Trexler, Rebecca S.	17 NOV 1879 R	13	492
James, James Henry	Stephenson, Elizabeth	27 SEP 1883	18	157
James, Jessie E.	Scott, Henry Winters	17 JAN 1883 R	17	254
James, John R.	Williams, Sarah J.	08 SEP 1881 R	15	478
James, Lafayette	Green, Sallie	18 OCT 1878 R	12	292
James, Lizzie	Clay, Henry	09 AUG 1878 L	12	162
James, Lucy	Parker, Thomas	14 APR 1884 L	18	507
James, Lula	Hunaker, Harry	28 SEP 1882 L	17	041
James, M.B.	Treece, N.M.	25 MAY 1880	14	286
James, Maggie	Fields, Samuel	01 SEP 1881 L	15	468
James, Maggie	Vigal, Richard	29 JAN 1881 L	15	170
James, Mary	Davenport, Christopher	01 MAY 1879 L	13	170
James, Mary E.	Fantroy, John	12 NOV 1878 R	12	296
James, Mary E.	Carroll, Henry	29 JAN 1880	14	041
James, Morris M.	Everton, Florence	30 APR 1880	14	247
James, Nellie M.	MacLellan, Harry H.	11 JUL 1885 R	20	320
James, Robert	Holmes, Mary	13 AUG 1878	12	165
James, Sarah	Carter, Thomas	21 MAY 1885 R	20	234
James, Sonnie	Dixon, Thomas	16 MAR 1882 L	16	279
James, William	Masterson, Rachael L.	12 DEC 1878 L	12	378
James, William	Sardo, Julia	07 JAN 1882 R	16	185
James, William	Braxton, Nora	16 SEP 1884 L	19	251
Jameson, Annie E.	Johnson, George H.	03 MAR 1885	20	095
Jameson, William P.	Murphy, Lula L.	19 AUG 1884 L	19	193
Jamieson, Ruth	King, James Alfred	02 SEP 1878	12	191
Jamison, Anna A.	Wilson, Frank L.	13 JAN 1880 L	14	103
Jamison, Clara	Phair, George F.	19 OCT 1881 L	16	034
Jamison, James Philip	Mahoney, Annie	12 AUG 1880 R	14	393
Jamison, Matilda	Countee, Charles Robert	02 OCT 1879 L	13	398
Janens, Lillie	Kidwell, Zeddie K.	21 DEC 1883 R	18	334
Janes, George	Bryan, Mary	15 JUL 1885 L	20	327
Janey, Samuel	Adams, Judy	29 OCT 1880 L	15	022
Janifer, George C.	Brown, Laura R.A.	03 JUL 1879	13	267
Janin, Edward	Morse, Helen	24 OCT 1877 L	11	153
Janin, Henry	Smith, May B.	29 OCT 1884 L	19	347
Jankey, Amelia	Glasco, David Benjamin	29 JAN 1884 R	18	400
Janney, Franklin	Loman, Jennie	14 FEB 1885 L	20	067
Jannifer, John	Hawkins, Annie	19 FEB 1879 L	13	067
Jannifer, Rosa	Contee, James B.	07 NOV 1883 L	18	239
Jannus, Frankland	Weightman, Emeline C.	25 OCT 1883 R	18	211
Janus, William H.	Turner, Susan	22 FEB 1883 L	17	317
Jarboe, George H.	Lacey, Martha J.	24 DEC 1881 L	16	156

D.C. Marriage Records Index, June 28, 1877 to October 19, 1885   237

Jarboe, James A.	Fry, Annie E.D.	06 NOV 1879 R	13	464
Jarboe, John H.	Johnson, Cynthia	22 MAR 1882 L	16	286
Jarboe, Snowden E.	Schneider, Emma	11 OCT 1885 R	20	473
Jardiner, Amos J.	Gibson, Nancy Ann	18 AUG 1885 L	20	376
Jarvis, Christopher	Fitchett, Cordie Jane	07 SEP 1881 R	15	474
Jarvis, John Fillis	Heath, Augusta Louise	25 DEC 1878 R	12	399
Jarvis, Mary	Beverly, Robert	09 MAR 1885 L	20	102
Jarvis, Thaddeus	Royston, Kate Janette	14 NOV 1877 R	11	185
Jarvis, Virginia Austin	Doyle, Burton Thomas	22 NOV 1881 R	16	084
Jarvis, William	Herbert, Georgie	23 NOV 1882 R	17	148
Jason, George	Queen, Theresa	13 AUG 1877 L	11	052
Jasper, Jennette E.	Gray, John W.	02 OCT 1884	19	281
Jasper, Martha C.	Moten, Charles L.	06 AUG 1878	12	157
Jasper, Mary Jane	Anderson, William R.	07 OCT 1878	12	226
Jasper, Morris	Wade, Mittie	12 SEP 1878	12	215
Jasper, Rachel	Morris, Henry E.	10 OCT 1877 R	11	115
Jasper, William C.	Dolan, Grace R.	30 JUN 1885 R	20	301
Javins, Harrison, Jr.	Devis, Sarah Jane	06 JAN 1880 R	14	080
Javins, Lillie	Herbert, Ernest	14 JUN 1883 L	17	491
Javins, Missouri	Simms, John	21 FEB 1884	18	435
Javins, Randolph	Taylor, Mary Ann	03 SEP 1878	12	195
Jay, Jane Minnesola	King, William Benjamin	28 APR 1880 R	14	238
Jay, Leonard Brewer	Green, Mabel	28 JAN 1884 R	18	398
Jean, Lina Essie	Pulies, Llewellyn Wm.	12 MAR 1885 R	20	108
Jedel, Hyman	Sinsheimer, Bertha	04 JUN 1878 R	12	081
Jefferis, Helen Mortimer	Easton, Edward Denison	24 MAY 1883 R	17	461
Jefferis, Ida F.	Fitzgerald, Jenkins A.	03 NOV 1882 R	17	109
Jefferson, Albert C.	Jones, Sophia	14 SEP 1882 L	17	021
Jefferson, Carrie	Brooks, Arthur J.	07 OCT 1880 L	14	479
Jefferson, Eliza	Jones, Henry	23 APR 1878 R	12	016
Jefferson, Elizabeth	Body, John H.	01 JUN 1882 L	16	388
Jefferson, Florence	Sampson, Edgar K.	03 MAR 1881 R	15	214
Jefferson, James	Lounds, Elizabeth	21 MAY 1885 R	20	233
Jefferson, John L.[7]	Gaskins, Susie E.	08 MAR 1884 R	18	463
Jefferson, Josephine	Stewart, Thomas	25 SEP 1880 R	14	460
Jefferson, Josephine C.	Berry, Enoch	10 DEC 1879 R	14	040
Jefferson, Kate	Norris, John	13 NOV 1879 L	13	482
Jefferson, Lafayette	Minor, Alice	28 MAY 1884 R	19	042
Jefferson, Samuel	Levey, Mary Jane	28 MAY 1885 L	20	244
Jefferson, Simon Peter	Bowman, Letha Virginia	03 OCT 1882 R	17	049
Jeffries, Anna Florence	Stout, Orrin Beech	10 DEC 1879 R	14	041
Jeffries, Henrietta Linn	Brown, William Lee	12 DEC 1878 R	12	373
Jeffries, James	Neger, Kale	29 SEP 1883 L	18	161
Jeffries, James H.	Neger, J. Kate	05 JUL 1884	19	114
Jeffries, John T.	Brissey, Louisa	23 JUN 1879 R	13	244
Jeffries, Lurie E.	Stanford, W.W.	22 MAY 1880 R	14	268
Jekel, Dora	Weigel, Henry	13 APR 1879	13	133
Jelka, Anthony F.	Garvey, Mary	12 AUG 1880 L	14	398
Jenifer, Benjamin	Johnson, Isabella	11 JUN 1883 L	17	485
Jenifer, Carrie	Wallace, James	28 DEC 1882 L	17	220
Jenifer, George	Thomas, Jennie	09 SEP 1880 R	14	424
Jenifer, Mary	Griffin, Tyson	27 AUG 1884 L	19	210
Jenkins, Annie	Hoyle, Henry J.	22 OCT 1878 R	12	286
Jenkins, Annie	Smallwood, William	05 MAR 1885 R	20	082
Jenkins, Annie E.	Smith, Frank	22 OCT 1878	12	285
Jenkins, Antonia Thornton	Converse, George Leroy, Jr.	12 OCT 1882 R	17	067

[7]This return #8,989, for a marriage performed 8 MAR 1884, is found bound amidst returns of early 1886.

Jenkins, Arthur	Gordon, Fannie C.	20 OCT 1881	16	036
Jenkins, Benjamin C.	Moudy, Naomi K.	29 JAN 1884 L	18	400
Jenkins, Charles	Adams, Elizabeth	06 MAY 1881	15	295
Jenkins, Daniel	Chase, Mary	23 DEC 1884 L	19	479
Jenkins, David E.	May, Marion E.	12 JUN 1884 L	19	081
Jenkins, Edgar M.	Littleford, Annie E.	22 JAN 1883 R	17	270
Jenkins, Edward	Davis, Annie	09 AUG 1877 R	11	046
Jenkins, Edward	Burch, Sidonia	18 MAY 1884	19	025
Jenkins, Elizabeth	Mason, William	15 FEB 1883	17	304
Jenkins, Emily	Suter, Alexander	18 DEC 1878 R	12	386
Jenkins, Emma E.	Berkley, Enos R.	23 APR 1882	16	330
Jenkins, Frederick	Singleton, Melda	30 APR 1879 R	13	167
Jenkins, Georgianna	Coleman, Charles A.	20 SEP 1885 R	20	429
Jenkins, Henry	Johnson, Isabella	11 SEP 1878 L	12	213
Jenkins, Hosanna	Baker, William H.	03 OCT 1878 R	12	245
Jenkins, James	Feester, Maggie	08 JUN 1878 R	12	092
Jenkins, John	Fantroy, Mary	31 MAY 1883 L	17	470
Jenkins, Joseph E.	Bowman, Ella F.	25 DEC 1883	18	335
Jenkins, Laura A.	Blincoe, Joseph	27 JUN 1878	12	117
Jenkins, Maggie	Dorsey, Daniel	23 JUL 1885 L	20	338
Jenkins, Margaret	Turner, John T.	16 DEC 1880 R	15	103
Jenkins, Maria	Brooks, Frank	29 MAR 1880	14	201
Jenkins, Maria	Nelson, Robert	30 APR 1885	20	198
Jenkins, Martha	Tolson, Charles S.	07 OCT 1880 R	14	477
Jenkins, Mary	Brown, Henry	01 SEP 1880 L	14	426
Jenkins, Mary A.	Meyerberg, Frederick	24 AUG 1885 R	20	385
Jenkins, Mary E.	Nalley, James T.	12 JUN 1884	19	081
Jenkins, Mary Josephine	Churn, Charles H.	25 SEP 1879 R	13	385
Jenkins, Mary, Mrs.	Bayliss, Robert Vinton	08 MAY 1884 R	19	004
Jenkins, Millie	Green, Robert H.	14 MAY 1883	17	436
Jenkins, Rebecca	Ray, William	08 SEP 1879	13	358
Jenkins, Robert	Strother, Rachael	15 MAY 1883 L	17	439
Jenkins, Roy C.	Belt, Annie R.	15 MAR 1882 R	16	278
Jenkins, Sarah Virginia	Williams, William Alber	27 OCT 1880 R	15	016
Jenkins, Susan	Smart, Frank	24 DEC 1879 R	14	070
Jenkins, Susannah	Wood, George Thomas	14 JUL 1877 R	11	012
Jenkins, Talbot M.	Banks, Matilda B.	06 NOV 1883 L	18	238
Jenkins, Thomas J.	Bowman, Mary	26 DEC 1883	18	343
Jenkins, Thomas T.	Burke, Jennie E.	06 DEC 1882 R	17	171
Jenkins, Tilman	Gray, Caroline	27 MAR 1884 R	18	484
Jenkins, Virginia U.	Greer, Robert Franklin	11 SEP 1883 R	18	124
Jenkins, William	Grimes, Laura J.	12 JAN 1881 R	15	148
Jenkins, William	Washington, Rosa	14 OCT 1885 L	20	480
Jenkins, William Francis	Harris, Jinnie	01 FEB 1883	17	283
Jenness, Maggie	Grady, James	14 SEP 1884	19	244
Jennifer, Edward	Jordan, Mary	28 APR 1880 R	14	229
Jenning, Mary Jane	Gray, George	27 MAY 1878 L	12	068
Jennings, Edward J.	McArdle, Mary D.	28 DEC 1880 L	15	128
Jennings, Ella Frances	Moore, John Benson	15 MAR 1882 R	16	277
Jennings, Emma	Bellfield, Benjamin B.	24 MAY 1883 L	17	460
Jennings, Felix A.	Johnson, Cordelia L.	08 AUG 1878 R	12	160
Jennings, Henry	Coates, Louisa	25 DEC 1877	11	262
Jennings, Joseph E.	Jones, Katie L.	14 JUL 1880 L	14	360
Jennings, Laura	Bellew, William R.	26 MAY 1884	19	037
Jennings, Lida W.	Hawley, Lucian	18 DEC 1877	11	242
Jennings, Mary	Johnson, James	29 MAY 1882 R	16	379
Jennings, Pug	Hargrove, Silas	13 AUG 1877 L	11	051
Jennings, R.B.	Rose, Kate	20 APR 1880	14	230

D.C. Marriage Records Index, June 28, 1877 to October 19, 1885 — 239

Jennings, Sarah A.	Harding, Hezekiah	08 SEP 1882 R	17	013
Jennings, Wm. Harrison	Tremble, Annie E.	24 AUG 1882	16	492
Jennison, Marcellina	Robison, James	08 JAN 1885 L	20	009
Jerman, M.G.	Jacobs, Ida M.	28 JUN 1883	18	025
Jernels, Laura S.	Thornton, James S.	24 APR 1883 L	17	408
Jeter, Bettie	Glass, Robert R.	19 JUN 1883 R	18	001
Jett, George M.	Wine, Ollie Rebecca	26 JUN 1879 R	13	253
Jett, Ida	Perry, Benjamin	24 SEP 1885 R	20	438
Jett, Janie Eliza	Ward, Charles E.	28 NOV 1878 R	12	354
Jett, Maria R.	Dodson, Frank D.	02 DEC 1884 L	19	431
Jett, Mary F.	Payne, Walter B.	31 MAR 1879 L	13	120
Jett, Rosa Brown	Robinson, Charles Wm.	01 OCT 1884 L	19	278
Jewell, Eugene P.	Towner, Edith	20 OCT 1884	19	319
Jewell, Ida M.	Bailey, Charles E.	17 OCT 1882 R	17	076
Jewell, Malvern H.	Belfils, Alice	05 MAR 1882	16	267
Jewell, Mary E.	Patterson, Augustus	15 FEB 1883 R	17	308
Jewricks, Georgia	Copeland, Soloman	21 MAR 1878 L	11	390
Jhonson, Archey	Clark, Hannah	06 APR 1885 R	20	146
Jimmerson, Richard	Smothers, Rosa	18 JUN 1878 L	12	103
Jinkins, Dennis	Malone, Martha E.	02 APR 1884 R	18	489
Jinkins, William A.	Miller, Mary A.	22 NOV 1881 R	16	083
Jinnerson, Georgiana	Robinson, Edward	17 FEB 1879 R	13	063
Jivinse, Samuel	McKnight, Florence	12 APR 1882 L	16	314
Joachim, John	Cordes, Friederika Karoline D.	29 APR 1883 R	17	419
Joachim, Olivia	Smithson, Charles Marion	24 DEC 1881 L	16	156
Jobson, Joseph Tyler	Spence, G. May	10 NOV 1880 R	15	041
Johannes, Corella Wynn	Seeger, Paul Augustus	30 MAR 1885 R	20	137
Johannes, John Martin	Turner, Catharine A.	03 JAN 1878 R	11	292
John, Lena Augusta	Cain, Joseph Guien	04 JUL 1883	18	019
John, Martha Pry	Slaughter, Edward	12 MAY 1881 R	15	304
Johns, Alice J.	Ford, James	09 FEB 1882 R	16	230
Johns, Jenny	Drummond, William N.	14 NOV 1880 R	15	046
Johns, John H.	Williams, Susan	27 OCT 1883 L	18	219
Johns, Lucy M.	Sanger, William P.S.	10 JUL 1877	11	014
Johns, Mary Elizabeth	Baker, Charles Thos. Morrison	01 JUN 1882 R	16	389
Johns, Thomas H.	Kent, Mary Ann	05 NOV 1878 R	12	309
Johnson, A.J.	Ford, Anna M.	11 APR 1882	16	310
Johnson, Abbie	Goodall, William	14 MAR 1878 R	11	382
Johnson, Abrauna	Taplet, W.A.	19 AUG 1880 L	14	407
Johnson, Ada	Simmons, Preston	20 MAR 1882 L	16	284
Johnson, Agnes	Grimes, Andrew	17 DEC 1883	18	318
Johnson, Agnes	Buckner, Randolph	26 DEC 1884 L	19	492
Johnson, Agnes C.	Keith, Wm. W.	23 SEP 1885	20	431
Johnson, Albert	Powers, Augusta	21 DEC 1882 L	17	202
Johnson, Albert	Stroud, Malvina	06 MAY 1884 L	19	008
Johnson, Aleck	Campbell, Emily	15 SEP 1881 L	15	485
Johnson, Alexander	Nevitt, Mary	27 SEP 1877	11	110
Johnson, Alexander	Smith, Lizzie	10 APR 1878 R	11	413
Johnson, Alexander	Bouldin, Josephine	06 OCT 1880	14	476
Johnson, Alexander	Tancil, Annie E.	25 DEC 1884 R	19	490
Johnson, Alice	Smith, Barney	05 AUG 1880 L	14	389
Johnson, Alice	Gannaway, Thomas H.	06 DEC 1883 L	18	304
Johnson, Alice	Nelson, Robert	01 OCT 1884 L	19	278
Johnson, Alonzo T.	Simpson, Alice	07 DEC 1881 L	16	116
Johnson, Anna	Allen, Joseph	01 JUL 1878 L	12	119
Johnson, Anna	Gant, George	15 MAY 1879 L	13	193
Johnson, Anna	Crockett, Alfred	15 SEP 1883 L	18	131
Johnson, Annie	Greenleaf, John Thomas	09 NOV 1877	11	177

Johnson, Annie	Millen, Robert	12 OCT 1878 L	12	269
Johnson, Annie	Price, William Henry	10 JAN 1878 R	11	296
Johnson, Annie	Smith, William	18 JUL 1878 L	12	140
Johnson, Annie	Taylor, Jerry	10 JUN 1880 R	14	316
Johnson, Annie	Osborn, James	03 FEB 1881 L	15	175
Johnson, Annie	Carter, George	09 DEC 1882 L	17	175
Johnson, Annie	Craig, Thomas	03 JUL 1884 R	19	118
Johnson, Annie	Jackson, Washington	11 AUG 1884 L	19	179
Johnson, Annie	Lomax, Daniel	24 DEC 1884 L	19	488
Johnson, Annie	Thompson, Phiny Cleophas	14 MAY 1884 R	19	020
Johnson, Annie	Underwood, Dave	28 MAY 1884 L	19	042
Johnson, Annie	Warren, Richard	20 AUG 1884 L	19	198
Johnson, Annie	Hall, Mack	11 AUG 1885	20	358
Johnson, Annie E.	Harris, Washington R.	14 APR 1881 R	15	233
Johnson, Annie E.	Brown, Thomas	26 APR 1883 R	17	415
Johnson, Annie E.	Sewell, J.W.	22 OCT 1883	18	207
Johnson, Annie M.	Tilman, Andrew	18 NOV 1880 L	15	056
Johnson, Annie R.	Wood, Daniel M.	27 DEC 1881	16	152
Johnson, At Lee	Becker, Helen C.	26 DEC 1882	17	208
Johnson, Bailey	Hughes, Ella	06 DEC 1882 L	17	170
Johnson, Barbara	Scott, Samuel	27 DEC 1881 R	16	150
Johnson, Barney	Bell, Fannie	25 JAN 1883 R	17	272
Johnson, Belle	Crandall, Milton R.	24 OCT 1879 R	13	427
Johnson, Benjamin	Smith, Eveline	16 DEC 1878 R	12	380
Johnson, Benjamin	Coleman, Lydia Anne	05 DEC 1878 R	12	361
Johnson, Benjamin	Peterson, Jane	19 AUG 1881 L	15	454
Johnson, Benjamin	Noxon, Eliza	31 JUL 1883	17	487
Johnson, Benjamin	Dickson, Mime	18 DEC 1883	18	323
Johnson, Benjamin	Adams, Katie	21 AUG 1884 R	18	314
Johnson, Benjamin F.	Freeman, Emma	09 SEP 1885 R	20	407
Johnson, Bernice	Barnes, Everard F.	25 SEP 1879 L	13	386
Johnson, Bertie	Ketner, James H.	24 JAN 1879 L	13	033
Johnson, Bessey	Martin, Thomas	06 OCT 1885 R	20	461
Johnson, Beverly	Roots, Anna	02 OCT 1884	19	277
Johnson, Birl	Smith, Emma	24 JAN 1879 R	13	026
Johnson, Caltiene, Mrs.	Page, Isaac	09 JAN 1879 R	12	2974
Johnson, Caroline	Campbell, Joseph	03 JAN 1883 L	17	234
Johnson, Carrie	Taylor, Harry	06 DEC 1877 R	11	223
Johnson, Carrie E.	Lewis, William	15 DEC 1881	16	133
Johnson, Carrie Eliza	Berry, Emory E.	20 SEP 1877 L	11	102
Johnson, Catharine F.	Trevitt, Clarence L.	27 JUN 1883 R	18	022
Johnson, Catherine	Page, Isaac	12 DEC 1877 L	11	232
Johnson, Catherine	Adams, George S.	19 MAR 1879 L	13	107
Johnson, Catherine	Morrison, Riddall	08 FEB 1881 R	15	180
Johnson, Catherine, Mrs.	Page, Albert	08 NOV 1882 R	17	118
Johnson, Celia	Henson, James	06 OCT 1879 L	13	406
Johnson, Charles	Thompson, Laura	12 MAY 1880 L	14	265
Johnson, Charles	Snead, Amelia	02 DEC 1880	15	079
Johnson, Charles	Washington, Sophia	17 NOV 1881 L	16	082
Johnson, Charles	Day, Patsy	22 MAR 1883 L	17	355
Johnson, Charles	Johnson, Matilda	06 AUG 1883	18	075
Johnson, Charles Edwin	Dorr, Emma Minnie	18 APR 1883 R	17	398
Johnson, Charles H.	Ford, Isabella	07 NOV 1878	12	311
Johnson, Charles H.	Brown, Corrie	19 NOV 1878 L	12	337
Johnson, Charles H.	Boulden, Charlotte	05 FEB 1879	13	044
Johnson, Charles H.	Hutchinson, Maggie E.	24 MAY 1882	16	375
Johnson, Charles Henry	Queen, Louisa	20 AUG 1884 L	19	195
Johnson, Charles Henry	Sullivan, Ivy Isabelle	29 OCT 1884	19	343

Johnson, Charles M.	Dolle, Mary E.	03 JAN 1881	15	047
Johnson, Charles M.	Dolle, Mary E.	03 JAN 1881 R	20	4767
Johnson, Charles N.	Thomas, Barbara V.	01 JAN 1884	18	357
Johnson, Charles Sweet	Miller, Mary Elizabeth	04 FEB 1885 R	20	051
Johnson, Charley	Dorsey, Matilda	03 JAN 1885 L	20	003
Johnson, Charlotte	Jones, John Wesley	28 NOV 1878 R	12	352
Johnson, Chester	Brian, Sophia	13 NOV 1878 R	12	324
Johnson, Christie	Chisley, John Henry	20 APR 1882	16	323
Johnson, Clara	Stevens, John	15 DEC 1879 L	14	048
Johnson, Clara E.	Bodine, Hiram D.	27 MAR 1883 R	17	360
Johnson, Clarence	Hennigan, Eliza	31 JAN 1884	18	396
Johnson, Connerway	Simmons, Fanny E.	06 JUN 1878 R	12	089
Johnson, Cordelia L.	Jennings, Felix A.	08 AUG 1878 R	12	160
Johnson, Corinne	Miller, George C.	31 MAY 1881 L	15	332
Johnson, Cynthina	Jarboe, John H.	22 MAR 1882 L	16	286
Johnson, Daniel	Carter, Sarah	25 JUN 1883 R	18	013
Johnson, Daniel D.	Wilson, Julia	05 SEP 1884	19	229
Johnson, Daniel Philip	Rollins, Evelina	09 DEC 1884 R	19	442
Johnson, David	Stewart, Tabby	04 SEP 1877 L	11	075
Johnson, Dennis	Bradford, Grace	19 MAY 1880 L	14	277
Johnson, Dennis	Taylor, Emily	12 APR 1884 L	18	505
Johnson, Dora	Sanders, Ambrose	08 JAN 1878 R	11	295
Johnson, Edith B.	Stewart, Edward	12 DEC 1883	18	312
Johnson, Edward	Ricketts, Julia A.	24 SEP 1878 L	12	233
Johnson, Edward	Kirby, Sarah	29 JUN 1881 R	15	381
Johnson, Edward	Germeroth, Mary	19 MAR 1883 R	17	339
Johnson, Edward	Brown, Charlotte	26 APR 1883 R	17	413
Johnson, Edward	Hammond, Virginia	21 NOV 1883 L	18	269
Johnson, Edward	Fletcher, Emma	20 AUG 1884	19	196
Johnson, Edward	Gaines, Emma	04 DEC 1884 R	19	436
Johnson, Edward N.	Mudd, Gertrude C.	23 APR 1884	18	529
Johnson, Edwin	Kendrick, Kate	24 SEP 1885 R	20	442
Johnson, Edwin J.	Bohn, Theresa Marie	26 MAY 1880	14	285
Johnson, Eliza	Williams, John	26 AUG 1877 R	11	062
Johnson, Eliza	Chase, William H.	21 MAY 1879	13	199
Johnson, Eliza	Hawkins, Thomas D.	24 MAR 1881 L	15	238
Johnson, Eliza Jane	Mason, Henry Douglass	15 DEC 1880 R	15	100
Johnson, Eliza Louisa	Nolin, Gabriel Emanuel	10 APR 1882 L	16	307
Johnson, Elizabeth	Daniels, Benjamin	13 NOV 1878 R	12	283
Johnson, Elizabeth	Johnson, Henry	08 OCT 1879 L	13	410
Johnson, Elizabeth Jane	Alexander, Thomas E.	14 MAY 1878	12	051
Johnson, Elizabeth L. Dora	Craig, Andrew Cyrus	30 JAN 1884 R	18	401
Johnson, Ella	Moore, Traverse	19 DEC 1878 R	12	389
Johnson, Ella	Payne, John William	03 JUL 1879 R	13	258
Johnson, Ella	Newman, Randall	16 APR 1885 R	20	168
Johnson, Ella R.	Keys, Montgomery B.	07 APR 1885 L	20	148
Johnson, Ellen T.	Febiger, John C., U.S.N.	01 JUN 1882	16	387
Johnson, Ellenora	Brown, Henry	18 SEP 1879 L	13	377
Johnson, Elvira	Mansfield, John	13 SEP 1883 R	18	113
Johnson, Emily	Clomas, Griffin	04 AUG 1885 R	20	335
Johnson, Emily L.	Johnson, James	25 OCT 1880	15	006
Johnson, Emma	Moss, John	06 SEP 1877 L	11	078
Johnson, Emma	Duckett, Samuel	27 FEB 1879 R	13	055
Johnson, Emma	Johnson, John	15 NOV 1882 L	17	131
Johnson, Emma	Duvall, Albert	22 DEC 1884 R	19	475
Johnson, Emma	Williams, Philip	07 FEB 1884 L	18	416
Johnson, Emma Jane	Padgett, Washington	08 JUN 1880 R	14	310
Johnson, Eugene C.	Lee, Florence T.	23 JAN 1884 R	18	138

Johnson, Eva	Gant, George S.	07 AUG 1879	13	312
Johnson, Eva	Slauder, Burgess	23 JAN 1884 L	18	390
Johnson, F.S.	Reed, W.R.	14 FEB 1882	16	241
Johnson, Fannie R.	Burgess, James H.	29 AUG 1883	18	103
Johnson, Fanny	Carter, Champ	02 APR 1878 R	11	401
Johnson, Fleming	Beverly, Delphia	25 JUL 1882 R	16	413
Johnson, Florence A.	Hughes, Eli H.	11 OCT 1882 L	17	065
Johnson, Frances	Smith, Richard	28 NOV 1878	12	353
Johnson, Francis	Stewart, Martha	05 MAR 1883 L	17	382
Johnson, Frank	Fuller, Helen	06 SEP 1877 L	11	080
Johnson, Frank	Scroggin, Mattie	12 MAR 1879 R	13	095
Johnson, Frank	Mack, Georgeanna	17 DEC 1881 R	16	137
Johnson, French	Jackson, Sarah	04 SEP 1883 R	18	109
Johnson, Gabriel	Eskridge, Eliza	31 AUG 1882 R	16	494
Johnson, Gabriel F., Dr.	Lowe, Nelly R.	25 OCT 1881 R	16	043
Johnson, Garrison	Johnson, Henrietta	21 NOV 1883 L	18	269
Johnson, George	Soden, Maggie	06 AUG 1878 R	12	158
Johnson, George	Perry, Mary	28 AUG 1879 R	13	340
Johnson, George	DeMiends, Tressey	21 SEP 1880 L	14	453
Johnson, George	Beall, Ann Eliza Wallingsforth	04 NOV 1882 R	17	111
Johnson, George	Arnold, Priscilla	15 MAR 1883 L	17	347
Johnson, George	Jones, Rachel	05 MAR 1883 R	17	325
Johnson, George	Jackson, Lizzie	15 NOV 1884	19	372
Johnson, George A.	Heath, Annie E.	06 DEC 1883	18	302
Johnson, George Alfred	Parker, Martha A.V.	16 JAN 1885 L	20	023
Johnson, George Allen	Freeman, Martha	06 SEP 1883 R	18	114
Johnson, George H.	Jameson, Annie E.	03 MAR 1885	20	095
Johnson, George W.	Posey, Mary A.	29 MAY 1883 R	17	467
Johnson, Georgiana	Robinson, Newton	23 DEC 1880 L	15	117
Johnson, Georgiana	Wilson, Benjamin	21 AUG 1881	16	442
Johnson, Gilbert	Breckenridge, Hattie	12 SEP 1885 R	20	412
Johnson, Hamilton	Adams, Sarah	30 AUG 1877 L	11	071
Johnson, Hannah	Brown, Robert	05 MAY 1883 R	17	430
Johnson, Hannah	Washington, Wesley	27 OCT 1884 L	19	339
Johnson, Harriet	Williams, William	30 NOV 1878 L	12	356
Johnson, Harriet C.	Green, William H.	27 NOV 1881 R	16	099
Johnson, Harrison	Berry, Rosena	20 AUG 1884 L	19	197
Johnson, Harry	Grimes, Maria	07 APR 1881	15	247
Johnson, Hattie	Jones, Peter	08 DEC 1881 R	16	123
Johnson, Hattie	Huitt, Churchwell H.	30 APR 1884	18	544
Johnson, Helen	Parker, George W.	18 JUL 1877 L	11	025
Johnson, Hennie	Shadrach, James	09 JUN 1878	12	093
Johnson, Hennie	Taylor, John	08 MAY 1879	13	181
Johnson, Henrietta	Peyton, Leonard	15 JUL 1878 L	12	135
Johnson, Henrietta	Thomas, Oscar C.	20 MAY 1878 R	12	060
Johnson, Henrietta	Lee, Albert	15 JAN 1880 R	14	107
Johnson, Henrietta	Johnson, Garrison	21 NOV 1883 L	18	269
Johnson, Henry	Jones, Mary	14 AUG 1879	13	323
Johnson, Henry	Johnson, Elizabeth	08 OCT 1879 L	13	410
Johnson, Henry	Humphreys, Martha	01 NOV 1880 R	15	023
Johnson, Henry	Smallwood, Nettie	19 AUG 1880 R	14	405
Johnson, Henry	Simonds, Margaret	07 AUG 1880 L	14	392
Johnson, Henry	Cook, Nellie M.	14 JUL 1881 R	15	400
Johnson, Henry	Brandum, Maggie	20 FEB 1882 R	16	250
Johnson, Henry	Radcliffe, Getrude	04 AUG 1882 L	16	469
Johnson, Henry	Dorsey, Maria Izenna	14 NOV 1883	18	252
Johnson, Henry	Stewart, Mary A.	12 APR 1884 L	18	504
Johnson, Henry	Warren, Emily	14 MAY 1885	20	221

Johnson, Henson	Hill, Maria	18 JAN 1881 L	15	153
Johnson, Hillary	Ages, Anna	05 MAR 1885	20	059
Johnson, Hiram	Lowe, Rebecca	27 MAR 1878 L	11	396
Johnson, Hiram	Cole, Ella	24 FEB 1883 L	17	320
Johnson, Hiram	Lou, Rebecca	18 FEB 1884 L	18	429
Johnson, Horace	Simms, Louisa	20 AUG 1880 L	14	409
Johnson, Howard	Shepherd, Mary A.	18 NOV 1879 R	13	483
Johnson, Ida	Bell, Enoch	13 MAY 1880	14	264
Johnson, Ida D.	Henry, George B.	20 JAN 1882 L	16	203
Johnson, Ida E.	Mitchell, Francis E.	10 NOV 1881 L	16	070
Johnson, Ida L.	Davison, Joseph C.	20 AUG 1882 R	16	486
Johnson, Ida L.	Bergling, Henry G.	26 JUN 1883 R	18	015
Johnson, Ida M.	Rupp, Edward C.	21 DEC 1882 L	17	203
Johnson, Irene	Shepherd, Peter Ezekiel	10 APR 1884 R	18	503
Johnson, Isaac	Mahoney, Elizabeth	07 OCT 1878 R	12	241
Johnson, Isaac	Williams, Sarah	06 JUL 1882	16	441
Johnson, Isaac	Warren, Jane	03 JUL 1884 R	19	119
Johnson, Isabella	Jenkins, Henry	11 SEP 1878 L	12	213
Johnson, Isabella	Jenifer, Benjamin	11 JUN 1883 L	17	485
Johnson, J. Frank	Schwartz, [Maggie] Janie	26 NOV 1884 R	19	411
Johnson, J. Hiram	Mann, Evie	21 JAN 1879	13	028
Johnson, J. Hiram	Trunnel, Lizzie W.	15 OCT 1883	18	191
Johnson, J.W.	Box, Martha (Carter)	21 JUN 1883 R	18	005
Johnson, J.W.	Henderson, Luvinia	15 JUN 1885	20	273
Johnson, Jacob A.	Posy, Amanda V.	27 MAR 1884 R	18	485
Johnson, James	Brown, Harriet	23 OCT 1877 R	11	150
Johnson, James	Jackson, Lizzie	20 AUG 1877 R	11	057
Johnson, James	Johnson, Virginia	12 APR 1879 L	13	137
Johnson, James	Johnson, Emily L.	25 OCT 1880	15	006
Johnson, James	Addison, Josephine	09 SEP 1880 L	14	438
Johnson, James	Taney, Elizabeth	07 FEB 1881 R	15	176
Johnson, James	Bowles, Virginia	12 MAY 1881 L	15	303
Johnson, James	Burden, Mary	04 NOV 1881 R	15	431
Johnson, James	Jennings, Mary	29 MAY 1882 R	16	379
Johnson, James	Budd, Rosie	05 JUL 1883 L	18	035
Johnson, James	Page, Mary	23 NOV 1883 L	18	274
Johnson, James	Lanham, Rebecca	12 NOV 1884 L	19	377
Johnson, James D.	Hawkins, Mary E.	28 JUN 1877	11	002
Johnson, James H.	Moten, Mildred	31 MAY 1881 L	15	332
Johnson, James Henry	Smith, Ella	16 FEB 1883 L	17	310
Johnson, James W.	Lee, Rosa	04 APR 1878 R	11	404
Johnson, Jane	Jones, John O.	14 MAY 1882 R	16	359
Johnson, Jefferson	Sevoy, Eliza	02 APR 1879 L	13	123
Johnson, Jennie	Robinson, William	27 FEB 1879 R	13	081
Johnson, Jennie	Gardner, Alexander	22 DEC 1881 L	16	149
Johnson, Jennie	Smith, Frank	02 NOV 1881	16	058
Johnson, Jerome A.	Jackson, Anna M.	30 NOV 1878 L	12	357
Johnson, Jerry F.	Perry, Mary	02 APR 1883 L	17	373
Johnson, John	Williams, Julia	30 JUL 1877	11	015
Johnson, John	Alexander, Mary Shahan	02 APR 1878 R	11	400
Johnson, John	Hutton, Sophia	20 MAY 1878 L	12	061
Johnson, John	Spencer, Annie	22 OCT 1878 L	12	285
Johnson, John	Alexander, Malinda	10 JUL 1878 R	13	272
Johnson, John	Brown, Eliza E.	26 FEB 1880 R	14	164
Johnson, John	Bumry, Martha	15 DEC 1881 R	16	132
Johnson, John	Johnson, Emma	15 NOV 1882 L	17	131
Johnson, John	Parker, Lizzie	14 MAY 1884 L	19	019
Johnson, John	Drummer, Leonad	11 MAR 1885	20	106

Johnson, John	Brooke, Kate	06 OCT 1885 R	20	460
Johnson, John Altheus	Hobbs, Mary Linda	12 SEP 1883 R	18	126
Johnson, John Clinton	Hume, Sue Ellen	14 OCT 1885 R	20	477
Johnson, John F.	Wallace, Josephine	11 DEC 1879 L	14	044
Johnson, John H.	Douglass, Jennie	22 AUG 1884	19	203
Johnson, John Henry	Simms, Mary	12 NOV 1877	11	179
Johnson, John Henry	Rowe, Mary	29 APR 1881	15	285
Johnson, John Henry	Fox, Sallie	24 APR 1882 L	16	332
Johnson, John J.	Webb, Fannie M.	19 JAN 1882	16	198
Johnson, John Randall	Chase, Mary Ann	22 AUG 1877 R	11	060
Johnson, John T.	Mims, Sarah	10 SEP 1884 L	19	240
Johnson, John Thomas	Coleman, Mary Louisa	19 FEB 1883 R	17	310
Johnson, John Wesley	Bowie, Rachel	10 NOV 1879	13	474
Johnson, John Wesley	Birney, Geogeanna	01 MAY 1882 R	16	343
Johnson, Jordan	Hord, Frankie	01 SEP 1881	15	487
Johnson, Joseph	Davis, Elizabeth	15 MAY 1879 L	13	191
Johnson, Joseph	Tyler, Amnimia	06 MAY 1882	16	345
Johnson, Joseph	Simms, Maria	15 OCT 1884 R	19	308
Johnson, Joseph H., Jr.	Smith, Maggie E.	20 SEP 1883 R	18	143
Johnson, Joseph H.	Ware, Georgianna A.	22 JUL 1885 L	20	337
Johnson, Joseph L.	Cook, Mollie E.	09 FEB 1882 R	16	233
Johnson, Josephine	Hensin, John H.	14 JUN 1883 R	17	023
Johnson, Josephine R.	Shaw, Spencer	23 OCT 1883	18	208
Johnson, Julia	Lewis, Creed	04 JUL 1878	12	124
Johnson, Julia	Bird, Harvey	09 OCT 1879 R	13	399
Johnson, Julia	McPherson, Peter	29 DEC 1884 L	19	495
Johnson, Julia A.	Clarke, William H.	11 DEC 1878 R	12	377
Johnson, Julia A.	Cumber, James H.	22 AUG 1882 L	16	491
Johnson, Julie	Thomas, Ralph	25 SEP 1879 L	13	388
Johnson, Kate	Barnes, Joseph H.	13 MAY 1884 L	19	017
Johnson, Kate A.	Ober, Albert N.	18 DEC 1880 L	15	109
Johnson, Keseiah	Banner, Edward	20 FEB 1879 R	13	067
Johnson, Kittie	Green, William	27 JUN 1884 L	19	107
Johnson, Lafayette	Thomas, Betsy	23 DEC 1880 R	15	120
Johnson, Laura	Anderson, John	24 APR 1879 L	13	159
Johnson, Laura	Williams, Albert	11 NOV 1880 L	15	091
Johnson, Laura	Lee, Charles Henry	16 OCT 1884	19	317
Johnson, Laura Ester Joyce	Baldwin, Leander	18 JAN 1881 R	15	153
Johnson, Laurie	Lancaster, C.H.	07 JUN 1880	14	308
Johnson, Lawson	Jackson, Annie	29 AUG 1880	14	418
Johnson, Leanna	Gaskins, Moses	15 MAR 1880 L	14	185
Johnson, Lee	Brooks, Lizzie	03 JAN 1884 L	18	364
Johnson, Lenorah	Smith, Eugene S.	24 DEC 1884 L	19	489
Johnson, Letitia	Wanzer, Thomas Wm.	06 MAY 1880 R	14	255
Johnson, Levi	Stewart, Mary	18 DEC 1880 L	15	108
Johnson, Lewis	Wallace, Hannah	04 NOV 1880 L	15	031
Johnson, Lewis H.	Johnson, Margaret A.	06 AUG 1885 R	20	339
Johnson, Lidy	Hawkens, Robert	13 DEC 1884 R	32	7900
Johnson, Lillie	Jones, Sager	05 JAN 1885 R	20	001
Johnson, Lina	Bosley, Cornelius	23 MAR 1881 L	15	236
Johnson, Lizzie	Dixon, Carter	02 JAN 1883 L	17	231
Johnson, Logan	Williams, Julia A.	11 AUG 1880 R	14	387
Johnson, Lola	Bruno, Harry	23 JUN 1883 L	18	011
Johnson, Louis C.	Evans, Sarah I.	27 JUN 1883	18	018
Johnson, Louisa	Washington, Albert	30 OCT 1879 R	13	453
Johnson, Louisa	Childs, Washington	21 APR 1881 R	15	268
Johnson, Lucinda	Stevenson, Charles	17 SEP 1884	19	246
Johnson, Lucius	Johnson, Miranda	07 JUL 1881 L	15	394

Johnson, Lucy	Payne, Lewis S.	05 DEC 1883 L	18	297
Johnson, Lucy	Nally, Wesley	27 JAN 1884	18	389
Johnson, Lucy	Wade, John B.	03 FEB 1885 L	20	050
Johnson, Lucy Jane	Giles, James H.	19 MAR 1879 L	13	109
Johnson, Lulie	Hopkins, Charles	15 APR 1881 L	15	258
Johnson, Lydia	Brown, Edward	12 SEP 1877 R	11	089
Johnson, Lydia	McPherson, Robert	01 DEC 1884 R	19	428
Johnson, Mag	Lee, Archy	22 DEC 1880 L	15	116
Johnson, Maggie	Vailor, Daniel E.	01 FEB 1883	17	284
Johnson, Maggie	Yeager, Samuel F.	11 DEC 1883	18	310
Johnson, Malinda	Garnett, Charles	01 MAR 1882 L	16	262
Johnson, Mamie T.	Eberly, August F.	23 JAN 1879 R	13	025
Johnson, Margaret	Snowden, Benjamin	14 MAY 1881 L	15	306
Johnson, Margaret A.	Parker, George W.	30 APR 1878 R	12	030
Johnson, Margaret A.	Johnson, Lewis H.	06 AUG 1885 R	20	339
Johnson, Marguarite	Wells, Benjamin F.	22 FEB 1883	17	317
Johnson, Maria	Queen, John	27 NOV 1878 L	12	351
Johnson, Maria	Simms, John	17 JUN 1878 L	12	101
Johnson, Maria B.	Brown, John M.	06 JAN 1879 R	13	007
Johnson, Maria L.	Kent, Elias	21 FEB 1878 R	11	348
Johnson, Maria L.	Lyons, Frank	11 FEB 1884 L	18	419
Johnson, Marian A.	Brown, Winfield S.	10 SEP 1879 R	13	362
Johnson, Mark	Norman, Mary	06 JAN 1882	16	178
Johnson, Marshall L.	Oliver, Martha	03 NOV 1879 L	13	460
Johnson, Martha A.	Coats, Charles H.	19 NOV 1884 R	19	393
Johnson, Martin	Reed, Sarah	17 DEC 1883 L	18	319
Johnson, Martin G.W.	Gibson, Pamelia M.J.	08 JUN 1878 L	12	092
Johnson, Mary	Morton, John	17 JUL 1877	11	024
Johnson, Mary	Williams, William	17 SEP 1877 L	11	096
Johnson, Mary	Fry, Robert	15 MAR 1878	11	383
Johnson, Mary	Bogel, Essick	20 OCT 1879 R	13	430
Johnson, Mary	Walker, Edward	03 NOV 1881	16	061
Johnson, Mary	Tyler, Robert	08 JUN 1881 R	15	348
Johnson, Mary	Robinson, Benjamin	06 DEC 1883 L	18	299
Johnson, Mary	Smith, Thomas H.	15 NOV 1883 L	18	258
Johnson, Mary	Gee, David	09 OCT 1884 L	19	298
Johnson, Mary	Griffin, Oliver	18 DEC 1884 L	19	471
Johnson, Mary	Lanes, Elias	09 AUG 1884 L	19	177
Johnson, Mary	Miller, Austin	18 SEP 1884 L	19	256
Johnson, Mary A.	Simpson, Henry B.	31 DEC 1884 R	19	511
Johnson, Mary Ann	Hall, Philip	09 DEC 1879 R	14	034
Johnson, Mary Anne	Walker, John	14 JUN 1881 R	21	5071
Johnson, Mary E.	Cooper, George W.	13 MAY 1879	13	187
Johnson, Mary E.	Hawkins, Richard	06 JAN 1880 L	14	090
Johnson, Mary E.	Harris, Preston P.	03 OCT 1883 R	18	166
Johnson, Mary E.	Henderson, Thomas	28 OCT 1884 L	19	342
Johnson, Mary Ellen	Chase, William	05 SEP 1885 R	20	400
Johnson, Mary Frances	Taylor, John Andrew	10 JUN 1884 R	19	072
Johnson, Mary Jane	Countee, Richard	30 JUN 1881 R	15	383
Johnson, Mary Rose	Watkins, Geo. Archibald	21 SEP 1881 R	15	494
Johnson, Mary V.	Ennels, William Matthew	05 MAY 1881 R	15	291
Johnson, Mary V.	McKnee, John T.	19 MAR 1884 R	18	475
Johnson, Matilda	Johnson, Charles	06 AUG 1883	18	075
Johnson, Mattie	Bryant, William	19 APR 1882 L	16	326
Johnson, Mattie	Lee, Henry C.	25 SEP 1884	19	270
Johnson, Mattie L.	Short, Thomas	31 DEC 1878	12	410
Johnson, May	Burton, Walter	03 MAR 1879	13	086
Johnson, Miles	Taylor, Mary	11 SEP 1877 R	11	085

D.C. Marriage Records Index, June 28, 1877 to October 19, 1885

Johnson, Miranda	Johnson, Lucius	07 JUL 1881 L	15	394
Johnson, Mollie M.	McKenney, William H.	19 MAR 1884 R	18	475
Johnson, Moses	Daniels, Emma	09 JAN 1879 R	13	005
Johnson, Moses	Carter, Millie	05 NOV 1884 L	19	361
Johnson, Musette	Hill, Reuben B.	20 APR 1880	14	228½
Johnson, Nancy	Smith, John	01 JUL 1878 R	12	113
Johnson, Nannie	Lonesome, Frank L.	28 FEB 1882 L	16	261
Johnson, Nathaniel	Moncure, Caroline	27 FEB 1879 R	13	075
Johnson, Nelson	Welden, Eliza	13 DEC 1882 L	17	182
Johnson, Nettie	Green, Edward	24 DEC 1883 L	18	336
Johnson, Nettie	Williams, Patrick	14 JUL 1885 L	20	325
Johnson, Norman	Powell, Addel A. [Rachel]	27 JUL 1883	18	062
Johnson, Olivia	Busy, George	05 APR 1879	13	127
Johnson, Olmstead	Bell, Elizabeth	25 OCT 1877 R	11	154
Johnson, Oscar	Montgomery, Ann	25 SEP 1879	13	367
Johnson, Patsey	Holmes, John	24 DEC 1877 L	11	266
Johnson, Peter	Menefee, Belle, Mrs.	16 DEC 1880	15	099
Johnson, Peter	Smallwood, Mary	17 SEP 1882 R	17	003
Johnson, Peter Henry	Tobin, Lizzie Beatrice	01 JUL 1882 L	16	433
Johnson, Philip	Chase, Jane	05 JUN 1882 L	16	394
Johnson, Rachel Ann	Brown, Thomas Isaac	11 NOV 1880 R	15	031
Johnson, Rachel Ann	Taylor, Geo. Washington	10 MAY 1884 L	19	014
Johnson, Reuben	Lockett, Margaret	06 JUN 1881 R	15	346
Johnson, Reuben R.W.	Tuckson, Martha E.	18 JUN 1882	16	414
Johnson, Reverdy C.	Willis, Anna	08 MAY 1879	13	182
Johnson, Richard	Kooms, Gwenett	02 APR 1879	13	124
Johnson, Richard	Payne, Susan	24 AUG 1882 L	16	493
Johnson, Richard	Nelson, Mary	15 OCT 1882	17	070
Johnson, Richard H.	Mangan, Rachel, Mrs.	06 JUN 1881 R	15	345
Johnson, Robert	Mason, Alice	02 MAY 1879 L	10	171
Johnson, Robert	Lucas, Elizabeth	03 DEC 1879	14	024
Johnson, Robert	Wise, Julia A.	19 JUL 1880 R	14	368
Johnson, Robert	Hardaway, Mary	29 MAY 1884	19	044
Johnson, Robert Edward	Tinney, Emma Jane	31 JAN 1882 L	16	216
Johnson, Robert Harris	Martin, Bettie Serene	14 MAR 1879 R	13	102
Johnson, Rosa	Logan, John	13 DEC 1877 L	11	235
Johnson, Rosa	Ford, Andrew	12 MAY 1881 L	15	304
Johnson, Rosa	Anderson, David	11 NOV 1884 R	19	373
Johnson, Ruben E.	Parker, John H.	21 MAY 1884 L	19	033
Johnson, Rubin	Moxley, Gertrude	28 OCT 1880 R	15	018
Johnson, Sadie F.	DeNeale, Franklin T.	28 SEP 1880 R	14	461
Johnson, Sallie	Turner, Benjamin	26 APR 1880	14	238
Johnson, Sallie	Burnham, Henry W.	27 SEP 1881 R	15	495
Johnson, Sallie	Newman, Joseph W.	24 SEP 1885	20	439
Johnson, Samuel	Bowers, Louisa	15 AUG 1877 R	11	056
Johnson, Samuel	Turner, Jane	15 JUN 1882 R	16	400
Johnson, Samuel	Kelly, Lillie May	05 NOV 1883 L	18	233
Johnson, Samuel	Watson, Eliza	08 OCT 1883 L	18	178
Johnson, Samuel	Queen, Mary	30 OCT 1884 L	19	350
Johnson, Sandy	Trammell, Mary	07 JAN 1884 L	18	367
Johnson, Sarah	Smith, John	28 NOV 1877 L	11	207
Johnson, Sarah	Shanklin, Mason	03 SEP 1878 L	12	194
Johnson, Sarah	Roan, Anderson	18 SEP 1879 R	13	375
Johnson, Sarah	Gipson, Alfred	31 MAY 1881 R	15	333
Johnson, Sarah	Douglass, William	19 MAY 1884 R	19	028
Johnson, Sarah	Motion, Edward	29 OCT 1884 R	19	348
Johnson, Sarah A.	Blue, Samuel	14 FEB 1881 L	15	189
Johnson, Sarah C.	Hill, William	01 JUN 1885	20	246

Johnson, Sarah E.	Phelps, Richard L.	23 SEP 1877	11	073
Johnson, Sarah E.	Ricketts, Marchant Oliver	25 AUG 1880 R	14	415
Johnson, Sarah E.	Martin, Albert L.	02 NOV 1881 L	16	057
Johnson, Sarah F.	Ford, William	26 NOV 1879	14	015
Johnson, Sarah Jane	Taylor, Dennis	15 OCT 1885	20	477
Johnson, Sidonia R.	Thompson, Thomas A.	31 JAN 1885 L	20	045
Johnson, Simeon F.	Stutzman, Cora M.	17 MAY 1883	17	446
Johnson, Smith	Terrell, Matilda	06 MAR 1879 R	13	092
Johnson, Sophia	Butler, Robert	28 FEB 1883 L	17	327
Johnson, Sophia C.	Douglass, Frederick	20 JAN 1885	20	029
Johnson, Stephen R.	Guire, Annie	03 APR 1883 L	17	375
Johnson, Susan	Strawther, Benjamin	24 OCT 1878 R	12	290
Johnson, Susan	Young, John	31 JAN 1878 L	11	324
Johnson, Susanne	Oldberg, Charles John Rudolph	19 SEP 1877 R	11	097
Johnson, Susie	Phillips, William	01 JAN 1878	11	288
Johnson, Susie	Green, John W.	27 SEP 1882 L	17	040
Johnson, Theophilus	Redinger, Pauline	11 APR 1882 L	16	308
Johnson, Thomas	King, Frances	26 MAY 1879	13	200
Johnson, Thomas	Poole, Martha	25 JUL 1879	13	286
Johnson, Thomas	Gibson, Elizabeth	27 MAY 1880	14	292
Johnson, Thomas	Calvert, Amelia	18 JAN 1881 L	15	152
Johnson, Thomas	Day, Fanny	27 MAY 1881 R	15	212
Johnson, Thomas	Barnes, Annie	06 FEB 1882 L	16	227
Johnson, Thomas	Hughes, Lottie	28 MAR 1883 L	17	366
Johnson, Thomas	Napier, Jennie	25 OCT 1883 R	18	214
Johnson, Thomas	Taylor, Mary	28 SEP 1883	18	123
Johnson, Thomas	Summerville, Mary E.	31 JAN 1884 L	18	403
Johnson, Thomas C.	Beall, Annie J.L.	14 JUN 1884 L	19	084
Johnson, Thomas C.	Norton, Harriet A.	31 DEC 1884 L	19	520
Johnson, Thomas E.	Kennedy, Susanna	28 FEB 1884 L	18	450
Johnson, Thomas M.	Tilley, Sarah E.	27 APR 1882	16	331
Johnson, Virginia	Johnson, James	12 APR 1879 L	13	137
Johnson, Walker	Morris, Charlotte	22 SEP 1877	11	105
Johnson, Walter S.	Woodward, Jennie Miller	27 MAY 1882 R	16	378
Johnson, Washington	Adams, Ellen	17 DEC 1877 L	11	239
Johnson, Washington	Countee, Laura	01 FEB 1883 R	17	285
Johnson, Wesley	Matson, Addie	28 JAN 1878 R	11	318
Johnson, Wesley S.	Williams, Mary C.	23 APR 1878 L	12	019
Johnson, Will W.	Sterne, Victoria	20 NOV 1882	17	136
Johnson, William	Bowie, Maria	10 JAN 1878 R	11	297
Johnson, William	Ellis, Jane	25 SEP 1880 L	14	459
Johnson, William	Harris, Fannie	17 DEC 1880 L	15	107
Johnson, William	Morgan, Josphine	09 DEC 1882 L	17	176
Johnson, William	Brown, Rachel	14 AUG 1883 L	18	086
Johnson, William	Welcome, Winnie	13 JUL 1884	19	132
Johnson, William	Jackson, Frances	01 JUL 1885 R	20	304
Johnson, William	Brown, Mary	01 OCT 1885 L	20	451
Johnson, William B.	White, Getrude A.	26 FEB 1880 R	14	165
Johnson, William B.	Roseweg, Ella N.	12 FEB 1883	17	302
Johnson, William E.	Nelson, Harvie H.	16 JUN 1880 R	14	315
Johnson, William, Elder	Pace, Pinkey	24 AUG 1885 R	20	384
Johnson, William H.	Boston, Adaline	27 SEP 1877 L	11	112
Johnson, William H.	Perry, Alice	04 DEC 1877	11	218
Johnson, William H.	Brent, Jennie D.	27 NOV 1877	11	197
Johnson, William H.	Marmaduke, Bee	09 JUN 1879 R	13	224
Johnson, William H.	Radebaugh, Mary J.	15 JUN 1880 R	14	319
Johnson, William H.	Wilson, Nora Lee	06 DEC 1882 R	17	169
Johnson, William H.	Banks, Sarah M.	10 JUL 1884 L	19	133

Johnson, William H.	Armstrong, Mary C.	14 OCT 1885 L	20	480
Johnson, William Henry	Jones, Elizabeth	15 JUL 1881 L	15	404
Johnson, William Henry	Brown, Eliza E.	27 AUG 1885	20	386
Johnson, William J.	Ritchie, Emma A.	28 SEP 1882 R	17	038
Johnson, William S.	Marks, Mary Frances	15 NOV 1883 L	18	257
Johnson, William T.	Smackum, Emma Jane	30 OCT 1879 R	13	432
Johnson, William Thomas	Bates, Mary	28 JUL 1881 R	15	422
Johnson, Willie	Davis, Thomas	27 SEP 1877	11	114
Johnson, Willis	Mills, Adelin	15 NOV 1883 L	18	258
Johnson, Willis	Harris, Nancy	15 DEC 1883 L	18	317
Johnson, Windsor	Nolan, Carrie	19 MAY 1881	15	318
Johnson, Winnie	Thomas, Lewis	07 APR 1885 L	20	151
Johnson, Wm. Crawford, Dr.	Gouverneur, Ruth Monroe	06 DEC 1882 R	17	168
Johnson, Wm. H.	Snyder, Florence H.	22 JUL 1885	20	336
Johnson, Wm. L.	Trunnell, M.E.	23 JUL 1883 L	18	058
Johnston, Ada H.	Weiss, William J.	23 DEC 1884 R	19	477
Johnston, Anna E. Barrett	Reinlein, Paul	06 OCT 1879 R	13	404
Johnston, Annie	Scott, Robert	23 OCT 1880 L	15	011
Johnston, Annie E.	Bury, George B.	18 JUN 1885 L	20	280
Johnston, Charles E.	Soper, Laura Hicks	22 OCT 1882 R	17	084
Johnston, Emma L.	Lewis, Richard H.	05 MAR 1878 L	11	373
Johnston, George M.	Garrett, Carrie E.	19 SEP 1883 R	18	142
Johnston, Georgianna	Thomas, John	19 JUN 1882 L	16	418
Johnston, Henry A.	Brooks, Eva S.	10 NOV 1880 R	15	041
Johnston, J.R.	Fairfax, Emma L.	14 JUN 1881 L	15	362
Johnston, James	Smith, Sallie	24 FEB 1880	14	164
Johnston, John Henry	Taylor, Millery	01 AUG 1884	19	163
Johnston, John Pierce	Van Vleck, Elizabeth C.	29 FEB 1880 R	14	169
Johnston, Kate Arlena	Bastianelli, Adrian	22 NOV 1882 R	17	138
Johnston, Lizzie Anne	Reynolds, William	12 APR 1883 R	17	391
Johnston, Margaret Stewart	Pratt, James Calcott	11 OCT 1880 R	18	187
Johnston, Margery M.	Ortlip, Charles J.	14 AUG 1879 R	13	321
Johnston, Mary	Stuart, Reuben	06 OCT 1882 L	17	058
Johnston, Mary A.	Seitz, Lawrence A.	02 SEP 1881 R	15	465
Johnston, Mary Ann	Monroe, David Lloyd	28 MAY 1878 L	12	070
Johnston, Mary E.	Hodgson, Thomas A.	13 DEC 1882 L	17	181
Johnston, Matthew B.	Clarkson, Cecilia M.	28 APR 1883 L	17	419
Johnston, Middleton	Jackson, Luena	07 AUG 1884	19	175
Johnston, Robert	Fuller, Minnie	15 NOV 1881	16	076
Johnston, Thomas H.	Dorsey, Carrie A.	22 JUL 1884 R	19	151
Johnston, Thurston B.	Stuart, Alice C.	17 OCT 1880 R	14	499
Johnston, Thurston B.	Stuart, Alice C.	14 OCT 1885 R	20	480
Johnston, W.J.	Flynn, Annie T.	09 DEC 1879 L	14	038
Johnston, William E.	Burr, Mary	15 OCT 1884	19	310
Johnston, William Henry	Lahey, Ellen	12 FEB 1882 R	16	237
Johnstone, Lidie McPherson	McCarty, Richard Jay	03 JAN 1882 R	16	178
Johnstone, W.B.	Harvard, M.E.S.	01 DEC 1881	16	110
Joice, H.L.	Perry, H.M.	12 OCT 1882	17	068
Joiner, Samuel	Harris, Maria	10 MAY 1882 L	16	355
Jolley, Jefferson D.	Owens, Annie Elizabeth	31 JUL 1882 R	16	462
Jonas, LeRoy D.	Haner, Etta G.	26 MAY 1885	20	241
Jones, Aaron	Jackson, Harriet	30 SEP 1885	20	449
Jones, Addie	Kelly, William	09 JAN 1879	13	012
Jones, Agnes	Henry, Washington	19 OCT 1880 R	14	493
Jones, Albert L.	Tylor, Anna M.	26 OCT 1882	17	087
Jones, Alexander	Lockner, Emma	18 NOV 1878	12	331
Jones, Alice	Smith, James	02 JUN 1878	12	077
Jones, Alice	Miller, George	12 OCT 1880 L	14	488

Jones, Alice C.	Bottriell, John W.	03 JUN 1879	13	216
Jones, Alice Cornelia	Gibbins, Chas. Matthew	09 OCT 1878	12	263
Jones, Alice Leeatha	Hall, Peter	11 SEP 1884 R	19	241
Jones, Allen	Wells, Nellie	02 JUL 1883 R	17	498
Jones, Alvin M.	Reed, Annie E.	10 MAR 1885	20	098
Jones, Andrew	Tasco, Annie E.	07 SEP 1880 R	14	434
Jones, Andrew Coles	Harris, Annie Lee	04 JUL 1881 R	15	386
Jones, Andrew J.	Bozeman, Ada A.	10 OCT 1883	18	185
Jones, Ann R.	Chase, Robert A.	26 APR 1879 R	13	158
Jones, Annie	Watson, Robert	27 FEB 1883 L	17	324
Jones, Annie B.	Lokey, James B.	06 JUL 1880	14	349
Jones, Annie E.	Poole, Wm. Thos.	14 APR 1880	14	221
Jones, Annie M.	Holland, Charles R.	06 MAR 1879 R	13	087
Jones, Annie N.	Gardner, William H.	13 OCT 1880 R	14	482
Jones, Anthony	Lawson, Charlotte	04 OCT 1880 L	14	472
Jones, Anthony	Pryor, Fannie E.	24 JAN 1884 L	18	394
Jones, Archie	Smith, Rosa E.	17 AUG 1882	16	485
Jones, Augustus	Williams, Elizabeth	21 AUG 1879 R	13	329
Jones, Barbara M.	Mitchell, John H.	06 OCT 1881 R	16	004
Jones, Beckie	Gordon, James G.	24 JAN 1883 L	17	274
Jones, Belmore	Weaver, Annie	24 DEC 1877	11	256
Jones, Benjamin A.	Williams, Anna E.	29 NOV 1883	18	280
Jones, Benjamin Franklin	Owens, Annie Eliza	10 DEC 1884 R	19	446
Jones, Bettie	Reed, Joseph Anditon	20 OCT 1881 R	16	039
Jones, Bettie	Harris, Frederick	23 APR 1884 R	18	528
Jones, Blake	Dyson, Sallie	28 DEC 1881 R	25	6108
Jones, Broadus H.	McCarty, Mary A.	01 NOV 1879 L	13	457
Jones, Carrie	Thornton, John C.	23 OCT 1878	12	287
Jones, Catharine	Bumbach, Amandus	24 JUL 1879 L	13	290
Jones, Catharine Ann	Warrick, Thomas Bolton	31 DEC 1878 R	12	409
Jones, Catherine	Moore, John H.	13 NOV 1879 L	13	479
Jones, Catherine C.	Holmes, George W.	04 MAR 1879 L	13	089
Jones, Celia	Lyles, Robert	13 NOV 1879 R	13	482
Jones, Celia Ann	Fowler, Walter	04 OCT 1881 R	15	505
Jones, Charity	Lockley, John	09 OCT 1885	20	471
Jones, Charles	Lowe, Laura	04 MAR 1878	11	369
Jones, Charles	Hall, Annie	18 OCT 1881	16	030
Jones, Charles W.	Anderson, Mary S.	27 DEC 1881 L	16	158
Jones, Charles Wash.	Carter, Mary	16 MAR 1885 L	20	115
Jones, Clement	Washington, Ida	12 NOV 1883 L	18	246
Jones, Creed	Offut, Susan	27 OCT 1879 R	13	445
Jones, Dallas	Lewis, Ailsey	16 OCT 1879 R	13	419
Jones, Daniel	Jones, Mary	14 NOV 1878 L	12	331
Jones, David	Hall, Josephine	06 DEC 1883 L	18	302
Jones, Dennis	Ross, Fannie	22 JUN 1882 R	16	402
Jones, Edmund	Peterson, Lucy	06 JUN 1878 L	12	088
Jones, Edward	Swear, Mary	26 OCT 1880 R	15	014
Jones, Edward	Finnell, Lucy	16 MAY 1885 R	20	225
Jones, Edwin D.	Lotz, Nancy J.	27 FEB 1884	18	447
Jones, Edwin F.	Seavers, Amy	10 JAN 1878	11	297
Jones, Edwin P.	Pettit, Mary Elizabeth	15 MAR 1883	17	349
Jones, Eliza A.	Mercer, John T.	01 DEC 1880 R	15	076
Jones, Elizabeth	Brooks, Levi	16 NOV 1881	16	074
Jones, Elizabeth	Johnson, William Henry	15 JUL 1881 L	15	404
Jones, Elizabeth A.	Davis, John, Rev.	03 OCT 1882	17	049
Jones, Elizabeth M.	Whidbee, John A.	09 APR 1884	18	502
Jones, Ella	Lewis, Frank	21 SEP 1877	11	103
Jones, Ella	Eimer, John Philip	09 JUL 1878	12	125

Jones, Ella	Morse, Oliver C.	22 JUN 1881 R	15	370
Jones, Ella B.	Stewart, John C.	29 OCT 1884	19	346
Jones, Ella T.	Dement, Edward N.	27 JUN 1882 R	16	425
Jones, Ellen	Burris, Benjamin	18 APR 1881	15	260
Jones, Elmira	Miller, John	01 MAR 1879 R	13	081
Jones, Emily	Page, Abraham	12 JUL 1877 R	11	006
Jones, Emily A.G.	Braunstein, Louis	18 SEP 1884	19	258
Jones, Emma	Ross, Aaron	18 DEC 1879 L	14	056
Jones, Emma	Cloyd, Alfred	31 MAY 1882 L	16	383
Jones, Emma B.	Stidham, Samuel H.	27 MAR 1883 L	17	362
Jones, Everet	Hunter, Louisa	02 APR 1879 L	13	124
Jones, Fannie E.	Williamson, John T.	19 NOV 1879 R	13	495
Jones, Fitzhugh C.	Meaneley, Irene B.	25 MAR 1885 R	20	132
Jones, Frances E.	Quinn, William	20 FEB 1878 R	11	348
Jones, Frances E.	Berry, Charles H.	03 NOV 1884 R	19	430
Jones, Francis A.	Burroughs, Mary A.	15 JAN 1880 R	14	103
Jones, Francis A.	Neal, Mary J.	03 FEB 1880 L	14	133
Jones, Frank W.	Bland, Irene	05 SEP 1885	20	400
Jones, Frank Y.	Ferguson, Ella M.	15 SEP 1885 R	20	418
Jones, G. Tucker	Fletcher, Inazella F.	01 JAN 1879	13	001
Jones, G.E.	Cosby, Leppie	20 NOV 1883 L	18	276
Jones, G.E.	Cosby, Teppie	26 NOV 1883 R	29	7111
Jones, George	Scott, Mary	31 MAR 1880 R	14	192
Jones, George	Farr, Clementia, Mrs.	06 DEC 1882 R	17	164
Jones, George	Easton, Lydia	13 FEB 1883 L	17	303
Jones, George A.	Smith, Mary E.	29 JAN 1878	11	320
Jones, George Alfred	Ford, Gerty	08 SEP 1881 L	15	477
Jones, George B.	Lincom, George A.	27 NOV 1881	16	094
Jones, George J.	Catlet, Lucy Ann	18 MAR 1879 L	13	103
Jones, George W.	Boswell, Elmira	09 APR 1880 R	14	218
Jones, George W.	Harper, Lurena E.	04 JUL 1882	16	432
Jones, George William	Crandy, Annie	04 SEP 1879 R	13	350
Jones, Georgianna	Lee, William Francis	11 AUG 1882 R	16	472
Jones, Georgie	Brooks, John E.	26 AUG 1879 R	13	336
Jones, Georgie	Collins, Lewis	11 MAR 1885 R	20	108
Jones, Gertrude	Jackson, William	24 JAN 1884	18	393
Jones, H. Clay	Crockett, Lillian Patton	21 NOV 1882 R	17	140
Jones, Harriet	Bird, Alexander	14 OCT 1880	14	493
Jones, Harriet	Countee, William	09 JUN 1881 L	15	354
Jones, Harrison	Newman, Maria	28 MAY 1885	20	238
Jones, Harry S.	Kellum, Virginia McC.	23 MAR 1883 R	17	356
Jones, Henrietta	Thompson, Samuel	16 MAY 1879 L	13	194
Jones, Henrietta	Ball, John Robert	19 SEP 1883 R	18	141
Jones, Henry	Jefferson, Eliza	23 APR 1878 R	12	016
Jones, Henry	Wood, Rachel Lovetta	04 JUN 1884 R	19	056
Jones, Henry	Ellis, Eliza	13 JUL 1885	20	322
Jones, Henry A.	Keazer, Ellen M.	18 JAN 1882	16	199
Jones, Herline	McPherson, Henry	18 OCT 1884 L	19	318
Jones, Hester	Lymon, John	15 SEP 1885 L	20	417
Jones, Hetty	Thomas, Charles	12 DEC 1877 R	11	231
Jones, Ida	Woodard, William	04 OCT 1877	11	040
Jones, Ida	Major, Richard	23 AUG 1881	15	455
Jones, Ida A.	Shreve, William O., Jr.	12 AUG 1878 L	12	164
Jones, Ida Mary	Jones, James Walter	23 SEP 1880 R	14	452
Jones, Isaac	Eiler, Mary	26 OCT 1881 R	22	5312
Jones, Isabella	Cox, Edward D.	25 MAY 1880 R	14	287
Jones, Isabella	Gaskins, William	24 JUN 1885 R	20	284
Jones, J. Moulton	Gardiner, Mary Alice	07 JUL 1885	20	314

Jones, James	Tolson, Ida	06 JAN 1880 L	14	092
Jones, James	Fuller, Catherine	29 AUG 1881 L	15	464
Jones, James	Patterson, Ida	12 JUL 1882 L	16	445
Jones, James	Billingsly, Ellen	05 JUL 1885 L	20	054
Jones, James	Hughes, Lilly	08 JAN 1885 R	20	009
Jones, James D.	Scott, Cornelia	05 JUN 1879 L	13	220
Jones, James L.	Rollins, Annie R.	14 SEP 1882 R	17	022
Jones, James W.	Woodyard, Ida M.	24 FEB 1885 L	20	084
Jones, James Walter	Jones, Ida Mary	23 SEP 1880 R	14	452
Jones, Jane	Arnold, George W.	21 JUN 1879 L	13	242
Jones, Jane	Codley, Archie	05 OCT 1885 L	20	456
Jones, Jeff	Gunnell, Laura	24 MAY 1883 R	17	461
Jones, John	Douglas, Emaline	08 AUG 1878	12	161
Jones, John	Washington, Ella	15 APR 1879 L	13	144
Jones, John	Dyer, Mary R.	11 NOV 1879 R	13	476
Jones, John	Stevenson, Eliza	05 JAN 1881 L	15	140
Jones, John	Turner, Alice	18 DEC 1882 L	17	189
Jones, John	McKern, Katie	22 JUN 1885 L	20	283
Jones, John Alfred	Simms, Josephine	04 JUL 1882	16	436
Jones, John H.	Hart, Mamie E.	29 NOV 1882 R	17	157
Jones, John Henry	Warren, Martha	11 JUN 1883	17	486
Jones, John J.	Bailey, Aimee E.	01 JUN 1878	12	079
Jones, John O.	Johnson, Jane	14 MAY 1882 R	16	359
Jones, John Robert	Kane, Mary	16 NOV 1882 R	17	131
Jones, John T.	Washington, Eliza, Mrs.	21 APR 1883	17	403
Jones, John Wesley	Johnson, Charlotte	28 NOV 1878 R	12	352
Jones, John William	Allen, Maria	10 MAR 1885 R	20	104
Jones, John Wm.	Hicks, Rosa	08 OCT 1884	19	292
Jones, Joseph	Lee, Mary	04 MAY 1882 L	16	350
Jones, Joseph	Fisher, Hattie	14 DEC 1882	17	183
Jones, Joseph J.	Holtzman, Catharine Celestine	02 OCT 1879 R	13	398
Jones, Judith A.	Clay, Hyrel A.	05 MAY 1879	13	174
Jones, Julia N.	Higginson, William L.	13 MAR 1885 L	20	140
Jones, Katie	Locket, John	03 AUG 1882	16	467
Jones, Katie L.	Jennings, Joseph E.	14 JUL 1880 L	14	360
Jones, Laura	Turner, Thomas	05 MAR 1879 L	13	091
Jones, Laura	Boswell, Samuel	04 MAR 1880 L	14	175
Jones, Lavinia	Pynn, Samuel	09 JAN 1879 L	13	012
Jones, Lelia	Coughlein, James	03 NOV 1884	19	356
Jones, Levi	Ellis, Mary C.	19 FEB 1878 L	11	347
Jones, Lewis	Burley, Hattie	10 MAR 1885 R	20	098
Jones, Lewis C.	Steuart, Maggie	11 NOV 1884 R	19	359
Jones, Lewis C.	Taylor, Rosa J.	29 SEP 1885	20	425
Jones, Lewis G.	Purks, Bettie G.	28 DEC 1884	19	495
Jones, Lizzie E.	Banks, William H.	02 JAN 1879	13	005
Jones, Lola C.	Miller, John L.	06 APR 1880 R	14	211
Jones, Lottie	Hamilton, Henry	08 AUG 1882 R	16	470
Jones, Louis	Fisher, Mary	10 MAY 1883 R	17	435
Jones, Louisa	Bass, Hamilton	13 SEP 1877 L	11	091
Jones, Lucy	Butler, Frank	19 JUN 1878	12	104
Jones, Lucy	Berryman, Robert	31 JUL 1879 R	13	296
Jones, Lucy	Thomas, Walter W.	12 JAN 1885 L	20	013
Jones, Lucy A.	Burch, Robert R.	07 NOV 1882 L	17	115
Jones, Lula S.	Perry, Fred C.	27 SEP 1877	11	113
Jones, Maggie E.	Baker, John L.	10 DEC 1884 L	19	449
Jones, Maggie V.	Morse, William A.	02 MAR 1885	33	8068
Jones, Margaret	Marshall, Vincent	13 SEP 1877 R	11	091
Jones, Margaret	Brown, Joseph	04 MAY 1885 R	20	203

Jones, Maria	Little, George W.	21 OCT 1880 R	15	008
Jones, Maria	Tilton, Peter G.	15 MAY 1884	19	024
Jones, Marian	Brown, Edward	09 MAR 1880 R	14	180
Jones, Marian	Garner, John W.	20 APR 1880	14	227
Jones, Martha	Early, William	20 AUG 1884	19	196
Jones, Martha Ann	Stewart, John	11 JUN 1885 L	20	269
Jones, Mary	Jones, Daniel	14 NOV 1878 L	12	331
Jones, Mary	Holling, Charles	14 APR 1879	13	142
Jones, Mary	Johnson, Henry	14 AUG 1879	13	323
Jones, Mary	Foster, Edward	28 MAR 1883	17	367
Jones, Mary C.	Cobb, Norvell H.	27 JAN 1880 R	14	121
Jones, Mary Catherine	Coleman, Alexander B.	30 NOV 1880 R	15	073
Jones, Mary E.	Nothey, John	12 MAY 1884	19	015
Jones, Mary Elizabeth	Morris, Charles	23 DEC 1882 L	17	207
Jones, Mary Elizabeth	Anderson, Thomas H.	03 OCT 1883	18	164
Jones, Mary Frances	Lewis, Peter	12 MAR 1879 R	13	097
Jones, Mary G.	Milburn, Lewis C.	17 FEB 1885	20	035
Jones, Mary M.	Smith, Robert F.	03 NOV 1880	15	025
Jones, Matthew	Blueit, Ella	29 MAY 1882 L	16	381
Jones, Mattie E.	Bell, Solon L.	02 DEC 1880 R	15	077
Jones, Melville E.	Taylor, Ellen M.C.	31 JUL 1879 R	13	301
Jones, Mollie J.	Thurston, William Henry	16 JUN 1881 R	15	363
Jones, Moses	Brown, Lucy Dora	25 AUG 1879	13	333
Jones, Nelson	Smith, Mary Jane	25 MAY 1881	15	325
Jones, Owen	Lee, Mary E.	21 AUG 1879	13	325
Jones, Owen W.	Birch, Mary Estelle	14 OCT 1885 R	20	483
Jones, P.B.	Cook, Mary E.	25 SEP 1879	13	500
Jones, Patsie	Payne, Lewis	09 OCT 1882 L	17	060
Jones, Peter	Lane, Louisa	23 SEP 1880 L	14	458
Jones, Peter	Johnson, Hattie	08 DEC 1881 R	16	123
Jones, Peter	Hawkins, Bettie	26 JUL 1883	18	062
Jones, Philip	Ioward, Emma	18 SEP 1883 L	18	139
Jones, R.C., Col.	O'Donnell, Mary, Mrs.	05 JUN 1884 L	19	063
Jones, Rachel	Johnson, George	05 MAR 1883 R	17	325
Jones, Richard H.	Norton, Minnie C.	17 MAY 1881 R	15	314
Jones, Richard R.	Clark, Mary M.	22 DEC 1877 L	11	259
Jones, Robert H.	Jackson, Louisa	08 JAN 1878	11	296
Jones, Robert W.	Sanders, Annie	10 MAR 1884 R	18	463
Jones, Roberta J.	Beck, Lyman Seely	02 NOV 1883 R	18	229
Jones, Roberta Jackson	Jones, William Elmore	19 APR 1881 R	15	264
Jones, Rosa L.	Nalle, John C.	27 MAR 1879	13	111
Jones, Rose	More, Frederick	21 SEP 1885 L	20	430
Jones, Sager	Johnson, Lillie	05 JAN 1885 R	20	001
Jones, Sallie	Holmes, Charles E.	14 JUN 1883 R	17	487
Jones, Sally	Gills, Charles	22 JAN 1880	14	104
Jones, Samuel	Taylor, Margaret	02 OCT 1877 R	11	119
Jones, Samuel	Taylor, Elizabeth	09 JUL 1878	12	130
Jones, Samuel	Payne, Nellie	22 MAR 1883 R	17	355
Jones, Samuel A.	Randall, Annie	26 JAN 1878 R	11	317
Jones, Samuel M.	Golden, Cornelia G.	21 JAN 1885	20	027
Jones, Sarah	Greenleaf, Tillman	23 MAR 1880 R	14	157
Jones, Sarah	Page, Horace	01 NOV 1883	18	225
Jones, Sarah	Wood, Nathaniel	03 NOV 1884 L	19	355
Jones, Sarah E.	Christian, Albert P.	22 MAR 1883 R	17	354
Jones, Sarena	White, Thomas	13 DEC 1883 L	18	316
Jones, Sidney	Mason, James	23 OCT 1884 L	19	335
Jones, Sina	Hankins, Jacob	16 JUN 1882 R	16	414
Jones, Sophia	Jefferson, Albert C.	14 SEP 1882 L	17	021

Jones, Susan	Smith, Jacob	27 NOV 1883 L	18	279
Jones, Sylvester	Hall, Annie	24 SEP 1885 L	20	441
Jones, Theophilus	Walker, Delia	21 DEC 1881 R	16	142
Jones, Thomas	Boyd, Louisa	12 NOV 1879	13	480
Jones, Thomas	Anderson, Annie	03 NOV 1882	17	108
Jones, Thomas	Haggin, Cassie M.	17 SEP 1884	19	255
Jones, Thomas A.	Hill, Rosa	13 OCT 1883 L	18	190
Jones, Thomas H.	Phillips, Lucy Duncan	16 NOV 1881 R	16	072
Jones, Thomas Henry	Moore, Alice	08 JUN 1885 L	20	260
Jones, Thomas L.	Light, Matilda	18 OCT 1885 R	20	492
Jones, Thomas Rozzel	Davis, Minnie Ellsworth	02 FEB 1882 R	16	218
Jones, Virginia	Mitchell, Charles A.	12 MAY 1880 L	14	268
Jones, Virginia E.	Hewitt, Samuel S.	05 AUG 1879 L	13	308
Jones, Virginia W.	Morton, William A.	23 DEC 1880 R	15	121
Jones, Walter	Meredith, Charity	25 DEC 1881 R	16	148
Jones, Walter S.	Simonds, Katie C.	18 DEC 1882 R	17	190
Jones, William	Porter, Lizzie	06 SEP 1878	12	203
Jones, William	Washington, Millie	09 DEC 1879	14	037
Jones, William	Northridge, Mary Jane	10 JAN 1880 R	14	100
Jones, William	Stewart, Mary Alice	13 APR 1881 L	15	256
Jones, William	Kiner, Rose	19 APR 1882 L	16	325
Jones, William Botts	Lamkin, Minnie V.	03 AUG 1882 R	16	466
Jones, William Elmore	Jones, Roberta Jackson	19 APR 1881 R	15	264
Jones, William F.	Merrick, Margaret	05 JUL 1877	11	008
Jones, William Francis	Carter, Lucy Ann	03 FEB 1881 R	15	176
Jones, William H.	Edwards, Louisa	22 AUG 1878 R	12	169
Jones, William H.	Thomas, Sarah	30 SEP 1882 L	17	045
Jones, William H.	Douglas, Frazier T.	27 NOV 1883 L	18	279
Jones, William H.	Smith, Emma J.	24 DEC 1884 R	19	486
Jones, William H.	Somerville, Annie	18 MAY 1885 L	20	228
Jones, William Henry	Chase, Sarah Frances	18 JUN 1880	14	325
Jones, William J.	Howlett, Ella	31 JAN 1883	17	280
Jones, William M.	Baylor, Sarah	19 JUN 1884 L	19	093
Jones, William T.	Keleher, Annie E.	26 SEP 1878 R	12	236
Jones, William Wright	Flournoy, Lettie Carrington	14 MAY 1883 R	17	437
Jones, Wm. F.	Williams, Mary Langdonia Va.	07 JUL 1881 L	15	395
Jones, Worthington L.	Cook, Alice E.	05 APR 1878 R	11	407
Jonscher, Robert Frederick	Mansell, Annie Eliz.	31 MAR 1884 R	18	487
Jonson, Mollie, Mrs.	Keith, Judge F.	15 FEB 1881 R	15	183
Jony, Pierre Louis	Craig, Alice Elizabeth	26 JUN 1879 R	13	253
Joost, Fanny Genevieve	Frederich, Leon L., M.D.	05 APR 1881 R	15	246
Jordan, Alexander	Parker, Mary	12 DEC 1883	18	350
Jordan, Alice	Wise, Nathan	02 JUN 1879	13	176
Jordan, Braxton	Russell, Lizzie	08 SEP 1881 R	15	476
Jordan, Cherry	Gantt, Susan	04 DEC 1877 L	11	219
Jordan, Edward L.	Stewart, Ella E.	18 MAY 1882 R	16	365
Jordan, George	Young, Isabella	03 MAR 1885 R	20	093
Jordan, Hannah E.	Jordan, John T.	22 APR 1879 R	13	154
Jordan, Ida Blanche	Dunnington, George G.	29 OCT 1884	19	346
Jordan, Ida Frances	Bouler, Charlie E.	19 MAY 1882	16	365
Jordan, Ida V.	Pemberton, Frank O.	13 AUG 1877	11	052
Jordan, Isabella	Reed, Charles Henry	10 SEP 1878 R	12	206
Jordan, James	Hurd, Lizzie	29 JAN 1884 L	18	401
Jordan, James	Mason, Katie	14 JUL 1884	19	138
Jordan, Jane	Wood, Charles	10 JAN 1884 L	18	373
Jordan, John L., Jr.	Lyons, Amanda	19 FEB 1879 L	13	067
Jordan, John T.	Jordan, Hannah E.	22 APR 1879 R	13	154
Jordan, Julia	Lee, James	09 AUG 1884 L	19	176

Name	Spouse	Date	Vol	Page
Jordan, Julia C.	Collier, Lewis C.	23 DEC 1879 R	14	061
Jordan, Lucie D.	Callis, Walter S.	10 APR 1885 R	20	159
Jordan, Margaret	Dye, Andrew	04 MAR 1879 R	13	087
Jordan, Margaret E.	Hall, Henry	12 MAY 1879 L	13	184
Jordan, Mary	Jennifer, Edward	28 APR 1880 R	14	229
Jordan, Mary Catharine	Sackson, Nathaniel	19 NOV 1884 R	19	094
Jordan, Mary E.	Fitzhugh, Samuel	02 AUG 1883 L	18	071
Jordan, Mary E.	Jackson, Henry Alfonso	03 JUN 1884 L	19	054
Jordan, Mary F.	Winfield, John	17 OCT 1878	12	274
Jordan, Mary Fannie	Jackson, Charles	02 JAN 1879 L	13	005
Jordan, Mary Susan	Venie, Samuel	11 JUN 1885 R	20	269
Jordan, R.S.	Harris, J.T.	10 SEP 1879 L	13	364
Jordan, Richard E.	Braunstein, Emma	02 MAR 1880 R	14	170
Jordan, Thomas	Robinson, Rosina	03 DEC 1882	17	164
Jordan, William	Bird, Ella	27 NOV 1877 R	11	203
Jordan, William	Schmidt, Kate	12 SEP 1878	12	212
Jorden, Mary	Smith, Richard	01 JAN 1880 R	16	3883
Jorden, William	Wood, Sarah	06 FEB 1884 R	30	7261
Jordon, Augustus	Smith, Mary L.	18 DEC 1880	15	110
Jordon, Harry B.	Brown, Alice E.	24 MAR 1880 L	14	195
Jordon, John W.	Merritt, Georgianna	08 NOV 1877 R	11	172
Jordon, Robert Thomas	King, Mary Ann	11 NOV 1880 R	15	044
Jose, Sarah E.	Stevens, Samuel	03 JUN 1885 R	20	252
Joseph, Frederick	Angel, Lottie	13 JUN 1882 R	16	408
Joseph, William B.	Downs, Lizzie	16 OCT 1882 R	17	073
Joshua, Ida	Jackson, James	11 OCT 1877 R	11	131
Joslin, Eva L.	Warner, Harry F.	22 AUG 1883	18	096
Jost, John B.	Hohbein, Annie	20 NOV 1883	18	264
Joswell, Fanny	Montello, Edward	21 APR 1879 R	13	153
Jouvenal, Clara C.M.	Steinle, Frederick	12 OCT 1884 R	19	300
Jouvenal, Emma	Fiedler, Madison	29 JAN 1882 R	16	214
Joy, Annie M.	Valk, Emory G.	15 NOV 1880 R	15	048
Joy, Bridget C.	Cross, John J.	14 JUN 1881 L	15	361
Joy, Charles H.	Tibbs, Mary E.	02 APR 1884 R	18	493
Joy, Edward F.	Cumberland, Ann Rebecca	10 MAR 1885 L	20	104
Joy, Johanna V.	Ragan, Francis J.	16 JUL 1881 L	15	404
Joy, John C.	Dutton, Lydia B.	04 OCT 1883 L	18	173
Joy, Julia	Sweeney, Michael	14 OCT 1885 L	20	482
Joy, Mollie E.	Ash, Thomas F.	04 APR 1881 L	15	245
Joyce, Annie W.	Gude, George	24 APR 1878 L	12	021
Joyce, Asa Addison	Wingate, Carrie Dail	19 OCT 1882 R	17	081
Joyce, Charlotte M.	Birckhead, Middleton	16 DEC 1880	15	107
Joyce, George W.	Wilson, Hattie A.	25 FEB 1882 R	16	259
Joyce, Leila	Roots, John	04 APR 1881 L	15	245
Joyce, Margaret	Anderson, Edward	22 NOV 1884 L	19	402
Joyce, Margaret A.	Simonton, John P.	15 OCT 1879 R	13	423
Joyce, Mary	Beale, Edward	13 MAY 1883 R	17	436
Joyce, Mary A.	Rodriguez, José Ignacio	14 APR 1884	18	506
Joyce, Mary J.	Tynan, John	13 NOV 1879	13	485
Joyce, Maurice	Nolan, Katie	04 JUN 1883 R	17	473
Joyner, Littleton J.	Derrick, Anna L.	12 AUG 1884	19	178
Judah, Rosa, Mrs.	Reichenberg, Aron	01 DEC 1881 L	16	106
Judd, Kate I.	Evans, Waring E.	04 OCT 1882 L	17	053
Judd, Laura L.	Eckloff, Randolph J.	07 MAY 1884 L	19	011
Juenemann, Amelia	Reh, Rudolph	21 MAY 1878 L	12	062
Juggins, Louis	Speed, Emma	18 SEP 1885	20	426
Julihn, M.L.	Higdon, Florence R.	06 OCT 1885 L	20	462
Julin, Mary	Kendrick, John	09 NOV 1881 L	16	068

Julius, Rosa L.	Laws, Richard M.	08 MAY 1878 R	12	043
Jullien, Frances E.	Brown, William M., Jr.	02 DEC 1880 R	15	082
Juna, Joshua	Williams, Hannah	03 JAN 1878	11	276
Junemann, George J.	Meter, Annie Agnes	29 DEC 1881	16	167
Junghaus, Joseph	McLain, Sarah F.	01 AUG 1880	14	380
Junifer, Georgiena	West, Eli	02 AUG 1877 L	11	038
Junken, Elizabeth M.	Benedict, James E.	22 NOV 1883 R	18	271
Just, George W.	Streb, Annie	22 MAY 1879 R	13	201
Juster, Gerritt	Höhlein, Margaretha	30 JAN 1879 R	13	038

K

Kaa, Carrie	Roth, P. Wm.	04 JAN 1880 R	14	087
Kadle, Arthur E.	Reid, Catherine	21 APR 1880 R	14	232
Kaelin, Mary A.L.	Howard, Francis	05 DEC 1880	15	081
Kaemmerer, Edith M.	Baltzley, Edwin	27 DEC 1883	18	341
Kahlert, Louisa	Hoeke, John	30 DEC 1879	14	081
Kahlert, William	Bluet, Mildred S.	16 NOV 1882 R	17	133
Kaiser, Adelaide G.	Brown, Silas M.	02 FEB 1881 R	15	171
Kaiser, Elizabeth D.	Yeabower, Christopher	10 SEP 1882 R	17	014
Kaiser, Emmer A.	Roth, Jacob	28 JUL 1885	20	343
Kaiser, Henrietta M.	Ockershausen, George	04 NOV 1880 R	15	027
Kaiser, John W.	Dunning, Mary Ann	25 JAN 1881 L	15	162
Kaiser, John William	Dunning, Mary Ann	05 JUN 1882 R	16	393
Kaiser, Louise	Lowe, Wm. R.	27 NOV 1877 L	11	205
Kaiser, Margaret Agnes	Spencer, Leonard G.	08 APR 1885	20	153
Kaiser, Pauline	William, Paul	15 JAN 1880 L	14	108
Kaiser, Sarah C.	Nevitt, James C.	10 MAY 1881 R	15	299
Kaiser, William S.	Tobe, Elizabeth A.	18 DEC 1884 R	19	467
Kaisling, C. Oscar	Wade, Beatrice E.	03 SEP 1885	20	396
Kalbfus, Charles H.	Mallory, Josephine A.	02 JUN 1884 R	19	049
Kaldenbach, James Henry	Clark, Mary Ann	12 AUG 1879 R	13	316
Kaldenbach, Robert J.	Ladson, Emily	29 NOV 1884 R	19	427
Kaldenbach, William E.	Vermillion, Lizzie L.	06 JAN 1881	15	142
Kancher, Theodore	Fitz, Mary C.	29 AUG 1878 L	12	185
Kane, Ellen	Driscoll, Cornelius	19 JUL 1877 L	11	026
Kane, Ellen E.	Shanahan, Daniel	25 NOV 1884 L	19	410
Kane, Emma E.	Matchett, Herbert H.	25 JUN 1879 R	13	252
Kane, Henrietta Virginia	Steward, Charles	21 JUN 1883 L	18	008
Kane, J.P.	McCarthy, E.E.	31 DEC 1879	13	500
Kane, James	Donn, Lillian V.	29 JAN 1879 R	13	038
Kane, John	Chase, Emma	26 APR 1878 R	12	018
Kane, Lizzie M.	Murphy, Jeremiah J.	06 SEP 1882 L	17	007
Kane, Margaret Anne	Sullivan, Edward Joseph	27 DEC 1878 L	12	415
Kane, Mary	Bennett, Richard	23 JUN 1881 L	15	376
Kane, Mary	Jones, John Robert	16 NOV 1882 R	17	131
Kane, Mary E.	Killigan, Thomas I.	24 SEP 1884 L	19	265
Kane, Mary Jane	Hart, Archie M.	11 DEC 1878 L	12	377
Kane, Sarah	Brown, James	29 JUL 1880 R	14	378
Kane, Thomas F.	Wright, Julia A.	10 FEB 1884 R	18	418
Kane, Winifred	McVarry, James	27 DEC 1881 L	16	162
Kaney, Shelton	Middleton, Jane C.	29 SEP 1884	19	261
Kanke, Cary W.	Phillips, Miriam E.	20 APR 1881 R	15	261
Kaplan, Dora	Schlomberg, Solomon	01 MAR 1883 L	17	328
Kappler, Gregory, Jr.	Cass, Kate	07 FEB 1878 L	11	331
Kappler, Gregory, Jr.	Karney, Ida V.	05 JUN 1884	19	062
Karcher, Louis	Mitchel, Mary	28 JAN 1879 R	13	036
Karney, Ida V.	Kappler, Gregory, Jr.	05 JUN 1884	19	062
Karr, Patrick	Cunningham, Mary	26 FEB 1878 L	11	357
Karr, Philip A.	Kline, Louisa	04 APR 1882 R	16	296
Karr, William Wesley	Parker, Emma Josephine	23 NOV 1881 R	16	091
Kaspar, William	McDonald, Mary	29 NOV 1881 R	16	103
Kasten, William	Houk, Julia	02 FEB 1879 R	13	041
Kates, Charles H.	Rasch, Maggie F.D.	25 JUN 1885	20	295
Kattell, John C.	Jackson, Annie P.	28 AUG 1879 R	13	340
Kattenberg, Minna	Brent, Louis	15 JUL 1882 R	16	449
Katz, Charley	Murphy, Margaret	02 APR 1879 L	13	125
Kauffman, Anna S.	Mattern, John Edwin	27 SEP 1879 R	13	389
Kauffman, Mary Emma	Fishback, William Owen	06 DEC 1877 R	11	221

D.C. Marriage Records Index, June 28, 1877 to October 19, 1885

Kauffman, Rudolph	Kennedy, Jessie	05 JAN 1882 R	16	181
Kaufman, Bertha	Hollander, Edward	15 OCT 1885 R	20	482
Kaufman, Bertha C.	Frank, Benjamin	14 OCT 1885 R	20	477
Kaufman, Treasa	Hollander, Justus	01 FEB 1882 R	16	217
Kaufmann, Heinrich	Schmerz, Lizzie	28 MAR 1880 R	14	200
Kaufmann, Lina	Raff, Elias	15 OCT 1879 R	13	413
Kay, Elizabeth	Brockenborough, Edmund T.	20 JUL 1878 L	12	143
Kayser, Florence G.	Woodley, Knight V.	20 MAY 1885 R	20	230
Keach, Roman F.	Wright, Eleanor W.	17 OCT 1878 R	12	280
Keady, Patrick	Maloney, Annie	16 MAY 1878 R	12	048
Kealey, Annie R.	Gardner, C. Clinton	08 AUG 1885 L	20	360
Kealey, James H.	Mawdsley, Mary J.	03 MAY 1881 L	15	288
Kean, John Taylor	Perry, Bessie Fronie	03 APR 1884 R	18	489
Keane, Julia	Connor, Patrick	16 JAN 1879 R	13	022
Keane, Patrick	Ford, Mary	05 FEB 1884 R	18	410
Kearney, Charles E.	Hamilton, Mary A.	23 DEC 1880 R	15	118
Kearney, Jeannett B.	Rossiter, Edward C.	30 JUN 1884	19	109
Kearney, John H.	King, Marion E.	28 SEP 1880	14	462
Kearney, Sarah C.	Aiken, George R.	14 MAY 1878	12	050
Kearon, Annie	Smith, Charles T.	24 JUN 1880 R	14	333
Keating, Chester B.	Burke, Clara J.	28 JUL 1878 R	12	146
Keating, Delia	Murphy, John	15 JUL 1877	11	022
Keating, Mary A.	Kelly, John T.	28 OCT 1878	12	294
Keating, Matthew	Simpson, Mary Elizabeth	20 MAY 1880	14	274
Keating, William C.	King, Priscilla R.	16 MAY 1882	16	361
Keatley, Annie E.	West, John R.	29 DEC 1881 R	16	169
Keazer, Ellen M.	Jones, Henry A.	18 JAN 1882	16	199
Kee, William J.	Simms, Annie	27 JAN 1885 L	20	039
Keech, Anna Eliza	Burr, Fredrick H.	15 MAR 1880 R	14	184
Keech, John Reeder	Hunt, Electa	31 MAY 1883	17	470
Keech, William Cyril	Bonney, Florence Estelle	16 JAN 1878	11	308
Keefe, Deborah	Hart, Joseph B.	07 APR 1885 L	20	150
Keefe, Elizabeth	Duvall, Samuel	29 APR 1885	20	196
Keefe, Jeremiah	Halpin, Bridget Adele	26 SEP 1883 L	18	156
Keefe, Joanna	Lovejoy, William	04 SEP 1878	12	197
Keefe, John	Regan, Mary A.	16 OCT 1884 L	19	315
Keefe, John J.	Falkner, Margaret A.	28 SEP 1878	12	239
Keefe, Maggie	Noone, P.R.	18 AUG 1884 L	19	191
Keefe, May E.	Simms, Robert F.	26 OCT 1880 R	15	013
Keefe, Owen T.	Sweeny, Ellen	18 JAN 1883	17	267
Keefer, Antoinette	Lavezzi, John	16 FEB 1880 R	14	154
Keefer, Joseph H.	McDonald, Virginia C.	20 OCT 1884	19	280
Keefer, Philip F.	Shipley, Mary L.	06 JUN 1881 L	15	346
Keely, Mary	Dunn, Peter	06 MAY 1882 L	16	352
Keenan, Florence	Taylor, Thorton	05 MAY 1882 L	16	351
Keenan, John Francis	Griner, Josephine	23 DEC 1881 R	16	154
Keenan, Mary	Colleton, Thomas	22 APR 1885	20	177
Keenan, Theresa	Ahern, John	15 AUG 1881 L	15	445
Keene, Charles Henry	Ertter, Sarah Jane	17 MAY 1880 R	14	272
Keene, Herbert N.	Gibson, Laura V.	25 OCT 1882	17	092
Keene, Mary Elizabeth	Hummer, John W.	10 JAN 1878 R	11	293
Keeney, Joseph	Edwards, Isabella S.	04 MAY 1884 R	19	003
Keeney, Joseph	Edwards, Isabella S.	03 MAY 1884 L	18	549
Keep, Mary E.	Hopson, Lucien	27 AUG 1885 R	20	390
Keese, John Henry	Hadley, Sarah E.	30 MAR 1882 R	16	294
Keese, Mary Jane	Beckett, Daniel C.	07 MAY 1884 L	19	010
Keese, Samuel	Cronan, Janey	20 AUG 1878	12	173
Keeseman, Lillie B.	Gallaher, Edmond M.	12 OCT 1885 L	20	476

Keeser, Margaret A.	Crown, William S.	20 OCT 1880	15	005
Keifer, Cora May	Kline, Scott M.	18 AUG 1885 L	20	375
Keifer, Elwood	Cole, Mary Aggness	05 OCT 1879 R	13	404
Keiley, Winifred	Edwards, George T.	18 JUL 1878 L	12	139
Keister, James H.	Nice, Laura E.	10 JAN 1884	18	371
Keith, David	Thornton, Anne	26 DEC 1878	12	255
Keith, Judge F.	Jonson, Mollie, Mrs.	15 FEB 1881 R	15	183
Keith, Mattie	Douglas, Henry H.	13 MAR 1879 R	13	101
Keith, Rosa A.	Mills, William F.	29 APR 1882 L	16	341
Keith, Wm. W.	Johnson, Agnes C.	23 SEP 1885	20	431
Keithely, Laura V.	Seitz, Joseph Franklin	14 APR 1879 L	13	141
Keithley, Anna G.	Tate, Harry	29 SEP 1880 R	14	465
Keithley, Arthur	Bury, Annie Eliz.	10 JUL 1885 R	20	319
Keithley, Franklin	Yeatman, Ella J.	01 SEP 1880 R	14	423
Keithley, John T.	Anderson, Catherine D.	26 APR 1882	16	338
Keithley, Josiah	Hutchinson, Emma Jane	15 JAN 1884 R	18	377
Keithly, William A.	Hurley, Josephine	05 SEP 1883 R	18	112
Keleher, Annie E.	Jones, William T.	26 SEP 1878 R	12	236
Keleher, Katie	Fox, Silas	23 DEC 1881 R	16	154
Keleher, Mary	Retterhouse, Ernest J.	10 JUL 1884 L	19	131
Keleher, Thomas	Shugrue, Mollie	07 JAN 1885 L	20	008
Keleher, Timothy J.	Wilson, Georgie, Mrs.	08 DEC 1881 R	16	122
Keli, James	Bros, Mary	06 JUL 1881 L	15	392
Keliher, Jams	Bresnan, Mary	28 MAR 1883 R	27	6598
Kell, James H.	Goss, Maud E.	19 SEP 1884	19	259
Kell, William Alfred	Morgan, Maggie Eliz.	14 DEC 1884 R	19	458
Kellain, Margaret E.	LaFleur, William C.	29 JUL 1879 L	13	297
Keller, Arthur C.	Newgent, Ida V.	03 JUN 1884 R	19	055
Keller, Conrad	Steinhope, Auguste	30 APR 1885 R	20	193
Keller, Elizabeth	Fauth, Charles	27 JUN 1882 L	16	427
Keller, James H.	Wenger, Rebecca	28 APR 1001 R	15	284
Keller, John L.	del Bondio, Texanita	05 DEC 1882 R	17	166
Keller, Kate	Grubbs, Augustine S.	17 OCT 1878	12	276
Keller, Lucie V.	Peregoy, William E.	14 JUL 1879 R	13	280
Keller, Margaret F., Mrs.	Atwell, John W.	23 OCT 1879	13	441
Keller, Mattie A.	Harrison, J.H.	27 FEB 1878	11	362
Keller, Mollie	Lindawood, J.J.	28 SEP 1882	17	042
Keller, Samuel P.	Butt, Eva E.	16 SEP 1884 L	19	252
Keller, Thomas White	Fant, Alice Norton	28 DEC 1882 R	17	221
Keller, William H.	Heinline, Amanda	23 FEB 1885 R	20	082
Kellerman, John	Gately, Mary Jane	13 APR 1885 L	20	161
Kellett, David	Whiteside, Rosy B.	12 OCT 1880	11	384
Kelley, Catharine	Shannon, Felix	19 DEC 1879 L	14	059
Kelley, Catharine B.	Reagan, William	25 FEB 1884 L	18	440
Kelley, Charles H.	Meadors, Sarah E.	19 DEC 1883	18	326
Kelley, David	Balluff, Annie	15 SEP 1885 L	20	417
Kelley, Howard M.	Sparklin, Alice Thomas	05 MAY 1884 R	18	549
Kelley, Howard M.	Sparklin, Alice A.	05 MAY 1884	19	004
Kelley, John Edward	Bankhead, Carry	26 JAN 1881 R	15	164
Kelley, John H.	Bonini, Jennie	04 OCT 1883	18	170
Kelley, Joseph Van Dorn	Hain, Ida	22 MAR 1883 R	17	351
Kelley, Kate McPherson	Clutter, Noah D.	19 MAR 1879 R	13	108
Kelley, Sarah Ann	Boyd, William F.	23 JAN 1884 R	18	391
Kells, Joseph M.	Rainey, Mary E.	14 DEC 1880 R	15	096
Kellum, Charles	Woolford, Henrietta	14 AUG 1878 L	12	167
Kellum, Katie E.	Got, Ching	06 NOV 1882 R	17	073
Kellum, Virginia McC.	Jones, Harry S.	23 MAR 1883 R	17	356
Kellum, Zed B.	Griffo, Mary	10 OCT 1882 L	17	062

D.C. Marriage Records Index, June 28, 1877 to October 19, 1885   259

Kellums, Belle	Taylor, Nicholas B.	12 MAR 1885	20	111
Kelly, Alice	Porter, David	10 OCT 1878 R	12	265
Kelly, Carrie	Imes, Simon	04 SEP 1883 L	18	110
Kelly, Catherine C.	Ahern, Laurence J.	03 SEP 1884 L	19	222
Kelly, Edward Bell	Lynch, Mary Ann, Mrs.	15 MAR 1883 R	17	343
Kelly, Elizabeth	Lindsey, James H., Rev.	09 JUL 1878 R	12	128
Kelly, Ellen	Miles, Ignatius	06 MAY 1880 L	14	256
Kelly, Fanny Wiggins	Gordon, William F.	05 MAY 1880 R	14	254
Kelly, George E.	Soper, Alice	27 AUG 1877 R	11	065
Kelly, Henrietta	Robinson, James	15 NOV 1883	18	248
Kelly, Henry H.	Simms, Adelaide E.	10 DEC 1879 R	14	040
Kelly, Irene A.	Denham, Lewis C.	12 OCT 1881 R	16	020
Kelly, James	Ahern, Josepheria T.	24 JUN 1884 L	19	099
Kelly, James	Betts, Mary	06 NOV 1884 L	19	366
Kelly, James F.	Sewell, Lizzie A.	15 AUG 1883	18	088
Kelly, John T.	Keating, Mary A.	28 OCT 1878	12	294
Kelly, Julia S.	Brock, William S.	15 DEC 1881 R	16	134
Kelly, Lillie May	Johnson, Samuel	05 NOV 1883 L	18	233
Kelly, Lizzie	Hart, William	11 SEP 1881	15	482
Kelly, Martha	Thomas, George	08 JUN 1880 L	14	310
Kelly, Mary Agnes	Hyde, William Edgar	27 JUN 1881 R	15	379
Kelly, Mary E.	Curriden, Samuel W.	19 OCT 1880 R	15	003
Kelly, Mary Louisa	Shelvy, James Henry	16 MAY 1878 R	12	057
Kelly, Mary M.	Barry, Clifton	13 APR 1882	16	298
Kelly, Nathan	Taylor, Sophia George	09 AUG 1883	18	082
Kelly, Peter C.	O'Neill, Kate	27 APR 1880 L	14	239
Kelly, Richard S.	Boose, Mary	12 APR 1882 R	16	313
Kelly, Sarah E.	Reding, John	08 MAR 1883 R	17	333
Kelly, T.J.	Sullivan, Mary	29 APR 1879 L	13	165
Kelly, Theophilus J.	Cooper, Virginia C.	13 AUG 1885 L	20	370
Kelly, Thomas S.	Smith, Belle W.	07 JUL 1879 R	13	270
Kelly, W.B.	Sisson, Harriet I.	19 NOV 1884 R	19	394
Kelly, William	Jones, Addie	09 JAN 1879	13	012
Kelly, William	Ashton, Nellie	30 DEC 1884 R	19	500
Kelly, William Benson	Greenwell, Annie Adelaide	29 NOV 1882 R	17	153
Kelly, William H.	White, Catherine	02 JUN 1879 L	13	213
Kelly, William O.	Scott, Anna E.	23 MAY 1883 R	17	453
Kelpy, Anthony	Carter, Adelaide	10 JAN 1881 R	15	145
Kelser, William W.	Brown, Nellie T.	25 SEP 1878 R	12	234
Kelsey, Moses	Norris, Hattie	09 JUN 1886	20	342
Kelsey, Philip P.	Holmes, Rosa Lee	27 NOV 1884 R	19	413
Keltin, James R.	Collins, Mittie	10 AUG 1881	15	439
Kelton, Grandison	Lomax, Julia	22 MAY 1883 L	17	456
Kemmauf, Maggie	Heunigs, Henry	30 NOV 1884	19	424
Kemon, Frank C.	Mackey, Katie E.	25 AUG 1881 L	15	459
Kemon, Helen S.	Carson, Adolph B.	08 APR 1884 R	18	500
Kemon, Solon C.	Pugh, Jennie	18 SEP 1877	11	098
Kemp, Amanda	Washington, Charles	17 JAN 1884 R	18	381
Kemp, Ann Eliza	King, John W.	08 AUG 1877	11	046
Kemp, Howard Mason	Reinke, Anna Elizabeth	22 MAR 1881 R	15	233
Kemp, James H.	Herbert, Anna	04 JAN 1883 L	17	239
Kemp, Julia A.	Butler, Charles E.	21 FEB 1878 R	11	350
Kemp, Martha J.	Rabbitt, William J.	18 MAR 1879 R	13	106
Kemp, Richard R.	Berry, Martha E.	28 DEC 1881 R	16	108
Kemp, Solomon	Smith, Lizzie	25 JUN 1885 R	20	288
Kemp, William A.	Forney, Annie K.	03 MAR 1881 L	15	213
Kempf, Julie	Coignet, Charles Eugene	28 SEP 1879	13	389
Kempter, Antoinetta	Zietler, William	02 AUG 1877	11	036

Kendall, George H.	White, Hattie L.	10 JUN 1884	19	073
Kendall, John	Able, Dulcie	30 APR 1879	13	168
Kendall, John B.	Hooker, Mary D.	31 JAN 1883	17	276
Kendall, Lilean	Russell, Philip Gray	17 DEC 1884 R	19	465
Kendall, Marie	Witmer, Calvin	13 MAY 1880 R	14	266
Kendick, Abraham L.	Mitchell, Ida	25 SEP 1881	15	497
Kendig, Isabelle Lawrence	Walker, Robert J.	04 JUN 1879 R	13	217
Kendig, Rosa G.	Wainwright, Dallas B.	25 MAY 1880 R	14	283
Kendig, Wilmot G.	Whaley, Laura Lee	30 NOV 1882 R	17	162
Kendler, Ellen Nora	Ricketts, George W.	18 NOV 1881 R	16	031
Kendrick, Abraham L.	Dentinger, Mary M.	04 SEP 1884	19	225
Kendrick, Amelia K.	Odenwald, Albert G.	18 JUL 1881 L	15	406
Kendrick, Charles M.	McKeever, Clara V.	11 JAN 1881 R	15	147
Kendrick, John	Julin, Mary	09 NOV 1881 L	16	068
Kendrick, John J.	Groves, Matilda	14 DEC 1881 R	16	130
Kendrick, Kate	Johnson, Edwin	24 SEP 1885 R	20	442
Kendrick, Lillie Walker	Spiller, Logan A.	05 JAN 1885 R	20	004
Kendrick, Mary E.	Campbell, John H.	06 FEB 1880 L	14	141
Kendrick, Mary L.	Dean, Richard L.	06 NOV 1883 L	18	234
Kendrick, Massena	Rye, Jane T.	10 MAY 1882 R	16	354
Kendrick, Thomas J.	Cannon, Mary A.	18 OCT 1882 R	17	080
Kendrick, William L.H.	Horsman, Martha A.	07 AUG 1884 L	19	173
Kenealy, Mary J.	Chase, Isaac Henry	25 NOV 1884 R	19	405
Kengla, E. Lorenzo	Varnell, Anna	17 MAR 1881	15	506
Kengla, George M.	Hazel, Addie Marie	05 MAY 1880 L	14	253
Kenneally, Mary M.	Murray, John	29 JUL 1885 L	20	345
Kennedy, Anna G.	Stormont, William T.	22 NOV 1881	16	087
Kennedy, Catharine	Bligh, John	31 JUL 1877 L	11	035
Kennedy, Ellen	Minnitt, Robert	30 AUG 1880 R	14	422
Kennedy, Fannie	Reed, James	12 OCT 1880 L	14	488
Kennedy, J.W.	Ready, Bridget	20 SEP 1880	14	451
Kennedy, James	Crawley, Bridget	26 SEP 1878 R	12	235
Kennedy, James	Hatto, Annie	02 OCT 1880	14	470
Kennedy, Jessie	Kauffman, Rudolph	05 JAN 1882 R	16	181
Kennedy, Julia	Callahan, Francis R.	13 FEB 1879	13	060
Kennedy, Mary E.	Guild, Alexander	23 APR 1879	13	157
Kennedy, Patrick	Collins, Honora	06 FEB 1880 L	14	140
Kennedy, Sarah	Violett, Edward Allen	05 JUN 1883	17	478
Kennedy, Susanna	Johnson, Thomas E.	28 FEB 1884 L	18	450
Kennedy, Susie E.	Browning, Frank Temple	11 JAN 1882 L	16	191
Kennedy, Theresa	Brown, Oscar J.	16 JUN 1879 L	13	234
Kennedy, Tillie E.	Toner, Edward T.	08 JUN 1882 R	16	401
Kennelly, Edward M.	Artes, Sophia	18 SEP 1882 L	17	025
Kenner, Hiram	Tolbert, Sidney	20 MAR 1880 R	14	190
Kenner, Preston E.	Thomas, Elizabeth	13 MAR 1879 R	13	101
Kenney, Edward C.	Morris, Louisa E.	14 FEB 1878 R	11	341
Kenney, Edward C.	Thompson, Jennie	02 JAN 1884 L	18	362
Kenney, James	Preston, Ida	08 JAN 1884 L	18	369
Kenney, John	Price, Fannie	05 JUL 1885 R	20	310
Kenney, John Manns	Fillins, Katie Eliz.	01 SEP 1885 R	20	392
Kenney, Martha	Brown, Edward	31 OCT 1878	12	301
Kenney, Peter	Weber, Louise	17 MAR 1879 L	13	104
Kenney, Sarah Jane	Braxton, Thomas	07 FEB 1883 R	17	299
Kenney, Thomas M.	Driscoll, Mary	16 MAY 1879	13	194
Kenney, Tucker	Black, Miranda	08 SEP 1883 L	18	118
Kenny, Edmund	Hall, Mary Susan	08 OCT 1878 L	12	259
Kenny, Michael P.	O'Hearn, Mary	22 APR 1880 R	14	233
Kenon, Peter Sophodes	Lesh, Clara J.	02 MAR 1882 R	16	262

Kent, Alexander	Gove, Caddie E.	24 JAN 1878	11	316
Kent, David	Simmons, Celia	09 JAN 1878 R	12	410
Kent, Douglas	Brashears, Ellen	18 DEC 1879 L	14	057
Kent, Elias	Johnson, Maria L.	21 FEB 1878 R	11	348
Kent, Georgiana	Duvall, Robert Edward	23 DEC 1884 L	19	477
Kent, Joseph	Edelin, Jane	30 JUN 1879 R	13	259
Kent, Lewis	Mildred, Washington	10 APR 1878 L	11	415
Kent, Lizzie F.	Mulligan, William G.	18 DEC 1879 R	14	055
Kent, Maria	Carter, James	12 JUL 1877 R	11	016
Kent, Mary Ann	Johns, Thomas H.	05 NOV 1878 R	12	309
Kent, Mary F.	Borden, Alanson	25 DEC 1877	11	259
Kent, Mary M.	Webster, Fletcher	25 DEC 1884 R	19	489
Kent, Matilda	Dogans, Henry	22 MAY 1880 L	14	282
Kent, William L.	Perry, Sarah C.	10 JUL 1882 R	16	443
Keogh, John M.	Cleary, Annie	29 JAN 1880 R	14	127
Keonig, Peter E.	Brightwell, Sarah Virginia	17 JUL 1884	19	144
Kepler, Lizzie F.	Hicks, Samuel H.	27 FEB 1878	11	360
Keppler, Annie	Lown, William G.	23 JAN 1884 R	18	391
Keppler, George H.	Koch, Catherine E.	11 FEB 1880 R	14	149
Kerin, James A.	Ford, Mary A.	06 JAN 1885 L	20	007
Kerkham, Robert E.	Barron, Gertrude	29 SEP 1881 R	15	507
Kern, Ada R.	Bennett, Francis A.	20 OCT 1881	16	033
Kern, Edward	Paxton, Kate V.	12 NOV 1879 R	13	478
Kern, George	Artis, Isabelle	19 MAR 1885	20	124
Kern, Henry P.	Koons, Carrie R.	29 APR 1879 R	13	163
Kernell, Harriet	Van Orden, John W.	26 FEB 1879	13	074
Kernill, John A.	Drescher, Eliza	24 JUN 1884 L	19	100
Kernner, Henry G.	Lanahan, Martha	09 JUN 1880	14	311
Kerper, Francis B.P.	Steadman, Ida E.	09 DEC 1880 R	15	090
Kerper, Lizzie	Flood, William F.	16 JUN 1884	19	085
Kerper, Mary O.	Padgett, Daniel E.	12 FEB 1884 R	18	421
Kerper, William D.	Smallwood, Annie J.	28 OCT 1880 L	15	019
Kerr, Caroline	Goodman, Richard D.	04 JUL 1885	20	309
Kerr, M. Rosetta	Lucas, George W.	11 DEC 1880 L	15	092
Kerr, Mary A.	Arrington, Andrew J.	23 OCT 1884 L	19	333
Kerr, Robert H.	Fitzgerald, Belle	07 AUG 1884	19	175
Kerr, William J.	Curren, Annie E.	11 JUN 1884	19	085
Kerrick, Charles C.	Hibbs, Bettie	08 JAN 1879 R	13	010
Kerrick, Edward	Clarke, Blanche	02 AUG 1883	18	071
Kerrick, Jennie	Richardson, J.W.	09 OCT 1879	13	413
Kerrick, Sue Franklin	Carroll, Patrick	12 MAY 1879 R	13	185
Kersey, Matilda J.	Billings, Rolland B.	30 OCT 1884 L	19	348
Kersey, Sallie E.	Edelin, Clayton A.	17 APR 1882 R	16	319
Kershaw, Agnes E.	Nott, Wilford E.	19 JAN 1881 R	15	156
Kerstin, Charles	Pattey, Ella	31 JAN 1883	17	280
Kesley, Lydia Smith	McElhinney, Wm. Ernest	01 SEP 1880 R	14	425
Kessler, Anna	Lynn, Duncan C.	20 SEP 1877	11	100
Kessler, Mary	Bernhardt, William	11 APR 1880	14	206
Ketcham, Ellis M.	Gilbert, Sallie S.	25 DEC 1884	19	487
Ketner, James H.	Johnson, Bertie	24 JAN 1879 L	13	033
Ketter, William	Shoemaker, Mary C.	19 NOV 1878	12	333
Kettler, Rosa D.	Weser, Benjamin F.	30 JUN 1883	18	027
Kettner, James D.	Linkins, Annie F.	10 AUG 1884	19	166
Kettner, Rachel V.	Thorne, Joshua S.	15 AUG 1877 R	11	052
Keuchet, Anthony	Staffregen, Elise	01 OCT 1883	18	164
Keve, John	Green, Virginia	15 JAN 1885 L	20	021
Key, Ernestine	Thomas, J.H.	19 MAR 1878 L	11	388
Key, Gillis	Smallwood, Mary Jane	06 FEB 1882 L	16	227

Name	Spouse	Date	Age	Ref
Key, Harriet Sellman	Renard, Jean Lean	15 DEC 1883 L	18	318
Key, Lucinda	Brooks, Peter	11 NOV 1878	12	321
Key, Mary	Thomas, Joseph	28 JUL 1882 R	16	238
Key, Norman	Riley, Jennie	14 OCT 1879 R	13	422
Key, Robert H.	Rawls, Sarah A.	01 JUL 1882 L	16	434
Key, Thornton	Lewis, Malvinia	12 AUG 1882 R	16	477
Key, William	Adams, Lucy Ann	20 OCT 1884 L	19	319
Keyes, Charles	Maddox, Laura	05 JUL 1880	14	347
Keyes, Charles W.	Tomlinson, Katie M.	02 FEB 1885 R	20	047
Keyes, Daniel	Robinson, Sarah A.	29 OCT 1884 L	19	344
Keyes, Margaret	Clarke, Robert	24 JUL 1882 L	16	455
Keyes, Mattie E.	Kuchling, Benjamin C.	08 JUN 1881 R	15	353
Keys, Carrie	Herbert, Pierson	15 MAY 1883 L	17	441
Keys, Clara M.	Houghton, Wilson H.	05 SEP 1877	11	074
Keys, Delia Ann	Harper, Edward	22 SEP 1885 L	20	434
Keys, Ellen	Harleston, Charles W.	30 MAY 1883 L	17	469
Keys, Emma	Bennett, John	30 MAR 1878 L	11	399
Keys, Henry	White, Mary Anna	24 JAN 1883 R	17	272
Keys, Julia A.	Frost, John W.	14 AUG 1879 R	13	320
Keys, Marion H.	Paxton, Hannah E.M.	05 DEC 1882	17	168
Keys, Mary E.	Ward, Robert E.	18 JUL 1883	18	048
Keys, Montgomery B.	Johnson, Ella R.	07 APR 1885 L	20	148
Keys, Nelson	Jackson, Margaret	12 JUN 1884	19	082
Keys, Virginia A.	Springmann, Samuel	18 DEC 1879 R	14	056
Keys, W.H.	Eastman, Annie	22 DEC 1884	19	476
Keys, William Henry	Lane, Harriet	13 JAN 1880 L	14	103
Keyser, Earl A.	Cassidy, Nellie L.	18 OCT 1882 R	17	079
Kibble, Alexander	Brightwell, Elizabeth	19 AUG 1879 R	13	325
Kibble, Columbus	Gilluly, Annie Catherine	27 JAN 1881 L	15	168
Kibble, John Morris	McGill, Cora Eugenia	06 OCT 1879 R	13	406
Kidd, Benjamin	Ragan, Annie	08 JUN 1885 R	20	260
Kidd, Fannie R.	Sands, Harvey A.	04 NOV 1880 R	15	032
Kidwell, Beauregard	Allen, Mary E.	14 NOV 1883 R	18	246
Kidwell, Charles G.	Connor, Maggie C.	28 APR 1884 L	18	539
Kidwell, Cordelia	O'Brien, James T.	15 MAR 1881 L	15	226
Kidwell, Eli S.	Thomas, Sallie E.	21 DEC 1880	15	112
Kidwell, George W.	McKenney, Annie E.	13 DEC 1882	17	181
Kidwell, Ida West	Hyde, George Augustus	08 FEB 1881	15	181
Kidwell, J.W.	Mann, Mattie A.	16 APR 1879 L	13	148
Kidwell, James E.	Thomas, Martha A.	14 AUG 1882 R	16	479
Kidwell, James W.	Docherty, Lizzie	24 APR 1884	18	533
Kidwell, Jennie E.	Willett, George B.	28 MAR 1883	17	364
Kidwell, John P.	McGinley, Margaret	28 DEC 1882 R	17	217
Kidwell, Joseph B.	Ward, Maria Frances	24 OCT 1881 R	16	039
Kidwell, Julia Ann	Ball, William T.	12 FEB 1880 R	14	149
Kidwell, Laura V.	Lanham, Alfred E.	27 DEC 1877	11	272
Kidwell, Mary	Barrett, Franklin	15 JAN 1884 R	18	374
Kidwell, Mary C.	Polen, Noble B.	17 MAR 1885 R	20	121
Kidwell, Sarah V.	Harding, John E.	03 MAY 1883 R	17	428
Kidwell, Virginia	Wiley, Ballentine	03 APR 1879 R	13	126
Kidwell, Zeddie K.	Janens, Lillie	21 DEC 1883 R	18	334
Kiefer, Rosa	Ruppel, Joseph	25 JAN 1880	14	112
Kiernan, Elizabeth	Gately, Patrick	27 JUL 1884	19	158
Kiesecker, Frederick	Webster, Katie M.	07 OCT 1880 R	14	481
Kiesecker, Leonora	Rouzer, George W.	19 OCT 1882 R	17	082
Kiesecker, William	Brelsford, Frances Cornelia	20 MAR 1880 R	14	191
Kleve, Isidor	Weiss, Rachel	15 JAN 1882 R	16	194
Kilbman, Margaret A.	Grissett, James A.	07 DEC 1881	16	115

D.C. Marriage Records Index, June 28, 1877 to October 19, 1885   263

Kilborn, Winnifred E.P.	Watson, William	17 SEP 1884 R	19	255
Kilburn, Catherine A.	Anderson, Joshua	25 JUN 1884	19	103
Kilby, Addie C.	Burchard, George C.	01 SEP 1885 R	20	394
Kiley, Hannah	Leonard, Francis	03 AUG 1879 R	13	303
Kilgour, Annie	McGrath, Henry	06 OCT 1885 R	20	463
Killafoyle, John J.	Carroll, Mary A.	02 JUN 1880 L	16	390
Killigan, Thomas I.	Kane, Mary E.	24 SEP 1884 L	19	265
Killmon, William H.	Mitchell, Emily R.	08 MAY 1879 R	13	181
Killpatrick, Ella J.	Dinwiddie, William A.	27 FEB 1878	11	356
Kilroy, John	Garnett, Sophia L. [Turner]	11 DEC 1884 R	19	439
Kilroy, Patrick	Callahan, Ella	28 NOV 1882 L	17	154
Kimball, Edwin S.	Cluss, Mary	10 DEC 1881 R	15	285
Kimball, Helen Knight	Wishart, William Wilson	19 MAR 1885 R	20	124
Kimball, Israel, Jr.	Lapham, Charlotte E.	17 JUL 1878 R	12	138
Kimball, William Wirt	Spencer, Esther Smith	18 JUL 1882 R	16	452
Kimling, Amelia	Walker, Donus A.	15 JAN 1880 R	14	090
Kimmell, Frank P.	Nally, Rebecca	09 FEB 1882 L	16	235
Kimmell, John Q.A.	Moon, Martie R.	15 AUG 1881 R	15	445
Kindrick, William H.	Berry, Anna E.	31 MAY 1881 L	15	331
Kindslow, Levi	Story, Eliza	14 NOV 1882 R	17	126
Kiner, Rose	Jones, William	19 APR 1882 L	16	325
Kines, Frances W.	Hoffman, Marie A.	18 MAY 1882 R	16	364
King, Abraham	Dyson, Lucy	29 NOV 1882	17	161
King, Alex	Henderson, Margaret Ellen	05 SEP 1885	20	406
King, Alexander S.	Callahan, Mary J.	13 FEB 1884 L	18	423
King, Alexander Simms	Mitchell, Florence B.	02 JUN 1879 L	13	214
King, Alfred	Williams, Lucy	26 JUN 1882 R	16	425
King, Alice	Bell, Dionysius	16 SEP 1885 R	20	421
King, Alice A.	Beck, John, Jr.	22 MAY 1884	19	035
King, Amanda J.	Thomas, Harry E.	11 SEP 1879 R	13	329
King, Annie	Bailey, Charles	25 FEB 1885	20	085
King, Annie	Norris, Lorenzo	23 APR 1885 R	20	185
King, Annie E.	Manuell, Milton G.	15 OCT 1885 R	20	452
King, Benjamin	Carter, Susan	01 APR 1880 R	14	196
King, Benjamin F.	Thompson, Katie V.	25 JUL 1878	12	143
King, Benjamin F.	Peverell, Elizabeth	14 DEC 1880	15	095
King, Borrows W.	Hauptman, Mary M.	15 DEC 1881 R	16	136
King, Charles	Jackson, Sarah E.	04 JUN 1884 L	19	060
King, Charles Henry	Talbert, Margaret E.	03 NOV 1881 L	16	061
King, Charles R.	Hamilton, Susie N.	17 APR 1884 L	18	517
King, Charlotte P.	Bushnell, Albert B.	13 SEP 1883	18	129
King, Clarence Elias	Thompson, Georgiana	07 DEC 1881 R	16	118
King, Clinton M.	Ourand, Evelyn C.	28 APR 1885	20	190
King, Cora D.	Fisher, Charles B.	16 NOV 1885	20	473
King, Edward E.	Bennett, Mary E.	02 APR 1878 L	11	402
King, Edward J.	Crane, Mary	08 FEB 1885	20	056
King, Eliza J.	Burnett, William H.	07 NOV 1878	12	311
King, Elizabeth	Conway, George	27 NOV 1877 L	11	206
King, Elizabeth	Beall, George I.	06 OCT 1883 R	18	174
King, Elizabeth	Green, William	08 SEP 1885 R	20	404
King, Eloise	Statham, Henry Thomas	15 OCT 1885 R	20	481
King, Emma	Brown, Henry	27 SEP 1883 R	18	158
King, Emma J.	Winchester, John E.B.	04 OCT 1880 R	14	471
King, Estella B.	Mead, Christopher	05 FEB 1878 R	11	328
King, Fannie E.	Goodman, Samuel	26 MAY 1881 R	15	327
King, Florence	Harmon, John D., Jr.	02 APR 1883 L	17	375
King, Florence E.	Pynchon, William McKibben	07 MAR 1883 L	17	337
King, Frances	Johnson, Thomas	26 MAY 1879	13	200

King, George	Carroll, Sarah	02 DEC 1878 L	12	357
King, George A.	Edmonston, Ada	14 JUN 1881 R	15	356
King, Gracie B.	Sisson, Samuel	27 AUG 1878 L	12	182
King, Hattie Maria	Proctor, Willie Worthington	22 JUL 1880 R	14	372
King, Henry	Webster, Catherine	26 DEC 1878 L	12	401
King, Henry B.	Mitchell, Emma M.	27 NOV 1879 R	14	013
King, Ida L.	Hebrew, John A.	19 JUL 1877	11	025
King, Ida Luvinia	Nosey, James	03 JUL 1882 R	16	435
King, Isaac Millard Filmore	Devileant, Annie E.	27 FEB 1883	17	324
King, J.E.	Ellis, Matilda C.	12 APR 1881 L	15	254
King, James	Lunsford, Mamie	27 MAR 1879	13	112
King, James	Tucker, Florence	09 JAN 1884 R	18	372
King, James	Jackson, Fannie W.	16 MAR 1885 L	20	116
King, James	Dorsey, Mary	09 JUL 1885 L	20	318
King, James Alfred	Jamieson, Ruth	02 SEP 1878	12	191
King, James B.	Rollins, Annie D.	03 JUN 1885 L	20	254
King, James E.	Collins, Barbara A.	03 JUL 1884 L	19	118
King, James W.	Brawner, Louisa P.	07 NOV 1878	12	312
King, Janie Y.	Ewin, James L.	14 DEC 1880 R	15	096
King, Jennie [Lewis]	Permillion, John Nelson	22 SEP 1885 R	20	432
King, Jno. Samuel	Gleason, Sarah	24 JAN 1884 L	18	394
King, John	Edinburg, Martha	09 SEP 1879 R	13	352
King, John	Robinson, Lovinia	02 OCT 1883 L	18	165
King, John	Turner, Maggie	13 AUG 1884	19	184
King, John Henry	Thompson, Susannah	09 JAN 1883 R	17	246
King, John J.	Brittain, Clara Belle	09 JAN 1885 R	19	516
King, John S.	Turben, Kate	18 OCT 1880 L	15	001
King, John T.	Moulton, Eliza	28 JUN 1878	12	114
King, John Thomas	Dick, Isabella C.	28 FEB 1878 L	11	363
King, John W.	Kemp, Ann Eliza	08 AUG 1877	11	046
King, John W.	Chaney, Mary	24 FEB 1881 L	15	203
King, Joseph E.	Brown, Ella	14 NOV 1878	12	331
King, Josephine	Fowler, Charles E.	19 NOV 1877 L	11	191
King, Katie A.	Huguley, James F.	29 OCT 1878	12	297
King, Laura Anne	Tayman, James Philip	17 DEC 1878	12	384
King, Laura J.	Osborn, Marion	04 MAR 1879 R	13	088
King, Laura V.	Boss, Stewart H.	18 NOV 1884 L	19	392
King, Laura V.	McGill, George E.	29 SEP 1885	20	424
King, Lewis	Rogers, Millie	31 JAN 1884	18	386
King, Lillie Lee	Pulman, Samuel	15 JUL 1885 R	20	326
King, Lillie M.	Creecy, William B.	25 DEC 1883 R	18	335
King, Lulu	Willett, Robert E.	18 MAR 1884 L	18	474
King, Margaret	Barry, William	16 AUG 1883	18	091
King, Margaret	Bell, Solomon	01 MAR 1883	17	329
King, Margaret J.	Norris, William R.	29 DEC 1883	18	354
King, Marion E.	Kearney, John H.	28 SEP 1880	14	462
King, Marion T.	Lusby, Samuel H.	07 MAR 1880 R	14	178
King, Martha Jane, Mrs.	Parker, Ludwell S.	25 JUN 1879	13	248
King, Mary	Bolden, Charles Francis	19 APR 1882 R	16	325
King, Mary Ann	Jordon, Robert Thomas	11 NOV 1880 R	15	044
King, Mary E.	Thorn, William A.	23 NOV 1881 L	16	092
King, Mary R.	Steuart, Bernard M.	16 JAN 1878 L	11	306
King, Matthew	Spencer, Catherine	25 JUN 1879 R	13	249
King, Michael	Hartnett, Bridget	13 NOV 1877 R	11	177
King, Mortimer Dorsey	Lee, Hattie Ann	01 JUN 1880 R	14	286
King, Nellie S.	Henderson, Asbury	23 AUG 1882 R	16	492
King, Priscilla R.	Keating, William C.	16 MAY 1882	16	361
King, R.F.	Braund, Alice B.	02 FEB 1880 L	14	132

King, Rebecca R.	Tayman, John S.	14 SEP 1880	14	442
King, Richard C.	Golden, Ida V.	16 OCT 1881 R	16	025
King, Robert	Lee, Lilly	27 JAN 1880	14	122
King, Robert C.	Weaver, Mary M.	11 OCT 1882 R	17	007
King, Rufus T.	Rollow, Anna M.	03 FEB 1879 R	13	044
King, Sarah	Day, Joseph	13 APR 1880 L	14	222
King, Sarah	Heider, William	01 DEC 1881 L	16	107
King, Sarah	Hunziker, Adolph	31 JUL 1884	19	163
King, Simon Peter	Crocket, Laura Virginia	13 OCT 1884 L	19	303
King, Theo. Ingalls	Hodgkins, Cora	04 FEB 1885 R	20	050
King, Thomas	Cross, Harriet T.	05 JUL 1877 R	11	009
King, Thomas	Thomas, Jane	06 MAR 1884 R	18	460
King, Thomas A.	Shipman, Martha E.	16 FEB 1882 R	16	246
King, Thomas O.	Ridgeway, Martha	15 OCT 1878	12	269
King, Walter J.	Pyles, Emeline	10 MAR 1885	20	103
King, William	Oten, Dora	01 AUG 1878 L	12	155
King, William Benjamin	Jay, Jane Minnesola	28 APR 1880 R	14	238
King, William Bruce	Gilbert, Edith Estelle	29 JUN 1885 R	20	298
King, William E.	Lout, Emma J.	02 SEP 1880 R	14	430
King, William Edward	Lewis, Jennie	26 MAY 1882 R	16	377
King, William F.	Crump, Cora V.	10 FEB 1879 R	13	052
King, William F.	Hurdle, Irene C.	17 APR 1879	13	148
King, William H.	Baily, Anna R.	19 DEC 1878	12	393
King, William H.	Givens, Mary, Miss	25 APR 1885 L	20	188
King, William, Jr.	Pond, Alice Hubbard	23 SEP 1880 R	14	458
Kingsbury, Roberta A.	Myers, Willard H.	05 NOV 1884 L	19	358
Kingsley, George P.	Mason, Abbie H.	12 JUN 1884	19	081
Kingsley, H.A.	Webster, Cora B.	01 NOV 1883 L	18	228
Kingston, Catherine	Murphy, William	01 JUL 1879 L	13	261
Kinkaid, Thomas Wright	Cassin, Virgina Lee	03 APR 1883 R	17	373
Kinne, Frank P.	Schoonmaker, Fannie S.	09 JUL 1877	11	013
Kinney, Beverly W.	Mason, Emma V.	02 JUL 1885 R	20	308
Kinsella, Thomas	Field, Emeline Van S.	19 MAY 1880 R	14	276
Kinsey, Joseph A.	Moynihan, Mary E.	27 DEC 1881 L	16	159
Kinsey, Kate B.	Brashear, M. Larn	25 OCT 1883	18	213
Kinsey, Laura A.	Smith, Charles A.	10 MAR 1881 R	15	222
Kinsley, Jane G.	Schroth, W.H.	04 AUG 1880 L	14	386
Kinsley, Lillian	Upperman, Horace Winston	23 DEC 1884 L	19	483
Kinsley, Louisa	Rothmund, Philip	23 AUG 1877	11	062
Kinslow, Charlotte	Hipkins, Moses	14 FEB 1884 R	18	422
Kinslow, Ida	Creegan, Michael	15 APR 1885 L	20	170
Kinstendorff, Charles A., Jr.	Hoff, Alice A.	23 FEB 1880	14	163
Kinzel, Christina	Haburk, Conrad	16 APR 1879 R	13	142
Kinzy, Isaac	Dyer, Abby	14 APR 1878 R	12	003
Kirbage, Emma	McCoy, Harvy	31 JAN 1885 R	20	044
Kirbey, Joseph C.	Cage, Catherine E.	08 APR 1884 R	18	499
Kirby, Amelia A.	Pfeil, Rudolph	21 OCT 1877	11	147
Kirby, Amelia A.	Letterer, John M.	03 DEC 1882	17	163
Kirby, Annie, Mrs.	Clinton, Edward	19 SEP 1881 R	15	483
Kirby, Flora C.	Dyer, Edward F.	12 JUL 1877 R	11	013
Kirby, Frank E.	Bremerman, Phoebe S.	15 MAY 1883 L	17	440
Kirby, Jenny C.	Roeser, Adolph	30 AUG 1882 R	16	495
Kirby, Laura Virginia	Earnest, Henry Taylor	23 OCT 1883 R	18	207
Kirby, Mary Kate	Mann, Richard Wise	17 AUG 1879 R	13	254
Kirby, Mary V.	Milstead, Robert A.	27 MAR 1884 R	18	483
Kirby, Samuel G., Jr.	French, Fannie M.	10 OCT 1882 R	17	060
Kirby, Sarah	Johnson, Edward	29 JUN 1881 R	15	381
Kirby, Sarah	Lancaster, Herbert	21 JUL 1881 R	15	410

Name	Spouse	Date		
Kirby, Susan V.	Brooke, Thomas H., Jr.	05 JUL 1884	19	126
Kirby, Thomas	Gingell, Alice	07 JUL 1885 L	20	057
Kirchner, Rosa K.	Mitchell, Clifton	23 NOV 1881 R	16	091
Kirk, George W.	Jackson, Irene	22 OCT 1878 R	12	286
Kirk, Kathirine A.	Stewart, John	11 OCT 1883	18	187
Kirk, Marian Frances	Henderson, John William	01 NOV 1882 R	17	104
Kirk, Nicholas J.	Schwing, Katie	29 APR 1884 R	18	539
Kirk, Sumner S.	Williamson, J. Rosa	01 JUL 1884	19	113
Kirkland, William W.	Kreamer, Rose V.	23 AUG 1883	18	096
Kirmamon, Jacob H.	Williams, Carrie L.V.	15 JAN 1885 L	20	020
Kiskadden, Annie E.	Adams, Perry M.	26 APR 1881 R	15	271
Kissner, Clara	Gude, Henry	21 JUL 1880 L	14	370
Kissner, Lawrence	Barber, Elenora	17 JUN 1879	13	233
Kissner, Mary Elizabeth	Miller, Daniel	04 JUN 1883 L	17	474
Kissner, Robert	Barshall, Fannie	01 FEB 1882	16	220
Kitchen, Nora	Routzhn, Charles	15 APR 1885 R	20	161
Kite, Cora L.	Graves, James P.	15 OCT 1883 R	18	193
Kite, Isaac Newton	Reid, Mary C.	07 OCT 1880 R	14	483
Kite, Thomas O.	Gailey, Annie	31 MAY 1881	15	334
Kittle, Susan	Warren, Julius	14 OCT 1879 L	13	421
Kittrick, Thornton	Marshall, Mary	16 JAN 1878 L	11	307
Kitzmiller, Martin	Plant, Alice J.	24 DEC 1878 L	12	399
Kizer, Sallie A.	Sweble, Charles F.	21 AUG 1879	13	327
Klabunde, Louisa	Deske, Karl	01 JAN 1881	15	125
Klaumburg, Annie	Wood, Edward	08 APR 1878 R	11	409
Klear, Kaspar	Vesta, Kate	13 JUN 1881 R	15	357
Klein, Amelia	Casten, Henry	25 SEP 1881 R	15	491
Klein, Valentine	Wagner, Anna	22 AUG 1878	12	176
Kleinberger, William	Heilprin, Henrietta	09 DEC 1879 L	14	036
Kleindienst, Joseph B.	Everts, Virginia	11 JUN 1885 L	20	269
Kleinhause, Susie E.	Briggs, Solomon R.	03 APR 1879 R	13	122
Klenk, John George	Ricks, Louisa C.	04 NOV 1879 R	13	463
Klino, James H.G.	Hartwick, Emma	07 APR 1880 R	14	214
Kline, Jane	Degges, Charles A.	14 AUG 1877 L	11	053
Kline, Louisa	Karr, Philip A.	04 APR 1882 R	16	296
Kline, Peter	Rogers, Jane H.	11 NOV 1877 R	11	175
Kline, Peter	Windsor, Margaret A.	20 APR 1882	16	328
Kline, Scott M.	Keifer, Cora May	18 AUG 1885 L	20	375
Klock, Henry Anderson	Rowzer, Julia A.	02 OCT 1883 R	18	164
Kloman, Annie M.	Neurath, John V.	20 JAN 1881 R	15	158
Klopfer, Harry C.	Blondel, Emma V.	26 MAR 1884 L	18	482
Klopfer, Laura Viriginia	Cook, John Waters	25 FEB 1880	14	166
Klopfer, Walter H.	Blondel, Maggie W.	28 DEC 1881 L	16	166
Klotz, Annie R.	Scherer, Charles H.	28 NOV 1882 L	17	151
Klotz, Fred R.	Scherer, Clara	20 MAY 1882 L	16	371
Klotz, Henry E.	Herman, Linda	03 OCT 1881	16	002
Klotz, Mary	Reed, Thomas	10 DEC 1877 L	11	228
Klueh, August	Ritz, Lucy	17 APR 1882 L	16	320
Klueh, Josephine	Popp, Oswold	11 OCT 1881	16	017
Klug, Elizabeth	Brahler, John H.	23 NOV 1880	15	059
Klug, Katie A.	Smith, Robert B.	25 NOV 1884 L	19	408
Klug, Lizzie Mary	Brahler, George W.	17 SEP 1885 L	20	425
Klug, Mary	Gramlich, John P.	25 SEP 1883	18	151
Knabe, Bertha	Linden, Edward C., Jr.	17 JUN 1885 R	20	271
Knabe, Karl Albert Theo.	Wagner, Josephine	12 APR 1885 R	20	151
Knapp, Gustav	Covington, Ellen T.	05 APR 1882 L	16	298
Knapp, John H.	Rightstine, E. Kate	14 MAY 1879 L	13	188
Knauff, Mary E.	Miller, Edgar L.	21 AUG 1880 R	14	410

D.C. Marriage Records Index, June 28, 1877 to October 19, 1885   267

Name	Spouse	Date	Vol	Page
Knauff, William Jacob	Snapp, Sarah Agnes	09 NOV 1880 R	15	038
Kneas, Adolph	Finly, Sarah H.	08 NOV 1881	16	067
Kneas, Pauline C.	O'Hare, Michael	23 DEC 1879 R	13	474
Kneesi, Fred W.	Stewart, Laura E.	16 APR 1880 L	14	226
Knemb, Rosa	Raymond, Albert M.	23 APR 1883	17	403
Knight, Anna Ruth	Howard, William Robert	26 MAR 1883 R	17	361
Knight, Annie E.	James, Charlie	29 APR 1879	13	156
Knight, Charles D.	Hannum, Jennie	20 FEB 1884	18	432
Knight, E.E.	Chapman, E.K.	12 MAY 1879 R	13	186
Knight, Emma Katie	McGee, Delavan	03 APR 1880 R	14	208
Knight, Jackson	Bishop, Mollie	31 OCT 1883	18	222
Knight, Lizzie G.	Brittain, Milton J.	31 JUL 1877 L	11	034
Knight, Marie Lillian	Hunt, William Franklin	07 NOV 1878 R	12	314
Knight, Mary K.	Pollard, J. Austin	22 JUN 1882 L	16	423
Knight, Virginia	McUllum, John	02 MAY 1883	17	428
Knighton, Michael	Downey, Hanna	24 DEC 1883 L	18	339
Knoch, Marie	Schoeltzel, Albert	26 MAR 1884	18	483
Knode, Thomas	Edson, Emma E.	02 AUG 1882 L	16	466
Knoor, William H.A.	Arpenstaen, Annie Oertele	15 DEC 1884 L	19	459
Knopp, Charles	Ogle, Mary A.	08 JUL 1879 R	13	273
Knott, Annie May	Woodward, Kirby Sedley	15 JAN 1885 L	20	019
Knott, Benjamin F.	Underwood, Annie C.	24 FEB 1879 L	13	073
Knott, Cora C.	West, Albert C.	25 JUN 1879 R	13	247
Knott, Isaiah	Goodrick, Martha	21 SEP 1878 L	12	230
Knott, James H.	Walter, Mary	05 JUL 1877 R	11	008
Knott, James William	Cheseldine, Annie Sophia	22 DEC 1881 R	16	149
Knott, Jennie V.	Donaldson, Thomas A.	25 APR 1885 L	20	189
Knott, John	Harden, Mary Jane	07 MAR 1878 L	11	376
Knott, John	Eglin, Mary E.	15 NOV 1880 R	14	500
Knott, John Francis	Hume, Jennie	01 SEP 1881 R	15	469
Knott, Linnie A.	Korts, Charles H.	06 OCT 1885 R	20	464
Knott, Margaret C.	Wise, Samuel C.	02 JUN 1884 L	19	049
Knott, Maria Frances	Piercynski, Joseph Charles	02 AUG 1883	18	072
Knott, Mary Jane	Randall, Robert Thomas	20 NOV 1884	19	399
Knott, William	Staton, Lottie	17 AUG 1882	16	485
Knowles, Alice Magruder	Taylor, John Phinney	03 MAY 1883 R	17	429
Knowles, David O.	Hogan, Mary	28 NOV 1880	15	064
Knowles, John B.	Sengstack, Ida	21 APR 1880 L	14	231
Knowles, Sarah E., Mrs.	Henley, Hamilton H.	07 JAN 1879 L	13	010
Knox, Anna Octavia	Parkins, Marrast, Con.	13 OCT 1883	18	192
Knox, Fannie	Colvin, John R.	24 DEC 1878 R	12	388
Knox, James	O'Neill, Mary	21 FEB 1878 L	11	352
Knox, M.B.	Hamilton, Ross	18 MAY 1885 L	20	228
Knox, Maude H.	Wheeley, George E.	04 MAR 1885 R	20	095
Knox, William Salsbury	Hamilton, Cora L.	14 OCT 1885 R	20	479
Koats, Charles A.	Clark, Lillie	25 FEB 1884 L	18	442
Kober, Charles	Broeker, Mary	10 JUL 1884	19	134
Koch, Adelaide M.	Murray, Walter Walls	26 FEB 1884	18	443
Koch, Barbara L.	Ruppert, John H.	03 OCT 1882 L	17	048
Koch, Catherine E.	Keppler, George H.	11 FEB 1880 R	14	149
Koch, Katie	Daughton, Dixon M.	24 OCT 1883	18	210
Koch, Margaret	Martin, William	14 SEP 1882	17	022
Koch, Mary E.	Prott, Frank J.	06 FEB 1882 L	16	226
Koch, William	Murray, Ella May	23 NOV 1880 R	15	062
Koch, William	Weigel, Sophia	28 MAY 1885	20	245
Koechling, Magnus	Robinson, Regina M.	29 MAY 1879 L	13	392
Koehler, Ferdinand	Ribnitzki, Pauline	09 APR 1882 R	16	305
Koehler, George	Holland, Estelle M.	30 SEP 1885 L	20	448

Koehler, John A.	Sonnemann, Caroline Dorothea	20 FEB 1879 R	13	064
Koehler, Louisa C.	Reilly, William B.	15 APR 1884 L	18	513
Koehler, William F.	France, Augusta Bertha	25 JUN 1885 R	20	293
Koenig, John M.	Dredge, Laura Virginia	20 JAN 1881 R	15	160
Koepf, Louise	Baurman, Augustus B.	24 MAR 1885	20	129
Koester, Lewis	Faubel, Alice H.	02 JUN 1879	13	213
Koetzner, Mary A.	Appich, John	18 JUN 1879	13	212
Kohl, Frank	Ruppert, Mary Annie	06 MAY 1878 L	12	038
Kohl, Mamie L.	Brown, Robert	13 OCT 1884 L	19	301
Kohl, Mary E.	Wedmann, Joseph C.	18 JAN 1881	15	154
Kohler, Friedrick	Michelbacher, Elisa, Mrs.	18 JAN 1880 R	14	111
Kohlert, Katie	Hoffman, Charles	25 JUN 1881 L	15	379
Kolb, Charles A.	Gasch, Lissetta M.	18 JUN 1884 R	19	089
Kolb, Dora S.	Oakham, Lemuel Wyatt	08 JUL 1878 L	12	127
Kolb, Edward L.	Goebel, Othilia	10 JUN 1884 R	19	073
Konig, Bertha	Detterer, Auguste	03 DEC 1877 L	11	215
Kookogey, Adah Naomi	Gibbons, George Walter	01 JAN 1884 R	18	349
Kookogey, Olivia R.	Pogenhoff, Frank W.	02 JAN 1885	20	002
Kooms, Gwenett	Johnson, Richard	02 APR 1879	13	124
Koon, Clara H.	Baxter, G.H.	24 APR 1878	12	022
Koon, Jennie L.	Chappel, Charles H.	24 APR 1878	12	021
Koons, Carrie R.	Kern, Henry P.	29 APR 1079 R	13	103
Koons, Charles Henry	Sammons, Lizzie E.	15 OCT 1884 R	19	308
Koons, Robert John W.	Brewster, Mary Walker	06 FEB 1883 R	17	291
Koontz, A.W.	Speck, Lillie D.	10 JUL 1878 R	12	131
Koontz, Anna D.	O'Donnell, John H	11 JUL 1882 R	16	444
Koontz, Marcellus	Pusey, Annie	07 APR 1878	11	410
Koontz, Margaret L.	Smith, Jesse A.	24 SEP 1878	12	230
Koontz, Medora	Dyer, John W.	01 MAR 1879	13	085
Koontz, Olivia W.	Smith, Frank H.	27 AUG 1884 L	19	209
Koontz, Thomas L.	Barron, Ada R.	07 FEB 1882 R	16	229
Koppen, William	Buecholer, Emilie	02 SEP 1885 R	20	393
Korster, Johana Buchsteiner	Heitmüller, Charles	10 MAR 1881 R	15	222
Korts, Charles H.	Knott, Linnie A.	06 OCT 1885 R	20	464
Kottmann, Henry	Godron, Barbara	21 MAR 1882	16	280
Kowaska, Josephine A. Ruth	Seward, William L.	06 DEC 1879 R	14	032
Kozel, Charles F.	Meinikheim, Anna C.	10 OCT 1881 R	16	016
Kozel, George	Tilp, Rose E.	15 APR 1879 R	13	146
Kozel, George Fredrick	Meyer, Katie M.	13 MAY 1885 R	20	220
Kracka, Bertha	Beckmann, August	20 JUN 1883	17	466
Kraemer, Charles	Scherger, Johanna E.	28 NOV 1880 R	15	069
Kraemer, John	Giesler, Julia	10 JAN 1883	17	248
Kraemer, William	Ewald, Rose	18 NOV 1877	11	188
Kraemmer, Lorenz Theodor	Graefe, Lena	19 AUG 1880 L	14	406
Krafft, Pertonilla	Rice, Henry D.	10 MAR 1885 R	20	105
Kraft, Clarence O.	Jackson, Mary V.	23 JAN 1882 L	16	205
Kraft, Henson C.	Heller, Annie	16 SEP 1883	18	133
Kraft, John	Colcasier, Hattie	17 OCT 1880 R	14	499
Kraft, Louise C.	Smith, Adolphus B.	24 NOV 1880 L	15	064
Kraft, Philip	Donovan, Annie C.	17 AUG 1880 R	14	403
Kraft, Philip C.	Huysman, Anna Maaria	05 NOV 1878 R	12	307
Kraft, Philip H.	Foreman, Hattie M.	30 OCT 1884 L	19	350
Kraft, William S.	Markland, Sallie	28 SEP 1885 R	20	445
Krahling, Herman	Daughton, Emma	16 OCT 1884 R	19	314
Kramer, Alois	Bauer, Dora	02 FEB 1882	16	219
Kramer, Frederika	Rihner, Caspar	14 MAR 1881 R	15	224
Kramer, George	Wood, Mary V.	31 AUG 1878 R	12	189
Kramer, J.C.	Duley, Ida W.	19 AUG 1880 L	14	408

Kramer, James Sewell, Jr.	Onward, Lillie K.	02 DEC 1881 R	16	129
Kramer, John J.	Talbot, Maggie A.	05 NOV 1879 L	13	465
Kramer, Mary D.	Barrett, Elbert G.	19 DEC 1883 L	18	328
Kraus, Annie	Mühler, Henry	16 JUL 1880 L	14	365
Kraus, Catherine L.	Graninger, Balthaser	09 SEP 1883	18	117
Kraus, Charles A.	Holland, Mollie E.	11 AUG 1884 L	19	179
Kraus, Katie	Paine, George Wm.	16 JUN 1881 R	15	365
Krause, Bertha L.	Dieterich, Fred G.	07 OCT 1879 R	13	406
Krause, Charles Adolph	Fraeler, Ella Marc.	11 JUN 1884 R	19	075
Krause, Franz	Hierling, Mary Adelaide	19 JUL 1884	19	147
Krause, John	Hurley, Addie	12 FEB 1884 R	18	422
Krause, Julia	Till, George B.	18 DEC 1883	18	314
Krause, Lizzie	Mercer, Harvey	02 JUL 1878 R	12	121
Krause, William	Conley, Annie	07 SEP 1885 L	20	402
Krauskopf, Katie M.	Glutting, Andrew F.	27 JAN 1885 R	20	036
Kreamer, Charles A.	Shoemaker, Ella N.	19 AUG 1884 L	19	193
Kreamer, Rose V.	Kirkland, William W.	23 AUG 1883	18	096
Kreamer, Samuel G.	Taylor, Elizza C.	03 OCT 1883	18	167
Krehling, Lizzie B.	Rocheweg, Charles D.	19 NOV 1882 R	17	134
Kreidler, Edward Allanson	Wells, Mary Dagworthy	24 OCT 1877 R	11	151
Kremer, C.H.	Devine, Julia C.	21 FEB 1884 L	18	435
Krepps, George W.	Yarber, Mamie	27 APR 1885	20	190
Krepps, Helen V.	Bergling, Bernard	14 NOV 1884 L	19	381
Kretschmann, Hugo	Shellhorn, Sophie	16 NOV 1881 R	16	073
Kreuter, William George	Artes, Mary	08 DEC 1879	14	035
Krey, Charles H.	Cook, Annie	27 NOV 1884 R	19	411
Krich, Charles	Leypold, Emma	09 NOV 1880 R	15	037
Krichelt, Mary C.	Weidman, John C.	30 JUN 1885	20	302
Krisman, Emma	Hill, William	18 JUL 1878 L	12	140
Krochel, Lena	Courtney, John R.	27 JAN 1879	13	035
Kroeling, Mary	Umhau, George M.	04 OCT 1880 L	14	472
Krogmann, Clement	Lochbeohler, Lena	17 APR 1882 L	16	320
Krone, Maria Lisette	Feldman, Christoph Frederick	17 OCT 1880 R	14	497
Kropp, Barbara	Kropp, Henry, Sr.	02 JUL 1882 R	16	433
Kropp, Henry, Jr.	Wetzel, Sallie J.	13 MAY 1885 R	20	218
Kropp, Henry, Sr.	Kropp, Barbara	02 JUL 1882 R	16	433
Krouse, Kentzing P.	Warren, Annie E.	29 SEP 1885 R	20	447
Krouse, Mary L.	Preston, John H.	04 JAN 1882 R	16	180
Krouse, Rose	Perkins, James T.	11 APR 1882 R	16	308
Krug, Mary Theresa	Wogonfield, Valentine C.	02 NOV 1881 R	16	058
Kruger, Charles William	Smith, Nettie G.	05 NOV 1884 R	19	362
Krumke, Carl	Ziegler, Babetta Wilhelmine	06 FEB 1878 L	11	330
Kübler, Carl August	Bechler, Maria	04 JUN 1884 R	19	061
Kuchling, Benjamin C.	Keyes, Mattie E.	08 JUN 1881 R	15	353
Kueberth, Barbara	Zimmerman, Alfred	18 JUN 1885 R	20	279
Kuebuer, Richard	Smith, Elizabeth	17 OCT 1878 R	12	270
Kuhblank, Emil	Colignon, Louise	21 JAN 1884 R	18	235
Kuhlman, Fredrick	Geier, Annie	18 SEP 1881	15	489
Kuhlman, Mary Louise	Hoffman, Ernest Emil	24 JAN 1878 R	11	316
Kuhlmann, Henry	Berger, Auguste	22 JUN 1881	15	369
Kuhn, Joseph	Schirmer, Mary	05 APR 1884 L	18	497
Kuhn, Lena	Gloom, John W.	14 OCT 1883	18	191
Kuhn, Louisa	Wesley, George W.	02 DEC 1883	18	290
Kuhn, Mary J.	Lowe, George R.	29 NOV 1877 L	11	212
Kuhn, Richard P.	Williams, Buenavista	03 MAR 1880	14	172
Kuker, Ludwig	Scott, Annie, Mrs.	04 JUN 1883 R	17	463
Kulle, Lizzie A.	Magill, Charles W.	09 JUN 1885	20	265
Kummer, Joseph	Watson, Addie T.	31 MAY 1879 L	13	213

Künzig, Fraziska	Bucigaluppi, John	06 JUN 1884	19	066
Kurchival, George W.	Merson, Lucretia Virginia	14 DEC 1882 R	17	183
Kurtz, Jane Mosher	Smoot, William Sothoron	29 NOV 1882 R	17	152
Kurtz, Lewis	Frankel, Friederika	25 MAY 1878 L	12	066
Kydd, Eleanor M.	Champlin, William	09 APR 1878	12	046
Kyle, Christopher C.	Spaulding, Mary H.	15 NOV 1883 L	18	256
Kyle, Emma G.	Carrico, William C.	14 SEP 1885 R	20	415
Kyle, James	Curtain, Ida	07 FEB 1878	11	333
Kyle, Mary E.	Nicholson, Charles M.	11 AUG 1879 R	13	297
Kyler, Mary Allen	Gray, George	14 MAR 1878	11	343
Kyler, William H.	Reed, Fannie	02 AUG 1884 L	19	166
Kyne, Bridget	Finley, Joseph James	10 JUL 1880 L	14	356
Kyne, Mamie A.	Connor, John F.	02 SEP 1884 L	19	221

L

La Fetra, Anna M.	Arberly, Abraham J.	13 AUG 1885	20	368
LaBarre, George Emanuel	Whitman, Emma	27 JUL 1883	18	061
Labor, Thomas	Shehan, Ellen	13 NOV 1877 L	11	182
Lacey, Carrie Virginia	Garrison, George Edward	14 APR 1884 R	18	506
Lacey, Edith E.	Power, J. Clyde	23 JUL 1884	19	153
Lacey, Eliza I.	Hester, J. Lester A.	28 AUG 1884	19	215
Lacey, Joseph	Posey, Emma	27 JUL 1882 L	16	428
Lacey, Julia R.	Lyddane, William W.	11 MAY 1881 R	15	303
Lacey, Lewis	Nelson, Anna	26 MAY 1880 L	14	291
Lacey, Lewis	Tolliver, Irene	11 APR 1882	16	306
Lacey, Martha J.	Jarboe, George H.	24 DEC 1881 L	16	156
Lacey, Mary Jane	Adamson, Richard Alvin	13 FEB 1879 R	13	059
Lacey, Richard M.	Smithson, Sarah O.	21 AUG 1877 R	11	061
Lacey, William B.	Marks, Martha	21 APR 1878 R	12	013
Lacey, William L.	Hurley, Mamie F.	02 MAY 1883 R	17	427
Lachmann, Mary	Harris, Michael	19 JUN 1883 L	18	004
Lackey, Elizabeth M.	Adams, James W.	03 MAY 1878 L	12	036
Lackey, Sally	Mack, John	18 JUL 1877	11	025
Lacy, Annie E.	Shaw, James A.	11 DEC 1879	14	035
Lacy, George	Ford, Annie	21 FEB 1883	17	316
Lacy, Jennie	Brown, Charles H.	27 MAY 1880 R	14	290
Lacy, Jennie R.	Hall, F.P.	08 JUL 1880	14	353
Lacy, Oliver	Baker, Mary Eliza	13 AUG 1883 L	18	084
Lacy, Sylvester S.	Jackson, Clara P.	30 MAR 1882 L	16	293
Lacy, Virginia	Hillman, Charles	15 SEP 1884	19	249
Ladd, Elizabeth	Mishaw, John	29 NOV 1877 R	11	207
Ladd, Story Butler	Paine, Eliza Brigham	18 DEC 1878 R	12	386
Ladson, Charles John	Rodier, Louisa Monroe	25 JUN 1885 R	20	293
Ladson, Emily	Kaldenbach, Robert J.	29 NOV 1884 R	19	427
Ladson, Henry James	Gregory, Hannah Lewis	22 OCT 1879 R	13	438
Ladson, Thomas Alfred	Voss, Alice May	10 MAY 1882 R	16	356
Lafayette, Pierce	Holmes, Nannie T.	27 DEC 1877	11	273
Lafelle, William P.	Stuart, Mary F.	06 OCT 1881 L	16	012
LaFleur, William C.	Kellain, Margaret E.	29 JUL 1879 L	13	297
LaFontaine, Mary	Law, John W.	05 APR 1884 L	18	496
Lafontine, Alice	Beatty, Charles A.	19 OCT 1877 L	11	146
Lahey, Ellen	Johnston, William Henry	12 FEB 1882 R	16	237
Lahey, Katie	Duehring, Edward, Jr.	16 OCT 1881 R	16	024
Lahey, Mary Catherine	Shelton, Joseph	12 DEC 1884 R	19	456
Lahey, Mollie	Crandall, Clarke P.	26 JAN 1885	20	036
Laignel, Marie	Cassell, Washington F.	25 JUN 1884 R	19	103
Lair, Martha A.	Duckett, James	19 DEC 1878	12	391
Lake, Annie	Goodno, Charles E.	26 MAR 1878 R	11	393
Lake, James Randall	Ballock, Kate	14 JUN 1882 R	16	408
Lake, William E.	Leech, Mary Alice	19 JUL 1878	12	142
Lake, Wilmot	Collins, Annie M.	08 JAN 1885 L	20	008
Lalley, Katie	Callaghan, Dennis	08 JUL 1879 L	13	274
Lamar, Martha Ann	Gwin, William	10 OCT 1877 R	11	129
Lamar, Sarah I.	Padgett, Joseph H.	25 AUG 1884 R	19	205
Lamb, Francis H.	Ewin, Deborah D.	20 MAY 1880	14	276
Lamb, Francis R.	Bailey, Lidia E.	23 FEB 1882	16	258
Lamb, Jennie M.	Clarvoe, R.G.	28 DEC 1882	17	220
Lamb, John Melvin, Dr.	Fischer, Pauline A.	08 SEP 1885 R	20	405
Lamb, Laura E.W.	Hammond, Willie D.	08 JUN 1885	20	261
Lamb, Mary A. Hunt	Schneider, William Ionian	04 FEB 1880 R	14	136
Lambert, Alice M. Williams	Cox, Samuel Henry	20 DEC 1880 R	15	112
Lambert, Connorn	Brown, Henry	05 DEC 1882 L	17	167

Lambert, Eugene	Martin, Caroline	06 DEC 1883 L	18	298
Lambert, Henry	Brown, Alice R.	02 JUL 1879 R	13	260
Lambert, Jefferson D.	Weadon, Sarah P.	01 OCT 1885	20	452
Lambert, Josephine	Cornwell, Thompson	15 OCT 1879 R	13	427
Lambie, Edward L.	Blau, Antoinette H.	02 FEB 1881 R	15	171
Lambourne, George F.	Dowell, Emma	08 NOV 1882 R	17	119
Lamkin, Alice V.	Hansen, John H.	12 OCT 1878	12	271
Lamkin, Minnie V.	Jones, William Botts	03 AUG 1882 R	16	466
Lamkins, Wilson	Wilson, Annie	12 DEC 1883 L	18	310
Lamont, John Charles	Clear, Mary Alline	16 SEP 1885 R	20	423
Lamson, Charles H.	Rickard, Mary C.	13 JAN 1884 R	18	374
Lanahan, John	McGinley, Mary	03 OCT 1878 L	12	251
Lanahan, Martha	Kernner, Henry G.	09 JUN 1880	14	311
Lanahan, Mary Elizabeth	Norris, Brison	27 JUN 1883 L	18	022
Lanam, George	Elsey, Louisa	13 MAR 1883	17	340
Lancaster, Agnes H.	Peters, Arthur S.	02 SEP 1879	13	345
Lancaster, Alfred	Pinkney, Laura	25 NOV 1879	14	004
Lancaster, Andrew Jackson	Heyl, Elizabeth Rebecca	30 JUL 1882 R	16	458
Lancaster, Augustus, Jr.	Harris, Katie	01 SEP 1885	20	394
Lancaster, Benjamin	Brooks, Isabella	13 OCT 1880 R	14	492
Lancaster, C.H.	Johnson, Laurie	07 JUN 1880	14	308
Lancaster, Catherine Bost, Mrs.	Mozee, William	02 FEB 1882 R	16	220
Lancaster, Cresey	Miller, Giles	19 JUL 1881	15	407
Lancaster, Henrietta	Carroll, Edward	30 JUN 1880 L	14	339
Lancaster, Henry Clay	Elliott, Annie S.	30 OCT 1882 R	17	100
Lancaster, Herbert	Kirby, Sarah	21 JUL 1881 R	15	410
Lancaster, Isaih	Freeman, Reah	16 DEC 1880 L	15	104
Lancaster, John	Bird, Florence	09 MAY 1881 L	15	297
Lancaster, John W.	Morris, Jennie	24 DEC 1878 L	12	398
Lancaster, Lucretia	Tinney, John T.	20 JAN 1880	14	113
Lancaster, Mary S.	Eliot, Llewellyn	15 APR 1885	20	169
Lancaster, Russell	Parker, Harriet	29 DEC 1884 L	19	498
Lancaster, Sarah E.	Giles, John M.	05 NOV 1879 L	13	465
Lanckton, Thomas W.	Ellett, Martha J.	06 SEP 1877	11	078
Lancster, John	Holmes, Mary	17 NOV 1881 R	16	084
Landic, Isaac	Teagle, Mary Jane	18 MAY 1882 L	16	366
Landig, Isaac	Scotlin, Victoria	21 FEB 1878 L	11	351
Landon, Cordelia A.	Crown, French C.	28 JAN 1885	20	042
Landon, G.W.	Barnett, K.J.	24 JUL 1879	13	292
Landon, Herbert	Mitchell, Maggie Frank	16 AUG 1883	18	089
Landon, Isaac	Burgess, Susan	07 JAN 1879 L	13	009
Landon, Joseph	Paris, Matilda	10 JAN 1878 R	11	299
Landram, Sarah L.	Bradley, Edward J.	10 AUG 1882 L	16	476
Landren, Lizzie	Day, Edward	12 JUN 1879 L	13	232
Landrick, Virginia	Bain, William V.	03 FEB 1879 L	13	043
Landrum, Blanche L.	Blakey, William O.	21 OCT 1884 R	19	327
Landvoigt, William H.	Arnold, Ezzie	14 MAR 1878 L	11	381
Lane, Abby	Rigney, Patrick	06 OCT 1879 L	13	407
Lane, Andrew Jackson	Brooks, Ella Geneva	13 OCT 1881 R	16	022
Lane, Ann Matilda	Mason, John A.	16 JAN 1883 R	17	259
Lane, Annie	Monroe, William Ignatius	22 APR 1879 L	13	154
Lane, Daniel	Clayton, Airy E.	13 MAY 1880 L	14	269
Lane, George W.	Ward, Virginia A.	08 NOV 1880 R	15	036
Lane, Hannah	Jackson, Lemuel	20 MAR 1879	13	110
Lane, Harriet	Keys, William Henry	13 JAN 1880 L	14	103
Lane, Louisa	Jones, Peter	23 SEP 1880 L	14	458
Lane, Louise	Warren, John	08 DEC 1884 L	19	441
Lane, Reuben	Ridgeley, Eliza Ann	28 MAR 1878	11	396

D.C. Marriage Records Index, June 28, 1877 to October 19, 1885

Lane, Robert Alexander	Coats, Jane	09 OCT 1877 R	10	2328
Lane, W. Aloysius	O'Connell, E.D.C.	04 JUL 1877 L	11	008
Lane, William	Daly, Margaret	15 OCT 1877 R	11	134
Lane, William	Thomas, Julia	21 DEC 1882 R	17	201
Lane, William Andrew	Cautions, Mary Eliza Sewall	21 APR 1881 R	15	258
Laner, Mary R.	Downs, Peter	05 FEB 1882	16	218
Lanes, Elias	Johnson, Mary	09 AUG 1884 L	19	177
Laney, John	Smith, Emma	22 MAR 1878 L	11	390
Laney, Julia	Patten, James M.	09 JUL 1885 R	20	318
Lang, Fannie Wing	Coffin, Edwin Chapin	30 APR 1878 R	12	027
Lang, Fanny	Roane, John William	20 MAY 1880 L	14	280
Lang, John	Patten, Lucy	26 MAR 1883 R	17	359
Lang, Oscar	Case, Marion Hill	18 JUL 1883	18	052
Lang, William	Harrison, Maggie E.	16 NOV 1879 R	13	488
Lang, William H.	Evans, Sallie	08 JAN 1880 R	14	096
Langdon, William	Weaver, Susie	15 JUL 1885	20	329
Lange, George William	Denham, Cora Virginia	18 JAN 1881 R	15	154
Langer, Joseph R.	Gurrath, Rosina, Mrs.	15 MAY 1881 R	15	305
Langhorn, Annie	Hooper, George	20 OCT 1882 L	17	083
Langhorne, Mary M.	McRae, G.F.	26 SEP 1884	19	270
Langley, Emma V.	Whitelow, Charles A.	30 APR 1879 L	13	169
Langley, Hattie A.	Lenman, Charles E.R.	28 JUN 1881 L	15	380
Langley, John H.	Berry, Mary H.	19 DEC 1878 R	12	386
Langley, Lizzie E.	Langley, William T.	01 DEC 1882 R	17	163
Langley, Lizzie S.	Harries, George H.	23 APR 1884	18	530
Langley, Lizzie T.	Drane, Thomas W.	03 APR 1878 L	11	416
Langley, Lucy M.	O'Brien, Eustace E.	17 MAR 1884 R	18	473
Langley, Margaret S., Mrs.	Mankin, George Henry	29 JAN 1878 R	11	321
Langley, Margaret S.	Barnett, William	15 JUN 1883 R	17	496
Langley, Mary	Stanici, Michael	16 FEB 1881 R	15	188
Langley, Preston F.B.	Burdine, Mary I.	10 JUN 1884 L	19	073
Langley, Richard Warren	Bowie, Annie S.	12 SEP 1878	12	209
Langley, Robert R.	O'Neill, Julia Webster	26 OCT 1880 R	15	015
Langley, Sarah E.S.	Maddox, Frederick	06 FEB 1884 R	18	412
Langley, Sue G.	LeFevre, H.W.	10 JAN 1883	27	6535
Langley, Treasia G.	Tippett, Marion A.	27 JUN 1883	18	020
Langley, Walter B.	Thurston, Harriet R.	16 OCT 1879 R	13	425
Langley, William T.	Langley, Lizzie E.	01 DEC 1882 R	17	163
Langry, Annie	Young, Luke	18 MAY 1878 L	12	058
Langston, Annie	Wallace, Richard	06 APR 1883	17	383
Langston, Lemuel	Brown, Mary Josephine	22 DEC 1877 L	11	260
Langston, Nettie D.	Napier, James C.	02 OCT 1878 R	12	247
Langston, Ralph E.	Jackson, Ann Mary	14 MAR 1881 L	15	224
Langston, Richard	Hill, Mildred C.	23 APR 1885 L	20	186
Langton, Henry	Ace, Annie	14 MAY 1885	20	223
Langworthy, S. Ransom	Cox, Gussie	16 JUN 1884 L	19	086
Langworthy, Villie M.	Harding, C.T.	02 JUN 1880 R	14	301
Lanham, Alfred E.	Kidwell, Laura V.	27 DEC 1877	11	272
Lanham, Columbus F.	Talbert, Sarah M.	05 SEP 1878 R	12	198
Lanham, Martha E.	Lucas, William E.	27 JAN 1880 R	14	021
Lanham, Rachel	Brown, John B.	02 JUL 1881 R	15	384
Lanham, Rebecca	Johnson, James	12 NOV 1884 L	19	377
Lanham, William	Loveless, Mary	23 JUN 1881 L	15	376
Lanhardt, Maggie M.	Sonder, Lewis F.	24 JUN 1885 L	20	289
Laning, Delia	Morten, Wyatt	02 SEP 1880 R	14	430
Lansburgh, Carrie	Jacobs, Harry H.	25 MAR 1885 R	20	129
Lansdale, Addie L.	Watt, John Henry	08 JUN 1881 R	15	351
Lansdale, Charlotte Bleecker	Lowber, Henry Sergeant	30 OCT 1884	19	336

Name	Spouse	Date	Vol	Page
Lansdale, Ella A.	Sayre, Calvin L.	24 APR 1880 R	14	237
Lantz, Franklin W.	Sherman, Mary L.	31 MAR 1885 R	20	138
Lanz, Alexander, Jr.	Miller, Dora	02 NOV 1879 R	13	458
Lanzing, Mary	Tasco, Charles E.	03 OCT 1884 L	19	284
Lapham, Charlotte E.	Kimball, Israel, Jr.	17 JUL 1878 R	12	138
Lapham, William R.	Cross, Lillie M.	24 APR 1879	13	159
Lapiter, Willis	Waters, Carrie	18 APR 1878 L	12	011
Laplace, Leonide	Viboud, Francois	11 NOV 1880 R	15	042
Larcombe, Samuel Thos.	Martin, Margaret Ellen	16 JUL 1883	18	049
Larkin, Attie A.	Brooks, Jackson D.	21 APR 1880 L	14	231
Larkin, Julia Villet	Finley, John Park	18 NOV 1879 R	13	492
Larkin, Verona Elflida	Pollock, Andrew Lyon	25 OCT 1879 R	13	442
Larkins, Lewis	Thorton, Lizzie	12 SEP 1881 R	15	481
Larman, Ellanora	Sherwood, Clarkson R.	04 DEC 1878 R	12	366
Larman, Emma G.	Coumbe, Oscar H.	14 SEP 1881 R	15	485
Larman, Margaret	Norris, Calvin C.J.	14 APR 1879	13	140
Larman, Melvie M.	Holton, Hoyt A.	16 JAN 1883 R	17	257
Larmer, Julia Ann	Miles, Nathan Edwards	01 FEB 1882 R	16	220
Larmier, Leonide Elise	Fortin, Leon Sosthenes	22 DEC 1880 R	15	113
Larner, Charles N.	Cox, Annie B.	09 DEC 1884	19	443
Larner, John Bell	Reed, Kate Louise	08 DEC 1880	15	087
Larrabee, Bertha E.L.	Gary, Robert Lee	26 JUN 1884 R	19	104
Larrabee, Clinton	Hush, Eliza Theresa	04 SEP 1880 L	14	432
Lasano, Anna M.	Downs, Samuel I.	29 DEC 1880 R	15	126
Lashhorn, Charles S.H.	DeNeale, Jeannett Y.	10 JUL 1884	19	131
Lasier, Thomas Jefferson	Emery, Ellen	23 OCT 1878 R	12	285
Lasser, Oscar	Carberry, M.A.	31 JUL 1882 L	16	463
Latchford, Mary Etta	Harrison, John Thomas	05 MAY 1880 R	14	251
Latham, Anna	Bingham, Lafayette	06 APR 1880 L	14	212
Latham, James	Robey, Elizabeth	18 MAR 1879 R	13	105
Latham, Leroy Minor	Talley, Sarah Jane	16 APR 1879 R	13	147
Lathan, Lydia	Baber, Daniel	21 JAN 1879	13	026
Lathrop, Flora Elizth.	Ballard, Augustus Warwick	30 MAR 1880 R	14	202½
Latimer, Charles M.N., Dr.	Waters, Stella E.	05 NOV 1883 L	18	232
Latimer, Chas. Marshall N.	Waters, Stella	06 OCT 1883 R	28	6981
Latimer, Clementine R.	Clarke, George R.	20 JUL 1885 R	20	315
Latimer, Frederick	Goodman, Mary	02 OCT 1879 R	13	400
Latimer, John W.	Richardson, Eliza R.	15 MAR 1881	15	225
Latimer, Mary P.	Evans, George H.	12 DEC 1877 L	11	231
Latimer, William James	Allen, Mary Ann	14 FEB 1878 R	11	340
Latnee, Lewis H.	Smith, Jane	03 OCT 1882	17	050
Laton, Annie	Ellis, Edward	07 AUG 1879 R	13	309
Latta, Jennie	Lowry, Robert	19 DEC 1878 R	12	389
Laub, Francis A.	Williams, Effie	04 FEB 1880	14	136
Laubach, H.J.	Watson, Laura V.	30 JAN 1884	18	402
Laubie, Kate B.	Weeks, Edward E.	08 AUG 1877 R	11	045
Lauck, Carrie	Schmidt, Henry	19 NOV 1878 L	12	335
Lauck, Horatio Jones	Donaldson, Lucy Dawes	13 MAR 1884 R	18	468
Lauder, Charles	Detrick, Irene	13 MAY 1884 L	19	015
Lauder, John W.	Vessey, Mary I.	16 NOV 1882 R	17	133
Lauer, Heinrich F.W.	Bergmann, Hedwig	24 APR 1881 R	15	257
Lauer, Josephine	Schneider, Joseph	16 FEB 1879	13	056
Laughlin, John T.	Booth, Mary L.	24 MAY 1880 R	14	284
Laughlin, Mary A.	Higgs, Wm. Thompson	13 DEC 1877 R	11	236
Laughlin, William H.	Butts, Fannie M.	12 JUN 1882 R	16	406
Laugley, Charles H.	Stamp, Margaret E.	25 AUG 1885 R	20	385
Lauman, John H.	Hartung, Teresa L.A.	13 SEP 1884	19	245
Launay, Jane	Buttet, George	22 AUG 1884 L	19	203

Name	Spouse	Date	Vol	Page
Lauphelmer, Michael	Goldsmith, Clara	16 OCT 1878 L	12	275
Laurence, Caroline	Miller, Isaac C.	16 DEC 1880 L	15	106
Laurenzi, Cesare	Arata, Madalena	12 APR 1880 R	14	221
Lauria, Maria L.	Gerardi, Vincenigo	22 NOV 1880 L	15	060
Laurie, Jane B. (Richardson)	Somers, Richard	24 DEC 1882 R	17	208
Lautenberger, Elizabeth	Mills, Malachi	11 SEP 1883	18	124
Lauxmann, Barbara	Scroggins, George W.	18 MAR 1885 R	20	122
Laveen, Laura	Bornheim, Moses	13 OCT 1880 R	14	490
Lavender, Ella	Nutter, Frank B.	04 JUL 1878 R	12	118
Lavezzi, John	Keefer, Antoinette	16 FEB 1880 R	14	154
Lavezzi, Joseph Sylvester	Burn, Mary V.	21 OCT 1880	15	008
Law, Abner W.	Sandy, Mary E.	31 DEC 1881 L	16	175
Law, Elsie G.A. Justice	Ryland, Edward Craft	09 JUL 1879 L	13	277
Law, John W.	LaFontaine, Mary	05 APR 1884 L	18	496
Law, Laura Harding	Giddings, William	13 JAN 1882	16	193
Lawerence, A.	West, Mary	22 DEC 1881 L	16	155
Lawkins, Rosa	Hamilton, Joseph	06 AUG 1883 L	18	075
Lawler, D.J.	Buckley, Margaret V.	15 AUG 1877 L	11	054
Lawler, Samuel	Carter, Louisa	21 DEC 1881 R	16	146
Lawlers, Lizza	Newton, Henson	22 JUL 1880 L	14	372
Lawless, Annie	Darr, Philip	20 OCT 1883 L	18	204
Lawlor, James	O'Brien, Johannah	15 JAN 1880 L	14	109
Lawlor, James	Butler, Mary	10 JAN 1880 L	14	098
Lawrence, Cordelia F.	Bogger, William	30 OCT 1877 L	11	160
Lawrence, Emma J.	Campbell, Thomas H.	06 JAN 1884	18	366
Lawrence, Flonia	Rigney, William	09 DEC 1884	19	443
Lawrence, George	McDermott, Katie	22 SEP 1884 L	19	263
Lawrence, Henrietta	Steward, William W.	06 JAN 1881	15	144
Lawrence, Henry	McElreavy, Margaret J.	05 MAR 1885 R	20	096
Lawrence, Ida S.	Moore, Frederick R.	09 APR 1879 R	13	131
Lawrence, Martha, Mrs.	Smith, Montgomery	31 JUL 1879 R	13	301
Lawrence, Nina Eliz.	Wilson, Joseph Wilson	03 JUN 1885 R	20	252
Lawrence, Sylvia	Bell, Joshua	22 NOV 1880 L	15	060
Lawrence, Thomas Henry	Hosman, Victoria	05 MAR 1882 R	16	268
Lawrence, Wayman C.	Gaines, Margaret Catherine	23 JUL 1884	19	152
Laws, Corrie L.	Clagett, Henry B.	16 JAN 1884 R	18	379
Laws, Grace	Walker, Champ Turner	06 AUG 1877 R	11	042
Laws, John E.	Dockett, Nora E.	20 SEP 1883 L	18	146
Laws, Lindsey	Worn, Ellen	31 DEC 1881 L	16	174
Laws, Medora P.	Bennett, Charles S.	15 NOV 1877 R	11	190
Laws, Richard M.	Julius, Rosa L.	08 MAY 1878 R	12	043
Laws, Spencer	Washington, Maggie, Mrs.	31 JUL 1881 R	15	424
Lawson, Ada	Cook, Geo. T.	17 AUG 1882 R	16	485
Lawson, Adam	Fountain, Mary E.	29 JUN 1880 L	14	338
Lawson, Albert	Garner, Nellie	10 JAN 1881 L	15	145
Lawson, Benjamin F.	Anderson, Elizabeth A. Garner	06 JUL 1880 R	14	348
Lawson, Charlotte	Jones, Anthony	04 OCT 1880 L	14	472
Lawson, Elizabeth	Miller, James	09 OCT 1883 L	18	181
Lawson, Ella	Gibson, David	30 JAN 1878	11	322
Lawson, Emeline	Pleasants, Joseph H.	22 JUN 1883 L	18	010
Lawson, Fleetwood	Banks, Mary	18 SEP 1884 L	19	260
Lawson, Frances	Gant, Frank	04 SEP 1882 R	17	002
Lawson, Henry W.	Wright, Mary L.	26 FEB 1883	17	319
Lawson, J. William	Garner, Effie G.	19 DEC 1883 L	18	326
Lawson, James H.	Gloyd, Lizzie S. Clagett	16 OCT 1883 R	18	195
Lawson, Jesse	Coakley, Rosetta E.	17 DEC 1884 R	19	465
Lawson, John E.	Garner, Agnes V.	24 FEB 1881 R	15	202
Lawson, John E.	Snowden, Elizabeth	28 APR 1884 L	18	538

Lawson, Julia	Dodson, James	09 SEP 1879 L	13	360
Lawson, Julia	Washington, George	08 JUL 1884 L	19	128
Lawson, Mark F.E.	Gassaway, Sarah	19 JUN 1884 R	19	091
Lawson, Melvina	Coats, Lewis	27 NOV 1877	11	200
Lawson, Peter	Ross, Hattie	14 JUN 1883	17	492
Lawson, Samuel	Reed, Sina Ann	28 APR 1884 L	18	536
Lawson, Virginia Beach	Rushman, Wm. Andrew	25 AUG 1880 R	14	417
Lawson, William	Dobbins, Ella	29 OCT 1879 L	13	452
Lawton, A. Bradley	Campbell, Rosa E.	22 APR 1884	18	522
Lawton, William T.	Grant, Electa S.	03 SEP 1878 L	12	196
Lay, John A.	Withers, Kittie E.	23 SEP 1885 R	20	437
Layton, Almanzer W.	Mundell, Annie E.	24 DEC 1884 R	19	491
Layton, Ellen R.	Rodgers, John W.	10 JUN 1880	14	317
Layton, Katie W.	Malcolm, Horatio G.	05 NOV 1883 R	18	231
Lazenberry, Charles B.	Morris, Isabella	13 OCT 1870 R	13	418
Lazenby, Sarah E.	Floyd, Charles J.	03 DEC 1878 L	12	362
Lazenby, Sarah Frances	Mockabee, Henry C.	10 APR 1878	11	414
Le Fevre, H.W.	Longley, Sue G.	10 JAN 1883	17	250
Leach, Adoniram Judson	Lewis, Mary Foster	25 DEC 1883 R	18	337
Leach, Mary E.	Town, Edward Daniel	06 MAR 1879 R	13	091
Leach, Phineas Block	Morgan, Henrietta Maria	15 APR 1879 R	13	138
Leach, Susie	Marconnier, John A.	25 SEP 1879 R	13	381
Leache, Robert Willett	Armistead, Mary Loudon	23 AUG 1877	11	063
Leahy, Nellie	Delahunty, John	01 FEB 1884 L	18	404
Leahy, William	Downey, Bridget L.	22 MAY 1884 L	19	034
Leake, Mary G.	Deitrick, John W.	16 FEB 1881 R	15	192
Leake, Willie A.	Marsh, Gallie M.	19 MAY 1884 R	19	030
Leamon, Robert	Simons, Amanda J.	23 MAR 1880 R	14	192
Leapley, P.F.	Duckett, Grace B.	10 JUL 1879	13	278
Lear, Frances	Banks, James	06 NOV 1878	12	312
Lear, Thomas T.B.	Robey, Lottie	25 OCT 1881 R	16	041
Learriel, Alexandria	Loogood, Adelaid Victoria	10 SEP 1884 L	19	239
Leary, Ella	Murray, Elias H.	12 SEP 1878 R	12	216
Leary, Louisa	Cook, William F.	21 APR 1885 L	20	177
Leary, Maggie E.	Wood, George O.	26 FEB 1884 L	18	444
Leary, Mary	Desmond, Jerry	26 APR 1883 L	17	414
Leasenby, Catharine	Gray, William F.	07 JUL 1879 R	13	263
Leason, Frances	Pulchin, Pasqua	10 AUG 1885 R	20	363
Leavers, Lafayette	Clements, Mary S.	18 JUN 1884	19	090
Leavy, Cary A.	Bone, Wallace G.	21 DEC 1882	17	199
Leavy, Nels	Biddle, Maggie	10 MAY 1878 L	12	047
Leavy, Patrick Joseph	Welch, Mary Ellen	14 OCT 1882 L	17	071
LeBarre, Mary Frances	Dorsey, John Thomas	19 JUN 1882 R	16	418
Lechlender, Mary	Norgle, George	05 MAY 1881 R	15	295
Lecomte, Alfred	Fred, Mathilda	10 MAY 1882 R	16	353
Lecount, Annie C.	West, David	13 OCT 1885 R	20	476
Leddey, Margaret	Monaghan, James	28 NOV 1877 L	11	208
Leddy, Catherine	Simmons, William D.	16 FEB 1885	20	068
Lederer, Linie	Buchert, William	01 MAR 1884 L	18	452
Lederer, Magdalene B.	Hettinger, Wm. L.	04 FEB 1883	17	287
Lee, Albert	Johnson, Henrietta	15 JAN 1880 R	14	107
Lee, Alexander	Herndon, Alice	21 MAY 1881 L	15	320
Lee, Alexander	Brown, Mary	24 SEP 1883 L	18	150
Lee, Alice Mary	Coleman, Thomas	03 JUL 1883 L	18	033
Lee, Amelia	Hopkins, James	25 AUG 1885 L	20	387
Lee, Ann	Poole, Scott	14 MAR 1878	11	383
Lee, Ann Elizabeth	Patterson, Abraham	31 JUL 1882	16	462
Lee, Anna	Grayson, George W.	06 DEC 1883 L	18	300

Lee, Anna E.	Piper, Samuel L.F.	29 APR 1885 L	20	197
Lee, Annie	Young, Benjamin F.	26 JUL 1878 R	12	147
Lee, Annie E.	Queen, John M.A.	13 FEB 1878	11	338
Lee, Archy	Johnson, Mag	22 DEC 1880 L	15	116
Lee, Caroline	Herbert, Clement	01 NOV 1877 R	11	165
Lee, Catherine	Murray, Harry	02 JUL 1881	15	386
Lee, Charity	Washington, Silas	28 APR 1880 L	14	241
Lee, Charles	Magruder, Catherine	24 APR 1880 R	14	237
Lee, Charles H.	Dyson, Nelly	11 MAR 1880 L	14	182
Lee, Charles H.	Silence, Annie W.	21 JUL 1881 R	15	232
Lee, Charles Henry	Johnson, Laura	16 OCT 1884	19	317
Lee, Cornelius William	Waller, Elizabeth	25 MAY 1882 L	16	377
Lee, Edward	Engel, Mary	13 JUL 1885 R	20	323
Lee, Elie	Armstrong, Gemima	06 AUG 1878 L	12	157
Lee, Eliza	Burgess, William	27 JUL 1878 L	12	149
Lee, Eliza	Matthews, James	01 MAR 1881	15	208
Lee, Elizabeth	Stewart, Edwin E.	18 OCT 1881 R	16	031
Lee, Ella Phillips	Parker, James Henry Shanks	23 NOV 1882 R	17	144
Lee, Elmer E.	Parker, Georgeanna	02 JUL 1883 L	18	030
Lee, Emery	Barns, Lucretia	09 OCT 1877 R	11	126
Lee, Emma Jane	Clark, Nelson	14 SEP 1878 R	12	217
Lee, Fanny	Terrill, Ambrose	03 OCT 1878	12	253
Lee, Florence T.	Johnson, Eugene C.	23 JAN 1884 R	18	138
Lee, Frank	Randolph, Martha	06 JUL 1885 L	20	311
Lee, George	Willis, Agnes	05 FEB 1880 R	14	134
Lee, George	Washington, Mary Susan	01 JUL 1880	14	343
Lee, George F.	Bales, Alice	05 JUN 1879 R	13	220
Lee, George H.	Smith, Marion T.	22 DEC 1877 R	11	247
Lee, George Henry	Bowman, Dora	31 DEC 1883 R	18	353
Lee, George Thomas	Brown, Matilda	13 DEC 1879 L	14	045
Lee, Gertrude L.	Moore, Charles W.H.	24 JAN 1883 R	17	271
Lee, Hannah	Locksey, Frank	13 JAN 1881 R	15	085
Lee, Harriet	Carr, John	11 JUL 1883 R	18	041
Lee, Hattie	Davis, Thomas	29 MAY 1885	20	237
Lee, Hattie Ann	King, Mortimer Dorsey	01 JUN 1880 R	14	286
Lee, Henrietta	Ellis, Herman L.	22 MAR 1883 R	17	340
Lee, Henry C.	Johnson, Mattie	25 SEP 1884	19	270
Lee, Herbert	Gaskins, Sarah Virginia	10 JUL 1884	19	130
Lee, Ida J.	McGhee, Martin L.	14 NOV 1883	18	251
Lee, Israel S.	Duffield, Harriet A.	27 AUG 1881	15	462
Lee, James	Jordan, Julia	09 AUG 1884 L	19	176
Lee, James Alexander	Williams, Henrietta	17 FEB 1880 R	14	150
Lee, Jane	Mack, Henry	20 JAN 1881	15	159
Lee, Jerry	Banks, Martha	26 OCT 1882 L	17	097
Lee, Jessie	Cleggett, William	01 FEB 1883 L	17	282
Lee, John	Smith, Elizabeth	28 FEB 1884 R	18	448
Lee, John	Diggs, Nancy	29 MAY 1885 L	20	247
Lee, John T.	Honest, Margaret	06 JAN 1881 R	15	141
Lee, John Washington	Martin, Martha Ellen	13 MAY 1880 R	14	270
Lee, John Wilson	Warren, Mary E.	06 SEP 1884	19	230
Lee, Julia	Tracey, John J.	12 SEP 1883	18	126
Lee, Julia Ann	Lucas, Edward	26 SEP 1878	12	236
Lee, Katherine W.	Moore, Edwin W.S.	23 FEB 1885 R	20	080
Lee, Lewis	Nervis, Elizabeth	27 DEC 1883 R	18	351
Lee, Lillian Beattrice	Malord, Charles Jerome	19 DEC 1883	18	327
Lee, Lilly	King, Robert	27 JAN 1880	14	122
Lee, Loretta	Butler, Henry	04 DEC 1878	12	368
Lee, Louisa A.	Smith, James H.	30 APR 1885 R	20	191

Lee, Lucretia	Haithman, William I.	20 DEC 1881 L	16	142
Lee, Lucretia	Myers, Robert	15 NOV 1883	18	259
Lee, Lula J.	Skillman, Bushrod W.	22 JUL 1879 R	13	287
Lee, Maggie Elizabeth	Plowden, Robert Henry	07 NOV 1883 L	18	241
Lee, Margaret M.	Savage, William	28 JUL 1881	15	422
Lee, Martha	Thomas, William H.	06 JUN 1878	12	085
Lee, Mary	Ward, Robert	04 DEC 1879 L	14	029
Lee, Mary	Crampton, William H.	25 JUL 1882 R	16	430
Lee, Mary	Jones, Joseph	04 MAY 1882 L	16	350
Lee, Mary	Thomas, Zephaniah	31 MAY 1882 L	16	384
Lee, Mary	Piffer, Robert	27 NOV 1884 L	19	423
Lee, Mary	Tolliver, James	01 SEP 1884 L	19	219
Lee, Mary A.	Hendley, William	07 APR 1878	11	410
Lee, Mary E.	Jones, Owen	21 AUG 1879	13	325
Lee, Mary E.	Crier, Henry A.	19 APR 1883 R	17	399
Lee, Mary Frances Per	Masi, Edward Pennaman	06 OCT 1881 R	16	010
Lee, Mary L.	Jackson, W.H.	02 APR 1884 L	18	492
Lee, Minerva	Sorrell, William	08 OCT 1882	17	054
Lee, Minnie A.	Buchanan, E. Key	30 APR 1880	14	207
Lee, Munroe	Duvall, Fannie	03 FEB 1885 L	20	051
Lee, Nancy	Whitley, Edward	09 DEC 1884 L	19	445
Lee, Oscar	Mason, Johanna, Mrs.	22 JUL 1870 R	12	144
Lee, Reuben	Moulton, Fannie Ellen	15 JUL 1884 R	19	139
Lee, Richard	Adams, Rebecca	03 SEP 1879 L	13	348
Lee, Richard Henry	Banks, Martha Ellen	08 NOV 1881 R	16	055
Lee, Richard J.	Powell, Mary M.	02 SEP 1880 R	14	426
Lee, Roland	Day, Jennie	08 AUG 1883 L	18	081
Lee, Rosa	Murray, William Henry	15 NOV 1877 R	11	187
Lee, Rosa	Johnson, James W.	04 APR 1878 R	11	404
Lee, Sallie	Coleman, Thomas	29 MAR 1883 R	17	366
Lee, Samuel	Hill, Lucretia	18 JUL 1878 L	12	141
Lee, Samuel	Goff, Letty Payne	17 SEP 1879 R	13	374
Lee, Samuel	Nelson, Mary M.	02 DEC 1879 R	14	023
Lee, Samuel	Drew, Katie	01 AUG 1883 L	18	069
Lee, Sarah	Dixon, John	30 MAY 1878	12	075
Lee, Sarah	Armstead, Bartlett	02 OCT 1884 L	19	284
Lee, Sarah	Hayes, John	29 JAN 1885 R	20	042
Lee, Sarah	Scott, James A.	15 JAN 1885 R	20	022
Lee, Sarah E.	Childress, John A.	04 OCT 1879 R	13	404
Lee, Spencer G.	Douglas, Margaret	09 AUG 1877 L	11	048
Lee, Thacker E.	Gates, Mary C.	23 JUL 1883	18	057
Lee, Thomas	Smith, Elizabeth	10 SEP 1878 L	12	208
Lee, Thomas	Hawkins, Mary C.	06 NOV 1883 R	18	237
Lee, Thomas	Bell, Christine	06 AUG 1885 L	20	359
Lee, Thomas R.	Sprigg, Minnie	13 SEP 1877 L	11	093
Lee, Thomas S.	Goree, Patsy	06 NOV 1878	12	310
Lee, Virginia	Countee, Philip	28 DEC 1882	17	221
Lee, William	Howard, Emma	18 DEC 1879 L	14	058
Lee, William	Stewart, Josephine	10 AUG 1880 L	14	396
Lee, William	McDaniel, Mildred J.	16 NOV 1881 L	16	080
Lee, William	Norris, Frances	18 AUG 1883	18	090
Lee, William	Gadsby, Mary Augusta	09 APR 1885 R	20	155
Lee, William	Holmes, Carrie	16 APR 1885 L	20	173
Lee, William Francis	Jones, Georgianna	11 AUG 1882 R	16	472
Lee, William H.	Green, Maggie	17 AUG 1880 L	14	404
Lee, William H.	Rucker, Mary	02 JUL 1885 L	20	307
Lee, William H.J.	Tillman, Mary E.	21 NOV 1881 L	16	087
Lee, William Henry	Iverson, Millie	03 NOV 1881 R	16	038

D.C. Marriage Records Index, June 28, 1877 to October 19, 1885   279

Lee, William P.R.	Stubbs, Nannie T.	09 SEP 1884	19	234
Lee, Willie	Griffin, Sarah E.	08 AUG 1885 R	20	360
Lee, Wm. H.	Washington, Adele	16 JAN 1883	17	261
Leebode, Lena	Gieseke, August	31 AUG 1878	12	189
Leech, Ella S.	Lewis, Frank M.	15 OCT 1878 R	12	272
Leech, Mary Alice	Lake, William E.	19 JUL 1878	12	142
Leech, Mary E.	Bradshaw, Aaron	25 JUN 1879 R	13	247
Leech, Mary Louise	Irwin, H. May	11 SEP 1879 R	13	366
Leeman, Elizabeth M.	Cunningham, George D.	15 AUG 1883 L	18	088
Lees, Clara L.	Nalley, Charles K.	05 FEB 1883 R	17	286
Leese, Emma E.	Miller, John	16 FEB 1881 R	15	192
Leese, Henry Watson	Luckett, Jennie C.	07 DEC 1881 R	15	475
Leesnitzer, Henry J.	Fridley, Sarah E.	26 NOV 1884	19	419
Lefevre, Louise H.	Stone, Thomas J.	12 AUG 1885 R	20	366
LeFevre, H.W.	Langley, Sue G.	10 JAN 1883	27	6535
Leftridge, Robert P.	Heathman, Maria L.	05 DEC 1878 R	12	359
Leftwich, Martha J.	Hill, William M.	04 JUN 1884 R	19	060
Lehman, Mary Helena	Davis, Joseph Gilbert	19 DEC 1878 R	12	373
Leib, Harrison	Ramsay, Mary Eleanor	25 APR 1878 R	12	020
Leigh, Lewis C.	Smith, Annie E.	15 AUG 1878	12	169
Leim, Mary A.	Arteuzer, Mathias	19 JAN 1884	18	384
Leimbach, Adam	Walker, Annie	26 DEC 1878 R	12	402
Leimberger, Lisetta	Sauter, John Casper	30 SEP 1877	11	110
Leisher, Kate L.	Wimmer, George	06 MAR 1883 L	17	334
Leitch, Alexander Archibald	Geddes, Maggie	20 OCT 1879 R	13	433
Leitch, John J.	Norris, Annie M.	19 DEC 1877	11	247
Leitch, Nannie G.	Ransom, William H.	20 APR 1881 R	15	265
Leland, Hester Annie	Gott, Frank Pierce	20 APR 1881 R	15	264
Leland, Theo F.	Curran, Rosanna	03 JUL 1878 L	12	123
Lemke, Cathenka	Weber, Caspar A.	01 SEP 1881 R	15	465
Lemke, Dora Maria Cathinka	Rose, Carl Diedrich Adolph	10 AUG 1882 R	16	474
Lemkul, Louis M.L.	Struven, Kate F.	08 APR 1882 L	16	305
Lemly, Rachel	Tyler, Reuben	20 APR 1885	20	174
Lemmon, Jesse R.	Rudd, Addie	07 SEP 1881	15	474
Lemmon, Wm. Lee	Bushie, Laura	25 MAY 1880 R	14	285
Lemon, Lizzie W.	Gordon, William H.	12 OCT 1883	18	186
Lemon, Martha	Schneider, Charles W.	22 APR 1882 R	16	329
Lemore, John	Gray, Sarah	05 JUL 1883	18	037
Lemore, Lavinia	Mason, Charles W.	07 NOV 1878	12	316
Lemos, Beverly R.	Fleet, Mary M.	21 APR 1881	15	265
Lenman, Charles E.R.	Langley, Hattie A.	28 JUN 1881 L	15	380
Lennon, John J.	Gallagher, Rosa	13 MAY 1884 R	19	017
Lennox, Frank	Colton, Maria	03 OCT 1878	12	248
Lenoir, Ida V.	Hopkins, Frederick W.	07 FEB 1881 R	15	179
Lenoir, Samuel H.	Schwier, Laura	30 MAR 1885 R	20	137
Lentbecher, Christian	Nehren, Margaret	01 MAR 1882 R	16	263
Lentz, Gustav Franc	Slaich, Lina Louisa	25 APR 1880 R	14	236
Lenz, George A.	Bremerman, Clara	21 OCT 1878 L	12	284
Leonard, Alfred L.	Venable, Sadie C.	21 MAY 1883 R	17	453
Leonard, Francis	Kiley, Hannah	03 AUG 1879 R	13	303
Leonard, Henrietta Louisa	Roach, Philip	26 NOV 1884 R	19	417
Leonard, John J.	Sullivan, Minnie	14 JAN 1884 L	18	375
Leonard, Katie	Petitt, Robert	11 JUN 1878 L	12	094
Leonard, Mary L.	Lloyd, Thomas L.	14 DEC 1879 R	14	047
Leonard, Mattie F.	Leonard, William N.	17 JUN 1881 L	15	366
Leonard, William	Doddrell, M. Ellen	27 AUG 1879 R	13	337
Leonard, William H.	Smith, Ada C. (Squires)	29 APR 1885 R	20	192
Leonard, William N.	Leonard, Mattie F.	17 JUN 1881 L	15	366

Leonberger, Hannah M.	Frankel, Andreas	23 JUN 1880 R	14	329
Leonberger, Henry	Thorn, Bertha M.	12 MAY 1880 L	14	267
Leonberger, John	Schmerz, Katie	05 OCT 1880 R	14	470
Leonhard, Harry	Vedder, Mary	08 JUL 1884	19	125
Lepley, William H.	Smith, Margaret E.	11 JAN 1883	17	248
Lepondré, Josephine	Rougnet, Raymond	03 JAN 1878	11	291
Lepper, Lina	Lerch, John J.B.	11 APR 1880 R	14	219
LePreux, Imogene	Standiford, Harry	07 JUL 1881 L	15	394
LePreux, Manning	French, Edith	14 AUG 1884	19	186
Leprew, Louis	Horner, Emma C.	16 DEC 1879 R	16	3836
Lerch, Anthony	Mergenthaler, Caroline	27 APR 1881 L	15	278
Lerch, George A.	Dieterich, Annie K.	07 APR 1885 R	20	149
Lerch, H.F.	Huth, Minnie	18 JUN 1879	13	222
Lerch, John Henry P.	Dilger, Hanna	02 MAY 1882 R	16	340
Lerch, John J.B.	Lepper, Lina	11 APR 1880 R	14	219
Lerch, Minnie E.	Hulien, Charles H.	20 NOV 1881 R	16	085
Lerch, Thomas J.	Hohbein, Kate	30 MAY 1880 R	14	294
LeRoy, William E.	Stump, Mary B.	17 NOV 1881	16	078
Lescalleet, Samuel M.	Umpleby, Mamie A.	11 SEP 1883	16	203
Lescalleit, Samuel M.	Umpely, Mamie A.	11 SEP 1883 R	28	6865
Lesch, Margaret	Meyer, John C.	18 OCT 1885	20	494
Lesh, Annette	Finch, Erastus M.	06 NOV 1879 R	13	469
Lesh, Clara J.	Kenon, Peter Sophodes	02 MAR 1882 R	16	262
Lesher, Mollie J.	Gittings, Wm. Thos.	30 NOV 1884 R	19	425
Lester, Elizabeth	Clark, Lemuel F.	18 SEP 1877 R	11	100
Lester, William	McAbee, Margaret	16 OCT 1878 R	12	278
Lester, William	Montgomery, Minnie Yardley	26 APR 1885	20	188
Letter, Emma	Burkley, Joseph	09 OCT 1879 R	13	412
Letterer, John M.	Kirby, Amelia A.	03 DEC 1882	17	163
Levels, James Henry	Williams, Martha	07 MAR 1881 R	15	217
Levey, Mary Jane	Jefferson, Samuel	28 MAY 1885 l	20	244
Levi, Fannie	Reese, Abraham E.	03 FEB 1878	11	319
Levi, Fannie	Bregstone, Miles	08 FEB 1885 R	20	057
Levi, Sarah	Samuel, Isidor W.	23 JAN 1880 L	14	118
Levy, Annie	McKanna, John	16 JAN 1884 L	18	358
Levy, Bettie	Smith, Alfred	01 MAR 1883 L	17	330
Levy, Henry	Green, Sarah A.	05 NOV 1878 L	12	308
Levy, Katie	Chorpenning, Harry W.	30 SEP 1878 R	12	240
Levy, Letitia	Young, Joseph	17 DEC 1884 R	19	461
Levy, Louisa	Dorsey, Richard	27 NOV 1879 R	14	016
Levy, Louisa M.	Stehley, John Z.	15 JUN 1884 L	19	087
Levy, Moses A.	Stern, Leah	12 JUN 1885 L	20	271
Levy, Nellie C.	Veihmeyer, J. Oliver	27 SEP 1883 L	18	159
Levy, Nelson	Love, Mary E.	31 MAY 1880 R	14	296
Levy, Rachel	Hodson, William M.	17 JUL 1878 L	12	137
Levy, Samuel	Peyser, Hessie	27 APR 1884 R	18	534
Levyman, Susie	Fields, William	03 SEP 1884	19	223
Lewis, Addison	Washington, Winnie	11 OCT 1884	19	288
Lewis, Agnes	Herndon, Moses	10 JUL 1884 L	19	134
Lewis, Ailsey	Jones, Dallas	16 OCT 1879 R	13	419
Lewis, Albert E.	Brinkley, Alice R.	26 NOV 1884 R	19	421
Lewis, Andrew	Hearns, Mary	19 MAY 1881 R	15	317
Lewis, Andrew	Penn, Annie	19 APR 1883 R	17	400
Lewis, Andrew L.	Taylor, Jennie V.	01 NOV 1884	19	352
Lewis, Anna M. Haslup	Hill, James W.	21 JUL 1880 R	14	371
Lewis, Annia	Lewis, Morton	15 DEC 1881 R	16	135
Lewis, Bettie	Smith, Reuben	30 JUL 1881 L	15	426
Lewis, Bettie R.	Ford, John T.	31 JUL 1879 R	13	297

Lewis, Birdie	Ashton, Lewis	02 DEC 1880 L	15	083
Lewis, Blanche D.	Walker, Harry B.	23 SEP 1880 L	14	460
Lewis, Caroline	Shaw, J.H.	26 FEB 1879 L	13	080
Lewis, Carrie Elizabeth	Gardner, William Henry	26 FEB 1880 R	14	163
Lewis, Carrie Virginia	Allen, Frank	25 OCT 1884	19	336
Lewis, Catherine	Smith, Reuben	23 NOV 1878 L	12	344
Lewis, Catherine	Askins, Isaac	13 DEC 1881 L	16	129
Lewis, Charles H.	Ross, Anna	04 MAR 1880	14	131
Lewis, Clara	Newman, John	18 DEC 1884 R	19	471
Lewis, Clarence H.	Adams, Sarah M.	10 FEB 1880 R	14	147
Lewis, Cora	Beander, Geo. Thomas	17 DEC 1878 R	12	384
Lewis, Cora B.	Blake, William F.	27 NOV 1884 R	19	420
Lewis, Creed	Johnson, Julia	04 JUL 1878	12	124
Lewis, David E.	Briggs, Rachel	29 MAR 1881 R	15	240
Lewis, Dio W.	Baum, Emmie C.	17 SEP 1885 R	20	421
Lewis, Edward	Green, Nancy	20 MAY 1878 R	12	016
Lewis, Edward	Ford, Mary	20 FEB 1879 L	13	070
Lewis, Edward	Ford, Alberta	08 JUN 1880 R	14	306
Lewis, Edward H.	Gorden, Ida C.	15 JAN 1885 L	20	022
Lewis, Eliza	Tibbs, Spencer	09 DEC 1880 L	15	089
Lewis, Elizabeth	Curtis, F.	10 APR 1878 L	11	415
Lewis, Ella V.	Farr, Clarke L.	19 DEC 1883	18	328
Lewis, Emily C.	Lloyd, William P.	23 JUN 1885	20	284
Lewis, Emma	Jackson, William	04 JUN 1878 R	12	083
Lewis, Evelina	Butler, James	20 JUN 1885 L	20	282
Lewis, Everett	Coleman, Nannie A.	02 DEC 1884 R	19	429
Lewis, F.L.	Rich, Katie	02 JAN 1880	14	082
Lewis, Fannie	Stilson, Frank	29 NOV 1883	18	281
Lewis, Fanny	Edwards, Ned	04 DEC 1878 L	12	367
Lewis, Frances A.	Queen, Charles H.	11 SEP 1883 R	18	118
Lewis, Frank	Jones, Ella	21 SEP 1877	11	103
Lewis, Frank M.	Leech, Ella S.	15 OCT 1878 R	12	272
Lewis, George	Berry, Eliza	17 OCT 1877	11	142
Lewis, George	Rogers, Maria	16 FEB 1879 R	13	056
Lewis, George	Bundy, Millie Jane	05 JAN 1882 L	16	184
Lewis, George Barnholt	Thompson, Florence	11 MAR 1885 R	20	106
Lewis, George E.	Spady, Sarah A.	25 JUN 1878	12	113
Lewis, George Henry	Stewart, Idell	05 FEB 1880 C	14	139
Lewis, George Henry	Parker, Isabel	12 JUN 1883 L	17	489
Lewis, George T.	Wallace, Helen M.	31 MAY 1878 L	12	077
Lewis, George T.	Smith, Rosa I.	04 OCT 1882	17	053
Lewis, Georgianna	Stewart, Horace	20 MAR 1879 L	13	111
Lewis, Harriet	Edmunds, Richard	18 MAR 1880 R	14	188
Lewis, Hattie	Wilson, Edward	17 JUL 1878 L	12	138
Lewis, Henry	Ellis, Mary A.	24 NOV 1881 L	16	098
Lewis, Henry F.	Brown, Alice	30 OCT 1883 L	18	222
Lewis, Ida	Fairfax, William T.	27 MAR 1878 L	11	394
Lewis, Ida V.	Bryan, John A.	28 APR 1882 R	16	334
Lewis, Isaiah	Burrell, Mary	28 FEB 1883 R	17	327
Lewis, James	Day, Harriet	16 APR 1878 L	12	006
Lewis, James	Smith, Frances	17 FEB 1882 L	16	247
Lewis, James H.	Marshall, Alice C.	03 FEB 1885 R	20	049
Lewis, James Hall	Donaldson, Anna Bruce	24 OCT 1882 R	17	087
Lewis, James Henry	Beard, Jeannette	16 FEB 1881 R	13	370
Lewis, James P., M.D.	Wilkey, Mary, Mrs.	30 JUN 1880 R	14	342
Lewis, Jeanette	Smith, Walter	16 FEB 1882 L	16	245
Lewis, Jennie	King, William Edward	26 MAY 1882 R	16	377
Lewis, Jennie	Campbell, Horace	27 JAN 1885	20	038

Lewis, John	Countee, Amy	25 JUL 1878 R	12	148
Lewis, John	Hill, Annie	19 MAR 1879 L	13	109
Lewis, John	Smith, Julia	28 JAN 1880 L	14	124
Lewis, John	Pullian, Marietta	14 OCT 1880 R	14	496
Lewis, John H.	Cunningham, Fannie	04 OCT 1883 R	18	172
Lewis, John K.	Matthews, Mary E.	02 FEB 1882	16	213
Lewis, John M., Jr.	Lewis, Sallie W.	11 JUN 1884 R	19	076
Lewis, John T.	Wade, Katie R.	18 SEP 1882 R	17	026
Lewis, John Yeuell	Moran, Jennie	07 MAY 1885 R	20	213
Lewis, Joseph	Griffith, Nancy	17 APR 1879	13	150
Lewis, Julius	Darnall, Sarah E.	20 DEC 1877 R	11	255
Lewis, Kate	Walker, Frank	26 JUN 1883 L	18	016
Lewis, Kate	Williams, Henry	15 NOV 1884 L	19	383
Lewis, Katharine Anna	Buechling, John B.	19 MAR 1878 L	11	386
Lewis, Laura Custiss	Oliffe, William Henry	01 JUL 1883	18	028
Lewis, Laura R.	Conner, James T.	07 JUL 1880 R	14	351
Lewis, Leonidas A.	Harri, Millie	05 SEP 1883	18	113
Lewis, Lewis	Crawford, Josephine	02 DEC 1884 L	19	432
Lewis, Lizzie D.	Hamilton, John	29 OCT 1882	17	099
Lewis, Louisa	Harris, Patrick	18 DEC 1884 R	32	7901
Lewis, Maggie E.	Lyne, Richard G.	14 MAR 1882 R	16	276
Lewis, Malvinia	Key, Thornton	12 AUG 1882 R	16	477
Lewis, Mars	Wilcoxon, Hattie B.	29 MAY 1880 L	14	296
Lewis, Mary	Holmes, Albert	12 SEP 1878 L	12	214
Lewis, Mary	Ross, Peter	01 JUL 1881 L	15	384
Lewis, Mary	Ward, Rebuel	08 AUG 1882 R	16	474
Lewis, Mary	Allen, Richard	19 SEP 1883 L	18	141
Lewis, Mary	Neal, Richard	11 DEC 1884 L	19	454
Lewis, Mary F., Mrs.	Withers, Thomas G.	22 SEP 1880 R	14	456
Lewis, Mary F.	Gilbert, John W.	10 MAR 1885 R	20	093
Lewis, Mary Foster	Leach, Adoniram Judson	25 DEC 1883 R	18	337
Lewis, Mary L.	Hackenyos, Charles W.	19 APR 1883 R	17	391
Lewis, Milwood Eddy	Carter, John Lewis	01 OCT 1884	19	278
Lewis, Morton	Lewis, Annia	15 DEC 1881 R	16	135
Lewis, Nancy A.	Cheese, Thomas	06 SEP 1884	19	231
Lewis, Nellie	Warder, Frank	14 OCT 1882	17	070
Lewis, Peter	Jones, Mary Frances	12 MAR 1879 R	13	097
Lewis, Peter	Cross, Jane	29 SEP 1880 L	14	464
Lewis, Peter	Madison, Sarah	13 APR 1881 L	15	255
Lewis, Philip	Taylor, Mary	08 SEP 1880 L	14	437
Lewis, Richard	Dorsey, Eliza	14 SEP 1882 L	17	021
Lewis, Richard	Alexander, Lizzie	10 DEC 1884	19	447
Lewis, Richard H.	Johnston, Emma L.	05 MAR 1878 L	11	373
Lewis, Robert	Beaver, Charlotte	27 JUN 1882 L	16	428
Lewis, Robert	Taylor, Mamie	09 APR 1885	20	155
Lewis, Robert	Whyte, Agnes V.	03 OCT 1885 L	20	455
Lewis, Robert Eldon	Cromwell, Mary Isabel	18 DEC 1883	18	320
Lewis, Sallie	Temple, John	29 DEC 1884 L	19	497
Lewis, Sallie W.	Lewis, John M., Jr.	11 JUN 1884 R	19	076
Lewis, Samuel	Williams, Nellie S.	28 DEC 1880 R	15	094
Lewis, Sophia	Harris, Patrick	05 DEC 1884	19	440
Lewis, Susan Alice	Hunster, Thomas Watkins	06 OCT 1880 R	14	475
Lewis, Thomas G.	West, Lena	08 SEP 1880	14	431
Lewis, Thomas J.	Taylor, Fannie	17 MAY 1882 R	16	364
Lewis, Victoria	Bowman, James	05 JUN 1884 L	19	063
Lewis, Virginia	Carter, William H.	01 OCT 1884	19	297
Lewis, Walter L.	Grinnell, Bettie E.	20 SEP 1882 L	17	030
Lewis, William	Thompson, Alice	08 JUL 1879	13	263

D.C. Marriage Records Index, June 28, 1877 to October 19, 1885

Lewis, William	Johnson, Carrie E.	15 DEC 1881	16	133
Lewis, William	Cison, Katie	17 MAR 1884	18	473
Lewis, William	Simms, Louisa	07 AUG 1884	19	129
Lewis, William	Winston, Mary	26 JUN 1884 L	19	105
Lewis, William A.	Steward, Mary F., Mrs.	13 DEC 1877 R	11	232
Lewis, William A.	Tyler, Mary	11 DEC 1884 L	19	452
Lewis, William F.	Selva, Fannie	07 JAN 1880	13	388
Lewis, William H.	Swailes, Alice	04 SEP 1879 L	13	352
Lewis, William H.	Crider, Genevieve A.	04 OCT 1883 R	18	172
Lewis, Wm. Frederick	Stelle, Mary Ann	05 MAR 1884 R	18	458
Leydecker, Email Gust. Theo.	Weissman, Caroline	30 APR 1883	17	422
Leyhan, John	Huddleston, Cordelia U.	12 DEC 1882 L	17	179
Leypold, Emma	Krich, Charles	09 NOV 1880 R	15	037
Leypoldt, Annie	Earl, Edward Frank	13 SEP 1885 R	20	412
Leypoldt, Christopher	Gates, Fanny	29 DEC 1877 L	11	279
Lias, Josephine	Robinson, William	06 SEP 1877 L	11	079
Lias, Nannie	Booker, William L.	02 APR 1883 R	17	372
Lias, Robert	Coates, Ellen	03 AUG 1881 R	15	428
Liddle, Mary Helen	Galbraith, William John	05 NOV 1882 R	17	112
Liesch, Mary	Adler, Edmund	16 SEP 1880 R	14	448
Liggan, Robert L.	Everett, Julia R.	08 AUG 1883	18	080
Liggons, Samuel C.	Mumford, Maria A.	04 MAY 1882 L	16	348
Light, Matilda	Jones, Thomas L.	18 OCT 1885 R	20	492
Light, Sarah E.	Ronsples, Francis E.	30 JUN 1885 L	20	301
Lightener, Lucy Anna	Snellings, John Samuel	19 NOV 1882 R	17	136
Lighter, Daniel Webster	Sparrow, Annie May	23 DEC 1880 R	15	119
Lightfoot, Annie	Buchanan, Charles T.	23 JUN 1881 R	15	378
Lightfoot, Laura L.	Cannon, William H.	23 JAN 1883 R	17	271
Lightfoot, Lavinia	Ray, Joseph	30 OCT 1882 L	17	102
Lightfoot, Ophelia	Scott, Joseph H.	20 NOV 1878 R	12	339
Lightfoot, William	Williams, Annie Lee	20 MAY 1882 R	16	369
Lilburn, Anna Maria Birch	Miles, James Henry, Dr.	08 DEC 1879 R	14	034
Lillard, Lizzie J.	Pulliam, George F.	27 JUL 1879	13	295
Lillebridge, Annie W.	Goodhue, Isaac W.	16 APR 1884 R	18	513
Lillie, Charles	Waters, Laura M.	16 DEC 1879 R	14	047
Lillie, Edwinia	Parke, Mart	20 NOV 1883	18	267
Lilly, Clara Alphonsa	Beale, Edward M.	04 JUN 1884 R	19	055
Lilly, Frank	Crummins, Annie	04 JUN 1878 R	12	084
Limberger, Henry	Schickler, Maggie	31 JUL 1880 R	14	380
Linch, Julia	Smith, George	03 SEP 1885 L	20	397
Lincoln, Frank J.	McDonald, Jennie	01 AUG 1878	12	154
Lincoln, James H.	Queen, Mary	09 AUG 1883 L	18	082
Lincoln, Mary	Sweeney, Richard	16 MAR 1885 R	20	117
Lincoln, Sally	Copely, Henry	17 JUL 1878	12	137
Lincom, George A.	Jones, George B.	27 NOV 1881	16	094
Lindawood, J.J.	Keller, Mollie	28 SEP 1882	17	042
Linde, Elise	Wolff, Albert	20 OCT 1883	18	205
Linden, Edward C., Jr.	Knabe, Bertha	17 JUN 1885 R	20	271
Linden, James F.	Hull, Bessie M.	31 DEC 1884 R	19	517
Lindsay, Maria Annie	Davenport, Christopher	2y DEC 1883 R	18	340
Lindsay, Walter Edzell	Turner, Florence Gunnell	12 JUN 1882 R	16	403
Lindsey, Charles	Brown, Vada	03 JAN 1884	18	360
Lindsey, James E.	Elliot, Fanny	09 JUN 1878	12	093
Lindsey, James H., Rev.	Kelly, Elizabeth	09 JUL 1878 R	12	128
Lindsey, Maggie B.	Glascock, Abner L.	27 AUG 1878	12	181
Lindsey, Maggie E.	Hopkins, Henry	05 JUL 1881 L	15	390
Lindsey, Mary Eliza	Howard, George	08 JAN 1880 R	14	093
Lindsey, Noble	Aitcheson, Kate	21 AUG 1878	12	175

Lindsey, Sarah E.	Whitemore, James H.	21 JUN 1882 L	16	421
Lindsley, Sarah A.	West, Clement R.	22 DEC 1881 R	16	153
Lingebach, Louise	Armbrecht, Augustus	06 NOV 1878	12	304
Lingenbaugh, Charles	Carpenter, Mary	27 SEP 1877 L	11	111
Link, Mary	Ruppert, Mathew	06 JAN 1880 R	14	089
Linken, Jennie B.	Tippet, Charles M.	14 NOV 1878 R	12	330
Linkhauer, John F.	Lord, Josephine W.	14 MAY 1883	17	436
Linkhow, J.C.	Cherry, M.E.	17 AUG 1880 R	14	403
Linkins, Alice Louisa	Cline, George Thomas	08 JUL 1878 R	12	129
Linkins, Ann Sophonia Brown	Nicholson, John Harrison	20 SEP 1881 R	15	488
Linkins, Annie F.	Kettner, James D.	10 AUG 1884	19	166
Linkins, Blanche	Ehrmantraut, Leonard A.	01 SEP 1885 L	20	396
Linkins, John R.	Bartley, Lillie A.	04 AUG 1879 R	13	305
Linkins, Joseph	Eliason, Annie O.	02 MAY 1883	17	427
Linkins, Mary	McStay, Henry	01 FEB 1882 R	16	218
Linkins, Peter Francis	Mercer, Annie	14 JUL 1881 R	15	400
Linkins, William W.	Eldridge, Lillian I.	08 JAN 1880 R	14	096
Linn, Thomas	Bell, Mary Jane	30 DEC 1880 R	15	131
Linney, John J.	Hutton, Katie B.	12 FEB 1879 L	13	057
Linney, Mary Agnes	Harris, Morgan B.	29 MAR 1880 R	14	200
Linquist, Charlotte M.	Williams, Matthew H.	27 MAY 1880 R	14	289
Linsey, Philip	Hill, Emma	24 SEP 1885 L	20	439
Linsley, Elizabeth	Falvey, William	16 JUL 1877	11	023
Linthicum, Amanda L.	Herron, James L.	09 MAR 1885 R	20	101
Linthicum, Benjamin F.	Cooper, Lottie E.	12 SEP 1884	19	243
Linthicum, Edwin S.	Burke, Sadie E.	11 MAR 1881	15	221
Linthicum, George F.	Smith, Ellenora C.	16 APR 1879 R	13	140
Linton, Bertha A.	Fitzhugh, Norman R., Jr.	01 OCT 1885 R	20	445
Linville, Annie H.	Baker, Harry C.	22 OCT 1878	12	284
Lipphard, Adolph	Twiford, Sarah	23 MAR 1885 R	20	128
Lipphard, Nellie	Smith, Charles H.	09 OCT 1885	20	457
Lipphard, Sophie M.	Rempp, Charles W.	04 JAN 1882 L	16	180
Lipphard, William A.	Bredekamp, Ellanora	16 JUL 1878 R	12	133
Lippincott, Charles D.	Reeves, Rebecca L.	16 OCT 1878	12	279
Lippold, Annie B.	Eckloff, Harry A.	14 DEC 1882 R	17	186
Lipscomb, Andrew A.	Harmon, Grace G.	21 SEP 1881	15	492
Lipscomb, James	Robinson, Lucy	17 FEB 1885	20	066
Lipscomb, John T.	Poore, Mary A.	16 FEB 1882	16	245
Lipscomb, Lizzie W.	Conti, John T.	26 MAY 1885 R	20	240
Lipscomb, Stanley	Powers, Celeste	05 JUL 1881 R	15	391
Lisber, Mary	Hollan, Alexander	02 JAN 1883	17	233
Lishear, Samuel Edward	Wiley, Annie Zelia	17 JAN 1880 R	14	052
Lisle, Mary	Ogden, Thomas	24 JUL 1878 R	12	146
Listman, Philip	Thomas, Lizzie	05 MAR 1884	18	457
Liston, Ellen	Edwards, William I.	29 JUN 1885 L	20	299
Liston, Maggie E.	Fitzgibbon, Edward J.	10 MAY 1881 L	15	300
Liston, Michael	Sheehy, Mary	08 APR 1880 L	14	214
Liston, Richard	Wright, Ellen	06 JAN 1880 R	14	089
Little, Charles F.	Duffy, Margaret C.	05 NOV 1879 R	13	466
Little, Frank T.	Wilmer, Katie	11 FEB 1880 R	14	146
Little, George W.	Jones, Maria	21 OCT 1880 R	15	008
Little, Joseph W.	Smith, Mina J.	27 DEC 1877	11	278
Little, Margaret Foyles	Sands, Lawrence	30 APR 1878 R	12	029
Little, S.M.	Owens, A.J.	15 OCT 1885 L	20	490
Little, Thomas A.	Mason, Jessie Q.	09 MAR 1885 R	20	103
Little, William	Marshall, Willie	23 DEC 1880 R	15	121
Littleford, Annie E.	Jenkins, Edgar M.	22 JAN 1883 R	17	270
Littleford, Catherine L.	Hill, Lloyd	03 FEB 1881	15	177

Littleford, James M.	Sears, Joanna	18 JAN 1883 R	17	268
Littleford, Martha Ann	White, Thomas	24 DEC 1877	11	267
Littles, Jennie	Howard, John H.	24 NOV 1884 L	19	404
Littleton, Charles Burras	Pfeiffer, Margaret	25 APR 1880 R	14	236
Litz, Annie A.	Reed, William	12 JAN 1881 R	15	148
Lively, John H.	Phillips, Mary	13 AUG 1883	18	084
Lively, Thomas	Brockenborough, Lettie	08 MAR 1881 L	15	219
Liverpool, James	Somerville, Josephine	12 MAY 1879 R	12	201
Liverpool, James	Taylor, Mary	27 DEC 1883	18	339
Livingston, Anna M.	Bagaley, Waterman Palmer	22 JAN 1878	11	313
Livingston, Annie M.	Bagaley, Wateman	05 NOV 1881	16	063
Livingston, Athenia	Bourn, James	26 MAR 1879 R	13	113
Livingston, Robert L.R.	Collison, Annie V.	29 NOV 1882	17	156
Livingston, Victoria V.	Gladden, Joseph	09 APR 1878	11	412
Livingstone, Catherine A.	Williams, Joseph	14 DEC 1880 R	15	095
Lloyd, Belle E.	McNickel, Hugh	24 JUN 1878 L	12	111
Lloyd, Eliza	McKeever, Sam	25 NOV 1880 R	15	065
Lloyd, Ella J.	Snead, George W.	05 MAR 1885 R	20	097
Lloyd, Francis B.	Rollins, Eolia	05 JUL 1884 L	19	123
Lloyd, Frederick Morgan	Clarke, Eliza	29 APR 1878 R	12	028
Lloyd, Mary F.	Newhall, Wm. H.	14 JUL 1880 R	14	361
Lloyd, Morris D.	Carpenter, Katie	03 FEB 1883 L	17	288
Lloyd, Nancy	Edwards, Alpheus L.	01 SEP 1881 L	15	468
Lloyd, Thomas	Hamilton, Cornelia	13 AUG 1879 R	13	312
Lloyd, Thomas L.	Leonard, Mary L.	14 DEC 1879 R	14	047
Lloyd, William H.	Mayhew, Katie	06 MAY 1880 R	14	257
Lloyd, William P.	Lewis, Emily C.	23 JUN 1885	20	284
Lloyd, William T.	Read, Ruth A.E.	12 SEP 1883	18	124
Loane, John T.S.	Spratt, Joanna	26 OCT 1879 R	13	443
Lobsinger, Annie Marg. Cath.	Marks, Henry W.	15 FEB 1883 R	17	301
Lochbehler, Laura	Goetzinger, Walter	15 FEB 1881	15	169
Lochbeohler, Lena	Krogmann, Clement	17 APR 1882 L	16	320
Lochboehler, Mary	Ostmamn, Bernard	29 JUN 1880	14	336
Lochboehler, Mary Mag.	Desio, Salvatore	22 SEP 1885 R	20	434
Lochte, Amelia	Wiseman, Joseph B.	15 FEB 1882 R	16	242
Lockard, Arabella	Padget, Buchannan	16 OCT 1878	12	279
Locket, John	Jones, Katie	03 AUG 1882	16	467
Lockett, Margaret	Johnson, Reuben	06 JUN 1881 R	15	346
Lockett, Scott	Bond, Maggie	16 FEB 1885 R	20	071
Lockhard, Emma E.	Armistead, Thomas H.	28 NOV 1877	11	206
Lockley, Cora	Spriggs, Richard	09 SEP 1879 L	13	361
Lockley, John	Jones, Charity	09 OCT 1885	20	471
Lockley, Lucy	Myers, Hyter	11 APR 1878 R	12	001
Lockley, Wm. H.	Dawes, Hattie E.	15 JAN 1880 R	14	107
Lockner, Emma	Jones, Alexander	18 NOV 1878	12	331
Locks, Albert A.	Dorsey, Sophia	15 JUN 1882 R	16	411
Locksey, Frank	Lee, Hannah	13 JAN 1881 R	15	085
Lockwood, Emma	Southern, John S.	01 NOV 1884 L	19	354
Lockwood, Florence	Booth, Charles Alfred	27 FEB 1878 R	11	359
Lockwood, John Henry	Shorter, Mary Catherine	18 SEP 1883 R	18	133
Lockwood, Julia	Orme, William B.	11 JUL 1879	13	226
Lockwood, Lillie M.	Brown, Benjamin F.	20 SEP 1883 R	18	146
Lockwood, Robert M.	Simpson, Etta	07 JUN 1878	12	087
Lodge, Katrine	Anderson, Andrew	23 APR 1881 L	15	270
Loeb, Meyer	Spanier, Leah	15 APR 1885 R	20	165
Loeckel, Ludwig	Beukert, Maria	10 AUG 1879 R	13	312
Loeffler, Annie Catharine	Simnacher, Adam	26 NOV 1884 L	19	414
Loeffler, Henry S.	Schlosser, Catherine Eva	19 OCT 1881 L	16	035

Loeflar, William A.	Stafford, Mary A.	11 NOV 1879 L	13	477
Loehr, J. Herman	Willett, Mary E.	28 JUL 1880 R	14	377
Loeliker, John	Deitemann, Emma	03 NOV 1877	11	166
Loes, Adam	Folkmann, Caroline	15 JUL 1882 R	16	442
Loewenthal, William	Dreifus, Sarah	20 MAR 1881 R	15	230
Lofty, Frank L.	Pifler, Jane A.	18 AUG 1885	20	376
Logan, Aldah Amelia	Dorsey, Moses A.	10 SEP 1883 L	18	122
Logan, Alice	Benton, John	10 FEB 1883 L	17	301
Logan, Alice Ann	Bentley, William Henry	11 JUL 1879 L	13	279
Logan, Alonzo T.	Miles, Mollie A.	22 NOV 1882	17	143
Logan, Emma L.	Meagher, Peter	29 MAY 1882 L	16	379
Logan, Georgianna	Jackson, J. Thornton	30 NOV 1882	17	150
Logan, John	Johnson, Rosa	13 DEC 1877 L	11	235
Logan, John	Cook, Sarah	26 AUG 1884 L	19	209
Logan, Mary M.	Williams, Henry A.	23 NOV 1883 R	18	264
Logan, Toliver	Brooks, Sarah	14 AUG 1884	19	186
Logans, Robert	Brooks, Susanna	19 JUN 1879	13	240
Lohman, Christina	Germuiller, Julius	27 JAN 1885 L	20	039
Lohman, Robert Lee	Stubener, Annie M.	14 JUL 1885 R	20	324
Lohmann, Anna Gesche	Luedermann, Herrmann Hein.	14 OCT 1882	17	071
Lohr, Charles G.	Moran, Tenie C.	11 OCT 1883 R	18	188
Lohr, Charles W.	Hoesch, Anna	17 NOV 1884 R	19	386
Lohr, Julia M.	Giacchetti, Joseph	20 JUN 1887 R	15	366
Lokey, David	Flick, Nettie B.	23 JAN 1884	18	391
Lokey, James B.	Jones, Annie B.	06 JUL 1880	14	349
Lomack, Lewis T., Jr.	Camper, Sarena A.	18 DEC 1883 L	18	323
Loman, Jennie	Janney, Franklin	14 FEB 1885 L	20	067
Lomax, Daniel	Johnson, Annie	24 DEC 1884 L	19	488
Lomax, Edward	Washington, Emma	24 APR 1882 R	16	331
Lomax, Elias	Miller, Christie	25 JUN 1884 L	19	102
Lomax, Henry	Gasaway, Henrietta	12 JUL 1883 L	18	045
Lomax, Jacob	Lyles, Sarah J.	09 NOV 1878 L	12	318
Lomax, Jerry L.	Raum, Mary Ellen	25 DEC 1879	14	071
Lomax, Julia	Kelton, Grandison	22 MAY 1883 L	17	456
Lomax, Julia	Briscoe, Moses	21 AUG 1884 L	19	198
Lomax, Lucy	Terrill, Tolliver	03 JAN 1878 L	11	292
Lomax, Maggie	Weaver, Richmond	22 SEP 1881 R	15	493
Lomax, Marian	Douglas, Harry R.	30 AUG 1884	19	216
Lomax, Mary Jane	Watkins, William	01 MAY 1883 L	17	425
Lomax, Moses	Hodge, Annie	01 AUG 1884	19	141
Lomax, William	Templeman, Lucy	18 APR 1885 L	20	174
Lombard, Andrew J.	Barbour, Susanna D.	31 OCT 1878 R	12	301
Lombardy, Charles	Hammer, Rosa	09 DEC 1879 R	14	038
Lomis, Isaac	Ellen, Mary	26 JUL 1881 L	15	416
Londerman, George F.	Green, Ida M.	16 JUN 1882	16	415
Lonesome, Frank L.	Johnson, Nannie	28 FEB 1882 L	16	261
Long, Ada B.	Cowan, Edward J.	28 AUG 1883 R	18	102
Long, Bettie A.	Humphreys, George W.	06 AUG 1885 L	20	358
Long, Edward F.	Harrigan, Kate E.	20 AUG 1883 L	18	095
Long, Esther	Hamilton, William	07 APR 1878	11	404
Long, Georgie	Saxton, Robert	02 JUL 1878 L	12	120
Long, Israel	Hilton, Annie E.	05 JUN 1882 R	16	394
Long, Julia	Collins, John	06 FEB 1883 L	17	297
Long, Lizzie Constance	Duryee, Sacket	09 OCT 1879 R	13	413
Long, Lizzie Constance	Duryee, Sacket	09 OCT 1879	13	414
Long, Mary F.	Ellis, Charles A.	24 NOV 1879 R	14	001
Long, Mary Jane	Wood, George	26 FEB 1881 L	15	204
Long, Mike	O'Keefe, Maggie	17 JAN 1881 L	15	152

D.C. Marriage Records Index, June 28, 1877 to October 19, 1885 287

Long, Philip P.	Dinges, Sarah C.	04 FEB 1884 R	18	409
Long, Rebecca	Conaway, John C.	18 MAY 1883 R	17	437
Long, Sallie	Dean, Walker	29 DEC 1883 R	18	348
Long, William	Sebastian, Alice	28 NOV 1878 R	12	353
Longhoff, William C.	Snellings, Nellie	12 DEC 1883 L	18	310
Longley, Sue G.	Le Fevre, H.W.	10 JAN 1883	17	250
Loogood, Adelaid Victoria	Learriel, Alexandria	10 SEP 1884 L	19	239
Loomis, Mabel	Todd, David Peck	05 MAR 1879 R	13	090
Looney, Julia	Coleman, Peter	05 NOV 1877	11	169
Loosé, Joseph L.	Ridley, Nellie Regina Stannard	16 SEP 1885	20	420
Lord, Ella D.	Benson, Elbert G.	20 AUG 1880 R	14	409
Lord, Isadora	Truell, Edwin M.	10 AUG 1883	18	093
Lord, Josephine W.	Linkhauer, John F.	14 MAY 1883	17	436
Lord, Katie M.	Eggleston, William H.	09 SEP 1884	19	234
Lord, Rose E.	Sherwood, James L.	12 DEC 1883	18	311
Lorman, Lizzie L.	Trainham, Edward B.	14 JAN 1885	20	017
Loskam, Barbara	Hollinger, Daniel	16 AUG 1880 R	14	401
Loth, Wilhelm	Günther, Caroline	20 JUL 1884	19	147
Lotz, Jeremiah Carpenter	Hartt, Lizzie J.	05 DEC 1877 R	11	219
Lotz, Nancy J.	Jones, Edwin D.	27 FEB 1884	18	447
Lou, Rebecca	Johnson, Hiram	18 FEB 1884 L	18	429
Loudon, John A.	Hickman, Ellen F.	07 AUG 1884	19	174
Loudon, Maria	Price, Noah	04 NOV 1880 R	15	029
Loudon, Onimeral	Herbert, John R.	29 NOV 1882 L	17	159
Lough, Augusta	McLain, John	28 AUG 1878 L	12	183
Loughlin, Frank	Barnes, Adelaide	06 OCT 1885 L	20	460
Louis, Ferderiand	Corbin, Augustine	02 JUL 1881 R	15	384
Lounds, Elizabeth	Jefferson, James	21 MAY 1885 R	20	233
Loury, George C.R.	Carter, Lena N.	23 JAN 1879	13	032
Lout, Emma J.	King, William E.	02 SEP 1880 R	14	430
Louvette, Ida May	Trammell, Joseph C.	12 FEB 1878 R	11	336
Love, Emmett Roberta	Sherwood, George L.	02 NOV 1879 R	13	450
Love, Hannah A.	Gaver, Henry	13 NOV 1879 R	13	483
Love, John P.	McHenry, Ida M.	11 AUG 1884	19	178
Love, Mary E.	Levy, Nelson	31 MAY 1880 R	14	296
Love, Mary Jane	Bailey, William H.	24 DEC 1884 R	19	487
Love, Virginia Lillian	Fullings, Frank Harrison	29 NOV 1882 R	17	158
Love, William	Harover, Emma J.	04 JUN 1884 R	19	055
Loveday, James P.	Thompson, Florence V.	03 DEC 1878 R	12	359
Lovejoy, Annie Ellen	Groves, William Henry	18 SEP 1879 R	13	376
Lovejoy, Emma Rebecca	DeVaughn, Luther	08 OCT 1884 L	19	293
Lovejoy, William	Keefe, Joanna	04 SEP 1878	12	197
Lovelace, Annie	DeVilliers, Francis	28 JUN 1883 R	18	024
Lovelace, Laura	Cater, Benjamin	28 AUG 1877	11	066
Loveless, Benjamin O.	Thomas, Nellie M.	12 NOV 1884	19	375
Loveless, Charles	Clemens, Mary Elizabeth	13 OCT 1885 R	20	475
Loveless, Fannie A.	Lusby, Charles E.	28 FEB 1884 R	18	447
Loveless, Georgia G.	Saur, Charles L.	29 AUG 1881 R	15	460
Loveless, James W.	Crehan, Margaret	07 SEP 1878 L	12	204
Loveless, John A.	O'Day, Annie	08 FEB 1882 R	16	230
Loveless, John T.	Barrett, Maggie F.	14 JUL 1882 L	16	448
Loveless, Margaret	Patterson, John T.	04 JUN 1881	15	344
Loveless, Mary	Lanham, William	23 JUN 1881 L	15	376
Loveless, Mary Ann	Fisher, George Everett	31 JUL 1881 R	15	425
Loveless, Sarah	Sillex, Thomas	26 MAY 1879 L	13	204
Lovett, Eliza	Buckner, Frederick	10 DEC 1883 L	18	306
Lovey, James	Thornton, Bertha	24 JUL 1884 L	19	154
Loving, Lloyd P.	Scott, Henrietta	10 JUL 1882 R	16	443

Loving, Robinson	Rothrock, Jeannie D.	16 OCT 1879 R	13	428
Low, A. Maurice	Baden, Annie W.	23 OCT 1884	19	329
Low, Ellen Virginia	Waugh, John	18 SEP 1884	19	256
Low, Harry Niles	Marshall, Louise Hammond	08 SEP 1885 R	20	405
Low, John	Tolson, Ella	24 AUG 1879 R	13	331
Low, Lemuel S.	Soper, Mary E.	23 APR 1884	18	527
Lowber, Henry Sergeant	Lansdale, Charlotte Bleecker	30 OCT 1884	19	336
Lowe, Earnest C.	Buckley, Rosa L.	26 JUN 1883	18	014
Lowe, Franklin	Wells, Mary V.	11 APR 1882 L	16	310
Lowe, George R.	Kuhn, Mary J.	29 NOV 1877 L	11	212
Lowe, Henry W.	Miles, Mary I.	16 FEB 1878 R	11	343
Lowe, Ida V.	Morgan, Milton I.	02 DEC 1884 R	19	432
Lowe, John R.	Sullivan, Ella E.	01 OCT 1879 R	13	397
Lowe, Laura	Jones, Charles	04 MAR 1878	11	369
Lowe, Laura May	Mangum, Thomas Henry	05 JUN 1883 R	17	475
Lowe, Lucy H.	Lyon, Thomas E.	13 FEB 1882	16	238
Lowe, Nelly R.	Johnson, Gabriel F., Dr.	25 OCT 1881 R	16	043
Lowe, Rebecca	Johnson, Hiram	27 MAR 1878 L	11	396
Lowe, Wm. R.	Kaiser, Louise	27 NOV 1877 L	11	205
Lowell, Emma N.	Boynton, Charles A.	12 MAY 1880 R	14	264
Lowenstein, Bettina	Lowenthal, Isidor	01 NOV 1883 R	18	225
Lowenthal, Isidor	Lowenstein, Bettina	01 NOV 1883 R	18	225
Lower, Cyras Benson	Hinton, Florence	08 NOV 1881 R	16	065
Lowery, William	Wren, Margaret	12 FEB 1884 R	18	421
Lowmax, Mary F.	Colvert, Enoch	22 SEP 1885	20	432
Lown, William G.	Keppler, Annie	23 JAN 1884 R	18	391
Lowndes, Loveanna	Hendley, Peter	11 AUG 1884	19	178
Lowrey, Maggie	Burton, John	10 SEP 1885 R	20	411
Lowry, M.K.	Pollard, Alelia	22 SEP 1883	18	148
Lowry, Mary Rosina	Morton, Joseph Bruce	02 OCT 1882 R	17	046
Lowry, Robert	Latta, Jennie	19 DEC 1878 R	12	389
Lowry, William H.	Davis, Mary M.	16 MAR 1881 L	15	228
Loyd, George W.	Truslow, Joanna	16 JAN 1884 L	18	379
Loyd, Lawrence	Dickerson, Fannie	06 SEP 1881 R	15	473
Lucas, Alice A.	Baughn, James N.	29 MAY 1882 R	16	379
Lucas, Catherine Jane	Anderson, Robert W.	12 MAR 1885 R	20	106
Lucas, Charles	Simms, Amanda	31 MAY 1883 R	17	465
Lucas, Edgar	Robinson, Annie	24 JUL 1884	19	156
Lucas, Edward	Lee, Julia Ann	26 SEP 1878	12	236
Lucas, Eliza	Williams, Taylor	06 SEP 1882 R	17	004
Lucas, Elizabeth	Johnson, Robert	03 DEC 1879	14	024
Lucas, George H.	Crangle, Nannie	01 OCT 1884	19	280
Lucas, George W.	Kerr, M. Rosetta	11 DEC 1880 L	15	092
Lucas, George William	Payne, Mary Catherine	03 MAR 1878	11	367
Lucas, Hannah A.	Buckner, Robert H.	10 SEP 1880	14	441
Lucas, Hattie L.	Queen, Richard D.	06 MAY 1878	12	039
Lucas, Henry	Williams, Lizzie	23 DEC 1884 L	19	482
Lucas, Ida M.	Roux, J. Mitchell	06 OCT 1885	20	463
Lucas, James	Smith, Sarah M.	30 APR 1879 L	13	166
Lucas, James	Walker, Julia	14 AUG 1884 L	19	185
Lucas, James Henry	Chyle, Maria	12 NOV 1884 L	19	375
Lucas, Josephine	Thompson, Joseph M.	05 JUN 1882 R	16	394
Lucas, Kate S.	Goodrick, William	26 NOV 1884 L	19	415
Lucas, Lillie C.	Nigle, Richard A.	18 OCT 1877	11	145
Lucas, Littleton T.	Starks, Maggie	16 MAY 1878 L	12	053
Lucas, Lottie	Yeatman, R.P.	04 SEP 1884	19	228
Lucas, Louisa	Berry, James P.	29 DEC 1884 L	19	499
Lucas, Louisa H.	Sheedy, Patrick F.	05 APR 1880 R	14	202

Lucas, Mamie A.	Milligan, Alexander H.	13 OCT 1880 R	14	490
Lucas, Maria	Gray, Samuel	16 MAR 1885 R	20	116
Lucas, Maria A.	Brooks, Thomas H.	11 DEC 1884 L	19	453
Lucas, Mary A.	Parks, Samuel	28 MAR 1878	11	398
Lucas, Mary E.	Carter, E.F.	05 JUN 1879 L	13	221
Lucas, Mary V.	Ross, John	03 JUL 1877 R	11	004
Lucas, Ophelia A.	Trice, James H.	15 JUN 1882 R	16	409
Lucas, Sadie V.	Bennett, C.F.	14 FEB 1883 R	17	306
Lucas, William A.	Minor, Matilda	04 APR 1885 R	20	202
Lucas, William E.	Lanham, Martha E.	27 JAN 1880 R	14	021
Lucas, Wm. Thomas	Rhodes, Mary Helen	02 MAY 1880 R	14	248
Luce, Robert	Harris, Jane	18 JUL 1885 L	20	331
Luchs, Augusta	Spear, Abraham	01 JUN 1879	13	209
Luchs, Joseph	Baum, Fannie	11 MAY 1879 R	13	183
Luckett, Annie	Scott, William A.	12 MAR 1885	20	108
Luckett, Celia	Murphy, Joseph R.	20 OCT 1884	19	322
Luckett, Ellen A.	Fellows, Barnard T.	19 FEB 1879 R	13	068
Luckett, Frank	Holliday, Henniretta	07 JUN 1882 L	16	399
Luckett, Harriet	Tyler, John A.W.W.	03 MAR 1880 L	14	174
Luckett, Harriet	Swann, John Albert	17 JAN 1883 R	17	110
Luckett, Jane	Cleveland, Burton	30 SEP 1877	11	115
Luckett, Jennie	Sayles, Aquilla	10 JAN 1883 R	17	249
Luckett, Jennie C.	Leese, Henry Watson	07 DEC 1881 R	15	475
Luckett, John F.	Robey, Sarah J.	14 JUN 1881 R	15	360
Luckett, Martha Cecilia	Polly, Joseph Edward	22 JUL 1877	11	028
Luckett, Sarah E.	Richardson, George T.	04 OCT 1884 R	19	287
Lucus, Mildred Anne	Spinks, John Edward	21 AUG 1879 R	13	329
Ludwig, Phebe Henrietta	Hall, Thomas L.	09 SEP 1885 R	20	407
Luedermann, Herrmann Hein.	Lohmann, Anna Gesche	14 OCT 1882	17	071
Luff, Charles H.	McNerhaney, Laura C.	08 JUN 1881	15	350
Lugenbeel, John W.	Flagler, Sarah P.	02 MAY 1885 L	20	201
Luke, Vyvyan	Daniel, Adelaide E.	07 DEC 1883	18	305
Lukes, Mary M.	Clark, Ferdinand	03 MAR 1880 R	14	171
Lukowitz, Antoinette von	Constantine, Al W.	16 MAY 1878 R	12	053
Lukowitz, Eli von	McLaughlin, Isabella	23 MAR 1878 R	11	391
Lumpkin, Alice	Anderson, William M.	11 DEC 1884 R	19	451
Lundy, Alice R.	Gregory, William B.	20 DEC 1877	11	256
Lung, Fred J.	Gill, Mary Emma	08 JUN 1881 R	15	352
Lunsford, Addie Edmonds	Hood, Charles Dennis	21 NOV 1883 R	18	268
Lunsford, Elizabeth R.	Archer, James A.	28 DEC 1882 L	17	217
Lunsford, Kate	Fennell, Robert A.	14 JAN 1882 L	16	195
Lunsford, Mamie	King, James	27 MAR 1879	13	112
Lupton, Jesse Monroe	Hart, Ettie	19 JAN 1881 R	15	157
Lusby, Annie G.	Bury, William T.	23 JUL 1878	12	145
Lusby, Annie R.	Snyder, John D.P.	19 AUG 1884	19	192
Lusby, Annie Victoria	Gray, Richard L.	10 DEC 1879 R	14	038
Lusby, Charles C.	Farrell, Helen C.	29 SEP 1883 L	18	161
Lusby, Charles E.	Loveless, Fannie A.	28 FEB 1884 R	18	447
Lusby, Charles F.	Lusby, Mary A.	24 JUL 1884 R	19	155
Lusby, George Washington	Mills, Nannie Lee	22 DEC 1881 R	16	147
Lusby, Ida	Mack, John Daaaniel	16 FEB 1885 R	20	069
Lusby, James E.	Curtin, Teresa B.	20 AUG 1884 L	19	195
Lusby, John N.	Mayhew, Alice	16 OCT 1884	19	311
Lusby, Lemuel Franklin	Beyer, Mary Magdalen	30 NOV 1881 R	16	106
Lusby, Maria Louisa	Rosette, John, Dr.	17 JUL 1884	19	144
Lusby, Mary A.	Lusby, Charles F.	24 JUL 1884 R	19	155
Lusby, Samuel H.	King, Marion T.	07 MAR 1880 R	14	178
Lusby, William T.	Angell, Annie	29 OCT 1878	12	295

Lustig, Charles	Plitt, Emma	21 NOV 1880 R	15	058
Luthy, Bertha	Mitchison, William J.	19 NOV 1883 R	18	263
Lutton, Jennie	Grant, Edward M.	17 MAR 1885 L	20	119
Lutz, Annie	Caspari, John	23 APR 1883 L	17	405
Lutz, Cora Barbara	Bushman, Joseph T.	01 JAN 1878	11	284
Lybrand, Harry Clay	Work, Kate Elizabeth	26 JAN 1882 R	16	212
Lybrand, Horace W.	Shipley, Margaret M.	21 APR 1885 L	20	181
Lyddane, Maggie C.	Varnell, Roizer J.	18 OCT 1881	16	029
Lyddane, Thomas O.	Scior, Mary Elizabeth	24 DEC 1877 R	11	264
Lyddane, William W.	Lacey, Julia R.	11 MAY 1881 R	15	303
Lyle, Charles	Bland, Dolly	16 JUL 1878 L	12	136
Lyle, Maud	Rosson, Abner A.	06 JAN 1881 L	15	142
Lyles, Agnes	Smith, Jesse	10 FEB 1885 L	20	062
Lyles, Alice	Wilson, William	13 MAR 1879 R	13	098
Lyles, Anna	Bruce, Lewis	08 AUG 1884	19	174
Lyles, Dennis	Mills, Margaret	28 SEP 1881 R	15	500
Lyles, Ellenora	Huntington, Peter	01 SEP 1881	15	468
Lyles, Fanny	Crawford, John J.	09 MAR 1882	16	270
Lyles, George L.	Denty, Annie C.	09 AUG 1877 L	11	048
Lyles, James H.	Oliver, Virginia P.	13 SEP 1877	11	093
Lyles, Ledger Benjamin	Garner, Julia	29 MAY 1879	13	195
Lyles, Lewis	Henison, Lucy	24 MAY 1879 L	13	203
Lyles, Mary A. (Goddard)	Perkins, Robert S.	21 MAY 1883 R	17	455
Lyles, Mary E.	Carpenter, Daniel W.	07 APR 1880	14	213
Lyles, Milton	Freeman, Anne	15 JAN 1878	11	303
Lyles, Richard	Hawkins, Lizzie	05 DEC 1881 L	16	113
Lyles, Robert	Jones, Celia	13 NOV 1879 R	13	482
Lyles, Sarah J.	Lomax, Jacob	09 NOV 1878 L	12	318
Lyles, Thomas	Brown, Susan	07 AUG 1879	13	309
Lyles, Virginia	Warfield, W. John	24 SEP 1070 R	12	231
Lymon, John	Jones, Hester	15 SEP 1885 L	20	417
Lynch, Catherine	Henning, Sidney	06 FEB 1879 R	13	050
Lynch, Catherine	Browner, John W.	01 NOV 1880 R	15	023
Lynch, Charles A.	Boyd, Mary Agnes	25 NOV 1879 R	14	004
Lynch, Emma J.	High, Henry	04 OCT 1877	11	122
Lynch, Flora B.	Burrhus Fredrick C., Jr.	03 JAN 1881 L	15	136
Lynch, Georgie	Webster, Charles R.	30 DEC 1881 R	16	105
Lynch, James F.	Curran, Nellie G.	20 JUN 1883 R	18	005
Lynch, James P.	Dowd, Julia M.	10 APR 1882 L	16	306
Lynch, James S.	Conway, Sarah Elizabeth	29 MAR 1884 L	18	486
Lynch, Jeremiah	Tracy, Sarah A.	20 AUG 1882 R	16	486
Lynch, John	Murphy, Mary Anne	24 FEB 1879	13	073
Lynch, John	Donnelly, Bridget	25 JUL 1885 L	20	340
Lynch, John Roy	Somerville, Ella Wickham	18 DEC 1884 R	19	468
Lynch, John T.	Malone, Mary	14 APR 1883 L	17	394
Lynch, Julia	Wheeler, James	25 NOV 1878	12	347
Lynch, Margaret	O'Flaherty, Edward	25 AUG 1877 R	11	064
Lynch, Martin	Casey, Mary	27 AUG 1883 L	18	127
Lynch, Mary Ann, Mrs.	Kelly, Edward Bell	15 MAR 1883 R	17	343
Lynch, Mary J.	Tippett, George L.	28 NOV 1882	17	153
Lynch, Michael A.	Murphy, Rose L.	24 FEB 1881 L	15	202
Lynch, Michael A.	Malone, Mary M.	25 MAY 1884	19	037
Lynch, Olivia Jessie	Baker, Julian George	31 JUL 1881 R	15	425
Lynch, Patrick	Ellis, Ella E.	06 NOV 1877 R	11	167
Lynch, Rosa G.	Troxell, Wm. H.	25 OCT 1883 L	18	215
Lynch, Thomas	Flanagan, Mary A.	16 SEP 1882 L	17	024
Lyne, John R.	Strother, Maria Belle	15 JUL 1877 R	11	019
Lyne, Richard G.	Lewis, Maggie E.	14 MAR 1882 R	16	276

Lynham, W.D.	Shiles, M.E.	04 MAY 1878	12	038
Lynn, Clarence A.	Thompson, Ella V.	17 JAN 1882	16	197
Lynn, Duncan C.	Kessler, Anna	20 SEP 1877	11	100
Lynn, Estella J.	Clarke, William D.	16 AUG 1882 L	16	482
Lynn, Florian M.	Hunt, John S.	06 AUG 1881 L	15	434
Lynn, Ida	Adamson, William	25 MAY 1885 R	20	238
Lynn, James W.	Allen, Lillian J.	21 FEB 1882	16	249
Lynn, Joseph A.	Underwood, Annie E.	04 JUN 1884 R	19	057
Lynn, Lucy M.	Clarke, Lucien A.	09 JUN 1880 R	14	314
Lynn, Lucy Maria	Payne, Melvin Mays	06 FEB 1878 R	11	327
Lynn, Mary E., Mrs.	Adams, Richard R.	04 DEC 1878	12	366
Lynn, Ocea A.	Clarke, Benjamin F.	12 JAN 1882	16	191
Lynn, Pammie	Eaton, Samuel Oscar	08 APR 1884 R	18	499
Lynn, Phebe	Bennett, William A.	22 JUL 1884	19	150
Lynn, Rena E.	Tansill, George W.	23 APR 1879 R	13	152
Lynn, Thomas H.	Brawner, Bettie E.	19 FEB 1880 R	14	160
Lyon, Alice J.	Young, Edward T.	01 APR 1882 R	16	294
Lyon, Anna L., Mrs.	Adams, William	09 NOV 1884	19	369
Lyon, Bettie	Henson, Llewellyn	11 JAN 1883 R	17	252
Lyon, Celestia G.	Garnett, George L.	08 AUG 1882 R	16	472
Lyon, Denis	Reynolds, Bessie	24 APR 1883 L	17	407
Lyon, Harriet Caldwell	Thomas, Wm. Provoost	30 APR 1884	18	541
Lyon, Horace Freeman	Ellis, Carrie Maria	26 JUL 1882 R	16	458
Lyon, Mary M.	Conrad, Charles T.	30 OCT 1878 R	12	300
Lyon, Thomas E.	Lowe, Lucy H.	13 FEB 1882	16	238
Lyons, Amanda	Jordan, John L., Jr.	19 FEB 1879 R	13	067
Lyons, Catherine	Cain, William	31 OCT 1877 L	11	162
Lyons, Daniel J.	Faley, Katie A.	06 JAN 1880 L	14	092
Lyons, Edgar E.	Wood, Agnes E.	15 DEC 1879 R	14	049
Lyons, Emma	Simms, William	20 MAR 1882 L	16	284
Lyons, Frank	Johnson, Maria L.	11 FEB 1884 L	18	419
Lyons, Johanna A.	Foley, William J.	24 DEC 1884 L	19	486
Lyons, John	George, Nettie E.	31 DEC 1884 L	19	512
Lyons, Lucy Ellen	Beaman, Mills	09 SEP 1879 L	13	361
Lyons, Maggie	Simms, James	08 SEP 1885	20	403
Lyons, Mary E., Mrs.	Hichew, John D.	21 DEC 1880 L	15	113
Lyons, Mary E.	Hayden, John T.W.	27 DEC 1882 R	17	216
Lyons, Philip W.	Davis, Alice Virginia	03 JAN 1884	18	365
Lyvers, Paris	Harris, Laura S.	05 APR 1882	16	300

M

Maag, Catharina	Meier, John	07 NOV 1878 L	12	313
Mabee, Charles K.	Wagner, Emma B.	28 MAR 1882 R	16	289
Mable, Henry	Holmes, Carrie	22 OCT 1885	20	496
Mabry, Victoria	Rousseau, Young	03 APR 1884 L	18	495
Macarty, Cornelius	O'Leary, Julia	16 APR 1880	14	226
Macauley, Charles Henry	Morris, Mary E.	03 JUL 1879 R	13	264
MacCarthy, Fannie	Stahl, Edward	29 JUL 1883	18	051
MacDonald, James Frankin	Warner, Ida Elizebeth	09 MAR 1881 R	15	221
Machenheimer, Charles Page, Dr.	Guinn, Annie Marie	25 OCT 1877 R	11	156
Machette, Henry C.	Granet, Adelaide	13 APR 1885	20	160
MacIntosh, Annie	Benton, J.H.	31 JAN 1885 L	20	046
Mack, Annie	Stewart, Robert	24 SEP 1879 R	13	384
Mack, Frank	Neale, Lue	19 DEC 1883 L	18	329
Mack, George	Hard, Margaret	16 JUN 1881 L	15	364
Mack, Georgeanna	Johnson, Frank	17 DEC 1881 R	16	137
Mack, Henry	Lee, Jane	20 JAN 1881	15	159
Mack, Jeanie	Orr, John	13 DEC 1881 L	16	128
Mack, John	Lackey, Sally	18 JUL 1877	11	025
Mack, John Daaaniel	Lusby, Ida	16 FEB 1885 R	20	069
Mack, Lane	Gray, Celia	06 JUN 1878 R	12	086
Mack, Mary	Wheeler, James W.	30 APR 1878 R	12	025
Mack, Mary E.	Houst, William R.	03 NOV 1880	15	026
Mack, Mary M.	Randolph, John	12 JAN 1882 L	16	192
Mack, Robert	Campbell, Annie	01 JAN 1878 R	11	283
Mack, Rose	Harris, Albert	18 APR 1878 R	12	002
Mack, Samuel H.	Clarke, Mary E.	03 JAN 1884 L	18	364
Mack, Sarah Ann	Stagenwalter, John A.	08 FEB 1885 R	20	055
Mack, Thomas	Rover, Maggie E.	02 FEB 1880	14	130
Mackabee, Martha	Esko, Kause	30 DEC 1884 L	19	501
Mackall, James Mc., Dr.	Evans, Nina Florence	30 APR 1880 R	14	282
Mackall, Joseph	Snowden, Eliza	13 NOV 1879 R	13	481
Mackall, Phillis	Gant, Charles	11 NOV 1880	15	043
Mackel, Charles	Cox, Ella	02 JAN 1878 L	11	286
Mackenzie, James B.	Harris, Katie	12 JAN 1880 R	14	102
Mackenzie, P.R.	Clarke, Luretta	16 JUL 1883	18	046
MacKenzie, John Stuart	Pierce, Fannie	20 NOV 1879 R	13	499
Mackey, Ada B.	Macnichol, Charles, Jr.	26 JAN 1882	16	211
Mackey, Ida B.	Webster, Addison A.	18 JUN 1882 R	16	416
Mackey, Jefferson	Allen, Letitia	02 AUG 1883	18	071
Mackey, Katie E.	Kemon, Frank C.	25 AUG 1881 L	15	459
Mackey, Margaret Ann	Wall, Walter Samuel	19 FEB 1885 R	20	079
Mackin, Annie	Becker, Michael H.	29 SEP 1880 L	14	465
Mackintosh, Augustus	Tumbin, Mary	18 MAR 1882	16	281
MacLellan, Harry H.	James, Nellie M.	11 JUL 1885 R	20	320
MacMurray, Blanche	McDonald, James K.	03 JUL 1877	11	007
MacNalty, William P.	Hill, Ida V.	01 MAY 1884 R	19	001
Macnamara, Kate	Boudren, James E.	25 NOV 1879	14	003
Macnamara, Thomas	Dealy, Honora	09 FEB 1885 L	20	059
Macnichol, Charles, Jr.	Mackey, Ada B.	26 JAN 1882	16	211
Maco, Lizzie	Rich, John	16 MAY 1878	12	056
Macon, Mary E.	Ford, Robert H.	13 DEC 1877	11	237
Macwell, Abram	Norris, Susan	30 MAY 1878 R	12	076
MacWill, Louisa E.	Harvey, Peyton	13 JAN 1880 R	14	090
Maddan, John	Hynes, Ellen	09 OCT 1880 L	14	484
Madden, William Henry	Tarlton, Sarah Jane	17 JAN 1883 R	17	261
Maddox, Annie C.	Magee, James W.	11 JUL 1883 R	18	043
Maddox, Annie M.	Teachum, Charles T.	04 MAY 1881 L	15	292

Name	Spouse	Date		
Maddox, Frederick	Langley, Sarah E.S.	06 FEB 1884 R	18	412
Maddox, Highland	Hayes, Marian T.	29 APR 1879	13	164
Maddox, James H.	Stone, Mary Ellen	13 SEP 1883	18	128
Maddox, Jane	Scroggins, John	05 MAY 1880 R	14	259
Maddox, Laura	Keyes, Charles	05 JUL 1880	14	347
Maddox, Laura W.	Dent, George	30 JUL 1885 R	20	346
Maddox, Mary	Donifer, John Davis	06 NOV 1883 L	18	238
Maddox, Virginia	Harold, Charles	26 JUN 1883 R	18	016
Maddox, W.M.	Davis, Harriet	27 FEB 1884	18	448
Maddox, William F.	Baillieux, Clementine M.	14 JUL 1884 L	19	137
Maddox, Willie A.	Hutcheson, John W.	14 JAN 1878 L	11	303
Mades, Catharine, Mrs.	Murphy, John	17 OCT 1878	12	268
Madigan, Bridget H.	Hepburn, Charles W.	04 FEB 1879 R	13	043
Madigan, John A.	Reilly, Katie	15 DEC 1880 L	15	100
Madigan, Mary A.	Stack, William P.	30 SEP 1884 L	19	277
Madison, Amanda	Jackson, Henry	09 OCT 1883 R	18	174
Madison, Elizabeth	Thomas, William	01 JUN 1880 L	14	299
Madison, James	Shillow, Joanna	19 DEC 1879 L	14	059
Madison, James A.	Harris, Samuel C.	19 JUL 1880 R	14	369
Madison, John C.	Scott, Emma	28 DEC 1881 R	16	136
Madison, Martha E.	Tillman, Richard A.	25 SEP 1878	12	234
Madison, Matilda M.	Smith, Yorick W.	16 FEB 1885 L	20	071
Madison, Rose	Griffin, Oliver	01 DEC 1877	11	214
Madison, Ryland R.	White, Carrie	25 AUG 1885	20	386
Madison, Sarah	Lewis, Peter	13 APR 1881 L	15	255
Magans, Robert	Ellis, May	13 SEP 1883 R	18	129
Magee, Anna Maria	Sexton, Daniel Joseph	17 SEP 1885 R	20	424
Magee, Bertie	Ely, Judson	14 AUG 1880 L	14	399
Magee, Catherine	Barnes, Lewis	02 DEC 1880 R	15	077
Magee, James W.	Maddox, Annie C.	11 JUL 1883 R	18	043
Magee, John	Haines, Bessie	13 DEC 1879 L	14	046
Magill, Charles W.	Kulle, Lizzie A.	09 JUN 1885	20	265
Magill, Jennie V.	Eliason, James U.	02 DEC 1883	18	290
Maginnis, Florence	Ferguson, J. Edwin	20 JUL 1884 L	19	148
Maginnis, Sarah E.	Tabler, Norval F.	21 APR 1885 R	20	176
Magor, Lewis	Butler, Fannie	18 FEB 1885 R	20	031
Magruder, Allan	Chase, Emma	23 DEC 1880 L	15	119
Magruder, Annie	Bell, James R.	22 FEB 1883 R	17	311
Magruder, Catherine	Lee, Charles	24 APR 1880 R	14	237
Magruder, Edward	Herold, Elizabeth Capitola	22 NOV 1883 R	18	272
Magruder, Eliza	Turner, Alexander	21 AUG 1879	13	311
Magruder, Elizabeth Ellen	Brown, John	08 MAR 1883 R	17	339
Magruder, Emma	Higgins, Lloyd	23 JUN 1878	12	110
Magruder, George C.W.	Marshall, Eleanor A.H.	08 FEB 1882 L	16	231
Magruder, George L., Dr.	Burns, Belle	21 NOV 1882 L	17	141
Magruder, Helen Ann	Blackwill, Americus	30 OCT 1877 R	11	157
Magruder, Henrietta	Brown, Charles H.	16 JAN 1879	13	023
Magruder, John H.	Slough, Sarah A.	16 OCT 1882	17	071
Magruder, John Rose	Cooke, Kate Moorhead	19 FEB 1879 L	13	066
Magruder, John Wm.	Magruder, Sarah Van Wyck	30 JUN 1885 R	20	299
Magruder, Jonathan	Bean, Sophronia J.	08 SEP 1880 R	14	438
Magruder, Laura Virginia	Nalley, John H.	20 APR 1881 R	15	266
Magruder, Lavinia	Baker, James S.	29 JUL 1883	18	064
Magruder, Louisa	Cooper, Nelson	06 SEP 1879 L	13	355
Magruder, Maria	Williams, John	04 SEP 1879	13	351
Magruder, Mary Elizabeth	Mason, Samuel T.	26 NOV 1877	11	203
Magruder, Samuel F.	Brooke, Annie F.	20 NOV 1884 L	19	398
Magruder, Sarah Van Wyck	Magruder, John Wm.	30 JUN 1885 R	20	299

Magruder, Sophia C.	Wicks, William H., Jr.	27 AUG 1885	20	389
Magruder, Walter F.	Evans, Helen M.	03 OCT 1877 R	11	120
Magruder, Walter F.	Dufief, Maggie W.	15 JAN 1885 L	20	020
Magruder, William	Brown, Mary	02 FEB 1882 L	16	223
Magruder, William H.	Brown, Emma J.	02 DEC 1879 L	14	022
Magruder, William Henry	Thomas, Hattie	06 DEC 1877 R	11	226
Magruder, William P.	Casey, Fannie	18 NOV 1878 R	12	333
Magruder, Willis B.	DeSaules, Susie H.	20 DEC 1883	18	331
Magruder, Zebedee B.	Houseman, Maggie L.	30 NOV 1882 R	17	162
Maguire, Alice E.	Hall, Julian M.	06 FEB 1883 L	17	294
Maguire, Francis A.	Holle, Anna Viola	15 FEB 1882 R	16	244
Maguire, Franck Z.	Raum, Maud	14 FEB 1885 R	20	066
Maguire, Fred. Leopold	Mattingly, Marie Boury	13 AUG 1885	20	366
Maguire, George A.	Soper, Marion R.	25 MAY 1884 R	19	036
Maguire, J. Frank	Roche, Ella H.	08 OCT 1879 R	13	409
Maguire, John	Farrell, Margaret E.	13 FEB 1879 R	13	060
Maguire, Mary	Simpson, John	25 NOV 1879 R	14	005
Maguire, Mary E.	Berry, Richard	21 FEB 1881 R	15	196
Mahagan, J. Robert	Dangler, Mattie P.	22 NOV 1882 L	17	144
Mahagan, Mary A.	Wheatley, Edward E.	29 JAN 1879 L	13	037
Mahaney, Barbara Ellen	Emberson, Noah R.	29 AUG 1878 R	12	186
Mahaney, Mary F.	Malone, Patrick	28 OCT 1884 L	19	341
Maher, Mary A.	Sanders, Frank C.	15 JAN 1885	20	022
Maher, Theresa Elliot	McComb, David Edward	28 AUG 1878 R	12	183
Mahler, Kate M.	Darr, Robert W.	14 OCT 1884	19	305
Mahloy, Julia	Clancy, Thomas	09 DEC 1880 L	15	089
Mahon, Mary A.	Merry, Pliny Case	28 NOV 1877 L	11	210
Mahoney, Annie	Jamison, James Philip	12 AUG 1880 R	14	393
Mahoney, Bub	Brown, Lou	29 MAY 1882 L	16	381
Mahoney, Elizabeth	Johnson, Isaac	07 OCT 1878 R	12	241
Mahoney, Emma	Allen, Edward	20 JUN 1878 L	12	108
Mahoney, Flora Elizabeth	Dond, James I.	17 DEC 1884	19	366
Mahoney, George	Fairfax, Mary	13 NOV 1884 R	19	380
Mahoney, Ida	Davidson, Thomas	06 SEP 1882 L	17	010
Mahoney, Isaac	Fountain, Susan	14 NOV 1877 R	11	182
Mahoney, Jackson S.	Gibson, Mary E.	28 OCT 1880 R	15	018
Mahoney, James	Marshall, Mary	21 NOV 1878 R	12	340
Mahoney, Jane	Stanton, Reuben	26 JUL 1881 R	15	416
Mahoney, John	Dorney, Johanna	15 MAY 1884 L	19	021
Mahoney, John Henry	Rollins, Letitia	25 APR 1883	17	411
Mahoney, Julia A.	Caldwell, Charles W.	05 SEP 1882 L	17	004
Mahoney, Kate	Trahey, John	13 MAY 1878 L	12	049
Mahoney, Katie H.	Green, George H.	16 MAY 1882 L	16	361
Mahoney, Margaret	McCarthy, John	10 APR 1880 L	14	220
Mahoney, Mary L.	Hawkins, George H.	07 NOV 1882 L	17	116
Mahoney, Mary Magdaline	Chadwick, Robert P.	21 AUG 1882	16	490
Mahoney, Mary V.	Horidan, Patrick	30 JUN 1884 L	19	110
Mahoney, William	Thompson, Minnie	13 JUN 1878	12	098
Mahoney, William	Allen, Charlotte	10 APR 1879 R	13	136
Mahony, Jennie	Donaldson, Silas	24 APR 1884	18	530
Mahorney, Clara D.	West, Edward C.	14 NOV 1881 L	16	074
Mahorney, Lue	Taylor, William	09 JUL 1879 L	13	276
Mahorney, Michael	Hurley, Catherine	26 JUN 1880 L	14	335
Maier, Katie	Skidmore, Jarret F.	08 JAN 1880 R	14	095
Maiers, Louis Henry	Street, Clara Evelina	12 SEP 1883 R	18	122
Mailhouse, Cecilia	Bachrach, Moses	16 NOV 1879 R	13	488
Main, Hial P.	Martin, Sarah Elizabeth	22 APR 1878 L	12	015
Main, Robert	Flynn, Nellie	24 DEC 1880 L	15	123

Mainz, Emma	Schiminger, George C.	02 SEP 1884	19	220
Maisak, George H.	Dowling, Mary A.	01 JUL 1884 L	19	114
Maish, Levi	Miller, Louise L.	30 OCT 1883 R	18	221
Maith, Mildreth	Carter, James	31 DEC 1879 L	14	085
Maitland, Lindley Hoffman	Stansbury, Virginia Ward	25 MAR 1882 R	16	289
Major, Annie S.	Dunawin, William H.	19 DEC 1878 R	12	389
Major, Jessie F.	Sengstack, Charles H.	19 JUL 1881 L	15	409
Major, Levia W.	Hurley, John W.	27 DEC 1877 L	11	277
Major, Richard	Jones, Ida	23 AUG 1881	15	455
Majors, Charles	Tine, Amanda	29 NOV 1881	16	102
Majors, Reuben	Matthews, Lizzie	02 OCT 1881	15	501
Makeley, Ada	Heise, Eli	20 APR 1884	18	502
Makell, Lemuel	Coleman, Annie	30 AUG 1881 L	15	465
Makely, Cassius E.	Fairfax, Victorine	20 DEC 1882	17	197
Makle, Brook	Brooks, Bettie	09 FEB 1884 L	18	417
Makle, Maria	Harris, James P.	14 NOV 1882 L	17	126
Makle, Mary	Parker, William A.	27 DEC 1882 L	17	215
Makley, Richard L.	Makley, Virginia L.	07 OCT 1885 R	20	467
Makley, Virginia L.	Makley, Richard L.	07 OCT 1885 R	20	467
Malad, Ella	Eaton, Reuben	09 JUN 1884 L	19	070
Malady, Mary	Smith, William	14 SEP 1881	15	460
Malatesta, Colomba L.	Cristofani, Felice	27 NOV 1880 L	15	070
Malatesta, Virginia	Bryan, Bernard, Jr.	10 MAR 1884 L	18	464
Malcolm, Horatio G.	Layton, Katie W.	05 NOV 1883 R	18	231
Malcolm, Sennie C. Mallicote	Thomas, John Truman	21 FEB 1882 R	16	252
Maley, John E.	Beach, Mary C.	12 JUN 1884 R	19	079
Malezieux, Marguerite	Campbell, John G., Hon.	20 MAY 1880	14	278
Malks, Richard C.	Reed, Mary Emma	28 NOV 1883	18	282
Malley, John O.	Brennan, Bridget Agnes	05 APR 1885	20	143
Malley, Thomas	Creegan, Ellen	01 OCT 1878 R	12	241
Mallonee, John P.	Foder, Blanche F.	26 SEP 1882	17	037
Mallonee, Mary Ida	Drach, John Henry, Dr.	13 JUN 1883 R	17	471
Mallonee, Oliver Winfield	Beavin, Luvina	08 JUL 1880	14	352
Mallory, Alfred Edward	Sherman, Ida Louise	25 APR 1881 R	15	272
Mallory, John	Dow, Sarah	14 MAY 1879	13	190
Mallory, Josephine A.	Kalbfus, Charles H.	02 JUN 1884 R	19	049
Mallory, Julia Ann	Thomas, Henry H.	20 DEC 1877 L	11	254
Malloy, Edwin	Briscoll, Mary Ann	18 MAR 1879 R	13	105
Malloy, Matthew	Quinn, Bridget	08 OCT 1881 L	16	015
Malone, Aloysius	Mattingly, Sallie R.	22 DEC 1881	16	153
Malone, Delia	Short, John	27 OCT 1883 L	18	217
Malone, Edward E.	Gunnell, Catherine	18 AUG 1877 L	11	056
Malone, George	Maloney, Mary	02 SEP 1884 L	19	221
Malone, Isabella A.	Ahern, James	30 APR 1883 L	17	423
Malone, Louisa T. Allen	Shoemaker, Edward James	31 DEC 1879 R	14	083
Malone, Margaret E.	Farr, Richard R.	12 FEB 1879	13	058
Malone, Margaret M.	McNamara, Patrick H.	25 APR 1878	12	024
Malone, Martha E.	Jinkins, Dennis	02 APR 1884 R	18	489
Malone, Mary	Lynch, John T.	14 APR 1883 L	17	394
Malone, Mary M.	Lynch, Michael A.	25 MAY 1884	19	037
Malone, Patrick	Mahaney, Mary F.	28 OCT 1884 L	19	341
Malone, William J.	Brooke, Alice	09 FEB 1881 R	15	185
Maloney, A.T.	Sheehan, Daniel	31 JUL 1882 L	16	463
Maloney, Annie	Keady, Patrick	16 MAY 1878 R	12	048
Maloney, Annie M.	Dorsey, Morgan J.	14 JUL 1881 R	15	401
Maloney, Elbert S.	Mills, Nannie B.	26 JUN 1879 R	13	250
Maloney, Hanora Ellen	Horrigan, Dennis	23 FEB 1879 R	13	072
Maloney, James	Maloy, Katherine	06 JAN 1880 L	14	093

Maloney, James	Murphy, Kate	28 JAN 1882 L	16	214
Maloney, Julia	Pitts, William H.	01 FEB 1883 L	17	284
Maloney, Maggie	Beyer, James V.	01 NOV 1883 L	18	226
Maloney, Margaret	Clancey, Daniel	03 MAY 1884 L	19	002
Maloney, Margaret	Clancey, Daniel	04 MAY 1884	18	548
Maloney, Mary	Spresser, Henry W.	05 SEP 1882 L	17	005
Maloney, Mary	Malone, George	02 SEP 1884 L	19	221
Maloney, Patrick	McCormick, Ellen F.	22 OCT 1884 L	19	330
Malord, Charles Jerome	Lee, Lillian Beattrice	19 DEC 1883	18	327
Maloy, Katherine	Maloney, James	06 JAN 1880 L	14	093
Maltby, Lewis C.	Thompson, Jane E.S.	11 SEP 1877	11	088
Maltby, Sidney	Hopkins, Sarah E.	30 AUG 1877 R	11	072
Malvan, Ella F.	Conaway, William H.	12 FEB 1884	18	419
Malvin, Virginia	Young, Robert	24 MAR 1884	18	480
Mamminger, Gesina	Schule, Adolph	04 JAN 1885	19	485
Manakee, Lizzie	Sparrow, John C.	13 JAN 1885	20	014
Manchino, Rosario	Giardina, Francesca Pavola	10 NOV 1883 L	18	245
Mandews, Horace	Matthews, Emily B.	09 APR 1885 R	20	143
Mandul, Berry	Barns, Sarah	01 OCT 1878	12	245
Manfield, Eliza	Hamond, William T.	23 JUN 1880 R	14	333
Mangan, Agnes	Cunningham, Harry T.	05 FEB 1883 L	17	292
Mangan, John	Riley, Mollie A.	19 JAN 1882 L	16	202
Mangan, Rachel, Mrs.	Johnson, Richard H.	06 JUN 1881 R	15	345
Mangan, Sarah	Schwier, Henry	03 SEP 1885 L	20	398
Mangan, Timothy	Fitzgerald, Ella	23 MAR 1884	18	479
Mangon, Benjamin Franklin	White, Elizabeth	22 DEC 1881 R	16	151
Mangum, Edith May	Mangum, Robert Collin	22 AUG 1881 R	15	455
Mangum, Ida L.	Raybold, Wallace	15 MAR 1879	13	102
Mangum, James H.	Shry, Minnie	24 SEP 1883 L	18	151
Mangum, John	Grissett, Mary E.	20 JAN 1879	13	024
Mangum, John Thomas	Brown, Martha Virginia	04 MAY 1878 L	12	037
Mangum, Rachel Sophia	Hamilton, Ana H.	22 NOV 1883 L	18	271
Mangum, Robert Collin	Mangum, Edith May	22 AUG 1881 R	15	455
Mangum, Thomas Henry	Lowe, Laura May	05 JUN 1883 R	17	475
Mangum, William H.	Boyd, Nellie R.	17 OCT 1877 R	11	142
Mangun, Marvelda	Shaw, Franklin	07 FEB 1878 R	11	329
Mangurr, William K.	Smoot, May	03 FEB 1885	20	048
Manikheim, John G.	Powake, Joana	07 APR 1885	20	212
Manion, Maggie	Hutcherson, John F.	03 JUN 1880 R	14	304
Manion, Mary	Hartnett, William	20 JUN 1881 L	15	367
Manjue, Mary	Olmstead, Albert	03 NOV 1884 L	19	356
Mankin, George B.	Flack, Florence A.	12 JUN 1884 R	19	078
Mankin, George Henry	Langley, Margaret S., Mrs.	29 JAN 1878 R	11	321
Mankin, Henry D.	Dent, Catherine F.	29 DEC 1881 L	15	509
Mankin, Minnie	Tucker, A. Dallas	27 FEB 1878	11	360
Mankin, Mollie L.	Hutchison, Charles L.	25 JAN 1882 R	16	209
Mankins, George E.	Steinberger, Elizabeth Hess	07 JUN 1880 R	14	230
Mann, Benjamin Frank	Stromberger, Lissie M.	24 DEC 1880 R	15	123
Mann, Evie	Johnson, J. Hiram	21 JAN 1879	13	028
Mann, Franklin P.	Divine, Fannie	09 AUG 1877	11	048
Mann, Hesta L.	Harley, John A.	23 APR 1884	18	528
Mann, James Defrees	Ray, Kate Leslie	07 JAN 1885 R	20	006
Mann, Mattie A.	Kidwell, J.W.	16 APR 1879 L	13	148
Mann, Richal M.	Savoy, Edward A.	15 JUL 1880 L	14	363
Mann, Richard Wise	Kirby, Mary Kate	17 AUG 1879 R	13	254
Mann, Sarah E.	Wilson, Joseph L.	29 DEC 1884 R	19	497
Mann, William Walter	Prater, Martha C.	31 DEC 1884	19	469
Mann, Wm. E.	Anthony, Mary E.	16 DEC 1884 R	19	458

Manning, Alex. E.	Coghill, Malvina	18 MAR 1880 R	14	188
Manning, Anna Belle	Glidden, Charles	13 SEP 1877 R	11	092
Manning, Bernard	Hollin, Delia	09 DEC 1884 L	19	442
Manning, Bertha A.	Wagner, William H.	14 MAR 1882 R	16	276
Manning, Charlotte Thruston	Ridgely, Frank Inloes	04 OCT 1881 R	16	006
Manning, James	Myers, Anna Eliza	09 JUN 1878	12	091
Manning, James Forrest	Graham, Florence Louise	15 SEP 1884 L	19	248
Manning, John Henry	Parker, Mary	14 OCT 1884 L	19	305
Manning, Payton	Bullock, Sousan	03 JUN 1880 R	14	304
Mannix, John B.	Casey, Ellen E.	26 JUN 1880 L	14	335
Mansell, Amy Priscilla	Arth, John William	20 FEB 1882 R	16	244
Mansell, Annie Eliz.	Jonscher, Robert Frederick	31 MAR 1884 R	18	487
Mansfield, Alice R.	Burrows, J. Lemuel	15 MAR 1885 R	20	112
Mansfield, Charles H.	Bailey, Mary E.	07 MAR 1879 L	13	093
Mansfield, Charles P.	Roach, Mollie E.	04 OCT 1882 L	17	052
Mansfield, Charles S.	Robertson, Carrie	07 AUG 1884	19	176
Mansfield, Edward	Conley, Lottie A.	15 MAR 1885 R	20	112
Mansfield, Ella E.	Chrisman, Benjamin F.	21 MAY 1882 R	16	370
Mansfield, Emma C.	Gees, Richard H.	10 MAY 1879 R	13	184
Mansfield, John	Johnson, Elvira	13 SEP 1883 R	18	113
Mansfield, John R.	Bruehl, Clara A.	08 APR 1880 R	14	214
Mansfield, Josephine E.	Swain, Benedict	07 DEC 1881 R	15	507
Mansfield, Philip	Buckley, Alice S.	27 JUN 1883 R	17	488
Mansfield, Walter N.	Hall, Martha L.	15 FEB 1882 R	16	243
Manson, Joseph Oscaar	Harkness, Kate Elizabeth	12 APR 1882 R	16	313
Mantley, Joseph C.	Soper, Fannie	09 JUN 1885	20	264
Mantrow, Thos. Alexander	Broadus, Rosa Ann	04 DEC 1879 L	14	031
Manual, Johnson W.	Richardson, Anna	10 MAR 1882 L	16	273
Manuell, Milton G.	King, Annie E.	15 OCT 1885 R	20	452
Mapes, Rose C.	Reilly, Lewis W.	16 APR 1884 L	18	515
Marbury, Helen	Stephenson, Henry	11 SEP 1878	12	213
Marbury, Malvina	Green, Riburn	01 DEC 1880 L	15	076
Marceron, Bernice B.	Crawford, George A.	13 JUL 1877 L	11	049
Marceron, Bernice B.	Crawford, George A.	21 AUG 1877	11	164
Marche, Thomas Everett	Cross, Alice R.	12 OCT 1882 R	17	069
Marchie, Annie	Travis, Augustus	08 JUN 1880 L	14	310
Marconnier, John A.	Leach, Susie	25 SEP 1879 R	13	381
Marcus, Rebecca	Harris, Abraham	05 NOV 1877	11	168
Marcy, Matilda	Beach, Walter L.	04 JUN 1878	12	085
Marden, Lillie	Wiltherger, Frank	24 NOV 1884 L	19	406
Marden, William A.	Shaw, Ella C.	22 APR 1885 L	20	182
Marders, Ada	Taylor, George H.	23 MAR 1881	15	231
Mareau, Fred. G.	Helm, Corrina L.	03 JUN 1884	19	053
Marias, William	Hart, Lillian P.	26 DEC 1883	18	341
Maring, Delos T.	Hewitt, Ida W.	14 JAN 1885	20	018
Marion, Hazel	Van Praag, Solomon	06 JUN 1885 R	20	258
Mark, William	Stewart, Harriet	15 MAY 1884 L	19	022
Markell, Charles F.	Allen, Lillian E.	08 AUG 1878 L	12	159
Markes, Lucy	Slaughter, Cain	19 DEC 1883	18	327
Markin, Maggie C.	Sommer, John Henry	01 SEP 1885 L	20	395
Markland, Sallie	Kraft, William S.	28 SEP 1885 R	20	445
Markley, Emma A.	Burns, J. Eldridge	30 APR 1884 R	18	544
Marks, Annie	Coffman, Delman J.	04 JUN 1879 R	13	218
Marks, Annie E.	Seebach, Fred	15 APR 1885 L	20	171
Marks, Edwina Pierrepont	Chamberlin, William Nelson	25 OCT 1880 R	15	010
Marks, Ella	Pennifill, Joseph C.	05 OCT 1880 L	14	473
Marks, Eva H.	Holmes, William J.	04 JUN 1884 L	19	059
Marks, Henry W.	Lobsinger, Annie Marg. Cath.	15 FEB 1883 R	17	301

Marks, Joseph	Bowie, Celia	06 MAY 1884 R	19	009
Marks, Maggie	Moreland, William	18 MAY 1878 L	12	059
Marks, Martha	Lacey, William B.	21 APR 1878 R	12	013
Marks, Mary Frances	Johnson, William S.	15 NOV 1883 L	18	257
Marks, Medora	Smoote, James B.	24 JUN 1884	19	100
Markward, Celia	Hammack, William M.	04 APR 1882 L	16	299
Markward, Geo. Clinton	Clements, Clara V.	10 OCT 1877	11	130
Markward, George A.	Hutchinson, Belle	12 JUN 1879 R	13	230
Marll, John S.	Graham, Elizabeth	27 JUL 1881 R	15	421
Marlon, Jane	Stuteley, Alonzo	24 SEP 1885 R	20	440
Marlow, Charles	Williams, Laura	18 JUL 1878	12	142
Marlow, Cornelia	Barnes, Henry C.	08 FEB 1881 L	15	182
Marlow, Kate	Ware, Lloyd	16 DEC 1884 L	19	461
Marlow, Sarah Elizabeth	Hawkins, Geo. Samuel	14 OCT 1879 R	13	420
Marmaduke, Bee	Johnson, William H.	09 JUN 1879 R	13	224
Marmaduke, Jos. Berkeley	Sandy, Alice M.	28 APR 1881 R	15	282
Marmion, Robert A.	Paul, Beatrice	07 OCT 1885	20	465
Marmion, William V.	McLellan, Caroline W.	01 JUL 1880 R	14	345
Marnaker, Josephine	Hendley, James William	20 DEC 1877	11	251
Marneaux, Marguarite	Hughes, Joseph	28 APR 1880 R	14	239
Maroni, Malachi N.	McLane, Lizzie	25 FEB 1878 R	11	355
Marr, Jennie W.	Wake, Charles N.	30 OCT 1878 R	12	298
Marr, R. Josephine	Dent, Milton C.	12 FEB 1879 R	13	058
Marrs, Carrie E.	Wilson, James R.	26 NOV 1884	19	418
Mars, Alice	Chew, Abraham	13 SEP 1877 L	11	090
Mars, George A.	Scott, Susannah	30 OCT 1882 R	17	100
Mars, Lulu	Henderson, William	21 FEB 1883 L	17	315
Mars, Maggie	Mars, William	11 JUN 1884 R	19	069
Mars, William	Jackson, Matilda	03 DEC 1879 R	13	001
Mars, William	Mars, Maggie	11 JUN 1884 R	19	069
Marschauer, Annie	Disney, Frank	10 MAY 1885	20	215
Marsden, Ella	Meredith, Benj. Franklin Leigh	20 OCT 1879 R	13	433
Marsden, Frank L.	Carraher, Mary E.	27 SEP 1883 L	18	157
Marsden, Julia	Hill, Levi	20 FEB 1879 R	13	071
Marsden, Lillie J.	Eimer, Charles G.	15 AUG 1881 R	15	442
Marsh, Anne Ruth	Tolman, Albert Joseph	10 OCT 1883 R	18	183
Marsh, Blanche W.	Cawood, Thos. Marion	03 NOV 1884 R	19	355
Marsh, Fannie H.	McAnally, Joseph F.	11 DEC 1884 R	19	455
Marsh, Flora Lavinia	Stake, Charles Thomas	18 SEP 1883 R	18	135
Marsh, Frank A.	Hillman, Clara	18 JUN 1884	19	090
Marsh, Gallie M.	Leake, Willie A.	19 MAY 1884 R	19	030
Marsh, Rosa E.	Chaney, Andrew W.	24 DEC 1877	11	262
Marshal, Charles W.	Matthews, Mary E.	20 MAY 1880	14	278
Marshal, Isaac	Dotson, Mary	11 JAN 1883 L	17	252
Marshal, John	Wilson, Carrie [Ware]	25 JUN 1884 R	19	102
Marshal, Rebecca	Grove, Berkley	26 MAY 1880 R	14	291
Marshal, William	Pinkney, Lettie	28 DEC 1878 L	12	405
Marshal, William	Tyler, Annie	17 JUN 1880	14	319
Marshall, Ada H.	Mitchell, James W.	06 JUN 1883 R	17	479
Marshall, Alice C.	Lewis, James H.	03 FEB 1885 R	20	049
Marshall, Anna C.	Greene, John W.	03 FEB 1885 R	20	049
Marshall, Arianna Elizabeth	Ward, George Carlin	19 NOV 1883 R	18	261
Marshall, Cecelia	Harris, Lorenzo	11 APR 1883 L	17	391
Marshall, Daisy E.	Robey, Randolph	09 NOV 1882 L	17	122
Marshall, Eleanor A.H.	Magruder, George C.W.	08 FEB 1882 L	16	231
Marshall, Ella	Davis, Samuel	07 JUN 1882	16	399
Marshall, Emma	Jackson, William	29 DEC 1884 L	19	498
Marshall, Evan	Shorter, Henry	10 JAN 1880 L	14	098

Name	Spouse	Date	Vol	Page
Marshall, F.M.	Sadler, A.G.	20 DEC 1877 L	11	248
Marshall, Fanny	Collins, Robert	08 JUL 1879 L	13	275
Marshall, Frank	Bennett, Annie	21 JUL 1877 L	11	028
Marshall, George	McNulty, Katie	06 NOV 1884 R	19	361
Marshall, Hannah E.	Palmer, John H.	12 JUL 1883	18	045
Marshall, Harriet A.	Burley, C. St. Clair	24 NOV 1882 L	17	148
Marshall, Henry	Ford, Belle	25 OCT 1877 L	11	155
Marshall, Ignatius A.	Hawkins, Mary Olivia	28 OCT 1879 R	13	444
Marshall, James	Richardson, Adelaide	23 APR 1883 L	17	405
Marshall, John	Imwald, Mary A.	07 OCT 1879 R	13	408
Marshall, Joseph A.	Cross, Mary E.	07 APR 1884 R	18	493
Marshall, Joseph M.	Allen, Sophie I.	30 JUN 1880 L	14	340
Marshall, Josephine	Thomas, Robert	09 AUG 1877 R	11	043
Marshall, Julia	Smith, Henry	14 DEC 1881 L	16	132
Marshall, Katie E.	Francis, Henry E.	01 MAR 1880	14	169
Marshall, Laura	Bolden, Samuel Henry	01 JUL 1884 L	19	115
Marshall, Lizzie E.	Chidister, Thomas E.	25 SEP 1878 R	12	235
Marshall, Louis	Pitcher, Mary	27 AUG 1885	20	387
Marshall, Louisa	Warren, Alexander	11 JAN 1881 L	15	146
Marshall, Louise Hammond	Low, Harry Niles	08 SEP 1885 R	20	405
Marshall, Lucinda	Craddle, William	20 OCT 1885	20	492
Marshall, Maria	Butler, James	15 JAN 1883 L	17	257
Marshall, Martha	Myers, Henry	20 APR 1882	16	327
Marshall, Mary	Kittrick, Thornton	16 JAN 1878 L	11	307
Marshall, Mary	Mahoney, James	21 NOV 1878 R	12	340
Marshall, Mary	Douglass, Lewis	09 JUN 1879 L	13	224
Marshall, Mary	Reed, Philip	22 JAN 1879 L	13	029
Marshall, Mary	Washington, Joseph	07 DEC 1883 L	18	305
Marshall, Susanna	Curtis, John Henry	13 NOV 1884	19	373
Marshall, Vincent	Jones, Margaret	13 SEP 1877 R	11	091
Marshall, Vincent	Harrison, Hattie	24 MAR 1883 L	17	358
Marshall, William H.	Aller, Ophelia	06 MAR 1879 R	13	054
Marshall, William J.	Corse, Julie Grenville	02 JUN 1879 R	13	212
Marshall, Willie	Little, William	23 DEC 1880 R	15	121
Marston, Alfred P.	Sullivan, Alice A.	29 OCT 1879 R	13	449
Marston, George	Carey, Julia	16 JUL 1879 R	13	283
Marten, Cora Z.	Hill, James Henry	16 NOV 1882 R	17	124
Martens, William	Dreyer, Mary	27 MAY 1883	17	463
Martin, Albert L.	Johnson, Sarah E.	02 NOV 1881 L	16	057
Martin, Alice C.	Miller, John Henry	27 NOV 1884	19	415
Martin, Anna D.	Bailey, Levi J.	04 JUL 1878	12	121
Martin, Bernard	Hales, Martha P.	01 NOV 1879 R	13	459
Martin, Bertie F.	Nightzer, Wallace D.	03 SEP 1885 R	20	398
Martin, Bettie Serene	Johnson, Robert Harris	14 MAR 1879 R	13	102
Martin, Caroline	Lambert, Eugene	06 DEC 1883 L	18	298
Martin, Clem P.	Riley, Mary Virginia	08 SEP 1881 L	15	479
Martin, Cyrus F.	Martin, Sarah J.	27 DEC 1883 L	18	347
Martin, Edward	Brooks, Mary	21 JUL 1880 R	14	370
Martin, Eliza V.	Sparks, Charles	14 JUL 1885 R	20	321
Martin, Elizabeth	Robinson, William	24 MAY 1880	14	283
Martin, Elizabeth	Moffatt, Charles	23 JUL 1883	18	057
Martin, Emma Catharine	Williams, George Edward	21 JUL 1883	18	055
Martin, Emma E.	Rückert, William Edward	02 FEB 1880 R	14	129
Martin, Fannie	Seal, George A.	18 SEP 1878 R	12	226
Martin, Fannie Louise	Danforth, James A.	06 MAY 1879 R	13	177
Martin, George	Baker, Fannie	20 MAY 1880 R	14	279
Martin, George E.	Smith, Maggie E.	21 JAN 1880	14	116
Martin, George E.	Geisendaffer, Lucy M.	22 DEC 1884 R	19	482

Martin, Griffin S.	Whittaker, Catherine	14 SEP 1880 R	14	444
Martin, Hillray	Boston, Julia	15 JAN 1885	20	020
Martin, Ida	Coster, Stephen K.	30 MAY 1879 R	12	412
Martin, J.M.	Greer, Fannie	11 MAY 1881 L	15	301
Martin, James	Moore, Mary C.	18 NOV 1879 R	13	489
Martin, James A.	Ouraud, Addie Rosalie	01 JUL 1880 R	14	344
Martin, James, Jr.	Simpson, M. Addie	08 NOV 1877	11	172
Martin, Jessie Lee	Tycer, Henry T.	18 OCT 1881 L	16	032
Martin, John	Bell, Mary	16 SEP 1878 L	12	219
Martin, John	Booth, Margaret A.	08 SEP 1880 R	14	437
Martin, John R.	Nicholson, Georgia	14 AUG 1881 R	15	443
Martin, Kate C.	Daly, James A.	20 JUL 1883 L	18	054
Martin, Kate C.	Daley, James A.	04 AUG 1883	18	074
Martin, Katie E.	Caldwell, John T.	07 APR 1883 L	17	386
Martin, Laura L.	Atkinson, R.W.	05 JUL 1881 R	15	389
Martin, Lewis	Adam, Lucretia	10 SEP 1878 L	12	208
Martin, Lillie B.	Godman, S.C.	27 MAR 1884	18	485
Martin, Lizzie	Coxen, Thomas E.	06 SEP 1880 L	14	433
Martin, Lizzie	Fall, Martin	10 JUN 1883 R	17	485
Martin, Luther J.	Goodwin, Mattie J.	18 OCT 1882 R	17	078
Martin, Mack	Sinkfield, Josephine	10 MAY 1883 L	17	433
Martin, Maggie	Thomas, Luther	24 MAR 1881 R	15	237
Martin, Maggie E.	Belcher, Lucius C.	14 MAR 1881 R	15	224
Martin, Margaret Ellen	Larcombe, Samuel Thos.	16 JUL 1883	18	049
Martin, Martha Ellen	Lee, John Washington	13 MAY 1880 R	14	270
Martin, Mary	Colbert, Frank	23 JAN 1879 R	13	028
Martin, May M.	O'Meara, John D.	24 MAY 1882 L	16	375
Martin, Millard F.	Fales, Minnie E.	20 MAY 1878	12	060
Martin, Mollie Mildred	Wright, Charles	11 AUG 1885	20	365
Martin, Nellie Geraldine	Everett, John Coleman, Dr.	26 AUG 1885 R	20	008
Martin, R.H.	Harris, Millie W.	29 NOV 1881	16	101
Martin, Robert	Payne, Malinda	25 MAR 1880 R	14	183
Martin, Samuel E.	Cockrell, Lizzie	02 JUL 1878	12	121
Martin, Sarah	Brooks, Eli	09 MAR 1882 L	16	272
Martin, Sarah	Dennis, Alexander	29 SEP 1885 L	20	447
Martin, Sarah E.	Reynolds, Walter B.	06 NOV 1877	11	170
Martin, Sarah Elizabeth	Main, Hial P.	22 APR 1878 L	12	015
Martin, Sarah J.	Martin, Cyrus F.	27 DEC 1883 L	18	347
Martin, Sidney	Goodwin, Eliza	10 DEC 1881 R	16	124
Martin, Thomas	Johnson, Bessey	06 OCT 1885 R	20	461
Martin, Thomas A.	Mason, Offie	11 OCT 1882	17	067
Martin, William	Douglass, Frances	02 MAR 1882 R	16	266
Martin, William	Koch, Margaret	14 SEP 1882	17	022
Martin, William Franklin	Gray, Laura Louisa	27 JUN 1881 R	15	380
Marting, Mary A.	Pulman, C.O.	20 AUG 1885	20	381
Martyne, Susie S.J.L.	Fleming, Harry	18 NOV 1883	18	260
Marx, Marx	Freirick, Clara	07 MAY 1882 R	16	349
Marx, Moses	Schmidt, Jennie	13 MAY 1885 R	20	218
Maryman, Annie I.	Smith, C.B.	21 AUG 1884 L	19	199
Maryman, Harriet E.	Hammett, Charles N.	23 NOV 1881 L	16	092
Masi, Edward Pennaman	Lee, Mary Frances Per	06 OCT 1881 R	16	010
Maske, August	Welcker, Mary	05 SEP 1877 L	11	076
Maske, Henrietta	Ratke, Albert	20 SEP 1883	18	144
Maske, Wilhelmina	Radtke, William	25 NOV 1884	19	404
Mason, Abbie H.	Kingsley, George P.	12 JUN 1884	19	081
Mason, Alexander	Hill, Elizabeth A.	11 MAR 1885 L	20	107
Mason, Alice	Johnson, Robert	02 MAY 1879 L	13	171
Mason, Alice M.	Drury, John S.	15 APR 1884 L	18	512

D.C. Marriage Records Index, June 28, 1877 to October 19, 1885

Mason, Allen	Miner, Emma	26 JUL 1883	18	061
Mason, Amos	Brown, Mary	26 JUN 1879 R	13	252
Mason, Amos	Davis, Sibbie	26 NOV 1884 L	19	414
Mason, Carrie	Wilks, Joseph	24 DEC 1880 L	15	123
Mason, Carrie C.	Gardner, James R.	28 APR 1885 L	20	194
Mason, Catherine Germond	Proctor, John M.	03 NOV 1879 R	13	460
Mason, Celia	Taylor, Charles[ß]	10 JUN 1879 R	13	225
Mason, Charles	Grandison, Eliza	21 APR 1884 L	18	523
Mason, Charles A.	Herbert, Emma M.	19 JAN 1880	14	111
Mason, Charles W.	Lemore, Lavinia	07 NOV 1878	12	316
Mason, Charles W.	Brown, Sarah Elizabeth	14 AUG 1879	13	322
Mason, Edward	Harris, Annie	26 MAY 1881 L	15	329
Mason, Ellen	Day, William	28 AUG 1884 L	19	212
Mason, Emma V.	Kinney, Beverly W.	02 JUL 1885 R	20	308
Mason, Essie	Waters, Daniel	03 SEP 1878 L	12	196
Mason, F.M.	Brooker, Laura	29 MAR 1883 L	17	369
Mason, George H.	Carr, Lula M.	02 MAR 1878 L	11	370
Mason, Henry Douglass	Johnson, Eliza Jane	15 DEC 1880 R	15	100
Mason, Isaiah	Dunmore, Elizabeth	22 DEC 1878	12	394
Mason, James	Jones, Sidney	23 OCT 1884 L	19	335
Mason, Jennette	Reed, James W.	09 OCT 1884 L	19	297
Mason, Jessie Q.	Little, Thomas A.	09 MAR 1885 R	20	103
Mason, Johanna, Mrs.	Lee, Oscar	22 JUL 1878 R	12	144
Mason, John A.	Lane, Ann Matilda	16 JAN 1883 R	17	259
Mason, John H.	Dorsey, Margaret	30 OCT 1881	16	052
Mason, John Sanford	Wilson, Cornelia Marie Keller	08 MAR 1881 R	15	218
Mason, Katie	Adams, Aaron	21 APR 1881 L	15	269
Mason, Katie	Jordan, James	14 JUL 1884	19	138
Mason, Laura	Harris, Frank	02 NOV 1881 R	15	467
Mason, Lizzie	White, Richard	23 NOV 1882 L	17	146
Mason, Lucy	Bouldin, Joseph	14 DEC 1882 L	17	184
Mason, Lula S.	Smith, A. Thomas	08 OCT 1884	19	287
Mason, Maria Margareth	Bernharth, Jessy	16 JUL 1878 L	12	136
Mason, Mary	Ford, Henry	15 DEC 1881 R	16	112
Mason, Melinda	Woodroe, Charles	28 DEC 1882	17	219
Mason, Nannie M.	Ross, William F.	27 AUG 1877 L	11	068
Mason, Offie	Martin, Thomas A.	11 OCT 1882	17	067
Mason, Rebecca	Rome, William	28 OCT 1877	11	157
Mason, Richard	Hedgman, Sarah	24 MAY 1879	13	206
Mason, Richard	Fowler, Margaret V.	02 SEP 1879 R	13	346
Mason, Robert	Simmons, Eliza E.	05 MAY 1885 L	20	205
Mason, Samuel	Carter, Winnie Ann	20 NOV 1877 L	11	193
Mason, Samuel	Carter, Polly	24 AUG 1881 L	15	456
Mason, Samuel T.	Magruder, Mary Elizabeth	26 NOV 1877	11	203
Mason, Samuel Tufton	Shannon, Harriett B.	20 NOV 1880 R	21	5108
Mason, Sarah	Yancey, Jacob	29 MAR 1881 L	15	242
Mason, Sol Labran	Green, Rebecca	25 FEB 1885 L	20	085
Mason, Virginia Fairfax	Howland, Edwin P.	15 OCT 1877 R	11	135
Mason, William	Moore, Cecelia	28 DEC 1882 L	17	222
Mason, William	Jenkins, Elizabeth	15 FEB 1883	17	304
Mason, William	Gross, Alice	21 SEP 1885 R	20	431
Mason, William B.	Richards, Jessie	27 DEC 1883 R	18	351
Mason, William H.	Thomas, Mary E.	22 DEC 1881	16	143
Masses, Sadie M.	Patrick, John H.	24 OCT 1877	11	152
Massey, Emma	Jackson, Andrew	16 SEP 1880	14	449
Massey, Eva	Mockabee, John T.	21 FEB 1878 L	11	353

[ß]Return gives name of groom as Charles Mason.

Massey, Helen	Beach, Frank	07 FEB 1881 R	15	180
Massey, James H.	Parke, Victoria M.	12 NOV 1879 R	13	478
Massey, James L.	Clark, Susie V.	26 MAY 1880 R	14	291
Massey, Lilian Duncan	Wright, Frederick Parker	20 NOV 1879 R	13	497
Massey, Lola	Campbell, George W.	05 OCT 1885 R	20	456
Massey, Mida Wilmot	Wiltberger, Charles H., Jr.	01 DEC 1881 L	16	107
Massey, Rachel	Parker, Robert H.	30 MAY 1882 R	16	354
Massie, Byron	Cash, Katie	22 OCT 1883	18	205
Masson, James E.W.	Ellart, Margaret	08 MAY 1878 R	12	042
Masten, Ed S.	Cox, Mollie E.	04 MAR 1885	20	094
Masterem, John	Selden, Mary A.E.	16 SEP 1883	18	127
Masterson, D.W.	Douglas, E.E.	07 JUL 1885	20	313
Masterson, Lucretia	Moore, Allen	09 FEB 1878	11	334
Masterson, Rachael L.	James, William	12 DEC 1878 L	12	378
Mastin, Charles E.	Wood, Mary M.	16 JUL 1884	19	142
Mastin, James S.	Passeno, Amanda F.	13 JUL 1878	12	133
Maston, Philip	Taylor, Mary Elizabeth	08 JUN 1880 L	14	311
Matchett, Elizabeth	Volz, Anthony	10 FEB 1881 R	15	186
Matchett, Herbert H.	Kane, Emma E.	25 JUN 1879 R	13	252
Mateer, Annie E., Mrs.	Williams, George	12 JAN 1880 R	17	4077
Mathaney, Thomas H.	Bowen, Sallie E.	19 AUG 1880 R	14	409
Matheney, Sarah E.	Gist, Elmer F.	06 AUG 1885	20	360
Mathers, James W.	Duffey, Catherine	18 AUG 1884	19	190
Mathers, Louisa A.	Norris, John W.	15 OCT 1885 R	20	486
Mathes, Mary Louisa	Coleman, Robert	15 OCT 1885	20	442
Mathews, Charles	Mathews, Eliza	12 NOV 1884 L	19	376
Mathews, Cornelia A.	Simons, Walter H.	09 DEC 1879 R	14	035
Mathews, Eliza	Mathews, Charles	12 NOV 1884 L	19	376
Mathews, Jennie S.	Bartlett, Phoenix	14 NOV 1883 R	18	254
Mathews, Lydia	Goss, Thomas J.	28 MAY 1878	12	071
Mathews, Mary E.	Simms, Tyler Lindy	11 DEC 1879	14	039
Mathews, Robert A.	Summers, Matilda A.	12 FEB 1885 R	20	065
Mathews, Sarah	Wallace, Daniel	15 JAN 1885 L	20	021
Mathiot, Estelle	Stirling, Archibald	08 JUL 1884	19	126
Mathiot, Harry B.	Davis, Effie V.	04 JUN 1884	19	053
Matlock, Josie F.	Fridley, William H.	17 SEP 1878 R	12	221
Matney, Jennie	Brooks, Daniel	12 APR 1884	18	464
Matney, Thomas H.	Holtzman, Flora	27 MAY 1880	14	293
Matson, Addie	Johnson, Wesley	28 JAN 1878 R	11	318
Mattern, John Edwin	Kauffman, Anna S.	27 SEP 1879 R	13	389
Mattern, P. Adolf	Oppermann, Johanna	03 JUL 1884	19	119
Matthews, Alice	Forman, John	05 JUL 1881 R	15	390
Matthews, Amanda	Crawford, Nathan	12 APR 1883 R	17	392
Matthews, Annie	Matthews, James	15 JUN 1878 L	12	100
Matthews, Annie	William, James	05 FEB 1878 R	11	317
Matthews, Annie	Munroe, Samuel	06 SEP 1883 L	18	114
Matthews, Beale	Strong, Clarissa	12 JUL 1880	14	357
Matthews, Carter	Beckett, Catherine	26 JUL 1884 L	19	158
Matthews, Charles	Gay, Hattie	30 APR 1884 L	18	545
Matthews, Cora W.	Taylor, Charles W.	25 NOV 1878 L	12	345
Matthews, Edward	Flaherty, Johanna	12 MAR 1884	18	466
Matthews, Ella	Butler, David	14 JUN 1882 L	16	410
Matthews, Ellen	Scott, Abraham	27 NOV 1884	19	418
Matthews, Emily B.	Mandews, Horace	09 APR 1885 R	20	143
Matthews, Etta	Minor, Thaddeus	29 JUN 1881 R	15	355
Matthews, George	Gray, Elizabeth	06 JAN 1879 L	13	007
Matthews, Georgetta	Anderson, Ira Imri	25 JAN 1882	16	207
Matthews, Hattie	Vail, Benjamin, Jr.	16 SEP 1885 R	20	418

Matthews, Helen	Robinson, William	23 NOV 1882	17	147
Matthews, Helen	Dixon, Aaron	08 JAN 1884	18	455
Matthews, Henrietta	Smothers, George M.	20 NOV 1884 L	19	398
Matthews, Henry	Smith, Adeline	09 AUG 1879 R	13	311
Matthews, Ida	Jackson, Fenton	18 JUN 1885 R	20	281
Matthews, James	Matthews, Annie	15 JUN 1878 L	12	100
Matthews, James	Lee, Eliza	01 MAR 1881	15	208
Matthews, John	Harris, Maggie	02 AUG 1883	18	072
Matthews, John	McNally, Bridget	15 SEP 1883 L	18	132
Matthews, John N.	Folie, Agnes	27 MAR 1885 L	20	135
Matthews, John T.	Burke, Fanny E.	27 SEP 1877 L	11	113
Matthews, Joseph O.	Bullard, Mary E.	22 MAY 1879 R	15	3724
Matthews, Josephine E.	Brown, Oscar	13 NOV 1884	19	381
Matthews, Joshua	Stewart, Marion F.	06 JAN 1881 R	15	139
Matthews, Joshua	Bowles, Sarah	20 NOV 1882 L	17	137
Matthews, Julia Ann	Pratt, Isaiah	13 SEP 1882 L	17	019
Matthews, Lizzie	Shorter, Robert	04 SEP 1879	13	353
Matthews, Lizzie	Majors, Reuben	02 OCT 1881	15	501
Matthews, Lucy A.	Clark, George	27 FEB 1879 L	13	083
Matthews, Lulu	Jackson, Joseph	08 DEC 1884 R	19	441
Matthews, Maria	Armstrong, James	28 JUN 1880 L	14	336
Matthews, Marie	Faulkner, Albert	03 SEP 1884 L	19	222
Matthews, Martha	Peyton, Albert	10 SEP 1879 L	13	361
Matthews, Mary	Chase, James	05 JUN 1883 L	17	475
Matthews, Mary E.	Marshal, Charles W.	20 MAY 1880	14	278
Matthews, Mary E.	Lewis, John K.	02 FEB 1882	16	213
Matthews, Mary Francis	Chapman, Richard	28 JUN 1877	11	003
Matthews, Matilda	Moulton, Edward	06 SEP 1877 L	11	079
Matthews, Matilda	Hall, Woolsey P.	16 APR 1879 R	13	147
Matthews, Moses A.	Gordon, Mary Elizabeth	03 JUL 1884	19	121
Matthews, Nellie	Pirie, William	02 NOV 1882	17	109
Matthews, Rebecca	Mitchell, John E.	06 DEC 1881 L	16	114
Matthews, Reuben	Dickson, Patsy	05 APR 1883 R	17	381
Matthews, Robert	Bassfield, Emma	14 DEC 1882 R	17	186
Matthews, Robert	Peyton, Julia	05 OCT 1885	20	457
Matthews, Samuel	Moulden, Mary	29 MAR 1883 R	17	370
Matthews, Sarah	Crump, Carlisle F.	15 JUL 1879 R	13	282
Matthews, Sarah L.	Taylor, Fairfax H.	30 OCT 1884 L	19	348
Matthews, Sophia	Henson, Robert	10 DEC 1881 L	16	123
Matthews, Stephen T.M.	Forrest, Julia V.	14 OCT 1878 R	12	270
Matthews, William	Russell, Mary	22 APR 1880 L	14	235
Matthews, William	Nugent, Parry	06 DEC 1880 R	15	086
Matthews, William	Fletcher, Mariah	26 JUN 1884 R	19	101
Matthews, William E.	Bozeman, Euretta B.	03 JAN 1883	17	236
Matthias, Sallie J.	Evans, John R.	22 DEC 1884 R	19	475
Mattice, Emmitt L.	McKelden, Fanny B.	20 MAR 1884	18	477
Mattill, Henry	Ball, Mary	10 JUL 1880 L	14	355
Mattingly, Eliza	Hines, William	24 FEB 1885 R	20	081
Mattingly, Henry	Williams, Sarah	13 OCT 1883	18	188
Mattingly, Joseph S.	Codrick, Cora A.	17 MAY 1881 L	15	313
Mattingly, Josephine	Barnes, John F.	16 OCT 1884 L	19	311
Mattingly, Lena	West, Frank	03 MAY 1880 L	14	251
Mattingly, Marie Boury	Maguire, Fred. Leopold	13 AUG 1885	20	366
Mattingly, Mary	Follin, Thomas	10 DEC 1880	15	083
Mattingly, Orland F.	Skerving, Anna M.	24 JUN 1885 R	20	291
Mattingly, Robert F.	Scott, Sallie E.	17 SEP 1878 R	12	222
Mattingly, Rosa Lee	Foust, James F.	27 MAY 1885	20	242
Mattingly, Sallie R.	Malone, Aloysius	22 DEC 1881	16	153

Maubry, Ella	Beattie, James A.	25 AUG 1885	20	387
Maupin, Clara L.	Sheltin, Thomas M.	19 AUG 1885	20	380
Mauro, Philip	Rockwood, Emily Johnston	07 JUN 1881 R	15	345
Maury, Fontaine	Blacklock, Elizabeth Va.	06 JUN 1885 R	20	257
Mavrans, Annie Josephine	Harrison, George W.	25 DEC 1878 R	12	395
Mawdsley, Mary J.	Kealey, James H.	03 MAY 1881 L	15	288
Maxfield, Joseph	Robinson, Mary	17 JUL 1883 L	18	050
Maxfield, Margeret E.	McKelleget, Wm.	31 MAY 1880	14	297
Maxson, Frank O.	Van Doren, Evelyn M.	24 DEC 1877	11	269
Maxson, Louis Wm.	Bohrer, Minnie R.	25 DEC 1884 R	19	483
Maxwell, Catherine F.	Thomas, William E.	18 JAN 1884 L	18	384
Maxwell, Emma R.	Hall, Lewis K.	12 MAY 1880	14	266
May, Allie	Baxter, George O.	11 FEB 1884	18	418
May, Annie	Busher, John H.	06 MAR 1878	11	371
May, Arcie A.	Cillcapio, Andrew J.	10 SEP 1884	19	238
May, David	Humphreys, Kate	06 DEC 1884 R	19	437
May, Edward L.	Geary, Margaret J.	18 MAY 1879	13	194
May, Elizabeth	Davis, Franklin R.	10 NOV 1880	15	034
May, Elizabeth B.	Roswag, Charles F.	16 AUG 1885	20	371
May, Elizabeth Boss	Curtiss, John Klink	28 OCT 1878 R	12	291
May, Frank P.	O'Hare, Annie K.	14 OCT 1878 L	12	272
May, George C.	Dennis, Ida V.	13 JAN 1883 L	17	255
May, George C.	Hammond, Addie Ursula	06 SEP 1883 R	18	110
May, James B.	Bispham, Lou H.	22 NOV 1877	11	198
May, John G.	Dammann, Emma O.	28 OCT 1881 L	16	051
May, Marion E.	Jenkins, David E.	12 JUN 1884 L	19	081
May, Mary Elizabeth	Reckert, Charles George	14 OCT 1884 L	19	304
May, Sarah M.	Schladt, Joseph	23 FEB 1879	13	072
Mayfield, Mercer B.	Blundon, Kate M.	23 SEP 1885	20	437
Mayhew, Alice	Lusby, John N.	16 OCT 1884	19	311
Mayhew, Georgie	Bryan, R. Hughlett	04 DEC 1882	17	165
Mayhew, James	Taylor, Alice	15 MAY 1879 R	13	164
Mayhew, Katie	Lloyd, William H.	06 MAY 1880 R	14	257
Mayhugh, Frances	Duvall, Manadier Mason	10 NOV 1884 R	19	368
Mayhugh, Roxy	Tobia, Frank	26 DEC 1883	18	345
Mayhugh, Sallie	Sherwood, Elias	18 JAN 1883	17	264
Maynard, Elizabeth E.	Burke, James Henry	17 MAY 1882 L	16	364
Maynard, Lucy	Contee, George	17 MAY 1883	17	447
Mayne, Laura C.	House, Joseph S.	01 NOV 1880 L	15	024
Mayo, George W.	Broach, Alice	14 AUG 1882	16	478
Mayo, Minnie A.	Ambroselli, Joseph B.	08 OCT 1878	12	260
Mays, Georgeanna, Mrs.	Gordon, Charles H.	22 NOV 1884 R	19	402
Mays, William	Watson, Maggie	25 DEC 1877 R	11	266
Mazur, Lorenz	Shay, Mary	07 MAY 1885 L	20	211
McAbee, M. Broderick	Bentley, Nellie B.	12 SEP 1877	11	089
McAbee, Margaret	Lester, William	16 OCT 1878 R	12	278
McAbee, Tempe	Tuxon, Edward	02 MAR 1882	16	256
McAdam, William Alfred	Senter, Mary Isabel	10 OCT 1883 R	18	184
McAllister, John Ferguson	Ashby, Rebecca J. (Harris)	24 JUL 1882 R	16	455
McAllister, Mary Frances	Richmond, Walter Stanley	23 DEC 1880 R	15	115
McAllister, Narametta Stallings	Oliver, William H.	08 DEC 1879 R	14	034
McAllister, Richard	Bagaley, Sarah Elizabeth	21 APR 1879 R	13	152
McAllister, Richard, Jr.	Saunders, Mary I.	08 OCT 1885 R	20	466
McAllister, Thomas A.	Flaherty, Margaret C.	08 FEB 1882 R	16	232
McAllister, Willie T.	Dull, Samuel R.	26 JUN 1882 L	16	425
McAnally, Joseph F.	Marsh, Fannie H.	11 DEC 1884 R	19	455
McArdle, Kate	O'Toole, Michael	22 JAN 1884 L	18	388

D.C. Marriage Records Index, June 28, 1877 to October 19, 1885   305

McArdle, Mary D.	Jennings, Edward J.	28 DEC 1880 L	15	128
McAuley, George Robert	Voss, Delia M.	21 JAN 1884 R	18	387
McAuley, Richard Charles	Van Syckle, Mary Carman	18 DEC 1879 R	14	053
McAuliff, Nellie	Huhn, William	17 NOV 1884 L	19	387
McAuliffe, John	O'Leary, Margaret	15 SEP 1884 L	19	246
McAuliffe, Katie	Golly, Benjamin	05 OCT 1878	12	255
McAuliffe, Mary	Ellis, William Francis	14 SEP 1879 R	13	298
McAvoy, George F.	Chapman, E. Rose	26 NOV 1884 L	19	416
McBee, Elias Alexander	Corse, Mary Eltinge	18 FEB 1882 R	16	320
McBee, Randolph	Blackiston, Minnie D.	19 JUL 1877 R	11	026
McBlair, Charles Ridgely	Parr, Florence May	17 FEB 1885 R	20	074
McBride, James	Meyer, Margaret A.	17 DEC 1877 L	11	239
McBride, Maggie	Howard, James	13 MAR 1883 L	17	341
McBride, Mary E.	Miller, George W.	22 SEP 1885 R	20	430
McBride, Patrick	Doggett, Melvinia	11 JUN 1884	19	077
McCabe, James A.	Connell, Mary Agnes	08 AUG 1881 R	15	435
McCabe, Maria	Ballinger, William H.	13 OCT 1884 L	19	303
McCabe, Mary E.	Buckman, John Harrison	02 SEP 1881 R	15	469
McCabe, Sarah	Solawry, Benjamin	10 JAN 1882 L	16	189
McCaffney, Hugh R.	Sherwood, Kate E.	17 JUL 1884	19	145
McCaffrey, Katie	Foley, Daniel P.	24 SEP 1882 R	17	035
McCaffrey, Thomas	O'Neill, Katie	10 MAR 1881	15	219
McCallan, Honora	Connor, James	03 AUG 1880	14	382
McCallister, Charles D.	Brown, Josephine N.	12 AUG 1882 R	16	478
McCallum, Margaret M.	Ortlip, Charles John	24 SEP 1884	19	265
McCalman, Peter	Gabriel, Elizabeth Ann	14 AUG 1883 L	18	086
McCann, Bridget E.	Smith, Peter A.	26 NOV 1879 L	14	013
McCann, Julia	Talbot, Chris J.	30 SEP 1884 L	19	276
McCann, Michael H.	Cook, Sarah J.	03 DEC 1881 L	16	112
McCargo, Peyton R.	Hodges, Ida D.	22 SEP 1881 R	15	494
McCarroll, Ann	Shea, James	26 JUL 1881 L	15	417
McCarteney, Charles M.	Cragin, Annette F.	30 APR 1878	12	031
McCarter, Sarah	Hoban, Henry	22 JUN 1881 L	15	373
McCarthy, Christopher	Reedy, Mary	28 NOV 1883 L	18	282
McCarthy, Daniel	Reilley, Mary	05 NOV 1879 R	13	462
McCarthy, E.E.	Kane, J.P.	31 DEC 1879	13	500
McCarthy, Jerome J.	Bernard, Mary J.	22 SEP 1879 R	13	380
McCarthy, John	Mahoney, Margaret	10 APR 1880 L	14	220
McCarthy, John	Grogan, Mary	03 MAY 1884 L	18	550
McCarthy, John B.	Crosby, Nellie C.	29 JUN 1883	18	026
McCarthy, John J.	Cranston, Sallie M.	17 MAY 1881 R	15	310
McCarthy, Justin J.	O'Connor, Mary E.	13 SEP 1879 L	13	369
McCarthy, Kate A.	Spellman, J.F.	22 APR 1879 L	13	155
McCarthy, Margaret	Callaghan, Richard	12 JUL 1885 L	20	321
McCarthy, Mary	O'Leary, Jeremiah	05 FEB 1880	14	137
McCarthy, Patrick	Sullivan, Mary	14 NOV 1882	17	125
McCarthy, Sophia A.	Glancy, John P.	08 OCT 1883 L	18	177
McCarthy, William	Sullivan, Johanna	06 NOV 1879 L	13	469
McCartney, Alice	Ahern, William J.	29 JUN 1880 R	14	337
McCartney, Bernard T.	Beane, Lizzie M.	06 JUL 1879 R	13	269
McCartney, Ellen C.	Sullivan, Thomas Joseph	04 DEC 1878 L	12	367
McCartney, Peter	Fletcher, Annie C.	05 JAN 1882 R	16	184
McCarty, Anna	O'Connor, Jeremiah	25 DEC 1878 R	12	397
McCarty, Louisa B.	Peters, George H.	18 JUN 1878	12	102
McCarty, Mary A.	Jones, Broadus H.	01 NOV 1879 L	13	457
McCarty, Mary L.	Daley, John C.	29 MAY 1883 L	17	467
McCarty, Richard Jay	Johnstone, Lidie McPherson	03 JAN 1882 R	16	178
McCathran, Benjamin F.	Carroll, Hannora	29 APR 1883 R	17	421

Name	Spouse	Date	Vol	Page
McCathran, F.C.	Hall, A.L.	01 AUG 1881 L	15	429
McCathran, Maggie	Guest, George W.	11 MAR 1880 R	14	182
McCauley, Benjamin Franklin	Stuart, Annie	03 APR 1881 R	15	244
McCauley, Bettie C.	Clements, Stephen A.	04 OCT 1882 L	17	051
McCauley, Daniel L.	Dugan, Rachel A.	21 OCT 1884 L	19	327
McCauley, Joseph	Russell, Harriet	13 NOV 1880	15	046
McCauley, Kate	Forrester, Peter	01 JAN 1878	11	285
McCauley, Maggie	Nichols, Harland A.	30 AUG 1883 L	18	105
McCauliffe, Kate D.W.	Dove, James	14 OCT 1880	14	494
McCauslen, Nellie H.	Browning, Ringgold W.	03 JUL 1885	20	308
McCaw, Sallie Pelham	Wheeler, William M.	21 AUG 1877 R	11	057
McCellicett, Laura	Cleveland, Wm. H.	23 DEC 1879	14	061
McCeney, John S.	Hyatt, Helen M.	12 MAR 1884 R	18	467
McChesner, Ellsworth E.	Teasdale, Lola M.	29 NOV 1882	17	160
McChesney, Algernon R.	Hein, Agnes W.	08 MAY 1885 R	20	210
McChesney, Alice V.	Gilliland, James C.	08 NOV 1883 L	18	242
McChesney, Junius Baylor	Grove, Virginia May	30 APR 1884 R	18	547
McChesney, Kate H.	Swart, William W.	23 JUN 1885 L	20	286
McChesney, Mary Alice	Brown, Harry B.	12 JUN 1884	19	079
McClain, Winnifred Ward	Rheims, Robert L.	13 OCT 1879	13	417
McClanahan, Bettie	West, William Lovel	13 AUG 1883	18	085
McCleary, Andrew H.	Holland, Mary C.	02 MAR 1883 R	17	330
McCleary, Maggie W.	Cate, Holmes	26 AUG 1879 R	13	337
McClees, Sallie Endicott	Gittings, Jedidiah, Jr.	27 OCT 1880 R	15	017
McClellan, George Robert	Connor, Mary Catherine	21 JUN 1879 R	13	285
McClellan, Lizzie E., Mrs.	Wood, Foster P.	31 MAY 1882	16	385
McClelland, James Robert	Cady, Bridget Ellen	08 JUL 1884 L	19	129
McClelland, John, Capt.	Draper, Annie G.	06 JAN 1881	15	144
McClelland, Kate	Peck, Charles T.	18 APR 1878	12	009
McClelland, Lola	Haller, Nicholas	06 MAR 1878 R	11	374
McClelland, Mamie C.	Reynolds, John W.	21 FEB 1885	20	083
McClery, Marion	Dryan, Henry Lewis	15 OCT 1878 R	12	271
McCliesh, Henry I.	Sauers, Kate	21 JAN 1883	17	270
McClintock, John M.	Conrad, Annie	07 JAN 1884 R	18	367
McClosky, Rose A.	Bennett, George A.	22 SEP 1881 L	15	495
McCloud, George	Somers, Sarah Walker	25 SEP 1878 R	12	205
McClure, Alfred J.	Cutler, Louise F.	01 JAN 1880	14	083
McClure, Austin Wade	Swann, Jessie Haney	23 DEC 1879 R	14	027
McClure, William J.	Gessford, Ida V.	30 OCT 1879 R	13	456
McCollam, Edward F.W.	Chaney, Emma E.	22 MAY 1883	17	456
McCollum, H.A.	Hill, Mary	21 AUG 1877	11	061
McComb, David Edward	Maher, Theresa Elliot	28 AUG 1878 R	12	183
McCondach, James	Grinder, Bettie	15 NOV 1882	17	129
McConike, Isabella G.	Grove, Elijah F.	05 MAR 1879 R	13	092
McConley, Charles	Posey, Rebecca	16 MAR 1884 R	18	471
McConnell, Elizabeth Campbell	Merryman, John H.	09 OCT 1883 R	18	181
McConnell, Mary A.	Walsh, Walter E.	19 NOV 1877 R	11	192
McCorkle, Simpson	Shepherd, Millie A.	11 DEC 1884 R	19	452
McCormick, Ellen F.	Maloney, Patrick	22 OCT 1884 L	19	330
McCormick, Ellen Morgan	Fisher, William Thomas	12 SEP 1877 L	11	090
McCormick, Julia R.	Day, Lewis W.	22 MAR 1882 R	16	286
McCormick, Mary E.	Graves, Lewis H.	15 NOV 1883	18	258
McCormick, Matilda	Brightwell, John W.	07 NOV 1882	17	113
McCormick, Michael George	Hammersly, Laura	26 JAN 1885 L	20	036
McCormick, Millard P.	Guilford, Lottie	11 APR 1882	16	303
McCourt, Lizzie Bonduel	Tabor, Horace A.W.	01 MAR 1883 L	17	329
McCoy, Augustus	Fleming, Roberta	23 APR 1880	14	236
McCoy, Ellen Espy	Bartley, Thomas W.	17 SEP 1878 L	12	223

McCoy, Fannie E.	Ridgway, George A.	04 JUN 1880 L	14	305
McCoy, Georgianna	Wallace, Jerry	31 MAR 1885 L	20	139
McCoy, Harvy	Kirbage, Emma	31 JAN 1885 R	20	044
McCoy, J. Findley	Parks, Annie A.	16 OCT 1878	12	277
McCoy, Joseph Melville	Peterson, Eunice Ella	28 JAN 1885	20	028
McCoy, Mary Jane	Wright, Daniel Pratt	29 JAN 1879 R	13	036
McCoy, Mollie	Jackson, James	09 JAN 1879	13	013
McCoy, Rachel	Hanson, John	28 NOV 1877	11	211
McCoy, Richard	Ricks, Catherine	15 JUN 1883 R	17	493
McCoy, William	Chisley, Elizabeth	06 MAY 1882	16	351
McCoy, William A.	Snyder, Virginia A.	08 SEP 1883 R	18	119
McCrestle, Annie	Webster, Charles S.	26 SEP 1883	18	149
McCrossin, Henry	Murphy, Kate E.	20 JUN 1883	18	004
McCubbin, Edward	Haven, Priscilla	27 MAR 1879	13	116
McCubbin, Mary Geneva	Hoover, Edward C.	16 AUG 1881 R	15	448
McCuen, John	Sutton, Jennie E.	05 JUL 1884	19	122
McCuller, Peter C.	Ager, Josey L.	22 NOV 1881 L	16	088
McCulloch, George M. Dallas	Devine, Kate A.	16 OCT 1879 R	13	428
McCulloch, Kitty	Center, Henry R.	17 APR 1879 R	13	150
McCullough, Ruth Buckley	Garrett, Jesse L.	09 JAN 1881 R	15	145
McCullough, Wesley E.M.	Stewart, Agnes M.	29 NOV 1883	18	287
McCullum, George T.	Sanders, Lola B.	07 DEC 1883	18	305
McCullum, Lizzie	Holmes, Armstead	08 APR 1884 L	18	500
McCully, Emma E.	Cameron, Theodore R.	18 SEP 1884	19	258
McCurdy, Katie B.	Mullin, Philip E.	18 JAN 1882	16	199
McCutcheon, Mary	Soper, Charles P.	11 JUN 1878	12	096
McDaniel, George	Pinn, Maria	16 SEP 1879	13	372
McDaniel, John	Bell, Mary	26 NOV 1884 L	19	412
McDaniel, Marian Jackson	Codrick, Frederick Milton	15 MAR 1882 R	16	278
McDaniel, Martha A., Mrs.	Poole, Edwin W.	11 OCT 1877 R	11	132
McDaniel, Mildred J.	Lee, William	16 NOV 1881 L	16	080
McDaniel, Robert	Shands, Fanny	04 NOV 1880 L	15	032
McDaniel, Rosa	Twine, John	15 NOV 1883	18	249
McDaniel, Sarah C.	Waring, Charles S.	20 APR 1878	12	012
McDaniel, William D.	Prather, Flora R.	09 SEP 1884	19	237
McDermot, Emma J.	Wamaling, Charles T.	14 SEP 1879 R	13	368
McDermot, Mary Ann	Hatcher, Edward W.	06 OCT 1881 R	16	007
McDermott, Bridget	Reed, James H.	18 JUN 1884	19	091
McDermott, Dorothea	Chester, John C.	10 OCT 1879 R	13	415
McDermott, Eliza	Feeney, William J.	04 AUG 1885 L	20	351
McDermott, Frank P.	McKeever, Anna V.	16 SEP 1884 L	19	250
McDermott, George	Cumberland, Susie	19 APR 1882 L	16	324
McDermott, Julia	Donohue, Columbus C.	19 OCT 1879 R	13	432
McDermott, Katie	Lawrence, George	22 SEP 1884 L	19	263
McDermott, Maggie V.	Stowell, Frederick G.	19 JAN 1882	16	199
McDermott, Peter D.	Byrns, Maria	23 FEB 1884 L	18	440
McDevitt, Annie W.	Epping, Carl A.	07 AUG 1883 L	18	077
McDevitt, John J.	Sullivan, Fannie	10 MAY 1883 R	17	247
McDonald, Alice	Work, William J.	12 SEP 1883 L	18	125
McDonald, Alice V.	Ricks, William	25 APR 1881 L	15	270
McDonald, Bridget D.	Duhneen, John F.	09 AUG 1881 L	15	437
McDonald, Harry A.	Shreve, Lillian E.	23 MAY 1878	12	064
McDonald, James F.	Graves, Sallie A.	14 FEB 1878 L	11	340
McDonald, James K.	MacMurray, Blanche	03 JUL 1877	11	007
McDonald, Jennie	Lincoln, Frank J.	01 AUG 1878	12	154
McDonald, John D.	Daniels, Rosa A.	24 OCT 1883 L	18	210
McDonald, Joseph E.	Barnard, Josephine F.	12 JAN 1881	15	146
McDonald, Judson R.	Dunnington, Mary H.	02 NOV 1880	15	024

McDonald, Lizzie S.	Brandt, Adam	04 FEB 1884	18	408
McDonald, Mary	Kaspar, William	29 NOV 1881 R	16	103
McDonald, Mary A.	Fister, William H.	04 NOV 1881	16	062
McDonald, Mary Ann	Ford, Oscar Irven	19 MAY 1881 L	15	319
McDonald, Mary Bell	Myers, John Solon	05 DEC 1877	11	219
McDonald, Mary E.	Yost, William H.	29 APR 1885 L	20	196
McDonald, Mary Loreno	McElfresh, Henry Millard	29 MAR 1881 R	15	242
McDonald, Mattie	Hawkins, Barclay	23 APR 1885 L	20	186
McDonald, Pierce	Hackett, Mary Ann	06 JUN 1879 L	13	222
McDonald, Robert	Quealy, Delie T.	26 DEC 1877 L	11	269
McDonald, Virginia C.	Keefer, Joseph H.	20 OCT 1884	19	280
McDonnell, Ella	Clarke, John T.	15 SEP 1881 L	15	486
McDonnell, Katie	Norwood, George A.	23 APR 1878 L	12	017
McDonogh, Mary	Collins, John	08 SEP 1883 L	18	120
McDonough, Annie L.	Crown, John A.	27 MAR 1878 R	11	395
McDonough, Patrick	Collins, Johannah	13 FEB 1879 R	13	057
McDowell, Dan	Campbell, Julia	01 NOV 1881 L	16	056
McDowell, Hattie M.	Hunt, John	06 JUN 1882 R	16	396
McDowell, James H.	Pusey, Louanna	04 OCT 1877 R	11	123
McDowell, Will A.	Warren, Lula A.	30 JAN 1882 L	16	215
McElfresh, Frances E.	Rainey, Francis H.	29 JAN 1879 L	13	037
McElfresh, Frank Spindler	Chappell, Minnie Jennetta	12 FEB 1884 R	18	420
McElfresh, Henry Millard	McDonald, Mary Loreno	29 MAR 1881 R	15	242
McElfresh, John J.S.	Finley, Kate Palmer	10 OCT 1882 L	17	062
McElfresh, Rose E.	Brown, Henry T.	15 APR 1885 R	20	167
McElfresh, Vannetta C.	Boggs, Cyrus E.	29 JUN 1878	12	118
McElhinney, Charles Andrews	Schoepf, Millie Kesley	15 OCT 1879 R	13	424
McElhinney, Mollie C.	Peterson, Augustus	31 JAN 1878 L	11	323
McElhinney, Wm. Ernest	Kesley, Lydia Smith	01 SEP 1880 R	14	425
McElreavy, Margaret J.	Lawrence, Henry	05 MAR 1885 R	20	096
McEntee, Elizabeth	Hawkins, Abraham	11 AUG 1881 L	15	441
McEntee, Laura E.	Honesty, James	03 JUN 1878	12	082
McEwing, Henry	Pearson, Julia F.	02 APR 1885 L	20	142
McFadden, Sarah Hays	Thornton, George Taylor	26 NOV 1879 R	14	015
McFarland, Charles E.	Youngs, Allice	05 OCT 1885	20	459
McFarland, Sidney M.	Hogan, Mary	03 JUN 1885 L	20	255
McFarland, W.E.	Giddings, Rosa E.	12 NOV 1879 R	13	480
McFaul, Anna	Gaghan, John	12 SEP 1883	18	128
McFaul, Annie S.	Soaper, William	28 OCT 1878 L	12	294
McFermillion, Mary	Thompson, James	05 DEC 1877 L	11	220
McGann, Rachel L.	Moreland, Enoch C.	09 DEC 1879 L	14	037
McGarr, John R.	Healy, Ellen	05 FEB 1881 R	15	178
McGarraghy, Mary Reddy	Dant, Thomas E.	21 FEB 1882 R	16	252
McGarver, Margaret	Gallagher, Timothy A.	03 DEC 1879 L	14	027
McGarvey, Ellen	Gallagher, James	25 FEB 1879 L	13	078
McGee, Delavan	Knight, Emma Katie	03 APR 1880 R	14	208
McGee, Edward	Cole, Nettie C., Mrs.	17 APR 1879 R	13	149
McGee, George Francis	Carter, Mary Ellen	15 SEP 1879 R	13	369
McGee, James F.	Corcoran, Lizzie A.	08 NOV 1882 L	17	116
McGee, Katie	Thecker, Alonzo	02 FEB 1879	13	042
McGee, Patrick	Donahue, Mary	19 FEB 1884	18	431
McGeorge, John F.	Rebman, Virginia A.	29 JUL 1881 R	15	424
McGettigan, James	Walsh, Mary	07 SEP 1878 L	12	203
McGhee, Lizzie F.	Rowe, Thomas R.	28 JUN 1877 L	11	001
McGhee, Martin L.	Lee, Ida J.	14 NOV 1883	18	251
McGhee, Mary B.	Ricketts, Edward	23 JUL 1879	13	291
McGill, Cora Eugenia	Kibble, John Morris	06 OCT 1879 R	13	405
McGill, Emma L.	Cox, Wm. Washington	21 JUN 1881 R	15	373

D.C. Marriage Records Index, June 28, 1877 to October 19, 1885

Name	Spouse	Date	Vol	Page
McGill, Emma T.	Cushing, Frank H.	10 JUL 1882	16	442
McGill, George E.	Thompson, Anna E.	26 FEB 1884 L	18	444
McGill, George E.	King, Laura V.	29 SEP 1885	20	424
McGill, Harriet A.	Barker, Nelson	06 DEC 1877 L	11	224
McGill, Harriet V.	Evans, Charles P.	15 JUN 1878 L	12	100
McGill, Mary Janet	Taylor, George F., Dr.	19 DEC 1882 R	17	191
McGill, Molly	Seaton, Peter G.	26 DEC 1881	16	157
McGilvray, Ida	Forbes, Nestor H., Jr.	25 AUG 1877	11	065
McGinily, Elizabeth J.	Dimmick, Edgar C.	17 SEP 1884	19	254
McGinley, Margaret	Kidwell, John P.	28 DEC 1882 R	17	217
McGinley, Mary	Lanahan, John	03 OCT 1878 L	12	251
McGinley, Michael M.	Worthington, Kate N.	23 APR 1878 R	12	018
McGinn, Robert Wright	Hall, Lillian Hammond	19 MAR 1881 R	15	233
McGinniss, Richard M.	Miller, Mary E.	17 OCT 1885	20	495
McGirr, Ella Aloysia	Watson, James Allen	09 MAR 1880 R	14	177
McGoing, Lucinda	Thomas, Robert Henry	20 FEB 1883 L	17	313
McGolerich, Mary	Austin, Edward	23 SEP 1879 R	13	383
McGrade, Laura Virginia	Wyatt, George M.	01 JAN 1884 L	18	359
McGrath, Catherine	Chase, Augustus	14 MAR 1881 L	15	225
McGrath, Eliza	Wren, Daniel	19 AUG 1883	18	093
McGrath, Henry	Kilgour, Annie	06 OCT 1885 R	20	463
McGrath, Richard	Foley, Catherine C.	27 JUN 1883 L	18	018
McGrath, Richard	Foley, Catharine C.	14 APR 1884 L	18	507
McGrath, Wallock	Bowie, Armenia	15 FEB 1884 R	18	426
McGraw, F.J.	Seiler, Katie A.	06 AUG 1884	19	171
McGraw, Honora	Cady, Matthew	04 JUN 1884	19	052
McGraw, Mary	Flynn, Thomas	28 JUL 1884 L	19	160
McGraw, Mary Louise	Clements, Charles A.	26 JAN 1881 R	15	166
McGregor, Inez	Green, John Marshall	10 MAY 1885 R	20	215
McGrew, Agnes Eliz.	Wickersham, Morris Dickinson	04 JAN 1883 R	17	234
McGrew, Grace Annie	Monypeny, William, Jr.	08 APR 1884 R	18	499
McGruder, Susan	Wilson, Charles Henry	14 OCT 1878	12	271
McGuigan, John J.	Tincher, Georgie F.	05 OCT 1879 R	13	379
McGuigan, Mary	Swagart, Columbus L.	30 MAR 1885 R	20	136
McGuire, Blanche S.	Brown, John R.	08 SEP 1880 L	14	436
McGuire, Gertrude	O'Rouke, Joseph	26 DEC 1884 R	19	492
McGuire, John	Ganley, Kate A.	07 JUL 1881	15	394
McHale, Anthony	Barry, Julia	04 NOV 1883	18	291
McHenry, Ida M.	Love, John P.	11 AUG 1884	19	178
McHenry, Mamie E.	Blackburn, Henry H.	10 OCT 1878	12	267
McHugh, Charles M.	Flurry, Sarah Frances	22 JAN 1878 R	11	311
McHugo, James	Sullivan, Mary	21 SEP 1882 L	17	033
McInerny, Dennis	O'Day, Catherine	08 OCT 1883 L	18	176
McInteer, Arthur L.	Shacklette, Virginia A.	29 JUN 1885 R	20	299
McIntire, Annie Laura	Gallagher, William T.	02 OCT 1877 R	11	116
McIntire, Henry	Parrish, Lizzie	24 DEC 1877 R	11	267
McIntosh, Arabella F.	Head, Benjamin Franklin	25 AUG 1880 R	14	416
McIntosh, Charles R.	True, Ida V.	03 JAN 1882 L	16	179
McIntosh, Mary Claiborne Stevens	Chase, Walter Edward	06 MAY 1884 R	19	007
McIntosh, Mary Ruth	Williams, Thomas Burr	17 JUL 1877	11	023
McIntryre, Thomas F.	Cadey, Julia	08 APR 1885	20	153
McInturf, Mary E.	Moss, Elverton	14 JUL 1884 L	19	136
McInturff, Emily W.	Cage, Lemuel P.	01 DEC 1879 L	14	021
McInturff, Emily W.	Cage, Leonard P.	02 DEC 1879 R	14	017
McIntyre, Bernard	Bradford, Ida F.	09 AUG 1881	15	436
McIntyre, John H.	Shoemaker, Catharine V.	18 FEB 1884 L	18	430
McIntyre, Mary Agnes	Talbot, William N.	11 AUG 1883 L	18	083
McIntyre, Michael	Steimer, Margaret	30 AUG 1882 L	16	496

McIntyre, Robert	Smith, Elizabeth B.	20 MAY 1881 L	15	319
McKanna, John	Levy, Annie	16 JAN 1884 L	18	358
McKean, Theodore F.	Newton, Sarah A.	08 JAN 1879 R	13	008
McKee, Georgie Brubaker	Barrett, Theodore H.	05 JUN 1879 R	13	219
McKee, Lillian B.	Rice, Nathan E.	05 OCT 1881 R	16	008
McKee, Martha J.	Allen, Clarence G.	20 OCT 1884	19	317
McKeever, Anna V.	McDermott, Frank P.	16 SEP 1884 L	19	250
McKeever, Clara V.	Kendrick, Charles M.	11 JAN 1881 R	15	147
McKeever, Edwin K.	Smith, Elisa Bell	16 OCT 1884	19	312
McKeever, Mary A.	Walling, William L.	03 NOV 1883	18	230
McKeever, Sam	Lloyd, Eliza	25 NOV 1880 R	15	065
McKeever, William	Stuart, Alice	30 JUN 1879 L	13	259
McKelden, Fanny B.	Mattice, Emmitt L.	20 MAR 1884	18	477
McKelden, Mary W.	Adams, Manning J.	18 DEC 1884	19	467
McKelleget, Wm.	Maxfield, Margeret E.	31 MAY 1880	14	297
McKenna, Joseph M.	Goodrich, Ida	30 OCT 1879 R	13	451
McKenna, Laura	Broman, Andrew	27 NOV 1877 R	11	205
McKenney, Annie	Forrester, George H.	05 AUG 1884 L	19	167
McKenney, Annie E.	Kidwell, George W.	13 DEC 1882	17	181
McKenney, Bettie	Cole, Harry	08 SEP 1880 L	14	435
McKenney, Charles E.	Harley, Jane A.	21 APR 1882	16	327
McKenney, Clara E.	Barnes, Louie M.	17 SEP 1878 R	12	221
McKenney, Edgar	Ringgold, Josephine	15 AUG 1884 L	19	189
McKenney, Elizabeth	White, Thomas	14 JUN 1883 L	17	494
McKenney, George B.	Pollard, Sarah	20 NOV 1879 L	13	497
McKenney, Jared	McKnight, Mary	24 DEC 1877 L	11	267
McKenney, John	Campbell, Elizabeth	17 SEP 1878 L	12	222
McKenney, Lizzie	Barrett, John W.	30 JUN 1880	14	337
McKenney, Louise	Roy, Stewart	25 APR 1883	17	411
McKenney, Martha E.	Howard, Alexander E.	16 OCT 1878	12	276
McKenney, Mary	Newby, William H.	30 AUG 1882 R	16	496
McKenney, Mary J.	Gettinger, Jamoo O.	28 DEC 1882 R	17	220
McKenney, Mollie	Clift, James B.	07 MAR 1882 R	16	269
McKenney, Stephen	Holmes, Maria	14 DEC 1882 R	17	182
McKenney, William H.	Johnson, Mollie M.	19 MAR 1884 R	18	475
McKenney, William R.	Pickrell, Clara I.	02 DEC 1878 R	12	358
McKenny, Martha	Cook, Alexander J.	01 NOV 1877	11	165
McKenny, Sarah A.	Bohrer, Marion Willett	16 SEP 1879 R	13	371
McKenzie, Alexander	Guinand, Alice E.	12 APR 1882 R	16	312
McKenzie, Cannetta	Brooks, Charles	22 NOV 1883 L	18	272
McKenzie, Charlotte E.K.V.	Randolph, Robert P.V.	11 OCT 1883 L	18	188
McKenzie, Kate	Barbour, Anderson H.	22 MAR 1882	16	287
McKenzie, Lambert J.H.	McPherson, Sarah S.	06 AUG 1884	19	172
McKeon, Robert W.	Blair, Regina Agnes	22 SEP 1884 L	19	265
McKerichar, Mary S.	Halley, John E.	23 FEB 1882 R	16	258
McKern, Katie	Jones, John	22 JUN 1885 L	20	283
McKernan, Thomas	Shields, Margaret	19 SEP 1883 R	18	140
McKim, Harriet Hutchins	Haddaway, Charles A.	15 OCT 1884	19	309
McKinney, Benjamin F.	Truman, Annie Virginia	15 SEP 1885 R	20	416
McKinney, Christopher C.	Miller, Lena M.	26 MAY 1880	14	288
McKinney, William W.	Bateman, Laura L.	29 MAR 1884 R	18	486
McKinzie, Little L.	Post, William E.	05 NOV 1883	18	232
McKnee, John T.	Johnson, Mary V.	19 MAR 1884 R	18	475
McKnee, Victoria V.	Ford, Frank B.	19 MAR 1884 R	18	475
McKnew, Nina	Ashby, William Todd	18 APR 1883 R	17	397
McKnew, Thomas Willson	Fisher, Bertha Virginia	16 JUN 1885 R	20	275
McKnew, Wm. Harrison	Higgins, Ida	22 NOV 1882 R	17	143
McKnight, Cassius	Hall, Rachel	14 JUL 1883 L	18	047

McKnight, Florence	Jivinse, Samuel	12 APR 1882 L	16	314
McKnight, John	Dunn, Annie	27 DEC 1884 R	19	495
McKnight, Katie Dickson	Ourdan, Vincent LeComte	30 DEC 1879 R	14	079
McKnight, Martha V.	Rhodrick, Elbridge P.	23 SEP 1879 R	13	381
McKnight, Mary	McKenney, Jared	24 DEC 1877 L	11	267
McKnight, Robert	Spence, Susie	04 OCT 1884 L	19	287
McLain, John	Lough, Augusta	28 AUG 1878 L	12	183
McLain, Portus B.	Rowe, Inez E.	16 JUN 1882	16	415
McLain, Sarah F.	Junghaus, Joseph	01 AUG 1880	14	380
McLane, Anne	Cropper, John	22 NOV 1881 R	16	086
McLane, John	Cannon, Mary	31 AUG 1880 L	14	424
McLane, Lizzie	Maroni, Malachi N.	25 FEB 1878 R	11	355
McLaughlin, Charles	Hearty, Sarah	27 APR 1882	16	339
McLaughlin, Eleanor E.	Ellery, Stephen B.	28 FEB 1881 R	15	206
McLaughlin, Isabella	Lukowitz, Eli von	23 MAR 1878 R	11	391
McLaughlin, James A.	Elms, Lida A.	26 JUL 1881 R	15	419
McLaughlin, John	Cole, Jessie R.	07 DEC 1881 R	16	115
McLaughlin, Lida A.	French, Clarence E.	04 JUN 1884 R	19	057
McLaughlin, Mary J.	Frain, John N.	24 JUN 1881 R	15	377
McLaughlin, William J.	Yoe, Ella D.	06 JUL 1882 R	16	439
McLean, Bettie	Moreland, Thomas	14 JAN 1879 R	13	018
McLean, Carrie	Weed, John J.	23 JUL 1884	19	153
McLean, George H.	Germond, Laura V.	01 SEP 1877 R	11	073
McLean, John R.	Beale, Emily T.	06 OCT 1884 L	19	289
McLean, John W.	Coon, Rosa	16 OCT 1883 R	18	195
McLean, Richard	Campbell, D. Kate	21 APR 1884 L	18	523
McLellan, Caroline W.	Marmion, William V.	01 JUL 1880 R	14	345
McLeod, Ambrosia M.	Herbert, W.A.	14 AUG 1877 L	11	053
McLeod, Angus A.	Evans, Mary R.	05 OCT 1882 R	17	057
McLeod, Edwin Markham	Gilmore, Mary Leonard	02 NOV 1882 R	17	107
McLeod, Minnie C.	Helmsen, Charles J.	12 DEC 1882	17	179
McLoughlin, Maggie M.	Smith, Orlando F.	02 OCT 1882 R	17	048
McMahon, Annie A.	Fitzgerald, Michael J.	20 AUG 1884 L	19	194
McMahon, Catharine	Schotter, Frederic Edward	28 AUG 1879 R	13	342
McMahon, Catherine	Conners, Michael	16 OCT 1878 L	12	275
McMahon, John W.	Gardiner, Columbia R.	24 JUL 1883	18	059
McMahon, William J.	Gordon, Harriet S.	19 DEC 1877 L	11	250
McMann, Ellen	Hunt, James	02 MAR 1882 L	16	264
McMann, Mary	Shea, Alfred D.	31 DEC 1884 L	19	518
McMaster, Susie L.	Wells, Henry L.	26 JAN 1881 R	15	165
McMeanes, Mary A.	Hawkins, John L.	13 MAR 1880	14	184
McMeen, Robert	Parker, Annie E.	14 MAR 1878	11	382
McMenamin, Richard	Phillips, Alice	05 MAY 1880 R	14	251
McMichael, Alexander Ausle	Jackson, Robie St. Clair	19 JUL 1882 R	16	451
McMichael, William C.	Roberts, Armienia E.	02 FEB 1881 R	15	175
McMillan, Alexander	Gillem, Caroline St. Clair	16 JAN 1883	17	259
McMillan, Mary Elizabeth	Thurton, John W.	06 JAN 1885 R	20	004
McMorran, Samuel	Crofoot, Carrie V.	03 JAN 1884 R	18	364
McMullen, Margaret	Montgomery, Thomas	07 NOV 1881 L	16	066
McMurphy, Mahlon	Russeau, Lelia M.	09 MAR 1885	20	101
McMurray, Dora L.	Steele, Marshall A.	17 NOV 1879 R	13	492
McMurray, Hattie R.	O'Brien, Daniel	05 SEP 1878 R	12	207
McMurray, Robert A.	Davis, Carrie A. Harnes, Mrs.	21 OCT 1880 R	14	495
McNall, Lena	Ormes, DeForrest P.	04 JUL 1879 R	13	269
McNally, Annie E.	Deeble, Silas W.	24 JUL 1879 L	13	292
McNally, Belle	Moriarty, Patrick	17 MAY 1885 R	20	223
McNally, Bridget	Matthews, John	15 SEP 1883 L	18	132
McNally, Francis	Noonan, Margaret	31 MAR 1880 L	14	204

McNally, John E.	Torney, Emma V.	19 MAR 1885 L	20	126
McNally, Rachel	Williams, John	30 MAY 1885 L	20	248
McNally, Richard	Connell, Sue A.	30 AUG 1880 L	14	422
McNally, Thomas	Gonzenbach, Susie D.	06 DEC 1877	11	224
McNally, Valentine	Eliot, Catharine Llewellin	17 OCT 1883 L	18	199
McNalty, William P.	Hill, Ida V.	01 MAY 1884 L	18	546
McNamara, Annie, Mrs.	Hesson, William	26 AUG 1879 R	13	307
McNamara, Emma T.	Morgan, William G.	11 OCT 1884 L	19	301
McNamara, M.T.	Gross, Maggie E.	29 DEC 1882 L	17	223
McNamara, Mary	Allen, David	30 APR 1885 L	20	200
McNamara, Patrick E.	Griffin, Mary T.	01 OCT 1884 L	19	279
McNamara, Patrick H.	Malone, Margaret M.	25 APR 1878	12	024
McNamara, William	Davis, Sarah A.E.	19 OCT 1885 L	20	497
McNamara, Winifred	Shanahan, Michael	11 DEC 1877 R	11	229
McNaney, Edward	Donohue, Bridget	12 MAY 1880	14	264
McNantz, Emma Louisa	Repetti, Fredrick Francis	19 OCT 1880 R	15	003
McNealy, John R.	Rennoe, Roberta	23 SEP 1885	20	438
McNeil, Jennett	Newton, Henry D.	09 APR 1885 R	20	137
McNerhaney, Laura C.	Luff, Charles H.	08 JUN 1881	15	350
McNerhany, Emily L.	Genella, William B.	03 DEC 1879 R	14	023
McNery, Kate	Collins, Michael	11 FEB 1881 L	15	186
McNew, Frank O.	Baird, Sarah	22 OCT 1884	19	321
McNickel, Hugh	Lloyd, Belle E.	24 JUN 1878 L	12	111
McNiel, John	Gutridge, Mary Jane	10 OCT 1882	17	063
McNulty, Katie	Marshall, George	06 NOV 1884 R	19	361
McNulty, Lillie M.	Robey, Thomas E.	10 APR 1883	17	387
McNulty, Patrick	Mergen, Minnie	19 SEP 1877	11	096
McNunty, F.	Crosor, Julies C.	09 DEC 1878	12	371
McPhee, Thomas L.	Wilkerson, Mary A.	01 JUL 1885	20	303
McPherson, Agnes	Calvert, William F.	18 JUL 1878 L	12	140
McPherson, Dorsey Mahon	DeLand, Ida May	29 DEC 1880 R	15	130
McPherson, Ella	Connell, Dennis	22 NOV 1881 R	16	089
McPherson, Henry	Miller, Erline C.	22 SEP 1884 L	19	262
McPherson, Henry	Jones, Herline	18 OCT 1884 L	19	318
McPherson, James	Watkins, Alverta	07 APR 1885 R	20	150
McPherson, Janet D.	Coon, Byron C.	29 APR 1879 L	13	165
McPherson, Julia	Bouldin, Robert	05 JUL 1881 L	15	388
McPherson, Kate	Traver, Norman L.	21 NOV 1878 L	12	341
McPherson, Kate	Berkeley, Guy	15 MAY 1879 R	13	185
McPherson, Lewis Edwin	Myers, Flora B. (Spangler)	28 AUG 1883 R	18	103
McPherson, Maria	Ricks, James	08 SEP 1881 L	15	478
McPherson, Mary A.	Sis, John H.	27 JUL 1880	14	375
McPherson, Peter	Johnson, Julia	29 DEC 1884 L	19	495
McPherson, Richard	Carter, Lucy A.	02 OCT 1884	19	283
McPherson, Robert	Johnson, Lydia	01 DEC 1884 R	19	428
McPherson, Sarah S.	McKenzie, Lambert J.H.	06 AUG 1884	19	172
McProuty, William L.	Campbell, Norah	28 NOV 1883 L	18	282
McPynchon, William	Offutt, L.E., Mrs.	18 OCT 1877	11	242
McQuay, William	Davis, Sarah	17 MAR 1881 R	15	228
McQueen, David William	Davis, Mary Ann	26 FEB 1880 R	14	166
McQueen, Hoel Lawrence	Pratt, Caroline Outerbridge	07 NOV 1878 R	12	310
McQueen, James G.	Phillips, Sallie M.	03 MAY 1879 R	13	163
McQuin, George H.	Cranage, Mary Elizabeth	20 APR 1881 R	15	261
McRae, Edward W.	Connell, Lizzie	23 DEC 1884 L	19	478
McRae, G.F.	Langhorne, Mary M.	26 SEP 1884	19	270
McReynolds, Curren T.	Gresham, Sarah	29 DEC 1881 R	16	131
McReynolds, Mary J.	Stacy, Robert H.	16 NOV 1882 L	17	131
McShane, William	Rogers, Ada	01 MAR 1882 R	16	263

D.C. Marriage Records Index, June 28, 1877 to October 19, 1885   313

McSherry, Helen Nicholson	Shriver, B. Franklin	20 FEB 1878	11	349
McStay, Henry	Linkins, Mary	01 FEB 1882 R	16	218
McSween, Mary	Witherbee, Walter E.	28 MAY 1878 L	12	069
McUlaff, Patrick	Wolf, Kate	02 JAN 1878 L	11	290
McUllum, John	Knight, Virginia	02 MAY 1883	17	428
McVarrey, Mary Ann	Brown, Michael J.	04 NOV 1877 R	11	165
McVarry, James	Kane, Winifred	27 DEC 1881 L	16	162
McVarry, Katie	Collins, Michael	16 MAY 1881 L	15	311
McVarry, Michael L.	Carmody, Hanorah	30 APR 1879 R	13	167
McVay, Charlotte	Halleck, William Filmore	14 NOV 1882 R	17	124
McVeigh, George H.	James, Ada	04 SEP 1884	19	226
McWill, William H.	Chase, Lizzie Ambush	28 APR 1880 R	14	239
McWilliams, Ada L.	Schnopp, Dammair	16 OCT 1878	12	277
Meacham, Charles E.	Quigley, Mary E.	15 NOV 1882 L	17	130
Meacham, Mary Emma	Helmick, Howard Franklin	03 DEC 1883	18	292
Mead, Ann Maria	Dyer, James W.	02 JUL 1878	12	118
Mead, Annie	Gibson, Joshua E.	20 MAY 1882 R	16	370
Mead, Christopher	King, Estella B.	05 FEB 1878 R	11	328
Mead, Elgar J.	Howard, Rosa E.	01 JUN 1878	12	078
Mead, James	Brown, Mary	08 AUG 1882 L	16	474
Mead, John H.	Corcoran, Sarah	15 MAY 1879 L	13	191
Mead, John H.	Cockerill, Sarah	10 JAN 1880 L	14	099
Mead, Losanna	Sweat, John B.	17 SEP 1882	17	288
Mead, Lucy	Ross, Alexander	21 OCT 1880	15	008
Mead, Thaddeus	Perkins, Sarah Caroline "Kate"	25 DEC 1881 R	16	127
Meade, Eugene Carlton	Neale, Adelaide Eloise	21 NOV 1880 R	15	058
Meade, Julia A.	Cunningham, George A.	21 JAN 1884 L	18	387
Meader, Emma R.	Tupper, Charles A.	24 MAR 1880 R	14	193
Meader, Henry I.	Dunan, Molly O.	17 APR 1882 R	16	319
Meador, Elizabeth R.	Darlington, Joseph J.	21 JUL 1885	20	333
Meadors, Sarah E.	Kelley, Charles H.	19 DEC 1883	18	326
Meads, Ida Virginia	Pritchard, Stephen Meredith	04 JUN 1884 R	19	057
Meads, Lizzie G.	Balderston, Joseph W.	30 MAY 1883 R	17	467
Meads, Mary M.	Padgett, James	13 OCT 1880	14	490
Meagher, Francis	Carter, Andromeda C.	17 JUL 1882	16	447
Meagher, Peter	Logan, Emma L.	29 MAY 1882 L	16	379
Mealey, Thomas S.	Bird, Mary E.	01 DEC 1881	16	117
Meals, Ella Blanche	Reinecke, Otto Charles Louis	19 JAN 1881 R	15	158
Meals, Mary Grace	Merillat, Charles E.	18 FEB 1885 R	20	075
Meaneley, Irene B.	Jones, Fitzhugh C.	25 MAR 1885 R	20	132
Meaney, Michael	Welsh, Mary	12 MAY 1878	12	039
Means, John W.	Anadale, Sarah F.	07 NOV 1877	11	171
Means, Lewis E.	Reiley, Katie S.	27 OCT 1881 R	16	049
Means, Marian M.	Bozzell, Charles S.	28 APR 1881	15	279
Mearns, Charles T.F.	Stout, Clara V.	13 DEC 1883	18	312
Mears, Mariana B.	Fant, Joseph N.	02 FEB 1880 L	14	130
Mechan, Carrie	Pfluger, George J.	14 JAN 1885 R	20	018
Meckel, Niclaus	Ruppert, Annie	15 FEB 1881	15	189
Meddow, Marthy E.	Nash, Henry E.	22 JUL 1881 L	15	413
Meder, Virginia	Sampson, John W.	14 OCT 1883 R	18	191
Medford, Alonzo W.	Medford, Sarah	09 JAN 1882 R	16	187
Medford, Daniel	Boone, Eliza Ann	03 APR 1883	17	376
Medford, Sarah	Medford, Alonzo W.	09 JAN 1882 R	16	187
Medford, William C.	Fuller, Ruth H.	28 SEP 1881	15	500
Medley, George	Westin, Rebecca	13 JUN 1878	12	090
Medley, George D.	Ball, Carrie E.V.	14 OCT 1885 R	20	485
Medlock, Annie	Chew, Lemuel	27 JAN 1881 L	15	168

Meeds, Carrie V.	Denham, William	20 MAR 1882 L	16	284
Meeds, Mary	Delaney, Edward	21 OCT 1884	19	321
Meeker, Alice	Day, David P.	17 JUL 1879	13	282
Meekins, Rachel	Wells, Augustus	29 AUG 1881 L	15	464
Meeks, Arrene	Davis, Lewis Henry	19 NOV 1878 L	12	336
Meeks, George W.	Deacon, Virginia Lee	18 FEB 1882	16	247
Meeks, Georgiana	Scott, John	08 SEP 1885 R	20	403
Meeks, John	Ross, Margaret	02 OCT 1879 R	13	400
Meeks, Martha	Bounds, Evan	14 OCT 1877 R	11	136
Meeks, Sandy	Cooper, Mary	21 JUN 1883 R	18	010
Meeks, Susan	Thompson, John	20 AUG 1878 L	12	174
Meeny, Ann	Connor, Patrick	02 NOV 1878	12	411
Megby, Frank	Bodine, Rose E.	17 DEC 1884 R	19	463
Megeath, Marietta F.	Tyler, John J.	28 DEC 1879 R	14	077
Megginson, Mamie F.	Moon, D. Willie	13 MAY 1880	14	262
Mehring, Emma	DeAtley, Benjamin F.	18 DEC 1884 R	19	472
Mehrling, Mary E.	Donsion, William B.	20 JUN 1878	12	107
Meier, Ezekiel	Thäter, Catherina	26 AUG 1878	12	180
Meier, Henry	Ruebsam, Lizzie C.	26 MAY 1885 R	20	240
Meier, John	Maag, Catharina	07 NOV 1878 L	12	313
Meiggs, Georgie C.	Cox, J.P.	17 AUG 1880	14	403
Meigs, John Forsythe, Jr.	Rodgers, Jane Perry	27 APR 1881	15	275
Meinekhein, George	Connell, Maggie	07 JUL 1881 R	15	392
Meiners, John H.	Schmertz, Rebecca	25 MAR 1883	17	358
Meinikheim, Anna C.	Kozel, Charles F.	10 OCT 1881 R	16	016
Meintel, Joseph W.	Gaegler, Barbara E.	22 DEC 1882 L	17	204
Meitzler, William H.	Perkins, Henrietta	16 OCT 1882 R	17	074
Melbourne, Delia	Whinery, Thomas	08 JUN 1881 R	15	349
Melia, Mary	Trahey, John	06 DEC 1883 L	18	299
Mellen, George H.	Warner, Mary A.	23 SEP 1878 L	12	231
Mellin, William A.	Ellis, Annie	11 AUG 1881 L	15	441
Mellny, Kate M.	Smith, George W.	02 JUL 1879 R	13	266
Molontree, John Andrew	Tunnia, Fannie Flora	30 MAR 1885 R	20	135
Meloy, James	Donahue, Mary	08 DEC 1878	12	372
Melson, Annie E.	Bean, Thaddeus	19 NOV 1879 R	13	494
Melson, John E.	Thompson, Margaret E.	20 SEP 1885 R	20	428
Melton, A.L.	Holler, Amelia	28 DEC 1880 R	15	128
Melton, Hattie	Turner, George	04 JUL 1884	19	123
Melville, Robert L.	Thomas, Henrietta	03 JUN 1882 L	16	392
Memmert, Louisa S.	Wagner, Henry G.	02 OCT 1883	18	166
Menagh, Preston S.	Curtis, Mary Bell	02 SEP 1885	20	394
Mendehall, James B.	Mitchell, Sallie P.	24 DEC 1879 R	14	071
Menefee, Belle, Mrs.	Johnson, Peter	16 DEC 1880	15	099
Menhorn, Caroline Matilda	Bowen, Burton Lee	13 JUN 1882 R	16	408
Mennier, Louis	Ervenbeck, Margaret	29 APR 1879 R	13	163
Mercer, Annie	Linkins, Peter Francis	14 JUL 1881 R	15	400
Mercer, Cyrus	Taliaferro, Cordelia	03 AUG 1882 L	16	467
Mercer, Delia	Jackson, Henry	19 NOV 1884 L	19	395
Mercer, Fenton	Chatman, Annie	08 MAR 1883 R	17	334
Mercer, George H.	Reed, Judah	20 APR 1883 L	17	402
Mercer, George H.	Murphy, Mary A.	15 NOV 1884	19	383
Mercer, George P.	Dwilley, Mary S.	05 OCT 1882	17	055
Mercer, Harvey	Krause, Lizzie	02 JUL 1878 R	12	121
Mercer, John T.	Jones, Eliza A.	01 DEC 1880 R	15	076
Mercer, Sadie	Ewell, William Henry	05 JAN 1881 R	15	140
Merchant, Richard F.	Speak, Annie F.	05 SEP 1877 R	11	076
Mercy, Charles E.	Adams, Annie	14 JUL 1877 L	11	019
Mercy, Wallace	Turner, Gracie	13 FEB 1878 R	11	339

Merdoc, Frederick	Greenhow, Catharine	14 JAN 1884	18	371
Meredith, Ann E.	Whitney, C.N.	01 JAN 1884	18	357
Meredith, Benj. Franklin Leigh	Marsden, Ella	20 OCT 1879 R	13	433
Meredith, Charity	Jones, Walter	25 DEC 1881 R	16	148
Meredith, Charles	Baptist, Jennie	08 NOV 1883 L	18	243
Meredith, Charles H.	Queenan, Linda	29 DEC 1880 L	15	130
Meredith, Charlotte	Bateman, John Thomas	21 FEB 1883 R	17	314
Meredith, David	Morris, Katie	19 APR 1882	16	322
Meredith, Gustave A.	Dipert, Annie Leonora	04 JUL 1881 R	15	385
Meredith, John Henry	Hill, Mary Jane	21 NOV 1878 L	12	341
Meredith, John P.	Hammacher, Catherine E.	25 JUL 1883	18	059
Meredith, Josephine	Carrington, Charles	03 JUL 1885 L	20	309
Meredith, Lawson	Pickett, Rosa	24 OCT 1881 L	16	040
Meredith, Mitchell Thos.	Mulling, Annie	11 MAR 1885 L	20	107
Meredith, Peter B.	Brooks, Annie E.	17 DEC 1884 L	19	466
Meredith, Rodger	Donnelly, Annie	27 DEC 1883 L	18	349
Meredith, William Henry	Minor, Ella	09 APR 1880 R	14	217
Mergen, Minnie	McNulty, Patrick	19 SEP 1877	11	096
Mergenthaler, Caroline	Lerch, Anthony	27 APR 1881 L	15	278
Meridith, Henry	Hamilton, Charlotte	18 JAN 1881 L	15	154
Merillat, Charles E.	Dew, Etta	21 DEC 1881 L	16	143
Merillat, Charles E.	Meals, Mary Grace	18 FEB 1885 R	20	075
Merillat, Charlotte Amy	Edelin, Robley Dunglison	22 APR 1885 R	20	180
Merity, Martha	Sommerville, Richard	22 JUL 1884	19	145
Mero, Colin Lambert	Pettit, Lizzie	19 DEC 1881 R	16	140
Merredith, Alice A.	Robinson, Cipio H.	10 SEP 1885	20	409
Merrick, Adelaide Emily	Munn, Clarence Emerson	30 JUN 1885 R	20	300
Merrick, Caleb Cornwell	Howard, Harriet (Gandy)	29 JUN 1883 R	18	014
Merrick, Edwin	Hill, Georgianna	04 AUG 1883	18	070
Merrick, Margaret	Jones, William F.	05 JUL 1877	11	008
Merrill, Anna D.	Merwin, Charles H.	07 MAY 1878	12	041
Merrill, Harriet Edith	Sweet, Reuben Thomas	16 JUL 1883	18	047
Merrill, John B.	Gibson, Ida K.	16 DEC 1880 R	15	101
Merrill, Lucy Frances	Drennan, Daniel Ogilvie	22 MAY 1884 R	19	031
Merrill, Luella B.	Draper, Amos G.	16 JUN 1879	13	233
Merriman, Lillian Reed	Berry, Albert Gleaves	28 SEP 1881 R	15	498
Merrit, Aline T.	Merrit, William A.	04 SEP 1878 L	12	198
Merrit, William A.	Merrit, Aline T.	04 SEP 1878 L	12	198
Merritt, Bettie E.	Bell, Walter E.	23 DEC 1884 R	19	481
Merritt, Georgianna	Jordon, John W.	08 NOV 1877 R	11	172
Merritt, Louisa	Polk, Matthias	04 MAR 1880 R	14	175
Merritt, Washington C.	Henderson, Clara C.	26 JUN 1883 R	18	015
Merry, Pliny Case	Mahon, Mary A.	28 NOV 1877 L	11	210
Merryman, John H.	McConnell, Elizabeth Campbell	09 OCT 1883 R	18	181
Merryman, Kate L.	Dodds, James	11 DEC 1884	19	454
Merson, Lucretia Virginia	Kurchival, George W.	14 DEC 1882 R	17	183
Merten, Annie	Otto, Henry G.	07 OCT 1882	17	058
Merten, Henry	Behr, Eva Maria	27 JAN 1878	11	315
Mertz, William Corrigan	Israel, Ida Ella	21 JAN 1879 R	13	029
Merwin, Charles H.	Merrill, Anna D.	07 MAY 1878	12	041
Meserole, M.L., Mrs.	Brown, A.H.	02 MAY 1878	12	036
Messer, Andrew	Vouck, Jane A.	30 APR 1883	17	422
Messer, George B.	Smithley, Annie E.	10 APR 1879 L	13	134
Messer, Helen	Roseberry, George W.	26 SEP 1877	11	108
Messer, William	Sayers, Catherine C.	17 JUL 1879 R	13	285
Messiah, Martha	Garner, Harry	20 DEC 1880	15	111
Messler, Cornelius N.	Bowles, Ruth	23 JUL 1883	18	056
Metcalf, Francis S.	Herzberger, Mary	18 SEP 1880 L	14	451

Metcalfe, Annie Hodge	Crocker, Willis Francis	05 NOV 1879 R	13	465
Meter, Annie Agnes	Junemann, George J.	29 DEC 1881	16	167
Meter, Charles	Synch, Ella	08 DEC 1881 L	16	119
Metonhall, Hattie S.	Minor, William F	21 NOV 1882 L	17	139
Mettert, Joseph G., Jr.	Cropper, Mary E.B.	27 MAY 1882 R	16	380
Metzgar, Charles Watson	Gill, Mary Virginia	11 APR 1883 R	17	390
Meyenberg, Pauline	Hansen, John	02 SEP 1878 L	12	192
Meyer, Annie	Wise, Charles E.	16 FEB 1885 L	20	069
Meyer, Edward F.	Gettings, Mary E.	20 MAY 1885	20	231
Meyer, Ernest H.	Rothstein, Anna Elizabeth	03 FEB 1884 R	18	402
Meyer, Ida Louisa Carolina	Bergmann, Henry Hermann	27 DEC 1879 R	14	069
Meyer, Johann Heinrich	Heitmüller, Augusta D.A.	10 FEB 1885 R	20	063
Meyer, John C.	Lesch, Margaret	18 OCT 1885	20	494
Meyer, Joseph	Vaughan, Emma L.	09 SEP 1884	19	235
Meyer, Joseph	Rubenstein, Pauline	15 MAR 1885 R	20	111
Meyer, Katie M.	Kozel, George Fredrick	13 MAY 1885 R	20	220
Meyer, Margaret A.	McBride, James	17 DEC 1877 L	11	239
Meyerberg, Frederick	Jenkins, Mary A.	24 AUG 1885 R	20	385
Meyers, Annie H.	Hodgkins, J.S.	21 FEB 1880	14	162
Meyers, Henrietta	Beach, Frank L.	01 SEP 1880 L	14	425
Meyers, Henrietta	Beach, Frank L.	08 SEP 1881 L	15	477
Meyers, Katie M.	Corcoran, W.L.	28 NOV 1883 R	18	283
Meyers, Solomon	Wise, Bertha	08 JUL 1881 L	15	396
Meyers, William R.	Auguste, Gertrude	16 OCT 1884	19	316
Michaels, John Walter	Steirs, Mary Whitcomb	17 JUL 1878	12	136
Michaelson, George H.	Petsch, Bertha	05 SEP 1884 L	19	230
Michel, Adam	Feile, Magdalena	31 JUL 1883 L	18	067
Michel, George	Baltz, Mary	29 JAN 1884 R	18	398
Michel, William F.	Zells, Maggie E.	02 MAR 1882 R	16	263
Michelbacher, Elisa, Mrs.	Kohler, Friedrick	18 JAN 1880 R	14	111
Michler, Rebecca	Giles, George H.	14 FEB 1878	11	340
Mickens, Harrison	Sands, Susan	17 MAR 1881 L	15	229
Mickins, Harrison	Rubinson, Martha	21 APR 1884	18	522
Mickins, Josephine	Barber, Henry	06 MAR 1878	11	371
Middeldorff, Casper	Schmidt, Bertha B.	06 NOV 1883 L	18	237
Middledorf, Lizzie	Theck, William	24 NOV 1878	12	344
Middleton, Annie M.	Wesley, John	16 DEC 1880 L	15	104
Middleton, Arthur E.	Ober, Carrie R.	08 OCT 1884	19	290
Middleton, Edward	Bailey, Catherine	22 JUN 1880	14	330
Middleton, Florence	Ingraham, Thomas	25 APR 1878 L	12	024
Middleton, George	Dodson, Hernetta	21 JAN 1880 R	14	117
Middleton, Henry M.	Coles, Mary V.	30 APR 1885 R	20	201
Middleton, Jane C.	Kaney, Shelton	29 SEP 1884	19	261
Middleton, Kittie V.	Wilson, James P.	12 JUN 1885 R	20	272
Middleton, Maria	Shepherd, Hannibal	15 SEP 1881	15	484
Middleton, Mary	Henson, John	29 MAR 1883 R	17	371
Middleton, Mary E.	Earley, Frederick D.	12 JUN 1879 R	13	229
Middleton, Mary Isabel	Butler, William H.	05 SEP 1883	18	110
Middleton, Robert Levi	Williamson, Cora Ann	19 DEC 1882 R	17	188
Middleton, Robert Parker	Fowler, Florence Virginia	08 NOV 1877 R	11	174
Middleton, S. Agnes	Aitken, George	14 OCT 1880 R	14	493
Middleton, Samuel	Brown, Maria L.	27 AUG 1884 L	19	211
Middleton, Walter	Hawkins, Sarah J.	02 MAR 1880 L	14	171
Middleton, William Eliot	Whitwell, Anna Wood	15 NOV 1877 R	11	183
Middleton, William P.	Blackwell, Anne E.	11 OCT 1881 R	16	018
Miele, Augustine	Rupertus, Charles	03 DEC 1884 R	19	434
Mifflin, Alice F.	Crubaugh, Wesley W.	01 JAN 1884	18	355
Mihm, George	Rupp, Augusta	29 JUL 1878 L	12	151

D.C. Marriage Records Index, June 28, 1877 to October 19, 1885   317

Name	Spouse	Date	Vol	Page
Milburn, Charles	Hawkins, Georgie	23 FEB 1881 L	15	201
Milburn, Charles H.	Edelin, Josephine	08 JAN 1885 L	20	010
Milburn, Elizabeth	Miller, Wesley	30 JAN 1885 L	20	044
Milburn, Jennie	Wallace, Alonzo	21 DEC 1879	14	059
Milburn, Lewis C.	Jones, Mary G.	17 FEB 1885	20	035
Milburn, Mary	Carroll, William	08 NOV 1877 L	11	176
Milburn, Page	Woodward, Nannie R.	02 DEC 1880	15	078
Milburn, Thomas	Hall, Mary	30 OCT 1882	17	056
Mildred, Washington	Kent, Lewis	10 APR 1878 L	11	415
Miles, Alice	Harris, Joseph C.	17 MAR 1881 L	15	229
Miles, George	Carter, Eliza	02 JUL 1883 L	18	029
Miles, George Edward	Perkins, Solustus Celestia	04 MAR 1880	14	177
Miles, Ignatius	Kelly, Ellen	06 MAY 1880 L	14	256
Miles, James F.	Rabitt, Emma C.	29 NOV 1883	18	284
Miles, James Henry, Dr.	Lilburn, Anna Maria Birch	08 DEC 1879 R	14	034
Miles, John	Turner, Jennie	04 AUG 1885 L	20	353
Miles, John D.	Brown, Rose	31 JAN 1880 R	14	128
Miles, John Vincent	Hayslock, Maria	01 SEP 1880	14	421
Miles, Julia	Hamilton, Charles	28 JAN 1884 L	18	398
Miles, Katie	Nichols, Clinton	17 JAN 1884	18	383
Miles, Margaret Eliz. Hilton	Parsons, James J.	10 SEP 1881 L	15	480
Miles, Martha	Parker, John Henry	13 SEP 1883 R	18	118
Miles, Mary	Thompson, George	09 OCT 1877 R	11	126
Miles, Mary I.	Lowe, Henry W.	16 FEB 1878 R	11	343
Miles, Mollie A.	Logan, Alonzo T.	22 NOV 1882	17	143
Miles, Nathan Edwards	Larmer, Julia Ann	01 FEB 1882 R	16	220
Miles, Richard E.	Clark, Mary	30 OCT 1883	18	221
Miles, Robert	Chris, Julia	15 FEB 1881 L	15	191
Miles, William	Davis, Jane	06 MAR 1878 L	11	373
Milford, Eliza A.	Wilson, Morris	07 MAR 1882	16	269
Mililice, Tony	Chase, Amelia	02 MAR 1880 R	14	170
Millar, Fannie P.	Cocking, Joseph	27 DEC 1883 R	18	332
Millar, Sallie Dunbar	Giddings, William Virginius	06 JUN 1883 R	17	478
Millen, Robert	Johnson, Annie	12 OCT 1878 L	12	269
Miller, Abram J.	Over, Anna R.	24 JUN 1884	19	097
Miller, Adam	Aufrecht, Caroline	18 NOV 1880 R	15	052
Miller, Albert G.	Denham, Mary Josephine	26 DEC 1882 R	17	216
Miller, Alexander	Henderson, Ella	06 NOV 1877	11	171
Miller, Anna May	Archibald, William	30 SEP 1885	20	448
Miller, Annie M.	Hurdle, Charles H.[9]	11 MAY 1880 L	14	263
Miller, Augusta D.	Bode, Richard	11 JAN 1881	15	147
Miller, Austin	Johnson, Mary	18 SEP 1884 L	19	256
Miller, Benjamin A.	Walter, Lizzie	02 MAY 1881	16	001
Miller, Caroline	Thompson, William Perry	26 SEP 1877 R	11	108
Miller, Catherine	Wilson, Henry Louis	25 MAY 1885 R	20	239
Miller, Charles	Murray, Malinda	24 MAY 1878 R	12	050
Miller, Charles	Seins, Barbara	02 SEP 1880	14	427
Miller, Charles	Norris, Eliza	25 SEP 1882 R	17	037
Miller, Charles G.	Ridgeway, Mary A.	26 FEB 1883 R	16	410
Miller, Christie	Lomax, Elias	25 JUN 1884 L	19	102
Miller, Dan	Rollins, Annie	11 JUN 1884 R	19	072
Miller, Daniel	Kissner, Mary Elizabeth	04 JUN 1883 L	17	474
Miller, Daniel	Hamilton, Fannie E.	28 JUL 1884	19	160
Miller, Dora	Lanz, Alexander, Jr.	02 NOV 1879 R	13	458
Miller, Douglass G.	Davidson, Sophie P.	28 MAR 1881	15	240
Miller, Edgar L.	Knauff, Mary E.	21 AUG 1880 R	14	410

[9] May 11th 1880. This license is issued without my consent or knowledge-- I protest against it. /signed/ Charles H. Hurdle.

Miller, Edith	Butler, Charles	04 MAR 1882 L	16	267
Miller, Edward H.	Herfurth, Theresa	12 MAR 1882	16	270
Miller, Edwin	Bartholomae, Emma	13 FEB 1878 L	11	339
Miller, Eleanora	Burgess, John J.A.	07 DEC 1882 L	17	174
Miller, Eliza G.	Wilcox, Walter R.	12 JAN 1882	16	191
Miller, Elizabeth	Watson, Thomas C.	27 AUG 1881 R	15	461
Miller, Ella M.W.	Allnutt, Joseph T.	02 SEP 1885 R	20	397
Miller, Ella May	Searle, Frank W.	24 APR 1878	12	022
Miller, Ellen	Cheney, Thomas	03 NOV 1881	16	061
Miller, Emanuel	Birch, Isabella	11 NOV 1882	17	115
Miller, Erline C.	McPherson, Henry	22 SEP 1884 L	19	262
Miller, Fannie K.	Andrews, William T.	21 JUL 1883	18	055
Miller, Francis	Straub, Frances	23 JUN 1885 L	20	284
Miller, Francis, Jr.	Hurdle, Hester	18 MAR 1882 L	16	282
Miller, George	Jones, Alice	12 OCT 1880 L	14	488
Miller, George	Fauntleroy, Rachel	06 FEB 1883 R	17	294
Miller, George C.	Johnson, Corinne	31 MAY 1881 L	15	332
Miller, George W.	Wilson, Ella S.	21 JAN 1880 R	14	117
Miller, George W.	McBride, Mary E.	22 SEP 1885 R	20	430
Miller, Giles	Lancaster, Cresey	19 JUL 1881	15	407
Miller, Harriet N.	Driver, Golden	24 SEP 1881 L	15	496
Miller, Helen	Clifford, Thomas	14 AUG 1878 L	12	166
Miller, Henry	Miller, Louisa	04 FEB 1878 L	11	326
Miller, Henry	Scott, Florence Louisa	10 SEP 1881 R	15	322
Miller, Henry	Crummey, Emma	28 FEB 1883 R	17	326
Miller, Henry T.	Bush, Mattie E.	16 NOV 1883 L	18	260
Miller, Ida Beale	Tevis, Joshua	24 APR 1878 R	12	020
Miller, Isaac C.	Laurence, Caroline	16 DEC 1880 L	15	106
Miller, Jacob	Turner, Georgianna	11 SEP 1882 R	17	023
Miller, James	Lawson, Elizabeth	09 OCT 1883 L	18	181
Miller, James Edgar	Jacobs, Ida May	02 MAR 1881 R	15	211
Miller, James M	Frank, Mary A.	30 NOV 1878 R	12	356
Miller, Jerry	Dobbins, Emma	31 AUG 1880 R	14	423
Miller, John	Hughey, Mary	07 MAR 1878	11	366
Miller, John	Jones, Elmira	01 MAR 1879 R	13	081
Miller, John	Davis, Mollie E.	27 FEB 1879	13	073
Miller, John	Leese, Emma E.	16 FEB 1881 R	15	192
Miller, John	Weisge, Rose	29 JAN 1882 R	15	071
Miller, John Henry	Townshend, Elizabeth Pitts	01 JAN 1883 R	17	224
Miller, John Henry	Martin, Alice C.	27 NOV 1884	19	415
Miller, John L.	Jones, Lola C.	06 APR 1880 R	14	211
Miller, John Thomas	Downs, Mary E.	20 MAY 1879 R	13	198
Miller, John W.	Harvey, Isabella	20 MAY 1884	19	038
Miller, Joseph M.	Thomas, Mary E.	26 FEB 1878 L	11	358
Miller, Kate G.	Sewall, William G.	21 JUL 1885	20	309
Miller, Katie	Waterholder, Fred. Wm.	07 JUL 1881	15	395
Miller, Lena C.	Fitzhugh, Joseph D.	16 JAN 1885	20	025
Miller, Lena M.	McKinney, Christopher C.	26 MAY 1880	14	288
Miller, Leonard D.	Fowcus, Martha A.	08 JUL 1885 R	20	316
Miller, Lillie L.	Constantine, G.W.	11 APR 1878 R	12	001
Miller, Louisa	Miller, Henry	04 FEB 1878 L	11	326
Miller, Louise L.	Maish, Levi	30 OCT 1883 R	18	221
Miller, Maggie	Arnold, David C.	31 AUG 1882 L	17	001
Miller, Maggie	Arnold, David C.	31 AUG 1882 R	16	500
Miller, Margaret Regina	Sheckels, James Borrows	26 OCT 1881 R	16	045
Miller, Mary A.	Jinkins, William A.	22 NOV 1881 R	16	083
Miller, Mary D.	Grant, Donald S.	10 FEB 1878	11	335
Miller, Mary E.	McGinniss, Richard M.	17 OCT 1885	20	495

Name	Spouse	Date	Vol	Page
Miller, Mary Eleanor	Edmonston, Samuel Sherwood	03 NOV 1880	15	026
Miller, Mary Elizabeth	Johnson, Charles Sweet	04 FEB 1885 R	20	051
Miller, Mary F.	Posey, Francis B.	17 DEC 1879 L	14	054
Miller, Mary K. McPherson	Gulick, James H.	28 APR 1878 R	12	026
Miller, Mary Margaret Short	Vebusch, John Henry	03 SEP 1878 R	12	193
Miller, Mary Theresa	Bessler, Frank Bonifox	17 FEB 1882 L	16	247
Miller, Matilda	Moore, Roger W.	04 NOV 1878 R	12	307
Miller, Minerva Rose	Crawford, John James	21 NOV 1882 R	17	138
Miller, Nelson	Brown, Hettie E.	07 JAN 1883 R	17	240
Miller, Nelson	Carrick, Martha Is. Va.	07 OCT 1885 R	20	466
Miller, Perry R.	Baldwin, Chricelia	21 MAY 1884 L	19	033
Miller, Rhetta	Shoemaker, Charles F.	08 SEP 1881 R	15	476
Miller, Richard	Bell, Joanna	22 APR 1878 L	12	019
Miller, Richard A.	Beall, Annie J.	17 NOV 1884	19	388
Miller, Roy Lena, Mrs.	Roy, Austen	26 DEC 1878 L	12	403
Miller, Sarah	Reeves, James Edward	14 MAR 1882 R	16	276
Miller, Sarah Stanley	Owens, Charles Forrest	26 DEC 1878 R	12	403
Miller, Shelton	Washington, Mary	20 NOV 1877 R	11	184
Miller, Shelton	Payne, Carrie	26 JUN 1884 R	19	100
Miller, Stephen A.	Sonder, Adeline V.	29 JUN 1881	15	382
Miller, Susanna	Carter, Churchill	07 MAY 1884 L	19	011
Miller, Thomas	Freeman, Julia Ann	17 DEC 1879	14	054
Miller, Thomas	Heitmuller, Mary L.H.	20 SEP 1883 L	18	145
Miller, Thomas F.	Wade, Annie Eliz.	29 JUL 1885 R	20	344
Miller, Thomas H.	Hunter, Rose A.	13 AUG 1879 L	13	320
Miller, Timothy	Atkins, Alice	06 NOV 1880	15	034
Miller, Webster	Baylor, Gussie	12 JAN 1882 R	16	187
Miller, Wesley	Milburn, Elizabeth	30 JAN 1885 L	20	044
Miller, William	Heine, Maria	24 APR 1879 R	13	157
Miller, William A.	Thomas, Carrie M.	04 FEB 1885	20	052
Miller, William Edward	Vogelson, Ida Mary	12 APR 1882 R	16	312
Miller, William H.	Reisinger, Mary L.	30 OCT 1884	19	349
Miller, William H.	Boyer, Margaret	20 OCT 1884 L	19	322
Miller, Wm. H.	Vermillion, Julia M.	05 FEB 1885 L	20	053
Milligan, Alexander H.	Lucas, Mamie A.	13 OCT 1880 R	14	490
Milliken, N. Byron	Sinclair, Mary J.	05 MAY 1885	20	203
Millington, Willis Eugene	Peggs, Jennie Susis	08 SEP 1882 R	17	013
Mills, Adelin	Johnson, Willis	15 NOV 1883 L	18	258
Mills, Annie	Henry, C.O.	08 SEP 1877	11	083
Mills, Annie E.	Hendley, Julian P.	05 OCT 1882 R	17	057
Mills, Annie Mary	Taylor, William	21 APR 1884	18	521
Mills, Benjamin	Ford, Harriet	10 FEB 1881 R	15	185
Mills, Clarence	Ratliff, Mary E.	02 DEC 1879 R	14	022
Mills, Cornelia A.	Thompson, Granville S.	15 FEB 1879 R	13	061
Mills, Ella	Woods, Horace	10 NOV 1881 R	16	070
Mills, Ella L.	Floyd, John B.	07 JUN 1880 R	14	308
Mills, Ellen Florence	Boswell, John B.	18 OCT 1883 R	18	201
Mills, Emma	Progatzky, Otto Charles	23 MAR 1880 R	14	186
Mills, Evalina	Adams, William	10 AUG 1881 R	15	433
Mills, Fanny E.	Yeatman, George W.	14 NOV 1883	18	252
Mills, Flora Ellen	Ennis, James Edward	21 JUL 1881 R	15	412
Mills, George	Datcher, Emily	12 APR 1879 L	13	139
Mills, George	Arnold, Eliza	08 OCT 1880 L	14	483
Mills, George Albert	Rowland, Nellie R.	16 AUG 1883 R	18	091
Mills, Jane	Nelson, Robert	19 JAN 1882 R	16	202
Mills, John Sedwick	Nichols, Annie Cecilia	14 NOV 1882 R	17	125
Mills, Kate	Palmer, John	25 MAY 1885	20	238
Mills, Katie F.	Burlingame, Frederick H.	04 AUG 1884	19	166

Mills, Lavinia	Hayne, James Henry	04 OCT 1882 R	17	051
Mills, Malachi	Lautenberger, Elizabeth	11 SEP 1883	18	124
Mills, Margaret	Lyles, Dennis	28 SEP 1881 R	15	500
Mills, Mary	Hudlow, James	02 FEB 1878	11	324
Mills, Mary Anna	Traylor, George Archer	04 FEB 1880 R	14	135
Mills, Mary Lela [Pool]	Sessford, Joseph Stone F.	07 FEB 1884 R	18	415
Mills, Matilda	Bryan, Edward	27 FEB 1879 R	13	083
Mills, Nannie B.	Maloney, Elbert S.	26 JUN 1879 R	13	250
Mills, Nannie Lee	Lusby, George Washington	22 DEC 1881 R	16	147
Mills, Robert	Rhody, Sarah C. [Fry]	16 JUN 1884 R	19	084
Mills, Roberta F.	Sesch, William	11 OCT 1882 R	17	066
Mills, Theodore A.	Friedrich, Mary Elizabeth	29 NOV 1877 R	11	210
Mills, Virginia	Chalk, George F.	20 JAN 1880	14	112
Mills, William	Taylor, Martha A.	24 FEB 1881 L	15	202
Mills, William F.	Keith, Rosa A.	29 APR 1882 L	16	341
Mills, William H.	Hemming, Annie F.	27 MAY 1885 L	20	242
Millstead, James E.	Thomas, Margaret E.	13 OCT 1881	16	021
Milocich, Louis	Ratto, Theresa M.	07 NOV 1878 L	12	315
Milstead, Dora E.	Sutherland, Theodore A.	08 JUL 1878 L	12	128
Milstead, Emma	Harold, John	02 APR 1878 L	11	401
Milstead, Hillery	Perry, Maria	12 MAR 1885 L	20	110
Milstead, K.A.A.	Teeple, D.H.	30 OCT 1879	13	455
Milstead, Robert A.	Kirby, Mary V.	27 MAR 1884 R	18	483
Milstead, W. Edward	Bean, Carrie V.	23 JAN 1878 L	11	315
Milsterd, J.T.	Thomas, Mollie	06 DEC 1883	18	299
Milton, William	Tyler, Mary	13 JUL 1885	20	322
Mims, Sarah	Johnson, John T.	10 SEP 1884 L	19	240
Mindeleff, Victor	Randall, Jessie Louise	02 APR 1883 R	17	374
Minear, Clara C.	Boudinot, Elias Cornelius	16 APR 1885 R	20	173
Miner, Belle	Gray, Town	16 JUN 1885	20	274
Miner, David	Alexander, Sarah	22 DEC 1881 L	16	151
Miner, Emma	Mason, Allen	26 JUL 1883	18	061
Miner, Frank	Munt, Victoria	26 JUN 1878 L	12	114
Miner, Georgianna	Williams, John W.	06 MAY 1884	18	548
Miner, Georgianna	Williams, John W.	06 MAY 1884 R	19	003
Miner, Jennie	Gavit, Allen	19 APR 1884 R	18	519
Miner, Maggie	Pritchard, John H.	02 JUN 1881 L	15	340
Miner, Patsy	Gater, William	17 MAR 1879 L	13	105
Miner, Sarah	Williams, Theodore	27 APR 1881	15	279
Miner, Thomas	Fisher, Margaret	02 JUL 1879	13	264
Mines, James M.	Hall, Mary Lizzie	02 JUN 1881 L	15	341
Mines, Sarah	Parker, Ashford	11 JUN 1885 R	20	267
Mines, Solomon E.	Pollott, Frances	02 SEP 1880 R	14	429
Mines, William Parker	Williams, Julia	01 AUG 1878 R	12	155
Minick, John B.	Clampitt, Katie M.	15 SEP 1880 L	14	446
Minnick, Lydia C.	Atchison, Welford C.	22 DEC 1881 R	16	153
Minnis, George W.	Douglass, Mary E.	13 JUL 1882 L	16	447
Minnis, J.W.	Harrison, Sarah R.	11 MAY 1880	14	262
Minnis, Richard	Delany, Ellen	02 APR 1878	11	402
Minnis, Thomas M.	Brooks, Rosetta	29 APR 1879 R	13	162
Minniter, Lizzie C.	Funtner, Samuel E.	15 MAR 1880	14	185
Minnitt, Robert	Kennedy, Ellen	30 AUG 1880 R	14	422
Minor, Alice	Jefferson, Lafayette	28 MAY 1884 R	19	042
Minor, Allena	Smith, John Edward	06 APR 1884 R	18	497
Minor, Ella	Meredith, William Henry	09 APR 1880 R	14	217
Minor, Emily	Webster, Charles Fenton	14 MAY 1879 L	13	190
Minor, Eugene P.	Herbert, Hattie C.	16 OCT 1885 L	20	491
Minor, Fairfax Catlett	West, Roberta Lemmon	13 APR 1882 R	16	314

Minor, George	Cox, Harriet A.	26 FEB 1880 L	14	168
Minor, Henry	Dorsey, Mary Ann	10 JUL 1880 R	14	354
Minor, Isabella	Carroll, Richard H.	01 OCT 1878	12	244
Minor, James	Shilloo, Josephine	26 JAN 1880 R	14	121
Minor, James	Robinson, Ellen	28 JUN 1881 L	15	380
Minor, James	Friendrick, Lottie	05 AUG 1885 L	20	356
Minor, John Thomas	Beales, Amanda	08 SEP 1879 R	13	348
Minor, Laura	Payne, John Thomas	03 MAY 1881 R	15	291
Minor, Maria	Green, Israel	03 SEP 1883 L	18	107
Minor, Matilda	Lucas, William A.	04 APR 1885 R	20	202
Minor, Millie	Bailey, Howard T.	03 JUN 1884 L	19	052
Minor, Thaddeus	Matthews, Etta	29 JUN 1881 R	15	355
Minor, Thomas N.	Dorsey, Ida M.	31 DEC 1877	11	282
Minor, William	Gray, Mary	28 MAY 1885 R	20	246
Minor, William F	Metonhall, Hattie S.	21 NOV 1882 L	17	139
Minter, Theophilus F.	Downs, Ida V.	02 OCT 1884	19	283
Minyburg, Amelia	Murphy, John	12 SEP 1878 R	12	214
Minz, Rebecca	Oppenheimer, Hertz	21 AUG 1884 L	19	200
Mirick, Emily	Farless, Benjamin A.	22 JUN 1881	15	373
Mishaw, John	Ladd, Elizabeth	29 NOV 1877 R	11	207
Miskell, John H.	Moran, Lily Maud	28 JUL 1885	20	343
Miskell, Sarah F.	Wood, Charles W.	12 MAR 1885	20	109
Miskell, William A.	Farr, Zadie L.	03 AUG 1880 R	14	384
Mister, Frederick M.	Cuvillier, Maggie	01 DEC 1879 R	14	020
Mitchel, Edwin	Sims, Susan	23 NOV 1878 L	12	343
Mitchel, Elise A.	Hoban, James	28 JUL 1880 R	14	376
Mitchel, Mary	Karcher, Louis	28 JAN 1879 R	13	036
Mitchell, Abraham	Dyson, Mary Cordelia	03 APR 1885 R	20	136
Mitchell, Alice	Clark, Samuel	31 MAR 1880	14	202
Mitchell, Andrew J.	Stone, Fannie J.	25 SEP 1885	20	442
Mitchell, Annie	Coats, Robert	25 SEP 1884 L	19	268
Mitchell, Bettie	Conway, Jeremiah	18 SEP 1884 L	19	260
Mitchell, Catharine	Smiley, William F.	01 APR 1884 R	18	490
Mitchell, Charles	Scott, Malinda	26 MAY 1884 R	19	039
Mitchell, Charles A.	Jones, Virginia	12 MAY 1880 L	14	268
Mitchell, Clifton	Kirchner, Rosa K.	23 NOV 1881 R	16	091
Mitchell, Ella	Taylor, Peter	14 MAY 1879 R	13	178
Mitchell, Ellen C.	Bassford, John N.	05 DEC 1883	18	295
Mitchell, Emily R.	Killmon, William H.	08 MAY 1879 R	13	181
Mitchell, Emma M.	King, Henry B.	27 NOV 1879 R	14	013
Mitchell, Filmore	Hayre, Mary E.	22 OCT 1883 R	18	204
Mitchell, Florence B.	King, Alexander Simms	02 JUN 1879 L	13	214
Mitchell, Francis E.	Johnson, Ida E.	10 NOV 1881 L	16	070
Mitchell, Geo. Wash.	Currell, Virginia F.	16 SEP 1880	14	450
Mitchell, George	West, Sallie A.	26 JUL 1882	16	457
Mitchell, Ida	Kendick, Abraham L.	25 SEP 1881	15	497
Mitchell, Ida R.	Foulkes, George L.	06 AUG 1883	18	076
Mitchell, Isaiah	Stratton, Margaret	05 AUG 1879 R	13	308
Mitchell, Isaiah	Contee, Lucinda S.	20 JAN 1881	15	159
Mitchell, Isham	Thomas, Catherine	05 JAN 1882 R	16	182
Mitchell, James W.	Marshall, Ada H.	06 JUN 1883 R	17	479
Mitchell, Jennie	Webb, Gilbert	14 MAY 1885 L	20	221
Mitchell, Jennie A.	Harbin, James T.	23 SEP 1882 L	17	034
Mitchell, Jennie C.V.	Sanderson, Charles Edward	29 NOV 1883	18	285
Mitchell, John A.	Hardester, Mollie E.	26 MAR 1885 R	20	134
Mitchell, John E.	Matthews, Rebecca	06 DEC 1881 L	16	114
Mitchell, John H.	Jones, Barbara M.	06 OCT 1881 R	16	004
Mitchell, Joseph	Washington, Caroline	16 APR 1885 L	20	172

Mitchell, Joseph Franklin	Thomas, Florence Thomson	02 FEB 1885 R	20	046
Mitchell, Kate	Windsor, John H.	21 DEC 1881 L	16	145
Mitchell, Laura Eunice (Collier)	Colston, Ralph Edward	27 JUN 1883 R	18	020
Mitchell, Maggie	Campbell, Benjamin S.	06 DEC 1882 L	17	171
Mitchell, Maggie Frank	Landon, Herbert	16 AUG 1883	18	089
Mitchell, Mary	Foster, J. William	15 APR 1880 R	14	224
Mitchell, Patrick H.	Fitzgerald, Annie Y.	18 NOV 1884 L	19	391
Mitchell, Peter	Cages, Sarah Maria	04 DEC 1881 R	16	111
Mitchell, R.A.	Parris, R.T.	27 MAY 1880 R	14	293
Mitchell, Sallie P.	Mendehall, James B.	24 DEC 1879 R	14	071
Mitchell, Sarah	Randall, George	05 MAY 1881 R	15	295
Mitchell, Sarah	Harrison, William	18 JAN 1882 R	16	200
Mitchell, Sarah Wilmot	Deffinbaugh, B.W.	27 NOV 1878 R	12	347
Mitchell, Susan Brown	Aiken, Matthew	06 NOV 1879 R	13	463
Mitchell, Susan S.	Thomas, Wm. B.	22 DEC 1881 R	16	139
Mitchell, Zachariah	Walker, Carrie	07 JUN 1879 L	13	222
Mitchellmore, Katie	Hererford, R.W.	26 FEB 1885	20	088
Mitchison, William J.	Luthy, Bertha	19 NOV 1883 R	18	263
Mittag, Thomas E.	Gehr, Lou A.	03 JUN 1881 R	15	342
Mobley, Howard S.	Smeltzer, Nora B.	04 MAR 1884	18	456
Mockabee, Edward M.	Wood, Josephine A.	07 OCT 1880 L	14	480
Mockabee, Elizabeth	Dines, Joseph	07 NOV 1882 R	17	114
Mockabee, Frank	Denny, Mary	22 DEC 1877 L	11	260
Mockabee, Henry C.	Lazenby, Sarah Frances	10 APR 1878	11	414
Mockabee, John T.	Massey, Eva	21 FEB 1878 L	11	353
Mockabee, Susie A.	Boyce, Walter J.	08 OCT 1877	11	125
Mockabee, William	Carroll, Clara E.	07 JUN 1884	19	068
Mocobee, William A.	Thurston, Addie	28 APR 1880 L	14	242
Moens, Frank	Betts, Susan	31 JUL 1879 R	13	302
Moffat, Daniel J.	Williamson, Joanna	17 JUN 1879 R	13	235
Moffatt, Charles	Martin, Elizabeth	23 JUL 1883	18	057
Moffett, Henrietta	Fletcher, Joseph	25 APR 1882 R	16	329
Moffett, Henry O.	Stofiel, Sarah I.	20 NOV 1879 R	13	495
Moffitt, Maggie C.	Smith, Ephraim	26 AUG 1884	19	189
Moffitt, Stephen	Green, Gracie A.	12 AUG 1879 R	13	317
Mohler, Herrman	Buhler, Katherine	06 MAR 1885	20	126
Mohler, Jacob Rupert	Hester, Gertrude	18 JAN 1881 R	15	152
Molan, John F.	Verry, Elizabeth	22 JAN 1885 L	20	034
Moland, Thomas	Steward, Mary Ann	30 SEP 1879 L	13	394
Molfenter, William	Englehardt, Catherine	31 MAY 1884 L	19	048
Mollard, Jennie	Stevens, Henry L.	30 DEC 1882 R	17	226
Moloch, Thomas R.	Tarlton, Joanna	30 NOV 1881 L	16	105
Mommberger, Lena B.	Morken, Henry	16 APR 1882	16	315
Monaghan, James	Leddey, Margaret	28 NOV 1877 L	11	208
Monahan, Eleanor Augusta	Evans, Frederick Walter	26 JUL 1882 R	16	459
Monahan, Ella J.	Hannan, Frank	27 NOV 1884 L	19	423
Monahan, John	Dinneen, Nellie	09 JUL 1884 L	19	131
Monahan, Julia	Huff, John	04 DEC 1882	17	153
Moncue, Scott	Smith, Mary	06 DEC 1881 L	16	115
Moncure, Caroline	Johnson, Nathaniel	27 FEB 1879 R	13	075
Moncure, Lilla J.	Ashby, Richard	31 OCT 1878	12	304
Monday, Lavinia	Palmer, George W.	21 DEC 1882 R	17	181
Money, Laura J.	Walker, Benjamin F.	17 FEB 1881 R	15	193
Money, Nathaniel B.	Beall, Ida M.	14 FEB 1882 L	16	239
Money, Valvia D.	Cross, Charles T.	26 APR 1881 R	15	273
Monihan, Johanna	Quill, James	01 NOV 1878	12	411
Monroe, Annie J.	Quarles, Charles W.	11 SEP 1877	11	086
Monroe, Charles	Bailey, Janie	25 MAY 1882	16	376

D.C. Marriage Records Index, June 28, 1877 to October 19, 1885

Monroe, David Lloyd	Johnston, Mary Ann	28 MAY 1878 L	12	070
Monroe, Elizabeth Miranda	Robey, William Alfred	10 OCT 1878 R	12	258
Monroe, Frank	Jackson, Susan	06 FEB 1883 R	17	294
Monroe, James	Imes, Cecelia	26 NOV 1884 L	19	420
Monroe, Lewis	Davis, Annie	19 SEP 1880	14	440
Monroe, Lou	Turner, George	10 AUG 1885 L	20	362
Monroe, Louise	Pope, Emanuel	19 APR 1883 L	17	400
Monroe, Martha	Penn, Douglass	25 DEC 1878 R	12	398
Monroe, Mary	Coats, Ananias	06 OCT 1878	12	253
Monroe, Mary	Wilson, Thomas	24 APR 1879 R	13	157
Monroe, Mary E.	Howard, William	17 NOV 1881	16	080
Monroe, Morgan L.	Cox, Maggie L.	18 AUG 1885	20	498
Monroe, Rebecca M.	Nash, Charles Francis	15 JAN 1881 R	15	151
Monroe, Richard H.	Brown, Mary V.	03 OCT 1883 R	18	168
Monroe, Richmond	Bayliss, Mary E.	15 JAN 1878 R	10	2460
Monroe, William Ignatius	Lane, Annie	22 APR 1879 L	13	154
Montague, Benjamin F., Dr.	Gardner, Gussie B.	07 JUL 1879 L	13	273
Montague, Julia C.	Herbert, Charles C.	19 FEB 1879 L	13	068
Montague, Pierre La	Patterson, Katharine P.	29 OCT 1884	19	340
Montague, William	Harris, Rachel	23 MAY 1883 R	17	458
Monteiro, Margaret	Berry, H.A.	10 FEB 1884 L	18	418
Monteith, Emma	Chinn, James	12 JUN 1882 R	16	405
Montello, Edward	Joswell, Fanny	21 APR 1879 R	13	153
Montgomery, Ann	Johnson, Oscar	25 SEP 1879	13	367
Montgomery, Anna	Coates, Singleton	10 JAN 1880 L	14	100
Montgomery, C.F.	Cole, Alice M.	04 NOV 1879 L	13	463
Montgomery, Ella J.	Weyrich, John F.	17 NOV 1880 L	15	052
Montgomery, George	Nelson, Mary E.	09 NOV 1880 R	15	039
Montgomery, Henry P.	Brown, Emma V.	06 MAR 1879	13	093
Montgomery, Isaac	Carter, Susan	14 AUG 1884 L	19	185
Montgomery, James A.	Wilkerson, Sallie	16 AUG 1881 R	15	447
Montgomery, James H., Jr.	Robey, Georgianna Grace	25 FEB 1884 R	18	442
Montgomery, Mary Adams	Ross, George	31 JUL 1881 R	15	417
Montgomery, Mary Emily	Fechet, Eugene Oscar	03 DEC 1879 R	14	026
Montgomery, Minnie Yardley	Lester, William	26 APR 1885	20	188
Montgomery, Thomas	McMullen, Margaret	07 NOV 1881 L	16	066
Montgomery, William	Wood, Louisa	28 JUL 1879 L	13	295
Monypeny, William, Jr.	McGrew, Grace Annie	08 APR 1884 R	18	499
Moodey, Helen Quamer	Coolidge, James Abernethy	04 MAY 1880 R	14	253
Moody, Ella L.	Watkins, C.J.	04 JUL 1881	15	387
Moody, Maggie A.	O'Connors, Timothy	27 JUN 1885 R	20	296
Mook, Margaret	Ebert, Joseph C.	16 SEP 1885 L	20	422
Moon, D. Willie	Megginson, Mamie F.	13 MAY 1880	14	262
Moon, Florence	Frazier, McHenry Grafton	13 JUN 1885 R	20	272
Moon, Martie R.	Kimmell, John Q.A.	15 AUG 1881 R	15	445
Mooney, Bernard	Campbell, Mary Jane	30 JUN 1884 L	19	110
Mooney, Thomas H.	Barrett, Norah	26 NOV 1880 L	15	068
Mooney, William	Gibson, Jane	11 JUN 1884 L	19	078
Moonshine, Lena	Emmett, John	30 OCT 1882 L	17	101
Moor, Jacob	Chapman, Ella	29 NOV 1878	12	355
Moor, Lizzie	Winston, William S.	11 NOV 1878 L	12	321
Moore, Abner L.	Chenault, Ann Elizabeth	14 JUL 1879	13	281
Moore, Adlade	Burke, Daniel J.	18 MAR 1884 R	18	476
Moore, Alexander	Bowen, Maria	11 AUG 1880 L	14	397
Moore, Alexander Christopher	Shehan, Mary	31 AUG 1882 R	16	498
Moore, Alexexander	Moten, Nettie	23 DEC 1879 R	14	055
Moore, Alfred	Poindexter, Hattie	03 AUG 1885 R	20	349
Moore, Alice	Perkins, Robert	15 AUG 1882 L	16	480

Moore, Alice	Hardy, Richard	09 JUL 1885 L	20	319
Moore, Alice	Jones, Thomas Henry	08 JUN 1885 L	20	260
Moore, Alice R.	Deeton, Andrew D.	08 SEP 1879	13	357
Moore, Allen	Masterson, Lucretia	09 FEB 1878	11	334
Moore, Amelia H.	Ellery, George H.	06 SEP 1881	15	471
Moore, Ann	Allen, Alfred	28 DEC 1880	15	125
Moore, Anna	Barker, Charles A.	03 NOV 1881 R	16	060
Moore, Anna M.	Boyer, Andrew J.	14 OCT 1885	20	483
Moore, Annie B.	Wysham, William E.	13 JUN 1881 R	15	357
Moore, Barbara E.	Mullikin, Richard T.	08 NOV 1883 R	18	233
Moore, Capitola	Price, John J.	26 AUG 1884	19	206
Moore, Catherine C.	Norris, John	14 OCT 1880 L	14	494
Moore, Cecelia	Mason, William	28 DEC 1882 L	17	222
Moore, Charles T.	Carroll, Mary Ellen	29 JUN 1882 R	16	432
Moore, Charles W.H.	Lee, Gertrude L.	24 JAN 1883 R	17	271
Moore, Douglass	Hulse, Florence C.	18 JAN 1881 R	15	155
Moore, Edwin W.S.	Lee, Katherine W.	23 FEB 1885 R	20	080
Moore, Elvie	Jackson, Andrew	05 APR 1881	15	247
Moore, Fred	Berry, Lucy C.	09 FEB 1883	17	291
Moore, Frederick R.	Lawrence, Ida S.	09 APR 1879 R	13	131
Moore, George	Offutt, Sallie	30 JUN 1884 L	19	112
Moore, George D.	Robinson, Mary J.	23 JUN 1878	12	095
Moore, George D.	Skinner, Annie D.	10 FEB 1879	13	045
Moore, George D.	Simms, Emma Lee	04 SEP 1883 R	18	111
Moore, Hattie A.	Tracy, Raudolph H.	29 OCT 1884	19	345
Moore, Ida	Nelson, Thomas	06 DEC 1879 L	14	032
Moore, Ida C.	Estler, Theodore W.	26 JUN 1884 R	19	106
Moore, Isaac J.	Bryan, Annie A.	18 SEP 1879 R	13	378
Moore, Jacob G.	Adams, Fannie W.	18 SEP 1883 R	18	135
Moore, James	Seeton, Mary Virginia	21 DEC 1881 R	16	148
Moore, James H.	Dorsey, Frances	28 JUL 1881 R	15	423
Moore, Jane	Tyler, John	07 OCT 1878 L	12	256
Moore, Jennie	Henry, William	02 NOV 1880	15	025
Moore, Jennie T.	Morris, George G.	25 AUG 1884	19	206
Moore, Jessie L.	Birch, Philip Wilbur	15 JUN 1883 R	17	496
Moore, John Benson	Jennings, Ella Frances	15 MAR 1882 R	16	277
Moore, John G.	Shine, Anna M.	24 MAR 1883 L	17	359
Moore, John G.T.	Schnaebel, Julia	29 OCT 1882	17	098
Moore, John H.	Jones, Catherine	13 NOV 1879 L	13	479
Moore, Josaphene	Gillott, Joseph L.	18 DEC 1879	14	057
Moore, Joseph	Scott, Laura	31 DEC 1881	16	072
Moore, Joseph B.	Hile, Margaret	09 NOV 1879 R	13	486
Moore, Joseph J.	Padgett, Laura Virginia	05 NOV 1880 L	15	033
Moore, Josephine Elizabeth	Club, Edward	26 AUG 1884 R	19	207
Moore, Juba B.	Tenney, Robert B.	29 JAN 1878	11	320
Moore, Kate	Roberts, William Florian	01 JUN 1882 R	16	384
Moore, Lannia	Brown, Charles H.	27 SEP 1883 R	18	156
Moore, Laura	Day, George W.	29 APR 1879 R	13	162
Moore, Laura	Washington, Joshua	11 JAN 1883 L	17	251
Moore, Leopold Fred.	Chambers, Georgie Delrean	05 SEP 1883	18	109
Moore, M.S.	Wilson, Alfred	16 SEP 1884	19	233
Moore, Madison	Brannum, Sally	20 OCT 1883 L	18	203
Moore, Maggie	Perkins, Robert S.	04 APR 1878	11	406
Moore, Marcus	Tyler, Pathenia [Dotson]	15 APR 1883 R	17	394
Moore, Margaret A.	Hill, Edward	23 MAY 1883	17	457
Moore, Maria	Smothers, John F.	28 SEP 1885 L	20	446
Moore, Marl	Butts, Jennie L.	25 JAN 1880 R	14	119
Moore, Mary	Tenney, Dennis	27 MAY 1879 L	13	208

Moore, Mary	West, Alfred	19 FEB 1880 R	14	159
Moore, Mary	Ellwood, Thomas	04 AUG 1882 L	16	469
Moore, Mary	Simmons, Daniel M.	26 JUN 1884 R	19	107
Moore, Mary C.	Martin, James	18 NOV 1879 R	13	489
Moore, Mary R.	Robertson, Walter	28 SEP 1882 L	17	040
Moore, Mollie Whaley	Crane, George Francis	26 MAY 1881 R	15	326
Moore, Morgan M.	Bush, Kate G.	02 JAN 1880 R	14	087
Moore, Primus	Davis, Mary Ann	26 NOV 1880 RL	15	068
Moore, Rebecca O.	Duvall, J. Walter	09 JUL 1878	12	129
Moore, Roger W.	Miller, Matilda	04 NOV 1878 R	12	307
Moore, Rosa	Frazier, Lewis	16 DEC 1878 L	12	382
Moore, S. Jeanette	Stevens, Henry Eugene	01 FEB 1882 R	16	219
Moore, Sallie	Campbell, Cornelius	15 DEC 1880 R	15	098
Moore, Sarah E.	Simpson, William Alex.	14 APR 1880	14	222
Moore, Sarah Francis	Watson, Thomas Alexander	12 FEB 1879 R	13	056
Moore, Sarah Josephine	Orndorff, Lunsford G.	30 APR 1879 R	13	167
Moore, Sarah M.	Davidson, Alexander S.	23 MAY 1883 L	17	457
Moore, Solomon	Robinson, Sarah	15 JUN 1882	16	405
Moore, Squire	Brown, Annie	30 JUL 1879 R	13	299
Moore, Thomas	Dorsey, Jennie	20 NOV 1882 L	17	152
Moore, Thomas J.	Talburtt, Ellen Ruth	19 JAN 1882 R	16	200
Moore, Traverse	Johnson, Ella	19 DEC 1878 R	12	389
Moore, Violetta	Sydnor, Baldwin R.	23 MAY 1882 L	16	373
Moore, Virginia M.	Cole, Charles N.	14 APR 1879 L	13	143
Moorehead, Maggie W.	Rhodes, Willis O.	20 FEB 1882 R	16	250
Mopkins, Harris	Thompson, Anna	18 DEC 1879 L	14	057
Moran, Agnes	Stuart, Gibbons	13 AUG 1883 L	18	085
Moran, Alexander F.	Noyes, Alice	26 APR 1883	17	409
Moran, Elasah French	Eliot, Leila Rebecca	12 OCT 1884	19	301
Moran, Elizabeth	Frey, Jacob	31 DEC 1878 L	12	410
Moran, Elizabeth	White, William C.	19 APR 1881 R	15	263
Moran, Frank M.	Draper, Annie E., Mrs.	17 AUG 1884 R	19	191
Moran, Horatio H.	Hill, Melinda E.	15 MAR 1883 L	17	348
Moran, J. Milton	Clements, M. Rosalie	13 OCT 1885 L	20	478
Moran, Jennie	Lewis, John Yeuell	07 MAY 1885 R	20	213
Moran, John A.	Stockett, Isabella	01 OCT 1884 L	19	280
Moran, John W.	Garrison, Virginia	20 JUL 1881 R	15	409
Moran, Josephine	Howard, Beverly W.	18 DEC 1884 L	19	468
Moran, Lily Maud	Miskell, John H.	28 JUL 1885	20	343
Moran, Mary E.	Shea, Daniel E.	15 JUN 1882 R	16	412
Moran, Mary Elizabeth	Bailey, William	05 NOV 1883	18	233
Moran, May	Avery, Frank T.	24 JUL 1879 R	13	291
Moran, Nellie	Spaight, Daniel	18 DEC 1882 R	17	190
Moran, Rosa E.	Nutwell, James W.	12 JAN 1882 R	16	192
Moran, Tenie C.	Lohr, Charles G.	11 OCT 1883 R	18	188
Moran, William H.	Downing, Belle	09 APR 1879	13	131
Morant, Ellen	Nuvelle, James G.	21 NOV 1881 R	16	087
More, Frederick	Jones, Rose	21 SEP 1885 L	20	430
More, Martin	Costello, Margaret	26 APR 1882 L	16	335
Morehouse, Mary J. White	Gee, Samuel P.	28 SEP 1882 R	16	495
Moreland, Enoch C.	McGann, Rachel L.	09 DEC 1879 L	14	037
Moreland, John H.	Wilkinson, Anna Rebecca	21 AUG 1879	13	328
Moreland, Mary L.	Cox, Robert W.	19 NOV 1881 L	16	085
Moreland, Thomas	McLean, Bettie	14 JAN 1879 R	13	018
Moreland, William	Marks, Maggie	18 MAY 1878 L	12	059
Morell, Clara	Parkhurst, George A.	31 JAN 1885	20	045
Morency, Annie W.S.	Phipps, Thomas E.	14 JUN 1881 L	15	361
Morewood, George Palmer	Harris, Phoebe	25 MAY 1882 R	16	376

Name	Spouse	Date		
Morgan, Alice	Carroll, Dennis	30 OCT 1877	11	161
Morgan, Annie Tobitha	Dorsey, Clifton S.	04 JUN 1881 R	15	339
Morgan, Catherine	Thomas, Arry	26 NOV 1879 R	14	008
Morgan, Eleanora D.	Speer, Emory	14 JUL 1881 L	15	401
Morgan, Elizabeth J.	Stinemetz, Samuel W.	15 JAN 1879 R	13	017
Morgan, Frances	Briscoe, William	01 FEB 1881 L	15	172
Morgan, George	Jackson, Ada	12 MAY 1881	15	296
Morgan, George G.W.	Daines, Matilda	22 DEC 1877 R	11	227
Morgan, Henrietta Maria	Leach, Phineas Block	15 APR 1879 R	13	138
Morgan, Ida M.	Wight, George A.	09 DEC 1880	15	088
Morgan, James E.	Brown, Nellie E.	16 DEC 1880 L	15	105
Morgan, John	Skinner, Maggie	11 DEC 1883	18	309
Morgan, John R.	Wendel, Magdelena	09 SEP 1885	20	406
Morgan, Josphine	Johnson, William	09 DEC 1882 L	17	176
Morgan, Katie	Webb, Frank B.	29 MAY 1879	13	210
Morgan, Lizzie	Broom, Andrew J.	17 AUG 1882 L	16	483
Morgan, Lizzie Lawton	Beck, James Hopkins	21 FEB 1884 R	18	437
Morgan, Maggie Eliz.	Kell, William Alfred	14 DEC 1884 R	19	458
Morgan, Margaret M.	Bond, Charles T.	12 SEP 1878	12	215
Morgan, Mary Margaret	Henderson, James H.	06 NOV 1881 R	16	064
Morgan, Milton I.	Lowe, Ida V.	02 DEC 1884 R	19	432
Morgan, Morris A.	Evely, Mary A.	08 JAN 1880	14	097
Morgan, Richard	Hattoo, Annie	01 JUN 1881 L	15	336
Morgan, Richard	Clark, Julia	21 DEC 1881	16	142
Morgan, Richard W.	Coates, Emma B.	23 JUN 1880 R	14	332
Morgan, Thomas	Hardin, Margaret	21 SEP 1881	15	492
Morgan, Thomas H.	Raegan, Rosa G.	17 JUN 1878	12	088
Morgan, William G.	McNamara, Emma T.	11 OCT 1884 L	19	301
Morgan, William H.	Wilson, Annie	08 NOV 1883 L	18	243
Morgan, Wm. P.	Bryan, Carrie P.	29 JAN 1880 R	14	128
Moriarty, Josephine E.	Hartnett, John	21 NOV 1878 R	12	338
Moriarty, Patrick	McNally, Belle	17 MAY 1885 R	20	223
Moriarty, Richard	Hyde, May	28 MAY 1884 L	19	043
Morken, Henry	Mommberger, Lena B.	16 APR 1882	16	315
Morland, Laura	Small, Charles H.	02 JUL 1882	16	427
Mormann, Edwin	Sewfert, Mary E.	20 FEB 1879	13	071
Morrice, Lizzie, Mrs.	Gillingham, Henry R.	30 SEP 1879 R	13	393
Morrill, Mary J.	Smith, J. Clement	12 JUN 1880 R	14	317
Morris, Charles	Jones, Mary Elizabeth	23 DEC 1882 L	17	207
Morris, Charles D.	Quarles, Adele F.	25 NOV 1880 R	15	067
Morris, Charlotte	Johnson, Walker	22 SEP 1877	11	105
Morris, Ellenor B.	Finley, William L.	15 OCT 1884	19	306
Morris, Frances	Williams, Thomas	10 APR 1879 L	13	136
Morris, George A.	Bailey, Guinette	29 JUL 1879 R	13	298
Morris, George G.	Moore, Jennie T.	25 AUG 1884	19	206
Morris, Henry	Carpenter, Louisa Victoria	10 APR 1879 R	13	128
Morris, Henry E.	Jasper, Rachel	10 OCT 1877 R	11	115
Morris, Isabella	Lazenberry, Charles B.	13 OCT 1879 R	13	418
Morris, James	Haines, Laura	15 OCT 1877	11	132
Morris, James H.	Buckner, Hellen	10 APR 1879 L	13	135
Morris, James P.	Burch, Lizzie	10 OCT 1881	14	501
Morris, Jennie	Lancaster, John W.	24 DEC 1878 L	12	398
Morris, Jennie	Howard, William	30 AUG 1883 R	18	104
Morris, Jessie P.	Hynes, Thomas	04 AUG 1882	16	465
Morris, Jim	Washington, Mary Frances	09 APR 1879 L	13	133
Morris, John	Smith, Annie	17 NOV 1884 L	19	387
Morris, John	Groshon, Nettie A.	09 JUN 1885 R	20	263
Morris, John E.	Strong, Maria S.	16 MAY 1878	12	056

Morris, John P.	Pendleton, E.H.	27 APR 1881	15	278
Morris, John W.	Stotsenburg, Alice R., Mrs.	12 APR 1880	14	218
Morris, Katie	Meredith, David	19 APR 1882	16	322
Morris, Katie V.	Swiggard, John F.	06 JUN 1885	20	259
Morris, Louisa E.	Kenney, Edward C.	14 FEB 1878 R	11	341
Morris, Lucy E.	Taylor, William	02 MAY 1885 L	20	202
Morris, Maria	Chase, David	14 DEC 1882 L	17	184
Morris, Martha	Butler, Madison	15 APR 1884	18	511
Morris, Martha, Mrs.	Damens, John Andrew	02 NOV 1882 R	16	384
Morris, Mary E.	Macauley, Charles Henry	03 JUL 1879 R	13	264
Morris, Mary Virginia	Shirley, George W.	26 JUL 1882 R	16	426
Morris, Nehemiah	Ducket, Lucy	26 AUG 1884 L	19	207
Morris, Rebecca	Harris, Samuel H.	25 MAR 1880 R	14	197
Morris, Richard K.	Queen, Lucy	01 APR 1879 L	13	121
Morris, Susie	Price, John H.	06 MAY 1880 L	14	257
Morris, Thomas L.	Burrage, Mary E.	28 AUG 1878 R	12	184
Morris, Thornton	Smith, Julia	26 NOV 1884	19	414
Morris, Virginia	Perrie, Augustus Lepreaux	20 JUN 1882 R	16	420
Morris, William	Gross, Mamie V.	15 APR 1885 R	20	170
Morris, William H.	Smith, Julia	09 MAY 1884 L	19	013
Morris, William T.	Owens, Medora A.	28 AUG 1884	19	213
Morrison, Charles Clifford	Dunn, Emma Mary Louisa	30 APR 1879	13	164
Morrison, Emma M.	Byington, George Richmond	03 APR 1878 R	11	404
Morrison, Harriet R.	Gorham, Aaron S.	17 MAR 1881 L	15	229
Morrison, Joseph	Pleasants, Annie E.	20 DEC 1882 R	17	196
Morrison, Lizzie	Brown, William	19 JUN 1883 L	18	002
Morrison, Margaret A.	Whipple, David R.	05 FEB 1878	11	288
Morrison, Mary E.	Chrissinger, William, Dr.	06 DEC 1883	18	304
Morrison, Mary Ellen	Bates, William J.	03 AUG 1885	20	348
Morrison, Mary F.	Short, Sidney H.	26 JUL 1881	15	417
Morrison, Mary Isabella	Thompson, John	18 SEP 1882 R	17	025
Morrison, Riddall	Johnson, Catherine	08 FEB 1881 R	15	180
Morrison, Rosina R.	Davidson, William J.	12 APR 1883 R	17	381
Morrison, Ross W.	Ward, Annie E.	07 APR 1884	18	498
Morrison, Samuel	Radcliffe, Manie	01 JAN 1885 R	19	513
Morrison, William F.	Stanton, Savantine Gerty	07 NOV 1880 R	15	028
Morrow, Alice V.	Cooke, Robert R.	03 OCT 1883 R	18	161
Morrow, Annie L.	Obold, Sebastian F.	30 DEC 1884 L	19	504
Morrow, George T., Jr.	Smith, Lena Grace	15 JUN 1885 L	20	275
Morrow, Harriet A.	Mulcahy, Michael A.	29 DEC 1878 R	12	406
Morrow, James	Bowman, Imogene	27 OCT 1881	16	048
Morrow, James P.	Burrows, Fannie C.	26 DEC 1883	18	277
Morrow, Katherine	Stafford, James	17 OCT 1878 L	12	279
Morrow, Thomas	Quailley, Elizabeth	15 APR 1879 L	13	143
Morrow, Thomas G.	Birch, Bessie	06 JUN 1883 L	17	479
Morrow, William Nelson	Burley, Mary Lizzie	05 OCT 1879 R	13	403
Morse, Alexander Porter	Clarke, Ellen M.	17 APR 1883	17	397
Morse, Bryan Hebert	Ringwalt, Elizabeth Price	03 SEP 1884	19	217
Morse, Fannie S.	Perrie, Walter Thomas	09 JAN 1884 R	18	371
Morse, Helen	Janin, Edward	24 OCT 1877 L	11	153
Morse, Marx	Eichberg, Kate (Morse)	27 AUG 1885 R	20	390
Morse, Mary A.	Davis, Joseph M.T.	30 JAN 1883 R	17	279
Morse, Oliver C.	Jones, Ella	22 JUN 1881 R	15	370
Morse, William A.	Jones, Maggie V.	02 MAR 1885	33	8068
Morsell, Annie	Blair, John [the Baptist]	01 NOV 1884 L	19	386
Morsell, Robert L.	Beach, Martha F.	12 NOV 1877	11	178
Morsell, William A.	Hodges, Clara W.	10 SEP 1883	18	123
Morten, Wyatt	Laning, Delia	02 SEP 1880 R	14	430

Mortimer, Harmonia	Tyler, George W.	23 DEC 1879 R	14	063
Mortimer, Missouri O.	Bailey, Theodore	26 MAR 1879 R	13	113
Mortimore, Emma	Tyler, William	17 JUL 1883 R	18	051
Morton, A.H.	Hudson, M.E.	16 OCT 1879	13	429
Morton, Alice	Bates, Mason	18 SEP 1879 R	13	377
Morton, Arthur Austerfield	Polson, Kitty Tucker	31 DEC 1883 R	18	332
Morton, Jennie	Gains, Richard	28 APR 1880 R	14	240
Morton, John	Johnson, Mary	17 JUL 1877	11	024
Morton, John Henry	Tolliver, Bertha	17 APR 1878 R	12	012
Morton, Joseph Bruce	Lowry, Mary Rosina	02 OCT 1882 R	17	046
Morton, Martha	Drew, Robert	24 AUG 1880 L	14	412
Morton, May E.	White, Maximo	27 MAY 1880 R	14	287
Morton, Peter	Jackson, Susie	30 APR 1885 R	20	200
Morton, Rena	Beal, James A.	24 OCT 1883 L	18	212
Morton, Robert	Fields, Susan	18 FEB 1878	12	227
Morton, Viney	Carter, William	28 FEB 1878 L	11	366
Morton, William A.	Jones, Virginia W.	23 DEC 1880 R	15	121
Morton, Willie	Walker, John W.	03 JUN 1880 R	14	298
Morwood, Agnes V.	Cain, John T.	09 SEP 1885 L	20	407
Mosby, Frances	Smith, Joseph H.	09 AUG 1877 L	11	049
Mosby, Joseph	Jackson, Jane	09 DEC 1880 R	15	089
Mosby, Joseph	Skinner, Sarah Ann	28 DEC 1882 R	17	213
Moseby, John	Fletcher, Rebecca	05 SEP 1878	12	199
Moseby, Thomas L.	Goodman, Cordelia E.	29 OCT 1878 L	12	298
Moseley, Ardella	Berryman, Wilson W.	04 DEC 1879 L	14	030
Moseley, Nancy	Beckwith, John	13 DEC 1877 L	11	234
Moseley, Sophia	Briscoe, Alexander	09 JUL 1878 L	12	130
Mosely, George C.	Barriere, Fannie	23 FEB 1883 R	17	319
Moser, Christian	Fisher, Annie	09 DEC 1879 L	14	037
Moser, Teresa	Sanford, Edward E.	09 MAY 1883 R	17	433
Moses, S. Preston, Jr.	Bryan, Carrie P.	01 JUN 1880 L	14	299
Mosher, Mary M.	Chase, Constantine	06 APR 1878 R	11	409
Mosher, Theodore, Lt.	Colegate, Augusta McBlair	28 NOV 1877 L	11	206
Mosley, Lucy Floyd	Russell, Charles Wells	19 FEB 1880 R	14	154
Moss, Annie	Thronton, Henry	22 OCT 1884	19	329
Moss, Elverton	McInturf, Mary E.	14 JUL 1884 L	19	136
Moss, George W.	Allabach, Gertrude B.	12 FEB 1878 R	11	338
Moss, John	Johnson, Emma	06 SEP 1877 L	11	078
Moten, Annie	Gray, Madison	14 DEC 1881 L	16	130
Moten, Charles L.	Jasper, Martha C.	06 AUG 1878	12	157
Moten, Edith	Barnes, Henry Francis	01 AUG 1882	16	461
Moten, Harriet A., Mrs.	White, Peter B.	29 NOV 1877 R	11	207
Moten, Lucy A.	Stanard, David	23 DEC 1880 R	15	114
Moten, Mildred	Johnson, James H.	31 MAY 1881 L	15	332
Moten, Nettie	Moore, Alexexander	23 DEC 1879 R	14	055
Moten, S.B.	Isaacs, S.J.	26 JUL 1880 L	14	375
Moten, Sarah	Ridout, John Henry	26 NOV 1883 L	18	277
Moten, Sylvester B.	Isaacs, Sarah Jane	01 AUG 1880 R	14	303
Mothersead, Charles C.	Garrett, Laura V.	31 JUL 1879 R	13	302
Motion, Edward	Johnson, Sarah	29 OCT 1884 R	19	348
Motley, Nellie	Olden, Frank J.	22 JUL 1879 R	13	289
Moton, Armstead	Harris, Mary A.	06 DEC 1877 R	11	225
Motz, Werner Carl	Bruehl, Emilie Charlotte	19 APR 1880 R	14	227
Mouch, Anna Catherine	Prelle, Fritz	20 NOV 1878 L	12	339
Moudy, Naomi K.	Jenkins, Benjamin C.	29 JAN 1884 L	18	400
Moulden, Charlotte R.	Thomas, Frank	04 JAN 1881 R	15	129
Moulden, Lillia E.	Allen, Cyrus M.	08 FEB 1882 R	16	232
Moulden, Mary	Matthews, Samuel	29 MAR 1883 R	17	370

Moulder, John N.	Trouland, Jennie	17 FEB 1883 L	17	310
Mouldin, David	Williams, Annie Eliza	02 MAR 1882	16	261
Moulding, Anna	Hayes, Frank	24 SEP 1881 R	22	5285
Moulton, Alice	Nolan, Charles Thomas	17 JUN 1883	17	500
Moulton, Charles	Jackson, Rebecca	25 DEC 1879	14	064
Moulton, Edward	Matthews, Matilda	06 SEP 1877 L	11	079
Moulton, Eliza	King, John T.	28 JUN 1878	12	114
Moulton, Emma	Wood, Jesse	29 AUG 1878	12	185
Moulton, Fannie Ellen	Lee, Reuben	15 JUL 1884 R	19	139
Moulton, Henry	Smith, Cynthia	17 JUL 1879 L	13	284
Moulton, Laurelia L.	Branson, William A.	03 DEC 1884 L	19	435
Moulton, Lucy	Webster, Joel	28 AUG 1879 R	13	344
Moulton, Mary	Woodward, Edward	03 AUG 1878 L	12	156
Mount, Ellen	Brown, Charles	02 MAY 1883 R	17	423
Mount, William J.	Golding, Harriet L.	22 JUN 1880 R	14	329
Mountjoy, Anthony	Curtis, Christiana	11 SEP 1884 L	19	242
Mountjoy, Catherine H.	Blanton, George W.	16 SEP 1880 R	14	449
Mountjoy, David	Robinson, Bettie	30 SEP 1885 L	20	449
Mowbray, Frank de	Evans, French S.	31 MAR 1885 R	20	138
Moxley, Alice	Anderson, Stephen	07 JUN 1882	16	369
Moxley, Charles	Drummer, Martha	05 FEB 1885	20	060
Moxley, Florence R.	Pattison, Frank H.	10 DEC 1884 L	19	448
Moxley, Gertrude	Johnson, Rubin	28 OCT 1880 R	15	018
Moxley, Ida B.	Drury, George W.	06 MAR 1883 R	17	332
Moxley, Lloyd	Towler, Maria	20 NOV 1884 R	19	399
Moxley, Mary E.	Mulloy, James Eugene	27 NOV 1881 R	16	089
Moynihan, Catherine	Boyd, Milton P.	08 OCT 1881 R	16	014
Moynihan, Cornelius J.	Reichert, Katie F.	14 APR 1885	20	162
Moynihan, Mary E.	Kinsey, Joseph A.	27 DEC 1881 L	16	159
Mozee, William	Lancaster, Catherine Bost, Mrs.	02 FEB 1882 R	16	220
Mudd, Anna C.	Carter, Charles F.	25 SEP 1879 R	13	387
Mudd, Daniel H.	Benson, Mary	07 APR 1883 L	17	385
Mudd, Ernest F.	Hardesty, Anna J.	06 JUN 1878 L	12	090
Mudd, Gertrude C.	Johnson, Edward N.	23 APR 1884	18	529
Mudd, Hattie	Fowler, Ambrose	17 FEB 1878	11	344
Mudd, John F.	Butler, Louisa	02 SEP 1882	17	002
Mudd, Rufus H.	Fearson, Ella S.	19 JUN 1882 L	16	418
Mudd, William H.	Early, Martha Jane	16 JUN 1881 R	15	317
Muddiman, Anne E.	Benner, George L.	21 MAY 1884 R	19	030
Muddiman, Laura Gertrude	Watson, John Mark	05 DEC 1878 R	12	369
Mueller, Heinrich, Jr.	Garner, Mollie F.	13 MAY 1880 R	14	269
Mueller, Lany	Thompson, J. Ashley	23 MAY 1882 R	16	373
Muggles, Kate	Salser, Frank	31 DEC 1879 R	14	082
Mugler, Hamlet M.	Guy, Minnie	08 JAN 1883 R	17	243
Mühler, Henry	Kraus, Annie	16 JUL 1880 L	14	365
Muhlhofer, Emma E.	Whitacre, Joseph D.	06 MAY 1885	20	209
Muir, Mabel Olive	Howell, James Notley	01 SEP 1880 R	14	424
Mulcahy, Mary E.	Harman, William H.	15 NOV 1879 L	13	489
Mulcahy, Michael A.	Morrow, Harriet A.	29 DEC 1878 R	12	406
Muldary, Catharine	Prosser, Erastus S.	23 JAN 1878	11	315
Muldoon, Celia T.	Payne, James F.	18 OCT 1882 L	17	080
Muldoon, E.F.	Powers, Annie M.	29 DEC 1879	14	078
Muldoon, Mamie E.	Voigt, William O.	24 SEP 1884 L	19	267
Mulfinger, Conrad	Sparrow, Flora	23 JUN 1885 R	20	288
Mulhall, Joseph	Sullivan, Maggie	03 AUG 1885 L	20	348
Mulhare, Joseph F.	Burke, Maggie A.	23 AUG 1884 L	19	205
Mulholland, John	Buckley, Mary M.	28 JAN 1880 R	14	124
Mullen, Annie	White, Brandie	23 JUN 1879 R	13	245

Name	Spouse	Date	Vol	Page
Mullen, Daniel P.	Coffey, Margaret A.	14 OCT 1879 R	13	420
Mullen, John	Washington, Matilda	25 MAY 1878	12	063
Mullen, John T.	Bernard, Cornelia C.	16 MAY 1878	12	054
Mullen, Luther P.	Russell, Frankie A.	14 APR 1885 R	20	164
Muller, Henry Joseph	Summers, Ida	18 MAY 1885 R	20	227
Müller, Alice	Stanze, Christian	26 DEC 1882 L	17	212
Müller, Charles	Wilson, Martha, Mrs.	15 MAY 1884 R	19	021
Müller, Christian	Sommersfeld, Juliana Augusta	19 MAR 1882 R	16	281
Müller, Kathinka	Brachhoogel, Udo	12 JAN 1878 L	11	302
Mullican, John E.	Bloudon, Martha Jane	10 FEB 1880 R	14	144
Mullican, Marian C.	Saunders, Charles S.	15 MAY 1884	19	022
Mulligan, William G.	Kent, Lizzie F.	18 DEC 1879 R	14	055
Mulliken, Martha Virginia	Wines, Guy Woodworth	23 NOV 1881 L	16	093
Mulliken, Mary O.	Wilcox, Andrew C.	24 FEB 1879 L	13	074
Mullikin, Richard T.	Moore, Barbara E.	08 NOV 1883 R	18	233
Mullin, Edward J.	Foos, Kate V.	29 NOV 1882 R	17	156
Mullin, Kate R.	Walter, James T.	27 JAN 1880 L	14	123
Mullin, Mary	Frain, Michael	05 MAY 1879 R	13	173
Mullin, Mollie M.	Gaskins, Charles H.	12 OCT 1880 R	14	487
Mullin, Philip E.	McCurdy, Katie B.	18 JAN 1882	16	199
Mulling, Annie	Meredith, Mitchell Thos.	11 MAR 1885 L	20	107
Mullintree, Sarah E.	Taylor, Charles W.	27 JUN 1878	12	111
Mullory, Frank P.	O'Brien, Sarah	05 OCT 1881 L	16	010
Mulloy, James Eugene	Moxley, Mary E.	27 NOV 1881 R	16	089
Mulquin, Mary A.	Caton, George D.	30 OCT 1879 L	13	454
Mulvahill, Mary E.	Hauf, John L.	21 MAY 1883 R	17	454
Mumford, Emma	Clute, Charles P.	17 MAR 1885	20	118
Mumford, J.C.	Oswill, Sarah	16 APR 1878 L	12	009
Mumford, Maria A.	Liggons, Samuel C.	04 MAY 1882 L	16	348
Mumford, Moses	Gray, Georgianna	08 MAR 1881 L	15	220
Mumma, Mary Alice	Roberts, Theophilus D.	16 OCT 1878 R	12	204
Mumper, Harvey J.	Trout, Lydia A.	24 DEC 1879	14	070
Munday, Cary P.	Wilkins, Kate V.	28 SEP 1885 R	20	444
Munday, Ellen	Spencer, Richard	11 SEP 1879 R	13	350
Mundell, Annie E.	Layton, Almanzer W.	24 DEC 1884 R	19	491
Mundell, Benjamin M.	Rose, Catherine	06 MAY 1879 R	13	177
Mundell, Mary Martha	Fonda, Charles Bradford	25 OCT 1882 R	17	093
Mundell, Samuel R.	Newton, Mary	29 NOV 1878 L	12	355
Mundheim, Albert K.	Rothberg, Paulina	08 MAY 1883 R	17	432
Mundlein, Charlotte	Hellriegel, Michael	22 MAY 1879	13	201
Mundy, Florence V.	Sims, Eudeliene A.	09 NOV 1881 R	16	068
Mundy, William H.	Willis, Malinda C.	05 APR 1882 R	16	302
Munford, Elijah	Clark, Susie	04 FEB 1885 R	20	047
Mungen, Theodore	Hennicke, Helen J.	28 JUN 1878	12	116
Munn, Clarence Emerson	Merrick, Adelaide Emily	30 JUN 1885 R	20	300
Munro, David M.	Ranney, Elizabeth B.	08 DEC 1880	15	084
Munro, Mary Catherine	Hill, Alexander P., Jr.	25 APR 1883	17	406
Munroe, Alice Broom	Winlock, William Crawford	02 JUN 1883 R	17	472
Munroe, Edward	Talbot, Emeline	04 MAR 1879	13	088
Munroe, Elizabeth	Wells, James	26 DEC 1877 L	11	270
Munroe, Ella	Beller, James H.	29 NOV 1882 R	17	157
Munroe, Grace Ellen	Turner, Chapman	05 MAY 1884 L	19	005
Munroe, Jennie	Butler, Isaac	21 AUG 1882 R	17	033
Munroe, Samuel	Matthews, Annie	06 SEP 1883 L	18	114
Munroe, Sarah	Payne, Samuel	01 MAR 1884	18	453
Munroe, Thomas Eugene	Chamblin, Manie	24 SEP 1885 R	20	439
Munson, Ollie	Ellicott, Charles P.	19 DEC 1881 R	16	137
Munt, Victoria	Miner, Frank	26 JUN 1878 L	12	114

Munzinger, Charles	Sergeon, Catharine R.	06 NOV 1884 R	19	367
Murchant, Fannie M.	Donaldson, Naaman	24 FEB 1881	15	203
Murdock, David B.	Williams, Annie E.	20 JAN 1885 L	20	028
Murdock, John B.	Pennebaker, Phoebe	18 NOV 1880	15	056
Murdock, Laura V.	Church, Joseph B.	06 JUN 1882	16	395
Murdock, Mary Eliz.	England, Robert Ezra	17 FEB 1885 R	20	072
Murdock, Robert A.	Henderson, Janie M.	12 DEC 1878	12	377
Murphey, Bridget	Fitan, James	08 JAN 1884 L	18	368
Murphey, Florence S.	Hoyt, Frederick A.	03 APR 1883 L	17	377
Murphy, Amanda	Dorsey, Thomas	21 JAN 1880 L	14	114
Murphy, Annie	Dunn, Dennis	19 FEB 1878 L	11	349
Murphy, Annie	Geier, Bernard J.	19 SEP 1882 L	17	028
Murphy, Annie	Greer, Marcus	04 JUN 1884 R	19	056
Murphy, Annie	Donovan, Jeremiah E.	26 SEP 1885 L	20	443
Murphy, Arthur, Jr.	Nokes, Florence K.	05 JUN 1883 R	17	476
Murphy, Augusta	Thurston, Frederick	07 MAY 1883 L	17	431
Murphy, Charles Wash.	Worthan, Kate McCathran	02 MAR 1885 R	33	8069
Murphy, Elizabeth	Murphy, John	09 JUL 1881 L	15	397
Murphy, Hannah A.	Wise, Charles B.	06 OCT 1880 L	14	478
Murphy, Ida M.	Golden, John Arthur	13 JAN 1882 R	16	193
Murphy, Isbell Neal	Benson, Richard J.	22 APR 1880 R	14	233
Murphy, James	Roan, Hannah	01 MAY 1880 L	14	248
Murphy, James J.	Farrington, Mary A.	11 DEC 1879 L	14	044
Murphy, Jeremiah J.	Kane, Lizzie M.	06 SEP 1882 L	17	007
Murphy, John	Keating, Delia	15 JUL 1877	11	022
Murphy, John	Mades, Catharine, Mrs.	17 OCT 1878	12	268
Murphy, John	Minyburg, Amelia	12 SEP 1878 R	12	214
Murphy, John	Murphy, Elizabeth	09 JUL 1881 L	15	397
Murphy, John	Wines, Ada Hise	17 AUG 1881 L	15	450
Murphy, Joseph	Trammell, Ida Lee	15 JAN 1882	16	194
Murphy, Joseph	Parker, Mary Ann	25 SEP 1884 L	19	269
Murphy, Joseph C.	O'Connor, Mary	29 NOV 1884 L	19	426
Murphy, Joseph R.	Luckett, Celia	20 OCT 1884	19	322
Murphy, Josephine	Cardew, William H.	24 MAY 1881 L	15	323
Murphy, Julia E.	Benson, Thomas E.	18 JAN 1883	17	263
Murphy, Kate	Maloney, James	28 JAN 1882 L	16	214
Murphy, Kate E.	McCrossin, Henry	20 JUN 1883	18	004
Murphy, Katie	Norton, Daniel	09 DEC 1882 L	17	176
Murphy, Katta	Tumelety, Hugh B.	17 JAN 1878 L	11	310
Murphy, Kossuth M.	Schutter, Clara M.	22 FEB 1883 R	17	314
Murphy, Lillie	Scheerer, John S.	01 NOV 1882 R	17	105
Murphy, Lula L.	Jameson, William P.	19 AUG 1884 L	19	193
Murphy, Maggie A.	O'Connor, Michael J.	30 JUL 1883 L	18	066
Murphy, Mamie	Dyer, Andrew Stanislaus	16 MAY 1882 L	16	362
Murphy, Margaret	Katz, Charley	02 APR 1879 L	13	125
Murphy, Mary	Schreiver, Philip	02 OCT 1879 R	13	398
Murphy, Mary A.	Mercer, George H.	15 NOV 1884	19	383
Murphy, Mary Anne	Lynch, John	24 FEB 1879	13	073
Murphy, Mary E.	Douglass, Ambrose M.	22 DEC 1877	11	258
Murphy, Mary E.	Collins, George W.	30 JUN 1882 R	16	432
Murphy, Mary Henrietta Luvina	Bailey, John Wm.	20 FEB 1883	17	312
Murphy, Mary J.	Chism, Tilly A.	18 MAR 1879 L	13	106
Murphy, Mary Morrissey	Clarke, Albert S.	27 NOV 1879 R	14	017
Murphy, Mildred	Taylor, Richard	16 DEC 1884 R	19	462
Murphy, Nellie A.	Harrington, David J.	16 APR 1884 R	18	514
Murphy, Nellie B.	Harding, Thomas H.	17 OCT 1882 L	17	075
Murphy, Nellie C.	Roche, William E.	05 FEB 1883 L	17	291
Murphy, Rose	Ready, Michael	02 JUL 1878 L	12	120

Name	Spouse	Date		
Murphy, Rose L.	Lynch, Michael A.	24 FEB 1881 L	15	202
Murphy, William	Carroll, Catharine	20 MAY 1879 R	13	197
Murphy, William	Kingston, Catherine	01 JUL 1879 L	13	261
Murphy, William	Walker, Nellie M.	13 JUN 1882 R	16	409
Murphy, Wm. Augustus	Hunt, Georgia Anna	08 APR 1885 R	20	149
Murray, Addie	Jackson, Andrew	11 FEB 1880	14	147
Murray, Alice E.	Dant, Edward E.	09 SEP 1885	20	435
Murray, Annie O.	Smith, Albert	12 OCT 1881	16	003
Murray, Augusta L.	Foster, Ross H.	12 MAY 1884	19	014
Murray, Catherine	Richardson, James	04 OCT 1881 R	16	004
Murray, Charles D.	Hammond, Ella J.	05 AUG 1884 R	19	168
Murray, Clare	Postley, Charles E.	27 DEC 1881 R	16	140
Murray, Clarence	Dean, Frances	01 JUN 1882 L	16	388
Murray, Daniel	Evans, Anna J.	02 APR 1879	13	121
Murray, Elias H.	Leary, Ella	12 SEP 1878 R	12	216
Murray, Elizabeth	Russell, John R.	23 NOV 1881	16	071
Murray, Ella May	Koch, William	23 NOV 1880 R	15	062
Murray, Emma Jackson	Seeny, James	20 NOV 1879 R	13	499
Murray, Emma Louisa	Myers, Adam	22 MAY 1881 R	15	320
Murray, George E.	Spratley, Virginia Mills	01 JAN 1884 R	18	353
Murray, George E.	Hatcher, Jeannette W.	25 APR 1884 R	18	533
Murray, George William	Spalding, Mary A.	08 OCT 1885	20	473
Murray, H.T.	Tolson, K.M.	23 MAY 1883 R	17	459
Murray, Harry	Lee, Catherine	02 JUL 1881	15	386
Murray, J. Harry	Tucker, Julia T.	19 APR 1882 L	16	324
Murray, James A.	Cage, Jeannette M.	15 MAY 1881	15	307
Murray, John	Humphreys, Mary	20 MAR 1882	16	281
Murray, John	Kenneally, Mary M.	29 JUL 1885 L	20	345
Murray, Lewis W.	Wilson, Sophia S.	29 DEC 1881 L	16	169
Murray, Malinda	Miller, Charles	24 MAY 1878 R	12	050
Murray, Margaret A.	Finegan, John	28 SEP 1885 L	20	444
Murray, Margaret J.	Allen, George	07 MAR 1881	15	217
Murray, Margaret Rachel	Widmyer, Thomas Walter	07 NOV 1881 R	16	065
Murray, Mary	Hilton, James H.	16 JAN 1878 L	11	305
Murray, Mary	Grady, William E.	29 MAR 1881 R	15	241
Murray, Mary	Barton, William W.	03 JUL 1883 L	18	034
Murray, Mary A.	Cassidy, Edward F.	17 APR 1884 R	18	517
Murray, Mary C.	Cloey, James F.	18 DEC 1883	18	324
Murray, Mary Emory	Norris, William	15 OCT 1879 R	13	423
Murray, Maud M.	Downs, Thomas B.	23 FEB 1881 R	15	199
Murray, Oscar	Silas, Caroline	04 OCT 1884 L	19	286
Murray, Owen	Cady, Mary J.	30 JUL 1881 L	15	427
Murray, Philip	Peel, Jane	02 OCT 1882 L	17	047
Murray, Rosa	Jackson, John H.	23 NOV 1882 L	17	145
Murray, Ruth	Collett, John H.	22 JUN 1882 L	16	422
Murray, Spencer, Jr.	Myers, Maggie E.	11 SEP 1879	13	359
Murray, Virginia	Brooks, Henson	05 DEC 1884 L	19	437
Murray, Walter Walls	Koch, Adelaide M.	26 FEB 1884	18	443
Murray, William Henry	Lee, Rosa	15 NOV 1877 R	11	187
Murray, William J.	Forsberg, Helen	14 MAY 1878 R	12	050
Murry, Ellen	Fletcher, Henry	29 JAN 1880 R	14	122
Muse, Annie	Taylor, Philip A.	05 JUL 1883 L	18	036
Muse, Fannie	Weaver, George O.	25 OCT 1877	11	156
Muse, William	Hipkins, Penny	27 AUG 1880	14	419
Muse, William Henry	Briant, Margaret Eliza	20 SEP 1880	14	452
Musgrove, Ella M.	Gates, George W.	12 DEC 1880 R	15	092
Mutersbaugh, Georgie Etta	Brubaker, Jonas M.	25 NOV 1879 R	14	004
Myer, William	Newman, Hannah	08 OCT 1878 R	12	257

Myers, Adam	Murray, Emma Louisa	22 MAY 1881 R	15	320
Myers, Alice	Smith, Charles	10 JUN 1879 R	13	223
Myers, Alice A.	Peirce, Wilbert	13 FEB 1879	13	059
Myers, Anna Eliza	Manning, James	09 JUN 1878	12	091
Myers, Annie	Shorter, William	25 JUL 1882 R	16	440
Myers, Charles	Myers, Ida	05 AUG 1885 R	20	355
Myers, Edward E.	Cook, Violet E.	03 SEP 1884	19	220
Myers, Elizabeth	Reilley, P.S.	24 MAY 1885	20	235
Myers, Ellis Gregg	Fletcher, Franzeona M.	31 DEC 1883 R	18	356
Myers, Evelyn F.	Travers, Olivia H.	19 APR 1879 R	13	151
Myers, Flora B. (Spangler)	McPherson, Lewis Edwin	28 AUG 1883 R	18	103
Myers, Fred	Wagner, Emma	23 NOV 1883	18	273
Myers, Genevive E.	Evans, Charles Alfred	26 NOV 1879 R	14	011
Myers, Henrietta B.	Dixon, William S.	11 JUN 1884 R	19	076
Myers, Henry	Marshall, Martha	20 APR 1882	16	327
Myers, Hyter	Lockley, Lucy	11 APR 1878 R	12	001
Myers, Ida	Myers, Charles	05 AUG 1885 R	20	355
Myers, J.P.	Donnelly, Helen L.	24 JAN 1880 L	14	119
Myers, Janie Frances	Cheseldine, Aug. Dunn.	05 JUN 1884 R	19	061
Myers, John Solon	McDonald, Mary Bell	05 DEC 1877	11	219
Myers, Joseph	Nickens, Eliza	03 MAR 1884 L	18	454
Myers, Joseph H.	Dean, Malisha A.	27 JUL 1881 R	15	420
Myers, Kate	Nicholson, W.H.	31 OCT 1881	15	462
Myers, Katie	Cline, John William	04 MAY 1878	12	036
Myers, Katie H.	Emmert, John H.	06 APR 1881 L	15	249
Myers, Leonora B.	Smith, Walter R.	26 FEB 1885	20	086
Myers, Lucy L.	Cruit, John W.	08 JAN 1884	18	369
Myers, Maggie E.	Murray, Spencer, Jr.	11 SEP 1879	13	359
Myers, Margaret	Bransom, John James	24 OCT 1883	18	208
Myers, Maria	Sands, Joseph	07 FEB 1878	11	332
Myers, Marion Isabelle	Paine, Frederick Henry	17 FEB 1885 R	20	073
Myers, Mary	Clark, Henry	04 APR 1878	11	403
Myers, Mary	Tyler, James	09 JUN 1879 L	13	224
Myers, Mary	Stern, Myer	15 MAR 1881	15	227
Myers, Mary	Barrett, Michael	16 JUN 1883 L	17	497
Myers, Mary Eveline	DeLacy, William H.	20 FEB 1884 R	18	434
Myers, Robert	Lee, Lucretia	15 NOV 1883	18	259
Myers, Sadie G.	Barnes, Charles H.	10 FEB 1884 R	18	411
Myers, Susie P.	Higgins, Lucius Cornelius	06 NOV 1879 R	13	464
Myers, Thomas	Eden, Carrie V.	14 JUL 1881	15	396
Myers, Wallace E.	Sedgwick, Elizabeth	26 NOV 1880 L	15	068
Myers, Washington O.	Starliper, Elsie	27 OCT 1883 R	18	219
Myers, Willard H.	Kingsbury, Roberta A.	05 NOV 1884 L	19	358
Myers, William	Powers, Lavina	20 MAY 1885 L	20	230
Myers, Zachary	Payne, Sarah	08 APR 1880	14	216
Mygatt, Lois	Wilcox, John F.	10 NOV 1881 L	16	070
Mylins, Mary L.	Babendreier, Fred L.	17 SEP 1885 R	20	425

N

Nace, Charles L.	Hoover, Clara E.	16 AUG 1882 R	16	482
Nachman, Hannah	Clark, Morris	18 JAN 1882 R	16	197
Naddy, Maggie J.	Creagh, James F.	08 MAY 1882 L	16	352
Nadin, Arthur	Hablemann, Annie M.	19 JUL 1880 R	14	367
Naecker, Ludwig	Isemann, Sophie	03 JUN 1879	13	217
Nagel, Charles	Walker, Ida L.	27 OCT 1880 R	15	015
Nailor, Richard Thomas	Taylor, Mary Eugenia	27 DEC 1883	18	349
Nairn, Mary J.	Heiberger, Franz J.	03 SEP 1878 R	12	194
Nalle, Agnes M.	Riley, Jerome R.	28 AUG 1877	11	069
Nalle, Edward G.	Ward, Finetta	18 OCT 1882 R	17	079
Nalle, John C.	Jones, Rosa L.	27 MAR 1879	13	111
Nalley, Charles K.	Campbell, Ella B.	29 SEP 1881 L	15	510
Nalley, Charles K.	Lees, Clara L.	05 FEB 1883 R	17	286
Nalley, Florence J.	Walls, George N.	24 JAN 1883 R	17	272
Nalley, Isabella R.	Whalley, William H.	02 AUG 1882 L	16	466
Nalley, James E.	Harper, Mary E.	21 APR 1885 L	20	178
Nalley, James T.	Jenkins, Mary E.	12 JUN 1884	19	081
Nalley, John H.	Magruder, Laura Virginia	20 APR 1881 R	15	266
Nalley, Kathrin	Draeger, George	11 MAR 1878 L	11	377
Nalley, Mary A.	Reisenburg, William	12 NOV 1883 R	18	247
Nalley, Mary Ellen	Baker, Charles	21 OCT 1877	11	147
Nalley, Matilda	Granery, Michael	13 DEC 1882 R	17	182
Nalley, Nona C.	Farrell, J.	30 DEC 1884 L	19	506
Nalley, Wm. W.	Parker, Katie V.	08 NOV 1883 R	18	242
Nalls, Bryant B.	Brown, Josephine	21 JAN 1879 R	13	025
Nally, Maggie	Cole, Fred W.	30 APR 1884 R	18	545
Nally, Rebecca	Kimmell, Frank P.	09 FEB 1882 L	16	235
Nally, Wesley	Johnson, Lucy	27 JAN 1884	18	389
Napflie, Pauline	Sink, Frederick	02 JUN 1883 R	17	452
Napier, Edward A.	Bowles, Belle A.	23 JUL 1883	18	056
Napier, James C.	Langston, Nettie D.	02 OCT 1878 R	12	247
Napier, Jennie	Johnson, Thomas	25 OCT 1883 R	18	214
Napoleon, Louis	Wallace, Louisa	16 JUL 1885 R	20	324
Nappel, Annie	Howard, George L.	13 MAR 1882 L	16	275
Narl, Henry	Bell, Rachel A.	02 DEC 1884	19	429
Nary, Sarah	Conway, William	10 AUG 1882 R	16	475
Nash, Alice V.	Sullivan, William J.	14 AUG 1884	19	187
Nash, Annie	Webster, William	13 SEP 1877	11	087
Nash, Annie	Doleman, Charles M.	20 MAR 1880 R	14	190
Nash, Candus Ann	Chinn, Henry W.	29 NOV 1877	11	213
Nash, Charles Francis	Monroe, Rebecca M.	15 JAN 1881 R	15	151
Nash, Edward	Taylor, Anne R.	30 JUN 1877 L	11	003
Nash, Emma J.	Gill, Albert E.	30 JUL 1877 L	11	034
Nash, Frances	Donnelly, James	25 JAN 1879 R	13	034
Nash, Frances F.	Wylie, James H.	23 JUL 1878 L	12	145
Nash, George J.	Coggins, Ella E.	28 NOV 1882 R	17	154
Nash, George W.	Shugrue, Julia	09 AUG 1879 L	13	314
Nash, Henry E.	Meddow, Marthy E.	22 JUL 1881 L	15	413
Nash, James R.	America, Sallie Y.	18 JUN 1879 R	13	237
Nash, Jesse	Watson, Annie	29 DEC 1881 L	16	172
Nash, John W.	Watson, Martha	27 JUN 1884 R	19	083
Nash, Martha	Ragan, J.M.	02 SEP 1877 R	11	043
Nash, Melvina	Banks, John	16 SEP 1880 R	14	448
Nash, Mollie	Harding, George W.	17 OCT 1882	17	077
Nash, Nicholas M.	Armstrong, Ella V.	30 JAN 1882 R	16	215
Nash, Susie	Davis, Lon S.	26 OCT 1881	16	046
Nash, Thomas J.	Pierman, Bettie C.	09 OCT 1883 L	18	182

D.C. Marriage Records Index, June 28, 1877 to October 19, 1885   335

Name	Spouse	Date		
Nash, Willie	Going, Mildred	25 JUL 1882	16	457
Nass, Carlena	Goebel, George	12 SEP 1878	12	211
Nass, Katie	Schench, Charles D.	17 SEP 1884	19	252
Nasser, Emily Virginia	Bremmer, William	19 OCT 1880 R	14	491
Nathanson, Edward	Behrend, Rebecca	12 JUN 1883 R	17	482
Nau, Andrew Henry	Walterholter, Anna Mary Augusta	27 MAR 1878 L	11	395
Nauck, Arthur A.	Walter, Sophia Catherine	28 MAY 1878 R	12	071
Naughton, Nellie L.	Welsh, John A.	08 OCT 1882	17	057
Naughton, Patrick	Driscoll, Ellen	11 JUN 1885 L	20	270
Nave, Carrie N.	Parker, Charles H.	22 JUN 1882	16	422
Naylor, Amanda	Contee, Robert	14 JUN 1881 L	15	359
Naylor, Charles E.	Gieseking, Amelia H.	14 APR 1885 R	20	163
Naylor, Jane Elizabeth	Gittings, William Edward	09 JAN 1882 R	16	186
Naylor, Janie L.	Strum, Gustave P.	15 FEB 1881 R	15	190
Naylor, Lulie	Scott, Frank T.	04 JAN 1882 L	16	180
Naylor, Maggie A.	Edmonston, Robert O.	06 APR 1880 L	14	212
Naylor, William J.	Robinson, Elizabeth B.	06 JUN 1882	16	397
Neal, Ary Anna	Neal, Daniel	12 MAR 1878	11	378
Neal, Asbury	Griffin, Lucy	04 MAY 1880	14	252
Neal, Benjamin F.	Bundy, Emma	03 JUL 1879 R	13	258
Neal, Daniel	Neal, Ary Anna	12 MAR 1878	11	378
Neal, Emma	Harrison, James W.	12 JUN 1879	13	229
Neal, Fannie	Carter, Enoch	20 OCT 1881 L	16	037
Neal, Georgie	Hill, Willie F.	01 JAN 1880 R	14	076
Neal, Horatio	Collins, Julia E.	22 MAY 1883	17	455
Neal, Lewis Wm. Henry	Foster, Mary Frances	31 AUG 1885 L	20	393
Neal, Maria	Young, James	15 DEC 1879 R	14	049
Neal, Martha	Wess, Charles T.	02 AUG 1884	19	165
Neal, Mary J.	Jones, Francis A.	03 FEB 1880 L	14	133
Neal, P.D.	Crabbe, Cornelius C.	26 JUN 1878	12	114
Neal, Richard	Lewis, Mary	11 DEC 1884 L	19	454
Neal, Robert	Vane, Sarah	05 MAY 1881 R	15	292
Neal, Sophia E.	Fleetwood, Moses	08 MAY 1879	13	180
Neal, William	Stuart, Eliza	19 JUL 1884	19	147
Neale, Adelaide Eloise	Meade, Eugene Carlton	21 NOV 1880 R	15	058
Neale, Charles A.	Beaman, Addie M.	09 JAN 1883 L	17	246
Neale, Francis D.	Tolson, Rose Armatage Carter B.	16 FEB 1885 R	20	067
Neale, Ida F.	Charles, W.B.	27 FEB 1878 L	11	361
Neale, Jane	Simmons, Zachariah	11 JUN 1885 L	20	267
Neale, Julia V.	Clarke, Charles, M.D.	17 MAY 1883 R	17	446
Neale, Lue	Mack, Frank	19 DEC 1883 L	18	329
Neale, Mary Ellen	Russell, John C.	15 MAR 1883 L	17	345
Neale, Richard A.	Parker, Mary A.	30 MAY 1883 R	17	452
Nealy, Sid H.	Goff, Caroline E.	25 MAY 1881 R	15	326
Nebb, John	Weber, Louise [Perrot]	23 MAR 1885 R	20	115
Neenan, Katie A.	Dwire, Edward F.	29 APR 1885 R	20	195
Neenan, Stephen J.	Byrns, Teresa	15 MAY 1883 L	17	443
Neff, Kate F.	Ruppert, Frank J.	21 NOV 1882 L	17	141
Neger, Caroline E. Geiger	Eickel, Henry	01 DEC 1880 R	15	074
Neger, J. Kate	Jeffries, James H.	05 JUL 1884	19	114
Neger, Kale	Jeffries, James	29 SEP 1883 L	18	161
Nehren, Margaret	Lentbecher, Christian	01 MAR 1882 R	16	263
Neidfeldt, Carrie M.	Barnaclo, William Alphonso	18 JUN 1881 R	15	367
Neidomanski, Fred J.	Hulien, Ella	29 JUL 1878	12	149
Neilson, Julia	Poindexter, William M.	06 OCT 1881	16	011
Neilson, Louis	Rodgers, Anne Perry	28 OCT 1880 R	14	486
Neitzey, Augustus	Benhardt, Catharine	05 AUG 1885	20	354
Nellie, Conner	Selucius, Garfield	03 JAN 1881 L	15	135

Nelligan, Mary	Hughes, John	19 SEP 1878 L	12	228
Nelson, Andrew	Struder, Mary A.	01 MAY 1883 R	17	423
Nelson, Anna	Lacey, Lewis	26 MAY 1880 L	14	291
Nelson, Annie	Bundy, William Henry	07 JUN 1881 L	15	349
Nelson, Annie	Robinson, Cornelius	05 JUL 1882 L	16	439
Nelson, Augustus	Brown, Lucy	10 JAN 1878 R	11	300
Nelson, Caroline, Mrs.	Walters, James	14 AUG 1879 R	13	317
Nelson, Charles E.	Clore, Elizabeth J.	21 AUG 1879 L	13	330
Nelson, Edmonia	Gunnell, Joshua	27 MAR 1878 L	11	393
Nelson, Ella	Flemons, Ross	04 MAR 1885 R	20	094
Nelson, Ellen	Groves, George	21 JUN 1883 L	18	007
Nelson, Estella	Barnes, Andrew	19 JUN 1884 R	19	091
Nelson, Eva	Green, John	21 OCT 1879 L	13	434
Nelson, George H.	Griemsbey, Emma J.	01 JUN 1882	16	386
Nelson, George W.	Parker, Louisa	08 JUL 1870	13	274
Nelson, Georgiana V.	Townsend, Thornton	12 SEP 1878 R	12	193
Nelson, Hannah	Seals, Ferdinand	31 JUL 1885 L	20	347
Nelson, Harry	Williams, Laura	23 DEC 1882	17	204
Nelson, Harvie H.	Johnson, William E.	16 JUN 1880 R	14	315
Nelson, Hattie	Dale, Charley	28 JUN 1883 R	18	023
Nelson, Henry	Brannan, Susan	23 AUG 1877 L	11	063
Nelson, Ira C.	Grubbs, Emma W.	06 MAY 1885 R	20	208
Nelson, James B.	Clements, Eleanor	16 MAY 1878 L	12	052
Nelson, John	Wright, Ann	30 DEC 1879 R	14	080
Nelson, John Benjamin	Hall, Dora Lee	28 AUG 1884	19	214
Nelson, Julius	Bradford, Julia	06 JUL 1882 L	16	440
Nelson, Lewis	Dickerson, Julia	12 JUN 1879 L	13	232
Nelson, Lucy	Smith, Albert	28 AUG 1879 R	13	332
Nelson, Margaret A.	Howlin, Patrick Henry	02 FEB 1880 R	14	130
Nelson, Mary	Robertson, Charles	12 JUN 1879 L	13	230
Nelson, Mary	Jackson, Samuel	22 JUN 1880 R	14	328
Nelson, Mary	Johnson, Richard	15 OCT 1882	17	070
Nelson, Mary	Rivers, Randall	30 NOV 1882 R	17	160
Nelson, Mary Ann	Bruce, John Thomas	22 DEC 1879 R	14	066
Nelson, Mary E.	Montgomery, George	09 NOV 1880 R	15	039
Nelson, Mary Jane	Gordon, G.W.	08 DEC 1881 L	16	121
Nelson, Mary L.	Taliaferro, George W.	29 APR 1878	12	028
Nelson, Mary M.	Lee, Samuel	02 DEC 1879 R	14	023
Nelson, Mary Susan	Dade, Daniel B.	15 FEB 1879 R	13	061
Nelson, Missouri C.	Arnold, William H.	01 AUG 1881 L	15	429
Nelson, Parker A.	Anderson, Laura A.	23 DEC 1878	12	394
Nelson, Peter	Hennessy, Martha	29 APR 1882 L	16	340
Nelson, Phillip	Blair, Emma	15 APR 1879	13	142
Nelson, Robert	Webb, Leddy	19 SEP 1878	12	227
Nelson, Robert	Mills, Jane	19 JAN 1882 R	16	202
Nelson, Robert	Johnson, Alice	01 OCT 1884 L	19	278
Nelson, Robert	Jenkins, Maria	30 APR 1885	20	198
Nelson, Samuel	Tasker, Sarah	27 JUL 1882 R	16	460
Nelson, Sarah A.	Bell, William W.	06 SEP 1883	18	115
Nelson, Sarah Jane	Hawkins, Robert H.	26 JUL 1884	19	159
Nelson, Thomas	Moore, Ida	06 DEC 1879 L	14	032
Nelson, Walter	Syas, Anne	03 MAR 1882 R	16	266
Nelygan, Henry	Burke, Annie	20 APR 1878 L	12	013
Nephutt, Andrew	Brockhaus, Anna	08 JAN 1882	16	186
Nervis, Catherine	Reed, Thompson	21 OCT 1879 R	13	436
Nervis, Elizabeth	Lee, Lewis	27 DEC 1883 R	18	351
Nesler, Mary	Schleger, Frederick	14 JUN 1884 L	19	084
Nesmith, Frank E.	Watson, Emma Lulu	24 FEB 1882 R	16	258

Nessenson, Sophia	Bredekamp, Henry	28 FEB 1884	18	449
Nessi, Ulderico	Zimmer, Mary	05 DEC 1881 L	16	114
Nessline, Lizzie	Heeter, Uriah	02 DEC 1877 R	11	213
Netter, David	Peyton, Evelena	07 SEP 1882 R	17	013
Neuchter, Katherine	Hoffman, Fred	15 OCT 1883	18	193
Neuhaus, Ido	Immore, Dorothea	27 DEC 1879 R	16	3886
Neujahr, Maggie A.	Blinkard, William W.	24 APR 1879 R	13	158
Neumann, Margaretta	Becker, Diederich	27 OCT 1877 L	11	158
Neumeister, Conrad	Zeidler, Catherine	24 NOV 1884 L	19	405
Neumeyer, Lora E.	Tennesson, John Thomas	16 JUN 1879	13	232
Neurath, John V.	Kloman, Annie M.	20 JAN 1881 R	15	158
Neurath, Louisa	Otto, Henry Louis	10 DEC 1884 R	19	447
Neven, William Henry	Fisher, Barbara	12 FEB 1878 L	11	337
Neverson, Actia Virginia	Ricks, William	28 AUG 1879	13	341
Nevet, William	Gantt, Agnes	07 JUL 1884	19	125
Nevill, Mary A.	Weaver, Joseph A.	14 SEP 1885 L	20	413
Nevin, Mary	Connor, Martin	28 JAN 1878 L	11	319
Nevins, Cecile	Ions, Robert A.	05 SEP 1879 R	13	354
Nevitt, James C.	Kaiser, Sarah C.	10 MAY 1881 R	15	299
Nevitt, Mary	Johnson, Alexander	27 SEP 1877	11	110
New, John P.	Crist, Amelia C.	24 JAN 1882 R	16	207
Newby, William H.	McKenney, Mary	30 AUG 1882 R	16	496
Newcomer, Frank	Brandlinger, Lizzie	26 MAY 1879 R	13	205
Newell, Charles	Harris, Lucy	14 SEP 1877	11	094
Newgent, Ida V.	Keller, Arthur C.	03 JUN 1884 R	19	055
Newhall, Wm. H.	Lloyd, Mary F.	14 JUL 1880 R	14	361
Newham, Thomas J.	Bresnahan, Katie E.	13 MAY 1878 L	12	049
Newland, Andrew	Bessler, Bertha	17 MAR 1885 L	20	118
Newman, Annie A.	Hitnor, William	10 FEB 1885 L	20	060
Newman, Annie Elizabeth	Banks, William Henry	01 MAY 1883 R	17	425
Newman, Anthony W.	Turner, Georgia	25 SEP 1877 L	11	106
Newman, Benjamin F.	Shipman, Eliza	27 JUN 1882 R	16	428
Newman, Charles	Harris, Matilda	17 OCT 1883 R	18	197
Newman, Dennis E.	Blackstine, Margaret A.	29 APR 1880	14	246
Newman, Elizabeth	Davis, William H.	30 DEC 1880 L	15	134
Newman, George J.	Gentner, Mary B.	15 JAN 1884 R	18	377
Newman, Hannah	Myer, William	08 OCT 1878 R	12	257
Newman, Henry	Beach, Annie A.	10 NOV 1879 R	13	474
Newman, Johanna M.	Tiverny, John A.	09 SEP 1885	20	408
Newman, John	Lewis, Clara	18 DEC 1884 R	19	471
Newman, John H.	Haney, Annie V.	07 JUN 1883	17	479
Newman, Joseph W.	Johnson, Sallie	24 SEP 1885	20	439
Newman, Maria	Jones, Harrison	28 MAY 1885	20	238
Newman, Mary	Car, George	28 JUL 1881 R	15	423
Newman, Minnie	Fleming, Abraham	29 NOV 1877 R	11	209
Newman, Oscar B.	Tait, Mary C.	02 JUL 1884 L	19	117
Newman, Randall	Johnson, Ella	16 APR 1885 R	20	168
Newman, Richard P.	Brown, Fannie	15 OCT 1885 L	20	490
Newman, Robert	Harley, Irene	06 FEB 1883 L	17	293
Newman, Wesley	Thomas, Berta L.	22 JAN 1880 R	14	118
Newman, Wm. George	Tiverny, Clara Marcellene	11 JUN 1885 R	20	268
Newmeyer, Solomon	Blumenthal, Hannah	15 JAN 1882 R	16	188
Newmyer, Hattie	Harris, Reuben	01 SEP 1880 R	14	425
Newmyer, Louis	Bensinger, May	22 NOV 1882 R	17	139
Newmyer, Mamie	Engel, David L.	17 SEP 1878 R	12	219
Newton, Bessie	Bryant, George H.	19 JUN 1883	18	002
Newton, Celestine D.	Haynie, Marian F.	02 MAR 1882 R	16	265
Newton, Francis	Brown, Josephine	06 MAY 1880 R	14	256

Newton, Frank E.	Graves, Gertrude L.	02 JUL 1883 L	18	030
Newton, Henry D.	McNeil, Jennett	09 APR 1885 R	20	137
Newton, Henson	Lawlers, Lizza	22 JUL 1880 L	14	372
Newton, James B.	Rice, Fannie B.	20 APR 1881 R	15	264
Newton, John Alexander	Jackson, Florence	30 MAR 1882 R	16	288
Newton, John W.	Highfield, Mary E.	09 JUN 1884 L	19	068
Newton, Marshall	Gaskin, Frances	25 JUL 1885 L	20	340
Newton, Mary	Mundell, Samuel R.	29 NOV 1878 L	12	355
Newton, Mary A.	Reed, Robert L.	14 NOV 1877 L	11	185
Newton, May Ellis	Smallwood, Richard Lydstone	27 NOV 1883	18	278
Newton, Samuel F.	Steele, Alida	17 JAN 1883 L	17	265
Newton, Sarah A.	McKean, Theodore F.	08 JAN 1879 R	13	008
Newton, Sarah J.	Dent, Samuel	07 FEB 1882 R	16	229
Niblack, William Caldwell	Herr, Fannie	10 FEB 1880 R	14	145
Nice, Laura E.	Keister, James H.	10 JAN 1884	18	371
Nice, William A.	Despeaux, Carrie Virginia	12 DEC 1881 R	16	125
Nichell, Mary	Twaddell, Charles P.	28 JAN 1884	18	396
Nicholas, Ada M.	Weigle, Louis	27 JUN 1885	20	298
Nicholas, James L.	Bouldin, Indiana F.	15 AUG 1877 L	11	055
Nicholas, Limus M.	Winn, Hannah	14 AUG 1879 L	13	319
Nicholas, Mary	Holmes, William	19 OCT 1880 R	14	486
Nicholas, Otway	Blackwell, Emma	14 MAY 1878 R	12	055
Nicholas, Sarah, Mrs.	Sutton, Alfred	25 SEP 1882 R	17	018
Nichols, Alice E.	Hines, Albert E.	06 MAY 1885	20	208
Nichols, Annie Cecilia	Mills, John Sedwick	14 NOV 1882 R	17	125
Nichols, Annie J.	Selby, Charles H.	08 SEP 1883	18	120
Nichols, Clinton	Miles, Katie	17 JAN 1884	18	383
Nichols, Cora	Watts, Sidney James	27 MAY 1885 R	20	241
Nichols, Edmond S.	Humphreys, Annie E.	20 AUG 1885 L	20	380
Nichols, Ensign	Tiffany, Alvira	13 FEB 1878	11	339
Nichols, Eva	Ingraham, John	10 AUG 1884 R	19	175
Nichols, George W.	Shoemaker, Ella F.	09 JAN 1883	17	247
Nichols, Harland A.	McCauley, Maggie	30 AUG 1883 L	18	105
Nichols, Julius	Herbert, Lucy	01 OCT 1885 L	20	453
Nichols, Kate	Green, John R.	10 JUL 1879 L	13	278
Nichols, Katie Mary	Spalding, Howard Joseph	07 JUL 1885 R	20	316
Nichols, Katie R.	Conner, John W.	06 MAY 1884	19	006
Nichols, Lizzie	Day, Andrew Edward	24 DEC 1882 R	17	206
Nichols, Mary E.	Harris, James H.	12 JAN 1879	13	015
Nichols, Sarah	Curtis, James	29 NOV 1883	18	285
Nichols, Sarah E.	Renney, John H.	14 OCT 1879 R	13	409
Nichols, Susie L.	Short, George R.	19 JAN 1881	15	157
Nichols, Theodore	Bock, Ella	05 MAR 1884 L	18	459
Nichols, Theodore	Rock, Ellen	14 MAY 1884 L	19	021
Nichols, Thomas	Smith, Rachel A.	17 OCT 1881 L	16	137
Nichols, Thomas	Collins, Amelia H.	12 OCT 1885 L	20	476
Nicholson, Augustus Archibald	Clarke, Katherine Phillips	25 JUN 1879 R	13	249
Nicholson, Augustus L.	Davidsson, Maggie	27 OCT 1883 L	18	217
Nicholson, Charles M.	Kyle, Mary E.	11 AUG 1879 R	13	297
Nicholson, David	Shomo, Annie Laurie	25 OCT 1882 R	17	091
Nicholson, George	Brown, Caroline	13 SEP 1879	13	367
Nicholson, George	Blue, Sophy	28 APR 1884 R	18	535
Nicholson, Georgia	Martin, John R.	14 AUG 1881 R	15	443
Nicholson, Helen M.	Cooke, Pitt	28 APR 1881 R	15	276
Nicholson, James F.	Schwenk, Cara C.A.	06 OCT 1885	20	459
Nicholson, Jennie	Reed, George	17 JUL 1882	16	450
Nicholson, John Harrison	Linkins, Ann Sophonia Brown	20 SEP 1881 R	15	488
Nicholson, Joseph	Thomas, Lulu May	04 DEC 1879 R	14	010

Nicholson, Joshua Banks	White, Emma J.	23 JUN 1885 R	20	286
Nicholson, Mary A.	Thompson, William A.	03 DEC 1883	18	293
Nicholson, Millard Fillmore	White, Fannie May	02 JAN 1884 R	18	363
Nicholson, Philip Walter	Carroll, Carrie	20 MAY 1884 R	19	029
Nicholson, Reginald F.	Heap, Annie Ellen	05 JUL 1877 R	11	006
Nicholson, Sarah A.	Fraas, John M.	21 FEB 1878 L	11	351
Nicholson, W.H.	Myers, Kate	31 OCT 1881	15	462
Nicholson, William	Wise, Henrietta	25 NOV 1884 R	19	400
Nick, Mary E.	Conner, Marshal R.	19 OCT 1880 R	15	003
Nickens, Eliza	Myers, Joseph	03 MAR 1884 L	18	454
Nickens, Henry	Roan, Fannie	20 AUG 1879 L	13	327
Nickens, Julia	Fowles, Thomas	07 MAR 1878 L	11	375
Nickens, L.T.	Hatton, Sophia	29 MAY 1879	13	211
Nickens, Rodolph D.	Wilson, Martha	09 AUG 1881 L	15	436
Nickins, Annie	Quander, Joseph	29 JAN 1880 R	14	127
Nickson, Lucy A.	Queen, Lewis	15 SEP 1877 L	11	094
Nicodemus, Charles V.	Drury, Louise Marie	27 MAY 1879 R	13	205
Nicodemus, Conrad R.	Tenley, Margaret A.	03 APR 1879 R	13	123
Niebel, August	Ommert, Anna Barbara	18 MAR 1885	20	117
Niebuhr, Dora	Elmenreich, Hermann	30 JAN 1884 R	18	395
Niemanm, Fritz	Philipp, Barbara	01 MAY 1882	16	342
Niermann, Margaret Ellen	Hall, James Hiram Barney	13 OCT 1880 R	14	489
Nightingale, Emily	Daly, Walter H.	29 APR 1880 R	14	245
Nightingale, John A.	Bailey, Ida	02 JUN 1882 R	16	390
Nightzer, Wallace D.	Martin, Bertie F.	03 SEP 1885 R	20	398
Nigle, Richard A.	Lucas, Lillie C.	18 OCT 1877	11	145
Niland, Bridget	Reynolds, Joseph Randolph	02 JAN 1881	15	132
Niland, Bridget	O'Neil, Lawrence	16 FEB 1885 L	20	067
Nilant, Mary	Cook, Mark	10 AUG 1878 L	12	163
Nissen, Hartig	Peterson, Helene	12 AUG 1884 L	19	182
Nitzel, Charles A.	Caton, Jennie A.	13 AUG 1879 L	13	319
Nixer, Fred W.	Tatspaugh, M. Virginia	05 JUN 1879	13	211
Nixon, Frank	Washington, Minnie	18 SEP 1884	19	257
Nixon, Penny E.	Jackson, John H.	08 JAN 1880 R	14	097
Nixon, William G.	Andrews, Helen	02 JUN 1881	15	335
Noack, Augusta	Rowe, Rudolph Carl	27 FEB 1879 R	13	055
Noah, Morris Sampson	Bock, Louise	05 JUL 1880 R	14	347
Noakes, George Washington	Gordon, Mary Jane Arnold	04 FEB 1878 R	11	328
Noble, Emma L.	Clagett, Maurice J.	28 OCT 1884	19	340
Noble, Horace E.	Cary, Louisa M.	06 SEP 1883 R	18	117
Noble, J.A.	Riley, Alice V.	24 SEP 1884 L	19	266
Noble, Julia Moore Mrs.	Spaininburg, John E.	02 AUG 1878 R	12	156
Noel, John Snider	Burke, Ada Marie	18 OCT 1882	17	077
Noel, Joseph	Willis, Lucy	30 JUN 1880 R	14	340
Noerr, Susie C.	Irwin, John	09 FEB 1881	15	174
Nokes, Florence K.	Murphy, Arthur, Jr.	05 JUN 1883 R	17	476
Nokes, George T.	Smith, Mary	31 OCT 1882 R	17	102
Nokes, Mary H.	Cox, Owen A.	17 SEP 1885 R	20	427
Nolan, Carrie	Johnson, Windsor	19 MAY 1881	15	318
Nolan, Charles Thomas	Moulton, Alice	17 JUN 1883	17	500
Nolan, Edward	Tuttle, Josephine	25 DEC 1877 R	11	266
Nolan, Elizabeth	Carrick, Joseph C.	20 APR 1882 L	16	328
Nolan, James	Simpson, Mary, Mrs.	28 OCT 1878 R	12	241
Nolan, John	Williams, Catherine	02 JUL 1885 L	20	307
Nolan, John T.	Talbert, Agnes M.	31 MAY 1882	16	382
Nolan, John W.	Holmes, Annie Laura	09 DEC 1880 R	14	331
Nolan, Katie	Joyce, Maurice	04 JUN 1883 R	17	473
Nolan, Laura A.	Trexler, Eugene B.	08 JUL 1879	13	276

Nolan, Sarah A., Mrs.	Reed, Lewis H.	04 FEB 1884	18	407
Noland, Elizabeth	Jackson, Frank	16 DEC 1880 R	15	102
Noland, John Edward	Diggs, Cornelia Almira	11 NOV 1878 R	12	319
Noland, Samuel D.	Buil, Mary Elizabeth	13 SEP 1877 L	11	092
Noland, Walter F.	Graham, Florence J.	06 NOV 1884	19	364
Nolen, Ella M.	Hawkins, Isaac S.	07 DEC 1880 L	15	086
Nolen, William Geo.	Howell, Grace	12 SEP 1883 R	18	128
Nolin, Elizabeth	Woodward, William	11 APR 1878	11	413
Nolin, Gabriel Emanuel	Johnson, Eliza Louisa	10 APR 1882 L	16	307
Noll, Eve A.	Stiffler, George	19 JUL 1880 L	14	368
Noll, Henrietta Catherine	Schuerman, Samuel Clarke	22 JUN 1879 R	13	243
Noll, Lena	Shellhorn, Chris	11 APR 1885 R	20	159
Nolte, Margaretta	Rohde, William	04 NOV 1884	19	358
Nolte, Mary L.	Gerhold, John F.	26 AUG 1879 R	13	336
Noon, Katie	Hadfeld, Harry	29 MAR 1880 R	14	198
Noonan, Bridget	Cady, Patrick	11 MAY 1882 L	16	358
Noonan, Honora	Crowe, Peter	26 NOV 1884 L	19	418
Noonan, James H.	Cottingham, Maggie	23 JUN 1885 L	20	287
Noonan, Margaret	McNally, Francis	31 MAR 1880 L	14	204
Noonan, Matthias	Gavoin, Margaret	26 NOV 1881 L	16	099
Noonan, Michael	Shanahan, Mary	24 AUG 1881 L	15	457
Noone, P.R.	Keefe, Maggie	18 AUG 1884 L	19	191
Noordzy, Harry C.	Gormley, Mary	20 AUG 1884 L	19	194
Norbeck, Bertha C.	Werner, John William	12 NOV 1878 R	12	325
Norcom, Fanny E.	Smith, Benjamin F.	02 OCT 1877 R	11	117
Nord, Alexander G.	Williams, Sarah E.	01 MAY 1878 R	12	030
Nordenstrahl, Thor	Hamilton, Charlotte, Mrs.	04 NOV 1882 R	17	106
Nordlinger, Hannah	Rice, Solomon	12 SEP 1883 R	18	125
Norfleet, Mildred	Bisbee, Horace F.	13 MAY 1884	19	018
Norfolk, Buddy	Gray, Lena	30 SEP 1879 R	13	391
Norfolk, Charles K.	Barry, Mary S.	05 AUG 1885	20	355
Norfolk, Martha Ann Swayne	Edelen, Joshua T.	22 APR 1980 R	14	232
Norglo, George	Lechlender, Mary	05 MAY 1881 R	15	295
Norman, Christopher	William, Pinkey	20 DEC 1877 R	11	246
Norman, Frances	Bryan, Nathaniel	30 JAN 1884 L	18	402
Norman, Hattie	Ewing, John Wm.	16 JUL 1885 R	20	330
Norman, Lucy E.	Daly, Frederick F.	03 JUN 1882 L	16	392
Norman, Mary	Johnson, Mark	06 JAN 1882	16	178
Norman, William	Brook, Nancy	24 OCT 1878	12	288
Normon, Rosie	Tyler, George W.	14 APR 1884 L	18	506
Norris, Amos	Brown, Marion	11 JAN 1883 R	17	254
Norris, Annie M.	Leitch, John J.	19 DEC 1877	11	247
Norris, Brison	Lanahan, Mary Elizabeth	27 JUN 1883 L	18	022
Norris, Calvin C.J.	Larman, Margaret	14 APR 1879	13	140
Norris, Eliza	Miller, Charles	25 SEP 1882 R	17	037
Norris, Eliza Jane	Chum, John H.	19 JUL 1881 R	15	407
Norris, Elizabeth E.	Thompson, John H.	23 FEB 1882 R	16	257
Norris, Frances	Lee, William	18 AUG 1883	18	090
Norris, Harrison	Tolliver, Frances	15 SEP 1885 L	20	416
Norris, Hattie	Kelsey, Moses	09 JUN 1886	20	342
Norris, Henry J.	Albaugh, Mollie A.M.	28 APR 1884 R	18	536
Norris, Hiram	Ware, Harriet	31 DEC 1881 R	16	172
Norris, Jane	Bell, William H.	08 JUL 1880	14	352
Norris, John	Jefferson, Kate	13 NOV 1879 L	13	482
Norris, John	Moore, Catherine C.	14 OCT 1880 L	14	494
Norris, John W.	Mathers, Louisa A.	15 OCT 1885 R	20	486
Norris, Lizzie	West, Thomas	08 JUN 1882 L	16	400
Norris, Lorenzo	King, Annie	23 APR 1885 R	20	185

Norris, Louisa	Slater, Emanuel	16 SEP 1884	19	248
Norris, Martha F.	Field, George W.	16 SEP 1879 L	13	373
Norris, Matilda	Winfield, Robert	21 DEC 1882 R	17	190
Norris, Millard A.	Farrell, Katie	11 OCT 1885	20	474
Norris, Nimrod	West, Josephine	10 MAR 1881 R	15	219
Norris, Reuben	Barton, Mary	09 NOV 1879	13	468
Norris, Sarah Jane	Dent, Samuel F.	11 SEP 1880 R	14	441
Norris, Susan	Macwell, Abram	30 MAY 1878 R	12	076
Norris, William	Murray, Mary Emory	15 OCT 1879 R	13	423
Norris, William P.	Corley, Nellie A.	11 JUN 1885 L	20	270
Norris, William R.	King, Margaret J.	29 DEC 1883	18	354
Norriss, Jacob	Carston, Maggie	20 NOV 1879 R	13	496
Norriss, Mary Jane	Gass, Frederick William	19 JUN 1879	13	240
North, George	Graham, Eliza, Mrs.	01 NOV 1882 L	17	104
North, Sarah Elizabeth	Smith, William	22 MAY 1884 L	19	035
Northern, Clara	Rowell, Ambrose E.	20 APR 1881 R	15	266
Northridge, Mary Jane	Jones, William	10 JAN 1880 R	14	100
Nortin, Emma	Younger, Edward C., Jr.	19 AUG 1885 R	20	377
Norton, A. Howard	Freeman, Mary Teresa	08 DEC 1879 L	14	033
Norton, Adele	Bladen, Andrew	10 JUN 1879 L	13	226
Norton, Charles Edward	Henderson, Lina M.	25 FEB 1884 L	18	441
Norton, Charles Henry	Robertson, Elizabeth	24 JUL 1884 L	19	155
Norton, Daniel	Murphy, Katie	09 DEC 1882 L	17	176
Norton, Ella R.	Risdon, John R.	17 JUL 1880 L	14	366
Norton, Emma	Smith, James O.	08 AUG 1881	15	415
Norton, Fannie	Spencer, Thomas	01 JUL 1884 L	19	115
Norton, Harriet A.	Johnson, Thomas C.	31 DEC 1884 L	19	520
Norton, John T.	Gilman, Laura V.	04 APR 1878	11	399
Norton, Minnie C.	Jones, Richard H.	17 MAY 1881 R	15	314
Norton, Rebecca	Sheckles, Charles R.	26 MAR 1883 L	17	362
Norton, Robert H.	Butler, Mary A.	01 OCT 1879 R	13	395
Norton, William Henry	Sinclair, Fannie	26 FEB 1882	16	259
Norton, Willie E.	Fitton, Mary S.	26 NOV 1884	19	413
Norvell, Elvira R.	Page, Charles L.	03 JUN 1879 R	13	217
Norwood, George A.	McDonnell, Katie	23 APR 1878 L	12	017
Nosey, James	King, Ida Luvinia	03 JUL 1882 R	16	435
Nothey, John	Jones, Mary E.	12 MAY 1884	19	015
Nott, Wilford E.	Kershaw, Agnes E.	19 JAN 1881 R	15	156
Nott, William T.	Bland, Allie F.	03 OCT 1878	12	242
Nourse, Mamie W.	Brooks, Thomas B.	23 DEC 1879 R	14	068
Nourse, Mary Adelaide	Solberg, Ludwig Thorval	01 AUG 1880 R	14	381
Nourse, Mary Jane	Gray, Cornelius	09 JAN 1878 L	11	297
Nowell, Hettie F.	Stallings, George W.	05 DEC 1881	16	113
Nowland, Mary Lee	Hill, Thomas O.L.	02 APR 1883 R	17	374
Noxon, Eliza	Johnson, Benjamin	31 JUL 1883	17	487
Noyes, Albert	Collins, Mary	27 SEP 1880 L	14	461
Noyes, Alice	Moran, Alexander F.	26 APR 1883	17	409
Noyes, Clarence	Duguid, Isabella	28 SEP 1881	15	499
Noyes, Florence M.	Van Vleek, Eugene A.	29 APR 1885 R	20	197
Noyes, Galveston	Carter, Berta Verginia	26 SEP 1883 R	18	155
Noyes, Henrietta	Poist, Robert C.	27 OCT 1880 L	15	017
Noyes, Joseph	Show, Henrietta	07 OCT 1881	16	013
Noyes, Marian Bingham	Pierce, Martin Wilbur	08 JUL 1878 L	12	127
Nuckols, Clarence Pend.	Hope, Lady Blanche	06 JAN 1885 R	20	005
Nugent, Henry	Taylor, Lucy	05 OCT 1886	20	146
Nugent, Maria Louisa	Bowers, Jordan	30 DEC 1878 R	12	407
Nugent, Nelly Ann Maria	Taylor, William	18 SEP 1879	13	376
Nugent, Parry	Matthews, William	06 DEC 1880 R	15	086

Nunes, William Joseph	Fenton, Julia G.	31 DEC 1882 R	17	224
Nunnally, Josie H.	Sharp, Charles H.	10 MAR 1885 R	20	105
Nuskey, Katie	Parkinson, Charles H.	06 MAY 1879 R	13	175
Nuthall, John T.	Dove, Eugenia C.	17 SEP 1877 R	11	097
Nutt, Ella	Henson, Yarmouth	18 DEC 1884	19	473
Nutt, Laura	Crawley, Nathaniel	23 JUL 1885 R	20	338
Nutter, Frank B.	Lavender, Ella	04 JUL 1878 R	12	118
Nutwell, James W.	Moran, Rosa E.	12 JAN 1882 R	16	192
Nuvelle, James G.	Morant, Ellen	21 NOV 1881 R	16	087
Nyce, Ella C.	Cooper, John A.	19 AUG 1878 R	12	171

O

O'Brien, Cordelia E.	Birch, Richard	09 OCT 1884	19	296
O'Brien, Daniel	McMurray, Hattie R.	05 SEP 1878 R	12	207
O'Brien, Dennis	O'Connors, Mary	24 DEC 1879 L	14	073
O'Brien, Edward M.	Seip, Martha E.	25 FEB 1879	13	077
O'Brien, Eustace E.	Langley, Lucy M.	17 MAR 1884 R	18	473
O'Brien, Hanora	Sandstrum, William	05 FEB 1879 R	13	046
O'Brien, James	Hughes, Maggie	06 APR 1883 L	17	383
O'Brien, James T.	Kidwell, Cordelia	15 MAR 1881 L	15	226
O'Brien, Jennie	Brown, Edward F.	20 DEC 1881 R	16	141
O'Brien, Johannah	Lawlor, James	15 JAN 1880 L	14	109
O'Brien, John	Campbell, Margaret	25 NOV 1877	11	201
O'Brien, John	Robinson, Ann	25 NOV 1880	15	061
O'Brien, Joseph	Hornity, Ellen	08 SEP 1885 L	20	404
O'Brien, Julia Anne	Birch, Jacob	16 OCT 1878	12	276
O'Brien, Kate	Dunnovan, Daniel	11 JUN 1877	11	005
O'Brien, Lizzie	Walker, George S.	01 JAN 1878 R	11	285
O'Brien, Mary	Sullivan, John	22 NOV 1884 L	19	403
O'Brien, Missouri	Allman, James J.	06 JUN 1885 L	20	259
O'Brien, Richard	O'Neil, Mary	05 JAN 1881 L	15	141
O'Brien, Richard A.	Burroughs, Mary	02 JUL 1883 L	18	028
O'Brien, Sarah	Mullory, Frank P.	05 OCT 1881 L	16	010
O'Brien, William	Holloran, Mary	26 FEB 1878	11	357
O'Brien, William	Brown, Annie Cooney	07 MAR 1880 R	14	176
O'Brien, William T.	Biggins, Catharine	10 OCT 1883 R	18	181
O'Byrne, Rosa A.	Braendel, Fredolino	05 JUN 1878 L	12	086
O'Connell, Annie L.	Fealy, Patrick A.	07 OCT 1882 L	17	059
O'Connell, E.D.C.	Lane, W. Aloysius	04 JUL 1877 L	11	008
O'Connell, Jeremiah	Roberts, Margaret	25 JUL 1882 L	16	456
O'Connell, John C.	Reirdon, Honora	11 MAY 1881 L	15	302
O'Connell, Maggie J.	Baldwin, John W.	31 JUL 1880 L	14	381
O'Connell, Michael	Bresnahan, Margaret	22 JAN 1885 L	20	033
O'Connell, Nora	Daly, Eugene	14 MAY 1882 R	16	360
O'Connell, Patrick B.	Coughlin, Mary E.	03 OCT 1882	17	050
O'Conner, Minnie	Truxell, Francis William	18 MAY 1881	15	315
O'Connor, Bridget	Hawkins, John H.	30 MAR 1880	14	202½
O'Connor, Eugene A.	Hayes, Florence L.	17 OCT 1878 R	12	281
O'Connor, James	Young, Arabella	07 SEP 1882 R	17	012
O'Connor, James L.	Griffin, Catherine	07 DEC 1880	15	085
O'Connor, Jane	O'Neal, Andrew	22 OCT 1883 L	18	205
O'Connor, Jeremiah	McCarty, Anna	25 DEC 1878 R	12	397
O'Connor, Jeremiah J.	Barry, Mary M.	16 OCT 1882 R	17	074
O'Connor, Katie E.	Boyle, Patrick A.	04 FEB 1883 R	17	283
O'Connor, Maggie	White, Franklin Pierce	06 AUG 1884	19	170
O'Connor, Mary	Murphy, Joseph C.	29 NOV 1884 L	19	426
O'Connor, Mary E.	McCarthy, Justin J.	13 SEP 1879 L	13	369
O'Connor, Michael	Davis, Ella	26 AUG 1884 L	19	209
O'Connor, Michael J.	Murphy, Maggie A.	30 JUL 1883 L	18	066
O'Connors, Mary	O'Brien, Dennis	24 DEC 1879 L	14	073
O'Connors, Timothy	Moody, Maggie A.	27 JUN 1885 R	20	296
O'Day, Annie	Loveless, John A.	08 FEB 1882 R	16	230
O'Day, Catherine	McInerny, Dennis	08 OCT 1883 L	18	176
O'Day, Delia	Berry, John	03 MAY 1881	15	290
O'Day, John J.	Biggin, Mary Jane	22 APR 1884 L	18	526
O'Dea, Annie	Robertson, J.F.	15 DEC 1879 L	14	048
O'Dea, Kate	Welch, Patrick	05 FEB 1880	14	139
O'Dea, Martin	Donohue, Kate	04 FEB 1883 R	17	283
O'Dea, Michael	Connor, Julia	21 OCT 1884	19	324

O'Dea, Patrick	Tobin, Annie A.	16 SEP 1880 L	14	449
O'Donnell, Henry	Barry, Mary	03 DEC 1877 R	11	210
O'Donnell, John H	Koontz, Anna D.	11 JUL 1882 R	16	444
O'Donnell, John Henry	Wayland, Sarah Madeleine	08 SEP 1877	11	082
O'Donnell, Mary, Mrs.	Jones, R.C., Col.	05 JUN 1884 L	19	063
O'Donnell, Thomas	Simmons, Ella	18 MAY 1885 L	20	227
O'Donnoghue, Mary E.	Aitkenhead, Wilfred C.	14 JAN 1879 R	13	017
O'Donnoghue, William F.	Wieskie, Mary E.	05 OCT 1879 R	13	402
O'Donoghue, Dennis	Sullivan, Bridget A.	18 OCT 1882 L	17	081
O'Donoghue, Martin J.	Gallagher, Kate	11 NOV 1879 R	13	475
O'Dowd, Katie	Whiteford, William S.	12 APR 1882 R	16	311
O'Dowd, Maggie	Demonet, George H.	06 MAY 1885	20	207
O'Dwyer, William G.	Beckman, Mary E.	03 JUL 1883 R	18	031
O'Farrell, Ida M.	Burke, William	21 FEB 1882 R	16	248
O'Field, Maggie	Turner, Samuel W.	07 AUG 1878	12	159
O'Flaherty, Edward	Lynch, Margaret	25 AUG 1877 R	11	064
O'Grady, Patrick	Tucker, Penelope	24 SEP 1885	20	441
O'Hagan, James T.	Curtin, Elizabeth A.	12 DEC 1882 L	17	178
O'Hare, Annie K.	May, Frank P.	14 OCT 1878 L	12	272
O'Hare, Catherine J.	Tolson, Alfred C.	13 NOV 1878 L	12	327
O'Hare, Edward	Georges, Louise	03 JUN 1885	20	247
O'Hare, John	Dove, Mary	23 OCT 1878 L	12	287
O'Hare, Maggie	Callow, Robert	30 MAY 1880 R	14	295
O'Hare, Mary E.N.	Burke, Frank P.	06 MAR 1883 L	17	335
O'Hare, May E.	Burke, Patrick	01 MAR 1883 L	17	330
O'Hare, Michael	Kneas, Pauline C.	23 DEC 1879 R	13	474
O'Hearn, Mary	Kenny, Michael P.	22 APR 1880 R	14	233
O'Holloran, Helena M.	Cross, Henry C.	20 NOV 1877 R	11	194
O'Keefe, Maggie	Long, Mike	17 JAN 1881 L	15	152
O'Laughlin, Bridget	Frayser, John	13 JUL 1883 L	18	046
O'Leary, David	Allen, Margaret A.	18 AUG 1881	15	452
O'Leary, Jeromiah	McCarthy, Mary	05 FEB 1880	14	137
O'Leary, Julia	Macarty, Cornelius	16 APR 1880	14	226
O'Leary, Margaret	McAuliffe, John	15 SEP 1884 L	19	246
O'Leary, Mary	Davis, Roger	23 AUG 1882 L	16	492
O'Leary, Mary E.	Cullinan, Martin F.	11 FEB 1885	20	064
O'Meara, John D.	Martin, May M.	24 MAY 1882 L	16	375
O'Neal, Andrew	O'Connor, Jane	22 OCT 1883 L	18	205
O'Neal, John	Donahue, Ellen	31 MAR 1883 L	17	372
O'Neal, Mary Ellen	Smith, Henry	22 AUG 1881 L	15	455
O'Neal, William	Carroll, Annie J.	27 SEP 1883 R	18	147
O'Neil, James J.	Byrne, Mary	07 NOV 1878 L	12	315
O'Neil, Julia C.	Smith, Henry M.	17 FEB 1878	11	344
O'Neil, Lawrence	Niland, Bridget	16 FEB 1885 L	20	067
O'Neil, Mary	O'Brien, Richard	05 JAN 1881 L	15	141
O'Neil, William	Thomas, Josephine	05 JUL 1877 R	11	010
O'Neill, Edward	Gallivair, Bridget	18 AUG 1880 L	14	405
O'Neill, John J.	Goddin, Rosalie W.	01 DEC 1881 L	16	108
O'Neill, Julia Webster	Langley, Robert R.	26 OCT 1880 R	15	015
O'Neill, Kate	Haley, Edward	20 JAN 1878	11	311
O'Neill, Kate	Kelly, Peter C.	27 APR 1880 L	14	239
O'Neill, Katie	McCaffrey, Thomas	10 MAR 1881	15	219
O'Neill, Martin	Cunningham, Mary	25 APR 1881 L	15	271
O'Neill, Mary	Knox, James	21 FEB 1878 L	11	352
O'Rork, Charles E.	Burnett, Etta	04 JUL 1881	15	387
O'Rouke, Joseph	McGuire, Gertrude	26 DEC 1884 R	19	492
O'Shaughnessy, Thomas	Quirk, Ellen	20 AUG 1878 L	12	173
O'Shea, J. Boyle	Welch, Ella	03 JUL 1879 R	13	267

O'Shurland, George C.	Hagerty, Lizzie C.	13 MAY 1878 L	12	049
O'Toole, Michael	McArdle, Kate	22 JAN 1884 L	18	388
Oakham, Lemuel Wyatt	Kolb, Dora S.	08 JUL 1878 L	12	127
Oakland, Catherine	Burgess, Charles A.	21 JUL 1881 L	15	412
Oar, Anna Martha	Henry, Wilmore John	04 OCT 1881 R	16	007
Oatman, Nellie Louise	Burke, Charles Sumner	31 DEC 1879 R	14	082
Ober, Albert N.	Johnson, Kate A.	18 DEC 1880 L	15	109
Ober, Carrie R.	Middleton, Arthur E.	08 OCT 1884	19	290
Oberteuffer, Herman F.	Fitch, May Perkins	30 JAN 1883 L	17	278
Oberteuffer, William G.	Fox, Roberta K.	05 MAR 1884 L	18	458
Obey, Daniel F., Jr.	Stewart, Jennie C.	11 MAR 1880 L	14	183
Obinger, John	Babikow, Augusta	07 JUN 1880 L	14	307
Obold, Sebastian F.	Morrow, Annie L.	30 DEC 1884 L	19	504
Occhionero, Nicolino	Papa, Carmela	21 AUG 1880 L	14	411
Ochard, James F.	Harris, Sarah V.	15 SEP 1880 L	14	445
Oches, Mollie M.	Crouch, Edwin D.	05 NOV 1879 R	13	467
Ockershausen, Caroline	Seipp, John H.	20 SEP 1885 R	20	428
Ockershausen, George	Kaiser, Henrietta M.	04 NOV 1880 R	15	027
Ockershausen, Henry	Haneke, Christine	12 JUN 1879	13	230
Ockershausen, William	Rheb, Caroline	03 OCT 1878 R	12	250
Oda, Minnie	Brown, Alex	27 DEC 1883	18	346
Odare, Belle	Van Bramer, James	17 MAR 1885	20	109
Odel, Mary E.	Duesberry, Americus B.	28 APR 1883 L	17	418
Odelions, Frank	Carter, Emma	18 JUL 1881 L	15	408
Odell, Matie M.	Harper, T. Dennis	07 AUG 1877 L	11	044
Oden, Anthony	Jackson, Lucy	06 NOV 1884	19	363
Oden, Emma	Smothers, Sylvester	29 JUN 1885 L	20	300
Oden, Hanna	Williams, John R.	20 SEP 1878	12	218
Oden, Maggie	Holmes, Thomas	04 FEB 1878 L	11	326
Oden, Marian C.	Bell, John M.	21 FEB 1878 R	11	352
Oden, Thomas William	Taylor, Mary Elizabeth	06 MAY 1880 R	14	258
Odenhall, Ellen	Broderick, Dennis	04 DEC 1879 R	14	027
Odenwald, Albert G.	Kendrick, Amelia K.	18 JUL 1881 L	15	406
Oder, Benjamin Franklin	Wright, Jennie	15 APR 1880 R	14	225
Oderick, Jane	Wesley, Charles	19 APR 1879 L	13	151
Odrick, John W.	Green, Ellen L.	17 JAN 1884 R	18	383
Oelrich, Sophie	Seebode, Friderich	22 JUN 1881	15	369
Oeser, Margaretha	Schotterer, Charles	29 JUN 1879 R	13	255
Ofenstein, John	Reigel, Teresa B.	07 OCT 1880	14	476
Offerman, August	Shipman, Miranda C.	24 JUN 1879 R	13	246
Offertt, Mary Eliza	Randolph, Nathaniel	15 OCT 1879 L	13	419
Offield, Mary E.	Beall, George M.	05 APR 1881	15	247
Offut, Susan	Jones, Creed	27 OCT 1879 R	13	445
Offutt, Charles Alphonse	Gilbert, Caroline Saltillo	26 NOV 1884 R	19	417
Offutt, Dorsey W.	Hunter, Rebecca K.	23 FEB 1881 L	15	199
Offutt, Elvira C.	Robinson, John D.	25 MAR 1884 L	18	481
Offutt, Frank	Cumbach, Mary	26 NOV 1884 L	19	412
Offutt, George Warren	Tribby, Gertrude V.	24 JAN 1882 R	16	206
Offutt, Henry	Gilmore, Ida	17 FEB 1885 R	20	073
Offutt, James	Bundy, Mary	04 JUL 1882	16	436
Offutt, L.E., Mrs.	McPynchon, William	18 OCT 1877	11	242
Offutt, Lucy	Young, Spencer	31 JUL 1877 L	11	034
Offutt, Sallie	Moore, George	30 JUN 1884 L	19	112
Offutt, Wesley	Hascus, Hennie	12 JUL 1877	11	018
Ogden, Annabel	Page, Harvey L.	30 APR 1879	13	160
Ogden, C.W.	Tenley, A.V.	09 JUN 1881 R	15	354
Ogden, David M.	Parkhurst, Minerva A.	15 APR 1880 R	14	223
Ogden, John	Baldwin, Mary Ann, Mrs.	15 AUG 1882 R	16	464

Ogden, John W.	Day, Catherine E.	06 SEP 1877	11	078
Ogden, Leonard R.W.	Fowler, Annie S.	18 MAR 1880 L	14	187
Ogden, Martha	Davis, James	28 OCT 1880 L	15	021
Ogden, Thomas	Lisle, Mary	24 JUL 1878 R	12	146
Ogdon, Emma	Carrol, Robert C.	13 MAR 1884 R	18	471
Ogilvie, Marion J.	French, William E.P.	03 MAR 1880	14	176
Ogle, Albert C.	Anthony, Sallie L.	26 DEC 1877 L	11	268
Ogle, Annie Cora	Bryant, Frank	17 APR 1879	13	149
Ogle, Elizabeth	Durkin, John	22 APR 1882 L	16	330
Ogle, Harry	Dwyer, Bettie	02 JUN 1881 L	15	341
Ogle, Ida Louise	Rixey, Edward Richard	23 OCT 1884 L	19	334
Ogle, John R.	Woody, Annie	05 FEB 1879	13	047
Ogle, Mary A.	Knopp, Charles	08 JUL 1879 R	13	273
Ogle, Mary Elizabeth	Beall, Geo. Washington	17 JAN 1878 L	11	310
Ogleton, John	Williams, Eliza	04 APR 1878 L	11	407
Oker, Sophie	Barkley, John A.	05 JUN 1881	15	343
Olcott, Wareham Harry	Hedrick, Alice	10 MAR 1884 R	18	463
Oldberg, Charles John Rudolph	Johnson, Susanne	19 SEP 1877 R	11	097
Olden, Elizabeth	Howard, Charles H.	10 SEP 1878	12	207
Olden, Frank J.	Motley, Nellie	22 JUL 1879 R	13	289
Olden, Fred	Fergusson, Amanda	23 AUG 1883 L	18	097
Olden, John W.	Disney, Emma J.	09 SEP 1884	19	236
Olds, Catherine M.	Hamilton, Stanislaus M.	28 SEP 1880 L	14	463
Oliffe, William Henry	Lewis, Laura Custiss	01 JUL 1883	18	028
Olin, James H.	Harris, Annie	16 SEP 1884	19	253
Olive, Bunyan	Wineberger, Sallie	01 JUL 1885 L	20	305
Oliver, Alexander Weems	Allen, Charlotte Virginia	26 DEC 1882 R	17	212
Oliver, Elizabeth	Booth, Moses Z.	24 NOV 1880 L	15	064
Oliver, Francis R.	Barker, Elsie	02 OCT 1885	20	452
Oliver, Jennette B.	Giese, Francis J.	07 JUL 1881 L	15	393
Oliver, Lambert	Savage, Margaret E.	05 SEP 1883 R	18	112
Olivor, Lucy B.	Walker, Samuel T.	23 DEC 1880 R	15	117
Oliver, Maggie	Cox, Owen Augustus	05 FEB 1879	13	046
Oliver, Martha	Johnson, Marshall L.	03 NOV 1879 L	13	460
Oliver, Melinda	Queen, William	21 FEB 1881	15	195
Oliver, Mollie B.	Reiter, John H.	28 DEC 1877	11	278
Oliver, Mollie E.	Walker, John E.	15 AUG 1882 R	16	479
Oliver, Octavia	Darne, R.H.	05 MAY 1881	15	291
Oliver, Virginia P.	Lyles, James H.	13 SEP 1877	11	093
Oliver, William H.	McAllister, Narametta Stallings	08 DEC 1879 R	14	034
Ollifer, Sarah Louisa	Garner, Stephen G.	18 DEC 1877 R	11	240
Olmstead, Albert	Manjue, Mary	03 NOV 1884 L	19	356
Olmstead, John F.	Hutchinson, Catherine Abbott	08 NOV 1882	17	117
Olmstead, Melancthon A.	Willis, Ella L.	27 DEC 1882	17	214
Olsen, Johan Frederik	Digelé, Marie Luise	08 MAY 1884 L	19	012
Olverson, Alice Robinson	Hall, Charles William	07 JUN 1883	17	483
Oman, Barney	Hill, Lucy Ann	31 MAR 1879 L	13	118
Ommert, Anna Barbara	Niebel, August	18 MAR 1885	20	117
Omohumdro, Carrie Thornley	Thornley, Andrew Glassell	26 APR 1882 R	16	337
Omohundro, William R.	Hurdle, Bettie C.	13 DEC 1881 R	16	128
Oneal, Kate	Scott, William H.	10 OCT 1878 L	12	266
Only, Bertha W.	Branson, Louis Whitman	02 FEB 1885 R	19	451
Onward, Lillie K.	Kramer, James Sewell, Jr.	02 DEC 1881 R	16	129
Oppenheimer, Hertz	Minz, Rebecca	21 AUG 1884 L	19	200
Oppenheimer, Ida	Stern, Solomon	16 MAR 1884 R	18	472
Oppenheimer, Rose	Heine, Edward	18 NOV 1883 R	18	249
Oppermann, Johanna	Mattern, P. Adolf	03 JUL 1884	19	119
Oppermann, Maria Katharina	Herzog, Friedrich	23 FEB 1880 R	14	161

Orange, Malinda	Powell, David	28 APR 1881 L	15	281
Orbella, Cesare P.	Greenwell, Alice	31 MAY 1882 L	16	383
Ordril, Antonio	Retagala, Josephena	23 AUG 1883 L	18	097
Ordvil, John	Ritalierra, Johanna	21 FEB 1880 L	14	161
Orem, George W.	Yeatman, Alice V.	05 DEC 1883	18	296
Orleman, Lillie	Spitzka, Henry F.	17 MAY 1883	17	449
Orme, James W.	Chery, Ella Carnana	31 JUL 1882 R	16	461
Orme, William B.	Lockwood, Julia	11 JUL 1879	13	226
Ormes, DeForrest P.	McNall, Lena	04 JUL 1879 R	13	269
Ormsbee, Mary Ellen	Binns, John Alexander	20 FEB 1881 R	15	195
Orndorff, Lunsford G.	Moore, Sarah Josephine	30 APR 1879 R	13	167
Orndorff, Susie Irene	Parker, Frank Van Syckel	19 SEP 1877 R	11	101
Orr, Emma J.	Wetherall, James A.	28 AUG 1877	11	069
Orr, John	Mack, Jeanie	13 DEC 1881 L	16	128
Orrison, Oscar J.	Sebastian, Rebecca	14 MAR 1878 L	11	381
Ortlip, Charles J.	Johnston, Margery M.	14 AUG 1879 R	13	321
Ortlip, Charles John	McCallum, Margaret M.	24 SEP 1884	19	265
Orton, Willie E.	Voy, Lizzie	06 DEC 1882 L	17	170
Osbern, Ada	Huth, Charles H.	18 DEC 1884	19	464
Osborn, Alfred G.	Beall, Annie C.	06 OCT 1885	20	459
Osborn, Eugene Ernest	Gibbs, Ada Nettie	27 AUG 1879	13	338
Osborn, James	Johnson, Annie	03 FEB 1881 L	15	175
Osborn, James B.	Wood, Sarah A.	30 DEC 1884 L	19	505
Osborn, Kate	West, Jonas	23 JUN 1884	19	097
Osborn, Marion	King, Laura J.	04 MAR 1879 R	13	088
Osborn, Mildred E.	Eglin, Robert B.	08 OCT 1885 L	20	472
Osborn, William B.	Tourney, Mary E.	06 JUN 1881 L	15	347
Osborne, Bertha A.	Holt, George W., Jr.	10 NOV 1884 L	19	372
Osborne, Lizzie E.	Gonter, William M.	06 FEB 1883 L	17	296
Osborne, Mary A.	Colbert, Nicholas A.	27 APR 1882 R	16	336
Osburn, Sarah J.	Robey, James T.	19 JUL 1885	20	332
Osgood, Kate Clifton	Holmes, William Henry	17 OCT 1883 R	18	196
Ossire, Julia A.	Greaves, James T.	07 AUG 1879	13	311
Osterman, John F.	Daley, Annie	07 JUN 1882 L	16	399
Ostmamn, Bernard	Lochboehler, Mary	29 JUN 1880	14	336
Ostrander, Mary E.	Thompson, D. Darby	15 DEC 1881 L	16	135
Oswald, Louis Oscar	Arnold, Anne Mary	19 OCT 1885 R	20	496
Oswell, Katie	Ash, Frank	03 DEC 1878 R	12	363
Oswill, Sarah	Mumford, J.C.	16 APR 1878 L	12	009
Oswold, Helen	Butler, Orlando Robinson	19 MAR 1880 R	14	189
Oten, Dora	King, William	01 AUG 1878 L	12	155
Otis, Anna Maria	Winston, Isaac	19 SEP 1882	17	026
Otis, Harriet Elizabeth	Abbott, George Albert	20 MAR 1883	17	352
Otis, Susie T.	Scott, Thomas A.	15 MAR 1883	17	346
Otis, William	Harley, Laura	05 JUL 1883	18	038
Otler, Hellen Elizabeth	Chalker, Chas. Webster	25 JUL 1878	12	148
Ott, Annie	Zeigler, Albert	23 JUL 1882	16	426
Ott, George G.	Anderson, Susie C.	18 DEC 1877 L	11	243
Ott, Joseph W.	Hartbrecht, Josephine E.	12 MAY 1885 L	20	217
Otto, Alexander	Roof, Rachel A.	03 DEC 1878 R	12	363
Otto, Henry G.	Merten, Annie	07 OCT 1882	17	058
Otto, Henry Louis	Neurath, Louisa	10 DEC 1884 R	19	447
Ouden, Lewis	Hamilton, Ellen	30 JAN 1883 L	17	279
Ourand, Annie E.	Randall, Charles H.	28 APR 1883 L	17	417
Ourand, Evelyn C.	King, Clinton M.	28 APR 1885	20	190
Ourand, Thomas D.D.	Godey, Rachel E.	15 NOV 1883	18	257
Ouraud, Addie Rosalie	Martin, James A.	01 JUL 1880 L	14	344
Ourdan, Vincent LeComte	McKnight, Katie Dickson	30 DEC 1879 R	14	079

Over, Anna R.	Miller, Abram J.	24 JUN 1884	19	097
Overall, Fannie L.	Burns, William G.	17 OCT 1883	18	195
Overall, Lena	Smith, Clarendon	25 AUG 1880 R	14	414
Overlander, Adeline	Wright, William	01 MAY 1878	12	032
Overton, Charles H.	Atkinson, Cora A.	04 FEB 1878 R	11	325
Overton, Emma J.	Grandison, Henry	03 OCT 1884 L	19	285
Owden, William C.	Diggs, Elizabeth	12 AUG 1879 R	13	316
Owen, Franklin B.	Shea, Nellie V.	28 MAY 1885 L	20	247
Owen, George	Fry, Sarah F.	27 SEP 1877 R	11	107
Owen, Helen G.	Cox, John F.	23 OCT 1883 R	18	208
Owen, Wm. Henry	Talbert, Frances	15 JAN 1880	14	108
Owens, A.J.	Little, S.M.	15 OCT 1885 L	20	490
Owens, Alice M.	Bailey, Henry	28 JAN 1879	13	036
Owens, Annie	Smith, Edward	15 MAY 1879 L	13	193
Owens, Annie Eliza	Jones, Benjamin Franklin	10 DEC 1884 R	19	446
Owens, Annie Elizabeth	Jolley, Jefferson D.	31 JUL 1882 R	16	462
Owens, Annie S.	Fowler, Gilbert J.	08 JAN 1883 L	17	242
Owens, Cecilia	Owens, John H.	08 JAN 1884 R	18	368
Owens, Charles Forrest	Miller, Sarah Stanley	26 DEC 1878 R	12	403
Owens, Charles P.	Shaw, Sarah J.	04 DEC 1881 R	16	113
Owens, Edmund W.	Bryan, Mary I. Augustin	04 DEC 1878 R	12	364
Owens, Evens	Taylor, Florence C.	12 DEC 1878 R	12	378
Owens, Gertrude	Hogg, William S.	11 MAR 1885	20	104
Owens, Helen	Plater, Jesse	22 JUL 1884	19	151
Owens, Ida Emma	Owens, William Henry	06 APR 1880 R	14	209
Owens, James C.	Hughes, Mary A.	08 DEC 1883 L	18	306
Owens, James F.	Howarth, Lillie P.	16 JAN 1879 R	13	021
Owens, John H.	Brodiecamp, Matilda	10 JUN 1882 L	16	404
Owens, John H.	Owens, Cecilia	08 JAN 1884 R	18	368
Owens, Lula V.	Smith, James C.	17 MAY 1881 L	15	313
Owens, Lydia O.	Andrews, Frank	21 FEB 1881	15	197
Owens, Margaret G.	Tucker, Benjamin L.	10 MAY 1870 L	13	184
Owens, Marshall	Dent, Annie Ellen	28 JUN 1883	18	018
Owens, Mary	Frank, Cornelius A.	05 AUG 1885	20	356
Owens, Mary Catherine	Owens, Robert Henry	01 OCT 1878 R	12	242
Owens, Medora A.	Morris, William T.	28 AUG 1884	19	213
Owens, Minnie	Simpson, George	05 JUN 1884 R	19	054
Owens, Nettie R.	Reamy, Thomas M.L.	29 OCT 1884	19	343
Owens, Olivia Jane	Dunham, Edward Jay	03 MAR 1880 R	14	172
Owens, Rebecca	Humphrey, John	27 AUG 1885	20	388
Owens, Robert Henry	Owens, Mary Catherine	01 OCT 1878 R	12	242
Owens, Samuel H.	Chambers, Maggie E.	19 FEB 1885 R	20	077
Owens, Sarah J.	August, Benjamin E.	14 OCT 1884 L	19	306
Owens, Susan	Wallace, Frank	16 DEC 1880 R	15	101
Owens, William Henry	Owens, Ida Emma	06 APR 1880 R	14	209
Owings, G.A.	Hall, Ada E.	04 DEC 1882	17	165
Owings, James H.	Becker, Anna M.	10 NOV 1878 R	12	317
Owings, Lizzie Mortimer Craabster	Smallwood, Benjamin Franklin	05 DEC 1878 R	12	368
Owings, Thomas H.	Bosley, Ada A.	01 APR 1882 L	16	295
Oxley, Edgar F.	Vinson, Sarah E.	01 SEP 1884	19	219
Oxley, Mary Amelia	Woodburn, James Lyon	20 JUL 1880 R	14	370

P

Pabst, Amelia F.	Schwarz, Frank	14 APR 1881 R	15	257
Pace, Emma D.	Hall, Charles W.	22 OCT 1884	19	328
Pace, Pinkey	Johnson, William, Elder	24 AUG 1885 R	20	384
Pace, Thomas H.	Wood, Lelia W.	04 MAR 1884	18	457
Pachmayer, John M.	Garmeroth, Caroline	17 DEC 1878 R	12	379
Packenham, Philip	Connors, Mary Jane	05 MAY 1881 L	15	294
Padget, Buchannan	Lockard, Arabella	16 OCT 1878	12	279
Padgett, Annie M.	Talbert, R. Thomas	27 DEC 1882 R	17	214
Padgett, Charles E.	Stant, Ella M.	05 JUN 1881	15	344
Padgett, Charles Edward	Bahrs, Joanna Heneretta	15 OCT 1878 L	12	273
Padgett, Charles Logan	Smith, Jennie Eliza	18 FEB 1879 R	13	066
Padgett, Daniel E.	Kerper, Mary O.	12 FEB 1884 R	18	421
Padgett, Fannie G.	Pistorio, F.D.	06 NOV 1877 R	11	169
Padgett, Fannie McClelland	Bohlyer, George	07 DEC 1880 R	15	028
Padgett, Ida Adelaide	Flagg, William	16 APR 1878 R	12	007
Padgett, James	Meads, Mary M.	13 OCT 1880	14	490
Padgett, James E.	Berry, Ida M.	24 MAY 1880	14	284
Padgett, James E.	Heyde, Helen W.	15 DEC 1880 R	15	099
Padgett, Jonathan Francis	Dowbiggin, Agnes	06 OCT 1885 R	20	464
Padgett, Joseph H.	Lamar, Sarah I.	25 AUG 1884 R	19	205
Padgett, Katie	Butts, Charles	29 SEP 1878 R	12	240
Padgett, Laura Virginia	Moore, Joseph J.	05 NOV 1880 L	15	033
Padgett, M.M.	Smith, J.P.	02 JAN 1878	11	289
Padgett, Margaret Louisa	Bladen, George William	26 MAR 1879 R	13	116
Padgett, Millard Filmore	Duffey, Sarah Jane	16 JUL 1877 R	11	022
Padgett, Rebecca	Clements, James H.	24 NOV 1880	15	067
Padgett, Robert L.	Dempsey, Ann C.	19 MAR 1885 R	20	123
Padgett, Washington	Johnson, Emma Jane	08 JUN 1880 R	14	310
Padgett, William B.	Sweeney, Sadie C.	22 MAY 1878	12	063
Padgett, William L.	Carroll, Kate	23 FEB 1881 R	15	199
Padgett, William R.	Darmstead, Teny	05 OCT 1880 R	14	475
Page, Abraham	Jones, Emily	12 JUL 1877 R	11	006
Page, Albert	Johnson, Catherine, Mrs.	08 NOV 1882 R	17	118
Page, Alice M.	Waters, Leon W.	23 JUN 1884	19	097
Page, Arthur	Rollen, Emma	07 DEC 1882 L	17	173
Page, Charles F.	Vermillion, E., Mrs.	10 NOV 1883 L	18	245
Page, Charles G.	Young, Virginia	09 OCT 1884	19	296
Page, Charles L.	Norvell, Elvira R.	03 JUN 1879 R	13	217
Page, Ellen O.	Bolden, Wilson	15 JAN 1880 R	14	109
Page, Fletcher S.	Tyson, Emma J.	02 JAN 1884	18	362
Page, George F.	Wills, India E.	01 JUL 1879 R	13	259
Page, Grace D.	Estes, Dana	10 NOV 1884	19	354
Page, Harvey L.	Ogden, Annabel	30 APR 1879	13	160
Page, Henry C.	Barber, Carrie	20 SEP 1883 L	18	144
Page, Horace	Jones, Sarah	01 NOV 1883	18	225
Page, Isaac	Johnson, Catherine	12 DEC 1877 L	11	232
Page, Isaac	Davis, Maria	24 OCT 1878 R	12	290
Page, Isaac	Johnson, Caltiene, Mrs.	09 JAN 1879 R	12	2974
Page, James Henry	West, Mary Jane	24 MAR 1885 L	20	130
Page, John	Hunter, Hester	02 OCT 1879 R	13	396
Page, Junius	Smith, Eliza	01 MAR 1879 L	13	085
Page, Louisa	Fitzhugh, James S.	17 FEB 1881 L	15	193
Page, Lucy	Brown, George W.	26 DEC 1881 L	16	159
Page, Mary	Johnson, James	23 NOV 1883 L	18	274
Page, Mary Virginia	Cornwell, John L.	15 MAY 1883 R	17	440
Page, Robert	Wood, Sarah	15 MAR 1879	13	103
Page, Robert M.	Thompson, Addie R.	14 SEP 1878 L	12	218

Page, Rosa	Cook, James	12 AUG 1885 R	20	363
Page, Sarah	Yookam, George	23 FEB 1885 R	20	081
Page, Thos.	Jackson, Margarett	10 JUN 1880 L	14	314
Page, W.B.	Reed, Ella V.	10 AUG 1885	20	364
Page, Washington Edw.	Getty, Caroline	07 APR 1885 R	20	144
Page, Will Freneau	Underwood, Lettie Bailey	07 JUL 1879 R	13	271
Page, William H.	Cole, Susan E.	05 SEP 1878 L	12	201
Page, William H.	Tingsley, Hattie H.	14 MAR 1883 R	17	342
Paglissi, Josefina	Rallo, Francisco P.	08 OCT 1878 R	12	254
Paige, Charles H.	Faunce, Margaret E.	09 NOV 1882 R	17	122
Paine, Eliza Brigham	Ladd, Story Butler	18 DEC 1878 R	12	386
Paine, Frederick Henry	Myers, Marion Isabelle	17 FEB 1885 R	20	073
Paine, George Wm.	Kraus, Katie	16 JUN 1881 R	15	365
Paine, Henry C.	Skinner, Martha M.	11 MAR 1884 L	18	465
Paine, John	Jackson, Mary	13 MAR 1879	13	097
Paine, Lillie	Brown, John	01 APR 1880 L	14	204
Paine, Lucy	Saunders, Peter	15 APR 1878 L	12	004
Paine, Lucy	Dawes, Frederick	07 FEB 1881	15	179
Paine, Martha	Booker, Moses	25 DEC 1881 R	16	156
Paine, Martha	Brown, Joseph	06 DEC 1883 L	18	300
Paine, Melvina	Spriggs, James	02 JAN 1879 L	13	002
Paine, Nannie	Gant, Benjamin	12 JUL 1880 L	14	358
Paine, Robert E.	Hill, Mary W.	23 SEP 1878 L	12	230
Paine, Sarah	Reintzel, Powhattan J.	28 JUL 1883	18	065
Paine, Sumner Cummings	Coffin, Helen Olcott	27 FEB 1878 R	11	358
Painter, Katie E.	Richardson, Thomas E.	03 FEB 1880	14	135
Palmer, Alice V.	Bridges, Benjamin, Jr.	29 APR 1880 R	14	244
Palmer, Anne Mumford	Fell, Edward Nelson	25 MAY 1885 R	20	239
Palmer, Annie	Stewart, Anthony	31 OCT 1878	12	302
Palmer, Annie E.	Presgraves, Thomas L.	15 DEC 1880 R	15	097
Palmer, Charles	Gray, Julia Eliza	07 APR 1881 L	15	250
Palmer, Charles Ernest	Berry, Elizabeth	10 AUG 1881 R	15	438
Palmer, Clinton C.	Chase, Josephine A.	29 APR 1881 L	15	285
Palmer, Eliza	Roten, Charles	26 AUG 1880 R	14	419
Palmer, George W.	Monday, Lavinia	21 DEC 1882 R	17	181
Palmer, Henry	Hurd, Margaret	10 SEP 1885 L	20	411
Palmer, James Hervey	Hughes, Sarah Ann	27 DEC 1877 R	11	276
Palmer, Jennie F.	Clark, Norris A.	30 SEP 1884 L	19	276
Palmer, John	Mills, Kate	25 MAY 1885	20	238
Palmer, John H.	Marshall, Hannah E.	12 JUL 1883	18	045
Palmer, John M.	Broden, Mary	19 JUL 1880 R	14	342
Palmer, John M.	Griffin, Hannah	12 SEP 1884 L	19	242
Palmer, Juliet	Adam, Charles Fox Frederick	29 NOV 1877 R	11	209
Palmer, Katie O.	Randall, Edward Gustave	15 FEB 1882 R	16	240
Palmer, Laura R.	Bagby, George W.	25 FEB 1885 L	20	085
Palmer, Lucy	Triplet, Urias	18 MAR 1879 L	13	106
Palmer, Mary Letitia	Cole, George Heath	16 JUL 1881	15	405
Palmer, Philip C.	Anderson, Maggie L.	17 NOV 1884	19	386
Palmer, Susan Bonaparte	Swift, Eben	17 MAY 1880 R	14	273
Palmer, Victoria B.	Harryman, William D.	02 FEB 1885 R	20	048
Palmer, Zadock	Robinson, Mary E.	30 NOV 1882 R	17	152
Pangle, Annie M.	Summers, Richard H.	06 JUN 1882 R	16	398
Pankens, Ellen	Ashburn, Roland	17 NOV 1880 R	15	052
Papa, Carmela	Occhionero, Nicolino	21 AUG 1880 L	14	411
Papa, Maria	Delcandio, Francesco	21 JAN 1882 L	16	204
Parater, Rose Anna	Walton, Edward	27 AUG 1883 R	18	099
Paret, John Francis	Burnside, Alice Edgehill	29 APR 1884 R	18	536
Paret, Peter	Whitemore, Frances M.	10 OCT 1883 R	18	183

Parham, Ellsworth C.	Casassa, Agnes R.	23 MAY 1878	12	064
Parham, John	French, Amanda	15 JUL 1885 R	20	325
Parham, Lydia S.	Forsberg, Helge	07 JUL 1879 R	13	271
Paris, Matilda	Landon, Joseph	10 JAN 1878 R	11	299
Park, Ella	Williams, James	14 JUN 1882 L	16	410
Park, Henrietta	Jackson, Thomas R.	10 FEB 1880 R	14	144
Park, Virginia	Teneson, James M.	13 AUG 1879 R	13	318
Parke, Alice M.	Shadd, Furmann J.	26 DEC 1882 R	17	205
Parke, Mart	Lillie, Edwinia	20 NOV 1883	18	267
Parke, Victoria M.	Massey, James H.	12 NOV 1879 R	13	478
Parker, Albert	Smith, Mary	04 OCT 1883 L	18	171
Parker, Alfred	White, Sarah	06 JAN 1880 R	14	091
Parker, Alfred Curtis	Fuller, Minnie Harriet	26 FEB 1885 R	20	087
Parker, Alice R.	Plant, Piercy A.	14 OCT 1885 R	20	485
Parker, Andrew	Clemmonds, Katy	02 AUG 1881 R	15	430
Parker, Anna	Douglas, John	28 FEB 1881 L	15	208
Parker, Annie	Davidge, James	26 APR 1881 L	15	275
Parker, Annie	Gill, Joseph A.	19 JUL 1881 L	15	409
Parker, Annie	Hammond, Henry	12 OCT 1881 L	16	018
Parker, Annie E.	McMeen, Robert	14 MAR 1878	11	382
Parker, Ashford	Mines, Sarah	11 JUN 1885 R	20	267
Parker, Carrie	Wilkerson, Charles	29 MAY 1879 L	13	210
Parker, Charles	Brent, Mary	07 NOV 1877 R	11	170
Parker, Charles F.	Ball, Mary F.	29 MAY 1878	12	072
Parker, Charles H.	Nave, Carrie N.	22 JUN 1882	16	422
Parker, Charles W.	Harding, Jennie	05 OCT 1880 R	14	475
Parker, Charles W.	Hunaker, Mary E.	30 SEP 1882 L	17	044
Parker, Columbia	Brooks, Henry	16 JUN 1879 R	13	198
Parker, Edward F.	Hamilton, Lelia	29 NOV 1882	17	151
Parker, Elijah	Washington, Jennie	15 MAY 1881	15	305
Parker, Eliza Ann	Houst, William	10 JAN 1878 R	11	298
Parker, Ella	Coleman, Richard	30 MAY 1879 R	13	203
Parker, Ellen	Primus, Lewis H.	07 NOV 1878	12	314
Parker, Emma J.	Smallwood, Philipp S.W.	19 DEC 1883	18	327
Parker, Emma Josephine	Karr, William Wesley	23 NOV 1881 R	16	091
Parker, Esau	Thomas, M. Ann	07 APR 1885 R	20	152
Parker, Fanny	Vincent, William	03 MAY 1881	15	286
Parker, Florence L.	Fanning, William H.	17 MAR 1885	20	120
Parker, Frances	Cook, James Henry	11 DEC 1879 R	14	043
Parker, Frances, Mrs.	Brooks, John	20 MAR 1882 L	16	283
Parker, Francis D.	Carr, Sebina C.	18 NOV 1880 R	15	055
Parker, Frank Van Syckel	Orndorff, Susie Irene	19 SEP 1877 R	11	101
Parker, George T.	Turner, Nellie M.	10 OCT 1885	20	474
Parker, George W.	Johnson, Helen	18 JUL 1877 L	11	025
Parker, George W.	Johnson, Margaret A.	30 APR 1878 R	12	030
Parker, Georgeanna	Lee, Elmer E.	02 JUL 1883 L	18	030
Parker, Harriet	Battle, John	21 JUN 1883 L	18	009
Parker, Harriet	Lancaster, Russell	29 DEC 1884 L	19	498
Parker, Helena Jacqueline	Thomas, Vincent Butler	19 JAN 1878	11	305
Parker, Henrietta	Willis, William A.	05 MAY 1881 R	15	294
Parker, Isabel	Lewis, George Henry	12 JUN 1883 L	17	489
Parker, Isabella	Carroll, Oden	08 APR 1883 R	17	384
Parker, Jackson	Gibbs, Fanny	24 DEC 1877	11	263
Parker, James	Turner, Ann	29 AUG 1877 L	11	070
Parker, James	Alexander, Eliza	05 OCT 1882	17	056
Parker, James Henry Shanks	Lee, Ella Phillips	23 NOV 1882 R	17	144
Parker, Jane	Dosier, Albert	30 JUL 1879 L	13	299
Parker, John B.	Wilson, Elizabeth P.	23 JAN 1879 R	13	033

Name	Spouse	Date	Vol	Page
Parker, John E.	Davidson, Margaret A.	29 FEB 1884 R	18	452
Parker, John H.	Duncan, Annie E.	05 JUN 1883 R	17	476
Parker, John H.	Johnson, Ruben E.	21 MAY 1884 L	19	033
Parker, John Henry	Miles, Martha	13 SEP 1883 R	18	118
Parker, John S.	Royce, Mary E.	17 JUN 1885 R	20	276
Parker, John T.	Carlin, Mary Ann	05 JUL 1877	11	009
Parker, John W.	Scott, Laura E.	19 NOV 1878 R	12	335
Parker, Julia	Stevenson, Robert	31 MAY 1881 L	15	332
Parker, Julia A.	Carter, James A.	09 DEC 1880 R	15	081
Parker, Kate	Huff, Randolph	04 NOV 1880 L	15	031
Parker, Kate E.	Cochran, Joseph	04 AUG 1883	18	073
Parker, Katie V.	Nalley, Wm. W.	08 NOV 1883 R	18	242
Parker, Lizzie	Taylor, Joseph	28 DEC 1882 R	17	216
Parker, Lizzie	Johnson, John	14 MAY 1884 L	19	019
Parker, Louisa	Nelson, George W.	08 JUL 1879	13	274
Parker, Louise Alfretta	Humphrey, Fred H.	15 JAN 1880 R	14	105
Parker, Ludwell S.	King, Martha Jane, Mrs.	25 JUN 1879	13	248
Parker, Mahala	Richardson, John	17 JUL 1882 L	16	450
Parker, Maria	Branson, Fred Douglass	28 JUN 1883 L	18	024
Parker, Marietta Matilda Wilkins	Bones, Thomas Arthur	20 MAR 1881 R	15	231
Parker, Martha A.	Fantleroy, Richard H.	06 JAN 1881 R	15	143
Parker, Martha A.V.	Johnson, George Alfred	16 JAN 1885 L	20	023
Parker, Mary	Carpenter, Eli	16 AUG 1880 L	14	401
Parker, Mary	Jordan, Alexander	12 DEC 1883	18	350
Parker, Mary	Manning, John Henry	14 OCT 1884 L	19	305
Parker, Mary	Sexton, Nicholas J.	01 JUL 1885	20	304
Parker, Mary A.	Neale, Richard A.	30 MAY 1883 R	17	452
Parker, Mary Amelia	Dodge, William Waldo	26 APR 1883	17	414
Parker, Mary Ann	Watkins, Henry	14 OCT 1877	11	129
Parker, Mary Ann	Murphy, Joseph	25 SEP 1884 L	19	269
Parker, Mary E.	Burgess, William	18 FEB 1883 R	17	301
Parker, Mary J.	Smith, Robert H.	21 JUN 1882 R	16	419
Parker, Mary L.	Henson, Frank E.	24 NOV 1884 L	19	406
Parker, Melinda	Harper, Thomas	12 OCT 1881 R	16	019
Parker, Miles	Hamilton, Frances	21 AUG 1884 L	19	202
Parker, Minnie M.	West, William A.	22 JUL 1878 L	12	144
Parker, Octavia	Ferguson, J.C., M.D.	30 JUN 1880	14	341
Parker, Page	Gibson, Matilda	27 DEC 1877	11	278
Parker, Rebecca	Williams, John H.	22 JUL 1879 L	13	289
Parker, Richard H.	Greenleaf, Letitia	15 NOV 1883 R	18	259
Parker, Richard T.	Pond, Lilly Virginia	20 OCT 1884 L	19	323
Parker, Robert H.	Massey, Rachel	30 MAY 1882 R	16	354
Parker, Robert H.	Darnall, Katie A.	25 NOV 1884	19	407
Parker, Rosa	Bryant, James Derby	30 AUG 1878 L	12	187
Parker, Sally	Foreman, Alexander	30 OCT 1877 R	11	155
Parker, Sarah E.	Davis, George W.	02 DEC 1879 R	14	021
Parker, Sarah J.	Cook, Franklin	15 APR 1884 R	18	511
Parker, Sarah J.	Henson, James E.	02 SEP 1884 L	19	220
Parker, Susie	Williams, Peter	17 FEB 1881 R	15	193
Parker, Sydney	Swan, Lucy Ann	02 OCT 1883 R	18	163
Parker, Thomas	Ford, Lavinia	30 APR 1878 R	12	027
Parker, Thomas	James, Lucy	14 APR 1884 L	18	507
Parker, Virginia	Vanniaer, John Ernest	02 MAR 1881 R	15	210
Parker, Virginia W. (Calhoun)	Wetmore, Henry S.	01 NOV 1881 R	15	506
Parker, Walter	Clarke, Ella	12 DEC 1883	18	308
Parker, William	Allen, Harriet	28 SEP 1882 R	17	039
Parker, William	Brown, Henrietta	03 JUN 1884 L	19	053
Parker, William	Young, Sophia	16 OCT 1884 L	19	316

D.C. Marriage Records Index, June 28, 1877 to October 19, 1885 — 353

Parker, William A.	Makle, Mary	27 DEC 1882 L	17	215
Parker, William H.	Washington, Carrie E.	29 NOV 1878 L	12	355
Parker, William H.	Quonn, Florence Isadore	24 APR 1884 R	18	532
Parker, William H.F.	Bell, Mary Q. Ella	03 NOV 1881	16	059
Parker, William Henry	Fenwick, Sarah	16 DEC 1878 R	12	358
Parker, William M.	Jackson, Eliza	20 NOV 1879 R	13	473
Parker, William T.	Cox, Mary	03 MAR 1879 L	13	085
Parker, William T.	Dudley, Alice A.	25 JAN 1883 R	17	244
Parkhurst, Benjamin	Slentz, Lillie E.	16 SEP 1884 L	19	250
Parkhurst, George A.	Morell, Clara	31 JAN 1885	20	045
Parkhurst, Mabel A.	Barrett, Wm. Claude	15 APR 1884 R	18	509
Parkhurst, Minerva A.	Ogden, David M.	15 APR 1880 R	14	223
Parkins, Marrast, Con.	Knox, Anna Octavia	13 OCT 1883	18	192
Parkinson, Charles H.	Nuskey, Katie	06 MAY 1879 R	13	175
Parks, Annie A.	McCoy, J. Findley	16 OCT 1878	12	277
Parks, Frederick James	Bangs, Annie Eliza	20 OCT 1877	11	147
Parks, Janie	Porter, Rufus H., Rev.	05 MAR 1879 R	13	090
Parks, Mary	Turner, Plummer	18 JUN 1885 L	20	279
Parks, Samuel	Lucas, Mary A.	28 MAR 1878	11	398
Parks, William	Ritchie, Lizzie	15 MAR 1881	15	226
Parks, William S.	Whitcomb, Leora A.	10 DEC 1884	19	446
Parley, Julia Ann	Cooper, James	05 JUL 1884	19	124
Parlon, Patrick	Whiteley, Catharine	23 NOV 1879 R	14	001
Parr, Dora L.	Wigfield, Douglas N.	27 APR 1881	15	275
Parr, Florence May	McBlair, Charles Ridgely	17 FEB 1885 R	20	074
Parr, Mary C.	Smith, Frank	16 OCT 1878 R	12	244
Parris, Bertha	Stevens, John	12 SEP 1883 L	18	125
Parris, Joseph	Edmonston, Elizabeth Linger	20 NOV 1879 R	13	490
Parris, Mildred A.	Richardson, Wm. M.	31 AUG 1881 L	15	466
Parris, R.T.	Mitchell, R.A.	27 MAY 1880 R	14	293
Parrish, Lizzie	McIntire, Henry	24 DEC 1877 R	11	267
Parrott, Abner A.	Copp, Walter S.	19 SEP 1881	15	490
Parrott, Jane E.	Reed, David S.	09 JUL 1882	16	442
Parrott, Ralph	Walker, Mary Ann Paynter	24 DEC 1879 R	14	071
Parsley, Margaret Victor	Donald, John Wm.	09 SEP 1880	14	439
Parsly, George Robert	Shaloe, Delia	23 MAR 1880 L	14	195
Parsons, Francis H.	Fisher, Sophia S.	03 JUN 1880 R	14	300
Parsons, James J.	Miles, Margaret Eliz. Hilton	10 SEP 1881 L	15	480
Parsons, John	Thomas, Mary S.	27 JAN 1885 R	20	037
Parsons, Joseph Hepburn	Emerson, Lillie E.	12 JAN 1883 R	17	255
Parsons, Julia	Daly, William B.	13 JAN 1881 L	15	151
Parsons, Starr	Wroe, Mamie V.	19 NOV 1884 L	19	397
Partrick, Alfred W.	Wise, Nellie P.	13 SEP 1882 R	17	017
Partridge, Charlotte P.	Herron, J. Whit	25 DEC 1877	11	265
Partridge, Susie	Thompson, Charles W.	13 SEP 1884 L	19	245
Paschal, Bessie Duval	Wright, Edward M.	07 MAR 1878 R	11	375
Pascuccio, Grazia	Amoroso, Alfonso	01 JUN 1880 L	14	298
Passeno, Amanda F.	Mastin, James S.	13 JUL 1878	12	133
Passeno, Frank V.	Ritter, Fannie L.	16 OCT 1880 R	14	497
Passeno, Isabelle May	Balinger, Richard Clinton	30 SEP 1885 R	20	450
Patch, Joseph	Wood, Elizabeth Morton	04 AUG 1877 R	11	041
Pate, William A.	Atkinson, Fannie E.	06 FEB 1883 L	17	296
Patram, Thomas W.	Bryant, Catherine	05 DEC 1883 L	18	295
Patrick, John H.	Masses, Sadie M.	24 OCT 1877	11	152
Patron, Mary E.	Wrenn, Walter D.	09 SEP 1884	19	234
Patten, Ellen D.	Carter, William B., Rev.	01 JUL 1884	19	111
Patten, James M.	Laney, Julia	09 JUL 1885 R	20	318
Patten, John W.	French, Mary	26 MAY 1880 R	14	286

Patten, Lucy	Lang, John	26 MAR 1883 R	17	359
Patten, Mary Emma	Porter, Charles W.	05 JUN 1883	17	477
Patterson, Abraham	Lee, Ann Elizabeth	31 JUL 1882	16	462
Patterson, Abraham	Hawkins, Laura	17 JUL 1884	19	144
Patterson, Adolphus	Warick, Mary	15 JUL 1879 L	13	281
Patterson, Annie Elizabeth	Thomas, William	20 OCT 1884 L	19	323
Patterson, Augustus	Jewell, Mary E.	15 FEB 1883 R	17	308
Patterson, Harriet	Winslow, Francis	17 OCT 1881	16	025
Patterson, Ida	Jones, James	12 JUL 1882 L	16	445
Patterson, Ida Minetta	Gatewood, James W.	05 APR 1883 R	17	378
Patterson, James	Vann, Jennie	26 APR 1879 L	13	161
Patterson, John T.	Loveless, Margaret	04 JUN 1881	15	344
Patterson, Katharine P.	Montague, Pierre La	29 OCT 1884	19	340
Patterson, Margaret	Culton, John R.	27 AUG 1877	11	067
Patterson, Walter B.	Cate, Nellie F.	21 FEB 1884	18	436
Patterson, William E.	Campbell, Henrietta	23 JUL 1884 R	19	473
Patterson, William Hart	Evans, Georgie	13 JAN 1881 R	15	150
Pattey, Ella	Kerstin, Charles	31 JAN 1883	17	280
Pattison, Frank H.	Moxley, Florence R.	10 DEC 1884 L	19	448
Patton, Amelia A.	Pryor, Robert R.	16 AUG 1877	11	056
Patton, Mildred A.	Runk, Alden A.	16 MAR 1885 R	20	114
Patton, Sarah	Ceals, Frank	14 MAR 1882	16	275
Patton, Thomas	Thomas, Catherine	14 FEB 1881 L	15	188
Paul, Beatrice	Marmion, Robert A.	07 OCT 1885	20	465
Paul, Henry M.	Gray, Augusta A.	27 AUG 1878 R	12	179
Paul, James	Burnes, Susie M.R.	18 FEB 1879 R	13	064
Paul, Joseph	Snell, Elva Antoinette	30 APR 1884 R	18	543
Paul, Joseph R.	Cartwright, Harriet A.	30 DEC 1884 L	19	503
Paul, Nicholas	Berry, Eliza	01 SEP 1884	19	215
Paulding, Anna Caroline	Ray, Robert Clary	29 SEP 1881 R	15	500
Paulding, Helen Offley	Douglass, Macdonald	05 OCT 1881 R	16	005
Paxson, Westwood F.	Skirving, Carrie T.	15 FEB 1881 R	15	190
Paxton, George C.	Sherwood, Anna B.	23 NOV 1881	16	097
Paxton, George M.	Goodrich, Elizabeth R.	18 MAY 1882	16	365
Paxton, Hannah E.M.	Keys, Marion H.	05 DEC 1882	17	168
Paxton, James A.	Chappell, Ida H.	10 JAN 1880 R	14	096
Paxton, John	Reed, Hattie A.	26 NOV 1882	17	228
Paxton, John	Reed, Hattie M.	18 JUN 1883	17	500
Paxton, Joseph	Wolford, Ann Maria	10 SEP 1884	19	238
Paxton, Kate V.	Kern, Edward	12 NOV 1879 R	13	478
Paxton, Mary C.	Gilkeson, Henry B.	18 NOV 1884	19	390
Paxton, Richard L.	Pyles, Sarah E.	22 NOV 1882	17	143
Paxton, William	Williard, Mary Ella	03 DEC 1884 R	19	436
Payne, A.U.	Welch, Jeanette A.	21 MAY 1884 L	19	032
Payne, Albert	Allen, Catherine	20 FEB 1879 L	13	071
Payne, Andrew L.	Wendell, Annie C.	22 MAY 1883 L	17	455
Payne, Anna Rose	Dashields, Robert Benjamin	20 JUN 1880 R	14	322
Payne, Carrie	Miller, Shelton	26 JUN 1884 R	19	100
Payne, Charles A.	Davis, Mary V.	03 DEC 1878 R	12	362
Payne, Charles W.	Strother, Jennie E.	26 AUG 1878 R	12	179
Payne, Eliza	Pyles, James	05 MAY 1881	15	293
Payne, Elizabeth	Bailey, William	30 AUG 1880	14	423
Payne, Emma	Gassaway, Richard	06 OCT 1880	14	470
Payne, Emma	Robinson, David Albert	14 DEC 1882	17	184
Payne, Emma C.	Clark, James R.	06 SEP 1877 R	11	081
Payne, F.L.	White, Mary E.	05 MAR 1879	13	090
Payne, George R.	Fant, Nellie L.	25 DEC 1879	14	075
Payne, George W.	Chase, Mary L.	16 JUL 1884	19	142

D.C. Marriage Records Index, June 28, 1877 to October 19, 1885   355

Name	Spouse	Date		
Payne, George W.	Fitzpatrick, Susie	21 JUL 1885 R	34	8410
Payne, Gibson	Cole, Annie M.	14 JUL 1881	15	402
Payne, Ida	Brown, Reason	15 OCT 1885 R	20	489
Payne, Inman Horner, Jr.	Pendleton, Wilhelmina Eliz.	25 JUN 1885 R	20	291
Payne, James	Brook, Caroline	19 JUL 1877 L	11	027
Payne, James	Washington, Virginia E.	05 DEC 1878 L	12	370
Payne, James	Williams, Fanny	23 DEC 1884 L	19	480
Payne, James F.	Muldoon, Celia T.	18 OCT 1882 L	17	080
Payne, James H.	Dean, Katie	31 MAY 1878	12	078
Payne, Jane	Butler, William	28 AUG 1879 R	13	341
Payne, John T.	Foster, Mary E.	24 APR 1883 R	17	407
Payne, John Thomas	Minor, Laura	03 MAY 1881 R	15	291
Payne, John William	Johnson, Ella	03 JUL 1879 R	13	258
Payne, Julia Ann	Simms, John H.	20 JUL 1885 L	20	026
Payne, Lewis	Jones, Patsie	09 OCT 1882 L	17	060
Payne, Lewis S.	Johnson, Lucy	05 DEC 1883 L	18	297
Payne, Lineas	Jackson, Hattie	04 OCT 1884 L	19	285
Payne, Lucy	Phearson, Charles H.	28 FEB 1879 R	13	082
Payne, Maggie	Taylor, Robert	16 JUN 1881 R	15	359
Payne, Malinda	Martin, Robert	25 MAR 1880 R	14	183
Payne, Margaret	Slater, Thomas	06 MAY 1879 L	13	176
Payne, Martha	Brown, Arthur	18 DEC 1884 L	19	472
Payne, Mary	Wormley, John	15 NOV 1877	11	109
Payne, Mary	Wilson, William	12 OCT 1882 R	17	069
Payne, Mary C.	Hurdle, Thomas T.	22 JAN 1885 L	20	034
Payne, Mary Catherine	Lucas, George William	03 MAR 1878	11	367
Payne, Mary Elizabeth	Shaw, Clark G.	23 OCT 1884	19	321
Payne, Mary L.	Burke, James W.	11 DEC 1879 R	14	045
Payne, Mary Lucretia	Eaglin, William Francis	22 MAY 1882 L	16	372
Payne, Medora Lee	Cook, James E.	27 SEP 1884	19	271
Payne, Melvin Mays	Lynn, Lucy Maria	06 FEB 1878 R	11	327
Payne, Nannie E.	Howarth, John Thomas	20 JUN 1883 R	17	498
Payne, Nellie	Jones, Samuel	22 MAR 1883 R	17	355
Payne, Rebecca	Heiter, James	14 FEB 1878 L	12	099
Payne, Robert	Walker, Caroline	07 JAN 1879 R	13	009
Payne, Robert L.	Greer, Effie	12 MAR 1883	17	340
Payne, Roberta	Rose, Frederick	19 MAR 1885 R	20	125
Payne, Samuel	Munroe, Sarah	01 MAR 1884	18	453
Payne, Samuel H.	Benton, Mary P.	30 OCT 1878 R	12	299
Payne, Sarah	Myers, Zachary	08 APR 1880	14	216
Payne, Sarah	Elliott, Franklin	29 MAY 1884 L	19	046
Payne, Sarah E.	Ellis, John D.	09 OCT 1879	13	414
Payne, Sarah Emma	Waugh, Albert Philip	09 FEB 1882 R	16	232
Payne, Sarah V., Mrs.	Beach, Sanford A.	13 DEC 1880	15	093
Payne, Susan	Johnson, Richard	24 AUG 1882 L	16	493
Payne, Walter B.	Jett, Mary F.	31 MAR 1879 L	13	120
Payne, Wesley	Sewell, Barbara A.	11 JUL 1884	19	104
Payne, William H.	Day, Mary Elizabeth, Mrs.	24 NOV 1878 R	12	343
Payne, William Joseph	Scott, Jane	28 FEB 1878 R	11	363
Payne, William L.	Franklin, Rosabella M.J.	10 JAN 1880 L	14	099
Payton, Emma	Smithson, Bud	05 MAR 1884 L	18	460
Peabody, James Harper	Rapelje, Ellie Mortimer	25 FEB 1884 R	18	439
Peach, Helen M.	Chilton, Joseph C.	14 JUL 1884	19	137
Peach, Rebecca A.	Hall, William W.	25 AUG 1881 L	15	458
Peach, Thomas F.	Hughes, Louisa T.	11 JUL 1877	11	015
Peacock, Delilah	Thompson, Joseph	14 DEC 1880 R	15	094
Peacock, Sallie B.	Burr, Thomas Washington	27 SEP 1881 R	15	499
Peak, Ellen	Smith, Mathews N.	06 JAN 1879 L	13	007

Peake, Bertha	Davis, Harrison	08 JUL 1885 R	20	316
Peake, Charles P.	Connolly, Theresa M.	01 NOV 1880 R	15	023
Peake, James A.	Hunter, Mabel M.	12 APR 1883 L	17	392
Peake, Mary Ella	Surdez, Edouard A.	03 MAY 1885 R	20	187
Peake, Mary L.	Anderson, James F.	21 OCT 1879 R	13	435
Peale, Nancy	Iverson, Soloman	31 JAN 1878 R	11	322
Pear, Ella	Buck, Thomas O.	30 MAR 1880 R	14	203
Pearce, Sarah	Clark, Allen C.	21 NOV 1882 R	17	142
Pearce, Stanley	Herman, Louise	24 DEC 1884 R	19	485
Pearce, William H.	Wiggin, Fredelina A.	22 MAR 1881 R	15	234
Pearman, John N.	Harris, Annie C.	16 JUL 1883	18	048
Pearson, Ella Frances	Zeir, Jacob B.	02 NOV 1882 R	17	107
Pearson, George W.	Edmonston, Kate E.	13 DEC 1877	11	237
Pearson, Julia F.	McEwing, Henry	02 APR 1885 L	20	142
Pearson, Lottie	Plowden, Jesse	11 APR 1882 L	16	308
Peck, Anna	Coleman, Anderson	03 JUL 1879	13	262
Peck, Charles T.	McClelland, Kate	18 APR 1878	12	009
Peck, Georgia M.	Hazel, Frank	15 AUG 1880 R	14	399
Peck, Laura	Crumpton, Jacob	05 MAY 1885	20	206
Peck, Melvin D.	Dell, Maggie H.	29 MAY 1878 R	12	073
Peck, Nancy	Contee, Solomon	01 DEC 1883 L	18	291
Peck, Ophelia Gertrude	Clark, Joseph Edward	21 AUG 1884	19	202
Peck, William H.	Hansbrough, Maria	28 APR 1880 L	14	240
Peckelton, William	Reynolds, Nettie	11 JAN 1879 L	13	015
Peckham, Willimine W.	Bromley, Frank C.	30 OCT 1884	19	344
Peed, James	Hawkins, Sarah Jane	31 DEC 1881	16	165
Peed, James	Wilson, Agnes	08 APR 1883 R	17	386
Peed, L.A.	Carter, J.W.	21 JUN 1883	18	009
Peehsa, Wilhelmine	Ebert, Julius	14 MAY 1885 L	20	222½
Peeksa, Wilhelmina	Ebert, Julius	16 MAY 1885	20	231
Peel, Jane	Murray, Philip	02 OCT 1882 L	17	047
Peggs, Jennie Susis	Millington, Willis Eugene	08 SEP 1882 R	17	013
Peirce, Wilbert	Myers, Alice A.	13 FEB 1879	13	059
Pelham, Martha Rosa	Suit, S. Taylor	04 SEP 1883 R	18	111
Pellum, Julia	Reed, Harrison	17 AUG 1885	20	373
Pelouze, Frank H.	Davis, Maggie	23 APR 1879 R	13	156
Pelouze, Kate	Collins, John B.J.	25 OCT 1880 L	15	012
Pelouze, Minnie E.	Cutler, William Gifford	20 SEP 1882 R	17	027
Pelton, Guy R.	Scoville, Angelina S.	21 JAN 1879 R	13	027
Pelton, Jane, Mrs.	Foley, Theophilus	23 JUL 1881 R	15	414
Pemberton, Frank O.	Jordan, Ida V.	13 AUG 1877	11	052
Pendleton, Almiles	Booze, Mary Agnes	14 MAY 1880	14	271
Pendleton, Amanda	Carter, Frank	24 MAY 1882 R	16	374
Pendleton, Charles E.	Goodwin, Kitty W.	26 AUG 1882 R	16	493
Pendleton, E.H.	Morris, John P.	27 APR 1881	15	278
Pendleton, Frank	Phillips, Louisa	25 NOV 1880	15	073
Pendleton, John	Frieland, Mahala	09 MAY 1885 L	20	215
Pendleton, John Richardson	Goodhart, Adelaide	20 AUG 1879 R	13	324
Pendleton, Louisa M.	Holl, Eugene A.	19 DEC 1883	18	324
Pendleton, Louisa V.	Wilkes, Edward	08 MAY 1879 R	13	179
Pendleton, Muscoe R.	Jackson, Jennie	13 SEP 1884 L	19	244
Pendleton, Muscow	Carpenter, Annie	22 JUL 1882 L	16	454
Pendleton, Theodore	Roane, Martha	18 MAY 1882 L	16	368
Pendleton, Thornton	Pinkney, Priscilla, Mrs.	20 AUG 1885 R	20	378
Pendleton, Wilhelmina Eliz.	Payne, Inman Horner, Jr.	25 JUN 1885 R	20	291
Penfield, Jessie Mary	Hazard, Robert Houston	19 OCT 1882 R	17	082
Penhallow, Charles Sherburne	Coffin, Mary	28 APR 1881 R	15	277
Penn, Annie	Lewis, Andrew	19 APR 1883 R	17	400

Name	Spouse	Date	Vol	Page
Penn, Charles T.	Burch, Rosie	04 SEP 1877 L	11	074
Penn, Delaware	Dunlap, Martha E.	13 JUN 1881 L	15	357
Penn, Douglass	Monroe, Martha	25 DEC 1878 R	12	398
Penn, George Edward	Sauerwald, Jennie	28 OCT 1879 R	13	446
Penn, Grace	Callahan, Adolphus W.	02 NOV 1877	11	164
Penn, Isaiah G.	Brooks, Bellzora	12 APR 1882	16	311
Penn, James H.	Gibson, Annie E.	05 SEP 1878 L	12	202
Penn, Janie E.	Glassgow, William M.	07 NOV 1883	18	240
Penn, Jennie	Fremont, George W.	17 OCT 1885	20	483
Penn, Jesse	Bolls, Margaret	31 OCT 1878 R	12	299
Penn, Victorine	Cole, Patrick Henry	30 DEC 1879 R	14	079
Penn, William Henry	White, Adelaide	10 OCT 1878 R	12	267
Pennebaker, Phoebe	Murdock, John B.	18 NOV 1880	15	056
Pennell, Andrew	Hutton, Della T.	24 DEC 1879 R	14	070
Pennie, John C.	York, Alida S.	19 FEB 1884 R	18	429
Pennifill, Joseph C.	Marks, Ella	05 OCT 1880 L	14	473
Pennifill, Sarah A.	Wells, James	02 JUN 1883	17	472
Pennill, Nancy Ann	Alton, John Wesley	13 NOV 1877 L	11	181
Pennington, Mary C.	Hallock, Edward D.	01 DEC 1880 L	15	078
Pentland, Robert Watson	Quinn, Annie M.	26 NOV 1884 R	19	421
Pentz, John J.	Boteler, Mary B.	24 NOV 1880	15	066
Peoples, Cary Henry	Davis, Emma Jane	02 OCT 1884	19	257
Pepper, Mary J.	Donovan, John J.	03 MAY 1883 R	17	429
Peregoy, Henry H.	Duer, Virgio A.	06 DEC 1883 L	18	301
Peregoy, William E.	Keller, Lucie V.	14 JUL 1879 R	13	280
Perkins, Daniel W.	Fletcher, Nellie M.	12 FEB 1884 R	18	421
Perkins, Edwy	Hewitt, Etta M.	30 MAY 1884	19	047
Perkins, Helen	Saunders, Frank	02 DEC 1880 R	15	082
Perkins, Henrietta	Meitzler, William H.	16 OCT 1882 R	17	074
Perkins, James T.	Krouse, Rose	11 APR 1882 R	16	308
Perkins, Marion	Rhodes, W.	31 MAR 1881 R	15	243
Perkins, Nannie G.	Perkins, Wilber C.	07 NOV 1883 R	18	238
Perkins, Robert	Moore, Alice	15 AUG 1882 L	16	480
Perkins, Robert S.	Moore, Maggie	04 APR 1878	11	406
Perkins, Robert S.	Lyles, Mary A. (Goddard)	21 MAY 1883 R	17	455
Perkins, Sarah Caroline "Kate"	Mead, Thaddeus	25 DEC 1881 R	16	127
Perkins, Solustus Celestia	Miles, George Edward	04 MAR 1880	14	177
Perkins, Thomas	Hand, Mary J.	30 JUN 1878	12	117
Perkins, Wilber C.	Perkins, Nannie G.	07 NOV 1883 R	18	238
Perkins, William F.	Purinton, Alice Josephine	29 AUG 1877 L	11	070
Perks, Rosa	Gerhold, Henry	13 OCT 1881	16	013
Permillion, John	Walker, Susan	27 FEB 1881 R	15	203
Permillion, John Nelson	King, Jennie [Lewis]	22 SEP 1885 R	20	432
Pernell, William L.	Bennett, Mary C.	30 DEC 1881 R	16	164
Perrie, Augustus Lepreaux	Morris, Virginia	20 JUN 1882 R	16	420
Perrie, James C.	Allen, Matilda E.	22 OCT 1884	19	329
Perrie, Walter Thomas	Morse, Fannie S.	09 JAN 1884 R	18	371
Perrine, Lewis, Jr.	Slack, Harriet Addie	05 DEC 1883	18	293
Perrott, George	Trunnel, Mary E.	19 JUN 1883 R	18	003
Perrott, Minnie J.	Columbus, John B.	19 OCT 1885 L	20	498
Perry, Alice	Johnson, William H.	04 DEC 1877	11	218
Perry, Annie Lee	Bradley, James H.	06 AUG 1885 R	20	357
Perry, Benjamin	Jett, Ida	24 SEP 1885 R	20	438
Perry, Benjamin Oliver	Greenwood, Alice McGuire	10 MAY 1883 R	17	434
Perry, Bessie Fronie	Kean, John Taylor	03 APR 1884 R	18	489
Perry, Carrie	Harris, Charles	10 NOV 1881	16	028
Perry, Catherine	Cole, Jerry	27 DEC 1883	18	350
Perry, Clement S.	Wallace, Mary L.	09 JAN 1883 L	17	244

Name	Spouse	Date	Vol	Page
Perry, Daniel	Queen, Annie	07 MAY 1880 L	14	259
Perry, Daniel E.	Fox, Nella	21 AUG 1884	19	200
Perry, Edgar J.	Wright, Mary Alice	08 OCT 1884	19	292
Perry, Ellen	Robertson, John	24 DEC 1879	14	069
Perry, Erasmus	Everly, Rebecca	13 MAR 1884 R	18	469
Perry, Fannie V.	Polkinhorn, Charles R.	15 SEP 1883	18	132
Perry, Fred C.	Jones, Lula S.	27 SEP 1877	11	113
Perry, Georgia	Wood, Harry	14 NOV 1877 L	11	184
Perry, H.M.	Joice, H.L.	12 OCT 1882	17	068
Perry, Henson	Turner, Ella	08 MAY 1883	17	432
Perry, Ida	Williams, Allen	11 AUG 1879 L	13	315
Perry, James A.	Baldwin, Agnes B.	27 FEB 1878	11	362
Perry, James M.	Bowie, Agnes W.	26 APR 1883 R	17	415
Perry, James Summers	Ward, Ida Elmer	22 SEP 1881 R	15	494
Perry, Jane	Bailey, Levi	07 JAN 1880 R	14	086
Perry, Jesse	Waters, Louisa	07 OCT 1880 R	14	472
Perry, John W.	Godey, Katie M.	19 DEC 1878	12	390
Perry, Lewis P.	Firth, Fannie P.	24 DEC 1880 R	15	122
Perry, Lizzie	Bowman, John	29 DEC 1880 R	15	130
Perry, Maria	Milstead, Hillery	12 MAR 1885 L	20	110
Perry, Maria D.	Hurst, Robert J.	21 JUL 1881 R	15	413
Perry, Marshal B.	Seal, Emma V.	25 FEB 1884	18	440
Perry, Mary	Johnson, George	28 AUG 1879 R	13	340
Perry, Mary	Thomas, Frederick	07 MAY 1879 L	13	178
Perry, Mary	Johnson, Jerry F.	02 APR 1883 L	17	373
Perry, Mary	Daily, Edward	11 APR 1885 L	20	160
Perry, Mary Catharine	Diggs, Meredith Smith	15 NOV 1882 R	17	127
Perry, Mary Eliza	Williamson, Samuel Stuart	20 JUN 1882 R	16	420
Perry, Mary Elizabeth	Caldwell, Joseph W.L.	31 AUG 1883 R	18	106
Perry, Philip	Warren, Mary Frances	16 AUG 1881 R	15	446
Perry, Reason	Taylor, Jane	21 NOV 1883 R	18	265
Perry, Sarah C.	Kent, William L.	10 JUL 1882 R	16	443
Perry, William	Hickman, Sarah	16 APR 1881 L	15	259
Perry, William	Holmes, Maria	06 NOV 1884	19	368
Peters, Abraham	Chase, Minnie	01 APR 1882	16	463
Peters, Arthur S.	Lancaster, Agnes H.	02 SEP 1879	13	345
Peters, Bettie	Hobelmann, Herman	22 JAN 1880 R	14	115
Peters, Charles A.	Rest, Rosa M.	24 JUN 1885	20	285
Peters, Conrad F.	Cool, Annie	14 FEB 1884 R	18	425
Peters, Eliza	Boyd, Harry F.	23 JUL 1881 L	15	415
Peters, George H.	McCarty, Louisa B.	18 JUN 1878	12	102
Peters, Harry	Brooks, Patsey A.	24 NOV 1884 L	19	405
Peters, Jesse David Bright	Watson, Willianna	02 FEB 1881 R	15	173
Peters, John B.	Christopher, Louise	28 JUL 1883 R	18	064
Peters, Louisa R.	Stevenson, Richard	02 OCT 1879	13	400
Peters, Rudolph	Williams, Gertie	03 DEC 1879 R	14	022
Peters, William	Doggett, Fannie A.	20 NOV 1879 L	13	497
Peters, Winnie G.	Dinguid, John T.	20 APR 1885 R	20	175
Petersen, Charles W.	Pruette, Florence J.	01 DEC 1880	15	075
Petersen, Christian Fred. Peter	Georgii, Eugenia Anna Frederika	01 MAR 1883 L	17	328
Petersen, Ferdinand	Tew, Emily L.	12 MAY 1880 R	14	268
Peterson, Augustus	McElhinney, Mollie C.	31 JAN 1878 L	11	323
Peterson, David	Carter, Martha C.	22 FEB 1882 R	16	257
Peterson, Ellen	Jackson, Philip	22 MAY 1884 R	19	032
Peterson, Emma	Ether, Robert Morton	26 DEC 1877 L	11	268
Peterson, Eunice Ella	McCoy, Joseph Melville	28 JAN 1885	20	028
Peterson, Helene	Nissen, Hartig	12 AUG 1884 L	19	182
Peterson, Jane	Johnson, Benjamin	19 AUG 1881 L	15	454

D.C. Marriage Records Index, June 28, 1877 to October 19, 1885   359

Peterson, Janet West	Bowman, Samuel Stillman	13 OCT 1884 R	19	302
Peterson, Lucy	Eglin, James	19 NOV 1877 R	11	191
Peterson, Lucy	Jones, Edmund	06 JUN 1878 L	12	088
Peterson, Robert	Sonneman, Emma	28 OCT 1883 R	18	215
Petignat, Augusta	Goheens, Frank	16 JAN 1883 R	17	225
Petit, J.F.	Warren, Clara Belle	10 JUN 1884 R	19	075
Petitt, Alfred	Rodgers, Annie	01 JUN 1881 R	15	336
Petitt, David L.	Green, Julia Ada	25 JAN 1881 R	15	163
Petitt, Elizabeth	Devers, John W.	10 AUG 1880 R	14	395
Petitt, James W.	Abbot, Edna	03 OCT 1878	12	253
Petitt, Lorenzo	Rodgers, Emma	19 DEC 1882 R	17	192
Petitt, Norman	Williamson, Mary	15 DEC 1880	15	097
Petitt, Robert	Leonard, Katie	11 JUN 1878 L	12	094
Petrola, Celestia	Simpson, Thomas C.	23 NOV 1881	16	096
Petrola, Mary L.	Soulé, Jules E.	17 JAN 1883	17	260
Petsch, Bertha	Michaelson, George H.	05 SEP 1884 L	19	230
Pettes, Mary E.	Ryan, J.C.	14 AUG 1880	14	399
Pettet, H. Anne	Rogers, William Henry	03 OCT 1878	12	250
Pettey, Fannie	Dixon, Frank	10 JUN 1884	19	075
Petteys, Nellie	Adams, Mason P., Dr.	16 JUN 1880	14	324
Pettiford, Edmonia	Harris, Moses	11 NOV 1880 R	15	044
Pettis, Charlotte	Walters, John	14 OCT 1882 L	17	072
Pettis, William	Phillips, Betty	23 AUG 1877 R	11	059
Pettit, Amelia L.	Copeland, Guild Anderson	30 APR 1885 R	20	195
Pettit, Aura V.	Robinson, David H.	04 MAR 1878 L	11	368
Pettit, Elias	Gorahm, Ann Virginia	02 JUL 1885 R	20	306
Pettit, Emily B.	Bailey, Bernard	02 MAR 1881 R	15	207
Pettit, Henry S.	Tinley, Charity A.	25 AUG 1881 R	15	458
Pettit, Jackson	Thompson, Mary E.	24 APR 1884	18	531
Pettit, Lizzie	Mero, Colin Lambert	19 DEC 1881 R	16	140
Pettit, Margaret	Rodgers, James E.	01 MAY 1879 L	13	171
Pettit, Mary Elizabeth	Jones, Edwin P.	15 MAR 1883	17	349
Pettit, Mary Jefferson	Harrison, William Henry	20 SEP 1879 R	13	380
Pettit, Viemma	Davis, Lycurgus F.	23 MAR 1880	14	192
Pettitt, Elmira E.	Weaver, John B.	01 JAN 1879 L	13	003
Pettitt, Madge	Thompson, William H.	07 FEB 1881 R	15	180
Petty, Edward W.	Walker, Mary F.	28 SEP 1882 R	17	041
Petty, Henry S.	Hodges, Margaret E.	12 JUL 1877 R	11	016
Petty, Littleton M.	Woodyard, Annie E.	03 OCT 1881 L	16	003
Peverell, Elizabeth	King, Benjamin F.	14 DEC 1880	15	095
Peverill, Thomas	Duncan, Lizzie	13 FEB 1878 R	11	337
Peyser, Henry	Stein, Rose	12 SEP 1884 L	19	242
Peyser, Hessie	Levy, Samuel	27 APR 1884 R	18	534
Peyser, Sarah	Garner, William	01 FEB 1885 R	20	044
Peyton, Albert	Matthews, Martha	10 SEP 1879 L	13	361
Peyton, Alexander	Jackson, Addealia	29 SEP 1880 R	14	451
Peyton, Cunningham	Sherman, Beulah Walden	30 APR 1883 R	17	422
Peyton, Evelena	Netter, David	07 SEP 1882 R	17	013
Peyton, Fountain	Powell, Caroline	15 APR 1884	18	510
Peyton, J. Harvey	Price, Rosa B.	03 JUN 1885 R	20	253
Peyton, John Francis	Tatspaugh, Laura Ella	07 AUG 1877 R	11	039
Peyton, Josephus S.	Sullivan, Lesley	21 SEP 1881 R	15	496
Peyton, Julia	Matthews, Robert	05 OCT 1885	20	457
Peyton, Leonard	Johnson, Henrietta	15 JUL 1878 L	12	135
Peyton, Mary	Russell, Clarence	01 NOV 1881 R	16	054
Peyton, Randolph V.	White, Mary J.	18 JUL 1878 R	12	138
Peyton, Sarah	Beckley, Charles	22 APR 1885 L	20	184
Peyton, Walter S.	Randolph, Harriet Louisa	17 JUN 1881 R	15	365

Peyton, William Henry	Green, Julia	10 JUL 1883	18	042
Pezzati, Marie Louise Josephine	Schaap, Christian Henry	04 FEB 1880 R	14	101
Pfaff, Hannah	Schimdt, George	09 OCT 1881	15	301
Pfahrer, Elise	Holer, Emil	13 FEB 1879 R	13	060
Pfanz, George A.	Voigt, Mary M.A.	14 AUG 1884 L	19	185
Pfaumann, Laura E.	Furrer, Jacob A.	16 NOV 1879 R	13	486
Pfeiffer, Annetta A.	Herold, Charles	13 NOV 1877 L	11	181
Pfeiffer, Elizabeth Madaline	Baur, Joseph Anton	26 OCT 1879 R	13	442
Pfeiffer, Frederick	White, Catherine	11 SEP 1882 L	17	015
Pfeiffer, Margaret	Littleton, Charles Burras	25 APR 1880 R	14	236
Pfeil, John K., Jr.	Guiss, Amelia	11 MAY 1879 R	13	183
Pfeil, Louisa K.	Goetz, George W.	17 MAR 1878	11	384
Pfeil, Rudolph	Kirby, Amelia A.	21 OCT 1877	11	147
Pfeil, Sophie M.	Fry, Samuel B.	08 APR 1879 R	13	131
Pfiel, John K., Jr.	Burns, Lizzie	01 MAY 1882	16	344
Pfister, Henry	Steiwer, Helena	08 SEP 1879 R	13	355
Pfisterer, Kate	Wicker, William H.	08 JAN 1885 L	20	008
Pfitzmaier, Mary	Bauer, Louis	15 JAN 1880 R	14	105
Pflasterer, Francis	Dixon, Josephine	04 DEC 1883	18	294
Pfluger, George J.	Mechan, Carrie	14 JAN 1885 R	20	018
Pfluger, Katie R.	Clements, Charles A.	14 JAN 1885 R	20	017
Pfluger, Lizzie	Green, Charles	09 JUN 1879	13	225
Phair, George F.	Jamison, Clara	19 OCT 1881 L	16	034
Phair, Jane L.	Hall, John F.	06 DEC 1883 L	18	300
Phair, John H.	Croasdale, Marion S.	13 FEB 1879 R	13	058
Phair, Thomas Elwood	Boss, Anna Estelle	25 JUN 1879 R	13	245
Phearson, Charles H.	Payne, Lucy	28 FEB 1879 R	13	082
Pheatt, Harvey D.	Taylor, Josephine E.	24 SEP 1884	19	266
Phelan, James	Early, Mary L.	15 OCT 1881 R	16	024
Phelps, Annie	Tyeryar, Frank	10 JUN 1880 L	14	316
Phelps, Annie Bell	West, John D.	18 MAR 1884 L	18	476
Phelps, Annie C.	Steurnagle, Adam A.	17 OCT 1882 L	17	076
Phelps, Charles M.H.	Sprightley, Erin C.	27 MAR 1884 R	18	484
Phelps, Ellen Virginia Sibley	Beard, Julian Mortimer	30 DEC 1884	19	500
Phelps, George B.	Finney, Mary M.J.	08 JUN 1880 R	14	309
Phelps, J.W.	Green, Mary A.	16 JUL 1881 L	15	406
Phelps, Joseph A.	Baeschlin, Carrie	17 FEB 1885 L	20	072
Phelps, Richard L.	Johnson, Sarah E.	23 SEP 1877	11	073
Phelps, Sally Maynadier	Brown, Sewellon Alden	05 FEB 1880 R	14	138
Phenix, James	Fisher, Alice V.	25 DEC 1877 R	11	263
Phenix, Sallie	Hill, William Cocoran	23 OCT 1877 R	11	149
Phenix, Samuel	Copper, Lydia	06 JUN 1878	12	091
Philipp, Barbara	Niemanm, Fritz	01 MAY 1882	16	342
Philips, Anna	Ford, Joseph	10 SEP 1884 L	19	239
Phillip, Charles M.	Posey, Rosie M.	13 DEC 1881	16	126
Phillippi, Mane Josephine	Brod, Charles Emile	16 AUG 1880 R	14	400
Phillips, Alice	McMenamin, Richard	05 MAY 1880 R	14	251
Phillips, Alice	Brice, Robert	14 OCT 1885 R	20	482
Phillips, Betty	Pettis, William	23 AUG 1877 R	11	059
Phillips, Edward	Bombray, Elsie	25 SEP 1879 L	13	385
Phillips, Emily R.	Gleason, Henry M.	27 DEC 1882 L	17	215
Phillips, James E.	Divine, Mary E.	16 NOV 1880 R	15	049
Phillips, James R.	Yunghein, Annie	15 AUG 1884	19	187
Phillips, Jane	Roland, John W.	10 MAR 1879 R	13	095
Phillips, Jane, Mrs.	Dyson, John E.	03 DEC 1879 R	14	020
Phillips, John	Clark, Susie	23 JUN 1881 R	15	378
Phillips, John J.	Cunningham, Carrie R.	28 JAN 1885 R	20	024
Phillips, Josephine	Souder, Amos F.	21 SEP 1881 R	15	493

Phillips, Louisa	Pendleton, Frank	25 NOV 1880	15	073
Phillips, Lucy Duncan	Jones, Thomas H.	16 NOV 1881 R	16	072
Phillips, Lucy E.	Horan, Joseph H.	27 MAY 1884 L	19	041
Phillips, Malvina	Dine, Daniel	23 MAY 1885 R	20	232
Phillips, Mamie	Wood, Carroll B.	01 SEP 1884 R	19	218
Phillips, Mary	Lively, John H.	13 AUG 1883	18	084
Phillips, Mary C.	Tilling, John H.	30 JAN 1883 L	17	278
Phillips, Mary E.	Herbert, Edward H.	21 AUG 1884	19	199
Phillips, Miriam E.	Kanke, Cary W.	20 APR 1881 R	15	261
Phillips, Robert A.	Barbour, Mary Imogene	27 DEC 1880 L	15	127
Phillips, Sallie M.	McQueen, James G.	03 MAY 1879 R	13	163
Phillips, Samuel	Braxton, Fanny	11 APR 1878 R	12	001
Phillips, Susie	Withers, Sheldon	26 MAY 1881	15	329
Phillips, William	Johnson, Susie	01 JAN 1878	11	288
Phillipson, Anne Walker	Bagley, Thomas	31 OCT 1878 R	12	303
Philp, John	Pittenger, S. Anna	29 DEC 1880 R	15	129
Philp, Mansel B.	Friel, Emily	06 JUN 1880	14	306
Phipps, John L.	Sears, Josie A.	18 JAN 1883 L	17	267
Phipps, Robert	Bowman, Annie	10 MAY 1883	17	434
Phipps, Thomas E.	Morency, Annie W.S.	14 JUN 1881 L	15	361
Phoenix, Richard	Jackson, Julia	03 AUG 1878 L	12	156
Phoenix, Sylvester	Coats, Laura	24 OCT 1882 L	17	089
Pickett, Robert	Wiley, Jennie C.	27 NOV 1879 R	14	008
Pickett, Rosa	Meredith, Lawson	24 OCT 1881 L	16	040
Pickett, Willis Minor	Washington, Araminta	07 MAR 1878 R	11	367
Pickrell, Carrie Salome	Green, Edward Harris, Dr.	17 DEC 1884 R	19	457
Pickrell, Clara I.	McKenney, William R.	02 DEC 1878 R	12	358
Pickrell, James R.	Willet, Virginia Frances	05 AUG 1885	20	353
Pieper, August K.H.	Schelstedt, Anna Helene	22 JUN 1878 R	12	110
Pierce, Annie J.	Bland, John H.	28 APR 1881 L	15	276
Pierce, Charles B.	Bailey, Calista	25 OCT 1877 L	11	155
Pierce, Clark Sweet	Crumpsey, Laura J.	07 MAR 1883 R	17	331
Pierce, Fannie	MacKenzie, John Stuart	20 NOV 1879 R	13	499
Pierce, Ignatius H.	Velhmeyer, Emma Elizabeth	25 FEB 1878 L	11	356
Pierce, James Edward	Smith, Laura Virginia	23 OCT 1877 R	11	150
Pierce, James F.	Harris, Elizabeth	07 JUL 1879 L	13	272
Pierce, James F.	Taylor, Virgie E.	23 APR 1884	18	528
Pierce, James H.	Ives, Ella K.	04 OCT 1881	16	003
Pierce, John W.	Stewart, Laura	02 DEC 1880 L	15	079
Pierce, Joseph H.	Hull, Evaline W.	09 SEP 1884 L	19	235
Pierce, M.C.	Hicks, Susie	09 JUN 1879 L	13	225
Pierce, Martin Wilbur	Noyes, Marian Bingham	08 JUL 1878 L	12	127
Pierce, William J.	Spicer, Annie	15 NOV 1881 R	16	076
Pierce, William T.	Taylor, Ida May	06 JUL 1882 R	16	438
Pierce, William W.	Brown, Emma V.	26 OCT 1880 R	15	011
Piercynski, Joseph Charles	Knott, Maria Frances	02 AUG 1883	18	072
Pierman, Bettie C.	Nash, Thomas J.	09 OCT 1883 L	18	182
Pierre, John A.	Taylor, Carrie E.	20 APR 1882 R	16	324
Pierson, Charles O.	Till, Ida M., Mrs.	03 NOV 1880 R	15	029
Pierson, Ida M.	Bruce, Henry T.	31 MAY 1882 R	16	382
Pierson, Mary	Harrison, William	13 OCT 1883	18	189
Piexotto, Daniel L.M.	Solomons, Ida J.	21 JAN 1880 R	14	114
Piffer, Robert	Lee, Mary	27 NOV 1884 L	19	423
Pifferling, Zelinda	Bass, Louis	25 OCT 1884 L	19	337
Pifler, Jane A.	Lofty, Frank L.	18 AUG 1885	20	376
Pike, Annie C.	Rollins, George F.	16 MAR 1878 R	11	385
Pike, Charles A.	Heisey, Mary L.	27 SEP 1882 L	17	040
Pike, William H.	Dunn, Mary	01 JUL 1884 L	19	113

Pilkerton, Alexander	Furlong, Emma	07 OCT 1879 L	13	407
Pilkington, Thomas	Wright, Ella	24 DEC 1883 R	18	338
Pillage, Annie Elizabeth	Darr, John Francis	19 JUN 1881 R	15	368
Pillsbeaury, Mary E.	Della, Henry T.	12 JUN 1878 R	12	097
Pinckney, Gabriella	Brown, Isaac	16 AUG 1881 L	15	447
Pinckney, Georgiana	Carter, Charles	30 OCT 1879 R	13	453
Pinckney, Hanson	Butler, Jane	29 OCT 1879 R	13	449
Pindle, Diana	Ennis, Albert	21 DEC 1883 L	18	334
Pindle, Jerome	Dyrerg, Mollie	25 FEB 1884 R	18	438
Pindle, Rebecca	Smoot, Henry	13 MAY 1880	14	269
Pinggold, Hester	Hopkins, Wesley	29 NOV 1883	18	286
Pinion, Rachel	Carter, Frank	18 FEB 1884 R	18	430
Pinkard, Robert O.	Boswell, Josephine	26 FEB 1880 L	14	167
Pinkerton, David C.	Hall, Sallie Evelyn	23 DEC 1880	15	117
Pinkett, Benjamin	Bagby, Nettie	13 JUN 1878 L	12	097
Pinkett, Mary Eliz.	Alexander, Abraham Lin.	05 AUG 1885 R	20	354
Pinkney, Eugene K.	Gross, Mary M.	10 JUL 1878	12	132
Pinkney, Joseph W.	Smoot, Annetta	03 JAN 1883 L	17	236
Pinkney, Laura	Lancaster, Alfred	25 NOV 1879	14	004
Pinkney, Lettie	Marshal, William	28 DEC 1878 L	12	405
Pinkney, Martha	West, Nelson	21 MAY 1885 L	20	233
Pinkney, Priscilla, Mrs.	Pendleton, Thornton	20 AUG 1885 R	20	378
Pinkney, Rachel	Clagett, William	10 JUN 1878 L	12	094
Pinkney, Susan	Allen, James T.	11 JUL 1881 L	15	398
Pinkus, Rosa	Herzog, Joseph	18 MAR 1885 R	20	121
Pinkwood, Emanuel	Galway, Kate	19 JUL 1877 R	11	027
Pinn, David	Shelton, Sallie F.	25 MAY 1880 R	14	285
Pinn, Hannah	Bailey, Addison	01 MAY 1878	12	031
Pinn, Maria	McDaniel, George	16 SEP 1879	13	372
Pinn, Mary	Brown, Albert	02 DEC 1880 R	15	077
Pinn, Strother	Washington, Laura	10 DEC 1878 L	12	375
Piper, Henry	Plumer, Cora Annie	22 NOV 1882 R	17	137
Piper, Samuel L.F.	Lee, Anna E.	29 APR 1885 L	20	197
Pipsico, Letitia	Clark, Edward	05 MAR 1878 L	11	372
Pirie, William	Matthews, Nellie	02 NOV 1882	17	109
Pistorio, Eliza C.	Hudson, George	28 OCT 1879 R	13	445
Pistorio, Emma	Robertson, James P.	08 NOV 1877 R	11	174
Pistorio, F.D.	Padgett, Fannie G.	06 NOV 1877 R	11	169
Pistorio, John N.	Wheeler, Lizzie M.	16 OCT 1879 R	13	430
Pistorio, Josephine	Williams, George A.	31 DEC 1880 L	15	134
Pitcher, Edward	Williams, Annie	01 OCT 1885 R	20	448
Pitcher, Mary	Marshall, Louis	27 AUG 1885	20	387
Pitchlynn, Thomas	Dorsey, Grace M.	12 JAN 1881	15	149
Pittenger, S. Anna	Philp, John	29 DEC 1880 R	15	129
Pitts, Helen	Douglass, Frederick	24 JAN 1884 R	18	395
Pitts, Laban W.	Bass, Marian C.	12 MAR 1884	18	466
Pitts, William H.	Maloney, Julia	01 FEB 1883 L	17	284
Place, Charles H.	Bouldin, Agnes	10 APR 1885 R	20	151
Plant, Alice J.	Kitzmiller, Martin	24 DEC 1878 L	12	399
Plant, George H.	Chase, Henrietta P.	02 JUN 1879	13	215
Plant, Josephine A.	Stewart, William McC.	05 SEP 1877 L	11	077
Plant, Laura V.	Wagoner, Samuel E.	28 JUN 1879 L	13	256
Plant, Louisa	Hawkins, Lewis	19 NOV 1878 L	12	337
Plant, Piercy A.	Parker, Alice R.	14 OCT 1885 R	20	485
Plaskett, Emma T.	Springman, Joseph M.	20 DEC 1877 R	11	250
Plaskett, Joseph	Heflin, Lucy	31 OCT 1879 R	13	457
Plater, Benjamin	Ford, Fannie	04 MAY 1882 L	16	348
Plater, Henry	Ford, Maggie	27 FEB 1882 R	16	260

Plater, Jesse	Owens, Helen	22 JUL 1884	19	151
Plater, Martha	Diggs, William	23 JUL 1880 R	14	362
Plater, Mayhew	Brockenbrough, Alice Bland	29 NOV 1883	18	280
Plater, Sarah	Williams, Welford	20 DEC 1877 L	11	251
Plato, William	Smith, Alice	05 DEC 1883	18	294
Platt, Emily	Hastings, Russell	19 JUN 1878	12	103
Platt, William	Bradbury, Maggie Bross	02 NOV 1877 R	11	164
Player, Milton W.	Turner, Sallie V.	28 JUN 1883 R	18	022
Pleasant, Sallie	Buchanan, Israel	15 NOV 1877	11	187
Pleasants, Annie E.	Morrison, Joseph	20 DEC 1882 R	17	196
Pleasants, Charles L.	Brown, Sallie W.	29 MAY 1882 R	16	380
Pleasants, Emily	Simms, John F.	08 JUN 1880 L	14	312
Pleasants, Evie J.	Willis, Peter D.	23 OCT 1880 R	15	010
Pleasants, James H.	Stamps, Laura	16 APR 1878	12	006
Pleasants, Joseph H.	Lawson, Emeline	22 JUN 1883 L	18	010
Pleasants, Katie	Bushnell, T. Howard	18 MAY 1878 L	12	058
Pleasants, Margaret Cassandra	Carman, Jesse Seaman	27 OCT 1881 R	16	046
Pletsch, Rosa	Howard, George B.	17 DEC 1883 L	18	319
Plitt, August	Voehl, Louisa	14 FEB 1882	16	239
Plitt, Emma	Lustig, Charles	21 NOV 1880 R	15	058
Plowden, James H.	Howard, Martha C.	13 MAR 1882 L	16	275
Plowden, Jesse	Pearson, Lottie	11 APR 1882 L	16	308
Plowden, Robert Henry	Lee, Maggie Elizabeth	07 NOV 1883 L	18	241
Plowman, Jesse W.	Davis, Nona	09 APR 1881 R	15	252
Plowman, Jesse W.	Grimes, Jennie V.	09 SEP 1883 R	18	119
Plumer, Cora Annie	Piper, Henry	22 NOV 1882 R	17	137
Plummer, Daniel	Stewart, Mary Alice	18 JUN 1885	20	279
Plummer, Elizabeth Jane	Winslow, James H.	19 DEC 1877 L	11	246
Plummer, Julia Ella	Fearson, Charles Dallas	03 JUN 1879 F	13	214
Plummer, Mary	Brown, Isaac	20 JUL 1880	14	369
Plummer, Mary	Redmond, Francis	02 SEP 1884 L	19	221
Plummer, Milton	Gibson, Alice	03 OCT 1878 L	12	251
Plummmer, Mollie H.	Pumphrey, Charles B.	10 SEP 1878	12	211
Plunkett, Frank	Hurdel, Ella C.	16 NOV 1878 L	12	332
Poch, Wilhelm	Auth, Paulina	17 JUN 1882	16	417
Pocher, Simon	Giles, Elizabeth	05 SEP 1878	12	199
Podiaski, B.F.	Schneider, Annie Mary	15 SEP 1881 L	15	485
Poffenberger, Martin L.	Frye, Elizabeth G.	06 JUN 1883 R	17	480
Pogenhoff, Frank W.	Kookogey, Olivia R.	02 JAN 1885	20	002
Poggensee, Johannah Martha	Bachschmid, Paul	04 SEP 1883 R	18	109
Poindexter, Hattie	Moore, Alfred	03 AUG 1885 R	20	349
Poindexter, James Green	Williams, Elizabeth	01 JUN 1882 L	16	387
Poindexter, Julia A.	Barnes, Elzy	04 NOV 1880 R	15	030
Poindexter, Katie	Alexander, Lewis	03 JAN 1881 R	14	300
Poindexter, Sarah	Braxton, John	13 FEB 1885 R	20	041
Poindexter, William M.	Neilson, Julia	06 OCT 1881	16	011
Poist, Robert C.	Noyes, Henrietta	27 OCT 1880 L	15	017
Poland, Fanny D.	Allison, Charles H.	19 JUN 1884 R	19	093
Pole, Samuel Boyce	Christine, Katie Josephine	02 SEP 1880 R	14	427
Polen, Noble B.	Kidwell, Mary C.	17 MAR 1885 R	20	121
Polen, William H.	Smith, Laura Virginia	28 MAR 1882 R	16	291
Polglase, Emma G.	Dungan, Ezekial S.	13 APR 1878	12	003
Polk, Madeleine Tascar	Buell, Augustus C.	11 MAR 1878 R	11	376
Polk, Matthias	Merritt, Louisa	04 MAR 1880 R	14	175
Polkinhorn, Charles R.	Perry, Fannie V.	15 SEP 1883	18	132
Polkinhorn, Joseph H.	Stubblefield, Grace T.	14 NOV 1882 R	17	129
Pollard, Alelia	Lowry, M.K.	22 SEP 1883	18	148
Pollard, Griffin	Fields, Louisa	26 MAY 1880 L	14	288

Pollard, Griffith	Fields, Louvinia	02 JAN 1878 L	11	287
Pollard, J. Austin	Knight, Mary K.	22 JUN 1882 L	16	423
Pollard, James	White, Mary	13 OCT 1885	20	479
Pollard, Sarah	McKenney, George B.	20 NOV 1879 L	13	497
Pollard, Thomas	Bryan, Maggie	15 JUL 1880	14	363
Pollock, Andrew Lyon	Larkin, Verona Elflida	25 OCT 1879 R	13	442
Pollock, Anne Louise	Baker, John	21 JUN 1881 R	15	369
Pollock, Mary Agnes	Vermillion, James Franklin	17 MAY 1883 R	17	447
Pollock, Virginia, Mrs.	Williams, Dennis	23 NOV 1882 L	17	145
Pollott, Frances	Mines, Solomon E.	02 SEP 1880 R	14	429
Polly, Ida R.	White, William K.	30 JUL 1878 L	12	151
Polly, Joseph Edward	Luckett, Martha Cecilia	22 JUL 1877	11	028
Polson, Kitty Tucker	Morton, Arthur Austerfield	31 DEC 1883 R	18	332
Polston, James Edward	Coleman, Lucy Ann	06 DEC 1877	11	222
Pomeroy, Harry M.	Rickard, Carrie A.	11 JUL 1884	19	135
Pomeroy, James S.	Clements, Mary Ida	26 DEC 1883 R	18	344
Pomeroy, John F.	Seaton, Mollie F.	06 MAY 1884	19	007
Pommeresher, Emma	Ralph, Adolph	28 SEP 1882 L	17	042
Pond, Alice Hubbard	King, William, Jr.	23 SEP 1880 R	14	458
Pond, Lilly Virginia	Parker, Richard T.	20 OCT 1884 L	19	323
Pony, Martha	Clark, Gabriel	08 NOV 1877	11	175
Pool, Benjamin G.	Chase, Fannie R.	20 DEC 1882 R	17	194
Pool, Mary W.	Fluehart, John C.	22 JAN 1879 R	13	031
Pool, Wm. Alex	Evans, Emma	14 SEP 1881 R	14	233
Poole, Dorsey W.	Stanley, Mary V.	15 NOV 1877 L	11	186
Poole, E.C.	Bell, R.R.	08 NOV 1883	18	244
Poole, Edwin W.	McDaniel, Martha A., Mrs.	11 OCT 1877 R	11	132
Poole, George	Davis, Minnie	18 MAY 1882 L	16	367
Poole, Katie A.	Conrad, Robert W.	30 SEP 1878 R	12	243
Poole, Maria A.	Young, Charles H.	14 JUN 1884	19	083
Poole, Martha	Johnson, Thomas	25 JUL 1879	13	286
Poole, Scott	Lee, Ann	14 MAR 1878	11	383
Poole, Wm. Thos.	Jones, Annie E.	14 APR 1880	14	221
Poor, Ada T.	Cotter, Joseph W.	26 JAN 1882 L	16	211
Poor, Annie Cunningham	Glover, Charles Carroll	10 JAN 1878 R	11	300
Poor, Clara N.	Pyles, William H.	16 MAY 1878 L	12	052
Poore, Bushard W.	Barnaclo, Alice	10 JUN 1882	16	403
Poore, Josephine	Somerville, Fred N.	16 FEB 1882	16	245
Poore, Mary	Allen, George W.	21 JAN 1878 L	11	311
Poore, Mary A.	Lipscomb, John T.	16 FEB 1882	16	245
Pope, Emanuel	Monroe, Louise	19 APR 1883 L	17	400
Pope, Frederick C.	Whitney, Susan, Mrs.	08 JUN 1882 R	16	401
Pope, Frederick C.	Jack, Sophia C.	18 DEC 1884 L	19	472
Pope, Georgie	Richardson, Frederick	22 OCT 1884	19	325
Pope, Minnie B.	Davis, Edward F.	03 FEB 1881	15	177
Pope, N.Q.	Cassell, Lou A.	03 APR 1878 R	11	405
Popkins, Ella F.	Ennis, Edward	10 JUN 1884	19	074
Popkins, Sarah A.	Tucker, Richard W.	11 APR 1883 R	17	390
Popp, Oswold	Klueh, Josephine	11 OCT 1881	16	017
Porter, Adalaide	Henson, Thomas Bruce	26 FEB 1885 R	20	083
Porter, Adeline	Skiner, Richard H.	07 NOV 1878	12	316
Porter, Alice	Burks, Nelson	19 FEB 1884 L	18	430
Porter, Blanche	Southworth, Richmond J.	23 MAR 1878 L	11	391
Porter, Charles, Capt.	Wilkins, Carrie E.	24 APR 1879 R	13	155
Porter, Charles W.	West, Maggie	22 MAR 1880 R	14	191
Porter, Charles W.	Patten, Mary Emma	05 JUN 1883	17	477
Porter, Charlotte A.	Taylor, George P.	29 JUN 1882 R	16	427
Porter, David	Kelly, Alice	10 OCT 1878 R	12	265

Porter, Harvey J.	Glenn, Minnie Sherburne	29 FEB 1884	18	449
Porter, Ida V.	Rodier, James LaCoste	15 MAY 1879 L	13	192
Porter, Jane	Gilbert, Isaac	15 JAN 1879 L	13	018
Porter, Jermain G.	Snowden, Emily B.	03 JUL 1879 R	13	256
Porter, John	Young, Mary	15 SEP 1883	18	131
Porter, Lizzie	Jones, William	06 SEP 1878	12	203
Porter, Magga	Greene, Clinton	07 OCT 1883 R	18	220
Porter, Margaret Ann	Dyer, Nathaniel	27 OCT 1880 R	15	016
Porter, Mary A.	Douglass, William O.	04 AUG 1885	20	352
Porter, Rufus H., Rev.	Parks, Janie	05 MAR 1879 R	13	090
Porter, Sophia	Taliaferro, Loudon	26 DEC 1878 R	12	402
Porter, Susie E.	Harley, John J.	06 SEP 1882 L	17	009
Porter, Thomas	Ashton, Emma	30 JUL 1885	20	345
Porter, Thomas K.	Goodrich, Elizabeth Elliot	22 JAN 1879	13	030
Porter, Venora E.	Buckingham, William E.	14 JUL 1885 R	20	323
Porter, William R.	Burns, Sallie	27 JAN 1885 R	20	038
Portis, Laura	Shely, James Wm.	07 OCT 1885 R	20	467
Portlock, Fannie	Dines, Philip	15 JUN 1885	20	271
Posey, Annie	Smith, Harrison	02 MAY 1878 R	12	034
Posey, Annie Eliza	Ford, Frederick	04 OCT 1885 R	20	454
Posey, Benjamin Hunter	Taylor, Katie Lee	22 MAY 1882 R	16	371
Posey, Emma	Lacey, Joseph	27 JUL 1882 L	16	428
Posey, Francis A.	Bender, Catharine A.	02 JUL 1883 L	18	030
Posey, Francis B.	Miller, Mary F.	17 DEC 1879 L	14	054
Posey, Ida P.	Streets, Frank W.	05 DEC 1877 L	11	222
Posey, Isaac H.	Williams, M. Margaret	28 JUN 1882 L	16	429
Posey, John A.	White, Annie	01 NOV 1882 R	17	106
Posey, Mary A.	Johnson, George W.	29 MAY 1883 R	17	467
Posey, Mary L.	Sturgis, John R.	12 FEB 1883	17	303
Posey, Rebecca	McConley, Charles	16 MAR 1884 R	18	471
Posey, Rosie M.	Phillip, Charles M.	13 DEC 1881	16	126
Possey, J'An	Dyson, John	01 NOV 1883 R	18	229
Post, Chas. C.	Speer, Minnie S.	16 NOV 1878 R	12	332
Post, William E.	McKinzie, Littie L.	05 NOV 1883	18	232
Postell, Porcher	Barnes, Agnes R.	02 NOV 1884	19	353
Posthwait, Clara D.	Elliot, Charles A.	07 OCT 1878 L	12	257
Postley, Charles E.	Murray, Clare	27 DEC 1881 R	16	140
Posy, Amanda V.	Johnson, Jacob A.	27 MAR 1884 R	18	485
Potbury, William Enos	Thomas, Amelia Christina	23 JUN 1885	20	287
Potee, Robert L.	Cavis, Belle	06 APR 1885 R	20	145
Potee, Thomas	Wenzel, Catherine	19 MAR 1878	11	387
Potmer, Lizzie	Smoot, Karl	11 JUL 1880 R	14	352
Potter, Edward	Rogers, Alice	23 JUL 1884	19	152
Potter, John William	Williams, Fannie M.	18 SEP 1884 L	19	260
Potter, Susan Virginia	Clair, Edward G.	11 DEC 1877 L	11	230
Potts, Bertha L.	Henderson, C.W.	21 JUL 1885	20	337
Potts, Mary Jane	Wilson, Robert	09 JAN 1882 R	16	186
Poutsch, John Thomas	Stallings, Jane Eliza Sherwood	11 NOV 1880 R	15	045
Powake, Joana	Manikheim, John G.	07 APR 1885	20	212
Powell, Addel A. [Rachel]	Johnson, Norman	27 JUL 1883	18	062
Powell, Alice	Slade, Roman	05 JUL 1884	19	123
Powell, Caroline	Peyton, Fountain	15 APR 1884	18	510
Powell, Charles H.	Wallace, Catherine	14 MAY 1885 R	20	156
Powell, Charles M.	Watson, Fannie J.	10 AUG 1885	20	362
Powell, Charles R.	Wright, Jennie E.	25 APR 1883	17	417
Powell, Dallas	Simpson, Bettie	29 MAR 1882 R	16	293
Powell, David	Orange, Malinda	28 APR 1881 L	15	281
Powell, Edward	Smith, Ellen	23 JUN 1880 L	14	331

Name	Spouse	Date	Vol	Page
Powell, Ella	Chase, Greenbury	07 SEP 1877 R	11	070
Powell, Ella	Chase, Greenbury	29 OCT 1877 R	09	2164
Powell, Evelina	Hamilton, Charles	17 SEP 1885 L	20	424
Powell, George	Ridgley, Arabella	13 DEC 1879	14	047
Powell, Georgie W.	Tyler, Lacklan	02 NOV 1878 R	12	306
Powell, Harriet	Watson, James H.	14 FEB 1878 R	11	341
Powell, Irene F.	Walker, Herbert T.	29 MAY 1879 L	13	209
Powell, Jacob	Thompson, Fannie	31 MAY 1881 L	15	334
Powell, Malinda	Champ, Charles P.	24 APR 1884 R	18	515
Powell, Martha Ann	Proctor, Richard	16 JAN 1882 L	16	196
Powell, Mary	Branham, Samuel	29 DEC 1877 L	11	280
Powell, Mary	Edmonds, James	20 MAY 1884 L	19	028
Powell, Mary M.	Lee, Richard J.	02 SEP 1880 R	14	426
Powell, Nancy	Hitchins, Owen	14 MAR 1885 R	20	113
Powell, Robert C.	Gray, Hattie	22 JUL 1879	13	288
Powell, Samuel	Horton, Margaret Elizabeth	15 JUN 1885	20	273
Powell, Sarah	Russel, Robert	24 OCT 1878	12	290
Powell, Sarah J.	White, Theodore F.	16 MAR 1878	11	383
Powell, Tobias	Coombs, Mary	30 SEP 1880 L	14	466
Powell, Wm. H.	Green, Harriet	11 MAY 1882 L	16	357
Powels, Sallie	Thomas, William	03 DEC 1878 R	12	350
Power, Ann L.	Williams, Watkins H.	16 DEC 1878 L	12	383
Power, J. Clyde	Lacey, Edith E.	23 JUL 1884	19	153
Power, Robert H., Dr.	French, Dorathea B.	17 AUG 1881 R	15	449
Powers, Annie M.	Muldoon, E.F.	29 DEC 1879	14	078
Powers, Augusta	Johnson, Albert	21 DEC 1882 L	17	202
Powers, Celeste	Lipscomb, Stanley	05 JUL 1881 R	15	391
Powers, Cora	Atwell, John W.	15 MAY 1883 R	17	443
Powers, John S.	Armistead, Rose A.	11 JUN 1884	19	077
Powers, Lavina	Myers, William	20 MAY 1885 L	20	230
Powers, Mary F.	Sewel, Josiah	07 JUN 1879	13	223
Powers, Sophie Jane	Goodrick, Samuel	03 DEC 1879 R	14	023
Powers, William	Starud, Rachel Ann	29 NOV 1882 L	17	158
Pozner, Mary	Auth, John	09 OCT 1877	11	124
Pracht, George Hermann	Scharfe, Lizzie	12 MAY 1880 R	14	267
Pralle, George William	Tegeler, Anna Sophia	30 OCT 1883 R	18	220
Prater, Lucy	Riggs, Washington Edward	20 MAY 1880 R	14	276
Prater, Martha C.	Mann, William Walter	31 DEC 1884	19	469
Prater, Mary E.	Stewart, C. McK.	27 MAY 1895	14	180
Prater, Rachael A.	Davis, William	05 DEC 1881	16	109
Prather, Annie Darius	Briscoe, Benjamin Franklin	25 SEP 1879 R	13	384
Prather, Beatrice	Frailey, Robert T.	01 JUL 1885 R	20	302
Prather, Catharine Edmonia	Roberson, Peter Asbury	20 OCT 1884 R	19	319
Prather, Charles S.	Barrett, Hannah M.	09 SEP 1884 L	19	235
Prather, Flora R.	McDaniel, William D.	09 SEP 1884	19	237
Prather, Ida	Saunders, George	12 FEB 1878	11	337
Prather, Ida Kate	Harvey, Charles A., Jr.	25 DEC 1879 R	14	073
Prather, Jesse J.	Hodgen, Annie M.	06 JUL 1885 R	20	056
Prather, Jessie M.	Jacobs, George M.	15 AUG 1885	20	371
Pratt, Caroline Outerbridge	McQueen, Hoel Lawrence	07 NOV 1878 R	12	310
Pratt, Isaiah	Matthews, Julia Ann	13 SEP 1882 L	17	019
Pratt, James Calcott	Johnston, Margaret Stewart	11 OCT 1883 R	18	187
Pratt, Nellie	Wall, Edward J.	02 JUN 1884 R	19	045
Pratt, William B.	Taylor, Sue B.	28 AUG 1883	18	098
Preall, Andrew J.	Higby, Celinda	12 JUN 1883	17	488
Preinkert, Fred C.B.	Taylor, Mary J.	03 MAY 1882	16	345
Preinkert, John P.	Taylor, Alice Ward	08 OCT 1885	20	471
Prelle, Fritz	Mouch, Anna Catherine	20 NOV 1878 L	12	339

D.C. Marriage Records Index, June 28, 1877 to October 19, 1885

Preller, Mary Irene	Ciscle, George E.	28 OCT 1884 L	19	341
Prendeville, Kate	Shughrue, John	13 NOV 1882	17	123
Prentiss, Eunice A.	Caulfield, Charles J.	17 JUL 1880 R	14	366
Presbrey, Frank Spencer	Cohen, Emma	12 JUN 1878 R	12	095
Prescott, Clara C.	Hogan, Leonard T.	22 OCT 1884	19	320
Prescott, Mary Frances	Vaughan, William W., Jr.	25 DEC 1882	17	205
Presgrave, Eugene W.	Bradshaw, Ida C.	27 FEB 1883 L	17	322
Presgraves, Frank	Walker, Gerice	19 JAN 1882 L	16	202
Presgraves, Thomas L.	Palmer, Annie E.	15 DEC 1880 R	15	097
Preston, Anne	Jacobs, Henry	21 JUN 1881 R	15	370
Preston, Clarence	Washington, Annie	07 SEP 1883 L	18	117
Preston, Ida	Kenney, James	08 JAN 1884 L	18	369
Preston, John H.	Krouse, Mary L.	04 JAN 1882 R	16	180
Preston, Oliver J.	Shugrue, Maggie	09 AUG 1879 L	13	313
Preston, Samuel	Smith, M.	18 JUL 1881	15	395
Preston, Samuel Henry H.	Robinson, Magdeline Rosetta	12 AUG 1879	13	316
Price, Abram	Ramsey, Sarah	20 DEC 1884 R	19	474
Price, Albert Sidney Johnson	Brown, Katie	28 MAY 1884 R	19	041
Price, Alice	Gant, Daniel E.	06 JUN 1878 R	12	089
Price, Aurelia	Dove, Henry	10 MAR 1880 L	14	182
Price, Basil	Countee, Mary Jane	05 AUG 1880	14	388
Price, Bettie	Green, Lewis	03 APR 1882	16	296
Price, Bettie	Alexander, Albert	05 JUN 1884 R	19	064
Price, C.C.	Hodgkin, M.A.	02 JAN 1878	11	289
Price, Charles P.	Watkins, Virginia	12 JUL 1881	15	400
Price, Edward	Ship, Trittie Ann	17 NOV 1883 L	18	262
Price, Edwin F.	Bell, Katie G.	06 DEC 1882	17	169
Price, Fannie	Kenney, John	05 JUL 1885 R	20	310
Price, Fannie F.	Smith, George W.	22 NOV 1877 L	11	198
Price, Florence E.	Richards, Lewis H.	11 OCT 1881	16	017
Price, Francis	Williams, Laura B.	11 SEP 1878 L	12	212
Price, Frederick M.	Quigley, Julia A.	13 MAY 1885 L	20	219
Price, George W.	Fitzgerald, Ella	09 FEB 1885 L	20	058
Price, Ida B.	Thompson, Charles W.	26 JUL 1883	18	062
Price, Jacob	Foster, Annie	16 DEC 1881 R	16	134
Price, Jane	Butler, Buck	24 JUN 1885 L	20	290
Price, Janie	Schafer, Phillip	27 AUG 1884 L	19	211
Price, John	Coleman, Caroline	04 MAR 1878 L	11	369
Price, John H.	Morris, Susie	06 MAY 1880 L	14	257
Price, John J.	Moore, Capitola	26 AUG 1884	19	206
Price, John S.	Ensor, Rachel A.	13 NOV 1878 R	12	326
Price, Kate R.	Tennent, John G.	24 APR 1882 L	16	331
Price, Lemuel	Jackson, Catharine	19 JUN 1879 R	13	196
Price, Margaret E.	Thompson, Middleton	04 JUN 1878 L	12	082
Price, Mary	Ward, Amanuel	11 DEC 1878 L	12	376
Price, Mollie B.	French, James W.	31 OCT 1883 R	18	224
Price, Nannie	Carr, Allen	14 FEB 1884 R	18	424
Price, Noah	Loudon, Maria	04 NOV 1880 R	15	029
Price, Rena	Cooksey, Francis B.	18 OCT 1880	14	498
Price, Robert R.	Ruppert, Kate M.	20 FEB 1882 L	16	249
Price, Rosa A.	Duvall, George W.	19 AUG 1882 R	16	487
Price, Rosa B.	Peyton, J. Harvey	03 JUN 1885 R	20	253
Price, Sandonia	Cox, William T.	18 FEB 1885	20	074
Price, Thomas W.	Benson, Rosetta L.	21 DEC 1882 L	17	200
Price, William	Smith, Amelia	25 APR 1878 R	12	017
Price, William Henry	Johnson, Annie	10 JAN 1878 R	11	296
Price, William Paschal	Wood, William Ann	23 SEP 1882 L	17	034
Priddy, E.O. Clifford	Bloomer, Eliza S.	18 JUL 1878	12	139

Name	Spouse	Date		
Priddy, John Edward	Robertson, Ruth	28 SEP 1883	18	101
Pridgeon, Mary Virginia	Broune, William E.	04 AUG 1885 L	20	350
Priest, Lucy	Dorcas, Jackson	13 AUG 1885 L	20	369
Priest, Nannie E.	Shamwell, James H.	23 DEC 1882 L	17	207
Prigg, Ada Ball	Coe, Walker Peyton Conway	25 MAR 1885 R	20	131
Primus, Lewis H.	Parker, Ellen	07 NOV 1878	12	314
Primus, Lucy	Wood, James Henry	05 MAY 1884 R	19	008
Prince, Fannie	Smith, Walter	19 JUL 1877 R	11	026
Prince, James P.	Robinson, Harriet	04 SEP 1883 L	18	108
Prince, John A.	Webster, Emily F.	30 JUN 1880 L	14	339
Prince, Laura	Taylor, Robert	09 OCT 1880 L	14	484
Prince, Martha	Dinquid, William Alphonse	12 FEB 1880 R	14	151
Prior, William	Jackson, L.J.	18 JUL 1878	12	142
Pritchard, George J.	Dutton, Leila V.	08 OCT 1884	19	294
Pritchard, Jessie R.	Gates, Walter N.	15 SEP 1885 R	20	419
Pritchard, John H.	Miner, Maggie	02 JUN 1881 L	15	340
Pritchard, Stephen Meredith	Meads, Ida Virginia	04 JUN 1884 R	19	057
Pritchet, Mattie	Hall, Lutha	20 SEP 1878	12	228
Pritchett, M. Blanche	Gordan, Charles H.	26 FEB 1878	11	358
Pritchett, Mary E.	Selby, William S.	16 JAN 1879 R	13	022
Proctor, Abr. M.	Ashford, Annie E.	09 JUN 1880 R	14	313
Proctor, Arthur B.	Gibbons, Mary E.	10 JUN 1885 R	20	266
Proctor, Cordelia	Butler, Delozier Jerry	28 JUL 1880 L	14	377
Proctor, Daniel Brads.	Glasgow, Ann Elizabeth	16 OCT 1877	11	137
Proctor, Eliza	Henderson, Joseph	27 OCT 1884	19	339
Proctor, Ellen	Rogers, Joseph	18 JUN 1885 L	20	280
Proctor, Emma J.	Burr, Charles E.	26 MAR 1885 R	20	133
Proctor, Fannie A.	Stephens, Edward A.	09 OCT 1882 R	17	060
Proctor, George	Taylor, Fanny	06 SEP 1883 R	18	114
Proctor, George Thomas	Wallace, Lavinia	19 FEB 1880 R	14	158
Proctor, Henry	Turner, Lydia	26 AUG 1880 R	14	411
Proctor, James	Darron, Elizabeth	20 OCT 1883 R	18	200
Proctor, James	Crittenton, Mary	26 MAR 1885 L	20	134
Proctor, John M.	Mason, Catherine Germond	03 NOV 1879 R	13	460
Proctor, Lewis	Collins, Jennie	02 JUL 1884 R	19	116
Proctor, Martha	Higgins, Reason	21 NOV 1878 L	12	341
Proctor, Mary	Emory, Albert	02 APR 1885	20	142
Proctor, Mary E.	Smith, Robert J.	05 OCT 1881 R	16	011
Proctor, Mary Ellen	Colbert, James	07 NOV 1879 L	13	472
Proctor, Richard	Powell, Martha Ann	16 JAN 1882 L	16	196
Proctor, Rose	Adams, George S.	01 NOV 1881 R	16	054
Proctor, Samuel	Harris, Alice A.	13 OCT 1877 L	11	134
Proctor, Sylvester	Thompson, Kittie Anne	10 DEC 1878 R	12	374
Proctor, Virginia	Smith, Edward	23 OCT 1884 L	19	334
Proctor, William	Christian, Lucy Ellen	17 NOV 1881	16	083
Proctor, Willie Worthington	King, Hattie Maria	22 JUL 1880 R	14	372
Progatzky, Otto Charles	Mills, Emma	23 MAR 1880 R	14	186
Prosise, Ida Virginia	Fowler, Frank Stephen	28 SEP 1881 R	15	499
Prosperi, Adelaide Aug.	Cridler, Thomas Wilbur	26 FEB 1885 R	20	087
Prosperi, Fredrick	House, Jennie	11 JUN 1878 R	12	102
Prosperi, James H.	Walsh, Mamie	24 DEC 1883 L	18	340
Prosser, Erastus S.	Muldary, Catharine	23 JAN 1878	11	315
Prott, Frank J.	Koch, Mary E.	06 FEB 1882 L	16	226
Prout, Alice	Godson, George	17 DEC 1879	14	050
Prout, Ellen Teresa	Corcoran, Richard J.	23 JAN 1884 L	18	392
Prout, Emma C.	Vernon, Charles E.	29 OCT 1878	12	297
Provis, William	Holston, Dora	23 JUL 1878 L	12	145
Provoo, Lizzie E.	Satterwhite, Jefferson D.	27 DEC 1883 R	18	347

Pruette, Florence J.	Petersen, Charles W.	01 DEC 1880	15	075
Prufer, William J.	Harris, Sadie F.	10 SEP 1878	12	208
Pryer, John W.	Smith, Amand	27 DEC 1883 L	18	347
Pryor, Alice	Eskridge, Osborne	16 DEC 1882	17	188
Pryor, Ellsworth	Braxton, Louisa N.	23 AUG 1884	19	204
Pryor, Emily	Custis, Henry	07 DEC 1881 L	16	119
Pryor, Fannie E.	Jones, Anthony	24 JAN 1884 L	18	394
Pryor, Joseph	Winters, Rebecca	25 DEC 1884 R	19	480
Pryor, Julia E. Anderson	Clifton, John	28 AUG 1879 R	13	342
Pryor, Maria	Robinson, Daniel	02 APR 1883	17	288
Pryor, Mary Virginia	Spencer, James H.	21 APR 1881 R	15	268
Pryor, Robert	Smith, Emma	31 MAR 1879	13	119
Pryor, Robert James	Hall, Josephine	09 FEB 1884 L	18	416
Pryor, Robert R.	Patton, Amelia A.	16 AUG 1877	11	056
Pryor, Thomas D.	Siggers, Kate Virginia	17 AUG 1885 R	20	374
Pugh, Jennie	Kemon, Solon C.	18 SEP 1877	11	098
Pugh, Sallie S.	Elliot, Albert D.	09 SEP 1884	19	231
Pugh, Thomas O.	Darby, Hattie	03 OCT 1882 R	17	050
Pulchin, Pasqua	Leason, Frances	10 AUG 1885 R	20	363
Pulies, Llewellyn Wm.	Jean, Lina Essie	12 MAR 1885 R	20	108
Pulitzer, Joseph	Davis, Kate	19 JUN 1878	12	106
Pullen, Janie T.	Hopkins, Edward E.	31 JAN 1883	17	281
Pullen, John Fountani	Clark, Ann Jordan	10 JUL 1880 L	14	355
Pullett, John Edward	Snowden, Mary Emily	26 NOV 1879 L	14	010
Pulley, Perry W.	Coakley, Seraphine F.	18 OCT 1881 R	16	032
Pulliam, George F.	Lillard, Lizzie J.	27 JUL 1879	13	295
Pullian, Marietta	Lewis, John	14 OCT 1880 R	14	496
Pullman, Edgar J.	Haines, Emma N.	30 DEC 1883	18	354
Pulman, C.O.	Marting, Mary A.	20 AUG 1885	20	381
Pulman, Henry B.	Downey, Susie L.	20 NOV 1884	19	399
Pulman, Samuel	King, Lillie Lee	15 JUL 1885 R	20	326
Pumphrey, Charles B.	Plummmer, Mollie H.	10 SEP 1878	12	211
Pumphrey, Columbus	Condie, Charlotte	18 FEB 1880 R	14	158
Pumphrey, Edward	Hayes, Hester Edith	16 AUG 1883	18	090
Pumphrey, Emma A.	Hogan, John F.	26 DEC 1877 R	11	265
Pumphrey, Frank	Bradley, Lulu	26 FEB 1884 L	18	445
Pumphrey, Laura C.	Towne, Frank H.	01 OCT 1878	12	244
Pumphrey, Martha	Weedon, Lee Poyntz	14 APR 1885 L	20	165
Pumphrey, Mary F.	White, M.F.	11 JUL 1885	20	320
Pumphrey, R.H.	Riggs, Mamie G.	14 NOV 1881 L	16	074
Pumphrey, Robert H.	Soper, Mollie	12 MAY 1881	15	305
Pundexter, Geo. Wallace	Yowles, Harriet	03 JUN 1880 R	14	305
Purcell, Benjamin F.	Cook, Louisa	08 APR 1884	18	501
Purcell, Ellen J.	Quackenbush, George	11 OCT 1877 R	11	131
Purcell, James H.	Davis, Alice C.	28 OCT 1884	19	343
Purcell, John Fleet	Duvall, Sarah A. Grandell	26 JUN 1879 R	13	253
Purcell, Mahlon	Filler, Maud	23 FEB 1881 R	15	200
Purcell, Thomas P.	Harrin, Mary A.	29 JUN 1882	16	430
Purdum, J. Rufus	Hall, Sarah A.	01 MAY 1883 R	17	420
Purdy, John E.	Reed, Mary E.	30 AUG 1883	18	106
Purdy, John W. Larman	Balcher, Elizabeth	18 SEP 1879 R	13	376
Purington, Joseph W.	Hodgson, Laura C.	11 MAY 1881	15	302
Purinton, Alice Josephine	Perkins, William F.	29 AUG 1877 L	11	070
Purks, Bettie G.	Jones, Lewis G.	28 DEC 1884	19	495
Purks, William Plumer	Stengel, Mary	08 AUG 1881 L	15	436
Purman, David Gray	Secor, Marilla E.	19 AUG 1880 R	14	408
Purman, Louis C.	Barrett, Carrie L.	26 AUG 1880 L	14	418
Purner, Lillie M.	Quinter, William E.	05 FEB 1884 R	18	410

Puruer, Ferdinand	Yost, Amelia	11 AUG 1884	19	168
Purvis, Joseph P.	Purvis, Julia Lee	04 DEC 1882 R	17	166
Purvis, Julia Lee	Purvis, Joseph P.	04 DEC 1882 R	17	166
Pusey, Annie	Koontz, Marcellus	07 APR 1878	11	410
Pusey, Louanna	McDowell, James H.	04 OCT 1877 R	11	123
Putnam, Benjamin	Fishback, Sallie	19 JUN 1878 R	12	110
Putner, William S.	Almond, Maggie	08 JUL 1882 R	16	443
Puvogel, Diedrich	Ellerbruck, Dora	08 SEP 1882	17	014
Pye, Mary C.	Colbert, Edward N.	29 JAN 1883 L	17	277
Pyles, Annie	Finn, John F.	17 MAR 1884	18	473
Pyles, Barbara Ellen	Dorsey, Thomas Edward	24 JUL 1879 R	13	290
Pyles, Emeline	King, Walter J.	10 MAR 1885	20	103
Pyles, Frances R.	Van Gruder, Frank	29 JAN 1883 R	17	277
Pyles, Francis T.	Ryan, Catherine S.	10 FEB 1880 L	14	145
Pyles, James	Payne, Eliza	05 MAY 1881	15	293
Pyles, John T.	Tenley, Annie H.	07 NOV 1883	18	240
Pyles, Lula R.	Turton, William E.	07 DEC 1882 L	17	172
Pyles, Mary Elizabeth	Burrows, George Francis	08 DEC 1880 R	15	087
Pyles, Sarah E.	Paxton, Richard L.	22 NOV 1882	17	143
Pyles, William H.	Poor, Clara N.	16 MAY 1878 L	12	052
Pyncheon, William McKibben	King, Florence E.	07 MAR 1883 L	17	337
Pynn, Samuel	Jones, Lavinia	09 JAN 1879 L	13	012
Pywell, Ella E.	Shipley, Maurice E.	18 OCT 1880 R	14	500
Pywell, Emma C.	Rea, Thomas F.	13 MAR 1878	11	379
Pywell, Francis E.	Weitzel, Louisa M.	14 AUG 1879 R	13	318

Q

Quackenbush, Geo. D.	Boyle, Ellen	30 SEP 1880	14	464
Quackenbush, George	Purcell, Ellen J.	11 OCT 1877 R	11	131
Quailley, Elizabeth	Morrow, Thomas	15 APR 1879 L	13	143
Qualtrough, Edward Francis	Ray, Leila	06 NOV 1879 R	13	467
Quander, Charles Henry	Bell, Amanda A.R.	18 DEC 1878	12	385
Quander, Joseph	Nickins, Annie	29 JAN 1880 R	14	127
Quander, William	Allen, Ann	30 AUG 1883 R	18	106
Quann, Edward T.	Richards, Dora F.	29 DEC 1883 L	18	353
Quantville, Julia M.	Walker, Joseph W.S.	23 DEC 1881 L	16	154
Quarles, Adele F.	Morris, Charles D.	25 NOV 1880 R	15	067
Quarles, Charles W.	Monroe, Annie J.	11 SEP 1877	11	086
Quarles, Henry	Davis, Pracilla	31 DEC 1883 L	18	356
Quarles, Robert	Richards, Emma	23 DEC 1882 L	17	206
Quarles, William	Washington, Laura	06 DEC 1877 L	11	225
Quealy, Delie T.	McDonald, Robert	26 DEC 1877 L	11	269
Queen, Ann	Queen, Sam	17 JUL 1880 L	14	366
Queen, Annie	Davis, George	09 AUG 1877 R	11	045
Queen, Annie	Perry, Daniel	07 MAY 1880 L	14	259
Queen, Annie M.	Dorum, James S.	16 JUL 1884	19	141
Queen, Catharine	Biggs, William E.	01 JUL 1884 L	19	114
Queen, Chailley	Bell, Fannie	01 JUL 1880 R	14	343
Queen, Charles	Davis, Alice	01 JUN 1878	12	079
Queen, Charles H.	Lewis, Frances A.	11 SEP 1883 R	18	118
Queen, Eliza V.	Collins, William F.	03 JUL 1883 R	18	033
Queen, Fannie M.	Barlow, Alfred	24 FEB 1883 R	17	320
Queen, Florence	Wade, Marcellus	07 AUG 1880 L	14	391
Queen, Frank	Brooks, Alcena	25 FEB 1881 R	15	204
Queen, James	Scott, Martha	15 SEP 1885	20	420
Queen, John	Johnson, Maria	27 NOV 1878 L	12	351
Queen, John M.A.	Lee, Annie E.	13 FEB 1878	11	338
Queen, Lewis	Nickson, Lucy A.	15 SEP 1877 L	11	094
Queen, Louisa	Johnson, Charles Henry	20 AUG 1884 L	19	195
Queen, Lucy	Morris, Richard K.	01 APR 1879 L	13	121
Queen, Lydia Ann	Ford, Richard	11 SEP 1879	13	365
Queen, Martha	Walter, Joseph	30 JUL 1880 L	14	379
Queen, Mary	Lincoln, James H.	09 AUG 1883 L	18	082
Queen, Mary	Cram, N.D.	13 MAR 1884	18	469
Queen, Mary	Johnson, Samuel	30 OCT 1884 L	19	350
Queen, Mary A.	Rye, David A.	01 MAY 1882 R	16	341
Queen, Richard D.	Lucas, Hattie L.	06 MAY 1878	12	039
Queen, Sam	Queen, Ann	17 JUL 1880 L	14	366
Queen, Samuel	Ward, Ann W.	20 OCT 1881 R	16	029
Queen, Samuel Fitch	Green, Cathey, Mrs.	09 NOV 1882 R	25	6176
Queen, Susannah	Simms, Henry	13 DEC 1877	11	236
Queen, Theresa	Jason, George	13 AUG 1877 L	11	052
Queen, William	Bell, Emily	29 AUG 1878 L	12	188
Queen, William	Oliver, Melinda	21 FEB 1881	15	195
Queenan, Edward	Warrick, Annie	30 MAR 1880	14	199
Queenan, Linda	Meredith, Charles H.	29 DEC 1880 L	15	130
Queene, Charles	Boas, Rachel	21 JUL 1884 L	19	149
Quenan, Mary Nettie	Coates, Lewis, Maj.	04 MAY 1881 R	15	292
Quenzel, Charles A.H.	Fockler, S. Eugenia	27 NOV 1882 R	17	150
Quesenberry, Alice	Bruce, Edwin	21 SEP 1882 L	17	032
Quesenbery, Taylor	Green, Charlotte	28 FEB 1878	11	364
Quiet, Carrie	Russell, Edward	15 MAR 1883 R	17	345
Quiet, Sallie	Rease, Joseph	15 MAR 1883 R	17	344
Quigley, Julia A.	Price, Frederick M.	13 MAY 1885 L	20	219

Quigley, Maggie	Carr, William E.	16 FEB 1882 L	16	246
Quigley, Mary E.	Williams, Charles G.	30 SEP 1879 R	13	392
Quigley, Mary E.	Meacham, Charles E.	15 NOV 1882 L	17	130
Quigley, Mollie E.	Bayliss, William F.	22 APR 1885	20	183
Quill, Anna	Fantroy, Cornealous	05 SEP 1881 R	22	5286
Quill, James	Monihan, Johanna	01 NOV 1878	12	411
Quill, John P.	Soper, Lizza	02 SEP 1884 L	19	219
Quince, Josephine	Beckett, James	02 DEC 1880 L	15	079
Quinlan, Timothy	Foley, Catherine	29 MAY 1882 L	16	381
Quinlan, William T.	Riley, Georgia A.	16 MAY 1878 R	12	054
Quinn, Annie	Donnelly, Francis P.	17 JAN 1878	11	301
Quinn, Annie	Ryan, Joseph C.	08 JUL 1878	12	129
Quinn, Annie M.	Pentland, Robert Watson	26 NOV 1884 R	19	421
Quinn, Bridget	Malloy, Matthew	08 OCT 1881 L	16	015
Quinn, Daniel P.	Conrad, Sallie M.	11 SEP 1885 R	20	412
Quinn, Florence	Eils, Bette Edward Julius	01 NOV 1877 R	11	163
Quinn, John	Holtzman, Annie M.	16 MAY 1881 L	15	309
Quinn, Sallie	Whiteford, John H.	08 DEC 1879 R	14	033
Quinn, William	Smith, Mary	17 SEP 1877 L	11	096
Quinn, William	Jones, Frances E.	20 FEB 1878 R	11	348
Quinn, William	Grandin, M. Gussie	14 JUN 1883 R	17	490
Quinter, Mary Ann	Bowman, William J.	25 SEP 1884 L	19	269
Quinter, Washington D.	Senter, Alvina M.	15 AUG 1878	12	169
Quinter, William E.	Purner, Lillie M.	05 FEB 1884 R	18	410
Quirk, Ellen	O'Shaughnessy, Thomas	20 AUG 1878 L	12	173
Quisenbery, Joseph L.	Augustine, Bell	24 DEC 1878 R	12	400
Quistorff, Hellen Louise	Harbeck, Theodore	11 AUG 1885 R	20	364
Quivers, Mary	Shanklin, Matthew	09 JUL 1878 R	12	131
Quonn, Addie	Gains, Frank	27 JUN 1885 R	20	297
Quonn, Florence Isadore	Parker, William H.	24 APR 1884 R	18	532

R

Raab, Antoinette	Handrup, Ferdinand A.	23 JUN 1883 L	18	011
Rabbe, Margaretha	Bohn, August	11 SEP 1881	15	479
Rabbitt, James E.	Cissel, Emily Virginia	29 NOV 1882 R	17	155
Rabbitt, Ellenor	Zumborg, Herman H.	12 NOV 1884 L	19	377
Rabbitt, Emma	Cross, Richard W.	29 AUG 1883 R	18	103
Rabbitt, Samuel P.	Eggensberger, Veronica	28 APR 1884 R	18	538
Rabbitt, William J.	Kemp, Martha J.	18 MAR 1879 R	13	106
Rabe, William	Weinandt, Lena	24 NOV 1877 L	11	201
Rabitt, Emma C.	Miles, James F.	29 NOV 1883	18	284
Rackey, William Henry	Eimer, Lizzie	17 NOV 1884 R	19	389
Radcliffe, Getrude	Johnson, Henry	04 AUG 1882 L	16	469
Radcliffe, Manie	Morrison, Samuel	01 JAN 1885 R	19	513
Raddick, Archibald DeG.	Williams, Eliza E., Mrs.	16 NOV 1880 R	14	328
Radebaugh, Mary J.	Johnson, William H.	15 JUN 1880 R	14	319
Raderly, Kate	Widmire, John	13 AUG 1878 L	12	165
Radey, Ellen	Riley, Edward	14 MAY 1881 L	15	306
Radford, Sophia Adelaide	DeMeissner, Wladimir	20 NOV 1878 R	12	333
Radtke, William	Maske, Wilhelmina	25 NOV 1884	19	404
Rady, Alice	Tennent, Christopher	02 JUN 1881 L	15	339
Rady, Henry	Ashton, Alice	18 SEP 1883 L	18	140
Raegan, Rosa G.	Morgan, Thomas H.	17 JUN 1878	12	088
Raff, Elias	Kaufmann, Lina	15 OCT 1879 R	13	413
Raff, Isabell	Cahn, Felix	14 OCT 1877 R	11	134
Ragan, Annie	Kidd, Benjamin	08 JUN 1885 R	20	260
Ragan, Columbus	Scott, Lottie	21 AUG 1877 R	11	060
Ragan, Daniel	Desmond, Katie	10 SEP 1884 L	19	240
Ragan, Francis J.	Joy, Johanna V.	16 JUL 1881 L	15	404
Ragan, J.M.	Nash, Martha	02 SEP 1877 R	11	043
Ragan, John	Riley, Annie	06 JAN 1878 R	12	361
Ragan, John W.	Reeves, Mary S.	16 OCT 1877 R	11	140
Ragan, Mary Jane	Becker, Edward	09 FEB 1880	14	145
Ragan, Patrick	Sheehy, Nellie	30 JUN 1885 L	20	301
Raid, Roseanna	Worthington, Henry	19 MAR 1878 L	11	387
Raiede, Hester	Strather, Thomas H.	01 MAY 1882	16	344
Raife, Aurelia A.	Thomas, A.A.	11 DEC 1884 L	19	453
Railey, Robert M.	Bender, Matilda A.	06 OCT 1880 L	14	478
Raine, Alice L.	Wortham, J.E.	28 NOV 1877 L	11	212
Raines, Amos G.	Snelling, Sarah E.	11 AUG 1884 R	19	177
Raines, Edward M.	Hayes, Florence B.	19 OCT 1883 R	18	203
Raines, Eliza	Wills, John E.	15 JUL 1884	19	139
Raines, Oswald Wm.	Scott, Susan	19 AUG 1885 R	20	378
Rainey, Catherine	Atchison, William	30 DEC 1879 L	14	078
Rainey, Charles	Ehrhardt, Kate	18 NOV 1880 L	15	055
Rainey, Ferdinand	Brooks, Emma	25 JUN 1879 R	13	247
Rainey, Francis H.	McElfresh, Frances E.	29 JAN 1879 L	13	037
Rainey, Isabel	Hemsley, William H.	10 DEC 1878 L	12	375
Rainey, Mary E.	Kells, Joseph M.	14 DEC 1880 R	15	096
Rains, William R.	Garrison, Martha C.	06 MAY 1883	17	430
Rainsford, Charlotte Mary	Farrington, Frederick	24 JAN 1882 R	16	204
Raitz, Frank W.	Thompson, Frances May	10 SEP 1883 R	18	123
Rakeman, Agnes	Willenbucher, Wm. Chris.	27 NOV 1884 R	19	408
Raley, James B.	Tucker, Emma M.	19 MAY 1881 L	15	318
Raley, Maria	Repetti, Anthony	13 SEP 1877 L	11	088
Rall, Susie	Hesen, Harmon O.	21 APR 1885	20	178
Rallo, Francisco P.	Paglissi, Josefina	08 OCT 1878 R	12	254
Ralph, Adolph	Pommeresher, Emma	28 SEP 1882 L	17	042
Ramby, Samuel H.	Selby, Fannie	14 MAY 1884 R	19	020

Ramey, Daniel	Scott, Annie E.	02 JUL 1885 L	20	306
Ramey, Elizabeth C.	Sanford, Robert	23 NOV 1882	17	146
Ramey, John W.	Hanover, Sarah E.	08 JUN 1882	16	400
Rammling, Anna	Wagner, Julius	03 MAY 1885 R	20	184
Ramsay, Dennis McCarty	Hill, Louise L.	13 FEB 1880 R	14	152
Ramsay, Mary Eleanor	Leib, Harrison	25 APR 1878 R	12	020
Ramsberg, Sammuel	Hildebrand, Mary	06 OCT 1880 L	14	476
Ramsburg, Eliza Emma	Greenfield, William W.	06 FEB 1879 R	13	048
Ramsey, John H.	Graves, Lizzie S.	10 SEP 1879 R	13	362
Ramsey, Sarah	Price, Abram	20 DEC 1884 R	19	474
Ramsey, William	Skinner, Annie	16 OCT 1883 R	18	175
Ramsey, William H.	Duffey, Mary A.	25 SEP 1879 R	13	383
Randall, Annie	Jones, Samuel A.	26 JAN 1878 R	11	317
Randall, Charles	Dummer, Anna	10 SEP 1878 L	12	210
Randall, Charles	Scott, Lizzie	19 JUL 1883	18	053
Randall, Charles H.	Ourand, Annie E.	28 APR 1883 L	17	417
Randall, Charles S.	Hawthorne, Emma	02 AUG 1880 R	14	381
Randall, Churchill	Whitening, Emma	13 JUN 1884 L	19	082
Randall, Clara G. Gassaway	Hindmarsh, Henry Edward	16 NOV 1881 R	16	079
Randall, Davy A.	Walker, Elizabeth	23 JUL 1881 L	15	414
Randall, Edward Gustave	Palmer, Katie O.	15 FEB 1882 R	16	240
Randall, Francis G.	Carpenter, Annie E.	03 JUL 1883	18	032
Randall, George	Mitchell, Sarah	05 MAY 1881 R	15	295
Randall, George	Inslee, Hannah Armstrong	20 SEP 1882	17	029
Randall, Jessie Louise	Mindeleff, Victor	02 APR 1883 R	17	374
Randall, Julia	Carter, Morton	30 MAY 1882	16	378
Randall, Laura	Dixon, Samuel	05 MAR 1879 L	13	091
Randall, Robert Thomas	Knott, Mary Jane	20 NOV 1884	19	399
Randall, Silas S.	Shanklin, Maggie	21 APR 1881 R	15	268
Randall, William	Coleman, Julia	15 DEC 1877 R	11	238
Randall, William	Hill, Mary	19 NOV 1882	17	135
Randolph, Edmonia	Walker, Jacob B.	20 OCT 1882 R	17	006
Randolph, Ella	Ridgely, Charles C.	15 DEC 1880 R	15	097
Randolph, Harriet Louisa	Peyton, Walter S.	17 JUN 1881 R	15	365
Randolph, Henry	Garrison, Mary Emma	15 JAN 1879	13	019
Randolph, John	Mack, Mary M.	12 JAN 1882 L	16	192
Randolph, Martha	Lee, Frank	06 JUL 1885 L	20	311
Randolph, Nathaniel	Offertt, Mary Eliza	15 OCT 1879 R	13	419
Randolph, Robert P.V.	McKenzie, Charlotte E.K.V.	11 OCT 1883 L	18	188
Rank, Elizabeth	Ruland, George	14 OCT 1882	17	072
Rankin, James W.	Shanahan, Annie J.	29 APR 1884	18	529
Rankin, Mary F.	Goulder, Harvey D.	11 NOV 1878 R	12	320
Rankins, Disco	Roy, Bertie	17 OCT 1878 R	12	277
Rankins, Elizabeth Jane	Davis, Samuel	24 AUG 1880	14	413
Rankins, Emeline	Dorsey, Richard P.	30 SEP 1878 R	12	243
Ranney, Elizabeth B.	Munro, David M.	08 DEC 1880	15	084
Rannie, James	Weer, Mary J.	30 JUN 1881	15	383
Ransel, Georgetta W.	Cladwell, Benjamin M.	17 SEP 1878	12	222
Ransom, John Wm.	Bellefille, Charlotte	17 OCT 1882	17	075
Ransom, William H.	Leitch, Nannie G.	20 APR 1881 R	15	265
Ranson, Lou	Jackson, Henry	27 NOV 1879 R	14	012
Rapelje, Ellie Mortimer	Peabody, James Harper	25 FEB 1884 R	18	439
Rapp, Francis	Weisky, Mary	16 SEP 1879 L	13	371
Rasch, Maggie F.D.	Kates, Charles H.	25 JUN 1885	20	295
Rasor, Sarah	Giles, William	21 OCT 1882	17	084
Ratcliff, Richard A.	Harbaugh, Christina	13 OCT 1883 L	18	190
Ratcliffe, Conway B.	Coates, Mollie A.	25 JUL 1885 R	20	341
Rathvon, Robert Hind.	Davis, Ida Eliz.	19 NOV 1884 R	19	395

Ratke, Albert	Maske, Henrietta	20 SEP 1883	18	144
Ratliff, Mary E.	Mills, Clarence	02 DEC 1879 R	14	022
Ratry, Mary	Burke, Michael	23 FEB 1878 L	11	355
Ratte, Annie	Cassasa, Joseph	26 JUL 1879	13	293
Ratto, Theresa M.	Milocich, Louis	07 NOV 1878 L	12	315
Rauber, Jacob	Angle, Ella	05 JAN 1882 L	16	183
Raum, George	Harron, Elizabeth M.	26 MAY 1881 R	15	328
Raum, Grace	Taylor, Charles C.	10 JUN 1885	20	266
Raum, Henry	Barr, Annie Isadora	27 MAY 1880 R	14	294
Raum, Mary Ellen	Lomax, Jerry L.	25 DEC 1879	14	071
Raum, Maud	Maguire, Franck Z.	14 FEB 1885 R	20	066
Raum, William	Taylor, Marcellena	15 APR 1884	18	511
Raun, Emma Louise	Robinson, Henry Duvall	16 OCT 1880 R	14	498
Raun, George W.	Sydnor, Anna	16 APR 1881 L	15	259
Raun, Yutta C.	Reinhardt, Charles, Jr.	27 OCT 1881 R	16	050
Raurer, Catherine	Hauser, J.W.	16 DEC 1879 L	14	050
Ravené, Bertha	Bessels, Emil, Dr.	20 JUN 1885 L	20	282
Rawles, George	Towles, Isabella	19 MAR 1885	20	125
Rawlings, Annie E.	Barthlomeai, Albert S.	26 NOV 1883 L	18	276
Rawlings, Eliza	Davis, Elias	30 JUN 1881 R	15	350
Rawlings, James	Bowie, Mary	11 MAR 1878	11	376
Rawlings, Jennie E.	House, Thomas L.	15 NOV 1881 R	16	077
Rawlings, Margaret Anne	Stuart, Augustus	17 FEB 1879 L	13	063
Rawlings, Margaret R.	Thompson, George L.	19 MAR 1878	11	387
Rawlings, Mary E.	Eaton, W. Frank I.	09 SEP 1884	19	237
Rawlings, Nellie A.	Burgess, William R.	05 NOV 1883 L	18	231
Rawls, Mary F.	Hall, James	11 DEC 1879 R	14	042
Rawls, Sarah A.	Key, Robert H.	01 JUL 1882 L	16	434
Ray, Alverta	Smith, Edward S.	16 NOV 1881 L	16	081
Ray, Charles G.	Jacobs, Mary E.	05 FEB 1879 L	13	047
Ray, Ella	Howe, Frank H.	18 JUN 1879 R	13	235
Ray, Emory F.C.	Ward, Lizzie	27 MAR 1884	18	483
Ray, Florence	Dartt, James F.	19 MAY 1881	15	316
Ray, Frank P.	Bopp, Mary R.	18 MAY 1883	17	451
Ray, George Elmore	Bender, Carrie Monroe	16 DEC 1882 R	17	187
Ray, Gertrude T.	Blundon, Lewis A.	05 OCT 1885 L	20	458
Ray, Hester	Day, Daniel	15 JUL 1882 R	16	448
Ray, Joseph	Lightfoot, Lavinia	30 OCT 1882 L	17	102
Ray, Kate Leslie	Mann, James Defrees	07 JAN 1885 R	20	006
Ray, Leila	Qualtrough, Edward Francis	06 NOV 1879 R	13	467
Ray, Lewis B.	Treinor, Ella Hadley	26 DEC 1881	16	155
Ray, Lillie Dale	Strother, Peter F.	15 NOV 1877 R	11	186
Ray, Mamie R.	Harrison, George F.E.	13 FEB 1882	16	236
Ray, Robert Clary	Paulding, Anna Caroline	29 SEP 1881 R	15	500
Ray, William	Jenkins, Rebecca	08 SEP 1879	13	358
Ray, William	Chapman, Celia	21 NOV 1883 L	18	270
Raybold, Lizzie T.	Hudson, William H.	18 JUN 1884	19	090
Raybold, Rebecca	Saterfield, John	10 FEB 1879	13	052
Raybold, Wallace	Mangum, Ida L.	15 MAR 1879	13	102
Rayfield, Eva H.	Bitting, Charles Carroll	18 FEB 1880 R	14	157
Raymond, Albert M.	Knemb, Rosa	23 APR 1883	17	403
Raymond, Ellen	Shreves, Charles	30 AUG 1878 R	12	188
Raymond, Stephen	James, Anne Price	20 NOV 1877 R	11	174
Rayner, Susie Polk	Glennan, Arthur H., Dr.	28 APR 1881 R	15	279
Raynolds, Alice C.	Ritchie, David W.	13 OCT 1881 R	16	020
Raynor, Eddie	Davis, William H.	26 APR 1883	17	413
Raynor, Edward	Winfield, Annie E.	11 NOV 1884	19	374
Raynor, Martin	Carver, Luellen	10 OCT 1879 R	13	407

Rea, Thomas F.	Pywell, Emma C.	13 MAR 1878	11	379
Reaagan, Josie A.	Reagan, Timothy B.	26 FEB 1884 L	18	444
Read, Daniel	Dallas, Mary	26 OCT 1882 R	17	097
Read, Mary Anna	Bates, Emory H.	14 NOV 1878 R	12	330
Read, Ruth A.E.	Lloyd, William T.	12 SEP 1883	18	124
Readin, Mary	Scott, Charles	18 NOV 1880 R	15	054
Readings, Rose	Chase, William	26 DEC 1883 L	18	350
Ready, Bridget	Kennedy, J.W.	20 SEP 1880	14	451
Ready, Catherine	Doherty, John H.	21 FEB 1879 L	13	072
Ready, George L.	Wagner, Regina	27 SEP 1877 L	11	113
Ready, Julian H.	Schwabe, Maggie	20 AUG 1882	16	488
Ready, Maurice J.	Head, Ethelberta	27 OCT 1883 L	18	217
Ready, Michael	Murphy, Rose	02 JUL 1878 L	12	120
Reagan, Annie	Roche, John A.	29 JUN 1882 L	16	431
Reagan, Bertie C.	Shreve, Samuel F.	05 MAY 1884 L	19	005
Reagan, Margaret A.	Barrett, James P.	11 NOV 1884 L	19	373
Reagan, Patrick F.	Barrett, Elizabeth	20 SEP 1879 R	15	3508
Reagan, Timothy B.	Reaagan, Josie A.	26 FEB 1884 L	18	444
Reagan, William	Kelley, Catharine B.	25 FEB 1884 L	18	440
Ream, Vinnie	Hoxie, Richard Leveridge, Lt.	28 MAY 1878	12	067
Reamer, Frank	Davis, Anne	15 OCT 1878	12	274
Reamy, Annie L.	Bartlett, James W.	00 OCT 1883 R	18	175
Reamy, R.H.	Sanford, Emma J.	06 DEC 1883 L	18	298
Reamy, Thomas M.L.	Owens, Nettie R.	29 OCT 1884	19	343
Reamy, William D.	Combs, Sallie C.	23 APR 1878	12	015
Reardon, Agnes B.	Franklin, J. Chauncey	15 JUN 1885 L	20	275
Reardon, George Evett	Fant, Mary Emilie	13 NOV 1878 R	12	338
Reardon, Julia	Gallagher, James	11 JUN 1883 L	17	486
Reardon, Thomas	DeNeale, Annie E.	29 MAR 1880 L	14	200
Rease, Joseph	Quiet, Sallie	15 MAR 1883 R	17	344
Rebecca, Lizzie	Ritenhour, Henry	30 DEC 1878 L	12	408
Rebman, Virginia A.	McGeorge, John F.	20 JUL 1881 R	16	424
Reckert, Charles George	May, Mary Elizabeth	14 OCT 1884 L	19	304
Reckie, John	Wilding, Elizabeth	01 JUL 1881 R	15	361
Reckweg, Lena S.	Schmidt, John H.	19 OCT 1879 R	13	431
Rector, Catherine J.	Harrison, William S.	25 JUL 1882	16	456
Rector, Edward B.	Foley, Eva R.	25 JUL 1882	16	457
Rector, Martha	Haley, John	15 APR 1885 R	20	167
Red, Alice C.	Galloway, Basil P.	28 DEC 1882	17	218
Red, Maria	Adams, Thomas	28 JUL 1877 L	11	033
Red, Reuben	Todd, Gabrella	13 MAY 1884 L	19	017
Redcroft, Scott	Clark, Mary	12 SEP 1878 L	12	216
Redd, Floretta	Gaither, Henry	29 NOV 1882 L	17	159
Redd, William H.	Brown, Nellie	06 NOV 1879 L	13	472
Redder, W. Pierce	Beavers, Leona W.	15 AUG 1878 L	12	170
Reddick, J.F.	Campbell, Mary T.	20 SEP 1877 R	11	101
Reddick, Mary Ellen (Dean)	Wilson, David Russell	29 DEC 1884 L	19	496
Reddick, Rose, Mrs.	Davis, Albert	03 JUL 1879 R	13	266
Redding, Anna	Collins, John	01 MAR 1878 R	11	361
Redding, Margaret Ann Evans	Batts, George M.	30 JUL 1879 R	13	298
Reder, Caroline	Hoffmann, George N.	27 DEC 1881	16	162
Redin, Charlotte	Simms, Alexander	10 DEC 1878 L	12	376
Reding, John	Kelly, Sarah E.	08 MAR 1883 R	17	333
Redinger, Pauline	Johnson, Theophilus	11 APR 1882 L	16	308
Redman, Alice	Carrol, Richard	04 FEB 1879	13	045
Redman, Arthur F.	Beckett, Hattie	27 OCT 1882 L	17	098
Redman, Basil	Jackson, Mary	20 DEC 1878 R	12	385
Redman, Betta	Redman, James	18 AUG 1883 L	18	094

Redman, James	Redman, Betta	18 AUG 1883 L	18	094
Redman, John	Young, Jane	16 OCT 1880 L	14	498
Redman, Martha J.	Adams, Nicholas J.	07 NOV 1878 R	12	310
Redmines, Kate	Slye, William W.	27 OCT 1881 R	16	047
Redmon, James Lewis	Collins, Maria Virginia	29 OCT 1879 R	13	451
Redmond, Francis	Plummer, Mary	02 SEP 1884 L	19	221
Redmond, Richard	Alexander, Fannie	05 FEB 1879 L	13	046
Redon, E. Alice	Fisburne, B.P., Dr.	01 JUN 1881	15	336
Redthka, Mina	Finn, William J.	12 SEP 1884 L	19	243
Reed, Ada L.	White, John S.	06 MAY 1878	12	040
Reed, Alexander	Brown, Martha	22 SEP 1877	11	095
Reed, Amanda	Bostick, Peter	17 JAN 1884 R	18	383
Reed, Anna Bell	Boyd, William G.	21 FEB 1883	17	315
Reed, Annie	Tinker, George F.	24 SEP 1885	20	438
Reed, Annie E.	Jones, Alvin M.	10 MAR 1885	20	098
Reed, Bushrad W.	Burlingame, Fannie M.	21 OCT 1884	19	326
Reed, Catharine	Hilleary, George C.	27 JUN 1883 L	18	021
Reed, Charles Henry	Jordan, Isabella	10 SEP 1878 R	12	206
Reed, David S.	Parrott, Jane E.	09 JUL 1882	16	442
Reed, Eliza	Brooks, John Thomas	19 JUL 1877	11	027
Reed, Ella V.	Page, W.B.	10 AUG 1885	20	364
Reed, Fannie	Kyler, William H.	02 AUG 1884 L	19	166
Reed, George	Nicholson, Jennie	17 JUL 1882	16	450
Reed, George W.	Ball, Mary E.	17 JAN 1882	16	196
Reed, Harrison	Pellum, Julia	17 AUG 1885	20	373
Reed, Hattie A.	Paxton, John	26 NOV 1882	17	228
Reed, Hattie M.	Paxton, John	18 JUN 1883	17	500
Reed, Henry	Davis, Lizzie	22 SEP 1879 R	13	380
Reed, James	Kennedy, Fannie	12 OCT 1880 L	14	488
Reed, James H.	McDermott, Bridget	18 JUN 1884	19	091
Reed, James Henry	Brown, Eliza	11 OCT 1883	18	186
Reed, James W.	Rucker, Laura A.	20 NOV 1879 R	13	498
Reed, James W.	Mason, Jennette	09 OCT 1884 L	19	297
Reed, Jane C.	Doyle, George E.	25 AUG 1881 L	15	459
Reed, John D.	Sewell, Anna	04 JAN 1882 L	16	183
Reed, John F.	Bailey, Alice	18 OCT 1883	18	193
Reed, John N.	Summerton, Addie	04 JUL 1880 R	14	347
Reed, Joseph Anditon	Jones, Bettie	20 OCT 1881 R	16	039
Reed, Judah	Mercer, George H.	20 APR 1883 L	17	402
Reed, Julia S.	Green, Edward C.	05 JUL 1883 L	18	035
Reed, Kate Louise	Larner, John Bell	08 DEC 1880	15	087
Reed, Laura A.	Bradley, Henry H.	15 FEB 1881 R	15	190
Reed, Lewis H.	Nolan, Sarah A., Mrs.	04 FEB 1884	18	407
Reed, Lizzie A.	Collins, John	10 MAY 1881	15	300
Reed, Mamie E.	Ball, Andrew F.	31 JAN 1882 L	16	217
Reed, Mary E.	Purdy, John E.	30 AUG 1883	18	106
Reed, Mary Emma	Malks, Richard C.	28 NOV 1883	18	282
Reed, Mattie (Arnold)	Rumsey, Joseph C.	17 JAN 1883 R	17	263
Reed, Millie	Simms, Daniel	20 JAN 1883 R	17	268
Reed, Philip	Marshall, Mary	22 JAN 1879 L	13	029
Reed, Robert L.	Newton, Mary A.	14 NOV 1877 L	11	185
Reed, Sarah	Johnson, Martin	17 DEC 1883 L	18	319
Reed, Sina Ann	Lawson, Samuel	28 APR 1884 L	18	536
Reed, Thomas	Klotz, Mary	10 DEC 1877 L	11	228
Reed, Thomas Randolph	Diggs, Ann Eliza	16 MAY 1881 R	15	310
Reed, Thompson	Nervis, Catherine	21 OCT 1879 R	13	436
Reed, W.R.	Johnson, F.S.	14 FEB 1882	16	241
Reed, William	Slater, Mary	14 MAR 1878	11	380

Reed, William	Chase, Susan	09 JUL 1880 R	14	354
Reed, William	Litz, Annie A.	12 JAN 1881 R	15	148
Reed, William	Estes, Martha	09 SEP 1884	19	232
Reed, Wm. H.	Heck, Nettie	06 OCT 1885 R	20	457
Reeder, Alice	Ross, Jacob	19 JUL 1877 R	11	028
Reedy, John	Welch, Nora	31 AUG 1881	15	466
Reedy, Mary	McCarthy, Christopher	28 NOV 1883 L	18	282
Reely, Mary, Mrs.	Jackson, Jesse Lewis	28 MAY 1881 R	15	325
Reese, Abraham E.	Levi, Fannie	03 FEB 1878	11	319
Reese, Elizabeth Virginia	Taylor, Matthew, Dr.	07 SEP 1882 R	17	011
Reese, Harriet E.	Herbert, Charles R.	15 AUG 1880 R	14	392
Reese, John	Bayliss, Clara V.	13 OCT 1879 R	13	418
Reese, John Wm. Henry	Brown, Eliza	06 APR 1883 L	17	384
Reese, Theoliver	Duvall, Susan D.	07 AUG 1879 R	13	310
Reese, William K.	Bartley, Minnie H.	11 OCT 1877 R	11	130
Reeside, Edwin	Steinbrenner, Marie Josephine	15 OCT 1885 R	20	487
Reeve, Manette Lansing	Valk, William E.	07 MAY 1885 R	20	207
Reeves, Adelaide L.	Richards, James	21 MAY 1881	15	320
Reeves, Archie	Tutt, Kate	12 MAY 1881 R	15	265
Reeves, Barbara	Boyer, Richard	22 MAR 1882 R	16	286
Reeves, Ella	Bowie, Samuel	10 OCT 1882 L	17	063
Reeves, Ida M.	Whalley, Samuel	27 DEC 1883 L	18	346
Reeves, Isaac S.K.	Young, Henrietta Maria	16 APR 1879 R	13	143
Reeves, James C.	Fraser, M. Agnes	16 SEP 1885	20	422
Reeves, James E.	Dickerson, Jennie	06 SEP 1880	14	433
Reeves, James Edward	Miller, Sarah	14 MAR 1882 R	16	276
Reeves, Lucy E.	Taylor, George P.	01 DEC 1881 R	16	107
Reeves, Martha	Robertson, William Henry	26 MAY 1880 R	14	281
Reeves, Mary C.	Green, Richard	27 JAN 1884 R	18	387
Reeves, Mary S.	Ragan, John W.	16 OCT 1877 R	11	140
Reeves, Rebecca L.	Lippincott, Charles D.	16 OCT 1878	12	279
Reeves, Rosa B.	Carter, Benjamin G.	07 MAY 1884	19	011
Reeves, Sarah	Adams, David	23 DEC 1884 R	19	481
Reeves, William	Terrell, Rosa	10 JUL 1884	19	134
Regan, Betty	Shepherd, John	29 SEP 1877 L	11	115
Regan, Edward	Gainer, Marsella	24 MAR 1883 L	17	358
Regan, John E.F.	Connor, Mary A.	04 JUN 1878 L	12	084
Regan, Margaret	Spiess, Louis	15 APR 1877 L	11	248
Regan, Mary A.	Keefe, John	16 OCT 1884 L	19	315
Regnier, Charles N.	Fischer, Emma K.	07 APR 1880 R	14	209
Reh, Rudolph	Juenemann, Amelia	21 MAY 1878 L	12	062
Rehling, Wilhelm Fred. Heinrich	Thilow, Laura Antonie	09 JUL 1881	15	397
Rehner, Caspar C.	Twiford, Susie E.	22 MAR 1881 R	15	235
Reichenbach, Flora	White, Charles, Jr.	24 OCT 1882 R	17	088
Reichenberg, Aron	Judah, Rosa, Mrs.	01 DEC 1881 L	16	106
Reichert, Katie F.	Moynihan, Cornelius J.	14 APR 1885	20	162
Reid, Anna Laura	Corning, Albert Edward	18 MAR 1885 R	20	123
Reid, Catherine	Kadle, Arthur E.	21 APR 1880 R	14	232
Reid, Eugenius N.	Bayliss, Margaret A.	15 SEP 1884 L	19	247
Reid, Mary C.	Kite, Isaac Newton	07 OCT 1880 R	14	483
Reid, Robert A.C.	Campbell, Marg. Cornelia	02 JAN 1878 L	11	286
Reidrick, Harriet	Hepburn, John H.	05 DEC 1877 R	11	222
Reidy, Mary E.	Walsh, Thomas	02 SEP 1878 R	12	190
Reigel, Teresa B.	Ofenstein, John	07 OCT 1880	14	476
Reight, Emma	Brown, Charles E.	16 FEB 1884 L	18	428
Reihl, James A.	Stone, Amelia V.	28 JAN 1884	18	397
Reiley, Annie Elizabeth	Shimer, Reuben L.	15 SEP 1885 R	20	417
Reiley, Gertrude	Darden, Andrew J.	06 DEC 1884	19	439

Reiley, Katie S.	Means, Lewis E.	27 OCT 1881 R	16	049
Reilley, Lizzie V.	Schlosser, Henry W.	19 JUL 1885 R	20	332
Reilley, Mary	McCarthy, Daniel	05 NOV 1879 R	13	462
Reilley, P.S.	Myers, Elizabeth	24 MAY 1885	20	235
Reilly, Dennis	Ash, Maria A.	03 NOV 1880 R	15	027
Reilly, James	Day, Mary O.	23 NOV 1881 L	16	096
Reilly, Katie	Madigan, John A.	15 DEC 1880 L	15	100
Reilly, Lewis W.	Mapes, Rose C.	16 APR 1884 L	18	515
Reilly, Maggie	Connell, Jeremiah T.	24 FEB 1879	13	075
Reilly, William B.	Koehler, Louisa C.	15 APR 1884 L	18	513
Reinburg, Honora	Chapman, Edward	09 APR 1885 L	20	156
Reinburg, Mary A.	Schenck, Charles August	19 JUL 1881	15	406
Reinecke, Otto Charles Louis	Meals, Ella Blanche	19 JAN 1881 R	15	158
Reiner, Caspar	Sanders, Lizzie T.	20 MAY 1879 L	13	197
Reinhardt, Charles, Jr.	Raun, Yutta C.	27 OCT 1881 R	16	050
Reinhardt, Henry C.	Hueter, Susie C.	20 SEP 1883 L	18	145
Reinhardt, Rebecca	Grosendorf, John	29 DEC 1877 L	11	280
Reinhart, Daniel	Field, Bessie	12 NOV 1884 R	19	378
Reinhart, William L.	Cloud, Martha P.	18 APR 1883	17	399
Reinke, Anna Elizabeth	Kemp, Howard Mason	22 MAR 1881 R	15	233
Reinlein, Paul	Johnston, Anna E. Barrett	06 OCT 1879 R	13	404
Reintzel, Powhattan J.	Paine, Sarah	28 JUL 1883	18	065
Reirdon, Honora	O'Connell, John C.	11 MAY 1881 L	15	302
Reisenburg, William	Nalley, Mary A.	12 NOV 1883 R	18	247
Reiser, William F.	Bladen, Alice E.	13 APR 1882 L	16	314
Reisinger, John E.	Riddle, Lillie	16 JUL 1884	19	142
Reisinger, Mary L.	Miller, William H.	30 OCT 1884	19	349
Reiss, Benjamin W.	Van Syckel, Josephine A.	28 DEC 1882 R	17	218
Reiss, J.H.H.	Dixon, Jennie A.	07 JUL 1885	20	315
Reiss, William	Stuart, Cedonia M.	19 FEB 1878	11	347
Reiter, John H.	Oliver, Mollie B.	28 DEC 1877	11	278
Reith, Mary Frances	Schell, Leonard	05 OCT 1878 L	12	256
Reithmüller, Louisa	Heffer, Daniel	15 AUG 1878	12	167
Reitzer, Emma J. Nixon	Ridgely, Franklin W.	08 SEP 1881 R	15	478
Relye, Ella	Coogan, Thomas E.	05 JUL 1884 L	19	122
Remingham, Mary	Beadle, Henry M.	06 NOV 1880 L	15	035
Remington, William H.	Tucker, Matilda L.L.	20 FEB 1878	11	345
Remmington, George A.	Watts, Jerusha A.	27 OCT 1883	18	219
Rempp, Charles W.	Lipphard, Sophie M.	04 JAN 1882 L	16	180
Remus, Hannah	Woodro, Henry	02 DEC 1880 R	15	082
Renard, Jean Lean	Key, Harriet Seliman	15 DEC 1883 L	18	318
Renaud, Edward	Whelpley, Blanche Ella	19 MAY 1880	14	227½
Renick, E.I.	Turpin, Annie C.	03 JUL 1884	19	117
Rennert, Edward	Berkeley, Kate	13 JUN 1885 R	20	272
Renney, John H.	Nichols, Sarah E.	14 OCT 1879 R	13	409
Rennoe, Chapman	Davis, Fannie	13 SEP 1877 R	11	093
Rennoe, Fannie E.	Williams, James S.	17 JUN 1884	19	086
Rennoe, Maggie	Sampsell, Baron D.	27 DEC 1877 L	11	277
Rennoe, Roberta	McNealy, John R.	23 SEP 1885	20	438
Renoe, Arthur	Harron, Ella	20 JUN 1883	18	004
Renshaw, Jennie N.	Wollard, William Spencer	05 JAN 1883 R	17	282
Renshawe, John H.	Winslow, Annie M.	15 APR 1878	12	005
Repetti, Anthony	Raley, Maria	13 SEP 1877 R	11	088
Repetti, Fredrick Francis	McNantz, Emma Louisa	19 OCT 1880 R	15	003
Repetti, Joseph A.	Smith, Victoria M.	25 NOV 1879 R	14	006
Repp, Charles	Schenck, Mary	04 SEP 1881 R	15	462
Rest, Mary	Wittmer, Fritz	06 MAY 1881 R	14	334
Rest, Rosa M.	Peters, Charles A.	24 JUN 1885	20	285

Retagala, Josephena	Ordril, Antonio	23 AUG 1883 L	18	097
Retaliata, Joseph A.	Becraft, Clara E.	21 AUG 1885 L	20	382
Retrick, John	Singlton, Fannie	18 NOV 1884 R	19	390
Rettagliutii, Maria	Douden, Bertolomeo	03 APR 1878 L	11	403
Retterhouse, Ernest J.	Keleher, Mary	10 JUL 1884 L	19	131
Reuss, William	Schaefer, Emily	18 FEB 1878 L	11	346
Rex, Samuel	Allen, Martha	04 OCT 1883 R	18	153
Rex, Virginia	Gibson, Sandy	27 AUG 1885 L	20	390
Reyburn, Elizabeth	Stockbridge, Geo. Herbert	27 NOV 1884 R	19	407
Reynaldo, James	Willis, Sallie	04 NOV 1884	19	357
Reynolds, Agnes	Bain, William V.	25 SEP 1883 R	18	154
Reynolds, Archie	Beverly, Julia	29 JAN 1885 L	20	043
Reynolds, Bessie	Lyon, Denis	24 APR 1883 L	17	407
Reynolds, Charles Leslie	Cowling, Frances Ann	08 JUN 1880 R	14	311
Reynolds, Edward	Walters, Sarah Jane, Mrs.	17 APR 1882	16	321
Reynolds, Elizabeth	Williams, George	11 DEC 1879	14	043
Reynolds, Ellie V.	Wallace, William J.B.	10 DEC 1879 R	14	040
Reynolds, Henry W.	Caton, Mary A.	23 AUG 1884 L	19	204
Reynolds, James W.	Gibbs, Mary W.	17 SEP 1885	20	427
Reynolds, Jarett	Harris, Eliza	21 JUL 1885 L	20	336
Reynolds, Jerry	Harrod, Sarah	03 APR 1884	18	493
Reynolds, John R.	Sheele, Alice M.	27 JUL 1881 L	15	420
Reynolds, John W.	McClelland, Mamie C.	24 FEB 1885	20	083
Reynolds, Joseph Randolph	Niland, Bridget	02 JAN 1881	15	132
Reynolds, Nettie	Peckelton, William	11 JAN 1879 L	13	015
Reynolds, Richard H.	Davis, Anna L.	07 NOV 1883	18	240
Reynolds, Samuel C.A.	Brown, Jane	15 MAY 1878	12	051
Reynolds, Sarah E.	Burrows, Otto M.	28 FEB 1884	18	450
Reynolds, Walter B.	Martin, Sarah E.	06 NOV 1877	11	170
Reynolds, William	Bolan, Mary Margaret	20 AUG 1882	16	488
Reynolds, William	Johnston, Lizzie Anne	12 APR 1883 R	17	391
Reynolds, Wm. Edward	Collins, Minnie Gertrude	09 MAR 1885 R	20	100
Rheb, Caroline	Ockershausen, William	03 OCT 1878 R	12	250
Rheb, Sophia	Haase, Wilhelm August	12 MAR 1878	11	378
Rheem, Louise Rosine	Hensey, Alex. Thomas	19 FEB 1885 R	20	078
Rhees, Fannie A.	Burket, Joseph U.	04 JUN 1884	19	056
Rheims, Robert L.	McClain, Winnifred Ward	13 OCT 1879	13	417
Rhoads, Ida C.	Wolff, Robert	31 DEC 1881 L	16	173
Rhoden, Robert	Grinnell, Harriet	12 FEB 1885 L	20	065
Rhodes, Cora	Crump, Armistead	23 NOV 1882 R	17	114
Rhodes, Ella	Boyd, William	06 JUL 1885 L	20	312
Rhodes, Hannah	Handy, Thomas	23 OCT 1882 L	17	085
Rhodes, Julia	Dyson, Henson	21 NOV 1877	11	198
Rhodes, Lena	Franklin, William	30 JUL 1884	19	162
Rhodes, Lillian F.	Blake, Daniel F.	25 OCT 1882	17	092
Rhodes, Margaret	Dyson, Henry	16 SEP 1884	19	259
Rhodes, Martha E.	Dorsey, Moses H.	26 NOV 1878	12	348
Rhodes, Mary Helen	Lucas, Wm. Thomas	02 MAY 1880 R	14	248
Rhodes, W.	Perkins, Marion	31 MAR 1881 R	15	243
Rhodes, Willis O.	Moorehead, Maggie W.	20 FEB 1882 R	16	250
Rhodrick, Elbridge P.	McKnight, Martha V.	23 SEP 1879 R	13	381
Rhody, Sarah C. [Fry]	Mills, Robert	16 JUN 1884 R	19	084
Rhone, Mary	Davis, Patrick	14 MAR 1885 L	20	113
Riani, Gandenzio	Castafneto, Maria	27 OCT 1881 L	16	050
Ribnitzkey, Annie	Colné, Charles C.	30 MAR 1880 R	14	201
Ribnitzki, Pauline	Koehler, Ferdinand	09 APR 1882 R	16	305
Rice, Cephas	Ashton, Mary	14 AUG 1884	19	184
Rice, Fannie B.	Newton, James B.	20 APR 1881 R	15	264

D.C. Marriage Records Index, June 28, 1877 to October 19, 1885

Rice, Henry D.	Burnside, Lizzie M.	13 OCT 1881 R	16	021
Rice, Henry D.	Krafft, Pertonilla	10 MAR 1885 R	20	105
Rice, Ida J.	Sherman, John	16 APR 1879	13	147
Rice, John	Croueberg, Anna	21 MAR 1882 L	16	285
Rice, Nathan E.	McKee, Lillian B.	05 OCT 1881 R	16	008
Rice, Regina	Fleishman, Lehman	03 OCT 1880 R	14	466
Rice, Solomon	Nordlinger, Hannah	12 SEP 1883 R	18	125
Rice, Susie M.	Tucker, John F.	07 NOV 1883 L	18	241
Rich, Bertha	Ullman, Morris	14 SEP 1881 L	15	484
Rich, Claybourn	Brown, Henrietta	25 DEC 1884	19	491
Rich, Georgie	Jackson, Edward	21 FEB 1884 L	18	436
Rich, John	Maco, Lizzie	16 MAY 1878	12	056
Rich, Joseph	Buckner, Eliza	31 AUG 1881 L	15	466
Rich, Katie	Lewis, F.L.	02 JAN 1880	14	082
Rich, Mary	Richards, Charles Henry	02 JUL 1880 L	14	346
Rich, Susan Ann	Dorsey, Alfred	24 JAN 1883 L	17	273
Rich, Washington	Cox, Mary	27 MAY 1885 R	20	243
Richard, Archibald	Foster, Jennie Elizabeth	21 APR 1882 R	16	328
Richard, Carter	Chapman, Olivia	22 APR 1882 L	16	329
Richard, Marion Genevieve	Chase, Lincoln Melville	25 SEP 1882 R	17	036
Richards, Alfred A.	Conley, Julia	10 DEC 1880 L	15	090
Richards, Anna S.	Van Alstyne, Thos. Butler	07 MAY 1879 R	13	178
Richards, Annie Bradocks	Brooks, George H.	07 JUL 1878 R	12	125
Richards, Benjamin R.	Bremmehl, Lillie	14 OCT 1877	11	131
Richards, Charles Henry	Rich, Mary	02 JUL 1880 L	14	346
Richards, Dora F.	Quann, Edward T.	29 DEC 1883 L	18	353
Richards, Emma	Quarles, Robert	23 DEC 1882 L	17	206
Richards, James	Reeves, Adelaide L.	21 MAY 1881	15	320
Richards, James	Dunmore, Ellen	24 OCT 1883 R	18	211
Richards, Jessie	Mason, William B.	27 DEC 1883 R	18	351
Richards, John	Sweetney, Betsey	24 JAN 1883 L	17	273
Richards, Lewis H.	Price, Florence E.	11 OCT 1881	16	017
Richards, Louisa	Capps, James S.	08 SEP 1879 R	13	357
Richards, Mary M.	Whittlessy, William H.	20 DEC 1881 L	16	141
Richards, Rosa E.	Anderson, Robert L.	20 NOV 1879 R	13	495
Richards, Thomas L.	Webster, Emma I.	10 DEC 1879 R	14	039
Richards, William M.	Crawford, Kate	28 APR 1885 R	20	194
Richardson, Adelaide	Marshall, James	23 APR 1883 L	17	405
Richardson, Alice	Young, John F.	21 AUG 1882	16	489
Richardson, Alice R.	Harris, Shepherd Augustus	28 APR 1881 R	15	284
Richardson, Anna	Manual, Johnson W.	10 MAR 1882 L	16	273
Richardson, Annie	Hill, James	08 SEP 1881 R	15	471
Richardson, Annie	Evans, Robert	08 OCT 1885	20	470
Richardson, Attrell	Simms, Lulu E.	13 NOV 1884 L	19	381
Richardson, Burley	Cole, Sarah	09 OCT 1881 R	16	014
Richardson, Charles	Jackson, Maggie	28 AUG 1879 R	13	343
Richardson, Charles	Simms, Lucinda	15 JAN 1880 L	14	075
Richardson, Charley E.	Cardwell, Martha L.	10 JUL 1884	19	132
Richardson, Cora J.	Hardy, Francis B.	16 DEC 1884 R	19	461
Richardson, Daniel	Sample, Maria	10 JUN 1879	13	227
Richardson, Eliza	Dorsey, Charles W.H.	13 MAR 1879 R	13	086
Richardson, Eliza R.	Latimer, John W.	15 MAR 1881	15	225
Richardson, Frederick	Pope, Georgie	22 OCT 1884	19	325
Richardson, George T.	Luckett, Sarah E.	04 OCT 1884 R	19	287
Richardson, Gracie Ann	Robinson, Ruffin	20 AUG 1885 R	20	382
Richardson, Harry	Cox, Harriet	07 NOV 1884 R	19	358
Richardson, J.F.	Carrington, Mollie	18 SEP 1877	11	098
Richardson, J.W.	Kerrick, Jennie	09 OCT 1879	13	413

Richardson, James	Murray, Catherine	04 OCT 1881 R	16	004
Richardson, James L.	Diener, A. Laberta	18 NOV 1884	19	393
Richardson, John	Parker, Mahala	17 JUL 1882 L	16	450
Richardson, John Francis	Carroll, Mary E.	23 FEB 1878 L	11	354
Richardson, John R.	Towers, Mary A.	11 DEC 1882 L	17	177
Richardson, Julia	Honesty, William	04 AUG 1881	15	433
Richardson, Julia A.	Whiting, Wm. M.	08 OCT 1879	13	466
Richardson, Julia C.	Brooks, William H.	09 MAY 1882 R	16	354
Richardson, Julia M.	Whiting, Wm. M.	27 JUN 1879 L	13	255
Richardson, Lizzie	Buchanan, William Henry	10 FEB 1885 L	20	060
Richardson, Maggie B.	Rodgers, William H.	21 OCT 1882	17	084
Richardson, Maggie L.	Dobson, John W.	07 OCT 1878	12	259
Richardson, Margaret	Brooking, Peter G.	08 SEP 1881 L	15	479
Richardson, Mary	Clark, Thomas	12 MAY 1880 R	14	258
Richardson, Mary Ellen	Harris, E. Samuel	05 DEC 1878 R	12	369
Richardson, Mary S.	Smith, Parker	30 MAR 1879 R	13	118
Richardson, Nellie P.	Fulmer, John A.	30 APR 1884 R	18	540
Richardson, Nettie	Young, Neal	11 FEB 1880 R	14	146
Richardson, Ocella	Wilson, Andrew	25 MAR 1881	15	239
Richardson, Richard	Scott, Susan	26 FEB 1885 L	20	086
Richardson, Thomas E.	Painter, Katie E.	03 FEB 1880	14	135
Richardson, Thomas E.	Dawson, Zernah	01 NOV 1884	19	353
Richardson, Willard S.	Dailey, Annie M.	29 JUL 1884 L	19	161
Richardson, William	Washington, Kate	10 JUL 1884	19	125
Richardson, William H.	Gill, Laura V.	08 APR 1878	11	411
Richardson, William H.	Ellis, Ella E.	10 MAR 1885 R	20	105
Richardson, William H.	Fry, Ida L.	25 JUN 1885	20	290
Richardson, William L.	Blackmen, Elizabeth	11 APR 1878 R	11	411
Richardson, Wm. M.	Parris, Mildred A.	31 AUG 1881 L	15	466
Richelson, Fannie	Harris, Morris	06 JAN 1883 L	17	240
Richey, Stephen O.	Blair, Minna	15 NOV 1884 R	19	384
Richmond, Walter Stanley	McAllister, Mary Frances	23 DEC 1880 R	15	115
Richson, Thomas	Burke, Eliza	05 MAR 1885 R	20	097
Richter, Carl	Siebert, Selma	18 MAR 1879 R	13	107
Richter, Joseph	Buckley, Johanna	15 SEP 1879 L	13	370
Richter, Mary A.	Hammer, William	12 OCT 1878 L	12	267
Rick, Alois	Englett, Josephine	05 OCT 1878	12	254
Rick, Katie	Schultze, William	16 NOV 1879 R	13	488
Rick, Lottie C.	Zier, Philip R.	14 APR 1885 R	20	166
Rickard, Carrie A.	Pomeroy, Harry M.	11 JUL 1884	19	135
Rickard, Daniel H.	Robertson, Mary E.	29 APR 1884 R	18	542
Rickard, Mary C.	Lamson, Charles H.	13 JAN 1884 R	18	374
Rickes, Lorenz	Gassmann, Elizabeth Diana, Mrs.	07 JAN 1883 R	17	239
Ricketts, Charles W.	Titus, Laura C.	25 JUL 1878 R	12	144
Ricketts, Edward	McGhee, Mary B.	23 JUL 1879	13	291
Ricketts, Ella	Green, William Burton	11 JAN 1883	17	253
Ricketts, Emeline	Caywood, John B.	07 OCT 1880 R	14	480
Ricketts, George W.	Kendler, Ellen Nora	18 NOV 1881 R	16	031
Ricketts, John A.	Ball, Barbara	23 JUN 1881	15	375
Ricketts, Julia A.	Johnson, Edward	24 SEP 1878 L	12	233
Ricketts, Laura V.	Carrington, Campbell	12 SEP 1877	11	085
Ricketts, Marchant Oliver	Johnson, Sarah E.	25 AUG 1880 R	14	415
Ricketts, Margaret M.	Fitzgerald, George	03 MAY 1881 L	15	289
Ricketts, Richard	Hyatt, Margaret A., Mrs. [Eliz.]	18 FEB 1879 R	13	065
Ricketts, William	Smith, Elizabeth C.	09 NOV 1881 R	16	069
Ricks, Catherine	McCoy, Richard	15 JUN 1883 R	17	493
Ricks, James	McPherson, Maria	08 SEP 1881 L	15	478
Ricks, John	Donner, Susan	31 MAY 1883 R	17	470

Ricks, Julia	Burgess, Jacob	27 JUL 1877 L	11	033
Ricks, Lena	Jackson, Edward	02 DEC 1880 R	15	083
Ricks, Louisa C.	Klenk, John George	04 NOV 1879 R	13	463
Ricks, William	Neverson, Actia Virginia	28 AUG 1879	13	341
Ricks, William	McDonald, Alice V.	25 APR 1881 L	15	270
Ricks, William C.	Batley, Georgie A.	05 JUL 1884	19	124
Riddle, Harriet	Davis, Henry Edgar	17 JAN 1882 R	16	196
Riddle, Lillie	Reisinger, John E.	16 JUL 1884	19	142
Riddle, Mary P.	Jacobs, Charles P.	02 OCT 1883	18	162
Riddles, Alice	Sedgwick, Israel	11 JUL 1878	12	133
Ridenour, Charles Howard	Hosmer, Jessie	16 AUG 1882 R	16	481
Ridenour, Florence	Irwin, James	08 JUN 1882	16	398
Rideout, Eliza	Jackson, William	25 MAR 1880 R	14	183
Rider, Charles J.	Waugh, Emma A.	30 OCT 1879 L	13	455
Rider, Willie J.	Stanford, Sammuel M.	11 DEC 1880 L	15	091
Ridgeley, Eliza Ann	Lane, Reuben	28 MAR 1878	11	396
Ridgeley, Ida	Williams, Cornelius F.	04 OCT 1883	18	170
Ridgely, Bessie	Walton, Joe Richardson	19 MAR 1878 R	11	384
Ridgely, Charles C.	Randolph, Ella	15 DEC 1880 R	15	097
Ridgely, Ellen	Wood, Thomas	29 JUL 1879	13	296
Ridgely, Frank Inloes	Manning, Charlotte Thruston	04 OCT 1881 R	16	006
Ridgely, Franklin W.	Reitzer, Emma J. Nixon	08 SEP 1881 R	15	478
Ridgely, Mary Stella	Beach, Daniel Webster	19 JUN 1879 R	13	238
Ridgeway, Hayden	Dove, Mary J.	21 NOV 1882 R	17	142
Ridgeway, Martha	King, Thomas O.	15 OCT 1878	12	269
Ridgeway, Mary A.	Miller, Charles G.	26 FEB 1883 R	16	410
Ridgeway, William Henry	Ewer, Mary Ella	09 AUG 1877	11	050
Ridgley, Arabella	Powell, George	13 DEC 1879	14	047
Ridgley, Florence	Holmes, Milo	23 SEP 1884	19	264
Ridgley, Mary E.	Chase, William A.	15 SEP 1881 L	15	486
Ridgway, George A.	McCoy, Fannie E.	04 JUN 1880 L	14	305
Ridgway, George T.	Hill, Ida	05 SEP 1883	18	112
Ridley, Nellie Regina Stannard	Loosé, Joseph L.	16 SEP 1885	20	420
Ridout, Abraham	Winns, Lucinda	15 NOV 1883	18	255
Ridout, John Henry	Moten, Sarah	26 NOV 1883 L	18	277
Ries, Julia	Haggenmaker, James M.	16 FEB 1880 R	14	153
Rietmüller, Lizzie	Freedman, Charles	31 DEC 1878 R	12	409
Riggins, Samuel	Atkinson, Ada	01 SEP 1883 L	18	107
Riggle, Emily	Snead, Edward	02 JUL 1881 R	15	385
Riggles, Anna M.	Hopkins, Ira W.	07 JUL 1885 R	20	315
Riggles, Galusha A.	Schneider, Annie R.	16 SEP 1879 R	13	371
Riggles, Hannah E.	Erney, Charles A.	18 OCT 1877	11	142
Riggles, Molly	Arnold, Henry F.	21 MAY 1884	19	031
Riggs, Isabella	Copeland, Thomas	30 DEC 1879 R	14	081
Riggs, Mamie G.	Pumphrey, R.H.	14 NOV 1881 L	16	074
Riggs, Washington Edward	Prater, Lucy	20 MAY 1880 R	14	276
Righter, John Henry	Shepherd, Annie	24 DEC 1880 R	15	122
Rightstine, E. Kate	Knapp, John H.	14 MAY 1879 L	13	188
Rigner, Firmer	Fletcher, Roseanna	18 MAY 1884 R	19	026
Rigney, Charles Wesley	Smith, Lucy Ann	10 DEC 1884	19	448
Rigney, Patrick	Lane, Abby	06 OCT 1879 L	13	407
Rigney, William	Lawrence, Flonia	09 DEC 1884	19	443
Rigney, William	Field, Lucy	01 JUL 1885 R	20	305
Rihner, Caspar	Kramer, Frederika	14 MAR 1881 R	15	224
Riley, Alice V.	Noble, J.A.	24 SEP 1884 L	19	266
Riley, Annie	Ragan, John	06 JAN 1878 R	12	361
Riley, Annie E.	Wayson, Charles A.	04 FEB 1883	17	287
Riley, Araminta	Cross, William R.E.	14 FEB 1883 R	17	304

Riley, Delia	Anderson, James W.	13 SEP 1883	18	130
Riley, Edgar B.	Drury, Hattie E.	27 SEP 1883 R	18	154
Riley, Edward	Radey, Ellen	14 MAY 1881 L	15	306
Riley, Gabriel	Ware, Annie	06 MAY 1884	18	471
Riley, Georgia A.	Quinlan, William T.	16 MAY 1878 R	12	054
Riley, Henry C.	Duvall, Florence A.	11 JAN 1882 R	16	190
Riley, James	Casey, Mary	11 AUG 1883 L	18	083
Riley, Jennie	Key, Norman	14 OCT 1879 R	13	422
Riley, Jerome R.	Nalle, Agnes M.	28 AUG 1877	11	069
Riley, John	Sullivan, Maggie	16 AUG 1885 R	20	372
Riley, Joseph R.	Ryan, Annie	24 OCT 1882 R	17	088
Riley, Juliet Marie	Williams, Charles Phelps	26 APR 1883 R	17	412
Riley, Kate N.	Thompson, William Edward	21 FEB 1882 R	16	254
Riley, Laura C.	Burrows, John R.	10 JAN 1878 R	11	299
Riley, Lillian D.	West, Elliott S.	14 OCT 1880 R	14	495
Riley, Mary	Henderson, William T.	07 JUL 1885 L	20	314
Riley, Mary Virginia	Martin, Clem P.	08 SEP 1881 L	15	479
Riley, Mollie	Daniel, Fernando	23 SEP 1885 R	20	432
Riley, Mollie A.	Mangan, John	19 JAN 1882 L	16	202
Riley, Philip G.	Wenk, Elizabeth	30 NOV 1879	14	019
Riley, Pleasant	Sedgwick, Julia	26 JUL 1879	13	293
Riley, Richard R.	Cooke, Sarah J.	07 OCT 1884	19	288
Riley, Thomas	Curtin, Nettie M.	04 FEB 1884 R	18	405
Rinehart, Charles	Currier, Sallie Ella	09 MAY 1882 R	16	355
Ringgold, Basill S.	Scott, Carrie E.	31 OCT 1881 R	16	053
Ringgold, Edward	Ross, Fannie	29 OCT 1879 R	13	451
Ringgold, Elizabeth A. (Brennan)	Townsend, James P.	12 SEP 1882 R	17	015
Ringgold, Hortense Cisco	Stevens, Edward	20 SEP 1877 R	11	102
Ringgold, John	Slaughter, Louisa	04 DEC 1879 R	14	030
Ringgold, Josephine	McKenney, Edgar	15 AUG 1884 L	19	189
Ringgold, Marie C.	Waite, George W.	26 AUG 1877	11	065
Ringgold, Nellie D.	Browning, Arthur	06 NOV 1879 R	13	441
Ringwalt, Elizabeth Price	Morse, Bryan Hebert	03 SEP 1884	19	217
Riordan, Bartholomew	Sheehan, Ellen	03 JAN 1882 R	16	176
Riordan, Mary E.	Friess, Frederick W.	23 DEC 1881 L	16	155
Ripley, G.H.	Waters, Julia C.	12 DEC 1883 L	18	311
Ripperger, Edward W.	Williams, Jennie	03 DEC 1879 L	14	026
Risdon, John R.	Norton, Ella R.	17 JUL 1880 L	14	366
Riston, Charles Thos.	Carstens, Anna P.	03 JUN 1885 R	20	252
Ritalierra, Johanna	Ordvil, John	21 FEB 1880 L	14	161
Ritch, Henry	Willis, Mariah E.	22 NOV 1883	18	267
Ritchie, David W.	Raynolds, Alice C.	13 OCT 1881 R	16	020
Ritchie, Emma A.	Johnson, William J.	28 SEP 1882 R	17	038
Ritchie, Lizzie	Parks, William	15 MAR 1881	15	226
Ritenhour, Henry	Rebecca, Lizzie	30 DEC 1878 L	12	408
Rithmiller, Mary	Smith, Leonard Tauben	24 APR 1878	12	017
Rittenhouse, Charles E., Jr.	Goode, Helen Shaaff	16 FEB 1880 R	14	153
Ritter, Fannie L.	Passeno, Frank V.	16 OCT 1880 R	14	497
Ritter, John B.	Halfert, Katie	19 OCT 1885 L	20	495
Ritz, John	Flavin, Katie	21 NOV 1883 L	18	270
Ritz, Lucy	Klueh, August	17 APR 1882 L	16	320
Rivers, Jane	Brooks, William	26 SEP 1878	12	238
Rivers, John W.	Stevenson, Minnie	27 AUG 1879 L	13	339
Rivers, Randall	Nelson, Mary	30 NOV 1882 R	17	160
Rives, Lockwood Chafin	Douglass, Mary Huntington	28 MAY 1885 R	20	245
Rixey, Edward Richard	Ogle, Ida Louise	23 OCT 1884 L	19	334
Rixey, Eugenia A.	Smith, John W.	05 FEB 1884 R	18	409
Roach, Joseph E.	Hayes, Mary F.	23 MAY 1882	16	371

Roach, Mary E.	Dailey, John M.	30 SEP 1884 L	19	274
Roach, Mollie E.	Mansfield, Charles P.	04 OCT 1882 L	17	052
Roach, Philip	Leonard, Henrietta Louisa	26 NOV 1884 L	19	417
Roach, William H.	Houghton, Hattie M.	01 SEP 1880 R	14	426
Roache, Wm. F.	Tucker, Ella Virginia	30 DEC 1881 L	15	508
Roan, Anderson	Johnson, Sarah	18 SEP 1879 R	13	375
Roan, Fannie	Nickens, Henry	20 AUG 1879 L	13	327
Roan, Frances	Walker, Robert	28 FEB 1878	11	365
Roan, Hannah	Murphy, James	01 MAY 1880 L	14	248
Roan, Patrick	Hunter, Winnie Yardley	18 JUN 1884 R	19	089
Roan, Rosetta	Trice, Isaac	15 AUG 1879 L	13	323
Roane, Carrie	Ham, Jeemes	25 SEP 1883 L	18	152
Roane, John William	Lang, Fanny	20 MAY 1880 L	14	280
Roane, Martha	Pendleton, Theodore	18 MAY 1882 L	16	368
Roase, Jane	Canavin, James	01 NOV 1883 L	18	291
Robb, Clara	Williams, Charles N.	22 AUG 1884 L	19	204
Roberson, Ida	Cosman, Charles T.	29 AUG 1878 L	12	185
Roberson, Peter Asbury	Prather, Catharine Edmonia	20 OCT 1884 R	19	319
Roberson, Thomas Gordon	Brown, Jennie Catherine	25 APR 1883 R	17	409
Roberts, Annie	Coleman, Thomas Emery	03 MAR 1882 R	16	266
Roberts, Annie	Hammond, Robert	27 JUL 1882 R	16	317
Roberts, Armienia E.	McMichael, William C.	02 FEB 1881 R	15	175
Roberts, Bettie L.	Carter, Robert	30 DEC 1879 R	16	3865
Roberts, Edward	Underwood, Sarah	25 OCT 1879 R	13	442
Roberts, Emily	Davis, George H.	27 JUL 1880 R	14	376
Roberts, George	Green, Annie	29 MAY 1879 R	13	210
Roberts, Isabella	Williams, Joseph James	04 JUL 1885	20	310
Roberts, John S.	Crampton, Sophie C.	06 DEC 1883	18	301
Roberts, John T.	Della, Lillie	08 SEP 1881 L	15	476
Roberts, Joseph M.	Berry, Marcellena O.	29 SEP 1879 R	13	391
Roberts, Madeleine Rosalie	Cooper, Robert Simpson	10 JAN 1883 R	17	245
Roberts, Margaret	O'Connell, Jeremiah	25 JUL 1882 L	16	456
Roberts, Mary E.	Gheen, John S.	06 MAY 1880 R	14	003
Roberts, Mittie	Beagle, James	04 APR 1885 R	20	144
Roberts, Richard H.	Cleveland, Annie M.	03 APR 1879 R	13	127
Roberts, Richford R.	Simmons, Josie	25 DEC 1884 R	19	488
Roberts, Theophilus D.	Mumma, Mary Alice	16 OCT 1878 R	12	264
Roberts, William Florian	Moore, Kate	01 JUN 1882 R	16	384
Robertson, Addie	Alexander, Grant	03 MAY 1879 R	13	173
Robertson, Agnes	Smith, Elijah	15 OCT 1877	11	136
Robertson, Alfred B.	Watson, Emma Letitia	18 MAR 1879 R	13	107
Robertson, Carrie	Mansfield, Charles S.	07 AUG 1884	19	176
Robertson, Charles	Nelson, Mary	12 JUN 1879 L	13	230
Robertson, Daniel	Hoffman, Emma F.	04 JUL 1879 R	13	268
Robertson, Elizabeth	Norton, Charles Henry	24 JUL 1884 L	19	155
Robertson, George	Herbert, Martha	12 JUL 1877 R	11	017
Robertson, Henry	Sanders, Rebecca	04 OCT 1877 L	11	121
Robertson, Henry	Hamill, Ida Malvina	29 MAY 1881 R	15	330
Robertson, Ida I.	Rockwell, Willis G.	08 JUN 1884	19	067
Robertson, Isaac	West, Jane	18 SEP 1877 R	11	092
Robertson, Isaac Holborn	Winder, Annie Louisa	06 APR 1885 R	20	144
Robertson, J.F.	O'Dea, Annie	15 DEC 1879 L	14	048
Robertson, James P.	Pistorio, Emma	08 NOV 1877 R	11	174
Robertson, John	Perry, Ellen	24 DEC 1879	14	069
Robertson, John	Brown, Amelia A.	14 FEB 1884 L	18	427
Robertson, John Walter	Frederick, Julia Ann	10 OCT 1880 R	14	484
Robertson, Lina	Hawkins, Robert	04 DEC 1884	19	438
Robertson, Martha	Harris, Mason	03 JUL 1879	13	265

Robertson, Mary E.	Rickard, Daniel H.	29 APR 1884 R	18	542
Robertson, Mary Lizzie	Veitch, William Henry	14 MAR 1880 R	14	184
Robertson, Morris	Roundtree, Sally	29 MAR 1878	11	391
Robertson, Rachel	Bond, Edwin Hilton	20 DEC 1883	18	325
Robertson, Rosetta	Bland, Joseph	23 JUL 1884 L	19	151
Robertson, Ruth	Priddy, John Edward	28 SEP 1883	18	101
Robertson, Sarah R.R.	Wood, William	04 AUG 1885	20	350
Robertson, Walter	Moore, Mary R.	28 SEP 1882 L	17	040
Robertson, William E.	Hooper, Mary J.	20 APR 1883	17	402
Robertson, William F.	Barr, Frances A.	19 APR 1884	18	520
Robertson, William H.	Grant, Mamie	20 MAY 1885 L	20	230
Robertson, William Henry	Reeves, Martha	26 MAY 1880 R	14	281
Robeson, Charles	Green, Jennie	18 DEC 1879 R	14	056
Robey, Amanda E.	Coates, James	21 AUG 1882	16	489
Robey, Elizabeth	Latham, James	18 MAR 1879 R	13	105
Robey, Ella Virginia	Cahill, William	29 OCT 1878 L	12	297
Robey, Francis	Stansbury, Emma	26 AUG 1880	14	415
Robey, Georgianna Grace	Montgomery, James H., Jr.	25 FEB 1884 R	18	442
Robey, Grace M.	Smith, Samuel	20 OCT 1881 R	16	041
Robey, James T.	Osburn, Sarah J.	19 JUL 1885	20	332
Robey, John	Williams, Ida	25 JUN 1881 R	15	379
Robey, John Thomas	Davis, Lizzie	30 JUN 1885	20	302
Robey, Laura V.	Duvall, William A.	28 NOV 1877 R	11	208
Robey, Lottie	Lear, Thomas T.B.	25 OCT 1881 R	16	041
Robey, Lucien E.	Bresnahan, Johanna A.	23 JUN 1884 L	19	096
Robey, Mary E.	Ash, Frank Thomas	25 DEC 1878 R	12	395
Robey, Mary E.	Adams, George W.	16 OCT 1882 L	17	073
Robey, Mary Virginia	Adams, George W.	29 JUN 1881 R	15	331
Robey, Randolph	Marshall, Daisy E.	09 NOV 1882 L	17	122
Robey, Rosa D.	Jacob, John W.	19 JAN 1885 L	20	026
Robey, Sarah J.	Luckett, John F.	14 JUN 1881 R	15	360
Robey, Sarah L.	Talbott, James E.	14 FEB 1878 L	11	341
Robey, Thomas E.	McNulty, Lillie M.	10 APR 1883	17	387
Robey, Virginia E.	Bell, William S.	27 DEC 1881 R	16	160
Robey, William Alfred	Monroe, Elizabeth Miranda	10 OCT 1878 R	12	258
Robinon, Charles Henry	Ford, Agnes Lutetia	20 DEC 1882 R	17	202
Robinson, Ada	Roden, Robert	16 MAR 1882	16	274
Robinson, Ada V.	Wetzel, James A.	01 DEC 1877	11	214
Robinson, Agnes E.	Turner, John R.	07 OCT 1885	20	468
Robinson, Alfred S.	Bennett, Helen May	03 JUL 1882 R	16	216
Robinson, Amelia	Sprigs, Isaac	27 NOV 1878 L	12	351
Robinson, Amelia	Allen, Notley	17 FEB 1880 L	14	155
Robinson, Andrew J.	Ashton, Maggie L.	11 FEB 1880 R	14	148
Robinson, Ann	O'Brien, John	25 NOV 1880	15	061
Robinson, Anna B.	Green, Spencer	21 JAN 1879 R	13	027
Robinson, Annie	Carter, Strawther	09 DEC 1880 R	15	085
Robinson, Annie	Lucas, Edgar	24 JUL 1884	19	156
Robinson, Annie J.	Eager, Francis H.	26 NOV 1884	19	422
Robinson, Benjamin	Johnson, Mary	06 DEC 1883 L	18	299
Robinson, Bernard	Hirschfield, Rose	18 JAN 1885 R	20	023
Robinson, Bettie	Mountjoy, David	30 SEP 1885 L	20	449
Robinson, Bettie B.	Jackson, Andrew	24 FEB 1880	14	165
Robinson, C. Blanche	Harvey, B. Fenwick	03 OCT 1881 L	16	004
Robinson, Caroline	Conway, Shadrach	16 NOV 1878 R	12	237
Robinson, Caroline B.	Heflin, Henry W.	01 APR 1885	20	140
Robinson, Catharine	Wheeler, Bud	31 JAN 1883 R	17	257
Robinson, Catherine	Banks, John F.	15 NOV 1881 R	16	077
Robinson, Charles	White, Ellen	31 OCT 1878 R	12	302

D.C. Marriage Records Index, June 28, 1877 to October 19, 1885

Robinson, Charles	Carrol, Mary	14 NOV 1878	12	330
Robinson, Charles G.	Britt, Mary A.	19 MAY 1880 R	14	274
Robinson, Charles J.	Burch, Ellen	13 NOV 1879 L	13	484
Robinson, Charles Wm.	Jett, Rosa Brown	01 OCT 1884 L	19	278
Robinson, Cipio H.	Merredith, Alice A.	10 SEP 1885	20	409
Robinson, Columbus	Davis, Ellen	04 MAR 1880 L	14	176
Robinson, Cornelius	Nelson, Annie	05 JUL 1882 L	16	439
Robinson, Daisy Lee	Wood, William H.	02 DEC 1880 R	15	080
Robinson, Daniel	Pryor, Maria	02 APR 1883	17	288
Robinson, David Albert	Payne, Emma	14 DEC 1882	17	184
Robinson, David H.	Pettit, Aura V.	04 MAR 1878 L	11	368
Robinson, Edie	Carter, Robert Daniel	24 JAN 1878 L	11	316
Robinson, Edward	Jinnerson, Georgiana	17 FEB 1879 R	13	063
Robinson, Eliza	Dorsey, Nathaniel	08 OCT 1884 L	19	294
Robinson, Eliza Fox	Holmes, Warren	02 DEC 1880 R	15	075
Robinson, Eliza Jane	Washington, Bob	01 AUG 1878 L	12	153
Robinson, Elizabeth B.	Naylor, William J.	06 JUN 1882	16	397
Robinson, Ellen	Minor, James	28 JUN 1881 L	15	380
Robinson, Emma	Smith, Robert P.	02 JUN 1879 L	13	215
Robinson, Fannie	Robinson, Peter H.	18 DEC 1877 L	11	241
Robinson, Fannie B.	Willis, Charles B.	06 MAR 1879 R	13	093
Robinson, Fannie H.	Dreyfuss, Jacob	03 NOV 1880 R	15	029
Robinson, Gabriel	Williams, Betty	08 AUG 1877 L	11	045
Robinson, George S.	Campbell, Kate	04 AUG 1882	16	464
Robinson, Georgie	Duncan, Thomas	30 DEC 1882	17	225
Robinson, Hannah	Day, Andrew	15 OCT 1885 R	20	488
Robinson, Harriet	Prince, James P.	04 SEP 1883 L	18	108
Robinson, Hattie Bladen	Diggs, Robert William	17 FEB 1881 R	15	194
Robinson, Helen M.	Shepherd, Jno. Hooper	17 SEP 1879 R	13	374
Robinson, Henrietta	Roots, Walter	14 APR 1885 L	20	164
Robinson, Henry	Bates, Mollie	09 OCT 1880 L	14	485
Robinson, Henry	Clagett, Bettie	18 SEP 1882	17	026
Robinson, Henry	Jackson, Rozetta	06 DEC 1883 L	18	297
Robinson, Henry Duvall	Raun, Emma Louise	16 OCT 1880 R	14	498
Robinson, Henry S.	Conkling, Frances Helen	13 NOV 1883 R	18	250
Robinson, Hiram	Jackson, Elizabeth	04 JAN 1882 R	16	182
Robinson, Horace	Webb, Betty	18 MAR 1878 L	11	386
Robinson, Ida V.	Frazier, Arthur F.	20 MAR 1883 R	17	352
Robinson, Isaac	Honesty, Mary Ann, Mrs.	16 DEC 1880 R	15	100
Robinson, Isabella	Bell, Thomas P.	03 NOV 1881	16	059
Robinson, James	Hardy, Mary S.	01 DEC 1880 R	15	074
Robinson, James	Kelly, Henrietta	15 NOV 1883	18	248
Robinson, James	Robinson, Lizzie	13 JUN 1884 R	19	069
Robinson, James F.	Goddard, Mary A.	18 SEP 1878	12	225
Robinson, James, Rev.	Thornton, Mary, Mrs.	02 OCT 1879 R	13	397
Robinson, Johanna	Taylor, William S.	09 FEB 1882 L	16	235
Robinson, John	Gardener, Margaret	01 JUL 1879 L	13	260
Robinson, John D.	Offutt, Elvira C.	25 MAR 1884 L	18	481
Robinson, John W.	Dove, Mamie C.	12 JUL 1880 L	14	357
Robinson, Joseph T.	Bartel, Priscilla	16 JAN 1878 L	11	306
Robinson, Joshua	Armstrong, Susie	21 FEB 1882 R	16	254
Robinson, Julia	Coleman, Lawerence	06 JUN 1882 L	16	397
Robinson, Kate	Van Kamp, A.P.	11 NOV 1879 R	13	476
Robinson, Lee	Bates, Bertie	20 DEC 1877 R	11	252
Robinson, Lewis	Brown, Frances	07 APR 1881 L	15	251
Robinson, Lillie J.	Fitzgerald, Edward D.	18 JAN 1883	17	265
Robinson, Lizzie	Cooper, Joseph H.	05 MAY 1878 R	12	037
Robinson, Lizzie	Robinson, James	13 JUN 1884 R	19	069

Robinson, Lovinia	King, John	02 OCT 1883 L	18	165
Robinson, Lucian D.	Slaughter, Sophie C.	13 NOV 1883 R	18	247
Robinson, Lucy	Lipscomb, James	17 FEB 1885	20	066
Robinson, Lucy M.	Woodyear, William H.J.	16 MAR 1885 R	20	116
Robinson, Magdeline Rosetta	Preston, Samuel Henry H.	12 AUG 1879	13	316
Robinson, Marion E.	Gray, Charles B.	26 MAY 1880 R	14	289
Robinson, Martha	Mickins, Harrison	21 APR 1884	18	522
Robinson, Martha	Charlton, William	31 AUG 1885 L	20	392
Robinson, Martha J.	Anderson, John E.	08 MAY 1883	17	432
Robinson, Mary	Maxfield, Joseph	17 JUL 1883 L	18	050
Robinson, Mary	Taylor, Johnson	02 JAN 1884 R	18	363
Robinson, Mary E.	Palmer, Zadock	30 NOV 1882 R	17	152
Robinson, Mary E.	Venner, Robert	16 NOV 1882 R	17	134
Robinson, Mary J.	Moore, George D.	23 JUN 1878	12	095
Robinson, Mary Jane	Sullivan, Philip	09 DEC 1878 L	12	374
Robinson, Molly	Gray, Robert H.	15 JAN 1880 R	14	105
Robinson, Nannie A.	Finch, Edwin Jr.	03 OCT 1882 R	17	049
Robinson, Nathaniel	Scott, Isabella	15 NOV 1877 L	11	190
Robinson, Newton	Johnson, Georgiana	23 DEC 1880 L	15	117
Robinson, Patsy L.	Tippitt, Clarence D.	27 JAN 1881 L	15	167
Robinson, Peter H.	Robinson, Fannie	18 DEC 1877 L	11	241
Robinson, Priscilla	Webb, Joseph	18 SEP 1883 L	18	137
Robinson, R. Brannon	Carr, J. Gertrude	02 SEP 1880 R	14	428
Robinson, Regina M.	Koechling, Magnus	29 SEP 1879 L	13	392
Robinson, Richard	Dyson, Eliza	03 SEP 1884	19	223
Robinson, Richmond	Tilghman, Susie	27 SEP 1877 R	11	106
Robinson, Robert E.	Brown, Louisa Alberta	22 AUG 1878 R	12	147
Robinson, Rosina	Jordan, Thomas	03 DEC 1882	17	164
Robinson, Ruffin	Richardson, Gracie Ann	20 AUG 1885 R	20	382
Robinson, Samuel	Davis, Olive	04 JUN 1878 R	12	081
Robinson, Samuel R.	Willett, Mary C.	18 DEC 1881 R	16	138
Robinson, Sara Eaton Gregg	Clark, George Washington	15 DEC 1880 R	15	098
Robinson, Sarah	Bellford, James	12 SEP 1882 L	17	017
Robinson, Sarah	Moore, Solomon	15 JUN 1882	16	405
Robinson, Sarah A.	Keyes, Daniel	29 OCT 1884 L	19	344
Robinson, Sarah, Mrs.	Carrington, Jacob	12 APR 1881	15	251
Robinson, Scipio	Duckett, Ida C.	14 APR 1885 L	20	165
Robinson, Spencer	Jackson, Maria	20 SEP 1882 L	17	031
Robinson, Susie	Green, Andrew	18 MAY 1880 R	14	273
Robinson, Thomas M.	Griffin, Nellie	20 AUG 1884 L	19	197
Robinson, Warner	Davenport, Belle	24 JUL 1884	19	156
Robinson, Wash. W.	Green, Mollie	12 MAY 1880 R	14	266
Robinson, William	Lias, Josephine	06 SEP 1877 L	11	079
Robinson, William	Johnson, Jennie	27 FEB 1879 R	13	081
Robinson, William	Callbut, Rebecca	08 JUL 1880 R	14	348
Robinson, William	Martin, Elizabeth	24 MAY 1880	14	283
Robinson, William	Harris, Charity Tinney	23 MAY 1881 R	15	321
Robinson, William	Matthews, Helen	23 NOV 1882	17	147
Robinson, William	Holmes, Mary	17 DEC 1884 L	19	464
Robinson, William	Chew, Sarah	03 FEB 1885 L	20	049
Robinson, William F.	Emicks, Mary	22 MAR 1883 R	17	354
Robinson, William H.	Shelton, Caroline	28 JUN 1884 L	19	108
Robinson, William H.	Dodson, Julia A.	23 OCT 1884 L	19	332
Robinson, William H.	Stewart, Rosetta	14 DEC 1884 R	19	452
Robinson, William Henry	Thomas, Fannie	14 JUL 1881 R	15	403
Robison, Asbury	Henderson, Mary	01 JAN 1880 R	14	087
Robison, Hagar	Day, George	20 FEB 1883 L	17	314
Robison, Henry	Ellison, Margaret	02 OCT 1884	19	283

D.C. Marriage Records Index, June 28, 1877 to October 19, 1885

Robison, James	Jennison, Marcellina	08 JAN 1885 L	20	009
Robison, Richard	Campbell, Mary	27 JUN 1878 R	12	116
Robrecht, Frank	Hensley, Martha A., Mrs.	22 FEB 1884 R	18	437
Robrecht, Mary E.	Bailey, Levi J.	17 MAY 1882	16	363
Robson, John	Toney, Catharine	28 AUG 1877 L	11	068
Robson, mary Ann	Brown, Joshua A.	23 JUN 1883 L	18	012
Roby, Gracie A.	Scott, Thomas E.	19 DEC 1881	16	030
Rocca, John B.	Cassosa, Louisa	14 JAN 1883	17	256
Rochbuck, Clarrisa B.	Brown, Horace	10 JUN 1880 R	14	312
Roche, Anna M.	DeRemer, James R.	14 JUL 1885	20	324
Roche, Ella H.	Maguire, J. Frank	08 OCT 1879 R	13	409
Roche, John A.	Reagan, Annie	29 JUN 1882 L	16	431
Roche, Josephine	Sciardi, Autoni	25 APR 1881 L	15	270
Roche, Katie A.	Brosnan, John	30 MAY 1878 L	12	076
Roche, Maggie	Comer, Peter	05 NOV 1881 L	16	063
Roche, Nellie B.	Fuse, Charles B.	14 JUL 1877 L	11	020
Roche, William E.	Murphy, Nellie C.	05 FEB 1883 L	17	291
Roche, William J.	Daily, Mary E.	16 FEB 1885 R	20	068
Rocheweg, Charles D.	Krehling, Lizzie B.	19 NOV 1882 R	17	134
Rock, Ellen	Nichols, Theodore	14 MAY 1884 L	19	021
Rock, Laura Cecilia	Accardi, Adrian J.P.	02 OCT 1877 R	11	119
Rockafellow, Andrew D.	Hardy, Louisa	30 MAY 1878	12	073
Rockett, George T.	Clubb, Sophia	22 APR 1884	18	524
Rockett, William R.	Satterfield, Mary L.	23 JUL 1883	18	043
Rockey, Emma	Hilton, Abraham L.	07 JUN 1885	20	258
Rockwell, Willis G.	Robertson, Ida I.	08 JUN 1884	19	067
Rockwood, Emily Johnston	Mauro, Philip	07 JUN 1881 R	15	345
Roden, Robert	Robinson, Ada	16 MAR 1882	16	274
Rodgers, Alexander	Cameron, Virginia Rolette	11 JAN 1883	17	238
Rodgers, Anne Perry	Neilson, Louis	28 OCT 1880 R	14	486
Rodgers, Annie	Petitt, Alfred	01 JUN 1881 R	15	336
Rodgers, Emma	Petitt, Lorenzo	19 DEC 1882 R	17	192
Rodgers, George H.	Doggett, Susie	03 NOV 1880	15	027
Rodgers, James	Yates, Maria	02 NOV 1878 L	12	304
Rodgers, James E.	Pettit, Margaret	01 MAY 1879 L	13	171
Rodgers, Jane Perry	Meigs, John Forsythe, Jr.	27 APR 1881	15	275
Rodgers, John W.	Layton, Ellen R.	10 JUN 1880	14	317
Rodgers, Lafayette	Turner, Annie	11 OCT 1882 R	17	062
Rodgers, Mark J.	Ross, Louisa V.	16 FEB 1884	18	426
Rodgers, Mary Agnes	Wade, Thomas Leonard	04 NOV 1882 L	17	111
Rodgers, Rebecca Ann	Baggott, Levi	26 DEC 1882 R	17	210
Rodgers, William H.	Richardson, Maggie B.	21 OCT 1882	17	084
Rodier, Effie	Boughton, Wilfred E.	12 NOV 1884	19	376
Rodier, Emma Elizabeth	Burket, Lincoln	05 AUG 1881 L	15	434
Rodier, Frances Louise	Adams, Hamilton	28 FEB 1881 L	15	205
Rodier, Iola E.	Braddock, Denton Scott	28 JUL 1885 R	20	343
Rodier, James LaCoste	Porter, Ida V.	15 MAY 1879 L	13	192
Rodier, Louisa Monroe	Ladson, Charles John	25 JUN 1885 R	20	293
Rodier, Mattie K.	Suthard, Charles M.	18 JUL 1883	18	053
Rodier, Joseph S.	Schladt, Annie	12 NOV 1883 L	18	248
Rodriguez, José Ignacio	Joyce, Mary A.	14 APR 1884	18	506
Roe, Mattie E.	Smith, William H.	28 APR 1885 L	20	192
Roeser, Adolph	Kirby, Jenny C.	30 AUG 1882 R	16	495
Rofe, Wyatt	Smith, Harriet	22 AUG 1878 R	12	175
Rogers, Ada	McShane, William	01 MAR 1882 R	16	263
Rogers, Alice	Potter, Edward	23 JUL 1884	19	152
Rogers, Archibald I.	Shellhorn, Bertha	19 AUG 1885	20	377
Rogers, Bettie	Wright, Gustave B.	18 AUG 1881 R	15	452

Rogers, Ella	Hafner, Augustus P.	06 DEC 1883	18	303
Rogers, Harriet, Mrs.	Smith, Andrew Washington	07 JUN 1879 R	13	135
Rogers, Ida May	Waters, William O.	13 DEC 1883 L	18	316
Rogers, Jane H.	Kline, Peter	11 NOV 1877 R	11	175
Rogers, Joseph	Proctor, Ellen	18 JUN 1885 L	20	280
Rogers, Joseph I.	Durse, Elizabeth	26 DEC 1878 R	12	358
Rogers, Laura	Sims, Charles H.	29 OCT 1878	12	295
Rogers, Louisianna	Arundell, Charles A.	26 AUG 1884	19	208
Rogers, Lydia A.	Wilson, Robert	06 DEC 1883 L	18	298
Rogers, Maria	Lewis, George	16 FEB 1879 R	13	056
Rogers, Mary Ann, Mrs.	Dixon, George	06 JUL 1880 L	14	349
Rogers, Millie	King, Lewis	31 JAN 1884	18	386
Rogers, Nellie Marmaduke	Spence, Thomas B.	07 MAR 1881 R	15	218
Rogers, Robert Cummins	Fvans, Madge Randolph	24 MAR 1885 R	20	127
Rogers, Thomas L.	Brown, Rosa L.	02 JUN 1884	19	051
Rogers, William E.	Smith, Louise G.	20 OCT 1882 L	17	083
Rogers, William Henry	Pettet, H. Anne	03 OCT 1878	12	250
Rogers, William Isaac	Curtis, Leonora Clara	15 MAY 1878 R	12	048
Rohde, William	Nolte, Margaretta	04 NOV 1884	19	358
Rokenheiser, Elizabeth L.	America, Joseph P.	20 JUL 1884	19	146
Rokes, Emerson	Soper, Broxie B.	21 FEB 1882	16	249
Roland, Ida L.	Saxton, John R.	31 OCT 1882 R	17	102
Roland, John W.	Phillips, Jane	10 MAR 1879 R	13	095
Roland, Laura V.	Smith, Willard F.	06 JAN 1883 L	17	241
Roland, Mary	Thomas, James	09 AUG 1881 L	15	437
Roland, Rachel E.	Berry, William H.	06 SEP 1878 R	12	202
Rolfe, Kate	Hailey, Thomas	27 MAY 1880 R	14	290
Rollen, Emma	Page, Arthur	07 DEC 1882 L	17	173
Rollings, John Henry	Chamberlain, Mary E.	26 JUL 1881 L	15	419
Rollins, Annie	Miller, Dan	11 JUN 1884 R	19	072
Rollins, Annie D.	King, James B.	03 JUN 1885 L	20	254
Rollins, Annie R.	Jones, James L.	14 SEP 1882 R	17	022
Rollins, Caroline Alice	Henson, Albert Tiberias	25 SEP 1879 R	13	388
Rollins, Charles	Ducket, Odelia	23 FEB 1882 R	16	256
Rollins, Charles Franklin	Thompson, Sarah Jane Elizabeth	02 JUL 1877	11	005
Rollins, Daniel	Dabney, Mamie	27 NOV 1883 L	18	278
Rollins, Eolia	Lloyd, Francis B.	05 JUL 1884 L	19	123
Rollins, Evelina	Johnson, Daniel Philip	09 DEC 1884 R	19	442
Rollins, Fanny J.	Brown, Nathan	05 DEC 1877	11	220
Rollins, George F.	Pike, Annie C.	16 MAR 1878 R	11	385
Rollins, Isaac	Jackson, Mary O.	21 DEC 1882	17	203
Rollins, Letitia	Mahoney, John Henry	25 APR 1883	17	411
Rollins, Lewis F.	Gunnell, Carrie	31 AUG 1885	20	393
Rollins, Maggie Ann	Ward, Moses Columbus	27 FEB 1883 R	17	323
Rollins, Maria	Floyd, Robert	29 NOV 1878 R	12	346
Rollins, Mary	Graham, Oscar	19 DEC 1883	18	325
Rollins, Oliver	Clements, Margaret	22 APR 1879 R	13	152
Rollins, Tiny	Thompson, Walter	15 SEP 1880 R	14	445
Rollins, William	Bell, Jane Ann	20 DEC 1882 L	17	199
Rollins, William Henry	Beach, Annie Laura	11 JUL 1882 R	16	444
Rollow, Anna M.	King, Rufus T.	03 FEB 1879 R	13	044
Romain, Arthur	German, Emma J.	21 SEP 1877 L	11	104
Rome, William	Mason, Rebecca	28 OCT 1877	11	157
Rone, Levi	White, Ellen	02 AUG 1877 R	11	037
Ronspies, Francis E.	Light, Sarah E.	30 JUN 1885 L	20	301
Ronz, Johanna	Gatto, Joseph	16 MAR 1879 R	13	095
Roof, Rachel A.	Otto, Alexander	03 DEC 1878 R	12	363
Roones, Florence B.	Solger, Julius	22 NOV 1881 L	16	090

Rooney, Maggie	Dugan, Stephen	10 FEB 1878 R	11	335
Roony, Morris	Hunt, Taresa	05 FEB 1884 L	18	411
Roosa, Margaret T.	Wyman, Albert J.	15 JUL 1877 R	11	021
Roose, Mary C.	Connell, George E.	21 APR 1880 R	14	231
Root, Harriet C.	Fielding, William S.	03 AUG 1882 R	16	468
Roots, Anna	Johnson, Beverly	02 OCT 1884	19	277
Roots, Fannie	Burnett, John T.	09 SEP 1885 R	20	408
Roots, Howard	Carr, Lucy	24 JUL 1877 R	11	029
Roots, John	Joyce, Leila	04 APR 1881 L	15	245
Roots, Walter	Robinson, Henrietta	14 APR 1885 L	20	164
Rorey, Henry C.	Rorey, Mary Catherine Gregg	22 JAN 1878 R	11	314
Rorey, Mary Catherine Gregg	Rorey, Henry C.	22 JAN 1878 R	11	314
Rose, Carl Diedrich Adolph	Lemke, Dora Maria Cathinka	10 AUG 1882 R	16	474
Rose, Catherine	Mundell, Benjamin M.	06 MAY 1879 R	13	177
Rose, Edith	Beall, William W.	15 NOV 1877 L	11	186
Rose, Frederick	Payne, Roberta	19 MAR 1885 R	20	125
Rose, Hetty A.	Stunkel, Edward T.	06 APR 1880	14	210
Rose, Kate	Jennings, R.B.	20 APR 1880	14	230
Rose, Virginia C.	Walter, Henry S.	13 OCT 1880 R	14	492
Rose, William	Washington, Rosetta	13 DEC 1877	11	235
Rose, William L.	Barron, Mattie	18 JUL 1883	18	052
Rose, Willis	Brown, Joanna F.	27 OCT 1881 L	16	051
Roseberry, Annie S.	Young, John M.	24 DEC 1878 R	12	397
Roseberry, Carrie Iola	Talbot, Edward Henry	10 FEB 1884 R	18	417
Roseberry, George W.	Messer, Helen	26 SEP 1877	11	108
Rosell, Henry	Jackson, Ella	26 SEP 1883	18	148
Rosenbaum, Rosa H.	Ellis, Lewis Y.	18 NOV 1879	13	494
Rosenberg, Emma	Frank, Ferdinand	28 FEB 1883 R	17	321
Rosenberg, Fannie	Hofheimer, Alexander T.	18 AUG 1880 R	14	402
Rosenberg, Hanna	Auerbach, Carl	02 JUN 1878 R	12	067
Rosenbusch, Lewis C.	Volkman, E.H.	28 AUG 1883	18	101
Rosendale, Henry	Sellner, Dora	03 AUG 1879 R	13	303
Rosengun, Lena	Williams, William H.	11 DEC 1878	12	374
Rosenthal, Felix Louis	Samstag, Emma	05 MAR 1885 R	20	094
Rosenthall, Charles	DeHaan, Jennie	19 MAY 1879 R	13	195
Rosette, John, Dr.	Lusby, Maria Louisa	17 JUL 1884	19	144
Roseway, Susan	Stewart, Charles	19 JUN 1880 R	14	326
Roseweg, Ella N.	Johnson, William B.	12 FEB 1883	17	302
Rosher, Emma	Gibbs, Aaron	03 JUL 1879 R	13	268
Rosier, John T.	Dorsey, Elizabeth	04 MAR 1878 L	11	368
Rosier, Mary	Gilmore, George	11 SEP 1879 R	13	364
Ross, Aaron	Jones, Emma	18 DEC 1879 L	14	056
Ross, Alexander	Mead, Lucy	21 OCT 1880	15	008
Ross, Anna	Lewis, Charles H.	04 MAR 1880	14	131
Ross, Anna Rebecca	Colbert, James F.	25 DEC 1884	19	440
Ross, Ben	White, Allis	26 FEB 1882 R	23	5653
Ross, Benjamin	Turner, Elmina	07 FEB 1882	16	227
Ross, Charles H.	Smith, Frances A.	20 JAN 1885	20	026
Ross, Eliza Alice	Thomas, George W.	14 JUL 1881 R	15	401
Ross, Elizabeth	Jackson, James William	27 SEP 1877	11	111
Ross, Elizabeth	Brown, Richard	04 APR 1881	15	245
Ross, Fannie	Ringgold, Edward	29 OCT 1879 R	13	451
Ross, Fannie	Jones, Dennis	22 JUN 1882 R	16	402
Ross, Fannie Cole	Watts, Edward C.	27 OCT 1879 R	13	445
Ross, Fannie M.	Chapman, Charles W.	24 OCT 1880	15	011
Ross, Fanny	Franklin, James	15 DEC 1877 R	11	238
Ross, Fanny	Burley, John	04 OCT 1881	16	005
Ross, George	Montgomery, Mary Adams	31 JUL 1881 R	15	417

Ross, Hattie	Lawson, Peter	14 JUN 1883	17	492
Ross, Henry L.	Cross, Emma G.	01 NOV 1883 L	18	227
Ross, Hestor Ann	Wood, William Henry	09 MAY 1881 L	15	297
Ross, Jacob	Reeder, Alice	19 JUL 1877 R	11	028
Ross, James	Fendrick, Sarah	09 FEB 1882 L	16	234
Ross, James	Hudson, Nettie Bell	28 MAR 1883 L	17	366
Ross, John	Lucas, Mary V.	03 JUL 1877 R	11	004
Ross, John	Washington, Sallie Ann	03 SEP 1879 R	13	327
Ross, John R.	Elliot, Cecilia M.	20 FEB 1879 L	13	069
Ross, John Robert	Shane, Mary Ann	19 APR 1880 L	14	228
Ross, John Thomas deHavilland	Young, Louisa Latham	26 JUN 1879 R	13	246
Ross, Laura D.	Carrington, David C.	16 APR 1879	13	140
Ross, Lemuel	Bradley, Mary Emma	04 DEC 1877 L	11	218
Ross, Lottie	Dabney, James H.	09 MAY 1878 L	12	045
Ross, Louisa V.	Rodgers, Mark J.	16 FEB 1884	18	426
Ross, Lucy E.	Green, Richard	17 OCT 1877 R	11	140
Ross, Margaret	Meeks, John	02 OCT 1879 R	13	400
Ross, Mary C.	Hicks, Henry	29 SEP 1885	20	429
Ross, Peter	Lewis, Mary	01 JUL 1881 L	15	384
Ross, Rachel	Whitney, Thomas	24 MAR 1885	20	130
Ross, Smith E.	Woodfall, Louisa	30 SEP 1879 R	13	390
Ross, Thomas	Barber, Ella	03 JUN 1880 R	14	303
Ross, Thomas B.	Wood, Ida M.	28 MAY 1878 L	12	069
Ross, Tillman G.	Thomas, Sarah E.	03 APR 1882 L	16	295
Ross, William F.	Mason, Nannie M.	27 AUG 1877 L	11	068
Ross, William F.	Bird, Cornelia	04 NOV 1884	19	351
Rossi, Eugene	Carter, Eliza R.	17 FEB 1885	20	065
Rossiter, Edward C.	Kearney, Jeannett B.	30 JUN 1884	19	109
Rosson, Abner A.	Lyle, Maud	06 JAN 1881 L	15	142
Roswag, Charles F.	May, Elizabeth B.	16 AUG 1885	20	371
Rotchford, Annie	Head, James M.	17 DEC 1879 R	14	053
Roten, Charles	Palmer, Eliza	26 AUG 1880 R	14	110
Roten, Louisa	Wood, John William	01 DEC 1881 R	16	109
Roth, Annie	Stump, Joseph	20 MAY 1885 R	20	231
Roth, Annie M.	Fitzgerald, John P.	28 APR 1884 L	18	537
Roth, Frances	Willers, William	05 JUN 1878 L	12	086
Roth, Jacob	Kaiser, Emmer A.	28 JUL 1885	20	343
Roth, Julius	Campbell, Harriet Rebecca	08 MAY 1881 R	15	296
Roth, P. Wm.	Kaa, Carrie	04 JAN 1880 R	14	087
Rothbeger, Annie	Vaeth, Philip	26 JUL 1881	15	416
Rothberg, Paulina	Mundheim, Albert K.	08 MAY 1883 R	17	432
Rothenburg, Hugo	Sauer, Hedwig	15 MAY 1885 L	20	224
Rothery, Eva	Salmon, John	26 SEP 1880 R	14	459
Rothmund, Philip	Kinsley, Louisa	23 AUG 1877	11	062
Rothrock, Hamilton Irving	Groff, Bessie	04 DEC 1884	19	433
Rothrock, Jeannie D.	Loving, Robinson	16 OCT 1879 R	13	428
Rothsehn, Margaret	Güthler, Max	21 AUG 1881 R	15	453
Rothstein, Anna Elizabeth	Meyer, Ernest H.	03 FEB 1884 R	18	402
Rott, Elizabeth	Weiske, Benjamin	09 NOV 1878 L	12	318
Rotto, Kata	Sears, Harry M.	16 AUG 1885 R	20	370
Rotto, Stephen	Vannattar, Mollie	17 NOV 1883 L	18	261
Roub, Philip	Green, Mary Alice	29 MAR 1883 R	17	369
Roudabush, Fannie B.	Suter, John R.	05 NOV 1884	19	364
Rougnet, Raymond	Lepondré, Josephine	03 JAN 1878	11	291
Roundtree, Sally	Robertson, Morris	29 MAR 1878	11	391
Rouse, Charles William	Warner, Lizzie S.	26 MAR 1881 L	15	239
Rousseau, Young	Mabry, Victoria	03 APR 1884 L	18	495
Routh, John	Bates, Jeanie M., Mrs.	20 JAN 1881 R	15	160

Routzhn, Charles	Kitchen, Nora	15 APR 1885 R	20	161
Roux, J. Mitchell	Lucas, Ida M.	06 OCT 1885	20	463
Rouzer, George W.	Kiesecker, Leonora	19 OCT 1882 R	17	082
Rover, Maggie E.	Mack, Thomas	02 FEB 1880	14	130
Rowe, Emily	Bollison, Roderick	04 DEC 1878	12	363
Rowe, Henry H.	Scrimger, Bettie A.	13 NOV 1878 R	12	327
Rowe, Inez E.	McLain, Portus B.	16 JUN 1882	16	415
Rowe, Lavinia B.	Faerber, Julius I.	17 MAR 1885 R	20	119
Rowe, Mary	Edmunds, Richard	24 OCT 1877 L	11	152
Rowe, Mary	Johnson, John Henry	29 APR 1881	15	285
Rowe, Rudolph Carl	Noack, Augusta	27 FEB 1879 R	13	055
Rowe, Thomas R.	McGhee, Lizzie F.	28 JUN 1877 L	11	001
Rowell, Ambrose E.	Northern, Clara	20 APR 1881 R	15	266
Rowland, J. Shannon	Teel, S. Julia	03 DEC 1884 L	19	433
Rowland, Nellie R.	Mills, George Albert	16 AUG 1883 R	18	091
Rowley, Charles P.	Arnold, Lillie	07 SEP 1878 R	12	204
Rowzee, Annie M.	Turner, W.R.	11 DEC 1883	18	308
Rowzee, Charles R.	Ferry, Julia N.	20 JAN 1881 R	15	157
Rowzee, William S.	Hughes, Clara W.	04 MAY 1878	11	406
Rowzel, Edward G.	Jackson, Estelle E.	11 NOV 1879	13	477
Rowzer, Julia A.	Klock, Henry Anderson	02 OCT 1883 R	18	164
Roy, Austen	Miller, Roy Lena, Mrs.	26 DEC 1878 L	12	403
Roy, Bertie	Rankins, Disco	17 OCT 1878 R	12	277
Roy, Ned	Watson, Rosanna	01 APR 1878 L	13	122
Roy, Stewart	McKenney, Louise	25 APR 1883	17	411
Royce, C.L.	Ubhoff, Lillie	27 AUG 1881 L	15	463
Royce, Mary E.	Parker, John S.	17 JUN 1885 R	20	276
Roye, Ella	Washington, Marshall	17 APR 1884 R	18	519
Royston, Kate Janette	Jarvis, Thaddeus	14 NOV 1877 R	11	185
Rozer, Henrietta Frances	Adams, Charles Frederic	05 AUG 1885 R	20	351
Rubbeins, Carrie M.	Tuttle, Columbus	26 SEP 1885 R	20	443
Rubenstein, Pauline	Meyer, Joseph	15 MAR 1885 R	20	111
Rubinstein, Minnie	Feldman, Shiman	27 SEP 1885 R	20	443
Ruckcer, Ella G.	Green, William E.	15 NOV 1882 L	17	128
Rucker, Laura A.	Reed, James W.	20 NOV 1879 R	13	498
Rucker, Martha	Delany, Thomas	21 SEP 1881 R	15	492
Rucker, Mary	Lee, William H.	02 JUL 1885 L	20	307
Rückert, William Edward	Martin, Emma E.	02 FEB 1880 R	14	129
Rudd, Addie	Lemmon, Jesse R.	07 SEP 1881	15	474
Rudd, Laura M.	Hall, James D.	20 JUL 1884	19	143
Rudd, Sarah V.	Carlin, Jno. Frank	16 AUG 1881 R	15	447
Rudhart, Anna	Hebsacker, Robert	29 OCT 1882	17	099
Ruebsam, Lizzie C.	Meier, Henry	26 MAY 1885 R	20	240
Rueth, John M.	Rueth, Mary Anna	19 FEB 1884 L	18	431
Rueth, Mary Anna	Rueth, John M.	19 FEB 1884 L	18	431
Ruff, Miriam E.	Small, John Henry, Jr.	11 OCT 1882 R	17	064
Ruffin, Matilda Catharine	Harryday, Stephen Daniel	01 JUN 1880 R	14	289
Ruffins, Benjamin	Green, Susan	23 FEB 1878 R	11	342
Ruffins, Louisa Miles	Baylor, James	29 SEP 1882 R	17	044
Ruhl, Anna	Behrens, Ernst	29 SEP 1885 R	20	446
Ruick, Emil A.H.	Thurow, Louise E.W.	14 SEP 1885	20	414
Rükert, Joseph	Emmert, Christine	25 JUN 1884 R	19	104
Ruland, George	Rank, Elizabeth	14 OCT 1882	17	072
Rummels, Sarah	Ball, David	17 JAN 1880	14	110
Rumpf, Lewis	Ferguson, Anna Laura	24 JUL 1883	18	058
Rumsey, Joseph C.	Reed, Mattie (Arnold)	17 JAN 1883 R	17	263
Rumsey, Mary Katherine	Winsinger, William	24 FEB 1885 R	20	083
Runby, L.	Faunce, Annie	07 NOV 1881	16	064

Runk, Alden A.	Patton, Mildred A.	16 MAR 1885 R	20	114
Runnells, Maria	Harlan, Thomas	08 MAR 1883 R	17	338
Runnells, Sarah McClellan	Ferry, James Thomas	17 JUL 1883 R	18	050
Ruoff, Charles H.	Stowell, Carrie L.	06 OCT 1885 R	20	461
Ruoff, Julia Spencer	Flint, Charles	02 OCT 1878 R	12	248
Rupenacker, Christina	Weis, Adam	04 DEC 1878 L	12	364
Rupertus, Charles	Miele, Augustine	03 DEC 1884 R	19	434
Rupertus, Henry	Schneider, Marther	28 JAN 1884 R	18	397
Rupertus, William	Schneider, Bertha	05 OCT 1880 R	14	474
Rupp, Albert E.	Coster, Susie E.	04 OCT 1880 L	14	471
Rupp, Augusta	Mihm, George	29 JUL 1878 L	12	151
Rupp, Edward C.	Johnson, Ida M.	21 DEC 1882 L	17	203
Rupp, John N.	Garrett, Katie	07 JUN 1881 L	15	348
Rupp, Louise W.	Van Syckel, Geo. W.E.	21 JUL 1880 L	14	371
Rupp, William H.	Harkness, Cora P.	20 NOV 1878 R	12	338
Ruppel, Joseph	Kiefer, Rosa	25 JAN 1880 R	14	112
Ruppel, Josephine	Huhn, Henry	14 NOV 1878 L	12	329
Ruppert, Annie	Meckel, Niclaus	15 FEB 1881	15	189
Ruppert, Frank J.	Neff, Kate F.	21 NOV 1882 L	17	141
Ruppert, Henry J.	Cord, Louise	20 NOV 1883 L	18	265
Ruppert, John H.	Koch, Barbara L.	03 OCT 1882 L	17	048
Ruppert, Kate M.	Price, Robert R.	20 FEB 1882 L	16	249
Ruppert, Katie	Bottomley, Louis	23 AUG 1882 R	16	446
Ruppert, Mary Annie	Kohl, Frank	06 MAY 1878 L	12	038
Ruppert, Mary E.	Anders, John A.	31 MAY 1885	20	154
Ruppert, Mathew	Link, Mary	06 JAN 1880 R	14	089
Rupprecht, Richard	Bicking, Augusta	07 APR 1885 R	20	143
Rushman, Wm. Andrew	Lawson, Virginia Beach	25 AUG 1880 R	14	417
Russ, Charles	Berkley, Rosetta	16 AUG 1879 L	13	324
Russ, Geneva M.	Graham, John W.	11 NOV 1878 L	12	322
Russeau, Lelia M.	McMurphy, Mahlon	09 MAR 1885	20	101
Russel, Florence	Daly, Martin	29 APR 1881	15	286
Russel, Robert	Powell, Sarah	24 OCT 1878	12	290
Russel, Susan Frances	Talbot, Dennison C.	14 MAR 1881 L	15	223
Russell, Benj. Theodore	Collison, Catherine Alice	09 NOV 1882	17	120
Russell, Charles	Stewart, Maria	06 APR 1880	14	210
Russell, Charles	Anderson, Amy	20 JUN 1882 L	16	420
Russell, Charles Wells	Mosley, Lucy Floyd	19 FEB 1880 R	14	154
Russell, Clarence	Peyton, Mary	01 NOV 1881 R	16	054
Russell, Cora J.	Buckley, Phillip Maury	16 JAN 1879 R	13	019
Russell, Daniel	Hall, Harriet	16 JAN 1885 L	20	023
Russell, Edward	Quiet, Carrie	15 MAR 1883 R	17	345
Russell, Edward M.	Gould, Ellen L.	06 DEC 1877 R	11	220
Russell, Frankie A.	Mullen, Luther P.	14 APR 1885 R	20	164
Russell, Harriet	McCauley, Joseph	13 NOV 1880	15	046
Russell, John	Snowden, Mary Ellen	09 MAR 1885 L	20	102
Russell, John C.	Neale, Mary Ellen	15 MAR 1883 L	17	345
Russell, John R.	Murray, Elizabeth	23 NOV 1881	16	071
Russell, Laura R.S.C.	Dulin, John F.	20 AUG 1879 R	13	325
Russell, Lizzie	Jordan, Braxton	08 SEP 1881 R	15	476
Russell, Mary	Matthews, William	22 APR 1880 L	14	235
Russell, Mary V.	Simons, John T.	21 FEB 1882 L	16	255
Russell, Patrick	Dudley, Mary	17 AUG 1883 L	18	092
Russell, Philip Gray	Kendall, Lilean	17 DEC 1884 R	19	465
Rust, Ella	Smith, James Moncure	26 APR 1881 R	15	272
Rustin, William H.	Woodward, Maria	15 APR 1884 L	18	510
Ruth, John H.	Ruth, Teresa	07 FEB 1885 L	20	057
Ruth, Teresa	Ruth, John H.	07 FEB 1885 L	20	057

Rüth, John M.	Weigand, Monica	13 AUG 1878 L	12	166
Rutherford, Annie	Farden, James D.	10 SEP 1884	19	236
Rutherford, J.A.	Williamson, M.V.	22 MAY 1879	13	202
Rutherford, Jennie	Westling, Charles E.	15 AUG 1881	15	446
Rutherford, Mary A.	Ireland, Robert	02 AUG 1877 L	11	038
Ryal, Ferdinand	Ellis, Lucy A.C.	02 SEP 1880 R	14	421
Ryan, Annie	Riley, Joseph R.	24 OCT 1882 R	17	088
Ryan, Annie	Cusick, William	02 JAN 1883 L	17	232
Ryan, C.W.	Welch, Pattie L.	13 DEC 1879 R	14	046
Ryan, Catherine S.	Pyles, Francis T.	10 FEB 1880 L	14	145
Ryan, Ella C.	Burgess, John B.	01 JUN 1881 L	15	337
Ryan, J.C.	Pettes, Mary E.	14 AUG 1880	14	399
Ryan, James	Ryan, Nellie	30 AUG 1881 L	15	464
Ryan, Joseph	Herbertons, Emmy	19 AUG 1885 L	20	377
Ryan, Joseph C.	Quinn, Annie	08 JUL 1878	12	129
Ryan, Lydia	Ensor, Harry G.	20 JAN 1885	20	027
Ryan, Mary A.	Cleavland, Luther	08 JAN 1884 L	18	369
Ryan, Mary Cecelia	Scott, Cephas Watkins	26 NOV 1879 R	14	007
Ryan, Mary E.	Twomey, John	29 OCT 1879 R	13	447
Ryan, Michael	Whitney, Lizzie Ann	22 AUG 1878 L	12	177
Ryan, Nellie	Ryan, James	30 AUG 1881 L	15	464
Ryan, Patrick	Devine, Mary	08 JUL 1877	11	003
Ryan, Thomas F.	French, Mary E.	13 OCT 1881 L	16	023
Ryan, William S.	Handley, Margaret L.	25 DEC 1883 R	18	336
Ryder, Frances E.	Voss, Charles H.	18 AUG 1881 L	15	451
Ryder, Josephine	Adams, Wesley	20 NOV 1879 R	13	498
Rye, David A.	Queen, Mary A.	01 MAY 1882 R	16	341
Rye, Jane T.	Kendrick, Massena	10 MAY 1882 R	16	354
Rye, John	Donaldson, Ida B.	14 SEP 1880 R	14	443
Rye, Mary McElfresh	Fichter, George	03 MAR 1880	14	175
Ryer, Henry C.	Ashby, Mary A.	15 AUG 1881 R	15	446
Ryland, Edward Craft	Law, Elsie G.A. Justice	09 JUL 1879 L	13	277
Ryon, John T.	Espey, Maria V.	24 OCT 1882 L	17	090
Ryon, Millard F.	Simpson, Lillie	07 FEB 1883	17	299

S

Sabel, George W.	Whittemore, Henrietta J.	02 MAY 1881	15	287
Sabin, Harriet Brooks	Wells, Leon H.	30 JUN 1885 R	20	303
Sabine, Adeleide W.	Clark, Prentiss M.	11 MAR 1884 L	18	465
Sabine, Andrew, Dr.	Brown, Nannie C.	28 OCT 1879 R	13	444
Sachs, Jacob	Caplan, Fannie	27 MAY 1883 R	17	462
Sackson, Nathaniel	Jordan, Mary Catharine	19 NOV 1884 R	19	094
Saddler, Ida	Wright, Charles	11 JUN 1879 R	13	169
Saddler, William D.	Herbert, Jennie A.	08 JUN 1882 R	16	401
Sadler, A.G.	Marshall, F.M.	20 DEC 1877 L	11	248
Sadler, Harry Warren	DeWees, Irene	14 SEP 1881 R	15	484
Saffee, Emma L.	Hall, Martimore S.	16 JUL 1884	19	136
Saffel, Albin F.	Allen, Annie May	28 SEP 1882	17	043
Saffel, Mary Margaretta	Thompson, Wilbert Grant	13 FEB 1883 R	17	302
Saffell, Annie T.	Cushman, Frederick A.	17 JAN 1885 L	20	025
Saffold, Milton Whiting	Benson, Sarah E.L., Mrs.	15 DEC 1882 R	17	187
Safoe, Francis	Shambaugh, Annie	01 JUL 1884 L	19	115
Sage, Harriet R.	Dwyer, Henry	18 MAY 1880	14	272
Sailes, William	Walker, Molly	29 AUG 1878 L	12	186
Saks, Rebecca	Heckheimer, Abraham	17 MAR 1878 R	11	380
Salas, Augustus Ramon	Whitehead, Valeria Berrien	24 DEC 1884 R	19	479
Salb, Charles F.	Burke, Mariah A.	02 JUN 1884 R	19	050
Sale, Ida Lee	Craig, A. Franklin	07 OCT 1878 R	12	259
Sale, Leonard D.	Jackson, Annie E.	06 OCT 1885	20	454
Sales, Bettie	James, George H.	31 JAN 1885 L	20	046
Sales, Julia	Henry, William	01 DEC 1877 L	11	214
Salf, Julia Ann	Armistead, Wm. Christ.	26 JUL 1877 R	11	032
Salinas, Anna E.	Ford, Robert H.	21 APR 1878 R	12	013
Salinger, Fred	Cohen, Rachel	11 JAN 1880 R	14	099
Salisbury, John W.	Turner, Inez E.	06 SEP 1877 L	11	080
Salisbury, William H.	Allen, Mary Elizabeth	08 JAN 1883	17	243
Sallaba, Henry R.	Devlin, Mary C.	29 APR 1880 R	14	246
Salmon, John	Rothery, Eva	26 SEP 1880 R	14	459
Salmon, Joseph H.	Hayes, Helena Cole	25 NOV 1878 R	12	342
Salor, Nettie Aanna	Boswell, Ignatius	04 DEC 1879 R	14	028
Salsbury, Mary	Dwyer, Thomas D.	16 MAY 1883 L	17	445
Salser, Frank	Muggles, Kate	31 DEC 1879 R	14	082
Salter, Samuel T.	Whiting, Hortense E.	28 MAR 1881 R	15	241
Saltmer, George H.	Grubb, Mary A.	19 DEC 1877	11	245
Saltzer, James E.	Boyd, Mattie V.	22 NOV 1881 L	16	088
Salusbury, John M.	Bronson, Maggie	27 DEC 1877	11	276
Salzig, Katie P.	Gerhardt, Julius I.	04 SEP 1881	15	470
Salzmann, Mary S.	Brown, David	22 JAN 1878 L	11	313
Samilton, William S.	Thompson, E.M.	11 SEP 1879 L	13	366
Sammons, James E.	Flaherty, Mollie	15 OCT 1877	11	136
Sammons, Joseph H.	Dubant, Hattie	11 FEB 1885 R	20	061
Sammons, Lizzie E.	Koons, Charles Henry	15 OCT 1884 R	19	308
Sammons, William E.	Wheeler, Lottie E.	04 DEC 1878 R	12	365
Sample, Maria	Richardson, Daniel	10 JUN 1879	13	227
Sampsell, Baron D.	Rennoe, Maggie	27 DEC 1877 L	11	277
Sampson, Edgar K.	Jefferson, Florence	03 MAR 1881 R	15	214
Sampson, John W.	Meder, Virginia	14 OCT 1883 R	18	191
Sampson, Mary	Hawkins, William Henry	07 OCT 1884	19	291
Samstag, Emma	Rosenthal, Felix Louis	05 MAR 1885 R	20	094
Samtain, Emma	Scott, Albert	27 DEC 1877 R	11	274
Samuel, Isidor W.	Levi, Sarah	23 JAN 1880 L	14	118
Samuel, James Edward	Thomas, Katie M.	18 DEC 1884 R	19	469
Sanborn, Daniel	Weaver, Alice	29 SEP 1882 R	17	043

Sandek, Elizabeth V.	Stern, Leopold	05 JUN 1884 R	19	045
Sanders, Ambrose	Johnson, Dora	08 JAN 1878 R	11	295
Sanders, Amelia	Bolden, Charles	26 JUN 1878 R	12	109
Sanders, Ann	Simpson, Charles Wm.	08 JUN 1881 R	15	348
Sanders, Annie	Jones, Robert W.	10 MAR 1884 R	18	463
Sanders, Annie M.	Fortune, Isaiah	05 SEP 1884	19	169
Sanders, Belle A.	Day, John W.	22 MAR 1884 L	18	478
Sanders, Charles	Coleman, Malvina	08 DEC 1877 L	11	227
Sanders, Charles	Barnes, Mary E.	15 JAN 1880 R	14	107
Sanders, Clements	Berry, Carrie	21 DEC 1880 R	15	112
Sanders, Emma A.	Carroll, Patrick H.	26 AUG 1879 L	13	338
Sanders, Eunice Wentworth	Hughes, Bernard Richard	31 DEC 1884 R	19	509
Sanders, Frank C.	Maher, Mary A.	15 JAN 1885	20	022
Sanders, George	Day, Hannah	30 JUN 1883 L	18	027
Sanders, Harrison	Bodin, Lucy J.	11 AUG 1883 L	18	083
Sanders, Jane	Ball, Benjamin	15 AUG 1882 L	16	480
Sanders, Lizzie T.	Reiner, Caspar	20 MAY 1879 L	13	197
Sanders, Lola B.	McCullum, George T.	07 DEC 1883	18	305
Sanders, Mary A.	Clinkett, Isaac E.	10 MAY 1881 L	15	301
Sanders, Mary E.	Sanford, James O.	20 DEC 1883	18	329
Sanders, Mollie	Bowie, Ethelbert	23 OCT 1878	12	287
Sanders, Phillis	Towles, Daniel	27 DEC 1877	11	272
Sanders, Rebecca	Robertson, Henry	04 OCT 1877 L	11	121
Sanders, Robert W.	Boatman, Mary J.	20 DEC 1883 R	18	331
Sanders, Stephen	Jackson, Anna	16 JAN 1878 L	11	308
Sanders, William	Spradling, Emma	21 JAN 1885	20	031
Sanders, Zachanah T.	Angel, Maria I.	13 MAY 1880	14	270
Sanderson, Charles Edward	Mitchell, Jennie C.V.	29 NOV 1883	18	285
Sanderson, Edward	Trautman, Lena	24 OCT 1878	12	282
Sanderson, John Thomas	Curran, Helen Givin	15 OCT 1878 R	12	274
Sanderson, Maggie E.	Twitchell, Lousville	19 JUN 1878	12	105
Sandford, Edward E.	Swope, Maggie	09 FEB 1882	16	224
Sands, Ellsworth	Burke, Dora	01 AUG 1882	16	464
Sands, Frederic Parker	Simpson, Julia Elizabeth	19 NOV 1884 R	19	388
Sands, Harvey A.	Kidd, Fannie R.	04 NOV 1880 R	15	032
Sands, Johnny	Coleman, Annie	17 JUN 1884 L	19	088
Sands, Joseph	Myers, Maria	07 FEB 1878	11	332
Sands, Joseph R.	Gibson, Louisa P.	04 APR 1878 R	11	405
Sands, Lawrence	Little, Margaret Foyles	30 APR 1878 R	12	029
Sands, Lulu G.	Vandervort, William E.	21 MAY 1883 L	17	454
Sands, Mary Diffendiffer	Spencer, William Henry	03 MAR 1880 R	14	174
Sands, Mary, Mrs.	Farquhar, Patrick	27 DEC 1882	17	213
Sands, Susan	Mickens, Harrison	17 MAR 1881 L	15	229
Sandstrum, William	O'Brien, Hanora	05 FEB 1879 R	13	046
Sandy, Alice M.	Marmaduke, Jos. Berkeley	28 APR 1881 R	15	282
Sandy, Mary E.	Law, Abner W.	31 DEC 1881 L	16	175
Sanford, Alice Ada	Henning, Aloysius	26 APR 1882 R	16	337
Sanford, Amanda	Hickey, Patrick	13 FEB 1884	18	422
Sanford, Charles E.	Burke, Mollie E.	24 APR 1884 L	18	532
Sanford, Edward E.	Moser, Teresa	09 MAY 1883 R	17	433
Sanford, Emma J.	Reamy, R.H.	06 DEC 1883 L	18	298
Sanford, James O.	Sanders, Mary E.	20 DEC 1883	18	329
Sanford, John M.	Stockholm, Rosa	11 MAR 1878	11	377
Sanford, Mamie E.	Biddle, Hiram R.	24 OCT 1878 R	12	288
Sanford, Mary E.	Beach, James H.	10 OCT 1883 R	18	184
Sanford, Mary Elizabeth	Hunter, William Henry	17 DEC 1877 R	11	241
Sanford, Mary F.	Allan, Charles, Dr.	08 NOV 1883	18	243
Sanford, Robert	Ramey, Elizabeth C.	23 NOV 1882	17	146

Sanger, William P.S.	Johns, Lucy M.	10 JUL 1877	11	014
Sangston, William R.	Davis, Marian R.	22 APR 1879 R	12	412
Sanner, Harry	Bridget, Emma	05 OCT 1880 R	14	474
Sanner, Jerome F.	Emerson, Eudosia Sutor	20 SEP 1879 R	13	382
Sanno, Emma J.	Bell, Robert, Jr.	22 OCT 1877	11	148
Sansberry, Elizabeth T.	Webster, Stephen J.	30 JAN 1879 L	13	040
Sansbury, James A.	Trice, Maimie E.	28 JAN 1885 R	20	041
Santain, Susie	Talbot, William	18 APR 1883	17	398
Sanzio, D.E.	Herbert, Ella L.	10 OCT 1882 R	17	064
Sapp, Sallie	Boudurant, Henry	08 JUN 1885	20	260
Sappington, Turner	Hunter, Selina	03 NOV 1881 R	16	048
Sardo, Annie Clay	Sheehy, James S.	22 FEB 1881 L	15	198
Sardo, Julia	James, William	07 JAN 1882 R	16	185
Sargeant, John L.	Hamilton, Lydia J.	17 FEB 1884 R	18	428
Sargent, Charles H.	Whelan, Eliza Bella Booker	03 APR 1879 R	13	126
Sargent, George W.	Wilkerson, Annie M.	23 JUN 1881 L	15	374
Sargent, Nathan	Hill, Mary Isabel	26 APR 1879 R	13	161
Sartain, John W.	Wright, Maggie Skinner	13 NOV 1879 R	13	484
Sasscer, Riley E.	Smith, Hellen J.	18 JUL 1882	16	449
Saterfield, John	Raybold, Rebecca	10 FEB 1879	13	052
Satterfield, Laura V.	Smith, Parker S.	19 OCT 1885 R	20	497
Satterfield, Mary L.	Rockett, William R.	23 JUL 1883	18	043
Satterwhite, Jefferson D.	Provoo, Lizzie E.	27 DEC 1883 R	18	347
Sauer, Caroline M.	Schultze, Augustus L.	03 MAY 1885	20	202
Sauer, Carry M.	Forrest, William H.	20 SEP 1878 L	12	229
Sauer, Charles L.	French, Adah B.	05 MAY 1880 R	14	254
Sauer, Emma	Haag, Gustave E.	31 JAN 1880 R	14	129
Sauer, Hedwig	Rothenburg, Hugo	15 MAY 1885 L	20	224
Sauer, Margaretha	Wahausen, Charles	21 JAN 1879	13	028
Sauer, Peter G.	Jackson, Elizabeth	29 APR 1880	14	246
Sauers, Kate	McCliesh, Henry I.	21 JAN 1883 R	17	270
Sauerwald, Jennie	Penn, George Edward	28 OCT 1879 R	13	416
Saul, Frances E.	Frigon, Louis T.	11 FEB 1879	13	052
Sauls, Emma	Cleveland, Caleb	06 MAR 1879 R	13	087
Saunders, Abram Warrick	Ellis, Emma Eubank	09 MAY 1885 R	20	216
Saunders, Charles S.	Mullican, Marian C.	15 MAY 1884	19	022
Saunders, Christopher W.	Carter, Annisetta	13 AUG 1883	18	084
Saunders, Frank	Perkins, Helen	02 DEC 1880 R	15	082
Saunders, George	Prather, Ida	12 FEB 1878	11	337
Saunders, James	Ball, Sarah C.	04 MAR 1880 R	14	178
Saunders, James M.	Fairfax, Lucy M.	27 JUL 1882 R	16	440
Saunders, James Thornton	Gibbons, Sarah Alice	15 MAY 1881 R	15	308
Saunders, John	Fulton, Elizabeth	08 JAN 1885 L	20	010
Saunders, Lorin M.	Green, Mary C.	16 NOV 1881	16	081
Saunders, Margaret J.	Hailstock, Charles J.	18 NOV 1884 L	19	391
Saunders, Mary	Davis, John	28 AUG 1879	13	343
Saunders, Mary I.	McAllister, Richard, Jr.	08 OCT 1885 R	20	466
Saunders, Page	Evans, Laura J.	27 FEB 1884 L	18	446
Saunders, Peter	Paine, Lucy	15 APR 1878 L	12	004
Saunders, Richard	Spencer, Emily	13 MAY 1884 R	19	018
Saunders, Roberta J.	Dabney, Frank W.	04 JUL 1883 L	18	035
Saunders, Thornton	Carroll, Martha	04 SEP 1879 R	13	350
Saunders, Walter Turner	Boyd, Mary Jane	03 FEB 1880 R	14	131
Saunders, Willie Iren	Unkel, Alfred C.	24 MAY 1881 R	15	323
Sauntry, Jeremiah	Campbell, Mary	26 NOV 1879 L	14	012
Saur, Charles L.	Loveless, Georgia G.	29 AUG 1881 R	15	460
Saur, Emma	Hammer, George H.	28 NOV 1877	11	212
Saur, Katie	Yeatman, Wm. Henry	22 APR 1884 R	18	520

D.C. Marriage Records Index, June 28, 1877 to October 19, 1885

Saur, William F.	Goss, Mary G.	09 MAY 1885	20	214
Saurwald, Frederick H.	Speckmon, Jordena	12 APR 1884 L	18	505
Sauter, John Casper	Leimberger, Lisetta	30 SEP 1877	11	110
Sautter, Karl Albert	Schaible, Sophia Menger	04 MAR 1880 R	14	173
Savage, Hattie B.	White, William H.	20 JUL 1885 L	20	333
Savage, James W.	Glover, Cora J.	18 OCT 1881 R	16	028
Savage, Margaret E.	Oliver, Lambert	05 SEP 1883 R	18	112
Savage, Mary H.	Simms, Samuel B.	18 NOV 1880 L	15	056
Savage, Susie	Bohrer, Wm. P.	03 NOV 1884 L	19	354
Savage, William	Lee, Margaret M.	28 JUL 1881	15	422
Savoy, Edward A.	Mann, Richal M.	15 JUL 1880 L	14	363
Savoy, Frank	Curtis, Mary Ellen	11 OCT 1883 R	18	189
Savoy, Mary C.	Dade, Charles T.	22 SEP 1884	19	262
Savoy, Samuel W.	Dufee, Charlotte	09 FEB 1881 L	15	184
Savoy, Sarah C.	Evans, Lewis S.	03 AUG 1881	16	117
Sawnders, Edward	Cooper, Alice	22 DEC 1881 R	16	152
Sawtelle, Leston D.	Sheeter, Willie M.	10 APR 1879 R	13	137
Sawyer, Frederick Adolphus	Schwartz, Mary Eunice Mansfield	19 AUG 1880 R	14	405
Sawyers, Kincaid	Clark, Lizzie Pauline	21 DEC 1881 R	16	147
Saxton, John R.	Roland, Ida L.	31 OCT 1882 R	17	102
Saxton, Robert	Long, Georgie	02 JUL 1878 L	12	120
Saxty, Mamie	Shiles, Charles W.	02 APR 1879 L	13	123
Sayers, Catherine C.	Messer, William	17 JUL 1879 R	13	285
Sayers, Franklin P.	Atchison, Eliza	16 DEC 1884	19	463
Sayles, Aquilla	Luckett, Jennie	10 JAN 1883 R	17	249
Sayles, Hattie	Jackson, Edmund	06 JUN 1883	17	478
Sayles, James H.	Waters, Mary H.	05 JUN 1884	19	063
Sayles, Mary	Harris, Richard	27 JUN 1879 R	13	242
Sayles, Payton	Wallace, Lucy	11 OCT 1883 R	18	185
Sayre, Calvin L.	Lansdale, Ella A.	24 APR 1880 R	14	237
Sayres, Susie	Dean, John T.	04 MAR 1884	18	457
Scaggs, Alice	Brown, Fillmore	17 NOV 1884 R	19	389
Scaggs, Edward O.	Hughes, Marian	05 NOV 1877 L	11	169
Scaggs, Emma L.	Everett, Robert	08 MAY 1879	13	181
Scaggs, James F.	Whitmore, Alice M.	13 MAR 1879 R	13	098
Scaggs, M. Georgette	Cox, James L.	21 AUG 1878	12	174
Scaggs, Willie E.	Gordon, Sallie E.	10 APR 1884	18	503
Scala, William Franklin	Armour, Isabel Louise	20 DEC 1877 L	11	255
Scales, Adeline	Dorsey, Nicholas	30 OCT 1882	17	100
Scanlan, Bridget	Sheehan, John Francis	03 JAN 1882 R	16	176
Scanlan, Kate	Gahell, Henry	29 OCT 1883 L	18	221
Scanlan, Katherine	Young, Francis M.	04 OCT 1884	19	286
Scanlon, Patrick	Curtin, Katie F.	10 SEP 1879	13	363
Scarff, M. Alice	Bates, Edward T.	12 JUL 1882 R	16	446
Scarff, Margaret J.	Brooks, William F.	14 JUN 1882 R	16	411
Scarff, Martha Emma	Collins, Homer Krum	01 OCT 1878 R	12	246
Schaap, Christian Henry	Pezzati, Marie Louise Josephine	04 FEB 1880 R	14	101
Schaefer, Emily	Reuss, William	18 FEB 1878 L	11	346
Schaefer, George M.	Arendes, Mary	26 NOV 1884 L	19	412
Schaefer, Gustav	Cade, Alice	10 MAR 1879	13	094
Schaefer, Josephine	Tuomey, George	06 NOV 1883 L	18	237
Schaeffer, E.M.	Drury, Rose M.	18 OCT 1882	17	076
Schaeffer, George C.	Harrold, J.	08 JUN 1881 R	15	352
Schaeffer, Ida Louise	Williams, Charles E.	16 JUN 1885	20	274
Schaeffer, John Shelton	Shoemaker, Annie E.	08 SEP 1884	19	232
Schafer, Charles Francis	Schutter, Esther Jean	29 APR 1879 R	13	165
Schafer, Emma Elise	Exel, Christian	25 APR 1883 R	17	411
Schafer, Henry William	Davis, Lily V.	21 SEP 1881 R	15	489

Schafer, Phillip	Price, Janie	27 AUG 1884 L	19	211
Schaffer, George	Shombert, Mary	29 OCT 1882 R	17	093
Schaffer, John	Williams, Louraine	05 SEP 1882 L	17	005
Schaffert, Christine	Umhau, Christian F.	14 OCT 1884	19	304
Schaffert, John Leonhard	Alt, Kate	09 FEB 1879 R	13	051
Schafhirt, Rebecca	Stauf, William A.	27 OCT 1884	19	340
Schaible, Sophia Menger	Sautter, Karl Albert	04 MAR 1880 R	14	173
Schambra, Edward L.	Erberbach, Matilda W.	08 SEP 1880	14	438
Schaper, John	Howard, Alice R.	19 JUN 1883	18	003
Scharfe, Lizzie	Pracht, George Hermann	12 MAY 1880 R	14	267
Scharr, George Gottlob	Fuersinger, Mary Louise	31 JUL 1879 R	13	301
Scheckell, Ida J.	Fenton, Charles B.	11 JUL 1883 R	18	044
Scheel, Margaret W.	Allison, John H.	16 DEC 1879	14	051
Scheerer, John S.	Murphy, Lillie	01 NOV 1882 R	17	105
Scheffer, Julius Caesar	Fisher, Charlotte Muir	10 APR 1878 R	11	414
Scheide, Christian	Weimertz, Sarah	19 MAY 1883	17	452
Scheider, John	Wolfraum, Louisa	13 OCT 1879 L	13	416
Scheitlin, Annie M.	Hoover, Dickerson Naylor	17 SEP 1879 R	13	374
Scheitlin, Rudolph	Hilton, Hattie M.	15 OCT 1881 R	16	027
Schell, Leonard	Reith, Mary Frances	05 OCT 1878 L	12	256
Schelstedt, Anna Helene	Pieper, August K.H.	22 JUN 1878 R	12	110
Schembeck, Emanuel	Hoffa, Lena	17 OCT 1883 R	18	199
Schench, Charles D.	Nass, Katie	17 SEP 1884	19	252
Schenck, Charles August	Reinburg, Mary A.	19 JUL 1881	15	406
Schenck, Eliz. Catherine	Eberly, George Lewis	12 NOV 1878	12	322
Schenck, John D.M.	Seabode, Minnie	04 OCT 1885 R	20	455
Schenck, Katie	Schickler, Andrew	26 DEC 1880 R	15	122
Schenck, Katie S.	Steinle, John	25 MAY 1884 R	19	036
Schenck, Mary	Repp, Charles	04 SEP 1881 R	15	462
Scheppach, Katie	Zinser, Joseph	26 FEB 1882 R	16	259
Scheppoch, Margeretha	Sobatka, Franz	07 JUL 1878 R	12	126
Scherble, Gottlob	Allmendinger, Christine	25 SEP 1884 L	19	267
Scherer, Charles H.	Klotz, Annie R.	28 NOV 1882 L	17	151
Scherer, Clara	Klotz, Fred R.	20 MAY 1882 L	16	371
Scherger, Johanna E.	Kraemer, Charles	28 NOV 1880 R	15	069
Scherger, Wilhelmina E.	Widmayer, William G.	22 MAR 1885 R	20	127
Schick, Jacob	Voegler, Elenora	21 JUL 1879 R	13	287
Schickler, Andrew	Schenck, Katie	26 DEC 1880 R	15	122
Schickler, Christian	Springer, Elizabeth	07 NOV 1878	12	313
Schickler, Katie	Bauer, Andrew	24 MAR 1879	13	112
Schickler, Maggie	Limberger, Henry	31 JUL 1880 R	14	380
Schickler, Sophia	Hering, August	30 MAY 1883	17	466
Schifaly, Amelia	Beron, John	30 APR 1879	13	168
Schifner, Catherine L.	Hinke, Carl M.W.	23 APR 1883	17	404
Schilling, Frederike Fielindas	Wirsching, Caspar	17 JUN 1883 R	18	489
Schimdt, George	Pfaff, Hannah	09 OCT 1881	15	301
Schiminger, George C.	Mainz, Emma	02 SEP 1884	19	220
Schinault, Ida Lee	Trice, Hilard	12 JAN 1880	14	101
Schirmer, Mary	Kuhn, Joseph	05 APR 1884 L	18	497
Schiskler, Mary	Jaeschke, Charles	01 JUL 1883	18	028
Schissler, Laura A.	Smith, James E.	10 JAN 1883 R	17	242
Schladt, Annie	Rodler, Joseph S.	12 NOV 1883 L	18	248
Schladt, Joseph	May, Sarah M.	23 FEB 1879	13	072
Schlegel, Lottie M.	Boernstein, Henry N.	21 DEC 1881 R	16	146
Schleger, Frederick	Nesler, Mary	14 JUN 1884 L	19	084
Schleicher, Elizabeth Tinsley	Stockdale, Fletcher Summerfield	10 JUL 1877 R	11	012
Schlenker, Elizabeth	Welsh, Alonzo	24 JUL 1884	19	156
Schlerogt, Lizzie	Howard, William J.	18 JAN 1883 R	17	266

D.C. Marriage Records Index, June 28, 1877 to October 19, 1885   401

Schlesinger, Samuel	Singer, Lina	15 JAN 1884 R	18	376
Schleucher, Mary	Gennori, Joseph	08 AUG 1885 R	20	359
Schley, James McCannon	Welch, Guinilda Hall	18 OCT 1881 R	16	029
Schlichting, Henry A.	Dean, Anna	01 NOV 1883 L	18	227
Schlomberg, Solomon	Kaplan, Dora	01 MAR 1883 L	17	328
Schlorb, George L.	Donalson, Mary Ella	02 JUN 1885	20	249
Schlorb, Katie	Bricker, Joseph W.	18 JUN 1883 R	17	498
Schlosser, Catherine Eva	Loeffler, Henry S.	19 OCT 1881 L	16	035
Schlosser, Henry W.	Reilley, Lizzie V.	19 JUL 1885 R	20	332
Schlosser, James F.E.	Dunn, Mary Ellen	05 DEC 1884 L	19	438
Schlosser, Peter	Varnell, Katie	30 JUL 1881 L	15	426
Schlosser, William H.	Avery, Georgianna	14 DEC 1882 R	17	185
Schloz, Christian	Englehart, Annie	20 OCT 1884 R	19	320
Schlueter, Otto	Schretzenmeyer, Kate	10 NOV 1882 L	17	123
Schmalhoff, William L.	Carley, Kate E.	02 OCT 1882 R	17	046
Schmertz, Rebecca	Meiners, John H.	25 MAR 1883	17	358
Schmerz, Katie	Leonberger, John	05 OCT 1880 R	14	470
Schmerz, Lizzie	Kaufmann, Heinrich	28 MAR 1880 R	14	200
Schmid, Alexander	Gentner, Mary Virginia	05 AUG 1885 R	20	357
Schmid, Amelia	Xander, Andreas G.	13 JUL 1884	19	135
Schmid, Edward S.	Finkmann, Elizabeth C.	15 MAY 1883 R	17	440
Schmid, Ernst	Altschuh, Perdita	16 JAN 1883 L	17	260
Schmid, Katie	Tayman, James H.	02 DEC 1884 L	19	430
Schmid, Madelina Christina	Tudge, William W.	14 NOV 1877 L	11	185
Schmidt, August	Franz, Ernestine	02 APR 1882 R	16	290
Schmidt, Bertha B.	Middeldorff, Casper	06 NOV 1883 L	18	237
Schmidt, Bertha E.	Thomson, Frederick	11 OCT 1882 R	17	067
Schmidt, Charles G.L.	Hanover, Minnie	11 SEP 1881	15	470
Schmidt, Emily	Zoller, Emil Bruno	17 JUL 1877	11	024
Schmidt, Henry	Lauck, Carrie	19 NOV 1878 L	12	335
Schmidt, Jennie	Marx, Moses	13 MAY 1885 R	20	218
Schmidt, John H.	Reckweg, Lena S.	19 OCT 1879 R	13	431
Schmidt, Kate	Jordan, William	12 SEP 1878	12	212
Schmidt, Robert	Geiger, Babette	19 JUN 1879 L	13	241
Schmidtman, Hermann	Ewald, Louise	26 NOV 1882 R	17	148
Schmitt, Ewold	Hesselbach, Fanny	13 OCT 1881 L	16	022
Schmitt, Helena	Terney, Fred. Charles	12 AUG 1878 L	12	163
Schmitt, Magnus H.	Waters, Mary V.	31 DEC 1884	19	507
Schmuck, Sophia	Cook, Matthew	08 APR 1882 L	16	304
Schnaebel, Julia	Moore, John G.T.	29 OCT 1882	17	098
Schnaebele, Jacob	Westenmeier, Mary	28 FEB 1883	17	325
Schnebel, William	Walter, Lena	16 MAR 1884 R	18	472
Schneider, Annie Mary	Podiaski, B.F.	15 SEP 1881 L	15	485
Schneider, Annie R.	Riggles, Galusha A.	16 SEP 1879 R	13	371
Schneider, Bertha	Rupertus, William	05 OCT 1880 R	14	474
Schneider, Carmillo	Arrata, Vittoria	29 JUN 1880 L	14	338
Schneider, Charles W.	Lemon, Martha	22 APR 1882 R	16	329
Schneider, Emma	Jarboe, Snowden E.	11 OCT 1885 R	20	473
Schneider, George W.	Brocker, Jennie	17 MAR 1884 R	18	473
Schneider, Giosephina	Coda, Andrea	28 AUG 1880 L	14	419
Schneider, Gottlieb	Berk, Katherina	20 JUL 1884	19	146
Schneider, Harry M.	Taff, Elizabeth G.	30 SEP 1879 R	13	392
Schneider, Ida J.	Davis, Harry C.	09 OCT 1882 R	17	061
Schneider, John F.	Imhof, Karoline	13 JUN 1882 R	16	409
Schneider, Joseph	Lauer, Josephine	16 FEB 1879	13	056
Schneider, Lavinia M.	Carter, Robert B.	28 MAR 1884 L	18	486
Schneider, Louis H.	Brooks, Emma Adelle	17 JAN 1883	17	263
Schneider, Margaretha	Schurmann, Emil Hermann	02 MAR 1885 R	33	8111

Schneider, Marther	Rupertus, Henry	28 JAN 1884 R	18	397
Schneider, Mary E.	Trego, William Willett	06 JUL 1882 R	16	441
Schneider, Mary F.	Adams, Arthur C.	15 APR 1879 R	13	146
Schneider, Rosa E.	Engel, George W.	14 OCT 1885 R	20	484
Schneider, William Ionian	Lamb, Mary A. Hunt	04 FEB 1880 R	14	136
Schneiderwin, Elizabeth	Donn, Frank C.	13 NOV 1879 L	13	485
Schnepler, Joseph	Alman, Katie	30 SEP 1882 L	17	045
Schnopp, Dammair	McWilliams, Ada L.	16 OCT 1878	12	277
Schnopp, John Adam	Crown, Mary M.	28 DEC 1880 R	15	126
Schockey, Lucy M.	Shaw, Benjamin F.	22 SEP 1880 R	14	455
Schoelkopf, Heinrich	Wolfrey, Victoria	07 OCT 1884	19	290
Schoeltzel, Albert	Knoch, Marie	26 MAR 1884	18	483
Schoelung, Bettie	Weicker, Frederick	29 JAN 1884	18	400
Schoenberg, Katie	Werner, August	16 SEP 1881 R	15	487
Schoenborn, Mary A.	Jaegle, Joseph A.	26 SEP 1885 L	20	444
Schoenecker, Josephine	Gardner, J. Anthony	31 DEC 1884	19	519
Schoepf, Millie Kesley	McElhinney, Charles Andrews	15 OCT 1879 R	13	424
Schoepflen, Katharina	Groener, Charles	27 DEC 1877	11	275
Schofield, William S.	Carney, Mary	04 JUN 1878 R	12	085
Schonberger, Charles N.	Steinhardt, Ida, Mrs.	29 JUL 1882 L	16	461
Schooler, Maggie L.	Clark, Charles C.	06 SEP 1883 L	18	116
Schooley, Elmer E.	Cooney, Mollie	08 OCT 1885 R	20	471
Schooley, Henry Moore	Woltz, India	10 JAN 1883 R	17	250
Schoonmaker, Fannie S.	Kinne, Frank P.	09 JUL 1877	11	013
Schorb, Carl	Schüessler, Lina	28 APR 1885 R	20	193
Schotter, Frederic Edward	McMahon, Catharine	28 AUG 1879 R	13	342
Schotterer, Charles	Oeser, Margaretha	29 JUN 1879 R	13	255
Schreiner, Mary K.	Smith, J. Curtis	24 DEC 1884	19	491
Schreiver, Philip	Murphy, Mary	02 OCT 1879 R	13	398
Schrepler, Catherine	Guy, James T.	15 APR 1885 L	20	171
Schretzenmeyer, Kate	Schlueter, Otto	10 NOV 1882 L	17	123
Schreyer, George	Downey, Alice F.	27 OCT 1881 L	16	049
Schreyer, Lillie E.	Waters, Charles M.	28 APR 1880 R	14	241
Schroder, Gerrit Henry	Dierkopf, Louisa (Reiter)	08 APR 1884 R	18	464
Schroeder, George G.	Benke, Annie A.	18 JAN 1885	20	014
Schroeder, Seaton	Wainwright, Maria C.B.	16 JAN 1879 R	13	019
Schroth, Hannah	Stewart, John	14 OCT 1885 L	20	481
Schroth, Mary	Toole, James	15 JUN 1882 R	16	412
Schroth, W.H.	Kinsley, Jane G.	04 AUG 1880 L	14	386
Schuchmacher, Theodore	Weigman, Nettie	02 MAR 1882	16	265
Schuerman, Samuel Clarke	Noll, Henrietta Catherine	22 JUN 1879 R	13	243
Schuermann, Carl Wm.	Calvert, Rose Antoinette	09 DEC 1879 R	14	036
Schüessler, Lina	Schorb, Carl	28 APR 1885 R	20	193
Schuh, Mary	Washney, Michael	15 SEP 1885 R	20	416
Schule, Adolph	Mamminger, Gesina	04 JAN 1885	19	485
Schuler, Joseph A.	Vogel, Mary E.	29 APR 1884	18	541
Schulteis, John H.J.	Snyder, Agnes Marie	16 APR 1883	17	395
Schultz, Barbara E.	Ammann, Henry E.	03 JAN 1883 L	17	235
Schultz, Charles A.	Duehring, Rosa	05 APR 1885 R	20	145
Schultz, Clara Angusta	Engelhardt, Frank	12 MAR 1884 R	18	462
Schultz, Henry W.	Dean, Katie E.	25 NOV 1879 L	14	006
Schultz, Ludwig E.	Breeze, Caroline	25 MAY 1884 R	19	036
Schultze, Augustus L.	Sauer, Caroline M.	03 MAY 1885	20	202
Schultze, Lucie C.	Boehmer, George H.	03 NOV 1878	12	305
Schultze, William	Rick, Katie	16 NOV 1879 R	13	488
Schulz, Annie	Brill, Louis	05 JUN 1882	16	391
Schulz, Elizabeth	Behler, Paulus	13 JAN 1885 R	20	011
Schulz, Margareta	Unger, William O.	15 JUL 1884 L	19	139

Schurmann, Emil Hermann	Schneider, Margaretha	02 MAR 1885 R	33	8111
Schuster, Emelie	Villemez, Louis	30 MAR 1880 R	14	201
Schutter, Clara M.	Murphy, Kossuth M.	22 FEB 1883 R	17	314
Schutter, Esther Jean	Schafer, Charles Francis	29 APR 1879 R	13	165
Schutzbach, John	Wagner, Annie	23 NOV 1879 R	14	001
Schwab, Hermann Caspar	Baldwin, Mary	04 JUN 1885 R	20	256
Schwabe, Maggie	Ready, Julian H.	20 AUG 1882	16	488
Schwalenberg, Frank A.	Shephard, Elizabeth	06 APR 1885 L	20	147
Schwank, Hattie M.	Wood, William H.	28 JAN 1880	14	120
Schwartz, Bertha E.	Troll, Fred'k N.	02 OCT 1877	11	114
Schwartz, John	Strickling, Annie	19 SEP 1877 L	11	101
Schwartz, Justina J.	Douglass, Floyd	31 DEC 1877 L	11	284
Schwartz, Mary Eunice Mansfield	Sawyer, Frederick Adolphus	19 AUG 1880 R	14	405
Schwartz, Rachel	Baron, Bernard	10 AUG 1880 R	14	390
Schwartz, [Maggie] Janie	Johnson, J. Frank	26 NOV 1884 R	19	411
Schwarz, Frank	Pabst, Amelia F.	14 APR 1881 R	15	257
Schwarz, Louis A.	Grape, Anna Wilhelmi	27 APR 1885 R	20	189
Schweinshant, Francis	Byrne, Maria Teresa	15 JAN 1882 R	16	194
Schweitzer, Rosa E.	Calhoun, Robert W.	15 APR 1879 R	13	145
Schweizer, William T.	Carter, Mary E.	15 OCT 1883	18	192
Schwemke, Mary	Bernau, Louis	30 NOV 1882 R	17	146
Schwenk, Cara C.A.	Nicholson, James F.	06 OCT 1885	20	459
Schwerdtmann, Ludolph	Grube, Minna	04 SEP 1885	20	399
Schwier, Henry	Mangan, Sarah	03 SEP 1885 L	20	398
Schwier, Laura	Lenoir, Samuel H.	30 MAR 1885 R	20	137
Schwiering, Augustus E.L.	Hasselbusch, Lottie W.D.	17 APR 1883 R	17	396
Schwiering, Elizabeth	Forney, Andrew H.	04 JUN 1884 R	19	058
Schwigert, Edward C.	Huysman, Elizabeth V.C.	19 MAY 1885 L	20	229
Schwing, Katie	Kirk, Nicholas J.	29 APR 1884 R	18	539
Sciardi, Autoni	Roche, Josephine	25 APR 1881 L	15	270
Sciardi, Joseph	Verner, Caterina	07 FEB 1882 R	16	228
Scior, Ella G.	Holtzman, Robert C.	20 NOV 1877 R	11	192
Scior, Mary Elizabeth	Lyddane, Thomas O.	24 DEC 1877 R	11	264
Scipieo, Charles William	Braxton, Martha	15 MAR 1883 L	17	347
Scofield, John Cowles	Clark, Florence Lathin	18 MAR 1885 R	20	121
Scoggin, Blanche C.	Hope, William E.	14 SEP 1885	20	413
Scotlin, Victoria	Landig, Isaac	21 FEB 1878 L	11	351
Scott, Abraham	Matthews, Ellen	27 NOV 1884	19	418
Scott, Addie	Branson, Thomas	22 MAR 1878	11	389
Scott, Albert	Samtain, Emma	27 DEC 1877 R	11	274
Scott, Albert	Beckett, Laura	13 DEC 1877	11	234
Scott, Alexander	Skippon, Alice V.	03 SEP 1878 L	12	194
Scott, Alexander	Hawkins, Alice	26 AUG 1882	16	494
Scott, Anna E.	Kelly, William O.	23 MAY 1883 R	17	453
Scott, Annie	Warren, Julius	03 OCT 1878 L	12	252
Scott, Annie C.	Auguste, George G.	19 NOV 1879 R	13	496
Scott, Annie E.	Ramey, Daniel	02 JUL 1885 L	20	306
Scott, Annie, Mrs.	Kuker, Ludwig	04 JUN 1883 R	17	463
Scott, Aquilla D.	Hainey, Susie A.	05 JAN 1881 R	15	137
Scott, Ary	Burley, Richard T.	19 JUN 1879 R	13	239
Scott, Barbara	Stewart, C.F.	20 OCT 1879 L	13	433
Scott, Benjamin	Taylor, Ella	03 DEC 1884 R	18	362
Scott, Carrie	Hawking, William J.	04 DEC 1882 R	17	121
Scott, Carrie	Watkins, Charles	29 FEB 1884 L	18	451
Scott, Carrie E.	Ringgold, Basill S.	31 OCT 1881 R	16	053
Scott, Catherine	Warick, Alfred	02 FEB 1882	16	223
Scott, Cephas Watkins	Ryan, Mary Cecelia	26 NOV 1879 R	14	007
Scott, Charity	Humphreys, George	26 OCT 1880 L	15	014

Scott, Charles	Readin, Mary	18 NOV 1880 R	15	054
Scott, Charles D.	Childs, Ella	13 SEP 1879 R	13	368
Scott, Charley	Booze, Alice	05 JUN 1878 L	12	087
Scott, Clifton B.	Clark, Jane C.	09 FEB 1882 R	16	234
Scott, Cornelia	Jones, James D.	05 JUN 1879 L	13	220
Scott, Daniel	Warters, A.L.	13 JUN 1878 L	12	098
Scott, David W.	Duncan, Amanda A.G.	30 AUG 1884	19	216
Scott, Edward D.	Hewlett, Aronella Molyneaux	16 FEB 1882 R	16	246
Scott, Eliza	Fields, James	16 OCT 1884 L	19	311
Scott, Emma	Campbell, George	25 FEB 1880 R	14	120
Scott, Emma	Madison, John C.	28 DEC 1881 R	16	136
Scott, Emma	Dreer, Thomas	26 NOV 1884 R	19	420
Scott, Emma Florence	Speider, Charles Edwin	20 APR 1885	20	176
Scott, Epsey	Davis, Charles E.	30 SEP 1880 R	14	467
Scott, Eva	Cook, Joseph	07 NOV 1877 L	11	173
Scott, Fannie	Harris, Willis	09 OCT 1879 L	13	412
Scott, Fannie	Jackson, Philip M.	04 DEC 1880 L	15	084
Scott, Fannie	Herbert, Ananias	27 SEP 1883 L	18	159
Scott, Florence Louisa	Miller, Henry	10 SEP 1881 R	15	322
Scott, Frances Virginia	America, George Edward	15 JUN 1881 R	15	362
Scott, Frank	Hutton, Margaret	28 JUN 1883	18	024
Scott, Frank T.	Naylor, Lulie	04 JAN 1882 L	16	180
Scott, Frank T.	Barnes, Annie	22 JAN 1882	16	198
Scott, George A.	Butler, Jennie	27 DEC 1881 L	16	160
Scott, George W.	Adams, Hattie	09 MAR 1882 R	16	272
Scott, Georgianna	Holmes, Alfred	14 JUN 1882 L	16	411
Scott, Harriet	Gant, Willis	03 MAR 1880 L	14	173
Scott, Harry	Steele, Kate	04 MAR 1880	12	415
Scott, Henrietta	Loving, Lloyd P.	10 JUL 1882 R	16	443
Scott, Henry	Addison, Mary Lizzie	28 MAY 1885	20	246
Scott, Henry E.	Henderson, Lottie	03 OCT 1879 R	13	403
Scott, Henry Winters	James, Jessie C.	17 JAN 1883 R	17	254
Scott, Isaac W.	Smith, Jane E.	08 OCT 1883 R	18	177
Scott, Isabella	Robinson, Nathaniel	15 NOV 1877 L	11	190
Scott, James	Jackson, Sarah Jane	23 JUL 1883 L	18	057
Scott, James	Barnes, Sarah	25 JUN 1885	20	294
Scott, James A.	Lee, Sarah	15 JAN 1885 R	20	022
Scott, James E.	Davis, Pinkey A.	27 APR 1882	16	339
Scott, James H.	Dickson, Amanda	27 NOV 1884	19	410
Scott, Jane	Payne, William Joseph	28 FEB 1878 R	11	363
Scott, Jesse	Strokes, Mary	18 SEP 1879 L	13	378
Scott, John	Geddes, Jane	29 NOV 1877 R	11	209
Scott, John	Meeks, Georgiana	08 SEP 1885 R	20	403
Scott, John A.	Thomas, Alberta	13 FEB 1882 R	16	238
Scott, John A.	Harper, Clara M.	15 JUN 1882	16	413
Scott, John Fortune	Gibson, Elizabeth	28 JUL 1881	15	424
Scott, John R.	West, Emma S.	08 NOV 1882 L	17	117
Scott, John Wesley	Hunt, Ellen Ann	08 OCT 1885 R	20	469
Scott, Joseph	Coats, Louisa	14 OCT 1880 L	14	496
Scott, Joseph	Brown, Mary	21 JUL 1885	20	334
Scott, Joseph H.	Lightfoot, Ophelia	20 NOV 1878 R	12	339
Scott, Joseph H.	Ulster, Mary [Halstead]	30 MAR 1883 R	17	367
Scott, Josephine	Gant, Edward A., Jr.	25 OCT 1882	17	091
Scott, Josephine	Howe, John D.	29 SEP 1884	19	271
Scott, Kate A.	Emmons, Howard O.	06 APR 1880	14	211
Scott, Laura	Wise, Thomas H.	26 SEP 1877 R	11	107
Scott, Laura	Moore, Joseph	31 DEC 1881	16	072
Scott, Laura E.	Parker, John W.	19 NOV 1878 R	12	335

Scott, Lizzie	Cahill, Fielding	24 NOV 1881 R	16	093
Scott, Lizzie	Randall, Charles	19 JUL 1883	18	053
Scott, Lottie	Ragan, Columbus	21 AUG 1877 R	11	060
Scott, Louisa	Synder, John	27 DEC 1881 L	16	163
Scott, Malinda	Mitchell, Charles	26 MAY 1884 R	19	039
Scott, Martha	Queen, James	15 SEP 1885	20	420
Scott, Mary	Smallwood, William	23 JUN 1878 R	12	098
Scott, Mary	Welsh, John	23 OCT 1879 R	13	438
Scott, Mary	Jones, George	31 MAR 1880 R	14	192
Scott, Mary Elizabeth	Wheeler, Patrick	02 JAN 1878 L	11	291
Scott, Mary F.	Underwood, George R.	29 NOV 1883	18	281
Scott, Mary T.	Hunter, Horace	19 FEB 1885 R	20	078
Scott, R. Thomas	Gaegler, Rosa J.	10 AUG 1882 L	16	476
Scott, Robert	William, Hatty	29 AUG 1878 R	12	186
Scott, Robert	Johnston, Annie	23 OCT 1880 L	15	011
Scott, Robert D.	Henry, Maggie	16 NOV 1882 R	17	132
Scott, Robert D.	Ford, Delia	06 MAR 1884 L	18	460
Scott, Rochester	Hampton, Alice	08 AUG 1885 R	20	347
Scott, Rosa	Seals, George William	05 AUG 1884 L	19	169
Scott, Sallie E.	Mattingly, Robert F.	17 SEP 1878 R	12	222
Scott, Samuel	Johnson, Barbara	27 DEC 1881 R	16	150
Scott, Samuel B.	Soper, Ellen Douglass	27 FEB 1878 R	11	361
Scott, Sarah Jane	Taylor, Samuel	24 AUG 1885	20	385
Scott, Sarah R.	Sebastian, John W.	14 FEB 1883	17	304
Scott, Susan	Richardson, Richard	26 FEB 1885 L	20	086
Scott, Susan	Raines, Oswald Wm.	19 AUG 1885 R	20	378
Scott, Susannah	Mars, George A.	30 OCT 1882 L	17	100
Scott, Thomas	Hamilton, Eliza	05 JUL 1881	15	391
Scott, Thomas	Taylor, Catharine B.	02 OCT 1884	19	282
Scott, Thomas A.	Otis, Susie T.	15 MAR 1883	17	346
Scott, Thomas E.	Roby, Gracie A.	19 DEC 1881	16	030
Scott, W.H.	Fields, Laura A.	16 MAR 1880	14	185
Scott, Wilfred	Smith, Mary C.	09 AUG 1877 R	11	043
Scott, William	Irving, Carrie	02 NOV 1880 L	15	025
Scott, William	Carrison, Eva	22 JAN 1884 L	18	389
Scott, William A.	Luckett, Annie	12 MAR 1885	20	108
Scott, William H.	Oneal, Kate	10 OCT 1878 L	12	266
Scott, William Henry	Shanklin, Amanda	19 JUN 1882 R	16	416
Scott, William, Jr.	Taite, Anna	08 MAY 1879	13	182
Scouter, Gavin	Bookman, Ella A.	16 SEP 1878	12	220
Scoville, Angelina S.	Pelton, Guy R.	21 JAN 1879 R	13	027
Scriber, George W.	Barnes, Minnie	23 JAN 1882	16	205
Scrimger, Bettie A.	Rowe, Henry H.	13 NOV 1878 R	12	327
Scrivener, John T.	Trunnel, Margaret	17 JAN 1882	16	197
Scrivener, Mamie C.	Simpson, Ellsworth T.	04 FEB 1885 L	20	051
Scrivener, Mary J.	Sparks, Charles W.	15 DEC 1884	19	460
Scrivener, Theodore A.	Catis, Kate	19 JUL 1877	11	019
Scriver, Mary	Green, Thomas	21 NOV 1878 L	12	342
Scroggin, Catherine	Skinner, Sylvester	13 AUG 1878	12	166
Scroggin, Mattie	Johnson, Frank	12 MAR 1879 R	13	095
Scroggins, Agnes	Gillison, Lanzy	18 FEB 1880 R	14	148
Scroggins, George W.	Lauxmann, Barbara	18 MAR 1885 R	20	122
Scroggins, Indiana M.	Addis, Charles M.	18 JUN 1879 R	13	234
Scroggins, John	Maddox, Jane	05 MAY 1880 R	14	259
Scroggins, Nannie R.	Cannon, George E.	07 OCT 1885 R	20	465
Scroggins, Oscar	Wade, Milly Ann	11 JAN 1881 R	15	121
Scudder, Charles W.	Talley, Priscilla	27 NOV 1884 R	19	411
Scully, Annie	Driscoll, Cornelius	16 JAN 1879 R	13	023

Seabode, Minnie	Schenck, John D.M.	04 OCT 1885 R	20	455
Seal, Alice M.	Clay, Cassius H.	17 FEB 1885	20	077
Seal, Emma V.	Perry, Marshal B.	25 FEB 1884	18	440
Seal, George A.	Martin, Fannie	18 SEP 1878 R	12	226
Seals, Ferdinand	Nelson, Hannah	31 JUL 1885 L	20	347
Seals, Franklin	Jackson, Kate	24 JUN 1885	20	290
Seals, George William	Scott, Rosa	05 AUG 1884 L	19	169
Seaman, Matthew	Stewart, Martha	19 SEP 1885 L	20	429
Searle, Allan R.	Doniphan, Florence	02 FEB 1882	16	221
Searle, Charles Robinson	Doughty, Cecelia	02 JAN 1884 R	18	360
Searle, Frank W.	Miller, Ella May	24 APR 1878	12	022
Searle, Lodoiska Elizabeth	Allen, John Ethan	04 OCT 1881 R	16	006
Sears, Carry M.	Willis, Cornelius D.	03 SEP 1885 R	20	398
Sears, Harry M.	Rotto, Kata	16 AUG 1885 R	20	370
Sears, Joanna	Littleford, James M.	18 JAN 1883 R	17	268
Sears, Josie A.	Phipps, John L.	18 JAN 1883 L	17	267
Sears, Malvina DePratt	Snowden, James Alex.	28 JUN 1882 L	16	429
Sease, William H.	Hutson, Katie J.	13 FEB 1881	15	178
Seaton, Augusta B.	Timberlake, George A.	10 SEP 1879 R	13	363
Seaton, Constance Gertrude	Carrington, Thomas A.	06 MAR 1878 L	11	374
Seaton, Frederick A.	Dorsey, Hannah E.	07 JUN 1883	17	482
Seaton, Hiram	Garrison, Laura Virginia	12 JUN 1878 L	12	097
Seaton, Mollie F.	Pomeroy, John F.	06 MAY 1884	19	007
Seaton, Peter G.	McGill, Molly	26 DEC 1881	16	157
Seavers, Amy	Jones, Edwin F.	10 JAN 1878	11	297
Seay, Richard B.	Hunter, Viola B.	18 SEP 1882 R	17	008
Sebastian, Alice	Long, William	28 NOV 1878 R	12	353
Sebastian, Edward B.	Dyer, Mary E.R.	03 JAN 1878 R	11	291
Sebastian, John W.	Scott, Sarah R.	14 FEB 1883	17	304
Sebastian, Nettie L.	Walker, John S.	13 OCT 1882	17	068
Sebastian, Nicholas	Ball, Mary Elizabeth	15 FEB 1880	14	147
Sebastian, Rebecca	Orrison, Oscar J.	14 MAR 1878 L	11	381
Sebree, William E.	Faunce, Mary L.	23 JAN 1879 R	13	032
Sebree, Wm. E.	Cunningham, Ida C.	20 NOV 1883 R	18	265
Secor, Marilla E.	Purman, David Gray	19 AUG 1880 R	14	408
Sedgwick, Baker	Clark, Mary Ida	06 JUN 1878 R	12	089
Sedgwick, Elizabeth	Myers, Wallace E.	26 NOV 1880 L	15	068
Sedgwick, Israel	Riddles, Alice	11 JUL 1878	12	133
Sedgwick, Julia	Riley, Pleasant	26 JUL 1879	13	293
Sedgwick, Noah E.	Sinkfield, Emma L.	19 NOV 1878 L	12	334
Seebach, Fred	Marks, Annie E.	15 APR 1885 L	20	171
Seebo, Charles W.	Heiliger, Minnie M.M.	22 AUG 1880 R	14	410
Seebode, Friderich	Oelrich, Sophie	22 JUN 1881	15	369
Seebring, Francis A.	Hickenlooper, Carrie	21 OCT 1884	19	324
Seeger, Paul Augustus	Johannes, Corella Wynn	30 MAR 1885 R	20	137
Seely, Charles M.	Simms, Eleanor B.	11 MAR 1881	15	223
Seems, Caroline	Harris, Alfred	18 OCT 1883 R	18	199
Seeny, James	Murray, Emma Jackson	20 NOV 1879 R	13	499
Seeton, Mary Virginia	Moore, James	21 DEC 1881 R	16	148
Seevers, Ella	Howard, Sidney	23 DEC 1879 R	14	065
Sefton, Ida Constance	Clum, Andrew Herbert Wade	02 DEC 1878 R	12	357
Seibert, Delia	Christopher, Joseph B.	21 MAY 1884	19	032
Seidenspinner, Josephine	Crowley, William B.	28 JUN 1877 L	11	002
Seiler, Katie A.	McGraw, F.J.	06 AUG 1884	19	171
Seiler, Marg. Joh. Aug.	Turner, Lewis	02 MAR 1882 R	16	264
Seins, Barbara	Miller, Charles	02 SEP 1880	14	427
Seip, Martha E.	O'Brien, Edward M.	25 FEB 1879	13	077
Seipp, John H.	Ockershausen, Caroline	20 SEP 1885 R	20	428

Name	Spouse	Date	Vol	Page
Seitz, Charles N.	Fitzgerald, Ellen L.	16 OCT 1879	13	419
Seitz, Clinton A.	Hunter, Mollie R.	05 NOV 1884 L	19	362
Seitz, Joseph Franklin	Keithely, Laura V.	14 APR 1879 L	13	141
Seitz, Lawrence A.	Johnston, Mary A.	02 SEP 1881 R	15	465
Selby, Bettie E.	Brown, Ambrose M.	25 JUN 1885 R	20	292
Selby, Charles E.	Thompson, Elizabeth	12 AUG 1879 R	13	303
Selby, Charles H.	Nichols, Annie J.	08 SEP 1883	18	120
Selby, Fannie	Ramby, Samuel H.	14 MAY 1884 R	19	020
Selby, Hallie D.	Thomas, Edward	11 JAN 1883 R	17	251
Selby, Ida Amelia	Howard, Robert S.	15 NOV 1880 R	15	048
Selby, Ida M.	Gallagher, John H.	29 NOV 1884	19	425
Selby, Jacob S.	Shorter, Sarah	07 NOV 1878	12	308
Selby, Richard B.	Thornton, Lydia	20 AUG 1885 R	20	381
Selby, Susie R.	Shelton, Benjamin F.	11 JAN 1883 R	17	252
Selby, William H.	Church, Fannie	28 FEB 1878 R	11	366
Selby, William S.	Pritchett, Mary E.	16 JAN 1879 R	13	022
Selden, George	Singleton, Hattie	04 FEB 1884	18	404
Selden, Mary	Thomas, Henry	26 DEC 1882 R	17	211
Selden, Mary A.E.	Masterem, John	16 SEP 1883	18	127
Selden, Robert	Taper, Mary	13 MAR 1879 L	13	100
Selecman, James A.	Clarke, Julia F.	04 JUN 1884	19	058
Self, Robert W.	Beal, Ruberta Thrift	05 DEC 1877 R	11	223
Selinger, Julius	Cohen, Augusta	11 JUN 1884 R	19	074
Sell, Frank A.	Doyle, Katie E.	30 JUL 1881 L	15	426
Sellman, Frank B.	Smith, Mary Jane	04 DEC 1884 R	19	427
Sellner, Adam	Weil, Anna	04 JAN 1881	15	136
Sellner, Dora	Rosendale, Henry	03 AUG 1879 R	13	303
Seltman, William B.	Biddle, Eliza	17 JUN 1880 L	14	326
Selucius, Garfield	Nellie, Conner	03 JAN 1881 L	15	135
Selva, Fannie	Lewis, William F.	07 JAN 1880	13	388
Selvey, Mary Jane	Diggs, Henson	13 NOV 1883 R	18	247
Selvy, Joshua	Budd, Christiana	11 DEC 1884 R	19	450
Selvy, Sarah Ross	Williams, John	15 APR 1880 R	14	225
Selzle, Charles	Shea, Johanna (Wilson)	24 AUG 1879 R	13	340
Sembly, Thomas H.	Simmms, Rachel A.	27 AUG 1885	20	389
Semkens, Henry Milton	Glover, Blanche Meade	14 JUN 1883 R	17	491
Semly, William	Wheeler, Mary	22 APR 1884 L	18	526
Semmes, James Hall	Dennison, Minnesota	17 OCT 1881 R	16	026
Semmes, Mary	Fletcher, William	29 AUG 1882 L	16	495
Semple, Frank Buchanan	Brown, Annie Steele	07 FEB 1882 R	16	226
Semple, Lucinda	Horton, Lewis	08 JUL 1884	19	129
Sengstack, Charles H.	Major, Jessie F.	19 JUL 1881 L	15	409
Sengstack, Ida	Knowles, John B.	21 APR 1880 L	14	231
Senkind, Friederike Juliane Maria	Eberly, John A.	30 DEC 1877 R	11	279
Senter, Alvina M.	Quinter, Washington D.	15 AUG 1878	12	169
Senter, Mary Isabel	McAdam, William Alfred	10 OCT 1883 R	18	184
Sergeon, Catharine R.	Munzinger, Charles	06 NOV 1884 R	19	367
Serra, Henry A.	Smith, Catherine	17 APR 1878 R	12	008
Serrin, Cora C.	Dessez, Charles E.	06 NOV 1884	19	365
Serrin, David Dallas	Wiles, Mary A.	23 DEC 1884 R	19	478
Serrin, Ella Catharine	Feast, John, Jr.	06 NOV 1883 R	18	234
Serrin, Jabez W.	Wallower, Lyda M.	11 FEB 1879 R	13	053
Serrin, Marion V.	Hines, Albert B.	28 APR 1881 R	15	283
Sesch, William	Mills, Roberta F.	11 OCT 1882 R	17	066
Sesko, Charles	Waters, Jeminia	05 JUL 1881 L	15	388
Sessford, Joseph Stone F.	Mills, Mary Lela [Pool]	07 FEB 1884 R	18	415
Settle, Edwin B.	Greenlaw, Marian B.	15 OCT 1884 R	19	307
Settles, Mary Ellen	Dean, Henry	21 MAY 1885	20	232

Seufferle, Wm. Lowndes	Helmuth, Emma Christine	10 FEB 1885 R	20	059
Seuter, Albert	Gurley, Martha	15 DEC 1877 R	11	237
Severs, John	Hill, Lena	04 AUG 1882	16	465
Seville, Dorsey F.	Butler, Ella A.	28 JAN 1881 L	15	169
Sevoy, Eliza	Johnson, Jefferson	02 APR 1879 L	13	123
Sewall, Columbus	Smith, Elizabeth	26 APR 1883 L	17	413
Sewall, William G.	Miller, Kate G.	21 JUL 1885	20	309
Seward, Simon	Flaith, Louisa (Knell), Mrs.	10 JUN 1885 R	20	251
Seward, William L.	Kowaska, Josephine A. Ruth	06 DEC 1879 R	14	032
Sewel, Josiah	Powers, Mary F.	07 JUN 1879	13	223
Sewell, Anna	Reed, John D.	04 JAN 1882 L	16	183
Sewell, Annie E.	Hatton, Charles E.S.	21 DEC 1881 L	16	144
Sewell, Barbara A.	Payne, Wesley	11 JUL 1884	19	104
Sewell, J.P.	Donaldson, M.V.	03 OCT 1879 L	13	402
Sewell, J.W.	Johnson, Annie E.	22 OCT 1883	18	207
Sewell, James B.	Branham, Ella	28 APR 1881	15	277
Sewell, Jeanie A.	Duvall, George W.	08 JUL 1878	12	127
Sewell, John Fletcher	Clevenger, Elizabeth Kate	04 JUL 1880 R	14	260
Sewell, Katie Alice	Wade, Robert Hamilton	14 OCT 1885	20	478
Sewell, Laura V.	Skinner, Charles L.	31 DEC 1877	11	282
Sewell, Lizzie A.	Kelly, James F.	15 AUG 1883	18	088
Sewell, Mary	Smith, George C.	04 JUL 1885	20	295
Sewell, Sallie	Chisley, Richard T.	06 JUL 1879 R	13	271
Sewell, Susanna	Watts, William	04 APR 1883	17	379
Sewell, Thomas J.	Clark, Emma J.	19 JUL 1880 L	14	368
Sewfert, Mary E.	Mormann, Edwin	20 FEB 1879	13	071
Sexton, Daniel Joseph	Magee, Anna Maria	17 SEP 1885 R	20	424
Sexton, Ella C.	Hammack, William L.	23 OCT 1882 L	17	086
Sexton, Mary	Van Ness, Herbert M.	02 AUG 1880 R	14	383
Sexton, Nicholas J.	Parker, Mary	01 JUL 1885	20	304
Seyboldt, Cora	Thurn, Herman	04 SEP 1880 L	14	432
Seybolt, Lucy J. (Davis)	Egood, Lemuel	09 JUN 1885 R	20	263
Seyholt, Laura L.	Dunham, Samuel C.	29 APR 1885 L	20	198
Seymour, Arthur	Bell, Ida	12 SEP 1878	12	213
Seymour, Ella T.	Grier, Ralph H.	07 JUN 1881 R	15	345
Seymour, Ida McLean	Babbitt, Charles E.	17 AUG 1882 R	16	484
Seymour, Ida R.	Wilcox, Andrew D.	09 FEB 1882 L	16	233
Shackelford, Ella	Sutherland, Thomas E.	30 JUL 1880 R	14	378
Shackelford, Mary Ellen	Dye, Henry	06 NOV 1883 D	18	235
Shackelford, William M.	Carver, Margaret	13 NOV 1878 R	12	325
Shackford, Katie	Whitlock, James E.	17 SEP 1884	19	253
Shackleford, Bage	Calvert, Annie L.	15 JAN 1880 R	14	104
Shackleford, Lloyd M.	Bradley, Maria L.	02 JAN 1883 R	17	230
Shacklett, Carrie V.	Goods, James W.	14 JAN 1885	20	017
Shacklett, Nelson T.	Tolson, Cora A.	17 SEP 1877	11	098
Shacklette, Virginia A.	McInteer, Arthur L.	29 JUN 1885 R	20	299
Shad, Elizabeth C.	Ingle, John	18 JUN 1878 L	12	104
Shadd, Furmann J.	Parke, Alice M.	26 DEC 1882 R	17	205
Shade, Mary A.	Boston, George W.	26 JUN 1884 L	19	105
Shadrach, James	Johnson, Hennie	09 JUN 1878	12	093
Shaffer, John	Waggner, Eliza	01 JUN 1878 L	12	079
Shaffer, Mary J.	Duggan, John	31 AUG 1882 L	16	500
Shaffer, William Coss	Thomas, Mary M.	23 JAN 1884 R	18	392
Shaley, Mary Elen	Coburn, Charles Eli	26 FEB 1881 L	15	205
Shalloo, Marie A.	Coburn, Turley	25 JUN 1879 L	13	249
Shaloe, Delia	Parsly, George Robert	23 MAR 1880 L	14	195
Shambaugh, Annie	Safoe, Francis	01 JUL 1884 L	19	115
Shamwell, Charles H.	Ellison, Eliza Ann	10 NOV 1877 L	11	178

D.C. Marriage Records Index, June 28, 1877 to October 19, 1885

Shamwell, James H.	Priest, Nannie E.	23 DEC 1882 L	17	207
Shamwell, Lewis	Campbell, Florence	25 OCT 1884 L	19	337
Shanahan, Annie J.	Rankin, James W.	29 APR 1884	18	529
Shanahan, Daniel	Kane, Ellen E.	25 NOV 1884 L	19	410
Shanahan, Mary	Considine, John	01 SEP 1877 L	11	073
Shanahan, Mary	Blenck, William	17 MAY 1878 L	12	057
Shanahan, Mary	Noonan, Michael	24 AUG 1881 L	15	457
Shanahan, Michael	McNamara, Winifred	11 DEC 1877 R	11	229
Shanahan, Thomas	Cuddihy, Mary	18 APR 1881 R	15	252
Shanahan, Winnie	Conners, Daniel	30 NOV 1881 L	16	103
Shands, Booker F.	Walker, Victoria	02 OCT 1884 L	19	282
Shands, Elverton A.	Hoover, Annie C.	19 FEB 1884 R	18	431
Shands, Fanny	McDaniel, Robert	04 NOV 1880 L	15	032
Shane, Franklin	Williams, Annie	01 MAY 1883 L	17	424
Shane, Maggie	Cain, Cornelius	09 MAY 1880 R	14	260
Shane, Mary Ann	Ross, John Robert	19 APR 1880 L	14	228
Shankland, Anna	Gaines, George	06 MAR 1878	11	373
Shanklin, Amanda	Scott, William Henry	19 JUN 1882 R	16	416
Shanklin, Maggie	Randall, Silas S.	21 APR 1881 R	15	268
Shanklin, Mason	Johnson, Sarah	03 SEP 1878 L	12	194
Shanklin, Matthew	Quivers, Mary	09 JUL 1878 R	12	131
Shanklin, Richard	Campbell, Winnie	25 APR 1883 L	17	412
Shannon, Felix	Kelley, Catharine	19 DEC 1879 L	14	059
Shannon, Harriett B.	Mason, Samuel Tufton	20 NOV 1880 R	21	5108
Shannon, Mary C.	Bibb, William D.	01 APR 1885	20	140
Shannon, William A.	Berry, Agnes	11 OCT 1882	17	065
Sharp, Charles H.	Nunnally, Josie H.	10 MAR 1885 R	20	105
Sharp, George Andrew	Taylor, Mary Susan	21 MAY 1878	12	062
Sharp, Paul	Evans, Celia	15 OCT 1879 L	13	427
Sharpe, Caroline	Hollister, George H.	20 OCT 1877 L	11	148
Sharpless, Frank	Barrick, Annie M.	22 FEB 1882 R	16	255
Sharrets, Grayson W.	Sharrets, Maude A.	08 MAY 1878	12	044
Sharrets, Maude A.	Sharrets, Grayson W.	08 MAY 1878	12	044
Shattuck, Minnie A.	Houghton, Arthur J.	06 OCT 1880 R	14	471
Shattuck, Nettie F.	Wohlfarth, George F.	01 SEP 1883 L	18	107
Shauer, J.S.	Coriell, Octavia, Mrs.	07 APR 1883 R	17	385
Shaw, Benjamin F.	Schockey, Lucy M.	22 SEP 1880 R	14	455
Shaw, Charles E.	Stanton, Bettie	15 MAR 1885 R	20	110
Shaw, Clark G.	Payne, Mary Elizabeth	23 OCT 1884	19	321
Shaw, Daniel	Snowden, Clara	12 APR 1881 R	15	254
Shaw, Ella C.	Marden, William A.	22 APR 1885 L	20	182
Shaw, Francis	Jackson, Margaret	24 FEB 1881 R	16	170
Shaw, Franklin	Mangun, Marvelda	07 FEB 1878 R	11	329
Shaw, J.H.	Lewis, Caroline	26 FEB 1879 L	13	080
Shaw, James A.	Lacy, Annie E.	11 DEC 1879	14	035
Shaw, Laura Belle	Halliday, Francis A., Dr.	21 DEC 1881	16	144
Shaw, Louisa	Francis, George W.C.	14 AUG 1883	18	087
Shaw, Maria	Washington, Charles	01 FEB 1879 L	13	041
Shaw, Mary E.	Thompson, William M.E.	11 NOV 1880 L	15	044
Shaw, Richard A.	Hutchinson, Lucy A.	07 MAR 1878	11	375
Shaw, Sarah	Bailey, James S.	20 OCT 1884 L	19	323
Shaw, Sarah E.	Bowles, Lee P.	13 NOV 1884	19	380
Shaw, Sarah J.	Owens, Charles P.	04 DEC 1881 R	16	113
Shaw, Spencer	Johnson, Josephine R.	23 OCT 1883	18	208
Shaw, Susannah	Carter, George W.	12 JUN 1879	13	231
Shaw, Thomas E.	Williams, Mary	05 APR 1883 R	17	378
Shaw, Victoria D.	Alexander, Nathan H.	21 DEC 1882	17	200
Shaw, Wesley	Smith, Cora	13 OCT 1881 R	16	021

Shaw, William H.	Gibson, Nannie	07 NOV 1884	19	368
Shay, Annie A.	Goddard, William R.	05 JUL 1877 L	11	010
Shay, Mary	Mazur, Lorenz	07 MAY 1885 L	20	211
Shay, William	Frain, Sallie	04 MAR 1882 L	16	267
Shea, Alfred D.	McMann, Mary	31 DEC 1884 L	19	518
Shea, Daniel E.	Moran, Mary E.	15 JUN 1882 R	16	412
Shea, James	McCarroll, Ann	26 JUL 1881 L	15	417
Shea, Johanna (Wilson)	Selzle, Charles	24 AUG 1879 R	13	340
Shea, Mary	Fitzgerald, Edward	02 DEC 1877 R	11	193
Shea, Nellie V.	Owen, Franklin B.	28 MAY 1885 L	20	247
Sheaer, Elizabeth	Wagner, John	16 FEB 1882 R	16	244
Sheahan, Daniel S.	Downey, Mary A.	03 FEB 1883 R	17	287
Sheahan, Mary	Cunningham, Mark	28 APR 1883 L	17	420
Shealds, James	Wright, Mary	09 NOV 1878 L	12	317
Sheckells, Annie J.	Brooke, John W.	30 OCT 1877 R	11	160
Sheckells, Augustus C.	Wilcox, Mary C.	19 NOV 1878	12	334
Sheckells, Chester	Watkins, Agnes E.	24 DEC 1877	11	260
Sheckels, James Borrows	Miller, Margaret Regina	26 OCT 1881 R	16	045
Sheckels, William Henry	Busher, Lizzie	08 NOV 1882 L	17	119
Sheckles, Charles R.	Norton, Rebecca	26 MAR 1883 L	17	362
Shedd, James J.	Stutz, Adelaide M.	04 NOV 1884	19	360
Shedrick, James Andrew	Barnes, Helen	21 JAN 1885 L	20	032
Sheedy, Patrick F.	Lucas, Louisa H.	05 APR 1880 R	14	202
Sheehan, Daniel	Maloney, A.T.	31 JUL 1882 L	16	463
Sheehan, Ellen	Riordan, Bartholomew	03 JAN 1882 R	16	176
Sheehan, John Francis	Scanlan, Bridget	03 JAN 1882 R	16	176
Sheehan, Mary Ann	Hagan, James	10 NOV 1883 L	18	245
Sheehy, Henry	Brodracht, Marie E.	18 JUL 1883	18	051
Sheehy, James S.	Sardo, Annie Clay	22 FEB 1881 L	15	198
Sheehy, Mary	Liston, Michael	08 APR 1880 L	14	214
Sheehy, Nellie	Ragan, Patrick	30 JUN 1885 L	20	301
Sheehy, Nora	Driscoll, Humphrey	27 JUN 1885 L	20	290
Sheehy, Norah	Burke, Richard O'H.	20 JAN 1881 R	15	156
Sheele, Alice M.	Reynolds, John R.	27 JUL 1881 L	15	420
Sheeter, Willie M.	Sawtelle, Leston D.	10 APR 1879 R	13	137
Shehan, Ellen	Labor, Thomas	13 NOV 1877 L	11	182
Shehan, Mary	Moore, Alexander Christopher	31 AUG 1882 R	16	498
Shehan, Mary A.	Doyle, Thomas F.	28 OCT 1879 L	13	448
Sheid, Harry	Hawkshaw, Mary Josephine	15 AUG 1883	18	089
Sheid, John T., Jr.	Bushing, Augusta	02 MAY 1878 R	12	035
Sheid, William R.	Wise, Laura	08 APR 1884 R	18	496
Sheild, Alfred Prentis	Burfoot, Ellen Catharine	26 SEP 1879 R	13	389
Shekel, A.B., Dr.	Everard, Mary A.	09 OCT 1877 L	11	128
Shellhorn, Bertha	Rogers, Archibald I.	19 AUG 1885	20	377
Shellhorn, Chris	Noll, Lena	11 APR 1885 R	20	159
Shellhorn, Sophie	Kretschmann, Hugo	16 NOV 1881 R	16	073
Sheltin, Thomas M.	Maupin, Clara L.	19 AUG 1885	20	380
Shelton, Annie	Barnes, Edgar	24 JUN 1879 L	13	246
Shelton, Benjamin F.	Selby, Susie R.	11 JAN 1883 R	17	252
Shelton, Caroline	Robinson, William H.	28 JUN 1884 L	19	108
Shelton, Dennis	Wingfield, Susan	18 JUN 1879	13	236
Shelton, George H.	Sommerville, Claratine	17 NOV 1884 L	19	387
Shelton, Heston	Snellins, Hopie	11 JAN 1885 R	20	011
Shelton, James B.	Austin, Mary V.	12 APR 1882 R	16	309
Shelton, James C.	Strickhart, Mary Louise	05 MAR 1878 L	11	372
Shelton, James S.	Herbert, Eliza J.	05 FEB 1878	11	326
Shelton, John R.	Fairall, Mary E.	29 MAY 1878	12	074
Shelton, Joseph	Lahey, Mary Catherine	12 DEC 1884 R	19	456

Shelton, Julia	Crowther, William	09 OCT 1879 R	13	415
Shelton, Kaokie	Brown, David	17 NOV 1884 L	19	388
Shelton, Mary J.	Foster, Frank	23 FEB 1881 L	15	200
Shelton, Robert	Burnaw, Martha	22 APR 1880	14	224
Shelton, Sallie F.	Pinn, David	25 MAY 1880 R	14	285
Shelton, Virginia Florence	Timberlake, Richard Claybrook	02 JUN 1884 R	19	050
Shelvy, James Henry	Kelly, Mary Louisa	16 MAY 1878 R	12	057
Shely, James Wm.	Portis, Laura	07 OCT 1885 R	20	467
Shenton, Raymond	Gillingham, Cora	05 DEC 1878 R	12	370
Shepard, Catharine M.	Works, Winfield T.	09 APR 1883	17	384
Shepard, Charles	Summers, Florence I.	15 NOV 1882 L	17	127
Shepard, James H.	Browning, Maggie E.	07 JUN 1883 R	17	481
Shepard, Mark	Fairfax, Rosie L.	30 SEP 1884	19	273
Shepard, William H.	Tramell, Rachel Ann	24 JAN 1883 R	17	273
Shephard, Elizabeth	Schwalenberg, Frank A.	06 APR 1885 L	20	147
Shepherd, Aaron	Thompson, Sarah E.	15 OCT 1878 L	12	273
Shepherd, Annie	Righter, John Henry	24 DEC 1880 R	15	122
Shepherd, Arthur	Wharton, Mary America	08 AUG 1878 L	12	161
Shepherd, Elizabeth	Carter, Stephen	26 SEP 1885 L	20	088
Shepherd, Emma K.	Cole, John T.	27 FEB 1882	16	260
Shepherd, Hannibal	Middleton, Maria	15 SEP 1881	15	484
Shepherd, Henderson	Edwards, Sarah E.	06 DEC 1882 R	17	169
Shepherd, Jane F.	Childs, Frank H.	29 SEP 1879 R	13	390
Shepherd, Jno. Hooper	Robinson, Helen M.	17 SEP 1879 R	13	374
Shepherd, John	Regan, Betty	29 SEP 1877 L	11	115
Shepherd, John H.	Butler, Cora V.	08 FEB 1883 L	17	300
Shepherd, Lucelia Helen	Williams, James	28 FEB 1884	18	451
Shepherd, Lucy Ellen	Burgess, Henry Edwin	13 DEC 1884 R	19	457
Shepherd, Mary A.	Johnson, Howard	18 NOV 1879 R	13	483
Shepherd, Mary E.	Sullivan, Daniel	09 JAN 1881 R	15	144
Shepherd, Millie A.	McCorkle, Simpson	11 DEC 1884 R	19	452
Shepherd, Peter Ezekiel	Johnson, Irene	10 APR 1884 R	18	503
Shepherd, Samuel	Brant, Alice	18 JUL 1883	18	052
Shepherd, Silas	Wood, Annie K.	07 JUN 1883 R	17	480
Shepperson, Ida	Gessford, William T.	21 AUG 1883	18	095
Shepperson, James F.	Donaldson, Blanche E.	02 JUL 1884	19	116
Shepperson, James S.	Williams, Emma F.	04 SEP 1879 L	13	351
Shepperson, Jennie	Eckoff, Frederick T.	18 DEC 1883	18	324
Sherick, Sadie M.	Smith, Edward H.	28 AUG 1884	19	214
Sheridan, Charles F.	Berry, Annie	22 NOV 1884 L	19	401
Sheriff, Ebbie	Hatton, Maggie	29 NOV 1881 R	16	100
Sheriff, Nannie E.	Hayne, Daniel H.	23 AUG 1884	19	205
Sherlock, Robert	Edelin, Esther Jane	04 MAY 1880 R	14	250
Sherman, Beulah Walden	Peyton, Cunningham	30 APR 1883 R	17	422
Sherman, Cora	Welford, Charles	01 DEC 1881 L	16	110
Sherman, Eleanor Mary	Thackara, Alexander Montgomery	05 MAY 1880 R	14	249
Sherman, Florence Gertrude	Whittlesey, Walter R.	03 MAR 1881 F	15	213
Sherman, George S.	Dement, Annie V., Mrs.	07 FEB 1884 R	18	414
Sherman, Gussie E.	Bradley, Henry J.	06 NOV 1883	18	234
Sherman, Ida Louise	Mallory, Alfred Edward	25 APR 1881 R	15	272
Sherman, John	Corbin, Ann	25 MAR 1879	13	099
Sherman, John	Rice, Ida J.	16 APR 1879	13	147
Sherman, Mary L.	Lantz, Franklin W.	31 MAR 1885 R	20	138
Sherman, Roger M.	Drake, Mary Inman	28 FEB 1885 R	20	089
Shermans, Lenora C.	Williams, Beverly W.	13 SEP 1884	19	244
Sherran, John	Washington, Caroline Martha	22 NOV 1884 L	19	402
Sherry, James P.	Cotter, Annie C.	01 OCT 1879 R	13	394
Sherwin, Frank Remington	Dickerson, Louise	03 JUL 1883 R	18	025

Sherwood, Anna B.	Paxton, George C.	23 NOV 1881	16	097
Sherwood, Clarkson R.	Larman, Ellanora	04 DEC 1878 R	12	366
Sherwood, Columbus F.	Edwards, Josephine S.	21 SEP 1882 R	17	032
Sherwood, Elias	Mayhugh, Sallie	18 JAN 1883	17	264
Sherwood, Ella G.	Etter, Walter	29 AUG 1881 L	15	463
Sherwood, George L.	Love, Emmett Roberta	02 NOV 1879 R	13	450
Sherwood, Henry	Harvey, Ella M.	27 MAY 1879	13	207
Sherwood, James C.	Burrows, Ella M.	22 JUN 1880 R	14	330
Sherwood, James Edward	Burroughs, Evannah	10 OCT 1878 R	12	266
Sherwood, James L.	Lord, Rose E.	12 DEC 1883	18	311
Sherwood, Kate E.	McCaffney, Hugh R.	17 JUL 1884	19	145
Sherwood, Katie	Ward, William G.	25 JUL 1878 L	12	148
Sherwood, Lewis W.	Weaver, Mary L.	05 MAR 1883 R	17	325
Sherwood, Morgan A.	Hurdle, Pinky	13 DEC 1877 R	11	236
Sherzer, Charles P.	Betts, E.A.	26 DEC 1883 R	18	343
Sherzer, John	Weaver, Annie	23 MAR 1882	16	288
Shetler, Charles	Sorrell, Emma	06 FEB 1878 R	11	329
Shewalter, Addie V.	Fleet, Mozart B.	08 OCT 1878	12	261
Shieber, William F.	Bates, Lillie M.	03 SEP 1883 L	18	108
Shields, Anna	Harris, Robert	24 MAR 1879	13	110
Shields, Catherine	Barrett, Michael	22 JUL 1879 R	13	288
Shields, Eleas	Blair, Bettie	17 FEB 1885 R	20	069
Shields, Elizabeth Howard	Gurley, William Brooks	09 OCT 1879	13	412
Shields, Josie A.	Graham, Wesley F.	12 MAR 1884	18	467
Shields, Margaret	McKernan, Thomas	19 SEP 1883 R	18	140
Shields, Marian D.	Carter, John	21 AUG 1879	13	328
Shields, Mary Jane	Dawson, Lynch	29 AUG 1878 R	12	179
Shields, Rachel T.	Agnor, Theodore T.	27 OCT 1881 L	16	048
Shields, Sarah E.	Asterline, George	15 NOV 1882 L	17	129
Shields, William	Henderson, Catherine	18 AUG 1881 R	15	451
Shields, William H.	Smith, Ellen	20 JUL 1878 R	12	147
Shiflet, John S.	Walker, Martha R.	23 DEC 1870 R	14	000
Shiles, Charles W.	Saxty, Mamie	02 APR 1879 L	13	123
Shiles, Isabella	Butcher, Joseph	16 DEC 1880 R	15	102
Shiles, M.E.	Lynham, W.D.	04 MAY 1878	12	038
Shillen, Mollie A.	Craig, William	03 NOV 1881 R	16	059
Shillenn, Harriet Wynn	Harrison, Fillmore	30 AUG 1881 R	15	463
Shillinglaw, James G.	Gannon, Annie	05 AUG 1884 L	19	170
Shilloo, Josephine	Minor, James	26 JAN 1880 R	14	121
Shillow, Joanna	Madison, James	19 DEC 1879 L	14	059
Shimer, Reuben L.	Reiley, Annie Elizabeth	15 SEP 1885 R	20	417
Shine, Anna M.	Moore, John G.	24 MAR 1883 L	17	359
Shinn, Mattie	Van Vleck, William	19 FEB 1885 R	20	076
Ship, Trittie Ann	Price, Edward	17 NOV 1883 L	18	262
Shipe, Frank H.	Higgins, Maimie H.	30 APR 1879 R	13	169
Shipe, William R.	Howard, Katie H.	09 APR 1885 L	20	156
Shipley, Annie E.	Thomas, Jonathan J.	10 SEP 1878	12	209
Shipley, Charles E.	Ehrmantraut, Mary	22 JUN 1880 L	14	330
Shipley, Enos A.	Edelin, Mary A.	24 MAY 1881 R	15	324
Shipley, Fernando	Jackson, Anna	10 SEP 1877 L	11	084
Shipley, Fernando	Thornton, Frances	07 OCT 1885	20	463
Shipley, Fourose	Griffith, Mary C.	29 JUL 1883	18	065
Shipley, John	Graham, Rebecca	20 DEC 1877 R	11	250
Shipley, John R.	Gillis, Narcissa J.	27 FEB 1879 R	13	084
Shipley, Margaret M.	Lybrand, Horace W.	21 APR 1885 L	20	181
Shipley, Mary Jane	Davis, Frisby Francis	06 JUL 1879 R	13	260
Shipley, Mary L.	Keefer, Philip F.	06 JUN 1881 L	15	346
Shipley, Maurice E.	Pywell, Ella E.	18 OCT 1880 R	14	500

Shipman, Eliza	Newman, Benjamin F.	27 JUN 1882 R	16	428
Shipman, Frank	Howser, Ida	26 JUN 1883 R	18	017
Shipman, Martha E.	King, Thomas A.	16 FEB 1882 R	16	246
Shipman, Mary E.	Boswell, William H.	30 JUL 1883 L	18	066
Shipman, Miranda C.	Offerman, August	24 JUN 1879 R	13	246
Shipman, Nellie	Ball, Marshel T.	08 AUG 1881 L	15	435
Shipman, Washington E.	Henderson, Sarah A.	04 SEP 1883 R	18	108
Shirley, George W.	Morris, Mary Virginia	26 JUL 1882 R	16	426
Shirley, James Woodford	Brodie, Jenettie A.	18 DEC 1877 R	11	245
Shirley, John D.	Trammel, Zillia Ann	31 MAY 1882 R	16	383
Shirley, Maggie Lee	Trammell, John Henry	01 FEB 1885 R	20	035
Shoemaker, Annie E.	Schaeffer, John Shelton	08 SEP 1884	19	232
Shoemaker, Catharine V.	McIntyre, John H.	18 FEB 1884 L	18	430
Shoemaker, Charles F.	Miller, Rhetta	08 SEP 1881 R	15	476
Shoemaker, David W.	Auters, Kate V.	29 MAR 1883 L	17	371
Shoemaker, Edith L.	Cox, Robert Lee	25 OCT 1877	11	153
Shoemaker, Edward James	Malone, Louisa T. Allen	31 DEC 1879 R	14	083
Shoemaker, Eliza	Davidson, John Frank	06 DEC 1877 R	11	217
Shoemaker, Elizabeth Jane	Carr, Ashel	08 APR 1884 L	18	500
Shoemaker, Ella F.	Nichols, George W.	09 JAN 1883	17	247
Shoemaker, Ella N.	Kreamer, Charles A.	19 AUG 1884 L	19	193
Shoemaker, George W.	Wilson, Corlanthea H.E.	02 AUG 1881 R	15	430
Shoemaker, Ida	Ellis, James R.	06 JUL 1885 L	20	313
Shoemaker, Isaac W.	Carroll, Mary A.	03 APR 1879 L	13	125
Shoemaker, Jennie	Holroyd, Arthur E.	03 DEC 1881 L	16	111
Shoemaker, Leila	Brewster, Robert J.W.	19 OCT 1885 R	20	493
Shoemaker, Lizzie E.	Coon, William Henry	24 MAR 1885 R	20	129
Shoemaker, Mary A.B.	Wall, John H.	27 MAR 1878	11	392
Shoemaker, Mary C.	Ketter, William	19 NOV 1878	12	333
Shoemaker, Wm. Alfred	Cobb, Mary C.	13 MAR 1879	13	098
Shombert, Mary	Schaffer, George	29 OCT 1882 R	17	093
Shomo, Annie Laurie	Nicholson, David	25 OCT 1882 R	17	091
Shomo, Eva Frances (DeLand)	Shomo, Harvey Lemon	23 DEC 1884 R	19	483
Shomo, Harvey Lemon	Shomo, Eva Frances (DeLand)	23 DEC 1884 R	19	483
Shomo, Oscar V.	Hutton, Lola C.	06 AUG 1884 R	19	172
Shoop, Frances M.	Smith, William E.	05 FEB 1883 R	17	286
Shores, Annette	Taylor, Henry	14 OCT 1879 R	13	423
Short, Agnes	Ward, Thomas	03 JAN 1884 L	18	365
Short, Alfred	Stewart, Eliza	03 SEP 1877 R	11	069
Short, George R.	Nichols, Susie L.	19 JAN 1881	15	157
Short, John	Malone, Delia	27 OCT 1883 L	18	217
Short, Rebecca C.	Grant, James L.	15 SEP 1879 R	13	369
Short, Robert	Swink, Susan	23 JAN 1880 L	14	119
Short, Sadie	Febrey, Wallace A.	21 JUN 1883 L	18	008
Short, Sidney H.	Morrison, Mary F.	26 JUL 1881	15	417
Short, Thomas	Johnson, Mattie L.	31 DEC 1878	12	410
Shortell, John H.	Thompson, Emma E.	03 MAY 1881 L	15	289
Shorter, Amelia	Williams, Ludwell	07 JAN 1885 L	20	007
Shorter, Annie	Bush, Thomas Oliver	20 SEP 1885	20	426
Shorter, Charles	Carroll, Julia	14 MAY 1885	20	222
Shorter, Charles Henry	Hurley, Isabella	11 MAR 1879 L	13	096
Shorter, Charles Marshall	Holmes, Mary Elizabeth	14 OCT 1880 R	14	487
Shorter, Henry	Marshall, Evan	10 JAN 1880 L	14	098
Shorter, Margaret	Batson, Henson	24 DEC 1877	11	264
Shorter, Mary	Blackstone, Henry	21 DEC 1877 L	11	257
Shorter, Mary Catherine	Lockwood, John Henry	18 SEP 1883 R	18	133
Shorter, Nathan	Smith, Sarah	02 NOV 1882 R	17	079
Shorter, Rebecca	Smith, Thomas H.	28 SEP 1882 L	17	041

Shorter, Rebecca Ann	Hall, Charles	10 JUL 1879 R	13	273
Shorter, Richard	Wilson, Susie	16 AUG 1881 R	15	448
Shorter, Robert	Matthews, Lizzie	04 SEP 1879	13	353
Shorter, Sarah	Selby, Jacob S.	07 NOV 1878	12	308
Shorter, William	Myers, Annie	25 JUL 1882 R	16	440
Show, Henrietta	Noyes, Joseph	07 OCT 1881	16	013
Shrader, Houston D., Dr.	Amos, Mollie S.	29 MAR 1881	15	241
Shreeve, Mary Virginia	Dye, Lucius Cary	15 NOV 1883 R	18	257
Shreve, J.W.	Berry, Julia A.	08 JUN 1881	15	351
Shreve, John W.	Donaldson, Laura	05 JAN 1882	16	179
Shreve, Lillian E.	McDonald, Harry A.	23 MAY 1878	12	064
Shreve, Robert	Donalson, Anna	28 FEB 1884 R	18	448
Shreve, Samuel F.	Reagan, Bertie C.	05 MAY 1884 L	19	005
Shreve, Walter E.	Harrington, Mary I.	02 OCT 1878 R	12	247
Shreve, William O., Jr.	Jones, Ida A.	12 AUG 1878 L	12	164
Shreves, Ben	Harrington, Nannie V.	19 JUN 1880 L	14	327
Shreves, Charles	Raymond, Ellen	30 AUG 1878 R	12	188
Shreves, Charles Henry	Shrode, Minnie	10 MAY 1881 R	15	299
Shriver, B. Franklin	McSherry, Helen Nicholson	20 FEB 1878	11	349
Shrode, Minnie	Shreves, Charles Henry	10 MAY 1881 R	15	299
Shry, Minnie	Mangum, James H.	24 SEP 1883 L	18	151
Shryock, Carrie Biddle	Briggs, Alfred Benthall	08 AUG 1882 R	16	471
Shubkagel, William Henry	Bull, Clara Matilda	23 MAR 1882 R	16	288
Shue, Minnie J.	Bowman, Frank Hubbard	05 JUL 1884 R	19	122
Shughrue, John	Prendeville, Kate	13 NOV 1882	17	123
Shugrue, Julia	Nash, George W.	09 AUG 1879 L	13	314
Shugrue, Maggie	Preston, Oliver J.	09 AUG 1879 L	13	313
Shugrue, Mollie	Keleher, Thomas	07 JAN 1885 L	20	008
Shultz, John A.	Hall, Rosa A.	29 NOV 1884	19	337
Shumaker, Jane E.	Hough, Hector T.C.	24 MAR 1880 R	14	198
Shumate, Bettie	Holtzclaw, Lucien Dade	14 AUG 1883	18	086
Shunt, Jane Findley	Evans, Richard Kennon	11 NOV 1880 R	15	045
Shunt, Jane Lindley	Evans, Robert Kennon, Lt.	11 NOV 1880	15	039
Shupe, Laura	DeGrange, J. William	23 FEB 1880 R	14	159
Shuster, Ernest Alvin	Gray, Katharine	15 DEC 1879 R	14	046
Shutt, J.C.	Brown, Susie A.	02 JUL 1878	12	126
Shweitzer, Kate	Sweitzer, George J.	25 NOV 1883	18	274
Shyrock, J.F.	Walker, Mary	01 JAN 1880 R	14	086
Sibley, Samuel M.	Thorn, Catherine E.	30 JAN 1882	16	214
Sickle, Eli	Fisher, Hannah	18 OCT 1885 R	20	491
Sidman, George D.	Brown, Francene L.	24 JUN 1885 R	20	286
Sidney, Lizzie	Brooks, Joseph	09 DEC 1879 L	14	036
Sidney, Washington P.	White, Julia	17 SEP 1885 R	20	426
Sieber, Frederick	Frilling, Johanna	09 AUG 1885 R	20	361
Siebert, J.M.	Hollohan, Mary	21 MAY 1878 L	12	062
Siebert, Selma	Richter, Carl	18 MAR 1879 R	13	107
Siegel, Charles	Thomas, Ella	07 OCT 1880 L	14	480
Siegel, Clara	Sondheimer, Julius	11 MAY 1879 R	13	182
Siep, Louisa	Tinkler, William T.	04 NOV 1878 R	12	306
Siggers, Kate Virginia	Pryor, Thomas D.	17 AUG 1885 R	20	374
Silance, Florence G.	Turner, William H.	20 MAY 1885 R	20	232
Silas, Caroline	Murray, Oscar	04 OCT 1884 L	19	286
Silence, Annie W.	Lee, Charles H.	21 JUL 1881 R	15	232
Silence, George P.	Brady, Elizabeth Ann	08 MAY 1880 R	14	259
Sillex, Thomas	Loveless, Sarah	26 MAY 1879 L	13	204
Silver, John	Beam, Ophelia	05 FEB 1884	18	406
Silver, William	Thompson, Nellie	27 DEC 1882	17	201
Silvers, Lulu A.	Dorian, Marion	02 OCT 1882 R	17	046

Silvey, Robert W.	Jackson, Ann Eliza	05 APR 1882 R	16	293
Sim, John Wesley	Gant, Ann	23 MAY 1885 L	20	236
Sim, L.E.	Diggs, Lucy	04 AUG 1885 R	20	350
Simm, James T.	Finch, Jerusa K.	30 JUL 1881 L	15	427
Simmens, Lizzie	Tanner, John W.	18 SEP 1884	19	257
Simmes, Bennett Barton	Fitzhugh, Lulu Bright	21 SEP 1880	14	455
Simmes, Charlotte	Thomas, Daniel	15 DEC 1881	16	135
Simmes, Mary Elizabeth	George, Charles Andrew	24 MAY 1882 L	16	374
Simmms, Rachel A.	Sembly, Thomas H.	27 AUG 1885	20	389
Simmons, Allie E.	Haislip, William Walter	12 FEB 1884	18	420
Simmons, Amanda	Cole, George	05 SEP 1878 L	12	201
Simmons, Annie	Cole, Barney	03 FEB 1882 L	16	225
Simmons, Annie Laurie	Decker, Wm. Odey Hudson	20 APR 1884 R	18	503
Simmons, Celia	Kent, David	09 JAN 1878 R	12	410
Simmons, Daniel M.	Moore, Mary	26 JUN 1884 R	19	107
Simmons, Edward E.	Gaines, Jennie A.	14 JUL 1885 L	20	326
Simmons, Eliza E.	Mason, Robert	05 MAY 1885 L	20	205
Simmons, Eliza Ellen	Smith, Charles Harrison	19 DEC 1880 R	15	110
Simmons, Ella	O'Donnell, Thomas	18 MAY 1885 L	20	227
Simmons, Emma	Ashford, Henry C.	16 FEB 1880 L	14	156
Simmons, Fanny E.	Johnson, Connerway	06 JUN 1878 L	12	089
Simmons, Frank W.	Thomas, Lillie Fisher	14 MAY 1884	19	008
Simmons, George Clarkson	Clements, Amanda	24 NOV 1884 R	19	403
Simmons, George H.	Gross, Sarah	25 MAR 1884 L	18	481
Simmons, John Benjamin	Finagin, Margaret Cath.	03 OCT 1880 R	14	468
Simmons, John Thomas	Boston, Josephine	18 JUL 1882	16	451
Simmons, Josephine L.	Thompson, John H.	26 NOV 1884 R	19	422
Simmons, Josie	Roberts, Richford R.	25 DEC 1884 R	19	488
Simmons, Katie Lee	Dean, Ward H.	01 JUN 1884	19	048
Simmons, Leo	Braselman, Helen Marr	10 NOV 1884 R	19	370
Simmons, Lloyd A.	Doyle, Laura F.	09 OCT 1883 R	18	178
Simmons, Lucinda	Dyson, William	13 JAN 1881 R	15	150
Simmons, Maria	Dorsey, Wm. Edward	31 OCT 1877 L	11	163
Simmons, Mary A.	Dabney, Charles	18 SEP 1883 L	18	137
Simmons, Melinda	Braxton, Washington	21 AUG 1878 R	12	183
Simmons, Miles	Burk, Ellen J.	18 JAN 1884 R	18	384
Simmons, Preston	Johnson, Ada	20 MAR 1882 L	16	284
Simmons, Robert B.	Smith, Mary Frances	15 SEP 1880 R	14	442
Simmons, Susie	White, Robert	29 MAY 1884 R	19	029
Simmons, Walter L.	Calhoun, Etta E.	22 JUL 1884 L	19	150
Simmons, William	Green, Louisa	05 OCT 1878 R	12	252
Simmons, William D.	Leddy, Catherine	16 FEB 1885	20	068
Simmons, Zachariah	Neale, Jane	11 JUN 1885 L	20	267
Simmons, Zachariah E.	Jackson, Sarah M.	21 JAN 1879 R	13	027
Simms, Addie C.	Sinclair, Walter F.	24 MAR 1880 R	14	191
Simms, Adelaide E.	Kelly, Henry H.	10 DEC 1879 R	14	040
Simms, Alexander	Redin, Charlotte	10 DEC 1878 L	12	376
Simms, Alexander	Honesty, Martha	27 JUL 1883	18	064
Simms, Alice R.	Green, John	29 AUG 1879 L	13	344
Simms, Amanda	Lucas, Charles	31 MAY 1883 R	17	465
Simms, Annie	Anderson, Nathan	03 MAY 1878	12	035
Simms, Annie	Kee, William J.	27 JAN 1885 L	20	039
Simms, Annie S.	Thomas, George W.	29 NOV 1884	19	424
Simms, Charles E.	Green, Catharine E.	29 NOV 1883 L	18	286
Simms, Charles Henry	Bruce, Elizabeth	09 NOV 1878 L	12	319
Simms, Clayton Edmonston	Woodley, Amy Elizabeth	08 FEB 1881 R	15	183
Simms, Daniel	Reed, Millie	20 JAN 1883 R	17	268
Simms, Edward	Vincent, Martha	21 FEB 1878	11	345

Simms, Eleanor B.	Seely, Charles M.	11 MAR 1881 R	15	223
Simms, Elijah	Washington, Jane	09 FEB 1880 L	14	143
Simms, Emma Lee	Moore, George D.	04 SEP 1883 R	18	111
Simms, Estella Virginia	Wilson, Thomas	24 DEC 1878 L	12	400
Simms, Frank M.	Gleason, Sarah	06 MAY 1885 R	20	209
Simms, Geo. Jos. Martin	Coleman, Julia	26 SEP 1878 L	12	237
Simms, Henry	Queen, Susannah	13 DEC 1877	11	236
Simms, Henry	Thompson, Caroline	06 JUL 1882 L	16	441
Simms, Hester	Ward, David	21 JAN 1885 L	20	032
Simms, Ida R.	Birch, William Taylor	27 NOV 1878 R	12	349
Simms, James	Lyons, Maggie	08 SEP 1885	20	403
Simms, James B.	Bodenseck, Katy S.	14 APR 1878	12	411
Simms, James H.	Bradford, Emily M.	21 NOV 1884 L	19	400
Simms, Jane	Carroll, William	09 OCT 1884 L	19	298
Simms, Jane R.	Diggs, Louis	02 OCT 1884 L	19	282
Simms, Janett	Dyson, Sarah	13 DEC 1883 L	18	316
Simms, Jimmy	Butler, Catherine	25 MAY 1880 L	14	287
Simms, John	Johnson, Maria	17 JUN 1878 L	12	101
Simms, John	Hawkins, May	08 MAY 1880 L	14	260
Simms, John	Javins, Missouri	21 FEB 1884	18	435
Simms, John	Caldwell, Mary	22 APR 1885	20	179
Simms, John F.	Pleasants, Emily	08 JUN 1880 L	14	312
Simms, John H.	Payne, Julia Ann	20 JUL 1885 L	20	026
Simms, John T.	Craig, Charlotte C.	29 SEP 1879 R	13	331
Simms, John T.	Brown, Maggie	17 JAN 1884 L	18	382
Simms, John Wesley	Henson, Mary E.	14 DEC 1882	17	185
Simms, Josephine	Jones, John Alfred	04 JUL 1882	16	436
Simms, Louisa	Johnson, Horace	20 AUG 1880 L	14	409
Simms, Louisa	Lewis, William	07 AUG 1884	19	129
Simms, Lucinda	Richardson, Charles	15 JAN 1880 L	14	075
Simms, Lulu E.	Richardson, Attrell	13 NOV 1884 L	19	381
Simms, Margaret A.	Taylor, Thomas B.	02 FEB 1880 R	14	102
Simms, Maria	Johnson, Joseph	15 OCT 1884 R	19	308
Simms, Martha Ann	Winslow, J.H.	28 APR 1883 L	17	419
Simms, Mary	Johnson, John Henry	12 NOV 1877	11	179
Simms, Mary	Wells, John	27 MAR 1879	13	117
Simms, Mary	Hill, Daniel	08 SEP 1880 L	14	435
Simms, Mary	Smith, Ambrose	22 DEC 1880	15	116
Simms, Mary	Young, George	07 FEB 1881	15	181
Simms, Mary	Bacey, Richard	02 APR 1885	20	141
Simms, Maurice A.	Henderson, Mary V.	03 FEB 1883 L	17	290
Simms, Nancy	Simms, Robert	29 AUG 1885	20	392
Simms, nannie	Briscoe, Charles M.	20 JUN 1883	18	007
Simms, Rachel, Mrs.	Curtis, Clifton Henry	29 SEP 1880 R	14	462
Simms, Robert	Simms, Nancy	29 AUG 1885	20	392
Simms, Robert F.	Keefe, May E.	26 OCT 1880 R	15	013
Simms, Rosa R.	Davis, William B.T.	19 OCT 1881	16	035
Simms, Rose	Bush, Arthur Augustus	08 SEP 1885 L	20	405
Simms, Samuel	Birch, Mary	10 JAN 1882	16	187
Simms, Samuel B.	Savage, Mary H.	18 NOV 1880 L	15	056
Simms, Simon	Armistead, Mary	27 OCT 1883 R	18	190
Simms, Susan I.	Buckland, Daniel	29 JUL 1878 L	12	151
Simms, Tyler Lindy	Mathews, Mary E.	11 DEC 1879	14	039
Simms, Wallace	Carroll, Lucy	03 JUN 1879	13	216
Simms, William	Cole, Canterbury	09 JUL 1879 R	13	277
Simms, William	Lyons, Emma	20 MAR 1882 L	16	284
Simms, Winnie	Herbert, Levi	20 DEC 1877 L	11	252
Simnacher, Adam	Loeffler, Annie Catharine	26 NOV 1884 L	19	414

Simonds, Anna M.	Griffin, Robert W.	24 NOV 1880 R	15	065
Simonds, Katie C.	Jones, Walter S.	18 DEC 1882 R	17	190
Simonds, Louisa	Davis, Henry	16 AUG 1880 L	14	401
Simonds, Margaret	Johnson, Henry	07 AUG 1880 L	14	392
Simonds, Mary A.H.	Darnall, Percival Y.	18 JUL 1880 R	14	365
Simons, Amanda J.	Leamon, Robert	23 MAR 1880 R	14	192
Simons, Bettie Lewis	Garrrison, John	12 JUL 1881 R	15	399
Simons, Francis	Douglass, Annie Rebecca	27 NOV 1879 R	14	009
Simons, Gaylord C.	Hobbs, Susan J.	20 JAN 1879 R	13	026
Simons, Henry A.	Emmerich, L. Blanche	20 FEB 1879	13	070
Simons, John T.	Russell, Mary V.	21 FEB 1882 L	16	255
Simons, Samuel H.	Ashford, Florence V.	06 MAY 1879 R	13	176
Simons, Walter H.	Mathews, Cornelia A.	09 DEC 1879 R	14	035
Simons, Wellington F.	Gough, Marietta	29 JAN 1884 L	18	399
Simonton, John P.	Joyce, Margaret A.	15 OCT 1879 R	13	423
Simpson, Adelaide H.	Walker, John H.	08 NOV 1880 R	15	036
Simpson, Alice	Johnson, Alonzo T.	07 DEC 1881 L	16	116
Simpson, Alice	Corry, Robert	29 MAR 1883 L	17	368
Simpson, Annie L.	Bond, Elmer H.	28 OCT 1884 L	19	341
Simpson, Bettie	Powell, Dallas	29 MAR 1882 R	16	293
Simpson, Celia	Brown, Samuel	09 JAN 1879 R	13	013
Simpson, Charity	Blackstone, Walter	21 JAN 1878 L	11	312
Simpson, Charles Washington	Detweiler, Ada	28 FEB 1883 R	17	324
Simpson, Charles Wm.	Sanders, Ann	08 JUN 1881 R	15	348
Simpson, Charlotte Ann	Tubman, Benjamin	01 MAY 1884 R	18	542
Simpson, Christopher H.	Simpson, Rosa W.	29 NOV 1883	18	289
Simpson, Ellsworth T.	Scrivener, Mamie C.	04 FEB 1885 L	20	051
Simpson, Elmer E.	Brown, Libbie G.	21 MAY 1884	19	031
Simpson, Emma J.	Troth, Horace E.	25 DEC 1879	14	074
Simpson, Etta	Lockwood, Robert M.	07 JUN 1878	12	087
Simpson, Fannie M.	Bender, Harry F.	01 AUG 1883	18	069
Simpson, George	Owens, Minnie	05 JUN 1884 R	19	054
Simpson, Henry B.	Johnson, Mary A.	31 DEC 1884 R	19	511
Simpson, Henry Kedglie	Gray, Mary Ella	23 APR 1884 R	18	530
Simpson, Henry T., Sq.	Smallwood, Hannah E.	03 DEC 1884 R	19	435
Simpson, James C.	Garland, Hattie E.	29 JAN 1883 L	17	276
Simpson, James T.	Allen, Elizabeth J.	03 SEP 1878	12	191
Simpson, Jennie	Swetnem, C.F.	21 APR 1885 R	20	180
Simpson, John	Maguire, Mary	25 NOV 1879 R	14	005
Simpson, Julia Elizabeth	Sands, Frederic Parker	19 NOV 1884 R	19	388
Simpson, Laurette	Chartters, William S.	31 MAY 1882	16	382
Simpson, Lillie	Ryon, Millard F.	07 FEB 1883	17	299
Simpson, Lloyd	Hill, Bettie	04 MAR 1880 R	14	174
Simpson, M. Addie	Martin, James, Jr.	08 NOV 1877	11	172
Simpson, Mary A.	Bubb, Frederick L.	10 JUL 1883	18	040
Simpson, Mary Elizabeth	Keating, Matthew	20 MAY 1880	14	274
Simpson, Mary Elizabeth	Hurdle, James Richard	25 AUG 1884 L	19	206
Simpson, Mary, Mrs.	Nolan, James	28 OCT 1878 R	12	241
Simpson, Mattie M.	Brown, Wilson E.	17 NOV 1879 R	13	490
Simpson, Nathaniel W.	Walstrum, Cora A.	28 MAR 1883 R	17	365
Simpson, Philip H., Jr.	Humphries, Kate F.	03 MAY 1882 L	16	346
Simpson, R. Louise	Cohen, William K.	17 JUN 1884	19	087
Simpson, Rosa W.	Simpson, Christopher H.	29 NOV 1883	18	289
Simpson, Silas E.	Fairfax, Susie C.	19 MAR 1883 R	17	351
Simpson, Theodore Henry	Tipton, Neenah	01 NOV 1878 R	12	303
Simpson, Thomas C.	Petrola, Celestia	23 NOV 1881	16	096
Simpson, W I.	Duvall, Lizzie	31 MAY 1881 R	15	333
Simpson, William Alex.	Moore, Sarah E.	14 APR 1880	14	222

Name	Spouse	Date	Vol	Page
Simpson, William G.	Horseman, Nettie	30 SEP 1882 R	17	044
Sims, Charles H.	Rogers, Laura	29 OCT 1878	12	295
Sims, Eudeliene A.	Mundy, Florence V.	09 NOV 1881 R	16	068
Sims, Frederick G.	Adams, Annie R.	16 JAN 1878	11	306
Sims, Henry	Bacon, Sarah	31 MAR 1879 L	13	119
Sims, Manuel	Wright, Agnes	24 APR 1879	13	158
Sims, Susan	Mitchel, Edwin	23 NOV 1878 L	12	343
Sims, Thomas J.	Towsey, Lula L.	13 MAY 1884	19	016
Sims, Thomas Judson	Graham, Matilda	25 MAR 1885 L	20	131
Simson, Jean E.C.	Suter, Charles E.	27 OCT 1877 R	11	158
Sincell, Emma Margaret	Crews, Enos	16 APR 1884 R	18	516
Sinclair, Fannie	Norton, William Henry	26 FEB 1882	16	259
Sinclair, Lucy	Hunter, George W.	21 MAY 1884 L	19	030
Sinclair, Mary J.	Milliken, N. Byron	05 MAY 1885	20	203
Sinclair, Walter F.	Simms, Addie C.	24 MAR 1880 R	14	191
Singer, Lina	Schlesinger, Samuel	15 JAN 1884 R	18	376
Singleton, Adelaide	Snowden, Norris	01 FEB 1884 L	18	404
Singleton, Hattie	Selden, George	04 FEB 1884	18	404
Singleton, Mariah	Chase, Joseph	15 MAY 1884 R	19	022
Singleton, Melda	Jenkins, Frederick	30 APR 1879 R	13	167
Singleton, William H.	Duvall, Ina N.	23 JUL 1885 R	20	338
Singlton, Fannie	Retrick, John	18 NOV 1884 R	19	390
Sink, Frederick	Napflie, Pauline	02 JUN 1883 R	17	452
Sinkfield, Emma L.	Sedgwick, Noah E.	19 NOV 1878 L	12	334
Sinkfield, Josephine	Martin, Mack	10 MAY 1883 L	17	433
Sinsheimer, Bertha	Jedel, Hyman	04 JUN 1878 R	12	081
Sinton, Esther	Fitzgerald, David	09 APR 1878	11	409
Sion, John H.	Garrison, Nettie	23 SEP 1885	20	436
Sioussa, John E.	Goddard, Maggie E.	22 DEC 1879 L	14	061
Sipe, Andrew Gibbon Corouther	Bosworth, Maria Ryan (Jones)	28 MAY 1883 R	17	464
Sipes, John H.	Hill, Eliza B.	15 JUN 1883 R	17	485
Siple, Maud Virginia	Slaven, Harry F.	14 APR 1885	20	100
Sirine, Fred'k E.	Dunlop, Florence	15 DEC 1883 L	18	321
Sirine, Frederick E.	Dunlop, Florence	16 DEC 1884	18	550
Sis, John H.	McPherson, Mary A.	27 JUL 1880	14	375
Sisco, Henrietta	Elliott, Josiah	09 OCT 1883 L	18	180
Sisk, James H.	Cockrell, Elnora	27 JAN 1885	20	040
Sisson, Armstead C.	Atkinson, Annie E.	15 MAY 1879 L	13	191
Sisson, Armstead C.	Ceas, Ella M.	07 JUN 1883 R	17	484
Sisson, Charlotte D.	Waters, Hugh	27 OCT 1881 R	16	047
Sisson, Harriet I.	Kelly, W.B.	19 NOV 1884 R	19	394
Sisson, Sallie	Taylor, James W.	21 DEC 1882 R	17	199
Sisson, Samuel	King, Gracie B.	27 AUG 1878 L	12	182
Skeel, Clarence M.	Townsend, Gertrude C.	20 JUN 1878	12	107
Skeel, Gertrude C.	Taylor, Russell B.	24 APR 1883	17	407
Skerrett, Annie Louise	Hullfish, Henry Augustus	18 APR 1883 R	17	398
Skerving, Anna M.	Mattingly, Orland F.	24 JUN 1885 R	20	291
Skidmore, Jarret F.	Maier, Katie	08 JAN 1880 R	14	095
Skidmore, John T.	Crowe, Sallie B.	10 NOV 1880 R	15	043
Skidmore, Mary	Carney, William	18 JAN 1883 L	17	267
Skidmore, Patrick H.	Butler, Mary A.	06 APR 1880 L	14	212
Skidmore, Samuel Charles	Hill, Henrietta	25 AUG 1880	14	415
Skillman, Bushrod W.	Lee, Lula J.	22 JUL 1879 R	13	287
Skillman, Sadie B.	Veirs, S.J.	11 DEC 1880 L	15	091
Skillman, Walter Lee	Sloper, Cornelia	06 MAY 1885	20	208
Skiner, Richard H.	Porter, Adeline	07 NOV 1878	12	316
Skinner, Ann M.	Watson, Robert W.	01 AUG 1880 R	14	379
Skinner, Annie	Ramsey, William	16 OCT 1883 R	18	175

Skinner, Annie D.	Moore, George D.	10 FEB 1879	13	045
Skinner, Charles	Brooks, Lovely	27 DEC 1877 L	11	275
Skinner, Charles L.	Sewell, Laura V.	31 DEC 1877	11	282
Skinner, Eustace J.	Elder, Maggie F.	26 JAN 1885 R	20	037
Skinner, Horan L.	Clark, C.J., Mrs.	10 NOV 1880	15	040
Skinner, James	Duckett, Dennis	11 DEC 1879 R	14	032
Skinner, Jane	Skinner, Mills	14 APR 1879 L	13	139
Skinner, John M.	Waters, Flora	12 NOV 1884 L	19	377
Skinner, Julia	Church, Charles D.	20 APR 1880	14	229
Skinner, Laura V.	Cox, James L.	28 JUL 1881 R	15	421
Skinner, Maggie	Morgan, John	11 DEC 1883	18	309
Skinner, Martha M.	Paine, Henry C.	11 MAR 1884 L	18	465
Skinner, Mary A.	Harbin, John H.	29 DEC 1884 R	19	499
Skinner, Mills	Skinner, Jane	14 APR 1879 L	13	139
Skinner, Miriam	Fugitt, Eugene	18 JAN 1885	20	025
Skinner, Roswell M.	Wheeler, Laura V.	24 APR 1878	12	021
Skinner, Sarah Ann	Mosby, Joseph	28 DEC 1882 R	17	213
Skinner, Sylvester	Scroggin, Catherine	13 AUG 1878	12	166
Skinner, Thomas E.	Gass, Georgeanna D.	08 APR 1884	18	501
Skinner, William L.	Cherry, Susan M.	23 MAY 1878 L	12	064
Skippon, Alice V.	Scott, Alexander	03 SEP 1878 L	12	194
Skirving, Carrie T.	Paxson, Westwood F.	15 FEB 1881 R	15	190
Slack, Harriet Addie	Perrine, Lewis, Jr.	05 DEC 1883	18	293
Slack, Lizzie H.	Harrison, Edward M.	28 FEB 1883 R	17	326
Slack, Olivia M.	Havener, Marion I.	03 JAN 1883	17	234
Slack, Thomas A.	Washington, Mary	03 DEC 1877 L	11	216
Slacum, Novella	Hough, Samuel J.	01 MAY 1883 R	17	424
Slade, Francis H.	Strong, Amelia M.	06 MAY 1880	14	253
Slade, Jesse B.	Carter, Sarah A.	17 MAR 1881 L	15	230
Slade, Laura E.	Thomas, George Robert	16 SEP 1885 L	20	423
Slade, Roman	Powell, Alice	05 JUL 1884	19	123
Slaich, Lina Louisa	Lentz, Gustav Franc	25 APR 1880 R	14	236
Slaker, Adam	Sprigg, Ada Russell	30 DEC 1879 R	14	077
Slater, Catherine	Commodore, Holdsworth	28 JUL 1881 R	15	418
Slater, Effie L.	Hickman, Etchison H.	06 OCT 1885 R	20	458
Slater, Emanuel	Norris, Louisa	16 SEP 1884	19	248
Slater, James W. [John]	Bowman, Emma	02 APR 1878 R	11	401
Slater, Jeremiah	Watkins, Mary	29 MAY 1880 R	14	295
Slater, John W.	Brown, F. Oskie	20 OCT 1882 L	17	083
Slater, Mary	Reed, William	14 MAR 1878	11	380
Slater, Stephen	Colbert, Lizzie	12 JUN 1884 R	19	025
Slater, Thomas	Payne, Margaret	06 MAY 1879 L	13	176
Slater, William C.	Hines, Ellen	24 SEP 1878	12	232
Slater, Wm. P.	Emmerman, Mary	17 NOV 1877 R	11	191
Slattery, Daniel	Burns, Mary Ann	02 OCT 1877 L	11	118
Slauder, Burgess	Johnson, Eva	23 JAN 1884 L	18	390
Slaughter, Cain	Markes, Lucy	19 DEC 1883	18	327
Slaughter, Daniel	Thomas, Lucy	18 AUG 1884	19	191
Slaughter, Edward	John, Martha Pry	12 MAY 1881 R	15	304
Slaughter, Emma	Walker, John	01 SEP 1878	12	188
Slaughter, John	Taylor, Mary	17 APR 1879 R	13	151
Slaughter, Louisa	Ringgold, John	04 DEC 1879 R	14	030
Slaughter, Louisa	Hanson, James	04 OCT 1883	18	168
Slaughter, Lucy	Washington, Burrell	08 DEC 1884 L	19	440
Slaughter, Martha A.	Smith, William H.	15 APR 1878 R	12	003
Slaughter, Sophie C.	Robinson, Lucian D.	13 NOV 1883 R	18	247
Slaughter, William	Douglass, Jane	23 JUN 1881 L	15	377
Slaven, Harry F.	Siple, Maud Virginia	14 APR 1885	20	163

Slee, Robert H.S.	Barnett, Lou M.	25 NOV 1881 R	16	099
Sleigh, Hannah Putnam	Frey, Isacac	05 JUN 1883 R	17	474
Slentz, Lillie E.	Parkhurst, Benjamin	16 SEP 1884 L	19	250
Slick, John E.	Bowles, Otella A.	31 JAN 1878 R	11	323
Slick, John E.	Clark, Rosa	30 NOV 1881	16	104
Slingerland, E.J.	Gant, Ellen	15 AUG 1878	12	168
Slingland, Hester E.	Wood, Robert H.	14 SEP 1882 L	17	020
Sloan, John	Chenoweth, Elizabeth Crawford	14 NOV 1881 R	16	073
Sloane, John	Burkins, Catherine	20 OCT 1881 L	16	038
Sloane, Mary S.	Gist, George W.	29 MAY 1878	12	076
Sloper, Cornelia	Skillman, Walter Lee	06 MAY 1885	20	208
Slosson, Irene	Donaldson, Walter Alexander	08 FEB 1882 R	16	231
Slough, Sarah A.	Magruder, John H.	16 OCT 1882	17	071
Sluper, Bertha J.	Burch, George Robert	26 NOV 1884 R	19	404
Slye, John A.	Coleman, Adele A.	15 MAY 1884 L	19	024
Slye, William W.	Redmines, Kate	27 OCT 1881 R	16	047
Slyer, Ella Virginia	Duvall, Emelius Lafere	27 FEB 1879 R	13	081
Smackum, Emma Jane	Johnson, William T.	30 OCT 1879 R	13	432
Smackum, John P.	Dent, Georgie	28 NOV 1878 R	12	350
Smackum, John T.	Callaman, Frances M.	13 DEC 1883 L	18	317
Small, Charles H.	Morland, Laura	02 JUL 1882	16	427
Small, Emma Frances	Cahill, Patrick	28 JUN 1879 R	13	240
Small, Georgie A.	Haynes, George A.	16 JUN 1883 R	17	497
Small, John Henry, Jr.	Ruff, Miriam E.	11 OCT 1882 R	17	064
Small, Joseph Edward	Brown, Martha Louisa	08 NOV 1882 R	17	118
Small, Reuben A.	Douglass, Isabella V.	03 JAN 1883	17	235
Smallwood, Annie J.	Kerper, William D.	28 OCT 1880 L	15	019
Smallwood, Annie L.	Welch, John H.	13 JAN 1885 L	20	014
Smallwood, Benjamin Franklin	Owings, Lizzie Mortimer Craabster	05 DEC 1878 R	12	368
Smallwood, Cornelia F.	Hickman, Lewis W.	27 FEB 1884	18	447
Smallwood, Hannah E.	Simpson, Henry T., Sq.	03 DEC 1884 R	19	435
Smallwood, Howard	Dominee, Alice	30 JAN 1884 R	18	397
Smallwood, James	James, Amanda	02 AUG 1879 L	13	304
Smallwood, John T.	Carroll, Harriet L.	30 OCT 1884	19	349
Smallwood, Joseph A.	Grier, Sarah (Robinson)	27 DEC 1881 R	16	145
Smallwood, Joseph H.	Crier, Sarah	25 DEC 1882 L	17	209
Smallwood, Lovina	Cole, Jeremiah	13 NOV 1879 L	13	482
Smallwood, Mary	Johnson, Peter	17 SEP 1882 L	17	003
Smallwood, Mary E.	Webster, Frederick T.	27 APR 1885 L	20	191
Smallwood, Mary Jane	Key, Gillis	06 FEB 1882 L	16	227
Smallwood, Mary R.	Stohbel, Charles H.	05 APR 1879 R	13	129
Smallwood, Nettie	Johnson, Henry	19 AUG 1880 R	14	405
Smallwood, Philipp S.W.	Parker, Emma J.	19 DEC 1883	18	327
Smallwood, Richard Lydstone	Newton, May Ellis	27 NOV 1883	18	278
Smallwood, Sarah S.	Gaither, Harry	24 DEC 1884 L	19	484
Smallwood, Theresa	Hyson, Frank	01 JAN 1880 R	14	085
Smallwood, Thomas	Taylor, Elizabeth E.	23 MAY 1883	17	458
Smallwood, William	Dyson, Mary A.	05 SEP 1877 R	11	077
Smallwood, William	Scott, Mary	23 JUN 1878 R	12	098
Smallwood, William	Jenkins, Annie	05 MAR 1885 R	20	082
Smallwood, William H.	Honesty, Martha Celina	13 NOV 1884 L	19	379
Smallwood, Wm. Henry	Brown, Mary	05 AUG 1880 L	14	388
Smallwood, Wm. Henry	Tyler, Susie	05 OCT 1881 R	16	009
Smart, Alice	Holmes, Charles	08 JUL 1878 R	12	126
Smart, Frank	Jenkins, Susan	24 DEC 1879 R	14	070
Smart, John H.	Tubmon, Ella	13 DEC 1883 L	18	315
Smart, John Pearson	Hicks, Ida Matilda	19 JAN 1882 R	16	201
Smart, William E.	Tidmarsh, Sarah E.	25 OCT 1883 R	18	210

Smellie, Robert	Hogan, Fannie Austin	23 DEC 1877 R	11	258
Smeltzer, Nora B.	Mobley, Howard S.	04 MAR 1884	18	456
Smetnam, Mary E.	Burke, George H.	12 DEC 1883	18	311
Smiles, James	Gibson, Hattie E.	14 NOV 1881 R	16	067
Smiley, William F.	Mitchell, Catharine	01 APR 1884 R	18	490
Smilie, C.C.	Fortune, T.T.	21 FEB 1878 L	11	353
Smith, A. Thomas	Mason, Lula S.	08 OCT 1884	19	287
Smith, Abram M.	Haskins, Susie A.	21 DEC 1881 L	16	149
Smith, Ada C. (Squires)	Leonard, William H.	29 APR 1885 R	20	192
Smith, Addie C.	Geckel, Peter	07 APR 1879	13	129
Smith, Adeline	Matthews, Henry	09 AUG 1879 R	13	311
Smith, Adolphus B.	Kraft, Louise C.	24 NOV 1880 L	15	064
Smith, Aggie E.	Jackson, D.B.	18 JUN 1883 L	17	499
Smith, Agnes	Webb, Henry L.	19 SEP 1878 L	12	228
Smith, Albert	Nelson, Lucy	28 AUG 1879 R	13	332
Smith, Albert	Murray, Annie O.	12 OCT 1881	16	003
Smith, Albert	Berry, Mary	19 SEP 1883 R	18	142
Smith, Albert	Chum, Florence	24 DEC 1884 L	19	489
Smith, Albert L.	Thompson, A.F.	21 MAR 1881 L	15	232
Smith, Alexander	Baker, Louisa	18 AUG 1881 L	15	451
Smith, Alfred	Levy, Bettie	01 MAR 1883 L	17	330
Smith, Alice	Plato, William	05 DEC 1883	18	294
Smith, Alice	Jackson, Randolph	22 MAY 1884	19	034
Smith, Amand	Pryer, John W.	27 DEC 1883 L	18	347
Smith, Ambrose	Simms, Mary	22 DEC 1880	15	116
Smith, Amelia	Price, William	25 APR 1878 R	12	017
Smith, Amelia	Butler, George W.	15 JAN 1879 L	13	021
Smith, Amelia Jones, Mrs.	Clements, Joseph C.	12 APR 1881 R	15	255
Smith, Andrew Washington	Rogers, Harriet, Mrs.	07 JUN 1879 R	13	135
Smith, Anna	Datcher, Thomas Henry	31 DEC 1881 R	16	171
Smith, Anna Deroy	Wetmore, Charles A.	05 APR 1879 R	13	128
Smith, Anna E.	Jackson, Richard J.	03 OCT 1878	12	254
Smith, Annie	Hellmuth, Martin	09 JUL 1878	12	112
Smith, Annie	Smith, Henry	13 SEP 1878 L	12	217
Smith, Annie	Davis, Samuel	16 NOV 1882	17	132
Smith, Annie	Streets, Forrest	23 DEC 1882 L	17	208
Smith, Annie	Hoppkins, Moses	12 NOV 1883 R	18	248
Smith, Annie	Morris, John	17 NOV 1884 L	19	387
Smith, Annie	Winston, Albert	19 MAR 1884 L	18	477
Smith, Annie E.	Leigh, Lewis C.	15 AUG 1878	12	169
Smith, Annie F.	Chandler, Oliver M.	09 APR 1878	11	416
Smith, Annie T.K.	Condon, Edward M.	10 SEP 1880 R	14	440
Smith, Annie V.	Ceiss, John L.	03 NOV 1882	17	110
Smith, Annie Virginia	Washington, James E.	14 JUN 1880 R	14	318
Smith, Arthur B.	Taylor, Lillie A.	17 DEC 1879 R	14	051
Smith, Arthur G.	Humes, Ida	01 MAY 1878 L	12	033
Smith, Artie	Swales, George W.	30 NOV 1882	17	162
Smith, Barbara	Burke, Lawrence W.	22 MAY 1879 L	13	201
Smith, Barbara E.	Smith, John	10 SEP 1879	13	351
Smith, Barney	Johnson, Alice	05 AUG 1880 L	14	389
Smith, Belle W.	Kelly, Thomas S.	07 JUL 1879 R	13	270
Smith, Benjamin	Champ, Isabella	25 JUL 1877 L	11	031
Smith, Benjamin F.	Norcom, Fanny E.	02 OCT 1877 R	11	117
Smith, Benjamin F.	Bond, Emma L.	20 JUN 1883	18	001
Smith, Bertha	Gray, James	05 MAR 1883	17	321
Smith, C.B.	Maryman, Annie I.	21 AUG 1884 L	19	199
Smith, Carrie L.	Brent, William H.	04 AUG 1881	15	420
Smith, Catherine	Serra, Henry A.	17 APR 1878 R	12	008

Smith, Catherine	Brooks, James	02 AUG 1883	18	067
Smith, Charles	Homes, Frances	25 FEB 1879 L	13	078
Smith, Charles	Myers, Alice	10 JUN 1879 R	13	223
Smith, Charles	Smith, Mary	30 JUN 1884	19	108
Smith, Charles A.	Kinsey, Laura A.	10 MAR 1881 R	15	222
Smith, Charles B.	Harris, Mamie M.	06 SEP 1882 R	17	009
Smith, Charles Carrington	Howard, Mary A.	21 AUG 1878 R	12	175
Smith, Charles Coltman	Dangler, Susie Lovina	19 MAY 1885 R	20	229
Smith, Charles H.	Lipphard, Nellie	09 OCT 1885	20	457
Smith, Charles Harrison	Simmons, Eliza Ellen	19 DEC 1880 R	15	110
Smith, Charles T.	Kearon, Annie	24 JUN 1880 R	14	333
Smith, Charles W.	Cumberland, Mary Frances	26 MAY 1879 R	13	204
Smith, Charles W.	Beetly, Mary M.	08 JUL 1880 R	14	353
Smith, Charley	Wilkerson, Sarah	19 DEC 1878	12	390
Smith, Charlotte	Hayden, Andrew	04 OCT 1880 R	14	469
Smith, Clarence B.	Cronin, Katie A.	15 OCT 1881 L	16	027
Smith, Clarendon	Overall, Lena	25 AUG 1880 R	14	414
Smith, Cora	Shaw, Wesley	13 OCT 1881 R	16	021
Smith, Cornelia	Tyler, Robert	12 SEP 1881	15	482
Smith, Cynthia	Moulton, Henry	17 JUL 1879 L	13	284
Smith, Daisy Ethelberta	Alexander, Chas. Wm.	05 OCT 1885 R	20	456
Smith, Daniel	Stuart, Jeannett	19 FEB 1883 R	17	305
Smith, Daniel	Tabb, Belle	27 JUL 1885 L	20	342
Smith, David	Williams, Emma	03 APR 1883 L	17	376
Smith, David R.	Harris, Emma C.	31 DEC 1882 R	17	227
Smith, Dolly	Brown, Lewis	14 AUG 1882	14	019
Smith, Dorothea	Dunlap, Leander	23 DEC 1880 R	15	118
Smith, E.G.	Bayliss, C.B.	20 JUN 1882	16	419
Smith, Edmond F.	Browning, Mary E.	11 FEB 1884 R	18	413
Smith, Edward	Woods, Sarah	18 DEC 1877 R	11	244
Smith, Edward	Gant, Mary Anne	07 OCT 1878	12	255
Smith, Edward	Owens, Annie	16 MAY 1879 L	13	103
Smith, Edward	Dotry, Annie	13 NOV 1883 L	18	250
Smith, Edward	Bolling, Alice	16 JAN 1884 L	18	382
Smith, Edward	Proctor, Virginia	23 OCT 1884 L	19	334
Smith, Edward H.	Sherick, Sadie M.	28 AUG 1884	19	214
Smith, Edward S.	Ray, Alverta	16 NOV 1881 L	16	081
Smith, Elias	Braxton, Annie	04 OCT 1884 L	19	285
Smith, Elijah	Robertson, Agnes	15 OCT 1877	11	136
Smith, Elisa Bell	McKeever, Edwin K.	16 OCT 1884	19	312
Smith, Eliza	Page, Junius	01 MAR 1879 L	13	085
Smith, Eliza	Churchwell, Elias	12 DEC 1882	17	176
Smith, Elizabeth	Brown, John	21 DEC 1877 R	11	256
Smith, Elizabeth	Kuebuer, Richard	17 OCT 1878 R	12	270
Smith, Elizabeth	Lee, Thomas	10 SEP 1878 L	12	208
Smith, Elizabeth	Sullivan, Fielding F.	18 AUG 1881 L	15	454
Smith, Elizabeth	Sewall, Columbus	26 APR 1883 L	17	413
Smith, Elizabeth	Brown, John	18 MAR 1884 R	18	468
Smith, Elizabeth	Lee, John	28 FEB 1884 R	18	448
Smith, Elizabeth B.	McIntyre, Robert	20 MAY 1881 L	15	319
Smith, Elizabeth C.	Ricketts, William	09 NOV 1881 R	16	069
Smith, Ella	Johnson, James Henry	16 FEB 1883 L	17	310
Smith, Ella	Tubman, William K.	11 DEC 1883	18	307
Smith, Ellen	Shields, William H.	20 JUL 1878 R	12	147
Smith, Ellen	Turner, John	04 SEP 1879 L	13	352
Smith, Ellen	Powell, Edward	23 JUN 1880 L	14	331
Smith, Ellen	Jackson, A.D.	03 MAY 1881 L	15	290
Smith, Ellen M.	Hempstone, Snowden Lee	28 DEC 1880	15	124

D.C. Marriage Records Index, June 28, 1877 to October 19, 1885   423

Name	Spouse	Date	Vol	Page
Smith, Ellenora C.	Linthicum, George F.	16 APR 1879 R	13	140
Smith, Emeline Franter	Evans, Richard Penhallow	15 JUN 1880 R	14	322
Smith, Emma	Laney, John	22 MAR 1878 L	11	390
Smith, Emma	Johnson, Birl	24 JAN 1879 R	13	026
Smith, Emma	Pryor, Robert	31 MAR 1879	13	119
Smith, Emma	Williams, John	27 DEC 1881 L	16	163
Smith, Emma	Davis, George	02 JUL 1883 L	18	029
Smith, Emma	White, Samuel Ambrose	21 NOV 1883 R	18	263
Smith, Emma	Carroll, Wesley	05 FEB 1885	20	053
Smith, Emma E.	Denning, James L.	03 APR 1884 L	18	495
Smith, Emma J.	Jones, William H.	24 DEC 1884 R	19	486
Smith, Emma Lee	Dempsey, Joseph A.	08 SEP 1885 R	20	261
Smith, Enoch	Greenleaf, Betsy	15 FEB 1882 L	16	243
Smith, Ephraim	Moffitt, Maggie C.	26 AUG 1884	19	189
Smith, Etta	Taylor, Gabriel	02 JAN 1879	13	003
Smith, Eugene S.	Johnson, Lenorah	24 DEC 1884 L	19	489
Smith, Eulalie	Harper, William Mercer	25 JAN 1881 R	15	163
Smith, Eveline	Johnson, Benjamin	16 DEC 1878 R	12	380
Smith, Evelyn B.	Davis, Sandy A.	11 DEC 1884 R	19	449
Smith, Fannie E.	Cady, William R.	13 JAN 1881	15	149
Smith, Fannie V.	Tilghman, James H.	05 DEC 1878	12	369
Smith, Fanny F.	Williams, David G.	25 MAR 1885 R	20	131
Smith, Frances	Lewis, James	17 FEB 1882 L	16	247
Smith, Frances A.	Ross, Charles H.	20 JAN 1885	20	026
Smith, Francis E.	Stack, Annie T.	17 MAY 1883 L	17	449
Smith, Francis Littruite	Walker, Rose	05 JUN 1882 R	16	390
Smith, Frank	Parr, Mary C.	16 OCT 1878 R	12	244
Smith, Frank	Jenkins, Annie E.	22 OCT 1878	12	285
Smith, Frank	Johnson, Jennie	02 NOV 1881	16	058
Smith, Frank	Grice, Arie	20 MAR 1882 L	16	283
Smith, Frank	Williams, Mary E.	16 MAR 1882 L	16	280
Smith, Frank B.	Dyer, Grace King	25 NOV 1880 R	15	067
Smith, Frank H.	Koontz, Olivia W.	27 AUG 1884 L	19	209
Smith, Frank St. C.	Clarke, Daisy Octavia	08 NOV 1882 R	17	116
Smith, Fred	Briscoe, Henrietta	20 JUN 1881 L	15	368
Smith, Fred Percy	Dove, Lida Lawrence	25 NOV 1884 R	19	406
Smith, Geo. W.	Graves, Mary E.	02 NOV 1879 R	13	459
Smith, George	Boon, Emma	04 SEP 1878 L	12	199
Smith, George	Steward, Anna	20 NOV 1878	12	339
Smith, George	Connor, Susan	31 MAY 1879	13	206
Smith, George	Ganzhoon, Lizzie	11 DEC 1883	18	309
Smith, George	Linch, Julia	03 SEP 1885 L	20	397
Smith, George B.	Dickson, Lettie	02 JUN 1880	14	302
Smith, George B.	Tenley, Josephine	15 DEC 1881 R	16	133
Smith, George B.	Wane, Lucy C.	25 OCT 1884 R	19	338
Smith, George C.	Sewell, Mary	04 JUL 1885	20	295
Smith, George E.	Allen, Mary E.	12 JUL 1881	15	398
Smith, George Edward	Ward, Mary	13 NOV 1884 L	19	378
Smith, George F.	Thour, Elizabeth	04 SEP 1879 L	13	349
Smith, George N.R.	Cooper, Mary Ann	09 AUG 1880 L	14	394
Smith, George P., Jr.	Erpenbeck, Katharine	28 JUL 1880 R	14	376
Smith, George W.	Price, Fannie F.	22 NOV 1877 L	11	198
Smith, George W.	Crouch, Margaret	20 JUN 1878	12	106
Smith, George W.	Mellny, Kate M.	02 JUL 1879 R	13	265
Smith, Georgiana	Austin, Samuel M.	17 DEC 1879 L	14	052
Smith, Georgianna	Adams, Samuel W.	16 NOV 1882	17	133
Smith, Gertrude Frazier	Castello, Dan, Jr.	10 OCT 1883 L	18	183
Smith, Hamilton	Tolliver, Millie	12 JAN 1882 R	16	193

Smith, Hannah	Goings, Lewis	26 NOV 1884 L	19	417
Smith, Harriet	Rofe, Wyatt	22 AUG 1878 R	12	175
Smith, Harriet A.	Humphreys, Lee	28 JUN 1883 R	18	023
Smith, Harrison	Posey, Annie	02 MAY 1878 R	12	034
Smith, Harry Burton	Cocke, Grace Russell	10 APR 1882 R	16	307
Smith, Hartway	Harris, Viola	12 JUN 1884	19	080
Smith, Hattie	Gales, Everett	17 JAN 1885 L	20	024
Smith, Hattie Estelle	Grose, Daniel Charles	25 MAY 1881 R	15	326
Smith, Helen	Fenton, Joseph B.	01 MAR 1881 R	15	206
Smith, Helen	Clark, Joseph	06 APR 1885	20	147
Smith, Hellen J.	Sasscer, Riley E.	18 JUL 1882	16	449
Smith, Henry	Brooks, Annie	20 DEC 1877 R	11	252
Smith, Henry	Smith, Annie	13 SEP 1878 L	12	217
Smith, Henry	Eldridge, Nellie	26 DEC 1878 R	12	395
Smith, Henry	O'Neal, Mary Ellen	22 AUG 1881 L	15	455
Smith, Henry	Marshall, Julia	14 DEC 1881 L	16	132
Smith, Henry	Brooks, Mary	19 MAY 1884 R	19	028
Smith, Henry	Jackson, Lucy J.	30 AUG 1885 L	20	391
Smith, Henry F.	Crawford, Carrie R.	13 MAR 1879 R	13	101
Smith, Henry H.	Tramble, Mary Virginia	03 AUG 1881 L	15	431
Smith, Henry M.	O'Neil, Julia C.	17 FEB 1878	11	344
Smith, Henry Randolph	Foster, Flora	16 OCT 1883 R	18	196
Smith, Henson	Coleman, Julia	25 DEC 1884 R	19	479
Smith, Hillary	Taylor, Jennie	13 JUL 1881 L	15	399
Smith, Hillary	Baskerville, Ada V.	12 JAN 1885 R	20	013
Smith, Hodena	Blantaker, Lewis	24 DEC 1879 L	14	068
Smith, Hugh M.	Wood, Louisa	23 JUN 1885	20	285
Smith, Ida May	Causten, George P.	24 OCT 1878	12	289
Smith, Isabella	Sorrell, John W.	26 FEB 1878 L	11	359
Smith, Isadore M.	Thurston, John H.	19 FEB 1878	11	346
Smith, J. Clement	Morrill, Mary J.	12 JUN 1880 R	14	317
Smith, J. Curtis	Schreiner, Mary K.	24 DEC 1884	19	491
Smith, J.E.	Thorn, Cora V.	27 FEB 1884	18	443
Smith, J.G.	Taylor, E.J.	21 NOV 1883	18	269
Smith, J.P.	Padgett, M.M.	02 JAN 1878	11	289
Smith, J.W.	Welsh, Kate A.	20 JUN 1882 L	16	421
Smith, Jacob	Gordon, Ellen	30 OCT 1879 L	13	456
Smith, Jacob	Jones, Susan	27 NOV 1883 L	18	279
Smith, Jacob C.	Thompson, Catherine	11 NOV 1881 L	16	072
Smith, James	Holmes, Maggie	20 NOV 1877 L	11	195
Smith, James	Jones, Alice	02 JUN 1878	12	077
Smith, James	Strickhardt, Wilhelmina	01 SEP 1878	12	187
Smith, James	Harley, Lizzie	21 JUL 1885 R	20	327
Smith, James	Dorsey, Isabella	06 OCT 1885 L	20	462
Smith, James A.	Green, Marion C.	22 MAY 1879 L	13	202
Smith, James C.	Owens, Lula V.	17 MAY 1881 L	15	313
Smith, James E.	Schissler, Laura A.	10 JAN 1883 R	17	242
Smith, James H.	Hunter, Hattie J.	24 SEP 1883 R	18	150
Smith, James H.	Craig, Josephine	23 DEC 1884 R	19	444
Smith, James H.	Lee, Louisa A.	30 APR 1885 R	20	191
Smith, James Henry	Fox, Ella Leonora	15 DEC 1884 R	19	459
Smith, James Moncure	Rust, Ella	26 APR 1881 R	15	272
Smith, James Nelson	Ames, Rosa	05 AUG 1879 L	13	306
Smith, James O.	Norton, Emma	08 AUG 1881	15	415
Smith, James S.F.	Hodson, Lizzie A.	03 MAR 1881	15	211
Smith, James T.	Clarke, Addie	08 JUN 1884	19	065
Smith, Jane	Latnee, Lewis H.	03 OCT 1882	17	050
Smith, Jane E.	Scott, Isaac W.	08 OCT 1883 R	18	177

D.C. Marriage Records Index, June 28, 1877 to October 19, 1885   425

Smith, Jay B.	Farnsworth, Wealthey A.	14 DEC 1880	15	096
Smith, Jennie Eliza	Padgett, Charles Logan	18 FEB 1879 R	13	066
Smith, Jennie H.	Benter, Maximillian A.	10 APR 1883 R	17	388
Smith, Jeremiah	Banks, Nellie I.	25 MAR 1880	14	197
Smith, Jerry	Williams, Mary	17 AUG 1881 L	15	450
Smith, Jesse	Lyles, Agnes	10 FEB 1885 L	20	062
Smith, Jesse A.	Koontz, Margaret L.	24 SEP 1878	12	230
Smith, Jesse T.	Hopkins, Utah E.	02 APR 1885 R	20	141
Smith, John	Johnson, Sarah	28 NOV 1877 L	11	207
Smith, John	Johnson, Nancy	01 JUL 1878 R	12	113
Smith, John	Thornton, Ann	04 JUN 1879 L	13	219
Smith, John	Smith, Barbara E.	10 SEP 1879	13	351
Smith, John	Berry, Annie	30 JUN 1881 R	15	316
Smith, John	Corbley, Mary	14 JUN 1881 L	15	358
Smith, John	Allen, Mary E.	29 JUN 1882 R	16	431
Smith, John Condit	Swearingen, Sarah Henderson	15 MAY 1883 R	17	438
Smith, John Edward	Minor, Allena	06 APR 1884 R	18	497
Smith, John F.	Gieseke, Emilie	14 SEP 1880 R	14	443
Smith, John F.	Taylor, Isabella	07 FEB 1884	18	414
Smith, John G.	Eckert, Lizzie E.	08 JUL 1885 L	20	317
Smith, John H.	Turner, Eliza Ann	16 APR 1880	14	221
Smith, John H.	Jackson, Mary Elizabeth	20 DEC 1882 L	17	198
Smith, John H.P.	Homer, Lizzie L.	07 JUN 1884	19	067
Smith, John James	Washington, Lavinia	17 DEC 1883 L	18	320
Smith, John Michael	Welsh, Ella Teresa	14 APR 1882 L	16	316
Smith, John Phillip	Gibson, Julia Ann	03 JUL 1878 R	12	122
Smith, John T.	Faunce, Mary A.	19 MAR 1883 L	17	349
Smith, John W.	Rixey, Eugenia A.	05 FEB 1884 R	18	409
Smith, John W.H.	Bruce, Katie	08 APR 1880 R	14	217
Smith, Jordan	Ball, Henrietta	19 MAR 1879 R	13	103
Smith, Joseph	Wren, Dora	06 NOV 1881	16	034
Smith, Joseph	Booth, Elizabeth	28 NOV 1883 L	18	283
Smith, Joseph H.	Mosby, Frances	09 AUG 1877 L	11	049
Smith, Joseph T.	Acton, Josephine	05 JUN 1884 L	19	064
Smith, Josephine	Thompson, George	21 JUL 1879 R	13	284
Smith, Josephine	Douglass, William Edw.	05 JUL 1881	15	389
Smith, Josephine	Holland, Daniel	29 NOV 1882 L	17	161
Smith, Julia	Lewis, John	28 JAN 1880 L	14	124
Smith, Julia	Morris, William H.	09 MAY 1884 L	19	013
Smith, Julia	Morris, Thornton	26 NOV 1884	19	414
Smith, Julius K.	Squires, Rose J.	09 APR 1885 R	20	158
Smith, Katie W.	Godey, Edward	03 DEC 1878 R	12	361
Smith, Laura	Gross, Soloman	10 SEP 1877 R	11	083
Smith, Laura Virginia	Pierce, James Edward	23 OCT 1877 R	11	150
Smith, Laura Virginia	Polen, William H.	28 MAR 1882 R	16	291
Smith, Lena	Crewe, John	07 DEC 1881 L	16	119
Smith, Lena	Crandall, Milton R.	14 APR 1885 L	20	164
Smith, Lena Grace	Morrow, George T., Jr.	15 JUN 1885 L	20	275
Smith, Leonard Tauben	Rithmiller, Mary	24 APR 1878	12	017
Smith, Lewis	Brown, Fannie	07 AUG 1880	14	392
Smith, Lewis	Bowen, Mary	31 MAR 1884 R	30	7296
Smith, Lewis H.	Dutch, Martha	05 MAR 1884 R	18	458
Smith, Lillie	Carter, Harrison	02 JUN 1884	19	048
Smith, Lillie E.	Allen, Marcellus	26 MAR 1885 R	20	133
Smith, Lizzie	Johnson, Alexander	10 APR 1878 R	11	413
Smith, Lizzie	Edwards, George	27 SEP 1883	18	159
Smith, Lizzie	Walker, George W.	18 DEC 1883 L	18	323
Smith, Lizzie	Kemp, Solomon	25 JUN 1885 R	20	288

Smith, Lizzie M.	Barnhouse, Isaac P.	30 JAN 1878	11	322
Smith, Lloyd	Wilkes, Catherine	05 JUL 1882 L	16	438
Smith, Louise G.	Rogers, William E.	20 OCT 1882 L	17	083
Smith, Lucinda	Brown, Richard	05 OCT 1882 R	17	056
Smith, Lucy	Watson, Frank	18 AUG 1881 R	15	452
Smith, Lucy	Gray, Robert	05 FEB 1885 L	20	053
Smith, Lucy Ann	Rigney, Charles Wesley	10 DEC 1884	19	448
Smith, Lucy W.	Brown, Robert	22 JAN 1885 R	20	028
Smith, M.	Preston, Samuel	18 JUL 1881	15	395
Smith, Maggie E.	Martin, George E.	21 JAN 1880	14	116
Smith, Maggie E.	Johnson, Joseph H., Jr.	20 SEP 1883 R	18	143
Smith, Maggie L.	Atkinson, Elmer E.	06 MAR 1880 L	14	179
Smith, Maggie Lee	Fryatt, Henry Clay	22 MAY 1882 R	16	368
Smith, Malvina	Crawford, William	05 MAR 1883 L	17	332
Smith, Manuel	Henderson, Luvenia	22 SEP 1878 R	12	172
Smith, Marandar C.	Bailey, James E.	27 OCT 1880	14	123
Smith, Margaret	Somerville, Ezekiel	02 APR 1881	15	244
Smith, Margaret Ann	Bock, Henry Michael	28 MAR 1880 R	14	199
Smith, Margaret E.	Lepley, William H.	11 JAN 1883	17	248
Smith, Maria	Jackson, Thomas	22 AUG 1878 R	12	176
Smith, Maria	Taplin, James	25 NOV 1884 L	19	407
Smith, Marion T.	Lee, George H.	22 DEC 1877 R	11	247
Smith, Marshall L.	Archer, Agnes L.	07 OCT 1884 L	19	291
Smith, Martha	Jacobs, Norman	07 OCT 1882 R	17	059
Smith, Martha	Carter, James	17 MAY 1883 R	17	448
Smith, Mary	Quinn, William	17 SEP 1877 L	11	096
Smith, Mary	Twine, James	02 SEP 1879	13	346
Smith, Mary	Haynes, Henry	16 FEB 1880	14	155
Smith, Mary	Moncue, Scott	06 DEC 1881 L	16	115
Smith, Mary	Nokes, George T.	31 OCT 1882 R	17	102
Smith, Mary	Parker, Albert	04 OCT 1883 L	18	171
Smith, Mary	Smith, Charles	30 JUN 1884	19	108
Smith, Mary C.	Scott, Wilfred	09 AUG 1877 R	11	043
Smith, Mary E.	Jones, George A.	29 JAN 1878	11	320
Smith, Mary E.	Brooks, Alex. H.	06 MAY 1880 R	14	255
Smith, Mary E.	Campbell, Moses Alexa.	04 MAY 1885 L	20	204
Smith, Mary Ellen	Fisher, John Henry	08 DEC 1881 R	16	120
Smith, Mary Frances	Carter, John Wesley	04 OCT 1880 L	14	473
Smith, Mary Frances	Simmons, Robert B.	15 SEP 1880 R	14	442
Smith, Mary G.	Strother, Robert J.	21 MAR 1882 L	16	285
Smith, Mary J.	Bradley, George W.	25 OCT 1882	17	094
Smith, Mary J.E.	Hardister, James A.	22 SEP 1880 L	14	455
Smith, Mary Jane	Jones, Nelson	25 MAY 1881	15	325
Smith, Mary Jane	Sellman, Frank B.	04 DEC 1884 R	19	427
Smith, Mary L.	Jordon, Augustus	18 DEC 1880	15	110
Smith, Mary L.	Brown, William H.	15 FEB 1883 R	17	307
Smith, Mathews N.	Peak, Ellen	06 JAN 1879 L	13	007
Smith, Mattie	Brown, Hodge	20 SEP 1882 L	17	030
Smith, May B.	Janin, Henry	29 OCT 1884 L	19	347
Smith, May M.	Hawkins, John D.	18 DEC 1879 L	14	055
Smith, Middleton	Van Hook, Mine	03 APR 1884	18	359
Smith, Millie E.	Jackson, Joseph S.	30 OCT 1879 R	13	455
Smith, Mina J.	Little, Joseph W.	27 DEC 1877	11	278
Smith, Mollie	Hahn, Charles	03 AUG 1881 R	15	431
Smith, Monita Wederstradt	Gill, Herbert A.	27 JUN 1882	16	429
Smith, Montgomery	Lawrence, Martha, Mrs.	31 JUL 1879 R	13	301
Smith, Moses	Cannoday, Ann Eliza	27 DEC 1881	16	158
Smith, Moses H.	Brown, Mallie M.	30 JAN 1883 R	17	279

D.C. Marriage Records Index, June 28, 1877 to October 19, 1885   427

Smith, Nannie	Warren, Milford	09 SEP 1882 L	17	015
Smith, Nathan A.C.	Heitinger, Lena C.	08 AUG 1882	16	473
Smith, Nettie G.	Kruger, Charles William	05 NOV 1884 R	19	362
Smith, Orlando F.	McLoughlin, Maggie M.	02 OCT 1882 R	17	048
Smith, Parker	Richardson, Mary S.	30 MAR 1879 R	13	118
Smith, Parker S.	Satterfield, Laura V.	19 OCT 1885 R	20	497
Smith, Peter A.	McCann, Bridget E.	26 NOV 1879 L	14	013
Smith, Philip	Thompson, Mary	08 OCT 1878 L	12	262
Smith, Rachel A.	Nichols, Thomas	17 OCT 1881 L	16	137
Smith, Rebecca	Smith, Robert	10 JAN 1880	14	098
Smith, Rebecca	Ward, Robert	16 MAR 1885 L	20	117
Smith, Rebecca E.	Constantine, Adolphus C., Jr.	07 FEB 1882	16	228
Smith, Reuben	Lewis, Catherine	23 NOV 1878 L	12	344
Smith, Reuben	Lewis, Bettie	30 JUL 1881 L	15	426
Smith, Richard	Johnson, Frances	28 NOV 1878	12	353
Smith, Richard	Jorden, Mary	01 JAN 1880 R	16	3883
Smith, Richard	Branson, Hannah	04 APR 1881 L	15	246
Smith, Richard T., Capt.	Barker, George A. (Blundon)	19 JAN 1882 R	16	203
Smith, Robert	Smith, Rebecca	10 JAN 1880	14	098
Smith, Robert	Frazier, Fanny	29 JUL 1884	19	162
Smith, Robert B.	Klug, Katie A.	25 NOV 1884 L	19	408
Smith, Robert F.	Jones, Mary M.	03 NOV 1880	15	025
Smith, Robert H.	Parker, Mary J.	21 JUN 1882 R	16	419
Smith, Robert H.	Forrest, Laura	25 JUL 1883 L	18	098
Smith, Robert J.	Proctor, Mary E.	05 OCT 1881 R	16	011
Smith, Robert M.	Harman, Rosalie	22 FEB 1880 R	14	161
Smith, Robert P.	Robinson, Emma	02 JUN 1879 L	13	215
Smith, Rosa	Chinn, B.W.	02 MAY 1878 L	12	034
Smith, Rosa E.	Jones, Archie	17 AUG 1882	16	485
Smith, Rosa I.	Lewis, George T.	04 OCT 1882	17	053
Smith, Rose	Deery, Thomas	28 APR 1878 R	12	014
Smith, Sallie	Johnston, James	24 FEB 1880	14	164
Smith, Sallie V.	Gray, William L.	05 JUN 1884	19	066
Smith, Samuel	Brooks, Phobe	03 MAR 1881 R	15	212
Smith, Samuel	Robey, Grace M.	20 OCT 1881 R	16	041
Smith, Samuel	Green, Lucy	03 MAR 1885 L	20	092
Smith, Samuel A.	Grimes, Katie	06 NOV 1879 R	13	468
Smith, Samuel W.	Hagemeyer, Clara E.	02 JAN 1883	17	230
Smith, Sarah	Bell, Robert	18 OCT 1877 R	11	143
Smith, Sarah	Aldrich, Francis	17 AUG 1881 R	15	450
Smith, Sarah	Shorter, Nathan	02 NOV 1882 R	17	079
Smith, Sarah	Ford, George	28 JUN 1883	18	019
Smith, Sarah C.	Dorsey, Albert	10 JUL 1884 L	19	133
Smith, Sarah E., Mrs.	DeKrafft, John W.	13 MAR 1879	13	099
Smith, Sarah E.	Hawkins, H. Cray	29 MAY 1884	19	044
Smith, Sarah Elizabeth	Aldrich, Ossian F.	31 MAY 1880 R	14	194
Smith, Sarah Jane	Wye, Charles	09 DEC 1884 L	19	445
Smith, Sarah M.	Lucas, James	30 APR 1879 L	13	166
Smith, Sarah V.	Cooksey, Charles E.	21 OCT 1879 R	13	436
Smith, Serena	Coleman, Nelson	30 DEC 1880 L	15	133
Smith, Silas	Branagan, Mary	10 NOV 1880 R	15	040
Smith, Steward J.	Spicer, Mary E.	04 NOV 1884 R	19	357
Smith, Thomas	Guyvers, Louisa	21 NOV 1882 R	17	140
Smith, Thomas D.	Hatton, Eliza J.	25 MAR 1879	13	113
Smith, Thomas H.	Shorter, Rebecca	28 SEP 1882 L	17	041
Smith, Thomas H.	Johnson, Mary	15 NOV 1883 L	18	258
Smith, Thomas J.	Callan, Catherine C.	25 AUG 1880 R	14	412
Smith, Timothy	Bowman, Susan	26 FEB 1884	18	439

Smith, Victoria	Jackson, Frank	08 APR 1880 L	14	216
Smith, Victoria M.	Repetti, Joseph A.	25 NOV 1879 R	14	006
Smith, Virginia J.	Turner, Byron P.	13 AUG 1879 L	13	318
Smith, Walter	Prince, Fannie	19 JUL 1877 R	11	026
Smith, Walter	Lewis, Jeanette	16 FEB 1882 L	16	245
Smith, Walter R.	Myers, Leonora B.	26 FEB 1885	20	086
Smith, Wendell A.	Arnold, Katie A.	20 JUN 1883	18	003
Smith, Willard F.	Roland, Laura V.	06 JAN 1883 L	17	241
Smith, William	Crawford, Mary	29 DEC 1877 L	11	280
Smith, William	Johnson, Annie	18 JUL 1878 L	12	140
Smith, William	Alexander, Sarah	26 NOV 1879 R	14	002
Smith, William	Malady, Mary	14 SEP 1881	15	460
Smith, William	Wright, Amanda	23 NOV 1881 L	16	093
Smith, William	Campbell, Amelia	26 APR 1884 L	18	534
Smith, William	North, Sarah Elizabeth	22 MAY 1884 L	19	035
Smith, William	Wood, Mary	02 OCT 1884	19	281
Smith, William	Taylor, Mary A.E.	27 JAN 1890	19	188
Smith, William E.	Wood, Ella	10 OCT 1877	11	127
Smith, William E.	Shoop, Frances M.	05 FEB 1883 R	17	286
Smith, William Edward	Bell, Florence Serena	31 JAN 1881 R	15	170
Smith, William F.	Wodehouse, Julia	16 DEC 1878 R	12	382
Smith, William H.	Slaughter, Martha A.	15 APR 1878 R	12	003
Smith, William H.	Roe, Mattie E.	28 APR 1885 L	20	192
Smith, William Henry	Wells, Anna Elizabeth	23 SEP 1880 R	14	458
Smith, William P.	Turbin, Bertie	24 SEP 1885	20	436
Smith, Wilson	Coleman, Mildred	08 JAN 1883 L	17	243
Smith, Wm. C.	Cole, Mary A.	14 JUL 1885 R	20	326
Smith, Yorick W.	Madison, Matilda M.	16 FEB 1885 L	20	071
Smithley, Annie E.	Messer, George B.	10 APR 1879 L	13	134
Smithson, Ann Eliza	Weggeman, Frances H.	26 OCT 1882 R	17	088
Smithson, Bud	Payton, Emma	05 MAR 1884 L	18	460
Smithson, Charles Marion	Joachim, Olivia	24 DEC 1881 L	16	156
Smithson, Daniel C.	Burr, Nellie M.	13 FEB 1884	18	423
Smithson, Ida V.	Cooksey, Charles W.	14 NOV 1882	17	125
Smithson, Lydia A.	Eastburn, Gibbons S.	16 JUL 1885 R	20	312
Smithson, Sarah O.	Lacey, Richard M.	21 AUG 1877 R	11	061
Smithson, Susie A.	Wilkerson, William A.	29 SEP 1880 L	14	465
Smoot, Annetta	Pinkney, Joseph W.	03 JAN 1883 L	17	236
Smoot, Cordelia V.	Cross, George W.	09 JAN 1884 R	18	372
Smoot, Emma L.	Garvin, Madison A.	27 JAN 1880 L	14	123
Smoot, George L.	Bruce, Lucy J.	15 MAR 1885	20	112
Smoot, Henry	Pindle, Rebecca	13 MAY 1880	14	269
Smoot, Henry	Stewart, Mary E.	17 JUN 1885	20	249
Smoot, Hobart A.	Cowling, Emma J.	30 APR 1878	12	026
Smoot, Karl	Potmer, Lizzie	11 JUL 1880 R	14	352
Smoot, Mary P.	Dorsey, Joseph H.	26 DEC 1884 R	19	492
Smoot, May	Mangurr, William K.	03 FEB 1885	20	048
Smoot, Rosa E.	Hardy, Samuel F.	29 OCT 1884 L	19	344
Smoot, William Sothoron	Kurtz, Jane Mosher	29 NOV 1882 R	17	152
Smoote, James B.	Marks, Medora	24 JUN 1884	19	100
Smothers, Charity E.	Batson, John	12 FEB 1880 R	14	151
Smothers, George M.	Matthews, Henrietta	20 NOV 1884 L	19	398
Smothers, John F.	Moore, Maria	28 SEP 1885 L	20	446
Smothers, Joseph E.	Brown, Alice	10 JUL 1883 L	18	042
Smothers, Kitty	Gant, Paul	09 AUG 1877 R	11	047
Smothers, Rosa	Jimmerson, Richard	18 JUN 1878 L	12	103
Smothers, Sylvester	Oden, Emma	29 JUN 1885 L	20	300
Smothers, Thomas	Thomas, Sarah	06 AUG 1879 L	13	309

D.C. Marriage Records Index, June 28, 1877 to October 19, 1885

Snapp, Mollie E.	Downey, Jesse A.	19 DEC 1880 R	15	108
Snapp, Sarah Agnes	Knauff, William Jacob	09 NOV 1880 R	15	038
Snead, Amelia	Johnson, Charles	02 DEC 1880	15	079
Snead, Edward	Riggle, Emily	02 JUL 1881 R	15	385
Snead, George W.	Lloyd, Ella J.	05 MAR 1885 R	20	097
Sneden, Cordelia J.	Woodruff, George H.	15 OCT 1883	18	192
Sneed, Nora V.	Cohen, C. Henry	28 DEC 1882 R	17	219
Snell, Elva Antoinette	Paul, Joseph	30 APR 1884 R	18	543
Snell, James	Bell, Priscilla	27 OCT 1881 L	16	049
Snell, Maggie	Burton, Edward	21 OCT 1884 L	19	325
Snell, Margaret Ella	Walters, John	14 AUG 1879 R	13	322
Snelling, Andrew T.	Whitford, Clara E.	25 FEB 1879 R	13	076
Snelling, Ellie Eugenia	Crawford, Wm. Stewart	17 MAR 1885 R	20	118
Snelling, George E.	Anderson, Nellie E.	25 DEC 1880 R	15	124
Snelling, Sarah E.	Raines, Amos G.	11 AUG 1884 R	19	177
Snelling, Walter Comonfort	Hornor, Alice Lee	20 OCT 1879 R	13	432
Snellings, John Samuel	Lightener, Lucy Anna	19 NOV 1882 R	17	136
Snellings, Nellie	Longhoff, William C.	12 DEC 1883 L	18	310
Snellins, Hopie	Shelton, Heston	11 JAN 1885 R	20	011
Sniffen, William K.	Webb, Lillie M.	02 OCT 1883	18	166
Sniffin, Edward A.	Walters, Ella V.	22 APR 1884	18	525
Snight, Frederick H.	Webster, Emma F.	05 MAR 1878 L	11	370
Snow, Arnold	Cole, Mary L.E.	11 OCT 1881 R	16	016
Snow, Catharine	Bell, John	17 OCT 1878 R	12	281
Snow, Harriet	Anderson, Dennis	03 JUL 1884 L	19	121
Snow, Lillian A.	Whitely, Albert	30 NOV 1882 R	17	151
Snowden, Ada S.	Hays, Charles Bogue	16 APR 1878 R	12	004
Snowden, Benjamin	Johnson, Margaret	14 MAY 1881 L	15	306
Snowden, Clara	Shaw, Daniel	12 APR 1881 R	15	254
Snowden, Danie Webster, Dr.	Butler, Carrie	13 MAY 1880 R	14	270
Snowden, Edward	Harris, Amelia	17 MAY 1878	12	057
Snowden, Eliza	Mackall, Joseph	13 NOV 1879 R	13	481
Snowden, Eliza Ann	Christian, Leander	25 DEC 1879	14	062
Snowden, Elizabeth	Lawson, John E.	28 APR 1884 L	18	538
Snowden, Emily B.	Porter, Jermain G.	03 JUL 1879 R	13	256
Snowden, Frances	Diggs, Aaron	17 JUL 1879	13	274
Snowden, Geo. Wash.	Stepner, Eliza	27 FEB 1879	13	074
Snowden, Georgianna	Denton, Noyes	16 MAY 1878 L	12	055
Snowden, Gurden	Ambrose, Mamie Virginia	08 MAR 1883 L	17	338
Snowden, Henry	Dorsey, Catherine	05 MAY 1879	11	233
Snowden, Henry	Dosey, Catherine	05 MAY 1879 R	13	3189
Snowden, Henry	Butler, Lizzie	16 JUL 1879 R	13	282
Snowden, Henry	Easter, Louisa Frances	18 DEC 1884 L	19	469
Snowden, Ignatius	Duffy, Rebecca	21 OCT 1884 L	19	324
Snowden, James Alex.	Sears, Malvina DePratt	28 JUN 1882 L	16	429
Snowden, James R.	Fisher, Alice	07 JUN 1883 L	17	481
Snowden, John	Jackson, Sadie	13 AUG 1877 L	11	051
Snowden, John	Green, Lottie	12 MAY 1881 R	15	303
Snowden, Mary Ellen	Russell, John	09 MAR 1885 L	20	102
Snowden, Mary Emily	Pullett, John Edward	26 NOV 1879 L	14	010
Snowden, Norris	Singleton, Adelaide	01 FEB 1884 L	18	404
Snowden, Rebecca	West, Charles F.	07 JUL 1883 R	18	039
Snowden, Richard	Francis, Matilda	02 JAN 1883 R	17	223
Snowden, Samuel	Harris, Sophronia	05 JUN 1883	17	476
Snowden, Thomas	Thomas, Lucy	21 MAY 1885 L	20	234
Snowden, Walter	Collins, Alice A.	04 NOV 1879 L	13	462
Snowden, Wm. Albert	Henderson, Anne	08 MAR 1881	15	220
Snowdon, Anna	Carter, Horace	27 SEP 1883 L	18	158

Snowdon, Mary	Bell, Pinkney	24 OCT 1883 L	18	209
Snowdon, Mary Ellen	Hurbert, Thomas William	26 JUL 1883 L	18	063
Snyder, Agnes Marie	Schulteis, John H.J.	16 APR 1883	17	395
Snyder, Dora N.	Spotts, Wells W.	12 OCT 1880 R	14	489
Snyder, Fannie C.	Appler, Charles W.	04 DEC 1878 R	12	365
Snyder, Florence H.	Johnson, Wm. H.	22 JUL 1885	20	336
Snyder, James	West, Mary	01 NOV 1883 R	18	228
Snyder, John D.P.	Lusby, Annie R.	19 AUG 1884	19	192
Snyder, John F.	Cunningham, Leanora	09 JAN 1879 R	13	014
Snyder, Lilia	Thyson, W. Frank	23 APR 1878	12	019
Snyder, Maria	Hawkins, Cornelius	05 JUN 1883 R	17	457
Snyder, Thomas L.	Fox, Sofia C.	24 JAN 1884 R	18	393
Snyder, Virginia A.	McCoy, William A.	08 SEP 1883 R	18	119
Snyder, William Tayloe	Hammond, Marie Louise	26 MAR 1883 R	17	360
Soaper, William	McFaul, Annie S.	28 OCT 1878 L	12	294
Sobatka, Franz	Scheppoch, Margeretha	07 JUL 1878 R	12	126
Soden, Maggie	Johnson, George	06 AUG 1878 R	12	158
Sohn, Anna N.	Düvel, Friedrich Aug. Chris.	21 SEP 1883	18	147
Sohn, Elise	Exel, Leonhard	04 MAY 1882 L	16	350
Solawry, Benjamin	McCabe, Sarah	10 JAN 1882 L	16	189
Solberg, Ludwig Thorval	Nourse, Mary Adelaide	01 AUG 1880 R	14	381
Solger, Julius	Roones, Florence B.	22 NOV 1881 L	16	090
Soloman, Robert	Busey, Louisa	20 JAN 1879 R	13	025
Solomon, Emma J., Mrs.	Weltz, James L.	06 AUG 1882	16	470
Solomon, George Washington	Tasker, Jennie	06 NOV 1879	13	467
Solomon, Milanie	Broche, Gustavus	02 MAY 1883	17	426
Solomons, Ida J.	Piexotto, Daniel L.M.	21 JAN 1880 R	14	114
Solus, Charlie	Davis, Agnes	05 JAN 1882 L	16	184
Somby, Belle M.	Ease, William H.S.	06 DEC 1877	11	226
Somers, Richard	Laurie, Jane B. (Richardson)	24 DEC 1882 R	17	208
Somers, Sarah Walker	McCloud, George	25 SEP 1878 R	12	205
Somersville, Olivia	Jackson, James	16 MAY 1878	12	055
Somerville, Annie	Jones, William H.	18 MAY 1885 L	20	228
Somerville, Ella Wickham	Lynch, John Roy	18 DEC 1884 R	19	468
Somerville, Ezekiel	Smith, Margaret	02 APR 1881	15	244
Somerville, Fred N.	Poore, Josephine	16 FEB 1882	16	245
Somerville, G. Alex	Brown, Alice	23 DEC 1879 R	14	066
Somerville, Josephine	Liverpool, James	12 MAY 1879 R	12	201
Somerville, Mary A.	Thompson, Bartley B.	07 FEB 1878 R	11	332
Somerville, Robert H.	Thomas, C.A., Mrs.	26 DEC 1877	11	200
Somerville, Rosa	Clark, John	31 JUL 1879 R	13	294
Sommer, John Henry	Markin, Maggie C.	01 SEP 1885 L	20	395
Sommer, Kate L.	Allvine, John F.	10 JUN 1884	19	071
Sommers, Alice	Young, Sostman	28 JAN 1883 R	17	274
Sommers, Joseph	Blumenthal, Henrietta	01 MAR 1885 R	20	089
Sommers, Uriah	Course, Julia	07 AUG 1877 L	11	044
Sommersfeld, Juliana Augusta	Müller, Christian	19 MAR 1882 R	16	281
Sommerville, Claratine	Shelton, George H.	17 NOV 1884 L	19	387
Sommerville, Richard	Merity, Martha	22 JUL 1884	19	145
Sommners, Frank Pierce	Hill, Helena Marie	28 FEB 1881 R	15	207
Sonder, Adeline V.	Miller, Stephen A.	29 JUN 1881	15	382
Sonder, Lewis F.	Lanhardt, Maggie M.	24 JUN 1885 L	20	289
Sondheimer, Julius	Siegel, Clara	11 MAY 1879 R	13	182
Sonneman, Emma	Peterson, Robert	28 OCT 1883 R	18	215
Sonnemann, Caroline Dorothea	Koehler, John A.	20 FEB 1879 R	13	064
Sonnemann, Theodore	Essex, Jannie	20 DEC 1881 L	16	140
Sonnemann, William	Cowarding, Eugenia	02 APR 1884	18	491
Sonnenschmidt, Charles W.	Cook, Mary Virginia Scrivner	20 MAY 1882 R	16	369

D.C. Marriage Records Index, June 28, 1877 to October 19, 1885   431

Sonomon, Emma	Boyd, Augustus	12 JAN 1882 L	16	192
Soper, Albert	Soper, Rebecca	13 OCT 1879 R	13	417
Soper, Alice	Kelly, George E.	27 AUG 1877 R	11	065
Soper, Broxie B.	Rokes, Emerson	21 FEB 1882	16	249
Soper, Charles P.	McCutcheon, Mary	11 JUN 1878	12	096
Soper, Edward	Casseen, Annie	26 AUG 1879 R	13	333
Soper, Elizabeth	Carter, Wilbur E.	09 OCT 1877	11	128
Soper, Elizabeth	Allen, Oley	01 AUG 1878	12	154
Soper, Ellen Douglass	Scott, Samuel B.	27 FEB 1878 R	11	361
Soper, Emma	Hazel, John T.	04 OCT 1877	11	121
Soper, Emma	Barnes, Columbus	24 JUN 1880	14	334
Soper, Fannie	Barnes, Aloysius	16 OCT 1879	13	431
Soper, Fannie	Mantley, Joseph C.	09 JUN 1885	20	264
Soper, Gracie E.	Whiting, Joseph G.	15 OCT 1879	13	421
Soper, Julia E.	Hardell, Robert C.	16 NOV 1880 L	15	050
Soper, Laura Hicks	Johnston, Charles E.	22 OCT 1882 R	17	084
Soper, Lizza	Quill, John P.	02 SEP 1884 L	19	219
Soper, Maggie	Barnes, William H.	18 DEC 1877 L	11	244
Soper, Marion R.	Maguire, George A.	25 MAY 1884 R	19	036
Soper, Mary E.	Diggs, William J.	20 JUL 1881 L	15	411
Soper, Mary E.	Low, Lemuel S.	23 APR 1884	18	527
Soper, Mary I.	Garden, Peter G.	03 OCT 1877	11	120
Soper, Mollie	Pumphrey, Robert H.	12 MAY 1881	15	305
Soper, Rebecca	Soper, Albert	13 OCT 1879 R	13	417
Sorrel, Sandy	Burke, Louisa	07 OCT 1880 R	14	481
Sorrell, Annie E.	Grigsby, Milton T.	08 APR 1885 R	20	154
Sorrell, Emma	Shetler, Charles	06 FEB 1878 R	11	329
Sorrell, John W.	Smith, Isabella	26 FEB 1878 L	11	359
Sorrell, Thomas A.	Willis, Severene Elizabeth	02 FEB 1885 L	20	048
Sorrell, Welford	Wood, Rosie W.	27 MAY 1885	20	242
Sorrell, William	Lee, Minerva	08 OCT 1882	17	054
Sosick, Maggie	Desio, Girolamo	01 OCT 1877 L	11	117
Souder, Amos F.	Phillips, Josephine	21 SEP 1881 R	15	493
Souder, John W.	Ceas, Fannie M.	12 OCT 1881 L	16	019
Souder, William Charles	DeGraw, Elizabeth Pauline	15 DEC 1880	15	101
Soulé, Jules E.	Petrola, Mary L.	17 JAN 1883	17	260
Sousa, George W.	Spry, Cora A.	09 OCT 1884	19	295
Southall, Ella C.	Braselman, Joseph R.	24 SEP 1878 R	12	232
Southall, Louisa T.	Holmes, Benjamin T.	20 DEC 1877 R	11	242
Southall, Mary Whitfield	James, George Watson	07 JAN 1879 R	13	010
Southard, Harry Codding	Hess, Julie Caroline	08 APR 1885 R	20	149
Southard, John F.	Grieve, Mary E.	01 MAY 1882 R	16	343
Southerland, Richard	Jackson, Mary	06 NOV 1878 L	12	312
Southern, John S.	Lockwood, Emma	01 NOV 1884 L	19	354
Southword, Joseph	Spriggs, Mary A.	23 FEB 1885 R	20	080
Southworth, Harrison	Banks, Nannie E.	14 MAY 1879	13	189
Southworth, Richmond J.	Porter, Blanche	23 MAR 1878 L	11	391
Sowers, Henry	White, Bonnie	14 NOV 1883 L	18	251
Spaar, Annie Margaret	Sparrow, James Thos.	23 SEP 1885 R	20	437
Spady, Sarah A.	Lewis, George E.	25 JUN 1878	12	113
Spaight, Daniel	Moran, Nellie	18 DEC 1882 R	17	190
Spaight, Mary	Burdine, William A.	12 FEB 1883	17	302
Spaininburg, John E.	Noble, Julia Moore Mrs.	02 AUG 1878 R	12	156
Spalding, Howard Joseph	Nichols, Katie Mary	07 JUL 1885 R	20	316
Spalding, John H.	Davis, Bettie L.	26 APR 1881 L	15	274
Spalding, Mary A.	Murray, George William	08 OCT 1885	20	473
Spalding, Sarah Annie Davidson	Burkhardt, John George	03 MAY 1880 R	14	249
Spalding, Wm. L.	Thompson, Annie W.	02 JUN 1882 R	16	391

Spanier, Leah	Loeb, Meyer	15 APR 1885 R	20	165
Spanier, Sarah	Friedlander, Harry	22 JUL 1885 R	20	334
Sparklin, Alice A.	Kelley, Howard M.	05 MAY 1884	19	004
Sparklin, Alice Thomas	Kelley, Howard M.	05 MAY 1884 R	18	549
Sparks, Alfred R.	Steinbaugh, Katie	17 NOV 1881	16	082
Sparks, Charles	Martin, Eliza V.	14 JUL 1885 R	20	321
Sparks, Charles W.	Scrivener, Mary J.	15 DEC 1884	19	460
Sparks, Ella E.	Williams, Rege	09 APR 1879 R	13	132
Sparks, Lorenzo	Carpenter, Emma	26 SEP 1882 R	17	037
Sparks, Philip	Jackson, Ellen	24 SEP 1877 L	11	105
Sparks, Richard M.	Grantham, Joanna M.	25 SEP 1883	18	152
Sparrow, Addie	Young, James	17 DEC 1883 L	18	320
Sparrow, Annie May	Lighter, Daniel Webster	23 DEC 1880 R	15	119
Sparrow, Basil	Ward, Madalina Louisa	26 JUL 1879 L	13	294
Sparrow, Flora	Mulfinger, Conrad	23 JUN 1885 R	20	288
Sparrow, James Thos.	Spaar, Annie Margaret	23 SEP 1885 R	20	437
Sparrow, John C.	Manakee, Lizzie	13 JAN 1885	20	014
Sparrow, Rosa	Dodson, Peter A.	22 AUG 1878	12	178
Sparrow, W.N.	Weller, S.R.	15 JUN 1880	14	323
Sparrow, William	Harmon, Amelia	06 JUL 1880	14	350
Sparshott, Alfred	Delong, Vina	04 JUN 1883 R	17	472
Sparshott, Frank C.	Garrett, Cornelia A.	17 JAN 1883	17	264
Spates, Charles W.	Wood, Mary V.	05 MAY 1881 L	15	294
Spates, Henrietta C.	Chick, Henry C.	30 NOV 1878 L	12	356
Spates, Lula Alvernon	Trundle, John Horatio	24 MAY 1882 R	16	375
Spates, Minnette V.	Spear, Luther W.	15 OCT 1884	19	307
Spatz, Ludavig	Auth, Columba	28 NOV 1879	14	018
Spaulding, Daniel J.	Hall, Sarah Jane	17 OCT 1881	16	028
Spaulding, Fannie	Griswold, Dwight T.	24 AUG 1882 L	16	493
Spaulding, James J.	Campbell, Katie A.	01 SEP 1885 L	20	395
Spaulding, John Celestine	Thomas, Fannie	23 SEP 1879	13	381
Spaulding, Mary H.	Kyle, Christopher C.	15 NOV 1883 L	18	256
Spaulding, Patrick H.	Flaherty, Mary A.	07 APR 1884 L	18	498
Speak, Annie F.	Merchant, Richard F.	05 SEP 1877 R	11	076
Speake, John William, Jr.	Bernhard, Katie Genevieve	21 MAR 1883 R	17	353
Speake, Rufus Henry	Bliss, Amelia Ann	16 APR 1878 R	12	008
Speakes, Charlotte	Henson, William H.	15 JAN 1880 R	14	108
Speaks, Edward	Cooper, Mary J.	15 NOV 1881	16	076
Speaks, Jennie	White, Adolphus	20 SEP 1879	13	379
Speaks, Julia A.	Waters, John F.	25 DEC 1878 R	12	398
Spear, Abraham	Luchs, Augusta	01 JUN 1879	13	209
Spear, Luther W.	Spates, Minnette V.	15 OCT 1884	19	307
Speck, Lillie D.	Koontz, A.W.	10 JUL 1878 R	12	131
Speckman, Fredericka	Enselman, Christopher	23 DEC 1877	11	257
Speckmon, Jordena	Saurwald, Frederick H.	12 APR 1884 L	18	505
Speed, Emma	Juggins, Louis	18 SEP 1885	20	426
Speed, William	Waters, Isabel	23 MAR 1881 L	15	237
Speer, Emory	Morgan, Eleanora D.	14 JUL 1881 L	15	401
Speer, Kittie L.	Cramer, Benjamin D.	10 OCT 1883 R	18	185
Speer, Minnie S.	Post, Chas. C.	16 NOV 1878 R	12	332
Speer, William F.	Hammond, Katie	10 JUL 1882 R	16	444
Speiden, Annie R.	Worthington, Charles E.	20 MAY 1880 R	14	280
Speiden, Margaret R.	Wheatley, David	21 MAR 1881 L	15	232
Speider, Charles Edwin	Scott, Emma Florence	20 APR 1885	20	176
Spellman, J.F.	McCarthy, Kate A.	22 APR 1879 L	13	155
Spence, Adolphus N.	Turner, Sarah E.	17 NOV 1880 R	15	051
Spence, Cyrus	Tolliver, Adelina Virginia	22 JUN 1880 R	14	329
Spence, G. May	Jobson, Joseph Tyler	10 NOV 1880 R	15	041

Spence, Grace	Friess, John Henry	13 SEP 1879 R	13	368
Spence, Susie	McKnight, Robert	04 OCT 1884 L	19	287
Spence, Thomas B.	Rogers, Nellie Marmaduke	07 MAR 1881 R	15	218
Spence, William W.	Walker, Alice M.	20 OCT 1880 R	15	005
Spencer, Agnes	Tolson, James	23 DEC 1879 R	14	067
Spencer, Alice	Clements, John T.	29 APR 1880 R	14	245
Spencer, Annie	Johnson, John	22 OCT 1878 L	12	285
Spencer, Catherine	Harron, Leighton Greg.	04 DEC 1877 R	11	217
Spencer, Catherine	King, Matthew	25 JUN 1879 R	13	249
Spencer, Charles	Gastoll, Mary C.	05 JUN 1880 L	14	305
Spencer, Emily	Saunders, Richard	13 MAY 1884 R	19	018
Spencer, Esther Smith	Kimball, William Wirt	18 JUL 1882 R	16	452
Spencer, Frank A.	Arnold, Mary S.	29 NOV 1884 L	19	425
Spencer, James D.	Walters, Virginia	18 DEC 1880 L	15	109
Spencer, James H.	Pryor, Mary Virginia	21 APR 1881 R	15	268
Spencer, John E.	Fisher, Isabella	15 SEP 1885	20	418
Spencer, Leonard G.	Kaiser, Margaret Agnes	08 APR 1885	20	153
Spencer, Rachel	Vass, Spencer	03 JAN 1884 L	18	365
Spencer, Richard	Munday, Ellen	11 SEP 1879 R	13	350
Spencer, Thomas	Norton, Fannie	01 JUL 1884 L	19	115
Spencer, William Henry	Sands, Mary Diffendiffer	03 MAR 1880 R	14	174
Spicer, Annie	Pierce, William J.	15 NOV 1881 R	16	076
Spicer, Catherine Ann	Starr, William J.	27 MAR 1882 L	16	289
Spicer, Mary E.	Smith, Steward J.	04 NOV 1884 R	19	357
Spier, George W.	Hesselbach, Olga M.	20 JAN 1883 L	17	269
Spiess, Louis	Regan, Margaret	15 APR 1877 L	11	248
Spiess, Marie L.	Gersdorff, Charles A.	05 AUG 1884	19	165
Spiggs, Richard	Jackson, Josephine	20 DEC 1877	11	251
Spignul, Mary Lillian	Waters, Somerset R.	17 OCT 1883 R	18	198
Spiller, Logan A.	Kendrick, Lillie Walker	05 JAN 1885 R	20	004
Spilman, George N.	Fields, Mary R.	24 SEP 1883 R	18	149
Spindle, Ida M.	Stinemetz, Anthony	10 JUN 1882 R	16	404
Spindle, Susan Marcella	Garnett, Riter Case	12 DEC 1881 R	16	126
Spindler, William F.	Held, Mary	26 MAY 1884 R	19	039
Spinks, John Edward	Lucus, Mildred Anne	21 AUG 1879 R	13	329
Spinks, Richard Moody	Taylor, Kittie	11 MAY 1882 L	16	358
Spinning, Dewitt C.	Corson, Annie	20 MAR 1883 R	17	353
Spitzka, Henry F.	Orleman, Lillie	17 MAY 1883	17	449
Spotts, Charles	Corbin, Elizabeth	29 OCT 1877 L	11	159
Spotts, Wells W.	Snyder, Dora N.	12 OCT 1880 R	14	489
Spottswood, Maria	Flood, James	21 FEB 1882 L	16	255
Spradling, Emma	Sanders, William	21 JAN 1885	20	031
Spratley, Virginia Mills	Murray, George E.	01 JAN 1884 R	18	353
Spratt, Joanna	Loane, John T.S.	26 OCT 1879 R	13	443
Spresser, Henry W.	Maloney, Mary	05 SEP 1882 L	17	005
Sprigg, Ada Russell	Slaker, Adam	30 DEC 1879 R	14	077
Sprigg, Annie Florence	Hendrix, Thomas J.	10 JUL 1878 R	12	132
Sprigg, Minnie	Lee, Thomas R.	13 SEP 1877 L	11	093
Spriggs, Ben	West, Catherine	09 AUG 1884 L	19	177
Spriggs, George W.	Talbret, Mary	08 DEC 1881 R	16	123
Spriggs, Grace Anna	Hillary, William	15 APR 1880 L	14	224
Spriggs, James	Paine, Melvina	02 JAN 1879 L	13	002
Spriggs, James H.	Williams, Annie	09 JUN 1880 L	14	313
Spriggs, Mary	Gant, Joseph	20 OCT 1879 R	13	425
Spriggs, Mary A.	Southword, Joseph	23 FEB 1885 R	20	080
Spriggs, Peter	Gant, Sarah	01 JAN 1884 R	18	223
Spriggs, Richard	Lockley, Cora	09 SEP 1879 L	13	361
Spriggs, William	Dodson, Addie	18 APR 1882 L	16	322

Sprightley, Erin C.	Phelps, Charles M.H.	27 MAR 1884 R	18	484
Sprigs, Clara	Gerah, George	27 NOV 1878 L	12	350
Sprigs, Isaac	Robinson, Amelia	27 NOV 1878 L	12	351
Springer, Elizabeth	Schickler, Christian	07 NOV 1878	12	313
Springer, Horace P.	Halloran, Jennie B.	02 FEB 1879 R	13	042
Springman, Joseph M.	Plaskett, Emma T.	20 DEC 1877 R	11	250
Springmann, Rose V.	Bacon, Arthur A.	23 OCT 1879 R	13	441
Springmann, Samuel	Keys, Virginia A.	18 DEC 1879 R	14	056
Springsteen, Ahram F.	Combs, Emma J.	22 JUL 1885 L	20	336
Spry, Cora A.	Sousa, George W.	09 OCT 1884	19	295
Spry, James R.	Weaver, Mary	03 NOV 1884	19	355
Spurlock, Eliza	Ellis, Moses	19 OCT 1880 R	15	004
Squals, James	Braxton, Eliza	20 NOV 1883 R	18	252
Squires, Fannie E.	Haller, Nicholas T.	21 APR 1885	20	178
Squires, Rose J.	Smith, Julius K.	09 APR 1885 R	20	158
Srays, Kate	Brown, Edward	03 NOV 1881 L	16	058
Ssstiertz, Anna Maria Wilh.	Voigt, George	31 JUL 1879 L	13	300
St. Clair, Gilbert	Atherton, Emma Frances	20 OCT 1877 L	11	146
St. Clair, William W.	Durity, Ida V.	06 JUN 1878 R	12	088
St. John, Ada	Ehrnantraut, Edward	02 MAY 1881	15	286
St. John, J.F.	Chapman, Alice J.	23 OCT 1884 L	19	333
St. Lawrence, Philip A.	Davis, Susan A.	26 AUG 1879 L	13	336
Stack, Annie T.	Smith, Francis E.	17 MAY 1883 L	17	449
Stack, William P.	Madigan, Mary A.	30 SEP 1884 L	19	277
Stackpole, Edward C.	Delarue, Beulah	30 DEC 1884 R	19	501
Stacy, Adaline A.	Creswell, Francis McC.	26 MAR 1884 L	18	482
Stacy, Robert H.	McReynolds, Mary J.	16 NOV 1882 L	17	131
Stadler, Maggie	Crouch, Walter Francis	27 MAY 1879 L	13	207
Stadman, Alice Mary	Fling, James A.	03 SEP 1885 R	20	397
Stafford, James	Morrow, Katherine	17 OCT 1878 L	12	279
Stafford, Mary A.	Loeflar, William A.	11 NOV 1879 L	13	477
Stafford, Octavis	Thompson, Rudolph P.	12 JUN 1884	19	079
Staffregen, Elise	Keuchet, Anthony	01 OCT 1883	18	164
Stagenwalter, John A.	Mack, Sarah Ann	08 FEB 1885 R	20	055
Stahl, Edward	MacCarthy, Fannie	29 JUL 1883	18	051
Stahle, Mary	Vogelgesang, Daniel V.	16 MAR 1879 R	13	102
Stake, Charles Thomas	Marsh, Flora Lavinia	18 SEP 1883 R	18	135
Stallings, Blanche E.	Upperman, Charles H.	05 MAR 1879 L	13	089
Stallings, George W.	Nowell, Hettie F.	05 DEC 1881	16	113
Stallings, Jane Eliza Sherwood	Poutsch, John Thomas	11 NOV 1880 R	15	045
Stallings, John S.	Cooley, Lillie F.	31 MAY 1881 R	15	333
Stamp, Margaret E.	Laugley, Charles H.	25 AUG 1885 R	20	385
Stamper, Mary E.	Cragin, Harry W.	20 JAN 1880	14	111
Stamps, Laura	Pleasants, James H.	16 APR 1878	12	006
Stanard, David	Moten, Lucy A.	23 DEC 1880 R	15	114
Stanard, Sallie	Frost, William H.	12 SEP 1878	12	218
Stancliff, Annie Clark	Ayres, Chauncey Lewis	04 JUL 1883 R	18	034
Standard, Alice	Ferguson, William	18 SEP 1883 R	18	139
Standard, Charles H.	Dixson, Fannie	23 JUN 1881 R	15	375
Standard, William	Howard, Emily	05 MAR 1878 L	11	372
Standiford, Harry	LePreux, Imogene	07 JUL 1881 L	15	394
Stanford, Edward H.	Bryan, Annie E.	11 JUN 1885	20	270
Stanford, Sammuel M.	Rider, Willie J.	11 DEC 1880 L	15	091
Stanford, W.W.	Jeffries, Lurie E.	22 MAY 1880 R	14	268
Stanhope, Ida J.	Chapin, Charles T.	11 JUN 1882 R	16	404
Stanici, Michael	Langley, Mary	16 FEB 1881 R	15	188
Stanley, Amelia K.	Andrews, Reuben H.	30 JAN 1879 R	13	040
Stanley, Marshal	Ewell, Mary	08 AUG 1877 L	11	046

D.C. Marriage Records Index, June 28, 1877 to October 19, 1885

Name	Spouse	Date	Vol	Page
Stanley, Mary V.	Poole, Dorsey W.	15 NOV 1877 L	11	186
Stanmore, Harriet	Hieth, James	03 JUL 1882 L	16	435
Stansbury, Charles F.	Hunter, Irene	30 APR 1879 L	13	166
Stansbury, Emma	Robey, Francis	26 AUG 1880	14	415
Stansbury, John	White, Emma	24 JUN 1879 R	13	170
Stansbury, Kate Mason Moffet	Tyler, Walter Bowie	05 SEP 1878 R	12	193
Stansbury, Susanna R.	Allen, Nathaniel	18 SEP 1879 R	13	375
Stansbury, Virginia Ward	Maitland, Lindley Hoffman	25 MAR 1882 R	16	289
Stansell, Dwight Daniel	Hunter, Lydia McElfresh	25 JUN 1878 R	12	111
Stant, Ella M.	Padgett, Charles E.	05 JUN 1881	15	344
Stant, George W.	Brown, Ida E.	06 SEP 1880 R	14	429
Stant, Rosella	Boothe, George C.	16 JUL 1877	11	021
Stant, William	Trumbull, Emma S.	21 MAY 1880 L	14	281
Stanton, Annie	Hawkins, Charles	20 FEB 1882 L	16	251
Stanton, Bettie	Shaw, Charles E.	15 MAR 1885 R	20	110
Stanton, Edward G.	Farrelly, Mary J.	14 APR 1879 R	13	141
Stanton, Eleanor Adams	Bush, James Clark	08 JAN 1880 R	14	095
Stanton, Elias M., Rev.	Gibbs, Catherine E., Mrs.	07 SEP 1882 R	17	011
Stanton, Elizabeth	Walker, James H.	06 NOV 1879 R	13	466
Stanton, Francis M.	Warner, Clara L.	25 SEP 1878 R	12	234
Stanton, Frank	Broadus, Elizabeth	31 MAR 1885 L	20	139
Stanton, Leonidas Wellington	Weiter, Louisa Cora	29 DEC 1878 R	12	405
Stanton, Lucy	White, James	28 DEC 1882 R	17	207
Stanton, Philip	Thomas, Matilda, Mrs.	08 JUN 1880 R	14	309
Stanton, Reuben	Mahoney, Jane	26 JUL 1881 R	15	416
Stanton, Rose	Brown, Robert	10 JAN 1883	17	249
Stanton, Savantine Gerty	Morrison, William F.	07 NOV 1880 R	15	028
Stanton, Sophia	Gallagher, James	25 FEB 1884 L	18	441
Stanton, Thomas	Farmer, Mary	15 MAR 1881 L	15	225
Stanton, Thomas J.	Gibbons, Mary	26 NOV 1879 L	14	014
Stanwood, Robert Given	Bowker, Frances Drummond	08 APR 1879 R	13	130
Stanze, Christian	Müller, Alice	26 DEC 1882 L	17	212
Staples, Annie M.	Crismond, James	26 MAR 1883 R	17	359
Staples, Ida M.	Stelle, Thomas S.	18 SEP 1878 R	12	224
Starde, Henry	Tyler, Millie	21 OCT 1879 R	13	435
Stargardter, Leopold	Goldstein, Rachel Annah	04 OCT 1885 R	20	454
Starke, Mary A.	Streb, Henry L.	13 JUN 1883	17	491
Starks, Arthur	Thompson, Hennie	05 JUL 1877	11	011
Starks, Maggie	Lucas, Littleton T.	16 MAY 1878 L	12	053
Starliper, Elsie	Myers, Washington O.	27 OCT 1883 R	18	219
Starr, Alfred A.	Heinlein, Rosie C.	07 FEB 1881 R	15	181
Starr, William J.	Spicer, Catherine Ann	27 MAR 1882 L	16	289
Starters, Sarah	Berry, Fred	23 JUN 1881	15	377
Starud, Rachel Ann	Powers, William	29 NOV 1882 L	17	158
Starvit, Maggie	Hawkins, Wilson	26 DEC 1883	18	341
Statesman, Daniel	Wallace, Lizzie	17 SEP 1879 L	13	373
Statesman, Margaret	Walls, William A.	01 MAR 1881	15	209
Statham, Henry Thomas	King, Eloise	15 OCT 1885 R	20	481
Staton, Lottie	Knott, William	17 AUG 1882	16	485
Staub, Amandos	Bean, Lillie	15 AUG 1884 L	19	188
Staub, Jacob F.	Stone, Elizabeth A.	09 APR 1878 L	11	412
Stauf, William A.	Schafhirt, Rebecca	27 OCT 1884	19	340
Stausburg, Isabella	Stebbins, Harry Osmyn	19 JUL 1884	19	141
Stead, Robert	Force, Mary	10 APR 1882 R	16	306
Steadman, Ida E.	Kerper, Francis B.P.	09 DEC 1880 R	15	090
Steadman, William H.	Denamore, Mary G.	31 AUG 1884	19	216
Stearn, Emma J.	Artz, Samuel	18 MAY 1880 R	14	275
Stebbins, Harry Osmyn	Stausburg, Isabella	19 JUL 1884	19	141

Stecher, Joseph	Buesher, Mary	26 JAN 1882 L	16	211
Steel, Annie	Hoagland, John H.	27 NOV 1879 L	14	017
Steel, Annie Eliza	Hoagland, John Henry	07 JAN 1880 R	14	141
Steel, John T.	Albriton, Ida Virginia	04 APR 1878	11	405
Steel, T.M.	Hyde, Nettie	27 SEP 1883	18	158
Steele, Alida	Newton, Samuel F.	17 JAN 1883 L	17	265
Steele, Annie M.	Burrus, Robert	01 MAR 1881 L	15	209
Steele, Caroline H.	Addison, Arthur D.	21 FEB 1882 L	16	253
Steele, Charles N.	Dement, Mary E.	08 JUN 1885	20	262
Steele, James	Eddingberg, Rebecca	04 NOV 1884 L	19	359
Steele, Jennie	Sutton, James T.	19 MAY 1878	12	059
Steele, John E.	Tucker, Anna L.	10 AUG 1879 R	13	314
Steele, Kate	Scott, Harry	04 MAR 1880	12	415
Steele, Katharine Barney	Appleby, Geo. Franklin	28 JUL 1885 R	20	344
Steele, Marshall A.	McMurray, Dora L.	17 NOV 1879 R	13	492
Steele, Minnie Ann	Brent, William R.	14 APR 1881 L	15	258
Steele, Rachel Jane	Floyd, Frank Brooks	23 DEC 1879 R	14	066
Steele, Rush C.	Buckingham, Virginia	16 NOV 1881 R	16	081
Steele, Willmer	Eagan, Annie E.	24 SEP 1883 L	18	151
Stegmaier, George W.	Grady, Annie M.	13 OCT 1878 R	12	268
Stehley, John Z.	Levy, Louisa M.	15 JUN 1884 L	19	087
Steimer, Margaret	McIntyre, Michael	30 AUG 1882 L	16	496
Stein, George W.	Truseheim, Annie	23 APR 1878 L	12	018
Stein, Jacob	Hechinger, Julia	11 SEP 1881 R	15	481
Stein, Mary E.	Walter, Charles	11 JUN 1878 L	12	094
Stein, Otto J.H.	Beckman, Josephine	02 OCT 1880	14	469
Stein, Rose	Peyser, Henry	12 SEP 1884 L	19	242
Steinbaugh, Katie	Sparks, Alfred R.	17 NOV 1881	16	082
Steinberger, Elizabeth Hess	Mankins, George E.	07 JUN 1880 R	14	230
Steinbrenner, Marie Josephine	Reeside, Edwin	15 OCT 1885 R	20	487
Steiner, Annie M.	Hutcherson, Wm. Andrew	07 OCT 1884	19	291
Steiner, Lena	Fuelling, William L.	14 JUL 1880 R	14	360
Steinert, William	Bailey, Fannie	11 SEP 1884 L	19	241
Steinhardt, Ida, Mrs.	Schonberger, Charles N.	29 JUL 1882 L	16	461
Steinhope, Auguste	Keller, Conrad	30 APR 1885 R	20	193
Steinle, Frederick	Jouvenal, Clara C.M.	12 OCT 1884 R	19	300
Steinle, John	Schenck, Katie S.	25 MAY 1884 R	19	036
Steinle, Rosa Bertha	Gieseking, Fredrick C.	12 FEB 1884 R	18	420
Steinmann, Louise	York, Frank	12 AUG 1885 L	20	366
Steinmeyer, Josephine	Hammond, George W.	06 FEB 1880 R	14	133
Steinmeyer, William E.	Howison, Ella I.	27 DEC 1881	16	158
Steirs, Mary Whitcomb	Michaels, John Walter	17 JUL 1878	12	136
Steiver, Henry	Deckman, Elizabeth	03 OCT 1878 L	12	250
Steiwer, Helena	Pfister, Henry	08 SEP 1879 R	13	355
Stelle, Mary Ann	Lewis, Wm. Frederick	05 MAR 1884 R	18	458
Stelle, Thomas S.	Staples, Ida M.	18 SEP 1878 R	12	224
Stello, Louisa	Berger, Henry	11 SEP 1878 L	12	206
Stellwagen, Edward James	Fisher, Charlotte Margaret	29 SEP 1880 R	14	462
Stellwagen, Elise	Ducat, Arthur Charles, Jr.	15 AUG 1885 R	20	370
Stengel, Mary	Purks, William Plumer	08 AUG 1881 L	15	436
Stenger, Charles Robert	Addis, Georgia Eugenia	15 OCT 1879 L	13	424
Stenz, George F.	Zange, Mary M.E.	26 OCT 1880 L	15	014
Stephen, Alfred H.	Yibbie, Malvina	03 APR 1879 L	13	122
Stephen, Annie Louise	Fowler, John H.A.	07 JUN 1881 L	15	350
Stephens, Dora	Collins, Thomas J.	04 SEP 1884	19	230
Stephens, Edward A.	Proctor, Fannie A.	09 OCT 1882 R	17	060
Stephens, Horace	Conoway, Lizzie	01 FEB 1879 L	13	041
Stephens, Judson Williams Wade	Willett, Henrietta Virginia	11 JUN 1879	13	228

Stephens, Lewis Charles	Hughes, Carrie Melissa	16 JAN 1879 R	13	020
Stephens, Linda W.	Huckstep, W.W.	13 DEC 1884	19	458
Stephens, William H.	Donaldson, Laura F.	04 JUN 1878	12	082
Stephenson, Annie	Gant, George	26 AUG 1879 L	13	337
Stephenson, Augustus	Tinney, Ellen	28 NOV 1878 L	12	354
Stephenson, Elizabeth	James, James Henry	27 SEP 1883	18	157
Stephenson, Ella Rebecca	Downing, Thomas Myers	01 JAN 1878	11	285
Stephenson, Henry	Marbury, Helen	11 SEP 1878	12	213
Stephenson, Joseph G.	Abell, Leila Kate	27 JAN 1881 R	15	165
Stephenson, Nannie G.	Yancey, William T.	25 APR 1883	17	408
Stephenson, Thomas P.	White, Clara B.	06 OCT 1880 L	14	478
Stephinson, Catherine	Butler, John	06 SEP 1880 L	14	433
Stepner, Eliza	Snowden, Geo. Wash.	27 FEB 1879	13	074
Stepney, Franklin	Browne, Julia Janet	24 APR 1883 L	17	406
Stepney, Mary	Brooks, James	10 MAR 1885 R	20	058
Steptoe, Arthur	Thomas, Annie G.	25 OCT 1877 L	11	156
Steptowe, Alfred C.	Williams, Martha M.	14 FEB 1884	18	423
Sterling, Anna	Guthridge, Jules	20 OCT 1884 L	19	320
Sterling, Daniel G.	Bridgman, Harriett M.	13 AUG 1884	19	183
Sterling, Julia H.	Hill, Horace L.	03 MAR 1883 L	17	331
Sterling, Mary E.	Hodgdon, Micah W.	15 SEP 1881 L	15	487
Stern, Leah	Levy, Moses A.	12 JUN 1885 L	20	271
Stern, Leopold	Sandek, Elizabeth V.	05 JUN 1884 R	19	045
Stern, Louis	Gusdorf, Fannie	12 OCT 1879	13	414
Stern, Myer	Myers, Mary	15 MAR 1881	15	227
Stern, Selina	Brown, Julius	03 JUN 1883 R	17	471
Stern, Solomon	Oppenheimer, Ida	16 MAR 1884 R	18	472
Sterne, Charles M.	Davis, Mary L.	22 FEB 1883 R	17	317
Sterne, Susie	Harper, John H.	20 NOV 1882	17	136
Sterne, Victoria	Johnson, Will W.	20 NOV 1882	17	136
Sterns, Charles E.	Sylvester, Emma	01 JAN 1880 R	14	085
Steuart, Bernard M.	King, Mary R.	16 JAN 1878 L	11	306
Steuart, Katie	Fegan, James M.	22 APR 1884 L	18	524
Steuart, Maggie	Jones, Lewis C.	11 NOV 1884 R	19	359
Steuart, Maria Hunter	Davis, Edmund Walter	30 NOV 1880 R	15	072
Steurnagle, Adam A.	Phelps, Annie C.	17 OCT 1882 L	17	076
Stevens, Agnes V.	Hughlett, Julius	29 MAR 1885	20	136
Stevens, Agnes Vadieux	Hughlett, Julius	01 JUL 1885 R	20	303
Stevens, Alice C.	Vail, Stephen	25 JAN 1882	16	206
Stevens, Alphonso	Fairlamb, Fannie	12 JUN 1882 R	16	407
Stevens, Anna E.	Watts, Aaron B.	09 JUN 1885	20	259
Stevens, Edward	Ringgold, Hortense Cisco	20 SEP 1877 R	11	102
Stevens, Henry Eugene	Moore, S. Jeanette	01 FEB 1882 R	16	219
Stevens, Henry L.	Mollard, Jennie	30 DEC 1882 R	17	226
Stevens, Henry M.	Barnes, Elizabeth A.	18 JAN 1883 R	17	268
Stevens, John	Johnson, Clara	15 DEC 1879 L	14	048
Stevens, John	Parris, Bertha	12 SEP 1883 L	18	125
Stevens, John T.	Donegan, Mary	15 JUN 1882 L	16	413
Stevens, Julia M.	Daniel, Edward B.	17 OCT 1877 R	11	138
Stevens, Lizzie Adelaide	Douglas, Ranald	20 MAY 1882 R	16	339
Stevens, Lyndon Hoyt	Taylor, Louisa Warren	08 JAN 1884	18	368
Stevens, Mary C.H.	Fitch, Charles H.	26 APR 1882 R	16	332
Stevens, Minnie Franklin	Warfield, Lorenzo Gastavus	25 NOV 1881 L	16	098
Stevens, Samuel	Jose, Sarah E.	03 JUN 1885 R	20	252
Stevens, William K.	Watt, Bettie A.	25 OCT 1882	17	090
Stevens, William Presley	Bullock, Emma Spottswood	16 AUG 1879 R	13	324
Stevenson, Charles	Johnson, Lucinda	17 SEP 1884	19	246
Stevenson, Eliza	Jones, John	05 JAN 1881 L	15	140

Stevenson, Eugene	Hornblower, Helen	11 JUN 1884 R	19	070
Stevenson, Millie	Williams, Morris	03 MAR 1884 L	18	456
Stevenson, Minnie	Rivers, John W.	27 AUG 1879 L	13	339
Stevenson, Richard	Peters, Louisa R.	02 OCT 1879	13	400
Stevenson, Robert	Parker, Julia	31 MAY 1881 L	15	332
Stevenson, Sarah E.	Williams, Charles	30 JUN 1881	15	383
Stevenson, William	Bell, Laura	26 JUN 1884 L	19	106
Steward, Anna	Smith, George	20 NOV 1878	12	339
Steward, Charles	Kane, Henrietta Virginia	21 JUN 1883 L	18	008
Steward, Charles	Fisher, Alvina	30 AUG 1884 L	19	215
Steward, Edward	Flemmons, Harriet	08 MAY 1879 R	13	175
Steward, Emily	Williams, Cornelius	21 OCT 1879	13	435
Steward, Frances	Stoddard, Daniel	23 OCT 1883 L	18	209
Steward, Jannie	Wood, Albert	17 MAY 1884 L	19	026
Steward, Jennie	Bell, James Alfred	05 FEB 1879 L	13	047
Steward, John	Tolliver, Lizzie	16 MAY 1881 L	15	308
Steward, John	Jackson, Hattie	11 AUG 1882	16	477
Steward, John	Butler, Jennie	23 SEP 1884 L	19	263
Steward, Louisa	Bailey, William	21 JAN 1885	20	033
Steward, Lucinda	Wallace, Toliver	18 OCT 1883	18	202
Steward, Mary Ann	Moland, Thomas	30 SEP 1879 L	13	394
Steward, Mary F., Mrs.	Lewis, William A.	13 DEC 1877 R	11	232
Steward, William W.	Lawrence, Henrietta	06 JAN 1881	15	144
Steward, William W.	Duncan, Charity A.	15 NOV 1882	17	128
Stewart, Agnes M.	McCullough, Wesley E.M.	29 NOV 1883	18	287
Stewart, Anna	Berry, John	28 NOV 1882 R	17	154
Stewart, Annie	Brown, William	30 JAN 1879 L	13	039
Stewart, Anthony	Palmer, Annie	31 OCT 1878	12	302
Stewart, C. McK.	Prater, Mary E.	27 MAY 1895	14	180
Stewart, C.F.	Scott, Barbara	20 OCT 1879 L	13	433
Stewart, Caleb	Grimes, Sarah C.	11 DEC 1877 R	11	230
Stewart, Carrie	Willard, George	27 JUN 1883 R	18	014
Stewart, Charles	Roseway, Susan	19 JUN 1880 R	14	326
Stewart, Charlotte	Thomas, Walter A.	14 OCT 1880 L	14	494
Stewart, Columbus	Canty, Lizzie	08 FEB 1882 L	16	231
Stewart, Daniel H.	Banneker, Ettie	12 MAY 1885	20	015
Stewart, Dora	Ford, Saulsbury	14 FEB 1882 L	16	240
Stewart, Edward	Johnson, Edith B.	12 DEC 1883	18	312
Stewart, Edward	Ayes, Julia	11 JAN 1885 R	20	004
Stewart, Edwin E.	Lee, Elizabeth	18 OCT 1881 R	16	031
Stewart, Eliza	Short, Alfred	03 SEP 1877 R	11	069
Stewart, Eliza	Thomas, George W.	15 SEP 1877 L	11	095
Stewart, Elizabeth	Grayson, Charles B.	03 MAR 1879 L	13	086
Stewart, Ella E.	Jordan, Edward L.	18 MAY 1882 R	16	365
Stewart, Frank	Tewell, Caroline	28 MAY 1885 R	20	241
Stewart, George	Bombray, Lucy	29 NOV 1878 R	12	351
Stewart, George, Jr.	Jackson, Rachel	09 SEP 1880 R	14	439
Stewart, Harriet	Mark, William	15 MAY 1884 L	19	022
Stewart, Henry	Chase, Martha	20 OCT 1879 L	13	434
Stewart, Henry	Contee, Mary	03 SEP 1885	20	399
Stewart, Horace	Lewis, Georgianna	20 MAR 1879 L	13	111
Stewart, Idell	Lewis, George Henry	05 FEB 1880 C	14	139
Stewart, James	Allen, Josephene	03 JUL 1883	18	031
Stewart, James Robert	Williams, Mary E.	24 JUL 1884 L	19	158
Stewart, Jennie	Anderson, George W.	06 APR 1882 L	16	302
Stewart, Jennie C.	Obey, Daniel F., Jr.	11 MAR 1880 L	14	183
Stewart, John	Hammett, Susan Lydia	17 MAY 1883 R	17	448
Stewart, John	Kirk, Kathirine A.	11 OCT 1883	18	187

D.C. Marriage Records Index, June 28, 1877 to October 19, 1885

Stewart, John	Jones, Martha Ann	11 JUN 1885 L	20	269
Stewart, John	Schroth, Hannah	14 OCT 1885 L	20	481
Stewart, John C.	Jones, Ella B.	29 OCT 1884	19	346
Stewart, John T.	Carrick, Ella F.	21 JAN 1882 L	16	204
Stewart, John T.	Brooks, Janie W.	20 AUG 1884	19	194
Stewart, John Thomas	Dowd, Johanna Sullivan	01 JAN 1879 R	12	393
Stewart, Josephine	Lee, William	10 AUG 1880 L	14	396
Stewart, Josephine Adger	Ball, George W.	28 APR 1881 R	15	274
Stewart, Laura	Pierce, John W.	02 DEC 1880 L	15	079
Stewart, Laura E.	Kneesi, Fred W.	16 APR 1880 L	14	226
Stewart, Lizzie	Cooper, John	31 JUL 1880	14	380
Stewart, Lucy	Carter, Walter	13 MAY 1884	19	007
Stewart, Maria	Russell, Charles	06 APR 1880	14	210
Stewart, Marion F.	Matthews, Joshua	06 JAN 1881 R	15	139
Stewart, Marrie	Gray, John	06 FEB 1878 R	11	321
Stewart, Martha	Butcher, Henry	02 JAN 1879 L	13	004
Stewart, Martha	Johnson, Francis	05 MAR 1883 L	17	382
Stewart, Martha	Seaman, Matthew	19 SEP 1885 L	20	429
Stewart, Mary	Burton, John	13 AUG 1878 R	12	157
Stewart, Mary	Johnson, Levi	18 DEC 1880 L	15	108
Stewart, Mary A.	Johnson, Henry	12 APR 1884 L	18	504
Stewart, Mary Alice	Jones, William	13 APR 1881 L	15	256
Stewart, Mary Alice	Plummer, Daniel	18 JUN 1885	20	279
Stewart, Mary E.	Smoot, Henry	17 JUN 1885	20	249
Stewart, Mary J.	Thornton, William	29 MAR 1879 R	13	118
Stewart, Mary K.	Hemingway, Charles B.	03 NOV 1883 L	18	231
Stewart, Minty	Hall, Oden	15 OCT 1885 R	20	489
Stewart, Rebecca	Bettus, John	10 SEP 1883 L	18	120
Stewart, Robert	Mack, Annie	24 SEP 1879 R	13	384
Stewart, Rosa	White, Peyton U.	24 JUL 1879 R	13	288
Stewart, Rosetta	Robinson, William H.	14 DEC 1884 R	19	452
Stewart, Samuel Hamilton	Trussler, Virginia	11 SEP 1879 R	13	365
Stewart, Sarah E.	Fredick, Amasa C.	19 OCT 1881 R	16	033
Stewart, Tabby	Johnson, David	04 SEP 1877 L	11	075
Stewart, Thomas	Jefferson, Josephine	25 SEP 1880 R	14	460
Stewart, Thomas	Young, Ida	02 JUN 1881 L	15	340
Stewart, Thomas E.	Williams, Bettie E.	20 MAR 1884 L	18	478
Stewart, William	West, Fannie	22 SEP 1881 R	15	495
Stewart, William A.	Donaldson, Emma E.	14 APR 1881 R	15	257
Stewart, William Henry	Burrel, Elizabeth	17 APR 1878	12	007
Stewart, William McC.	Plant, Josephine A.	05 SEP 1877 L	11	077
Stewart, Wm. Thomas	Turner, Ella	05 JUL 1885 L	20	205
Stickell, S.E.	Sutton, S.J.	29 MAY 1879 L	13	211
Stickney, Mary Kingsford	Taylor, Lewis Rodney	24 OCT 1882 R	17	091
Stidham, Samuel H.	Jones, Emma B.	27 MAR 1883 L	17	362
Stiebeling, Elisabetha	Bischoff, Charles H.	16 JUL 1882 R	17	449
Stiebeling, Philipp	Stiebeling, Sophia	24 MAY 1885 R	20	236
Stiebeling, Sophia	Stiebeling, Philipp	24 MAY 1885 R	20	236
Stieff, John C.	Witters, S. Elizabeth	27 FEB 1883 R	17	323
Stier, Margaret H.	Cooper, George S.	26 SEP 1884	19	267
Stierman, Joseph	Goldstein, Bertha	25 MAR 1883 R	17	357
Stiffler, George	Noll, Eve A.	19 JUL 1880 L	14	368
Stilson, Frank	Lewis, Fannie	29 NOV 1883	18	281
Stilwell, Anna M.	Colman, Charles D.	29 MAY 1879 R	13	209
Stine, Roberta K.	Witmer, A.H.	30 OCT 1884	19	351
Stinemetz, Anthony	Spindle, Ida M.	10 JUN 1882 R	16	404
Stinemetz, Irene D.	Dulin, Thaddeus C.	17 MAY 1882 R	16	362
Stinemetz, Samuel W.	Morgan, Elizabeth J.	15 JAN 1879 R	13	017

Stiner, Ella A.	Hough, Caldwell C.	15 APR 1884	18	519
Stinzing, John P.	Bernard, Annette C.	15 SEP 1880	14	445
Stinzing, Mary L.	DeMoll, Theodore G.	15 OCT 1879 R	13	426
Stirling, Archibald	Mathiot, Estelle	08 JUL 1884	19	126
Stith, J.P.	Cox, Minnie	02 JUN 1880 L	14	301
Stith, Paul J.	Farmer, Ida	18 MAY 1881 R	15	315
Stith, Rosie	Tyas, Joseph	16 APR 1891	19	027
Stockbridge, Geo. Herbert	Reyburn, Elizabeth	27 NOV 1884 R	19	407
Stockdale, Fletcher Summerfield	Schleicher, Elizabeth Tinsley	10 JUL 1877 R	11	012
Stockett, Charles A.	Howe, Catherine C.	06 FEB 1879 R	13	048
Stockett, Isabella	Moran, John A.	01 OCT 1884 L	19	280
Stockett, William A.	Dusing, Sophronia	04 SEP 1884	19	229
Stockholm, Rosa	Sanford, John M.	11 MAR 1878	11	377
Stocks, Anthony A.	Grant, Julia D.	14 JUL 1879 R	13	280
Stockton, Lucy B.	Harris, Walter S.	23 APR 1885 R	20	187
Stoddard, Daniel	Steward, Frances	23 OCT 1883 L	18	209
Stoddard, John G.	Hudson, Jamie E.	04 APR 1881 L	15	246
Stoddard, Josiah C.	Wilson, Lucy Lee	12 APR 1885	20	367
Stoddard, Minnie V.	Treadway, Decatur B.	09 SEP 1885	20	410
Stoddard, Nathaniel	Wallace, Susan Elizabeth	24 MAR 1881 R	15	238
Stoddart, Armat	Berlin, Grace M.	24 MAR 1881 R	15	238
Stoddart, Joseph Kennard	Winter, Hattie	27 JUN 1883	18	017
Stoeper, Lissi	Von Apel, Philip	28 AUG 1878	12	164
Stofer, Mary	Brand, Edward James	09 MAR 1882 R	16	271
Stofiel, Sarah I.	Moffett, Henry C.	20 NOV 1879 R	13	495
Stohbel, Charles H.	Smallwood, Mary R.	05 APR 1879 R	13	129
Stokes, George W.R.	Gartrell, Ella Harkness	20 DEC 1883	18	328
Stokes, Sewell Lewis	Fisher, Helen	15 OCT 1885 R	20	488
Stokes, William Brown	Hosman, Ida May	03 JAN 1883 R	17	233
Stoks, Emmet	Gray, Anna	09 OCT 1879 R	13	391
Stollager, Carrie	Hammett, John A.	27 AUG 1883	18	100
Stone, Alfred	Burrows, Nettie	30 MAY 1885 L	20	248
Stone, Amelia V.	Reihl, James A.	28 JAN 1884	18	397
Stone, Charles Allston	Wood, Liley	09 JUL 1879 R	13	272
Stone, Elizabeth A.	Staub, Jacob F.	09 APR 1878 L	11	412
Stone, Elizabeth J.	Croggan, William N.	14 OCT 1879 L	13	421
Stone, Elizabeth Newton	Douglass, George Lyon	04 JUN 1878 R	12	080
Stone, Emma	Harding, John	16 JUL 1885	20	331
Stone, Fannie J.	Mitchell, Andrew J.	25 SEP 1885	20	442
Stone, Jay	Barber, Ida Belle	05 OCT 1881 R	16	005
Stone, John W.	Truslow, Annie J.	03 JUL 1884 L	19	120
Stone, Lottie M.	Daily, Patrick R.	13 DEC 1882 R	17	180
Stone, Lucinda Ridgely	Halleck, William Edward	26 NOV 1878 R	12	348
Stone, Mary	Farley, James	08 APR 1880 L	14	215
Stone, Mary Ellen	Maddox, James H.	13 SEP 1883	18	128
Stone, Oliver	Fornshill, Julia	05 AUG 1877	11	041
Stone, Oscar F.	Hackley, Lucy A.	08 MAY 1878 R	12	043
Stone, Sallie E.	Beach, Benjamin F.	17 FEB 1884	18	427
Stone, Thomas J.	Lefevre, Louise H.	12 AUG 1885 R	20	366
Stone, Thomas Ritchie	Whitney, Lelia	22 JAN 1885 R	20	034
Stone, William Jay	Bates, Nelly M.	14 MAY 1881 R	15	307
Storer, Laura Lorraine	Hack, Oliver Clarence	26 SEP 1880 R	14	460
Storey, Mary F.	Turner, Samuel T.	25 APR 1885 L	20	188
Storey, Robert	Walsh, Elizabeth	11 AUG 1881 R	15	440
Storks, Robert	Wheeler, Mary	24 MAY 1883	17	451
Storm, Annie W.	Wood, Lexious A.	12 SEP 1882 R	17	016
Stormont, William T.	Kennedy, Anna G.	22 NOV 1881	16	087
Storms, Mary	Wait, Hulbert H.	22 APR 1880 L	14	235

Story, Eliza	Kindslow, Levi	14 NOV 1882 R	17	126
Story, James	Grinder, Ida	01 JAN 1878	11	284
Story, Jane	Cornwell, Newton	06 JUL 1879 R	13	270
Story, Joseph W.	Dean, Annie L.	13 MAY 1884 R	19	015
Story, William	Watson, Celestine	02 JUL 1879 R	13	265
Story, William	Thorn, Massie	26 JUN 1879 R	13	255
Stotsenburg, Alice R., Mrs.	Morris, John W.	12 APR 1880	14	218
Stotts, Jesse	Hartley, Jennie	07 APR 1881 L	15	250
Stouffer, Anna May	Hall, Albert Green	03 APR 1883	17	372
Stouffer, Mary	Connell, Robert	03 APR 1883 R	17	375
Stout, Clara V.	Mearns, Charles T.F.	13 DEC 1883	18	312
Stout, Orrin Beech	Jeffries, Anna Florence	10 DEC 1879 R	14	041
Stover, John	Grover, Martha	31 OCT 1877 L	11	161
Stowell, Carrie L.	Ruoff, Charles H.	06 OCT 1885 R	20	461
Stowell, Frederick G.	McDermott, Maggie V.	19 JAN 1882	16	199
Straib, Johanna	Young, William	27 DEC 1877	11	273
Straightner, Perry Wm.	Diggs, Matilda	05 AUG 1882 L	16	469
Straitner, William	Diggs, Matilda	31 DEC 1883 R	18	355
Stranahan, G.N.	Amiss, Melvilla J.	01 OCT 1878	12	246
Strange, George	Fitzhugh, Roberta	05 FEB 1879	13	043
Strasburger, Bertha	Hirsh, Morris	16 SEP 1884 L	19	253
Strasburger, Myer	Bensinger, Emma	03 JAN 1883 R	17	231
Strather, Thomas H.	Raiede, Hester	01 MAY 1882	16	344
Stratton, Charles W.	Woodroof, Emma	06 SEP 1882 R	17	006
Stratton, Ella	Wells, Charles E.	26 JUL 1881	15	418
Stratton, Jennie	Abbott, Ernest E.	22 AUG 1885 R	20	361
Stratton, Margaret	Mitchell, Isaiah	05 AUG 1879 R	13	308
Straub, Frances	Miller, Francis	23 JUN 1885 L	20	284
Straub, Maggie	Freeman, Frank	30 SEP 1879 L	13	393
Straub, Rosa H.	Taylor, Henry	05 JUL 1881 L	15	390
Strauss, David	Herman, Bertha	11 APR 1880 R	14	215
Strauthers, Warren	Bowie, Maggie	17 FEB 1885 R	20	075
Strawther, Benjamin	Johnson, Susan	24 OCT 1878 R	12	290
Streaker, Mary Genila	Harrington, Charles Albert	06 JUN 1882 R	16	396
Streamer, Lewis P.	Van Riswick, Lillie	05 NOV 1880	15	033
Streamer, Marie B.	Evans, John D.	26 JUL 1881 R	15	415
Streamer, Mollie J.	Teachum, John K.	11 MAY 1880	14	265
Streb, Annie	Just, George W.	22 MAY 1879 R	13	201
Streb, Henry L.	Starke, Mary A.	13 JUN 1883	17	491
Streb, Magadalena	Glick, John H.F.	16 APR 1879 R	13	144
Streeks, Andrew	Cox, Mary C.	14 NOV 1880 R	15	047
Streeks, Emma L.	Anderson, Edgar S.	18 MAR 1884	18	476
Street, Clara Evelina	Maiers, Louis Henry	12 SEP 1883 R	18	122
Street, Daniel B.	Gatehell, Addie	22 JUL 1885	20	335
Street, Peter W.	Baker, Eliza Ellen	05 NOV 1884 L	19	365
Street, Walter	Frazier, Harriet	19 MAY 1881 L	15	318
Streets, Amelia	Homstead, Henry	07 OCT 1884 L	19	290
Streets, Cora	Corbin, John	05 AUG 1880 L	14	389
Streets, Forrest	Smith, Annie	23 DEC 1882 L	17	208
Streets, Frank W.	Posey, Ida P.	05 DEC 1877 L	11	222
Streets, John H.	Coleman, Mary Malvina	19 DEC 1878 R	12	390
Streets, Martha	Collins, Douglas	02 SEP 1879 R	13	338
Strickhardt, Wilhelmina	Smith, James	01 SEP 1878	12	187
Strickhart, Mary Louise	Shelton, James C.	05 MAR 1878 L	11	372
Strickling, Annie	Schwartz, John	19 SEP 1877 L	11	101
Striker, John B.	White, Annie E.	06 DEC 1878	12	371
Strine, William R.	Daily, Hattie B.	12 SEP 1879	13	367
Stringfellow, James W.	Bowers, Eliza Frances	15 NOV 1883	18	255

Strobel, Agnes A.	Eiker, James M.	29 OCT 1878 R	12	296
Strobel, Frederick W.	Thomas, Mary E.	28 JUN 1880 L	14	335
Strobel, Margaretta	Engel, Christian	30 JAN 1879	13	039
Stroder, John	Harris, Rosetta	20 DEC 1884	19	474
Strodus, Charles	Hawkins, Maggie	10 APR 1882 L	16	307
Strokes, Mary	Scott, Jesse	18 SEP 1879 L	13	378
Stromberger, Lissie M.	Mann, Benjamin Frank	24 DEC 1880 R	15	123
Strong, Amelia M.	Slade, Francis H.	06 MAY 1880	14	253
Strong, Clarissa	Matthews, Beale	12 JUL 1880	14	357
Strong, Lidia Eudore	Corbett, Charles F.	11 JAN 1879 R	13	014
Strong, Maria S.	Morris, John E.	16 MAY 1878	12	056
Strong, Mary	Warde, Daly	30 MAR 1878	11	398
Strother, Catherine M.E.	Washington, George	05 FEB 1880 L	14	138
Strother, James William	Wales, Lucinda	10 APR 1878 R	11	413
Strother, Jennie E.	Payne, Charles W.	26 AUG 1878 R	12	179
Strother, Maria Belle	Lyne, John R.	15 JUL 1877 R	11	019
Strother, Nathan	Sutton, Priscilla	08 AUG 1879 R	13	313
Strother, Peter F.	Ray, Lillie Dale	15 NOV 1877 R	11	186
Strother, Rachael	Jenkins, Robert	15 MAY 1883 L	17	439
Strother, Robert J.	Smith, Mary G.	21 MAR 1882 L	16	285
Strother, Sarah Virginia	Donaldson, Webster Clay	26 JAN 1880 R	14	112
Strothers, James	Bailey, Marietta	02 JUL 1885	20	305
Stroud, Harry Richard Skerrett	Warder, Mary Ellen	24 DEC 1877 R	11	258
Stroud, Malvina	Johnson, Albert	06 MAY 1884 L	19	008
Stroud, William D.	Eliot, Mary J.	15 NOV 1877	11	188
Struder, Mary A.	Nelson, Andrew	01 MAY 1883 R	17	423
Strum, Gustave P.	Naylor, Janie L.	15 FEB 1881 R	15	190
Struven, Kate F.	Lemkul, Louis M.L.	08 APR 1882 L	16	305
Stuart, Addie	Green, Francis	27 AUG 1878	12	181
Stuart, Alice	McKeever, William	30 JUN 1879 L	13	259
Stuart, Alice C.	Johnston, Thurston B.	17 OCT 1880 R	14	499
Stuart, Alice G.	Johnston, Thurston B.	14 OCT 1885 R	20	480
Stuart, Annie	McCauley, Benjamin Franklin	03 APR 1881 R	15	244
Stuart, Augustus	Rawlings, Margaret Anne	17 FEB 1879 L	13	063
Stuart, Benjamin S.	Hunter, Mary C.	22 OCT 1877 R	11	149
Stuart, Cedonia M.	Reiss, William	19 FEB 1878	11	347
Stuart, Charles J.	Young, Anna	05 MAY 1885	20	206
Stuart, Cora	Fickling, Austin	01 OCT 1877	11	116
Stuart, Eliza	Neal, William	19 JUL 1884	19	147
Stuart, George W.	Evans, Jennie L.	20 JUL 1882 R	16	448
Stuart, Gibbons	Moran, Agnes	13 AUG 1883 L	18	085
Stuart, Henry	Thompson, Susan	15 MAY 1879 R	13	188
Stuart, Ida M.	Blackman, Samuel Stockton	18 SEP 1883 R	18	140
Stuart, Isabella	Crawford, Albert	30 DEC 1880 L	15	134
Stuart, Jeannett	Smith, Daniel	19 FEB 1883 R	17	305
Stuart, John	Ignon, Lizzie	19 NOV 1878	12	334
Stuart, Mary F.	Lafelle, William P.	06 OCT 1881 L	16	012
Stuart, Reuben	Johnston, Mary	06 OCT 1882 L	17	058
Stuart, Sidonia	Ball, Robert	03 APR 1884 L	18	495
Stuart, William	Hannal, Georgiana	19 JUN 1884 R	19	092
Stubblefield, Grace T.	Polkinhorn, Joseph H.	14 NOV 1882 R	17	129
Stubbs, Edward	Brown, Nancy Ann	27 DEC 1877	11	274
Stubbs, Edward C.	Blake, Frances	16 OCT 1879 R	13	429
Stubbs, Nannie T.	Lee, William P.R.	09 SEP 1884	19	234
Stubener, Annie M.	Lohman, Robert Lee	14 JUL 1885 R	20	324
Studds, Laura A.	Brawner, George W.	10 NOV 1881 R	16	071
Stump, Joseph	Roth, Annie	20 MAY 1885 R	20	231
Stump, Mary B.	LeRoy, William E.	17 NOV 1881	16	078

Stumpf, Edward	Beltz, Paulina	19 SEP 1880 R	14	448
Stumpf, Mary	Widmann, Charles	09 DEC 1884 R	19	444
Stunkel, Edward T.	Rose, Hetty A.	06 APR 1880	14	210
Sturgeon, E.B.	Young, Annie L.	26 JUL 1877	11	031
Sturgeon, John F.	Winstead, M. Louise	01 JUN 1881 R	15	335
Sturgis, John R.	Posey, Mary L.	12 FEB 1883	17	303
Sturgis, Joseph	Connell, Ida R.	12 OCT 1879	13	416
Stuteley, Alonzo	Marlon, Jane	24 SEP 1885 R	20	440
Stutley, Thomas H.	Trice, Ardelia	09 JUN 1885 R	20	262
Stutz, Adelaide M.	Shedd, James J.	04 NOV 1884	19	360
Stutz, Anna Maria Babette	Eslin, George McClellan	12 AUG 1885 R	20	364
Stutzman, Annie G.	Boardman, Myron	02 OCT 1878	12	249
Stutzman, Cora M.	Johnson, Simeon F.	17 MAY 1883	17	446
Stweart, Cordelia	Hall, John T.	13 MAR 1884 L	18	470
Sudduth, Joseph A.	Carter, Mary	19 MAR 1879	13	108
Suit, Charles J.	Francis, Martha E.	21 JUN 1883	18	008
Suit, Ella	Tolson, Arthur	07 NOV 1878 R	12	305
Suit, George Tyler	Word, Blanche Aileen	11 JAN 1883 R	17	254
Suit, James E.	Ellis, Mary	10 FEB 1878	11	333
Suit, John E.	Watts, Jane E.	17 DEC 1884 R	19	467
Suit, John F.	Sullivan, Cecelia	11 AUG 1880 L	14	397
Suit, Mary S.	Yost, Augustus	23 MAR 1880 R	14	193
Suit, S. Taylor	Pelham, Martha Rosa	04 SEP 1883 R	18	111
Suit, William G.	Yost, Fannie	02 NOV 1882 R	17	108
Sulavan, Ella	Hogans, John J.	16 OCT 1880 L	14	499
Sullivan, Abby	Hudlow, Samuel	23 JUL 1878	12	146
Sullivan, Alice A.	Marston, Alfred P.	29 OCT 1879 R	13	449
Sullivan, Annie	Boland, Patrick	14 OCT 1885 L	20	484
Sullivan, Bridget A.	O'Donoghue, Dennis	18 OCT 1882 L	17	081
Sullivan, Cecelia	Suit, John F.	11 AUG 1880 L	14	397
Sullivan, Charles	Cox, Mary Ann Elizabeth	05 DEC 1883 L	18	297
Sullivan, Daniel	Shepherd, Mary E.	09 JAN 1881 R	15	144
Sullivan, Daniel J.	Eisenbeiss, Bertha J.R.	19 JUN 1880 L	14	327
Sullivan, Edward Joseph	Kane, Margaret Anne	27 DEC 1878 L	12	415
Sullivan, Elizabeth J.	Wells, George T.	13 NOV 1878 R	12	328
Sullivan, Ella E.	Lowe, John R.	01 OCT 1879 R	13	397
Sullivan, Ellen	Habram, John	02 OCT 1882 R	17	048
Sullivan, Eugene F.	Driscoll, Ellen V.	15 MAY 1883	17	443
Sullivan, Fannie	McDevitt, John J.	10 MAY 1883 R	17	247
Sullivan, Fielding F.	Smith, Elizabeth	18 AUG 1881 L	15	454
Sullivan, Florence Patten	Duffie, John Smiley	12 JUL 1883	18	042
Sullivan, George N.	Cleary, Kate	05 JUN 1879	13	221
Sullivan, Hannah	Carroll, John William	18 JUL 1879 R	13	281
Sullivan, Hannah	Sullivan, John	20 JAN 1884 R	18	385
Sullivan, Henry E.	Allen, Mary A.	11 APR 1885 L	20	160
Sullivan, Ivy Isabelle	Johnson, Charles Henry	29 OCT 1884	19	343
Sullivan, James Edward	Young, Annie	28 JUL 1878 R	12	150
Sullivan, Jennie	Sweitzer, Henry	13 DEC 1878 R	12	376
Sullivan, Jeremiah	Connor, Mary	15 APR 1885 L	20	171
Sullivan, Joe	Deviny, Edward	16 JUL 1881 L	15	404
Sullivan, Johanna	McCarthy, William	06 NOV 1879 L	13	469
Sullivan, John	Fuller, Johanna	07 JUL 1883 L	18	039
Sullivan, John	Sullivan, Hannah	20 JAN 1884 R	18	385
Sullivan, John	O'Brien, Mary	22 NOV 1884 R	19	403
Sullivan, John J.	Bennett, Annie E.	17 OCT 1877 L	11	143
Sullivan, John J.	Fahey, Delia L.	06 NOV 1878 R	12	163
Sullivan, John W.	Callohan, Ellen	18 APR 1878	12	010
Sullivan, Julia	Williams, Charles	11 FEB 1882 L	16	236

Sullivan, Katie	Booth, Joseph	13 JUL 1878 L	12	134
Sullivan, Lesley	Peyton, Josephus S.	21 SEP 1881 R	15	496
Sullivan, Maggie	Coon, Frank W.	05 SEP 1882 L	17	006
Sullivan, Maggie	Mulhall, Joseph	03 AUG 1885 L	20	348
Sullivan, Maggie	Riley, John	16 AUG 1885 R	20	372
Sullivan, Maggie F.	Crawford, Joel B.	17 AUG 1880 L	14	402
Sullivan, Maggie M.	Sydnor, Richard M.	08 JUL 1884 L	19	130
Sullivan, Marcus Wm.	Chenoweth, Jennie	03 JUN 1878 R	12	081
Sullivan, Margaret	Bolac, Henry	13 MAY 1885 L	20	217
Sullivan, Mary	Kelly, T.J.	29 APR 1879 L	13	165
Sullivan, Mary	Barry, Patrick	10 SEP 1881 R	15	480
Sullivan, Mary	McCarthy, Patrick	14 NOV 1882	17	125
Sullivan, Mary	McHugo, James	21 SEP 1882 L	17	033
Sullivan, Mary Ann	Doyle, John P.	19 AUG 1878	12	173
Sullivan, Mary E.	Harrington, Daniel	16 APR 1879 L	13	148
Sullivan, Mary E.	Herbert, Albert A.	15 FEB 1882 L	16	242
Sullivan, Mary F.	Swan, John Q.	25 FEB 1879 R	13	076
Sullivan, Michael	Harrington, Julia	03 APR 1883 L	17	377
Sullivan, Michael	Casey, Mary	08 FEB 1885	20	055
Sullivan, Michael P.	Fitzpatrick, Mary E.	26 SEP 1883	18	155
Sullivan, Millard Fillmore	Ferry, Laura Isabella	01 JAN 1882 R	16	175
Sullivan, Minnie	Leonard, John J.	14 JAN 1884 L	18	375
Sullivan, Nannie	Fuller, John J.	31 DEC 1881 L	16	174
Sullivan, Nellie T.	Goodwin, John J.	16 MAY 1883 R	17	444
Sullivan, Patrick	Sullivan, Sarah E.	29 APR 1884 R	18	541
Sullivan, Philip	Robinson, Mary Jane	09 DEC 1878 L	12	374
Sullivan, Sarah E.	Sullivan, Patrick	29 APR 1884 R	18	541
Sullivan, Thomas F.	Cotter, Mary	10 JAN 1884	18	372
Sullivan, Thomas Joseph	McCartney, Ellen C.	04 DEC 1878 L	12	367
Sullivan, W.F.	Butler, Loie M.	01 APR 1884	18	490
Sullivan, William	Edmonds, Kate	12 SEP 1885 R	20	408
Sullivan, William J.	Barron, Florence L., Mrs.	10 JUN 1884	19	072
Sullivan, William J.	Nash, Alice V.	14 AUG 1884	19	187
Suman, James Luther	Weaver, Clara Lizzie	14 FEB 1883 R	17	306
Suman, Teresa A.R.	Gonzenbach, Charles H.	18 OCT 1877	11	137
Sumby, Dennis	Thomas, Sarah	12 AUG 1884	19	182
Sumby, John	Brown, Sarah	14 APR 1884 R	18	504
Sumby, Samson	Anderson, Fanny	28 MAY 1885 L	20	244
Summers, Alice Sophronia	Davison, George Alfred	27 NOV 1877 R	11	202
Summers, Catherine L.	Beck, Jacob J.	22 NOV 1880 L	15	059
Summers, Edward W.	Burgess, Mary Hannah	07 AUG 1877 R	11	044
Summers, Florence I.	Shepard, Charles	15 NOV 1882 L	17	127
Summers, Ida	Muller, Henry Joseph	18 MAY 1885 R	20	227
Summers, Laura Amelia	Weast, Hiram Webster	23 DEC 1879 L	14	067
Summers, Mary E.	Tolson, Henry N.	21 AUG 1877 R	11	058
Summers, Matilda A.	Mathews, Robert A.	12 FEB 1885 R	20	065
Summers, Richard H.	Pangle, Annie M.	06 JUN 1882 R	16	398
Summers, Thomas F.	Whaley, Margaret A.	29 SEP 1880 R	14	464
Summerscales, Elizabeth	Fallon, John T.	22 APR 1879 L	13	154
Summerton, Addie	Reed, John N.	04 JUL 1880 R	14	347
Summerville, Georgeana	Diggs, Richard E.N.	27 DEC 1883	18	342
Summerville, John F.	Inloins, Margaret Etta	24 SEP 1885 L	20	440
Summerville, Mary E.	Johnson, Thomas	31 JAN 1884 L	18	403
Summerville, William H.	Escott, Annie	14 NOV 1883 R	18	251
Summons, Jennie	Fanning, John W.	15 NOV 1881 L	16	079
Sunderland, Hattie	Turrell, George	28 OCT 1878 R	12	295
Sunderland, Natalie Louise	Verdi, Tullio Suzzara	14 OCT 1882 L	17	072
Sunderland, Rosalie	Day, Orrin	30 OCT 1878 R	12	300

Surdez, Edouard A.	Peake, Mary Ella	03 MAY 1885 R	20	187
Susco, Charles	Gray, Virginia	22 JUN 1884	19	096
Suter, Alexander	Jenkins, Emily	18 DEC 1878 R	12	386
Suter, Charles E.	Simson, Jean E.C.	27 OCT 1877 R	11	158
Suter, Harry C.	Wagner, Georgia P.	09 JUN 1882 R	16	402
Suter, John R.	Roudabush, Fannie B.	05 NOV 1884	19	364
Suthard, Charles M.	Rodier, Mattie K.	18 JUL 1883	18	053
Suthard, Sallie A.	Deeton, George B.	02 JAN 1878 R	11	288
Sutherland, Alcinda	Beach, Frederick	21 AUG 1884	19	201
Sutherland, James Buchanan	Beach, Zera Rose	29 MAR 1883 R	17	370
Sutherland, Mobeary	Able, Roxie Ann	25 SEP 1879	13	387
Sutherland, Moses H.	Farrar, R. Blanche	25 APR 1882 R	16	332
Sutherland, Theodore A.	Milstead, Dora E.	08 JUL 1878 L	12	128
Sutherland, Thomas E.	Shackelford, Ella	30 JUL 1880 R	14	378
Sutherland, Virginia A.	Bryant, Thomas H.	30 MAR 1880 R	14	203
Sutphen, Hattie Minnetta	Symmes, Henry Cleves	09 MAY 1882 R	16	353
Suttle, C. Broaddus	Bagby, William W.	24 FEB 1880 R	14	165
Suttle, James D.	Brosshan, Mary D.	13 JAN 1883 L	17	256
Suttle, William H.	Bruce, Emma J.	24 MAY 1885 R	20	237
Sutton, Alfred	Nicholas, Sarah, Mrs.	25 SEP 1882 R	17	018
Sutton, Edward H.	Treadwell, Sarah	07 NOV 1879	13	472
Sutton, Eveline	English, Benjamin S.	06 JAN 1885 R	20	006
Sutton, James T.	Steele, Jennie	19 MAY 1878	12	059
Sutton, Jennie E.	McCuen, John	05 JUL 1884	19	122
Sutton, John Suter	Cady, Emma Cleveland	13 OCT 1877 R	11	132
Sutton, Kate R.	Battenfield, John E.	16 OCT 1884	19	313
Sutton, Priscilla	Strother, Nathan	08 AUG 1879 R	13	313
Sutton, Robert G.	Fearson, Lizzie	19 OCT 1882 R	17	080
Sutton, S.J.	Stickell, S.E.	29 MAY 1879 L	13	211
Sutton, Susan Isabella	Davis, George W.	04 FEB 1884 R	18	406
Swagart, Columbus L.	McGuigan, Mary	30 MAR 1885 R	20	136
Swailes, Alice	Lewis, William H.	04 SEP 1879 L	13	352
Swain, Augusta	Alexander, Douglass B.	17 SEP 1878	12	224
Swain, Benedict	Mansfield, Josephine E.	07 DEC 1881 R	15	507
Swain, Elizabeth Ann	Creamer, Samuel L.	24 OCT 1877 L	11	153
Swales, George W.	Smith, Artie	30 NOV 1882	17	162
Swales, Janet	Coleman, William	14 FEB 1878 R	11	336
Swales, Wesley	Coleman, Mary	11 MAY 1882	16	356
Swallow, Charlotte Jane Cawthorn	Clancy, Frank Willey	30 OCT 1879	13	452
Swan, John Q.	Sullivan, Mary F.	25 FEB 1879 R	13	076
Swan, Laura Ellen	Hawkins, Charles Allen	15 DEC 1879 L	14	048
Swan, Lucy Ann	Parker, Sydney	02 OCT 1883 R	18	163
Swan, Lula A.	Dunning, John W.	06 NOV 1879	13	470
Swan, Moses M.	Carroll, Emma	18 FEB 1879 L	13	064
Swann, Celia	Bond, Samuel	19 NOV 1877	11	189
Swann, Jessie Haney	McClure, Austin Wade	23 DEC 1879 R	14	027
Swann, John	Tillman, Mary	12 JUN 1879	13	231
Swann, John Albert	Luckett, Harriet	17 JAN 1883 R	17	110
Swann, Maria	Gordon, Anderson	15 APR 1882 R	16	317
Swann, Richard J.	Brooks, Annie P.	26 DEC 1877 R	11	270
Swann, Thomas	Fleming, Amanda	08 DEC 1880 L	15	087
Swann, William F.	Butler, Emma E.	15 MAY 1884	19	023
Swarn, James Nelson	Jackson, Martha Ann, Mrs.	26 SEP 1882 R	17	038
Swart, J.H.	Harrison, Florence	06 NOV 1879 R	13	471
Swart, Laura B.	Wunder, William Henry	28 OCT 1879 R	13	448
Swart, William W.	McChesney, Kate H.	23 JUN 1885 L	20	286
Swear, Mary	Jones, Edward	26 OCT 1880 R	15	014
Swearingen, Henry Hartmell	Hubbard, Valeria E.	15 DEC 1880 R	19	4700

Swearingen, Sarah Henderson	Smith, John Condit	15 MAY 1883 R	17	438
Sweat, John B.	Mead, Losanna	17 SEP 1882	17	288
Sweatmn, Isabella, Mrs.	Contine, Charles R.	11 NOV 1879 R	16	3776
Sweble, Charles F.	Kizer, Sallie A.	21 AUG 1879	13	327
Sweeney, A.A.	Brown, Sarah Jane	02 JAN 1878	11	290
Sweeney, Alice H.	Sweeney, Harry B.	22 APR 1885 R	20	183
Sweeney, George	Gray, Isabella Frances	03 JUL 1877 L	11	007
Sweeney, Harry B.	Sweeney, Alice H.	22 APR 1885 R	20	183
Sweeney, Hattie C.	Cleveland, Elijah	01 FEB 1882	16	217
Sweeney, John J.	Wharfield, Martha Ellen	25 FEB 1879 R	13	077
Sweeney, John T.	Sweeney, Ruth V.	09 OCT 1883 L	18	182
Sweeney, Michael	Joy, Julia	14 OCT 1885 L	20	482
Sweeney, Mollie J.	Cleveland, Philip B.	20 APR 1885 R	20	173
Sweeney, Richard	Lincoln, Mary	16 MAR 1885 R	20	117
Sweeney, Ruth V.	Sweeney, John T.	09 OCT 1883 L	18	182
Sweeney, Sadie C.	Padgett, William B.	22 MAY 1878	12	063
Sweeny, Bertie	Graham, John Robert	01 JAN 1884 R	18	360
Sweeny, Ellen	Keefe, Owen T.	18 JAN 1883	17	267
Sweet, Austin C.	Wyman, Hester A.	30 APR 1885 L	20	201
Sweet, Reuben Thomas	Merrill, Harriet Edith	16 JUL 1883	18	047
Sweetman, George Jay	Fischer, Florence	01 FEB 1884	18	405
Sweetney, Betsey	Richards, John	24 JAN 1883 L	17	273
Sweetnin, Augustus	Butler, Theresa	11 JAN 1881 L	15	146
Sweetnin, Lewis	Grant, Mary	06 APR 1882	16	301
Sweitzer, George J.	Shweitzer, Kate	25 NOV 1883	18	274
Sweitzer, Henry	Sullivan, Jennie	13 DEC 1878 R	12	376
Sweitzer, John	Brusecke, Annie	09 OCT 1884	19	296
Swetmamn, Ecca R.	Ford, Mollie T.	03 FEB 1881 L	15	175
Swetnam, Thomas R.	Ford, Patty C.	03 FEB 1881 L	15	176
Swetnem, C.F.	Simpson, Jennie	21 APR 1885 R	20	180
Swift, Eben	Palmer, Susan Bonaparte	17 MAY 1880 R	14	273
Swift, Joseph	Crawford, Mary R.	04 AUG 1880	14	386
Swift, Mary	Wootson, Maurice	04 NOV 1884 L	19	360
Swiggard, John F.	Morris, Katie V.	06 JUN 1885	20	259
Swinborne, John	Hall, Margaret	11 DEC 1884 R	19	454
Swing, Nora Maud	Fuller, Miles	27 MAY 1884 R	19	039
Swingle, Morgan	Hodgkins, S. Elizabeth	16 OCT 1884	19	313
Swink, Susan	Short, Robert	23 JAN 1880 L	14	119
Switzer, Charles J.	Dowd, Eva E.	14 MAY 1884 R	19	019
Switzer, Maggia	Zelbernagel, Wladystaw	10 OCT 1883 L	18	186
Swope, Kate	Barry, James	10 DEC 1877 L	11	228
Swope, Maggie	Sandford, Edward E.	09 FEB 1882	16	224
Sword, Robert B.	Donnelly, Mary T.	14 APR 1879 L	13	139
Syas, Anne	Nelson, Walter	03 MAR 1882 R	16	266
Sydenstricker, Oliver P.	Grimes, Josephine A.	26 NOV 1878	12	345
Sydnor, Anna	Arnold, Edgar	22 JUL 1880 L	14	372
Sydnor, Anna	Raun, George W.	16 APR 1881 L	15	259
Sydnor, Baldwin R.	Moore, Violetta	23 MAY 1882 L	16	373
Sydnor, Emma J.	Helm, Edwin L.	10 JUN 1884	19	071
Sydnor, Richard M.	Sullivan, Maggie M.	08 JUL 1884 L	19	130
Syford, George H.	Culbertson, Josephine	11 FEB 1885	20	063
Sylvester, Emma	Sterns, Charles E.	01 JAN 1880 R	14	085
Symanoskie, Joseph	Wasney, Annie	09 FEB 1880 R	14	143
Symcox, Frances	Daniel, Alonzo	18 DEC 1883	18	317
Symmes, Henry Cleves	Sutphen, Hattie Minnetta	09 MAY 1882 R	16	353
Synch, Ella	Meter, Charles	08 DEC 1881 L	16	119
Syncox, James T.	Able, Selone	13 SEP 1883	18	129
Syncox, Sophie	Taylor, Robert	04 MAY 1880 R	14	252

Synder, John	Scott, Louisa	27 DEC 1881 L	16	163
Syphax, Annie	Costin, James	28 JUN 1883 R	18	023
Syphax, Julia W.	Boston, William S.	26 OCT 1882	17	096
Syphax, Mary Ellinor	Brodie, Albert K.	05 APR 1881 R	15	248
Szegedy, Henry W.	Wells, Florence L.	30 OCT 1880 L	15	022

T

Taaff, Bridget	Byrne, Dennis	04 JUN 1884 L	19	059
Tabb, Belle	Smith, Daniel	27 JUL 1885 L	20	342
Tabler, Norval F.	Maginnis, Sarah E.	21 APR 1885 R	20	176
Tabor, Horace A.W.	McCourt, Lizzie Bonduel	01 MAR 1883 L	17	329
Tadoldi, Mary A.	Gantt, Edward L.	29 JAN 1880 R	14	126
Taff, Elizabeth G.	Schneider, Harry M.	30 SEP 1879 R	13	392
Taggart, Hugh T.	Jackson, Annie M.	15 OCT 1877 L	11	181
Tait, Andrew	Tait, Lucy	31 JUL 1885	20	346
Tait, Ella	Foster, John	22 AUG 1877 L	11	061
Tait, Lucy	Tait, Andrew	31 JUL 1885	20	346
Tait, Mary Ann	Harris, Benjamin F.	30 DEC 1880 L	15	132
Tait, Mary C.	Newman, Oscar B.	02 JUL 1884 L	19	117
Tait, Sarah Ann	Faulk, James E.	29 DEC 1881 L	16	168
Taite, Anna	Scott, William, Jr.	08 MAY 1879	13	182
Taite, Emma J.	Holtzclaw, Chas. Taylor	10 AUG 1881 L	15	439
Taite, Mary E.	Holtzclaw, C. Taylor	11 JUL 1877	11	016
Talbert, Agnes M.	Nolan, John T.	31 MAY 1882	16	382
Talbert, Frances	Owen, Wm. Henry	15 JAN 1880	14	108
Talbert, Harry	Holroyd, Julia	25 NOV 1884	19	409
Talbert, James J.	Winterhuth, Mary E.	16 SEP 1879	13	372
Talbert, Margaret E.	King, Charles Henry	03 NOV 1881 L	16	061
Talbert, Perry	Cockrill, Fannie	10 AUG 1880	14	396
Talbert, R. Thomas	Padgett, Annie M.	27 DEC 1882 R	17	214
Talbert, Rosie	Williams, James	17 JUN 1879	13	235
Talbert, Sarah E.	Denny, William H.	08 JAN 1879 R	13	011
Talbert, Sarah M.	Lanham, Columbus F.	05 SEP 1878 R	12	198
Talbot, Chris J.	McCann, Julia	30 SEP 1884 L	19	276
Talbot, Dennison C.	Russel, Susan Frances	14 MAR 1881 L	15	223
Talbot, Edmund R.	Burgess, Elizabeth	17 AUG 1882 R	16	481
Talbot, Edward Henry	Roseberry, Carrie Iola	10 FEB 1884 R	18	417
Talbot, Ellon	Tennyson, F.J.N.G.	24 SEP 1881 L	15	496
Talbot, Emeline	Munroe, Edward	04 MAR 1879	13	088
Talbot, Gracie	Washington, Richard R.	02 APR 1884	18	488
Talbot, Horace	Black, Frankie	04 SEP 1879 R	13	349
Talbot, James Robert	Dove, Margaret R.	17 JAN 1878 R	11	302
Talbot, John M.	Guy, Rosa B.	30 SEP 1880	14	467
Talbot, Lizzie E.	Collins, Edgar A.	12 APR 1880	14	219
Talbot, Maggie A.	Kramer, John J.	05 NOV 1879 L	13	465
Talbot, Mary A.	Cropsey, James Clement	22 JUN 1880 R	14	328
Talbot, Mary Jane	Crampton, James C.	14 AUG 1883	18	087
Talbot, William	Williams, Matilda	08 FEB 1878 L	11	334
Talbot, William	Santain, Susie	18 APR 1883	17	398
Talbot, William N.	McIntyre, Mary Agnes	11 AUG 1883 L	18	083
Talbott, James E.	Robey, Sarah L.	14 FEB 1878 L	11	341
Talbott, Virginia	Bailey, William Jenks	08 FEB 1883 R	17	298
Talbret, Mary	Spriggs, George W.	08 DEC 1881 R	16	123
Talburt, Isaac	Holmes, Annie	14 MAR 1884 R	18	469
Talburtt, Ellen Ruth	Moore, Thomas J.	19 JAN 1882 R	16	200
Talcott, A.B.	Goff, Doretta F.	13 FEB 1878	11	338
Talent, Arthur	Connell, Laura	15 JUL 1878 R	12	135
Taliaferro, Anna S.	Allen, William	26 FEB 1878	11	357
Taliaferro, Cordelia	Mercer, Cyrus	03 AUG 1882 L	16	467
Taliaferro, George W.	Nelson, Mary L.	29 APR 1878	12	028
Taliaferro, Jacob	Willis, Maggie	15 APR 1885 L	20	167
Taliaferro, Loudon	Porter, Sophia	26 DEC 1878 R	12	402
Taliaferro, Retta	Belfield, William E.	20 DEC 1882	17	198
Taliaferro, Thomas T.	Budd, Mary Jane	14 NOV 1877 L	11	184

Talifero, Agnes	Taylor, Samuel	15 MAY 1880 L	14	272
Talioferro, William	Coleman, Mary	13 NOV 1878	12	327
Talks, Arthur T.	Crissey, Sallie E.	22 JAN 1884 R	18	388
Tallant, John M.	Davis, Ella V.	08 FEB 1883 R	17	300
Tallent, Sarah Virginia	Collins, Charles Henry	26 JUN 1879 R	13	250
Talley, Priscilla	Scudder, Charles W.	27 NOV 1884 R	19	411
Talley, Sarah Jane	Latham, Leroy Minor	16 APR 1879 R	13	147
Talliaferno, Delia	Gant, James	04 MAY 1880 L	14	252
Talliaferro, Matilda	Winslow, Jerry	18 OCT 1883 R	18	201
Taltavull, Edith E.	Boteler, Edward M.	24 NOV 1880	15	063
Taltavull, Peter A.	Brinkley, Minnie J.	15 JUL 1885 L	20	328
Tamkin, Edwin	Clem, Lizzie	11 AUG 1880 R	14	398
Tancil, Annie E.	Johnson, Alexander	25 DEC 1884 R	19	490
Taney, Elizabeth	Johnson, James	07 FEB 1881 R	15	176
Tanner, Harriet Louisa	Harvey, Jacob Henry	20 AUG 1883 R	18	094
Tanner, John W.	Simmens, Lizzie	18 SEP 1884	19	257
Tanner, Millard Fillmore	Conkling, Annie Mary Wise	17 FEB 1885 R	20	071
Tansill, George W.	Lynn, Rena E.	23 APR 1879 R	13	152
Taper, Mary	Selden, Robert	13 MAR 1879 L	13	100
Taplet, W.A.	Johnson, Abrauna	19 AUG 1880 L	14	407
Taplett, Emma F.	Tyler, John H.	30 NOV 1880 L	15	073
Taplett, John	Franklin, Rachel	02 FEB 1881 L	15	174
Taplin, James	Smith, Maria	25 NOV 1884 L	19	407
Tapscott, Murray	Colvin, Katherine	09 SEP 1885 L	20	410
Tarkington, Joseph Asbury	Yeatman, Elva Meredith	14 JAN 1885 R	20	019
Tarlton, Joanna	Moloch, Thomas R.	30 NOV 1881 R	16	105
Tarlton, Sarah Jane	Madden, William Henry	17 JAN 1883 R	17	261
Tarr, Louisa J.	Gourley, James	03 OCT 1881 R	16	002
Tasca, Cressy	Boulden, Samuel	10 APR 1879	13	132
Tasco, Annie E.	Jones, Andrew	07 SEP 1880 R	14	434
Tasco, Charles E.	Lanzing, Mary	03 OCT 1884 R	19	284
Tasco, Margaret	Baynum, William	11 AUG 1880 R	14	397
Tasco, Martha	Jackson, Wayneboro	17 APR 1884 R	18	510
Tasco, Rebecca Ann	Butler, William Henry	05 JUN 1883 R	17	477
Tasker, Alice	Caldbert, Robert R.	16 OCT 1884 L	19	314
Tasker, Barbara	Ennis, Thomas	12 OCT 1877 L	11	133
Tasker, Jennie	Solomon, George Washington	06 NOV 1879	13	467
Tasker, Lucy, Mrs.	Holmes, Peter	18 OCT 1877 R	11	139
Tasker, Sarah	Nelson, Samuel	27 JUL 1882 R	16	460
Tate, Ella	Hunt, William	04 AUG 1885 L	20	352
Tate, Harry	Keithley, Anna G.	29 SEP 1880 R	14	465
Tatspaugh, Laura Ella	Peyton, John Francis	07 AUG 1877 R	11	039
Tatspaugh, M. Virginia	Nixer, Fred W.	05 JUN 1879	13	211
Tatum, Kate V. [Miller]	Bennett, George T.	03 MAY 1883 R	17	427
Taulman, Dan'l Jay	Clark, Victoria	11 MAR 1885 R	20	107
Tavener, Mary V.	Darnell, Reuben	28 APR 1885	20	193
Tayler, Lewis	Carick, Fannie	09 JUN 1884 R	19	070
Tayloe, Mary A.	Wheeler, George C.	16 OCT 1884 R	19	314
Taylor, Adalaide C.	Collins, Charles C.	06 FEB 1879	13	049
Taylor, Alice	Mayhew, James	15 MAY 1879 R	13	164
Taylor, Alice	Boston, Nathaniel	22 APR 1880	14	234
Taylor, Alice M.	White, Henry	04 MAR 1879	13	088
Taylor, Alice Ward	Preinkert, John P.	08 OCT 1885	20	471
Taylor, Ann	Brooks, Philip	18 MAR 1884 L	18	474
Taylor, Anne R.	Nash, Edward	30 JUN 1877 L	11	003
Taylor, Annie	Hollman, Alfred	08 AUG 1879 R	13	310
Taylor, Annie E.	Williams, Charles H.	15 MAR 1885	20	115
Taylor, Arthur	Brooks, Emma	13 AUG 1877 R	11	036

Taylor, Bartlett	Fisher, Annie	03 DEC 1877 L	11	215
Taylor, Bettie Ambler	Brooke, Albert	01 DEC 1881 R	16	105
Taylor, Carrie C.	Braxton, John W.	14 NOV 1878 R	12	313
Taylor, Carrie E.	Pierre, John A.	20 APR 1882 R	16	324
Taylor, Catharine B.	Scott, Thomas	02 OCT 1884	19	282
Taylor, Catherine	Campbell, John H.	07 AUG 1883 L	18	078
Taylor, Charles	Goldin, Rosa	26 SEP 1877 R	11	109
Taylor, Charles C.	Raum, Grace	10 JUN 1885	20	266
Taylor, Charles H.	Beal, Josephine	23 DEC 1878 R	12	393
Taylor, Charles Henry	Edelin, Virginia	14 SEP 1885	20	414
Taylor, Charles W.	Mullintree, Sarah E.	27 JUN 1878	12	111
Taylor, Charles W.	Matthews, Cora W.	25 NOV 1878 L	12	345
Taylor, Charles[10]	Mason, Celia	10 JUN 1879 R	13	225
Taylor, Charlotte	Brent, William Henry	29 NOV 1880	15	071
Taylor, Chloe Ann	Washington, George	18 SEP 1879 R	13	370
Taylor, Clara S.	Brooks, James N.	16 MAY 1885 L	20	225
Taylor, Cora Lee	Collins, Charles H.	07 MAY 1885 R	20	099
Taylor, Dennis	Johnson, Sarah Jane	15 OCT 1885	20	477
Taylor, E. Winston	Herbert, C. Victoria	09 JAN 1879	13	011
Taylor, E.J.	Smith, J.G.	21 NOV 1883	18	269
Taylor, Edward	Gaskins, Mollie	11 JAN 1878 R	11	287
Taylor, Eleanora	Beckwith, Francis E.	18 OCT 1880 R	15	001
Taylor, Eliza L.	White, Fred W.	06 SEP 1877 L	11	081
Taylor, Elizabeth	Jones, Samuel	09 JUL 1878	12	130
Taylor, Elizabeth	Connell, Samuel S.	18 APR 1883 R	17	399
Taylor, Elizabeth E.	Smallwood, Thomas	23 MAY 1883	17	458
Taylor, Elizza C.	Kreamer, Samuel G.	03 OCT 1883	18	167
Taylor, Ella	Scott, Benjamin	03 DEC 1884 R	18	362
Taylor, Ella P.	Brandebury, Henry F.	11 JUN 1885	20	265
Taylor, Ellen M.C.	Jones, Melville E.	31 JUL 1879 R	13	301
Taylor, Emily	Johnson, Dennis	12 APR 1884 L	18	505
Taylor, Emily M.	Taylor, James W.	10 SEP 1878 L	12	207
Taylor, Emma	Taylor, Richard	27 FEB 1879 R	13	080
Taylor, Emma	Harrison, William	24 JUL 1880 L	14	374
Taylor, Emma	Taylor, George	28 JUL 1881	15	423
Taylor, Emma Philippa	Wheatley, Joseph Moody	22 FEB 1881 R	15	198
Taylor, Erasmus Spencer	Fortune, Delia T.	16 JAN 1879 R	13	014
Taylor, Fairfax H.	Matthews, Sarah L.	30 OCT 1884 L	19	348
Taylor, Fannie	Boyce, Stansbury	11 DEC 1882	17	177
Taylor, Fannie	Lewis, Thomas J.	17 MAY 1882 R	16	364
Taylor, Fannie	White, James W.	25 JAN 1883 L	17	275
Taylor, Fanny	Brown, John	08 MAY 1878	12	040
Taylor, Fanny	Proctor, George	06 SEP 1883 R	18	114
Taylor, Florence C.	Owens, Evens	12 DEC 1878 R	12	378
Taylor, Frances	Dozier, Edward	02 SEP 1880 R	14	428
Taylor, Frances	Harris, Russell	28 DEC 1882 L	17	222
Taylor, Frances A.	Taylor, Lewis B.	10 JUL 1880 R	14	356
Taylor, Gabriel	Smith, Etta	02 JAN 1879	13	003
Taylor, Geo. Washington	Johnson, Rachel Ann	10 MAY 1884 L	19	014
Taylor, George	Taylor, Emma	28 JUL 1881	15	423
Taylor, George E.	Berry, Julia H.	05 MAY 1884 R	19	005
Taylor, George F., Dr.	McGill, Mary Janet	19 DEC 1882 R	17	191
Taylor, George H.	Marders, Ada	23 MAR 1881	15	231
Taylor, George M.	Albers, Annie D.	31 OCT 1883	18	224
Taylor, George P.	Reeves, Lucy E.	01 DEC 1881 R	16	107
Taylor, George P.	Porter, Charlotte A.	29 JUN 1882 R	16	427

[10] Return gives name of groom as Charles Mason.

D.C. Marriage Records Index, June 28, 1877 to October 19, 1885

Taylor, George W.	Denham, Lizzie E.	12 APR 1882 R	16	313
Taylor, Harry	Johnson, Carrie	06 DEC 1877 R	11	223
Taylor, Henrietta Van Patten	Babcock, Stephen	10 JUL 1878	12	130
Taylor, Henry	Shores, Annette	14 OCT 1879 R	13	423
Taylor, Henry	Harris, Florence O.	18 JAN 1881	15	153
Taylor, Henry	Straub, Rosa H.	05 JUL 1881 L	15	390
Taylor, Henry	Ashton, Martha	10 AUG 1882 L	16	475
Taylor, Ida Burnley	Chenery, James Harris	25 JAN 1882 R	16	208
Taylor, Ida Hilton	Holcombe, John Hite Lee	27 APR 1881 R	15	274
Taylor, Ida May	Pierce, William T.	06 JUL 1882 R	16	438
Taylor, Isabella	Smith, John F.	07 FEB 1884	18	414
Taylor, James E.	Crampton, Mary E.	24 DEC 1883	18	337
Taylor, James Lockerman	Dyer, Anne Mason	24 OCT 1877 R	11	152
Taylor, James R.	Young, Frances M.	27 MAR 1878 R	11	394
Taylor, James W.	Turner, Inez E.	06 SEP 1877	11	081
Taylor, James W.	Taylor, Emily M.	10 SEP 1878 L	12	207
Taylor, James W.	Sisson, Sallie	21 DEC 1882 R	17	199
Taylor, James W.P.	Curry, Mary E.	02 OCT 1881 R	16	001
Taylor, Jane	Perry, Reason	21 NOV 1883 R	18	265
Taylor, Jenettie	Childs, George B.	08 AUG 1883	18	078
Taylor, Jennie	Smith, Hillary	13 JUL 1881 L	15	399
Taylor, Jennie V.	Lewis, Andrew L.	01 NOV 1884	19	352
Taylor, Jerry	Johnson, Annie	10 JUN 1880 R	14	316
Taylor, Jesse	Bush, Mary	09 SEP 1880 R	14	440
Taylor, John	Johnson, Hennie	08 MAY 1879	13	181
Taylor, John	Evans, Mary Louisa	21 FEB 1881 L	15	196
Taylor, John	Thomas, Phyllis	19 DEC 1882 L	17	193
Taylor, John	Dorsey, Annie	29 DEC 1883 L	18	352
Taylor, John Andrew	Johnson, Mary Frances	10 JUN 1884 R	19	072
Taylor, John Phinney	Knowles, Alice Magruder	03 MAY 1883 R	17	429
Taylor, John W.	Brown, Martha	21 OCT 1880 L	15	009
Taylor, John W.	Bunnell, Annie Elizabeth	13 NOV 1884 R	19	379
Taylor, John Wm.	Blakey, Gertrude B.	30 APR 1884 R	18	545
Taylor, Johnson	Robinson, Mary	02 JAN 1884 R	18	363
Taylor, Joseph	Parker, Lizzie	28 DEC 1882 R	17	216
Taylor, Joseph	Corbin, Susan	03 APR 1884 R	18	494
Taylor, Josephine E.	Pheatt, Harvey D.	24 SEP 1884	19	266
Taylor, Julia Jane	Tennyson, David T.	07 SEP 1877 R	11	080
Taylor, Katie Lee	Posey, Benjamin Hunter	22 MAY 1882 R	16	371
Taylor, Kittie	Spinks, Richard Moody	11 MAY 1882 L	16	358
Taylor, Lewis	Davis, Susie	08 MAY 1884 L	19	012
Taylor, Lewis B.	Taylor, Frances A.	10 JUL 1880 R	14	356
Taylor, Lewis Rodney	Stickney, Mary Kingsford	24 OCT 1882 R	17	091
Taylor, Lillie A.	Smith, Arthur B.	17 DEC 1879 R	14	051
Taylor, Lizzie	Wood, Frank	14 MAR 1885 L	20	114
Taylor, Louisa	Jackson, Arthur	16 DEC 1880 L	15	103
Taylor, Louisa Warren	Stevens, Lyndon Hoyt	08 JAN 1884	18	368
Taylor, Lucy	Brown, Henry	05 JAN 1878 L	11	293
Taylor, Lucy	Nugent, Henry	05 OCT 1886	20	146
Taylor, Lucy J.	Howard, Oscar D.	20 NOV 1879	13	498
Taylor, Maggie	Anholt, Fredevich W.	08 SEP 1878	12	203
Taylor, Maggie	Tyler, George	31 AUG 1882 L	16	499
Taylor, Maggie	Tyler, George	31 AUG 1882 L	17	001
Taylor, Mamie	Lewis, Robert	09 APR 1885	20	155
Taylor, Mamie E.	White, John R.	09 OCT 1877 L	11	128
Taylor, Marcellena	Raum, William	15 APR 1884	18	511
Taylor, Margaret	Jones, Samuel	02 OCT 1877 R	11	119
Taylor, Maria C.	Green, Willis H.	16 SEP 1879 R	13	372

Name	Spouse	Date	Vol	Page
Taylor, Martha A.	Mills, William	24 FEB 1881 L	15	202
Taylor, Mary	Johnson, Miles	11 SEP 1877 R	11	085
Taylor, Mary	Slaughter, John	17 APR 1879 R	13	151
Taylor, Mary	Cross, Charles	20 AUG 1880 L	14	410
Taylor, Mary	Lewis, Philip	08 SEP 1880 L	14	437
Taylor, Mary	Johnson, Thomas	28 SEP 1883	18	123
Taylor, Mary	Liverpool, James	27 DEC 1883	18	339
Taylor, Mary	Vincent, Charles	04 SEP 1884 L	19	226
Taylor, Mary A.E.	Smith, William	27 JAN 1890	19	188
Taylor, Mary Ann	Javins, Randolph	03 SEP 1878	12	195
Taylor, Mary E.	Hurdle, Joseph	11 NOV 1879 R	13	475
Taylor, Mary Elizabeth	Maston, Philip	08 JUN 1880 L	14	311
Taylor, Mary Elizabeth	Oden, Thomas William	06 MAY 1880 R	14	258
Taylor, Mary Eugenia	Nailor, Richard Thomas	27 DEC 1883	18	349
Taylor, Mary J.	Preinkert, Fred C.B.	03 MAY 1882	16	345
Taylor, Mary J.	Bruce, Robert E.	18 AUG 1885 L	20	375
Taylor, Mary Susan	Sharp, George Andrew	21 MAY 1878	12	062
Taylor, Mary [Watkins]	Washington, George	22 DEC 1879 R	14	063
Taylor, Matthew, Dr.	Reese, Elizabeth Virginia	07 SEP 1882 R	17	011
Taylor, Matthews	Burrell, Jane	29 JUL 1880 L	14	377
Taylor, McKensie	Cole, Alice	27 MAY 1884 L	19	042
Taylor, Millery	Johnston, John Henry	01 AUG 1884	19	163
Taylor, Nero	Crump, Sarah	29 MAR 1883 R	17	365
Taylor, Nicholas B.	Kellums, Belle	12 MAR 1885	20	111
Taylor, Peter	Mitchell, Ella	14 MAY 1879 R	13	178
Taylor, Philip A.	Muse, Annie	05 JUL 1883 L	18	036
Taylor, R.W.	Allen, Sarah A.	02 JUL 1883 L	18	029
Taylor, Rebecca	Gant, Edward	23 DEC 1884 L	19	481
Taylor, Richard	Taylor, Emma	27 FEB 1879 L	13	080
Taylor, Richard	Murphy, Mildred	16 DEC 1884 R	19	462
Taylor, Robert	Syncox, Sophie	04 MAY 1880 R	14	252
Taylor, Robert	Prince, Laura	09 OCT 1880 L	14	484
Taylor, Robert	Payne, Maggie	16 JUN 1881 R	15	359
Taylor, Robert	Branson, Clara B.	02 APR 1883	17	374
Taylor, Robert V.	Briney, Elizabeth C.	20 MAY 1878 L	12	059
Taylor, Rosa	Clinton, Charles C.	08 AUG 1883 L	18	081
Taylor, Rosa J.	Jones, Lewis C.	29 SEP 1885	20	425
Taylor, Russell B.	Skeel, Gertrude C.	24 APR 1883	17	407
Taylor, S.B., Jr.	Dawson, Clara	10 OCT 1882 R	17	065
Taylor, Sallie	Adams, William	14 MAY 1883	17	442
Taylor, Sallie Ann	Brogden, Josiah	05 SEP 1878 R	12	202
Taylor, Samuel	Talifero, Agnes	15 MAY 1880 L	14	272
Taylor, Samuel	Scott, Sarah Jane	24 AUG 1885	20	385
Taylor, Sarah	Henderson, Henry	28 DEC 1881 L	16	166
Taylor, Sarah Ann	Diven, Thomas M.	12 APR 1883	17	385
Taylor, Sarah E.	Delaney, Alexander	02 MAR 1878 L	11	367
Taylor, Sarah Elizabeth	Courtney, Frederick W.	01 JAN 1879 R	12	408
Taylor, Selina	Dent, Henry	27 NOV 1879 R	14	003
Taylor, Sophia George	Kelly, Nathan	09 AUG 1883	18	082
Taylor, Stephen	Fletcher, Mary	15 AUG 1878	12	164
Taylor, Sue B.	Pratt, William B.	28 AUG 1883	18	098
Taylor, Thomas B.	Simms, Margaret A.	02 FEB 1880 R	14	132
Taylor, Thornton	Brooks, Mary	23 OCT 1884 L	19	335
Taylor, Thorton	Keenan, Florence	05 MAY 1882 L	16	351
Taylor, Violet	Childs, George H.	06 AUG 1884 L	19	172
Taylor, Virgie E.	Pierce, James F.	23 APR 1884	18	528
Taylor, Will B.	Davis, Fannie L.	02 JAN 1884 R	18	361
Taylor, William	Nugent, Nelly Ann Maria	18 SEP 1879	13	376

Taylor, William	Mahorney, Lue	09 JUL 1879 L	13	276
Taylor, William	Mills, Annie Mary	21 APR 1884	18	521
Taylor, William	Gardener, Martha	24 MAR 1884 L	18	480
Taylor, William	Morris, Lucy E.	02 MAY 1885 L	20	202
Taylor, William G.	Browne, Carrie J.	26 AUG 1879 R	13	299
Taylor, William H.	Waters, Mary	06 DEC 1877 R	11	221
Taylor, William N.	Wilborn, Lula A.	03 SEP 1884	19	224
Taylor, William S.	Robinson, Johanna	09 FEB 1882 L	16	235
Taylor, William Wirt	Heitzmann, Rosalie	15 JUL 1878	12	134
Taylor, Winifred A.	Gibson, Thomas H.	23 MAY 1885 L	20	237
Taylor, Winnie	Yates, James L.	27 MAY 1879 R	13	207
Tayman, James H.	Schmid, Katie	02 DEC 1884 R	19	430
Tayman, James Philip	King, Laura Anne	17 DEC 1878	12	384
Tayman, John S.	King, Rebecca R.	14 SEP 1880	14	442
Tayman, Zedock	Gallahan, Annie	21 OCT 1884	19	326
Tchlosser, William T.	Bingham, Emma V.	27 AUG 1884	19	212
Teachum, Annie E.	Burrows, George E.	23 MAR 1880 R	14	194
Teachum, Charles T.	Maddox, Annie M.	04 MAY 1881 L	15	292
Teachum, John K.	Streamer, Mollie J.	11 MAY 1880 R	14	265
Teagle, Abelinda	Gillam, Richard	21 MAY 1877	11	248
Teagle, Edward	Godrow, Lena	21 FEB 1882	16	250
Teagle, Mary Jane	Landic, Isaac	18 MAY 1882 L	16	366
Teasdale, Lola M.	McChesner, Ellsworth E.	29 NOV 1882	17	160
Tebbs, Carrie V.	Harris, James	01 AUG 1878	12	150
Teel, James H.	Butler, Anne	20 NOV 1882 R	17	135
Teel, S. Julia	Rowland, J. Shannon	03 DEC 1884 L	19	433
Teeple, D.H.	Milstead, K.A.A.	30 OCT 1879	13	455
Tegeler, Anna Sophia	Pralle, George William	30 OCT 1883 R	18	220
Temple, Emma	Henderson, Joseph	23 JAN 1879 L	13	032
Temple, John	Lewis, Sallie	29 DEC 1884 L	19	497
Templeman, Lucy	Lomax, William	18 APR 1885 L	20	174
Teneson, James M.	Park, Virginia	13 AUG 1879 R	13	318
Tenley, A.V.	Ogden, C.W.	09 JUN 1881 R	15	354
Tenley, Andrew F.	Brewer, Fanny	13 NOV 1881 R	16	064
Tenley, Annie H.	Pyles, John T.	07 NOV 1883	18	240
Tenley, Hattie V.	Duvall, William T., Jr.	25 JUN 1884	19	102
Tenley, Josephine	Smith, George B.	15 DEC 1881 R	16	133
Tenley, Margaret A.	Nicodemus, Conrad R.	03 APR 1879 R	13	123
Tenley, William A.	Hunnaker, Katie	07 MAR 1881 R	15	218
Tenly, Georgie I.	Carter, Richard W., Jr.	04 OCT 1883 L	18	169
Tennent, Christopher	Rady, Alice	02 JUN 1881 L	15	339
Tennent, John G.	Price, Kate R.	24 APR 1882 L	16	331
Tennesson, John Thomas	Neumeyer, Lora E.	16 JUN 1879	13	232
Tenney, Dennis	Moore, Mary	27 MAY 1879 L	13	208
Tenney, John E.	Willis, Susan J.	14 FEB 1884 L	18	424
Tenney, Robert B.	Moore, Juba B.	29 JAN 1878	11	320
Tennis, Ida	Tomlinson, Edward	21 SEP 1882	17	032
Tenny, John	Harris, Mary	27 OCT 1883 L	18	218
Tennyson, Ada T.	Arundell, James T.	22 APR 1884	18	521
Tennyson, David T.	Taylor, Julia Jane	07 SEP 1877 R	11	080
Tennyson, F.J.N.G.	Talbot, Ellen	24 SEP 1881 L	15	496
Tentman, Mary	Blair, Pat	02 MAY 1884 L	19	002
Tentman, Mary	Blair, Pat	02 MAY 1884 L	18	547
Terflinger, George W.	Williams, Ernestine F.	17 MAY 1881 R	15	311
Terne, F. Addie	Walker, W. Frank	03 DEC 1884	19	435
Terney, Fred. Charles	Schmitt, Helena	12 AUG 1878 L	12	163
Terrell, David	Bias, Lucinda	27 JUL 1877 L	11	033
Terrell, Matilda	Johnson, Smith	06 MAR 1879 R	13	092

Terrell, Rosa	Reeves, William	10 JUL 1884	19	134
Terrell, Rosamund G.	Eskridge, Edgar Peyton	26 APR 1884 R	18	533
Terrell, Scott	Hill, Eliza	26 NOV 1879 L	14	009
Terrill, Ambrose	Lee, Fanny	03 OCT 1878	12	253
Terrill, David B.	Gaskin, Caroline	07 MAR 1879 L	13	094
Terrill, Mary L.	Anderson, James Wm.	17 MAY 1881 R	15	312
Terrill, Silas	Gilchrist, Annie E.	07 JAN 1879 R	13	009
Terrill, Tolliver	Lomax, Lucy	03 JAN 1878 L	11	292
Terry, Ames	Huebner, Richard	06 NOV 1883 L	18	235
Terry, Bessie	Duvall, Alfred	23 FEB 1878 L	11	354
Terry, Eliza	Davis, John Wm. Henry	13 AUG 1885 R	20	368
Terry, Ella	Williams, Willis	22 MAR 1881 L	15	235
Terry, Lawrence	Brown, Lydia	20 DEC 1877 R	11	244
Terry, Mary	Harris, Elijah	10 MAY 1881 R	15	298
Terry, Sarah Ellen	Addison, Nathan	27 JAN 1881 R	15	168
Terry, Willie	Clark, Charles H.	01 JAN 1884 R	18	359
Teuly, Albert C.	Hardy, Annie	27 APR 1881 L	15	277
Tevis, Joshua	Miller, Ida Beale	24 APR 1878 R	12	020
Tew, Emily L.	Petersen, Ferdinand	12 MAY 1880 R	14	268
Tewell, Caroline	Stewart, Frank	28 MAY 1885 R	20	241
Thackara, Alexander Montgomery	Sherman, Eleanor Mary	05 MAY 1880 R	14	249
Thäter, Catherina	Meier, Ezekiel	26 AUG 1878	12	180
Thaxter, Warren P.	Whitcomb, Sophie H. (Dwinels)	06 JAN 1885 R	20	005
Thayer, Ella V.	Alexander, Edgar May	26 JAN 1881 R	15	164
Thayer, Helen	Hutcheson, David	11 SEP 1883	18	121
Theck, William	Middledorf, Lizzie	24 NOV 1878	12	344
Thecker, Alonzo	McGee, Katie	02 FEB 1879	13	042
Thecker, Mary J.	Finch, Paul	04 AUG 1877 L	11	040
Theilkuhl, Rosa L.	Jaeger, Henry	25 JUN 1884	19	103
Thelon, Etienne Joseph	Anderson, Annie	07 JUN 1882 R	16	397
Thiede, Louise E.	Ashman, William	01 AUG 1884	19	164
Thiel, Anna Martha	Duehring, August F.C.	02 JUL 1878 L	12	120
Thiel, Niclaus	Binnix, Roberta	29 OCT 1878 L	12	296
Thilow, Laura Antonie	Rehling, Wilhelm Fred. Heinrich	09 JUL 1881	15	397
Thockmorton, Charles	Green, Lucinda	06 APR 1881	15	249
Thom, George	Cooksey, Katie	21 AUG 1879 R	13	331
Thom, Katie C.	Wood, Thomas N.	17 OCT 1882 L	17	075
Thom, William G.B.	Everett, Rosanna	26 JAN 1885 R	20	037
Thoma, Charlotte	Corcoran, Jesse A.	24 DEC 1883 R	18	337
Thoma, Frank	Dubois, Juliette	26 MAR 1883	17	353
Thoma, Lena	Hoffman, Henry	02 SEP 1880 L	14	429
Thomas, A.A.	Raife, Aurelia A.	11 DEC 1884 L	19	453
Thomas, Aaron	Thomas, Alice	17 AUG 1878 L	12	171
Thomas, Agnes	Henderson, James H.	26 FEB 1878	11	360
Thomas, Alberta	Scott, John A.	13 FEB 1882 R	16	238
Thomas, Alfred H.	Doleman, Eliza	29 SEP 1884 L	19	272
Thomas, Alice	Thomas, Aaron	17 AUG 1878 L	12	171
Thomas, Amelia Christina	Potbury, William Enos	23 JUN 1885	20	287
Thomas, Annie	Cook, Richard	04 SEP 1878 L	12	198
Thomas, Annie	Harris, Philip B.	04 JUN 1878	12	083
Thomas, Annie C.	Garner, Lafayette J.	07 JUL 1880	14	351
Thomas, Annie E.	Thomas, Charles H.	16 JAN 1884 L	18	382
Thomas, Annie G.	Steptoe, Arthur	25 OCT 1877 L	11	156
Thomas, Annie, Mrs.	Harris, Philip B.	04 JUN 1879 R	14	3256
Thomas, Arry	Morgan, Catherine	26 NOV 1879 R	14	008
Thomas, Augusta	Carroll, Robert	07 FEB 1883 L	17	298
Thomas, Barbara Ann	Ward, Wesley	16 DEC 1880 R	15	106
Thomas, Barbara V.	Johnson, Charles N.	01 JAN 1884	18	357

Thomas, Benjamin	Chase, Eliza	16 MAR 1880 R	14	186
Thomas, Berta L.	Newman, Wesley	22 JAN 1880 R	14	118
Thomas, Bertie	Hardick, Henry	16 DEC 1884 L	19	460
Thomas, Betsy	Johnson, Lafayette	23 DEC 1880 R	15	120
Thomas, C.A., Mrs.	Somerville, Robert H.	26 DEC 1877	11	200
Thomas, Carrie	Twine, Andrew	15 NOV 1882 L	17	128
Thomas, Carrie M.	Miller, William A.	04 FEB 1885	20	052
Thomas, Catherine	Patton, Thomas	14 FEB 1881 L	15	188
Thomas, Catherine	Mitchell, Isham	05 JAN 1882 R	16	182
Thomas, Charles	Jones, Hetty	12 DEC 1877 R	11	231
Thomas, Charles H.	Thomas, Annie E.	16 JAN 1884 L	18	382
Thomas, Charles R.	Thomas, Emma L.	22 OCT 1884	19	330
Thomas, Charley	Tyler, Rose	14 SEP 1881 L	15	483
Thomas, Charlotte S.	Howard, John	02 DEC 1881 L	16	111
Thomas, Christine Elise	Frazier, J. Arthur	27 OCT 1881 R	16	045
Thomas, Clara	Brooks, Lewis	16 NOV 1880	15	049
Thomas, Daniel	Akers, Maggie	15 APR 1878 R	12	004
Thomas, Daniel	Simmes, Charlotte	15 DEC 1881	16	135
Thomas, David	Grayson, Lavinia	15 OCT 1883 R	18	194
Thomas, David W.	Hogans, Mary H.	26 NOV 1878 R	12	346
Thomas, Dennis	Brooks, Eliza	01 SEP 1881 R	15	467
Thomas, Dennis	Washington, Sidney Ann	22 NOV 1884 L	19	401
Thomas, Edith	Webb, Elijah	03 MAR 1881	15	212
Thomas, Edward	Selby, Hallie D.	11 JAN 1883 R	17	251
Thomas, Edward H.	Bond, Lillie K.	27 JUL 1884	19	159
Thomas, Edward Hildt	Wheelock, Frances A.	17 DEC 1884 R	19	462
Thomas, Eliza	Contee, Marcellus	29 SEP 1877 L	11	114
Thomas, Eliza Ann	Jackson, William	10 APR 1879	13	136
Thomas, Elizabeth	Thomas, Henry	26 NOV 1878	12	348
Thomas, Elizabeth	Kenner, Preston E.	13 MAR 1879 R	13	101
Thomas, Ella	Siegel, Charles	07 OCT 1880 L	14	480
Thomas, Ella	Burgdorf, Charles	03 DEC 1883 L	18	292
Thomas, Elvira	Barton, Albert	14 APR 1885 L	20	166
Thomas, Emma L.	Thomas, Charles R.	22 OCT 1884	19	330
Thomas, Fannie	Spaulding, John Celestine	23 SEP 1879	13	381
Thomas, Fannie	Robinson, William Henry	14 JUL 1881 R	15	403
Thomas, Fannie	Brown, Isaac	18 MAY 1882	16	366
Thomas, Florence Thomson	Mitchell, Joseph Franklin	02 FEB 1885 R	20	046
Thomas, Frank	Todd, Sarah	14 JAN 1878 L	11	303
Thomas, Frank	Vena, Sarah Alice	09 MAY 1878	12	047
Thomas, Frank	Moulden, Charlotte R.	04 JAN 1881 R	15	129
Thomas, Fred	Davis, Mary	26 AUG 1885 L	20	388
Thomas, Frederick	Perry, Mary	07 MAY 1879 L	13	178
Thomas, Geo. Williams	Day, Sarah Frances	03 JUL 1882	16	436
Thomas, George	Harding, Katie	08 JUL 1878 L	12	128
Thomas, George	Kelly, Martha	08 JUN 1880 L	14	310
Thomas, George	Henry, Mary Jane	27 SEP 1881 L	15	498
Thomas, George Robert	Slade, Laura E.	16 SEP 1885 L	20	423
Thomas, George W.	Stewart, Eliza	15 SEP 1877 L	11	095
Thomas, George W.	Ross, Eliza Alice	14 JUL 1881 R	15	401
Thomas, George W.	Simms, Annie S.	29 NOV 1884	19	424
Thomas, George Washington	Thomas, Harriet N.	01 MAY 1879	13	171
Thomas, H.A.	Woodward, Laura	13 MAR 1878	11	380
Thomas, Harriet Ann	Dent, James W.	28 JUN 1879	13	257
Thomas, Harriet N.	Thomas, George Washington	01 MAY 1879	13	171
Thomas, Harry E.	King, Amanda J.	11 SEP 1879 R	13	329
Thomas, Hattie	Magruder, William Henry	06 DEC 1877 R	11	226
Thomas, Helen Alfreda	Flint, Albert Stowell	22 OCT 1884 R	19	330

Thomas, Hellen	Epperson, William	25 DEC 1884	19	484
Thomas, Henrietta	Melville, Robert L.	03 JUN 1882 L	16	392
Thomas, Henry	Contee, Ann	05 JAN 1878	11	270
Thomas, Henry	Thomas, Elizabeth	26 NOV 1878	12	348
Thomas, Henry	Bell, Mary	18 OCT 1880 L	14	500
Thomas, Henry	Selden, Mary	26 DEC 1882 R	17	211
Thomas, Henry	Hannah, Susie	29 OCT 1883 R	18	220
Thomas, Henry H.	Mallory, Julia Ann	20 DEC 1877 L	11	254
Thomas, Hugh	Edwards, Helen	27 MAR 1879	13	117
Thomas, Isaac	Cosey, Jane J.	18 JUN 1878 L	12	103
Thomas, Isabella	Carter, Horace	10 FEB 1885 L	20	061
Thomas, J.E.	Bradburn, C.E.	10 MAR 1880 L	14	181
Thomas, J.H.	Key, Ernestine	19 MAR 1878 L	11	388
Thomas, J.M.F.A.	Barnard, Lucy A.	24 JUL 1879	13	292
Thomas, James	Brown, Addie	13 JUL 1878 L	12	134
Thomas, James	Roland, Mary	09 AUG 1881 L	15	437
Thomas, James	Butler, Frances	23 OCT 1884 L	19	334
Thomas, James H.	Webster, Alice R.	07 MAR 1883 R	17	336
Thomas, James L.	Harris, Gracie	13 MAR 1884	18	470
Thomas, James M.	Beach, Anna	11 DEC 1884	19	451
Thomas, Jane	King, Thomas	06 MAR 1884 R	18	460
Thomas, Jane T.	Coppar, Richard R.	19 DEC 1878	12	383
Thomas, Janie E.	Griffin, Wm. H.	09 MAR 1883	17	339
Thomas, Jennie	Gray, William H.	23 MAY 1878 L	12	065
Thomas, Jennie	Jenifer, George	09 SEP 1880 R	14	424
Thomas, Joe	Colville, Melvina	31 DEC 1879 L	14	084
Thomas, John	Johnston, Georgianna	19 JUN 1882 L	16	418
Thomas, John	Wiggins, Kate	09 DEC 1884 R	19	442
Thomas, John I.B.	Fox, Lucinda	11 SEP 1878	12	212
Thomas, John Truman	Malcolm, Sennie C. Mallicote	21 FEB 1882 R	16	252
Thomas, John W.	Hunter, Marion V.	02 JAN 1883 R	17	231
Thomas, John Wesley	Willis, Maggio	03 JUL 1879	13	267
Thomas, Jonathan J.	Shipley, Annie E.	10 SEP 1878	12	209
Thomas, Joseph	Key, Mary	28 JUL 1882 R	16	238
Thomas, Joseph B.	Cooksey, Charlotte G.	06 AUG 1884	19	171
Thomas, Joseph B.	Cooper, M. Charlotte	13 AUG 1884	19	181
Thomas, Josephine	O'Neil, William	05 JUL 1877 R	11	010
Thomas, Josephine F.	Curtin, Oliver	10 JUL 1884	19	132
Thomas, Julia	Ashton, Joseph	12 JAN 1882	16	170
Thomas, Julia	Lane, William	21 DEC 1882 R	17	201
Thomas, Justus	Bumbrey, Eliza	05 JUL 1879	13	270
Thomas, Katie M.	Samuel, James Edward	18 DEC 1884 R	19	469
Thomas, Lemuel	Bell, Sophia	08 OCT 1878 L	12	260
Thomas, Lemuel	Willis, Rosa	24 DEC 1879 L	14	072
Thomas, Lewis	Wright, Dollie	14 JUL 1884	19	137
Thomas, Lewis	Johnson, Winnie	07 APR 1885 L	20	151
Thomas, Lillie Fisher	Simmons, Frank W.	14 MAY 1884	19	008
Thomas, Lizzie	Campbell, Peter	27 AUG 1883 L	18	100
Thomas, Lizzie	Listman, Philip	05 MAR 1884	18	457
Thomas, Louisa	Dorsey, Joseph	27 NOV 1879 R	14	016
Thomas, Lucinda	Armistead, Leland	26 MAY 1879 L	13	205
Thomas, Lucy	Dorsey, Henry	26 SEP 1879 R	15	3523
Thomas, Lucy	Slaughter, Daniel	18 AUG 1884	19	191
Thomas, Lucy	Snowden, Thomas	21 MAY 1885 L	20	234
Thomas, Lulu May	Nicholson, Joseph	04 DEC 1879 R	14	010
Thomas, Luther	Martin, Maggie	24 MAR 1881 R	15	237
Thomas, M. Ann	Parker, Esau	07 APR 1885 R	20	152
Thomas, Maggie E.	Gibbs, Charles E.	02 JAN 1879 R	13	002

Thomas, Mamie E.	Bostic, John A.	24 OCT 1883	18	211
Thomas, Margaret E.	Millstead, James E.	13 OCT 1881	16	021
Thomas, Margaret J.	Hill, John	31 JUL 1883 L	18	068
Thomas, Maria	Carter, Daniel	21 FEB 1878 L	11	351
Thomas, Martha A.	Kidwell, James E.	14 AUG 1882 R	16	479
Thomas, Mary	Williams, James	27 AUG 1883 L	18	100
Thomas, Mary	Williams, Joseph	01 FEB 1883 L	17	285
Thomas, Mary Ann	Brown, Samuel	10 SEP 1883 R	18	122
Thomas, Mary Catherine	Waters, William	02 JUL 1878	12	119
Thomas, Mary E.	Miller, Joseph M.	26 FEB 1878 L	11	358
Thomas, Mary E.	Strobel, Frederick W.	28 JUN 1880 L	14	335
Thomas, Mary E.	Mason, William H.	22 DEC 1881	16	143
Thomas, Mary E.	Williams, James R.	20 DEC 1884 L	19	474
Thomas, Mary Ellen	Crawford, Griffin	20 JUN 1884 R	19	095
Thomas, Mary M.	Shaffer, William Coss	23 JAN 1884 R	18	392
Thomas, Mary S.	Parsons, John	27 JAN 1885 R	20	037
Thomas, Mary Virginia	Butler, Frank G.	13 FEB 1882 R	16	239
Thomas, Matilda	Butler, Joseph	15 JUL 1880	14	362
Thomas, Matilda	Harper, James	12 FEB 1881 L	15	187
Thomas, Matilda, Mrs.	Stanton, Philip	08 JUN 1880 R	14	309
Thomas, Michael B.	Cook, Mary	12 APR 1881 L	15	255
Thomas, Minnie	Grain, Thomas	06 MAY 1879 L	13	175
Thomas, Mollie	Jackson, Andrew	16 JUN 1881 L	15	364
Thomas, Mollie	Milsterd, J.T.	06 DEC 1883	18	299
Thomas, Nancy	Gardner, Alexander	14 NOV 1883	18	136
Thomas, Nathan	Woodward, Jane	14 DEC 1878 R	12	380
Thomas, Nellie M.	Loveless, Benjamin O.	12 NOV 1884	19	375
Thomas, Oscar C.	Johnson, Henrietta	20 MAY 1878 R	12	060
Thomas, Philip	Thompson, Charlotte Ann	29 JAN 1885	20	043
Thomas, Phyllis	Taylor, John	19 DEC 1882 L	17	193
Thomas, Ralph	Johnson, Julie	25 SEP 1879 L	13	388
Thomas, Robert	Marshall, Josephine	09 AUG 1877 R	11	043
Thomas, Robert	Butler, Sarah	08 JAN 1879 R	13	004
Thomas, Robert	Davis, Rebecca	14 JUN 1883	17	495
Thomas, Robert	Cooper, Carrie	18 MAY 1885 R	20	219
Thomas, Robert	Carpenter, Sarah	08 JUL 1885 L	20	317
Thomas, Robert Henry	McGoing, Lucinda	20 FEB 1883 L	17	313
Thomas, Rosa	Goodman, Isham C.	06 JUL 1883 R	17	486
Thomas, Rose	Wharton, William A.	06 FEB 1883 L	17	295
Thomas, Sallie E.	Kidwell, Eli S.	21 DEC 1880	15	112
Thomas, Sarah	Hanna, Robert	03 SEP 1879 L	13	348
Thomas, Sarah	Smothers, Thomas	06 AUG 1879 L	13	309
Thomas, Sarah	Farmer, James	22 DEC 1881	16	143
Thomas, Sarah	Jones, William H.	30 SEP 1882 L	17	045
Thomas, Sarah	Sumby, Dennis	12 AUG 1884	19	182
Thomas, Sarah A.V.	Thompson, Solomon H.	11 MAY 1885 L	20	216
Thomas, Sarah E.	Ross, Tillman G.	03 APR 1882 L	16	295
Thomas, Susan	Cooper, Morris	23 JAN 1879 R	13	031
Thomas, Susan	Gould, Samuel	23 MAR 1882	16	278
Thomas, Susan	Carter, Horace	09 JAN 1883 L	17	245
Thomas, Susie	Wedick, Harman	14 JAN 1884	18	375
Thomas, Thomas	West, Maria	31 OCT 1878 L	12	303
Thomas, Victoria	Ballard, James H.	14 APR 1880 L	14	222
Thomas, Vincent Butler	Parker, Helena Jacqueline	19 JAN 1878	11	305
Thomas, Walker	Catlet, Cassie	08 DEC 1884 L	19	439
Thomas, Walter A.	Stewart, Charlotte	14 OCT 1880 L	14	494
Thomas, Walter S.	Brooks, Anastatia E.	12 FEB 1880 R	14	150
Thomas, Walter W.	Jones, Lucy	12 JAN 1885 L	20	013

Thomas, Wilemon	Carter, Mary E.	27 JUL 1882 L	16	459
Thomas, William	Powels, Sallie	03 DEC 1878 R	12	350
Thomas, William	Hudson, Esther	21 JUL 1879 L	13	287
Thomas, William	Dent, Cornelia	23 SEP 1879	13	358
Thomas, William	Madison, Elizabeth	01 JUN 1880 L	14	299
Thomas, William	Patterson, Annie Elizabeth	20 OCT 1884 L	19	323
Thomas, William	Harris, Annie	24 SEP 1885 R	20	428
Thomas, William A.	Albinson, Annie M.	04 JUN 1878	12	083
Thomas, William E.	Dorsett, Laura Louisa	24 DEC 1879 R	14	073
Thomas, William E.	Maxwell, Catherine F.	18 JAN 1884 L	18	384
Thomas, William H.	Lee, Martha	06 JUN 1878	12	085
Thomas, William H.W.	Brown, Louisa	02 APR 1879 L	13	124
Thomas, William R.	Hayward, Delia	28 AUG 1883 R	18	101
Thomas, William W.	Thompson, Laura V.	06 DEC 1877 L	11	224
Thomas, Winnie	Davis, Lloyd T.	13 AUG 1884 L	19	184
Thomas, Wm. Arthur	Giddings, Mamie Anna	16 OCT 1885 R	20	489
Thomas, Wm. B.	Mitchell, Susan S.	22 DEC 1881 R	16	139
Thomas, Wm. G.	Wedge, Rosaline	06 JUL 1885	20	312
Thomas, Wm. Provoost	Lyon, Harriet Caldwell	30 APR 1884	18	541
Thomas, Wm. T.	Williams, Letitia B.	08 NOV 1883	18	226
Thomas, Zephaniah	Lee, Mary	31 MAY 1882 L	16	384
Thomason, Frank D.	Beau, Diana M.	24 NOV 1881	16	095
Thompkins, Robert	Bowman, Ann	24 MAY 1879 R	13	204
Thompson, A.F.	Smith, Albert L.	21 MAR 1881 L	15	232
Thompson, Addie R.	Page, Robert M.	14 SEP 1878 L	12	218
Thompson, Agnes E.	Gleason, James A.	05 MAR 1878 R	11	370
Thompson, Alexander	Townley, Kate	09 APR 1878 R	11	411
Thompson, Alice	Lewis, William	08 JUL 1879	13	263
Thompson, Alice	Anderson, Edward	03 DEC 1883 L	18	293
Thompson, Alice V.	Etchison, Thomas H.	15 DEC 1881 R	16	136
Thompson, Anna	Mopkins, Harris	18 DEC 1879 L	14	057
Thompson, Anna E	McGill, George E.	26 FEB 1884 L	18	444
Thompson, Annie	Carroll, William A.	09 APR 1881 R	15	235
Thompson, Annie W.	Spalding, Wm. L.	02 JUN 1882 R	16	391
Thompson, Augustus	Brice, Maude	04 MAR 1884 R	18	456
Thompson, Aurelia	Hart, John Cornelius	09 MAY 1878 R	12	046
Thompson, Bartley B.	Somerville, Mary A.	07 FEB 1878 R	11	332
Thompson, Bertha	Frazier, William Henry	28 JUL 1881 L	15	422
Thompson, Caroline	Simms, Henry	06 JUL 1882 L	16	441
Thompson, Catherine	Smith, Jacob C.	11 NOV 1881 L	16	072
Thompson, Charles	White, Annie	26 JUN 1879	13	251
Thompson, Charles W.	Price, Ida B.	26 JUL 1883	18	062
Thompson, Charles W.	Partridge, Susie	13 SEP 1884 L	19	245
Thompson, Charlotte Ann	Thomas, Philip	29 JAN 1885	20	043
Thompson, Clara B.	German, William G.	27 JUN 1883	18	017
Thompson, Clay	Warren, Abbie B.	17 OCT 1879 L	13	434
Thompson, Clay	Warren, Abbie B.	17 OCT 1879 R	13	431
Thompson, D. Darby	Ostrander, Mary E.	15 DEC 1881 L	16	135
Thompson, E.M.	Samilton, William S.	11 SEP 1879 L	13	366
Thompson, Eliza	Carter, Edward	23 NOV 1882 R	17	130
Thompson, Elizabeth	Hoffman, George W.	11 MAY 1878 L	12	048
Thompson, Elizabeth	Selby, Charles E.	12 AUG 1879 L	13	303
Thompson, Ella V.	Lynn, Clarence A.	17 JAN 1882	16	197
Thompson, Emma	Clark, Charles	28 MAR 1878 R	11	397
Thompson, Emma	Winslow, William F.	03 APR 1880	14	208
Thompson, Emma E.	Shortell, John H.	03 MAY 1881 L	15	289
Thompson, Fannie	Powell, Jacob	31 MAY 1881 L	15	334
Thompson, Florence	Lewis, George Barnholt	11 MAR 1885 R	20	106

D.C. Marriage Records Index, June 28, 1877 to October 19, 1885   459

Thompson, Florence V.	Loveday, James P.	03 DEC 1878 R	12	359
Thompson, Florida	Barry, Jeremiah	02 MAY 1880 R	14	247
Thompson, Frances D.	Davis, Jerome F.	05 JAN 1885 R	20	003
Thompson, Frances May	Raitz, Frank W.	10 SEP 1883 R	18	123
Thompson, Frederick	Gambrell, Madora	08 JAN 1884	18	370
Thompson, George	Miles, Mary	09 OCT 1877 R	11	126
Thompson, George	Smith, Josephine	21 JUL 1879 R	13	284
Thompson, George H.	Chaney, Martina	14 JUL 1879 L	13	280
Thompson, George L.	Rawlings, Margaret R.	19 MAR 1878	11	387
Thompson, George S.	Baxter, Annie	23 JUL 1884 R	19	152
Thompson, Georgiana	King, Clarence Elias	07 DEC 1881 R	16	118
Thompson, Granville S.	Mills, Cornelia A.	15 FEB 1879 R	13	061
Thompson, H. Owen	Wooldridge, Blanche	29 JUN 1883 L	18	026
Thompson, Hennie	Starks, Arthur	05 JUL 1877	11	011
Thompson, Henry S.	Tridell, Ella C.	12 SEP 1878 R	12	215
Thompson, Isaac	Wallace, Mary	15 OCT 1884	19	303
Thompson, J. Ashley	Mueller, Lany	23 MAY 1882 R	16	373
Thompson, James	McFermillion, Mary	05 DEC 1877 L	11	220
Thompson, James	Brown, Annie	08 DEC 1884 L	19	441
Thompson, James	Chester, Mary	16 JUL 1885 R	20	328
Thompson, James Albert	Cockrill, Eliza Victoria	20 SEP 1877 R	11	103
Thompson, James H.	Humphries, Lucy A.	06 JAN 1885 R	20	005
Thompson, Jane E.S.	Maltby, Lewis C.	11 SEP 1877	11	088
Thompson, Jennie	Kenney, Edward C.	02 JAN 1884 L	18	362
Thompson, Jerry	Jackson, Lucilia	04 JUN 1884 L	19	058
Thompson, John	Meeks, Susan	20 AUG 1878 L	12	174
Thompson, John	Morrison, Mary Isabella	18 SEP 1882 R	17	025
Thompson, John B.	Hobbs, Laura V.	24 FEB 1880 R	14	162
Thompson, John H.	Dawson, Frances E.	23 JUN 1879 L	13	243
Thompson, John H.	Norris, Elizabeth E.	23 FEB 1882 R	16	257
Thompson, John H.	Simmons, Josephine L.	26 NOV 1884 L	19	422
Thompson, John W.	Dorsey, Barbara Ellen	12 MAR 1878 R	11	379
Thompson, Joseph	Peacock, Delilah	14 DEC 1880 R	15	094
Thompson, Joseph M.	Lucas, Josephine	05 JUN 1882 R	16	394
Thompson, Josephine	Wheeler, George	27 MAR 1878	11	395
Thompson, Josephine	White, Eugene	28 APR 1884	18	538
Thompson, Kate	Cobin, John	25 DEC 1877 R	11	264
Thompson, Katie V.	King, Benjamin F.	25 JUL 1878	12	143
Thompson, Kittie Anne	Proctor, Sylvester	10 DEC 1878 R	12	374
Thompson, Laura	Johnson, Charles	12 MAY 1880 L	14	265
Thompson, Laura V.	Thomas, William W.	06 DEC 1877 L	11	224
Thompson, Lee	White, Mary	06 JAN 1880 L	14	091
Thompson, Lillie S.	Bergling, John	07 DEC 1881 L	16	117
Thompson, Louisa	Brown, T.R.	01 APR 1880 L	14	205
Thompson, Margaret E.	Melson, John E.	20 SEP 1885 R	20	428
Thompson, Marian V.	Clark, James A.	02 APR 1881 R	15	244
Thompson, Mary	Smith, Philip	08 OCT 1878 L	12	262
Thompson, Mary	Clements, John S.	09 APR 1884	18	502
Thompson, Mary	Thompson, Robert	28 AUG 1884 L	19	213
Thompson, Mary Antonia	Carlin, James S.	02 SEP 1880 R	14	427
Thompson, Mary E.	Beers, Harry C.	06 JUN 1881 L	15	347
Thompson, Mary E.	Pettit, Jackson	24 APR 1884	18	531
Thompson, Mary Olivia	Davis, George A.	03 JUL 1881 R	15	385
Thompson, Mary V. Ratcliff	Hands, Adam C.	30 SEP 1878 R	12	243
Thompson, Middleton	Price, Margaret E.	04 JUN 1878 L	12	082
Thompson, Minette	Babcock, Daniel A.	27 NOV 1878 L	12	353
Thompson, Minnie	Mahoney, William	13 JUN 1878	12	098
Thompson, Nellie	Silver, William	27 DEC 1882	17	201

Thompson, Niles Hibbard	Gannett, Lucy Gayton	05 DEC 1878 R	12	367
Thompson, Oliver Thos.	Gray, Adele Bertha	25 MAR 1885 R	20	132
Thompson, Phiny Cleophas	Johnson, Annie	14 MAY 1884 R	19	020
Thompson, Rebecca	Hughes, Benjamin F.	25 JUL 1885 L	20	340
Thompson, Richard L.	Graham, Emma G.	28 AUG 1883 L	18	102
Thompson, Robert	Thompson, Mary	28 AUG 1884 L	19	213
Thompson, Rudolph P.	Stafford, Octavis	12 JUN 1884	19	079
Thompson, Sallie E.	Brown, Andrew R.	08 OCT 1878 R	12	262
Thompson, Samuel	Jones, Henrietta	16 MAY 1879 L	13	194
Thompson, Sarah E.	Shepherd, Aaron	15 OCT 1878 L	12	273
Thompson, Sarah Jane Elizabeth	Rollins, Charles Franklin	02 JUL 1877	11	005
Thompson, Smith	Berry, Winnie	19 NOV 1884 R	19	396
Thompson, Solomon H.	Thomas, Sarah A.V.	11 MAY 1885 L	20	216
Thompson, Susan	Stuart, Henry	15 MAY 1879 R	13	188
Thompson, Susannah	King, John Henry	09 JAN 1883 R	17	246
Thompson, Susie E.	Anderson, H.P.	06 AUG 1877	11	042
Thompson, Thomas A.	Johnson, Sidonia R.	31 JAN 1885 L	20	045
Thompson, Vertie	Edmunds, Webster	25 MAR 1880 R	14	155
Thompson, Wales	Daniels, Mary	25 JAN 1882	16	208
Thompson, Walter	Rollins, Tiny	15 SEP 1880 R	14	445
Thompson, Wilbert Grant	Saffel, Mary Margaretta	13 FEB 1883 R	17	302
Thompson, William A.	Nicholson, Mary A.	03 DEC 1883	18	293
Thompson, William E.	Bryan, Sarah Savilla	28 MAY 1878	12	070
Thompson, William Edward	Riley, Kate N.	21 FEB 1882 R	16	254
Thompson, William H.	Pettitt, Madge	07 FEB 1881 R	15	180
Thompson, William M.E.	Shaw, Mary E.	11 NOV 1880 L	15	044
Thompson, William N.	Clarvoe, Mattie R.	04 AUG 1881 L	15	432
Thompson, William Perry	Miller, Caroline	26 SEP 1877 R	11	108
Thomson, Annie C.	Delavergne, Nathan E.	17 JUN 1880	14	326
Thomson, Charles P.	Barker, Mary	06 DEC 1883	18	304
Thomson, Frederick	Schmidt, Bertha E.	11 OCT 1882 R	17	067
Thomson, William	Cavis, Belle	07 FEB 1885 L	20	066
Thorn, Albert W.	Crager, Sarah S.	05 NOV 1879 R	13	464
Thorn, Annie Laura	Chipley, William R.	15 JUN 1880 R	14	319
Thorn, Bertha M.	Leonberger, Henry	12 MAY 1880 L	14	267
Thorn, Catherine E.	Sibley, Samuel M.	30 JAN 1882	16	214
Thorn, Cora V.	Smith, J.E.	27 FEB 1884	18	443
Thorn, Effie	Davies, Frank	18 OCT 1877	11	145
Thorn, Marion M.	Woodward, S.B.	15 JUN 1880 R	14	320
Thorn, Mary A.	Hawkins, Thomas F.	22 APR 1885 L	20	182
Thorn, Massie	Story, William	26 JUN 1879 R	13	255
Thorn, Olivia Jenkins	Donohoe, James W.	15 JAN 1879 L	13	018
Thorn, William A.	King, Mary E.	23 NOV 1881 L	16	092
Thorne, Joshua S.	Kettner, Rachel V.	15 AUG 1877 R	11	052
Thorne, S. Morris	Boyd, Mary	09 FEB 1882 R	16	234
Thornhill, Eliza	Jackson, William	17 MAR 1885 R	20	119
Thornhill, John	Jackson, Eliza	26 FEB 1881 R	15	204
Thornley, Andrew Glassell	Omohumdro, Carrie Thornley	26 APR 1882 R	16	337
Thornley, Jesse	Bennett, Martha	03 NOV 1881 R	16	057
Thornton, Ann	Smith, John	04 JUN 1879 L	13	219
Thornton, Anna	Williams, Richard	14 FEB 1883 R	17	307
Thornton, Anne	Keith, David	26 DEC 1878	12	255
Thornton, Bartley	Tierney, Catherine	16 OCT 1883	18	176
Thornton, Bertha	Lovey, James	24 JUL 1884 L	19	154
Thornton, Ella A.	Carlin, Thomas L.	29 DEC 1879	14	078
Thornton, Emma	West, Henry	02 FEB 1882 R	16	215
Thornton, Frances	Shipley, Fernando	07 OCT 1885	20	463
Thornton, George Taylor	McFadden, Sarah Hays	26 NOV 1879 R	14	015

Thornton, James S.	Jernels, Laura S.	24 APR 1883 L	17	408
Thornton, John C.	Jones, Carrie	23 OCT 1878	12	287
Thornton, John T.	Waldon, Lucy A.	30 JUN 1879 L	13	258
Thornton, Laura	Hamilton, Washington	16 JAN 1879	13	016
Thornton, Lee	Anderson, William Henry	03 MAY 1885	20	210
Thornton, Lydia	Selby, Richard B.	20 AUG 1885 R	20	381
Thornton, Mary A.	Burns, Joseph D.	28 OCT 1880	15	018
Thornton, Mary J.	Ford, James A.	28 MAY 1878 L	12	071
Thornton, Mary, Mrs.	Robinson, James, Rev.	02 OCT 1879 R	13	397
Thornton, Nellie	Anderson, William D.	12 APR 1881 R	15	254
Thornton, Reuben	Hunter, Annie	03 APR 1880 L	14	207
Thornton, Sallie	Jackson, James	31 OCT 1883 L	18	223
Thornton, William	Stewart, Mary J.	29 MAR 1879 R	13	118
Thorowgood, W.J.	Willett, Ada F.	28 APR 1881	15	281
Thorp, Eliza E.	Wesley, Joseph	19 APR 1883	17	401
Thorpe, Benjamin R.	Goddard, Ida	24 MAY 1883	17	461
Thorpe, Frances Isabelle	Clark, Williams Smith	09 MAY 1878 R	12	044
Thorton, Lizzie	Larkins, Lewis	12 SEP 1881 R	15	481
Thorton, Moses	Gottridge, Estella	16 MAY 1881 R	15	309
Thorton, Virginia	Anderson, Gillespie B.	20 OCT 1881	16	037
Thour, Elizabeth	Smith, George F.	04 SEP 1879 L	13	349
Thour, Margaret M.	Daly, William W.	21 NOV 1882 R	17	141
Threat, John H.	Jackson, Cornelia	06 DEC 1883 L	18	302
Thronton, Henry	Moss, Annie	22 OCT 1884	19	329
Throop, Laura W.	Burdett, John H.	07 OCT 1879 R	13	405
Thuringer, Joseph F.	Germeroth, Annie	20 DEC 1883	18	329
Thurm, Auguste Louise Agnes	Frieman, John W.	02 MAR 1880 R	14	159
Thurman, Selia	Boyd, Edwin W.	01 OCT 1884	19	279
Thurn, Herman	Seyboldt, Cora	04 SEP 1880 L	14	432
Thurow, Louise E.W.	Ruick, Emil A.H.	14 SEP 1885	20	414
Thurston, Addie	Mocobee, William A.	28 APR 1880 L	14	242
Thurston, Frederick	Murphy, Augusta	07 MAY 1883 L	17	431
Thurston, Harriet R.	Langley, Walter B.	16 OCT 1879 R	13	425
Thurston, John H.	Smith, Isadore M.	19 FEB 1878	11	346
Thurston, William Henry	Jones, Mollie J.	16 JUN 1881 R	15	363
Thurton, John W.	McMillan, Mary Elizabeth	06 JAN 1885 R	20	004
Thuston, Jno.	Williams, Lizzie	20 JUL 1880	14	359
Thyson, W. Frank	Snyder, Lilia	23 APR 1878	12	019
Tibb, Emanuel	Gross, Sarah	08 NOV 1881 R	16	066
Tibbals, Ralph C.	Wilkinson, Estella	18 APR 1881	15	216
Tibbetts, Nellie M.	Willis, Charles S.	02 OCT 1878	12	249
Tibble, Viney	Ellis, Daniel	14 JUL 1885 L	20	325
Tibbles, Charles H.	Young, Mary E.	27 NOV 1884 L	19	423
Tibbs, Annie L., Mrs.	Cavender, Joseph	14 JAN 1884 L	18	376
Tibbs, Betsy	Dozier, Jeremiah	02 SEP 1880 R	14	428
Tibbs, Henry	Bowles, Martha	04 JAN 1882 R	16	182
Tibbs, Mary	Washington, Richard	17 AUG 1882 R	16	483
Tibbs, Mary E.	Joy, Charles H.	02 APR 1884 R	18	493
Tibbs, Mary Jane	Hicks, Joseph	14 NOV 1883	18	254
Tibbs, Richard	Wickens, Viney	22 MAY 1879 R	13	202
Tibbs, Spencer	Lewis, Eliza	09 DEC 1880 L	15	089
Tibbs, Vivian	Hutchinson, Josephine Ann	15 MAR 1883 R	17	346
Tibbs, William A.	French, Henrietta	19 JUN 1885	20	280
Tice, William	Walker, Lettie	25 JAN 1883 L	17	275
Tichenor, Clarendon L.	Davis, Effie	05 AUG 1885 R	34	8427
Tidmarsh, Sarah E.	Smart, William E.	25 OCT 1883 R	18	210
Tiernan, John	Beyea, Georgianna C.	08 OCT 1879 R	13	410
Tierney, Catherine	Thornton, Bartley	16 OCT 1883	18	176

Tiffany, Alvira	Nichols, Ensign	13 FEB 1878	11	339
Tiffany, Walton Cuyler	Gilman, Julia	09 APR 1879 R	13	132
Tilghman, Charles	Clark, Mary	07 AUG 1884	19	173
Tilghman, James H.	Smith, Fannie V.	05 DEC 1878	12	369
Tilghman, Susie	Robinson, Richmond	27 SEP 1877 R	11	106
Till, George B.	Krause, Julia	18 DEC 1883	18	314
Till, Ida M., Mrs.	Pierson, Charles O.	03 NOV 1880 R	15	029
Tiller, Hattie L.	Tyree, Andrew W.	04 JUL 1881	15	386
Tillet, William	Howard, Emily J.	21 JAN 1880 R	14	115
Tillett, Eliza J.	Bayless, Ezra	23 APR 1885 R	20	185
Tillett, Hattie B.	Daniel, Lafayette W.	29 SEP 1880	14	466
Tillett, Lucy E.	Flaherty, Ananias	19 DEC 1882	17	192
Tillett, Sallie L.	Bayliss, William T.	02 JUL 1885 R	20	307
Tilley, Joseph R.	Brown, Annie	08 OCT 1879 L	13	411
Tilley, Sarah E.	Johnson, Thomas M.	27 APR 1882	16	331
Tilling, Annie M.	Walter, George W.	03 SEP 1878 R	12	195
Tilling, Ella	Alber, August	10 JUL 1878	12	132
Tilling, John H.	Phillips, Mary C.	30 JAN 1883 L	17	278
Tillman, Mary	Swann, John	12 JUN 1879	13	231
Tillman, Mary E.	Lee, William H.J.	21 NOV 1881 L	16	087
Tillman, Richard A.	Madison, Martha E.	25 SEP 1878	12	234
Tills, Ambrose	Bond, Rebecca	28 APR 1880 R	14	208
Tilman, Andrew	Johnson, Annie M.	18 NOV 1880 L	15	056
Tilp, Frederick	Breck, Annie C.	13 FEB 1879 R	13	055
Tilp, Rose E.	Kozel, George	15 APR 1879 R	13	146
Tilton, Peter G.	Jones, Maria	15 MAY 1884	19	024
Timberlake, George A.	Seaton, Augusta B.	10 SEP 1879 R	13	363
Timberlake, Richard Claybrook	Shelton, Virginia Florence	02 JUN 1884 R	19	050
Timmons, Emma L.	Bashears, Frank	24 AUG 1881 L	15	456
Timmons, Laura Ann	Timmons, Wallace M.	01 APR 1879 L	13	120
Timmons, Wallace M.	Timmons, Laura Ann	01 APR 1879 L	13	120
Timms, Jamoo B.	Budenseck, Katy S.	10 APR 1878 L	11	416
Tincher, Georgie F.	McGuigan, John J.	05 OCT 1879 R	13	379
Tinder, Fannie	Drummond, Sidney	19 NOV 1884	19	385
Tindle, Jacob E.	Yates, Emma	08 OCT 1885 R	20	468
Tine, Amanda	Majors, Charles	29 NOV 1881	16	102
Tines, Simon	Braxton, Ella M.	24 OCT 1878 L	12	292
Tines, Simon S.	Hood, Florence	25 SEP 1883 L	18	153
Tingsley, Hattie H.	Page, William H.	14 MAR 1883 R	17	342
Tinker, George F.	Reed, Annie	24 SEP 1885	20	438
Tinkler, William T.	Siep, Louisa	04 NOV 1878 R	12	306
Tinley, Charity A.	Pettit, Henry S.	25 AUG 1881 R	15	458
Tinney, A.B., Mrs.	Brown, Charles E.	20 MAR 1880 L	14	190
Tinney, Ellen	Stephenson, Augustus	28 NOV 1878 L	12	354
Tinney, Emma Jane	Johnson, Robert Edward	31 JAN 1882 L	16	216
Tinney, James Andrew	Williams, Ellen	15 OCT 1885	20	491
Tinney, John T.	Lancaster, Lucretia	20 JAN 1880	14	113
Tinney, Mary E.	Turner, James L.	18 NOV 1879	13	494
Tinsley, John	Baker, Mattie A.	24 JAN 1884 R	18	395
Tinsley, John C.	Barnes, Mary F.	29 AUG 1877 R	11	067
Tinsley, Rosa B.	Harris, Walter S.	10 SEP 1878 L	12	209
Tinsley, Sarah E.	Gibbons, Robert A.	27 NOV 1878 L	12	349
Tippet, Charles M.	Linken, Jennie B.	14 NOV 1878 R	12	330
Tippet, Susie	Zell, Charles	13 SEP 1877 R	11	090
Tippett, George L.	Lynch, Mary J.	28 NOV 1882	17	153
Tippett, Grace	Bernhard, E.J.	23 MAY 1883 L	17	460
Tippett, Marion A.	Langley, Treasia G.	27 JUN 1883	18	020
Tippett, Samuel F.	Ager, Emma J.	08 AUG 1884	19	176

Name	Spouse	Date		
Tippett, William B.	Hasler, Antonian B.	29 SEP 1884	19	271
Tippitt, Clarence D.	Robinson, Patsy L.	27 JAN 1881 L	15	167
Tipplet, Susie G.	Cook, Andrew	30 JAN 1881 R	15	170
Tipton, Neenah	Simpson, Theodore Henry	01 NOV 1878 R	12	303
Titus, Laura C.	Ricketts, Charles W.	25 JUL 1878 R	12	144
Tiverny, Clara Marcellene	Newman, Wm. George	11 JUN 1885 R	20	268
Tiverny, John A.	Newman, Johanna M.	09 SEP 1885	20	408
Tobe, Elizabeth A.	Kaiser, William S.	18 DEC 1884 R	19	467
Tobia, Frank	Mayhugh, Roxy	26 DEC 1883	18	345
Tobin, Annie A.	O'Dea, Patrick	16 SEP 1880 L	14	449
Tobin, James E.	Dowling, Jennie	13 MAY 1885 R	20	218
Tobin, Lizzie Beatrice	Johnson, Peter Henry	01 JUL 1882 L	16	433
Tobin, Mary E.	Casey, Patrick Jas.	26 OCT 1881 R	16	041
Tobin, Mary M.	Dove, Robert A.	11 OCT 1882 L	17	066
Todd, David Peck	Loomis, Mabel	05 MAR 1879 R	13	090
Todd, Edward Jesse	Durant, Mary Harper	27 DEC 1881 R	16	161
Todd, Gabrella	Red, Reuben	13 MAY 1884 L	19	017
Todd, Harriet	Harman, David	02 JAN 1882 R	16	176
Todd, Margaret J.	Jackson, Richard J.	15 JAN 1878 R	11	302
Todd, Mazie Brooke	Culver, Reuben Dillon	30 DEC 1883 R	18	352
Todd, Ralston L.	Young, Ella M.	27 FEB 1883 R	17	323
Todd, Sarah	Thomas, Frank	14 JAN 1878 L	11	303
Todd, Sarah P.	Alexander, Lewis W.	06 NOV 1878 R	12	311
Todd, William B.	Bond, R. Matilda	22 JAN 1885 R	20	033
Toepper, Louisa M.	Heitmuller, Ferdinand A.	23 JUN 1885 R	20	287
Tolbert, James	Barker, Soffie	07 JUN 1883 R	17	483
Tolbert, Sidney	Kenner, Hiram	20 MAR 1880 R	14	190
Tolbert, William	Haller, Eveline	15 JUN 1880 L	14	320
Tolbort, John F.	Blackson, Lucy	10 JAN 1878	11	294
Toler, Lucilia	Williams, Horace W.	15 MAY 1879	13	187
Toler, Philip	Harvey, Susan	02 NOV 1881 R	16	056
Toler, William	Vaughn, Henrietta	10 SEP 1879 R	13	363
Toles, Sarah E.	Hardy, William H.	05 DEC 1884 L	19	438
Toliver, Frank	Anderson, Amy	15 AUG 1883 L	18	088
Toliver, Maggie	Coves, John Willis	26 DEC 1883 R	18	345
Toliver, Mary	Griffin, Levi	05 JUL 1877 R	11	006
Toliver, Rosa	Conley, Frederick G.	10 APR 1884 R	18	498
Toliver, Shedrick	Davis, Sallie	06 JUN 1882 L	16	396
Tolley, Emily Jane	Carter, Charles Edward	10 NOV 1879 R	13	475
Tolliver, Adelina Virginia	Spence, Cyrus	22 JUN 1880 R	14	329
Tolliver, Alice V.	Furr, Eli C.	20 JUN 1878 L	12	106
Tolliver, Bertha	Morton, John Henry	17 APR 1878 R	12	012
Tolliver, Eliza	Benson, Isaac	15 AUG 1882	16	479
Tolliver, Frances	Norris, Harrison	15 SEP 1885 L	20	416
Tolliver, Irene	Lacey, Lewis	11 APR 1882	16	306
Tolliver, James	Lee, Mary	01 SEP 1884 L	19	219
Tolliver, James H.	Boone, Elizabeth E.	30 APR 1885	20	198
Tolliver, Josie	Gant, James W.	30 DEC 1880 R	15	092
Tolliver, Lizzie	Steward, John	16 MAY 1881 L	15	308
Tolliver, Mary	Wright, Philip	27 DEC 1877 R	11	274
Tolliver, Millie	Smith, Hamilton	12 JAN 1882 R	16	193
Tolliver, Rachel	Fields, Bailey	06 MAY 1880 L	14	257
Tolliver, Sallie	Bell, Matthew N.	05 APR 1883 R	17	382
Tolliver, Sarah	Harris, Archibald	04 JAN 1880 R	14	088
Tolliver, William	Clagett, Martha	22 SEP 1877	11	104
Tolliver, William P.R.	Atkinson, Rebecca	03 JUN 1885	20	255
Tolman, Albert Joseph	Marsh, Anne Ruth	10 OCT 1883 R	18	183
Tolman, Alice	Willoughby, Thaddeus D.	01 OCT 1885	20	451

Tolson, Alfred C.	O'Hare, Catherine J.	13 NOV 1878 L	12	327
Tolson, Amelia	Jackson, William	25 AUG 1879 R	13	326
Tolson, Annie E.	Herbert, Lawerence M.	27 DEC 1881 R	16	161
Tolson, Arthur	Suit, Ella	07 NOV 1878 R	12	305
Tolson, Carrie	Bell, John	24 AUG 1880	14	411
Tolson, Charles S.	Jenkins, Martha	07 OCT 1880 R	14	477
Tolson, Cora A.	Shacklett, Nelson T.	17 SEP 1877	11	098
Tolson, Ella	Low, John	24 AUG 1879 R	13	331
Tolson, Francis E.	Carter, Rosa L.	05 MAY 1881 R	15	293
Tolson, Hattie	Anderson, John V.	29 DEC 1884	19	497
Tolson, Henry N.	Summers, Mary E.	21 AUG 1877 R	11	058
Tolson, Henson	Winston, Frances Elizabeth	03 MAY 1883	17	428
Tolson, Ida	Jones, James	06 JAN 1880 L	14	092
Tolson, Isaac	Clagett, Alice	06 JAN 1883 R	17	241
Tolson, Isaac	Baker, Ellen	03 FEB 1885	20	050
Tolson, James	Spencer, Agnes	23 DEC 1879 R	14	067
Tolson, John F.	Green, Sarah Ann	14 DEC 1884 R	19	457
Tolson, K.M.	Murray, H.T.	23 MAY 1883 R	17	459
Tolson, Malvina	Hill, Thomas	04 SEP 1883 L	18	111
Tolson, Mary E.	Tracy, George N.	10 JUN 1879 R	13	226
Tolson, Rose Armatage Carter B.	Neale, Francis D.	16 FEB 1885 R	20	067
Tolson, Sarah	Henderson, James E.	26 FEB 1880 L	14	168
Tomlinson, Edward	Tennis, Ida	21 SEP 1882	17	032
Tomlinson, Katie M.	Keyes, Charles W.	02 FEB 1885 R	20	047
Toner, Edward T.	Kennedy, Tillie E.	08 JUN 1882 R	16	401
Toner, Rosannah	Hurley, James Dennis	07 JUL 1880 L	14	350
Toney, Catharine	Robson, John	28 AUG 1877 L	11	068
Toney, James Wm.	Clagett, Sarah Matilda	27 JUL 1882 R	16	459
Toodle, Susannah	Bell, Henry	17 NOV 1880 L	15	053
Toole, James	Schroth, Mary	15 JUN 1882 R	16	412
Toomey, Daniel D.	Wolfe, Katie	24 JUL 1883 L	18	058
Topley, Henry T.	Bellen, Maggie J.	29 JUN 1885 L	20	300
Torbert, Lilla W.	Dalrymple, James A.D.	20 DEC 1882 R	17	193
Torney, Emma V.	McNally, John E.	19 MAR 1885 L	20	126
Torrens, Mary C. Roy	Bodin, Henry Armand	23 JUL 1877 R	11	030
Torrey, Charles Henry	Ambrose, Mary Frances	02 JUL 1879 R	13	261
Torrey, William A.	Frazier, Adah S.	25 NOV 1879 R	14	002
Torreyson, William	Hughes, Jennie E.	21 JUN 1882 L	16	421
Toulson, Arthur Richard	Hilton, Mary Frances	15 DEC 1880 R	15	095
Tounay, Johanna	Britt, Pierce	04 OCT 1883 L	18	174
Tourney, Mary E.	Osborn, William B.	06 JUN 1881 L	15	347
Towers, Agnes May	Woodward, Oscar	20 OCT 1880	15	005
Towers, David I.	Waters, Mollie E.	16 FEB 1881 L	15	192
Towers, Lewis E.	Birth, Emma J. Wagner	18 JUL 1880 R	14	367
Towers, Marion D.	Crump, George A.	24 DEC 1882 R	17	203
Towers, Mary A.	Richardson, John R.	11 DEC 1882 L	17	177
Towers, Winfield Scott	Blanchard, Mary Lenthall	17 NOV 1880 R	15	051
Towler, Maria	Moxley, Lloyd	20 NOV 1884 R	19	399
Towles, Celia	Clark, William H.	25 MAR 1879 L	13	115
Towles, Daniel	Sanders, Phillis	27 DEC 1877	11	272
Towles, Henry O.	Bevans, Fannie E.	01 JUN 1882 R	16	386
Towles, Isabella	Rawles, George	19 MAR 1885	20	125
Towles, Jennie	Eskridge, Daniel	17 JAN 1878 R	11	307
Towles, Martha	Brookes, Stephen	16 DEC 1884	19	460
Towles, Sarah	Hardie, William H.	10 FEB 1885	33	8009
Town, Edward Daniel	Leach, Mary E.	06 MAR 1879 R	13	091
Towne, Frank H.	Pumphrey, Laura C.	01 OCT 1878	12	244
Towne, Phineas	Townly, Mary	03 JUL 1884	19	121

Towner, Edith	Jewell, Eugene P.	20 OCT 1884	19	319
Towner, Oscar T.	Frank, Mary Selina	15 NOV 1881 R	16	075
Townley, Charles T.	Cook, Mary F.	26 JUL 1883	18	061
Townley, Kate	Thompson, Alexander	09 APR 1878 R	11	411
Townley, Kate	Crocker, Edward A.	03 JUL 1882	16	435
Townley, Minnie S.	Willey, Charles F.	09 APR 1878 R	11	412
Townley, Sallie Edna	De Leon, George Henry	19 FEB 1880 R	14	160
Townly, Mary	Towne, Phineas	03 JUL 1884	19	121
Townsend, George Y.	Dodge, Neenah	16 OCT 1884	19	307
Townsend, Gertrude C.	Skeel, Clarence M.	20 JUN 1878	12	107
Townsend, Henry Clark	Goodall, Kate Hayes	23 APR 1879 R	13	155
Townsend, James P.	Ringgold, Elizabeth A. (Brennan)	12 SEP 1882 R	17	015
Townsend, Thornton	Nelson, Georgiana V.	12 SEP 1878 R	12	193
Townshend, Elizabeth Pitts	Miller, John Henry	01 JAN 1883 R	17	224
Townshend, Grafton C.D.	Walker, Alice A.	06 JAN 1880 R	14	089
Townshend, Willie Lumsdon	Gladding, Charles Davenport	25 SEP 1882 R	17	035
Towsey, Lula L.	Sims, Thomas J.	13 MAY 1884	19	016
Towson, Dorsey E.W.	Campbell, Blanche Kennedy	18 OCT 1883 R	18	201
Toy, Margaret	Gant, George	08 AUG 1883 L	18	080
Toy, Mary	Fitzhugh, Mary	06 MAR 1879 L	13	092
Toy, Sophie Anne	Jackson, John	20 FEB 1879 L	13	070
Toy, William	Barnes, Margaret	05 MAR 1878	11	371
Toyer, George Benjamin	Hall, Annie Mary	05 MAR 1885 R	20	089
Tracey, James	Buell, Alice V.	25 DEC 1878 R	12	391
Tracey, John J.	Lee, Julia	12 SEP 1883	18	126
Tracey, John T.	Fife, Mary A.	17 NOV 1882 L	17	134
Tracy, George N.	Tolson, Mary E.	10 JUN 1879 R	13	226
Tracy, Raudolph H.	Moore, Hattie A.	29 OCT 1884	19	345
Tracy, Sarah A.	Lynch, Jeremiah	20 AUG 1882 R	16	486
Tracy, W.H.	Barnes, Sarah O.	27 JUN 1883	18	019
Trader, Martha Elizabeth	Fitzmorris, John	18 APR 1881 L	15	259
Trahey, John	Mahoney, Kate	13 MAY 1878 L	12	049
Trahey, John	Melia, Mary	06 DEC 1883 L	18	299
Trailer, Mary E.	Howell, L.R.	01 MAR 1884 L	18	452
Trainham, Edward B.	Lorman, Lizzie L.	14 JAN 1885	20	017
Trainor, Eugene	Bresenhan, Hanorah	26 MAY 1885	20	240
Tramble, Mary Virginia	Smith, Henry H.	03 AUG 1881 L	15	431
Tramell, Lewis Thomas	Grimes, Amanda	28 FEB 1878 L	11	365
Tramell, Rachel Ann	Shepard, William H.	24 JAN 1883 R	17	273
Trammel, Zillia Ann	Shirley, John D.	31 MAY 1882 R	16	383
Trammell, Charles A.	Cornell, Maggie M.	27 JUN 1885	20	295
Trammell, Ida Lee	Murphy, Joseph	15 JAN 1882	16	194
Trammell, John Henry	Shirley, Maggie Lee	01 FEB 1885 R	20	035
Trammell, Joseph C.	Louvette, Ida May	12 FEB 1878 R	11	336
Trammell, Mary	Johnson, Sandy	07 JAN 1884 L	18	367
Trammell, Virginia D.	Trammell, Washington	14 FEB 1884 L	18	425
Trammell, Washington	Trammell, Virginia D.	14 FEB 1884 L	18	425
Trapp, Rosa	Elliott, Thomas H. McN.	27 JAN 1881 R	15	164
Trautman, Lena	Sanderson, Edward	24 OCT 1878	12	282
Traver, Norman L.	McPherson, Kate	21 NOV 1878 L	12	341
Travers, John C., Jr.	Barrow, Margaret E.	28 APR 1884 L	18	537
Travers, Margaret	Hutchison, Elijah	27 APR 1885 R	20	191
Travers, Olivia H.	Myers, Evelyn F.	19 APR 1879 R	13	151
Travis, Augustus	Marchie, Annie	08 JUN 1880 L	14	310
Travis, Dora	Harrison, John	30 JAN 1879	13	034
Travis, Maria	Brooks, John H.	23 DEC 1879 R	14	007
Travis, Phil	Brown, Susie	01 NOV 1883 R	18	226
Travis, Scipio	White, Eliza	26 OCT 1881	16	042

Name	Spouse	Date	Vol	Page
Traylor, George Archer	Mills, Mary Anna	04 FEB 1880 R	14	135
Traylor, Sarah E.	Case, Francis H.	23 OCT 1884	19	332
Treadway, Decatur B.	Stoddard, Minnie V.	09 SEP 1885	20	410
Treadwell, John	Farrow, Anna E.	19 OCT 1880	15	001
Treadwell, Sarah	Sutton, Edward H.	07 NOV 1879	13	472
Trede, Fretz	Gottsmann, Sophia M.	20 OCT 1878	12	282
Tredick, Fannie L.	Catlett, James M., Jr.	13 DEC 1881 R	16	127
Tredway, Catherine A.	Cartwright, Richard T.	05 APR 1880 R	14	209
Treece, N.M.	James, M.B.	25 MAY 1880	14	286
Trego, Albert	Carroll, Kate B.	07 NOV 1883 D	18	239
Trego, William Willett	Schneider, Mary E.	06 JUL 1882 R	16	441
Treiber, Ernst F.	Freudenberger, Catherine	29 AUG 1878 L	12	184
Treinor, Ella Hadley	Ray, Lewis B.	26 DEC 1881	16	155
Tremble, Annie E.	Jennings, Wm. Harrison	24 AUG 1882	16	492
Trescot, Stephen Barnwell	Worthington, Elizabeth	03 NOV 1880 R	15	022
Tretter, Maggie	Walter, Eugene L.	26 NOV 1884 R	19	415
Trevitt, Clarence L.	Johnson, Catharine F.	27 JUN 1883 R	18	022
Trew, Bushrod Washington	Divine, Virginia Wise	05 APR 1882 R	16	301
Trew, James Thomas	Billingsley, Mary Mildred	10 NOV 1877 R	11	170
Trexler, Eugene B.	Nolan, Laura A.	08 JUL 1879	13	276
Trexler, Rebecca S.	James, Henry C.	17 NOV 1879 R	13	492
Treynor, Katie May	Anderson, John Henry	14 OCT 1885 R	20	481
Tribble, Eustace C.	Wooddy, Anna J.	23 OCT 1884	19	332
Tribby, Charles E.	Davis, Katie S.	17 JUL 1885	20	328
Tribby, Gertrude V.	Offutt, George Warren	24 JAN 1882 R	16	206
Trice, Ardelia	Stutley, Thomas H.	09 JUN 1885 R	20	262
Trice, Hilard	Schinault, Ida Lee	12 JAN 1880	14	101
Trice, Isaac	Roan, Rosetta	15 AUG 1879 L	13	323
Trice, James H.	Lucas, Ophelia A.	15 JUN 1882 R	16	409
Trice, Maimie E.	Sansbury, James A.	28 JAN 1885 R	20	041
Trice, William	Dishman, Mary Ann	02 JUN 1879 L	13	214
Tricker, Annie Serena	Dante, Drancis	29 NOV 1883 L	18	287
Tridell, Ella C.	Thompson, Henry S.	12 SEP 1878 R	12	215
Trimble, Mary	Gaddis, Adam	12 JUN 1883 R	17	487
Triplet, James Edward	Fitzhugh, Annie Eliz.	13 AUG 1885 R	20	369
Triplet, Samuel	Young, Mary Jane	04 AUG 1877 L	11	041
Triplet, Urias	Palmer, Lucy	18 MAR 1879 L	13	106
Triplett, Cephas	Church, Maria	15 JUN 1880 L	14	320
Triplett, Emma	Ellis, George F.	20 JUL 1882	16	453
Triplett, Washington	Cross, Lucy	07 APR 1880 L	14	213
Tripp, Dwight Kasson	Williamson, Corinne	20 JAN 1881 R	15	156
Trissler, Hattie A.	Beall, James Lemuel	20 JAN 1885 R	20	029
Troll, Fred'k N.	Schwartz, Bertha E.	02 OCT 1877	11	114
Troth, Horace E.	Simpson, Emma J.	25 DEC 1879	14	074
Trotman, Hattie V.	Butty, Joseph	02 JUN 1881 R	15	341
Trott, Charles Vernon	Clark, Emma J.	08 NOV 1880 R	15	035
Trotter, Harriet E.	Hendley, James T.	27 DEC 1880 R	15	127
Trouland, Jennie	Moulder, John N.	17 FEB 1883 L	17	310
Troulard, Robert A.	Boegeholz, Emma G.	23 MAY 1883	17	458
Trout, Lydia A.	Mumper, Harvey J.	24 DEC 1879	14	070
Troxell, Wm. H.	Lynch, Rosa G.	25 OCT 1883 L	18	215
True, Alice Marian	Williamson, J.B.M.	15 MAY 1884	19	024
True, Edward R.	Bryan, Jeannie E.	10 SEP 1878 R	12	211
True, Ida V.	McIntosh, Charles R.	03 JAN 1882 L	16	179
True, Mabel	Bartles, Joseph	22 DEC 1883 D	18	333
Truell, Edwin M.	Lord, Isadora	10 AUG 1883	18	093
Truman, Annie Virginia	McKinney, Benjamin F.	15 SEP 1885 R	20	416
Truman, Mary	Williams, Jefferson	28 MAY 1879 L	13	208

D.C. Marriage Records Index, June 28, 1877 to October 19, 1885

Trumble, Samuel H.	Beach, Mary E.	19 JAN 1882 L	16	201
Trumbo, Louis	Bond, Leonia J.	01 JUL 1884	19	108
Trumbull, Emma S.	Stant, William	21 MAY 1880 L	14	281
Trundell, Rachel W.	Dawson, Americus	17 FEB 1885	20	072
Trundle, C. Newton	Boyer, Katie B.	13 OCT 1880 L	14	491
Trundle, John Horatio	Spates, Lula Alvernon	24 MAY 1882 R	16	375
Trunnel, Lizzie W.	Johnson, J. Hiram	15 OCT 1883	18	191
Trunnel, Margaret	Scrivener, John T.	17 JAN 1882	16	197
Trunnel, Mary E.	Perrott, George	19 JUN 1883 R	18	003
Trunnell, Amelia	Hutchinson, George Washington	13 MAR 1882 R	16	274
Trunnell, M.E.	Johnson, Wm. L.	23 JUL 1883 L	18	058
Trunnell, Thyson T.	Carr, Julia	07 AUG 1879 R	13	308
Truseheim, Annie	Stein, George W.	23 APR 1878 L	12	018
Trusheim, Caroline	Albinson, James Edwin	22 JUN 1882 R	16	423
Truslow, Annie J.	Stone, John W.	03 JUL 1884 L	19	120
Truslow, Joanna	Loyd, George W.	16 JAN 1884 L	18	379
Trussler, Virginia	Stewart, Samuel Hamilton	11 SEP 1879 R	13	365
Truxell, Francis William	O'Conner, Minnie	18 MAY 1881	15	315
Truxson, Susan K.	Wheeler, William B.	09 JUN 1880 L	14	312
Tubman, Benjamin	Simpson, Charlotte Ann	01 MAY 1884 R	18	542
Tubman, Elizabeth	Harrison, William H.	08 SEP 1885 R	20	404
Tubman, Frances	Butler, Robert	09 AUG 1885 R	20	360
Tubman, James R.	Ware, Viola	17 JUL 1884	19	143
Tubman, William K.	Smith, Ella	11 DEC 1883	18	307
Tubmon, Ella	Smart, John H.	13 DEC 1883 L	18	315
Tucker, A. Dallas	Mankin, Minnie	27 FEB 1878	11	360
Tucker, Alexander	Brown, Clara	28 NOV 1878	12	354
Tucker, Anna L.	Steele, John E.	10 AUG 1879 R	13	314
Tucker, B.L.	Conaway, M.	18 MAY 1881 L	15	315
Tucker, Benjamin L.	Owens, Margaret G.	10 MAY 1879 R	13	184
Tucker, Bessie	Follansbee, Lambert T.	16 AUG 1881 L	15	448
Tucker, Beverly, Capt.	Higginbottom, Lucy Jane	06 OCT 1881 R	16	011
Tucker, Carrie	Fletcher, William	20 JUL 1885 L	20	332
Tucker, Creed R.	Check, Susie B.	27 DEC 1883 R	18	348
Tucker, Ella	Carpenter, John	28 AUG 1877 R	11	063
Tucker, Ella Virginia	Roache, Wm. F.	30 DEC 1881 L	15	508
Tucker, Emma M.	Raley, James B.	19 MAY 1881 L	15	318
Tucker, Florence	King, James	09 JAN 1884 R	18	372
Tucker, Floyd W.	Ellis, Mary	29 JAN 1880 R	14	127
Tucker, George H.	Clarvoe, Mary Rose	16 OCT 1879 R	13	430
Tucker, John F.	Rice, Susie M.	07 NOV 1883 L	18	241
Tucker, Julia T.	Murray, J. Harry	19 APR 1882 L	16	324
Tucker, Margaret Rebecca	Hurley, Salem Henry	02 APR 1878	11	400
Tucker, Mary	Williams, Benjamin F.	12 SEP 1878 R	12	217
Tucker, Mary A.	Carpenter, George A.	07 SEP 1877 R	11	082
Tucker, Matilda	Hawkins, Horace	18 MAY 1881	15	314
Tucker, Matilda L.L.	Remington, William H.	20 FEB 1878	11	345
Tucker, Milton T.	Haight, Mary L.	15 OCT 1878	12	272
Tucker, Penelope	O'Grady, Patrick	24 SEP 1885	20	441
Tucker, Richard W.	Popkins, Sarah A.	11 APR 1883 R	17	390
Tucker, Robert A.	Wright, Maggie E.	06 SEP 1882 R	17	010
Tucker, Tarlton Webb	Carroll, Elizabeth Lucille	20 SEP 1883	18	141
Tuckson, Emma	Grantlin, Richard A.	01 FEB 1883 R	17	285
Tuckson, Martha E.	Johnson, Reuben R.W.	18 JUN 1882	16	414
Tudge, Charles	Vangruder, Emma	14 APR 1883	17	394
Tudge, William W.	Schmid, Madelina Christina	14 NOV 1877 L	11	185
Tullock, Seymour Wilcox	Hildrup, Jessie Sophia	22 NOV 1882 R	17	142
Tully, Annie E.	Evarts, Raymond M.	06 FEB 1884 R	18	413

Tully, Cora B.	Brown, Harry A.	31 MAR 1880 R	14	179
Tumbin, Mary	Mackintosh, Augustus	18 MAR 1882	16	281
Tumelety, Hugh B.	Murphy, Katta	17 JAN 1878 L	11	310
Tunia, William H.	Brown, Mary	13 MAY 1879	13	186
Tunis, Henry Clay	White, Viola	22 DEC 1880 R	15	115
Tunnia, Fannie Flora	Melontree, John Andrew	30 MAR 1885 R	20	135
Tuohy, Aloysius G.	Doyle, Annie	13 JUN 1882 R	16	407
Tuomey, George	Schaefer, Josephine	06 NOV 1883 L	18	237
Tupper, Aggie	Fitzgerald, Joseph R.	28 APR 1880	14	240
Tupper, Charles A.	Meader, Emma R.	24 MAR 1880 R	14	193
Tupper, Charlotte R.	Hawthorne, Hartwell K.	11 MAY 1884	19	014
Tupper, Silas	Williams, Martha	13 JAN 1881	15	147
Turben, Kate	King, John S.	18 OCT 1880 L	15	001
Turbin, Bertie	Smith, William P.	24 SEP 1885	20	436
Turnburke, Mary E.	Davis, Samuel	11 JUL 1885 L	20	320
Turner, Alexander	Magruder, Eliza	21 AUG 1879	13	311
Turner, Alice	Jones, John	18 DEC 1882 L	17	189
Turner, Alice E.	Waters, William H.	30 NOV 1884 R	19	426
Turner, Ann	Parker, James	29 AUG 1877 L	11	070
Turner, Annie	Rodgers, Lafayette	11 OCT 1882 R	17	062
Turner, Annie	Berg, Joseph S.	23 MAR 1883 L	17	357
Turner, Benjamin	Johnson, Sallie	26 APR 1880	14	238
Turner, Byron P.	Smith, Virginia J.	13 AUG 1879 L	13	318
Turner, Catharine A.	Johannes, John Martin	03 JAN 1878 R	11	292
Turner, Chapman	Munroe, Grace Ellen	05 MAY 1884 L	19	005
Turner, Charles H.	Walston, Mary L.	08 AUG 1878	12	160
Turner, Charles H.	Gaskins, Mary A.	30 OCT 1884 R	19	350
Turner, Charles L.	Burns, Lillie	22 JUL 1885 R	20	335
Turner, Charles Smoot	Clarke, Clara Ellen	25 APR 1878 R	12	020
Turner, Edward	Carpenter, Mattie	03 JUL 1884 L	19	120
Turner, Edwin	Alexander, Eliz. S., Mrs.	07 OCT 1885 R	20	467
Turner, Elias	Wanzer, Martha	20 JUL 1878	12	143
Turner, Eliza	Wright, Morris	15 MAY 1879 L	13	193
Turner, Eliza Ann	Smith, John H.	16 APR 1880	14	221
Turner, Elizabeth	Coates, Anthony	12 DEC 1878 R	12	379
Turner, Ella	Perry, Henson	08 MAY 1883	17	432
Turner, Ella	Stewart, Wm. Thomas	05 JUL 1885 L	20	205
Turner, Elmina	Ross, Benjamin	07 FEB 1882	16	227
Turner, Florence Gunnell	Lindsay, Walter Edzell	12 JUN 1882 R	16	403
Turner, Franklin P.	Brooks, Sarah	14 MAR 1883 L	17	343
Turner, George	Buckner, Priscilla	29 JUL 1880 R	14	378
Turner, George	Melton, Hattie	04 JUL 1884	19	123
Turner, George	Monroe, Lou	10 AUG 1885 L	20	362
Turner, Georgia	Newman, Anthony W.	25 SEP 1877 L	11	106
Turner, Georgianna	Miller, Jacob	11 SEP 1882 R	17	023
Turner, Gracie	Mercy, Wallace	13 FEB 1878 R	11	339
Turner, Henrietta	Ashton, Fred	20 JUN 1882 R	16	419
Turner, Inez E.	Salisbury, John W.	06 SEP 1877 L	11	080
Turner, Inez E.	Taylor, James W.	06 SEP 1877	11	081
Turner, Isaac	Brooks, Landonia	26 JUN 1879 L	13	252
Turner, J.A.D.	Wilson, Addie C.	16 APR 1885 R	20	172
Turner, James F.	Biggs, Wilhelmina	17 DEC 1884	19	464
Turner, James L.	Tinney, Mary E.	18 NOV 1879	13	494
Turner, Jane	Johnson, Samuel	15 JUN 1882 R	16	400
Turner, Jennie	Miles, John	04 AUG 1885 L	20	353
Turner, John	Smith, Ellen	04 SEP 1879 L	13	352
Turner, John R.	DeLyons, Rosa	20 AUG 1884 L	19	196
Turner, John R.	Robinson, Agnes E.	07 OCT 1885	20	468

D.C. Marriage Records Index, June 28, 1877 to October 19, 1885

Turner, John T.	Jenkins, Margaret	16 DEC 1880 R	15	103
Turner, Joseph W.	Boswell, Mary V.	05 JUL 1883	18	038
Turner, Lewis	Seiler, Marg. Joh. Aug.	02 MAR 1882 R	16	264
Turner, Louisa	Ward, William H.	17 FEB 1880	14	156
Turner, Louisa	Briscoe, James	13 JUN 1884 R	19	064
Turner, Louisa Virginia	Hayes, Joseph Capin	02 MAR 1882	16	261
Turner, Lucilia Helen	Clay, James Henry, Jr.	16 AUG 1882 L	16	482
Turner, Lucinda	Wood, Moses	02 DEC 1880 L	15	080
Turner, Lydia	Proctor, Henry	26 AUG 1880 R	14	411
Turner, Maggie	King, John	13 AUG 1884	19	184
Turner, Matilda	Diggs, Charlie	22 NOV 1883 R	18	273
Turner, Nellie M.	Parker, George T.	10 OCT 1885	20	474
Turner, Plummer	Parks, Mary	18 JUN 1885 L	20	279
Turner, Rebecca	Wilson, William	12 JUN 1884 L	19	080
Turner, Sallie V.	Player, Milton W.	28 JUN 1883 R	18	022
Turner, Sally	Carter, Addison	29 MAY 1878 L	12	073
Turner, Samuel T.	Storey, Mary F.	25 APR 1885 L	20	188
Turner, Samuel W.	O'Field, Maggie	07 AUG 1878	12	159
Turner, Sarah E.	Spence, Adolphus N.	17 NOV 1880 R	15	051
Turner, Stephen K.	Butler, Florence D.	16 FEB 1879 R	13	061
Turner, Susan	Janus, William H.	22 FEB 1883 L	17	317
Turner, Thomas	Jones, Laura	05 MAR 1879 L	13	091
Turner, Viola	Carter, L.T.	05 FEB 1878	11	328
Turner, W.R.	Rowzee, Annie M.	11 DEC 1883	18	308
Turner, William	Whiting, Eliza	27 JUN 1878 R	12	115
Turner, William H.	Silance, Florence G.	20 MAY 1885 R	20	232
Turner, William Thomas	Bowie, Matilda	15 SEP 1883 L	18	134
Turner, William W.	Woodgate, Maggie B.	09 JUN 1885	20	263
Turpin, Annie C.	Renick, E.I.	03 JUL 1884	19	117
Turpin, Perry B.	Daniel, Sallie W.	30 AUG 1882 L	16	497
Turpin, William B.	Gill, Elizabeth M.	15 NOV 1883 L	18	259
Turrell, George	Sunderland, Hattie	28 OCT 1878 R	12	295
Turton, Florence A.	Curtis, James M.	09 NOV 1882 L	17	121
Turton, William E.	Pyles, Lula R.	07 DEC 1882 L	17	172
Tutt, Kate	Reeves, Archie	12 MAY 1881 R	15	265
Tuttle, Columbus	Rubbeins, Carrie M.	26 SEP 1885 R	20	443
Tuttle, Josephine	Nolan, Edward	25 DEC 1877 R	11	266
Tuxon, Edward	McAbee, Tempe	02 MAR 1882	16	256
Twaddell, Charles P.	Nichell, Mary	28 JAN 1884	18	396
Twiford, Fannie	Wood, Charles E.E.	04 APR 1879 R	13	128
Twiford, Sarah	Lipphard, Adolph	23 MAR 1885 R	20	128
Twiford, Susie E.	Rehner, Caspar C.	22 MAR 1881 R	15	235
Twine, Andrew	Thomas, Carrie	15 NOV 1882 L	17	128
Twine, Ida E.	Upshaw, Arthur W.	20 SEP 1882	17	030
Twine, James	Smith, Mary	02 SEP 1879	13	346
Twine, John	Gaskins, Elizabeth	10 NOV 1879	13	473
Twine, John	McDaniel, Rosa	15 NOV 1883	18	249
Twitchell, Lousville	Sanderson, Maggie E.	19 JUN 1878	12	105
Twomey, John	Ryan, Mary E.	29 OCT 1879 R	13	447
Twomey, Mary Ellen	Dugan, John F.	24 JUL 1885 L	20	339
Twyman, Albert	Duncan, Lillie	07 FEB 1882 L	16	229
Tyas, Joseph	Stith, Rosie	16 APR 1891	19	027
Tycer, Henry T.	Martin, Jessie Lee	18 OCT 1881 L	16	032
Tyer, George	Bell, Chlora	25 DEC 1877 R	11	263
Tyeryar, Frank	Phelps, Annie	10 JUN 1880 L	14	316
Tyler, Amnimia	Johnson, Joseph	06 MAY 1882	16	345
Tyler, Annie	Brown, Thomas D.	04 DEC 1878 R	12	364
Tyler, Annie	Marshal, William	17 JUN 1880	14	319

Tyler, Catherine	Cleveland, J.D. Green	29 JAN 1878	11	318
Tyler, Clara W.	Boisseaux, C. Gray	16 NOV 1880 R	15	051
Tyler, Cora	Hawkins, Benjamin	08 SEP 1884 L	19	232
Tyler, Emma	Burrows, Campson	14 JUL 1880 R	14	359
Tyler, Estella	Chisley, David	09 APR 1883	17	387
Tyler, Frank	Worden, Winifred	24 SEP 1883	18	149
Tyler, George	Graham, Lizzie	10 APR 1879	13	134
Tyler, George	Taylor, Maggie	31 AUG 1882 L	16	499
Tyler, George	Taylor, Maggie	31 AUG 1882 L	17	001
Tyler, George S.	Calvert, Jennie	17 FEB 1880 L	14	156
Tyler, George W.	Mortimer, Harmonia	23 DEC 1879 R	14	063
Tyler, George W.	Normon, Rosie	14 APR 1884 L	18	506
Tyler, Henry	Young, Alice	14 MAR 1878	11	364
Tyler, Henry	Williams, Mary	03 APR 1879 L	13	126
Tyler, James	Myers, Mary	09 JUN 1879 L	13	224
Tyler, James Madison	Gurley, Laura	02 DEC 1884 L	19	430
Tyler, Jefferson	Walker, Susan	25 OCT 1882 R	16	333
Tyler, John	Moore, Jane	07 OCT 1878 L	12	256
Tyler, John	Finney, Sally	20 APR 1882 R	16	327
Tyler, John	Gordon, Margaret	21 JUN 1883	17	483
Tyler, John	Green, Mary	04 FEB 1885 L	20	052
Tyler, John A.W.W.	Luckett, Harriet	03 MAR 1880 L	14	174
Tyler, John H.	Taplett, Emma F.	30 NOV 1880 L	15	073
Tyler, John J.	Megeath, Marietta F.	28 DEC 1879 R	14	077
Tyler, Lacklan	Powell, Georgie W.	02 NOV 1878 R	12	306
Tyler, Mary	Garner, James E.	14 MAY 1878 L	12	051
Tyler, Mary	Lewis, William A.	11 DEC 1884 L	19	452
Tyler, Mary	Milton, William	13 JUL 1885	20	322
Tyler, Mary E.	Hall, Henry	27 JUN 1885 L	20	297
Tyler, Matilda	Winfield, Hennessey	10 MAY 1880 L	14	261
Tyler, Millie	Starde, Henry	21 OCT 1879 R	13	435
Tyler, Noble S.	Oladman, Mary Jane	25 FEB 1879 R	13	077
Tyler, Pathenia [Dotson]	Moore, Marcus	15 APR 1883 R	17	394
Tyler, Patsie	Huntington, Craven	22 FEB 1882 R	16	256
Tyler, Rebecca	Devers, Benjamin F.C.	28 MAR 1883 L	17	364
Tyler, Reuben	Lemly, Rachel	20 APR 1885	20	174
Tyler, Robert	Johnson, Mary	08 JUN 1881 R	15	348
Tyler, Robert	Smith, Cornelia	12 SEP 1881	15	482
Tyler, Rose	Thomas, Charley	14 SEP 1881 L	15	483
Tyler, Susie	Smallwood, Wm. Henry	05 OCT 1881 R	16	009
Tyler, Walter Bowie	Stansbury, Kate Mason Moffet	05 SEP 1878 R	12	193
Tyler, William	Mortimore, Emma	17 JUL 1883 R	18	051
Tyler, William Edward	Hill, Mamie F.	25 AUG 1883	18	098
Tylor, Anna M.	Jones, Albert L.	26 OCT 1882	17	087
Tylor, John H.	Jackson, Harriet	11 MAY 1885 R	20	213
Tynan, John	Joyce, Mary J.	13 NOV 1879	13	485
Tyre, Rosa, Mrs.	Bray, George	28 APR 1881 R	15	278
Tyree, Andrew W.	Tiller, Hattie L.	04 JUL 1881	15	386
Tyree, Henry	Cox, Elizabeth	21 JUN 1884 R	19	095
Tyree, William W.	Irving, Kate G.	28 OCT 1880 R	15	019
Tyson, Emma J.	Page, Fletcher S.	02 JAN 1884	18	362
Tyson, Mary Jane	Woods, James F.	12 JUL 1883	18	044

U

Ubhoff, Clara C.	Ely, Louis H.	15 JUN 1882 L	16	414
Ubhoff, Lillie	Royce, C.L.	27 AUG 1881 L	15	463
Uhfelder, Benjamin	Everett, Mary	20 JUL 1881 R	15	411
Ullman, Morris	Rich, Bertha	14 SEP 1881 L	15	484
Ulster, Mary [Halstead]	Scott, Joseph H.	30 MAR 1883 R	17	367
Umhan, M. Emilie	Werner, George L.	11 SEP 1883 R	18	121
Umhau, Christian F.	Schaffert, Christine	14 OCT 1884	19	304
Umhau, George M.	Kroeling, Mary	04 OCT 1880 L	14	472
Umhau, Margaret	Beck, August H.	12 DEC 1882	17	179
Umpleby, Mamie A.	Lescalleet, Samuel M.	11 SEP 1883	16	203
Umplely, Mamie A.	Lescalleit, Samuel M.	11 SEP 1883 R	28	6865
Underwood, Annie C.	Knott, Benjamin F.	24 FEB 1879 L	13	073
Underwood, Annie E.	Lynn, Joseph A.	04 JUN 1884 R	19	057
Underwood, Dave	Johnson, Annie	28 MAY 1884 L	19	042
Underwood, George R.	Scott, Mary F.	29 NOV 1883	18	281
Underwood, John C.	Godwin, Jean	22 OCT 1883 L	18	206
Underwood, Lettie Bailey	Page, Will Freneau	07 JUL 1879 R	13	271
Underwood, Sarah	Roberts, Edward	25 OCT 1879 R	13	442
Undith, Joanna Elizabeth	Hynson, William Thomas	03 JAN 1884	18	363
Unger, William O.	Schulz, Margareta	15 JUL 1884 L	19	139
Unkel, Alfred C.	Saunders, Willie Iren	24 MAY 1881 R	15	323
Upperman, Charles H.	Stallings, Blanche E.	05 MAR 1879 L	13	089
Upperman, Horace Winston	Kinsley, Lillian	23 DEC 1884 L	19	483
Upperman, Kate	Ashby, Irving G.	11 DEC 1879 R	14	041
Upperman, William B.	Boyd, Minnie A.	28 JUL 1879	13	295
Upshaw, Arthur W.	Twine, Ida E.	20 SEP 1882	17	030
Upsher, Albert	Buckner, Georgianna	13 MAY 1880 R	14	243
Upshur, James A.	Wright, Julia L.	14 JUN 1883 L	17	496
Upshur, Peter	Dorcas, Lucinda	05 JUL 1877 R	11	010
Upton, Annie Amelia	Harrison, Charles M.	21 DEC 1880	15	110
Upton, Cassius M.	Blodget, Carrie A.	14 MAY 1884 R	19	018
Upton, William H.	Bradley, Georgia L.	23 JUN 1881	15	376
Urich, Mary J.	Faber, Louis	09 JUL 1879 R	13	275
Urie, Mary C.	Coburn, Benjamin H.	24 OCT 1882 R	17	092
Utermehle, Augusta L.	Weisenborn, Albert N.C.	18 MAY 1882 R	16	367
Utt, Mary A.	Crooker, William L.	02 MAY 1878 R	12	033

V

Vaeth, Philip	Rothbeger, Annie	26 JUL 1881	15	416
Vail, Benjamin, Jr.	Matthews, Hattie	16 SEP 1885 R	20	418
Vail, Stephen	Stevens, Alice C.	25 JAN 1882	16	206
Vailor, Daniel E.	Johnson, Maggie	01 FEB 1883	17	284
Valentine, Annie A.	Edwards, George B.	21 NOV 1883	18	267
Valentine, Ida V.	Cane, John	03 JUL 1879 R	13	257
Valentine, John W.	DesVerney, Clara E.	10 JUL 1884	19	133
Valentine, Lewis Edmund	Wright, Catharine Mary	16 JAN 1879 R	13	023
Valiant, Theodore G.	Bell, Katie V.	30 APR 1878	12	030
Valk, Emory G.	Joy, Annie M.	15 NOV 1880 R	15	048
Valk, William E.	Reeve, Manette Lansing	07 MAY 1885 R	20	207
Vallen, Sarah	Harris, George W.	21 AUG 1884	19	199
Van Alstyne, Thos. Butler	Richards, Anna S.	07 MAY 1879 R	13	178
Van Arsdale, Joseph S.	Green, Anna P.	15 JAN 1879 R	13	017
Van Bramer, James	Odare, Belle	17 MAR 1885	20	109
Van Doren, Evelyn M.	Maxson, Frank O.	24 DEC 1877	11	269
Van Dyck, Rose	Brown, Charles L.	05 MAR 1884 R	18	459
Van Gruder, Frank	Pyles, Frances R.	29 JAN 1883	17	277
Van Gueder, Clara	Hutchinson, Geo. Wm.	10 SEP 1877 R	11	083
Van Hook, J. Clifford	Evans, Carrie Duror	10 JUL 1883	18	040
Van Hook, Mine	Smith, Middleton	03 APR 1884	18	359
Van Horn, Mary E.	Cook, Philip H.	23 JUL 1877 L	11	030
Van Horn, Mary E.	Been, Henry	10 JAN 1878 R	11	301
Van Horn, Mattie R.	Dwyer, Edwin	20 MAR 1882 R	16	282
Van Horn, Retta D.	Ellis, Henry P.	20 APR 1881 L	15	263
Van Horn, William G.	Boss, Sarah Virginia	05 MAR 1880 L	14	178
Van Kamp, A.P.	Robinson, Kate	11 NOV 1879 R	13	476
Van Metre, Mary Susan	Walters, George P.	19 FEB 1885 R	20	070
Van Ness, Herbert M.	Sexton, Mary	02 AUG 1880 R	14	383
Van Ness, Lizzie E.	Duvall, Benjamin F., Jr.	27 AUG 1884	19	210
Van Orden, John W.	Kernell, Harriet	26 FEB 1879	13	074
Van Pelt, Lydia Ann	Allen, F. Welton	03 MAY 1881	15	289
Van Pelt, Robert A.	Armentrout, Annie L.	07 FEB 1884	18	416
Van Praag, Solomon	Marion, Hazel	06 JUN 1885 R	20	258
Van Riswick, Lillie	Streamer, Lewis P.	05 NOV 1880	15	033
Van Riswick, Martina	Carr, William K.	04 JUN 1885	20	256
Van Sciver, Mary A. Courell	Friedrich, Ludolph H.	09 DEC 1880 R	15	090
Van Slyck, Mattie M.	Barnes, Raymond F.	07 DEC 1881 R	16	116
Van Slyke, Rachel	Chappell, Oliver F.	04 SEP 1884	19	227
Van Syckel, Geo. W.E.	Rupp, Louise W.	21 JUL 1880 L	14	371
Van Syckel, Josephine A.	Reiss, Benjamin W.	28 DEC 1882 R	17	218
Van Syckle, Mary Carman	McAuley, Richard Charles	18 DEC 1879 R	14	053
Van Vleck, Almeria S.	Williamson, L. Cabell	03 MAR 1880	14	172
Van Vleck, Elizabeth C.	Johnston, John Pierce	29 FEB 1880 R	14	169
Van Vleck, William	Shinn, Mattie	19 FEB 1885 R	20	076
Van Vleek, Eugene A.	Noyes, Florence M.	29 APR 1885 R	20	197
Van Winkle, Annie E.	Griffing, Edward B.	23 SEP 1884 L	19	264
Vanalstine, W.W.	Fulton, Mary	09 OCT 1881	16	013
Vance, Amanda	Foster, William N.	07 SEP 1881 R	15	472
Vanderbergh, Benjamin	Brumagin, Ella M.	25 FEB 1884 R	18	216
Vanderpool, Annie	Daley, Uriah	20 SEP 1883 L	18	145
Vandervort, William E.	Sands, Lulu G.	21 MAY 1883 L	17	454
VandeWater, Nellie G. Sherman	Byrnes, John Joseph	10 FEB 1880 R	14	144
Vandrow, Margaret	Wolf, William	06 DEC 1877 R	11	217
Vane, Sarah	Neal, Robert	05 MAY 1881 R	15	292
Vaner, Jeremiah	Wade, Mary L.	02 OCT 1877	11	118
Vangruder, Emma	Tudge, Charles	14 APR 1883	17	394

Name	Spouse	Date	Vol	Page
Vanhook, J. Clifford	Evans, Carrie D.	03 AUG 1882 L	16	468
Vanlentine, Maggie S.	Hawkins, Lewis C.	02 MAR 1881 L	15	210
Vann, Jennie	Patterson, James	26 APR 1879 L	13	161
Vannattar, Mollie	Rotto, Stephen	17 NOV 1883 L	18	261
Vanniaer, John Ernest	Parker, Virginia	02 MAR 1881 R	15	210
Varnell, Anna	Kengla, E. Lorenzo	17 MAR 1881	15	506
Varnell, Katie	Schlosser, Peter	30 JUL 1881 L	15	426
Varnell, Roizer J.	Lyddane, Maggie C.	18 OCT 1881	16	029
Varnell, Thomas O.	Freudenthal, Leonora Louise	09 NOV 1880	15	038
Vass, Hamilton	Wright, Mary	10 DEC 1884 R	19	448
Vass, Joseph	Willis, Frances	04 SEP 1877 L	11	076
Vass, Spencer	Spencer, Rachel	03 JAN 1884 L	18	365
Vaughan, Chaney	Brown, Edward P.	10 JAN 1878	11	299
Vaughan, Emma L.	Meyer, Joseph	09 SEP 1884	19	235
Vaughan, Maria	Cole, William Thomas	22 AUG 1885 R	20	383
Vaughan, Mary E.	Hampson, Charles	01 JUN 1885 R	20	250
Vaughan, Samuel J.	Davis, Martha J.	25 OCT 1882	17	094
Vaughan, Susan E.	Avery, John B.	02 APR 1884 L	18	492
Vaughan, William W., Jr.	Prescott, Mary Frances	25 DEC 1882	17	205
Vaughan, Willis H.	Willis, Jennie F.	07 FEB 1884 R	18	415
Vaughn, Henrietta	Toler, William	10 SEP 1879 R	13	363
Vebusch, John Henry	Miller, Mary Margaret Short	03 SEP 1878 R	12	193
Vedder, H. Adda	Willard, George F.B.	26 DEC 1883 R	18	343
Vedder, Mary	Leonhard, Harry	08 JUL 1884	19	125
Veener, Sophie	Waters, Henry	21 APR 1884 L	18	523
Veerhoff, W.H.	Asmussen, Louise	06 MAY 1878	12	033
Veige, Rosa	Bryan, W.S.	30 APR 1884	18	546
Veihmeyer, Emma Elizabeth	Pierce, Ignatius H.	25 FEB 1878 L	11	356
Veihmeyer, J. Oliver	Levy, Nellie C.	27 SEP 1883 L	18	159
Veirs, John H.	Gingell, Laura V.	16 OCT 1883 L	18	196
Veirs, S.J.	Skillman, Sadie B.	11 DEC 1880 L	15	091
Veitch, Robert L.	Walker, Margaret E.	29 APR 1885	20	195
Veitch, William Henry	Robertson, Mary Lizzie	14 MAR 1880 R	14	184
Vena, Sarah Alice	Thomas, Frank	09 MAY 1878	12	047
Venable, Kate	Gray, John H.	25 APR 1878	12	023
Venable, Sadie C.	Leonard, Alfred L.	21 MAY 1883 R	17	453
Veney, Emiline	Carter, John T.	10 MAY 1884 L	19	013
Venle, Samuel	Jordan, Mary Susan	11 JUN 1885 R	20	269
Venner, Robert	Robinson, Mary E.	16 NOV 1882 R	17	134
Verdi, Tullio Suzzara	Sunderland, Natalie Louise	14 OCT 1882 L	17	072
Vermillion, Charles F.	Hess, Mary Katie	03 APR 1884 R	18	489
Vermillion, E., Mrs.	Page, Charles F.	10 NOV 1883 L	18	245
Vermillion, Elijah	White, Mary Ellen	18 DEC 1879 R	14	058
Vermillion, James Fish	Crown, Mary Eugene	04 OCT 1883 R	18	171
Vermillion, James Franklin	Pollock, Mary Agnes	17 MAY 1883 R	17	447
Vermillion, Julia M.	Miller, Wm. H.	05 FEB 1885 L	20	053
Vermillion, Lizzie L.	Kaldenbach, William E.	06 JAN 1881	15	142
Verner, Caterina	Sciardi, Joseph	07 FEB 1882 L	16	228
Verneu, Elizabeth	Atzell, John Fred	03 FEB 1881 R	15	177
Vernon, Charles E.	Prout, Emma C.	29 OCT 1878	12	297
Verr, Kate	Disney, John Thomas	31 AUG 1879 R	13	344
Verry, Elizabeth	Molan, John F.	22 JAN 1885 L	20	034
Vertongen, Maria J.	Cox, William B.	31 OCT 1881 R	16	052
Vessels, Nancy	Allen, Barney	21 JUN 1884 L	19	096
Vessey, Mary I.	Lauder, John W.	16 NOV 1882 R	17	133
Vessey, Sallie Elizabeth	Golden, William Thomas	09 NOV 1882 R	17	117
Vessey, Sarah	Wohlforth, Edward S.	14 JUN 1883 L	17	492
Vesta, Kate	Klear, Kaspar	13 JUN 1881 R	15	357

Viboud, Francois	Laplace, Leonide	11 NOV 1880 R	15	042
Viedt, Amelia D.	Hornbach, William T.	28 OCT 1883	18	213
Viedt, Julius, Jr.	Zeh, Emma	28 MAR 1878 L	11	397
Viehmann, Catharine R.	Bontz, Fairfax	28 JUN 1883 L	18	025
Viehmeyer, John F.	Ernest, Mary Emma	15 MAY 1883 R	17	439
Viele, Katie	White, Jackson	13 OCT 1884 L	19	302
Vier, James	Brooks, Sophia	04 DEC 1879 R	14	028
Vierbuchen, John P.	Feldross, Annie M.	26 NOV 1884 R	19	416
Vigal, Richard	James, Maggie	29 JAN 1881 L	15	170
Vigle, Frank	Anderson, Julia	12 NOV 1878 R	12	299
Vigle, Henrietta	Hebren, Peter	15 SEP 1884	19	249
Vigle, Henry	Clark, Mary E.	18 SEP 1878	12	197
Vigle, William H.	Coalman, Annie E.	17 OCT 1878	12	266
Villemez, Louis	Schuster, Emelie	30 MAR 1880 R	14	201
Vincel, William D.	Hatton, Alice M.M.	24 SEP 1877 R	11	105
Vincent, Charles	Taylor, Mary	04 SEP 1884 L	19	226
Vincent, Martha	Simms, Edward	21 FEB 1878	11	345
Vincent, William	Parker, Fanny	03 MAY 1881	15	286
Vine, Alice	Hunter, Robert	06 JUN 1885	20	257
Vinson, Sarah E.	Oxley, Edgar F.	01 SEP 1884	19	219
Vinton, William	Bradley, Alice	25 OCT 1884 L	19	338
Violett, Alfred Lee	Everhart, Katie	19 AUG 1885	20	379
Violett, Edward Allen	Kennedy, Sarah	05 JUN 1883	17	478
Virts, Emma M.	Williams, Samuel L.	08 MAR 1882 R	16	270
Virts, Orra B.	George, John E.	13 DEC 1877	11	233
Vliet, Edgar	Halter, Christine Nellie	15 JUL 1880 R	14	360
Voegele, Alois	Weidmayer, Katharina	05 JAN 1882 R	16	177
Voegler, Elenora	Schick, Jacob	21 JUL 1879 R	13	287
Voehl, Louisa	Plitt, August	14 FEB 1882	16	239
Vogel, George	Brown, Georgianna	31 MAY 1880 R	14	297
Vogel, Maggie M.	Huth, Louis C.	18 MAR 1884 R	18	474
Vogel, Mary E.	Schuler, Joseph A.	29 APR 1884	18	541
Vogelgesang, Daniel V.	Stahle, Mary	16 MAR 1879 R	13	102
Vogelson, Ida Mary	Miller, William Edward	12 APR 1882 R	16	312
Voigt, Edward, Jr.	Haas, Lotta	26 MAR 1883 L	17	361
Voigt, George	Ssstiertz, Anna Maria Wilh.	31 JUL 1879 L	13	300
Voigt, Marie Johanna	Warder, Benton Lebanon	24 MAY 1880 R	14	282
Voigt, Mary M.A.	Pfanz, George A.	14 AUG 1884 L	19	185
Voigt, William O.	Muldoon, Mamie E.	24 SEP 1884 L	19	267
Volkman, E.H.	Rosenbusch, Lewis C.	28 AUG 1883	18	101
Voltz, Eliza	Cowen, Henry	07 MAR 1881 R	15	216
Volz, Anthony	Matchett, Elizabeth	10 FEB 1881 R	15	186
Von Apel, Philip	Stoeper, Lissi	28 AUG 1878	12	164
Von Nevta, George Oehlmann	Bruce, Minnie Maud	22 JAN 1880 R	14	117
Vosburgh, Annie E.	Canfield, Charles H.	14 OCT 1879	13	422
Voss, Alice May	Ladson, Thomas Alfred	10 MAY 1882 R	16	356
Voss, Charles H.	Ryder, Frances E.	18 AUG 1881 L	15	451
Voss, Delia M.	McAuley, George Robert	21 JAN 1884 R	18	387
Vosser, John	Burke, Katie E.	13 NOV 1882 L	17	123
Vouck, Jane A.	Messer, Andrew	30 APR 1883	17	422
Vowles, Annie A.	Gantt, Frederick R.	21 FEB 1881 L	15	197
Vowles, Beckie F.	Worden, Charles H.	28 APR 1881 R	15	283
Voy, Lizzie	Orton, Willie E.	06 DEC 1882 L	17	170
Vucinovich, Joseph	Fitzpatrick, Katie	08 DEC 1883	18	306

W

Wachter, Jacob W.	Wise, Janie	30 MAR 1879 R	13	117
Waddell, A.P.	Fleischmann, H.H.	26 NOV 1881 R	16	101
Waddey, Benjamin F.	Curtis, Ida M.	25 MAY 1878	12	066
Waddey, Hodgson B.	Dwyer, Laura F.	29 JUN 1881 R	15	382
Waddey, Sarah	Dorsey, Solomon	05 APR 1883 R	17	382
Waddy, Julia	Conaway, Alexander	17 NOV 1884	19	385
Wade, Alice L.	Adams, Richard A.	08 APR 1885	20	153
Wade, Annie Eliz.	Miller, Thomas F.	29 JUL 1885 R	20	344
Wade, Beatrice E.	Kaisling, C. Oscar	03 SEP 1885	20	396
Wade, Emma C.	Blanchard, William F.	11 AUG 1880 R	14	395
Wade, Frank	Brown, Carrie	03 DEC 1883 L	18	292
Wade, George A.	Button, Mary F. [Harris]	16 MAY 1883 R	17	446
Wade, Harrison	Brown, Sarah	26 MAY 1881 L	15	328
Wade, John B.	Johnson, Lucy	03 FEB 1885 L	20	050
Wade, Katie R.	Lewis, John T.	18 SEP 1882 R	17	026
Wade, Marcellus	Queen, Florence	07 AUG 1880 L	14	391
Wade, Mary L.	Vaner, Jeremiah	02 OCT 1877	11	118
Wade, Milly Ann	Scroggins, Oscar	11 JAN 1881 R	15	121
Wade, Mittie	Jasper, Morris	12 SEP 1878	12	215
Wade, Nannie L.	Evans, William M.	08 JAN 1883 R	17	242
Wade, Robert Hamilton	Sewell, Katie Alice	14 OCT 1885	20	478
Wade, Thomas Leonard	Rodgers, Mary Agnes	04 NOV 1882 L	17	111
Wade, William H.	Clopper, Ella C.	25 JUL 1879 R	13	293
Wadkins, Bell M.	Ellsworth, Henry L.	20 FEB 1883 R	17	313
Wadsworth, Edward	Clark, Alice	29 OCT 1878	12	294
Wagener, Kate	Calvert, Cecil	01 JUN 1881 R	15	334
Waggener, Norris M.	Blondelle, Eugenia	20 FEB 1878 L	11	350
Waggner, Eliza	Shaffer, John	01 JUN 1878 L	12	079
Wagner, Anna	Klein, Valentine	22 AUG 1878	12	176
Wagner, Annie	Schutzbach, John	23 NOV 1879 R	14	001
Wagner, Elizabeth C.	Beall, John W.	16 MAR 1882	16	280
Wagner, Emma	Myers, Fred	23 NOV 1883	18	273
Wagner, Emma B.	Mabee, Charles K.	28 MAR 1882 R	16	289
Wagner, Georgia P.	Suter, Harry C.	09 JUN 1882 R	16	402
Wagner, Henry G.	Memmert, Louisa S.	02 OCT 1883	18	166
Wagner, John	Sheaer, Elizabeth	16 FEB 1882 R	16	244
Wagner, John West	Browne, Sarah Lizzie	29 MAY 1878 R	12	074
Wagner, Josephine	Knabe, Karl Albert Theo.	12 APR 1885 R	20	151
Wagner, Julius	Rammling, Anna	03 MAY 1885 R	20	184
Wagner, Maggie M.	Bernalio, Frank J.	30 JUN 1884	19	111
Wagner, Regina	Ready, George L.	27 SEP 1877 L	11	113
Wagner, William H.	Manning, Bertha A.	14 MAR 1882 R	16	276
Wagoner, Samuel E.	Plant, Laura V.	28 JUN 1879 L	13	256
Wahansen, Anna Maria	Friederick, Friedrick Franz	15 JUL 1883	18	046
Wahausen, Charles	Sauer, Margaretha	21 JAN 1879	13	028
Wainwright, Dallas B.	Kendig, Rosa G.	25 MAY 1880 R	14	283
Wainwright, Maria C.B.	Schroeder, Seaton	16 JAN 1879 R	13	019
Wait, Hulbert H.	Storms, Mary	22 APR 1880 L	14	235
Waite, George W.	Ringgold, Marie C.	26 AUG 1877	11	065
Waite, John P.	Bohnhardt, Augusta A.	03 SEP 1878	12	195
Waites, Bessie	Frisby, Richard A.	31 MAY 1885 R	20	248
Wake, Charles N.	Marr, Jennie W.	30 OCT 1878 R	12	298
Wakeman, Stephen Herrick	James, Alice Louisa	07 APR 1885 R	20	148
Walace, Henry	Coleman, Hanna	24 OCT 1878	12	289
Walbridge, Louisa J.	Bryant, Napoleon B.	05 JUL 1877	11	009
Walbridge, Martha Maria	Dewar, Charles Alex.	15 MAR 1881 R	15	227
Walch, Clara H.	Fenton, Charles W.	21 DEC 1881 R	16	141

Walch, Katie	Coughlin, Daniel	16 FEB 1885 L	20	068
Walcott, Edith V.	Yates, William A.	26 APR 1883 R	17	412
Walde, Leona	Garges, Abraham	31 OCT 1881	16	053
Waldecker, William	Eichhorn, Eleanor M.	07 AUG 1883 L	18	077
Waldon, Lucy A.	Thornton, John T.	30 JUN 1879 L	13	258
Waldron, Edward	Baumbach, Mollie (Webber)	31 DEC 1881 R	16	173
Wales, Lucinda	Strother, James William	10 APR 1878 R	11	413
Walker, Alice	Elliott, John W.	17 MAY 1883 L	17	447
Walker, Alice A.	Townshend, Grafton C.D.	06 JAN 1880 R	14	089
Walker, Alice M.	Spence, William W.	20 OCT 1880 R	15	005
Walker, Angelina	Clark, Robert	06 JAN 1879 L	13	006
Walker, Anna C.	Ingle, Millard F.	15 NOV 1879 R	13	487
Walker, Anney	Ashton, Nathan	23 MAR 1882 R	16	253
Walker, Annie	Bowens, Randall	05 DEC 1878 L	12	370
Walker, Annie	Leimbach, Adam	26 DEC 1878 R	12	402
Walker, Annie	Bell, David H.	26 OCT 1882	17	098
Walker, Benjamin F.	Money, Laura J.	17 FEB 1881 R	15	193
Walker, Benjamin F.	Follin, Annie M.	26 APR 1883 R	17	415
Walker, Bettie	Jackson, James	04 JAN 1883 R	17	237
Walker, Bettie M.	Howes, Nicholas M.	24 NOV 1881 R	16	098
Walker, Carlile S.	Habermamn, Clara	10 AUG 1881 R	15	439
Walker, Caroline	Payne, Thomas	07 JAN 1879 R	13	009
Walker, Carrie	Mitchell, Zachariah	07 JUN 1879 L	13	222
Walker, Champ Turner	Laws, Grace	06 AUG 1877 R	11	042
Walker, Cora M.	Hayes, Frank L.	26 JUN 1884	19	101
Walker, Dabney	Dean, Rosa	27 JAN 1881 L	15	167
Walker, Delia	Jones, Theophilus	21 DEC 1881 R	16	142
Walker, Donus A.	Kimling, Amelia	15 JAN 1880 R	14	090
Walker, Edith Augusta	Gridley, Lucius Egbert	05 FEB 1880 R	14	138
Walker, Edward	Johnson, Mary	03 NOV 1881	16	061
Walker, Elizabeth	Randall, Davy A.	23 JUL 1801 L	15	414
Walker, Elizabeth M	Brooks, Henry J.	12 JUL 1877 R	11	015
Walker, Ella E.	Alexander, Joseph N.	20 JAN 1880 R	14	113
Walker, Ella M.	Crumbaugh, Edward	06 SEP 1877	11	079
Walker, Elmonia	Chephas, Bailey W.	13 NOV 1879 L	13	483
Walker, Emily	Carter, Lewis	20 SEP 1883 L	18	142
Walker, Emma J.	Hampton, John	25 JAN 1883	17	275
Walker, Fannie	Hoover, Arthur H.	28 SEP 1882	17	042
Walker, Fannie Gertrude	White, George Newton	15 JAN 1878 R	11	304
Walker, Florence O.	Hobbs, Frank B.	16 APR 1885 R	20	172
Walker, Francis M.	White, Minnie A.	17 JUN 1882	16	416
Walker, Frank	Lewis, Kate	26 JUN 1883 L	18	016
Walker, George	Barr, Jennie	07 APR 1881	15	250
Walker, George S.	O'Brien, Lizzie	01 JAN 1878 R	11	285
Walker, George W.	Smith, Lizzie	18 DEC 1883 L	18	323
Walker, Gerice	Presgraves, Frank	19 JAN 1882 L	16	202
Walker, Harry B.	Lewis, Blanche D.	23 SEP 1880 L	14	460
Walker, Henry	Cator, Martha Ann	11 MAR 1878 L	11	377
Walker, Henry	Campbell, Jennie	16 MAY 1882 L	16	361
Walker, Herbert T.	Powell, Irene F.	29 MAY 1879 L	13	209
Walker, Ida L.	Nagel, Charles	27 OCT 1880 R	15	015
Walker, Jacob B.	Randolph, Edmonia	26 OCT 1882 R	17	096
Walker, James H.	Cissel, Mary A.	03 OCT 1878	12	249
Walker, James H.	Stanton, Elizabeth	06 NOV 1879 R	13	466
Walker, James T.	Wells, Flora	01 MAY 1878	12	032
Walker, John	Slaughter, Emma	01 SEP 1878	12	188
Walker, John	Young, Mary	15 JUN 1881	15	353
Walker, John	Johnson, Mary Anne	14 JUN 1881 R	21	5071

D.C. Marriage Records Index, June 28, 1877 to October 19, 1885

Walker, John E.	Oliver, Mollie E.	15 AUG 1882 R	16	479
Walker, John H.	Simpson, Adelaide H.	08 NOV 1880 R	15	036
Walker, John S.	Sebastian, Nettie L.	13 OCT 1882	17	068
Walker, John W.	Morton, Willie	03 JUN 1880 R	14	298
Walker, Joseph E.	Clements, Cecilia V.	14 MAY 1879 R	13	188
Walker, Joseph S.	Faulkener, Mary A.	28 FEB 1885	20	090
Walker, Joseph W.S.	Quantville, Julia M.	23 DEC 1881 L	16	154
Walker, Julia	Lucas, James	14 AUG 1884 L	19	185
Walker, Leana	Wise, Charles W.	14 OCT 1880 L	14	495
Walker, Lettie	Tice, William	25 JAN 1883 L	17	275
Walker, Louisa	Williams, Henry	16 SEP 1879 L	13	373
Walker, Malvina	Williams, John Edward	22 JUL 1877	11	029
Walker, Margaret E.	Veitch, Robert L.	29 APR 1885	20	195
Walker, Martha	Cooper, Geo. Wash.	04 MAR 1880 R	14	177
Walker, Martha R.	Shiflet, John S.	23 DEC 1879 R	14	068
Walker, Mary	Ducket, Henry	18 DEC 1877 R	11	241
Walker, Mary	Shyrock, J.F.	01 JAN 1880 R	14	086
Walker, Mary	Ware, Albert	17 MAY 1883	17	450
Walker, Mary Ann Paynter	Parrott, Ralph	24 DEC 1879 R	14	071
Walker, Mary Emma	Donn, Millard Fillmore	05 OCT 1880 R	14	457
Walker, Mary F.	Petty, Edward W.	28 SEP 1882 R	17	041
Walker, Mary Jane	Adams, John T.	13 DEC 1879 L	14	045
Walker, Milly	Jackson, Dennis	23 NOV 1880 R	15	060
Walker, Molly	Sailes, William	29 AUG 1878 L	12	186
Walker, Nellie M.	Murphy, William	13 JUN 1882 R	16	409
Walker, Polly	Diggs, Samuel	03 JAN 1881 L	15	137
Walker, Robert	Roan, Frances	28 FEB 1878	11	365
Walker, Robert	Jackson, Cornelia	13 JUN 1878	12	099
Walker, Robert	Webster, Mary	01 JUL 1880 R	14	345
Walker, Robert	Dobson, Hattie	24 JUN 1882 L	16	424
Walker, Robert J.	Kendig, Isabelle Lawrence	04 JUN 1879 R	13	217
Walker, Rosa	Gibson, William	05 AUG 1880 R	14	388
Walker, Rose	Smith, Francis Littruite	05 JUN 1882 R	16	390
Walker, Sallie	Ware, William W.	16 OCT 1884 R	19	316
Walker, Samuel H.	Glascoe, Emma J.	07 OCT 1885 R	20	468
Walker, Samuel T.	Oliver, Lucy B.	23 DEC 1880 R	15	117
Walker, Sarah E.	Havener, Mason A.	12 DEC 1878 R	12	378
Walker, Stephen Miller	Franks, Julia Ann	16 DEC 1880 R	15	103
Walker, Susan	Gordon, William	12 FEB 1880 R	14	137
Walker, Susan	Permillion, John	27 FEB 1881 R	15	203
Walker, Susan	Tyler, Jefferson	25 OCT 1882 R	16	333
Walker, Victoria	Shands, Booker F.	02 OCT 1884 L	19	282
Walker, W. Frank	Terne, F. Addie	03 DEC 1884	19	435
Walker, William	Hickey, Ellen	28 MAY 1878 L	12	070
Walker, William	Carter, Bettie	15 SEP 1884 L	19	248
Walker, William	White, Katie	30 SEP 1884 L	19	275
Walker, William Henry	Ewell, Eliza	22 NOV 1880 R	15	053
Wall, Edward J.	Pratt, Nellie	02 JUN 1884 R	19	045
Wall, George W.	Crimmins, Mary E.	23 MAY 1883 L	17	459
Wall, Henry Wooford	Hall, Nora P.	06 JUN 1883	17	473
Wall, John H.	Shoemaker, Mary A.B.	27 MAR 1878	11	392
Wall, Mary E. Berry	Byrns, William F.	24 JUL 1882 R	16	454
Wall, Minnie	Brown, Wm. W.	03 NOV 1879 L	13	460
Wall, Rachel	Brown, Frank	19 DEC 1882 L	17	191
Wall, Susannah V.	Dunn, Winfield S.	05 JUN 1882 R	16	393
Wall, Walter Samuel	Mackey, Margaret Ann	19 FEB 1885 R	20	079
Wallace, Alonzo	Milburn, Jennie	21 DEC 1879	14	059
Wallace, Becky	Hughs, Lewis	23 JUN 1881 R	15	372

Wallace, Belle	Cole, James	26 FEB 1880 L	14	167
Wallace, Catherine	Powell, Charles H.	14 MAY 1885 R	20	156
Wallace, Charles	Harris, Lucinda	28 NOV 1877 L	11	208
Wallace, Courtenay Hamilton	Baker, Jesse M.	26 JAN 1882 R	16	210
Wallace, Daniel	Mathews, Sarah	15 JAN 1885 L	20	021
Wallace, Emma	Carter, Frederick	17 MAR 1885 R	20	120
Wallace, Fannie	Dare, Joseph W.	20 DEC 1882	17	196
Wallace, Frank	Owens, Susan	16 DEC 1880 R	15	101
Wallace, Hannah	Johnson, Lewis	04 NOV 1880 L	15	031
Wallace, Helen Leigh	Chew, Leonard Covington	17 APR 1879 R	13	146
Wallace, Helen M.	Lewis, George T.	31 MAY 1878 L	12	077
Wallace, James	Jenifer, Carrie	28 DEC 1882 L	17	220
Wallace, Jerry	McCoy, Georgianna	31 MAR 1885 L	20	139
Wallace, John	Watts, Rosa	15 SEP 1880 R	14	420
Wallace, Josephine	Johnson, John F.	11 DEC 1879 L	14	044
Wallace, Lavinia	Proctor, George Thomas	19 FEB 1880 R	14	158
Wallace, Lizzie	Statesman, Daniel	17 SEP 1879 L	13	373
Wallace, Louisa	Napoleon, Louis	16 JUL 1885 R	20	324
Wallace, Lucy	Sayles, Payton	11 OCT 1883 R	18	185
Wallace, Mary	Thompson, Isaac	15 OCT 1884	19	303
Wallace, Mary	Cook, George H.	15 JUL 1885 R	20	323
Wallace, Mary L.	Perry, Clement S.	09 JAN 1883 L	17	244
Wallace, Richard	Langston, Annie	06 APR 1883	17	383
Wallace, Sarah	Freeman, Thomas	17 OCT 1883 L	18	198
Wallace, Sarah G.	Fletcher, J. Harrison	16 OCT 1880 L	14	497
Wallace, Susan Elizabeth	Stoddard, Nathaniel	24 MAR 1881 R	15	238
Wallace, Thomas	Chase, Louisa	24 OCT 1878	12	291
Wallace, Toliver	Steward, Lucinda	18 OCT 1883	18	202
Wallace, Warren	Gillem, Eliza	08 OCT 1881	16	014
Wallace, William J.B.	Reynolds, Ellie V.	10 DEC 1879 R	14	040
Wallace, William S.	Broadis, Millie M	24 DEC 1877 L	11	261
Wallach, Richard L.	Fenwick, Alice G. (Evans)	28 MAY 1883 R	17	464
Wallen, Emma J.	Burch, David O.	31 DEC 1877	11	283
Waller, Eddie F.	Harris, Rickson T.	28 OCT 1880 R	15	021
Waller, Elizabeth	Lee, Cornelius William	25 MAY 1882 L	16	377
Wallich, John W.	Waters, Emma	09 OCT 1883 L	18	180
Walling, Annie L.	Beall, William J.	04 FEB 1884 L	18	408
Walling, Charles E.	Dean, Martha J.	03 JUN 1881 R	15	342
Walling, William L.	McKeever, Mary A.	03 NOV 1883	18	230
Wallingford, Mollie E.	Harris, William E.	04 OCT 1881 L	16	007
Wallis, Hattie C.	Graham, John T.	27 SEP 1877 L	11	112
Wallner, W.M.	Blenner, Rose	14 MAY 1883	17	438
Wallower, Lyda M.	Serrin, Jabez W.	11 FEB 1879 R	13	053
Walls, George N.	Nalley, Florence J.	24 JAN 1883 R	17	272
Walls, Patsey	Hall, Charles	06 MAR 1885 R	20	099
Walls, William A.	Statesman, Margaret	01 MAR 1881	15	209
Walsh, Alice C.	Walsh, George W.	26 SEP 1877 L	11	107
Walsh, Catharine Phelan	Barry, Michael	14 SEP 1880 R	14	444
Walsh, Daniel	Griffin, Catherine	26 MAY 1883 L	17	463
Walsh, Elizabeth	Storey, Robert	11 AUG 1881 R	15	440
Walsh, Elizabeth E.	Herbert, James J.	12 NOV 1879	13	479
Walsh, George M.	Crabbin, Mollie M.	24 JUL 1884	19	155
Walsh, George W.	Walsh, Alice C.	26 SEP 1877 L	11	107
Walsh, Harry H.	Beavers, Sadie W.	22 NOV 1881	16	085
Walsh, John E.	Englebright, Katie	03 OCT 1879 L	13	401
Walsh, Josephine	Anadale, Andrew M.	25 FEB 1884 L	18	441
Walsh, Maggie C.	Whyte, Warren M.	08 SEP 1879 L	13	359
Walsh, Mamie	Prosperi, James H.	24 DEC 1883 L	18	340

Walsh, Martin J.	Bobb, Rosa	05 MAR 1885 R	20	096
Walsh, Mary	McGettigan, James	07 SEP 1878 L	12	203
Walsh, Mary	Barrett, Michael J.	13 NOV 1884 L	19	380
Walsh, Mary A.	Young, Richard H.	25 APR 1882	16	333
Walsh, Mary E.	Halpin, James	08 JUL 1884 L	19	127
Walsh, Mary E.	Connor, Michael J.	04 APR 1885 L	20	145
Walsh, Mary L.	Ginnaty, James A.	07 JUL 1877 L	11	012
Walsh, Thomas	Reidy, Mary E.	02 SEP 1878 R	12	190
Walsh, Walter E.	McConnell, Mary A.	19 NOV 1877 R	11	192
Walsh, William	Brandt, Rosa G.	20 JUN 1883 L	18	006
Walsh, William J.	Gleason, Nellie C.	15 APR 1884 L	18	512
Walston, Mary L.	Turner, Charles H.	08 AUG 1878	12	160
Walstrum, Cora A.	Simpson, Nathaniel W.	28 MAR 1883 R	17	365
Waltemeyer, John S.	Howe, Josephine L.	25 NOV 1878 R	12	345
Walter, Charles	Stein, Mary E.	11 JUN 1878 L	12	094
Walter, Charles H.	Deakins, Alice	30 DEC 1882 R	17	224
Walter, Eugene L.	Tretter, Maggie	26 NOV 1884 R	19	415
Walter, Frederick	Hoffmann, Maria	11 NOV 1883	18	244
Walter, George W.	Tilling, Annie M.	03 SEP 1878 R	12	195
Walter, Henry S.	Rose, Virginia C.	13 OCT 1880 R	14	492
Walter, James T.	Mullin, Kate R.	27 JAN 1880 L	14	123
Walter, Joseph	Queen, Martha	30 JUL 1880 L	14	379
Walter, Joseph C.	Dearing, Sarah M., Mrs.	19 OCT 1884	19	318
Walter, Lena	Schnebel, William	16 MAR 1884 R	18	472
Walter, Lizzie	Miller, Benjamin A.	02 MAY 1881	16	001
Walter, Mary	Knott, James H.	05 JUL 1877 R	11	008
Walter, Regina M.	Bocock, James D.	30 NOV 1881 R	16	104
Walter, Sophia Catherine	Nauck, Arthur A.	28 MAY 1878 R	12	071
Walter, William J.	Donelly, Catharine A.	06 OCT 1884 L	19	288
Walterholter, Anna Mary Augusta	Nau, Andrew Henry	27 MAR 1878 L	11	395
Walters, Ella V.	Sniffin, Edward A.	22 APR 1884	18	525
Walters, George F.M.	Duvall, Katherine Hyde	04 SEP 1884	19	223
Walters, George P.	Van Metre, Mary Susan	19 FEB 1885 R	20	079
Walters, James	Nelson, Caroline, Mrs.	14 AUG 1879 R	13	317
Walters, John	Snell, Margaret Ella	14 AUG 1879 R	13	322
Walters, John	Pettis, Charlotte	14 OCT 1882 L	17	072
Walters, Lizzie	Brosius, George	01 JAN 1885 R	19	514
Walters, Louisa Davis	Barber, David	23 OCT 1879 R	13	439
Walters, Sarah Jane, Mrs.	Reynolds, Edward	17 APR 1882	16	321
Walters, Virginia	Spencer, James D.	18 DEC 1880 L	15	109
Walther, Rosalia	Huddleson, Willie Everett	01 DEC 1881 R	16	108
Walton, Edward	Parater, Rose Anna	27 AUG 1883 R	18	099
Walton, Joe Richardson	Ridgely, Bessie	19 MAR 1878 R	11	384
Walton, Julia C.	Carroll, William C.	22 SEP 1885 L	20	435
Walton, Louisa	Giesmar, Albert	07 DEC 1878 L	12	371
Walton, William Taylor	Wedge, Martha Elizabeth	06 FEB 1879	13	049
Waltz, Lena	Hohlpien, Mortin	08 JUL 1884	19	127
Walz, Matilda B.	Busher, Henry A.	28 OCT 1880	15	020
Wamaling, Charles T.	McDermot, Emma J.	14 SEP 1879 R	13	368
Wane, Lucy C.	Smith, George B.	25 OCT 1884 R	19	338
Wannall, Lizzie M.	Goodrich, Edward P.	07 OCT 1879 R	13	408
Wannall, William Tell	Downey, Mary Elizabeth	23 AUG 1883	18	096
Wannell, Henry Clay	Downey, Annie M.	17 MAR 1884 L	18	472
Wanner, Franz	Hohn, Christine	10 SEP 1877 L	11	084
Wanser, E.	Hunt, J.R.	19 DEC 1881 L	16	139
Wanstall, Frank B.	Barker, Mary E.	13 DEC 1880 R	15	093
Want, Admonia	Wilson, Ignatius	05 JUL 1883	18	036
Wanzer, Martha	Turner, Elias	20 JUL 1878	12	143

Wanzer, Thomas Wm.	Johnson, Letitia	06 MAY 1880 R	14	255
Ward, Amanuel	Price, Mary	11 DEC 1878 L	12	376
Ward, Ann W.	Queen, Samuel	20 OCT 1881 R	16	029
Ward, Annie E.	Morrison, Ross W.	07 APR 1884	18	498
Ward, Bertha	Watson, A.D.	09 JUN 1884	19	068
Ward, Bertha E.	Cook, Samuel F.	26 DEC 1878	12	403
Ward, Bessie Johnson	Doremus, Charles Avery, Dr.	04 AUG 1880 R	14	387
Ward, Bettie	Williams, Elijah M.	18 APR 1878 R	12	011
Ward, Charles E.	Jett, Janie Eliza	28 NOV 1878 R	12	354
Ward, David	Simms, Hester	21 JAN 1885 L	20	032
Ward, Finetta	Nalle, Edward G.	18 OCT 1882 R	17	079
Ward, George	Blackwell, Lavinia	22 JAN 1878 L	11	312
Ward, George Carlin	Marshall, Arianna Elizabeth	19 NOV 1883 R	18	261
Ward, Harriet E.	Bordon, Daniel L.	28 AUG 1883	18	102
Ward, Ida Elmer	Perry, James Summers	22 SEP 1881 R	15	494
Ward, Ignatus H.	Burrows, Sallie L.	03 MAR 1881	15	214
Ward, Jane Elizabeth	Hemsley, Luther	20 SEP 1881 L	15	491
Ward, Laura L.	Forrest, James F.	14 JUL 1879	13	276
Ward, Lizzie	Ray, Emory F.C.	27 MAR 1884	18	483
Ward, Madalina Louisa	Sparrow, Basil	26 JUL 1879 L	13	294
Ward, Maria Frances	Kidwell, Joseph B.	24 OCT 1881 R	16	039
Ward, Mary	Smith, George Edward	13 NOV 1884 L	19	378
Ward, Mary A.	Beverly, Richard H.	18 SEP 1883 L	18	138
Ward, Mary Frances	Carrick, William Everest	30 SEP 1879 R	13	382
Ward, Mattie J.	Gant, Charles B.	28 DEC 1882 L	17	219
Ward, Moses Columbus	Rollins, Maggie Ann	27 FEB 1883 R	17	323
Ward, Randolph G.	Brown, Belle M.	13 NOV 1882 L	17	124
Ward, Rebuel	Lewis, Mary	08 AUG 1882 R	16	474
Ward, Robert	Lee, Mary	04 DEC 1879 L	14	029
Ward, Robert	Smith, Rebecca	16 MAR 1885 L	20	117
Ward, Robert E.	Keys, Mary E.	10 JUL 1883	18	048
Ward, Rosa	Hunt, James Elias	14 AUG 1879 R	13	319
Ward, Samuel	Humphreys, Arcelia	16 JAN 1878	11	308
Ward, Sarah Ann	Hare, Francis G.	10 JAN 1883 R	17	246
Ward, Sophia	Harrison, William	08 MAY 1879	13	180
Ward, Thomas	Short, Agnes	03 JAN 1884 L	18	365
Ward, Thomas G.	Bunce, Mary	05 JUN 1878	12	087
Ward, Virginia A.	Lane, George W.	08 NOV 1880 R	15	036
Ward, Wesley	Thomas, Barbara Ann	16 DEC 1880 R	15	106
Ward, William E.	Banks, Anida Elizabeth	16 MAY 1878 L	12	056
Ward, William G.	Sherwood, Katie	25 JUL 1878 L	12	148
Ward, William H.	Turner, Louisa	17 FEB 1880	14	156
Ward, Wm., Dr.	Webb, Anna J.	01 FEB 1881 R	15	173
Warde, Daly	Strong, Mary	30 MAR 1878	11	398
Warden, Clifford	Warden, Lucy	27 OCT 1879	13	446
Warden, Lucy	Warden, Clifford	27 OCT 1879	13	446
Warden, Rachel V.	Howard, George W.	03 JUN 1879 R	13	216
Warden, Thomas	Waring, Louisa	09 JUL 1880 L	14	354
Warder, Benton Lebanon	Voigt, Marie Johanna	24 MAY 1880 R	14	282
Warder, Charles Edward	Evans, Catherine Wade	21 JAN 1880 R	14	115
Warder, Frank	Lewis, Nellie	14 OCT 1882	17	070
Warder, John W.	Byron, Annie	18 JUL 1883	18	050
Warder, Mary Eleanor	Guinniss, Guinn	10 FEB 1885 R	20	061
Warder, Mary Ellen	Stroud, Harry Richard Skerrett	24 DEC 1877 R	11	258
Wardon, David W.	Donaldson, Tillie E.K.	02 DEC 1884	19	431
Ware, Albert	Walker, Mary	17 MAY 1883	17	450
Ware, Alice	Dozier, Moses	10 SEP 1880 R	14	436
Ware, Annie	Riley, Gabriel	06 MAY 1884	18	471

Ware, Charles Howard	Bruce, Fannie E. Swift	07 AUG 1883	18	077
Ware, Emma	Day, James	03 DEC 1879 R	14	025
Ware, Georgianna A.	Johnson, Joseph H.	22 JUL 1885 L	20	337
Ware, Harriet	Norris, Hiram	31 DEC 1881 R	16	172
Ware, Joseph	Dickson, Mary	26 MAY 1884 R	19	037
Ware, Josephine A.	Cook, Frank W.	28 NOV 1881 R	16	066
Ware, Lloyd	Marlow, Kate	16 DEC 1884 L	19	461
Ware, Lucinda	Brooks, Albert	23 SEP 1880	14	456
Ware, Martha A.	Ellis, William B.	14 AUG 1883	18	087
Ware, Martha E.	Young, Henry	19 NOV 1884 L	19	396
Ware, Mary Jane	Henderson, Adam W.	19 MAY 1884	19	027
Ware, Rachel	Hill, Joseph	08 MAY 1882 R	16	346
Ware, Richard	Dirks, Isabel	02 JAN 1880 L	14	086
Ware, Sarah Ann	Hall, George	11 AUG 1881	15	440
Ware, Stephen	Coleman, Mary	25 APR 1882 L	16	334
Ware, Townley	Wilson, Carry	01 OCT 1879 R	13	396
Ware, Viola	Tubman, James R.	17 JUL 1884	19	143
Ware, William O.	Huston, Hannah D.	12 JUL 1877	11	017
Ware, William W.	Walker, Sallie	16 OCT 1884 R	19	316
Warfield, Catherine D.	Williams, John H.	01 JUL 1882	16	431
Warfield, Columbus	Beale, Alice	17 OCT 1878	12	280
Warfield, Harry L.	Allen, Lizzie	13 JUL 1885 R	20	321
Warfield, Ida	Clayton, Henry	26 JUN 1879 R	13	257
Warfield, Joshua D.	Cooke, Margaret E.	18 JAN 1883	17	255
Warfield, Lorenzo Gastavus	Stevens, Minnie Franklin	25 NOV 1881 L	16	098
Warfield, Maria Louisa	Zust, Jacob	09 NOV 1880	15	036
Warfield, Martha J.	Butler, William J.	29 AUG 1885	20	391
Warfield, Richard	Brown, Carrie	28 FEB 1881 R	15	207
Warfield, W. John	Lyles, Virginia	24 SEP 1878 R	12	231
Warfield, William	Washington, Nancy	08 DEC 1881 R	16	122
Warick, Alfred	Scott, Catherine	02 FEB 1882	16	223
Warick, Mary	Patterson, Adolphus	15 JUL 1879 L	13	281
Waring, Anna T.	Hays, Edward L.	18 NOV 1880 R	15	057
Waring, Charles S.	McDaniel, Sarah C.	20 APR 1878	12	012
Waring, James H.N.	Brown, Carrie A.	04 APR 1883 R	17	379
Waring, Louisa	Warden, Thomas	09 JUL 1880 L	14	354
Warmbold, Helen	Hanson, Charles L.	28 MAR 1883	17	364
Warner, Alford	Craig, Addie	03 OCT 1878 L	12	251
Warner, Clara L.	Stanton, Francis M.	25 SEP 1878 R	12	234
Warner, Harry F.	Joslin, Eva L.	22 AUG 1883	18	096
Warner, Henry W.	Williams, Harriet E.	12 NOV 1881 R	16	071
Warner, Ida Elizabeth	MacDonald, James Frankin	09 MAR 1881 R	15	221
Warner, James J.	Gatton, Ada	02 MAY 1881 L	15	288
Warner, Leslie	Burch, Catharine M.	30 NOV 1880	15	071
Warner, Lizzie S.	Rouse, Charles William	26 MAR 1881 L	15	239
Warner, Mary	Gross, James H.	11 NOV 1877 R	11	179
Warner, Mary A.	Mellen, George H.	23 SEP 1878 L	12	231
Warner, Watty	Conway, Louisa	10 JUL 1885 L	20	319
Warner, William	Williams, Sarah	16 JUL 1877 L	11	022
Warner, William	Campbell, Mary	11 APR 1878 L	12	002
Warren, Abbie B.	Thompson, Clay	17 OCT 1879 R	13	431
Warren, Abbie B.	Thompson, Clay	17 OCT 1879 L	13	434
Warren, Ada	Franklin, Benjamin	24 AUG 1878	12	178
Warren, Albert	Fletcher, Louisa	07 MAR 1885 L	20	099
Warren, Alexander	Marshall, Louisa	11 JAN 1881 L	15	146
Warren, Alice	Hall, Joseph	24 OCT 1883 R	18	209
Warren, Annie E.	Krouse, Kentzing P.	29 SEP 1885 R	20	447
Warren, Benjamin B.	Blanchard, Nellie McCay	17 JUN 1885 R	20	277

Warren, Clara Belle	Petit, J.F.	10 JUN 1884 R	19	075
Warren, Clora	Bell, Charles H.	30 JAN 1879 L	13	039
Warren, Columbus	Hicks, Julia	19 JAN 1882	16	201
Warren, Edward F.	Cord, Ida M.	07 JUL 1880 L	14	351
Warren, Emily	Johnson, Henry	14 MAY 1885	20	221
Warren, F.W.	Gross, Matilda	12 JUL 1877	11	020
Warren, George K.	Braxton, Ida J.	11 JUN 1884	19	076
Warren, Georgie	Douglas, Harry James	12 APR 1882 R	16	309
Warren, Jane	Johnson, Isaac	03 JUL 1884 R	19	119
Warren, Jessie May	Whallon, Eugene W.	15 AUG 1882 R	16	468
Warren, John	Honesty, Ida	02 OCT 1879 R	13	399
Warren, John	Lane, Louise	08 DEC 1884 L	19	441
Warren, John H.	Coffee, Cornelia Ann	04 APR 1882	16	299
Warren, Julius	Scott, Annie	03 OCT 1878 L	12	252
Warren, Julius	Kittle, Susan	14 OCT 1879 L	13	421
Warren, Julius	Diggs, Cora	05 APR 1883	17	380
Warren, Kate	Dyson, William R.	01 AUG 1878	12	153
Warren, Lizzie	Holland, James	21 DEC 1880 R	15	113
Warren, Louisa Malvina	Davies, Charles	30 AUG 1883 R	18	105
Warren, Lula A.	McDowell, Will A.	30 JAN 1882 L	16	215
Warren, Margaret	Brinkerhoff, Henry S.	18 SEP 1878 R	12	224
Warren, Margaret Gray	Holt, Thomas W.	22 APR 1885 R	20	185
Warren, Martha	Jones, John Henry	11 JUN 1883	17	486
Warren, Mary	Holden, Henry	23 OCT 1877 L	11	151
Warren, Mary	Wilson, Jacob H.	15 MAY 1880 R	14	271
Warren, Mary	Hickman, Henry	29 NOV 1883	18	287
Warren, Mary E.	Lee, John Wilson	06 SEP 1884	19	230
Warren, Mary Frances	Perry, Philip	16 AUG 1881 R	15	446
Warren, Milford	Smith, Nannie	09 SEP 1882 L	17	015
Warren, Richard	Johnson, Annie	20 AUG 1884 L	19	198
Warren, Robert	Gorham, Mary Victoria	05 AUG 1885 R	20	353
Warren, Samuel Donnis, Jr.	Bayard, Mabel	25 JAN 1883 R	17	270
Warren, Thomas	Williams, Louisa	07 FEB 1880 L	14	142
Warren, William	Driscoll, Louisa	26 OCT 1882	17	095
Warrick, Annie	Queenan, Edward	30 MAR 1880	14	199
Warrick, John B.	Hardy, Mary E.	21 OCT 1880 R	15	009
Warrick, Thomas Bolton	Jones, Catharine Ann	31 DEC 1878 R	12	409
Warrington, Ella	Hamm, Allen	22 JUN 1882 R	16	423
Warris, Beverly	Dorsey, Mary	03 MAR 1884 R	18	454
Wars, Lewis W.	Fauntleroy, Emma	30 JUL 1883 L	18	068
Warters, A.L.	Scott, Daniel	13 JUN 1878 L	12	098
Warth, Lizzie	Wrede, John A.	10 JUL 1883	18	041
Warwick, Alfred	Adams, Josephine	09 JAN 1878	11	249
Warwick, George L.	Driscole, Maggie Ellen	07 MAY 1883 L	17	431
Washburn, Dwight Hamilton	Allsworth, Ella Lillian	16 DEC 1882 R	17	187
Washburn, Ella	Wooster, Frank	26 DEC 1877	11	269
Washburn, Susie F.	Brooks, Clarke J.	19 SEP 1882 L	17	027
Washington, Adele	Lee, Wm. H.	16 JAN 1883	17	261
Washington, Albert	Johnson, Louisa	30 OCT 1879 R	13	453
Washington, Alexander	Gillem, Josephine	07 FEB 1878 L	11	331
Washington, Almira	Jackson, John Richard	09 AUG 1877	11	047
Washington, Almira	Burns, William H.	04 AUG 1885	20	352
Washington, Annie	Preston, Clarence	07 SEP 1883 L	18	117
Washington, Araminta	Pickett, Willis Minor	07 MAR 1878 R	11	367
Washington, Bob	Robinson, Eliza Jane	01 AUG 1878 L	12	153
Washington, Burrell	Slaughter, Lucy	08 DEC 1884 L	19	440
Washington, Caroline	Holly, Peter	29 MAR 1883 R	17	350
Washington, Caroline	Brooks, William B.	13 AUG 1884	19	183

Washington, Caroline	Mitchell, Joseph	16 APR 1885 L	20	172
Washington, Caroline Martha	Sherran, John	22 NOV 1884 L	19	402
Washington, Carrie	Henderson, Winslow	17 DEC 1884 L	19	466
Washington, Carrie	Goings, George W.	14 MAY 1885 L	20	223
Washington, Carrie E.	Parker, William H.	29 NOV 1878 L	12	355
Washington, Catherine	Whitney, James	14 JUN 1883 L	17	495
Washington, Cecelia	Evans, Champ	04 MAY 1882 R	16	349
Washington, Charles	Shaw, Maria	01 FEB 1879 L	13	041
Washington, Charles	Kemp, Amanda	17 JAN 1884 R	18	381
Washington, Charles	Adams, Louisa	10 JUN 1884 R	19	051
Washington, Charles L.	Williams, Louisa Frances	30 AUG 1877	11	072
Washington, Charlotte	Fontroy, Cornelius	02 MAY 1881 L	15	287
Washington, Cydonia	Anderson, Seymour	03 MAY 1883 L	17	429
Washington, Daniel L., Rev.	Aquilla, Celia Virginia	23 MAY 1883 L	17	460
Washington, Dora	Budd, Alexander	14 OCT 1884 R	19	304
Washington, Elenora	Davis, Henry P.	07 MAR 1881 R	15	217
Washington, Eliza	Alexander, James	08 NOV 1877 R	11	176
Washington, Eliza	White, John Shermon	31 AUG 1882 R	16	498
Washington, Eliza, Mrs.	Jones, John T.	21 APR 1883	17	403
Washington, Elizabeth	Holmes, Henry A.	18 MAR 1880 L	14	189
Washington, Elizabeth	Holmes, Alexander	19 MAY 1883 L	17	451
Washington, Ella	Brisco, Frank	07 NOV 1878	12	314
Washington, Ella	Jones, John	15 APR 1879 L	13	144
Washington, Ella	Williams, Samuel	25 APR 1879 L	13	160
Washington, Ella E.	Briscoe, Abraham L.	01 MAR 1883 R	17	328
Washington, Elmira	French, Edward E.	24 AUG 1881 R	15	457
Washington, Emily	Anderson, Alexander	03 SEP 1881 L	15	470
Washington, Emma	Watts, Henry	03 JAN 1881 R	15	137
Washington, Emma	Lomax, Edward	24 APR 1882 R	16	331
Washington, Emma	Dorsey, William	27 DEC 1884 R	19	494
Washington, George	Washington, Susan	12 APR 1879 L	13	137
Washington, George	Taylor, Chloe Ann	18 SEP 1879 R	13	370
Washington, George	Taylor, Mary [Watkins]	22 DEC 1879 R	14	063
Washington, George	Strother, Catherine M.E.	05 FEB 1880 L	14	138
Washington, George	Allison, Mary	17 AUG 1881 L	15	449
Washington, George	Harris, Lucinda	12 JUL 1883	18	044
Washington, George	Lawson, Julia	08 JUL 1884 L	19	128
Washington, George	Dorsey, Priscilla	21 JUN 1884 L	19	095
Washington, George	Campbell, Elizabeth	15 OCT 1884	19	308
Washington, George W.	Carter, Katie M.	16 SEP 1882 L	17	023
Washington, Harrison	White, Alice	16 MAY 1884 L	19	025
Washington, Henrietta	Day, James Henry	14 NOV 1882 L	17	126
Washington, Henry	Fender, Maria	30 AUG 1882 L	16	497
Washington, Ida	Jones, Clement	12 NOV 1883 L	18	246
Washington, James	Busey, Mary Ann	05 OCT 1882 R	17	055
Washington, James E.	Smith, Annie Virginia	14 JUN 1880 R	14	318
Washington, James H.	Webster, Margaret	15 OCT 1885 L	20	490
Washington, James O.	Williams, Josephine	02 SEP 1879	13	347
Washington, Jane	Simms, Elijah	09 FEB 1880 L	14	143
Washington, Jane Rebecca	Clark, William Henry	03 JUN 1885 L	20	254
Washington, Jennie	Parker, Elijah	15 MAY 1881	15	305
Washington, John	Herrit, Ella	12 FEB 1880 R	14	152
Washington, John	Brown, Lottie	15 APR 1881 R	15	256
Washington, John E.	Brown, Elizabeth	22 AUG 1878	12	177
Washington, Joseph	Marshall, Mary	07 DEC 1883 L	18	305
Washington, Joseph S.	Williams, Martha A.	29 OCT 1883 R	18	182
Washington, Josephine	Armstrong, Alexander	19 NOV 1884	19	391
Washington, Joshua	Moore, Laura	11 JAN 1883 L	17	251

D.C. Marriage Records Index, June 28, 1877 to October 19, 1885

Washington, Julia	Waters, Olmstead	19 SEP 1883	18	136
Washington, Julia A.	Jackson, Humphrey P.	02 DEC 1880 L	15	081
Washington, Julia Cady	Harbaugh, Edgar G.	10 DEC 1877	11	227
Washington, Kate	Richardson, William	10 JUL 1884	19	125
Washington, Kemp Wm.	Dotson, Laura E.	20 NOV 1877 R	11	192
Washington, Laura	Quarles, William	06 DEC 1877 L	11	225
Washington, Laura	Pinn, Strother	10 DEC 1878 L	12	375
Washington, Lavinia	Smith, John James	17 DEC 1883 L	18	320
Washington, Lee	Banks, Martha Ellen	13 NOV 1878 R	12	317
Washington, Lena	Grice, Edward	15 MAR 1883 R	17	342
Washington, Lewis	Allen, Mary	05 APR 1879 L	13	129
Washington, Lewis	Burton, Marian	08 SEP 1884 R	19	231
Washington, Louise	Berk, Nelson	16 FEB 1884 L	18	427
Washington, Lucinda	Digges, Samuel S.	24 DEC 1883 L	18	336
Washington, Maggie, Mrs.	Laws, Spencer	31 JUL 1881 R	15	424
Washington, Marshall	Roye, Ella	17 APR 1884 R	18	519
Washington, Mary	Miller, Shelton	20 NOV 1877 R	11	184
Washington, Mary	Slack, Thomas A.	03 DEC 1877 L	11	216
Washington, Mary	Chapman, Elijah	26 APR 1882 L	16	335
Washington, Mary E.	Carter, John	02 SEP 1878 L	12	192
Washington, Mary E.	Dawson, John Francis	23 MAR 1882	16	287
Washington, Mary E.	Carroll, William C.	16 SEP 1883	18	133
Washington, Mary E.	Gordon, Thomas M.	05 APR 1884	18	494
Washington, Mary F.	Wells, John	30 APR 1879 R	13	168
Washington, Mary F.	Freeman, Wm. Spencer	22 APR 1885 R	20	093
Washington, Mary Frances	Morris, Jim	09 APR 1879 L	13	133
Washington, Mary Susan	Lee, George	01 JUL 1880	14	343
Washington, Matilda	Mullen, John	25 MAY 1878	12	063
Washington, Millie	Jones, William	09 DEC 1879	14	037
Washington, Minnie	Nixon, Frank	18 SEP 1884	19	257
Washington, Nancy	Warfield, William	08 DEC 1881 R	16	122
Washington, Peyton	Bell, Jano E.	18 DEC 1884 L	19	470
Washington, Rebecca	Briggs, Orlando	27 DEC 1882 R	17	211
Washington, Richard	Tibbs, Mary	17 AUG 1882 R	16	483
Washington, Richard R.	Talbot, Gracie	02 APR 1884	18	488
Washington, Rosa	Jenkins, William	14 OCT 1885 L	20	480
Washington, Rosa Lee	Hambleton, Henry	03 NOV 1884	19	356
Washington, Rosetta	Rose, William	13 DEC 1877	11	235
Washington, Sallie Ann	Ross, John	03 SEP 1879 R	13	327
Washington, Sallie R.	Wenner, Jacob S.	21 OCT 1880	15	007
Washington, Sarah	Wrecks, Thomas L.	04 OCT 1877	11	120
Washington, Sidney Ann	Thomas, Dennis	22 NOV 1884 L	19	401
Washington, Silas	Lee, Charity	28 APR 1880 L	14	241
Washington, Sophia	Johnson, Charles	17 NOV 1881 L	16	082
Washington, Susan	Washington, George	12 APR 1879 L	13	137
Washington, Virginia E.	Payne, James	05 DEC 1878 L	12	370
Washington, Wesley	Johnson, Hannah	27 OCT 1884 L	19	339
Washington, Will	Williams, Katie	14 FEB 1884 L	18	426
Washington, William	Hall, Mary	10 DEC 1883 L	18	307
Washington, William H.	Colston, Annie V.	01 MAR 1881	15	209
Washington, Willis	Beckett, Florence E.	07 JAN 1880 R	14	094
Washington, Winnie	Lewis, Addison	11 OCT 1884	19	288
Washney, Michael	Schuh, Mary	15 SEP 1885 R	20	416
Wasmann, Dora	Fogle, George F.	23 OCT 1877	11	148
Wasney, Annie	Symanoskie, Joseph	09 FEB 1880 R	14	143
Wasney, J. Catherine	Gedney, Charles Deforest	05 FEB 1881 R	15	178
Wasney, Mary A.	Burke, Michael J.	02 JAN 1879 R	13	002
Wasselle, Lizzie G.	Arnold, Edmund C.	15 APR 1882 R	16	315

Wasser, Henry R.	Bruehl, Clara L.	13 AUG 1885 R	20	367
Waterholder, Fred. Wm.	Miller, Katie	07 JUL 1881	15	395
Waters, Ada	Bailey, Horace	24 FEB 1883 L	17	320
Waters, Alice	Basey, Richard	03 JUN 1879 R	13	218
Waters, Annah	Gregory, Charles Richmond	30 NOV 1881 R	16	103
Waters, Buena V.	Williams, John L.	13 DEC 1883	18	314
Waters, Carrie	Lapiter, Willis	18 APR 1878 L	12	011
Waters, Charles	Buckner, Lucinda A.	15 JAN 1880	14	100
Waters, Charles M.	Schreyer, Lillie E.	28 APR 1880 R	14	241
Waters, Daniel	Mason, Essie	03 SEP 1878 L	12	196
Waters, Eliza	Burgy, Emile	27 JUN 1882 R	16	426
Waters, Emma	Wallich, John W.	09 OCT 1883 L	18	180
Waters, Emmie W.	Eaton, Frank S.	28 SEP 1878 L	12	240
Waters, Eva S.	Clark, R. Bentley	15 SEP 1885 R	20	419
Waters, Fannie A.	Calver, Henry	17 DEC 1877	11	239
Waters, Flora	Skinner, John M.	12 NOV 1884 L	19	377
Waters, Henry	Carter, Mary E.	05 JUN 1882	16	393
Waters, Henry	Veener, Sophie	21 APR 1884 L	18	523
Waters, Hugh	Sisson, Charlotte D.	27 OCT 1881 R	16	047
Waters, Isabel	Speed, William	23 MAR 1881 R	15	237
Waters, Jeminia	Sesko, Charles	05 JUL 1881 L	15	388
Waters, John F.	Speaks, Julia A.	25 DEC 1878 R	12	398
Waters, John F.	Butler, Virginia V.	20 NOV 1883 R	18	266
Waters, John T.	Gerry, Fanny	12 JUL 1881 R	15	388
Waters, John W.	Hamilton, Clara	27 AUG 1885 L	20	389
Waters, Julia C.	Ripley, G.H.	12 DEC 1883 L	18	311
Waters, Laura M.	Lillie, Charles	16 DEC 1879 R	14	047
Waters, Lenore Tom	Duval, Everett Bennett	25 OCT 1881 R	15	504
Waters, Leon W.	Page, Alice M.	23 JUN 1884	19	097
Waters, Louisa	Perry, Jesse	07 OCT 1880 R	14	472
Waters, Maggie A.	Chesser, John E.	14 NOV 1883 R	18	254
Waters, Malinda	Fox, James Dallas	19 JUN 1879	13	239
Waters, Margaret	Wiggins, John	25 JUN 1885 R	20	294
Waters, Mary	Taylor, William H.	06 DEC 1877 R	11	221
Waters, Mary H.	Sayles, James H.	05 JUN 1884	19	063
Waters, Mary Josephine	Anderson, Charles Joseph	08 JUL 1880 R	14	350
Waters, Magnus V.	Schmitt, Magnus H.	31 DEC 1884	19	507
Waters, Minnie	Banks, John Mitchell	17 NOV 1881 L	16	082
Waters, Mollie E.	Towers, David I.	16 FEB 1881 L	15	192
Waters, Olmstead	Washington, Julia	19 SEP 1883	18	136
Waters, Somerset R.	Spignul, Mary Lillian	17 OCT 1883 R	18	198
Waters, Stella	Latimer, Chas. Marshall N.	06 OCT 1883 R	28	6981
Waters, Stella E.	Latimer, Charles M.N., Dr.	05 NOV 1883 L	18	232
Waters, William	Thomas, Mary Catherine	02 JUL 1878	12	119
Waters, William	Hughes, Martha	06 JUL 1881	15	391
Waters, William H.	Turner, Alice E.	30 NOV 1884 R	19	426
Waters, William Henry	Adams, Emma	17 JUN 1880 L	14	325
Waters, William O.	Rogers, Ida May	13 DEC 1883 L	18	316
Watkins, Agnes E.	Sheckells, Chester	24 DEC 1877	11	260
Watkins, Alverta	McPherson, James	07 APR 1885 R	20	150
Watkins, C.J.	Moody, Ella L.	04 JUL 1881	15	387
Watkins, Charles	Scott, Carrie	29 FEB 1884 L	18	451
Watkins, Geo. Archibald	Johnson, Mary Rose	21 SEP 1881 R	15	494
Watkins, George D.	Edwards, Ella	26 MAY 1881 L	15	327
Watkins, Henry	Parker, Mary Ann	14 OCT 1877	11	129
Watkins, J.C.	Watkins, W.O.	26 AUG 1880 R	14	416
Watkins, James	Bond, Maria, Mrs.	01 AUG 1878 R	12	153
Watkins, John	Beales, Mary	29 APR 1880 R	14	243

Watkins, Kate	Hayes, John	21 APR 1885 L	20	179
Watkins, Lucy	Bushroyd, Wesley	25 AUG 1880	14	414
Watkins, Lucy	Fisher, William	08 OCT 1885 L	20	470
Watkins, Mary	Slater, Jeremiah	29 MAY 1880 R	14	295
Watkins, Minnie E.	West, Robert L.	29 SEP 1881	15	503
Watkins, Virginia	Price, Charles P.	12 JUL 1881	15	400
Watkins, W.O.	Watkins, J.C.	26 AUG 1880 R	14	416
Watkins, William	Lomax, Mary Jane	01 MAY 1883 L	17	425
Watkins, Williams	Bowie, Carrie	10 AUG 1877 L	11	050
Watmough, Ellen Coxe	Griffith, Samuel H.	04 OCT 1883	18	167
Watson, A.D.	Ward, Bertha	09 JUN 1884	19	068
Watson, Addie T.	Kummer, Joseph	31 MAY 1879 L	13	213
Watson, Annie	Dickerson, Peter	13 FEB 1880 R	14	152
Watson, Annie	Nash, Jesse	29 DEC 1881 L	16	172
Watson, Annie Eliza	Gibson, Caleb	20 MAY 1879 R	13	196
Watson, Bettie	Ashton, Cornelius	31 DEC 1881 R	16	171
Watson, Celestine	Story, William	02 JUL 1879 R	13	265
Watson, E. Lavinia	Cator, Albert R.	23 NOV 1880	15	059
Watson, Eliza	Johnson, Samuel	08 OCT 1883 L	18	178
Watson, Emma Letitia	Robertson, Alfred B.	18 MAR 1879 R	13	107
Watson, Emma Lulu	Nesmith, Frank E.	24 FEB 1882 R	16	258
Watson, Emma Virginia	Edwood, Isaac	06 JUL 1882 R	16	439
Watson, Fannie	Farr, Middleton	11 SEP 1879 R	13	366
Watson, Fannie J.	Powell, Charles M.	10 AUG 1885	20	362
Watson, Frank	Smith, Lucy	18 AUG 1881 R	15	452
Watson, George	Harrison, Mary	20 NOV 1882 L	17	138
Watson, Harold	Arnold, Ella	27 NOV 1882 R	17	150
Watson, Ida E.	Harrison, George W.	03 JUN 1879 R	13	218
Watson, James	Bannan, Eliza	09 DEC 1882 L	17	175
Watson, James	Grayson, Alcinda	04 JAN 1883 R	17	237
Watson, James Allen	McGirr, Ella Aloysia	09 MAR 1880 R	14	177
Watson, James H.	Powell, Harriet	14 FEB 1878 R	11	341
Watson, John Mark	Muddiman, Laura Gertrude	05 DEC 1878 R	12	369
Watson, John Thomas	Green, Ella Virginia	26 MAY 1880 R	14	290
Watson, John W.	Grainer, Elizabeth	25 FEB 1885	20	086
Watson, Joseph	Castor, Mary E.	25 APR 1878	12	023
Watson, Julia	Jackson, Benjaamin	08 SEP 1884 L	19	233
Watson, Laura	Clark, Edward	06 DEC 1877 L	11	223
Watson, Laura V.	Laubach, H.J.	30 JAN 1884	18	402
Watson, Lucy Marion	Brodie, Charles Cameron	19 FEB 1883 R	17	312
Watson, Maggie	Mays, William	25 DEC 1877 R	11	266
Watson, Margaret	Allen, Henry	17 APR 1885 L	20	174
Watson, Martha	Nash, John W.	27 JUN 1884 R	19	083
Watson, Mary	Abel, Thomas	10 AUG 1885	20	363
Watson, Mary Jane	Carroll, David Winfield	07 SEP 1881 L	15	474
Watson, Mattie Leonore	Fisher, William Thos.	26 OCT 1881 R	16	045
Watson, Rebecca F.	Booker, Coleman	15 AUG 1878 L	12	170
Watson, Robert	Jones, Annie	27 FEB 1883 L	17	324
Watson, Robert W.	Skinner, Ann M.	01 AUG 1880 R	14	379
Watson, Rosa L.	Callon, William C.M.	28 JUN 1880 L	14	336
Watson, Rosanna	Roy, Ned	01 APR 1878 L	13	122
Watson, Thomas Alexander	Moore, Sarah Francis	12 FEB 1879 L	13	056
Watson, Thomas C.	Miller, Elizabeth	27 AUG 1881 R	15	461
Watson, W.C.	Bladon, Sallie A.	15 OCT 1884	19	309
Watson, Wharton B.	Douglas, Carrie	16 NOV 1881 R	16	080
Watson, William	Kilborn, Winnifred E.P.	17 SEP 1884 R	19	255
Watson, William H.	Greene, Emma J.	05 AUG 1880 R	14	383
Watson, William W.	Hannen, Maggie	09 SEP 1884 L	19	236

Watson, Willianna	Peters, Jesse David Bright	02 FEB 1881 R	15	173
Watt, Bettie A.	Stevens, William K.	25 OCT 1882	17	090
Watt, George	Fowler, Carrie R.	26 APR 1883	17	416
Watt, James Bell	Wilson, Emma D.	27 SEP 1883 R	18	155
Watt, John Henry	Lansdale, Addie L.	08 JUN 1881 R	15	351
Watts, Aaron B.	Stevens, Anna E.	09 JUN 1885	20	259
Watts, Anna	Diggs, Charles	14 MAR 1883 L	17	344
Watts, Annie Elizabeth	Fosque, Solomon Porterfield	15 DEC 1880 R	15	102
Watts, Edward C.	Ross, Fannie Cole	27 OCT 1879 R	13	445
Watts, Eliza	Fairbanks, William	21 AUG 1884 R	19	200
Watts, Georgie Cornelia	Brown, George Henry Johnson	26 FEB 1880 R	14	158
Watts, Henry	Jackson, Sarah	05 FEB 1878	11	327
Watts, Henry	Washington, Emma	03 JAN 1881 R	15	137
Watts, Jane E.	Suit, John E.	17 DEC 1884 R	19	467
Watts, Jerusha A.	Remmington, George A.	27 OCT 1883	18	219
Watts, John	Brown, Ella	25 DEC 1884	19	484
Watts, Mary E.	Brown, Isaac	10 JAN 1882 L	16	188
Watts, Richard	Carey, Jane	04 JUN 1879 L	13	219
Watts, Rosa	Wallace, John	15 SEP 1880 R	14	420
Watts, Samuel R.	Collins, Clara E.	19 NOV 1878	12	336
Watts, Sidney James	Nichols, Cora	27 MAY 1885 R	20	241
Watts, William	Sewell, Susanna	04 APR 1883	17	379
Waugh, Ada V.	Connor, John Fred.	14 MAY 1883 R	17	439
Waugh, Albert Philip	Payne, Sarah Emma	09 FEB 1882 R	16	232
Waugh, Clinton	Hill, Josephine	23 DEC 1880 R	15	119
Waugh, Emma A.	Rider, Charles J.	30 OCT 1879 L	13	455
Waugh, Harry	Duckett, Flora	04 JAN 1883 R	17	225
Waugh, John	Low, Ellen Virginia	18 SEP 1884	19	256
Waugh, Sallie R.	Adams, Amos S.	09 OCT 1879	13	411
Way, Fannie S.	Burton, Robert A.	11 FEB 1879 R	13	054
Wayland, Sarah Madeleine	O'Donnell, John Henry	08 SEP 1877	11	082
Wayman, Lewis	Wright, Elizabeth	24 OCT 1884 L	19	336
Wayne, Rachel Ann	Green, George Wm.	08 JUL 1877 R	11	011
Waynes, Henson	Ashton, Harriet A.E.	25 JUN 1885	20	292
Waynes, W.H.	Wicks, Alice	06 JAN 1881	15	142
Wayson, Charles A.	Riley, Annie E.	04 FEB 1883	17	287
Wayson, Edward	Fordham, Mary A.	15 MAR 1883	17	348
Weadon, Sarah P.	Lambert, Jefferson D.	01 OCT 1885	20	452
Weal, Mary Ann	Angell, Thomas	10 DEC 1884 R	19	445
Weast, Hiram Webster	Summers, Laura Amelia	23 DEC 1879 L	14	067
Weathers, Churchwell	Cleggett, Mary	17 NOV 1877 L	11	190
Weaver, Alice	Sanborn, Daniel	29 SEP 1882 R	17	043
Weaver, Annie	Jones, Belmore	24 DEC 1877	11	256
Weaver, Annie	Sherzer, John	23 MAR 1882	16	288
Weaver, Catharine	Werk, Flaurence	21 JUL 1883 L	18	055
Weaver, Charles H.	Cook, Alice J.	29 AUG 1883 R	18	104
Weaver, Clara Lizzie	Suman, James Luther	14 FEB 1883 R	17	306
Weaver, Egbert L.	Wright, Effie C.	17 JUL 1884	19	143
Weaver, Elizabeth	Whiting, Albert	24 MAY 1878	12	065
Weaver, George O.	Muse, Fannie	25 OCT 1877	11	156
Weaver, Jennie A.	Garner, William E.	10 APR 1878	11	414
Weaver, Jessie S.	Boss, Samuel D.	18 SEP 1883	18	136
Weaver, John B.	Pettitt, Elmira E.	01 JAN 1879 L	13	003
Weaver, John Henry	Deagle, Mary	10 JUN 1885	20	264
Weaver, Joseph A.	Nevill, Mary A.	14 SEP 1885 L	20	413
Weaver, Joseph F.	Yeatman, Emma	16 MAY 1883 R	17	444
Weaver, Joseph H.	Weaver, Mary	15 NOV 1884 R	19	382
Weaver, Lillie	Colvin, Thomas B.	10 JAN 1883	17	249

Weaver, Louisa Hunter	Gover, Robert Carey	19 APR 1880 R	14	227
Weaver, Lucy H.	Beall, Warren H.	18 JUL 1881 R	15	407
Weaver, Marie Ellen	Freeman, J.R.	26 NOV 1879	14	015
Weaver, Mary	Spry, James R.	03 NOV 1884	19	355
Weaver, Mary	Weaver, Joseph H.	15 NOV 1884 R	19	382
Weaver, Mary E.	Hall, Philip Thomas	30 APR 1878 R	12	031
Weaver, Mary L.	Sherwood, Lewis W.	05 MAR 1883 R	17	325
Weaver, Mary M.	King, Robert C.	11 OCT 1882 R	17	007
Weaver, Mary S.	Campbell, James	25 SEP 1884	19	269
Weaver, Richmond	Lomax, Maggie	22 SEP 1881 R	15	493
Weaver, Robert David	Yeabower, Mary A.R.	26 NOV 1879 R	14	011
Weaver, Sallie Elisabeth	Huysman, John Sidney	30 APR 1878 R	12	025
Weaver, Sarah Ann	Garner, Noah	30 JUL 1884	19	163
Weaver, Sarah Louise	Dawson, George C.	04 JAN 1883 R	17	238
Weaver, Susie	Langdon, William	15 JUL 1885	20	329
Weaver, Thomas A.	Buchanan, Mary J.	15 FEB 1881 R	15	191
Webb, Alice B.	Edwards, George A.	09 SEP 1879 R	13	360
Webb, Amanda	Jackson, Valdamar	22 OCT 1879 R	13	438
Webb, Anna J.	Ward, Wm., Dr.	01 FEB 1881 R	15	173
Webb, Asbury M.	Bridge, Anna H.	10 JUL 1883 L	18	041
Webb, Betty	Robinson, Horace	18 MAR 1878 L	11	386
Webb, Catharine A.	Buchanan, Charles H.	05 JUN 1884 L	19	065
Webb, Elijah	Thomas, Edith	03 MAR 1881	15	212
Webb, Ella M.D.	Carter, Henry	22 SEP 1880 R	14	456
Webb, Emma Jane	Hamersly, John Robert	25 AUG 1879	13	334
Webb, Fannie M.	Johnson, John J.	19 JAN 1882	16	198
Webb, Frank B.	Morgan, Katie	29 MAY 1879	13	210
Webb, Gilbert	Mitchell, Jennie	14 MAY 1885 L	20	221
Webb, Harriet	Gibson, Alfred	15 OCT 1883 R	18	194
Webb, Harry Edwin	Allen, Edith	23 MAY 1881 R	15	321
Webb, Henry L.	Smith, Agnes	19 SEP 1878 L	12	228
Webb, James W.	Edmunds, Hattie	12 OCT 1881 L	16	019
Webb, Joseph	Robinson, Priscilla	18 SEP 1883 L	18	137
Webb, Julia	Harlins, Winston	26 AUG 1884 L	19	208
Webb, Larica	Garland, James	24 MAY 1878	12	068
Webb, Leddy	Nelson, Robert	19 SEP 1878	12	227
Webb, Lillie M.	Sniffen, William K.	02 OCT 1883	18	166
Webb, Margaret	Barr, James H.	02 AUG 1881 R	15	428
Webb, Martha	Galleher, William R.	19 NOV 1883	18	262
Webb, William H.	Young, Louisa	22 FEB 1883	17	318
Webel, Charles	Donn, Katie C.	07 JUL 1885 L	20	314
Weber, Caspar A.	Lemke, Cathenka	01 SEP 1881 R	15	465
Weber, Emilie K.	Brinkmann, W. Henry	09 SEP 1885	20	406
Weber, George	Weiss, Anna	22 SEP 1885 L	20	433
Weber, John	Fritz, Katie	08 MAR 1883 R	17	338
Weber, John F.	Horgan, Kate C.	16 JUL 1885 L	20	330
Weber, Kate	Bailey, Richard H.	09 SEP 1885	20	410
Weber, Louise	Kenney, Peter	17 MAR 1879 L	13	104
Weber, Louise [Perrot]	Nebb, John	23 MAR 1885 R	20	115
Webster, Addison	Corbin, Joseph Anna	12 JUN 1879	13	206
Webster, Addison	Campbell, Martha	17 MAR 1881	15	230
Webster, Addison A.	Mackey, Ida B.	18 JUN 1882 R	16	416
Webster, Adele	Brown, Francis Milton	17 FEB 1881 R	15	194
Webster, Alice M.	Yost, Amos Smith	20 JAN 1881 R	15	160
Webster, Alice R.	Thomas, James H.	07 MAR 1883 R	17	336
Webster, Belle F.	Brown, Richard B.	14 NOV 1883	18	255
Webster, Benjamin F.	Flynn, Mary Ann	16 JUN 1877	11	309
Webster, Catherine	King, Henry	26 DEC 1878 L	12	401

Webster, Charles Albert	Woodburn, Elizabeth Estell	30 SEP 1878		12	238
Webster, Charles Fenton	Minor, Emily	14 MAY 1879	L	13	190
Webster, Charles R.	Lynch, Georgie	30 DEC 1881	R	16	105
Webster, Charles S.	McCrestle, Annie	26 SEP 1883		18	149
Webster, Cora B.	Kingsley, H.A.	01 NOV 1883	L	18	228
Webster, Ella M.	Beaver, Randolph W.	24 FEB 1885	R	20	081
Webster, Emily F.	Prince, John A.	30 JUN 1880	L	14	339
Webster, Emily Frances	Barrett, James D.	30 MAR 1882	R	16	290
Webster, Emma F.	Snight, Frederick H.	05 MAR 1878	L	11	370
Webster, Emma Grace	Blincoe, Albert F.	15 JUL 1884		19	140
Webster, Emma I.	Richards, Thomas L.	10 DEC 1879	R	14	039
Webster, Fletcher	Kent, Mary M.	25 DEC 1884	R	19	489
Webster, Frederick T.	Smallwood, Mary E.	27 APR 1885	L	20	191
Webster, James H.	Carroll, Mary E.	07 OCT 1877		11	123
Webster, Joel	Moulton, Lucy	28 AUG 1879	R	13	344
Webster, John Eddy	Holschuh, Josephine C.	22 JUN 1881	R	15	372
Webster, Katie E.	Clarkson, William G.H.	17 DEC 1879	R	14	053
Webster, Katie M.	Kiesecker, Frederick	07 OCT 1880	R	14	481
Webster, Maggie E.	Childs, Charles	28 APR 1884	R	18	537
Webster, Mannie	French, Fitzhugh	11 AUG 1882	L	16	476
Webster, Margaret	Washington, James H.	15 OCT 1885	L	20	490
Webster, Mary	Walker, Robert	01 JUL 1880	R	14	345
Webster, Mary Ellen	Coates, Christopher Columbus	02 JUL 1882	R	16	434
Webster, Rachel	Cross, Washington	06 JAN 1881	R	15	143
Webster, Stephen J.	Sansberry, Elizabeth T.	30 JAN 1879	L	13	040
Webster, William	Nash, Annie	13 SEP 1877		11	087
Webster, William Henry	Carter, Lucinda	18 DEC 1877	L	11	243
Wedge, Martha Elizabeth	Walton, William Taylor	06 FEB 1879		13	049
Wedge, Rosaline	Thomas, Wm. G.	06 JUL 1885		20	312
Wedick, Harman	Thomas, Susie	14 JAN 1884		18	375
Wedmann, Joseph C.	Kohl, Mary E.	18 JAN 1881		15	154
Weed, A.L.	Davis, Fannie L.	26 JUL 1881		15	418
Weed, Charlotte A.	Furnald, Francis P.	07 MAY 1885	R	20	211
Weed, John J.	McLean, Carrie	23 JUL 1884		19	153
Weeden, A.M.	Beall, A.V.	26 FEB 1878		11	359
Weeden, Ida V.	Cook, Sellman	12 OCT 1880		14	487
Weedon, John Henry	Arndt, Ruth	09 SEP 1884		19	149
Weedon, Lee Poyntz	Pumphrey, Martha	14 APR 1885	L	20	165
Weeks, Edward E.	Laubie, Kate B.	08 AUG 1877	R	11	045
Weeks, Margaret Reile	Wood, Arthur B.	31 MAR 1879	R	12	412
Weems, Annie	Williams, Isaac	12 JUL 1880		14	358
Weems, Benjamin	Williams, Emma	31 JAN 1882	R	16	205
Weems, Jerry	Graham, Ann	07 APR 1884	L	18	497
Weems, Mary	Bosley, Cornelius Henry	17 DEC 1878	L	12	385
Weems, Thomas	Garnet, Emma Lee	19 MAR 1883		17	351
Weer, Mary J.	Rannie, James	30 JUN 1881		15	383
Wege, Margaret, Mrs.	Bender, Charles	05 SEP 1879	L	13	354
Weggeman, Frances H.	Smithson, Ann Eliza	26 OCT 1882	R	17	088
Weicker, Frederick	Schoelung, Bettie	29 JAN 1884		18	400
Weide, George E.	Huneke, Minnie R.C.	28 MAY 1881	L	15	330
Weidman, John C.	Krichelt, Mary C.	30 JUN 1885		20	302
Weidmayer, Katharina	Voegele, Alois	05 JAN 1882	R	16	177
Weigand, Katherine	Glenn, William G.	19 FEB 1883	R	17	309
Weigand, Monica	Rüth, John M.	13 AUG 1878	L	12	166
Weigel, Henry	Jekel, Dora	13 APR 1879		13	133
Weigel, Sophia	Koch, William	28 MAY 1885		20	245
Weightman, Emeline C.	Jannus, Frankland	25 OCT 1883	R	18	211
Weigle, Louis	Nicholas, Ada M.	27 JUN 1885		20	298

Name	Spouse	Date	Vol	Page
Weigman, Nettie	Schuchmacher, Theodore	02 MAR 1882	16	265
Weil, Anna	Sellner, Adam	04 JAN 1881	15	136
Weil, Cornelia Jacoby	Clark, John Bullock, Jr.	10 NOV 1880 R	15	037
Weilacher, Louisa F.	Donovan, John P.	12 APR 1880 R	14	220
Weimertz, Sarah	Scheide, Christian	19 MAY 1883	17	452
Weims, Robert	Brown, Mary	12 APR 1883	17	393
Weinandt, Lena	Rabe, William	24 NOV 1877 L	11	201
Weiner, William G.	Fuller, A.M.	20 JUL 1881 L	15	410
Weis, Adam	Rupenacker, Christina	04 DEC 1878 L	12	364
Weisbacker, William	Coale, Annie May	28 JUN 1879 L	13	256
Weisenborn, Albert N.C.	Utermehle, Augusta L.	18 MAY 1882 R	16	367
Weisge, Rose	Miller, John	29 JAN 1882 R	15	071
Weisiger, Adelaide Amelia	Hasker, Charles Edmund	21 NOV 1877	11	193
Weiske, Benjamin	Rott, Elizabeth	09 NOV 1878 L	12	318
Weisky, Mary	Rapp, Francis	16 SEP 1879 L	13	371
Weiss, Anna	Weber, George	22 SEP 1885 L	20	433
Weiss, Rachel	Kieve, Isidor	15 JAN 1882 R	16	194
Weiss, William J.	Johnston, Ada H.	23 DEC 1884 R	19	477
Weissman, Caroline	Leydecker, Email Gust. Theo.	30 APR 1883	17	422
Weiter, Louisa Cora	Stanton, Leonidas Wellington	29 DEC 1878 R	12	405
Weitzel, Louisa M.	Pywell, Francis E.	14 AUG 1879 R	13	318
Welborne, Walter S.	Beckley, Ella B.	15 OCT 1884	19	310
Welch, Annie	Dougherty, Daniel	30 NOV 1877 L	11	213
Welch, Ella	O'Shea, J. Boyle	03 JUL 1879 R	13	267
Welch, Guinilda Hall	Schley, James McCannon	18 OCT 1881 R	16	029
Welch, Jeanette A.	Payne, A.U.	21 MAY 1884 L	19	032
Welch, John	Cleary, Katie	06 OCT 1885 L	20	460
Welch, John H.	Smallwood, Annie L.	13 JAN 1885 L	20	014
Welch, Josephine	Beach, James H.	10 APR 1884 R	18	504
Welch, Lena	Hicks, Robert L.	24 AUG 1885	20	384
Welch, Louisa	Hall, Thomas	03 JAN 1878 R	11	290
Welch, Mary Ellen	Leavy, Patrick Joseph	14 OCT 1882 L	17	071
Welch, Nora	Reedy, John	31 AUG 1881	15	466
Welch, Patrick	O'Dea, Kate	05 FEB 1880	14	139
Welch, Pattie L.	Ryan, C.W.	13 DEC 1879 R	14	046
Welcker, Mary	Maske, August	05 SEP 1877 L	11	076
Welcome, Winnie	Johnson, William	13 JUL 1884	19	132
Welden, Eliza	Johnson, Nelson	13 DEC 1882 L	17	182
Welford, Charles	Sherman, Cora	01 DEC 1881 L	16	110
Weller, M. Scott	Brown, Annie E.	13 MAY 1885 R	20	220
Weller, S.R.	Sparrow, W.N.	15 JUN 1880	14	323
Welling, Gevevieve	Wigfall, F. Halsey	08 SEP 1881 L	15	477
Wellman, Edwin H.	Graham, Sarah A.	17 JUN 1880 R	14	323
Wells, Albert H.	Fitnan, Laura V.	10 NOV 1884 L	19	371
Wells, Anna Elizabeth	Smith, William Henry	23 SEP 1880 R	14	458
Wells, Annie	Green, Joseph	31 OCT 1883 L	18	222
Wells, Augustus	Meekins, Rachel	29 AUG 1881 L	15	464
Wells, Benjamin F.	Johnson, Marguarite	22 FEB 1883	17	317
Wells, Beverly	Carey, Annie	04 JUL 1880 R	14	346
Wells, Charles C.	Cook, Jane E.	17 APR 1884	18	517
Wells, Charles E.	Stratton, Ella	26 JUL 1881	15	418
Wells, Charles W.	Dodge, Mary A.	25 AUG 1881	15	459
Wells, Cornelia Ann	Busey, Paris Worthington	18 AUG 1880 L	14	406
Wells, Daniel	Brooks, Carrie	07 MAR 1883 L	17	337
Wells, Eldridge Wash.	Fitzgerald, Martha	19 SEP 1881 L	15	490
Wells, Elizabeth	Jackson, John	26 MAY 1880 L	14	292
Wells, Elvira	Crammell, George W.	26 MAR 1885 L	20	133
Wells, Emma	Crampton, John	12 OCT 1884	19	298

Wells, Emma M.	Daniels, Walter W.	31 DEC 1877	11	283
Wells, Flora	Walker, James T.	01 MAY 1878	12	032
Wells, Florence L.	Szegedy, Henry W.	30 OCT 1880 L	15	022
Wells, George T.	Sullivan, Elizabeth J.	13 NOV 1878 R	12	328
Wells, Henry L.	McMaster, Susie L.	26 JAN 1881 R	15	165
Wells, Ida Lavinia	Drury, Charles Scott	05 NOV 1884 L	19	361
Wells, Ida Lavinia	Drury, Charles Scott	05 NOV 1884	19	362
Wells, Jacob R.	Gaines, Annie Elizabeth	09 NOV 1882	17	120
Wells, James	Munroe, Elizabeth	26 DEC 1877 L	11	270
Wells, James	Pennifill, Sarah A.	02 JUN 1883	17	472
Wells, John	Washington, Mary F.	30 APR 1879 R	13	168
Wells, John	Simms, Mary	27 MAR 1879	13	117
Wells, John Edward	Wood, Agnes	10 JAN 1878 R	11	298
Wells, Leon H.	Sabin, Harriet Brooks	30 JUN 1885 R	20	303
Wells, Lewis	Christon, Kate	05 JUN 1884 R	19	061
Wells, Lizzie	Jackson, Andrew	16 JUN 1881 R	15	365
Wells, Maria	DeLaney, Richard	31 JUL 1883 L	18	067
Wells, Mary Dagworthy	Kreidler, Edward Allanson	24 OCT 1877 R	11	151
Wells, Mary V.	Lowe, Franklin	11 APR 1882 L	16	310
Wells, Millard F.	Green, Annie B.	07 AUG 1883	18	074
Wells, Nellie	Jones, Allen	02 JUL 1883 R	17	498
Wells, Samuel	Hurst, Lucy Ann	13 NOV 1880 R	15	020
Wells, Thomas	Howard, Henrietta	28 AUG 1879 L	13	341
Wells, William H.	Fitzgerald, Catherine	02 JAN 1885 L	20	001
Wells, William H.	Greenfield, Christie	05 JUN 1885 L	20	257
Wells, William J.	Holland, Mary	02 OCT 1883 L	18	165
Wells, William L.	Davis, India	28 AUG 1877 L	11	068
Welsh, Alonzo	Schlenker, Elizabeth	24 JUL 1884	19	156
Welsh, Annie	Foley, Michael	27 DEC 1878 R	12	404
Welsh, Charles E.	Conroy, Katie A.	16 APR 1883 L	17	396
Welsh, Ella Teresa	Smith, John Michael	14 APR 1882 L	16	316
Welsh, Johanna	Barry, Patrick	08 OCT 1877	11	125
Welsh, John	Scott, Mary	23 OCT 1879 R	13	438
Welsh, John A.	Naughton, Nellie L.	08 OCT 1882	17	057
Welsh, John E.	Brown, Lizzie A.	12 MAR 1883 L	17	341
Welsh, Kate A.	Smith, J.W.	20 JUN 1882 L	16	421
Welsh, Mary	Meaney, Michael	12 MAY 1878	12	039
Welsh, Michael Raymond	Boyle, Mary Jane	21 NOV 1878 L	12	343
Welsh, William P.	Holson, Eliza A.	22 MAY 1882	16	372
Weltz, James L.	Solomon, Emma J., Mrs.	06 AUG 1882	16	470
Wendel, Magdelena	Morgan, John R.	09 SEP 1885	20	406
Wendel, Samuel O.	Wetzel, Agnes E.	06 NOV 1879 R	13	471
Wendell, Annie C.	Payne, Andrew L.	22 MAY 1883 L	17	455
Wendell, Mildred	Wickersham, George W.	17 SEP 1883 L	18	134
Wenger, Rebecca	Keller, James H.	28 APR 1881 R	15	284
Wenk, Elizabeth	Riley, Philip G.	30 NOV 1879	14	019
Wenner, Jacob S.	Washington, Sallie R.	21 OCT 1880	15	007
Wenner, Sallie J.	Hickman, Samuel T.	21 JUL 1885 R	20	334
Wenzel, Catherine	Potee, Thomas	19 MAR 1878	11	387
Wenzel, George W.	Crutchett, Sarah E.	11 NOV 1879 R	13	476
Werk, Flaurence	Weaver, Catharine	21 JUL 1883 L	18	055
Werner, August	Schoenberg, Katie	16 SEP 1881 R	15	487
Werner, Emily	Collins, John C.	16 MAY 1881 L	15	311
Werner, George L.	Umhan, M. Emilie	11 SEP 1883 R	18	121
Werner, John William	Norbeck, Bertha C.	12 NOV 1878 R	12	325
Werr, Mary	Jacobson, Jacob	31 DEC 1877 L	11	282
Wertheim, Isaac C.	Burton, Cora Ann	05 JUL 1879 R	13	269
Weser, Annie M.	Gordon, James A.	26 DEC 1883 L	18	342

Weser, Benjamin F.	Kettler, Rosa D.	30 JUN 1883	18	027
Wesley, Charles	Oderick, Jane	19 APR 1879 L	13	151
Wesley, George W.	Kuhn, Louisa	02 DEC 1883	18	290
Wesley, John	Middleton, Annie M.	16 DEC 1880 L	15	104
Wesley, Joseph	Thorp, Eliza E.	19 APR 1883	17	401
Wess, Charles T.	Neal, Martha	02 AUG 1884	19	165
West, Albert	Cober, Louisa Jane	15 JUL 1880	14	364
West, Albert C.	Knott, Cora C.	25 JUN 1879 R	13	247
West, Alfred	Moore, Mary	19 FEB 1880 R	14	159
West, Amos	Cross, Marian G.	17 APR 1882 L	16	318
West, Annie	Blair, George P.	07 APR 1879 R	13	130
West, Benjamin O.	Helvin, Jennie	04 DEC 1878 R	12	360
West, Caroline	Coggie, Frank	27 NOV 1882 R	17	149
West, Catherine	Spriggs, Ben	09 AUG 1884 L	19	177
West, Charles	Chase, Sophronia	02 AUG 1879 L	13	305
West, Charles F.	Snowden, Rebecca	07 JUL 1883 R	18	039
West, Christopher	Hornig, Rosa	11 MAY 1880 L	14	263
West, Clement R.	Lindsley, Sarah A.	22 DEC 1881 R	16	153
West, David	Lecount, Annie C.	13 OCT 1885 R	20	476
West, Edward C.	Mahorney, Clara D.	14 NOV 1881 L	16	074
West, Eli	Junifer, Georgiena	02 AUG 1877 L	11	038
West, Ella	Williams, James	05 NOV 1881 L	16	063
West, Elliott S.	Riley, Lillian D.	14 OCT 1880 R	14	495
West, Emily	Griggs, Newton	11 SEP 1877 R	11	129
West, Emma S.	Scott, John R.	08 NOV 1882 L	17	117
West, Fannie	Stewart, William	22 SEP 1881 R	15	495
West, Fannie	Harper, James	07 JUN 1883 L	17	481
West, Frances	Dick, William	26 JUN 1878	12	113
West, Francis	Calvert, Mary Jane	02 FEB 1882	16	223
West, Frank	Mattingly, Lena	03 MAY 1880 L	14	251
West, Frank	Brown, Melvina	02 FEB 1882 R	16	222
West, George W.	Claughton, Blanche	11 SEP 1877 L	11	087
West, Gertrude Morse	Guy, Frank Morsell	18 FEB 1879 R	13	065
West, Henry	Thornton, Emma	02 FEB 1882 R	16	215
West, Hezekiah	Haislip, Mary	27 DEC 1877 L	11	271
West, Jane	Robertson, Isaac	18 SEP 1877 R	11	092
West, John	Harris, Clara	07 SEP 1880 R	14	435
West, John D.	Phelps, Annie Bell	18 MAR 1884 L	18	476
West, John R.	Keatley, Annie E.	29 DEC 1881 R	16	169
West, Jonas	Osborn, Kate	23 JUN 1884	19	097
West, Joseph	Harrison, Mary J.	15 JAN 1878	11	305
West, Joseph	Brooks, Sarah	27 MAR 1879 R	13	104
West, Josephine	Norris, Nimrod	10 MAR 1881 R	15	219
West, Julia G.	Barker, John B.	16 FEB 1878 L	11	345
West, Julius	Ford, Hester Ann	26 FEB 1880	14	167
West, Laura	Gilbert, George	20 DEC 1877	11	253
West, Lena	Lewis, Thomas G.	08 SEP 1880	14	431
West, Lloyd	Bowens, Anna	10 MAY 1879	13	183
West, Maggie	Porter, Charles W.	22 MAR 1880 R	14	191
West, Maria	Thomas, Thomas	31 OCT 1878 L	12	303
West, Mary	Lawerence, A.	22 DEC 1881 L	16	155
West, Mary	Snyder, James	01 NOV 1883 R	18	228
West, Mary E.	Griffin, Thomas H.	26 DEC 1883 L	18	344
West, Mary Jane	Page, James Henry	24 MAR 1885 L	20	130
West, Matthew	Green, Mary	19 JUL 1883 L	18	054
West, Mollie E.	Crampton, James William	02 NOV 1882 R	17	107
West, Nellie G.	Burnett, Simon C.	30 JUL 1881 L	15	427
West, Nelson	Pinkney, Martha	21 MAY 1885 L	20	233

D.C. Marriage Records Index, June 28, 1877 to October 19, 1885 493

Name	Spouse	Date		
West, Nettie A.	Brown, J. Ingalls	15 FEB 1883 R	17	307
West, Rebecca	Bruce, Samuel	01 JAN 1883	17	226
West, Robert L.	Watkins, Minnie E.	29 SEP 1881	15	503
West, Roberta Lemmon	Minor, Fairfax Catlett	13 APR 1882 R	16	314
West, Russell	Jackson, Maria M.	10 MAR 1882 R	16	273
West, Sallie A.	Mitchell, George	26 JUL 1882	16	457
West, Sarah A.	Wilkenson, George F.	04 APR 1878	11	406
West, Susan A. Skinner	Wilson, Robert	09 NOV 1880 R	15	038
West, Susan Elizabeth	Bringas, Luis	22 DEC 1884 L	19	477
West, Thomas	Norris, Lizzie	08 JUN 1882 L	16	400
West, William	Williams, Nancy	15 JUL 1880 L	14	361
West, William A.	Parker, Minnie M.	22 JUL 1878 L	12	144
West, William Lovel	McClanahan, Bettie	13 AUG 1883	18	085
Westberg, Bertha M.	Foley, Michael P.	01 NOV 1883 R	18	227
Westenmeier, Mary	Schnaebele, Jacob	28 FEB 1883	17	325
Western, Clemnes	Anderson, Sarah	11 SEP 1882 R	17	016
Westin, Rebecca	Medley, George	13 JUN 1878	12	090
Westling, Charles E.	Rutherford, Jennie	15 AUG 1881	15	446
Westnedge, James	Bergmann, Etta M.	05 FEB 1885 R	20	054
Weston, Jeannette E.	Butterfield, George	23 DEC 1880 R	15	120
Wetherall, James A.	Orr, Emma J.	28 AUG 1877	11	069
Wetmore, Charles A.	Smith, Anna Deroy	05 APR 1879 R	13	128
Wetmore, Henry S.	Parker, Virginia W. (Calhoun)	01 NOV 1881 R	15	506
Wetzel, Agnes E.	Wendel, Samuel O.	06 NOV 1879 R	13	471
Wetzel, Charles J.	Droege, Wilhelmina C.	31 MAR 1884 R	18	487
Wetzel, James A.	Robinson, Ada V.	01 DEC 1877	11	214
Wetzel, John A.	Fletcher, Ida L.	14 APR 1884 L	18	508
Wetzel, Sallie J.	Kropp, Henry, Jr.	13 MAY 1885 R	20	218
Wex, Henry	Baker, Emma J.	24 OCT 1882 R	17	089
Weyrich, Annie D.	Dubaut, William M.	14 FEB 1884 R	18	424
Weyrich, John F.	Montgomery, Ella J.	17 NOV 1880 L	15	052
Weyrich, William H.	Eckloff, Kate C.	20 APR 1881 L	15	266
Whails, George	Cross, Kate	21 MAR 1882 R	16	268
Whalen, James W.	Duckett, Alice H.	19 APR 1881 L	15	262
Whalen, William	Writtoe, Martha	28 OCT 1878 L	12	293
Whaley, Laura Lee	Kendig, Wilmot G.	30 NOV 1882 R	17	162
Whaley, Lelia Virginia	Hutchison, Columbus P.	14 FEB 1882 R	16	242
Whaley, Margaret A.	Summers, Thomas F.	29 SEP 1880 R	14	464
Whalley, Samuel	Reeves, Ida M.	27 DEC 1883 L	18	346
Whalley, William H.	Nalley, Isabella R.	02 AUG 1882 L	16	466
Whallon, Eugene W.	Warren, Jessie May	15 AUG 1882 R	16	468
Wharfield, Martha Ellen	Sweeney, John J.	25 FEB 1879 R	13	077
Wharton, Mamie S.	Dickinson, Charles H.	12 NOV 1884 L	19	376
Wharton, Mary America	Shepherd, Arthur	08 AUG 1878 L	12	161
Wharton, William A.	Thomas, Rose	06 FEB 1883 L	17	295
Wharton, William M.	Evatt, Maggie L.	07 SEP 1882 R	17	011
Wheatley, David	Speiden, Margaret R.	21 MAR 1881 L	15	232
Wheatley, Edward E.	Mahagan, Mary A.	29 JAN 1879 L	13	037
Wheatley, John W.	Boaman, Lillie	17 FEB 1879 L	13	063
Wheatley, Joseph Moody	Taylor, Emma Philippa	22 FEB 1881 R	15	198
Wheeler, Albert	Jackson, Betsey	29 NOV 1877 R	11	204
Wheeler, Bud	Robinson, Catharine	31 JAN 1883 R	17	257
Wheeler, Charles S.	Downing, Elizabeth E.	28 JAN 1879 L	13	035
Wheeler, Charlotte Oram	Hilleary, Clarence Worthing	25 JAN 1882 R	16	206
Wheeler, Ella	Freeman, Charles	02 MAR 1881 L	15	211
Wheeler, F.M.	Brayton, S.W.	14 APR 1879 L	13	141
Wheeler, George	Thompson, Josephine	27 MAR 1878	11	395
Wheeler, George C.	Tayloe, Mary A.	16 OCT 1884 R	19	314

Wheeler, James	Lynch, Julia	25 NOV 1878	12 347
Wheeler, James	Courtis, Florence	04 NOV 1884 L	19 360
Wheeler, James W.	Mack, Mary	30 APR 1878 R	12 025
Wheeler, Langden P.	Bleecker, Cornelia	26 OCT 1881 R	16 046
Wheeler, Laura V.	Skinner, Roswell M.	24 APR 1878	12 021
Wheeler, Lizzie M.	Pistorio, John N.	16 OCT 1879 R	13 430
Wheeler, Lottie E.	Sammons, William E.	04 DEC 1878 R	12 365
Wheeler, M. Clara	Dashiell, George B.	22 JUL 1884 L	19 150
Wheeler, Mary	Storks, Robert	24 MAY 1883	17 451
Wheeler, Mary	Semly, William	22 APR 1884 L	18 526
Wheeler, Nicholas	Fisher, Sarah	18 APR 1878 R	11 2504
Wheeler, Patrick	Scott, Mary Elizabeth	02 JAN 1878 L	11 291
Wheeler, Robert	Hart, Dora	01 JUN 1885 L	20 250
Wheeler, Samuel	Woodfolk, Kate	30 JUN 1880 L	14 340
Wheeler, Thomas	Brown, Ella	25 MAR 1885	20 130
Wheeler, William B.	Truxson, Susan K.	09 JUN 1880 L	14 312
Wheeler, William M.	McCaw, Sallie Pelham	21 AUG 1877 R	11 057
Wheeley, George E.	Knox, Maude H.	04 MAR 1885 R	20 095
Wheelock, Frances A.	Thomas, Edward Hildt	17 DEC 1884 R	19 462
Whelan, Anna E.	Bartlett, William U.	02 JUL 1885 L	20 306
Whelan, Eliza Bella Booker	Sargent, Charles H.	03 APR 1879 R	13 126
Whelan, William T.	Crow, Susie W.	01 FEB 1882 L	16 219
Whelpley, Adeline	Flagg, Henry T.	15 NOV 1877	11 188
Whelpley, Blanche Ella	Renaud, Edward	19 MAY 1880	14 227½
Wherrett, William H.	Clark, Linda E.	10 FEB 1885	20 062
Whibking, Dora	Hadfield, Alexander	03 JUN 1881 L	15 343
Whiby, Mary	Howard, Mack	02 OCT 1885 R	20 450
Whidbee, John A.	Jones, Elizabeth M.	09 APR 1884	18 502
Whidnon, Jesse	Carter, Martha	27 NOV 1879 R	14 018
Whinery, Thomas	Melbourne, Delia	08 JUN 1881 R	15 349
Whipple, David R.	Morrison, Margaret A.	05 FEB 1878	11 288
Whipps, Adam, Jr.	Butler, Teresa	13 OCT 1884 L	19 302
Whipps, Sarah Elizabeth	Aitchoson, Robert	09 JUN 1884	19 069
Whitacre, Joseph D.	Muhlhofer, Emma E.	06 MAY 1885	20 209
Whitaker, Grenville A.	Clark, Laura S.	05 FEB 1880	14 137
Whitback, Emma	Daniel, William	25 SEP 1878	12 233
Whitcomb, James A.	Cammack, Virginia H.	23 APR 1882 R	16 330
Whitcomb, Leora A.	Parks, William S.	10 DEC 1884	19 446
Whitcomb, Sophie H. (Dwinels)	Thaxter, Warren P.	06 JAN 1885 R	20 005
White, Abner	Gant, Mary C.	25 FEB 1879 L	13 080
White, Adelaide	Penn, William Henry	10 OCT 1878 R	12 267
White, Adolphus	Speaks, Jennie	20 SEP 1879	13 379
White, Alice	Jackson, William H.	18 SEP 1883 R	18 139
White, Alice	Washington, Harrison	16 MAY 1884 L	19 025
White, Allis	Ross, Ben	26 FEB 1882 R	23 5653
White, Annie	Thompson, Charles	26 JUN 1879	13 251
White, Annie	Posey, John A.	01 NOV 1882 R	17 106
White, Annie E.	Striker, John B.	06 DEC 1878	12 371
White, Annie E.	Burgess, William	04 DEC 1879 R	14 031
White, Annie G.	Gibson, John E.	06 MAR 1883 R	17 333
White, Bonnie	Sowers, Henry	14 NOV 1883 L	18 251
White, Brandie	Mullen, Annie	23 JUN 1879 R	13 245
White, Carrie	Madison, Ryland R.	25 AUG 1885	20 386
White, Catherine	Kelly, William H.	02 JUN 1879 L	13 213
White, Catherine	Pfeiffer, Frederick	11 SEP 1882 L	17 015
White, Charles	Fauntleroy, Annie	18 MAY 1881 L	15 316
White, Charles, Jr.	Reichenbach, Flora	24 OCT 1882 R	17 088
White, Clara B.	Stephenson, Thomas P.	06 OCT 1880 L	14 478

White, David	Harris, Augusta	09 NOV 1877 R	11	177
White, Dennis E.	Baylor, Mary E.	08 JUN 1881	15	351
White, Eleanor	Grills, William A.	16 SEP 1884 L	19	249
White, Eliza	Travis, Scipio	26 OCT 1881	16	042
White, Eliza Fletcher	Chrisman, George William	14 MAY 1882 R	16	358
White, Elizabeth	Mangon, Benjamin Franklin	22 DEC 1881 R	16	151
White, Ellen	Rone, Levi	02 AUG 1877 R	11	037
White, Ellen	Robinson, Charles	31 OCT 1878 R	12	302
White, Emma	Stansbury, John	24 JUN 1879 R	13	170
White, Emma J.	Nicholson, Joshua Banks	23 JUN 1885 R	20	286
White, Eugene	Thompson, Josephine	28 APR 1884	18	538
White, Fannie May	Nicholson, Millard Fillmore	02 JAN 1884 R	18	363
White, Frances	Woodland, Daniel E.	28 MAR 1882 R	16	290
White, Frank H.	Beckert, Nellie C.	02 AUG 1880 R	14	382
White, Frank W.	Durham, Bridget A.	20 NOV 1884 R	19	378
White, Franklin Pierce	O'Connor, Maggie	06 AUG 1884	19	170
White, Fred W.	Taylor, Eliza L.	06 SEP 1877 L	11	081
White, George H.	Burrill, Susan	13 JUN 1881 L	15	358
White, George Newton	Walker, Fannie Gertrude	15 JAN 1878 R	11	304
White, Getrude A.	Johnson, William B.	26 FEB 1880 R	14	165
White, Hattie L.	Kendall, George H.	10 JUN 1884	19	073
White, Henry	Taylor, Alice M.	04 MAR 1879	13	088
White, Henry	Atkinson, Julia Ann	05 JAN 1882 L	16	183
White, Irene B.	Young, John C.	05 DEC 1877 L	11	221
White, Isabella	Foster, Edward	28 DEC 1882 R	17	157
White, Jackson	Viele, Katie	13 OCT 1884 L	19	302
White, James	Stanton, Lucy	28 DEC 1882 R	17	207
White, James W.	Taylor, Fannie	25 JAN 1883 L	17	275
White, John J.	Corcoran, Annie E.	22 FEB 1881 R	15	196
White, John M.	Ellis, Genevieve	29 NOV 1879 L	14	019
White, John R.	Taylor, Mamie E.	09 OCT 1877 L	11	128
White, John S.	Reed, Ada L.	06 MAY 1878	12	040
White, John Shermon	Washington, Eliza	31 AUG 1882 R	16	498
White, Julia	Sidney, Washington P.	17 SEP 1885 R	20	426
White, Julia Ann Elizabeth	Bond, James Henry G.	10 NOV 1880 R	15	033
White, Katherine	Coe, S.A.	17 JUL 1885	20	278
White, Katie	Walker, William	30 SEP 1884 L	19	275
White, Letitia Lettie	Cooley, Benjamin	14 NOV 1883 R	18	236
White, M. Carrie	Anderson, Richard D.	30 NOV 1881 L	16	104
White, M.F.	Pumphrey, Mary F.	11 JUL 1885	20	320
White, Margaret Crawford	Fridley, P.B.	31 AUG 1878 L	12	190
White, Mariah	Butler, George	05 AUG 1884	19	167
White, Martha A.	Henault, Robert Emile	29 NOV 1881 R	16	094
White, Mary	Thompson, Lee	06 JAN 1880 L	14	091
White, Mary	Pollard, James	13 OCT 1885	20	479
White, Mary Anna	Keys, Henry	24 JAN 1883 R	17	272
White, Mary E.	Payne, F.L.	05 MAR 1879	13	090
White, Mary E.	Crawford, William P.	20 JUL 1882 L	16	452
White, Mary Ellen	Vermillion, Elijah	18 DEC 1879 R	14	058
White, Mary G.	Fowler, William E.	15 AUG 1878	12	167
White, Mary J.	Peyton, Randolph V.	18 JUL 1878 R	12	138
White, Matilda	Beatty, Joseph	28 OCT 1879 R	13	449
White, Matilda	Fry, Dennis W.	06 SEP 1883 R	18	115
White, Maximo	Morton, May E.	27 MAY 1880 R	14	287
White, Minnie A.	Walker, Francis M.	17 JUN 1882	16	416
White, Oscar William	Green, Agnes Louisa	04 JUN 1883 R	17	473
White, Patsy	Brown, William H.	20 MAY 1880 L	14	279
White, Peter B.	Moten, Harriet A., Mrs.	29 NOV 1877 R	11	207

White, Peyton U.	Stewart, Rosa	24 JUL 1879 R	13	288
White, Richard	Gordon, Mary	31 DEC 1879 L	14	083
White, Richard	Mason, Lizzie	23 NOV 1882 L	17	146
White, Richard E.	Flaherty, Mary J.	08 NOV 1880	15	034
White, Robert	Simmons, Susie	29 MAY 1884 R	19	029
White, Sallie	Hill, Benjamin F.	26 MAR 1885 R	20	132
White, Samuel Ambrose	Smith, Emma	21 NOV 1883 R	18	263
White, Sarah	Howard, Frank	17 JAN 1878	11	309
White, Sarah	Parker, Alfred	06 JAN 1880 R	14	091
White, Simon	Brooks, Jennie E.	14 JUN 1883 R	17	495
White, Theodore F.	Powell, Sarah J.	16 MAR 1878	11	383
White, Thomas	Littleford, Martha Ann	24 DEC 1877	11	267
White, Thomas	Green, Susan	01 JUL 1878 R	12	119
White, Thomas	Carter, Henrietta	28 AUG 1881	15	438
White, Thomas	McKenney, Elizabeth	14 JUN 1883 L	17	494
White, Thomas	Jones, Sarena	13 DEC 1883 L	18	316
White, Viola	Tunis, Henry Clay	22 DEC 1880 R	15	115
White, Volney	Brothers, Alcenia E.	12 JUN 1884	19	082
White, William B.	Dodge, Alice M.	07 FEB 1883	17	298
White, William C.	Moran, Elizabeth	19 APR 1881 R	15	263
White, William F.	Williams, Kate L.	27 OCT 1880	15	017
White, William H.	Savage, Hattie B.	20 JUL 1885 L	20	333
White, William K.	Polly, Ida R.	30 JUL 1878 L	12	151
White, William L.	Dozier, Jennie	21 JAN 1885 L	20	030
White, William O.	Burkhardt, Tina C.	14 JUL 1881 L	15	403
Whiteford, John H.	Quinn, Sallie	08 DEC 1879 R	14	033
Whiteford, William S.	O'Dowd, Katie	12 APR 1882 R	16	311
Whitehead, Joel H.	Dyer, Elizabeth	24 AUG 1879	13	332
Whitehead, Valeria Berrien	Salas, Augustus Ramon	24 DEC 1884 R	19	479
Whitehouse, Lottie M.	Huntress, William F.	07 MAY 1885	20	179
Whitehurst, Manning E.	Crews, Rosa	15 JUL 1884	19	138
Whiteley, Catharine	Parlon, Patrick	23 NOV 1879 R	14	001
Whiteley, Mary B.	Dove, William M.	12 MAY 1880 R	14	263
Whitelow, Charles A.	Langley, Emma V.	30 APR 1879 L	13	169
Whitely, Albert	Snow, Lillian A.	30 NOV 1882 R	17	151
Whitemore, David B.	Hagar, Caroline	13 DEC 1881 R	16	127
Whitemore, Frances M.	Paret, Peter	10 OCT 1883 R	18	183
Whitemore, Henry H.	Cooksey, Ellen A.	05 APR 1881 R	15	248
Whitemore, James H.	Lindsey, Sarah E.	21 JUN 1882 L	16	421
Whitening, Emma	Randall, Churchill	13 JUN 1884 L	19	082
Whiteside, Rosy B.	Kellett, David	12 OCT 1880	11	384
Whitford, Clara E.	Snelling, Andrew T.	25 FEB 1879 R	13	076
Whiting, Albert	Weaver, Elizabeth	24 MAY 1878	12	065
Whiting, Allen	Gill, Frances	30 MAY 1881 R	15	331
Whiting, Amanda	Howard, Eli C.	25 APR 1878	12	023
Whiting, Amelia Ann	Frazier, Samuel L.	13 JUN 1882 R	16	343
Whiting, Benjamin C.	Goff, Mollie E.	05 APR 1882	16	301
Whiting, Eliza	Turner, William	27 JUN 1878 R	12	115
Whiting, Eliza Macomb	Fosdick, Dering	16 MAY 1882 R	16	360
Whiting, Flora	Diggs, Thomas J.	03 JUN 1880 L	14	304
Whiting, Frank	Hawkins, Matilda	13 JUL 1884	19	135
Whiting, Hortense E.	Salter, Samuel T.	28 MAR 1881 R	15	241
Whiting, Joseph G.	Soper, Gracie E.	15 OCT 1879	13	421
Whiting, Mahalah, Mrs.	Cook, Lewis	19 JAN 1881 R	15	155
Whiting, Mary Gray	Burnside, James Bradford	05 OCT 1882 R	17	052
Whiting, Philip	Bowie, Anna A.	22 MAR 1883 L	17	356
Whiting, Susan	Gaines, John	25 JUL 1880 R	14	295
Whiting, Wm. M.	Richardson, Julia M.	27 JUN 1879 L	13	255

D.C. Marriage Records Index, June 28, 1877 to October 19, 1885   497

Whiting, Wm. M.	Richardson, Julia A.	08 OCT 1879	13	466
Whitley, Catherine	Harrison, James	12 FEB 1881 L	15	187
Whitley, Edward	Lee, Nancy	09 DEC 1884 L	19	445
Whitley, Julia F.	Cotton, James S.W.	08 AUG 1883 L	18	079
Whitley, Mary	Clark, Horace	11 FEB 1885 L	20	064
Whitlock, James E.	Shackford, Katie	17 SEP 1884	19	253
Whitlow, John Andrew	Wilkerson, Annie Pattie	14 JUN 1880 R	14	318
Whitman, Emma	LaBarre, George Emanuel	27 JUL 1883	18	061
Whitmore, Alfred H.	Bowles, Carrie Grace	23 DEC 1882 L	17	206
Whitmore, Alice M.	Scaggs, James F.	13 MAR 1879 R	13	098
Whitmore, Domie A.	Whittington, M.V.B.	30 NOV 1880 R	15	070
Whitmore, Emma V.	Daniels, Ara M.	07 DEC 1882	17	174
Whitney, C.N.	Meredith, Ann E.	01 JAN 1884	18	357
Whitney, Carrie	Brown, Charles	01 NOV 1879 L	13	458
Whitney, Charles	Berkley, Maria	14 OCT 1880 R	14	492
Whitney, James	Washington, Catherine	14 JUN 1883 L	17	495
Whitney, Lelia	Stone, Thomas Ritchie	22 JAN 1885 R	20	034
Whitney, Lelia E.	Imbrie, J. Rankin	09 OCT 1877	11	124
Whitney, Lizzie Ann	Ryan, Michael	22 AUG 1878 L	12	177
Whitney, Marcella	Carroll, William	05 AUG 1879	13	307
Whitney, Mary	Davis, Lewis	27 DEC 1883 L	18	348
Whitney, Patrick	Heaney, Julia	20 MAY 1881 L	15	319
Whitney, Reuben M.	Wilcox, Mary M.	28 FEB 1881 L	15	206
Whitney, Susan, Mrs.	Pope, Frederick C.	08 JUN 1882 R	16	401
Whitney, Thomas	Ross, Rachel	24 MAR 1885	20	130
Whiton, Emma Sumner	Bonnelle, Frank Jackson	23 DEC 1880 R	15	114
Whittaker, Catherine	Martin, Griffin S.	14 SEP 1880 R	14	444
Whittemore, Henrietta J.	Sabel, George W.	02 MAY 1881	15	287
Whittey, Julia	Baylor, Allen	15 AUG 1885 L	20	371
Whittier, Clara O.	Cate, Fernando C.	18 MAY 1882	16	363
Whittington, M.V.B.	Whitmore, Domie A.	30 NOV 1880 R	15	070
Whittlesey, Walter R.	Sherman, Florence Gertrude	03 MAR 1881 F	15	213
Whittlessy, William H.	Richards, Mary M.	20 DEC 1881 L	16	141
Whitwell, Anna Wood	Middleton, William Eliot	15 NOV 1877 R	11	183
Whyte, Agnes V.	Lewis, Robert	03 OCT 1885 L	20	455
Whyte, Katie R.	Fahey, Daniel C.	18 NOV 1884	19	392
Whyte, Warren M.	Walsh, Maggie C.	08 SEP 1879 L	13	359
Wiber, Annah N., Mrs.	Bartlett, Fitz J.	15 FEB 1883	17	309
Wibert, Minnie B.	Corbett, Charles F.	30 MAY 1883	17	468
Wickens, Viney	Tibbs, Richard	22 MAY 1879 R	13	202
Wicker, William H.	Pfisterer, Kate	08 JAN 1885 L	20	008
Wickersham, George W.	Wendell, Mildred	17 SEP 1883 L	18	134
Wickersham, Morris Dickinson	McGrew, Agnes Eliz.	04 JAN 1883 R	17	234
Wicks, Alice	Waynes, W.H.	06 JAN 1881	15	142
Wicks, William H., Jr.	Magruder, Sophia C.	27 AUG 1885	20	389
Widdecombe, Thomas W.	Croghan, Cornelia	21 FEB 1878 L	11	352
Widmann, Charles	Stumpf, Mary	09 DEC 1884 R	19	444
Widmayer, Rosa Mary	Baltz, Henry Edward	27 APR 1885 R	20	189
Widmayer, William G.	Scherger, Wilhelmina E.	22 MAR 1885 R	20	127
Widmeyer, Thomas Walter	Murray, Margaret Rachel	07 NOV 1881 R	16	065
Widmire, John	Raderly, Kate	13 AUG 1878 L	12	165
Wiebking, Carlina W.M.	Dice, Robert McLelland	13 AUG 1885	20	368
Wiesemann, Lissie	Wonders, Andrew	13 JUL 1881	15	399
Wieskie, Mary E.	O'Donnoghue, William F.	05 OCT 1879 R	13	402
Wigfall, F. Halsey	Welling, Gevevieve	08 SEP 1881 L	15	477
Wigfield, Douglas N.	Parr, Dora L.	27 APR 1881	15	275
Wiggin, Fredelina A.	Pearce, William H.	22 MAR 1881 R	15	234
Wiggins, Alice	Blackwell, John	06 APR 1882	16	303

Name	Spouse	Date	Vol	Page
Wiggins, Benjamin	Dangerfield, carrie	20 AUG 1884 L	19	198
Wiggins, George H.	Holmes, Susan P.	03 MAR 1884 L	18	455
Wiggins, John	Waters, Margaret	25 JUN 1885 R	20	294
Wiggins, Kate	Thomas, John	09 DEC 1884 R	19	442
Wiggins, Mary	Burnett, James	27 JAN 1885 L	20	040
Wight, George A.	Morgan, Ida M.	09 DEC 1880	15	088
Wilborn, Lula A.	Taylor, William N.	03 SEP 1884	19	224
Wilbrand, Ernst	Bacchus, Anna	14 APR 1881 R	15	253
Wilbur, Bertha E.	Bowie, Hamilton	06 OCT 1885 R	20	464
Wilburn, Elisabeth	Bryant, William H.	06 MAR 1881 R	15	215
Wilburn, John William	Bowman, Ida Sophronia	24 SEP 1878 R	12	233
Wilcox, Andrew C.	Mulliken, Mary O.	24 FEB 1879 L	13	074
Wilcox, Andrew D.	Seymour, Ida R.	09 FEB 1882 L	16	233
Wilcox, Floie D.	Gregory, John R.	03 JUN 1883 R	17	474
Wilcox, John F.	Mygatt, Lois	10 NOV 1881 L	16	070
Wilcox, Mary C.	Sheckells, Augustus C.	19 NOV 1878	12	334
Wilcox, Mary E.	Bell, Joseph S.	16 MAY 1883	17	445
Wilcox, Mary M.	Whitney, Reuben M.	28 FEB 1881 L	15	206
Wilcox, Walter R.	Miller, Eliza G.	12 JAN 1882	16	191
Wilcoxon, Hattie B.	Lewis, Mars	29 MAY 1880 L	14	296
Wild, Alfred E.	Yung, Julia	27 MAY 1878	12	067
Wilding, Elizabeth	Reckie, John	01 JUL 1881 R	15	361
Wilernan, Miles H.	Bates, Emma F.	13 MAY 1885	20	217
Wiles, Ida	Homes, Thomas	16 JAN 1884 L	18	380
Wiles, Mary A.	Serrin, David Dallas	23 DEC 1884 R	19	478
Wiley, Annie Zelia	Lishear, Samuel Edward	17 JAN 1880 R	14	052
Wiley, Ballentine	Kidwell, Virginia	03 APR 1879 R	13	126
Wiley, E.F.	Harris, S.	31 MAR 1878	11	398
Wiley, Frances M.	Brown, George W.	05 AUG 1885	20	355
Wiley, Ida R.	Flinn, Michael W.	28 AUG 1880 R	14	421
Wiley, Jennie C.	Pickett, Robert	27 NOV 1879 R	14	008
Wiley, John T.	Hardy, Kate M.	27 SEP 1880	14	461
Wiley, Lena	Carter, John M.	01 FEB 1883	17	282
Wiley, Lucy	Hunter, John	23 MAR 1880 L	14	193
Wiley, Martha	Hicks, Reuben	10 MAY 1884 L	19	370
Wilhelmina, Henriette	Gahn, Henrick	16 AUG 1884 L	19	189
Wilkenson, George F.	West, Sarah A.	04 APR 1878	11	406
Wilker, James A.	Hamilton, Elizabeth Blanch	05 OCT 1885 R	20	455
Wilkerson, Annie M.	Sargent, George W.	23 JUN 1881 L	15	374
Wilkerson, Annie Pattie	Whitlow, John Andrew	14 JUN 1880 R	14	318
Wilkerson, Charles	Parker, Carrie	29 MAY 1879 L	13	210
Wilkerson, Edward O.	Greer, Everlyn	19 DEC 1878	12	392
Wilkerson, Everick	Wilson, Katie	19 OCT 1882 R	17	082
Wilkerson, Henry	Berry, Annie	09 OCT 1883 R	18	179
Wilkerson, Martha	Brown, Albert	29 DEC 1881 L	16	169
Wilkerson, Mary A.	McPhee, Thomas L.	01 JUL 1885	20	303
Wilkerson, Mollie C.	Cashell, George T.	23 MAY 1884	18	527
Wilkerson, Peter	Gaines, Annie	29 APR 1880 R	14	244
Wilkerson, Sallie	Montgomery, James A.	16 AUG 1881 R	15	447
Wilkerson, Sarah	Smith, Charley	19 DEC 1878	12	390
Wilkerson, Susie	Berry, George R.	12 OCT 1879 L	13	416
Wilkerson, Vincent	Harris, Vinsent	02 APR 1884 L	18	491
Wilkerson, William A.	Smithson, Susie A.	29 SEP 1880 L	14	465
Wilkes, Catherine	Smith, Lloyd	05 JUL 1882 L	16	438
Wilkes, Edward	Pendleton, Louisa V.	08 MAY 1879 R	13	179
Wilkey, Mary, Mrs.	Lewis, James P., M.D.	30 JUN 1880 R	14	342
Wilkins, Alonzo A.	Combs, Agatha B.	31 JAN 1883 R	17	280
Wilkins, Carrie E.	Porter, Charles, Capt.	24 APR 1879 R	13	155

Wilkins, Charles	Beam, Cora E.	05 JUL 1878	12	125
Wilkins, Franklin P.	Ball, Laurie J.	13 JAN 1881 R	15	150
Wilkins, John L.	Dieste, Kate M.	09 NOV 1880 R	15	040
Wilkins, Kate V.	Munday, Cary P.	28 SEP 1885 R	20	444
Wilkinson, Anna Rebecca	Moreland, John H.	21 AUG 1879	13	328
Wilkinson, Ella M.	Augell, George B.	02 FEB 1882	16	222
Wilkinson, Estella	Tibbals, Ralph C.	18 APR 1881	15	216
Wilkinson, Martha L.	Harvey, John B.	24 OCT 1882 R	17	086
Wilkinson, William H.	Green, Annie G.	23 MAY 1878 R	12	058
Wilkison, Charles C.	Bury, Mary I.	16 APR 1878 R	12	007
Wilks, Joseph	Mason, Carrie	24 DEC 1880 L	15	123
Willard, Alice R.	Barclay, Joseph J.	24 SEP 1884	19	266
Willard, George	Stewart, Carrie	27 JUN 1883 R	18	014
Willard, George F.	Donnell, Emma	08 AUG 1882	16	473
Willard, George F.B.	Vedder, H. Adda	26 DEC 1883 R	18	343
Willard, Lewis	Dangerfield, Eliza A.	14 AUG 1884	19	188
Willenbucher, Wm. Chris.	Rakeman, Agnes	27 NOV 1884 R	19	408
Willers, William	Roth, Frances	05 JUN 1878 L	12	086
Willet, Virginia Frances	Pickrell, James R.	05 AUG 1885	20	353
Willett, Ada F.	Thorowgood, W.J.	28 APR 1881	15	281
Willett, Ellen	Gibson, Peter	12 JUL 1879 R	13	279
Willett, George B.	Kidwell, Jennie E.	28 MAR 1883	17	364
Willett, Henrietta Virginia	Stephens, Judson Williams Wade	11 JUN 1879	13	228
Willett, Mary C.	Robinson, Samuel R.	18 DEC 1881 R	16	138
Willett, Mary E.	Loehr, J. Herman	28 JUL 1880 R	14	377
Willett, Robert E.	King, Lulu	18 MAR 1884 L	18	474
Wiley, Charles F.	Townley, Minnie S.	09 APR 1878 R	11	412
William, Hatty	Scott, Robert	29 AUG 1878 R	12	186
William, Henry A.	Beckman, Elizabeth	09 JUL 1883	18	040
William, James	Matthews, Annie	05 FEB 1878 R	11	317
William, Lucy	Ennis, Peter T.	21 FEB 1878 R	11	356
William, Paul	Kaiser, Pauline	15 JAN 1880 L	14	108
William, Pinkey	Norman, Christopher	20 DEC 1877 R	11	246
Williams, Agnes	Greenfield, James	07 MAR 1882 R	16	268
Williams, Albert	Johnson, Laura	11 NOV 1880 L	15	091
Williams, Alice	Armes, Aaron	17 APR 1878 L	12	010
Williams, Alice	Davis, John	26 APR 1880 L	14	237
Williams, Alice	Barnes, William	17 FEB 1885 L	20	075
Williams, Alice A.	Hunter, Edward B.	31 MAY 1883 L	17	471
Williams, Allen	Perry, Ida	11 AUG 1879 L	13	315
Williams, Anderson	Diggs, Annie	18 DEC 1884	19	470
Williams, Andrew	Grant, Maria	26 APR 1883 R	17	416
Williams, Andrew J.	Holt, Martha A.	29 NOV 1882 R	17	160
Williams, Ann E.	Bryant, George W.	30 OCT 1882 L	17	101
Williams, Anna Brown	Higgins, John deBree	07 FEB 1884 R	18	412
Williams, Anna E.	Jones, Benjamin A.	29 NOV 1883	18	280
Williams, Annie	Carroll, David	16 AUG 1877 R	11	054
Williams, Annie	Donaldson, Fillmore	23 DEC 1879 R	14	067
Williams, Annie	Gary, James	21 JUN 1879 R	13	242
Williams, Annie	Spriggs, James H.	09 JUN 1880 L	14	313
Williams, Annie	Shane, Franklin	01 MAY 1883 L	17	424
Williams, Annie	Pitcher, Edward	01 OCT 1885 R	20	448
Williams, Annie E.	Murdock, David B.	20 JAN 1885 L	20	028
Williams, Annie Eliza	Mouldin, David	02 MAR 1882	16	261
Williams, Annie Lee	Lightfoot, William	20 MAY 1882 R	16	369
Williams, Annie V.	Amidon, James M.	15 SEP 1880	14	447
Williams, Anthony	Dutch, Decy	06 FEB 1879	13	049
Williams, Augustus	Green, Caroline	17 DEC 1880 L	15	108

Williams, Augustus	Boarman, Elizabeth	20 DEC 1883 L	18	330
Williams, Benjamin F.	Tucker, Mary	12 SEP 1878 R	12	217
Williams, Bettie	Forbes, Dennis	28 OCT 1880	15	002
Williams, Bettie E.	Stewart, Thomas E.	20 MAR 1884 L	18	478
Williams, Betty	Robinson, Gabriel	08 AUG 1877 L	11	045
Williams, Beverly D.	Brown, Jane R.	12 DEC 1882	17	180
Williams, Beverly W.	Shermans, Lenora C.	13 SEP 1884	19	244
Williams, Buenavista	Kuhn, Richard P.	03 MAR 1880	14	172
Williams, Caleb	Gibson, Lizzie	29 JAN 1878	11	318
Williams, Caroline C.	Gally, Joseph E.	04 DEC 1877	11	216
Williams, Carrie L.V.	Kirmamon, Jacob H.	15 JAN 1885 L	20	020
Williams, Catherine	Beckett, Frank	03 AUG 1880	14	385
Williams, Catherine	Nolan, John	02 JUL 1885 L	20	307
Williams, Charles	Wolston, Lucy	08 DEC 1879 R	14	026
Williams, Charles	Stevenson, Sarah E.	30 JUN 1881	15	383
Williams, Charles	Sullivan, Julia	11 FEB 1882 L	16	236
Williams, Charles E.	Schaeffer, Ida Louise	16 JUN 1885	20	274
Williams, Charles G.	Quigley, Mary E.	30 SEP 1879 R	13	392
Williams, Charles H.	Claxton, Mary F.	12 AUG 1880	14	383
Williams, Charles H.	Jackson, Eliza	20 FEB 1884 L	18	433
Williams, Charles H.	Taylor, Annie E.	15 MAR 1885	20	115
Williams, Charles Henry	Gray, Julia Ann	22 DEC 1881 R	16	147
Williams, Charles N.	Robb, Clara	22 AUG 1884 L	19	204
Williams, Charles Phelps	Riley, Juliet Marie	26 APR 1883 R	17	412
Williams, Charlotte	Colston, William	11 JUL 1880	14	355
Williams, Clara E.	Ellis, George W.	13 AUG 1884	19	183
Williams, Cornelius	Steward, Emily	21 OCT 1879	13	435
Williams, Cornelius F.	Ridgeley, Ida	04 OCT 1883	18	170
Williams, David G.	Smith, Fanny F.	25 MAR 1885 R	20	131
Williams, Dennis	Pollock, Virginia, Mrs.	23 NOV 1882 L	17	145
Williams, Dora	Boston, Eugene	01 OCT 1885 L	20	453
Williams, Ed	Battle, Annie	20 DEC 1879 L	14	060
Williams, Edith C.	Brockwell, Roselle	29 SEP 1885 R	20	445
Williams, Edmonia	Hilbrandt, Alonzo E.	13 NOV 1877	11	180
Williams, Edward	Williams, Margaret	28 MAY 1881 R	15	298
Williams, Edward	Hawkins, Barbara	17 MAR 1881 R	15	228
Williams, Edward	Young, Emma	06 SEP 1883 L	18	116
Williams, Edward	Griffin, Annie	22 MAY 1884	19	035
Williams, Effie	Laub, Francis A.	04 FEB 1880	14	136
Williams, Elijah M.	Ward, Bettie	18 APR 1878 R	12	011
Williams, Eliza	Henson, William Henry	29 MAY 1878	12	074
Williams, Eliza	Ogleton, John	04 APR 1878 L	11	407
Williams, Eliza	Coleman, Charles	05 SEP 1882 L	17	006
Williams, Eliza Coleman	Butler, Simon	29 AUG 1880 R	14	420
Williams, Eliza E., Mrs.	Raddick, Archibald DeG.	16 NOV 1880 R	14	328
Williams, Elizabeth	Jones, Augustus	21 AUG 1879 R	13	329
Williams, Elizabeth	Poindexter, James Green	01 JUN 1882 L	16	387
Williams, Ella F.	Hoover, Andrew B.F.	11 DEC 1882 L	17	178
Williams, Ellen	Young, Thomas	01 JUL 1880 R	14	337
Williams, Ellen	Tinney, James Andrew	15 OCT 1885	20	491
Williams, Elzie	Jackson, Maria	02 JUN 1881 R	15	338
Williams, Emery W., Rev.	Chase, Ella V.	05 DEC 1882 R	17	167
Williams, Emma	Weems, Benjamin	31 JAN 1882 R	16	205
Williams, Emma	Smith, David	03 APR 1883 L	17	376
Williams, Emma	Dodson, Edwatd	27 JUN 1885 L	20	298
Williams, Emma F.	Shepperson, James S.	04 SEP 1879 L	13	351
Williams, Emma M.	Hodges, William H.	01 DEC 1880 L	15	078
Williams, Ernestine F.	Terflinger, George W.	17 MAY 1881 R	15	311

D.C. Marriage Records Index, June 28, 1877 to October 19, 1885   501

Williams, Fannie M.	Potter, John William	18 SEP 1884 L	19	260
Williams, Fanny	Payne, James	23 DEC 1884 L	19	480
Williams, Fanzy	Alton, Ann	17 MAR 1880	14	181
Williams, Flora Nettie	Grumley, Edward Clark	01 JUL 1883	18	027
Williams, Frank	Francis, Mary Ann	07 JUL 1882 R	16	362
Williams, George	Reynolds, Elizabeth	11 DEC 1879	14	043
Williams, George	Mateer, Annie E., Mrs.	12 JAN 1880 R	17	4077
Williams, George A.	Beaude, Julia	20 JUN 1878 L	12	107
Williams, George A.	Pistorio, Josephine	31 DEC 1880 L	15	134
Williams, George Edward	Martin, Emma Catharine	21 JUL 1883	18	055
Williams, Gertie	Peters, Rudolph	03 DEC 1879 R	14	022
Williams, Hannah	Juna, Joshua	03 JAN 1878	11	276
Williams, Harriet	Brown, John H.	26 MAY 1881	15	323
Williams, Harriet E.	Warner, Henry W.	12 NOV 1881 R	16	071
Williams, Hattie Belle	Hutchings, John Booker	01 JUL 1880 R	14	345
Williams, Henrietta	Garner, Henry	05 OCT 1877 R	11	123
Williams, Henrietta	Lee, James Alexander	17 FEB 1880 R	14	150
Williams, Henry	Wood, Ann	27 MAR 1878 R	11	394
Williams, Henry	Walker, Louisa	16 SEP 1879 L	13	373
Williams, Henry	Addision, Lizzie	03 NOV 1881	16	055
Williams, Henry	Lewis, Kate	15 NOV 1884 L	19	383
Williams, Henry A.	Logan, Mary M.	23 NOV 1883 R	18	264
Williams, Hester Eliza	Albee, Henry Worsle	04 FEB 1880 R	14	135
Williams, Horace W.	Toler, Lucilia	15 MAY 1879	13	187
Williams, Ida	Robey, John	25 JUN 1881 R	15	379
Williams, Isaac	Weems, Annie	12 JUL 1880	14	358
Williams, Isabella	Hackley, William H.	22 JUL 1880 L	14	373
Williams, J. Hale	Houston, Fanny S.	28 SEP 1878 R	12	247
Williams, Jacob	Young, Annie	30 AUG 1877	11	062
Williams, James	Grice, Josephine	22 NOV 1877 R	11	199
Williams, James	Talbert, Rosie	17 JUN 1879	13	235
Williams, James	West, Ella	05 NOV 1881 L	16	063
Williams, James	Park, Ella	14 JUN 1882 L	16	410
Williams, James	Thomas, Mary	27 AUG 1883 L	18	100
Williams, James	Shepherd, Lucelia Helen	28 FEB 1884	18	451
Williams, James H.	Harris, Alberta	10 JUN 1885 L	20	266
Williams, James R.	Thomas, Mary E.	20 DEC 1884 L	19	474
Williams, James S.	Rennoe, Fannie E.	17 JUN 1884	19	086
Williams, Jefferson	Truman, Mary	28 MAY 1879 L	13	208
Williams, Jennie	Ripperger, Edward W.	03 DEC 1879 L	14	026
Williams, Jesse	Combes, Alice	04 MAY 1879 R	13	172
Williams, John	Johnson, Eliza	26 AUG 1877 R	11	062
Williams, John	Hiltz, Maggie	24 APR 1878 L	12	022
Williams, John	Magruder, Maria	04 SEP 1879	13	351
Williams, John	Anderson, Ellen	28 OCT 1879 L	13	447
Williams, John	Selvy, Sarah Ross	15 APR 1880 R	14	225
Williams, John	Butler, Harriet, Mrs.	10 MAR 1881 R	15	187
Williams, John	Smith, Emma	27 DEC 1881 L	16	163
Williams, John	Clark, Sarah	28 DEC 1882 L	17	222
Williams, John	Carter, Polly [Dickson]	05 FEB 1883 R	17	290
Williams, John	McNally, Rachel	30 MAY 1885 L	20	248
Williams, John Edward	Walker, Malvina	22 JUL 1877	11	029
Williams, John Edward	Dodson, Sarah	25 OCT 1881	16	042
Williams, John F.	Brown, Maggie	07 JUL 1885 L	20	313
Williams, John H.	Parker, Rebecca	22 JUL 1879 L	13	289
Williams, John H.	Brown, Mattie L.	03 JAN 1881 R	15	135
Williams, John H.	Warfield, Catherine D.	01 JUL 1882	16	431
Williams, John H.	Carter, Elizabeth	02 MAY 1883 L	17	426

Williams, John L.	Waters, Buena V.	13 DEC 1883	18	314
Williams, John M.	Armstrong, Jennie B.	04 SEP 1877	11	075
Williams, John M.	Herold, Mary A., Mrs.	02 APR 1878	11	403
Williams, John R.	Oden, Hanna	20 SEP 1878	12	218
Williams, John S.	Dilber, Lavinia	02 AUG 1883	18	005
Williams, John S.	Winfield, Nellie	04 MAY 1885 L	20	205
Williams, John T.	Donaldson, Ida N.	10 FEB 1880 R	14	140
Williams, John W.	Miner, Georgianna	06 MAY 1884	18	548
Williams, John W.	Miner, Georgianna	06 MAY 1884 R	19	003
Williams, Joseph	Livingstone, Catherine A.	14 DEC 1880 R	15	095
Williams, Joseph	Grayson, Eliza	23 NOV 1881 R	16	092
Williams, Joseph	Thomas, Mary	01 FEB 1883 L	17	285
Williams, Joseph	Gosham, Virginia	24 SEP 1883 L	18	148
Williams, Joseph C.	Jackson, Lucy	22 AUG 1882	16	491
Williams, Joseph James	Roberts, Isabella	04 JUL 1885	20	310
Williams, Josephine	Washington, James O.	02 SEP 1879	13	347
Williams, Julia	Johnson, John	30 JUL 1877	11	015
Williams, Julia	Mines, William Parker	01 AUG 1878 R	12	155
Williams, Julia	Archer, Henry S.	19 AUG 1885 R	20	378
Williams, Julia A.	Johnson, Logan	11 AUG 1880 R	14	387
Williams, Kate L.	White, William F.	27 OCT 1880	15	017
Williams, Katie	Washington, Will	14 FEB 1884 L	18	426
Williams, Laura	Marlow, Charles	18 JUL 1878	12	142
Williams, Laura	Benson, Clarence	30 MAR 1879 R	13	114
Williams, Laura	Columbus, Archibald C.	31 MAY 1882 R	16	385
Williams, Laura	Nelson, Harry	23 DEC 1882	17	204
Williams, Laura	Cremmer, Nelson	04 JAN 1885 R	20	002
Williams, Laura B.	Price, Francis	11 SEP 1878 L	12	212
Williams, Lena	Diggs, Thomas A.	01 APR 1884 L	18	488
Williams, Letitia B.	Thomas, Wm. T.	08 NOV 1883	18	226
Williams, Lettie	Cissel, Charles H.	29 SEP 1881 R	15	504
Williams, Lewis	Fisher, Amanda	13 AUG 1885 L	20	369
Williams, Lizzie	Thuston, Jno.	20 JUL 1880	14	359
Williams, Lizzie	Lucas, Henry	23 DEC 1884 L	19	482
Williams, Louisa	Warren, Thomas	07 FEB 1880 L	14	142
Williams, Louisa	Harris, John W.	06 AUG 1883 L	18	075
Williams, Louisa Frances	Washington, Charles L.	30 AUG 1877	11	072
Williams, Louraine	Schaffer, John	05 SEP 1882 L	17	005
Williams, Lucy	King, Alfred	26 JUN 1882 R	16	425
Williams, Ludwell	Shorter, Amelia	07 JAN 1885 L	20	007
Williams, Lylie H.	Cowie, Fred G.	16 NOV 1880 L	15	050
Williams, M. Margaret	Posey, Isaac H.	28 JUN 1882 L	16	429
Williams, Maggie Brown	Calvert, Charles Washington	10 FEB 1880 R	14	146
Williams, Malvina	Dogans, John	15 JAN 1880 L	14	106
Williams, Margaret	Williams, Edward	28 MAY 1881 R	15	298
Williams, Martha	Harris, Wesley	20 JUN 1878 L	12	108
Williams, Martha	Brown, Robert	07 APR 1881	15	251
Williams, Martha	Levels, James Henry	07 MAR 1881 R	15	217
Williams, Martha	Tupper, Silas	13 JAN 1881	15	147
Williams, Martha A.	Washington, Joseph S.	29 OCT 1883 R	18	182
Williams, Martha Custis	Carter, Samuel Powh., Capt.	03 OCT 1877	11	118
Williams, Martha Eliz. Bell	Chandler, Richard	19 FEB 1880 R	14	160
Williams, Martha M.	Steptowe, Alfred C.	14 FEB 1884	18	423
Williams, Mary	Tyler, Henry	03 APR 1879 L	13	126
Williams, Mary	Brandon, William	13 MAY 1880 R	14	218
Williams, Mary	Smith, Jerry	17 AUG 1881 L	15	450
Williams, Mary	Holmes, Washington	20 DEC 1882 L	17	198
Williams, Mary	Shaw, Thomas E.	05 APR 1883 R	17	378

Williams, Mary	Garner, Moten	02 MAR 1884 R	18	453
Williams, Mary	Williams, Willie	29 SEP 1884	19	273
Williams, Mary	Gundaker, Samuel W.	27 JAN 1885 R	20	015
Williams, Mary A.	Herbert, Nathan Francis	21 DEC 1882 R	17	200
Williams, Mary C.	Johnson, Wesley S.	23 APR 1878 L	12	019
Williams, Mary E.	Harris, William T.	23 NOV 1882 L	17	147
Williams, Mary E.	Smith, Frank	16 MAR 1882 L	16	280
Williams, Mary E.	Stewart, James Robert	24 JUL 1884 L	19	158
Williams, Mary E.	Hutchinson, David	16 MAY 1885 L	20	224
Williams, Mary Ildergerte	Ballauff, Robert Benedict	05 NOV 1884 L	19	363
Williams, Mary L., Mrs.	Davison, Edward W.	23 NOV 1881	16	097
Williams, Mary Langdonia Va.	Jones, Wm. F.	07 JUL 1881 L	15	395
Williams, Matilda	Talbot, William	08 FEB 1878 L	11	334
Williams, Matilda A.	Cottrell, Willard M.	29 OCT 1884	19	345
Williams, Matthew H.	Linquist, Charlotte M.	27 MAY 1880 R	14	289
Williams, Mima	Granger, Robert	25 SEP 1884	19	270
Williams, Monterey T.	Herbert, William E.	04 DEC 1883	18	294
Williams, Morris	Stevenson, Millie	03 MAR 1884 L	18	456
Williams, Nancy	West, William	15 JUL 1880 L	14	361
Williams, Nellie S.	Lewis, Samuel	28 DEC 1880 R	15	094
Williams, Patrick	Johnson, Nettie	14 JUL 1885 L	20	325
Williams, Paxton	Dixon, Nancy	04 JUL 1883 R	18	034
Williams, Peter	Parker, Susie	17 FEB 1881 R	15	193
Williams, Philip	Harris, Emma	20 MAY 1878 R	12	045
Williams, Philip	Johnson, Emma	07 FEB 1884 L	18	416
Williams, Rege	Sparks, Ella E.	09 APR 1879 R	13	132
Williams, Richard	Holly, Mary	05 DEC 1882 R	17	168
Williams, Richard	Thornton, Anna	14 FEB 1883 R	17	307
Williams, Richard F.	Beckett, Marcellina S.	29 JAN 1880 R	14	125
Williams, Richard Thos.	Holt, Ida Virginia	02 JUL 1879 R	13	264
Williams, Samuel	Washington, Ella	25 APR 1879 L	13	160
Williams, Samuel L.	Virts, Emma M.	08 MAR 1882 R	16	270
Williams, Sarah	Warner, William	16 JUL 1877 L	11	022
Williams, Sarah	Blake, William Reed	30 MAR 1880 R	14	195
Williams, Sarah	Johnson, Isaac	06 JUL 1882	16	441
Williams, Sarah	Mattingly, Henry	13 OCT 1883	18	188
Williams, Sarah E.	Nord, Alexander G.	01 MAY 1878 R	12	030
Williams, Sarah E.	Howard, William	18 APR 1881 L	15	260
Williams, Sarah J.	James, John R.	08 SEP 1881 R	15	478
Williams, Solomon	Brandon, Virginia	26 JAN 1882 L	16	212
Williams, Susan	Johns, John H.	27 OCT 1883 L	18	219
Williams, Taylor	Lucas, Eliza	06 SEP 1882 R	17	004
Williams, Theodore	Miner, Sarah	27 APR 1881	15	279
Williams, Thomas	Morris, Frances	10 APR 1879 L	13	136
Williams, Thomas	Woodyer, Mary	06 DEC 1880 L	15	084
Williams, Thomas Burr	McIntosh, Mary Ruth	17 JUL 1877	11	023
Williams, Thomas W.	Bryan, Ella	16 AUG 1884 L	19	190
Williams, Watkins H.	Power, Ann L.	16 DEC 1878 L	12	383
Williams, Welford	Plater, Sarah	20 DEC 1877 L	11	251
Williams, William	Johnson, Mary	17 SEP 1877 L	11	096
Williams, William	Johnson, Harriet	30 NOV 1878 L	12	356
Williams, William	Gassaway, Julia Ann	31 MAY 1881	15	243
Williams, William Alber	Jenkins, Sarah Virginia	27 OCT 1880 R	15	016
Williams, William E.	Houston, Ella G.	05 SEP 1882 R	17	003
Williams, William H.	Rosengun, Lena	11 DEC 1878	12	374
Williams, William H.	Ford, Alice	14 NOV 1883 R	18	246
Williams, William H.	Jackson, Mary A.	12 MAR 1884 R	18	467
Williams, Willie	Williams, Mary	29 SEP 1884	19	273

Williams, Willis	Terry, Ella	22 MAR 1881 L	15	235
Williams, Wilson	Cox, Susan	14 NOV 1878 R	12	180
Williams, Winnie	Barber, Allan	03 FEB 1882 L	16	224
Williams, Winston W.	Green, Betty A.L.	09 NOV 1882 R	17	122
Williamson, Alexander	Beach, Laura C.	26 DEC 1884 L	19	493
Williamson, Alice	Grooves, Lemuel	18 JUN 1880	14	327
Williamson, Charles H.	Dean, Willie K.	15 NOV 1880	15	048
Williamson, Cora Ann	Middleton, Robert Levi	19 DEC 1882 R	17	188
Williamson, Corinne	Tripp, Dwight Kasson	20 JAN 1881 R	15	156
Williamson, Ella	Clark, James	07 FEB 1883 R	17	299
Williamson, J. Rosa	Kirk, Sumner S.	01 JUL 1884	19	113
Williamson, J.B.M.	True, Alice Marian	15 MAY 1884	19	024
Williamson, J.C.	Eilenberger, Fannie R.	10 NOV 1880	15	041
Williamson, Joanna	Moffat, Daniel J.	17 JUN 1879 R	13	235
Williamson, John T.	Jones, Fannie E.	19 NOV 1879 R	13	495
Williamson, Julia	Brown, Frederick	24 JUL 1883 R	18	059
Williamson, L. Cabell	Van Vleck, Almeria S.	03 MAR 1880	14	172
Williamson, M.V.	Rutherford, J.A.	22 MAY 1879	13	202
Williamson, Mary	Petitt, Norman	15 DEC 1880	15	097
Williamson, Samuel Stuart	Perry, Mary Eliza	20 JUN 1882 R	16	420
Williamson, William A.	Dorsey, Clara V.	15 NOV 1881 R	16	075
Williard, Mary Ella	Paxton, William	03 DEC 1884 R	19	436
Willie, William W.	Chaney, Belle	25 JUL 1885 L	20	341
Willis, Agnes	Lee, George	05 FEB 1880 R	14	134
Willis, Alice J.	Hillery, Lewis W.	12 JUL 1880 L	14	356
Willis, Anna	Johnson, Reverdy C.	08 MAY 1879	13	182
Willis, Bettie	Barnes, William	11 JUN 1884 L	19	078
Willis, Blucher	Bullard, Maggie M.	25 OCT 1882	17	095
Willis, Charles B.	Robinson, Fannie B.	06 MAR 1879 R	13	093
Willis, Charles S.	Tibbetts, Nellie M.	02 OCT 1878	12	249
Willis, Cornelius D.	Sears, Carry M.	03 SEP 1885 R	20	398
Willis, Ella L.	Olmstead, Meiancthon A.	27 DEC 1882	17	214
Willis, Frances	Vass, Joseph	04 SEP 1877 L	11	076
Willis, George W.	Dorsey, Susan Annie	17 AUG 1885 L	20	374
Willis, Henry M.	Fowler, Fannie J.	07 OCT 1885 R	20	461
Willis, Jane	Davis, Philip	12 JUL 1877 L	11	017
Willis, Jennie F.	Vaughan, Willis H.	07 FEB 1884 R	18	415
Willis, Johanna	Ambush, Samuel	24 FEB 1880 R	14	164
Willis, John	Ellis, Betsey	26 AUG 1878	12	180
Willis, Lizzie	Chew, Robert	07 FEB 1884 L	18	415
Willis, Lucy	Noel, Joseph	30 JUN 1880 R	14	340
Willis, Maggie	Thomas, John Wesley	03 JUL 1879	13	267
Willis, Maggie	Taliaferro, Jacob	15 APR 1885 L	20	167
Willis, Malinda C.	Mundy, William H.	05 APR 1882 R	16	302
Willis, Mariah E.	Ritch, Henry	22 NOV 1883	18	267
Willis, Mary	Crockett, Alfred	16 JUN 1880 L	14	324
Willis, Peter D.	Pleasants, Evie J.	23 OCT 1880 R	15	010
Willis, Rosa	Thomas, Lemuel	24 DEC 1879 L	14	072
Willis, Sallie	Reynaldo, James	04 NOV 1884	19	357
Willis, Severene Elizabeth	Sorrell, Thomas A.	02 FEB 1885 L	20	048
Willis, Susan J.	Tenney, John E.	14 FEB 1884 L	18	424
Willis, Thomas	Zucker, Alcinda	27 APR 1885 R	20	190
Willis, William A.	Parker, Henrietta	05 MAY 1881 R	15	294
Willis, William J.	Bond, Carrie E.	14 MAY 1885	20	222
Williss, Rodolph	Cavis, Ada P.	27 SEP 1882	17	039
Willmore, Mary S.	Worthington, Horace	13 JUN 1882	16	405
Willoughby, Thaddeus D.	Tolman, Alice	01 OCT 1885	20	451
Wills, Caroline W.	Field, John M.	29 JAN 1880	14	126

Wills, Henry	Hawkins, Ella	27 DEC 1883	18	351
Wills, India E.	Page, George F.	01 JUL 1879 R	13	259
Wills, John E.	Raines, Eliza	15 JUL 1884	19	139
Wills, Samuel	Brooke, Susan	10 SEP 1884 L	19	239
Wills, Sarah	Dent, James H.	07 JUN 1883 L	17	484
Wills, Walter H.	Henry, Norma W., Mrs.	07 JAN 1882 R	16	185
Willson, John E.	Borland, Lillian B.	03 JUN 1885 R	20	251
Willson, Mary W.	Hollingshead, John S.	07 JAN 1879 R	13	008
Wilmer, Harry	Green, Lucy	14 AUG 1884 L	19	187
Wilmer, Katie	Little, Frank T.	11 FEB 1880 R	14	146
Wilmouth, Delphine	Brown, Harrison Bradley	19 OCT 1883 L	18	203
Wilson, Adaline Hester	Brooks, Henry	17 SEP 1884 L	19	254
Wilson, Addie C.	Turner, J.A.D.	16 APR 1885 R	20	172
Wilson, Agnes	Peed, James	08 APR 1883 R	17	386
Wilson, Alfred	Moore, M.S.	16 SEP 1884	19	233
Wilson, Alice Jane	Dodd, Richard Joseph	28 JUL 1885 R	20	344
Wilson, Almira G.	Ambler, Charles F.	16 JUN 1881 R	15	363
Wilson, Amelia	Jackson, W.H.	30 OCT 1879	13	454
Wilson, Amelia	Harris, John	26 JUL 1880 L	14	375
Wilson, Andrew	Richardson, Ocella	25 MAR 1881	15	239
Wilson, Annie	Lamkins, Wilson	12 DEC 1883 L	18	310
Wilson, Annie	Morgan, William H.	08 NOV 1883 L	18	243
Wilson, Annie F.	Alber, William	01 AUG 1878 L	12	155
Wilson, Annie G.	Bell, William R.	13 MAY 1880	14	271
Wilson, Augusta	Gill, Levi C.	05 FEB 1879 R	13	045
Wilson, Belle	Harris, William James	15 APR 1885 R	20	168
Wilson, Benjamin	Johnson, Georgiana	21 AUG 1881	15	442
Wilson, Burnet	Anderson, Pauline	08 JUL 1884	19	128
Wilson, Carrie [Ware]	Marshal, John	25 JUN 1884 R	19	102
Wilson, Carry	Ware, Townley	01 OCT 1879 R	13	396
Wilson, Charles C.	Buxton, Lillian B.	25 DEC 1880	15	124
Wilson, Charles Harrison	Doren, Margaret	30 MAR 1880 R	14	203
Wilson, Charles Henry	McGruder, Susan	14 OCT 1878	12	271
Wilson, Christiana	Hawkins, George	16 JUN 1883 L	17	497
Wilson, Corianthea H.E.	Shoemaker, George W.	02 AUG 1881 R	15	430
Wilson, Cornelia Marie Keller	Mason, John Sanford	08 MAR 1881 R	15	218
Wilson, David Russell	Reddick, Mary Ellen (Dean)	29 DEC 1884 R	19	496
Wilson, E.J.	Everett, Mary L.	07 AUG 1883 L	18	078
Wilson, Edward	Lewis, Hattie	17 JUL 1878 L	12	138
Wilson, Eleanor Caldwell	Borden, William N.	05 MAR 1885 R	20	097
Wilson, Elias	Allen, Marina	08 OCT 1880 L	14	483
Wilson, Elias	Hunter, Harriet	26 NOV 1884 R	19	421
Wilson, Eliza	Irving, Nelson	13 OCT 1885 R	20	478
Wilson, Elizabeth P.	Parker, John B.	23 JAN 1879 R	13	033
Wilson, Ella S.	Miller, George W.	21 JAN 1880 R	14	117
Wilson, Ellen	Epps, Harry	19 JUN 1878 R	12	105
Wilson, Ellen, Mrs.	Bell, James, Corp.	16 MAY 1881 L	15	310
Wilson, Ellen T.	Fitzgerald, Michael E.	13 APR 1884	18	505
Wilson, Emma D.	Watt, James Bell	27 SEP 1883 R	18	155
Wilson, Eva E.	Hamlin, Theodore R.	21 JUN 1881	15	367
Wilson, Evelina	Carter, Robert	25 MAR 1880 R	14	196
Wilson, Frank	Bell, Mary F.S.	10 JUL 1879	13	278
Wilson, Frank	Carroll, Mary E.	07 FEB 1883	17	295
Wilson, Frank L.	Jamison, Anna A.	13 JAN 1880 L	14	103
Wilson, George W.	Hurdle, Lulu May	21 AUG 1884	19	202
Wilson, Georgie, Mrs.	Keleher, Timothy J.	08 DEC 1881 R	16	122
Wilson, Hamilton M.	Holmes, Mary A.	08 DEC 1881 L	16	122
Wilson, Hattie A.	Joyce, George W.	25 FEB 1882 R	16	259

D.C. Marriage Records Index, June 28, 1877 to October 19, 1885

Wilson, Henry Louis	Miller, Catherine	25 MAY 1885 R	20	239
Wilson, Ignatius	Want, Admonia	05 JUL 1883	18	036
Wilson, Jacob F.	Gockeler, Emma	04 JUN 1884 R	19	059
Wilson, Jacob H.	Warren, Mary	15 MAY 1880 R	14	271
Wilson, James Charles	Young, Virginia Robinson	18 NOV 1880 R	15	057
Wilson, James P.	Edelin, Emma Florence	15 FEB 1879 R	13	062
Wilson, James P.	Middleton, Kittie V.	12 JUN 1885 R	20	272
Wilson, James R.	Marrs, Carrie E.	26 NOV 1884	19	418
Wilson, James W.	Hartley, Leanna	27 SEP 1881 R	15	497
Wilson, Jennie Boyd	Birmingham, William Otis	31 MAR 1885 R	20	138
Wilson, Jesse H.	Woodward, Lizzie A.	19 DEC 1877 R	11	245
Wilson, John	Day, Julia	20 FEB 1878	11	349
Wilson, John	Fields, Rebecca	28 FEB 1883	17	326
Wilson, John Edwin	Erickson, Lucy	07 APR 1885 R	20	152
Wilson, John Francis	Hall, Alice	03 JUL 1879 R	13	250
Wilson, John H.	Browning, Titia	01 MAR 1882 L	16	262
Wilson, John S.	Brown, Mary	09 NOV 1882 R	17	114
Wilson, John William	Witmer, Clara Sabilla	07 FEB 1879 R	13	051
Wilson, Joseph L.	Mann, Sarah E.	29 DEC 1884 R	19	497
Wilson, Joseph Wilson	Lawrence, Nina Eliz.	03 JUN 1885 R	20	252
Wilson, Joshua J.	Gandy, Mary Bell	21 AUG 1884 L	19	201
Wilson, Julia	Johnson, Daniel D.	05 SEP 1884	19	229
Wilson, Julius J.	Anderson, Alice	31 OCT 1878 L	12	301
Wilson, Katie	Wilkerson, Everick	19 OCT 1882 R	17	082
Wilson, Katy	Ellinger, George	29 AUG 1878 L	12	184
Wilson, Lavinia, Mrs.	Crumpton, John T.	03 FEB 1880 R	14	133
Wilson, Lillie Cora	Duvall, John William	16 FEB 1879	13	062
Wilson, Lucy Lee	Stoddard, Josiah C.	12 APR 1885	20	367
Wilson, Maggie	Jackson, Paul Ardean	30 DEC 1879 L	14	079
Wilson, Marcellus	Foley, Maggie	16 FEB 1878 L	11	343
Wilson, Martha	Nickens, Rodolph D.	09 AUG 1881 L	15	436
Wilson, Martha, Mrs.	Müller, Charles	15 MAY 1884 R	19	021
Wilson, Mary	Demaine, Henry	21 JAN 1880 R	14	114
Wilson, Mary	Jackson, Enoch	26 APR 1883 R	17	404
Wilson, Mary A.	Derricks, Waymon	19 APR 1881 L	15	262
Wilson, Mary E.	Bayliss, McElmer	31 JUL 1880 R	14	379
Wilson, Mary E.	Armstrong, George H.	30 APR 1885 R	20	199
Wilson, Mary Frances	Butler, John	15 APR 1885 L	20	169
Wilson, Morgan C.	Gray, Sarah	27 SEP 1877	11	110
Wilson, Morris	Milford, Eliza A.	07 MAR 1882	16	269
Wilson, Nora Lee	Johnson, William H.	06 DEC 1882 R	17	169
Wilson, Orrin S.	Dadmun, Elizabeth	19 DEC 1877 R	11	240
Wilson, Perry	Brond, Emilie	02 JUN 1885 R	20	283
Wilson, R.H.	Jackson, Jane	02 JUL 1884	19	113
Wilson, Robert	West, Susan A. Skinner	09 NOV 1880 R	15	038
Wilson, Robert	Potts, Mary Jane	09 JAN 1882 R	16	186
Wilson, Robert	Rogers, Lydia A.	06 DEC 1883 L	18	298
Wilson, Robert A.	Butler, Mary F.	16 MAR 1883	17	348
Wilson, Rosa L.	Blakey, William E.	12 JUN 1882 R	16	406
Wilson, Samuel Eston	Wyatt, Kate Harrison	22 SEP 1880 R	14	453
Wilson, Samuel S.	Andrews, Catherine R.	26 AUG 1882 L	16	494
Wilson, Solmon	Brady, Catherine	24 NOV 1881 L	16	097
Wilson, Sophia S.	Murray, Lewis W.	29 DEC 1881 L	16	169
Wilson, Susie	Shorter, Richard	16 AUG 1881 R	15	448
Wilson, Taylor	Harper, Georgianna C.	25 AUG 1883	18	092
Wilson, Thomas	Simms, Estella Virginia	24 DEC 1878 L	12	400
Wilson, Thomas	Monroe, Mary	24 APR 1879 R	13	157
Wilson, Thomas	Crompton, Alice	26 APR 1883 R	17	410

Wilson, Whitwell H.	Franklin, Jeannie Wood	17 AUG 1882 R	16	486
Wilson, William	Coombs, Sarah	21 JUN 1878 L	12	109
Wilson, William	Lyles, Alice	13 MAR 1879 R	13	098
Wilson, William	Hill, Charlotte	28 JUL 1879 L	13	296
Wilson, William	Bowman, Serena	06 NOV 1879	13	470
Wilson, William	Payne, Mary	12 OCT 1882 R	17	069
Wilson, William	Daniels, Harriet	12 JUN 1883 R	17	484
Wilson, William	Turner, Rebecca	12 JUN 1884 L	19	080
Wilson, William Henry	Green, Helen	26 JUL 1881 R	15	419
Wilson, William J.	Barnett, Alice M.	04 MAY 1882 L	16	349
Wilson, William L.	Cooper, Leah Virginia	28 APR 1884	18	539
Wilt, Jeremiah	Dyer, Martha A.	19 MAR 1883	17	350
Wiltberger, Charles H., Jr.	Massey, Mida Wilmot	01 DEC 1881 L	16	107
Wiltherger, Frank	Marden, Lillie	24 NOV 1884 L	19	406
Wimer, Augustus	Woody, Geraldine	14 AUG 1882	16	478
Wimmer, George	Leisher, Kate L.	06 MAR 1883 L	17	334
Wimsatt, William A.	Cleary, Florence Josephine	30 SEP 1879 R	13	393
Winans, William	Gray, Mary E. Alice	02 OCT 1879 R	13	401
Winbush, S.H.	Harris, Henrietta	19 AUG 1878 L	12	172
Winchester, John E.B.	King, Emma J.	04 OCT 1880 R	14	471
Winck, Louis	Eckhardt, Henrietta	21 APR 1881 R	15	260
Winckelman, Annie M.D.	Dyer, William Robert	30 NOV 1880 R	15	074
Winder, Annie Louisa	Robertson, Isaac Holborn	06 APR 1885 R	20	144
Winder, Charles Henry	Butler, Alice	26 MAR 1880 L	14	199
Windsor, Annie C.	Calvert, Dennis J.	20 JAN 1885 R	20	027
Windsor, Eugene	Ferguson, Fannie	10 NOV 1884 R	19	371
Windsor, Eva R.	Adams, Frank C.	20 NOV 1884 R	19	398
Windsor, John H.	Mitchell, Kate	21 DEC 1881 L	16	145
Windsor, Margaret A.	Kline, Peter	20 APR 1882	16	328
Windsor, Richard	Young, Annie	12 OCT 1883 L	18	189
Wine, Ollie Rebecca	Jett, George M.	26 JUN 1879 R	13	253
Wineberger, Sallie	Olive, Bunyan	01 JUL 1885 L	20	305
Wines, Ada Hise	Murphy, John	17 AUG 1881 L	15	450
Wines, Guy Woodworth	Mulliken, Martha Virginia	23 NOV 1881 L	16	093
Winfield, Annie E.	Raynor, Edward	11 NOV 1884	19	374
Winfield, Benjamin F.	Coats, Mary C.	06 FEB 1878 R	11	330
Winfield, Hennessey	Tyler, Matilda	10 MAY 1880 L	14	261
Winfield, John	Jordan, Mary F.	17 OCT 1878	12	274
Winfield, John	Jackson, Ellen	16 OCT 1884 L	19	315
Winfield, John Joseph	Glotzbach, Lizza	18 SEP 1883 L	18	138
Winfield, Martha	Baylor, William	18 FEB 1878	11	346
Winfield, Nellie	Williams, John S.	04 MAY 1885 L	20	205
Winfield, Robert	Norris, Matilda	21 DEC 1882 R	17	190
Winfrey, Rebecca	Burks, Charles	31 JUL 1877	11	035
Wingate, Carrie Dail	Joyce, Asa Addison	19 OCT 1882 R	17	081
Wingate, Oliver A.	Fisher, Mary B.	24 OCT 1882 L	17	089
Wingfield, Charles Louis	Worrell, Lee Alice	13 DEC 1884	19	456
Wingfield, Louise Violet	Cook, Theodore Freling	24 NOV 1881 R	16	096
Wingfield, Susan	Shelton, Dennis	18 JUN 1879	13	236
Winkler, Clara	Dent, Edward	09 APR 1883 R	17	386
Winkler, Mary E.	Collins, Thomas M.	09 AUG 1880 R	14	391
Winlock, William Crawford	Munroe, Alice Broom	02 JUN 1883 R	17	472
Winn, Elizabeth A.	Frost, Charles A.	13 AUG 1884	19	180
Winn, Hannah	Nicholas, Limus M.	14 AUG 1879 L	13	319
Winne, Annie	Elam, Daniel N.	17 JUL 1885	20	331
Winns, Lucinda	Ridout, Abraham	15 NOV 1883	18	255
Winsinger, William	Rumsey, Mary Katherine	24 FEB 1885 R	20	083
Winslow, Annie M.	Renshawe, John H.	15 APR 1878	12	005

Name	Spouse	Date	Vol	Page
Winslow, Francis	Patterson, Harriet	17 OCT 1881	16	025
Winslow, Frederick	Cooper, Mary	16 JUN 1879 L	13	233
Winslow, J.H.	Simms, Martha Ann	28 APR 1883 L	17	419
Winslow, James H.	Plummer, Elizabeth Jane	19 DEC 1877 L	11	246
Winslow, Jerry	Talliaferro, Matilda	18 OCT 1883 R	18	201
Winslow, William F.	Thompson, Emma	03 APR 1880	14	208
Winslow, Wm. Frederick	Buckner, Laura	06 AUG 1883	18	074
Winstead, M. Louise	Sturgeon, John F.	01 JUN 1881 R	15	335
Winston, Albert	Smith, Annie	19 MAR 1884 L	18	477
Winston, Frances Elizabeth	Tolson, Henson	03 MAY 1883	17	428
Winston, Isaac	Otis, Anna Maria	19 SEP 1882	17	026
Winston, Louisa	Ammons, Israel H.	10 OCT 1882 L	17	064
Winston, Mary	Lewis, William	26 JUN 1884 L	19	105
Winston, Matilda	Brown, Douglas	28 AUG 1879 R	13	343
Winston, Miles	Fisher, Rosalie	29 OCT 1880 R	15	021
Winston, William S.	Moor, Lizzie	11 NOV 1878 L	12	321
Winstrum, Christina	Dodson, Rufus H.	01 NOV 1882 R	17	104
Winter, Hattie	Stoddart, Joseph Kennard	27 JUN 1883	18	017
Winterhuth, Mary E.	Talbert, James J.	16 SEP 1879	13	372
Winters, Bernard M.	Bender, Lillie C.	05 JUN 1882 R	16	226
Winters, Charlotte	Hathman, Edward	13 SEP 1880 L	14	442
Winters, Elisabeth	Campbell, Archibald	06 OCT 1879 R	13	405
Winters, Humphreys	Clark, Martha	03 AUG 1880 L	14	385
Winters, Izetta	Dorsey, Wm. W.	12 NOV 1879 L	13	479
Winters, Mary A.	Harris, Joseph H.	25 FEB 1885	20	084
Winters, Rebecca	Pryor, Joseph	25 DEC 1884 R	19	480
Wirsching, Caspar	Schilling, Frederike Fielindas	17 JUN 1883 R	17	489
Wirtz, Matilda	Brunner, Samuel W.	20 JAN 1883 L	17	269
Wise, Albert M.	Hessian, Julia A.	19 OCT 1885 L	20	498
Wise, Bertha	Meyers, Solomon	08 JUL 1881 L	15	396
Wise, Caroline L.	Henry, John G.	18 DEC 1883	18	319
Wise, Catharine V.	Fegan, Hugh J.	18 FEB 1878 L	11	347
Wise, Charles	Boyd, Catharine	19 JUN 1884 L	19	094
Wise, Charles B.	Murphy, Hannah A.	06 OCT 1880 L	14	478
Wise, Charles E.	Meyer, Annie	16 FEB 1885 L	20	069
Wise, Charles W.	Walker, Leana	14 OCT 1880 L	14	495
Wise, Charlotte Everett	Hopkins, Archibald	14 NOV 1878 R	12	322
Wise, Clara Rose	Wrenn, Thomas J.	13 JUL 1885 L	20	322
Wise, Emma F.	Byrnes, Edward M.	21 AUG 1882 L	16	490
Wise, Henrietta	Nicholson, William	25 NOV 1884 R	19	400
Wise, Hester	Dowdy, Robert	14 MAR 1883 R	17	343
Wise, Hiram	Fry, Angelina	13 AUG 1884	18	509
Wise, James D.	Hunt, E. Blanche	14 FEB 1883	17	305
Wise, Janie	Wachter, Jacob W.	30 MAR 1879 R	13	117
Wise, Julia A.	Johnson, Robert	19 JUL 1880 R	14	368
Wise, Laura	Sheid, William R.	08 APR 1884 R	18	496
Wise, Lillie Lee	Balthis, French A.	19 SEP 1878 L	12	227
Wise, Nathan	Jordan, Alice	02 JUN 1879	13	176
Wise, Nellie P.	Partrick, Alfred W.	13 SEP 1882 R	17	017
Wise, Rosa J.	Bell, Thomas S.	04 OCT 1882 R	17	053
Wise, Sallie Ellen	Byrnes, Edward Malcolm	10 OCT 1878 R	12	264
Wise, Samuel C.	Knott, Margaret C.	02 JUN 1884 L	19	049
Wise, Thomas H.	Scott, Laura	26 SEP 1877 R	11	107
Wise, William	Cator, Annie M.	01 JUL 1880 L	14	343
Wise, William	Edwards, Ellen	23 NOV 1880	15	061
Wisely, Marsella	Crump, George D.	04 JUN 1880 L	14	306
Wiseman, Joseph B.	Lochte, Amelia	15 FEB 1882 R	16	242
Wiseman, Joseph B.	Coldensroth, Dora W.	21 FEB 1884 L	18	437

Wishart, William Wilson	Kimball, Helen Knight	19 MAR 1885 R	20	124
Wister, Philip	Ballenger, Maggie	15 MAY 1879 R	13	190
Witherbee, Walter E.	McSween, Mary	28 MAY 1878 L	12	069
Withers, Kittie E.	Lay, John A.	23 SEP 1885 R	20	437
Withers, Sheldon	Phillips, Susie	26 MAY 1881	15	329
Withers, Thomas G.	Lewis, Mary F., Mrs.	22 SEP 1880 R	14	456
Withington, Caroline F.	Clapp, William W.	01 FEB 1883	17	281
Witmer, A.H.	Stine, Roberta K.	30 OCT 1884	19	351
Witmer, Calvin	Kendall, Marie	13 MAY 1880 R	14	266
Witmer, Clara Sabilla	Wilson, John William	07 FEB 1879 R	13	051
Witters, S. Elizabeth	Stieff, John C.	27 FEB 1883 R	17	323
Wittmer, Fritz	Rest, Mary	06 MAY 1881 R	14	334
Wodehouse, Julia	Smith, William F.	16 DEC 1878 R	12	382
Wogonfield, Valentine C.	Krug, Mary Theresa	02 NOV 1881 R	16	058
Wohlfarth, George F.	Shattuck, Nettie F.	01 SEP 1883 L	18	107
Wohlforth, Edward S.	Vessey, Sarah	14 JUN 1883 L	17	492
Wolf, Florence A.	Gotthold, Frederick	12 JUN 1878	12	095
Wolf, Kate	McUlaff, Patrick	02 JAN 1878 L	11	290
Wolf, William	Vandrow, Margaret	06 DEC 1877 R	11	217
Wolfe, James M.	Cox, Jennie E.	25 MAY 1885 R	20	239
Wolfe, Jesse Hyatt	Hyatt, L. Dorcas	31 MAY 1878	12	078
Wolfe, Katie	Toomey, Daniel D.	24 JUL 1883 L	18	058
Wolff, Albert	Linde, Elise	20 OCT 1883	18	205
Wolff, Robert	Rhoads, Ida C.	31 DEC 1881 L	16	173
Wolford, Ann Maria	Paxton, Joseph	10 SEP 1884	19	238
Wolfraum, Louisa	Scheider, John	13 OCT 1879 L	13	416
Wolfrey, Victoria	Schoelkopf, Heinrich	07 OCT 1884	19	290
Wollard, William Spencer	Renshaw, Jennie N.	05 JAN 1883 R	17	282
Wolston, Lucy	Williams, Charles	08 DEC 1879 R	14	026
Woltz, Charles H.	Favill, Annie R.	02 JAN 1878	11	289
Woltz, India	Schooley, Henry Moore	10 JAN 1883 R	17	250
Wolz, Annie B.	Baumann, William C.	27 JUL 1879 R	13	294
Wonders, Andrew	Wiesemann, Lissie	13 JUL 1881	15	399
Wood, Agnes	Wells, John Edward	10 JAN 1878 R	11	298
Wood, Agnes E.	Lyons, Edgar E.	15 DEC 1879 R	14	049
Wood, Albert	Steward, Jannie	17 MAY 1884 L	19	026
Wood, Alice G. (Caton)	Guilford, Harry A.	30 DEC 1882 L	17	227
Wood, Ann	Williams, Henry	27 MAR 1878 R	11	394
Wood, Annie K.	Shepherd, Silas	07 JUN 1883 R	17	480
Wood, Arthur B.	Weeks, Margaret Reile	31 MAR 1879 R	12	412
Wood, Augustus	Wood, Jennie	01 SEP 1884 L	19	217
Wood, Carroll B.	Phillips, Mamie	01 SEP 1884 R	19	218
Wood, Catharine E.	Hazen, William P.C.	08 JAN 1878 R	11	295
Wood, Charles	Beall, Catherine	12 NOV 1877	11	179
Wood, Charles	Jordan, Jane	10 JAN 1884 L	18	373
Wood, Charles E.	Dixon, Effie V.	16 JAN 1884	18	381
Wood, Charles E.E.	Twiford, Fannie	04 APR 1879 R	13	128
Wood, Charles L.	Boyd, Lulie A.	05 MAR 1879	13	089
Wood, Charles M.	Day, Emma J.	15 JUN 1885 R	20	276
Wood, Charles W.	Miskell, Sarah F.	12 MAR 1885	20	109
Wood, Daniel M.	Johnson, Annie R.	27 DEC 1881	16	152
Wood, Edna	Gillen, John R.	30 NOV 1883 L	18	288
Wood, Edward	Klaumburg, Annie	08 APR 1878 R	11	409
Wood, Edward J.	Brown, Sarah E.	19 MAY 1881 R	15	317
Wood, Elizabeth	Gordon, Jerry	14 OCT 1878 R	12	284
Wood, Elizabeth Morton	Patch, Joseph	04 AUG 1877 R	11	041
Wood, Ella	Smith, William E.	10 OCT 1877	11	127
Wood, Ella	Dotson, John Wesley	17 NOV 1881 R	16	009

Wood, Fannie G.	Griggs, Charles A.	16 OCT 1881	16	027
Wood, Foster P.	McClellan, Lizzie E., Mrs.	31 MAY 1882	16	385
Wood, Frank	Taylor, Lizzie	14 MAR 1885 L	20	114
Wood, George	Long, Mary Jane	26 FEB 1881 L	15	204
Wood, George O.	Leary, Maggie E.	26 FEB 1884 L	18	444
Wood, George Thomas	Jenkins, Susannah	14 JUL 1877 R	11	012
Wood, Harry	Perry, Georgia	14 NOV 1877 L	11	184
Wood, Hattie E.	Brashears, James T.	20 FEB 1884	18	433
Wood, Ida M.	Ross, Thomas B.	28 MAY 1878 L	12	069
Wood, James Henry	Primus, Lucy	05 MAY 1884 R	19	008
Wood, Jennie	Wood, Augustus	01 SEP 1884 L	19	217
Wood, Jesse	Moulton, Emma	29 AUG 1878	12	185
Wood, John	Herbert, Henrietta, Mrs.	26 DEC 1883 L	18	344
Wood, John E.	Coleman, Sadie A.	21 APR 1885	20	181
Wood, John William	Roten, Louisa	01 DEC 1881 R	16	109
Wood, Josephine A.	Mockabee, Edward M.	07 OCT 1880 L	14	480
Wood, Katie	Bacon, Gus	10 JUL 1884	19	126
Wood, Lelia W.	Pace, Thomas H.	04 MAR 1884	18	457
Wood, Lexious A.	Storm, Annie W.	12 SEP 1882 R	17	016
Wood, Liley	Stone, Charles Allston	09 JUL 1879 R	13	272
Wood, Lizzie	Arnold, Robert	07 MAY 1885	20	207
Wood, Louisa	Montgomery, William	28 JUL 1879 L	13	295
Wood, Louisa	Smith, Hugh M.	23 JUN 1885	20	285
Wood, Maggie	Elbert, Jeremiah	08 FEB 1881 L	15	182
Wood, Maggie	Bannister, George	25 JUL 1882 R	16	455
Wood, Mary	Smith, William	02 OCT 1884	19	281
Wood, Mary Ellen	Clay, Andrus	26 JUL 1883 L	18	063
Wood, Mary J.	Hazle, John T.	16 OCT 1878 L	12	278
Wood, Mary M.	Mastin, Charles E.	16 JUL 1884	19	142
Wood, Mary V.	Kramer, George	31 AUG 1878 R	12	189
Wood, Mary V.	Spates, Charles W.	05 MAY 1881 L	15	294
Wood, Mollie	Hayden, Samuel Alexander	04 APR 1882 R	16	299
Wood, Moses	Turner, Lucinda	02 DEC 1880 L	15	080
Wood, Nathaniel	Jones, Sarah	03 NOV 1884 L	19	355
Wood, Rachel Lovetta	Jones, Henry	04 JUN 1884 R	19	056
Wood, Robert H.	Slingland, Hester E.	14 SEP 1882 L	17	020
Wood, Rosie W.	Sorrell, Welford	27 MAY 1885	20	242
Wood, Samuel A.	Bird, Minnie C.	04 APR 1883 L	17	378
Wood, Sarah	Page, Robert	15 MAR 1879	13	103
Wood, Sarah	Jorden, William	06 FEB 1884 R	30	7261
Wood, Sarah A.	Osborn, James B.	30 DEC 1884 L	19	505
Wood, Stan King	Hall, Lizzie F.	20 FEB 1884 R	18	432
Wood, Thomas	Ridgely, Ellen	29 JUL 1879	13	296
Wood, Thomas N.	Thom, Katie C.	17 OCT 1882 L	17	075
Wood, William	Robertson, Sarah R.R.	04 AUG 1885	20	350
Wood, William A.	Beatty, Sadie	23 DEC 1878 R	12	396
Wood, William Ann	Price, William Paschal	23 SEP 1882 L	17	034
Wood, William H.	Schwank, Hattie M.	28 JAN 1880	14	120
Wood, William H.	Robinson, Daisy Lee	02 DEC 1880 R	15	080
Wood, William Henry	Ross, Hestor Ann	09 MAY 1881 L	15	297
Wood, William N.	Bowman, Maggie E.	04 JUN 1885 L	20	256
Woodard, Isaiah	Dyson, Adella	02 MAY 1882	16	345
Woodard, Janette	Baker, Frank B.	28 MAY 1881 R	15	330
Woodard, Mary J.	Jackson, Frank A.	21 MAY 1883 R	17	453
Woodard, William	Jones, Ida	04 OCT 1877	11	040
Woodburn, Elizabeth Estell	Webster, Charles Albert	30 SEP 1878	12	238
Woodburn, James Lyon	Oxley, Mary Amelia	20 JUL 1880 R	14	370
Wooddy, Anna J.	Tribble, Eustace C.	23 OCT 1884	19	332

Woodfall, Louisa	Ross, Smith E.	30 SEP 1879 R	13	390
Woodfield, Sarah O.	Fugitt, Lemuel	30 NOV 1884	19	427
Woodfolk, Kate	Wheeler, Samuel	30 JUN 1880 L	14	340
Woodfolk, Martha	Buckner, Jacob	15 NOV 1877 L	11	189
Woodfork, Laura	Gordon, Anthony	23 DEC 1879 L	14	064
Woodgate, Maggie B.	Turner, William W.	09 JUN 1885	20	263
Woodjet, Doxy	Dewey, Thomas	09 NOV 1881 L	16	068
Woodland, Daniel E.	White, Frances	28 MAR 1882 R	16	290
Woodland, Katie	Crump, Edward	23 APR 1885	20	187
Woodley, Amy Elizabeth	Simms, Clayton Edmonston	08 FEB 1881 R	15	183
Woodley, Knight V.	Kayser, Florence G.	20 MAY 1885 R	20	230
Woodman, Francis Jos.	Cutler, Jennie Whitmore	30 JUN 1884	19	112
Woodro, Henry	Remus, Hannah	02 DEC 1880 R	15	082
Woodroe, Charles	Mason, Melinda	28 DEC 1882	17	219
Woodroof, Emma	Stratton, Charles W.	06 SEP 1882 R	17	006
Woodruff, George H.	Sneden, Cordelia J.	15 OCT 1883	18	192
Woods, Arthur Tannatt	DeKrafft, Harriet Scott	02 SEP 1884	19	217
Woods, Elizabeth M.	Brough, John H.	11 DEC 1884	19	450
Woods, Ella	Cavanaugh, Joseph	30 NOV 1883 L	18	288
Woods, Horace	Mills, Ella	10 NOV 1881 R	16	070
Woods, James F.	Tyson, Mary Jane	12 JUL 1883	18	044
Woods, Samuel M.	Acton, Mary E.	02 FEB 1885 L	20	047
Woods, Sarah	Smith, Edward	18 DEC 1877 R	11	244
Woods, Sarah	Coleman, Charles H.	09 OCT 1882 R	17	081
Woods, William	Cattell, Lizzie M.	12 DEC 1877	11	230
Woods, William Henry	Brown, Helen	27 MAR 1884 R	18	482
Woodward, Arthur	Addison, Maggie M.M.	05 MAY 1879 L	13	173
Woodward, Charles W.	Gill, Bettie L.	04 JUL 1881 R	15	387
Woodward, Edward	Moulton, Mary	03 AUG 1878 L	12	156
Woodward, Herbert E.	Dante, Verdie S.	03 JUN 1885	20	253
Woodward, Jane	Thomas, Nathan	14 DEC 1878 R	12	380
Woodward, Jennie Miller	Johnson, Walter S.	27 MAY 1882 R	16	378
Woodward, Kirby Sedley	Knott, Annie May	15 JAN 1885 L	20	019
Woodward, Laura	Thomas, H.A.	13 MAR 1878	11	380
Woodward, Lizzie A.	Wilson, Jesse H.	19 DEC 1877 R	11	245
Woodward, Maria	Rustin, William H.	15 APR 1884 L	18	510
Woodward, Mary E.	Griffin, James A.	20 NOV 1877	11	194
Woodward, Matthew	Hopkins, Sallie P.	17 OCT 1883 R	18	180
Woodward, Nannie R.	Milburn, Page	02 DEC 1880	15	078
Woodward, Oscar	Towers, Agnes May	20 OCT 1880	15	005
Woodward, S.B.	Thorn, Marion M.	15 JUN 1880 R	14	320
Woodward, William	Nolin, Elizabeth	11 APR 1878	11	413
Woodward, William	Graves, Mary E.	17 JAN 1883 R	17	262
Woodworth, Mary L.	Evans, Samuel B.	26 OCT 1879	13	443
Woody, Annie	Ogle, John R.	05 FEB 1879	13	047
Woody, Ellen Addie	Howard, George Francis	20 APR 1885 R	20	175
Woody, Ellen Annie	Crombaugh, Daniel	23 AUG 1881 L	15	456
Woody, George D.	Baker, Millie W.	30 DEC 1884	19	499
Woody, Geraldine	Wimer, Augustus	14 AUG 1882	16	478
Woodyard, Annie E.	Petty, Littleton M.	03 OCT 1881 L	16	003
Woodyard, Ida M.	Jones, James W.	24 FEB 1885 L	20	084
Woodyard, William H.L.	Carrle, Banks	22 MAR 1883 L	17	355
Woodyear, William H.J.	Robinson, Lucy M.	16 MAR 1885 R	20	116
Woodyer, Mary	Williams, Thomas	06 DEC 1880 L	15	084
Wooldridge, Blanche	Thompson, H. Owen	29 JUN 1883 L	18	026
Woolford, Henrietta	Kellum, Charles	14 AUG 1878 L	12	167
Wooster, Frank	Washburn, Ella	26 DEC 1877	11	269
Wootson, Maurice	Swift, Mary	04 NOV 1884 L	19	360

Worcester, Rosella	Ferguson, William	23 OCT 1877 R	11	150
Word, Blanche Aileen	Suit, George Tyler	11 JAN 1883 R	17	254
Worden, Charles H.	Vowles, Beckie F.	28 APR 1881 R	15	283
Worden, Olivia Steele	Busbee, Perrin	19 NOV 1879 R	13	490
Worden, Winifred	Tyler, Frank	24 SEP 1883	18	149
Work, Ida Georgianna	Boggs, William Benjamin	07 JUN 1882 R	16	398
Work, Kate Elizabeth	Lybrand, Harry Clay	26 JAN 1882 R	16	212
Work, William J.	McDonald, Alice	12 SEP 1883 L	18	125
Works, Winfield T.	Shepard, Catharine M.	09 APR 1883	17	384
Wormley, Fannie	Alexander, John Henry	28 JUL 1882	16	460
Wormley, Frances	Holland, Robert	05 MAR 1885 L	20	096
Wormley, John	Payne, Mary	15 NOV 1877	11	109
Worn, Ellen	Laws, Lindsey	31 DEC 1881 L	16	174
Worrell, Lee Alice	Wingfield, Charles Louis	13 DEC 1884	19	456
Worsham, Richard S.	Dobbins, Marietta	03 OCT 1881 R	16	001
Worster, Martha	Beach, George W.	02 JUL 1877	11	004
Wortham, J.E.	Raine, Alice L.	28 NOV 1877 L	11	212
Worthan, John L.	Dove, Mary E.	16 SEP 1880 R	14	450
Worthan, Kate McCathran	Murphy, Charles Wash.	02 MAR 1885 R	33	8069
Worthan, Miriam S.	Harbin, James S.	04 MAY 1878	12	037
Worthington, Charles E.	Speiden, Annie R.	20 MAY 1880 R	14	280
Worthington, Elizabeth	Trescot, Stephen Barnwell	03 NOV 1880 R	15	022
Worthington, Henry	Raid, Roseanna	19 MAR 1878 L	11	387
Worthington, Horace	Willmore, Mary S.	13 JUN 1882	16	405
Worthington, Juana	Barry, William H.	26 NOV 1883 L	18	277
Worthington, Kate N.	McGinley, Michael M.	23 APR 1878 R	12	018
Worthington, Kate V.	Healy, John P.	14 NOV 1884	19	382
Worthington, Lucy	Blackman, William F.	01 JUL 1884	19	112
Worthmiller, Jane Rebecca	Heffner, Francis Eugene	16 JAN 1879 R	13	016
Wracks, Allen	Holmes, Jane	28 NOV 1878	12	336
Wrecks, Thomas L.	Washington, Sarah	04 OCT 1877	11	120
Wrede, John A.	Warth, Lizzie	10 JUL 1883	18	041
Wren, Daniel	McGrath, Eliza	19 AUG 1883	18	093
Wren, Dora	Smith, Joseph	06 NOV 1881	16	034
Wren, Edward L.	Holland, Mary D.	22 FEB 1878	11	353
Wren, Julia T.	Furlong, Irwin	04 AUG 1879	13	305
Wren, Margaret	Lowery, William	12 FEB 1884 R	18	421
Wrenn, Arthur	Yates, Annie M.	29 SEP 1880 L	14	463
Wrenn, Thomas J.	Wise, Clara Rose	13 JUL 1885 L	20	322
Wrenn, Walter D.	Patron, Mary E.	09 SEP 1884	19	234
Wright, Abner O.	Humphrey, Lillian E.	05 DEC 1883	18	296
Wright, Agnes	Sims, Manuel	24 APR 1879	13	158
Wright, Amanda	Smith, William	23 NOV 1881 L	16	093
Wright, Ann	Nelson, John	30 DEC 1879 R	14	080
Wright, Catharine Mary	Valentine, Lewis Edmund	16 JAN 1879 R	13	023
Wright, Celia	Green, George	08 MAY 1880 R	14	261
Wright, Charles	Saddler, Ida	11 JUN 1879 R	13	169
Wright, Charles	Martin, Mollie Mildred	11 AUG 1885	20	365
Wright, Charles E.	Gillbritzer, Mary E.	15 APR 1879 R	13	145
Wright, Daniel Pratt	McCoy, Mary Jane	29 JAN 1879 R	13	036
Wright, Dollie	Thomas, Lewis	14 JUL 1884	19	137
Wright, Edward M.	Paschal, Bessie Duval	07 MAR 1878 R	11	375
Wright, Effie C.	Weaver, Egbert L.	17 JUL 1884	19	143
Wright, Effie W.	Gordon, Herbert C.	16 DEC 1884 R	19	462
Wright, Eleanor W.	Keach, Roman F.	17 OCT 1878 R	12	280
Wright, Elizabeth	Wayman, Lewis	24 OCT 1884 L	19	336
Wright, Ella	Pilkington, Thomas	24 DEC 1883 R	18	338
Wright, Ella Elizabeth	Brown, George Robert	15 MAR 1881 R	15	226

D.C. Marriage Records Index, June 28, 1877 to October 19, 1885

Wright, Ellen	Liston, Richard	06 JAN 1880 R	14	089
Wright, Frank B.	Crowley, Estella	27 OCT 1881	16	050
Wright, Frederick Parker	Massey, Lilian Duncan	20 NOV 1879 R	13	497
Wright, George	Hall, Mary Alice	06 APR 1878 L	11	408
Wright, Gustave B.	Rogers, Bettie	18 AUG 1881 R	15	452
Wright, Henry	Alles, Louisa Bass	05 MAR 1881 R	15	215
Wright, Jennie	Oder, Benjamin Franklin	15 APR 1880 R	14	225
Wright, Jennie E.	Powell, Charles R.	25 APR 1883	17	417
Wright, John H.	Carroll, Louisa	09 OCT 1877	11	125
Wright, John Henry	Chinn, Catherine	17 DEC 1878 L	12	383
Wright, Josephine A.	Hicks, Phillips E.	19 NOV 1884 L	19	397
Wright, Julia A.	Kane, Thomas F.	10 FEB 1884 L	18	418
Wright, Julia L.	Upshur, James A.	14 JUN 1883 L	17	496
Wright, Laura E.	Graham, Horace A.	09 AUG 1882 R	16	475
Wright, Lewis	Cogey, Eliza	01 DEC 1881 L	16	106
Wright, Lucy (Lawrence)	Eckels, William A.	21 AUG 1882 R	16	490
Wright, Maggie E.	Tucker, Robert A.	06 SEP 1882 R	17	010
Wright, Maggie Skinner	Sartain, John W.	13 NOV 1879 R	13	484
Wright, Marion Jeanitte	Fox, Gilbert D.	30 MAY 1878	12	075
Wright, Mary	Shealds, James	09 NOV 1878 L	12	317
Wright, Mary	Harkness, John A.	25 FEB 1879 R	13	079
Wright, Mary	Vass, Hamilton	10 DEC 1884 R	19	448
Wright, Mary A.	Drury, George A.	27 MAR 1883 L	17	363
Wright, Mary A.	Donald, R.B.	27 SEP 1883	18	160
Wright, Mary Alice	Perry, Edgar J.	08 OCT 1884	19	292
Wright, Mary L.	Lawson, Henry W.	26 FEB 1883	17	319
Wright, Morris	Turner, Eliza	15 MAY 1879 L	13	193
Wright, Nellie	Clark, J. Jerome	27 MAR 1883 L	17	363
Wright, Paul B.	Dillard, Annie W.	22 DEC 1878 R	12	397
Wright, Philip	Tolliver, Mary	27 DEC 1877 R	11	274
Wright, Robert F.	Barnes, Sadie A.	21 SEP 1878	12	205
Wright, Rosa V.	Brown, Benjamin H.	18 APR 1878	12	011
Wright, Samuel B.	Conway, Mary Frances	14 MAY 1884 R	19	019
Wright, Sarah	Hill, Charles	15 MAY 1882 R	16	359
Wright, Sarah	Downs, Joshua	18 SEP 1884	19	256
Wright, Sarah E.	Holmes, James O.	09 MAY 1878 L	12	047
Wright, Stephen H.	Cropper, Allie B.	28 DEC 1881	16	165
Wright, William	Overlander, Adeline	01 MAY 1878	12	032
Wright, William	Adams, Mary	09 MAR 1882 R	16	271
Wrightson, Annie Stewart	Dean, Charles Thomas	24 MAR 1885 L	20	128
Wrisley, Mary Louise	Broun, Charles Albert	25 MAY 1881 R	15	324
Writtoe, Martha	Whalen, William	28 OCT 1878 L	12	293
Wroe, Mamie V.	Parsons, Starr	19 NOV 1884 L	19	397
Wunder, William Henry	Swart, Laura B.	28 OCT 1879 R	13	448
Wunderlich, Barbara	Hiser, Daniel	28 AUG 1881	15	461
Wunderlich, Kate	Hiser, Paul, Jr.	15 MAY 1881	15	307
Wurdeman, J. Henry	Dyer, Sidney S.	26 SEP 1882	17	038
Wurtmiller, Rosa A.	Heffner, William C.	27 JAN 1881 L	15	167
Wyatt, Cullin	Hipkins, Bertie	20 DEC 1877 L	11	254
Wyatt, George M.	McGrade, Laura Virginia	01 JAN 1884 L	18	359
Wyatt, Kate Harrison	Wilson, Samuel Eston	22 SEP 1880 R	14	453
Wye, Charles	Smith, Sarah Jane	09 DEC 1884 L	19	445
Wye, James	Daniel, Celia	20 JUN 1879	13	244
Wylie, Geo. Washington	Condon, Mary E.	19 MAR 1885 R	20	124
Wylie, James H.	Nash, Frances F.	23 JUL 1878 L	12	145
Wyman, Albert J.	Roosa, Margaret T.	15 JUL 1877 R	11	021
Wyman, Hester A.	Sweet, Austin C.	30 APR 1885 L	20	201
Wysham, William E.	Moore, Annie B.	13 JUN 1881 R	15	357

X

Xander, Andreas G.	Schmid, Amelia	13 JUL 1884	19 135

Y

Yadley, Mary Ellen	Donohue, George A.	23 NOV 1884 R	19 403
Yancey, Elizabeth	Duffy, Thomas	09 OCT 1882	17 061
Yancey, Jacob	Mason, Sarah	29 MAR 1881 L	15 242
Yancey, William T.	Stephenson, Nannie G.	25 APR 1883	17 408
Yantis, Amelia R.	Derry, Absalom R.	19 FEB 1885 R	20 077
Yarber, Mamie	Krepps, George W.	27 APR 1885	20 190
Yarborough, Thomas S.	Bowie, Louisa	09 APR 1885	20 157
Yarmann, Gustav Oscar	Cook, Mahala Virginia	01 APR 1880 L	14 205
Yarnell, Robert S.	Butts, Hattie	24 DEC 1877 R	11 262
Yaste, H. Jane A.	Howard, James M.	12 AUG 1884	19 180
Yates, Ada B.	Cooksey, J. Walter	26 FEB 1884 L	18 445
Yates, Annie M.	Wrenn, Arthur	29 SEP 1880 L	14 463
Yates, Emma	Tindle, Jacob E.	08 OCT 1885 R	20 468
Yates, Henry P.	Brown, Alice V.	17 DEC 1879 L	14 052
Yates, James L.	Taylor, Winnie	27 MAY 1879 R	13 207
Yates, James W.	Baden, Susie V.	05 MAR 1884 L	18 459
Yates, John William	Graham, Tillie	12 FEB 1879 R	13 057
Yates, Maria	Rodgers, James	02 NOV 1878 L	12 304
Yates, Richard H.	Harper, Mamie F.	18 APR 1882 L	16 323
Yates, Thomas	Jackson, Mary	16 SEP 1880	14 450
Yates, William	Craig, Emma	27 NOV 1878 R	12 349
Yates, William A.	Walcott, Edith V.	26 APR 1883 R	17 412
Yeabower, Christopher	Kaiser, Elizabeth D.	10 SEP 1882 R	17 014
Yeabower, Louisa	Young, Philip	26 MAY 1880 R	14 288
Yeabower, Mary A.R.	Weaver, Robert David	26 NOV 1879 R	14 011
Yeager, Katie	Greaver, Jacob A	17 OCT 1883	18 107
Yeager, Samuel F.	Johnson, Maggie	11 DEC 1883	18 310
Yeakle, John A.	Caulder, Laura	21 MAY 1881 L	15 321
Yeatman, Alice V.	Orem, George W.	05 DEC 1883	18 296
Yeatman, Bernard	Davis, Mollie	21 JAN 1884 R	18 386
Yeatman, Edith Morgan	Collins, R. Walter	30 NOV 1879 R	14 020
Yeatman, Ella J.	Keithley, Franklin	01 SEP 1880 R	14 423
Yeatman, Elva Meredith	Tarkington, Joseph Asbury	14 JAN 1885 R	20 019
Yeatman, Emma	Weaver, Joseph F.	16 MAY 1883 R	17 444
Yeatman, George W.	Mills, Fanny E.	14 NOV 1883	18 252
Yeatman, Mattie H.	Durfee, George W.	13 AUG 1883	18 085
Yeatman, R.P.	Lucas, Lottie	04 SEP 1884	19 228
Yeatman, Wm. Henry	Saur, Katie	22 APR 1884 R	18 520
Yibbie, Malvina	Stephen, Alfred H.	03 APR 1879 R	13 122
Yockel, Mary Josephine	Brebaker, George Henry	12 JUN 1883 R	17 489
Yoder, Charles T.	Berry, Emma L.	20 AUG 1877	11 058
Yoe, Ella D.	McLaughlin, William J.	06 JUL 1882 R	16 439
Yookam, George	Page, Sarah	23 FEB 1885 R	20 081
Yoos, Mary C.	Harvey, William K.	19 DEC 1883	18 326
York, Alida S.	Pennie, John C.	19 FEB 1884 R	20 429
York, Emma E.	Hammer, Andersen	10 OCT 1883	18 184
York, Frank	Steinmann, Louise	12 AUG 1885 L	20 366
York, Jane	Jackson, Samuel	02 JUL 1879 L	13 263
York, Jane	Gardner, Jacob	25 OCT 1882 L	17 094
York, Mary Christine	Herfurth, John	03 MAR 1885	20 091
Yost, Amelia	Puruer, Ferdinand	11 AUG 1884	19 168
Yost, Amos Smith	Webster, Alice M.	20 JAN 1881 R	15 160

Yost, Augustus	Suit, Mary S.	23 MAR 1880 R	14	193
Yost, Estelle K.	Dent, Louis A.	03 JUN 1884	19	038
Yost, Fannie	Suit, William G.	02 NOV 1882 R	17	108
Yost, Josephine	Coethen, Alfred	06 JAN 1879 R	13	006
Yost, William H.	McDonald, Mary E.	29 APR 1885 L	20	196
Young, Abraham	Henry, Rachel	28 SEP 1885 L	20	446
Young, Alfred	Hill, Emma P.	18 OCT 1877 R	11	144
Young, Alice	Tyler, Henry	14 MAR 1878	11	364
Young, Alice	Elliott, John G.	16 OCT 1879	13	429
Young, Anderson	Brooks, Lucy Ellen	05 SEP 1882	17	004
Young, Anna	Stuart, Charles J.	05 MAY 1885	20	206
Young, Annie	Williams, Jacob	30 AUG 1877	11	062
Young, Annie	Sullivan, James Edward	28 JUL 1878 R	12	150
Young, Annie	Windsor, Richard	12 OCT 1883 L	18	189
Young, Annie	Botts, Thomas	31 MAR 1885 L	20	139
Young, Annie L.	Sturgeon, E.B.	26 JUL 1877	11	031
Young, Arabella	O'Connor, James	07 SEP 1882 R	17	012
Young, Arthur	French, Frances M.	02 JUL 1879 R	13	262
Young, Benjamin F.	Lee, Annie	26 JUL 1878 R	12	147
Young, Beverly	Givens, Annie	27 AUG 1879 L	13	339
Young, Caroline Virginia	Dodson, Henry	06 JAN 1880 L	14	093
Young, Catherine	Barton, Henry	25 APR 1882 L	16	334
Young, Charles E.	Gibney, Elizabeth (Gardner)	14 SEP 1885 R	20	414
Young, Charles H.	Poole, Maria A.	14 JUN 1884	19	083
Young, Chlory Ann	Bacey, Emanuel	02 AUG 1877 L	11	038
Young, Clement Chapman	Clarke, Fannie	14 JUN 1883 R	17	490
Young, Constantine W.	Hanford, Fannie Lawson	28 FEB 1882 R	16	260
Young, Cora L.	Ingram, Thomas G.	20 FEB 1884 L	18	433
Young, Edward T.	Lyon, Alice J.	01 APR 1882 R	16	294
Young, Eleanor B.	Desper, Sandy B.	17 JUL 1877	11	024
Young, Ella M.	Todd, Ralston L.	27 FEB 1883 R	17	323
Young, Emma	Williams, Edward	06 SEP 1883 L	18	116
Young, Emma J.	Carr, John W.	15 SEP 1880	14	446
Young, Fannie K.	Dorsey, Walter	07 FEB 1883	17	296
Young, Frances M.	Taylor, James R.	27 MAR 1878 R	11	394
Young, Francis M.	Scanlan, Katherine	04 OCT 1884	19	286
Young, Frederick	Butler, Theresa	19 MAR 1885 L	20	125
Young, George	Simms, Mary	07 FEB 1881	15	181
Young, George W.	Hines, Mary E.	23 JAN 1881 R	15	161
Young, Harry A.	Anderson, Addie	06 SEP 1883	18	115
Young, Henrietta Maria	Reeves, Isaac S.K.	16 APR 1879 R	13	143
Young, Henry	Everet, Georgie	28 NOV 1883 L	18	284
Young, Henry	Ware, Martha E.	19 NOV 1884 L	19	396
Young, Ida	Stewart, Thomas	02 JUN 1881 L	15	340
Young, Isaac	Hard, Mary	23 DEC 1879	14	062
Young, Isabella	Jordan, George	03 MAR 1885 R	20	093
Young, James	Neal, Maria	15 DEC 1879 R	14	049
Young, James	Cokey, Mary	20 MAY 1880 L	14	278
Young, James	Ashton, Massouria	14 JUN 1883 R	17	493
Young, James	Sparrow, Addie	17 DEC 1883 L	18	320
Young, James E.	Green, Mattie	16 JAN 1883 R	17	256
Young, James Edward	Hawkins, Georgiana	15 SEP 1883	18	131
Young, James Henry	Gibbons, Maggie Virginia	08 APR 1878 R	11	410
Young, Jane	Redman, John	16 OCT 1880 L	14	498
Young, John	Johnson, Susan	31 JAN 1878 L	11	324
Young, John	Buckman, Kittie	23 DEC 1879	14	062
Young, John	Gray, Fannie	14 APR 1880 L	14	223
Young, John C.	White, Irene B.	05 DEC 1877 L	11	221

Young, John F.	Richardson, Alice	21 AUG 1882	16	489
Young, John M.	Roseberry, Annie S.	24 DEC 1878 R	12	397
Young, John Taylor	Corrick, Jenny Amelia	02 JAN 1879 R	13	003
Young, Joseph	Levy, Letitia	17 DEC 1884 R	19	461
Young, Joshua T.	Butler, Sarah A.	11 MAR 1879 L	13	096
Young, Linnie M.	Bourne, Thomas C.	10 FEB 1881 R	15	183
Young, Lizzie	Hugo, Louis C.F.	09 MAR 1880 R	14	180
Young, Lizzie	Cook, Charles	06 MAR 1884 L	18	461
Young, Lottie	Howard, William C.	20 FEB 1878 L	11	350
Young, Lottie	Hampton, John W.	15 MAY 1884 R	19	020
Young, Louisa	Webb, William H.	22 FEB 1883	17	318
Young, Louisa Latham	Ross, John Thomas deHavilland	26 JUN 1879 R	13	246
Young, Luke	Langry, Annie	18 MAY 1878 L	12	058
Young, M.	Fran, William	24 MAY 1883	17	462
Young, Maggie	Berry, Smith	19 AUG 1885	20	379
Young, Maria	Hill, Sam	20 MAR 1883 L	17	352
Young, Maria L.	Burrell, William H.	29 MAY 1884	19	046
Young, Martha E.	Jackson, Melvin M.	13 OCT 1881 R	16	023
Young, Martha Jane	Garnett, James	26 OCT 1882	17	096
Young, Mary	Walker, John	15 JUN 1881	15	353
Young, Mary	Porter, John	15 SEP 1883	18	131
Young, Mary	Carter, William	25 MAR 1884 L	18	481
Young, Mary E.	Tibbles, Charles H.	27 NOV 1884 L	19	423
Young, Mary Ellen	Crampton, Thomas H.	17 DEC 1879 R	14	050
Young, Mary F.	Harper, Samuel A.	24 DEC 1877 L	11	265
Young, Mary Jane	Triplet, Samuel	04 AUG 1877 L	11	041
Young, Minnie E.	Berg, Julius O.	06 MAY 1880 R	14	255
Young, Mulberry	Green, Mary Ann	19 APR 1883 L	17	400
Young, Neal	Richardson, Nettie	11 FEB 1880 R	14	146
Young, Nettie, Mrs.	Ashton, George W.	23 DEC 1883 R	18	333
Young, Noah	Hipkins, Mariah	25 SEP 1884	19	263
Young, Philip	Yeahower, Louisa	26 MAY 1880 R	14	288
Young, Richard	Fairall, Mary M.	25 OCT 1882 R	17	086
Young, Richard H.	Walsh, Mary A.	25 APR 1882	16	333
Young, Robert	Malvin, Virginia	24 MAR 1884	18	480
Young, Robert D.	Ambler, Julia B.	05 NOV 1884	19	364
Young, Rosa A.	Dorsey, Elijah	05 JUN 1884 L	19	065
Young, Sarah	Brown, Samuel	10 OCT 1877 R	11	130
Young, Sarah	Cook, Thomas	14 JUN 1883 R	17	494
Young, Soloman	Bush, Amy Ann	19 MAR 1879 L	13	108
Young, Sophia	Parker, William	16 OCT 1884 L	19	316
Young, Sostman	Sommers, Alice	28 JAN 1883 R	17	274
Young, Spencer	Offutt, Lucy	31 JUL 1877 L	11	034
Young, Spencer	Fletcher, Henrietta	04 NOV 1879 L	13	461
Young, Tapley Webb	Glenn, Annie Grace	20 SEP 1882 R	17	029
Young, Thadeus S.	Dorsy, Sarah A.	14 MAR 1878 R	11	381
Young, Thomas	Williams, Ellen	01 JUL 1880 R	14	337
Young, Thomas C.	Bird, Alice	29 OCT 1884	19	347
Young, Virginia	Page, Charles G.	09 OCT 1884	19	296
Young, Virginia Robinson	Wilson, James Charles	18 NOV 1880 R	15	057
Young, William	Straib, Johanna	27 DEC 1877	11	273
Young, William	Harris, Ellen	07 OCT 1884 L	19	289
Young, William A.	Bailey, Mamie F.	11 DEC 1884 R	19	453
Younger, Edward C., Jr.	Nortin, Emma	19 AUG 1885 R	20	377
Younger, George L.	Gray, Mary Matilde	06 FEB 1879 R	13	050
Younger, Lucinda	Ellis, Frederick	31 OCT 1877 L	11	162
Youngs, Allice	McFarland, Charles E.	05 OCT 1885	20	459
Yowell, Jefferson Davis	Carpenter, Lillie Thomas	29 MAR 1882 R	16	292

Yowles, Harriet	Pundexter, Geo. Wallace	03 JUN 1880 R	14	305
Yung, Julia	Wild, Alfred E.	27 MAY 1878	12	067
Yungheln, Annie	Phillips, James R.	15 AUG 1884	19	187

Z

Zachary, George Wash.	Cumberland, Mary Roberta	14 NOV 1883 R	18	253
Zamzaw, Albert	Darlington, Gerturde	06 NOV 1883 L	18	236
Zange, Mary M.E.	Stenz, George F.	26 OCT 1880 L	15	014
Zanner, Margaret	Gering, John J.	28 NOV 1883	18	280
Zeh, Emma	Viedt, Julius, Jr.	28 MAR 1878 L	11	397
Zeh, Virginia P.	Brandenburg, Frederick H.	29 NOV 1881 R	16	102
Zeidler, Catherine	Neumeister, Conrad	24 NOV 1884 L	19	405
Zeigler, Albert	Ott, Annie	23 JUL 1882	16	426
Zeigler, Carrie	Howaldt, George J.	14 JUN 1884	19	083
Zeigler, Louisa E.	Buckley, Joseph F.	20 NOV 1878 R	12	337
Zeir, Jacob B.	Pearson, Ella Frances	02 NOV 1882 R	17	107
Zeirmann, George W.	Gown, Adaline	11 JUN 1878 L	12	096
Zeis, Adams	Cannon, Mary	21 APR 1885	20	176
Zelbernagel, Wladystaw	Switzer, Maggia	10 OCT 1883 L	18	186
Zelbernagle, Wladyas	Guess, Magretta	28 OCT 1878	12	293
Zell, Charles	Tippet, Susie	13 SEP 1877 R	11	090
Zell, Ella Susannah	English, William Henry	21 JUN 1881 R	15	370
Zeller, Margaret D.	Ganzhorn, George P.	03 FEB 1884 R	18	405
Zells, Emma J.	Berkley, Christopher	13 JAN 1880 R	14	102
Zells, Maggie E.	Michel, William F.	02 MAR 1882 R	16	263
Zelner, Ellen S.	Fenton, Edwin L.	21 OCT 1884 L	19	325
Zentgraf, Frank	Burkart, Tillie	07 JUN 1881	15	349
Zepp, James H.	Cole, Julia I.	11 NOV 1880 R	15	045
Zerega, Luigi	Burke, Delia	13 MAY 1879	13	187
Zevely, Bartram	Evans, Nina	30 JAN 1879 R	13	037
Zevely, Douglass	Fletcher, Nellie R.	17 OCT 1885 L	20	493
Zevely, Henry B.	Colt, Elizabeth	04 JAN 1883	17	236
Ziegler, Babetta Wilhelmine	Krumke, Carl	06 FEB 1878 L	11	330
Ziegler, Gottlieb	Hoffman, Augusta	30 SEP 1877	11	108
Zier, Philip R.	Rick, Lottie C.	14 APR 1885 R	20	166
Zietler, William	Kempter, Antoinetta	02 AUG 1877	11	036
Zimmer, Mary	Nessi, Ulderico	05 DEC 1881 L	16	114
Zimmerman, Alfred	Kueberth, Barbara	18 JUN 1885 R	20	279
Zimmerman, Minnie B.	Cady, Benjamin J.	08 AUG 1878	12	160
Zimmerman, William	Dennison, Annie L.	01 JUL 1880 R	14	342
Zimmerman, William M.	Burch, Jessie E.	01 DEC 1883	18	290
Zinser, Joseph	Scheppach, Katie	26 FEB 1882 R	16	259
Zitting, William F.	Hennige, Christina F.	04 OCT 1883	18	170
Zoller, Emil Bruno	Schmidt, Emily	17 JUL 1877	11	024
Zucker, Alcinda	Willis, Thomas	27 APR 1885 R	20	190
Zulauf, Edward	Eckenrode, Mary Jane	10 DEC 1883	18	307
Zulauf, Henry	Bussman, Sophie E.D.	25 JUN 1883 R	18	010
Zumborg, Herman H.	Rabbitt, Ellenor	12 NOV 1884 L	19	377
Zust, Jacob	Warfield, Maria Louisa	09 NOV 1880	15	036

Incomplete Records

[Blank], Margaret	Butler, Andrew	06 MAY 1880 L	14	256
[Blank], [Blank]	Corbin, J.	04 DEC 1878 L	12	368
[Unknown], James C.	[Unknown], Maggie J.	28 APR 1883 L	17	421
[Unknown], Maggie J.	[Unknown], James C.	28 APR 1883 L	17	421

Other Heritage Books by Wesley E. Pippenger:

Alexandria (Arlington) County, Virginia Death Records, 1853-1896

Alexandria City and Arlington County, Virginia Records Index: Vol. 1

Alexandria City and Arlington County, Virginia Records Index: Vol. 2

Alexandria County, Virginia Marriage Records, 1853-1895

Alexandria Virginia Marriage Index, January 10, 1893 to August 31, 1905

Alexandria, Virginia Marriages, 1870-1892

*Alexandria, Virginia Town Lots, 1749-1801
Together with the Proceedings of the Board of Trustees, 1749-1780*

Alexandria, Virginia Wills, Administrations and Guardianships, 1786-1800

Alexandria, Virginia 1808 Census (Wards 1, 2, 3, and 4)

Alexandria, Virginia Death Records, 1863-1896

Alexandria, Virginia Hustings Court Orders, Volume 1, 1780-1787

Connections and Separations: Divorce, Name Change and Other Genealogical Tidbits from the Acts of the Virginia General Assembly

Daily National Intelligencer *Index to Deaths, 1855-1870*

Daily National Intelligencer, *Washington, District of Columbia Marriages and Deaths Notices (January 1, 1851 to December 30, 1854)*

Dead People on the Move: Reconstruction of the Georgetown Presbyterian Burying Ground, Holmead's (Western) Burying Ground, and Other Removals in the District of Columbia

Death Notices from Richmond, Virginia Newspapers, 1841-1853

District of Columbia Ancestors, A Guide to Records of the District of Columbia

District of Columbia Death Records: August 1, 1874-July 31, 1879

District of Columbia Foreign Deaths, 1888-1923

District of Columbia Guardianship Index, 1802-1928

*District of Columbia Interments (Index to Deaths)
January 1, 1855 to July 31, 1874*

District of Columbia Marriage Licenses, Register 1: 1811-1858

District of Columbia Marriage Licenses, Register 2: 1858-1870

*District of Columbia Marriage Records Index
June 28, 1877 to October 19, 1885: Marriage Record Books 11 to 20*
Wesley E. Pippenger and Dorothy S. Provine

*District of Columbia Marriage Records Index
October 20, 1885 to January 20, 1892: Marriage Record Books 21 to 30*

District of Columbia Probate Records, 1801-1852

District of Columbia: Original Land Owners, 1791-1800

Early Church Records of Alexandria City and Fairfax County, Virginia

Georgetown, District of Columbia 1850 Federal Population Census (Schedule I) and 1853 Directory of Residents of Georgetown

Georgetown, District of Columbia Marriage and Death Notices, 1801-1838

Husbands and Wives Associated with Early Alexandria, Virginia (and the Surrounding Area), 3rd Edition, Revised

Index to District of Columbia Estates, 1801-1929

Index to Virginia Estates, 1800-1865 Volumes 4, 5 and 6

John Alexander, a Northern Neck Proprietor, His Family, Friends and Kin

Legislative Petitions of Alexandria, 1778-1861

Pippenger and Pittenger Families

Proceedings of the Orphan's Court, Washington County, District of Columbia, 1801-1808

The Georgetown Courier Marriage and Death Notices: Georgetown, District of Columbia, November 18, 1865 to May 6, 1876

The Georgetown Directory for the Year 1830: to which is appended, a Short Description of the Churches, Public Institutions, and the Original Charter of Georgetown, and Extracts of the Laws Pertaining to the Chesapeake and Ohio Canal Company

The Virginia Gazette and Alexandria Advertiser: Volume 1, September 3, 1789 to November 11, 1790

The Virginia Journal and Alexandria Advertiser: Volume I (February 5, 1784 to January 27, 1785)

Volume II (February 3, 1785 to January 26, 1786)

Volume III (March 2, 1786 to January 25, 1787)

Volume IV (February 8, 1787 to May 21, 1789)

The Washington and Georgetown Directory of 1853

Tombstone Inscriptions of Alexandria, Volumes 1-4

Other Heritage Books by Dorothy S. Provine:

Alexandria County, Virginia Free Negro Register, 1797-1861

Compensated Emancipation in the District of Columbia: Petitions under the Act of April 16, 1862

District of Columbia Free Negro Registers

District of Columbia Indentures of Apprenticeship, 1801-1893

District of Columbia Marriage Records Index June 28, 1877 to October 19, 1885: Marriage Record Books 11 to 20 Wesley E. Pippenger and Dorothy S. Provine

District of Columbia Marriage Records, 1870-1877

Index to District of Columbia Wills, 1921-1950

www.ingramcontent.com/pod-product-compliance
Lightning Source LLC
Chambersburg PA
CBHW051331230426
43668CB00010B/1227